CODE OF
REGULATI

M000201435

Title 41

Public Contracts and Property Management

Chapters 102 to 200

Revised as of July 1, 2019

Containing a codification of documents
of general applicability and future effect

As of July 1, 2019

Published by the Office of the Federal Register
National Archives and Records Administration
as a Special Edition of the Federal Register

Table of Contents

Cite this Code: CFR

To cite the regulations in this volume use title, part and section number. Thus, 41 CFR 102–2.5 *refers to title 41, part 102–2, section 5.*

Explanation

The Code of Federal Regulations is a codification of the general and permanent rules published in the Federal Register by the Executive departments and agencies of the Federal Government. The Code is divided into 50 titles which represent broad areas subject to Federal regulation. Each title is divided into chapters which usually bear the name of the issuing agency. Each chapter is further subdivided into parts covering specific regulatory areas.

Each volume of the Code is revised at least once each calendar year and issued on a quarterly basis approximately as follows:

Title 1 through Title 16...as of January 1
Title 17 through Title 27 ....as of April 1
Title 28 through Title 41 ....as of July 1
Title 42 through Title 50...as of October 1

The appropriate revision date is printed on the cover of each volume.

LEGAL STATUS

The contents of the Federal Register are required to be judicially noticed (44 U.S.C. 1507). The Code of Federal Regulations is prima facie evidence of the text of the original documents (44 U.S.C. 1510).

HOW TO USE THE CODE OF FEDERAL REGULATIONS

The Code of Federal Regulations is kept up to date by the individual issues of the Federal Register. These two publications must be used together to determine the latest version of any given rule.

To determine whether a Code volume has been amended since its revision date (in this case, July 1, 2019), consult the "List of CFR Sections Affected (LSA)," which is issued monthly, and the "Cumulative List of Parts Affected," which appears in the Reader Aids section of the daily Federal Register. These two lists will identify the Federal Register page number of the latest amendment of any given rule.

EFFECTIVE AND EXPIRATION DATES

Each volume of the Code contains amendments published in the Federal Register since the last revision of that volume of the Code. Source citations for the regulations are referred to by volume number and page number of the Federal Register and date of publication. Publication dates and effective dates are usually not the same and care must be exercised by the user in determining the actual effective date. In instances where the effective date is beyond the cut-off date for the Code a note has been inserted to reflect the future effective date. In those instances where a regulation published in the Federal Register states a date certain for expiration, an appropriate note will be inserted following the text.

OMB CONTROL NUMBERS

The Paperwork Reduction Act of 1980 (Pub. L. 96–511) requires Federal agencies to display an OMB control number with their information collection request.

Many agencies have begun publishing numerous OMB control numbers as amendments to existing regulations in the CFR. These OMB numbers are placed as close as possible to the applicable recordkeeping or reporting requirements.

PAST PROVISIONS OF THE CODE

Provisions of the Code that are no longer in force and effect as of the revision date stated on the cover of each volume are not carried. Code users may find the text of provisions in effect on any given date in the past by using the appropriate List of CFR Sections Affected (LSA). For the convenience of the reader, a "List of CFR Sections Affected" is published at the end of each CFR volume. For changes to the Code prior to the LSA listings at the end of the volume, consult previous annual editions of the LSA. For changes to the Code prior to 2001, consult the List of CFR Sections Affected compilations, published for 1949-1963, 1964-1972, 1973-1985, and 1986-2000.

"[RESERVED]" TERMINOLOGY

The term "[Reserved]" is used as a place holder within the Code of Federal Regulations. An agency may add regulatory information at a "[Reserved]" location at any time. Occasionally "[Reserved]" is used editorially to indicate that a portion of the CFR was left vacant and not accidentally dropped due to a printing or computer error.

INCORPORATION BY REFERENCE

What is incorporation by reference? Incorporation by reference was established by statute and allows Federal agencies to meet the requirement to publish regulations in the Federal Register by referring to materials already published elsewhere. For an incorporation to be valid, the Director of the Federal Register must approve it. The legal effect of incorporation by reference is that the material is treated as if it were published in full in the Federal Register (5 U.S.C. 552(a)). This material, like any other properly issued regulation, has the force of law.

What is a proper incorporation by reference? The Director of the Federal Register will approve an incorporation by reference only when the requirements of 1 CFR part 51 are met. Some of the elements on which approval is based are:

(a) The incorporation will substantially reduce the volume of material published in the Federal Register.

(b) The matter incorporated is in fact available to the extent necessary to afford fairness and uniformity in the administrative process.

(c) The incorporating document is drafted and submitted for publication in accordance with 1 CFR part 51.

What if the material incorporated by reference cannot be found? If you have any problem locating or obtaining a copy of material listed as an approved incorporation by reference, please contact the agency that issued the regulation containing that incorporation. If, after contacting the agency, you find the material is not available, please notify the Director of the Federal Register, National Archives and Records Administration, 8601 Adelphi Road, College Park, MD 20740-6001, or call 202-741-6010.

CFR INDEXES AND TABULAR GUIDES

A subject index to the Code of Federal Regulations is contained in a separate volume, revised annually as of January 1, entitled CFR INDEX AND FINDING AIDS. This volume contains the Parallel Table of Authorities and Rules. A list of CFR titles, chapters, subchapters, and parts and an alphabetical list of agencies publishing in the CFR are also included in this volume.

An index to the text of "Title 3—The President" is carried within that volume.

The Federal Register Index is issued monthly in cumulative form. This index is based on a consolidation of the "Contents" entries in the daily Federal Register.

A List of CFR Sections Affected (LSA) is published monthly, keyed to the revision dates of the 50 CFR titles.

REPUBLICATION OF MATERIAL

There are no restrictions on the republication of material appearing in the Code of Federal Regulations.

INQUIRIES

For a legal interpretation or explanation of any regulation in this volume, contact the issuing agency. The issuing agency's name appears at the top of odd-numbered pages.

For inquiries concerning CFR reference assistance, call 202–741–6000 or write to the Director, Office of the Federal Register, National Archives and Records Administration, 8601 Adelphi Road, College Park, MD 20740-6001 or e-mail *fedreg.info@nara.gov*.

SALES

The Government Publishing Office (GPO) processes all sales and distribution of the CFR. For payment by credit card, call toll-free, 866-512-1800, or DC area, 202-512-1800, M-F 8 a.m. to 4 p.m. e.s.t. or fax your order to 202-512-2104, 24 hours a day. For payment by check, write to: US Government Publishing Office – New Orders, P.O. Box 979050, St. Louis, MO 63197-9000.

ELECTRONIC SERVICES

The full text of the Code of Federal Regulations, the LSA (List of CFR Sections Affected), The United States Government Manual, the Federal Register, Public Laws, Public Papers of the Presidents of the United States, Compilation of Presidential Documents and the Privacy Act Compilation are available in electronic format via *www.govinfo.gov*. For more information, contact the GPO Customer Contact Center, U.S. Government Publishing Office. Phone 202-512-1800, or 866-512-1800 (toll-free). E-mail, *ContactCenter@gpo.gov*.

The Office of the Federal Register also offers a free service on the National Archives and Records Administration's (NARA) World Wide Web site for public law numbers, Federal Register finding aids, and related information. Connect to NARA's web site at *www.archives.gov/federal-register*.

The e-CFR is a regularly updated, unofficial editorial compilation of CFR material and Federal Register amendments, produced by the Office of the Federal Register and the Government Publishing Office. It is available at *www.ecfr.gov*.

OLIVER A. POTTS,
Director,
Office of the Federal Register.
July 1, 2019.

THIS TITLE

Title 41—PUBLIC CONTRACTS AND PROPERTY MANAGEMENT consists of Subtitle A—Federal Procurement Regulations System [Note]; Subtitle B—Other Provisions Relating to Public Contracts; Subtitle C—Federal Property Management Regulations System; Subtitle D is reserved for other provisions relating to property management, Subtitle E—Federal Information Resources Management Regulations System and Subtitle F—Federal Travel Regulation System.

As of July 1, 1985, the text of subtitle A is no longer published in the Code of Federal Regulations. For an explanation of the status of subtitle A, see 41 CFR chapters 1–100 (page 3).

Other government-wide procurement regulations relating to public contracts appear in chapters 50 through 100, subtitle B.

The Federal property management regulations in chapter 101 of subtitle C are government-wide property management regulations issued by the General Services Administration. In the remaining chapters of subtitle C are the *implementing* and *supplementing* property management regulations issued by individual Government agencies. Those regulations which implement chapter 101 are numerically keyed to it.

The Federal Travel Regulation System in chapters 300–304 of subtitle F is issued by the General Services Administration.

Title 41 is composed of four volumes. The chapters in these volumes are arranged as follows: Chapters 1–100, chapter 101, chapters 102–200, and chapter 201 to end. These volumes represent all current regulations codified under this title of the CFR as of July 1, 2019.

For this volume, Ann Worley was Chief Editor. The Code of Federal Regulations publication program is under the direction of John Hyrum Martinez, assisted by Stephen J. Frattini.

Title 41—Public Contracts and Property Management

(This book contains chapters 102 to 200)

1

Subtitle C—Federal Property Management Regulations System (Continued)

CHAPTER 102—FEDERAL MANAGEMENT REGULATION

SUBCHAPTER A—GENERAL

PART 102—GENERAL [RESERVED]

PART 102-2—FEDERAL MANAGEMENT REGULATION SYSTEM

Subpart A—Regulation System

AUTHORITY: 40 U.S.C. 486(c).

SOURCE: 64 FR 39085, July 21, 1999, unless otherwise noted.

Subpart A—Regulation System

GENERAL

§ 102–2.5 What is the Federal Management Regulation (FMR)?

The Federal Management Regulation (FMR) is the successor regulation to the Federal Property Management Regulations (FPMR). It contains updated regulatory policies originally found in the FPMR. However, it does not contain FPMR material that described how to do business with the General Services Administration (GSA). "How to" materials on this and other subjects are available in customer service guides, handbooks, brochures and Internet websites provided by GSA. (See § 102–2.125.)

§ 102–2.10 What is the FMR's purpose?

The FMR prescribes policies concerning property management and related administrative activities. GSA issues the FMR to carry out the Administrator of General Services' functional responsibilities, as established by statutes, Executive orders, Presidential memoranda, Circulars and bulletins issued by the Office of Management and Budget (OMB), and other policy directives.

§ 102–2.15 What is the authority for the FMR system?

The Administrator of General Services prescribes and issues the FMR under the authority of the Federal Property and Administrative Services Act of 1949, as amended, 40 U.S.C. 486(c), as well as other applicable Federal laws and authorities.

§ 102–2.20 Which agencies are subject to the FMR?

The FMR applies to executive agencies unless otherwise extended to Federal agencies in various parts of this chapter. The difference between the two terms is that Federal agencies include executive agencies plus establishments in the legislative or judicial branch of the Government. See paragraphs (a) and (b) of this section for the definitions of each term.

(a) *What is an executive agency?* An executive agency is any executive department or independent establishment in the executive branch of the Government, including any wholly-owned Government corporation. (See 40 U.S.C. 472(a).)

(b) *What is a Federal agency?* A Federal agency is any executive agency or any establishment in the legislative or judicial branch of the Government (except the Senate, the House of Representatives, and the Architect of the Capitol and any activities under that person's direction). (See 40 U.S.C. 472(b).)

§ 102–2.25 When are other agencies involved in developing the FMR?

Normally, GSA will ask agencies to collaborate in developing parts of the FMR.

§ 102–2.30 Where and in what formats is the FMR published?

Proposed rules are published in the FEDERAL REGISTER. FMR bulletins are published in looseleaf format. FMR interim and final rules are published in the following formats—

(a) FEDERAL REGISTER under the "Rules and Regulations" section.

(b) Loose-leaf. (See § 102–2.35.)

(c) Code of Federal Regulations (CFR), which is an annual codification of the general and permanent rules published in the FEDERAL REGISTER. The CFR is available on line and in a bound-volume format.

(d) Electronically on the Internet.

§ 102–2.35 How is the FMR distributed?

(a) A liaison appointed by each agency provides GSA with their agency's distribution requirements of the looseleaf version of the FMR. Agencies must submit GSA Form 2053, Agency Consolidated Requirements for GSA Regulations and Other External Issuances, to—General Services Administration, Office of Communications (X), 1800 F Street, NW., Washington, DC 20405.

(b) Order FEDERAL REGISTER and Code of Federal Regulations copies of FMR material through your agency's authorizing officer.

§ 102–2.40 May an agency issue implementing and supplementing regulations for the FMR?

Yes, an agency may issue implementing regulations (see § 102–2.50) to expand upon related FMR material and supplementing regulations (see § 102–2.55) to address subject material not covered in the FMR. The Office of the Federal Register assigns chapters in Title 41 of the Code of Federal Regulations for agency publication of implementing and supplementing regulations.

NUMBERING

§ 102–2.45 How is the FMR numbered?

(a) All FMR sections are designated by three numbers. The following example illustrates the chapter (it's always 102), part, and section designations:

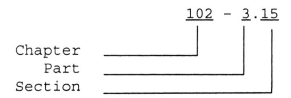

(b) In the looseleaf version, the month, year, and number of FMR amendments appear at the bottom of each page.

§ 102–2.50 How do I number my agency's implementing regulations?

The first three-digit number represents the chapter number assigned to your agency in Title 41 of the CFR. The part and section numbers correspond to FMR material. For example, if your agency is assigned Chapter 130 in Title 41 of the CFR and you are implementing § 102–2.60 of the FMR, your implementing section would be numbered § 130–2.60.

§ 102–2.55 How do I number my agency's supplementing regulations?

Since there is no corresponding FMR material, number the supplementing material "601" or higher. For example, your agency's supplementing regulations governing special services to states might start with § 130–601.5.

DEVIATIONS

§ 102–2.60 What is a deviation from the FMR?

A deviation from the FMR is an agency action or policy that is inconsistent with the regulation. (The deviation policy for the FPMR is in 41 CFR part 101–1.)

§ 102–2.65 When may agencies deviate from the FMR?

Because, it consists primarily of set policies and mandatory requirements, deviation from the FMR should occur infrequently. However, to address unique circumstances or to test the effectiveness of potential policy changes, agencies may be able to deviate from the FMR after following the steps described in § 102–2.80.

§ 102–2.70 What are individual and class deviations?

An individual deviation is intended to affect only one action. A class deviation is intended to affect more than one action (e.g., multiple actions, the actions of more than one agency, or individual agency actions that are expected to recur).

§ 102–2.75 What timeframes apply to deviations?

Timeframes vary based on the nature of the deviation. However, deviations cannot be open-ended. When consulting with GSA about using an individual or class deviation, you must set a timeframe for the deviation's duration.

§ 102–2.80 What steps must an agency take to deviate from the FMR?

(a) Consult informally with appropriate GSA program personnel to learn more about how your agency can work within the FMR's requirements instead of deviating from them. The consultation process may also highlight reasons why an agency would not be permitted to deviate from the FMR; e.g., statutory constraints.

(b) Formally request a deviation, if consultations indicate that your agency needs one. The head of your agency or a designated official should write to GSA's Regulatory Secretariat to the attention of a GSA official in the program office that is likely to consider the deviation. (See the FMR bulletin that lists contacts in GSA's program offices and § 102–2.90.) The written request must fully explain the reasons for the deviation, including the benefits that the agency expects to achieve.

§ 102–2.85 What are the reasons for writing to GSA about FMR deviations?

The reasons for writing are to:

(a) Explain your agency's rationale for the deviation. Before it can adequately comment on a potential deviation from the FMR, GSA must know why it is needed. GSA will compare your need against the applicable policies and regulations.

(b) Obtain clarification from GSA as to whether statutes, Executive orders, or other controlling policies, which may not be evident in the regulation, preclude deviating from the FMR for the reasons stated.

(c) Establish a timeframe for using a deviation.

(d) Identify potential changes to the FMR.

(e) Identify the benefits and other results that the agency expects to achieve.

§ 102–2.90 Where should my agency send its correspondence on an FMR deviation?

Send correspondence to: General Services Administration, Regulatory Secretariat (MVRS), Office of Governmentwide Policy, 1800 F Street, NW, Washington, DC 20405.

§ 102–2.95 What information must agencies include in their deviation letters to GSA?

Agencies must include:

(a) The title and citation of the FMR provision from which the agency wishes to deviate;

(b) The name and telephone number of an agency contact who can discuss the reason for the deviation;

(c) The reason for the deviation;

(d) A statement about the expected benefits of using the deviation (to the extent possible, expected benefits should be stated in measurable terms);

(e) A statement about possible use of the deviation in other agencies or Governmentwide; and

(f) The duration of the deviation.

§ 102–2.100 Must agencies provide GSA with a follow-up analysis of their experience in deviating from the FMR?

Yes, agencies that deviate from the FMR must also write to the relevant GSA program office at the Regulatory Secretariat's address (see § 102–2.90) to describe their experiences in using a deviation.

§ 102–2.105 What information must agencies include in their follow-up analysis?

In your follow-up analysis, provide information that may include, but should not be limited to, specific actions taken or not taken as a result of the deviation, outcomes, impacts, anticipated versus actual results, and the advantages and disadvantages of taking an alternative course of action.

§ 102–2.110 When must agencies provide their follow-up letters?

(a) For an individual deviation, once the action is complete.

(b) For a class deviation, at the end of each twelve-month period from the time you first took the deviation and at the end of the deviation period.

NON-REGULATORY MATERIAL

§ 102–2.115 What kinds of non-regulatory material does GSA publish outside of the FMR?

As GSA converts the FPMR to the FMR, non-regulatory materials in the FPMR, such as guidance, procedures, standards, and information, that describe how to do business with GSA, will become available in separate documents. These documents may include customer service guides, handbooks, brochures, Internet websites, and FMR bulletins. GSA will eliminate non-regulatory material that is no longer needed.

§ 102–2.120 How do I know whom to contact to discuss the regulatory requirements of programs addressed in the FMR?

Periodically, GSA will issue for your reference an FMR bulletin that lists program contacts with whom agencies can discuss regulatory requirements. At a minimum, the list will contain organization names and telephone numbers for each program addressed in the FMR.

§ 102–2.125 What source of information can my agency use to identify materials that describe how to do business with GSA?

The FMR establishes policy; it does not specify procedures for the acquisition of GSA services. However, as a service to users during the transition from the FPMR to the FMR and as needed thereafter, GSA will issue FMR bulletins to identify where to find information on how to do business with GSA. References include customer service guides, handbooks, brochures, Internet websites, etc.

Subpart B—Forms

§ 102–2.130 Where are FMR forms prescribed?

In any of its parts, the FMR may prescribe forms and the requirements for using them.

§ 102–2.135 How do agencies obtain forms prescribed by the FMR?

For copies of the forms prescribed by in the FMR, do any of the following:

(a) Write to us at: General Services Administration, National Forms and Publications Center (7CPN), Warehouse 4, Dock No. 1, 501 West Felix Street, Fort Worth, TX 76115.

(b) Send e-mail messages to: *NFPC@gsa-7FDepot.*

(c) Visit our web site at: *www.gsa.gov/ forms/forms.htm.*

Subpart C—Plain Language Regulatory Style

§ 102–2.140 What elements of plain language appear in the FMR?

The FMR is written in a "plain language" regulatory style. This style is easy to read and uses a question and answer format directed at the reader, active voice, shorter sentences, and, where appropriate, personal pronouns.

§ 102–2.145 To what do pronouns refer when used in the FMR?

Throughout its text, the FMR may contain pronouns such as, but not limited to, we, you, and I. When pronouns are used, each subchapter of the FMR will indicate whether they refer to the reader, an agency, GSA, or some other entity. In general, pronouns refer to who or what must perform a required action.

PART 102–3—FEDERAL ADVISORY COMMITTEE MANAGEMENT

Subpart A—What Policies Apply to Advisory Committees Established Within the Executive Branch?

Subpart B—How Are Advisory Committees Established, Renewed, Reestablished, and Terminated?

Subpart C—How Are Advisory Committees Managed?

AUTHORITY: Sec. 205(c), 63 Stat. 390 (40 U.S.C. 486(c)); sec. 7, 5 U.S.C., App.; and E.O. 12024, 3 CFR, 1977 Comp., p. 158.

SOURCE: At 66 FR 37733, July 19, 2001, unless otherwise noted.

Subpart A—What Policies Apply to Advisory Committees Established Within the Executive Branch?

§ 102–3.5 What does this subpart cover and how does it apply?

This subpart provides the policy framework that must be used by agency heads in applying the Federal Advisory Committee Act (FACA), as amended (or "the Act"), 5 U.S.C., App., to advisory committees they establish and operate. In addition to listing key definitions underlying the interpretation of the Act, this subpart establishes the scope and applicability of the Act, and outlines specific exclusions from its coverage.

§ 102–3.10 What is the purpose of the Federal Advisory Committee Act?

FACA governs the establishment, operation, and termination of advisory committees within the executive branch of the Federal Government. The Act defines what constitutes a Federal advisory committee and provides general procedures for the executive branch to follow for the operation of these advisory committees. In addition, the Act is designed to assure that the Congress and the public are kept informed with respect to the number, purpose, membership, activities, and cost of advisory committees.

§ 102–3.15 Who are the intended users of this part?

(a) The primary users of this Federal Advisory Committee Management part are:

(1) Executive branch officials and others outside Government currently involved with an established advisory committee;

(2) Executive branch officials who seek to establish or utilize an advisory committee;

(3) Executive branch officials and others outside Government who have decided to pursue, or who are already engaged in, a form of public involvement or consultation and want to avoid inadvertently violating the Act; and

(4) Field personnel of Federal agencies who are increasingly involved with

the public as part of their efforts to increase collaboration and improve customer service.

(b) Other types of end-users of this part include individuals and organizations outside of the executive branch who seek to understand and interpret the Act, or are seeking additional guidance.

§ 102–3.20 How does this part meet the needs of its audience?

This Federal Advisory Committee Management part meets the general and specific needs of its audience by addressing the following issues and related topics:

(a) *Scope and applicability.* This part provides guidance on the threshold issue of what constitutes an advisory committee and clarifies the limits of coverage by the Act for the benefit of the intended users of this part.

(b) *Policies and guidelines.* This part defines the policies, establishes minimum requirements, and provides guidance to Federal officers and agencies for the establishment, operation, administration, and duration of advisory committees subject to the Act. This includes reporting requirements that keep Congress and the public informed of the number, purpose, membership, activities, benefits, and costs of these advisory committees. These requirements form the basis for implementing the Act at both the agency and Governmentwide levels.

(c) *Examples and principles.* This part provides summary-level key points and principles at the end of each subpart that provide more clarification on the role of Federal advisory committees in the larger context of public involvement in Federal decisions and activities. This includes a discussion of the applicability of the Act to different decisionmaking scenarios.

§ 102–3.25 What definitions apply to this part?

The following definitions apply to this Federal Advisory Committee Management part:

Act means the Federal Advisory Committee Act, as amended, 5 U.S.C., App.

Administrator means the Administrator of General Services.

Advisory committee subject to the Act, except as specifically exempted by the Act or by other statutes, or as not covered by this part, means any committee, board, commission, council, conference, panel, task force, or other similar group, which is established by statute, or established or utilized by the President or by an agency official, for the purpose of obtaining advice or recommendations for the President or on issues or policies within the scope of an agency official's responsibilities.

Agency has the same meaning as in 5 U.S.C. 551(1).

Committee Management Officer ("CMO"), means the individual designated by the agency head to implement the provisions of section 8(b) of the Act and any delegated responsibilities of the agency head under the Act.

Committee Management Secretariat ("Secretariat"), means the organization established pursuant to section 7(a) of the Act, which is responsible for all matters relating to advisory committees, and carries out the responsibilities of the Administrator under the Act and Executive Order 12024 (3 CFR, 1977 Comp., p. 158).

Committee meeting means any gathering of advisory committee members (whether in person or through electronic means) held with the approval of an agency for the purpose of deliberating on the substantive matters upon which the advisory committee provides advice or recommendations.

Committee member means an individual who serves by appointment or invitation on an advisory committee or subcommittee.

Committee staff means any Federal employee, private individual, or other party (whether under contract or not) who is not a committee member, and who serves in a support capacity to an advisory committee or subcommittee.

Designated Federal Officer ("DFO"), means an individual designated by the agency head, for each advisory committee for which the agency head is responsible, to implement the provisions of sections 10(e) and (f) of the Act and any advisory committee procedures of the agency under the control and supervision of the CMO.

Discretionary advisory committee means any advisory committee that is established under the authority of an agency head or authorized by statute. An advisory committee referenced in general (non-specific) authorizing language or Congressional committee report language is discretionary, and its establishment or termination is within the legal discretion of an agency head.

Independent Presidential advisory committee means any Presidential advisory committee not assigned by the Congress in law, or by President or the President's delegate, to an agency for administrative and other support.

Non-discretionary advisory committee means any advisory committee either required by statute or by Presidential directive. A *non-discretionary advisory committee* required by statute generally is identified specifically in a statute by name, purpose, or functions, and its establishment or termination is beyond the legal discretion of an agency head.

Presidential advisory committee means any advisory committee authorized by the Congress or directed by the President to advise the President.

Subcommittee means a group, generally not subject to the Act, that reports to an advisory committee and not directly to a Federal officer or agency, whether or not its members are drawn in whole or in part from the parent advisory committee.

Utilized for the purposes of the Act, does not have its ordinary meaning. A committee that is not established by the Federal Government is *utilized* within the meaning of the Act when the President or a Federal office or agency exercises actual management or control over its operation.

§ 102–3.30 What policies govern the use of advisory committees?

The policies to be followed by Federal departments and agencies in establishing and operating advisory committees consistent with the Act are as follows:

(a) *Determination of need in the public interest.* A discretionary advisory committee may be established only when it is essential to the conduct of agency business and when the information to be obtained is not already available through another advisory committee or source within the Federal Government. Reasons for deciding that an ad-visory committee is needed may include whether:

(1) Advisory committee deliberations will result in the creation or elimination of (or change in) regulations, policies, or guidelines affecting agency business;

(2) The advisory committee will make recommendations resulting in significant improvements in service or reductions in cost; or

(3) The advisory committee's recommendations will provide an important additional perspective or viewpoint affecting agency operations.

(b) *Termination.* An advisory committee must be terminated when:

(1) The stated objectives of the committee have been accomplished;

(2) The subject matter or work of the committee has become obsolete by the passing of time or the assumption of the committee's functions by another entity;

(3) The agency determines that the cost of operation is excessive in relation to the benefits accruing to the Federal Government;

(4) In the case of a discretionary advisory committee, upon the expiration of a period not to exceed two years, unless renewed;

(5) In the case of a non-discretionary advisory committee required by Presidential directive, upon the expiration of a period not to exceed two years, unless renewed by authority of the President; or

(6) In the case of a non-discretionary advisory committee required by statute, upon the expiration of the time explicitly specified in the statute, or implied by operation of the statute.

(c) *Balanced membership.* An advisory committee must be fairly balanced in its membership in terms of the points of view represented and the functions to be performed.

(d) *Open meetings.* Advisory committee meetings must be open to the public except where a closed or partially-closed meeting has been determined proper and consistent with the exemption(s) of the Government in the Sunshine Act, 5 U.S.C. 552b(c), as the basis for closure.

(e) *Advisory functions only.* The function of advisory committees is advisory only, unless specifically provided by statute or Presidential directive.

§ 102–3.35 What policies govern the use of subcommittees?

(a) In general, the requirements of the Act and the policies of this Federal Advisory Committee Management part do not apply to subcommittees of advisory committees that report to a parent advisory committee and not directly to a Federal officer or agency. However, this section does not preclude an agency from applying any provision of the Act and this part to any subcommittee of an advisory committee in any particular instance.

(b) The creation and operation of subcommittees must be approved by the agency establishing the parent advisory committee.

§ 102–3.40 What types of committees or groups are not covered by the Act and this part?

The following are examples of committees or groups that are not covered by the Act or this Federal Advisory Committee Management part:

(a) *Committees created by the National Academy of Sciences (NAS) or the National Academy of Public Administration (NAPA).* Any committee created by NAS or NAPA in accordance with section 15 of the Act, except as otherwise covered by subpart E of this part;

(b) *Advisory committees of the Central Intelligence Agency and the Federal Reserve System.* Any advisory committee established or utilized by the Central Intelligence Agency or the Federal Reserve System;

(c) *Committees exempted by statute.* Any committee specifically exempted from the Act by law;

(d) *Committees not actually managed or controlled by the executive branch.* Any committee or group created by non-Federal entities (such as a contractor or private organization), provided that these committees or groups are not actually managed or controlled by the executive branch;

(e) *Groups assembled to provide individual advice.* Any group that meets with a Federal official(s), including a public meeting, where advice is sought from the attendees on an individual basis and not from the group as a whole;

(f) *Groups assembled to exchange facts or information.* Any group that meets with a Federal official(s) for the purpose of exchanging facts or information;

(g) *Intergovernmental committees.* Any committee composed wholly of full-time or permanent part-time officers or employees of the Federal Government and elected officers of State, local and tribal governments (or their designated employees with authority to act on their behalf), acting in their official capacities. However, the purpose of such a committee must be solely to exchange views, information, or advice relating to the management or implementation of Federal programs established pursuant to statute, that explicitly or inherently share intergovernmental responsibilities or administration (see guidelines issued by the Office of Management and Budget (OMB) on section 204(b) of the Unfunded Mandates Reform Act of 1995, 2 U.S.C. 1534(b), OMB Memorandum M–95–20, dated September 21, 1995, available from the Committee Management Secretariat (MC), General Services Administration, 1800 F Street, NW., Washington, DC 20405–0002);

(h) *Intragovernmental committees.* Any committee composed wholly of full-time or permanent part-time officers or employees of the Federal Government;

(i) *Local civic groups.* Any local civic group whose primary function is that of rendering a public service with respect to a Federal program;

(j) *Groups established to advise State or local officials.* Any State or local committee, council, board, commission, or similar group established to advise or make recommendations to State or local officials or agencies; and

(k) *Operational committees.* Any committee established to perform primarily operational as opposed to advisory functions. Operational functions are those specifically authorized by statute or Presidential directive, such as making or implementing Government decisions or policy. A committee designated operational may be covered by the Act if it becomes primarily advisory in nature. It is the responsibility of the administering agency to determine whether a committee is primarily operational. If so, it does not fall under the requirements of the Act and this part.

APPENDIX A TO SUBPART A OF PART 102–3—KEY POINTS AND PRINCIPLES

This appendix provides additional guidance in the form of answers to frequently asked questions and identifies key points and principles that may be applied to situations not covered elsewhere in this subpart. The guidance follows:

Key points and principles	Section(s)	Question(s)	Guidance
I. FACA applies to advisory committees that are either "established" or "utilized" by an agency.	102–3.25, 102–3.40(d), 102–3.40(f)	1. A local citizens group wants to meet with a Federal official(s) to help improve the condition of a forest's trails and quality of concessions. May the Government meet with the group without chartering the group under the Act? 2. May an agency official attend meetings of external groups where advice may be offered to the Government during the course of discussions? 3. May an agency official participate in meetings of groups or organizations as a member without chartering the group under the Act? 4. Is the Act applicable to meetings between agency officials and their contractors, licensees, or other "private sector program partners?"	A. The answer to questions 1, 2, and 3 is yes, if the agency does not either "establish" or "utilize" (exercise "actual management or control" over) the group. (i) Although there is no precise legal definition of "actual management or control," the following factors may be used by an agency to determine whether or not a group is "utilized" within the meaning of the Act: (a) Does the agency manage or control the group's membership or otherwise determine its composition? (b) Does the agency manage or control the group's agenda? (c) Does the agency fund the group's activities? (ii) Answering "yes" to any or all of questions 1, 2, or 3 does not automatically mean the group is "utilized" within the meaning of the Act. However, an agency may need to reconsider the status of the group under the Act if the relationship in question essentially is indistinguishable from an advisory committee established by the agency. B. The answer to question 4 is no. Agencies often meet with contractors and licensees, individually and as a group, to discuss specific matters involving a contract's solicitation, issuance, and implementation, or an agency's efforts to ensure compliance with its regulations. Such interactions are not subject to the Act because these groups are not "established" or "utilized" for the purpose of obtaining advice or recommendations.
II. The development of consensus among all or some of the attendees at a public meeting or similar forum does not automatically invoke FACA.	102–3.25, 102–3.40(d), 102–3.40(f)	1. If, during a public meeting of the "town hall" type called by an agency, it appears that the audience is achieving consensus, or a common point of view, is this an indication that the meeting is subject to the Act and must be stopped?	A. No, the public meeting need not be stopped. (i) A group must either be "established" or "utilized" by the executive branch in order for the Act to apply. (ii) Public meetings represent a chance for individuals to voice their opinions and/or share information. In that sense, agencies do not either "establish" the assemblage of individuals as an advisory committee or "utilize" the attendees as an advisory committee because there are no elements of either "management" or "control" present or intended.

Key points and principles	Section(s)	Question(s)	Guidance
III. Meetings between a Federal official(s) and a collection of individuals where advice is sought from the attendees on an individual basis are not subject to the Act.	102–3.40(e)	1. May an agency official meet with a number of persons collectively to obtain their individual views without violating the Act? 2. Does the concept of an "individual" apply only to "natural persons?"	A. The answer to questions 1 and 2 is yes. The Act applies only where a group is established or utilized to provide advice or recommendations "as a group." (i) A mere assemblage or collection of individuals where the attendees are providing individual advice is not acting "as a group" under the Act. (ii) In this respect, "individual" is not limited to "natural persons." Where the group consists of representatives of various existing organizations, each representative individually may provide advice on behalf of that person's organization without violating the Act, if those organizations themselves are not "managed or controlled" by the agency.
IV. Meetings between Federal, State, local, and tribal elected officials are not subject to the Act.	102–3.40(g)	1. Is the exclusion from the Act covering elected officials of State, local, and tribal governments acting in their official capacities also applicable to associations of State officials?	A. Yes. The scope of activities covered by the exclusion from the Act for intergovernmental activities should be construed broadly to facilitate Federal/State/local/tribal discussions on shared intergovernmental program responsibilities or administration. Pursuant to a Presidential delegation, the Office of Management and Budget (OMB) issued guidelines for this exemption, authorized by section 204(b) of the Unfunded Mandates Reform Act of 1995, 2 U.S.C. 1534(b). (See OMB Memorandum M–95–20, dated September 21, 1995, published at 60 FR 50651 (September 29, 1995), and which is available from the Committee Management Secretariat (MC), General Services Administration, 1800 F Street, NW, Washington, DC 20405–0002).
V. Advisory committees established under the Act may perform advisory functions only, unless authorized to perform "operational" duties by the Congress or by Presidential directive.	102–3.30(e), 102–3.40(k)	1. Are "operational committees" subject to the Act, even if they may engage in some advisory activities?	A. No, so long as the operational functions performed by the committee constitute the "primary" mission of the committee. Only committees established or utilized by the executive branch in the interest of obtaining advice or recommendations are subject to the Act. However, without specific authorization by the Congress or direction by the President, Federal functions (decisionmaking or operations) cannot be delegated to, or assumed by, non-Federal individuals or entities.

Key points and principles	Section(s)	Question(s)	Guidance
VI. Committees authorized by the Congress in law or by Presidential directive to perform primarily "operational" functions are not subject to the Act.	102–3.40(k)	1. What characteristics are common to "operational committees?" 2. A committee created by the Congress by statute is responsible, for example, for developing plans and events to commemorate the contributions of wildlife to the enjoyment of the Nation's parks. Part of the committee's role includes providing advice to certain Federal agencies as may be necessary to coordinate these events. Is this committee subject to FACA?	A. In answer to question 1, non-advisory, or "operational" committees generally have the following characteristics: (i) Specific functions and/or authorities provided by the Congress in law or by Presidential directive; (ii) The ability to make and implement traditionally Governmental decisions; and (iii) The authority to perform specific tasks to implement a Federal program. B. Agencies are responsible for determining whether or not a committee primarily provides advice or recommendations and is, therefore, subject to the Act, or is primarily "operational" and not covered by FACA. C. The answer to question 2 is no. The committee is not subject to the Act because: (i) Its functions are to plan and implement specific tasks; (ii) The committee has been granted the express authority by the Congress to perform its statutorily required functions; and (iii) Its incidental role of providing advice to other Federal agencies is secondary to its primarily operational role of planning and implementing specific tasks and performing statutory functions.

Subpart B—How Are Advisory Committees Established, Renewed, Reestablished, and Terminated?

§ 102–3.45 What does this subpart cover and how does it apply?

Requirements for establishing and terminating advisory committees vary depending on the establishing entity and the source of authority for the advisory committee. This subpart covers the procedures associated with the establishment, renewal, reestablishment, and termination of advisory committees. These procedures include consulting with the Secretariat, preparing and filing an advisory committee charter, publishing notice in the FEDERAL REGISTER, and amending an advisory committee charter.

§ 102–3.50 What are the authorities for establishing advisory committees?

FACA identifies four sources of authority for establishing an advisory committee:

(a) *Required by statute.* By law where the Congress establishes an advisory committee, or specifically directs the President or an agency to establish it (*non-discretionary*);

(b) *Presidential authority.* By Executive order of the President or other Presidential directive (*non-discretionary*);

(c) *Authorized by statute.* By law where the Congress authorizes, but does not direct the President or an agency to establish it (*discretionary*); or

(d) *Agency authority.* By an agency under general authority in title 5 of the United States Code or under other general agency-authorizing statutes (*discretionary*).

§ 102–3.55 What rules apply to the duration of an advisory committee?

(a) An advisory committee automatically terminates two years after its date of establishment unless:

(1) The statutory authority used to establish the advisory committee provides a different duration;

(2) The President or agency head determines that the advisory committee has fulfilled the purpose for which it was established and terminates the advisory committee earlier;

(3) The President or agency head determines that the advisory committee is no longer carrying out the purpose

for which it was established and terminates the advisory committee earlier; or

(4) The President or agency head renews the committee not later than two years after its date of establishment in accordance with § 102–3.60. If an advisory committee needed by the President or an agency terminates because it was not renewed in a timely manner, or if the advisory committee has been terminated under the provisions of § 102–3.30(b), it can be reestablished in accordance with § 102–3.60.

(b) When an advisory committee terminates, the agency shall notify the Secretariat of the effective date of the termination.

§ 102–3.60 What procedures are required to establish, renew, or reestablish a discretionary advisory committee?

(a) *Consult with the Secretariat.* Before establishing, renewing, or reestablishing a discretionary advisory committee and filing the charter as addressed later in § 102–3.70, the agency head must consult with the Secretariat. As part of this consultation, agency heads are encouraged to engage in constructive dialogue with the Secretariat. With a full understanding of the background and purpose behind the proposed advisory committee, the Secretariat may share its knowledge and experience with the agency on how best to make use of the proposed advisory committee, suggest alternate methods of attaining its purpose that the agency may wish to consider, or inform the agency of a pre-existing advisory committee performing similar functions.

(b) *Include required information in the consultation.* Consultations covering the establishment, renewal, and reestablishment of advisory committees must, as a minimum, contain the following information:

(1) *Explanation of need.* An explanation stating why the advisory committee is essential to the conduct of agency business and in the public interest;

(2) *Lack of duplication of resources.* An explanation stating why the advisory committee's functions cannot be performed by the agency, another existing committee, or other means such as a public hearing; and

(3) *Fairly balanced membership.* A description of the agency's plan to attain fairly balanced membership. The plan will ensure that, in the selection of members for the advisory committee, the agency will consider a cross-section of those directly affected, interested, and qualified, as appropriate to the nature and functions of the advisory committee. Advisory committees requiring technical expertise should include persons with demonstrated professional or personal qualifications and experience relevant to the functions and tasks to be performed.

§ 102–3.65 What are the public notification requirements for discretionary advisory committees?

A notice to the public in the FEDERAL REGISTER is required when a discretionary advisory committee is established, renewed, or reestablished.

(a) *Procedure.* Upon receiving notice from the Secretariat that its review is complete in accordance with § 102–3.60(a), the agency must publish a notice in the FEDERAL REGISTER announcing that the advisory committee is being established, renewed, or reestablished. For the establishment of a new advisory committee, the notice also must describe the nature and purpose of the advisory committee and affirm that the advisory committee is necessary and in the public interest.

(b) *Time required for notices.* Notices of establishment and reestablishment of advisory committees must appear at least 15 calendar days before the charter is filed, except that the Secretariat may approve less than 15 calendar days when requested by the agency for good cause. This requirement for advance notice does not apply to advisory committee renewals, notices of which may be published concurrently with the filing of the charter.

§ 102–3.70 What are the charter filing requirements?

No advisory committee may meet or take any action until a charter has been filed by the Committee Management Officer (CMO) designated in accordance with section 8(b) of the Act, or by another agency official designated by the agency head.

(a) *Requirement for discretionary advisory committees.* To establish, renew, or reestablish a discretionary advisory committee, a charter must be filed with:

(1) The agency head;

(2) The standing committees of the Senate and the House of Representatives having legislative jurisdiction of the agency, the date of filing with which constitutes the official date of establishment for the advisory committee;

(3) The Library of Congress, Anglo-American Acquisitions Division, Government Documents Section, Federal Advisory Committee Desk, 101 Independence Avenue, SE., Washington, DC 20540–4172; and

(4) The Secretariat, indicating the date the charter was filed in accordance with paragraph (a)(2) of this section.

(b) *Requirement for non-discretionary advisory committees.* Charter filing requirements for non-discretionary advisory committees are the same as those in paragraph (a) of this section, except the date of establishment for a Presidential advisory committee is the date the charter is filed with the Secretariat.

(c) *Requirement for subcommittees that report directly to the Government.* Subcommittees that report directly to a Federal officer or agency must comply with this subpart and include in a charter the information required by § 102–3.75.

§ 102–3.75 **What information must be included in the charter of an advisory committee?**

(a) *Purpose and contents of an advisory committee charter.* An advisory committee charter is intended to provide a description of an advisory committee's mission, goals, and objectives. It also provides a basis for evaluating an advisory committee's progress and effectiveness. The charter must contain the following information:

(1) The advisory committee's official designation;

(2) The objectives and the scope of the advisory committee's activity;

(3) The period of time necessary to carry out the advisory committee's purpose(s);

(4) The agency or Federal officer to whom the advisory committee reports;

(5) The agency responsible for providing the necessary support to the advisory committee;

(6) A description of the duties for which the advisory committee is responsible and specification of the authority for any non-advisory functions;

(7) The estimated annual costs to operate the advisory committee in dollars and person years;

(8) The estimated number and frequency of the advisory committee's meetings;

(9) The planned termination date, if less than two years from the date of establishment of the advisory committee;

(10) The name of the President's delegate, agency, or organization responsible for fulfilling the reporting requirements of section 6(b) of the Act, if appropriate; and

(11) The date the charter is filed in accordance with § 102–3.70.

(b) The provisions of paragraphs (a)(1) through (11) of this section apply to all subcommittees that report directly to a Federal officer or agency.

§ 102–3.80 **How are minor charter amendments accomplished?**

(a) *Responsibility and limitation.* The agency head is responsible for amending the charter of an advisory committee. Amendments may be either minor or major. The procedures for making changes and filing amended charters will depend upon the authority basis for the advisory committee. Amending any existing advisory committee charter does not constitute renewal of the advisory committee under § 102–3.60.

(b) *Procedures for minor amendments.* To make a minor amendment to an advisory committee charter, such as changing the name of the advisory committee or modifying the estimated number or frequency of meetings, the following procedures must be followed:

(1) *Non-discretionary advisory committees.* The agency head must ensure that any minor technical changes made to current charters are consistent with

the relevant authority. When the Congress by law, or the President by Executive order, changes the authorizing language that has been the basis for establishing an advisory committee, the agency head or the chairperson of an independent Presidential advisory committee must amend those sections of the current charter affected by the new statute or Executive order, and file the amended charter as specified in § 102–3.70.

(2) *Discretionary advisory committees.* The charter of a discretionary advisory committee may be amended when an agency head determines that technical provisions of a filed charter are inaccurate, or specific provisions have changed or become obsolete with the passing of time, and that these amendments will not alter the advisory committee's objectives and scope substantially. The agency must amend the charter language as necessary and file the amended charter as specified in § 102–3.70.

§ 102–3.85 How are major charter amendments accomplished?

Procedures for making major amendments to advisory committee charters, such as substantial changes in objectives and scope, duties, and estimated costs, are the same as in § 102–3.80, except that for discretionary advisory committees an agency must:

(a) Consult with the Secretariat on the amended language, and explain the purpose of the changes and why they are necessary; and

(b) File the amended charter as specified in § 102–3.70.

APPENDIX A TO SUBPART B OF PART 102–3—KEY POINTS AND PRINCIPLES

This appendix provides additional guidance in the form of answers to frequently asked questions and identifies key points and principles that may be applied to situations not covered elsewhere in this subpart. The guidance follows:

Key points and principles	Section(s)	Question(s)	Guidance
I. Agency heads must consult with the Secretariat prior to establishing a discretionary advisory committee.	102–3.60, 102–3.115	1. Can an agency head delegate to the Committee Management Officer (CMO) responsibility for consulting with the Secretariat regarding the establishment, renewal, or reestablishment of discretionary advisory committees?	A. Yes. Many administrative functions performed to implement the Act may be delegated. However, those functions related to approving the final establishment, renewal, or reestablishment of discretionary advisory committees are reserved for the agency head. Each agency CMO should assure that their internal processes for managing advisory committees include appropriate certifications by the agency head.
II. Agency heads are responsible for complying with the Act, including determining which discretionary advisory committees should be established and renewed.	102–3.60(a), 102–3.105	1. Who retains final authority for establishing or renewing a discretionary advisory committee?	A. Although agency heads retain final authority for establishing or renewing discretionary advisory committees, these decisions should be consistent with § 102–3.105(e) and reflect consultation with the Secretariat under § 102–3.60(a).

Key points and principles	Section(s)	Question(s)	Guidance
III. An advisory committee must be fairly balanced in its membership in terms of the points of view represented and the functions to be performed.	102–3.30(c), 102–3.60(b)(3)	1. What factors should be considered in achieving a "balanced" advisory committee membership?	A. The composition of an advisory committee's membership will depend upon several factors, including: (i) The advisory committee's mission; (ii) The geographic, ethnic, social, economic, or scientific impact of the advisory committee's recommendations; (iii) The types of specific perspectives required, for example, such as those of consumers, technical experts, the public at-large, academia, business, or other sectors; (iv) The need to obtain divergent points of view on the issues before the advisory committee; and (v) The relevance of State, local, or tribal governments to the development of the advisory committee's recommendations.
IV. Charters for advisory committees required by statute must be filed every two years regardless of the duration provided in the statute.	102–3.70(b)	1. If an advisory committee's duration exceeds two years, must a charter be filed with the Congress and GSA every two years?	A. Yes. Section 14(b)(2) of the Act provides that: Any advisory committee established by an Act of Congress shall file a charter upon the expiration of each successive two-year period following the date of enactment of the Act establishing such advisory committee.

Subpart C—How Are Advisory Committees Managed?

§ 102–3.90 What does this subpart cover and how does it apply?

This subpart outlines specific responsibilities and functions to be carried out by the General Services Administration (GSA), the agency head, the Committee Management Officer (CMO), and the Designated Federal Officer (DFO) under the Act.

§ 102–3.95 What principles apply to the management of advisory committees?

Agencies are encouraged to apply the following principles to the management of their advisory committees:

(a) *Provide adequate support.* Before establishing an advisory committee, agencies should identify requirements and assure that adequate resources are available to support anticipated activities. Considerations related to support include office space, necessary supplies and equipment, Federal staff support, and access to key decisionmakers.

(b) *Focus on mission.* Advisory committee members and staff should be fully aware of the advisory committee's mission, limitations, if any, on its duties, and the agency's goals and objectives. In general, the more specific an advisory committee's tasks and the more focused its activities are, the higher the likelihood will be that the advisory committee will fulfill its mission.

(c) *Follow plans and procedures.* Advisory committee members and their agency sponsors should work together to assure that a plan and necessary procedures covering implementation are in place to support an advisory committee's mission. In particular, agencies should be clear regarding what functions an advisory committee can perform legally and those that it cannot perform.

(d) *Practice openness.* In addition to achieving the minimum standards of public access established by the Act and this part, agencies should seek to be as inclusive as possible. For example, agencies may wish to explore the use of the Internet to post advisory committee information and seek broader input from the public.

(e) *Seek feedback.* Agencies continually should seek feedback from advisory committee members and the public regarding the effectiveness of the advisory committee's activities. At regular intervals, agencies should communicate to the members how their advice has affected agency programs and decisionmaking.

§102–3.100 What are the responsibilities and functions of GSA?

(a) Under section 7 of the Act, the General Services Administration (GSA) prepares regulations on Federal advisory committees to be prescribed by the Administrator of General Services, issues other administrative guidelines and management controls for advisory committees, and assists other agencies in implementing and interpreting the Act. Responsibility for these activities has been delegated by the Administrator to the GSA Committee Management Secretariat.

(b) The Secretariat carries out its responsibilities by:

(1) Conducting an annual comprehensive review of Governmentwide advisory committee accomplishments, costs, benefits, and other indicators to measure performance;

(2) Developing and distributing Governmentwide training regarding the Act and related statutes and principles;

(3) Supporting the Interagency Committee on Federal Advisory Committee Management in its efforts to improve compliance with the Act;

(4) Designing and maintaining a Governmentwide shared Internet-based system to facilitate collection and use of information required by the Act;

(5) Identifying performance measures that may be used to evaluate advisory committee accomplishments; and

(6) Providing recommendations for transmittal by the Administrator to the Congress and the President regarding proposals to improve accomplishment of the objectives of the Act.

§102–3.105 What are the responsibilities of an agency head?

The head of each agency that establishes or utilizes one or more advisory committees must:

(a) Comply with the Act and this Federal Advisory Committee Management part;

(b) Issue administrative guidelines and management controls that apply to all of the agency's advisory committees subject to the Act;

(c) Designate a Committee Management Officer (CMO);

(d) Provide a written determination stating the reasons for closing any advisory committee meeting to the public, in whole or in part, in accordance with the exemption(s) of the Government in the Sunshine Act, 5 U.S.C. 552b(c), as the basis for closure;

(e) Review, at least annually, the need to continue each existing advisory committee, consistent with the public interest and the purpose or functions of each advisory committee;

(f) Determine that rates of compensation for members (if they are paid for their services) and staff of, and experts and consultants to advisory committees are justified and that levels of agency support are adequate;

(g) Develop procedures to assure that the advice or recommendations of advisory committees will not be inappropriately influenced by the appointing authority or by any special interest, but will instead be the result of the advisory committee's independent judgment;

(h) Assure that the interests and affiliations of advisory committee members are reviewed for conformance with applicable conflict of interest statutes, regulations issued by the U.S. Office of Government Ethics (OGE) including any supplemental agency requirements, and other Federal ethics rules;

(i) Designate a Designated Federal Officer (DFO) for each advisory committee and its subcommittees; and

(j) Provide the opportunity for reasonable participation by the public in advisory committee activities, subject to §102–3.140 and the agency's guidelines.

§102–3.110 What are the responsibilities of a chairperson of an independent Presidential advisory committee?

The chairperson of an independent Presidential advisory committee must:

(a) Comply with the Act and this Federal Advisory Committee Management part;

(b) Consult with the Secretariat concerning the designation of a Committee Management Officer (CMO) and Designated Federal Officer (DFO); and

(c) Consult with the Secretariat in advance regarding any proposal to close any meeting in whole or in part.

§ 102–3.115 What are the responsibilities and functions of an agency Committee Management Officer (CMO)?

In addition to implementing the provisions of section 8(b) of the Act, the CMO will carry out all responsibilities delegated by the agency head. The CMO also should ensure that sections 10(b), 12(a), and 13 of the Act are implemented by the agency to provide for appropriate recordkeeping. Records to be kept by the CMO include, but are not limited to:

(a) *Charter and membership documentation.* A set of filed charters for each advisory committee and membership lists for each advisory committee and subcommittee;

(b) *Annual comprehensive review.* Copies of the information provided as the agency's portion of the annual comprehensive review of Federal advisory committees, prepared according to § 102–3.175(b);

(c) *Agency guidelines.* Agency guidelines maintained and updated on committee management operations and procedures; and

(d) *Closed meeting determinations.* Agency determinations to close or partially close advisory committee meetings required by § 102–3.105.

§ 102–3.120 What are the responsibilities and functions of a Designated Federal Officer (DFO)?

The agency head or, in the case of an independent Presidential advisory committee, the Secretariat, must designate a Federal officer or employee who must be either full-time or permanent part-time, to be the DFO for each advisory committee and its subcommittees, who must:

(a) Approve or call the meeting of the advisory committee or subcommittee;

(b) Approve the agenda, except that this requirement does not apply to a Presidential advisory committee;

(c) Attend the meetings;

(d) Adjourn any meeting when he or she determines it to be in the public interest; and

(e) Chair the meeting when so directed by the agency head.

§ 102–3.125 How should agencies consider the roles of advisory committee members and staff?

FACA does not assign any specific responsibilities to members of advisory committees and staff, although both perform critical roles in achieving the goals and objectives assigned to advisory committees. Agency heads, Committee Management Officers (CMOs), and Designated Federal Officers (DFOs) should consider the distinctions between these roles and how they relate to each other in the development of agency guidelines implementing the Act and this Federal Advisory Committee Management part. In general, these guidelines should reflect:

(a) *Clear operating procedures.* Clear operating procedures should provide for the conduct of advisory committee meetings and other activities, and specify the relationship among the advisory committee members, the DFO, and advisory committee or agency staff;

(b) *Agency operating policies.* In addition to compliance with the Act, advisory committee members and staff may be required to adhere to additional agency operating policies; and

(c) *Other applicable statutes.* Other agency-specific statutes and regulations may affect the agency's advisory committees directly or indirectly. Agencies should ensure that advisory committee members and staff understand these requirements.

§ 102–3.130 What policies apply to the appointment, and compensation or reimbursement of advisory committee members, staff, and experts and consultants?

In developing guidelines to implement the Act and this Federal Advisory Committee Management part at the agency level, agency heads must address the following issues concerning advisory committee member and staff appointments, and considerations with respect to uniform fair rates of compensation for comparable services, or expense reimbursement of members, staff, and experts and consultants:

(a) *Appointment and terms of advisory committee members.* Unless otherwise provided by statute, Presidential directive, or other establishment authority,

24

advisory committee members serve at the pleasure of the appointing or inviting authority. Membership terms are at the sole discretion of the appointing or inviting authority.

(b) *Compensation guidelines.* Each agency head must establish uniform compensation guidelines for members and staff of, and experts and consultants to an advisory committee.

(c) *Compensation of advisory committee members not required.* Nothing in this subpart requires an agency head to provide compensation to any member of an advisory committee, unless otherwise required by a specific statute.

(d) *Compensation of advisory committee members.* When an agency has authority to set pay administratively for advisory committee members, it may establish appropriate rates of pay (including any applicable locality pay authorized by the President's Pay Agent under 5 U.S.C. 5304(h)), not to exceed the rate for level IV of the Executive Schedule under 5 U.S.C. 5315, unless a higher rate expressly is allowed by another statute. However, the agency head personally must authorize a rate of basic pay in excess of the maximum rate of basic pay established for the General Schedule under 5 U.S.C. 5332, or alternative similar agency compensation system. This maximum rate includes any applicable locality payment under 5 U.S.C. 5304. The agency may pay advisory committee members on either an hourly or a daily rate basis. The agency may not provide additional compensation in any form, such as bonuses or premium pay.

(e) *Compensation of staff.* When an agency has authority to set pay administratively for advisory committee staff, it may establish appropriate rates of pay (including any applicable locality pay authorized by the President's Pay Agent under 5 U.S.C. 5304(h)), not to exceed the rate for level IV of the Executive Schedule under 5 U.S.C. 5315, unless a higher rate expressly is allowed by another statute. However, the agency head personally must authorize a rate of basic pay in excess of the maximum rate of basic pay established for the General Schedule under 5 U.S.C. 5332, or alternative similar agency compensation system. This maximum rate includes any appli-cable locality payment under 5 U.S.C. 5304. The agency must pay advisory committee staff on an hourly rate basis. The agency may provide additional compensation, such as bonuses or premium pay, so long as aggregate compensation paid in a calendar year does not exceed the rate for level IV of the Executive Schedule, with appropriate proration for a partial calendar year.

(f) *Other compensation considerations.* In establishing rates of pay for advisory committee members and staff, the agency must comply with any applicable statutes, Executive orders, regulations, or administrative guidelines. In determining an appropriate rate of basic pay for advisory committee members and staff, an agency must give consideration to the significance, scope, and technical complexity of the matters with which the advisory committee is concerned, and the qualifications required for the work involved. The agency also should take into account the rates of pay applicable to Federal employees who have duties that are similar in terms of difficulty and responsibility. An agency may establish rates of pay for advisory committee staff based on the pay these persons would receive if they were covered by the General Schedule in 5 U.S.C. Chapter 51 and Chapter 53, subchapter III, or by an alternative similar agency compensation system.

(g) *Compensation of experts and consultants.* Whether or not an agency has other authority to appoint and compensate advisory committee members or staff, it also may employ experts and consultants under 5 U.S.C. 3109 to perform work for an advisory committee. Compensation of experts and consultants may not exceed the maximum rate of basic pay established for the General Schedule under 5 U.S.C. 5332 (that is, the GS–15, step 10 rate, excluding locality pay or any other supplement), unless a higher rate expressly is allowed by another statute. The appointment and compensation of experts and consultants by an agency must be in conformance with applicable regulations issued by the U. S. Office of Personnel Management (OPM) (See 5 CFR part 304.).

(h) *Federal employees assigned to an advisory committee.* Any advisory committee member or staff person who is a Federal employee when assigned duties to an advisory committee remains covered during the assignment by the compensation system that currently applies to that employee, unless that person's current Federal appointment is terminated. Any staff person who is a Federal employee must serve with the knowledge of the Designated Federal Officer (DFO) for the advisory committee to which that person is assigned duties, and the approval of the employee's direct supervisor.

(i) *Other appointment considerations.* An individual who is appointed as an advisory committee member or staff person immediately following termination of another Federal appointment with a full-time work schedule may receive compensation at the rate applicable to the former appointment, if otherwise allowed by applicable law (without regard to the limitations on pay established in paragraphs (d) and (e) of this section). Any advisory committee staff person who is not a current Federal employee serving under an assignment must be appointed in accordance with applicable agency procedures, and in consultation with the DFO and the members of the advisory committee involved.

(j) *Gratuitous services.* In the absence of any special limitations applicable to a specific agency, nothing in this subpart prevents an agency from accepting the gratuitous services of an advisory committee member or staff person who is not a Federal employee, or expert or consultant, who agrees in advance and in writing to serve without compensation.

(k) *Travel expenses.* Advisory committee members and staff, while engaged in the performance of their duties away from their homes or regular places of business, may be allowed reimbursement for travel expenses, including per diem in lieu of subsistence, as authorized by 5 U.S.C. 5703, for persons employed intermittently in the Government service.

(l) Services for advisory committee members with disabilities. While performing advisory committee duties, an advisory committee member with disabilities may be provided services by a personal assistant for employees with disabilities, if the member qualifies as an individual with disabilities as provided in section 501 of the Rehabilitation Act of 1973, as amended, 29 U.S.C. 791, and does not otherwise qualify for assistance under 5 U.S.C. 3102 by reason of being a Federal employee.

APPENDIX A TO SUBPART C OF PART 102–3—KEY POINTS AND PRINCIPLES

This appendix provides additional guidance in the form of answers to frequently asked questions and identifies key points and principles that may be applied to situations not covered elsewhere in this subpart. The guidance follows:

Key points and principles	Section	Question(s)	Guidance
I. FACA does not specify the manner in which advisory committee members and staff must be appointed	102–3.105, 102–3.130(a)	1. Does the appointment of an advisory committee member necessarily result in a lengthy process?	A. No. Each agency head may specify those policies and procedures, consistent with the Act and this part, or other specific authorizing statute, governing the appointment of advisory committee members and staff. B. Some factors that affect how long the appointment process takes include: (i) Solicitation of nominations; (ii) Conflict of interest clearances; (iii) Security or background evaluations; (iv) Availability of candidates; and (v) Other statutory or administrative requirements. C. In addition, the extent to which agency heads have delegated responsibility for selecting members varies from agency to agency and may become an important factor in the time it takes to finalize the advisory committee's membership.

Key points and principles	Section	Question(s)	Guidance
II. Agency heads retain the final authority for selecting advisory committee members, unless otherwise provided for by a specific statute or Presidential directive	102–3.130(a)	1. Can an agency head select for membership on an advisory committee from among nominations submitted by an organization?	A. The answer to question 1 is yes. Organizations may propose for membership individuals to represent them on an advisory committee. However, the agency head establishing the advisory committee, or other appointing authority, retains the final authority for selecting all members.
		2. If so, can different persons represent the organization at different meetings?	B. The answer to question 2 also is yes. Alternates may represent an appointed member with the approval of the establishing agency, where the agency head is the appointing authority.
III. An agency may compensate advisory committee members and staff, and also employ experts and consultants	102–3.130(d), 102–3.130(e), 102–3.130(g)	1. May members and staff be compensated for their service or duties on an advisory committee? 2. Are the guidelines the same for compensating both members and staff? 3. May experts and consultants be employed to perform other advisory committee work?	A. The answer to question 1 is yes. (i) However, FACA limits compensation for advisory committee members and staff to the rate for level IV of the Executive Schedule, unless higher rates expressly are allowed by other statutes. (ii) Although FACA provides for compensation guidelines, the Act does not require an agency to compensate its advisory committee members. B. The answer to question 2 is no. The guidelines for compensating members and staff are similar, but not identical. For example, the differences are that: (i) An agency "may" pay members on either an hourly or a daily rate basis, and "may not" provide additional compensation in any form, such as bonuses or premium pay; while (ii) An agency "must" pay staff on an hourly rate basis only, and "may" provide additional compensation, so long as aggregate compensation paid in a calendar year does not exceed the rate for level IV of the Executive Schedule, with appropriate proration for a partial calendar year. C. The answer to question 3 is yes. Other work not part of the duties of advisory committee members or staff may be performed by experts and consultants. For additional guidance on the employment of experts and consultants, agencies should consult the applicable regulations issued by the U. S. Office of Personnel Management (OPM). (See 5 CFR part 304.)
IV. Agency heads are responsible for ensuring that the interests and affiliations of advisory committee members are reviewed for conformance with applicable conflict of interest statutes and other Federal ethics rules.	102–3.105(h)	1. Are all advisory committee members subject to conflict of interest statutes and other Federal ethics rules? 2. Who should be consulted for guidance on the proper application of Federal ethics rules to advisory committee members?	A. The answer to question 1 is no. Whether an advisory committee member is subject to Federal ethics rules is dependent on the member's status. The determination of a member's status on an advisory committee is largely a personnel classification matter for the appointing agency. Most advisory committee members will serve either as a "representative" or a "special Government employee" (SGE), based on the role the member will play. In general, SGEs are covered by regulations issued by the U. S. Office of Government Ethics (OGE) and certain conflict of interest statutes, while representatives are not subject to these ethics requirements.

Key points and principles	Section	Question(s)	Guidance
			B. The answer to question 2 is the agency's Designated Agency Ethics Official (DAEO), who should be consulted prior to appointing members to an advisory committee in order to apply Federal ethics rules properly.
V. An agency head may delegate responsibility for appointing a Committee Management Officer (CMO) or Designated Federal Officer (DFO); however, there may be only one CMO for each agency.	102–3.105(c), 102–3.105(i)	1. Must an agency's CMO and each advisory committee DFO be appointed by the agency head?	A. The answer to question 1 is no. The agency head may delegate responsibility for appointing the CMO and DFOs. However, these appointments, including alternate selections, should be documented consistent with the agency's policies and procedures.
		2. May an agency have more than one CMO?	B. The answer to question 2 also is no. The functions of the CMO are specified in the Act and include oversight responsibility for all advisory committees within the agency. Accordingly, only one CMO may be appointed to perform these functions. The agency may, however, create additional positions, including those in its subcomponents, which are subordinate to the CMO's agencywide responsibilities and functions.
VI. FACA is the principal statute pertaining to advisory committees. However, other statutes may impact their use and operations.	102–3.125(c)	1. Do other statutes or regulations affect the way an agency carries out its advisory committee management program?	A. Yes. While the Act provides a general framework for managing advisory committees Governmentwide, other factors may affect how advisory committees are managed. These include: (i) The statutory or Presidential authority used to establish an advisory committee; (ii) A statutory limitation placed on an agency regarding its annual expenditures for advisory committees; (iii) Presidential or agency management directives; (iv) The applicability of conflict of interest statutes and other Federal ethics rules; (v) Agency regulations affecting advisory committees; and (vi) Other requirements imposed by statute or regulation on an agency or its programs, such as those governing the employment of experts and consultants or the management of Federal records.

Subpart D—Advisory Committee Meeting and Recordkeeping Procedures

§ 102–3.135 What does this subpart cover and how does it apply?

This subpart establishes policies and procedures relating to meetings and other activities undertaken by advisory committees and their subcommittees. This subpart also outlines what records must be kept by Federal agencies and what other documentation, including advisory committee minutes and reports, must be prepared and made available to the public.

§ 102–3.140 What policies apply to advisory committee meetings?

The agency head, or the chairperson of an independent Presidential advisory committee, must ensure that:

(a) Each advisory committee meeting is held at a reasonable time and in a manner or place reasonably accessible to the public, to include facilities that are readily accessible to and usable by persons with disabilities, consistent with the goals of section 504 of the Rehabilitation Act of 1973, as amended, 29 U.S.C. 794;

(b) The meeting room or other forum selected is sufficient to accommodate advisory committee members, advisory committee or agency staff, and a reasonable number of interested members of the public;

(c) Any member of the public is permitted to file a written statement with the advisory committee;

(d) Any member of the public may speak to or otherwise address the advisory committee if the agency's guidelines so permit; and

(e) Any advisory committee meeting conducted in whole or part by a teleconference, videoconference, the Internet, or other electronic medium meets the requirements of this subpart.

§ 102–3.145 What policies apply to subcommittee meetings?

If a subcommittee makes recommendations directly to a Federal officer or agency, or if its recommendations will be adopted by the parent advisory committee without further deliberations by the parent advisory committee, then the subcommittee's meetings must be conducted in accordance with all openness requirements of this subpart.

§ 102–3.150 How are advisory committee meetings announced to the public?

(a) A notice in the FEDERAL REGISTER must be published at least 15 calendar days prior to an advisory committee meeting, which includes:

(1) The name of the advisory committee (or subcommittee, if applicable);

(2) The time, date, place, and purpose of the meeting;

(3) A summary of the agenda, and/or topics to be discussed;

(4) A statement whether all or part of the meeting is open to the public or closed; if the meeting is closed state the reasons why, citing the specific exemption(s) of the Government in the Sunshine Act, 5 U.S.C. 552b(c), as the basis for closure; and

(5) The name and telephone number of the Designated Federal Officer (DFO) or other responsible agency official who may be contacted for additional information concerning the meeting.

(b) In exceptional circumstances, the agency or an independent Presidential advisory committee may give less than 15 calendar days notice, provided that the reasons for doing so are included in the advisory committee meeting notice published in the FEDERAL REGISTER.

§ 102–3.155 How are advisory committee meetings closed to the public?

To close all or part of an advisory committee meeting, the Designated Federal Officer (DFO) must:

(a) *Obtain prior approval.* Submit a request to the agency head, or in the case of an independent Presidential advisory committee, the Secretariat, citing the specific exemption(s) of the Government in the Sunshine Act, 5 U.S.C. 552b(c), that justify the closure. The request must provide the agency head or the Secretariat sufficient time (generally, 30 calendar days) to review the matter in order to make a determination before publication of the meeting notice required by § 102–3.150.

(b) *Seek General Counsel review.* The General Counsel of the agency or, in the case of an independent Presidential advisory committee, the General Counsel of GSA should review all requests to close meetings.

(c) *Obtain agency determination.* If the agency head, or in the case of an independent Presidential advisory committee, the Secretariat, finds that the request is consistent with the provisions in the Government in the Sunshine Act and FACA, the appropriate agency official must issue a determination that all or part of the meeting be closed.

(d) *Assure public access to determination.* The agency head or the chairperson of an independent Presidential advisory committee must make a copy of the determination available to the public upon request.

§ 102–3.160 What activities of an advisory committee are not subject to the notice and open meeting requirements of the Act?

The following activities of an advisory committee are excluded from the procedural requirements contained in this subpart:

(a) *Preparatory work.* Meetings of two or more advisory committee or subcommittee members convened solely to gather information, conduct research, or analyze relevant issues and facts in preparation for a meeting of the advisory committee, or to draft position papers for deliberation by the advisory committee; and

(b) *Administrative work.* Meetings of two or more advisory committee or subcommittee members convened solely to discuss administrative matters of the advisory committee or to receive administrative information from a Federal officer or agency.

§ 102–3.165 How are advisory committee meetings documented?

(a) The agency head or, in the case of an independent Presidential advisory committee, the chairperson must ensure that detailed minutes of each advisory committee meeting, including one that is closed or partially closed to the public, are kept. The chairperson of each advisory committee must certify the accuracy of all minutes of advisory committee meetings.

(b) The minutes must include:

(1) The time, date, and place of the advisory committee meeting;

(2) A list of the persons who were present at the meeting, including advisory committee members and staff, agency employees, and members of the public who presented oral or written statements;

(3) An accurate description of each matter discussed and the resolution, if any, made by the advisory committee regarding such matter; and

(4) Copies of each report or other document received, issued, or approved by the advisory committee at the meeting.

(c) The Designated Federal Officer (DFO) must ensure that minutes are certified within 90 calendar days of the meeting to which they relate.

§ 102–3.170 How does an interested party obtain access to advisory committee records?

Timely access to advisory committee records is an important element of the public access requirements of the Act. Section 10(b) of the Act provides for the contemporaneous availability of advisory committee records that, when taken in conjunction with the ability to attend committee meetings, provide a meaningful opportunity to com-prehend fully the work undertaken by the advisory committee. Although advisory committee records may be withheld under the provisions of the Freedom of Information Act (FOIA), as amended, if there is a *reasonable expectation* that the records sought fall within the exemptions contained in section 552(b) of FOIA, agencies may not require members of the public or other interested parties to file requests for non-exempt advisory committee records under the request and review process established by section 552(a)(3) of FOIA.

§ 102–3.175 What are the reporting and recordkeeping requirements for an advisory committee?

(a) *Presidential advisory committee follow-up report.* Within one year after a Presidential advisory committee has submitted a public report to the President, a follow-up report required by section 6(b) of the Act must be prepared and transmitted to the Congress detailing the disposition of the advisory committee's recommendations. The Secretariat shall assure that these reports are prepared and transmitted to the Congress as directed by the President, either by the President's delegate, by the agency responsible for providing support to a Presidential advisory committee, or by the responsible agency or organization designated in the charter of the Presidential advisory committee pursuant to § 102–3.75(a)(10). In performing this function, GSA may solicit the assistance of the President's delegate, the Office of Management and Budget (OMB), or the responsible agency Committee Management Officer (CMO), as appropriate. Reports shall be consistent with specific guidance provided periodically by the Secretariat.

(b) *Annual comprehensive review of Federal advisory committees.* To conduct an annual comprehensive review of each advisory committee as specified in section 7(b) of the Act, GSA requires Federal agencies to report information on each advisory committee for which a charter has been filed in accordance with § 102–3.70, and which is in existence during any part of a Federal fiscal year. Committee Management Officers (CMOs), Designated Federal Officers

(DFOs), and other responsible agency officials will provide this information by data filed electronically with GSA on a fiscal year basis, using a Governmentwide shared Internet-based system that GSA maintains. This information shall be consistent with specific guidance provided periodically by the Secretariat. The preparation of these electronic submissions by agencies has been assigned interagency report control number (IRCN) 0304–GSA-AN.

(c) *Annual report of closed or partially-closed meetings.* In accordance with section 10(d) of the Act, advisory committees holding closed or partially-closed meetings must issue reports at least annually, setting forth a summary of activities and such related matters as would be informative to the public consistent with the policy of 5 U.S.C. 552(b).

(d) *Advisory committee reports.* Subject to 5 U.S.C. 552, 8 copies of each report made by an advisory committee, including any report of closed or partially-closed meetings as specified in paragraph (c) of this section and, where appropriate, background papers prepared by experts or consultants, must be filed with the Library of Congress as required by section 13 of the Act for public inspection and use at the location specified § 102–3.70(a)(3).

(e) *Advisory committee records.* Official records generated by or for an advisory committee must be retained for the duration of the advisory committee. Upon termination of the advisory committee, the records must be processed in accordance with the Federal Records Act (FRA), 44 U.S.C. Chapters 21, 29–33, and regulations issued by the National Archives and Records Administration (NARA) (see 36 CFR parts 1220, 1222, 1228, and 1234), or in accordance with the Presidential Records Act (PRA), 44 U.S.C. Chapter 22.

APPENDIX A TO SUBPART D OF PART 102–3—KEY POINTS AND PRINCIPLES

This appendix provides additional guidance in the form of answers to frequently asked questions and identifies key points and principles that may be applied to situations not covered elsewhere in this subpart. The guidance follows:

Key points and principles	Section(s)	Question(s)	Guidance
I. With some exceptions, advisory committee meetings are open to the public	102–3.140, 102–3.145(a), 102–3.155	1. Must all advisory committee and subcommittee meetings be open to the public?	A. No. Advisory committee meetings may be closed when appropriate, in accordance with the exemption(s) for closure contained in the Government in the Sunshine Act, 5 U.S.C. 552b(c). (i) Subcommittees that report to a parent advisory committee, and not directly to a Federal officer or agency, are not required to open their meetings to the public or comply with the procedures in the Act for announcing meetings. (ii) However, agencies are cautioned to avoid excluding the public from attending any meeting where a subcommittee develops advice or recommendations that are not expected to be reviewed and considered by the parent advisory committee before being submitted to a Federal officer or agency. These exclusions may run counter to the provisions of the Act requiring contemporaneous access to the advisory committee deliberative process.

Key points and principles	Section(s)	Question(s)	Guidance
II. Notices must be published in the FEDERAL REGISTER announcing advisory committee meetings	102–3.150	1. Can agencies publish a single FEDERAL REGISTER notice announcing multiple advisory committee meetings?	A. Yes, agencies may publish a single notice announcing multiple meetings so long as these notices contain all of the information required by § 102–3.150. (i) "Blanket notices" should not announce meetings so far in advance as to prevent the public from adequately being informed of an advisory committee's schedule. (ii) An agency's Office of General Counsel should be consulted where these notices include meetings that are either closed or partially closed to the public.

Key points and principles	Section(s)	Question(s)	Guidance
III. Although certain advisory committee records may be withheld under the Freedom of Information Act (FOIA), as amended, 5 U.S.C. 552, agencies may not require the use of FOIA procedures for records available under section 10(b) of FACA	102–3.170	1. May an agency require the use of its internal FOIA procedures for access to advisory committee records that are not exempt from release under FOIA?	A. No. Section 10(b) of FACA provides that: Subject to section 552 of title 5, United States Code, the records, reports, transcripts, minutes, appendixes, working papers, drafts, studies, agenda, or other documents which were made available to or prepared for or by each advisory committee shall be available for public inspection and copying at a single location in the offices of the advisory committee or the agency to which the advisory committee reports until the advisory committee ceases to exist. (i) The purpose of section 10(b) of the Act is to provide for the contemporaneous availability of advisory committee records that, when taken in conjunction with the ability to attend advisory committee meetings, provide a meaningful opportunity to comprehend fully the work undertaken by the advisory committee. (ii) Although advisory committee records may be withheld under the provisions of FOIA if there is a reasonable expectation that the records sought fall within the exemptions contained in section 552(b) of FOIA, agencies may not require members of the public or other interested parties to file requests for non-exempt advisory committee records under the request and review process established by section 552(a)(3) of FOIA. (iii) Records covered by the exemptions set forth in section 552(b) of FOIA may be withheld. An opinion of the Office of Legal Counsel (OLC), U.S. Department of Justice concludes that: FACA requires disclosure of written advisory committee documents, including predecisional materials such as drafts, working papers, and studies. The disclosure exemption available to agencies under exemption 5 of FOIA for predecisional documents and other privileged materials is narrowly limited in the context of FACA to privileged "inter-agency or intra-agency" documents prepared by an agency and transmitted to an advisory committee. The language of the FACA statute and its legislative history support this restrictive application of exemption 5 to requests for public access to advisory committee documents. Moreover, since an advisory committee is not itself an agency, this construction is supported by the express language of exemption 5 which applies only to inter-agency or intra-agency materials. (iv) Agencies first should determine, however, whether or not records being sought by the public fall within the scope of FACA in general, and section 10(b) of the Act in particular, prior to applying the available exemptions under FOIA. (See OLC Opinion 12 Op. O.L.C. 73, dated April 29, 1988, which is available from the Committee Management Secretariat (MC), General Services Administration, 1800 F Street, NW., Washington, DC 20405–0002.)

Key points and principles	Section(s)	Question(s)	Guidance
IV. Advisory committee records must be managed in accordance with the Federal Records Act (FRA), 44 U.S.C. Chapters 21, 29–33, and regulations issued by the National Archives and Records Administration (NARA) (see 36 CFR parts 1220, 1222, 1228, and 1234), or the Presidential Records Act (PRA), 44 U.S.C. Chapter 22	102–175(e)	1. How must advisory committee records be treated and preserved?	A. In order to ensure proper records management, the Committee Management Officer (CMO), Designated Federal Officer (DFO), or other representative of the advisory committee, in coordination with the agency's Records Management Officer, should clarify upon the establishment of the advisory committee whether its records will be managed in accordance with the FRA or the PRA. B. Official records generated by or for an advisory committee must be retained for the duration of the advisory committee. Responsible agency officials are encouraged to contact their agency's Records Management Officer or NARA as soon as possible after the establishment of the advisory committee to receive guidance on how to establish effective records management practices. Upon termination of the advisory committee, the records must be processed in accordance with the FRA and regulations issued by NARA, or in accordance with the PRA. C. The CMO, DFO, or other representative of an advisory committee governed by the FRA, in coordination with the agency's Records Management Officer, must contact NARA in sufficient time to review the process for submitting any necessary disposition schedules of the advisory committee's records upon termination. In order to ensure the proper disposition of the advisory committee's records, disposition schedules need to be submitted to NARA no later than 6 months before the termination of the advisory committee. D. For Presidential advisory committees governed by the PRA, the CMO, DFO, or other representative of the advisory committee should consult with the White House Counsel on the preservation of any records subject to the PRA, and may also confer with NARA officials.

Subpart E—How Does This Subpart Apply to Advice or Recommendations Provided to Agencies by the National Academy of Sciences or the National Academy of Public Administration?

§ 102–3.180 What does this subpart cover and how does it apply?

This subpart provides guidance to agencies on compliance with section 15 of the Act. Section 15 establishes requirements that apply only in connection with a funding or other written agreement involving an agency's use of advice or recommendations provided to the agency by the National Academy of Sciences (NAS) or the National Academy of Public Administration (NAPA), if such advice or recommendations were developed by use of a committee created by either academy. For purposes of this subpart, NAS also includes the National Academy of Engineering, the Institute of Medicine, and the National Research Council. Except with respect to NAS committees that were the subject of judicial actions filed before December 17, 1997, no part of the Act other than section 15 applies to any committee created by NAS or NAPA.

§ 102–3.185　What does this subpart require agencies to do?

(a) *Section 15 requirements.* An agency may not use any advice or recommendation provided to an agency by the National Academy of Sciences (NAS) or the National Academy of Public Administration (NAPA) under an agreement between the agency and an academy, if such advice or recommendation was developed by use of a committee created by either academy, unless:

(1) The committee was not subject to any actual management or control by an agency or officer of the Federal Government; and

(2) In the case of NAS, the academy certifies that it has complied substantially with the requirements of section 15(b) of the Act; or

(3) In the case of NAPA, the academy certifies that it has complied substantially with the requirements of sections 15(b) (1), (2), and (5) of the Act.

(b) *No agency management or control.* Agencies must not manage or control the specific procedures adopted by each academy to comply with the requirements of section 15 of the Act that are applicable to that academy. In addition, however, any committee created and used by an academy in the development of any advice or recommendation to be provided by the academy to an agency must be subject to both actual management and control by that academy and not by the agency.

(c) *Funding agreements.* Agencies may enter into contracts, grants, and cooperative agreements with NAS or NAPA that are consistent with the requirements of this subpart to obtain advice or recommendations from such academy. These funding agreements require, and agencies may rely upon, a written certification by an authorized representative of the academy provided to the agency upon delivery to the agency of each report containing advice or recommendations required under the agreement that:

(1) The academy has adopted policies and procedures that comply with the applicable requirements of section 15 of the Act; and

(2) To the best of the authorized representative's knowledge and belief, these policies and procedures substantially have been complied with in performing the work required under the agreement.

APPENDIX A TO SUBPART E OF PART 102–3—KEY POINTS AND PRINCIPLES

This appendix provides additional guidance in the form of answers to frequently asked questions and identifies key points and principles that may be applied to situations not covered elsewhere in this subpart. The guidance follows:

Key points and principles	Section(s)	Question(s)	Guidance
I. Section 15 of the Act allows the National Academy of Sciences (NAS) and the National Academy of Public Administration (NAPA) to adopt separate procedures for complying with FACA	102–3.185(a)	1. May agencies rely upon an academy certification regarding compliance with section 15 of the Act if different policies and procedures are adopted by NAS and NAPA?	A. Yes. NAS and NAPA are completely separate organizations. Each is independently chartered by the Congress for different purposes, and Congress has recognized that the two organizations are structured and operate differently. Agencies should defer to the discretion of each academy to adopt policies and procedures that will enable it to comply substantially with the provisions of section 15 of the Act that apply to that academy.
II. Section 15 of the Act allows agencies to enter into funding agreements with NAS and NAPA without the academies' committees being "managed" or "controlled"	102–3.185(c)	1. Can an agency enter into a funding agreement with an academy which provides for the preparation of one or more academy reports containing advice or recommendations to the agency, to be developed by the academy by use of a committee created by the academy, without subjecting an academy to "actual management or control" by the agency?	A. Yes, if the members of the committee are selected by the academy and if the committee's meetings, deliberations, and the preparation of reports are all controlled by the academy. Under these circumstances, neither the existence of the funding agreement nor the fact that it contemplates use by the academy of an academy committee would constitute actual management or control of the committee by the agency.

PART 102-4—NONDISCRIMINATION IN FEDERAL FINANCIAL ASSISTANCE PROGRAMS [RESERVED]

PART 102-5—HOME-TO-WORK TRANSPORTATION

Subpart A—General

AUTHORITY: 40 U.S.C. 121(c); 31 U.S.C. 1344(e)(1).

SOURCE: 65 FR 54966, Sept. 12, 2000, unless otherwise noted.

Subpart A—General

§ 102-5.5   Preamble.

(a) The questions and associated answers in this part are regulatory in effect. Thus compliance with the written text of this part is required by all to whom it applies.

(b) The terms "we," "I," "our," "you," and "your," when used in this part, mean you as a Federal agency, an agency head, or an employee, as appropriate.

§ 102-5.10   What does this part cover?

This part covers the use of Government passenger carriers to transport employees between their homes and places of work.

§ 102-5.15   Who is covered by this part?

This part covers Federal agency employees in the executive, judicial, and legislative branches of the Government, with the exception of employees of the Senate, House of Representatives, Architect of the Capitol, and government of the District of Columbia.

§ 102-5.20   Who is not covered by this part?

This part does not cover:

(a) Employees who use a passenger carrier in conjunction with official travel, including temporary duty (TDY) or relocation;

(b) Employees who are essential for the safe and efficient performance of intelligence, counterintelligence, protective services, or criminal law enforcement duties when designated in writing as such by their agency head; or

(c) Employees who use a passenger carrier for transportation between places of employment and mass transit facilities (*see, e.g.*, 41 CFR 102–34.210).

[65 FR 54966, Sept. 12, 2000, as amended at 75 FR 41995, July 20, 2010]

§ 102–5.25 What additional guidance concerning home-to-work transportation should Federal agencies issue?

Each Federal agency using Government passenger carriers to provide home-to-work transportation for employees who are essential for the safe and efficient performance of intelligence, counterintelligence, protective services, or criminal law enforcement duties should issue guidance concerning such use.

§ 102–5.30 What definitions apply to this part?

The following definitions apply to this part:

Agency head means the highest official of a Federal agency.

Clear and present danger means highly unusual circumstances that present a threat to the physical safety of the employee or their property when the danger is:

(1) Real; and

(2) Immediate or imminent, not merely potential; and

(3) The use of a Government passenger carrier would provide protection not otherwise available.

Compelling operational considerations means those circumstances where home-to-work transportation is essential to the conduct of official business or would substantially increase a Federal agency's efficiency and economy.

Emergency means circumstances that exist whenever there is an immediate, unforeseeable, temporary need to provide home-to-work transportation for those employees necessary to the uninterrupted performance of the agency's mission. (An emergency may occur where there is a major disruption of available means of transportation to or from a work site, an essential Government service must be provided, and there is no other way to transport those employees.)

Employee means a Federal officer or employee of a Federal agency, including an officer or enlisted member of the Armed Forces.

Federal agency means:

(1) A department (as defined in section 18 of the Act of August 2, 1946 (41 U.S.C. 5a));

(2) An executive department (as defined in 5 U.S.C. 101);

(3) A military department (as defined in 5 U.S.C. 102);

(4) A Government corporation (as defined in 5 U.S.C. 103(1));

(5) A Government controlled corporation (as defined in 5 U.S.C. 103(2));

(6) A mixed-ownership Government corporation (as defined in 31 U.S.C. 9101(2));

(7) Any establishment in the executive branch of the Government (including the Executive Office of the President);

(8) Any independent regulatory agency (including an independent regulatory agency specified in 44 U.S.C. 3502(10));

(9) The Smithsonian Institution;

(10) Any nonappropriated fund instrumentality of the United States; and

(11) The United States Postal Service.

Field work means official work requiring the employee's presence at various locations other than his/her regular place of work. (Multiple stops (itinerant-type travel) within the accepted local commuting area, limited use beyond the local commuting area, or transportation to remote locations that are only accessible by Government-provided transportation are examples of field work.)

Home means the primary place where an employee resides and from which the employee commutes to his/her place of work.

Home-to-work transportation means the use of a Government passenger carrier to transport an employee between his/her home and place of work.

Passenger carrier means a motor vehicle, aircraft, boat, ship, or other similar means of transportation that is owned (including those that have come into the possession of the Government by forfeiture or donation), leased, or rented (non-TDY) by the United States Government.

Work means any place within the accepted commuting area, as determined by the Federal agency for the locality involved, where an employee performs his/her official duties.

Subpart B—Authorizing Home-to-Work Transportation

§ 102–5.35 Who is authorized home-to-work transportation?

By statute, certain Federal officials are authorized home-to-work transportation, as are employees who meet certain statutory criteria as determined by their agency head. The Federal officials authorized by statute are the President, the Vice-President, and other principal Federal officials and their designees, as provided in 31 U.S.C. 1344(b)(1) through (b)(7). Those employees engaged in field work, or faced with a clear and present danger, an emergency, or a compelling operational consideration may be authorized home-to-work transportation as determined by their agency head. No other employees are authorized home-to-work transportation.

§ 102–5.40 May the agency head delegate the authority to make home-to-work determinations?

No, the agency head may not delegate the authority to make home-to-work determinations.

§ 102–5.45 Should determinations be completed before an employee is provided with home-to-work transportation?

Yes, determinations should be completed before an employee is provided with home-to-work transportation unless it is impracticable to do so.

§ 102–5.50 May determinations be made in advance for employees who respond to unusual circumstances when they arise?

Yes, determinations may be made in advance when the Federal agency wants to have employees ready to respond to:

(a) A clear and present danger;

(b) An emergency; or

(c) A compelling operational consideration.

NOTE TO § 102–5.50: Implementation of these determinations is contingent upon one of the three circumstances occurring. Thus, these may be referred to as "contingency determinations."

§ 102–5.55 How do we prepare determinations?

Determinations must be in writing and include the:

(a) Name and title of the employee (or other identification, if confidential);

(b) Reason for authorizing home-to-work transportation; and

(c) Anticipated duration of the authorization.

§ 102–5.60 How long are initial determinations effective?

Initial determinations are effective for no longer than:

(a) Two years for field work, updated as necessary; and

(b) Fifteen days for other circumstances.

§ 102–5.65 What procedures apply when the need for home-to-work transportation exceeds the initial period?

The agency head may approve unlimited subsequent determinations, when the need for home-to-work transportation exceeds the initial period, for no longer than:

(a) Two years each for field work, updated as necessary; and

(b) Ninety calendar days each for other circumstances.

§ 102–5.70 What considerations apply in making a determination to authorize home-to-work transportation for field work?

Agencies should consider the following when making a determination to authorize home-to-work transportation for field work:

(a) The location of the employee's home in proximity to his/her work and to the locations where non-TDY travel is required; and

(b) The use of home-to-work transportation for field work should be authorized only to the extent that such transportation will substantially increase the efficiency and economy of the Government.

§102–5.75 What circumstances do not establish a basis for authorizing home-to-work transportation for field work?

The following circumstances do not establish a basis for authorizing home-to-work transportation for field work:

(a) When an employee assigned to field work is not actually performing field work.

(b) When the employee's workday begins at his/her work; or

(c) When the employee normally commutes to a fixed location, however far removed from his/her official duty station (for example, auditors or investigators assigned to a defense contractor plant).

NOTE TO §102–5.75: For instances where an employee is authorized home-to-work transportation under the field work provision, but performs field work only on an intermittent basis, the agency shall establish procedures to ensure that a Government passenger carrier is used only when field work is actually being performed. Although some employees' daily work station is not located in a Government office, these employees are not performing field work. Like all Government employees, employees working in a "field office" are responsible for their own commuting costs.

§102–5.80 What are some examples of positions that may involve field work?

Examples of positions that may involve field work include, but are not limited to:

(a) Quality assurance inspectors;

(b) Construction inspectors;

(c) Dairy inspectors;

(d) Mine inspectors;

(e) Meat inspectors; and

(f) Medical officers on outpatient service.

NOTE TO §102–5.80: The assignment of an employee to such a position does not, of itself, entitle an employee to receive daily home-to-work transportation.

§102–5.85 What information should our determination for field work include if positions are identified rather than named individuals?

If positions are identified rather than named individuals, your determination

for field work should include sufficient information to satisfy an audit, if necessary. This information should include the job title, number, and operational level where the work is to be performed (e.g., five recruiter personnel or, positions at the Detroit Army Recruiting Battalion).

NOTE TO §102–5.85: An agency head may elect to designate positions rather than individual names, especially in positions where rapid turnover occurs.

§102–5.90 Should an agency consider whether to base a Government passenger carrier at a Government facility near the employee's home or work rather than authorize the employee home-to-work transportation?

Yes, situations may arise where, for cost or other reasons, it is in the Government's interest to base a Government passenger carrier at a Government facility located near the employee's home or work rather than authorize the employee home-to-work transportation.

§102–5.95 Is the comfort and/or convenience of an employee considered sufficient justification to authorize home-to-work transportation?

No, the comfort and/or convenience of an employee is not considered sufficient justification to authorize home-to-work transportation.

§102–5.100 May we use home-to-work transportation for other than official purposes?

No, you may not use home-to-work transportation for other than official purposes. However, if your agency has prescribed rules for the incidental use of Government vehicles (as provided in 31 U.S.C. note), you may use the vehicle in accordance with those rules in connection with an existing home-to-work authorization.

§102–5.105 May others accompany an employee using home-to-work transportation?

Yes, an employee authorized home-to-work transportation may share space in a Government passenger carrier with other individuals, provided that the passenger carrier does not travel additional distances as a result and such sharing is consistent with his/her Federal agency's policy. When a Federal agency establishes its space sharing policy, the Federal agency should consider its potential liability for and to those individuals. Home-to-work transportation does not extend to the employee's spouse, other relatives, or friends unless they travel with the employee from the same point of departure to the same destination, and this use is consistent with the Federal agency's policy.

Subpart C—Documenting and Reporting Determinations

§ 102–5.110 Must we report our determinations outside of our agency?

Yes, you must submit your determinations to the following Congressional Committees:

(a) Chairman, Committee on Governmental Affairs, United States Senate, Suite SD–340, Dirksen Senate Office Building, Washington, DC 20510–6250; and

(b) Chairman, Committee on Governmental Reform, United States House of Representatives, Suite 2157, Rayburn House Office Building, Washington, DC 20515–6143.

§ 102–5.115 When must we report our determinations?

You must report your determinations to Congress no later than 60 calendar days after approval. You may consolidate any subsequent determinations into a single report and submit them quarterly.

§ 102–5.120 What are our responsibilities for documenting use of home-to-work transportation?

Your responsibilities for documenting use of home-to-work transportation are that you must maintain logs or other records necessary to verify that any home-to-work transportation was for official purposes. Each agency may decide the organizational level at which the logs should be maintained and kept. The logs or other records should be easily accessible for audit and should contain:

(a) Name and title of employee (or other identification, if confidential) using the passenger carrier;

(b) Name and title of person authorizing use;

(c) Passenger carrier identification;

(d) Date(s) home-to-work transportation is authorized;

(e) Location of residence;

(f) Duration; and

(g) Circumstances requiring home-to-work transportation.

PARTS 102–6—102–30 [RESERVED]

SUBCHAPTER B—PERSONAL PROPERTY

PART 102–31—GENERAL [RESERVED]

PART 102–32—MANAGEMENT OF PERSONAL PROPERTY [RESERVED]

PART 102–33—MANAGEMENT OF GOVERNMENT AIRCRAFT

Subpart A—How These Rules Apply

Subpart B—Acquiring Government Aircraft and Aircraft Parts

Subpart C—Managing Government Aircraft and Aircraft Parts

MANAGEMENT/ADMINISTRATION

102–33.160 What standards must we establish or require (contractually, where applicable) for management/administration of our flight program?

OPERATIONS

102–33.165 What standards must we establish or require (contractually, where applicable) for operation of our flight program?

MAINTENANCE

102–33.170 What standards must we establish or require (contractually, where applicable) for maintenance of our Government aircraft?

TRAINING

102–33.175 What standards must we establish or require (contractually, where applicable) to train our flight program personnel?

SAFETY

102–33.180 What standards should we establish or require (contractually, where applicable) for aviation safety management?

102–33.185 What standards should we establish or require (contractually, where applicable) for responding to aircraft accidents and incidents?

ACCOUNTING FOR THE COSTS OF GOVERNMENT AIRCRAFT

102–33.190 What are the aircraft operations and ownership costs for which we must account?

102–33.195 Do we need an automated system to account for aircraft costs?

102–33.200 Must we periodically justify owning and operating Federal aircraft?

102–33.205 When we use our aircraft to support other executive agencies, must we recover the operating costs?

ACCOUNTING FOR THE USE OF GOVERNMENT AIRCRAFT

102–33.210 How do we account for the use of our Government aircraft?

102–33.215 May we use Government aircraft to carry passengers?

102–33.220 What are the responsibilities of our aviation program in justifying the use of a Government aircraft to transport passengers?

MANAGING AIRCRAFT PARTS

102–33.225 How must we manage aircraft parts?

102–33.230 May we use military FSCAP on non-military FAA-type certificated Government aircraft?

102–33.235 What documentation must we maintain for life-limited parts and FSCAP?

Subpart D—Disposing or Replacing of Government Aircraft and Aircraft Parts

OVERVIEW

102–33.240 What must we consider before disposing or replacing aircraft and aircraft parts?

102–33.245 May we report as excess, or replace (i.e., by exchange/sale), both operational and non-operational aircraft?

102–33.250 May we declassify aircraft?

102–33.255 Must we document FSCAP or life-limited parts installed on aircraft that we will report as excess or replace?

102–33.260 When we report as excess, or replace, an aircraft (including a declassified aircraft), must we report the change in inventory to the Federal Aviation Interactive Reporting System (FAIRS)?

REPORTING EXCESS FEDERAL AIRCRAFT

102–33.265 What must we do with aircraft that are excess to our needs?

102–33.270 What is the process for reporting an excess aircraft?

REPLACING AIRCRAFT THROUGH EXCHANGE/ SALE

102–33.275 What should we consider before replacing our aircraft through an exchange/sale?

102–33.280 What are our options if we need a replacement aircraft?

102–33.285 Do we need to include any special disclaimers in our exchange/sale agreements for non-certificated aircraft or aircraft that we have operated as public aircraft (i.e., not in compliance with 14 CFR)?

102–33.295 May we exchange/sell an aircraft through reimbursable transfer to another executive agency or conduct a negotiated sale at fixed price to a State Agency for Surplus Property (SASP)?

DISPOSING OF AIRCRAFT PARTS

102–33.300 What must we consider before disposing of aircraft parts?

102–33.305 May we report as excess, or replace, FSCAP and life-limited parts?

102–33.310 May we report as excess, or replace, unsalvageable aircraft parts?

102–33.315 What are the procedures for mutilating unsalvageable aircraft parts?

102–33.320 What must we do if we are unable to perform required mutilation of aircraft parts?

102–33.325 What documentation must we furnish with excess, surplus, or replaced parts when they are transferred, donated, exchanged, or sold?

Subpart E—Reporting Information on Government Aircraft

AUTHORITY: 40 U.S.C. 121(c); 31 U.S.C. 101 *et seq.*; Reorganization Plan No. 2 of 1970, 35 FR 7959, 3 CFR, 1066–1970 Comp., p. 1070; Executive Order 11541, 35 FR 10737, 3 CFR, 1966–1970 Comp., p. 939; and OMB Circular No. A–126 (Revised May 22, 1992), 57 FR 22150.

SOURCE: 79 FR 77336, Dec. 23, 2014, unless otherwise noted.

Subpart A—How These Rules Apply

GENERAL

§ 102–33.5 To whom do these rules apply?

(a) The rules in this part apply to all Federally-funded aviation activities of executive branch agencies of the U.S. Government who use Government aircraft to accomplish their official business, except for the exemptions listed in paragraph (b) of this section.

(b) The rules in this part do not apply to the following:

(1) The Armed Forces, except for:

(i) Section 102–33.25(e) and (g), which concern responsibilities related to the Interagency Committee for Aviation Policy (ICAP); and

(ii) Subpart D of this part, "Disposing of Government Aircraft and Aircraft Parts."

(2) The President or Vice President and their offices;

(3) Aircraft when an executive agency provides Government-furnished avionics for commercially owned or privately owned aircraft for the purposes of technology demonstration or testing; and

(4) Privately owned aircraft that agency personnel use for official travel (even though such use is Federally-funded).

§ 102–33.6 How are the terms "we," "you," "your," and "our" used in this part?

In this part, "we", "you", "your", and "our" refer to agency aviation managers or an executive agency.

§ 102–33.10 May we request approval to deviate from these rules?

(a) You may request approval to deviate from the rules in this part. See §§ 102–2.60 through 102–2.110 of this chapter for guidance on requesting a deviation. In most cases, GSA will respond to your written request within 30 days;

(b) GSA may not grant deviations from the requirements of OMB Circular A–126, "Improving the Management of Government Aircraft;" and

(c) You should consult with GSA's Aviation Policy Division before you request a deviation.

§ 102–33.15 How does this part relate to Title 14 of the Code of Federal Regulations?

This part does not supersede any of the regulations in 14 CFR Chapter I, "Federal Aviation Administration, Department of Transportation."

§ 102–33.20 What definitions apply to this part?

The following definitions apply to this part:

Acquire means to procure or otherwise obtain personal property, including by lease or rent.

Acquisition date means the date that the acquiring executive agency took responsibility for the aircraft, *e.g.*, received title (through purchase, exchange, or gift), signed a bailment agreement with the Department of Defense (DOD), took physical custody, received a court order, put into operational status an aircraft that is newly manufactured by the agency, or otherwise accepted physical transfer (*e.g.*, in the case of a borrowed aircraft).

Aircraft part means an individual component or an assembly of components that is used on aircraft.

Armed Forces mean the Army, Navy, Air Force, Marine Corps, and Coast Guard, including their regular and Reserve components and members serving without component status. For purposes of this part, the National Guard is also included in the Armed Forces.

Aviation life support equipment (ALSE) means equipment that protects flight crewmembers and others aboard an aircraft, assisting their safe escape, survival, and recovery during an accident or other emergency.

Aviation Policy Division is a division in the Office of Asset and Transportation Management, Office of Government-wide Policy, GSA. Contact the staff via the Aircraft Management Overview page at *http://www.gsa.gov/aviationpolicy*.

Crewmember means a person assigned to operate or assist in operating an aircraft during flight time. Crewmembers perform duties directly related to the operation of the aircraft (*e.g.*, as pilots, co-pilots, flight engineers, navigators) or duties assisting in operation of the aircraft (*e.g.*, as flight directors, crew chiefs, electronics technicians, mechanics). See also the terms and definitions for "Qualified non-crewmember" and "Passenger" in this section.

Criticality code means a single digit code that DOD assigns to military Flight Safety Critical Aircraft Parts (FSCAP) (see §§ 102–33.115 and 102–33.370).

Data plate means a fireproof plate that is inscribed with certain information required by 14 CFR part 45 (or for military surplus aircraft, as required by Military Specifications), and secured to an aircraft, aircraft engine, or propeller. The information must be marked by etching, stamping, engraving, or other approved method of fireproof marking. The plate must be attached in such a manner that it is not likely to be defaced or removed during normal service or lost or destroyed in an accident. Data plates are required only on certificated aircraft. However, non-certificated aircraft may also have data plates.

Declassify means to remove a lost, destroyed, or non-operational aircraft from the Federal aircraft inventory. Agencies may declassify only non-operational aircraft that they will retain for ground use only. Agencies must declassify an aircraft following the rules in §§ 102–33.415 and 102–33.420.

Disposal date means the date that the disposing executive agency relinquishes responsibility for an aircraft, for example, when the agency transfers title in the case of an exchange/sale; returns the aircraft to the lessor or bailer; declassifies it (for FAIRS, declassification is considered a "disposal" action, even though the agency retains the property); or relinquishes custody to another agency (*i.e.*, in the case of excess (transferred) or surplus (donated or sold) aircraft).

Donated aircraft means an aircraft disposed of as surplus by GSA through donation to a non-Federal government, a tax-exempt nonprofit entity, or other eligible recipient, following the rules in part § 102–37 (some agencies, for example DOD, may have independent donation authority.)

Exchange means to replace personal property by trade or trade-in with the supplier of the replacement property.

Exchange/sale means to exchange or sell non-excess, non-surplus personal property and apply the exchange allowance or proceeds of sale in whole or in part payment for the acquisition of similar property. See 40 U.S.C. 503.

Exclusive use means a condition under which an aircraft is operated for the sole benefit of the U.S. Government.

Executive agency means any executive department or independent establishment in the executive branch of the United States Government, including any wholly owned Government corporation. See 5 U.S.C. 105.

Federal Acquisition Service (FAS) means a component of GSA. FAS is or-

ganized by geographical regions. The FAS Property Management Division in GSA's Pacific Rim Region, 450 Golden Gate Ave., San Francisco, CA 94102–3434, has responsibility for disposing of excess and surplus aircraft.

Federal aircraft means manned or unmanned aircraft that an executive agency owns (*i.e.*, holds title to) or borrows for any length of time. Federal aircraft include—

(1) Bailed aircraft: Federal aircraft that is owned by one executive agency, but is in the custody of and operated by another executive agency under an agreement that may or may not include cost-reimbursement. Bailments are executive agency to executive agency agreements and involve only aircraft, not services;

(2) Borrowed aircraft: Aircraft owned by a non-executive agency and provided to an executive agency for use without compensation. The executive agency operates and maintains the aircraft;

(3) Forfeited aircraft: Aircraft acquired by the Government either by summary process or by order of a court of competent jurisdiction pursuant to any law of the United States;

(4) Loaned aircraft: Federal aircraft owned by an executive agency, but in the custody of a non-executive agency under an agreement that does not include compensation; and

(5) Owned aircraft: An aircraft for which title or rights of title are vested in an executive agency.

NOTE TO DEFINITION OF FEDERAL AIRCRAFT: When an executive agency loans or bails an aircraft that meets the criteria for Federal aircraft, the loaned or bailed aircraft is still considered a Federal aircraft in the owning agency's inventory, except when DOD is the owning agency of a bailed aircraft. In that case, the aircraft is recorded in the inventory of the bailee.

Federal Aviation Interactive Reporting System (FAIRS) is a management information system operated by GSA to collect, maintain, analyze, and report information on Federal aircraft inventories and cost and usage of Federal aircraft and CAS aircraft (and related services) (see §§ 102–33.395 through 102–33.440).

Flight Safety Critical Aircraft Part (FSCAP) means any aircraft part, assembly, or installation containing a critical characteristic whose failure, malfunction, or absence could cause a catastrophic failure resulting in loss or serious damage to the aircraft or an uncommanded engine shutdown resulting in an unsafe condition.

Full service contract means a contractual agreement through which an executive agency acquires an aircraft and related aviation services (*e.g.*, pilot, crew, maintenance, catering) for exclusive use. Aircraft hired under full service contracts are commercial aviation services (CAS), not Federal aircraft, regardless of the length of the contract.

Government aircraft means manned or unmanned aircraft operated for the exclusive use of an executive agency. Government aircraft include—

(1) Federal aircraft (see definition for "Federal aircraft" in this section); and

(2) Aircraft hired as commercial aviation services (CAS). CAS include—

(i) Leased aircraft for exclusive use for an agreed upon period of time (The acquiring executive agency operates and maintains the aircraft);

(ii) Capital lease aircraft for which the leasing agency holds an option to take title;

(iii) Charter aircraft for hire under a contractual agreement for one-time exclusive use that specifies performance (The commercial source operates and maintains a charter aircraft);

(iv) Rental aircraft obtained commercially under an agreement in which the executive agency has exclusive use for an agreed upon period of time (The executive agency operates, but does not maintain, a rental aircraft);

(v) Contracting for full services (*i.e.*, aircraft and related aviation services for exclusive use); or

(vi) Obtaining related aviation services (*i.e.*, services but not aircraft) by commercial contract, except those services acquired to support a Federal aircraft.

Governmental function means a Federally-funded activity that an executive agency performs in compliance with its statutory authorities.

Intelligence community means those agencies identified in the National Security Act, 50 U.S.C. 401a(4).

Inter-service support agreement (ISSA) means any agreement between two or more executive agencies (including the Department of Defense) in which one agency consents to perform aviation support services (*e.g.*, providing an aircraft and other aviation services or providing only services) for another agency with or without cost-reimbursement. An executive agency-to-executive agency agreement that involves only the use of an aircraft, not services, is a bailment, not an ISSA.

Life-limited part means any aircraft part that has an established replacement time, inspection interval, or other time-related procedure associated with it. For non-military parts, the FAA specifies life-limited part airworthiness limitations in 14 CFR 21.50, 23.1529, 25.1529, 27.1529, 29.1529, 31.82, 33.4, and 35.5, and on product Type Certificate Data Sheets (TCDS). Letters authorizing Technical Standards Orders (TSO) must also note or reference mandatory replacement or inspection of parts.

Military aircraft part means an aircraft part used on an aircraft that was developed by the Armed Forces (whether or not it carries an FAA airworthiness certificate).

Non-operational aircraft means a Federal aircraft that is not safe for flight and, in the owning executive agency's determination, cannot economically be made safe for flight. This definition refers to the aircraft's flight capability, not its mission-support equipment capability. An aircraft that is temporarily out of service for maintenance or repair and can economically be made safe for flight is considered an operational aircraft.

Official Government business in relation to Government aircraft—

(1) Includes, but is not limited to—

(i) Carrying crewmembers, qualified non-crewmembers, and cargo directly required for or associated with performing Governmental functions (including travel-related Governmental functions);

(ii) Carrying passengers authorized to travel on Government aircraft (see OMB Circular A–126); and

(iii) Training pilots and other aviation personnel.

(2) Does not include—

(i) Using Government aircraft for personal or political purposes, except for required use travel and space available travel as defined in OMB Circular A–126; or

(ii) Carrying passengers who are not officially authorized to travel on Government aircraft.

Operational aircraft means a Federal aircraft that is safe for flight or, in the owning executive agency's determination, can economically be made safe for flight. This definition refers to the aircraft's flight capability, not its mission-support capability. An aircraft temporarily out of service for maintenance or repair is considered an operational aircraft.

Original equipment manufacturer (OEM) means the person or company who originally designed, engineered, and manufactured, or who currently holds the data rights to manufacture, a specific aircraft or aircraft part. Parts produced under a Parts Manufacturer Approval (PMA) are not considered OEM parts, even though they can be acceptable replacement parts for OEM parts.

Passenger means a person flying on-board a Government aircraft who is officially authorized to travel and who is not a crewmember or qualified non-crewmember.

Performance indicator means a quantitative or qualitative term or value for reporting organizational activities and results, generally with respect to achieving specific goals related to outcomes, outputs, efficiency, and inputs. When applied to aircraft, performance indicators typically measure the effectiveness and efficiency of the processes involved with safely delivering aircraft services.

Production approval holder (PAH) means the person or company who holds a Production Certificate (PC), Approved Production Inspection System (APIS), Parts Manufacturer Approval (PMA), or Technical Standards Orders Authorization (TSOA), issued under provisions of 14 CFR part 21, Certification Procedures for Products and Parts, and who controls the design, manufacture, and quality of a specific aircraft part.

Qualified non-crewmember means an individual, other than a member of the crew, aboard an aircraft—

(1) Operated by an United States Government agency in the intelligence community; or

(2) Whose presence is required to perform or is associated with performing the Governmental function for which the aircraft is being operated (Qualified non-crewmembers are not passengers).

Registration mark means the unique identification mark that is assigned by the FAA and displayed on U.S.-registered Government aircraft (except Armed Forces aircraft). Foreign-registered aircraft hired as CAS will carry their national registration markings. Registration markings are commonly referred to as tail numbers.

Related aviation services contract means a commercial contractual agreement through which an executive agency hires aviation services only (not aircraft), *e.g.,* pilot, crew, maintenance, cleaning, dispatching, or catering.

Required use travel means use of a Government aircraft for the travel of an executive agency officer or employee where the use of the Government aircraft is required because of bona fide communications or security need of the agency or exceptional scheduling requirements. Required use travel must be approved as described in OMB Circular A–126.

Risk analysis and management means a systematic process for—

(1) Identifying risks and hazards associated with alternative courses of action involved in an aviation operation;

(2) Choosing from among these alternatives the course(s) of action that will promote optimum aviation safety;

(3) Assessing the likelihood and predicted severity of an injurious mishap within the various courses of action;

(4) Controlling and mitigating identified risks and hazards within the chosen course(s) of action; and

(5) Periodically reviewing the chosen course(s) of action to identify possible emerging risks and hazards.

Safe for flight means approved for flight and refers to an aircraft, aircraft engine, propeller, appliance, or part that has been inspected and certified to meet the requirements of applicable regulations, specifications, or standards. When applied to an aircraft that an executive agency operates under FAA regulations, safe for flight means "airworthy," *i.e.*, the aircraft or related parts meet their design specifications and are in a condition, relative to wear and deterioration, for safe operation. When applied to an aircraft that an executive agency uses, but does not operate under the FAA regulations, safe for flight means a state of compliance with military specifications or the executive agency's own Flight Program Standards, and as approved, inspected, and certified by the agency.

Safety Management System (SMS) means a formal, top-down business-like approach to managing safety risk. It includes systematic procedures, practices, and policies for the management of safety, safety risk management, safety policy, safety assurance, and safety promotion. For more information on SMS, refer to FAA Advisory Circular 120–92, "Safety Management Systems for Aviation Service Providers."

Senior Aviation Management Official (SAMO) means the person in an executive agency who is the agency's primary member of the Interagency Committee for Aviation Policy (ICAP). This person must be of appropriate grade and position to represent the agency and promote flight safety and adherence to standards.

Serviceable aircraft part means a part that is safe for flight, can fulfill its operational requirements, and is sufficiently documented to indicate that the part conforms to applicable standards/specifications.

Suspected unapproved part means an aircraft part, component, or material that any person suspects of not meeting the requirements of an "approved part." Approved parts are those that are produced in compliance with 14 CFR part 21, are maintained in compliance with 14 CFR parts 43 and 91, and meet applicable design standards. A part, component, or material may be suspect because of its questionable finish, size, or color; improper (or lack of) identification; incomplete or altered paperwork; or any other questionable indication. See detailed guidance in FAA Advisory Circular 21–29, "Detect-

ing and Reporting Suspected Unapproved Parts," available from the FAA at *http://www.faa.gov.*

Traceable part means an aircraft part whose manufacturer or production approval holder can be identified by documentation, markings/characteristics on the part, or packaging of the part. Non-military parts are traceable if you can establish that the parts were manufactured in accordance with or were previously determined to be airworthy under rules in 14 CFR parts 21 and 43. Possible sources for making a traceability determination could be shipping tickets, bar codes, invoices, parts marking (*e.g.*, PMA, TSO), data plates, serial/part numbers, manufacturing production numbers, maintenance records, work orders, etc.

Training means instruction for all flight program personnel (to include administrative, maintenance and dispatch personnel), which enables them to qualify initially for their positions and to maintain qualification for their positions over time.

NOTE: This instruction can apply to either public or civil missions as defined in the latest version of the FAA's Advisory Circular for Government aircraft operations.

Unmanned Aircraft Systems (UAS) means an unmanned aircraft and its associated elements related to safe operations, which may include but not be limited to control stations, data communications links, support equipment, payloads, flight termination systems, and launch/recovery equipment. The unmanned aircraft (UA) is the flying component of the system, flown by a pilot via a ground control system, or autonomously through the use of an on-board computer, communication links, and any additional equipment necessary for the unmanned aircraft to operate safely. The Federal Aviation Administration issues either an Airworthiness Directive (AD) or a Certificate of Authorization (COA) for the entire system, not just the flying component of the system. Reporting of UAS costs and flight hours is only required if the accumulated costs for acquisition and operations meets the agency's threshold for capitalization, and the UAS has a useful life of two years or more.

Unsalvageable aircraft part means an aircraft part that cannot be restored to a condition that is safe for flight because of its age, its physical condition, a non-repairable defect, insufficient documentation, or its non-conformance with applicable standards/specifications.

U.S. Government Aircraft Cost Accounting Guide (CAG) means guidance for the accounting of Government aircraft costs published by GSA and is based on the cost guidance within OMB Circular A–126, OMB Circular A–76, FAIRS, and the U.S. Government Standard General Ledger.

RESPONSIBILITIES

§ 102–33.25 What are our responsibilities under this part?

Under this part, your responsibilities are to—

(a) Acquire, manage, and dispose of Federal aircraft (see the definition of "Federal aircraft" in § 102–33.20) and acquire and manage Commercial Aviation Services (CAS) (see the definition for "CAS" in paragraph (2) of the definition of "Government aircraft" in § 102–33.20) as safely, efficiently, and effectively as possible consistent with the nature of your agency's aviation missions;

(b) Document and report the—

(1) Types and numbers of your Federal aircraft;

(2) Costs of acquiring and operating Government aircraft;

(3) Amount of time that your agency uses Government aircraft; and

(4) Accidents and incidents involving Government aircraft;

(c) Ensure that your Government aircraft are used only to accomplish your agency's official Government business;

(d) Ensure that all passengers traveling on your agency's Government aircraft are authorized to travel on such aircraft (see OMB Circular A–126);

(e) Appoint (by letter to the Deputy Associate Administrator, Office of Asset and Transportation Management, Office of Government-wide Policy, GSA) a Senior Aviation Management Official (SAMO), who will be your agency's primary member of the ICAP (this paragraph (e) applies to all executive agencies that use aircraft, including the Department of Defense (DOD), the Federal Aviation Administration (FAA), and the National Transpor-

tation Safety Board (NTSB), but excludes executive agencies that only hire aircraft occasionally for a specific flight). It is suggested that an agency's SAMO have:

(1) Experience as a pilot or crew member; or

(2) Management experience within an aviation operations management/flight program.

(f) Designate an official (by letter to the Deputy Associate Administrator, Office of Asset and Transportation Management, Office of Government-wide Policy, GSA) to certify the accuracy and completeness of information reported by your agency through FAIRS. (Armed Forces agencies, which include the DOD and the U.S. Coast Guard, are not required to report information to FAIRS.);

(g) Appoint representatives of the agency as members of ICAP subcommittees and working groups;

(h) Ensure that your agency's internal policies and procedures are consistent with the requirements of OMB Circulars A–126, A–76 and A–11, Federal Aviation Administration Advisory Circular 120–92, and this part; and

(i) Ensure that safety and other critical aviation program requirements are satisfied. Executive agencies that only hire aircraft occasionally for specific flights, must either:

(1) Establish an aviation program that complies with the requirements of OMB Circular A–126; or

(2) Hire those aircraft through an agency with a policy-compliant aviation program.

§ 102–33.30 What are the duties of an agency's Senior Aviation Management Official (SAMO)?

The duties of an agency's Senior Aviation Management Official (SAMO) are to—

(a) Represent the agency's views to the ICAP and vote on behalf of the agency as needed;

(b) Contribute technical and operational policy expertise to ICAP deliberations and activities;

(c) Serve as the designated approving official for FAIRS when the agency elects to have one person serve as both the SAMO and the designated official for FAIRS (DOD will not have a designated official for FAIRS); and

(d) Appoint representatives of the agency as members of ICAP subcommittees and working groups.

§ 102–33.35 How can we get help in carrying out our responsibilities?

To get help in carrying out your responsibilities under this part, you may—

(a) Call or write to GSA's Aviation Policy Division (see definition in § 102–33.20); or

(b) Find additional aviation program management information on the Internet at *http://www.gsa.gov/aviationpolicy.*

§ 102–33.40 What are some of GSA's responsibilities for Federal aviation management?

Under OMB Circular A–126, "Improving the Management and Use of Government Aircraft," (*http://www.whitehouse.gov/omb*) GSA's chief responsibilities for Federal aviation management are to maintain—

(a) A single office to carry out Governmentwide responsibilities for Government aircraft management, and publishing that policy;

(b) An interagency committee (*i.e.*, the ICAP), whose members represent the executive agencies that use Government aircraft to conduct their official business (including FAA and NTSB specifically) and advise and consult with GSA on developing policy for managing Government aircraft;

(c) A management information system to collect, analyze, and report information on the inventory, cost, usage, and safety of Government aircraft; and

(d) A set of performance indicators, policy recommendations, and guidance for the procurement, operation, and safety and disposal of Government aircraft.

NOTE TO § 102–33.40: See OMB Circular A–126 (*http://www.whitehouse.gov/omb*) for a complete listing of GSA's responsibilities related to Federal aviation.

Subpart B—Acquiring Government Aircraft and Aircraft Parts

OVERVIEW

§ 102–33.50 Under what circumstances may we acquire Government aircraft?

(a) When you meet the requirements for operating an in-house aviation program contained in OMB Circular A–76, "Performance of Commercial Activities" and OMB Circular A–11, "Preparation, Submission, and Execution of the Budget," Part 2, "Preparation and Submission of Budget Estimates," Section 25.5, "Summary of Requirements," Table 1, which refers to the Business Case for Acquisition and Maintenance of Aircraft, and Section 51.18, "Budgeting for the acquisition of capital assets," subparagraph (d) (Both circulars are available at *http://www.whitehouse.gov/omb*), you may—

(1) Acquire Federal aircraft when—

(i) Aircraft are the optimum means of supporting your agency's official business;

(ii) You do not have aircraft that can support your agency's official business safely (*e.g.*, in compliance with applicable safety standards and regulations) and cost-effectively;

(iii) No commercial or other Governmental source is available to provide aviation services safely (*i.e.*, in compliance with applicable safety standards and regulations) and cost-effectively; and

(iv) Congress has specifically authorized your agency to purchase, lease, or transfer aircraft and to maintain and operate those aircraft (see 31 U.S.C. 1343);

(2) Acquire Commercial Aviation Services (CAS) when—

(i) Aircraft are the optimum means of supporting your agency's official business; and

(ii) Using commercial aircraft and services is safe (*i.e.*, conforms to applicable laws, safety standards, and regulations) and is more cost effective than using Federal aircraft, aircraft from any other Governmental source, or scheduled air carriers.

(b) When acquiring aircraft, aircraft selection must be based on need, a strong business case, and life-cycle cost analysis, which conform to OMB Circular A–11, "Preparation, Submission, and Execution of the Budget," Part 2, "Preparation and Submission of Budget Estimates," Section 25.5, "Summary of Requirements," Table 1, which refers to the Business Case for Acquisition and Maintenance of Aircraft (*available at http://www.whitehouse.gov/omb*).

§ 102–33.55 Are there restrictions on acquiring Government aircraft?

Yes, you may not acquire—

(a) More aircraft than you need to carry out your official business;

(b) Aircraft of greater size or capacity than you need to perform your Governmental functions cost-effectively; or

(c) Federal aircraft that Congress has not authorized your agency to acquire or Federal aircraft or commercial aircraft and services for which you have not followed the requirements in OMB Circulars A–76 and A–11 (*available at http://www.whitehouse.gov/omb*).

§ 102–33.60 What methods may we use to acquire Government aircraft?

Following the requirements of §§ 102–33.50 and 102–33.55, you (or an internal bureau or sub-agency within your agency) may acquire Government aircraft by means including, but not limited to—

(a) Purchase;

(b) Borrowing from a non-Federal source;

(c) Bailment from another executive agency;

(d) Exchange/sale;

(e) Reimbursable transfer from another executive agency (see §§ 102–36.75 and 102–36.80);

(f) Transfer from another executive agency as approved by GSA;

(g) Reassignment from one internal bureau or subagency to another within your agency;

(h) Transfer of previously forfeited aircraft;

(i) Insurance replacement (*i.e.*, receiving a replacement aircraft);

(j) Capital lease;

(k) Rent or charter;

(l) Contract for full services (*i.e.*, aircraft plus crew and related aviation services) from a commercial source; or

(m) Inter-service support agreements with other executive agencies for aircraft and services.

§ 102–33.65 What is the process for acquiring Government aircraft?

Acquiring Government aircraft, as described in §§ 102–33.70 through 102–33.105, generally follows a three-step process:

(a) Planning;

(b) Budgeting; and

(c) Contracting.

PLANNING TO ACQUIRE GOVERNMENT
AIRCRAFT

§ 102–33.70 What directives must we follow when planning to acquire Government aircraft?

When planning to acquire Government aircraft, you must follow the requirements in—

(a) 31 U.S.C. 1343, "Buying and Leasing Passenger Motor Vehicles and Aircraft";

(b) OMB Circular A–126, "Improving the Management and Use of Government Aircraft" (*http://www.whitehouse.gov/omb*);

(c) OMB Circular A–11, Part 2, Section 25.5, Table 1, Business Case for Acquisition and Maintenance of Aircraft (*http://www.whitehouse.gov/omb*);

(d) OMB Circular A–76, "Performance of Commercial Activities" (*http://www.whitehouse.gov/omb*); and

(e) OMB Circular A–94, "Guidelines and Discount Rates for Benefit-Cost Analysis of Federal Programs" (*http://www.whitehouse.gov/omb*).

§ 102–33.75 What other guidance is available to us in planning to acquire Government aircraft?

You can find guidance for acquisition planning in:

(a) The "Aviation Planning Desk Guide" (available at *http://www.gsa.gov/aviationpolicy*) and

(b) OMB's "Capital Programming Guide," which is a supplement to OMB Circular A–11 (*http://www.whitehouse.gov/omb*).

OMB CIRCULAR A–76

§ 102–33.80 Must we comply with OMB Circular A–76 before we acquire Government aircraft?

Yes, before you acquire Government aircraft, you must comply with OMB Circular A–76 (*http:// www.whitehouse.gov/omb*). If you are acquiring Federal aircraft, you must ensure that the private sector cannot provide Government aircraft or related aviation services more cost-effectively than you can provide Federal aircraft and related services.

THE PROCESS FOR BUDGETING TO ACQUIRE GOVERNMENT AIRCRAFT

§ 102–33.90 What is the process for budgeting to acquire a Federal aircraft (including a Federal aircraft transferred from another executive agency)?

(a) The process for budgeting to acquire a Federal aircraft or to accept a Federal aircraft transferred from another executive agency requires that you have specific authority from Congress in your appropriation, as called for in 31 U.S.C. 1343, to—

(1) Purchase, capital lease, or lease a Federal aircraft and to operate and maintain it; or

(2) Accept a Federal aircraft transferred from another executive agency and to operate and maintain it.

(b) For complete information on budgeting to own Federal aircraft (*i.e.,* large purchase of a capital asset), see OMB Circular A–11, Part 2, Sections 25.1 and 51.18. Also see §§ 102–33.70 and 102–33.75.

§ 102–33.95 What is the process for budgeting to acquire Commercial Aviation Services (CAS)?

Except for leases and capital leases, for which you must have specific Congressional authorization as required by 31 U.S.C. 1343, you may budget to fund your CAS out of your agency's operating budget. Also see §§ 102–33.70 and 102–33.75.

CONTRACTING TO ACQUIRE GOVERNMENT AIRCRAFT

§ 102–33.100 What are our responsibilities when contracting to purchase or capital lease a Federal aircraft or to award a CAS contract?

In contracting to purchase or capital lease a Federal aircraft or to award a CAS contract, you must follow the Federal Acquisition Regulation (FAR) (48 CFR Chapter 1) unless your agency is exempt from following the FAR.

§ 102–33.105 What minimum requirements must we put into our CAS contracts?

At a minimum, your CAS contracts and agreements must require that any provider of CAS comply with—

(a) Civil standards in 14 CFR that are applicable to the type of operation(s) you are asking the contractor to conduct;

(b) Applicable military standards; or

(c) Your agency's Flight Program Standards (see §§ 102–33.140 through 102–33.185 for the requirements for Flight Program Standards).

ACQUIRING AIRCRAFT PARTS

§ 102–33.110 What are our responsibilities when acquiring aircraft parts?

When acquiring aircraft parts, you must:

(a) Acquire the parts cost-effectively and acquire only what you need;

(b) Inspect and verify that all incoming parts are documented as safe for flight prior to installation;

(c) Obtain all logbooks (if applicable) and maintenance records (for guidance on maintaining records for non-military parts, see Federal Aviation Administration (FAA) Advisory Circular 43–9C, "Maintenance Records," which is available from the FAA at *http:// www.faa.gov*);

(d) Plan for adequate storage and protection; and

(e) Refer to FAA Advisory Circular 21–29C, Change (2), "Detecting and Reporting Suspected Unapproved Parts" (*http://www.faa.gov*).

§ 102–33.115 Are there requirements for acquiring military Flight Safety Critical Aircraft Parts (FSCAP)?

Yes, when you acquire military Flight Safety Critical Aircraft Parts (FSCAP), you must—

(a) Accept FSCAP only when it is documented or traceable to its original equipment manufacturer. A part's DOD FSCAP Criticality Code should be marked or tagged on the part or appear on its invoice/transfer document (see § 102–33.375 for further explanation of the FSCAP Criticality Codes); and

(b) Not install undocumented, but traceable FSCAP until you have the parts inspected and recertified by the original equipment manufacturer or other FAA-approved facility (see § 102–33.370 on FSCAP and AC 20–142).

§ 102–33.120 Are there requirements for acquiring life-limited parts?

Yes, when you acquire new or used life-limited parts, you must—

(a) Identify and inspect the parts, ensuring that they have civil or military-certified documentation; and

(b) Mutilate and dispose of any expired life-limited parts (see § 102–33.370 on handling life-limited parts).

Subpart C—Managing Government Aircraft and Aircraft Parts

OVERVIEW

§ 102–33.125 If we use Federal aircraft, what are our management responsibilities?

If you use Federal aircraft, you are responsible for—

(a) Establishing agency-specific Flight Program Standards, as defined in §§ 102–33.140 through 102–33.185;

(b) Accounting for the cost of acquiring, operating, and supporting your aircraft;

(c) Accounting for the use of your aircraft;

(d) Maintaining and accounting for aircraft parts;

(e) Reporting inventory, cost, and utilization data (for reporting requirements, see subpart E of this part); and

(f) Properly disposing of aircraft and parts following §§ 102–33.240 through 102–33.375.

§ 102–33.130 If we hire CAS, what are our management responsibilities?

If you hire CAS, you are responsible for—

(a) Establishing agency-specific Flight Program Standards, as defined in §§ 102–33.140 through 102–33.185, as applicable, and requiring compliance with these standards in your contracts and agreements;

(b) Accounting for the cost of your aircraft and services hired as CAS;

(c) Accounting for the use of your aircraft hired as CAS; and

(d) Reporting the cost and usage data for your CAS hires (for reporting requirements, see subpart E of this part).

§ 102–33.135 Do we have to follow OMB Circular A–123, "Management Accountability and Control," for establishing management controls for our aviation program?

Yes, you must follow OMB Circular A–123, "Management's Responsibility for Accountability and Control" (*http://www.whitehouse.gov/omb*), when establishing management controls for your aviation program. The circular requires that you establish organizations, policies, and procedures to ensure that, among other things, your aviation program achieves its intended results and you use your resources consistently with your agency's missions.

ESTABLISHING FLIGHT PROGRAM STANDARDS

§ 102–33.140 What are Flight Program Standards?

Flight Program Standards are the minimum requirements that must be incorporated into your flight programs to ensure that your aircraft are operated safely, effectively, and efficiently. These requirements must:

(a) Be specific to your agency's aviation operations, including your CAS;

(b) Meet the requirements identified in §§ 102–33.155 through 102–33.185.

(c) Meet or exceed applicable civil or military rules (in particular 49 U.S.C. 40102(a)(37) and 40125), and applicable FAA regulations); and

(d) Incorporate risk management techniques when civil or military rules do not apply.

§ 102–33.145 Why must we establish Flight Program Standards?

You must establish Flight Program Standards because Title 14 of the Code of Federal Regulations (14 CFR) may not cover or address all aspects of your agency's flight program, such as non-certificated aircraft, high-risk operations, special personnel requirements, etc.

§ 102–33.150 What Federally-funded aviation activities of executive agencies are exempt from establishing Flight Program Standards under this part?

The following Federally-funded activities are exempt from establishing Flight Program Standards under this part:

(a) The Armed Forces (which includes the U.S. Coast Guard);

(b) Agencies in the Intelligence Community; and

(c) Entities outside the executive branch of the Federal Government when using aircraft loaned to them by an executive agency (that is, owned by an executive agency, but operated by and on behalf of the loanee) unless the loanee—

(1) Uses the aircraft to conduct official Government business; or

(2) Is required to follow §§ 102–33.140 through 102–33.185 under a Memorandum of Agreement governing the loan.

§ 102–33.155 How must we establish Flight Program Standards?

To establish Flight Program Standards, you must write, publish (as appropriate), implement, and comply with standards (specific to your agency), which establish or require (contractually, where applicable) policies and procedures for—

(a) Management/administration of your flight program (in this part, "flight program" includes CAS contracts);

(b) Operation of your flight program;

(c) Maintenance of your Government aircraft;

(d) Training for your flight program personnel;

(e) Safety of your flight program;

(f) Accident reporting and investigation as appropriate; and

(g) Reporting to FAIRS as required by this part.

MANAGEMENT/ADMINISTRATION

§ 102–33.160 What standards must we establish or require (contractually, where applicable) for management/administration of our flight program?

For management/administration of your flight program, you must establish or require (contractually, where applicable)—

(a) A management structure responsible for the administration, operation, safety, training, maintenance, and financial needs of your aviation operation (including establishing minimum requirements for these items for any commercial contracts); and

(b) Guidance describing the roles, responsibilities, and authorities of your flight program personnel, *e.g.,* managers, pilots and other crewmembers, flight safety personnel, maintenance personnel, administrative personnel and dispatchers.

OPERATIONS

§ 102–33.165 What standards must we establish or require (contractually, where applicable) for operation of our flight program?

For operation of your flight program, you must establish or require (contractually, where applicable)—

(a) Basic qualifications and currency requirements for your pilots and other crewmembers, maintenance personnel, administrative personnel and other mission-related personnel;

(b) Limitations on duty time and flight time for pilots and other crewmembers;

(c) Procedures to record and track flight time, duty time, training of crewmembers, and applicable medical requirements;

(d) Compliance with owning-agency or military safety of flight notices and operational bulletins;

(e) Flight-following procedures to notify management and initiate search and rescue operations for lost or downed aircraft;

(f) Dissemination, as your agency determines appropriate, of a disclosure statement to all crewmembers and qualified non-crewmembers who fly aboard your agency's Government aircraft (see Appendix A to this part);

(g) Creation of a manifest, at the origin of each flight, that contains the full names of all persons on board for each leg of flight, a point of contact for each person, and phone numbers for the points of contact;

(h) Documentation of any changes in the manifest by leg, and retention of manifests for two years from the time of flight;

(i) Procedures for reconciling flight manifests with persons actually on board and a method to test those procedures periodically;

(j) At the origin of each flight, preparation of a complete weight and balance computation and a cargo-loading manifest, and retention of this computation and manifest for 30 days from the date of flight;

(k) Appropriate emergency procedures and equipment for specific missions;

(l) Procedures to ensure that required Aviation Life Support Equipment (ALSE) is inspected and serviceable; and

(m) Procedures to implement a "risk assessment" before each flight and/or as frequently as necessary that include such items as weather, crew rest, type of flight (low level, Instrument Flight Rules (IFR), night, etc.) crew makeup, etc. This process should be accomplished in accordance with your agency's operations, flight dispatch, or flight following procedures/program.

MAINTENANCE

§ 102–33.170 What standards must we establish or require (contractually, where applicable) for maintenance of our Government aircraft?

For maintenance of your Government aircraft, you must establish or require (contractually, where applicable)—

(a) Procedures to record and track duty time and training of maintenance personnel;

(b) Aircraft maintenance and inspection programs that comply with whichever is most applicable among—

(1) Programs for ex-military aircraft;

(2) Manufacturers' programs;

(3) FAA-approved programs (*i.e.*, following the applicable parts of 14 CFR);

(4) FAA-accepted programs (*i.e.*, those following ICAP guides or similar programs that have been accepted by the FAA); or

(5) Your agency's self-prescribed programs;

(c) Compliance with owning-agency or military safety of flight notices, FAA airworthiness directives, advisory circulars and orders, or mandatory manufacturers' bulletins applicable to the types of aircraft, engines, propellers, and appliances you operate;

(d) Procedures for operating aircraft with inoperable instruments and equipment (*i.e.*, Minimum Equipment Lists and Configuration Deviation Lists);

(e) Technical support, including appropriate engineering documentation and testing, for aircraft, powerplant, propeller, or appliance repairs, modifications, or equipment installations;

(f) A quality control system for acquiring replacements, ensuring that the parts you acquire are suitable replacement parts and have the documentation needed to determine that they are safe for flight and are inspected and tested, as applicable;

(g) Procedures for recording and tracking maintenance actions; inspections; and the flight hours, cycles, and calendar times of life-limited parts and FSCAP; and

(h) The use of alternative aviation fuels in fleet aircraft to the maximum extent possible consistent with the availability of approved alternative fuels and aircraft operating procedures or manuals for those aircraft.

TRAINING

§ 102–33.175 What standards must we establish or require (contractually, where applicable) to train our flight program personnel?

You must establish or require (contractually, where applicable) the following standards to train your flight program personnel—

(a) An instructional program to train your flight program personnel, initially and on a recurrent basis, in their roles, responsibilities, authorities, and in the operational skills relevant to the types of operations that you conduct. Flight program personnel may include, *e.g.*, managers, pilots and other crewmembers, flight safety personnel, maintenance personnel, administrative personnel and dispatchers; and

(b) An instructional program that meets the specific requirements for safety manager training identified in § 102–33.180(a).

SAFETY

§ 102–33.180 What standards should we establish or require (contractually, where applicable) for aviation safety management?

You should establish or require (contractually, where applicable) the following aviation safety management standards:

(a) By June 30, 2015, a Safety Management System (SMS) that complies with the FAA's current Advisory Circular that addresses Safety Management Systems (SMS) or an equivalent internationally recognized SMS standard. The SMS should include:

(1) Policies that define clear roles and responsibilities for implementing an SMS. This includes ensuring that senior level management has the ultimate responsibility for your SMS. It also includes appointing members of management as qualified aviation safety managers and safety officers (*i.e.*, individuals who are responsible for an agency's aviation safety program, regardless of title), who should be—

(i) Experienced as pilots, crewmembers, maintenance personnel, or have experience in aviation management or aviation maintenance program management; and

(ii) Graduated or certificated from an aviation safety officer course provided by a recognized training provider and authority in aviation safety before appointment or within one year after appointment; and

(2) A program for preventing accidents, which includes—

(i) Measurable accident prevention procedures (*e.g.*, safety reviews, clear roles and responsibilities, operations and maintenance procedures, pilot and mechanic proficiency evaluations, fire drills, hazard analyses);

(ii) A procedure or system for disseminating accident-prevention information;

(iii) Safety training;

(iv) An aviation safety awards program that includes applying for the annual Federal Aviation Awards as appropriate;

(v) An annual review to ensure compliance with the GSA Gold Standard Program; and

(vi) A safety council or committee (applies to Federal aircraft-owning agencies);

(b) Procedures and processes for risk analysis and risk management that identify and mitigate hazards through formal administrative and engineering controls and provide recommendations to senior level managers for managing risk to an optimum level;

(c) Policies that require the use of independent, unbiased inspectors to verify compliance with the standards called for in this;

(d) Procedures for reporting unsafe operations to agency aviation safety officers and senior aviation safety managers without reprisal;

(e) A system to collect and report information on aircraft accidents and incidents (as required by 49 CFR part 830 and 41 CFR 102–33.445 and 102–33.450);

(f) Policies that identify clear standards for acceptable behavior; and

(g) A security program that includes—

(1) A designated security manager;

(2) A threat assessment process;

(3) Procedures for preventing and deterring unlawful acts;

(4) Procedures for responding to threats and unlawful acts;

(5) Security training for personnel; and

(6) Policies and procedures for a mail security plan that meet the mail security requirements contained in FMR 102–192, "Mail Management," Subpart C, "Security Requirements for All Agencies," §§ 102–192.70 through 102–192.80. Specifically, section 102–192.80 identifies topics that must be addressed in an agency's mail security plan, to include a plan to protect staff

and all other occupants of agency facilities from hazards that might be delivered in the mail, which would include an agency's use of aircraft for mail delivery.

§ 102–33.185 What standards must we establish or require (contractually, where applicable) for responding to aircraft accidents and incidents?

You must establish or require (contractually, where applicable) the following standards for responding to aircraft accidents and incidents:

(a) An aircraft accident/incident reporting policy to ensure that you will comply with the National Transportation Safety Board's (NTSB) regulations (located in 49 CFR parts 830 and 831), including notifying NTSB immediately when you have an aircraft accident or an incident as defined in 49 CFR 830.5. In addition, this policy must contain a method of notifying the U.S. General Services Administration of an accident or incident that was reported to the NTSB. Refer to §§ 102–33.445 and 102–33.450 for further information;

(b) An agency, bureau, or field level accident/incident response plan, modeled on the NTSB's "Federal Plan for Aviation Accidents Involving Aircraft Operated by or Chartered by Federal Agencies," and periodic disaster response exercises to test your plan. A copy of the NTSB's plan is available at *http://www.ntsb.gov*. The plan should also refer to or incorporate procedures (as outlined in FAA Advisory Circular 120–92) to identify the potential for accidents or incidents;

(c) Procedures (see 49 CFR 831.11) for participation as a party to NTSB accident or incident investigations involving aircraft that your agency either owns or hires, and for conducting parallel investigations, as appropriate;

(d) Training in investigating accidents/incidents for your agency's personnel who may be asked to participate in NTSB investigations or to conduct a parallel investigation; and

(e) Procedures for disseminating, in the event of an aviation disaster that involves one of your Government aircraft, information about eligibility for benefits contained in the disclosure statement in appendix A of this part to anyone injured, to the injured or deceased persons' points of contact (listed on the manifest), and to the families of injured or deceased crewmembers and qualified non-crewmembers.

NOTE TO § 102–33.185: This part does not supersede any of the regulations in 49 CFR parts 830 and 831. For definitions of terms and complete regulatory guidance on notifying the NTSB and reporting aircraft accidents and incidents, see 49 CFR parts 830 and 831.

ACCOUNTING FOR THE COSTS OF
GOVERNMENT AIRCRAFT

§ 102–33.190 What are the aircraft operations and ownership costs for which we must account?

You must account for the operations and ownership costs of your Government aircraft, including your Unmanned Aircraft Systems (UAS), as described in the "U.S. Government Aircraft Cost Accounting Guide" (CAG), available at (*http://www.gsa.gov/aviationpolicy*), which follows OMB Circular A–126 (*http://www.whitehouse.gov/omb*). To account for aircraft costs, you must do at least the following:

(a) Justify acquisitions to support the agency's aviation program;

(b) Justify the use of Government aircraft in lieu of commercially available aircraft, and the use of one Government aircraft in lieu of another;

(c) Develop a variable cost rate for each aircraft or aircraft type (*i.e.*, make and model) in your inventory;

(d) Recover the costs of operating Government aircraft;

(e) Determine the cost effectiveness of various aspects of agency aircraft programs; and

(f) Accumulate aircraft program costs following the procedures defined in the CAG, available at (*http://www.gsa.gov/aviationpolicy*).

§ 102–33.195 Do we need an automated system to account for aircraft costs?

(a) Yes, if you own Federal aircraft or operate bailed aircraft, you must maintain an automated system to account for aircraft costs by collecting the cost data elements required by FAIRS. The functional specifications and data definitions for a FAIRS-compliant system are described in the "Common Aviation Management Information Standard" (C–AMIS), which is available from the Aviation Policy Division. See §§ 102–33.395, 102–33.405, and 102–33.410 for more information on FAIRS, and §§ 102–33.455 and 102–33.460 for more information on C–AMIS.

(b) Agencies that use only CAS aircraft and do not have Federal aircraft must keep records adequate for reporting information through FAIRS, but are not required to have an automated system. See §§ 102–33.435 and 102–33.440 for the information on CAS that you must report through FAIRS.

§ 102–33.200 Must we periodically justify owning and operating Federal aircraft?

Yes, after you have held a Federal aircraft for five years, you must:

(a) Justify owning and operating the aircraft by reviewing your operations and establishing that you have a continuing need for the aircraft, using the procedures required in OMB Circular A–76 and OMB Circular A–11, Part 7, Appendix B, Budgetary treatment of lease-purchases and leases of capital assets; and

(b) Review the continuing need for each of your aircraft and the cost-effectiveness of your aircraft operations as directed by OMB Circulars A–11 and A–76, every five years.

§ 102–33.205 When we use our aircraft to support other executive agencies, must we recover the operating costs?

Yes, you must recover the following:

(a) Under 31 U.S.C. 1535 and other statutes, you may be required to recover the costs of operating aircraft in support of other agencies. Depending on the statutory authorities under which you acquired and operate your aircraft, you will use either of the following two methods for establishing the rates charged for using your aircraft:

(1) The variable cost recovery rate; or

(2) The full cost recovery rate.

(b) See the U.S. Government Aircraft Cost Accounting Guide (CAG) (*http:// www.gsa.gov/aviationpolicy*), for the definitions of "variable cost recovery rate" and "full cost recovery rate."

ACCOUNTING FOR THE USE OF GOVERNMENT AIRCRAFT

§ 102–33.210 How do we account for the use of our Government aircraft?

To account for the use of Government aircraft, including your Unmanned Aircraft Systems (UAS), you must document all flights and keep this documentation for two years after the date of the flight. For each flight, record the—

(a) Aircraft's registration mark;

(b) Owner and operator (the owner may not be the operator, as is the case when a CAS aircraft, owned commercially, is operated by U.S. Government personnel);

(c) Purpose of the flight (the Governmental function that the aircraft was dispatched to perform);

(d) Departure and destination points;

(e) Flight date(s) and times;

(f) Manifest (see § 102–33.165(g) and (h)); and

(g) Name(s) of the pilot(s) and crewmembers.

§ 102–33.215 May we use Government aircraft to carry passengers?

Yes, you may use Government aircraft to carry passengers with the following restrictions:

(a) You may carry passengers only on aircraft that you operate or require contractually to be operated in accordance with the rules and requirements in 14 CFR; and

(b) For certain kinds of travel, your agency must justify passengers' presence on Government aircraft. See OMB Circular A–126 and the Federal Travel Regulation (FTR) §§ 301–10.260 through 301–10.266, and 301–70.800 through 301–70.808, and 301–70.910 (41 CFR 301–10.260 through 301–10.266, 301–70.800 through 301–70.808, and 301–70.910) for complete information on authorizing travel and analyzing costs before authorizing travel on Government aircraft.

§ 102–33.220 What are the responsibilities of our aviation program in justifying the use of a Government aircraft to transport passengers?

After receiving a request from your agency, your aviation program's responsibilities in justifying the use of a

Government aircraft to transport passengers are to your travel approving authority:

(a) Cost estimates to assist in determining whether or not use of a Government aircraft to carry passengers is justified. See OMB Circular A–126 (*http://www.whitehouse.gov/omb*) for more information on justifying travel on Government aircraft. See also FTR §§ 301–10.260 through 301–10.266, and 301–70.800 through 301–70.808, and 301–70.910 (41 CFR 301–10.260 through 301–10.266, 301–70.800 through 301–70.808, and 301–70.910) for guidance on estimating the cost of using a Government aircraft. The cost of using a Government aircraft is—

(1) The variable cost of using a Federal aircraft;

(2) The amount your agency will be charged by a CAS provider; or

(3) The variable cost of using an aircraft owned by another agency as reported by the owning agency; and

(b) Information to assist in the analysis of alternatives to travel on Government aircraft. The information must include the following:

(1) If no follow-on trip is scheduled, all time required to position the aircraft to begin the trip and to return the aircraft to its normal base of operations;

(2) If a follow-on trip requires repositioning, the cost for the repositioning should be charged to the associated follow-on trip;

(3) If an aircraft supports a multi-leg trip (a series of flights scheduled sequentially), the use of the aircraft for the total trip may be justified by comparing the total variable cost of the entire trip to the commercial aircraft cost (including charter) for all legs of the trip; and

(4) The use of foreign aircraft as CAS is authorized when the agency has determined that an equivalent level of safety exists as compared to U.S. operations of a like kind. The safety of passengers shall be the overriding consideration for the selection of travel mode when comparing foreign sources of scheduled commercial airlines and CAS.

MANAGING AIRCRAFT PARTS

§ 102–33.225 How must we manage aircraft parts?

You must manage your aircraft parts by maintaining proper storage, protection, maintenance procedures, and records for the parts throughout their life cycles.

§ 102–33.230 May we use military FSCAP on non-military FAA-type certificated Government aircraft?

You may use dual-use military FSCAP on non-military aircraft operated under restricted or standard airworthiness certificates if the parts are inspected and approved for such installation by the FAA. See detailed guidance in FAA Advisory Circular 20–142, Change 1, "Eligibility and Evaluation of U.S. Military Surplus Flight Safety Critical Aircraft Parts, Engines, and Propellers" (*http://www.faa.gov*).

§ 102–33.235 What documentation must we maintain for life-limited parts and FSCAP?

For life-limited parts and FSCAP, you must hold and update the documentation that accompanies these parts for as long as you use or store them. When you dispose of life-limited parts or FSCAP, the up-to-date documentation must accompany the parts. (See § 102–33.370.)

Subpart D—Disposing or Replacing of Government Aircraft and Aircraft Parts

OVERVIEW

§ 102–33.240 What must we consider before disposing or replacing aircraft and aircraft parts?

Before disposing of aircraft and aircraft parts, you must first determine if the aircraft or parts are excess to your agency's mission or, if your aircraft or parts are not excess, if you will need replacements, as follows:

(a) If your aircraft/parts are . . .	And . . .	Then . . .
No longer needed to perform their mission(s) for your agency, i.e., they are excess to your needs,	You do not need to replace them,	You must report them to GSA as excess property (see 41 CFR 102–36.45(e)).

(b) If your aircraft/parts are . . .	And . . .	Then . . .
No longer suitable, or capable of performing their mission(s) for your agency,	You do need to replace them,	You may consider using the exchange/sale authority (see 41 CFR part 102–39).

§ 102–33.245 May we report as excess, or replace (i.e., by exchange/sale), both operational and non-operational aircraft?

Yes, you may report as excess, or replace both operational and non-operational aircraft by following the rules governing excess personal property and exchange/sale (see 41 CFR parts 102–36 and 102–39, respectively).

§ 102–33.250 May we declassify aircraft?

Yes, you may declassify aircraft (See §§ 102–33.415 and 102–33.420).

(a) A declassified aircraft is no longer considered an aircraft, but may be considered as a group of aircraft parts or other property for ground use only.

(b) You must retain documentation and traceability on all parts that are intended for use as replacement parts on other aircraft. You must carry such "aircraft parts or other property" on your property records under the appropriate Federal Supply Classification group(s) (e.g., miscellaneous property).

(c) For disposal of the property remaining after declassification of an aircraft, you must follow the property disposal regulations in 41 CFR parts 102–36, 102–37, 102–38 and 102–39.

§ 102–33.255 Must we document FSCAP or life-limited parts installed on aircraft that we will report as excess or replace?

Yes, you must comply with the documentation procedures described in § 102–33.370 if your aircraft and/or engines contain FSCAP or life-limited parts that you will report as excess or replace.

§ 102–33.260 When we report as excess, or replace, an aircraft (including a declassified aircraft), must we report the change in inventory to the Federal Aviation Interactive Reporting System (FAIRS)?

(a) Yes. When you report as excess or replace an aircraft you must report the change in inventory to FAIRS. For more information see § 102–33.405.

(b) Within 14 calendar days of the date you dispose of the aircraft, you must report—

(1) The disposal method (e.g., reassignment, inter-agency transfer, donation, sale as surplus or scrap, declassification, or exchange/sale);

(2) The disposal date; and

(3) The identity and type of recipient (e.g., State, educational institution, executive agency, commercial vendor).

REPORTING EXCESS FEDERAL AIRCRAFT

§ 102–33.265 What must we do with aircraft that are excess to our needs?

If aircraft are excess to your needs, you must:

(a) Reassign the aircraft within your agency if any of your sub-agencies can use the aircraft; or

(b) Report the aircraft as excess property to GSA (see 41 CFR part 102–36) if none of your sub-agencies can use the aircraft.

§ 102–33.270 What is the process for reporting an excess aircraft?

To report an excess aircraft, you must:

(a) Report electronically to GSA's Federal Disposal System GSAXcess® (http://gsaxcess.gov). For information on reporting excess property electronically, contact the Federal Acquisition Service (FAS), Pacific Rim Region (Region 9) at (415) 522–2777; and

(b) Submit a Standard Form (SF) 120, Report of Excess Personal Property (see § 102–2.135), to: General Services Administration, Federal Acquisition Service, Pacific Rim Region, 450 Golden Gate Avenue, 4th Floor West, San Francisco, CA, 94102–3434.

REPLACING AIRCRAFT THROUGH EXCHANGE/SALE

§ 102–33.275 What should we consider before replacing our aircraft through exchange/sale?

Before an exchange/sale of your aircraft, you should consider whether:

(a) You have a continuing need for similar property and that the property being exchanged or sold is not excess or surplus; and

(b) The exchange/sale meets all other requirements in 41 CFR part 102–39.

§ 102–33.280 What are our options if we need a replacement aircraft?

If you need to replace an aircraft, your options are—

(a) Negotiating and conducting an exchange transaction directly with an aircraft provider and obtaining credit toward the purchase of a replacement aircraft, following the procurement rules applicable to your agency; or

(b) Selling the aircraft and using the proceeds to offset the cost of purchasing a replacement aircraft, following 41 CFR part 102–39. Sales Centers (SC) that are currently authorized to conduct sales, as well as contact information for the GovSales Program Manager, are available on the GovSales Web site at *http://www.gsa.gov/portal/content/105020.*

§ 102–33.285 Do we need to include any special disclaimers in our exchange/sale agreements for non-certificated aircraft or aircraft that we have operated as public aircraft (i.e., not in compliance with 14 CFR)?

Yes, when you exchange/sell non-certificated aircraft or aircraft maintained as public aircraft, you must ensure that the exchange/sale offerings contain the following statement:

"*Warning to purchasers/recipients.* The aircraft you are purchasing or receiving in an exchange may not be in compliance with applicable Federal Aviation Administration (FAA) requirements. You are solely responsible for bringing the aircraft into compliance with 14 CFR Chapter I, or other applicable standards, by obtaining all necessary FAA inspections or modifications.

The purchaser/recipient agrees that the Government shall not be held liable for personal injuries to, disabilities of, or death of the purchaser/recipient, the purchaser's/recipient's employees, or to any other persons arising from or incident to the purchase of this aircraft, its use, or disposition. You will hold the Government harmless from any or all debts, liabilities, judgments, costs, demands, suits, actions, or claims of any nature arising from or incident to the purchase, use, or resale of this item. This aircraft may have been operated outside the limitations of 14 CFR Chapter I, and some type of inspection may be needed to determine its airworthiness prior to being flown. You should be aware of the items below prior to operating this aircraft.

• All civil and public aircraft must have a valid registration issued by the FAA as required by 14 CFR Chapter I.

• Civil aircraft must have a valid airworthiness certificate in order to operate in the U.S. airspace.

• In order for the aircraft to be eligible for a standard airworthiness certificate, the aircraft must conform to its FAA Type Certificate.

• Aircraft not having a valid airworthiness certificate may be eligible for a special FAA one-time flight permit to enable relocating the aircraft. Relocation can be for a number of reasons, including storage, repair, inspection, or public display. Any one-time flight approval is predicated on the aircraft being safe for flight.

• Individuals who purchase a surplus military (foreign or domestic) or foreign aircraft not having any type of FAA Type Certificate may be unable to obtain any type of airworthiness certificate or special flight permit.

• An aircraft with good maintenance and inspection records makes an airworthiness determination easier to ascertain. It is in your best interest to contact the nearest FAA Flight Standards District Office and discuss your responsibilities with respect to gaining an airworthiness determination. The location of your nearest FAA office may be obtained from the FAA's Web site (*http://www.faa.gov/*).

• When the aircraft is purchased for spare parts and the airframe is scrapped, you should declassify the aircraft (see § 102–33.420 for more information), complete the back of the aircraft's registration form and send it to: The FAA Aircraft Registration Branch, P.O. Box 25504, Oklahoma City, OK 73125–0504.''

§ 102–33.295 May we exchange/sell an aircraft through reimbursable transfer to another executive agency or conduct a negotiated sale at fixed price to a State Agency for Surplus Property (SASP)?

Yes, you may exchange/sell an aircraft through reimbursable transfer to another executive agency or conduct a negotiated sale at fixed price to a State Agency for Surplus Property (SASP) (see § 102–39.55 for more information).

NOTE TO § 102–33.295: Some agencies may also have special congressional authorization to recover costs.

DISPOSING OF AIRCRAFT PARTS

§ 102–33.300 What must we consider before disposing of aircraft parts?

Before disposing of aircraft parts, you must first determine if they are excess to your agency's mission requirements or, if the aircraft parts are not excess, if you will need replacements. The table in § 102–33.240 shows the differences between excess and replacement parts.

§ 102–33.305 May we report as excess, or replace, FSCAP and life-limited parts?

Yes, you may report as excess, or replace, FSCAP and life-limited parts, but they require special handling. See the tables in § 102–33.370.

§ 102–33.310 May we report as excess, or replace, unsalvageable aircraft parts?

No, you may not report unsalvageable aircraft parts as excess or exchange/sale them for replacements. You must mutilate unsalvageable parts. You may sell the mutilated parts only as scrap or report that scrap to GSA for sale.

§ 102–33.315 What are the procedures for mutilating unsalvageable aircraft parts?

When mutilating unsalvageable aircraft parts, you must—

(a) Destroy the data plates, remove the serial/lot/part numbers, and cut, crush, grind, melt, burn, or use other means to prevent the parts from being misidentified or used as serviceable aircraft parts. Call your regional FAA Flight Standards District Office for additional guidance;

(b) Ensure that an authorized official of your agency witnesses and documents the mutilation; and

(c) Retain a signed certification and statement of mutilation.

§ 102–33.320 What must we do if we are unable to perform required mutilation of aircraft parts?

If you are unable to perform the required mutilation of aircraft parts, you must turn the parts in to a Federal or Federally-approved facility for mutilation and proper disposition. Ensure that any contractor follows the provisions of § 102–33.315 for mutilating and disposing of the parts.

§ 102–33.325 What documentation must we furnish with excess, surplus or replaced parts when they are transferred, donated, or exchanged/sold?

When you transfer, donate, or exchange/sell excess, surplus or replaced parts, you must—

(a) Furnish all applicable labels, tags, and historical and modification records for serviceable aircraft parts;

(b) Mark mutilated parts as unsalvageable (mutilated parts may be sold only for scrap; see § 102–33.315); and

(c) Ensure that all available tags, labels, applicable historical data, life-histories, and maintenance records accompany FSCAP and life-limited parts and that FSCAP criticality codes (see § 102–33.375) are perpetuated on documentation (see § 102–33.330 for additional requirements).

REPORTING EXCESS AIRCRAFT PARTS

§ 102–33.330 What must we do with aircraft parts that are excess to our needs?

If aircraft parts are excess to your needs, you must:

(a) Reassign the aircraft parts within your agency if any of your sub-agencies can use the parts; or

(b) Report the excess parts to GSA, using Standard Form (SF) 120, "Report of Excess Personal Property" (see §102–2.135 for information to obtain this form). When reporting excess FSCAP, you must include the manufacturer's name, date of manufacture, part number, serial number, and the appropriate Criticality Code on the SF 120. For information on reporting excess property, refer to *http://gsaxcess.gov*. (See 41 CFR part 102–36 regarding disposal of excess property.)

§ **102–33.335 What are the receiving agency's responsibilities in the transfer of aircraft parts?**

An agency that receives transferred aircraft parts must:

(a) Verify that all applicable labels and tags and historical and modification records accompany all serviceable aircraft parts (*i.e.*, parts that are intended for flight use) that you receive. This requirement does not apply to parts for ground use only. See the tables in §102–33.370.

(b) Mutilate all transferred parts that you discover to be unsalvageable, and dispose of them properly, following the procedures in §102–33.315.

§ **102–33.340 What are GSA's responsibilities in disposing of excess and surplus aircraft parts?**

In disposing of excess aircraft parts, the GSA FAS office in your region:

(a) Reviews your SF 120, Report of Excess Personal Property (see §102–2.135 for information to obtain this form) for completeness and accuracy (of status, condition, and FSCAP and demilitarization codes if applicable); and

(b) Ensures that the following certification is included on disposal documents (*e.g.*, transfer orders or purchasers' receipts):

Because of the critical nature of the failure of aircraft parts and the resulting potential safety threat, recipients of aircraft parts must ensure that any parts installed on an aircraft meet applicable Federal Aviation Administration (FAA) requirements and must obtain required certifications. GSA makes no representation as to a part's conformance with the FAA requirements.

§ **102–33.345 What are the responsibilities of a State Agency for Surplus Property (SASP) in the donation of Federal Government aircraft parts?**

When a SASP accepts surplus Federal Government aircraft parts for donation, the SASP must:

(a) Review donation and transfer documents for completeness and accuracy, and ensure that the certification in §102–33.340 is included;

(b) Ensure that when the donee determines the part to be unsalvageable, the donee mutilates the part following the procedures in §102–33.315; and

(c) Ensure that the donee retains, maintains, and perpetuates all documentation for serviceable parts (parts intended for flight use).

REPLACING AIRCRAFT PARTS THROUGH EXCHANGE/SALE

§ **102–33.350 What do we need to consider for an exchange/sale of our aircraft parts?**

(a) When replacing aircraft parts through exchange/sale you—

(1) Do not need approval from GSA; and

(2) Must follow the provisions of this subpart and part 102–39 of this chapter.

(b) Replacement parts do not have to be for the same type or design of aircraft, but you must use the exchange allowance or sales proceeds to purchase aircraft parts to support your aviation program which meet the "similarity" requirement in 41 CFR part 102–39.

§ **102–33.355 May we exchange/sell aircraft parts through a reimbursable transfer to another executive agency or conduct a negotiated sale at fixed price to a State Agency for Surplus Property (SASP)?**

Yes, you may exchange/sell aircraft parts through a reimbursable transfer to another executive agency, or conduct a negotiated sale at fixed price to a SASP (see §102–39.55 for more information).

§ 102–33.360 What is the process for exchanging/selling aircraft parts for replacement?

(a) You or your agent (*i.e.*, another Federal agency or an authorized Sales Center) may transact an exchange/sale directly with a non-Federal source, or do a reimbursable transfer with another executive agency as long as you or your agent—

(1) Follow the provisions in this part and in 41 CFR part 102–39;

(2) Ensure that the applicable labels and tags, historical data and modification records accompany the parts at the time of sale, and that sales offerings on aircraft parts contain the following statement:

"*Warning to purchasers/recipients.* The aircraft parts you are purchasing or receiving in an exchange may not be in compliance with applicable Federal Aviation Administration (FAA) requirements. You are solely responsible for bringing the aircraft into compliance with 14 CFR Chapter I, or other applicable standards, by obtaining all necessary FAA inspections or modifications."

(3) Ensure that the following certification is signed by the purchaser/recipient and received by the Government before releasing parts to the purchaser/recipient:

"The purchaser/recipient agrees that the Government shall not be held liable for personal injuries to, disabilities of, or death of the purchaser/recipient, the purchaser's/recipient's employees, or to any other persons arising from or incident to the purchase of these aircraft parts, their use, or disposition. The purchaser/recipient shall hold the Government harmless from any or all debts, liabilities, judgments, costs, demands, suits, actions, or claims of any nature arising from or incident to the purchase, use, or resale of these aircraft parts.

These parts may have been used on aircraft that were operated outside the limitations of 14 CFR Chapter I, and some type of inspection may be needed to determine their airworthiness prior to being used on a recipient aircraft."

You should be aware of the following requirements prior to operating an aircraft with parts received from an exchange.

• All civil and public aircraft must have a valid registration issued by the FAA as required by 14 CFR Chapter I.

• Civil aircraft must have a valid airworthiness certificate in order to operate in U.S. airspace.

• In order for the aircraft to be eligible for a standard airworthiness certificate, the aircraft must conform to its FAA Type Certificate.

• Aircraft not having a valid airworthiness certificate may be eligible for a special FAA one-time flight permit to enable relocating the aircraft. Relocation can be for a number of reasons, perhaps including storage, repair, inspection, or public display. Any one-time flight approval is predicated on the aircraft being safe for flight.

• Individuals who purchase a surplus military (foreign or domestic) or foreign aircraft not having any type of FAA Type Certificate may be unable to obtain any type of airworthiness certificate or special flight permit.

• An aircraft with good maintenance and inspection records makes an airworthiness determination easier to ascertain. It is in your best interest to contact the nearest FAA Flight Standards District Office and discuss your responsibilities with respect to gaining an airworthiness determination. The location of your nearest FAA office may be obtained from the FAA's Web site (*http://www.faa.gov/*)."

(b) Authorized SCs can conduct sales of aircraft parts for you. SCs that are currently authorized to conduct sales, as well as contact information for the GovSales Program Manager, are available on the GovSales Web site at *http://www.gsa.gov/portal/content/105020*.

§ 102–33.365 Must we report exchange/sale of parts to FAIRS?

No, you don't have to report exchange/sale of parts to FAIRS. However, you must report the transactions to GSA as part of your agency's annual report (see 41 CFR part 102–39 Subpart C—Exchange/Sale Methods and Reports).

SPECIAL REQUIREMENTS FOR DISPOSING OF FLIGHT SAFETY CRITICAL AIRCRAFT PARTS (FSCAP) AND LIFE-LIMITED PARTS

§ 102–33.370 What must we do to dispose of military FSCAP and/or life-limited parts?

To dispose of military FSCAP and/or life-limited parts, you must use the following tables:

(a) Table 1 for disposing of uninstalled FSCAP and/or life-limited parts follows:

TABLE 1 FOR DISPOSING OF UNINSTALLED FSCAP AND/OR LIFE-LIMITED PARTS

(1) If an Uninstalled FSCAP (*i.e.*, not installed in an aircraft or engine)—		
(i) Is documented—	Then	(A) You may exchange/sale it or transfer it to another executive agency under 41 CFR parts 102–36 and 102–39; (B) GSA may donate it for flight use under 41 CFR part 102–37 of this subchapter; or (C) GSA may donate it for ground use only, after you mutilate and mark it, "FSCAP—NOT AIRWORTHY" (the State Agency for Surplus Property must certify that the part has been mutilated and marked before donation).
(ii) Is undocumented, but traceable to its original equipment manufacturer (OEM) or production approval holder (PAH)—	Then	(A) You may exchange/sell it only to the OEM or PAH under 41 CFR part 102–39; (B) GSA may transfer or donate it for flight use, but only by making it a condition of the transfer or donation agreement that the recipient will have the part inspected, repaired, and certified by the OEM or PAH before putting it into service (Note: You must mark parts individually to ensure that the recipient is aware of the part's service status); or (C) GSA may donate it for ground use only, after you mutilate and mark it, "FSCAP—NOT AIRWORTHY" (the State Agency for Surplus Property must certify that the part has been mutilated and marked before donation).
(iii) Is undocumented and untraceable, you must mutilate it, and—	Then	(A) GSA may transfer or donate it for ground use only, after you mark it, "FSCAP—NOT AIRWORTHY" (the State Agency for Surplus Property must certify that the part has been mutilated and marked before donation); or (B) You may sell it only for scrap under §§ 102–33.310 and 102–33.315.
(2) If an uninstalled life-limited part (*i.e.*, not installed in an aircraft or engine)—		
(i) Is documented with service life remaining—	Then	(A) You may exchange/sale it or transfer it to another executive agency under 41 CFR parts 102–36 and 102–39; (B) GSA may donate it for flight use under 41 CFR part 102–37; or (C) GSA may donate it for ground use only, after you mutilate and mark it, "EXPIRED LIFE-LIMITED—NOT AIRWORTHY" (the State Agency for Surplus Property must certify that the part has been mutilated and marked before donation).
(ii) Is documented with no service life remaining, or undocumented, GSA may not transfer it to another executive agency for flight use—	But	(A) GSA may transfer or donate it for ground use only, after you mutilate and mark it, "EXPIRED LIFE-LIMITED—NOT AIRWORTHY" (the State Agency for Surplus Property must certify that the part has been mutilated and marked before donation); or (B) You must mutilate it and may sell it only for scrap.

(b) Table 2 for disposing of installed FSCAP and/or life-limited parts follows:

TABLE 2 FOR DISPOSING OF INSTALLED FSCAP AND/OR LIFE-LIMITED PARTS

(1) If a FSCAP and/or life-limited part is installed in an aircraft or an engine, and it—		
(i) Is documented with service life remaining—	Then	(A) You may exchange/sale the aircraft or engine, or GSA may transfer the aircraft or engine to another executive agency under 41 CFR parts 102–36 and 102–39;
		(B) GSA may donate the aircraft or engine for flight use or ground use.
(ii) Is documented with no service life remaining—	Then	(A) You must remove and mutilate the part before you exchange/sale the aircraft or engine (see rules for disposing of uninstalled life-limited parts in Table 1 of this section). (Note: If an aircraft or engine is exchanged/sold to its OEM or PAH, you do not have to remove the expired life-limited part);
		(B) You must remove and mutilate the part before GSA may transfer or donate the aircraft or engine for flight use (see the rules for disposing of uninstalled FSCAP in Table 1 of this section). (Note: An internal engine part may be left installed, if you identify the part individually to ensure that the receiving agency is aware of the part's service status and, as a condition of the transfer or donation agreement, the receiving agency agrees to remove and mutilate the part before the engine is put into service. You must certify mutilation for transfers, and the State Agency for Surplus Property must certify that the part has been mutilated for donations); or
		(C) GSA may donate the aircraft or engine for ground use only, after you remove the part, mutilate and mark it "EXPIRED LIFE-LIMITED—NOT AIRWORTHY." (Note: An internal engine part may be left installed, if, as a condition of the donation agreement, the receiving agency agrees to remove and mutilate the part and mark it, and the State Agency for Surplus Property must certify that the part has been mutilated and marked).

§ 102–33.375 What is a FSCAP Criticality Code?

(a) A FSCAP Criticality Code is a code assigned by DOD to indicate the type of FSCAP: Code "F" indicates a standard FSCAP; Code "E" indicates a nuclear-hardened FSCAP.

(b) You must perpetuate a FSCAP Criticality Code on all property records and reports of excess. If the code is not annotated on the transfer document that you received when you acquired the part, you may contact the appropriate military service or query DOD's Federal Logistics Information System (FLIS) using the National Stock Number (NSN) or the part number (see *http://www.dlis.dla.mil/webflis*). For assistance in subscribing to the FLIS service, contact the WebFLIS Consumer Support Office, 1–877–352–2255.

Subpart E—Reporting Information on Government Aircraft

OVERVIEW

§ 102–33.380 Who must report information to GSA on Government aircraft?

You must report information to GSA on Government aircraft if your agency—

(a) Is an executive agency of the United States Government; and

(b) Owns, bails, borrows, loans, leases, rents, charters, or contracts for (or obtains by ISSA) Government aircraft.

§ 102–33.385 What Federally-funded aviation activities of executive agencies are exempt from the requirement to report information to GSA on Government aircraft?

The following Federally-funded activities are exempt from the requirement to report information to GSA on Government aircraft:

(a) The Armed Forces (which includes the U.S. Coast Guard); and

(b) Agencies in the Intelligence Community.

§ 102–33.390 What information must we report on Government aircraft?

You must report the following information to GSA (for information regarding how to report this information, see: *https://gsa.inl.gov/fairs/*):

(a) Inventory data on Federal aircraft, including your Unmanned Aircraft Systems (UAS), through FAIRS;

(b) Cost and utilization data on Federal aircraft, including your Unmanned Aircraft Systems (UAS), through FAIRS;

(c) Cost and utilization data on CAS aircraft and related aviation services (see definition of "Government aircraft" for more on CAS), through FAIRS;

(d) Accident and incident data (see § 102–33.445); and

(e) The results of standard competition studies in compliance with OMB Circular A–76 to justify purchasing, leasing, modernizing, replacing, or otherwise acquiring aircraft and related aviation services.

FEDERAL AVIATION INTERACTIVE REPORTING SYSTEM (FAIRS)

§ 102–33.395   What is FAIRS?

FAIRS is a management information system operated by GSA to collect, maintain, analyze, and report information on Federal aircraft inventories and cost and usage of Federal aircraft and CAS aircraft (and related aviation services). Users access FAIRS through a highly-secure Web site. The U.S. Government Aircraft Cost Accounting Guide (CAG) (see *http://www.gsa.gov/ aviationpolicy*) contains the business rules for using the system.

§ 102–33.400   How must we report to FAIRS?

You must report to FAIRS electronically through a secure Web interface to the FAIRS application on the Internet. For additional information see *https:// gsa.inl.gov/fairs/*.

§ 102–33.405   When must we report to FAIRS?

(a) You must report any changes in your Federal aircraft inventory within 14 calendar days of those changes.

(b) You must report cost and utilization data to FAIRS at the end of every quarter of the fiscal year (December 31, March 31, June 30, and September 30). However, you may submit your information to FAIRS on a daily, weekly, or monthly basis. To provide enough time to calculate your cost and utilization data, you may report any one quarter's cost and utilization in the following quarter, as follows:

Quarter	Submit
QTR 1—October 1–December 31	Federal inventory for QTR 1. Federal cost and utilization for previous QTR 4. CAS cost and utilization for previous QTR 4.
QTR 2—January 1–March 31	Federal inventory for QTR 2. Federal cost and utilization for QTR 1. CAS cost and utilization for QTR 1.
QTR 3—April 1–June 30	Federal inventory for QTR 3. Federal cost and utilization for QTR 2. CAS cost and utilization for QTR 2.
QTR 4—July 1–September 30	Federal inventory for QTR 4. Federal cost and utilization for QTR 3. CAS cost and utilization for QTR 3.

FEDERAL INVENTORY DATA

§ 102–33.410   What are Federal inventory data?

Federal inventory data includes:

(a) Information on each of the operational and non-operational Federal aircraft that you own, bail, borrow, or loan; and

(b) UAS as described in § 102–33.20.

§ 102–33.415   When may we declassify a Federal aircraft and remove it from our Federal aircraft inventory?

When an aircraft is lost or destroyed, or is otherwise non-operational and you want to retain it, you may declassify it and remove it from your Federal aircraft inventory. For further details, see §§ 102–33.250 and 102–33.420. See §§ 102–33.265 and 102–33.270 for reporting excess Federal aircraft.

§ 102–33.420   How must we declassify a Federal aircraft?

To declassify a Federal aircraft, you must—

(a) Send a letter to the Deputy Associate Administrator, Office of Asset and Transportation Management, Office of Government-wide Policy, General Services Administration, 1800 F

St. NW., Washington, DC 20405, that requests approval to declassify the aircraft and states that the aircraft is non-operational (which includes lost or destroyed). In this letter you must—

(1) Identify the Federal Supply Classification (FSC) group(s) that the declassified aircraft/parts will fall under, if applicable;

(2) Describe the condition of the aircraft (crash-damaged, unrecoverable, parts unavailable, etc.); and

(3) Include photographs as appropriate.

(b) Within 14 calendar days of receiving GSA's approval to declassify the aircraft, following 14 CFR 45.13, request approval from your local FAA Flight Standards District Office (FSDO) to remove the manufacturer's data plate;

(c) Within 14 calendar days of receiving approval from FAA to remove the data plate, inform GSA of FAA's approval, send the data plate by courier or registered mail to the FAA, as directed by your FSDO, and remove the certificate of airworthiness and the aircraft's registration form from the aircraft, complete the reverse side of the registration form, and send both documents to The FAA Aircraft Registration Branch, P.O. Box 25504, Oklahoma City, OK 73125–0504; and

(d) Update the FAIRS inventory record to reflect disposal status and update your personal property records, deleting the declassified aircraft from the aircraft category and adding it to another Federal Supply Classification group or groups, as appropriate.

FEDERAL AIRCRAFT COST AND
UTILIZATION DATA

§ 102–33.425 What Federal aircraft cost and utilization data must we report?

You must report certain costs for each of your Federal aircraft (including your UAS) and the number of hours that you flew each aircraft. In reporting the costs of your Federal aircraft, you must report both the amounts you paid as Federal costs, which are for services the Government provides, and the amounts you paid for commercial aviation services (CAS) in support of your Federal aviation program. For a list and definitions of the Federal aircraft cost and utilization data ele-

ments, see the U.S. Government Aircraft Cost Accounting Guide (CAG), which is available at *http://www.gsa.gov/aviationpolicy*.

§ 102–33.430 Who must report Federal aircraft cost and utilization data?

(a) Executive agencies, except the Armed Forces and agencies in the Intelligence Community, must report Federal cost and utilization data on all Federal aircraft; and

(b) Agencies should report Federal cost and utilization data for loaned aircraft only if Federal money was expended on the aircraft.

COMMERCIAL AVIATION SERVICES (CAS)
COST AND UTILIZATION DATA

§ 102–33.435 What CAS cost and utilization data must we report?

You must report:

(a) The costs and flying hours for each CAS aircraft you hire;

(b) The costs and contractual periods for related aviation services that you hire (by contract or through an Interservice support agreement (ISSA)).

NOTE TO § 102–33.435: You should not report related aviation services that you hire commercially in support of Federal aircraft. "Federal" aircraft are by definition owned aircraft. The agency that owns the aircraft is responsible for capturing all cost and utilization data and is required to report this data in GSA's FAIRS. See the U.S. Government Aircraft Cost Accounting Guide (CAG), which is available from GSA at *http://www.gsa.gov/aviationpolicy*.

§ 102–33.440 Who must report CAS cost and utilization data?

Executive agencies, except the Armed Forces and agencies in the Intelligence Community, must report CAS cost and utilization data. You must report CAS cost and utilization data if your agency makes payments to—

(a) Charter or rent aircraft;

(b) Lease or lease-purchase aircraft;

(c) Hire aircraft and related services through an ISSA or a full service contract; or

(d) Obtain related aviation services through an ISSA or by contract except when you use the services in support of Federal aircraft (see the Note at § 102–33.435).

ACCIDENT AND INCIDENT DATA

§ 102–33.445 What accident and incident data must we report?

You must report within 14 calendar days to GSA, Aviation Policy Division, 1800 F St. NW., Washington, DC 20405, all aviation accidents and incidents that your agency is required to report to the NTSB. You may also report other incident information. GSA and the ICAP will use the collected accident/incident information in conjunction with FAIRS' data, such as flying hours and missions, to calculate aviation safety statistics for the Federal aviation community and to share safety lessons-learned.

§ 102–33.450 How must we report accident and incident data?

You must report accident and incident data to GSA at *http://www.gsa.gov/ aviationpolicy* or call GSA's Aviation Policy Division and report the accident or incident telephonically.

COMMON AVIATION MANAGEMENT INFORMATION STANDARD (C–AMIS)

§ 102–33.455 What is C–AMIS?

The Common Aviation Management Information Standard (C–AMIS) is a guide to assist agencies in developing or modernizing their internal aviation management information systems. C–AMIS includes standard specifications and data definitions related to Federal aviation operations. C–AMIS is jointly written by the ICAP and GSA and available from GSA's Aviation Policy Division.

§ 102–33.460 What is our responsibility in relation to C–AMIS?

If you use a management information system to provide data to FAIRS by batch upload, you are responsible for ensuring that your system is C–AMIS-compliant (see § 102–33.195). For more information on compliance with C–AMIS, contact GSA's Aviation Policy Division at (202) 208–0519 or (202) 997–7274.

PERFORMANCE INDICATORS

§ 102–33.465 What is a performance indicator?

In addition to the definition in § 102–33.20, a performance indicator provides information (either qualitative or quantitative) on the extent to which the actual outcome of a policy, program, or initiative achieves the planned outcome.

§ 102–33.470 Must we develop performance indicators?

Yes, your agency must develop performance indicators in order to measure the degree to which key aviation program objectives are achieved. It is suggested that your performance indicators:

(a) Measure the contribution of the aviation program toward the accomplishment of the agency's mission;

(b) Support and justify aviation program budget requests; and

(c) Demonstrate the effectiveness and efficiency of the aviation program's performance.

§ 102–33.475 What are some examples of performance indicators that an agency can use?

Examples of performance indicators include, but are not limited to, a percentage increase or decrease:

(a) Of operations scheduling effectiveness;

(b) Of repeat system discrepancies over a specific period of time;

(c) In logistical response time for returned parts processing over a specified period of time;

(d) In lost man-hours due to personnel injuries;

(e) In aircraft turn-around time;

(f) In fuel expenditures for a given mission, location, or type/model/series of aircraft;

(g) In aircraft availability or non-availability rates;

(h) In full-mission-capable aircraft over a specific time period;

(i) In non-airworthy maintenance;

(j) In maintenance costs per flying hour; or

(k) In variable cost per passenger mile.

APPENDIX A TO PART 102–33—DISCLO-
SURE STATEMENT FOR CREW-
MEMBERS AND QUALIFIED NON-CREW-
MEMBERS FLYING ON BOARD GOVERN-
MENT AIRCRAFT OPERATED AS PUB-
LIC AIRCRAFT

Generally, an aircraft used exclusively for
the U.S. Government may be considered a
"public aircraft" as defined by Public Law
106–181 and 14 CFR Chapter I, provided it is
not a Government-owned aircraft transporting passengers or operating for commercial purposes. A public aircraft is not subject
to many Federal Aviation Regulations, including requirements relating to aircraft
certification, maintenance, and pilot certification. If the aircraft does not qualify as a
"public aircraft", then it is a civil aircraft
and must comply with all Federal Aviation
Regulations applicable to civil aircraft. If
you have any questions concerning whether
a particular flight will be a public aircraft
operation or a civil aircraft operation, you
should contact the agency sponsor of that
flight.

RIGHTS AND BENEFITS

You have certain rights and benefits in the
unlikely event you are injured or killed
while working aboard a Government-owned
or operated aircraft. Federal employees and
some private citizens are eligible for workers' compensation benefits under the Federal
Employees' Compensation Act (FECA). When
FECA applies, it is the sole remedy. For
more information about FECA and its coverage, consult with your agency's benefits
office or contact the Branch of Technical Assistance at the Department of Labor's Office
of Workers' Compensation Programs.

STATE OR FOREIGN LAWS

State or foreign laws may provide for product liability or "third party" causes of actions for personal injury or wrongful death.
If you have questions about a particular case
or believe you have a claim, you should consult with an attorney.

INSURANCE POLICIES

Some insurance policies may exclude coverage for injuries or death sustained while
working or traveling aboard a Government
or military aircraft or while within a combat
area. You may wish to check your policy or
consult with your insurance provider before
your flight. The insurance available to Federal employees through the Federal Employees Group Life Insurance Program does not
contain an exclusion of this type.

VICTIM RIGHTS

If you are the victim of an air disaster resulting from criminal activity, Victim and

Witness Specialists from the Federal Bureau
of Investigation (FBI) and/or the local U.S.
Attorney's Office will keep you or your family informed about the status of the criminal
investigation(s) and provide you or your
family with information about rights and
services, such as crisis intervention, counseling and emotional support. State crime
victim compensation may be able to cover
crime-related expenses, such as medical
costs, mental health counseling, funeral and
burial costs, and lost wages or loss of support. The Office for Victims of Crime (an
agency of the Department of Justice) and the
U.S. Attorneys Office are authorized by the
Antiterrorism Act of 1996 to provide emergency financial assistance to State programs
for the benefit of victims of terrorist acts or
mass violence.

FEDERAL EMPLOYEE

If you are injured or killed on the job during the performance of duty, including while
traveling or working aboard a Government
aircraft or other Government-owned or operated conveyance for official Government
business purposes, you and your family are
eligible to collect workers' compensation
benefits under FECA. You and your family
may not file a personal injury or wrongful
death suit against the United States or its
employees. However, you may have cause of
action against potentially liable third parties.

FAMILY MEMBER

You or your qualifying family member
must normally also choose between FECA
disability or death benefits, and those payable under your retirement system (either
the Civil Service Retirement System or the
Federal Employees Retirement System). You
may choose the benefit that is more favorable to you.

PRIVATE CITIZEN

Even if the Federal Government does not
regularly employ you, if you are rendering
personal service to the Federal Government
on a voluntary basis or for nominal pay, you
may be defined as a Federal employee for
purposes of FECA. If that is the case, you
and your family are eligible to receive workers' compensation benefits under FECA, but
may not collect in a personal injury or
wrongful death lawsuit against the United
States or its employees. You and your family
may file suit against potentially liable third
parties. Before you board a Government aircraft, you may wish to consult with the department or agency sponsoring the flight to
clarify whether you are considered a Federal
employee.

If the agency determines that you are not
a "Federal employee," you and your family

will not be eligible to receive workers' compensation benefits under FECA. If you are onboard the aircraft for purposes of official Government business, you may be eligible for workers' compensation benefits under state law. If an accident occurs within the United States, or its territories, its airspace, or over the high seas, you and your family may claim against the United States under the Federal Tort Claims Act or Suits in Admiralty Act. If you are killed aboard a military aircraft, your family may be eligible to receive compensation under the Military Claims Act, or if you are an inhabitant of a foreign country, under the Foreign Claims Act.

NOTE TO APPENDIX A TO PART 102-33: This disclosure statement is not all-inclusive. You should contact your agency's personnel office, or if you are a private citizen, your agency sponsor or point-of-contact for further assistance.

PART 102-34—MOTOR VEHICLE MANAGEMENT

Subpart A—General Provisions

Subpart B—Obtaining Fuel Efficient Motor Vehicles

Subpart C—Identifying and Registering Motor Vehicles

AUTHORITY: 40 U.S.C. 121(c); 40 U.S.C. 17503; 31 U.S.C. 1344; 49 U.S.C. 32917; E.O. 12375.

SOURCE: 74 FR 11871, Mar. 20, 2009, unless otherwise noted.

Subpart A—General Provisions

§ 102–34.5 What does this part cover?

This part governs the economical and efficient management and control of motor vehicles that the Government owns, leases commercially or leases through GSA Fleet. Agencies will incorporate appropriate provisions of this part into contracts offering Government-furnished equipment in order to ensure adequate control over the use of motor vehicles.

§102–34.10 What are the governing authorities for this part?

The authorities for the regulations in this part are 40 U.S.C. 121(c), 40 U.S.C. 17503, 31 U.S.C. 1344, 49 U.S.C. 32917, and E.O. 12375.

§102–34.15 Who must comply with these provisions?

All executive agencies must comply with the provisions of this part. The legislative and judicial branches are encouraged to follow these provisions.

§102–34.20 What motor vehicles are not covered by this part?

Motor vehicles not covered by this part are:

(a) Military design motor vehicles;

(b) Motor vehicles used for military field training, combat, or tactical purposes;

(c) Motor vehicles used principally within the confines of a regularly established military post, camp, or depot; and

(d) Motor vehicles regularly used by an agency to perform investigative, law enforcement, or intelligence duties, if the head of the agency determines that exclusive control of the vehicle is essential for effective performance of duties, although such vehicles are subject to subpart D and subpart J of this part.

§102–34.25 To whom do "we", "you", and their variants refer?

Unless otherwise indicated, use of pronouns "we", "you", and their variants throughout this part refer to you as an executive agency, as your agency's fleet manager, or as a motor vehicle user or operator, as appropriate.

§102–34.30 How do we request a deviation from the provisions of this part?

Refer to §§102–2.60 through 102–2.110 of this chapter for information on how to obtain a deviation from this part.

DEFINITIONS

§102–34.35 What definitions apply to this part?

The following definitions apply to this part:

Commercial design motor vehicle means a motor vehicle procurable from regular production lines and designed for use by the general public.

Commercial lease or lease commercially means obtaining a motor vehicle by contract or other arrangement from a commercial source for 120 continuous days or more. (Procedures for purchasing and leasing motor vehicles through GSA can be found in 41 CFR subpart 101–26.5).

Domestic fleet means all reportable motor vehicles operated in any State, Commonwealth, territory or possession of the United States, and the District of Columbia.

Foreign fleet means all reportable motor vehicles operated in areas outside any State, Commonwealth, territory or possession of the United States, and the District of Columbia.

Government motor vehicle means any motor vehicle that the Government owns or leases. This includes motor vehicles obtained through purchase, excess, forfeiture, commercial lease, or GSA Fleet lease.

Government-owned motor vehicle means any motor vehicle that the Government has obtained through purchase, excess, forfeiture, or otherwise and for which the Government holds title.

GSA Fleet lease means obtaining a motor vehicle from the General Services Administration Fleet (GSA Fleet).

Law enforcement motor vehicle means a light duty motor vehicle that is specifically approved in an agency's appropriation act for use in apprehension, surveillance, police or other law enforcement work or specifically designed for use in law enforcement. If not identified in an agency's appropriation language, a motor vehicle qualifies as a law enforcement motor vehicle only in the following cases:

(1) A passenger automobile having heavy duty components for electrical, cooling and suspension systems and at least the next higher cubic inch displacement or more powerful engine than is standard for the automobile concerned;

(2) A light truck having emergency warning lights and identified with markings such as "police;"

(3) An unmarked motor vehicle certified by the agency head as essential for the safe and efficient performance of intelligence, counterintelligence, protective, or other law enforcement duties; or

(4) A forfeited motor vehicle seized by a Federal agency that is subsequently used for the purpose of performing law enforcement activities.

Light duty motor vehicle means any motor vehicle with a gross motor vehicle weight rating (GVWR) of 8,500 pounds or less.

Light truck means a motor vehicle on a truck chassis with a gross motor vehicle weight rating (GVWR) of 8,500 pounds or less.

Military design motor vehicle means a motor vehicle (excluding commercial design motor vehicles) designed according to military specifications to directly support combat or tactical operations or training for such operations.

Motor vehicle means any vehicle, self propelled or drawn by mechanical power, designed and operated principally for highway transportation of property or passengers, but does not include a military design motor vehicle or vehicles not covered by this part (see § 102–34.20).

Motor vehicle identification (also referred to as "motor vehicle markings") means the legends "For Official Use Only" and "U.S. Government" placed on a motor vehicle plus other legends readily identifying the department, agency, establishment, corporation, or service by which the motor vehicle is used.

Motor vehicle markings (see definition of "Motor vehicle identification" in this section).

Motor vehicle purchase means buying a motor vehicle from a commercial source, usually a motor vehicle manufacturer or a motor vehicle manufacturer's dealership. (Procedures for purchasing and leasing motor vehicles through GSA can be found in 41 CFR subpart 101–26.5.)

Motor vehicle rental means obtaining a motor vehicle by contract or other arrangement from a commercial source for less than 120 continuous days.

Motor vehicles transferred from excess means obtaining a motor vehicle reported as excess and transferred with or without cost.

Owning agency means the executive agency that holds the vehicle title, manufacturer's Certificate of Origin, or is the lessee of a commercial lease. This term does not apply to agencies that lease motor vehicles from the GSA Fleet.

Passenger automobile means a sedan or station wagon designed primarily to transport people.

Reportable motor vehicles are any Government motor vehicles used by an executive agency or activity, including those used by contractors. Also included are motor vehicles designed or acquired for a specific or unique purpose, including motor vehicles that serve as a platform or conveyance for special equipment, such as a trailer. Excluded are material handling equipment and construction equipment not designed and used primarily for highway operation (e.g., if it must be trailered or towed to be transported).

Using agency means an executive agency that obtains motor vehicles from the GSA Fleet, commercial firms or another executive agency and does not hold the vehicle title or manufacturer's Certificate of Origin. However, this does not include an executive agency that obtains a motor vehicle by motor vehicle rental.

[74 FR 11871, Mar. 20, 2009, as amended at 76 FR 76623, Dec. 8, 2011]

Subpart B—Obtaining Fuel Efficient Motor Vehicles

§ 102–34.40 Who must comply with motor vehicle fuel efficiency requirements?

(a) Executive agencies operating domestic fleets must comply with motor vehicle fuel efficiency requirements for such fleets.

(b) This subpart does not apply to motor vehicles exempted by law or other regulations, such as law enforcement or emergency rescue work and foreign fleets. Other Federal agencies are encouraged to comply so that maximum energy conservation benefits may be realized in obtaining, operating, and managing Government motor vehicles.

§ 102–34.45 How are passenger automobiles classified?

Passenger automobiles are classified in the following table:

Sedan class	Station wagon class	Descriptive name
I	I	Subcompact.
II	II	Compact.
III	III	Midsize.
IV	IV	Large.
V	Limousine..	

§ 102–34.50 What size motor vehicles may we obtain?

(a) You may only obtain the minimum size of motor vehicle necessary to fulfill your agency's mission in accordance with the following considerations:

(1) You must obtain motor vehicles that achieve maximum fuel efficiency.

(2) Limit motor vehicle body size, engine size and optional equipment to what is essential to meet your agency's mission.

(3) With the exception of motor vehicles used by the President and Vice President and motor vehicles for security and highly essential needs, you must obtain midsize (class III) or smaller sedans.

(4) Obtain large (class IV) sedans only when such motor vehicles are essential to your agency's mission.

(b) Agencies must establish and document a structured vehicle allocation methodology to determine the appropriate size and number of motor vehicles (see FMR Bulletin B–9, located at *http://www.gsa.gov/bulletin*, for guidance).

§ 102–34.55 Are there fleet average fuel economy standards we must meet?

(a) Yes. 49 U.S.C. 32917 and Executive Order 12375 require that each executive agency meet the fleet average fuel economy standards in place as of January 1 of each fiscal year. The standards for passenger automobiles are prescribed in 49 U.S.C. 32902(b). The Department of Transportation publishes the standards for light trucks and amendments to the standards for passenger automobiles at *http://www.dot.gov*.

(b) These standards do not apply to military design motor vehicles, law enforcement motor vehicles, or motor vehicles intended for emergency rescue.

§ 102–34.60 How do we calculate the average fuel economy for Government motor vehicles?

You must calculate the average fuel economy for Government motor vehicles as follows:

(a) Because there are so many motor vehicle configurations, you must take an average of all light duty motor vehicles by category that your agency obtained and operated during the fiscal year.

(b) This calculation is the sum of such light duty motor vehicles divided by the sum of the fractions representing the number of motor vehicles of each category by model divided by the unadjusted city/highway mile-per-gallon ratings for that model. The unadjusted city/highway mile-per-gallon ratings for each make and model are published by the Environmental Protection Agency (EPA) for each model year and published at *http://www.fueleconomy.gov*.

(c) An example follows:

Light trucks:
(i) 600 light trucks acquired in a specific year. These are broken down into:
(A) 200 Six cylinder automatic transmission pick-up trucks, EPA rating: 24.3 mpg, plus
(B) 150 Six cylinder automatic transmission mini-vans, EPA rating: 24.8 mpg, plus
(C) 150 Eight cylinder automatic transmission pick-up trucks, EPA rating: 20.4 mpg, plus
(D) 100 Eight cylinder automatic transmission cargo vans, EPA rating: 22.2 mpg.

$$= \cfrac{600}{\cfrac{200}{24.3} + \cfrac{150}{24.8} + \cfrac{150}{20.4} + \cfrac{100}{22.2}}$$

$$= \cfrac{600}{8.2305 + 6.0484 + 7.3530 + 4.5045}$$

$$= \frac{600}{26.1364} = 22.9565 \text{ (Rounded to nearest 0.1 mpg.)}$$

(ii) Fleet average fuel economy for light trucks in this case is 23.0 mpg.

§ 102–34.65 How may we request an exemption from the fuel economy standards?

You must submit a written request for an exemption from the fuel economy standards to: Administrator, General Services Administration, ATTN: Deputy Associate Administrator, Office of Travel, Transportation and Asset Management (MT), Washington, DC 20405.

(a) Your request for an exemption must include all relevant information necessary to permit review of the request that the vehicles be exempted based on energy conservation, economy, efficiency, or service. Exemptions may be sought for individual vehicles or categories of vehicles.

(b) GSA will review the request and advise you of the determination within 30 days of receipt. Light duty motor vehicles exempted under the provisions of this section must not be included in calculating your fleet average fuel economy.

§ 102–34.70 What do we do with completed calculations of our fleet vehicle acquisitions?

You must maintain the average fuel economy data for each year's vehicle acquisitions on file at your agency headquarters in accordance with the National Archives and Records Administration, General Records Schedule 10, Motor Vehicle and Aircraft Maintenance and Operations Records, Item 4, Motor Vehicle Report Files. Exemption requests and their disposition must also be maintained with the average fuel economy files.

§ 102–34.75 Who is responsible for monitoring our compliance with fuel economy standards for motor vehicles we obtain?

Executive agencies are responsible for monitoring their own compliance with fuel economy standards for motor vehicles they obtain.

§ 102–34.80 Where may we obtain help with our motor vehicle acquisition plans?

For help with your motor vehicle acquisition plans, contact the: General Services Administration, ATTN: MT, Washington, DC 20405. E-mail: *vehicle.policy@gsa.gov.*

Subpart C—Identifying and Registering Motor Vehicles

MOTOR VEHICLE IDENTIFICATION

§ 102–34.85 What motor vehicles require motor vehicle identification?

All Government motor vehicles must display motor vehicle identification unless exempted under § 102–34.160, § 102–34.175 or § 102–34.180.

§ 102–34.90 What motor vehicle identification must we display on Government motor vehicles?

Unless exempted under § 102–34.160, § 102–34.175 or § 102–34.180, Government motor vehicles must display the following identification:

(a) "For Official Use Only";

(b) "U.S. Government"; and

(c) Identification that readily identifies the agency owning the vehicle.

§ 102–34.95   What motor vehicle identification must the Department of Defense (DOD) display on motor vehicles it owns or leases commercially?

Unless exempted under § 102–34.160, § 102–34.175 or § 102–34.180, the following must appear on motor vehicles that the DOD owns or leases commercially:

(a) "For Official Use Only"; and

(b) An appropriate title for the DOD component responsible for the vehicle.

§ 102–34.100   Where is motor vehicle identification displayed?

Motor vehicle identification is displayed as follows:

(a) *For most Government motor vehicles,* preferably on the official U.S. Government license plate. Some Government motor vehicles may display motor vehicle identification on a decal in the rear window, or centered on both front doors if the vehicle is without a rear window, or where identification on the rear window would not be easily seen.

(b) *For trailers,* on both sides of the front quarter of the trailer in a conspicuous location.

NOTE TO § 102–34.100: Each agency or activity that uses decals to identify Government motor vehicles is responsible for acquiring its own decals and for replacing them when necessary due to damage or wear.

§ 102–34.105   Before we sell a motor vehicle, what motor vehicle identification must we remove?

You must remove all motor vehicle identification before you transfer the title or deliver the motor vehicle.

LICENSE PLATES

§ 102–34.110   Must Government motor vehicles use Government license plates?

Yes, you must use Government license plates on Government motor vehicles, with the exception of motor vehicles exempted under § 102–34.160, § 102–34.175 or § 102–34.180.

§ 102–34.115   Can official U.S. Government license plates be used on motor vehicles not owned or leased by the Government?

No, official U.S. Government license plates may only be used on Government motor vehicles.

§ 102–34.120   Do we need to register Government motor vehicles?

If the Government motor vehicle displays U.S. Government license plates and motor vehicle identification, you do not need to register it in the jurisdiction where the vehicle is operated, however, you must register it in the Federal Government Motor Vehicle Registration System. GSA Fleet may register motor vehicles leased from GSA Fleet. Motor vehicles that have been exempted from the requirement to display official U.S. Government license plates under section § 102–34.160, § 102–34.175 or § 102–34.180 must be registered and inspected in accordance with the laws of the jurisdiction where the motor vehicle is regularly operated.

§ 102–34.125   Where may we obtain U.S. Government license plates?

You may obtain U.S. Government license plates for domestic fleets—

(a) By contacting: U.S. Department of Justice, UNICOR, Federal Prison Industries, Inc., 400 First Street, NW., Room 6010, Washington, DC 20534.

(b) For assistance with any issues involving license plates, contact the following office: General Services Administration, ATTN: MT, Washington, DC 20405. E-mail: *vehicle.policy@gsa.gov.*

NOTE TO § 102–34.125: GSA has established a Memorandum of Understanding (MOU) on behalf of all Federal agencies with Federal Prison Industries (UNICOR) for the procurement of official U.S. Government license plates. Each agency must execute an addendum to this MOU providing plate design and specific ordering and payment information before ordering license plates. Agency field activities should contact their national level Agency Fleet Manager for assistance.

§ 102–34.130   How do we display U.S. Government license plates on Government motor vehicles?

(a) Display official U.S. Government license plates on the front and rear of all Government motor vehicles. The exception is two-wheeled motor vehicles and trailers, which require rear license plates only.

(b) You must display U.S. Government license plates on the Government motor vehicle to which the license plates were assigned.

(c) Display the U.S. Government license plates until the Government motor vehicle is removed from Government service or is transferred outside the agency, or until the plates are damaged and require replacement. U.S. Government license plates shall only be used for one Government motor vehicle and shall not be reissued to another Government motor vehicle.

(d) For motor vehicles owned or commercially leased by DOD, also follow DOD regulations.

§ 102–34.135 What do we do about a lost or stolen license plate?

You must report the loss or theft of license plates as follows:

(a) *U.S. Government license plates.* Report to your local security office (or equivalent), local police, to GSA Fleet when a GSA Fleet leased motor vehicle is involved, and to the Federal Government Motor Vehicle Registration System.

(b) *District of Columbia or State license plates.* Report to your local security office (or equivalent) and either the District of Columbia Department of Transportation, or the State Department of Motor Vehicles, as appropriate.

§ 102–34.140 What records do we need to keep on U.S. Government license plates?

You must keep a central record of all U.S. Government license plates for Government motor vehicles. The GSA Fleet must also keep such a record for GSA Fleet vehicles. The record must:

(a) Identify the motor vehicle to which each set of plates is assigned; and

(b) List lost, stolen, destroyed, and voided license plate numbers.

§ 102–34.145 How are U.S. Government license plates coded?

U.S. Government license plate numbers will be preceded by a letter code that designates the owning agency for the motor vehicle. The agency letter codes are listed in GSA Bulletin FMR Bulletin B–11. (FMR bulletins are located at *http://www.gsa.gov/bulletin.*)

§ 102–34.150 How can we get a new license plate code designation?

To obtain a new license plate code designation, write to the: General Services Administration, ATTN: MT, Washington, DC 20405. E-mail: *vehicle.policy@gsa.gov.*

IDENTIFICATION EXEMPTIONS

§ 102–34.155 What are the types of motor vehicle identification exemptions?

The types of motor vehicle identification exemptions are:

(a) Limited exemption.

(b) Unlimited exemption.

(c) Special exemption.

§ 102–34.160 May we have a limited exemption from displaying U.S. Government license plates and other motor vehicle identification?

Yes. The head of your agency or designee may authorize a limited exemption to the display of U.S. Government license plates and motor vehicle identification upon written certification (see § 102–34.165). For motor vehicles leased from the GSA Fleet, send an information copy of this certification to the: General Services Administration, ATTN: GSA Fleet (QMDB), 2200 Crystal Drive, Arlington, VA 22202.

§ 102–34.165 What information must the limited exemption certification contain?

The certification must state that identifying the motor vehicle would endanger the security of the vehicle occupants or otherwise compromise the agency mission.

§ 102–34.170 For how long is a limited exemption valid?

An exemption granted in accordance with § 102–34.160 may last from one day up to 3 years. If the requirement for exemption still exists beyond 3 years, your agency must re-certify the continued exemption. For a motor vehicle leased from the GSA Fleet, send a copy of the re-certification to the: General Services Administration, ATTN: GSA Fleet (QMDB), 2200 Crystal Drive, Arlington, VA 22202.

§102–34.175 What motor vehicles have an unlimited exemption from displaying U.S. Government license plates and motor vehicle identification?

Motor vehicles used primarily for investigative, law enforcement, intelligence, or security duties have an unlimited exemption from displaying U.S. Government license plates and motor vehicle identification when identifying these motor vehicles would interfere with those duties.

§102–34.180 What agencies have a special exemption from displaying U.S. Government license plates and motor vehicle identification on some of their vehicles?

Motor vehicles assigned for the use of the President and the heads of executive departments specified in 5 U.S.C. 101 are exempt from the requirement to display motor vehicle identification.

§102–34.185 What license plates do we use on motor vehicles that are exempt from motor vehicle identification requirements?

For motor vehicles that are exempt from motor vehicle identification requirements, display the regular license plates of the State, Commonwealth, territory or possession of the United States, or the District of Columbia, where the motor vehicle is principally operated (see §102–34.120).

§102–34.190 What special requirements apply to exempted motor vehicles using District of Columbia or State license plates?

Your agency head must designate an official to authorize the District of Columbia (DC) or State motor vehicle department to issue DC license plates or State license plates for motor vehicles exempt from displaying U.S. Government license plates and motor vehicle identification. The agency head must provide the name and signature of that official to the DC Department of Transportation annually, or to the equivalent State vehicle motor vehicle department, as required. Agencies must pay DC and the States for these license plates in accordance with DC or State policy. Also, for motor vehicles leased from the GSA Fleet, send a list of the new plates to: General Services Admin-istration, ATTN: GSA Fleet (QMDB), 2200 Crystal Drive, Arlington, VA 22202.

§102–34.195 Must we submit a report concerning motor vehicles exempted under this subpart?

Yes. If asked, the head of each executive agency must submit a report concerning motor vehicles exempted under this subpart. This report, which has been assigned interagency report control number 1537–GSA–AR, should be submitted to the: General Services Administration, ATTN: MT, Washington, DC 20405. E-mail: *vehicle.policy@gsa.gov*.

Subpart D—Official Use of Government Motor Vehicles

§102–34.200 What is official use of Government motor vehicles?

Official use of a Government motor vehicle is using a Government motor vehicle to perform your agency's mission(s), as authorized by your agency.

§102–34.205 May I use a Government motor vehicle for transportation between my residence and place of employment?

No, you may not use a Government motor vehicle for transportation between your residence and place of employment unless your agency authorizes such use after making the necessary determination under 31 U.S.C. 1344 and part 102–5 of this title. Your agency must keep a copy of the written authorization within the agency and monitor the use of these motor vehicles.

§102–34.210 May I use a Government motor vehicle for transportation between places of employment and mass transit facilities?

Yes, you may use a Government motor vehicle for transportation between places of employment and mass transit facilities under the following conditions:

(a) The head of your agency must make a determination in writing, valid for one year, that such use is appropriate and consistent with sound budget policy, and the determination must be kept on file;

(b) There is no safe and reliable commercial or duplicative Federal mass transportation service that serves the same route on a regular basis;

(c) This transportation is made available, space provided, to other Federal employees;

(d) Alternative fuel vehicles should be used to the maximum extent practicable;

(e) This transportation should be provided in a manner that does not result in any additional gross income for Federal income tax purposes; and

(f) Motor vehicle ridership levels must be frequently monitored to ensure cost/benefit of providing and maintaining this transportation.

§ 102–34.215 May Government contractors use Government motor vehicles?

Yes, Government contractors may use Government motor vehicles when authorized in accordance with the Federal Acquisition Regulation (FAR), GSA Fleet procedures, and the following conditions:

(a) Government motor vehicles are used for official purposes only and solely in the performance of the contract;

(b) Government motor vehicles cannot be used for transportation between residence and place of employment, unless authorized in accordance with 31 U.S.C. 1344 and part 102–5 of this chapter; and

(c) Contractors must:

(1) Establish and enforce suitable penalties against employees who use, or authorize the use of, Government motor vehicles for unofficial purposes or for other than in the performance of the contract; and

(2) Pay any expenses or cost, without Government reimbursement, for using Government motor vehicles other than in the performance of the contract.

§ 102–34.220 What does GSA do if it learns of unofficial use of a Government motor vehicle?

GSA reports the matter to the head of your agency. The agency investigates and may, if appropriate, take disciplinary action under 31 U.S.C. 1349 or may report the violation to the Attorney General for prosecution under 18 U.S.C. 641.

§ 102–34.225 How are Federal employees disciplined for misuse of Government motor vehicles?

If an employee willfully uses, or authorizes the use of, a Government motor vehicle for other than official purposes, the employee is subject to suspension of at least one month or, up to and including, removal by the head of the agency (31 U.S.C. 1349).

§ 102–34.230 How am I responsible for protecting Government motor vehicles?

When a Government motor vehicle is under your control, you must:

(a) Park or store the Government motor vehicle in a manner that reasonably protects it from theft or damage; and

(b) Lock the unattended Government motor vehicle. (The only exception to this requirement is when fire regulations or other directives prohibit locking motor vehicles in closed buildings or enclosures.)

§ 102–34.235 Am I bound by State and local traffic laws?

Yes. You must obey all motor vehicle traffic laws of the State and local jurisdiction, except when the duties of your position require otherwise. You are personally responsible if you violate State or local traffic laws. If you are fined or otherwise penalized for an offense you commit while performing your official duties, but which was not required as part of your official duties, payment is your personal responsibility.

§ 102–34.240 Who pays for parking fees?

You must pay parking fees while operating a Government motor vehicle. However, you can expect to be reimbursed for parking fees incurred while performing official duties.

§ 102–34.245 Who pays for parking fines?

If you are fined for a parking violation while operating a Government motor vehicle, you are responsible for paying the fine and will not be reimbursed.

§ 102–34.250 Do Federal employees in Government motor vehicles have to use all safety devices and follow all safety guidelines?

Yes, Federal employees in Government motor vehicles have to use all provided safety devices including safety belts and follow all appropriate motor vehicle manufacturer safety guidelines.

Subpart E—Replacement of Motor Vehicles

§ 102–34.255 What are motor vehicle replacement standards?

Motor vehicle replacement standards specify the minimum number of years in use or miles traveled at which an executive agency may replace a Government-owned motor vehicle (see § 102–34.270).

§ 102–34.260 May we replace a Government-owned motor vehicle sooner?

Yes. You may replace a Government-owned motor vehicle if it needs body or mechanical repairs that exceed the fair market value of the motor vehicle. Determine the fair market value by adding the current market value of the motor vehicle plus any capitalized motor vehicle additions (such as a utility body or liftgate) or repairs. Your agency head or designee must review the replacement in advance.

§ 102–34.265 May we keep a Government-owned motor vehicle even though the standard permits replacement?

Yes. The replacement standard is a minimum only, and therefore, you may keep a Government-owned motor vehicle longer than shown in § 102–34.270 if the motor vehicle can be operated without excessive maintenance costs or substantial reduction in resale value.

§ 102–34.270 How long must we keep a Government-owned motor vehicle?

You must keep a Government-owned motor vehicle for at least the years or miles shown in the following table, unless it is no longer needed and declared excess:

TABLE OF MINIMUM REPLACEMENT STANDARDS

Motor vehicle type	Years [1]	Or miles [1]
Sedans/Station Wagons	3	60,000
Ambulances	7	60,000
Buses:		
Intercity	n/a	280,000
City	n/a	150,000
School	n/a	80,000
Trucks:		
Less than 12,500 pounds GVWR	6	50,000
12,500–23,999 pounds GVWR	7	60,000
24,000 pounds GVWR and over	9	80,000
4- or 6-wheel drive motor vehicles	6	40,000

[1] Minimum standards are stated in both years and miles; use whichever occurs first.

Subpart F—Scheduled Maintenance of Motor Vehicles

§ 102–34.275 What kind of maintenance programs must we have?

You must have a scheduled maintenance program for each motor vehicle you own or lease commercially. This requirement applies to domestic fleets, and is recommended for foreign fleets. The GSA Fleet will develop maintenance programs for GSA Fleet vehicles. The scheduled maintenance program must:

(a) Meet Federal and State emissions and safety standards;

(b) Meet manufacturer warranty requirements;

(c) Ensure the safe and economical operating condition of the motor vehicle throughout its life; and

(d) Ensure that inspections and servicing occur as recommended by the manufacturer or more often if local operating conditions require.

§ 102–34.280 What State inspections must we have for Government motor vehicles?

You must have the following State inspections for Government motor vehicles:

(a) Federally-mandated emissions inspections when required by the relevant State motor vehicle administration or State environmental department. Your agency must pay for these inspections if the fee is not waived. GSA Fleet will pay the cost of these inspections for motor vehicles leased from GSA Fleet; or

(b) For motor vehicles that display license plates issued by a State, Commonwealth, territory, or possession of the United States, motor vehicle safety inspections required by the relevant motor vehicle administration. Your agency must pay for these inspections unless the fee is waived. Payment for these inspections for motor vehicles leased from GSA Fleet is the responsibility of the using agency. Government motor vehicles that display official U.S. Government license plates do not require motor vehicle safety inspections.

§ 102–34.285 Where can we obtain help in setting up a maintenance program?

For help in setting up a maintenance program, contact the: General Services Administration, Attn: Motor Vehicle Policy, Washington, DC 20405. E-mail: *vehicle.policy@gsa.gov.*

Subpart G—Motor Vehicle Crash Reporting

§ 102–34.290 What forms do I use to report a crash involving a domestic fleet motor vehicle?

Use the following forms to report a domestic fleet crash. The forms should be carried in any domestic fleet motor vehicle.

(a) *Standard Form (SF) 91, Motor Vehicle Accident Report.* The motor vehicle operator should complete this form at the time and scene of the crash if possible, even if damage to the motor vehicle is not noticeable.

(b) *SF 94, Statement of Witness.* This form should be completed by any witness to the crash.

§ 102–34.295 To whom do we send crash reports?

Send crash reports as follows:

(a) If the motor vehicle is owned or commercially leased by your agency, follow your internal agency directives.

(b) If the motor vehicle is leased from GSA Fleet, report the crash to GSA in accordance with subpart 101–39.4 of this Title.

Subpart H—Disposal of Motor Vehicles

§ 102–34.300 How do we dispose of a domestic fleet motor vehicle?

After meeting the replacement standards under subpart E of this part, you may dispose of a Government-owned domestic fleet motor vehicle. Detailed instructions for the transfer of an excess motor vehicle to another Federal agency can be found in part 102–36 of this subchapter B, information for the donation of surplus of motor vehicles can be found in part 102–37 of this subchapter B, information for the sale of motor vehicles can be found in part 102–38 of this subchapter B, and information on exchange/sale authority can be found in part 102–39 of this subchapter B.

§ 102–34.305 What forms do we use to transfer ownership when selling a motor vehicle?

Use the following forms to transfer ownership:

(a) SF 97, The United States Government Certificate to Obtain Title to a Motor Vehicle, if both of the following apply:

(1) The motor vehicle will be retitled by a State, Commonwealth, territory or possession of the United States or the District of Columbia; and

(2) The purchaser intends to operate the motor vehicle on highways.

NOTE TO § 102–34.305(a)(2): Do not use SF 97 if the Government-owned motor vehicle is either not designed or not legal for operation on highways. Examples are construction equipment, farm machinery, and certain military-design motor vehicles and motor vehicles that are damaged beyond repair in crashes and intended to be sold as salvage only. Instead, use an appropriate bill of sale or award document. Examples are Optional Form 16, Sales Slip—Sale of Government Personal Property, and SF 114C, Sale of Government Property-Bid and Award.

(b) SF 97 is optional for foreign fleet motor vehicles because foreign governments may require the use of other forms.

NOTE TO § 102–34.305: The original SF 97 is printed on secure paper to identify readily any attempt to alter the form. The form is also pre-numbered to prevent duplicates. State motor vehicle agencies may reject certificates showing erasures or strikeovers.

§102–34.310 How do we distribute the completed Standard Form 97?

SF 97 is a 4-part set printed on continuous-feed paper. Distribute the form as follows:

(a) Original SF 97 to the purchaser or donee;

(b) One copy to the owning agency;

(c) One copy to the contracting officer making the sale or transfer of the motor vehicle; and

(d) One copy under owning agency directives.

Subpart I—Motor Vehicle Fueling

§102–34.315 How do we obtain fuel for Government motor vehicles?

You may obtain fuel for Government motor vehicles by using:

(a) A Government-issued charge card;

(b) A Government agency fueling facility; or

(c) Personal funds and obtaining reimbursement from your agency, if permitted by your agency. You must use the method prescribed by GSA Fleet to obtain fuel for vehicles leased from GSA fleet.

§102–34.320 What Government-issued charge cards may I use to purchase fuel and motor vehicle related services?

(a) You may use a fleet charge card specifically issued for this purpose. These cards are designed to collect motor vehicle data at the time of purchase. Where appropriate, State sales and motor fuel taxes may be deducted from fuel purchases by the fleet charge card services contractor before your agency is billed; otherwise you may need to request reimbursement from each State to which taxes were paid. The GSA contractor issued fleet charge card is the only Government-issued charge card that may be used for GSA Fleet motor vehicles. For further information on acquiring these fleet charge cards and their use, contact the: General Services Administration, ATTN: GSA SmartPay® (QMB), 2200 Crystal Drive, Arlington, VA 22202.

(b) You may use a Government purchase card if you do not have a fleet charge card or if the use of such a Government purchase card is required by your agency mission. However, the Government purchase card does not collect motor vehicle data nor does it deduct State sales and motor fuel taxes.

NOTE TO §102–34.320: OMB Circular A–123, Appendix B, contains additional specific guidance on the management, issuance, and usage of Government charge cards. The Appendix B guidance consolidates and updates current Governmentwide charge card program requirements and guidance issued by the Office of Management and Budget, GSA, Department of the Treasury, and other Federal agencies. Appendix B provides a single document to incorporate changes, new guidance, or amendments to existing guidance, and establishes minimum requirements and suggested best practices for Government charge card programs that may be supplemented by individual agency policy procedures.

§102–34.325 What type of fuel do I use in Government motor vehicles?

(a) Use the minimum grade (octane rating) of fuel recommended by the motor vehicle manufacturer when fueling Government motor vehicles, unless a higher grade of fuel is all that is available locally.

(b) Use unleaded gasoline in all foreign fleet motor vehicles designed to operate on gasoline unless:

(1) Such use would be in conflict with country-to-country or multi-national logistics agreements; or

(2) Such gasoline is not available locally.

(c) You must use alternative fuels in alternative fuel motor vehicles to the fullest extent possible as directed by regulations issued by the Department of Energy implementing the Energy Policy Act and related Executive Orders.

Subpart J—Federal Fleet Report

§102–34.330 What is the Federal Fleet Report?

The Federal Fleet Report (FFR) is an annual summary of Federal fleet statistics based upon fleet composition at the end of each fiscal year and vehicle use and cost during the fiscal year. The FFR is compiled by GSA from information submitted by Federal agencies.

The FFR is designed to provide essential statistical data for worldwide Federal motor vehicle fleet operations. Review of the report assists Government agencies, including GSA, in evaluating the effectiveness of the operation and management of individual fleets to determine whether vehicles are being utilized properly and to identify high cost areas where fleet expenses can be reduced. The FFR is posted on GSA's Motor Vehicle Management Policy Internet Web site (*http://www.gsa.gov/vehiclepolicy*).

§ 102–34.335 How do I submit information to the General Services Administration (GSA) for the Federal Fleet Report (FFR)?

(a) Annually, agencies must submit to GSA the information needed to produce the FFR through the Federal Automotive Statistical Tool (FAST), an Internet-based reporting tool. To find out how to submit motor vehicle data to GSA through FAST, consult the instructions from your agency fleet manager and read the documentation at *http://fastweb.inel.gov/*.

(b) Specific reporting categories, by agency, included in the FFR are—

(1) Inventory;

(2) Acquisitions;

(3) Operating costs;

(4) Miles traveled; and

(5) Fuel used.

NOTE TO § 102–34.335: The FAST system is also used by agency Fleet Managers to provide the Department of Energy with information required by the Energy Policy Act and related Executive Orders. In addition, the Office of Management and Budget (OMB) requires agency Fleet Managers and budget officers to submit annual agency motor vehicle budgeting information to OMB through FAST (see OMB Circular A–11, Preparation, Submission, and Execution of the Budget).

§ 102–34.340 Do we need a fleet management information system?

Yes, you must have a fleet management information system at the department or agency level that —

(a) Identifies and collects accurate inventory, cost, and use data that covers the complete lifecycle of each motor vehicle (acquisition, operation, maintenance, and disposal); and

(b) Provides the information necessary to satisfy both internal and external reporting requirements, including:

(1) Cost per mile;

(2) Fuel costs for each motor vehicle; and

(3) Data required for FAST (see § 102–34.335).

§ 102–34.345 What records do we need to keep?

You are responsible for developing and keeping adequate accounting and reporting procedures for Government motor vehicles. These will ensure accurate recording of inventory, cost, and operational data needed to manage and control motor vehicles, and will satisfy reporting requirements. You must also comply with the General Records Schedules issued by the National Archives and Records Administration (*http://www.archives.gov*).

Subpart K—Forms

§ 102–34.350 How do we obtain the forms prescribed in this part?

See § 102–2.135 of this chapter for how to obtain forms prescribed in this part.

PART 102–35—DISPOSITION OF PERSONAL PROPERTY

Sec.

102–35.5 What is the scope of the General Services Administration's regulations on the disposal of personal property?

102–35.10 How are these regulations for the disposal of personal property organized?

102–35.15 What are the goals of GSA's personal property regulations?

102–35.20 What definitions apply to GSA's personal property regulations?

102–35.25 What management reports must we provide?

102–35.30 What actions must I take or am I authorized to take regardless of the property disposition method?

AUTHORITY: 40 U.S.C. 121(c).

SOURCE: 72 FR 10085, Mar. 7, 2007, unless otherwise noted.

§ 102–35.5 What is the scope of the General Services Administration's regulations on the disposal of personal property?

The General Services Administration's personal property disposal regulations are contained in this part and in parts 102–36 through 102–42 of this subchapter B as well as in parts 101–42 and 101–45 of the Federal Property Management Regulations (FPMR)(41 CFR parts 101–42 and 101–45). With two exceptions, these regulations cover the disposal of personal property under the custody and control of executive agencies located in the United States, the U.S. Virgin Islands, American Samoa, Guam, Puerto Rico, the Northern Mariana Islands, the Federated States of Micronesia, the Marshall Islands, and Palau. The exceptions to this coverage are part 102–39 of this subchapter B, which applies to the replacement of all property owned by executive agencies worldwide using the exchange/sale authority, and §§102–36.380 through 102–36.400, which apply to the disposal of excess property located in countries and areas not listed in this subpart, i.e., foreign excess personal property. The legislative and judicial branches are encouraged to follow these provisions for property in their custody and control.

§ 102–35.10 How are these regulations for the disposal of personal property organized?

The General Services Administration (GSA) has divided its regulations for the disposal of personal property into the following program areas:

(a) Disposition of excess personal property (part 102–36 of this subchapter B).

(b) Donation of surplus personal property (part 102–37 of this subchapter B).

(c) Sale of surplus personal property (part 102–38 of this subchapter B).

(d) Replacement of personal property pursuant to the exchange/sale authority (part 102–39 of this subchapter B).

(e) Disposition of seized and forfeited, voluntarily abandoned, and unclaimed personal property (part 102–41 of this subchapter B).

(f) Utilization, donation, and disposal of foreign gifts and decorations (part 102–42 of this subchapter B).

(g) Utilization and disposal of hazardous materials and certain categories of property (part 101–42 of the Federal Property Management Regulations (FPMR), 41 CFR part 101–42).

§ 102–35.15 What are the goals of GSA's personal property regulations?

The goals of GSA's personal property regulations are to:

(a) Improve the identification and reporting of excess personal property;

(b) Maximize the use of excess property as the first source of supply to minimize expenditures for the purchase of new property, when practicable;

NOTE TO §102–35.15(b): If there are competing requests among Federal agencies for excess property, preference will be given to agencies where the transfer will avoid a new Federal procurement. A transfer to an agency where the agency will provide the property to a non-Federal entity for the non-Federal entity's use will be secondary to Federal use.

(c) Achieve maximum public benefit from the use of Government property through the donation of surplus personal property to State and local public agencies and other eligible non-Federal recipients;

(d) Obtain the optimum monetary return to the Government for surplus personal property sold and personal property sold under the exchange/sale authority; and

(e) Reduce management and inventory costs by appropriate use of the abandonment/destruction authority to dispose of unneeded personal property that has no commercial value or for which the estimated cost of continued care and handling would exceed the estimated sales proceeds (see FMR §§102–36.305 through 102–36.330).

§ 102–35.20 What definitions apply to GSA's personal property regulations?

The following are definitions of, or cross-references to, some key terms that apply to GSA's personal property regulations in the FMR (CFR parts 102–36 through 102–42). Other personal property terms are defined in the sections or parts to which they primarily apply.

Accountable Personal Property includes nonexpendable personal property whose expected useful life is two years or longer and whose acquisition value, as determined by the agency, warrants tracking in the agency's property records, including capitalized and sensitive personal property.

Accountability means the ability to account for personal property by providing a complete audit trail for property transactions from receipt to final disposition.

Acquisition cost means the original purchase price of an item.

Capitalized Personal Property includes property that is entered on the agency's general ledger records as a major investment or asset. An agency must determine its capitalization thresholds as discussed in Financial Accounting Standard Advisory Board (FASAB) Statement of Federal Financial Accounting Standards No. 6 Accounting for Property, Plant and Equipment, Chapter 1, paragraph 13.

Control means the ongoing function of maintaining physical oversight and surveillance of personal property throughout its complete life cycle using various property management tools and techniques taking into account the environment in which the property is located and its vulnerability to theft, waste, fraud, or abuse.

Excess personal property (see § 102–36.40 of this subchapter B).

Exchange/sale (see § 102–39.20 of this subchapter B).

Executive agency (see § 102–36.40 of this subchapter B).

Federal agency (see § 102–36.40 of this subchapter B).

Foreign gifts and decorations (for the definition of relevant terms, see § 102–42.10 of this subchapter B).

Forfeited property (see § 102–41.20 of this subchapter B).

Inventory includes a formal listing of all accountable property items assigned to an agency, along with a formal process to verify the condition, location, and quantity of such items. This term may also be used as a verb to indicate the actions leading to the development of a listing. In this sense, an inventory must be conducted using an actual physical count, electronic means, and/or statistical methods.

National property management officer means an official, designated in accordance with § 102–36.45(b) of this subchapter B, who is responsible for ensuring effective acquisition, use, and disposal of excess property within your agency.

Personal property (see § 102–36.40 of this subchapter B).

Property management means the system of acquiring, maintaining, using and disposing of the personal property of an organization or entity.

Seized property means personal property that has been confiscated by a Federal agency, and whose care and handling will be the responsibility of that agency until final ownership is determined by the judicial process.

Sensitive Personal Property includes all items, regardless of value, that require special control and accountability due to unusual rates of loss, theft or misuse, or due to national security or export control considerations. Such property includes weapons, ammunition, explosives, information technology equipment with memory capability, cameras, and communications equipment. These classifications do not preclude agencies from specifying additional personal property classifications to effectively manage their programs.

Surplus personal property (see § 102–37.25 of this subchapter B).

Utilization means the identification, reporting, and transfer of excess personal property among Federal agencies.

§ 102–35.25 What management reports must we provide?

(a) There are three reports that must be provided. The report summarizing the property provided to non-Federal recipients and the report summarizing exchange/sale transactions (see §§ 102–36.295 and 102–39.75 respectively of this subchapter B) must be provided every year (negative reports are required). In addition, if you conduct negotiated sales of surplus personal property valued over $5,000 in any year, you must report this transaction in accordance with § 102–38.115 (negative reports are not required for this report).

(b) The General Services Administration (GSA) may request other reports as authorized by 40 U.S.C. 506(a)(1)(A).

§ 102–35.30 What actions must I take or am I authorized to take regardless of the property disposition method?

Regardless of the disposition method used:

(a) You must maintain property in a safe, secure, and cost-effective manner until final disposition.

(b) You have authority to use the abandonment/ destruction provisions at any stage of the disposal process (see §§ 102-36.305 through 102-36.330 and § 102-38.70 of this subchapter B).

(c) You must implement policies and procedures to remove sensitive or classified information from property prior to disposal. Agency-affixed markings should be removed, if at all possible, prior to personal property permanently leaving your agency's control.

(d) Government-owned personal property may only be used as authorized by your agency. Title to Government-owned personal property cannot be transferred to a non-Federal entity unless through official procedures specifically authorized by law.

PART 102-36—DISPOSITION OF EXCESS PERSONAL PROPERTY

Subpart A—General Provisions

Subpart B—Acquiring Excess Personal Property For Our Agency

Subpart C—Acquiring Excess Personal Property for Non-federal Recipients

102–36.150 For which non-federal activities may we acquire excess personal property?

102–36.155 What are our responsibilities when acquiring excess personal property for use by a non-federal recipient?

102–36.160 What additional information must we provide on the SF 122 when acquiring excess personal property for non-federal recipients?

NON-APPROPRIATED FUND ACTIVITIES

102–36.165 Do we retain title to excess personal property furnished to a non-appropriated fund activity within our agency?

102–36.170 May we transfer personal property owned by one of our non-appropriated fund activities?

CONTRACTORS

102–36.175 Are there restrictions to acquiring excess personal property for use by our contractors?

COOPERATIVES

102–36.180 Is there any limitation/condition to acquiring excess personal property for use by cooperatives?

PROJECT GRANTEES

102–36.185 What are the requirements for acquiring excess personal property for use by our grantees?

102–36.190 Must we always pay 25 percent of the original acquisition cost when furnishing excess personal property to project grantees?

102–36.195 What type of excess personal property may we furnish to our project grantees?

102–36.200 May we acquire excess personal property for cannibalization purposes by the grantee?

102–36.205 Is there a limit to how much excess personal property we may furnish to our grantees?

Subpart D—Disposition of Excess Personal Property

102–36.210 Why must we report excess personal property to GSA?

REPORTING EXCESS PERSONAL PROPERTY

102–36.215 How do we report excess personal property?

102–36.220 Must we report all excess personal property to GSA?

102–36.225 Must we report excess related personal property?

102–36.230 Where do we send the reports of excess personal property?

102–36.235 What information do we provide when reporting excess personal property?

102–36.240 What are the disposal condition codes?

DISPOSING OF EXCESS PERSONAL PROPERTY

102–36.245 Are we accountable for the personal property that has been reported excess, and who is responsible for the care and handling costs?

102–36.250 Does GSA ever take physical custody of excess personal property?

102–36.255 What options do we have when unusual circumstances do not allow adequate time for disposal through GSA?

102–36.260 How do we promote the expeditious transfer of excess personal property?

102–36.265 What if there are competing requests for the same excess personal property?

102–36.270 What if a federal agency requests personal property that is undergoing donation screening or in the sales process?

102–36.275 May we dispose of excess personal property without GSA approval?

102–36.280 May we withdraw from the disposal process excess personal property that we have reported to GSA?

TRANSFERS WITH REIMBURSEMENT

102–36.285 May we charge for personal property transferred to another federal agency?

102–36.290 How much do we charge for excess personal property on a transfer with reimbursement?

REPORT OF DISPOSAL ACTIVITY

102–36.295 Is there any reporting requirement on the disposition of excess personal property?

102–36.300 How do we report the furnishing of personal property to non-federal recipients?

ABANDONMENT/DESTRUCTION

102–36.305 May we abandon or destroy excess personal property without reporting it to GSA?

102–36.310 Who makes the determination to abandon or destroy excess personal property?

102–36.315 Are there any restrictions to the use of the abandonment/destruction authority?

102–36.320 May we transfer or donate excess personal property that has been determined appropriate for abandonment/destruction without GSA approval?

102–36.325 What must be done before the abandonment/destruction of excess personal property?

102–36.330 Are there occasions when public notice is not needed regarding abandonment/destruction of excess personal property?

Subpart E—Personal Property Whose Disposal Requires Special Handling

102–36.335 Are there certain types of excess personal property that must be disposed of differently from normal disposal procedures?

AIRCRAFT AND AIRCRAFT PARTS

102–36.340 What must we do when disposing of excess aircraft?
102–36.345 May we dispose of excess Flight Safety Critical Aircraft Parts (FSCAP)?
102–36.350 How do we identify a FSCAP?
102–36.355 What are the FSCAP Criticality Codes?
102–36.360 How do we dispose of aircraft parts that are life-limited but have no FSCAP designation?

CANINES, LAW ENFORCEMENT

102–36.365 May we transfer or donate canines that have been used in the performance of law enforcement duties?

DISASTER RELIEF PROPERTY

102–36.370 Are there special requirements concerning the use of excess personal property for disaster relief?

FIREARMS

102–36.375 May we dispose of excess firearms?

FOREIGN EXCESS PERSONAL PROPERTY

102–36.380 Who is responsible for disposing of foreign excess personal property?
102–36.385 What are our responsibilities in the disposal of foreign excess personal property?
102–36.390 How may we dispose of foreign excess personal property?
102–36.395 How may GSA assist us in disposing of foreign excess personal property?
102–36.400 Who pays for the transportation costs when foreign excess personal property is returned to the United States?

GIFTS

102–36.405 May we keep gifts given to us from the public?
102–36.410 How do we dispose of a gift in the form of money or intangible personal property?
102–36.415 How do we dispose of gifts other than intangible personal property?
102–36.420 How do we dispose of gifts from foreign governments or entities?

HAZARDOUS PERSONAL PROPERTY

102–36.425 May we dispose of excess hazardous personal property?

MUNITIONS LIST ITEMS/COMMERCE CONTROL LIST ITEMS (MLIs/CCLIs)

102–36.430 May we dispose of excess Munitions List Items (MLIs)/Commerce Control List Items (CCLIs)?
102–36.435 How do we identify Munitions List Items (MLIs)/Commerce Control List Items (CCLIs) requiring demilitarization?

PRINTING EQUIPMENT AND SUPPLIES

102–36.440 Are there special procedures for reporting excess printing and binding equipment and supplies?

RED CROSS PROPERTY

102–36.445 Do we report excess personal property originally acquired from or through the American National Red Cross?

SHELF-LIFE ITEMS

102–36.450 Do we report excess shelf-life items?
102–36.455 How do we report excess shelf-life items?
102–36.460 Do we report excess medical shelf-life items held for national emergency purposes?
102–36.465 May we transfer or exchange excess medical shelf-life items with other Federal agencies?

VESSELS

102–36.470 What must we do when disposing of excess vessels?

Subpart F—Miscellaneous Disposition

102–36.475 What is the authority for transfers under "Computers for Learning"?

AUTHORITY: 40 U.S.C. 121(c).

SOURCE: 65 FR 31218, May 16, 2000, unless otherwise noted.

Subpart A—General Provisions

§ 102–36.5 What is the governing authority for this part?

Section 121(c) of title 40, United States Code, authorizes the Administrator of General Services to prescribe regulations as he deems necessary to carry out his functions under subtitle I of title 40. Section 521 of title 40 authorizes the General Services Administration (GSA) to prescribe policies to promote the maximum use of excess

Government personal property by executive agencies.

[71 FR 53571, Sept. 12, 2006]

§ 102–36.10 What does this part cover?

This part covers the acquisition, transfer, and disposal, by executive agencies, of excess personal property located in the United States, the U.S. Virgin Islands, American Samoa, Guam, Puerto Rico, the Federated States of Micronesia, the Marshall Islands, Palau, and the Northern Mariana Islands.

[65 FR 31218, May 16, 2000, as amended at 71 FR 53571, Sept. 12, 2006]

§ 102–36.15 Who must comply with the provisions of this part?

All executive agencies must comply with the provisions of this part. The legislative and judicial branches are encouraged to report and transfer excess personal property and fill their personal property requirements from excess in accordance with these provisions.

§ 102–36.20 To whom do "we", "you", and their variants refer?

Use of pronouns "we", "you", and their variants throughout this part refer to the agency.

§ 102–36.25 How do we request a deviation from these requirements and who can approve it?

See §§ 102–2.60 through 102–2.110 of this chapter to request a deviation from the requirements of this part.

§ 102–36.30 When is personal property excess?

Personal property is excess when it is no longer needed by the activities within your agency to carry out the functions of official programs, as determined by the agency head or designee.

§ 102–36.35 What is the typical process for disposing of excess personal property?

(a) You must ensure personal property not needed by your activity is offered for use elsewhere within your agency. If the property is no longer needed by any activity within your agency, your agency declares the property excess and reports it to GSA for possible transfer to eligible recipients, including federal agencies for direct use or for use by their contractors, project grantees, or cooperative agreement recipients. All executive agencies must, to the maximum extent practicable, fill requirements for personal property by using existing agency property or by obtaining excess property from other federal agencies in lieu of new procurements.

(b) If GSA determines that there are no federal requirements for your excess personal property, it becomes surplus property and is available for donation to state and local public agencies and other eligible non-federal activities. Title 40 of the United States Code requires that surplus personal property be distributed to eligible recipients by an agency established by each State for this purpose, the State Agency for Surplus Property.

(c) Surplus personal property not selected for donation is offered for sale to the public by competitive offerings such as sealed bid sales, spot bid sales, or auctions. You may conduct or contract for the sale of your surplus personal property, or have GSA or another executive agency conduct the sale on behalf of your agency in accordance with part 102–38 of this chapter. You must inform GSA at the time the property is reported as excess if you do not want GSA to conduct the sale for you.

(d) If a written determination is made that the property has no commercial value or the estimated cost of its continued care and handling would exceed the estimated proceeds from its sale, you may dispose of the property by abandonment or destruction, or donate it to public bodies.

[65 FR 31218, May 16, 2000, as amended at 71 FR 53571, Sept. 12, 2006]

DEFINITIONS

§ 102–36.40 What definitions apply to this part?

The following definitions apply to this part:

Commerce Control List Items (CCLIs) are dual use (commercial/military) items that are subject to export control by the Bureau of Export Administration, Department of Commerce. These items have been identified in the

U.S. Export Administration Regulations (15 CFR part 774) as export controlled for reasons of national security, crime control, technology transfer, and scarcity of materials.

Cooperative means the organization or entity that has a cooperative agreement with a federal agency.

Cooperative agreement means a legal instrument reflecting a relationship between a federal agency and a non-federal recipient, made in accordance with the Federal Grant and Cooperative Agreement Act of 1977 (31 U.S.C. 6301–6308), under any or all of the following circumstances:

(1) The purpose of the relationship is the transfer, between a federal agency and a non-federal entity, of money, property, services, or anything of value to accomplish a public purpose authorized by law, rather than by purchase, lease, or barter, for the direct benefit or use of the federal government.

(2) Substantial involvement is anticipated between the federal agency and the cooperative during the performance of the agreed upon activity.

(3) The cooperative is a state or local government entity or any person or organization authorized to receive federal assistance or procurement contracts.

Demilitarization means, as defined by the Department of Defense, the act of destroying the military capabilities inherent in certain types of equipment or material. Such destruction may include deep sea dumping, mutilation, cutting, crushing, scrapping, melting, burning, or alteration so as to prevent the further use of the item for its originally intended purpose.

Excess personal property means any personal property under the control of any federal agency that is no longer required for that agency's needs, as determined by the agency head or designee.

Exchange/sale property is property not excess to the needs of the holding agency but eligible for replacement, which is exchanged or sold under the provisions of part 102–39 of this chapter in order to apply the exchange allowance or proceeds of sale in whole or part payment for replacement with a similar item.

Executive agency means any executive department or independent establishment in the executive branch of the Government, including any wholly owned government corporation.

Fair market value means the best estimate of the gross sales proceeds if the property were to be sold in a public sale.

Federal agency means any executive agency or any establishment in the legislative or judicial branch of the government (except the Senate, the House of Representatives, and the Architect of the Capitol and any activities under his/her direction).

Flight Safety Critical Aircraft Part (FSCAP) is any aircraft part, assembly, or installation containing a critical characteristic whose failure, malfunction, or absence could cause a catastrophic failure resulting in engine shut-down or loss or serious damage to the aircraft resulting in an unsafe condition.

Foreign excess personal property is any U.S. owned excess personal property located outside the United States (U.S.), the U.S. Virgin Islands, American Samoa, Guam, Puerto Rico, the Federated States of Micronesia, the Marshall Islands, Palau, and the Northern Mariana Islands.

Grant means a type of assistance award and a legal instrument which permits a federal agency to transfer money, property, services or other things of value to a grantee when no substantial involvement is anticipated between the agency and the recipient during the performance of the contemplated activity.

GSAXcess® is GSA's website for reporting, searching and selecting excess personal property. For information on using GSAXcess®, access *http:// www.gsaxcess.gov.*

Hazardous personal property means property that is deemed a hazardous material, chemical substance or mixture, or hazardous waste under the Hazardous Materials Transportation Act (HMTA) (49 U.S.C. 5101), the Resource Conservation and Recovery Act (RCRA) (42 U.S.C. 6901–6981), or the Toxic Substances Control Act (TSCA) (15 U.S.C. 2601–2609).

Holding agency means the federal agency having accountability for, and generally possession of, the property involved.

Intangible personal property means personal property in which the existence and value of the property is generally represented by a descriptive document rather than the property itself. Some examples are patents, patent rights, processes, techniques, inventions, copyrights, negotiable instruments, money orders, bonds, and shares of stock.

Life-limited aircraft part is an aircraft part that has a finite service life expressed in either total operating hours, total cycles, and/or calendar time.

Line item means a single line entry, on a reporting form or transfer order, for items of property of the same type having the same description, condition code, and unit cost.

Munitions List Items (MLIs) are commodities (usually defense articles/defense services) listed in the International Traffic in Arms Regulation (22 CFR part 121), published by the U.S. Department of State.

Nonappropriated fund activity means an activity or entity that is not funded by money appropriated from the general fund of the U.S. Treasury, such as post exchanges, ship stores, military officers' clubs, veterans' canteens, and similar activities. Such property is not federal property.

Personal property means any property, except real property. For purposes of this part, the term excludes records of the federal government, and naval vessels of the following categories: battleships, cruisers, aircraft carriers, destroyers, and submarines.

Project grant means a grant made for a specific purpose and with a specific termination date.

Public agency means any State, political subdivision thereof, including any unit of local government or economic development district; any department, agency, or instrumentality thereof, including instrumentalities created by compact or other agreement between States or political subdivisions; multijurisdictional substate districts established by or pursuant to State law; or any Indian tribe, band, group, pueblo, or community located on a State reservation.

Related personal property means any personal property that is an integral part of real property. It is:

(1) Related to, designed for, or specifically adapted to the functional capacity of the real property and removal of this personal property would significantly diminish the economic value of the real property; or

(2) Determined by the Administrator of General Services to be related to the real property.

Salvage means property that has value greater than its basic material content but for which repair or rehabilitation is clearly impractical and/or uneconomical.

Scrap means property that has no value except for its basic material content.

Screening period means the period in which excess and surplus personal property are made available for excess transfer or surplus donation to eligible recipients.

Shelf-life item is any item that deteriorates over time or has unstable characteristics such that a storage period must be assigned to assure the item is issued within that period to provide satisfactory performance. Management of such items is governed by part 101–27, subpart 27.2, of this title and by DOD instructions, for executive agencies and DOD respectively.

Surplus personal property (surplus) means excess personal property no longer required by the Federal agencies as determined by GSA.

Surplus release date means the date when federal screening has been completed and the excess property becomes surplus.

Transfer with reimbursement means a transfer of excess personal property between Federal agencies where the recipient is required to pay, i.e. reimburse the holding agency, for the property.

Unit cost means the original acquisition cost of a single item of property.

United States means all the 50 States and the District of Columbia.

Vessels means ships, boats and craft designed for navigation in and on the water, propelled by oars or paddles, sail, or power.

[65 FR 31218, May 16, 2000, as amended at 71 FR 53571, Sept. 12, 2006]

RESPONSIBILITY

§ 102–36.45 What are our responsibilities in the management of excess personal property?

(a) Agency procurement policies should require consideration of excess personal property before authorizing procurement of new personal property.

(b) You are encouraged to designate national and regional property management officials to:

(1) Promote the use of available excess personal property to the maximum extent practicable by your agency.

(2) Review and approve the acquisition and disposal of excess personal property.

(3) Ensure that any agency implementing procedures comply with this part.

(c) When acquiring excess personal property, you must:

(1) Limit the quantity acquired to that which is needed to adequately perform the function necessary to support the mission of your agency.

(2) Establish controls over the processing of excess personal property transfer orders.

(3) Facilitate the timely pickup of acquired excess personal property from the holding agency.

(d) While excess personal property you have acquired is in your custody, or the custody of your non-Federal recipients and the government retains title, you and/or the non-Federal recipient must do the following:

(1) Establish and maintain a system for property accountability.

(2) Protect the property against hazards including but not limited to fire, theft, vandalism, and weather.

(3) Perform the care and handling of personal property. "Care and handling" includes completing, repairing, converting, rehabilitating, operating, preserving, protecting, insuring, packing, storing, handling, conserving, and transporting excess and surplus personal property, and destroying or rendering innocuous property which is dangerous to public health or safety.

(4) Maintain appropriate inventory levels as set forth in part 101–27 of this title.

(5) Continuously monitor the personal property under your control to assure maximum use, and develop and maintain a system to prevent and detect nonuse, improper use, unauthorized disposal, or destruction of personal property.

(e) When you no longer need personal property to carry out the mission of your program, you must:

(1) Offer the property for reassignment to other activities within your agency.

(2) Promptly report excess personal property to GSA when it is no longer needed by any activity within your agency for further reuse by eligible recipients.

(3) Continue the care and handling of excess personal property while it goes through the disposal process.

(4) Facilitate the timely transfer of excess personal property to other federal agencies or authorized eligible recipients.

(5) Provide reasonable access to authorized personnel for inspection and removal of excess personal property.

(6) Ensure that final disposition complies with applicable environmental, health, safety, and national security regulations.

§ 102–36.50 May we use a contractor to perform the functions of excess personal property disposal?

Yes, you may use service contracts to perform disposal functions that are not inherently governmental, such as warehousing or custodial duties. You are responsible for ensuring that the contractor conforms with the requirements of Title 40 of the United States Code and the Federal Management Regulation (41 CFR chapter 102), and any other applicable statutes and regulations when performing these functions.

[65 FR 31218, May 16, 2000, as amended at 71 FR 53571, Sept. 12, 2006]

§ 102–36.55 What is GSA's role in the disposition of excess personal property?

In addition to developing and issuing regulations for the management of excess personal property, GSA:

(a) Screens and offers available excess personal property to Federal agencies and eligible non-federal recipients.

(b) Approves and processes transfers of excess personal property to eligible activities.

(c) Determines the amount of reimbursement for transfers of excess personal property when appropriate.

(d) Conducts sales of surplus and exchange/sale personal property when requested by an agency.

(e) Maintains an automated system, GSAXcess®, to facilitate the reporting and transferring of excess personal property.

[65 FR 31218, May 16, 2000, as amended at 71 FR 53571, Sept. 12, 2006]

Subpart B—Acquiring Excess Personal Property For Our Agency

ACQUIRING EXCESS

§ 102–36.60 Who is eligible to acquire excess personal property as authorized by the Property Act?

The following are eligible to acquire excess personal property:

(a) Federal agencies (for their own use or use by their authorized contractors, cooperatives, and project grantees).

(b) The Senate.

(c) The House of Representatives.

(d) The Architect of the Capitol and any activities under his direction.

(e) The DC Government.

(f) Mixed-ownership government corporations as defined in 31 U.S.C. 9101.

§ 102–36.65 Why must we use excess personal property instead of buying new property?

Using excess personal property to the maximum extent practicable maximizes the return on government dollars spent and minimizes expenditures for new procurement. Before purchasing new property, check with the appropriate regional GSA Personal Property Management office or access GSAXcess® for any available excess personal property that may be suitable for your needs. You must use excess personal property unless it would cause serious hardship, be impractical, or impair your operations.

[65 FR 31218, May 16, 2000, as amended at 71 FR 53572, Sept. 12, 2006]

§ 102–36.70 What must we consider when acquiring excess personal property?

Consider the following when acquiring excess personal property:

(a) There must be an authorized requirement.

(b) The cost of acquiring and maintaining the excess personal property (including packing, shipping, pickup, and necessary repairs) does not exceed the cost of purchasing and maintaining new material.

(c) The sources of spare parts or repair/maintenance services to support the acquired item are readily accessible.

(d) The supply of excess parts acquired must not exceed the life expectancy of the equipment supported.

(e) The excess personal property will fulfill the required need with reasonable certainty without sacrificing mission or schedule.

(f) You must not acquire excess personal property with the intent to sell or trade for other assets.

§ 102–36.75 Do we pay for excess personal property we acquire from another federal agency under a transfer?

(a) No, except for the situations listed in paragraph (b) of this section, you do not pay for the property. However, you are responsible for shipping and transportation costs. Where applicable, you may also be required to pay packing, loading, and any costs directly related to the dismantling of the property when required for the purpose of transporting the property.

(b) You may be required to reimburse the holding agency for excess personal property transferred to you (i.e., transfer with reimbursement) when:

(1) Reimbursement is directed by GSA.

(2) The property was originally acquired with funds not appropriated from the general fund of the Treasury or appropriated therefrom but by law reimbursable from assessment, tax, or other revenue and the holding agency requests reimbursement. It is executive branch policy that working capital fund property shall be transferred without reimbursement.

(3) The property was acquired with appropriated funds, but reimbursement is required or authorized by law.

(4) You or the holding agency is the U.S. Postal Service (USPS).

(5) You are acquiring excess personal property for use by a project grantee that is a public agency or a nonprofit organization and exempt from taxation under 26 U.S.C. 501.

(6) You or the holding agency is the DC Government.

(7) You or the holding agency is a wholly owned or mixed-ownership government corporation as defined in the Government Corporation Control Act (31 U.S.C. 9101–9110).

§ 102–36.80 How much do we pay for excess personal property on a transfer with reimbursement?

(a) You may be required to reimburse the holding agency the fair market value when the transfer involves any of the conditions in § 102–36.75(b)(1) through (b)(4).

(b) When acquiring excess personal property for your project grantees (§ 102–36.75(b)(5)), you are required to deposit into the miscellaneous receipts fund of the U.S. Treasury an amount equal to 25 percent of the original acquisition cost of the property, except for transfers under the conditions cited in § 102–36.190.

(c) When you or the holding agency is the DC Government or a wholly owned or mixed-ownership Government corporation (§ 102–36.75(b)(6) or (b)(7)), you are required to reimburse the holding agency using fair value reimbursement. Fair value reimbursement is 20 percent of the original acquisition cost for new or unused property (i.e., condition code 1), and zero percent for other personal property. Where circumstances warrant, a higher fair value may be used if the agencies concerned agree. Due to special circumstances or the unusual nature of the property, the holding agency may use other criteria for establishing fair value if approved or directed by GSA. You must refer any disagreements to the appropriate regional GSA Personal Property Management office.

§ 102–36.85 Do we pay for personal property we acquire when it is disposed of by another agency under the exchange/sale authority, and how much do we pay?

Yes, you must pay for personal property disposed of under the exchange/sale authority, in the amount required by the holding agency. The amount of reimbursement is normally the fair market value.

SCREENING OF EXCESS

§ 102–36.90 How do we find out what personal property is available as excess?

You may use the following methods to find out what excess personal property is available:

(a) Check GSAXcess®, GSA's website for searching and selecting excess personal property. For information on GSAXcess®, access *http://www.gsaxcess.gov*.

(b) Contact or submit want lists to regional GSA Personal Property Management offices.

(c) Check any available holding agency websites.

(d) Conduct on-site screening at various federal facilities.

[65 FR 31218, May 16, 2000, as amended at 71 FR 53572, Sept. 12, 2006]

§ 102–36.95 How long is excess personal property available for screening?

The screening period for excess personal property is normally 21 calendar days. GSA may extend or shorten the screening period in coordination with the holding agency. For screening timeframes for government property in the possession of contractors see the Federal Acquisition Regulation (48 CFR part 45).

§ 102–36.100 When does the screening period start for excess personal property?

Screening starts when GSA receives the report of excess personal property (see § 102–36.230).

§ 102–36.105 Who is authorized to screen and where do we go to screen excess personal property on-site?

You may authorize your agency employees, contractors, or non-federal recipients that you sponsor to screen excess personal property. You may visit Defense Reutilization and Marketing Offices (DRMOs) and DOD contractor facilities to screen excess personal property generated by the Department of Defense. You may also inspect excess personal property at various civilian agency facilities throughout the United States.

§ 102–36.110 Do we need authorization to screen excess personal property?

(a) Yes, when entering a federal facility, federal agency employees must present a valid Federal ID. Non-federal individuals will need proof of authorization from their sponsoring federal agency in addition to a valid picture identification.

(b) Entry on some federal and contractor facilities may require special authorization from that facility. Persons wishing to screen excess personal property on such a facility must obtain approval from that agency. Contact your regional GSA Personal Property Management office for locations and accessibility.

§ 102–36.115 What information must we include in the authorization form for non-federal persons to screen excess personal property?

(a) For non-federal persons to screen excess personal property, you must provide on the authorization form:

(1) The individual's name and the organization he/she represents;

(2) The period of time and location(s) in which screening will be conducted; and

(3) The number and completion date of the applicable contract, cooperative agreement, or grant.

(b) An authorized official of your agency must sign the authorization form.

§ 102–36.120 What are our responsibilities in authorizing a non-federal individual to screen excess personal property?

You must do the following:

(a) Ensure that the non-federal screener certifies that any and all property requested will be used for authorized official purpose(s).

(b) Maintain a record of the authorized screeners under your authority, to include names, addresses and telephone numbers, and any additional identifying information such as driver's license or social security numbers.

(c) Retrieve any expired or invalid screener's authorization forms.

PROCESSING TRANSFERS

§ 102–36.125 How do we process a Standard Form 122 (SF 122), Transfer Order Excess Personal Property, through GSA?

(a) You must first contact the appropriate regional GSA Personal Property Management office to assure the property is available to you. Submit your request on a SF 122, Transfer Order Excess Personal Property, to the region in which the property is located. For the types of property listed in the table in paragraph (b) of this section, submit the SF 122 to the corresponding GSA regions. You may submit the SF 122 manually or transmit the required information by electronic media (GSAXcess®) or any other transfer form specified and approved by GSA.

(b) For the following types of property, you must submit the SF 122 to the corresponding GSA regions:

Type of property	GSA region	Location
Aircraft	9 FBP	San Francisco, CA 94102.
Firearms	7 FP–8	Denver, CO 80225.
Foreign Gifts	FBP	Washington, DC 20406.
Forfeited Property	3 FP	Washington, DC 20407.
Standard Forms	7 FMP	Ft. Worth, TX 76102.
Vessels, civilian	4 FD	Atlanta, GA 30365.
Vessels, DOD	3 FPD	Philadelphia, PA 19107.

[65 FR 31218, May 16, 2000; 65 FR 33889, May 25, 2000, as amended at 71 FR 53572, Sept. 12, 2006]

§ 102–36.130 What are our responsibilities in processing transfer orders of excess personal property?

Whether the excess is for your use or for use by a non-federal recipient that you sponsor, you must:

(a) Ensure that only authorized federal officials of your agency sign the

SF 122 prior to submission to GSA for approval.

(b) Ensure that excess personal property approved for transfer is used for authorized official purpose(s).

(c) Advise GSA of names of agency officials that are authorized to approve SF 122s, and notify GSA of any changes in signatory authority.

§ 102–36.135 How much time do we have to pick up excess personal property that has been approved for transfer?

Normally, you have 15 calendar days from the date of GSA allocation to pick up the excess personal property for transfer, and you are responsible for scheduling and coordinating the property removal with the holding agency. If additional removal time is required, you are responsible for requesting such additional removal time.

[74 FR 41060, Aug. 14, 2009]

§ 102–36.140 May we arrange to have the excess personal property shipped to its final destination?

Yes, when the holding agency agrees to provide assistance in preparing the property for shipping. You may be required to pay the holding agency any direct costs in preparing the property for shipment. You must provide shipping instructions and the appropriate fund code for billing purposes on the SF 122.

DIRECT TRANSFERS

§ 102–36.145 May we obtain excess personal property directly from another Federal agency without GSA approval?

Yes, but only under the following situations:

(a) You may obtain excess personal property that has not yet been reported to GSA, provided the total acquisition cost of the excess property does not exceed $10,000 per line item. You must ensure that a SF 122 is completed for the direct transfer and that an authorized official of your agency signs the SF 122. You must provide a copy of the SF 122 to the appropriate regional GSA office within 10 workdays from the date of the transaction.

(b) You may obtain excess personal property exceeding the $10,000 per line item limitation, provided you first contact the appropriate regional GSA Personal Property Management office for verbal approval of a prearranged transfer. You must annotate the SF 122 with the name of the GSA approving official and the date of the verbal approval, and provide a copy of the SF 122 to GSA within 10 workdays from the date of transaction.

(c) You are subject to the requirement to pay reimbursement for the excess personal property under a direct transfer when any of the conditions in § 102–36.75(b) applies.

(d) You may obtain excess personal property directly from another federal agency without GSA approval when that federal agency has statutory authority to dispose of such excess personal property and you are an eligible recipient.

Subpart C—Acquiring Excess Personal Property for Non-Federal Recipients

§ 102–36.150 For which non-federal activities may we acquire excess personal property?

Under the Property Act you may acquire and furnish excess personal property for use by your non-appropriated fund activities, contractors, cooperatives, and project grantees. You may acquire and furnish excess personal property for use by other eligible recipients only when you have specific statutory authority to do so.

§ 102–36.155 What are our responsibilities when acquiring excess personal property for use by a non-federal recipient?

When acquiring excess personal property for use by a non-federal recipient, your authorized agency official must:

(a) Ensure the use of excess personal property by the non-federal recipient is authorized and complies with applicable federal regulations and agency guidelines.

(b) Determine that the use of excess personal property will reduce the costs to the government and/or that it is in the government's best interest to furnish excess personal property.

(c) Review and approve transfer documents for excess personal property as the sponsoring Federal agency.

(d) Ensure the non-federal recipient is aware of his obligations under the FMR and your agency regulations regarding the management of excess personal property.

(e) Ensure the non-federal recipient does not stockpile the property but places the property into use within a reasonable period of time, and has a system to prevent nonuse, improper use, or unauthorized disposal or destruction of excess personal property furnished.

(f) Establish provisions and procedures for property accountability and disposition in situations when the government retains title.

(g) Report annually to GSA excess personal property furnished to non-federal recipients during the year (see § 102–36.295).

§ 102–36.160 What additional information must we provide on the SF 122 when acquiring excess personal property for non-federal recipients?

Annotate on the SF 122, the name of the non-federal recipient and the contract, grant or agreement number, when applicable, and the scheduled completion/expiration date of the contract, grant or agreement. If the remaining time prior to the expiration date is less than 60 calendar days, you must certify that the contract, grant or agreement will be extended or renewed or provide other written justification for the transfer.

NON-APPROPRIATED FUND ACTIVITIES

§ 102–36.165 Do we retain title to excess personal property furnished to a non-appropriated fund activity within our agency?

Yes, title to excess personal property furnished to a non-appropriated fund activity remains with the Federal Government and you are accountable for establishing controls over the use of such excess property in accordance with § 102–36.45(d). When such property is no longer required by the non-appropriated fund activity, you must reuse or dispose of the property in accordance with this part.

§ 102–36.170 May we transfer personal property owned by one of our non-appropriated fund activities?

Property purchased by a non-appropriated fund activity is not federal property. A non-appropriated fund activity has the option of making its privately owned personal property available for transfer to a federal agency, usually with reimbursement. If such reimbursable personal property is not transferred to another federal agency, it may be offered for sale. Such property is not available for donation.

[65 FR 31218, May 16, 2000, as amended at 65 FR 33778, May 25, 2000]

CONTRACTORS

§ 102–36.175 Are there restrictions to acquiring excess personal property for use by our contractors?

Yes, you may acquire and furnish excess personal property for use by your contractors subject to the criteria and restrictions in the Federal Acquisition Regulation (48 CFR part 45). When such property is no longer needed by your contractors or your agency, you must dispose of the excess personal property in accordance with the provisions of this part.

COOPERATIVES

§ 102–36.180 Is there any limitation/condition to acquiring excess personal property for use by cooperatives?

Yes, you must limit the total dollar amount of property transfers (in terms of original acquisition cost) to the dollar value of the cooperative agreement. For any transfers in excess of such amount, you must ensure that an official of your agency at a level higher than the officer administering the agreement approves the transfer. The federal government retains title to such property, except when provided by specific statutory authority.

PROJECT GRANTEES

§ 102–36.185 What are the requirements for acquiring excess personal property for use by our grantees?

You may furnish excess personal property for use by your grantees only when:

(a) The grantee holds a federally sponsored project grant;

(b) The grantee is a public agency or a nonprofit tax-exempt organization under section 501 of the Internal Revenue Code of 1986 (26 U.S.C. 501);

(c) The property is for use in connection with the grant; and

(d) You pay 25 percent of the original acquisition cost of the excess personal property, such funds to be deposited into the miscellaneous receipts fund of the U.S. Treasury. Exceptions to paying this 25 percent are provided in § 102–36.190. Title to property vests in the grantee when your agency pays 25 percent of the original acquisition cost.

§ 102–36.190 Must we always pay 25 percent of the original acquisition cost when furnishing excess personal property to project grantees?

No, you may acquire excess personal property for use by a project grantee without paying the 25 percent fee when any of the following conditions apply:

(a) The personal property was originally acquired from excess sources by your agency and has been placed into official use by your agency for at least one year. The federal government retains title to such property.

(b) The property is furnished under section 203 of the Department of Agriculture Organic Act of 1944 (16 U.S.C. 580a) through the U.S. Forest Service in connection with cooperative state forest fire control programs. The federal government retains title to such property.

(c) The property is furnished by the U.S. Department of Agriculture to state or county extension services or agricultural research cooperatives under 40 U.S.C. 483(d)(2)(E). The federal government retains title to such property.

(d) The property is not needed for donation under part 102–37 of this chapter, and is transferred under section 608 of the Foreign Assistance Act of 1961, as amended (22 U.S.C. 2358). Title to such property transfers to the grantee. (You need not wait until after the donation screening period when furnishing excess personal property to recipients under the Agency for International Development (AID) Development Loan Program.)

(e) The property is scientific equipment transferred under section 11(e) of the National Science Foundation (NSF) Act of 1950, as amended (42 U.S.C. 1870(e)). GSA will limit such transfers to property within Federal Supply Classification (FSC) groups 12, 14, 43, 48, 58, 59, 65, 66, 67, 68 and 70. GSA may approve transfers without reimbursement for property under other FSC groups when NSF certifies the item is a component of or related to a piece of scientific equipment or is a difficult-to-acquire item needed for scientific research. Regardless of FSC, GSA will not approve transfers of common-use or general-purpose items without reimbursement. Title to such property transfers to the grantee.

(f) The property is furnished in connection with grants to Indian tribes, as defined in section 3(c) of the Indian Financing Act (24 U.S.C. 1452(c)). Title passage is determined under the authorities of the administering agency.

[65 FR 31218, May 16, 2000, as amended at 71 FR 53572, Sept. 12, 2006]

§ 102–36.195 What type of excess personal property may we furnish to our project grantees?

You may furnish to your project grantees any property, except for consumable items, determined to be necessary and usable for the purpose of the grant. Consumable items are generally not transferable to project grantees. GSA may approve transfers of excess consumable items when adequate justification for the transfer accompanies such requests. For the purpose of this section, "consumable items" are items which are intended for one-time use and are actually consumed in that one time; e.g., drugs, medicines, surgical dressings, cleaning and preserving materials, and fuels.

§ 102–36.200 May we acquire excess personal property for cannibalization purposes by the grantees?

Yes, subject to GSA approval, you may acquire excess personal property for cannibalization purposes. You may be required to provide a supporting statement that indicates disassembly of the item for secondary use has greater benefit than utilization of the item in its existing form and cost savings to the government will result.

§ 102–36.205 Is there a limit to how much excess personal property we may furnish to our grantees?

Yes, you must monitor transfers of excess personal property so the total dollar amount of property transferred (in original acquisition cost) does not exceed the dollar value of the grant. Any transfers above the grant amount must be approved by an official at an administrative level higher than the officer administering the grant.

Subpart D—Disposition of Excess Personal Property

§ 102–36.210 Why must we report excess personal property to GSA?

You must report excess personal property to promote reuse by the government to enable federal agencies to benefit from the continued use of property already paid for with taxpayers' money, thus minimizing new procurement costs. Reporting excess personal property to GSA helps assure that the information on available excess personal property is accessible and disseminated to the widest range of reuse customers.

REPORTING EXCESS PERSONAL PROPERTY

§ 102–36.215 How do we report excess personal property?

Report excess personal property as follows:

(a) Electronically submit the data elements required on the Standard Form 120 (SF 120), Report of Excess Personal Property, in a format specified and approved by GSA; or

(b) Submit a paper SF 120 to the regional GSA Personal Property Management office.

§ 102–36.220 Must we report all excess personal property to GSA?

(a) Generally yes, regardless of the condition code, except as authorized in § 102–36.145 for direct transfers or as exempted in paragraph (b) of this section. Report all excess personal property, including excess personal property to which the government holds title but is in the custody of your contractors, cooperatives, or project grantees.

(b) You are not required to report the following types of excess personal property to GSA for screening:

(1) Property determined appropriate for abandonment/destruction (see § 102–36.305).

(2) Non-appropriated fund property (see § 102–36.165).

(3) Foreign excess personal property (see § 102–36.380).

(4) Scrap, except aircraft in scrap condition.

(5) Perishables, defined for the purposes of this section as any personal property subject to spoilage or decay.

(6) Trading stamps and bonus goods.

(7) Hazardous waste.

(8) Controlled substances.

(9) Nuclear Regulatory Commission-controlled materials.

(10) Property dangerous to public health and safety.

(11) Classified items or property determined to be sensitive for reasons of national security.

(c) Refer to part 101–42 of this title for additional guidance on the disposition of classes of property under paragraphs (b)(7) through (b)(11) of this section.

§ 102–36.225 Must we report excess related personal property?

Yes, you must report excess related personal property to the Office of Real Property, GSA, in accordance with part 102–75 of this chapter.

[65 FR 31218, May 16, 2000, as amended at 71 FR 53572, Sept. 12, 2006]

§ 102–36.230 Where do we send the reports of excess personal property?

(a) You must direct electronic submissions of excess personal property to GSAXcess® maintained by the Property Management Division (FBP), GSA, Washington, DC 20406.

(b) For paper submissions, you must send the SF 120 to the regional GSA Personal Property Management office for the region in which the property is located. For the categories of property listed in § 102–36.125(b), forward the SF 120 to the corresponding regions.

[65 FR 31218, May 16, 2000, as amended at 71 FR 53572, Sept. 12, 2006]

§ 102–36.235 What information do we provide when reporting excess personal property?

(a) You must provide the following data on excess personal property:

(1) The reporting agency and the property location.

(2) A report number (6-digit activity address code and 4-digit Julian date).

(3) 4-digit Federal Supply Class (use National Stock Number whenever available).

(4) Description of item, in sufficient detail.

(5) Quantity and unit of issue.

(6) Disposal Condition Code (see § 102–36.240).

(7) Original acquisition cost per unit and total cost (use estimate if original cost not available).

(8) Manufacturer, date of manufacture, part and serial number, when required by GSA.

(b) In addition, provide the following information on your report of excess, when applicable:

(1) Major parts/components that are missing.

(2) If repairs are needed, the type of repairs.

(3) Special requirements for handling, storage, or transportation.

(4) The required date of removal due to moving or space restrictions.

(5) If reimbursement is required, the authority under which the reimbursement is requested, the amount of reimbursement and the appropriate fund code to which money is to be deposited.

(6) If you will conduct the sale of personal property that is not transferred or donated.

§ 102–36.240 What are the disposal condition codes?

The disposal condition codes are contained in the following table:

Disposal condition code	Definition
1	New. Property which is in new condition or unused condition and can be used immediately without modifications or repairs.
4	Usable. Property which shows some wear, but can be used without significant repair.
7	Repairable. Property which is unusable in its current condition but can be economically repaired.
X	Salvage. Property which has value in excess of its basic material content, but repair or rehabilitation is impractical and/or uneconomical.
S	Scrap. Property which has no value except for its basic material content.

DISPOSING OF EXCESS PERSONAL PROPERTY

§ 102–36.245 Are we accountable for the personal property that has been reported excess, and who is responsible for the care and handling costs?

Yes, you are accountable for the excess personal property until the time it is picked up by the designated recipient or its agent. You are responsible for all care and handling charges while the excess personal property is going through the screening and disposal process.

§ 102–36.250 Does GSA ever take physical custody of excess personal property?

Generally you retain physical custody of the excess personal property prior to its final disposition. Very rarely GSA may consider accepting physical custody of excess personal property. Under special circumstances, GSA may take custody or may direct the transfer of partial or total custody to other executive agencies, with their consent.

§ 102–36.255 What options do we have when unusual circumstances do not allow adequate time for disposal through GSA?

Contact your regional GSA Personal Property Management office for any existing interagency agreements that would allow you to turn in excess personal property to a federal facility. You are responsible for any turn in costs and all costs related to transporting the excess personal property to these facilities.

§ 102–36.260 **How do we promote the expeditious transfer of excess personal property?**

For expeditious transfer of excess personal property you should:

(a) Provide complete and accurate property descriptions and condition codes on the report of excess to facilitate the selection of usable property by potential users.

(b) Ensure that any available operating manual, parts list, diagram, maintenance log, or other instructional publication is made available with the property at the time of transfer.

(c) Advise the designated recipient of any special requirements for dismantling, shipping/transportation.

(d) When the excess personal property is located at a facility due to be closed, provide advance notice of the scheduled date of closing, and ensure there is sufficient time for screening and removal of property.

§ 102–36.265 **What if there are competing requests for the same excess personal property?**

(a) GSA will generally approve transfers on a first-come, first-served basis. When more than one federal agency requests the same item, and the quantity available is not sufficient to meet the demand of all interested agencies, GSA will consider factors such as national defense requirements, emergency needs, avoiding the necessity of a new procurement, energy conservation, transportation costs, and retention of title in the government. GSA will normally give preference to the agency that will retain title in the Government.

(b) Requests for property for the purpose of cannibalization will normally be subordinate to requests for use of the property in its existing form.

§ 102–36.270 **What if a federal agency requests personal property that is undergoing donation screening or in the sales process?**

Prior to final disposition, GSA will consider requests from authorized federal activities for excess personal property undergoing donation screening or in the sales process. Federal transfers may be authorized prior to removal of the property under a donation or sales action.

§ 102–36.275 **May we dispose of excess personal property without GSA approval?**

No, you may not dispose of excess personal property without GSA approval except under the following limited situations:

(a) You may transfer to another federal agency excess personal property that has not yet been reported to GSA, under direct transfer procedures contained in § 102–36.145.

(b) You may dispose of excess personal property that is not required to be reported to GSA (see § 102–36.220(b)).

(c) You may dispose of excess personal property without going through GSA when such disposal is authorized by law.

§ 102–36.280 **May we withdraw from the disposal process excess personal property that we have reported to GSA?**

Yes, you may withdraw excess personal property from the disposal process, but only with the approval of GSA and to satisfy an internal agency requirement. Property that has been approved for transfer or donation or offered for sale by GSA may be returned to your control with proper justification.

TRANSFERS WITH REIMBURSEMENT

§ 102–36.285 **May we charge for personal property transferred to another federal agency?**

(a) When any one of the following conditions applies, you may require and retain reimbursement for the excess personal property from the recipient:

(1) Your agency has the statutory authority to require and retain reimbursement for the property.

(2) You are transferring the property under the exchange/sale authority.

(3) You had originally acquired the property with funds not appropriated from the general fund of the Treasury or appropriated therefrom but by law reimbursable from assessment, tax, or other revenue. It is current executive branch policy that working capital

fund property shall be transferred without reimbursement.

(4) You or the recipient is the U.S. Postal Service.

(5) You or the recipient is the DC Government.

(6) You or the recipient is a wholly owned or mixed-ownership government corporation.

(b) You may charge for direct costs you incurred incident to the transfer, such as packing, loading and shipping of the property. The recipient is responsible for such charges unless you waive the amount involved.

(c) You may not charge for overhead or administrative expenses or the costs for care and handling of the property pending disposition.

§ 102–36.290 How much do we charge for excess personal property on a transfer with reimbursement?

(a) You may require reimbursement in an amount up to the fair market value of the property when the transfer involves property meeting conditions in § 102–36.285(a)(1) through (a)(4).

(b) When you or the recipient is the DC Government or a wholly owned or mixed-ownership Government corporation (§ 102–36.285(a)(5) and (a)(6)), you may only require fair value reimbursement. Fair value reimbursement is 20 percent of the original acquisition cost for new or unused property (i.e., condition code 1), and zero percent for other personal property. A higher fair value may be used if you and the recipient agency agree. Due to special circumstances or the nature of the property, you may use other criteria for establishing fair value if approved or directed by GSA. You must refer any disagreements to the appropriate regional GSA Personal Property Management office.

REPORT OF DISPOSAL ACTIVITY

§ 102–36.295 Is there any reporting requirement on the disposition of excess personal property?

Yes, you must report annually to GSA personal property furnished in any manner in that year to any non-federal recipients, with respect to property obtained as excess or as property determined to be no longer required for the purposes of the appropriation from which it was purchased.

[65 FR 31218, May 16, 2000, as amended at 71 FR 53572, Sept. 12, 2006]

§ 102–36.300 How do we report the furnishing of personal property to non-federal recipients?

(a) Submit your annual report of personal property furnished to non-federal recipients, in letter form, to GSA, Office of Travel, Transportation, and Asset Management (MT), 1800 F Street, NW, Washington, DC 20405, within 90 calendar days after the close of each fiscal year. The report must cover personal property disposed during the fiscal year in all areas within the United States, the U.S. Virgin Islands, American Samoa, Guam, Puerto Rico, the Federated States of Micronesia, the Marshall Islands, Palau, and the Northern Mariana Islands. Negative reports are required.

(b) The report (interagency report control number 0154—GSA—AN) must reference this part and contain the following:

(1) Names of the non-federal recipients.

(2) Status of the recipients (contractor, cooperative, project grantee, etc.).

(3) Total original acquisition cost of excess personal property furnished to each type of recipient, by type of property (two-digit FSC groups).

[65 FR 31218, May 16, 2000, as amended at 71 FR 53572, Sept. 12, 2006]

ABANDONMENT/DESTRUCTION

§ 102–36.305 May we abandon or destroy excess personal property without reporting it to GSA?

Yes, you may abandon or destroy excess personal property when you have made a written determination that the property has no commercial value or the estimated cost of its continued care and handling would exceed the estimated proceeds from its sale. An item has no commercial value when it has neither utility nor monetary value (either as an item or as scrap).

§ 102–36.310 Who makes the determination to abandon or destroy excess personal property?

To abandon or destroy excess personal property, an authorized official of your agency makes a written finding that must be approved by a reviewing official who is not directly accountable for the property.

§ 102–36.315 Are there any restrictions to the use of the abandonment/destruction authority?

Yes, the following restrictions apply:

(a) You must not abandon or destroy property in a manner which is detrimental or dangerous to public health or safety. Additional guidelines for the abandonment/destruction of hazardous materials are prescribed in part 101–42 of this title.

(b) If you become aware of an interest from an entity in purchasing the property, you must implement sales procedures in lieu of abandonment/destruction.

§ 102–36.320 May we transfer or donate excess personal property that has been determined appropriate for abandonment/destruction without GSA approval?

In lieu of abandonment/destruction, you may donate such excess personal property only to a public body without going through GSA. A public body is any department, agency, special purpose district, or other instrumentality of a state or local government; any Indian tribe; or any agency of the federal government. If you become aware of an interest from an eligible non-profit organization (see part 102–37 of this chapter) that is not a public body in acquiring the property, you must contact the regional GSA Personal Property Management office and implement donation procedures in accordance with part 102–37 of this chapter.

[65 FR 31218, May 16, 2000, as amended at 71 FR 53572, Sept. 12, 2006]

§ 102–36.325 What must be done before the abandonment/destruction of excess personal property?

Except as provided in § 102–36.330, you must provide public notice of intent to abandon or destroy excess personal property, in a format and timeframe specified by your agency regulations (such as publishing a notice in a local newspaper, posting of signs in common use facilities available to the public, or providing bulletins on your website through the internet). You must also include in the notice an offer to sell in accordance with part 102–38 of this chapter.

§ 102–36.330 Are there occasions when public notice is not needed regarding abandonment/destruction of excess personal property?

Yes, you are not required to provide public notice when:

(a) The value of the property is so little or the cost of its care and handling, pending abandonment/destruction, is so great that its retention for advertising for sale, even as scrap, is clearly not economical;

(b) Abandonment or destruction is required because of health, safety, or security reasons; or

(c) When the original acquisition cost of the item (estimated if unknown) is less than $500.

[65 FR 31218, May 16, 2000, as amended at 65 FR 34983, June 1, 2000]

Subpart E—Personal Property Whose Disposal Requires Special Handling

§ 102–36.335 Are there certain types of excess personal property that must be disposed of differently from normal disposal procedures?

Yes, you must comply with the additional provisions in this subpart when disposing of the types of personal property listed in this subpart.

AIRCRAFT AND AIRCRAFT PARTS

§ 102–36.340 What must we do when disposing of excess aircraft?

(a) You must report to GSA all excess aircraft, regardless of condition or dollar value, and provide the following information on the SF 120:

(1) Manufacturer, date of manufacture, model, serial number.

(2) Major components missing from the aircraft, such as engines, electronics.

(3) Whether or not the:

(i) Aircraft is operational;

(ii) Data plate is available;

(iii) Historical and maintenance records are available;

(iv) Aircraft has been previously certificated by the Federal Aviation Administration (FAA) and/or has been maintained to FAA airworthiness standards;

(v) Aircraft was previously used for non-flight purposes (i.e., ground training or static display), and has been subjected to extensive disassembly and reassembly procedures for ground training, or repeated burning for fire-fighting training purposes.

(4) For military aircraft, indicate Category A, B, or C as designated by the Department of Defense (DOD), as follows:

Category of aircraft	Description
A	Aircraft authorized for sale and exchange for commercial use.
B	Aircraft previously used for ground instruction and/or static display.
C	Aircraft that are combat configured as determined by DOD.

NOTE TO § 102–36.340(a)(4): For additional information on military aircraft see Defense Materiel Disposition Manual, DOD 4160.21-M, accessible at *www.drms.dla.mil* under "Publications."

(b) When the designated transfer or donation recipient's intended use is for non-flight purposes, you must remove and return the data plate to GSA Property Management Branch (9FBP), San Francisco, CA 94102–3434 prior to releasing the aircraft to the authorized recipient. GSA will forward the data plates to FAA.

(c) You must also submit a report of the final disposition of the aircraft to the Federal Aviation Interactive Reporting System (FAIRS) maintained by the Office of Travel, Transportation, and Asset Management (MT), GSA, 1800 F Street, NW, Washington, DC 20405. For additional instructions on reporting to FAIRS, see part 102–33 of this chapter.

[65 FR 31218, May 16, 2000, as amended at 71 FR 53572, Sept. 12, 2006]

§ 102–36.345 May we dispose of excess Flight Safety Critical Aircraft Parts (FSCAP)?

Yes, you may dispose of excess FSCAP, but first you must determine whether the documentation available is adequate to allow transfer, donation, or sale of the part in accordance with part 102–33, subpart D, of this chapter. Otherwise, you must mutilate undocumented FSCAP that has no traceability to its original equipment manufacturer and dispose of it as scrap. When reporting excess FSCAP, annotate the manufacturer, date of manufacture, part number, serial number, and the appropriate Criticality Code on the SF 120, and ensure that all available historical and maintenance records accompany the part at the time of issue.

[65 FR 31218, May 16, 2000, as amended at 71 FR 53572, Sept. 12, 2006]

§ 102–36.350 How do we identify a FSCAP?

Any aircraft part designated as FSCAP is assigned an alpha Criticality Code, and the code is annotated on the original transfer document when you acquire the part. You must perpetuate the appropriate FSCAP Criticality Code on all personal property records. You may contact the Federal agency or Military service that originally owned the part for assistance in making this determination, or query DOD's Federal Logistics Information System (FLIS) using the National Stock Number (NSN) for the part. For assistance in subscribing to the FLIS service contact the FedLog Consumer Support Office, 800–351–4381.

§ 102–36.355 What are the FSCAP Criticality Codes?

The FSCAP Criticality Codes are contained in the following table:

FSCAP code	Description
E	FSCAP specially designed to be or selected as being nuclear hardened.
F	Flight Safety Critical Aircraft Part.

§ 102–36.360 How do we dispose of aircraft parts that are life-limited but have no FSCAP designation?

When disposing of life-limited aircraft parts that have no FSCAP designation, you must ensure that tags and labels, historical data, and maintenance records accompany the part on any transfers, donations or sales. For additional information regarding the disposal of life-limited parts with or without tags or documentation, refer to part 102–33 of this chapter.

[65 FR 31218, May 16, 2000, as amended at 71 FR 53572, Sept. 12, 2006]

CANINES, LAW ENFORCEMENT

§ 102–36.365 May we transfer or donate canines that have been used in the performance of law enforcement duties?

Yes, under 40 U.S.C. 555, when the canine is no longer needed for law enforcement duties, you may donate the canine to an individual who has experience handling canines in the performance of those official duties.

[65 FR 31218, May 16, 2000, as amended at 71 FR 53572, Sept. 12, 2006]

DISASTER RELIEF PROPERTY

§ 102–36.370 Are there special requirements concerning the use of excess personal property for disaster relief?

Yes, upon declaration by the President of an emergency or a major disaster, you may loan excess personal property to state and local governments, with or without compensation and prior to reporting it as excess to GSA, to alleviate suffering and damage resulting from any emergency or major disaster (Robert T. Stafford Disaster Relief and Emergency Assistance Act (42 U.S.C. 5121–5206) and Executive Order 12148 (3 CFR, 1979 Comp., p. 412), as amended). If the loan involves property that has already been reported excess to GSA, you may withdraw the item from the disposal process subject to approval by GSA. You may also withdraw excess personal property for use by your agency in providing assistance in disaster relief. You are still accountable for this property and your agency is responsible for developing

agencywide procedures for recovery of such property.

[65 FR 31218, May 16, 2000, as amended at 71 FR 53572, Sept. 12, 2006]

FIREARMS

§ 102–36.375 May we dispose of excess firearms?

Yes, unless you have specific statutory authority to do otherwise, excess firearms may be transferred only to those Federal agencies authorized to acquire firearms for official use. GSA may donate certain classes of surplus firearms to State and local government activities whose primary function is the enforcement of applicable federal, state, and/or local laws and whose compensated law enforcement officers have the authority to apprehend and arrest. Firearms not transferred or donated must be destroyed and sold as scrap. For additional guidance on the disposition of firearms refer to part 101–42 of this title.

FOREIGN EXCESS PERSONAL PROPERTY

§ 102–36.380 Who is responsible for disposing of foreign excess personal property?

Your agency is responsible for disposing of your foreign excess personal property, as provided by chapter 7 of title 40 of the United States Code.

[65 FR 31218, May 16, 2000, as amended at 71 FR 53572, Sept. 12, 2006]

§ 102–36.385 What are our responsibilities in the disposal of foreign excess personal property?

When disposing of foreign excess personal property you must:

(a) Determine whether it is in the interest of the U.S. Government to return foreign excess personal property to the U.S. for further re-use or to dispose of the property overseas.

(b) Ensure that any disposal of property overseas conforms to the foreign policy of the United States and the terms and conditions of any applicable Host Nation Agreement.

(c) Ensure that, when foreign excess personal property is donated or sold overseas, donation/sales conditions include a requirement for compliance with U.S. Department of Commerce and Department of Agriculture regulations when transporting any personal property back to the U.S.

(d) Inform the U.S. State Department of any disposal of property to any foreign governments or entities.

§102–36.390 How may we dispose of foreign excess personal property?

To dispose of foreign excess personal property, you may:

(a) Offer the property for re-use by U.S. Federal agencies overseas;

(b) Return the property to the U.S. for re-use by eligible recipients;

(c) Sell, exchange, lease, or transfer such property for cash, credit, or other property;

(d) Donate medical materials or supplies to nonprofit medical or health organizations, including those qualified under sections 214(b) and 607 of the Foreign Assistance Act of 1961, as amended (22 U.S.C. 2174, 2357); or

(e) Abandon, destroy or donate such property when you determine that it has no commercial value or the estimated cost of care and handling would exceed the estimated proceeds from its sale, in accordance with 40 U.S.C. 527. Abandonment, destruction or donation actions must also comply with the laws of the country in which the property is located.

[65 FR 31218, May 16, 2000, as amended at 71 FR 53572, Sept. 12, 2006]

§102–36.395 How may GSA assist us in disposing of foreign excess personal property?

You may request GSA's assistance in the screening of foreign excess personal property for possible re-use by eligible recipients within the U.S. GSA may, after consultation with you, designate property for return to the United States for transfer or donation purposes.

§102–36.400 Who pays for the transportation costs when foreign excess personal property is returned to the United States?

When foreign excess property is to be returned to the U.S. for the purpose of an approved transfer or donation under the provisions of 40 U.S.C. 521–529, 549, and 551, the Federal agency, State agency, or donee receiving the property is responsible for all direct costs involved in the transfer, which include packing, handling, crating, and transportation.

[65 FR 31218, May 16, 2000, as amended at 71 FR 53572, Sept. 12, 2006]

GIFTS

§102–36.405 May we keep gifts given to us from the public?

If your agency has gift retention authority, you may retain gifts from the public. Otherwise, you must report gifts you receive on a SF 120 to GSA. You must report gifts received from a foreign government in accordance with part 102–42 of this chapter.

[65 FR 31218, May 16, 2000, as amended at 71 FR 53572, Sept. 12, 2006]

§102–36.410 How do we dispose of a gift in the form of money or intangible personal property?

Report intangible personal property to GSA, Personal Property Management Division (FBP), Washington, DC 20406. You must not transfer or dispose of this property without prior approval of GSA. The Secretary of the Treasury will dispose of money and negotiable instruments such as bonds, notes, or other securities under the authority of 31 U.S.C. 324.

§102–36.415 How do we dispose of gifts other than intangible personal property?

(a) When the gift is offered with the condition that the property be sold and the proceeds used to reduce the public debt, report the gift to the regional GSA Personal Property Management office in which the property is located. GSA will convert the gift to money upon acceptance and deposit the proceeds into a special account of the U.S. Treasury.

(b) When the gift is offered with no conditions or restrictions, and your agency has gift retention authority, you may use the gift for an authorized official purpose without reporting to GSA. The property will then lose its identity as a gift and you must account for it in the same manner as Federal personal property acquired from authorized sources. When the property is no longer needed, you must report it as excess personal property to GSA.

(c) When the gift is offered with no conditions or restrictions, but your agency does not have gift retention authority, you must report it to the regional GSA Personal Property Management office. GSA will offer the property for screening for possible transfer to a federal agency or convert the gift to money and deposit the funds with U.S. Treasury. If your agency is interested in keeping the gift for an official purpose, you must annotate your interest on the SF 120 and also submit a SF 122.

§ 102–36.420 How do we dispose of gifts from foreign governments or entities?

Report foreign gifts on a SF 120 to GSA, Property Management Division (FBP), Washington, DC 20406, for possible transfer, donation or sale in accordance with the provisions of part 102–42 of this chapter.

[71 FR 53572, Sept. 12, 2006]

HAZARDOUS PERSONAL PROPERTY

§ 102–36.425 May we dispose of excess hazardous personal property?

Yes, but only in accordance with part 101–42 of this title. When reporting excess hazardous property to GSA, certify on the SF 120 that the property has been packaged and labeled as required. Annotate any special requirements for handling, storage, or use, and provide a description of the actual or potential hazard.

MUNITIONS LIST ITEMS/COMMERCE CONTROL LIST ITEMS (MLIs/CCLIs)

§ 102–36.430 May we dispose of excess Munitions List Items (MLIs)/Commerce Control List Items (CCLIs)?

You may dispose of excess MLIs/CCLIs only when you comply with the additional disposal and demilitarization (DEMIL) requirements contained in part 101–42 of this title. MLIs may require demilitarization when issued to any non-DoD entity, and will require appropriate licensing when exported from the U.S. CCLIs usually require export licensing when transported from the U.S.

§ 102–36.435 How do we identify Munitions List Items (MLIs)/Commerce Control List Items (CCLIs) requiring demilitarization?

You identify MLIs/CCLIs requiring demilitarization by the demilitarization code that is assigned to each MLI or CCLI. The code indicates the type and scope of demilitarization and/or export controls that must be accomplished, when required, before issue to any non-DOD activity. For a listing of the codes and additional guidance on DEMIL procedures see DOD Demilitarization and Trade Security Control Manual, DOD 4160.21–M–1.

PRINTING EQUIPMENT AND SUPPLIES

§ 102–36.440 Are there special procedures for reporting excess printing and binding equipment and supplies?

Yes, in accordance with 44 U.S.C. 312, you must submit reports of excess printing and binding machinery, equipment, materials, and supplies to the Public Printer, Government Printing Office (GPO), Customer Service Manager, 732 North Capitol Street, NW, Washington, DC 20401. If GPO has no requirement for the property, you must then submit the report to GSA.

[65 FR 31218, May 16, 2000, as amended at 71 FR 53572, Sept. 12, 2006]

RED CROSS PROPERTY

§ 102–36.445 Do we report excess personal property originally acquired from or through the American National Red Cross?

Yes, when reporting excess personal property which was processed, produced, or donated by the American National Red Cross, note "RED CROSS PROPERTY" on the SF 120 or report document. GSA will offer to return this property to the Red Cross if no other federal agency has a need for it. If the Red Cross has no requirement, the property continues in the disposal process and is available for donation.

SHELF-LIFE ITEMS

§ 102–36.450 Do we report excess shelf-life items?

(a) When there are quantities on hand, that would not be utilized by the expiration date and cannot be returned to the vendor for credit, you must report such expected overage as excess for possible transfer and disposal to ensure maximum use prior to deterioration.

(b) You need not report expired shelf-life items. You may dispose of property with expired shelf-life by abandonment/destruction in accordance with § 102–36.305 and in compliance with Federal, State, and local waste disposal and air and water pollution control standards.

§ 102–36.455 How do we report excess shelf-life items?

You must identify the property as shelf-life items by "SL", indicate the expiration date, whether the date is the original or an extended date, and if the date is further extendable. GSA may adjust the screening period based on re-use potential and the remaining useful shelf life.

§ 102–36.460 Do we report excess medical shelf-life items held for national emergency purposes?

When the remaining shelf life of any medical materials or supplies held for national emergency purposes is of too short a period to justify their continued retention, you should report such property excess for possible transfer and disposal. You must make such excess determinations at such time as to ensure that sufficient time remains to permit their use before their shelf-life expires and the items are unfit for human use. You must identify such items with "MSL" and the expiration date, and indicate any specialized storage requirements.

§ 102–36.465 May we transfer or exchange excess medical shelf-life items with other federal agencies?

Yes, you may transfer or exchange excess medical shelf-life items held for national emergency purposes with any other federal agency for other medical materials or supplies, without GSA approval and without regard to part 102–39 of this chapter. You and the transferee agency will agree to the terms and prices. You may credit any proceeds derived from such transactions to your agency's current applicable appropriation and use the funds only for the purchase of medical materials or supplies for national emergency purposes.

[65 FR 31218, May 16, 2000, as amended at 71 FR 53572, Sept. 12, 2006]

VESSELS

§ 102–36.470 What must we do when disposing of excess vessels?

(a) When you dispose of excess vessels, you must indicate on the SF 120 the following information:

(1) Whether the vessel has been inspected by the Coast Guard.

(2) Whether testing for hazardous materials has been done. And if so, the result of the testing, specifically the presence or absence of PCB's and asbestos and level of contamination.

(3) Whether hazardous materials clean up is required, and when it will be accomplished by your agency.

(b) In accordance with 40 U.S.C. 548, the Federal Maritime Administration (FMA), Department of Transportation, is responsible for disposing of surplus vessels determined to be merchant vessels or capable of conversion to merchant use and weighing 1,500 gross tons or more. The SF 120 for such vessels shall be forwarded to GSA for submission to FMA.

(c) Disposal instructions regarding vessels in this part do not apply to battleships, cruisers, aircraft carriers, destroyers, or submarines.

[65 FR 31218, May 16, 2000, as amended at 71 FR 53572, Sept. 12, 2006]

Subpart F—Miscellaneous Disposition

§ 102–36.475 What is the authority for transfers under "Computers for Learning"?

(a) The Stevenson-Wydler Technology Innovation Act of 1980, as amended (15 U.S.C. 3710(i)), authorizes federal agencies to transfer excess education-related federal equipment to educational institutions or nonprofit organizations for educational and research activities. Executive Order 12999 (3 CFR, 1996 Comp., p. 180) requires, to the extent permitted by law and where appropriate, the transfer of computer equipment for use by schools or nonprofit organizations.

(b) Each federal agency is required to identify a point of contact within the agency to assist eligible recipients, and to publicize the availability of such property to eligible communities. Excess education-related equipment may be transferred directly under established agency procedures, or reported to GSA as excess for subsequent transfer to potential eligible recipients as appropriate. You must include transfers under this authority in the annual Non-federal Recipients Report (See § 102-36.295) to GSA.

(c) The "Computers for Learning" website has been developed to streamline the transfer of excess and surplus Federal computer equipment to schools and nonprofit educational organizations. For additional information about this program access the "Computers for Learning" website, *http:// www.computers.fed.gov.*

PART 102-37—DONATION OF SURPLUS PERSONAL PROPERTY

Subpart E—Donations to Public Agencies, Service Educational Activities (SEAs), and Eligible Nonprofit Organizations

AUTHORITY: 40 U.S.C. 549 and 121(c).

SOURCE: 67 FR 2584, Jan. 18, 2002, unless otherwise noted.

Subpart A—General Provisions

§ 102–37.5 What does this part cover?

This part covers the donation of surplus Federal personal property located within a State, including foreign excess personal property returned to a State for handling as surplus property. For purposes of this part, the term State includes any of the 50 States, as well as the District of Columbia, the U.S. Virgin Islands, Guam, American Samoa, the Commonwealth of Puerto Rico, and the Commonwealth of the Northern Mariana Islands.

§ 102–37.10 What is the primary governing authority for this part?

Section 549 of title 40, United States Code, gives the General Services Administration (GSA) discretionary authority to prescribe the necessary regulations for, and to execute the surplus personal property donation program.

[67 FR 2584, Jan. 18, 2002, as amended at 71 FR 23868, Apr. 25, 2006]

§ 102–37.15 Who must comply with the provisions of this part?

You must comply with this part if you are a holding agency or a recipient of Federal surplus personal property approved by GSA for donation (e.g., a State agency for surplus property (SASP) or a public airport).

§ 102–37.20 How do we request a deviation from this part and who can approve it?

See §§ 102–2.60 through 102–2.110 of this chapter to request a deviation from the requirements of this part.

DEFINITIONS

§ 102–37.25 What definitions apply to this part?

The following definitions apply to this part:

Allocation means the process by which GSA identifies the SASP to receive surplus property on a fair and equitable basis, taking into account the condition of the property as well as the original acquisition cost of the property.

Cannibalization means to remove serviceable parts from one item of equipment in order to install them on another item of equipment.

Donee means any of the following entities that receive Federal surplus personal property through a SASP:

(1) A service educational activity (SEA).

(2) A public agency (as defined in appendix C of this part) which uses surplus personal property to carry out or promote one or more public purposes. (Public airports are an exception and are only considered donees when they elect to receive surplus property through a SASP, but not when they elect to receive surplus property through the Federal Aviation Administration as discussed in subpart F of this part.)

(3) An eligible nonprofit tax-exempt educational or public health institution (including a provider of assistance to homeless or impoverished families or individuals).

(4) A State or local government agency, or a nonprofit organization or institution, that receives funds appropriated for a program for older individuals.

Holding agency means the executive agency having accountability for, and generally possession of, the property involved.

Period of restriction means the period of time for keeping donated property in use for the purpose for which it was donated.

Screening means the process of physically inspecting property or reviewing lists or reports of property to determine whether property is usable or needed for donation purposes.

Service educational activity (SEA) means any educational activity designated by the Secretary of Defense as being of special interest to the armed forces; e.g., maritime academies or military, naval, Air Force, or Coast Guard preparatory schools.

Standard Form (SF) 123, Transfer Order Surplus Personal Property means the document used to request and document the transfer of Federal surplus personal property for donation purposes.

State means one of the 50 States, the District of Columbia, the U.S. Virgin Islands, Guam, American Samoa, the Commonwealth of Puerto Rico, and the Commonwealth of the Northern Mariana Islands.

State agency for surplus property (SASP) means the agency designated under State law to receive Federal surplus personal property for distribution to eligible donees within the State as provided for in 40 U.S.C. 549.

Surplus personal property (surplus property) means excess personal property (as defined in §102–36.40 of this chapter) not required for the needs of any Federal agency, as determined by GSA.

Surplus release date means the date on which Federal utilization screening of excess personal property has been completed, and the property is available for donation.

Transferee means a public airport receiving surplus property from a holding agency through the Federal Aviation Administration, or a SASP.

You, when used in subparts D and E of this part, means SASP, unless otherwise specified.

[67 FR 2584, Jan. 18, 2002, as amended at 71 FR 23868, Apr. 25, 2006; 79 FR 64514, Oct. 30, 2014]

DONATION OVERVIEW

§ 102–37.30 When does property become available for donation?

Excess personal property becomes available for donation the day following the surplus release date. This is the point at which the screening period has been completed without transfer to a Federal agency or other eligible recipient, and the GSA has determined the property to be surplus.

§ 102–37.35 Who handles the donation of surplus property?

(a) The SASPs handle the donation of most surplus property to eligible donees in their States in accordance with this part.

(b) The GSA handles the donation of surplus property to public airports under a program administered by the Federal Aviation Administration (FAA) (see subpart F of this part). The GSA may also donate to the American National Red Cross surplus property that was originally derived from or through the Red Cross (see subpart G of this part).

(c) Holding agencies may donate surplus property that they would otherwise abandon or destroy directly to public bodies in accordance with subpart H of this part.

§ 102–37.40 What type of surplus property is available for donation?

All surplus property (including property held by working capital funds established under 10 U.S.C. 2208 or in similar funds) is available for donation to eligible recipients, except for property in the following categories:

(a) Agricultural commodities, food, and cotton or woolen goods determined from time to time by the Secretary of Agriculture to be commodities requiring special handling with respect to price support or stabilization.

(b) Property acquired with trust funds (e.g., Social Security Trust Funds).

(c) Non-appropriated fund property.

(d) Naval vessels of the following categories: Battleships, cruisers, aircraft carriers, destroyers, and submarines.

(e) Vessels of 1500 gross tons or more which the Maritime Administration determines to be merchant vessels or capable of conversion to merchant use.

(f) Records of the Federal Government.

(g) Property that requires reimbursement upon transfer (such as abandoned or other unclaimed property that is found on premises owned or leased by the Government).

(h) Controlled substances.

(i) Items as may be specified from time to time by the GSA Office of Governmentwide Policy.

§ 102–37.45 How long is property available for donation screening?

Entities authorized to participate in the donation program may screen property, concurrently with Federal agencies, as soon as the property is reported as excess up until the surplus release date. The screening period is normally 21 calendar days, except as noted in § 102–36.95 of this chapter.

§ 102–37.50 What is the general process for requesting surplus property for donation?

The process for requesting surplus property for donation varies, depending on who is making the request.

(a) Donees should submit their requests for property directly to the appropriate SASP.

(b) SASPs and public airports should submit their requests to the appropriate GSA regional office. Requests must be submitted on a Standard Form (SF) 123, Transfer Order Surplus Personal Property, or its electronic equivalent. Public airports must have FAA certify their transfer requests prior to submission to GSA for approval. GSA may ask SASPs or public airports to submit any additional information required to support and justify transfer of the property.

(c) The American National Red Cross should submit requests to GSA as described in subpart G of this part when

obtaining property under the authority of 40 U.S.C. 551.

(d) Public bodies, when seeking to acquire property that is being abandoned or destroyed, should follow rules and procedures established by the donor agency (see subpart H of this part).

[67 FR 2584, Jan. 18, 2002, as amended at 79 FR 64514, Oct. 30, 2014]

§ 102–37.55 Who pays for transportation and other costs associated with a donation?

The receiving organization (the transferee) is responsible for any packing, shipping, or transportation charges associated with the transfer of surplus property for donation. Those costs, in the case of SASPs, may be passed on to donees that receive the property.

§ 102–37.60 How much time does a transferee have to pick up or remove surplus property from holding agency premises?

The transferee (or the transferee's agent) must remove property from the holding agency premises within 15 calendar days after being notified that the property is available for pickup, unless otherwise coordinated with the holding agency. If the transferee decides prior to pickup or removal that it no longer needs the property, it must notify the GSA regional office that approved the transfer request.

§ 102–37.65 What happens to surplus property that has been approved for transfer when the prospective transferee decides it cannot use the property and declines to pick it up?

When a prospective transferee decides it cannot use surplus property that has already been approved for transfer and declines to pick it up, the GSA regional office will advise any other SASP or public airport known to be interested in the property to submit a transfer request. If there is no transfer interest, GSA will release the property for other disposal.

§ 102–37.70 How should a transferee account for the receipt of a larger or smaller number of items than approved by GSA on the SF 123?

When the quantity of property received doesn't agree with that approved by GSA on the SF 123, the transferee should handle the overage or shortage as follows:

If . . .	And . . .	Then . . .
(a) More property is received than was approved by GSA for transfer.	The known or estimated acquisition cost of the line item(s) involved is $500 or more.	Submit a SF 123 for the difference to GSA (Identify the property as an overage and include the original transfer order number.)[1]
(b) Less property is received than was approved by GSA for transfer.	The acquisition cost of the missing item(s) is $500 or more.	Submit a shortage report to GSA, with a copy to the holding agency.[1]
(c) The known or estimated acquisition cost of the property is less than $500		Annotate on your receiving and inventory records, a description of the property, its known or estimated acquisition cost, and the name of the holding agency.

[1] Submit the SF 123 or shortage report to the GSA approving office within 30 calendar days of the date of transfer.

§ 102–37.75 What should be included in a shortage report?

The shortage report should include:

(a) The name and address of the holding agency;

(b) All pertinent GSA and holding agency control numbers, in addition to the original transfer order number; and

(c) A description of each line item of property, the condition code, the quantity and unit of issue, and the unit and total acquisition cost.

§ 102–37.80 What happens to surplus property that isn't transferred for donation?

Surplus property not transferred for donation is generally offered for sale under the provisions of part 102–38 of this chapter. Under the appropriate circumstances (see § 102–36.305 of this chapter), such property might be abandoned or destroyed.

[67 FR 2584, Jan. 18, 2002, as amended at 71 FR 23868, Apr. 25, 2006]

§ 102–37.85 Can surplus property being offered for sale be withdrawn and approved for donation?

Yes, surplus property being offered for sale may be withdrawn for donation if approved by GSA. GSA will not approve requests for the withdrawal of property that has been advertised or listed on a sales offering if that withdrawal would be harmful to the overall outcome of the sale. GSA will only grant such requests prior to sales award, since an award is binding.

Subpart B—General Services Administration (GSA)

§ 102–37.90 What are GSA's responsibilities in the donation of surplus property?

The General Services Administration (GSA) is responsible for supervising and directing the disposal of surplus personal property. In addition to issuing regulatory guidance for the donation of such property, GSA:

(a) Determines when property is surplus to the needs of the Government;

(b) Allocates and transfers surplus property on a fair and equitable basis to State agencies for surplus property (SASPs) for further distribution to eligible donees;

(c) Oversees the care and handling of surplus property while it is in the custody of a SASP;

(d) Approves all transfers of surplus property to public airports, pursuant to the appropriate determinations made by the Federal Aviation Administration (see subpart F of this part);

(e) Donates to the American National Red Cross property (generally blood plasma and related medical materials) originally provided by the Red Cross to a Federal agency, but that has subsequently been determined surplus to Federal needs (see subpart G of this part);

(f) Approves, after consultation with the holding agency, foreign excess personal property to be returned to the United States for donation purposes;

(g) Coordinates and controls the level of SASP and donee screening at Federal installations;

(h) Imposes appropriate conditions on the donation of surplus property having characteristics that require special handling or use limitations (see §102–37.455); and

(i) Keeps track of and reports on Federal donation programs (see §102–37.105).

§102–37.95 How will GSA resolve competing transfer requests?

In case of requests from two or more SASPs, GSA will use the allocating criteria in §102–37.100. When competing requests are received from public airports and SASPs, GSA will transfer property fairly and equitably, based on such factors as need, proposed use, and interest of the holding agency in having the property donated to a specific public airport.

§102–37.100 What factors will GSA consider in allocating surplus property among SASPs?

GSA allocates property among the SASPs on a fair and equitable basis using the following factors:

(a) Extraordinary needs caused by disasters or emergency situations.

(b) Requests from the Department of Defense (DOD) for DOD-generated property to be allocated through a SASP for donation to a specific service educational activity.

(c) Need and usability of property, as reflected by requests from SASPs. GSA will also give special consideration to requests transmitted through the SASPs by eligible donees for specific items of property. (Requests for property to be used as is will be given preference over cannibalization requests.)

(d) States in greatest need of the type of property to be allocated where the need is evidenced by a letter of justification from the intended donee.

(e) Whether a SASP has already received similar property in the past, and how much.

(f) Past performance of a SASP in effecting timely pickup or removal of property approved for transfer and making prompt distribution of property to eligible donees.

(g) The property's condition and its original acquisition cost.

(h) Relative neediness of each State based on the State's population and per capita income.

Subpart C—Holding Agency

§102–37.110 What are a holding agency's responsibilities in the donation of surplus property?

Your donation responsibilities as a holding agency begin when you determine that property is to be declared excess. You must then:

(a) Let GSA know if you have a donee in mind for foreign gift items or airport property, as provided for in §§102–37.525 and 102–42.95(h) of this chapter;

(b) Cooperate with all entities authorized to participate in the donation program and their authorized representatives in locating, screening, and inspecting excess or surplus property for possible donation;

(c) Set aside or hold surplus property from further disposal upon notification of a pending transfer for donation; (If GSA does not notify you of a pending transfer within 5 calendar days following the surplus release date, you may proceed with the sale or other authorized disposal of the property.)

(d) Upon receipt of a GSA-approved transfer document, promptly ship or release property to the transferee (or the transferee's designated agent) in accordance with pickup or shipping instructions on the transfer document;

(e) Notify the approving GSA regional office if surplus property to be picked up is not removed within 15 calendar days after you notify the transferee (or its agent) of its availability. (GSA will advise you of further disposal instructions.); and

(f) Perform and bear the cost of care and handling of surplus property pending its disposal, except as provided in § 102–37.115.

[67 FR 2584, Jan. 18, 2002, as amended at 67 FR 78732, Dec. 26, 2002]

§ 102–37.115   May a holding agency be reimbursed for costs incurred incident to a donation?

Yes, you, as a holding agency, may charge the transferee for the direct costs you incurred incident to a donation transfer, such as your packing, handling, crating, and transportation expenses. However, you may not include overhead or administrative costs in these charges.

§ 102–37.120   May a holding agency donate surplus property directly to eligible non-Federal recipients without going through GSA?

Generally, a holding agency may not donate surplus property directly to eligible non-Federal recipients without going through GSA, except for the situations listed in § 102–37.125.

§ 102–37.125   What are some donations that do not require GSA's approval?

(a) Some donations of surplus property that do not require GSA's approval are:

(1) Donations of condemned, obsolete, or other specified material by a military department or the Coast Guard to recipients eligible under 10 U.S.C. 2572, 10 U.S.C. 7306, 10 U.S.C. 7541, 10 U.S.C. 7545, and 14 U.S.C. 641a (see appendix A of this part for details). However, such property must first undergo excess Federal and surplus donation screening as required in this part and part 102–36 of this chapter;

(2) Donations by holding agencies to public bodies under subpart H of this part;

(3) Donations by the Small Business Administration (SBA) to small disadvantaged businesses under 13 CFR part 124 (although collaboration and agreement between the SBA, SASPs, and GSA is encouraged); and

(4) Donations by holding agencies of law enforcement canines to their handlers under 40 U.S.C. 555.

(b) You may also donate property directly to eligible non-Federal recipients under other circumstances if you have statutory authority to do so. All such donations must be included on your annual report to GSA under § 102–36.300 of this chapter.

[67 FR 2584, Jan. 18, 2002, as amended at 71 FR 23868, Apr. 25, 2006; 79 FR 64514, Oct. 30, 2014]

Subpart D—State Agency for Surplus Property (SASP)

§ 102–37.130   What are a SASP's responsibilities in the donation of surplus property?

As a SASP, your responsibilities in the donation of surplus property are to:

(a) Determine whether or not an entity seeking to obtain surplus property is eligible for donation as a:

(1) Public agency;

(2) Nonprofit educational or public health institution; or

(3) Program for older individuals.

(b) Distribute surplus property fairly, equitably, and promptly to eligible donees in your State based on their relative needs and resources, and ability to use the property, and as provided in your State plan of operation.

(c) Enforce compliance with the terms and conditions imposed on donated property.

§ 102–37.135   How does a SASP become eligible to distribute surplus property to donees?

In order to receive transfers of surplus property, a SASP must:

(a) Have a GSA-approved State plan of operation; and

(b) Provide the certifications and agreements as set forth in §§ 102–37.200 and 102–37.205.

STATE PLAN OF OPERATION

§ 102–37.140 What is a State plan of operation?

A State plan of operation is a document developed under State law and approved by GSA in which the State sets forth a plan for the management and administration of the SASP in the donation of property.

§ 102–37.145 Who is responsible for developing, certifying, and submitting the plan?

The State legislature must develop the plan. The chief executive officer of the State must submit the plan to the Administrator of General Services for acceptance and certify that the SASP is authorized to:

(a) Acquire and distribute property to eligible donees in the State;

(b) Enter into cooperative agreements; and

(c) Undertake other actions and provide other assurances as are required by 40 U.S.C. 549(e) and set forth in the plan.

[67 FR 2584, Jan. 18, 2002, as amended at 71 FR 23868, Apr. 25, 2006]

§ 102–37.150 What must a State legislature include in the plan?

The State legislature must ensure the plan conforms to the provisions of 40 U.S.C. 549(e) and includes the information and assurances set forth in Appendix B of this part. It may also include in the plan other provisions not inconsistent with the purposes of title 40 of the United States Code and the requirements of this part.

[67 FR 2584, Jan. 18, 2002, as amended at 71 FR 23868, Apr. 25, 2006]

§ 102–37.155 When does a plan take effect?

The plan takes effect on the date GSA notifies the chief executive officer of the State that the plan is approved.

§ 102–37.160 Must GSA approve amendments or modifications to the plan?

Yes, GSA must approve amendments or modifications to the plan.

§ 102–37.165 Do plans or major amendments require public notice?

Yes, proposed plans and major amendments to existing plans require general notice to the public for comment. A State must publish a general notice of the plan or amendment at least 60 calendar days in advance of filing the proposal with GSA and provide interested parties at least 30 calendar days to submit comments before filing the proposal.

§ 102–37.170 What happens if a SASP does not operate in accordance with its plan?

If a SASP does not operate in accordance with its plan, GSA may withhold allocation and transfer of surplus property until the nonconformance is corrected.

SCREENING AND REQUESTING PROPERTY

§ 102–37.175 How does a SASP find out what property is potentially available for donation?

(a) A SASP may conduct onsite screening at various Federal facilities, contact or submit want lists to GSA, or use GSA's or other agencies' computerized inventory system to electronically search for property that is potentially available for donation (see § 102–36.90 for information on GSAXcess).

(b) For the SASP (or a SASP's representative) to perform onsite screening, the screener must coordinate the onsite visit and screening with the individual holding agency or organization. The screener should ascertain the identification required and any special procedures for access to the facility or location.

[67 FR 2584, Jan. 18, 2002, as amended at 79 FR 64514, Oct. 30, 2014]

§§ 102–37.180—102–37.185 [Reserved]

§ 102–37.190 What records must a SASP maintain on authorized screeners?

You must maintain a current record of all individuals authorized to screen for your SASP, including their names, addresses, telephone numbers, qualifications to screen, and any additional identifying information such as driver's license or social security numbers.

In the case of donee screeners, you should place such records in the donee's eligibility file and review for currency each time a periodic review of the donee's file is undertaken.

§ 102–37.195 Does a SASP have to have a donee in mind to request surplus property?

Generally yes, you should have a firm requirement or an anticipated demand for any property that you request.

§ 102–37.200 What certifications must a SASP make when requesting surplus property for donation?

When requesting or applying for property, you must certify that:

(a) You are the agency of the State designated under State law that has legal authority under 40 U.S.C. 549 and GSA regulations, to receive property for distribution within the State to eligible donees as defined in this part.

(b) No person with supervisory or managerial duties in your State's donation program is debarred, suspended, ineligible, or voluntarily excluded from participating in the donation program.

(c) The property is usable and needed within the State by:

(1) A public agency for one or more public purposes.

(2) An eligible nonprofit organization or institution which is exempt from taxation under section 501 of the Internal Revenue Code (26 U.S.C. 501), for the purpose of education or public health (including research for any such purpose).

(3) An eligible nonprofit activity for programs for older individuals.

(4) A service educational activity (SEA), for DOD-generated property only.

(d) When property is picked up by, or shipped to, your SASP, you have adequate and available funds, facilities, and personnel to provide accountability, warehousing, proper maintenance, and distribution of the property.

(e) When property is distributed by your SASP to a donee, or when delivery is made directly from a holding agency to a donee pursuant to a State distribution document, you have determined that the donee acquiring the property is eligible within the meaning of the Property Act and GSA regulations, and that the property is usable and needed by the donee.

[67 FR 2584, Jan. 18, 2002, as amended at 71 FR 23868, Apr. 25, 2006]

§ 102–37.205 What agreements must a SASP make?

With respect to surplus property picked up by or shipped to your SASP, you must agree to the following:

(a) You will make prompt statewide distribution of such property, on a fair and equitable basis, to donees eligible to acquire property under 40 U.S.C. 549 and GSA regulations. You will distribute property only after such eligible donees have properly executed the appropriate certifications and agreements established by your SASP and/or GSA.

(b) Title to the property remains in the United States Government although you have taken possession of it. Conditional title to the property will pass to the eligible donee when the donee executes the required certifications and agreements and takes possession of the property.

(c) You will:

(1) Promptly pay the cost of care, handling, and shipping incident to taking possession of the property.

(2) During the time that title remains in the United States Government, be responsible as a bailee for the property from the time it is released to you or to the transportation agent you have designated.

(3) In the event of any loss of or damage to any or all of the property during transportation or storage at a place other than a place under your control, take the necessary action to obtain restitution (fair market value) for the Government. In the event of loss or damage due to negligence or willful misconduct on your part, repair, replace, or pay to the GSA the fair market value of any such property, or take such other action as the GSA may direct.

(d) You may retain property to perform your donation program functions, but only when authorized by GSA in accordance with the provisions of a cooperative agreement entered into with GSA.

(e) When acting under an interstate cooperative distribution agreement (see §102–37.335) as an agent and authorized representative of an adjacent State, you will:

(1) Make the certifications and agreements required in §102–37.200 and this section on behalf of the adjacent SASP.

(2) Require the donee to execute the distribution documents of the State in which the donee is located.

(3) Forward copies of the distribution documents to the corresponding SASP.

(f) You will not discriminate on the basis of race, color, national origin, sex, age, or handicap in the distribution of property, and will comply with GSA regulations on nondiscrimination as set forth in parts 101–4, subparts 101–6.2, and 101–8.3 of this title.

(g) You will not seek to hold the United States Government liable for consequential or incidental damages or the personal injuries, disabilities, or death to any person arising from the transfer, donation, use, processing, or final disposition of this property. The Government's liability in any event is limited in scope to that provided for by the Federal Tort Claims Act (28 U.S.C. 2671, *et seq.*).

[67 FR 2584, Jan. 18, 2002, as amended at 71 FR 23868, Apr. 25, 2006]

§ 102–37.210 Must a SASP make a drug-free workplace certification when requesting surplus property for donation?

No, you must certify that you will provide a drug-free workplace only as a condition for retaining surplus property for SASP use. Drug-free workplace certification requirements are found at part 105–68, subpart 105–68.6, of this title.

§ 102–37.215 When must a SASP make a certification regarding lobbying?

You are subject to the anti-lobbying certification and disclosure requirements in part 105–69 of this title when all of the following conditions apply:

(a) You have entered into a cooperative agreement with GSA that provides for your SASP to retain surplus property for use in performing donation functions or any other cooperative agreement.

(b) The cooperative agreement was executed after December 23, 1989.

(c) The fair market value of the property requested under the cooperative agreement is more than $100,000.

JUSTIFYING SPECIAL TRANSFER REQUESTS

§ 102–37.220 Are there special types of surplus property that require written justification when submitting a transfer request?

Yes, a SASP must obtain written justification from the intended donee, and submit it to GSA along with the transfer request, prior to allocation of:

(a) Aircraft and vessels covered by §102–37.455;

(b) Items requested specifically for cannibalization;

(c) Foreign gifts and decorations (see part 102–42 of this chapter);

(d) Items containing 50 parts per million or greater of polychlorinated biphenyl (see part 101–42 of this title);

(e) Firearms as described in part 101–42 of this title; and

(f) Any item on which written justification will assist GSA in making allocation to States with the greatest need.

§ 102–37.225 What information or documentation must a SASP provide when requesting a surplus aircraft or vessel?

(a) For each SF 123 that you submit to GSA for transfer of a surplus aircraft or vessel covered by §102–37.455 include:

(1) A letter of intent, signed and dated by the authorized representative of the proposed donee setting forth a detailed plan of utilization for the property (see §102–37.230 for information a donee has to include in the letter of intent); and

(2) A letter, signed and dated by you, confirming and certifying the applicant's eligibility and containing an evaluation of the applicant's ability to use the aircraft or vessel for the purpose stated in its letter of intent and any other supplemental information concerning the needs of the donee which supports making the allocation.

(b) For each SF 123 that GSA approves, you must include:

(1) Your distribution document, signed and dated by the authorized donee representative; and

(2) A conditional transfer document, signed by you and the intended donee, and containing the special terms and conditions prescribed by GSA.

§ 102-37.230 What must a letter of intent for obtaining surplus aircraft or vessels include?

A letter of intent for obtaining surplus aircraft or vessels must provide:

(a) A description of the aircraft or vessel requested. If the item is an aircraft, the description must include the manufacturer, date of manufacture, model, and serial number. If the item is a vessel, it must include the type, name, class, size, displacement, length, beam, draft, lift capacity, and the hull or registry number, if known;

(b) A detailed description of the donee's program and the number and types of aircraft or vessels it currently owns;

(c) A detailed description of how the aircraft or vessel will be used, its purpose, how often and for how long. If an aircraft is requested for flight purposes, the donee must specify a source of pilot(s) and where the aircraft will be housed. If an aircraft is requested for cannibalization, the donee must provide details of the cannibalization process (time to complete the cannibalization process, how recovered parts are to be used, method of accounting for usable parts, disposition of unsalvageable parts, etc.) If a vessel is requested for waterway purposes, the donee must specify a source of pilot(s) and where the vessel will be docked. If a vessel is requested for permanent docking on water or land, the donee must provide details of the process, including the time to complete the process; and

(d) Any supplemental information (such as geographical area and population served, number of students enrolled in educational programs, etc.) supporting the donee's need for the aircraft or vessel.

§ 102-37.235 What type of information must a SASP provide when requesting surplus property for cannibalization?

When a donee wants surplus property to cannibalize, include the following statement on the SF 123: "Line Item Number(s)____requested for cannibalization.''. In addition to including this statement, provide a detailed justification concerning the need for the components or accessories and an explanation of the effect removal will have on the item. GSA will approve requests for cannibalization only when it is clear from the justification that disassembly of the item for use of its component parts will provide greater potential benefit than use of the item in its existing form.

§ 102-37.240 How must a transfer request for surplus firearms be justified?

To justify a transfer request for surplus firearms, the requesting SASP must obtain and submit to GSA a letter of intent from the intended donee that provides:

(a) Identification of the donee applicant, including its legal name and complete address and the name, title, and telephone number of its authorized representative;

(b) The number of compensated officers with the power to apprehend and to arrest;

(c) A description of the firearm(s) requested;

(d) Details on the planned use of the firearm(s); and

(e) The number and types of donated firearms received during the previous 12 months through any other Federal program.

CUSTODY, CARE, AND SAFEKEEPING

§ 102-37.245 What must a SASP do to safeguard surplus property in its custody?

To safeguard surplus property in your custody, you must provide adequate protection of property in your custody, including protection against the hazards of fire, theft, vandalism, and weather.

§ 102-37.250 What actions must a SASP take when it learns of damage to or loss of surplus property in its custody?

If you learn that surplus property in your custody has been damaged or lost, you must always notify GSA and notify the appropriate law enforcement officials if a crime has been committed.

§ 102–37.255 Must a SASP insure surplus property against loss or damage?

No, you are not required to carry insurance on Federal surplus property in your custody. However, if you elect to carry insurance and the insured property is lost or damaged, you must submit a check made payable to GSA for any insurance proceeds received in excess of your actual costs of acquiring and rehabilitating the property prior to its loss, damage, or destruction.

DISTRIBUTION OF PROPERTY

§ 102–37.260 How must a SASP document the distribution of surplus property?

All SASPs must document the distribution of Federal surplus property on forms that are prenumbered, provide for donees to indicate the primary purposes for which they are acquiring property, and include the:

(a) Certifications and agreements in §§ 102–37.200 and 102–37.205; and

(b) Period of restriction during which the donee must use the property for the purpose for which it was acquired.

§ 102–37.265 May a SASP distribute surplus property to eligible donees of another State?

Yes, you may distribute surplus property to eligible donees of another State, if you and the other SASP determine that such an arrangement will be of mutual benefit to you and the donees concerned. Where such determinations are made, an interstate distribution cooperative agreement must be prepared as prescribed in § 102–37.335 and submitted to the appropriate GSA regional office for approval. When acting under an interstate distribution cooperative agreement, you must:

(a) Require the donee recipient to execute the distribution documents of its home SASP; and

(b) Forward copies of executed distribution documents to the donee's home SASP.

§ 102–37.270 May a SASP retain surplus property for its own use?

Yes, you can retain surplus property for use in operating the donation program, but only if you have a coopera-tive agreement with GSA that allows you to do so. You must obtain prior GSA approval before using any surplus property in the operation of the SASP. Make your needs known by submitting a listing of needed property to the appropriate GSA regional office for approval. GSA will review the list to ensure that it is of the type and quantity of property that is reasonably needed and useful in performing SASP operations. GSA will notify you within 30 calendar days whether you may retain the property for use in your operations. Title to any surplus property GSA approves for your retention will vest in your SASP. You must maintain separate records for such property.

SERVICE AND HANDLING CHARGES

§ 102–37.275 May a SASP accept personal checks and non-official payment methods in payment of service charges?

No, service charge payments must readily identify the donee institution as the payer (or the name of the parent organization when that organization pays the operational expenses of the donee). Personal checks, personal cashier checks, personal money orders, and personal credit cards are not acceptable.

§ 102–37.280 How may a SASP use service charge funds?

Funds accumulated from service charges may be deposited, invested, or used in accordance with State law to:

(a) Cover direct and reasonable indirect costs of operating the SASP;

(b) Purchase necessary equipment for the SASP;

(c) Maintain a reasonable working capital reserve;

(d) Rehabilitate surplus property, including the purchase of replacement parts;

(e) Acquire or improve office or distribution center facilities; or

(f) Pay for the costs of internal and external audits.

§ 102–37.285 May a SASP use service charge funds to support non-SASP State activities and programs?

No, except as provided in § 102–37.495, you must use funds collected from service charges, or from other sources such as proceeds from sale of undistributed property or funds collected from compliance cases, solely for the operation of the SASP and the benefit of participating donees.

DISPOSING OF UNDISTRIBUTED PROPERTY

§ 102–37.290 What must a SASP do with surplus property it cannot donate?

(a) As soon as it becomes clear that you cannot donate the surplus property, you should first determine whether or not the property is usable.

(1) If you determine that the undistributed surplus property is not usable, you should seek GSA approval to abandon or destroy the property in accordance with § 102–37.320.

(2) If you determine that the undistributed surplus property is usable, you should immediately offer it to other SASPs. If other SASPs cannot use the property, you should promptly report it to GSA for redisposal (i.e., disposition through retransfer, sale, or other means).

(b) Normally, any property not donated within a 1-year period should be processed in this manner.

§ 102–37.295 Must GSA approve a transfer between SASPs?

Yes, the requesting SASP must submit a SF 123, Transfer Order Surplus Personal Property, to the GSA regional office in which the releasing SASP is located. GSA will approve or disapprove the request within 30 calendar days of receipt of the transfer order.

§ 102–37.300 What information must a SASP provide GSA when reporting unneeded usable property for disposal?

When reporting unneeded usable property that is not required for transfer to another SASP, provide GSA with the:

(a) Best possible description of each line item of property, its current condition code, quantity, unit and total acquisition cost, State serial number, demilitarization code, and any special handling conditions;

(b) Date you received each line item of property listed; and

(c) Certification of reimbursement requested under § 102–37.315.

§ 102–37.305 May a SASP act as GSA's agent in selling undistributed surplus property (either as usable property or scrap)?

Yes, you may act as GSA's agent in selling undistributed surplus property (either as usable property or scrap) if an established cooperative agreement with GSA permits such an action. You must notify GSA each time you propose to conduct a sale under the cooperative agreement. You may request approval to conduct a sale when reporting the property to GSA for disposal instructions. If no formal agreement exists, you may submit such an agreement at that time for approval.

§ 102–37.310 What must a proposal to sell undistributed surplus property include?

(a) Your request to sell undistributed surplus property must include:

(1) The proposed sale date;

(2) A listing of the property;

(3) Location of the sale;

(4) Method of sale; and

(5) Proposed advertising to be used.

(b) If the request is approved, the GSA regional sales office will provide the necessary forms and instructions for you to use in conducting the sale.

§ 102–37.315 What costs may a SASP recover if undistributed surplus property is retransferred or sold?

(a) When undistributed surplus property is transferred to a Federal agency or another SASP, or disposed of by public sale, you are entitled to recoup:

(1) Direct costs you initially paid to the Federal holding agency, including but not limited to, packing, preparation for shipment, and loading. You will not be reimbursed for actions following receipt of the property, including unloading, moving, repairing, preserving, or storage.

(2) Transportation costs you incurred, but were not reimbursed by a donee, for initially moving the property from the Federal holding agency to your distribution facility or other point of receipt. You must document and certify the amount of reimbursement requested for these costs.

(b) Reimbursable arrangements should be made prior to transfer of the property. In the case of a Federal transfer, GSA will secure agreement of the Federal agency to reimburse your authorized costs, and annotate the amount of reimbursement on the transfer document. You must coordinate and make arrangements for reimbursement when property is transferred to another SASP. If you and the receiving SASP cannot agree on an appropriate reimbursement charge, GSA will determine appropriate reimbursement. The receiving SASP must annotate the reimbursement amount on the transfer document prior to its being forwarded to GSA for approval.

(c) When undistributed property is disposed of by public sale, GSA must approve the amount of sales proceeds you may receive to cover your costs. Generally, this will not exceed 50 percent of the total sales proceeds.

§ 102–37.320 Under what conditions may a SASP abandon or destroy undistributed surplus property?

(a) You may abandon or destroy undistributed surplus property when you have made a written finding that the property has no commercial value or the estimated cost of its continued care and handling would exceed the estimated proceeds from its sale. The abandonment or destruction finding must be sent to the appropriate GSA regional office for approval. You must include in the finding:

(1) The basis for the abandonment or destruction;

(2) A detailed description of the property, its condition, and total acquisition cost;

(3) The proposed method of destruction (burning, burying, etc.) or the abandonment location;

(4) A statement confirming that the proposed abandonment or destruction will not be detrimental or dangerous to public health or safety and will not infringe on the rights of other persons; and

(5) The signature of the SASP director requesting approval for the abandonment or destruction.

(b) GSA will notify you within 30 calendar days whether you may abandon or destroy the property. GSA will provide alternate disposition instructions if it disapproves your request for abandonment or destruction. If GSA doesn't

reply to you within 30 calendar days of notification, the property may be abandoned or destroyed.

COOPERATIVE AGREEMENTS

§ 102–37.325 With whom and for what purpose(s) may a SASP enter into a cooperative agreement?

Section 549(f) of title 40, United States Code allows GSA, or Federal agencies designated by GSA, to enter into cooperative agreements with SASPs to carry out the surplus property donation program. Such agreements allow GSA, or the designated Federal agencies, to use the SASP's property, facilities, personnel, or services or to furnish such resources to the SASP. For example:

(a) Regional GSA personal property management offices, or designated Federal agencies, may enter into a cooperative agreement to assist a SASP in distributing surplus property for donation. Assistance may include:

(1) Furnishing the SASP with available GSA or agency office space and related support such as office furniture and information technology equipment needed to screen and process property for donation.

(2) Permitting the SASP to retain items of surplus property transferred to the SASP that are needed by the SASP in performing its donation functions (see § 102–37.270).

(b) Regional GSA personal property management offices may help the SASP to enter into agreements with other GSA or Federal activities for the use of Federal telecommunications service or federally-owned real property and related personal property.

(c) A SASP may enter into a cooperative agreement with GSA to conduct sales of undistributed property on behalf of GSA (see § 102–37.305).

[67 FR 2584, Jan. 18, 2002, as amended at 71 FR 23868, Apr. 25, 2006]

§ 102–37.330 Must the costs of providing support under a cooperative agreement be reimbursed by the parties receiving such support?

The parties to a cooperative agreement must decide among themselves the extent to which the costs of the services they provide must be reimbursed. Their decision should be reflected in the cooperative agreement itself. As a general rule, the Economy Act (31 U.S.C. 1535) would require a Federal agency receiving services from a SASP to reimburse the SASP for those services. Since SASPs are not Federal agencies, the Economy Act would not require them to reimburse Federal agencies for services provided by such agencies. In this situation, the Federal agencies would have to determine whether or not their own authorities would permit them to provide services to SASPs without reimbursement. If a Federal agency is reimbursed by a SASP for services provided under a cooperative agreement, it must credit that payment to the fund or appropriation that incurred the related costs.

§ 102–37.335 May a SASP enter into a cooperative agreement with another SASP?

Yes, with GSA's concurrence and where authorized by State law, a SASP may enter into an agreement with an adjacent State to act as its agent and authorized representative in disposing of surplus Federal property. Interstate cooperative agreements may be considered when donees, because of their geographic proximity to the property distribution centers of the adjoining State, could be more efficiently and economically serviced by surplus property facilities in the adjacent State. You and the other SASP must agree to the payment or reimbursement of service charges by the donee and you also must agree to the requirements of § 102–37.205(e).

§ 102–37.340 When may a SASP terminate a cooperative agreement?

You may terminate a cooperative agreement with GSA 60-calendar days after providing GSA with written notice. For other cooperative agreements with other authorized parties, you or the other party may terminate the agreement as mutually agreed. You must promptly notify GSA when such other agreements are terminated.

AUDITS AND REVIEWS

§ 102–37.345 When must a SASP be audited?

For each year in which a SASP receives $500,000 or more a year in surplus property or other Federal assistance, it must be audited in accordance with the Single Audit Act (31 U.S.C. 7501–7507) as implemented by Office of Management and Budget (OMB) Circular A–133, "Audits of States, Local Governments, and Non-Profit Organizations" (for availability see 5 CFR 1310.3). GSA's donation program should be identified by Catalog of Federal Domestic Assistance number 39.003 when completing the required schedule of Federal assistance.

[67 FR 2584, Jan. 18, 2002, as amended at 71 FR 23868, Apr. 25, 2006]

§ 102–37.350 Does coverage under the single audit process in OMB Circular A–133 exempt a SASP from other reviews of its program?

No, although SASPs are covered under the single audit process in OMB Circular A–133, from time to time the Government Accountability Office (GAO), GSA, or other authorized Federal activities may audit or review the operations of a SASP. GSA will notify the chief executive officer of the State of the reasons for a GSA audit. When requested, you must make available financial records and all other records of the SASP for inspection by representatives of GSA, GAO, or other authorized Federal activities.

[67 FR 2584, Jan. 18, 2002, as amended at 71 FR 23868, Apr. 25, 2006]

§ 102–37.355 What obligations does a SASP have to ensure that donees meet Circular A–133 requirements?

SASPs, if they donate $500,000 or more in Federal property to a donee in a fiscal year, must ensure that the donee has an audit performed in accordance with Circular A–133. If a donee receives less than $500,000 in donated property, the SASP is not expected to assume responsibility for ensuring the donee meets audit requirements, beyond making sure the donee is aware that the requirements do exist. It is the donee's responsibility to identify and determine the amount of

Federal assistance it has received and to arrange for audit coverage.

[67 FR 2584, Jan. 18, 2002, as amended at 71 FR 23868, Apr. 25, 2006]

REPORTS

§ 102–37.360 What reports must a SASP provide to GSA?

(a) *Quarterly report on donations.* Submit a GSA Form 3040, State Agency Monthly Donation Report of Surplus Personal Property, to the appropriate GSA regional office by the 25th day of the month following the quarter being reported. (OMB Control Number 3090–0112 has been assigned to this form.) Forms and instructions for completing the form are available from your servicing GSA office.

(b) *Additional reports.* Make other reports GSA may require to carry out its discretionary authority to transfer surplus personal property for donation and to report to the Congress on the status and progress of the donation program.

LIQUIDATING A SASP

§ 102–37.365 What steps must a SASP take if the State decides to liquidate the agency?

Before suspending operations, a SASP must submit to GSA a liquidation plan that includes:

(a) Reasons for the liquidation;

(b) A schedule for liquidating the agency and the estimated date of termination;

(c) Method of disposing of property on hand under the requirements of this part;

(d) Method of disposing of the agency's physical and financial assets;

(e) Retention of all available records of the SASP for a 2-year period following liquidation; and

(f) Designation of another governmental entity to serve as the agency's successor in function until continuing obligations on property donated prior to the closing of the agency are fulfilled.

§ 102–37.370 Do liquidation plans require public notice?

Yes, a liquidation plan constitutes a major amendment of a SASP's plan of operation and, as such, requires public notice.

Subpart E—Donations to Public Agencies, Service Educational Activities (SEAs), and Eligible Nonprofit Organizations

§ 102–37.375 How is the pronoun "you" used in this subpart?

The pronoun "you," when used in this subpart, refers to the State agency for surplus property (SASP).

§ 102–37.380 What is the statutory authority for donations of surplus Federal property made under this subpart?

The following statutes provide the authority to donate surplus Federal property to different types of recipients:

(a) Section 549(d) of title 40, United States Code authorizes surplus property under the control of the Department of Defense (DOD) to be donated, through SASPs, to educational activities which are of special interest to the armed services (referred to in this part 102–37 as service educational activities or SEAs).

(b) Section 549(c)(3) of title 40, United States Code authorizes SASPs to donate surplus property to public agencies and to nonprofit educational or public health institutions, such as:

(1) Medical institutions.

(2) Hospitals.

(3) Clinics.

(4) Health centers.

(5) Drug abuse or alcohol treatment centers.

(6) Providers of assistance to homeless individuals.

(7) Providers of assistance to impoverished families and individuals.

(8) Schools.

(9) Colleges.

(10) Universities.

(11) Schools for the mentally disabled.

(12) Schools for the physically disabled.

(13) Child care centers.

(14) Radio and television stations licensed by the Federal Communications Commission as educational radio or educational television stations.

(15) Museums attended by the public.

(16) Libraries, serving free all residents of a community, district, State or region.

(17) Historic light stations as defined under section 308(e)(2) of the National Historic Preservation Act (16 U.S.C. 470w–7(e)(2)), including a historic light station conveyed under subsection (b) of that section, notwithstanding the number of hours that the historic light station is open to the public.

(c) Section 213 of the Older Americans Act of 1965, as amended (42 U.S.C. 3020d), authorizes donations of surplus property to State or local government agencies, or nonprofit organizations or institutions, that receive Federal funding to conduct programs for older individuals.

(d) Section 549(c)(3)(C) of title 40, United States Code authorizes SASPs to donate property to veterans organizations, for purposes of providing services to veterans (as defined in section 101 of title 38). Eligible veterans organizations are those whose:

(1) Membership comprises substantially veterans; and

(2) Representatives are recognized by the Secretary of Veterans Affairs under section 5902 of title 38.

[67 FR 2584, Jan. 18, 2002, as amended at 71 FR 23868, Apr. 25, 2006; 72 FR 12572, Mar. 16, 2007; 79 FR 64514, Oct. 30, 2014]

DONEE ELIGIBILITY

§ 102–37.385 Who determines if a prospective donee applicant is eligible to receive surplus property under this subpart?

(a) For most public and nonprofit activities, the SASP determines if an applicant is eligible to receive property as a public agency, a nonprofit educational or public health institution, or for a program for older individuals. A SASP may request GSA assistance or guidance in making such determinations.

(b) For applicants that offer courses of instruction devoted to the military arts and sciences, the Defense Department will determine eligibility to receive surplus property through the SASP as a service educational activity or SEA.

§ 102–37.390 What basic criteria must an applicant meet before a SASP can qualify it for eligibility?

To qualify for donation program eligibility through a SASP, an applicant must:

(a) Conform to the definition of one of the categories of eligible entities listed in § 102–37.380 (see appendix C of this part for definitions);

(b) Demonstrate that it meets any approval, accreditation, or licensing requirements for operation of its program;

(c) Prove that it is a public agency or a nonprofit and tax-exempt organization under section 501 of the Internal Revenue Code;

(d) Certify that it is not debarred, suspended, or excluded from any Federal program, including procurement programs; and

(e) Operate in compliance with applicable Federal nondiscrimination statutes.

§ 102–37.395 How can a SASP determine whether an applicant meets any required approval, accreditation, or licensing requirements?

A SASP may accept the following documentation as evidence that an applicant has met established standards for the operation of its educational or health program:

(a) A certificate or letter from a nationally recognized accrediting agency affirming the applicant meets the agency's standards and requirements.

(b) The applicant's appearance on a list with other similarly approved or accredited institutions or programs when that list is published by a State, regional, or national accrediting authority.

(c) Letters from State or local authorities (such as a board of health or a board of education) stating that the applicant meets the standards prescribed for approved or accredited institutions and organizations.

(d) In the case of educational activities, letters from three accredited or State-approved institutions that students from the applicant institution have been and are being accepted.

(e) In the case of public health institutions, licensing may be accepted as evidence of approval, provided the licensing authority prescribes the medical requirements and standards for the professional and technical services of the institution.

(f) The awarding of research grants to the institution by a recognized authority such as the National Institutes of Health, the National Institute of Education, or by similar national advisory council or organization.

§ 102–37.400 What type of eligibility information must a SASP maintain on donees?

In general, you must maintain the records required by your State plan to document donee eligibility (see appendix B of this part). For SEAs, you must maintain separate records that include:

(a) Documentation verifying that the activity has been designated as eligible by DOD to receive surplus DOD property.

(b) A statement designating one or more donee representative(s) to act for the SEA in acquiring property.

(c) A listing of the types of property that are needed or have been authorized by DOD for use in the SEA's program.

§ 102–37.405 How often must a SASP update donee eligibility records?

You must update donee eligibility records as needed, but no less than every 3 years, to ensure that all documentation supporting the donee's eligibility is current and accurate. Annually, you must update files for nonprofit organizations whose eligibility depends on annual appropriations, annual licensing, or annual certification. Particular care must be taken to ensure that all records relating to the authority of donee representatives to receive and receipt for property, or to screen property at Federal facilities, are current.

§ 102–37.410 What must a SASP do if a donee fails to maintain its eligibility status?

If you determine that a donee has failed to maintain its eligibility status, you must terminate distribution of property to that donee, recover any usable property still under Federal restriction (as outlined in § 102–37.465),

and take any other required compliance actions.

§ 102–37.415 What should a SASP do if an applicant appeals a negative eligibility determination?

If an applicant appeals a negative eligibility determination, forward complete documentation on the appeal request, including your comments and recommendations, to the applicable GSA regional office for review and coordination with GSA headquarters. GSA's decision will be final.

CONDITIONAL ELIGIBILITY

§ 102–37.420 May a SASP grant conditional eligibility to applicants who would otherwise qualify as eligible donees, but have been unable to obtain approval, accreditation, or licensing because they are newly organized or their facilities are not yet constructed?

You may grant conditional eligibility to such an applicant provided it submits a statement from any required approving, accrediting, or licensing authority confirming it will be approved, accredited, or licensed. Conditional eligibility may be granted for a limited and reasonable time, not to exceed one year.

[67 FR 2584, Jan. 18, 2002, as amended at 79 FR 64514, Oct. 30, 2014]

§ 102–37.425 May a SASP grant conditional eligibility to a not-for-profit organization whose tax-exempt status is pending?

No, under no circumstances may you grant conditional eligibility prior to receiving from the applicant a copy of a letter of determination by the Internal Revenue Service stating that the applicant is exempt from Federal taxation under section 501 of the Internal Revenue Code.

§ 102–37.430 What property can a SASP make available to a donee with conditional eligibility?

You may only make available surplus property that the donee can use immediately. You may not make available property that will only be used at a later date, for example, after the construction of the donee's facility has been completed. If property is provided to the donee with conditional eligibility, and the conditional eligibility lapses (see § 102–37.420), the property must be returned to the SASP for redistribution or disposal.

[67 FR 2584, Jan. 18, 2002, as amended at 79 FR 64514, Oct. 30, 2014]

TERMS AND CONDITIONS OF DONATION

§ 102–37.435 For what purposes may donees acquire and use surplus property?

A donee may acquire and use surplus property only for the following authorized purposes:

(a) *Public purposes.* A public agency that acquires surplus property through a SASP must use such property to carry out or to promote one or more public purposes for the people it serves.

(b) *Educational and public health purposes, including related research.* A nonprofit educational or public health institution must use surplus property for education or public health, including research for either purpose and assistance to the homeless or impoverished. While this does not preclude the use of donated surplus property for a related or subsidiary purpose incident to the institution's overall program, the property may not be used for a nonrelated or commercial purpose.

(c) *Programs for older individuals.* An entity that conducts a program for older individuals must use donated surplus property to provide services that are necessary for the general welfare of older individuals, such as social services, transportation services, nutrition services, legal services, and multipurpose senior centers.

§ 102–37.440 May donees acquire property for exchange?

No, a donee may not acquire property with the intent to sell or trade it for other assets.

§ 102–37.445 What certifications must a donee make before receiving property?

Prior to a SASP releasing property to a donee, the donee must certify that:

(a) It is a public agency or a nonprofit organization meeting the requirements of the Property Act and/or regulations of GSA;

(b) It is acquiring the property for its own use and will use the property for authorized purposes;

(c) Funds are available to pay all costs and charges incident to the donation;

(d) It will comply with the nondiscrimination regulations issued under title VI of the Civil Rights Act of 1964 (42 U.S.C. 2000d–2000d–4), section 122 of title 40, United States Code, section 504 of the Rehabilitation Act of 1973 (29 U.S.C. 794), as amended, title IX of the Education Amendments of 1972 (20 U.S.C. 1681–1688), as amended, and section 303 of the Age Discrimination Act of 1975 (42 U.S.C. 6101–6107); and

(e) It isn't currently debarred, suspended, declared ineligible, or otherwise excluded from receiving the property.

[67 FR 2584, Jan. 18, 2002, as amended at 71 FR 23868, Apr. 25, 2006]

§ 102–37.450 What agreements must a donee make?

Before a SASP may release property to a donee, the donee must agree to the following conditions:

(a) The property is acquired on an "as is, where is" basis, without warranty of any kind, and it will hold the Government harmless from any or all debts, liabilities, judgments, costs, demands, suits, actions, or claims of any nature arising from or incident to the donation of the property, its use, or final disposition.

(b) It will return to the SASP, at its own expense, any donated property:

(1) That is not placed in use for the purposes for which it was donated within 1 year of donation; or

(2) Which ceases to be used for such purposes within 1 year after being placed in use.

(c) It will comply with the terms and conditions imposed by the SASP on the use of any item of property having a unit acquisition cost of $5,000 or more and any passenger motor vehicle or other donated item. (Not applicable to SEAs.)

(d) It agrees that, upon execution of the SASP distribution document, it has conditional title only to the property during the applicable period of restriction. Full title to the property will vest in the donee only after the donee has met all of the requirements of this part.

(e) It will comply with conditions imposed by GSA, if any, requiring special handling or use limitations on donated property.

(f) It will use the property for an authorized purpose during the period of restriction.

(g) It will obtain permission from the SASP before selling, trading, leasing, loaning, bailing, cannibalizing, encumbering or otherwise disposing of property during the period of restriction, or removing it permanently for use outside the State.

(h) It will report to the SASP on the use, condition, and location of donated property, and on other pertinent matters as the SASP may require from time to time.

(i) If an insured loss of the property occurs during the period of restriction, GSA or the SASP (depending on which agency has imposed the restriction) will be entitled to reimbursement out of the insurance proceeds of an amount equal to the unamortized portion of the fair market value of the damaged or destroyed item.

SPECIAL HANDLING OR USE CONDITIONS

§ 102–37.455 On what categories of surplus property has GSA imposed special handling conditions or use limitations?

GSA has imposed special handling or processing requirements on the property discussed in this section. GSA may, on a case-by-case basis, prescribe additional restrictions for handling or using these items or prescribe special processing requirements on items in addition to those listed in this section.

(a) *Aircraft and vessels.* The requirements of this section apply to the donation of any fixed- or rotary-wing aircraft and donable vessels that are 50 feet or more in length, having a unit acquisition cost of $5,000 or more, regardless of the purpose for which donated. Such aircraft or vessels may be donated to public agencies and eligible nonprofit activities provided the aircraft or vessel is not classified for rea-

sons of national security and any lethal characteristics are removed. The following table provides locations of other policies and procedures governing aircraft and vessels:

For. . .	See. . .
(1) Policies and procedures governing the donation of aircraft parts.	Part 102–33, subpart D, of this chapter.
(2) Documentation needed by GSA to process requests for aircraft or vessels.	§ 102–37.225.
(3) Special terms, conditions, and restrictions imposed on aircraft and vessels.	§ 102–37.460.
(4) Guidelines on preparing letters of intent for aircraft or vessels.	§ 102–37.230.

(b) *Alcohol.* (1) When tax-free or specially denatured alcohol is requested for donation, the donee must have a special permit issued by the Assistant Regional Commissioner of the appropriate regional office, Bureau of Alcohol, Tobacco, Firearms and Explosives (ATF), Department of the Justice, in order to acquire the property. Include the ATF use-permit number on the SF 123, Transfer Order Surplus Personal Property.

(2) You may not store tax-free or specially denatured alcohol in SASP facilities. You must make arrangements for this property to be shipped or transported directly from the holding agency to the designated donee.

(c) *Hazardous materials, firearms, and property with unsafe or dangerous characteristics.* For hazardous materials, firearms, and property with unsafe or dangerous characteristics, see part 101–42 of this title.

(d) *Franked and penalty mail envelopes and official letterhead.* Franked and penalty mail envelopes and official letterhead may not be donated without the SASP certifying that all Federal Government markings will be obliterated before use.

[67 FR 2584, Jan. 18, 2002, as amended at 71 FR 23868, Apr. 25, 2006]

§ 102–37.460 What special terms and conditions apply to the donation of aircraft and vessels?

The following special terms and conditions apply to the donation of aircraft and vessels:

(a) There must be a period of restriction which will expire after the aircraft or vessel has been used for the purpose stated in the letter of intent (see § 102–37.230) for a period of 5 years, except that the period of restriction for a combat-configured aircraft is in perpetuity.

(b) The donee of an aircraft must apply to the FAA for registration of an aircraft intended for flight use within 30 calendar days of receipt of the aircraft. The donee of a vessel must, within 30 calendar days of receipt of the vessel, apply for documentation of the vessel under applicable Federal, State, and local laws and must record each document with the U.S. Coast Guard at the port of documentation. The donee's application for registration or documentation must include a fully executed copy of the conditional transfer document and a copy of its letter of intent. The donee must provide the SASP and GSA with a copy of the FAA registration (and a copy of its FAA Standard Airworthiness Certificate if the aircraft is to be flown as a civil aircraft) or Coast Guard documentation.

(c) The aircraft or vessel must be used solely in accordance with the executed conditional transfer document and the plan of utilization set forth in the donee's letter of intent, unless the donee has amended the letter, and it has been approved in writing by the SASP and GSA and a copy of the amendment recorded with FAA or the U.S. Coast Guard, as applicable.

(d) In the event any of the terms and conditions imposed by the conditional transfer document are breached, title may revert to the Government. GSA may require the donee to return the aircraft or vessel or pay for any unauthorized disposal, transaction, or use.

(e) If, during the period of restriction, the aircraft or vessel is no longer needed by the donee, the donee must promptly notify the SASP and request disposal instructions. A SASP may not issue disposal instructions without the prior written concurrence of GSA.

(f) Military aircraft previously used for ground instruction and/or static display (Category B aircraft, as designated by DOD) or that are combat-configured (Category C aircraft) may not be donated for flight purposes.

(g) For all aircraft donated for non-flight use, the donee must, within 30 calendar days of receipt of the aircraft, turn over to the SASP the remaining aircraft historical records (except the records of the major components/life limited parts; e.g., engines, transmissions, rotor blades, etc., necessary to substantiate their reuse). The SASP in turn must transmit the records to GSA for forwarding to the FAA.

RELEASE OF RESTRICTIONS

§ 102–37.465 May a SASP modify or release any of the terms and conditions of donation?

You may alter or grant releases from State-imposed restrictions, provided your State plan of operation sets forth the standards by which such actions will be taken. You may not grant releases from, or amendments or corrections to:

(a) The terms and conditions you are required by the Property Act to impose on the use of passenger motor vehicles and any item of property having a unit acquisition cost of $5,000 or more.

(b) Any special handling condition or use limitation imposed by GSA, except with the prior written approval of GSA.

(c) The statutory requirement that usable property be returned by the donee to the SASP if the property has not been placed in use for the purposes for which it was donated within 1 year of donation or ceases to be used by the donee for those purposes within 1 year of being placed in use, except that:

(1) You may grant authority to the donee to cannibalize property items subject to this requirement when you determine that such action will result in increased use of the property and that the proposed action meets the standards prescribed in your plan of operation.

(2) You may, with the written concurrence of GSA, grant donees:

(i) A time extension to place property into use if the delay in putting the property into use was beyond the control and without the fault or negligence of the donee.

(ii) Authority to trade in one donated item for one like item having similar use potential.

§ 102–37.470 At what point may restrictions be released on property that has been authorized for cannibalization?

Property authorized for cannibalization must remain under the period of restriction imposed by the transfer/distribution document until the proposed cannibalization is completed. Components resulting from the cannibalization, which have a unit acquisition cost of $5,000 or more, must remain under the restrictions imposed by the transfer/distribution document. Components with a unit acquisition cost of less than $5,000 may be released upon cannibalization from the additional restrictions imposed by the State. However, these components must continue to be used or be otherwise disposed of in accordance with this part.

§ 102–37.475 What are the requirements for releasing restrictions on property being considered for exchange?

GSA must consent to the exchange of donated property under Federal restrictions or special handling conditions. The donee must have used the donated item for its acquired purpose for a minimum of 6 months prior to being considered for exchange, and it must be demonstrated that the exchange will result in increased utilization value to the donee. As a condition of approval of the exchange, the item being exchanged must have remained in compliance with the terms and conditions of the donation. Otherwise, § 102–37.485 applies. The item acquired by the donee must be:

(a) Made subject to the period of restriction remaining on the item exchanged; and

(b) Of equal or greater value than the item exchanged.

COMPLIANCE AND UTILIZATION

§ 102–37.480 What must a SASP do to ensure that property is used for the purpose(s) for which it was donated?

You must conduct utilization reviews, as provided in your plan of operation, to ensure that donees are using surplus property during the period of restriction for the purposes for which it was donated. You must fully document your efforts and report all instances of noncompliance (misuse or mishandling of property) to GSA.

§ 102–37.485 What actions must a SASP take if a review or other information indicates noncompliance with donation terms and conditions?

If a review or other information indicates noncompliance with donation terms and conditions, you must:

(a) Promptly investigate any suspected failure to comply with the conditions of donated property;

(b) Notify GSA immediately where there is evidence or allegation of fraud, wrongdoing by a screener, or nonuse, misuse, or unauthorized disposal or destruction of donated property;

(c) Temporarily defer any further donations of property to any donee to be investigated for noncompliance allegations until such time as the investigation has been completed and:

(1) A determination made that the allegations are unfounded and the deferment is removed.

(2) The allegations are substantiated and the donee is proposed for suspension or debarment; and

(d) Take steps to correct the noncompliance or otherwise enforce the conditions imposed on use of the property if a donee is found to be in noncompliance. Enforcement of compliance may involve:

(1) Ensuring the property is used by the present donee for the purpose for which it was donated.

(2) Recovering the property from the donee for:

(i) Redistribution to another donee within the State;

(ii) Transfer through GSA to another SASP; or

(iii) Transfer through GSA to a Federal agency.

(3) Recovering fair market value or the proceeds of disposal in cases of unauthorized disposal or destruction.

(4) Recovering fair rental value for property in cases where the property has been loaned or leased to an ineligible user or used for an unauthorized purpose.

(5) Disposing of by public sale property no longer suitable, usable, or necessary for donation.

§ 102–37.490 When must a SASP coordinate with GSA on compliance actions?

You must coordinate with GSA before selling or demanding payment of the fair market or fair rental value of donated property that is:

(a) Subject to any special handling condition or use limitation imposed by GSA (see § 102–37.455); or

(b) Not properly used within 1 year of donation or which ceases to be properly used within 1 year of being placed in use.

§ 102–37.495 How must a SASP handle funds derived from compliance actions?

You must handle funds derived from compliance actions as follows:

(a) *Enforcement of Federal restrictions.* You must promptly remit to GSA any funds derived from the enforcement of compliance involving a violation of any Federal restriction, for deposit in the Treasury of the United States. You must also submit any supporting documentation indicating the source of the funds and essential background information.

(b) *Enforcement of State restrictions.* You may retain any funds derived from a compliance action involving violation of any State-imposed restriction and use such funds as provided in your State plan of operation.

RETURNS AND REIMBURSEMENT

§ 102–37.500 May a donee receive reimbursement for its donation expenses when unneeded property is returned to the SASP?

When a donee returns unneeded property to a SASP, the donee may be reimbursed for all or part of the initial cost of any repairs required to make the property usable if:

(a) The property is transferred to a Federal agency or sold for the benefit of the U.S. Government;

(b) No breach of the terms and conditions of donation has occurred; and

(c) GSA authorizes the reimbursement.

§ 102–37.505 How does a donee apply for and receive reimbursement for unneeded property returned to a SASP?

If the donee has incurred repair expenses for property it is returning to a SASP and wishes to be reimbursed for them, it will inform the SASP of this. The SASP will recommend for GSA approval a reimbursement amount, taking into consideration the benefit the donee has received from the use of the property and making appropriate deductions for that use.

(a) If this property is subsequently transferred to a Federal agency, the receiving agency will be required to reimburse the donee as a condition of the transfer.

(b) If the property is sold, the donee will be reimbursed from the sales proceeds.

SPECIAL PROVISIONS PERTAINING TO SEAs

§ 102–37.510 Are there special requirements for donating property to SEAs?

Yes, only DOD-generated property may be donated to SEAs. When donating DOD property to an eligible SEA, SASPs must observe any restrictions the sponsoring Military Service may have imposed on the types of property the SEA may receive.

§ 102–37.515 Do SEAs have a priority over other SASP donees for DOD property?

Yes, SEAs have a priority over other SASP donees for DOD property, but only if DOD requests GSA to allocate surplus DOD property through a SASP for donation to a specific SEA. In such cases, DOD would be expected to clearly identify the items in question and briefly justify the request.

Subpart F—Donations to Public Airports

§ 102–37.520 What is the authority for public airport donations?

The authority for public airport donations is 49 U.S.C. 47151. 49 U.S.C. 47151 authorizes executive agencies to give priority consideration to requests from a public airport (as defined in 49 U.S.C. 47102) for the donation of surplus property if the Department of Transportation (DOT) considers the property appropriate for airport purposes and GSA approves the donation.

[67 FR 2584, Jan. 18, 2002, as amended at 71 FR 23868, Apr. 25, 2006]

§ 102–37.525 What should a holding agency do if it wants a public airport to receive priority consideration for excess personal property it has reported to GSA?

A holding agency interested in giving priority consideration to a public airport should annotate its reporting document to make GSA aware of this interest. In an addendum to the document, include the name of the requesting airport, specific property requested, and a brief description of how the airport intends to use the property.

§ 102–37.530 What are FAA's responsibilities in the donation of surplus property to public airports?

In the donation of surplus property to public airports, the Federal Aviation Administration (FAA), acting under delegation from the DOT, is responsible for:

(a) Determining the property requirements of any State, political subdivision of a State, or tax-supported organization for public airport use;

(b) Setting eligibility requirements for public airports and making determinations of eligibility;

(c) Certifying that property listed on a transfer request is desirable or necessary for public airport use;

(d) Advising GSA of FAA officials authorized to certify transfer requests and notifying GSA of any changes in signatory authority;

(e) Determining and enforcing compliance with the terms and conditions under which surplus personal property is transferred for public airport use; and

(f) Authorizing public airports to visit holding agencies for the purpose of screening and selecting property for transfer. This responsibility includes:

(1) Issuing a screening pass or letter of authorization to only those persons who are qualified to screen.

(2) Maintaining a current record (to include names, addresses, and telephone numbers, and additional identifying information such as driver's license or social security numbers) of screeners operating under FAA authority and making such records available to GSA upon request.

(3) Recovering any expired or invalid screener authorizations.

§ 102–37.535 What information must FAA provide to GSA on its administration of the public airport donation program?

So that GSA has information on which to base its discretionary authority to approve the donation of surplus personal property, FAA must:

(a) Provide copies of internal instructions that outline the scope of FAA's oversight program for enforcing compliance with the terms and conditions of transfer; and

(b) Report any compliance actions involving donations to public airports.

Subpart G—Donations to the American National Red Cross

§ 102–37.540 What is the authority for donations to the American National Red Cross?

Section 551 of title 40, United States Code authorizes GSA to donate to the Red Cross, for charitable use, such property as was originally derived from or through the Red Cross.

[67 FR 2584, Jan. 18, 2002, as amended at 71 FR 23868, Apr. 25, 2006]

§ 102–37.545 What type of property may the American National Red Cross receive?

The Red Cross may receive surplus gamma globulin, dried plasma, albumin, antihemophilic globulin, fibrin foam, surgical dressings, or other products or materials it processed, produced, or donated to a Federal agency.

§ 102–37.550 What steps must the American National Red Cross take to acquire surplus property?

Upon receipt of information from GSA regarding the availability of surplus property for donation, the Red Cross will:

(a) Have 21 calendar days to inspect the property or request it without inspection; and

(b) Be responsible for picking up property donated to it or arranging and paying for its shipment.

§ 102–37.555 What happens to property the American National Red Cross does not request?

Property the Red Cross declines to request will be offered to SASPs for distribution to eligible donees. If such property is transferred, GSA will require the SASP to ensure that all Red Cross labels or other Red Cross identifications are obliterated or removed from the property before it is used.

Subpart H—Donations to Public Bodies in Lieu of Abandonment/Destruction

§ 102–37.560 What is a public body?

A public body is any department, agency, special purpose district, or other instrumentality of a State or local government; any Indian tribe; or any agency of the Federal Government.

§ 102–37.565 What is the authority for donations to public bodies?

Section 527 of title 40, United States Code authorizes the abandonment, destruction, or donation to public bodies of property which has no commercial value or for which the estimated cost of continued care and handling would exceed the estimated proceeds from its sale.

[67 FR 2584, Jan. 18, 2002, as amended at 71 FR 23868, Apr. 25, 2006]

§ 102–37.570 What type of property may a holding agency donate under this subpart?

Only that property a holding agency has made a written determination to abandon or destroy (see process in part 102–36 of this chapter) may be donated under this subpart. A holding agency may not donate property that requires destruction for health, safety, or security reasons. When disposing of hazardous materials and other dangerous property, a holding agency must comply with all applicable laws and regulations and any special disposal requirements in part 101–42 of this title.

§ 102–37.575 Is there a special form for holding agencies to process donations?

There is no special form for holding agencies to process donations. A holding agency may use any document that meets its agency's needs for maintaining an audit trail of the transaction.

§ 102–37.580 Who is responsible for costs associated with the donation?

The recipient public body is responsible for paying the disposal costs incident to the donation, such as packing, preparation for shipment, demilitarization (as defined in § 102–36.40 of this chapter), loading, and transportation to its site.

Subpart I—Transfer of Vehicle Title to a Donee

SOURCE: 79 FR 64514, Oct. 30, 2014, unless otherwise noted.

§ 102–37.585 In transferring donated surplus vehicles, what is the responsibility of the holding agency?

(a) The holding agency is responsible for preparing Standard Form 97, *The United States Government Certificate to Obtain Title to a Vehicle* (SF 97) upon notification by GSA that a donee has been identified. The SF 97 may be prepared by GSA if mutually agreed upon by the holding agency and GSA. The holding agency is designated as the "transferor."

(b) If the holding agency authorizes or requires any other entity, including a contractor or grantee, to complete this SF 97, the holding agency must first ensure compliance with the Paperwork Reduction Act.

(c) The SF 97 is a serially numbered, controlled form, stock number 7540–00–634–4047, which can be obtained by executive agencies from GSA Global Supply or online at *www.gsaglobalsupply.gsa.gov.* Proper precautions shall be exercised by the agency to prevent blank copies of the SF 97 from being obtained by unauthorized persons.

§ 102–37.590 In transferring donated surplus vehicles, what is the responsibility of the SASP?

The SASP is responsible for facilitating the transfer of the surplus vehicle to the donee in accordance with this part. The SASP should not sign the SF 97 as "transferee" unless the SASP is the donee.

§ 102–37.595 When transferring donated surplus vehicles, what is the responsibility of the donee?

The donee is responsible for processing the SF 97 in accordance with state licensing and titling authorities. The donee signs the SF 97 as "transferee" upon receipt of the surplus motor vehicle. The donee is responsible for notifying the SASP if a SF 97 is not provided by the Government.

§ 102–37.600 When does title to a surplus donated vehicle change hands?

Title to the vehicle rests with the holding agency until the SF 97 is signed by the donee upon receipt of the surplus motor vehicle. (If applicable under the terms of the donation, the title will be conditional until the end of the period of restriction).

APPENDIX A TO PART 102–37—
MISCELLANEOUS DONATION STATUTES

The following is a listing of statutes which authorize donations which do not require GSA's approval:

Statute: 10 U.S.C. 2572.
Donor Agency: Any military department (Army, Navy, and Air Force) or the Coast Guard.
Type of Property: Books, manuscripts, works of art, historical artifacts, drawings, plans, models, and condemned or obsolete combat material.
Eligible Recipients: Municipal corporations; soldiers' monument associations; museums, historical societies, or historical institutions of a State or foreign nation; incorporated museums that are operated and maintained for educational purposes only and the charters of which denies them the right to operate for profit; posts of the Veterans of Foreign Wars of the United States or of the American Legion or a unit of any other recognized war veterans' association; local or national units of any war veterans' association of a foreign nation which is recognized by the national government of that nation or a principal subdivision of that nation; and posts of the Sons of Veterans Reserve.

Statute: 10 U.S.C. 7306.
Donor Agency: Department of the Navy.
Type of Property: Any vessel stricken from the Naval Vessel Register or any captured vessel in the possession of the Navy.
Eligible Recipients: States, Commonwealths, or possessions of the United States; the District of Columbia; and not-for-profit or nonprofit entities.

Statute: 10 U.S.C. 7541.
Donor Agency: Department of the Navy.
Type of Property: Obsolete material not needed for naval purposes.
Eligible Recipients: Sea scouts of the Boy Scouts of America; Naval Sea Cadet Corps; and the Young Marines of the Marine Corps League.

Statute: 10 U.S.C. 7545.
Donor Agency: Department of the Navy.
Type of Property: Captured, condemned, or obsolete ordnance material, books, manuscripts, works of art, drawings, plans, and models; other condemned or obsolete material, trophies, and flags; and other material of historic interest not needed by the Navy.
Eligible Recipients: States, territories, commonwealths, or possessions of the United States, or political subdivisions or municipal corporations thereof; the District of Columbia; libraries; historical societies; educational institutions whose graduates or students fought in World War I or World War II; soldiers' monument associations; State museums; museums operated and maintained for educational purposes only, whose charter denies it the right to operate for profit; posts of the Veterans of Foreign Wars of the United States; American Legion posts; recognized war veterans' associations; or posts of the Sons of Veterans Reserve.

Statute: 14 U.S.C. 641(a).
Donor Agency: Coast Guard.
Type of Property: Obsolete or other material not needed for the Coast Guard.
Eligible Recipients: Coast Guard Auxiliary; sea scout service of the Boy Scouts of America; and public bodies or private organizations not organized for profit.

APPENDIX B TO PART 102–37—ELEMENTS OF A STATE PLAN OF OPERATION

The following is the information and assurances that must be included in a SASP's plan of operation:

STATE PLAN REQUIREMENTS

Regarding . . .	The plan must . . .
(a) Designation of a SASP	(1) Name the State agency that will be responsible for administering the plan. (2) Describe the responsibilities vested in the agency which must include the authorities to acquire, warehouse and distribute surplus property to eligible donees, carry out other requirements of the State plan, and provide details concerning the organization of the agency, including supervision, staffing, structure, and physical facilities. (3) Indicate the organizational status of the agency within the State governmental structure and the title of the State official who directly supervises the State agent.
(b) Operational authority	Include copies of existing State statutes and/or executive orders relative to the operational authority of the SASP. Where express statutory authority does not exist or is ambiguous, or where authority exists by virtue of executive order, the plan must include also the opinion of the State's Attorney General regarding the existence of such authority.
(c) Inventory control and accounting system.	(1) Require the SASP to use a management control and accounting system that effectively governs the utilization, inventory control, accountability, and disposal of property. (2) Provide a detailed explanation of the inventory control and accounting system that the SASP will use. (3) Provide that property retained by the SASP to perform its functions be maintained on separate records from those of donable property.
(d) Return of donated property	(1) Require the SASP to provide for the return of donated property from the donee, at the donee's expense, if the property is still usable as determined by the SASP; and (i) The donee has not placed the property into use for the purpose for which it was donated within 1 year of donation; or (ii) The donee ceases to use the property within 1 year after placing it in use. (2) Specify that return of property can be accomplished by: (i) Physical return to the SASP facility, if required by the SASP. (ii) Retransfer directly to another donee, SASP, or Federal agency, as required by the SASP. (iii) Disposal (by sale or other means) as directed by the SASP. (3) Set forth procedures to accomplish property returns to the SASP, retransfers to other organizations, or disposition by sale, abandonment, or destruction.
(e) Financing and service charges	(1) Set forth the means and methods for financing the SASP. When the State authorizes the SASP to assess and collect service charges from participating donees to cover direct and reasonable indirect costs of its activities, the method of establishing the charges must be set forth in the plan. (2) Affirm that service charges, if assessed, are fair and equitable and based on services performed (or paid for) by the SASP, such as screening, packing, crating, removal, and transportation. When the SASP provides minimal services in connection with the acquisition of property, except for document processing and other administrative actions, the State plan must provide for minimal charges to be assessed in such cases and include the bases of computation. (3) Provide that property made available to nonprofit providers of assistance to homeless individuals be distributed at a nominal cost for care and handling of the property. (4) Set forth how funds accumulated from service charges, or from other sources such as sales or compliance proceeds are to be used for the operation of the SASP and the benefit of participating donees. (5) Affirm, if service charge funds are to be deposited or invested, that such deposits or investments are permitted by State law and set forth the types of depositories and/or investments contemplated. (6) Cite State authority to use service charges to acquire or improve SASP facilities and set forth disposition to be made of any financial assets realized upon the sale or other disposal of the facilities. (7) Indicate if the SASP intends to maintain a working capital reserve. If one is to be maintained, the plan should provide the provisions and limitations for it. (8) State if refunds of service charges are to be made to donees when there is an excess in the SASP's working capital reserve and provide details of how such refunds are to be made, such as a reduction in service charges or a cash refund, prorated in an equitable manner.
(f) Terms and conditions on donated property.	(1) Require the SASP to identify terms and conditions that will be imposed on the donee for any item of donated property with a unit acquisition cost of $5,000 or more and any passenger motor vehicle. (2) Provide that the SASP may impose reasonable terms and conditions on the use of other donated property. If the SASP elects to impose additional terms and conditions, it should list them in the plan. If the SASP wishes to provide for amending, modifying, or releasing any terms or conditions it has elected to impose, it must state in the plan the standards it will use to grant such amendments, modifications or releases.

138

STATE PLAN REQUIREMENTS—Continued

Regarding . . .	The plan must . . .
	(3) Provide that the SASP will impose on the donation of property, regardless of unit acquisition cost, such conditions involving special handling or use limitations as GSA may determine necessary because of the characteristics of the property.
(g) Nonutilized or undistributed property.	Provide that, subject to GSA approval, property in the possession of the SASP which donees in the State cannot use will be disposed of by: (1) Transfer to another SASP or Federal agency. (2) Sale. (3) Abandonment or destruction. (4) Other arrangements.
(h) Fair and equitable distribution ...	(1) Provide that the SASP will make fair and equitable distribution of property to eligible donees in the State based on their relative needs and resources and ability to use the property. (2) Set forth the policies and detailed procedures for effecting a prompt, fair, and equitable distribution. (3) Require that the SASP, insofar as practicable, select property requested by eligible donees and, if requested by the donee, arrange for shipment of the property directly to the donee.
(i) Eligibility	(1) Set forth procedures for the SASP to determine the eligibility of applicants for the donation of surplus personal property. (2) Provide for donee eligibility records to include at a minimum: (i) Legal name and address of the donee. (ii) Status of the donee as a public agency or as an eligible nonprofit activity. (iii) Details on the scope of the donee's program. (iv) Proof of tax exemption under section 501 of the Internal Revenue Code if the donee is nonprofit. (v) Proof that the donee is approved, accredited, licensed, or meets any other legal requirement for operation of its program(s). (vi) Financial information. (vii) Written authorization by the donee's governing body or chief administrative officer designating at least one person to act for the donee in acquiring property. (viii) Assurance that the donee will comply with GSA's regulations on nondiscrimination. (ix) Types of property needed.
(j) Compliance and utilization	(1) Provide that the SASP conduct utilization reviews for donee compliance with the terms, conditions, reservations, and restrictions imposed by GSA and the SASP on property having a unit acquisition cost of $5,000 or more and any passenger motor vehicle. (2) Provide for the reviews to include a survey of donee compliance with any special handling conditions or use limitations imposed on items of property by GSA. (3) Set forth the proposed frequency of such reviews and provide adequate assurances that the SASP will take effective action to correct noncompliance or otherwise enforce such terms, conditions, reservations, and restrictions. (4) Require the SASP to prepare reports on utilization reviews and compliance actions and provide assurance that the SASP will initiate appropriate investigations of alleged fraud in the acquisition of donated property or misuse of such property.
(k) Consultation with advisory bodies and public and private groups.	(1) Provide for consultation with advisory bodies and public and private groups which can assist the SASP in determining the relative needs and resources of donees, the proposed utilization of surplus property by eligible donees, and how distribution of surplus property can be effected to fill existing needs of donees. (2) Provide details of how the SASP will accomplish such consultation.
(l) Audit	(1) Provide for periodic internal audits of the operations and financial affairs of the SASP. (2) Provide for compliance with the external audit requirements of Office of Management and Budget Circular No. A–133, "Audits of States, Local Governments, and Non-Profit Organizations" (available at *www.whitehouse.gov/OMB*), and make provisions for the SASP to furnish GSA with: (i) Two copies of any audit report made pursuant to the Circular, or with two copies of those sections that pertain to the Federal donation program. (ii) An outline of all corrective actions and scheduled completion dates for the actions. (3) Provide for cooperation in GSA or Comptroller General conducted audits.
(m) Cooperative agreements	If the SASP wishes to enter into, renew, or revise cooperative agreements with GSA or other Federal agencies: (1) Affirm the SASP's intentions to enter into cooperative agreements. (2) Cite the authority for entering into such agreements.
(n) Liquidation	Provide for the SASP to submit a liquidation plan prior to termination of the SASP activities if the State decides to dissolve the SASP.

STATE PLAN REQUIREMENTS—Continued

Regarding . . .	The plan must . . .
(o) Forms	Include copies of distribution documents used by the SASP.
(p) Records	Affirm that all official records of the SASP will be retained for a minimum of 3 years, except that: (1) Records involving property subject to restrictions for more than 2 years must be kept 1 year beyond the specified period of restriction. (2) Records involving property with perpetual restriction must be retained in perpetuity. (3) Records involving property in noncompliance status must be retained for at least 1 year after the noncompliance case is closed.

APPENDIX C TO PART 102–37—GLOSSARY OF TERMS FOR DETERMINING ELIGIBILITY OF PUBLIC AGENCIES AND NONPROFIT ORGANIZATIONS

The following is a glossary of terms for determining eligibility of public agencies and nonprofit organizations:

Accreditation means the status of public recognition that an accrediting agency grants to an institution or program that meets the agency's standards and requirements.

Accredited means approval by a recognized accrediting board or association on a regional, State, or national level, such as a State board of education or health; the American Hospital Association; a regional or national accrediting association for universities, colleges, or secondary schools; or another recognized accrediting association.

Approved means recognition and approval by the State department of education, State department of health, or other appropriate authority where no recognized accrediting board, association, or other authority exists for the purpose of making an accreditation. For an educational institution or an educational program, approval must relate to academic or instructional standards established by the appropriate authority. For a public health institution or program, approval must relate to the medical requirements and standards for the professional and technical services of the institution established by the appropriate authority.

Child care center means a public or nonprofit facility where educational, social, health, and nutritional services are provided to children through age 14 (or as prescribed by State law) and that is approved or licensed by the State or other appropriate authority as a child day care center or child care center.

Clinic means an approved public or nonprofit facility organized and operated for the primary purpose of providing outpatient public health services and includes customary related services such as laboratories and treatment rooms.

College means an approved or accredited public or nonprofit institution of higher learning offering organized study courses and credits leading to a baccalaureate or higher degree.

Conservation means a program or programs carried out or promoted by a public agency for public purposes involving directly or indirectly the protection, maintenance, development, and restoration of the natural resources of a given political area. These resources include but are not limited to the air, land, forests, water, rivers, streams, lakes and ponds, minerals, and animals, fish and other wildlife.

Drug abuse or alcohol treatment center means a clinic or medical institution that provides for the diagnosis, treatment, or rehabilitation of alcoholics or drug addicts. These centers must have on their staffs, or available on a regular visiting basis, qualified professionals in the fields of medicine, psychology, psychiatry, or rehabilitation.

Economic development means a program(s) carried out or promoted by a public agency for public purposes to improve the opportunities of a given political area for the establishment or expansion of industrial, commercial, or agricultural plants or facilities and which otherwise assist in the creation of long-term employment opportunities in the area or primarily benefit the unemployed or those with low incomes.

Education means a program(s) to develop and promote the training, general knowledge, or academic, technical, and vocational skills and cultural attainments of individuals in a community or given political area. Public educational programs may include public school systems and supporting facilities such as centralized administrative or service facilities.

Educational institution means an approved, accredited, or licensed public or nonprofit institution, facility, entity, or organization conducting educational programs or research for educational purposes, such as a child care center, school, college, university, school for the mentally or physically disabled, or an educational radio or television station.

Educational radio or television station means a public or nonprofit radio or television station licensed by the Federal Communications Commission and operated exclusively for noncommercial educational purposes.

Health center means an approved public or nonprofit facility that provides public health services, including related facilities such as diagnostic and laboratory facilities and clinics.

Historic light station means a historic light station as defined under section 308(e)(2) of the National Historic Preservation Act 16 U.S.C. 470w–7(e)2), including a historic light station conveyed under subsection (b) of that section, notwithstanding the number of hours that the historic light station is open to the public.

Homeless individual means:

(1) An individual who lacks a fixed, regular, and adequate nighttime residence, or who has a primary nighttime residence that is:

(i) A supervised publicly or privately operated shelter designed to provide temporary living accommodations (including welfare hotels, congregate shelters, and transitional housing for the mentally ill);

(ii) An institution that provides a temporary residence for individuals intended to be institutionalized; or

(iii) A public or private place not designed for, or ordinarily used as, a regular sleeping accommodation for human beings.

(2) For purposes of this part, the term *homeless individual* does not include any individual imprisoned or otherwise detained pursuant to an Act of the Congress or a State law.

Hospital means an approved or accredited public or nonprofit institution providing public health services primarily for inpatient medical or surgical care of the sick and injured and includes related facilities such as laboratories, outpatient departments, training facilities, and staff offices.

Library means a public or nonprofit facility providing library services free to all residents of a community, district, State, or region.

Licensed means recognition and approval by the appropriate State or local authority approving institutions or programs in specialized areas. Licensing generally relates to established minimum public standards of safety, sanitation, staffing, and equipment as they relate to the construction, maintenance, and operation of a health or educational facility, rather than to the academic, instructional, or medical standards for these institutions.

Medical institution means an approved, accredited, or licensed public or nonprofit institution, facility, or organization whose primary function is the furnishing of public health and medical services to the public or promoting public health through the conduct of research, experiments, training, or demonstrations related to cause, prevention, and methods of diagnosis and treatment of diseases and injuries. The term includes, but is not limited to, hospitals, clinics, alcohol and drug abuse treatment centers, public health or treatment centers, research and health centers, geriatric centers, laboratories, medical schools, dental schools, nursing schools, and similar institutions. The term does not include institutions primarily engaged in domiciliary care, although a separate medical facility within such a domiciliary institution may qualify as a *medical institution*.

Museum means a public or nonprofit institution that is organized on a permanent basis for essentially educational or aesthetic purposes and which, using a professional staff, owns or uses tangible objects, either animate or inanimate; cares for these objects; and exhibits them to the public on a regular basis (at least 1000 hours a year). As used in this part, the term *museum* includes, but is not limited to, the following institutions if they satisfy all other provisions of this definition: Aquariums and zoological parks; botanical gardens and arboretums; nature centers; museums relating to art, history (including historic buildings), natural history, science, and technology; and planetariums. For the purposes of this definition, an institution uses a professional staff if it employs at least one fulltime staff member or the equivalent, whether paid or unpaid, primarily engaged in the acquisition, care, or public exhibition of objects owned or used by the institution. This definition of *museum* does not include any institution that exhibits objects to the public if the display or use of the objects is only incidental to the primary function of the institution.

Nationally recognized accrediting agency means an accrediting agency that the Department of Education recognizes under 34 CFR part 600. (For a list of accrediting agencies, see the Department's web site at *http://www.ed.gov/admins/finaid/accred*)

Nonprofit means not organized for profit and exempt from Federal income tax under section 501 of the Internal Revenue Code (26 U.S.C. 501).

Parks and recreation means a program(s) carried out or promoted by a public agency for public purposes that involve directly or indirectly the acquisition, development, improvement, maintenance, and protection of park and recreational facilities for the residents of a given political area.

Program for older individuals means a program conducted by a State or local government agency or nonprofit activity that receives funds appropriated for services or programs for older individuals under the Older Americans Act of 1965, as amended, under title IV or title XX of the Social Security Act (42 U.S.C. 601 *et seq.*), or under titles VIII and X of the Economic Opportunity Act of

1964 (42 U.S.C. 2991 *et seq.*) and the Community Services Block Grant Act (42 U.S.C. 9901 *et seq.*).

Provider of assistance to homeless individuals means a public agency or a nonprofit institution or organization that operates a program which provides assistance such as food, shelter, or other services to homeless individuals.

Provider of assistance to impoverished families and individuals means a public or nonprofit organization whose primary function is to provide money, goods, or services to families or individuals whose annual incomes are below the poverty line (as defined in section 673 of the Community Services Block Grant Act) (42 U.S.C. 9902). Providers include food banks, self-help housing groups, and organizations providing services such as the following: Health care; medical transportation; scholarships and tuition assistance; tutoring and literacy instruction; job training and placement; employment counseling; child care assistance; meals or other nutritional support; clothing distribution; home construction or repairs; utility or rental assistance; and legal counsel.

Public agency means any State; political subdivision thereof, including any unit of local government or economic development district; any department, agency, or instrumentality thereof, including instrumentalities created by compact or other agreement between States or political subdivisions; multijurisdictional substate districts established by or pursuant to State law; or any Indian tribe, band, group, pueblo, or community located on a State reservation.

Public health means a program(s) to promote, maintain, and conserve the public's health by providing health services to individuals and/or by conducting research, investigations, examinations, training, and demonstrations. Public health services may include but are not limited to the control of communicable diseases, immunization, maternal and child health programs, sanitary engineering, sewage treatment and disposal, sanitation inspection and supervision, water purification and distribution, air pollution control, garbage and trash disposal, and the control and elimination of disease-carrying animals and insects.

Public health institution means an approved, accredited, or licensed public or nonprofit institution, facility, or organization conducting a public health program(s) such as a hospital, clinic, health center, or medical institution, including research for such programs, the services of which are available to the public.

Public purpose means a program(s) carried out by a public agency that is legally authorized in accordance with the laws of the State or political subdivision thereof and for which public funds may be expended. Public purposes include but are not limited to programs such as conservation, economic development, education, parks and recreation, public health, public safety, programs of assistance to the homeless or impoverished, and programs for older individuals.

Public safety means a program(s) carried out or promoted by a public agency for public purposes involving, directly or indirectly, the protection, safety, law enforcement activities, and criminal justice system of a given political area. Public safety programs may include, but are not limited to those carried out by:

(1) Public police departments.

(2) Sheriffs' offices.

(3) The courts.

(4) Penal and correctional institutions (including juvenile facilities).

(5) State and local civil defense organizations.

(6) Fire departments and rescue squads (including volunteer fire departments and rescue squads supported in whole or in part with public funds).

School (except schools for the mentally or physically disabled) means a public or nonprofit approved or accredited organizational entity devoted primarily to approved academic, vocational, or professional study and instruction, that operates primarily for educational purposes on a full-time basis for a minimum school year and employs a full-time staff of qualified instructors.

School for the mentally or physically disabled means a facility or institution operated primarily to provide specialized instruction to students of limited mental or physical capacity. It must be public or nonprofit and must operate on a full-time basis for the equivalent of a minimum school year prescribed for public school instruction for the mentally or physically disabled, have a staff of qualified instructors, and demonstrate that the facility meets the health and safety standards of the State or local government.

University means a public or nonprofit approved or accredited institution for instruction and study in the higher branches of learning and empowered to confer degrees in special departments or colleges.

Veterans Organizations means organizations eligible to receive Federal surplus property for purposes of providing services to veterans under 40 U.S.C. 549(c)(3)(C). Eligible veterans organizations are those whose (1) membership comprises substantially veterans (as defined under 38 U.S.C. 101); and (2) representatives are recognized by the Secretary of Veterans Affairs under 38 U.S.C. 5902. The Department of Veterans Affairs maintains a searchable Web site of recognized organizations. The address is *http://www.va.gov/ogc/apps/accreditation/index.asp.*

[67 FR 2584, Jan. 18, 2002, as amended at 71 FR 23868, Apr. 25, 2006; 72 FR 12572, Mar. 16, 2007; 79 FR 64515, Oct. 30, 2014]

AUTHORITY: 40 U.S.C. 545 and 40 U.S.C. 121(c).

SOURCE: 68 FR 51421, Aug. 26, 2003, unless otherwise noted.

Subpart A—General Provisions

§ 102–38.5 What does this part cover?

This part prescribes the policies governing the sale of Federal personal property, including—

(a) Surplus personal property that has completed all required Federal and/or donation screening; and

(b) Personal property to be sold under the exchange/sale authority.

NOTE TO § 102–38.5: You must follow additional guidelines in 41 CFR parts 101–42 and 101–45 of the Federal Property Management Regulations (FPMR) for the sale of personal property that has special handling requirements or property containing hazardous materials. Additional requirements for the sale of aircraft and aircraft parts are provided in part 102–33 of this chapter.

§ 102–38.10 What is the governing authority for this part?

The authority for the regulations in this part governing the sale of Federal personal property is 40 U.S.C. 541 through 548, 571, 573 and 574.

§ 102–38.15 Who must comply with these sales provisions?

All executive agencies must comply with the provisions of this part. The legislative and judicial branches are encouraged to follow these provisions.

§ 102–38.20 Must an executive agency follow the regulations of this part when selling all personal property?

Generally, yes, an executive agency must follow the regulations of this part when selling all personal property; however—

(a) Materials acquired for the national stockpile or supplemental stockpile, or materials or equipment acquired under section 303 of the Defense Production Act of 1950, as amended (50 U.S.C. App. 2093) are excepted from this part;

(b) The Maritime Administration, Department of Transportation, has jurisdiction over the disposal of vessels of 1,500 gross tons or more and determined by the Secretary to be merchant vessels or capable of conversion to merchant use;

(c) Sales made by the Secretary of Defense pursuant to 10 U.S.C. 2576 (Sale of Surplus Military Equipment to State and Local Law Enforcement and Firefighting Agencies) are exempt from these provisions;

(d) Foreign excess personal property is exempt from these provisions; and

(e) Agency sales procedures which are mandated or authorized under laws other than Title 40 United States Code are exempt from this part.

[73 FR 20802, Apr. 17, 2008]

§ 102–38.25 To whom do "we", "you", and their variants refer?

Unless otherwise indicated, use of pronouns "we", "you", and their variants throughout this part refer to the Sales Center responsible for the sale of the property.

[68 FR 51421, Aug. 26, 2003, as amended at 73 FR 20802, Apr. 17, 2008]

§ 102–38.30 How does an executive agency request a deviation from the provisions of this part?

Refer to §§ 102–2.60 through 102–2.110 of this chapter for information on how to obtain a deviation from this part. However, waivers which are distinct from the standard deviation process and specific to the requirements of the Federal Asset Sales (eFAS) initiative milestones (see subpart H of this part) are addressed in § 102–38.360.

[73 FR 20802, Apr. 17, 2008]

Definitions

§ 102–38.35 What definitions apply to this part?

The following definitions apply to this part:

Bid means a response to an offer to sell that, if accepted, would bind the bidder to the terms and conditions of the contract (including the bid price).

Bidder means any entity that is responding to or has responded to an offer to sell.

Estimated fair market value means the selling agency's best estimate of what the property would be sold for if offered for public sale.

Federal Asset Sales (eFAS) refers to the e-Government initiative to improve the way the Federal Government manages and sells its real and personal property assets. Under this initiative, only an agency designated as a Sales Center (SC) may sell Federal property, unless a waiver has been granted by the *eFAS* Planning Office in accordance with § 102–38.360. The *eFAS* initiative is governed and given direction by the *eFAS* Executive Steering Committee (ESC), with GSA as the managing partner agency.

Federal Asset Sales Planning Office (eFAS Planning Office) refers to the office within GSA assigned responsibility for managing the eFAS initiative.

Holding Agency refers to the agency in possession of personal property eligible for sale under this part.

Identical bids means bids for the same item of property having the same total price.

Migration Plan refers to the document a holding agency prepares to summarize its choice of SC(s) and its plan for migrating agency sales to the SC(s). The format for this document is determined by the eFAS ESC.

Personal property means any property, except real property. For purposes of this part, the term excludes records of the Federal Government, and naval vessels of the following categories:

(1) Battleships;

(2) Cruisers;

(3) Aircraft carriers;

(4) Destroyers; and

(5) Submarines.

Sales Center (SC) means an agency that has been nominated, designated, and approved by the eFAS ESC and the Office of Management and Budget (OMB) as an official sales solution for Federal property. The criteria for becoming an *SC*, the selection process, and the ongoing *SC* requirements for posting property for sale to the eFAS portal and reporting sales activity and performance data are established by the eFAS ESC and can be obtained from the eFAS Planning Office at GSA. The eFAS Planning Office may be contacted via e-mail at *FASPlanningOffice@gsa.gov*. *SCs* may utilize (and should consider) private sector entities as well as Government activities and are expected to provide exemplary asset management solutions in one or more of the following areas: on-line sales; off-line sales; and sales-related value added services. *SCs* will enter into agreements with holding agencies to sell property belonging to these holding agencies. A holding agency may employ the services of multiple *SCs* to maximize efficiencies.

State Agency for Surplus Property (SASP) means the agency designated under State law to receive Federal surplus personal property for distribution to eligible donees within the State as provided for in 40 U.S.C. 549.

State or local government means a State, territory, possession, political subdivision thereof, or tax-supported agency therein.

[68 FR 51421, Aug. 26, 2003, as amended at 73 FR 20802, Apr. 17, 2008]

RESPONSIBILITIES

§ 102–38.40 Who may sell personal property?

An executive agency may sell personal property (including on behalf of another agency when so requested) only if it is a designated Sales Center (SC), or if the agency has received a waiver from the eFAS Planning Office. An SC may engage contractor support to sell personal property. Only a duly authorized agency official may execute the sale award documents and bind the United States.

[73 FR 20802, Apr. 17, 2008]

§ 102–38.45 What are an executive agency's responsibilities in selling personal property?

An executive agency's responsibilities in selling personal property are to—

(a) Ensure the sale complies with the provisions of Title 40 of the U.S. Code, the regulations of this part, and any other applicable laws;

(b) Issue internal guidance to promote uniformity of sales procedures;

(c) Assure that officials designated to conduct and finalize sales are adequately trained;

(d) Be accountable for the care and handling of the personal property prior to its removal by the buyer; and

(e) Adjust your property and financial records to reflect the final disposition.

[68 FR 51421, Aug. 26, 2003, as amended at 73 FR 20803, Apr. 17, 2008]

§ 102–38.50 What must we do when an executive agency suspects violations of 40 U.S.C. 559, fraud, bribery, or criminal collusion in connection with the disposal of personal property?

If an executive agency suspects violations of 40 U.S.C. 559, fraud, bribery, or criminal collusion in connection with the disposal of personal property, the agency must—

(a) Refer the violations to the Inspector General of your agency and/or the

Attorney General, Department of Justice, Washington, DC 20530, for further investigation. You must cooperate with and provide evidence concerning the suspected violation or crime to the investigating agency assuming jurisdiction of the matter; and

(b) Submit to the General Services Administration (GSA), Property Management Division (FBP), 1800 F Street, NW., Washington, DC 20406, a report of any compliance investigations concerning such violations. The report must contain information concerning the noncompliance, including the corrective action taken or contemplated, and, for cases referred to the Department of Justice, a copy of the transmittal letter. A copy of each report must be submitted also to GSA, Personal Property Management Policy Division (MTP), 1800 F Street, NW., Washington, DC 20405.

[68 FR 51421, Aug. 26, 2003, as amended at 73 FR 20803, Apr. 17, 2008]

§ 102–38.55 What must we do when selling personal property?

When selling personal property, you must ensure that—

(a) All sales are made after publicly advertising for bids, except as provided for negotiated sales in §§ 102–38.100 through 102–38.125; and

(b) Advertising for bids must permit full and free competition consistent with the value and nature of the property involved.

§ 102–38.60 Who is responsible for the costs of care and handling of the personal property before it is sold?

The holding agency is responsible for the care and handling costs of the personal property until it is removed by the buyer, the buyer's designee, or an SC. The holding agency may request the SC to perform care and handling services in accordance with their agreement. When specified in the terms and conditions of sale, the SC may charge the buyer costs for storage when the buyer is delinquent in removing the property. The amount so charged may only be retained by the holding agency performing the care and handling in accordance with § 102–38.295.

[73 FR 20803, Apr. 17, 2008]

§ 102–38.65 What if we are or the holding agency is notified of a Federal requirement for surplus personal property before the sale is complete?

Federal agencies have first claim to excess or surplus personal property reported to the General Services Administration. When a bona fide need for the property exists and is expressed by a Federal agency, and when no like item(s) are located elsewhere, you or the holding agency must make the property available for transfer to the maximum extent practicable and prior to transfer of title to the property.

[68 FR 51421, Aug. 26, 2003, as amended at 73 FR 20803, Apr. 17, 2008]

§ 102–38.70 May the holding agency abandon or destroy personal property either prior to or after trying to sell it?

(a) Yes, the holding agency may abandon or destroy personal property either prior to or after trying to sell it, but only when an authorized agency official has made a written determination that—

(1) The personal property has no commercial value; or

(2) The estimated cost of continued care and handling would exceed the estimated sales proceeds.

(b) In addition to the provisions in paragraph (a) of this section, see the regulations at §§ 102–36.305 through 102–36.330 of this subchapter B that are applicable to the abandonment or destruction of personal property in general, and excess personal property in particular.

[68 FR 51421, Aug. 26, 2003, as amended at 73 FR 20803, Apr. 17, 2008]

Subpart B—Sales Process

METHODS OF SALE

§ 102–38.75 How may we sell personal property?

(a) You will sell personal property upon such terms and conditions as the head of your agency or designee deems proper to promote the fairness, openness, and timeliness necessary for the sale to be conducted in a manner most advantageous to the Government.

When you are selling property on behalf of another agency, you must consult with the holding agency to determine any special or unique sales terms and conditions. You must also document the required terms and conditions of each sale, including, but not limited to, the following terms and conditions, as applicable:

(1) Inspection.

(2) Condition and location of property.

(3) Eligibility of bidders.

(4) Consideration of bids.

(5) Bid deposits and payments.

(6) Submission of bids.

(7) Bid price determination.

(8) Title.

(9) Delivery, loading, and removal of property.

(10) Default, returns, or refunds.

(11) Modifications, withdrawals, or late bids.

(12) Requirements to comply with applicable laws and regulations. 41 CFR part 101–42 contains useful guidance addressing many of these requirements. You should also contact your agency's Office of General Counsel or environmental office to identify applicable Federal, State, or local environmental laws and regulations.

(13) Certificate of independent price determinations.

(14) Covenant against contingent fees.

(15) Limitation on Government's liability.

(16) Award of contract.

(b) Standard government forms (e.g., Standard Form 114 series) may be used to document terms and conditions of the sale.

(c) When conducting and completing a sale through electronic media, the required terms and conditions must be included in your electronic sales documentation.

[68 FR 51421, Aug. 26, 2003, as amended at 73 FR 20803, Apr. 17, 2008]

§ 102–38.80 Which method of sale should we use?

(a) You may use any method of sale provided the sale is publicly advertised and the personal property is sold with full and open competition. Exceptions to the requirement for competitive bids for negotiated sales (including fixed price sales) are contained in §§ 102–38.100 through 102–38.125. You must select the method of sale that will bring maximum return at minimum cost, considering factors such as—

(1) Type and quantity of property;

(2) Location of property;

(3) Potential market;

(4) Cost to prepare and conduct the sale;

(5) Available facilities; and

(6) Sales experience of the selling activity.

(b) Methods of sale may include sealed bid sales, spot bid sales, auctions, or negotiated sales and may be conducted at a physical location or through any electronic media that is publicly accessible.

COMPETITIVE SALES

§ 102–38.85 What is a sealed bid sale?

A sealed bid sale is a sale in which bid prices are kept confidential until bid opening. Bids are submitted either electronically or in writing according to formats specified by the selling agency, and all bids are held for public disclosure at a designated time and place.

§ 102–38.90 What is a spot bid sale?

A spot bid sale is a sale where immediately following the offering of the item or lot of property, bids are examined, and awards are made or bids rejected on the spot. Bids are either submitted electronically or in writing according to formats specified by the selling agency, and must not be disclosed prior to announcement of award.

§ 102–38.95 What is an auction?

An auction is a sale where the bid amounts of different bidders are disclosed as they are submitted, providing bidders the option to increase their bids if they choose. Bids are submitted electronically and/or by those physically present at the sale. Normally, the bidder with the highest bid at the close of each bidding process is awarded the property.

NEGOTIATED SALES

§ 102–38.100 What is a negotiated sale?

A negotiated sale is a sale where the selling price is arrived at between the seller and the buyer, subject to obtaining such competition as is feasible under the circumstances.

§ 102–38.105 Under what conditions may we negotiate sales of personal property?

You may negotiate sales of personal property when—

(a) The personal property has an estimated fair market value that does not exceed $15,000;

(b) The disposal will be to a State, territory, possession, political subdivision thereof, or tax-supported agency therein, and the estimated fair market value of the property and other satisfactory terms of disposal are obtained by negotiation;

(c) Bid prices after advertising are not reasonable and re-advertising would serve no useful purpose;

(d) Public exigency does not permit any delay such as that caused by the time required to advertise a sale;

(e) The sale promotes public health, safety, or national security;

(f) The sale is in the public interest under a national emergency declared by the President or the Congress. This authority may be used only with specific lot(s) of property or for categories determined by the Administrator of General Services for a designated period but not in excess of three months;

(g) Selling the property competitively would have an adverse impact on the national economy, provided that the estimated fair market value of the property and other satisfactory terms of disposal can be obtained by negotiation, e.g., sale of large quantities of an agricultural product that impact domestic markets; or

(h) Otherwise authorized by Title 40 of the U.S. Code or other law.

§ 102–38.110 Who approves our determinations to conduct negotiated sales?

The head of your agency (or his/her designee) must approve all negotiated sales of personal property.

§ 102–38.115 What are the specific reporting requirements for negotiated sales?

For negotiated sales of personal property, you must—

(a) In accordance with 40 U.S.C. 545(e), and in advance of the sale, submit to the oversight committees for the General Services Administration (GSA) in the Senate and House, explanatory statements for each sale by negotiation of any personal property with an estimated fair market value in excess of $15,000. You must maintain copies of the explanatory statements in your disposal files. No statement is needed for negotiated sales at fixed price or for any sale made without advertising when authorized by law other than 40 U.S.C. 545; and

(b) Report annually to GSA, Personal Property Management Policy Division (MTP), 1800 F Street, NW., Washington, DC, 20405, within 60 calendar days after the close of each fiscal year, a listing and description of all negotiated sales of personal property with an estimated fair market value in excess of $5,000. You may submit the report electronically or manually (see § 102–38.330).

§ 102–38.120 When may we conduct negotiated sales of personal property at fixed prices (fixed price sale)?

You may conduct negotiated sales of personal property at fixed prices (fixed price sale) under this section when:

(a) The items are authorized to be sold at fixed price by the Administrator of General Services, as reflected in GSA Bulletin FMR B–10 (located at *http://www.gsa.gov/fmrbulletin*). You may also contact the GSA Office of Travel, Transportation, and Asset Management (MT) at the address listed in § 102–38.115 to determine which items are on this list of authorized items;

(b) The head of your agency, or designee, determines in writing that such sales serve the best interest of the Government. When you are selling property on behalf of a holding agency, you must consult with the holding agency in determining whether a fixed price sale meets this criterion; and

(c) You must publicize such sales to the extent consistent with the value and nature of the property involved, and the prices established must reflect the estimated fair market value of the property. Property is sold on a first-come, first-served basis. You or the holding agency may also establish additional terms and conditions that must be met by the successful purchaser in accordance with § 102–38.75.

[73 FR 20803, Apr. 17, 2008]

§ 102–38.125 May we sell personal property at fixed prices to State agencies?

Yes, before offering to the public, you may offer the property at fixed prices (through the State Agencies for Surplus Property) to any States, territories, possessions, political subdivisions thereof, or tax-supported agencies therein, which have expressed an interest in obtaining the property. For additional information, see subpart G of this part.

ADVERTISING

§ 102–38.130 Must we publicly advertise sales of Federal personal property?

Yes, you must provide public notice of your sale of personal property to permit full and open competition.

§ 102–38.135 What constitutes a public advertisement?

Announcement of the sale using any media that reaches the public and is appropriate to the type and value of personal property to be sold is considered public advertising. You may also distribute mailings or flyers of your offer to sell to prospective purchasers on mailing lists. Public notice should be made far enough in advance of the sale to ensure adequate notice, and to target your advertising efforts toward the market that will provide the best return at the lowest cost.

§ 102–38.140 What must we include in the public notice on sale of personal property?

In the public notice, you must provide information necessary for potential buyers to participate in the sale, such as—

(a) Date, time and location of sale;

(b) General categories of property being offered for sale;

(c) Inspection period;

(d) Method of sale (i.e., spot bid, sealed bid, auction);

(e) Selling agency; and

(f) Who to contact for additional information.

PRE-SALE ACTIVITIES

§ 102–38.145 Must we allow for inspection of the personal property to be sold?

Yes, you must allow for an electronic or physical inspection of the personal property to be sold. You must allow prospective bidders sufficient time for inspection. If inspection is restricted to electronic inspections only, due to unusual circumstances prohibiting physical inspection, you must notify your General Services Administration Regional Personal Property Office in writing, with the circumstances surrounding this restriction at least 3 days prior to the start of the screening period.

§ 102–38.150 How long is the inspection period?

The length of the inspection period allowed depends upon whether the inspection is done electronically or physically. You should also consider such factors as the circumstances of sale, volume of property, type of property, location of the property, and accessibility of the sales facility. Normally, you should provide at least 7 calendar days to ensure potential buyers have the opportunity to perform needed inspections.

OFFER TO SELL

§ 102–38.155 What is an offer to sell?

An offer to sell is a notice listing the terms and conditions for bidding on an upcoming sale of personal property, where prospective purchasers are advised of the requirements for a responsive bid and the contractual obligations once a bid is accepted.

§ 102–38.160 What must be included in the offer to sell?

The offer to sell must include—

(a) Sale date and time;

(b) Method of sale;

(c) Description of property being offered for sale;

(d) Selling agency;

(e) Location of property;

(f) Time and place for receipt of bids;

(g) Acceptable forms of bid deposits and payments; and

(h) Terms and conditions of sale, including any specific restrictions and limitations.

§ 102–38.165 Are the terms and conditions in the offer to sell binding?

Yes, the terms and conditions in the offer to sell are normally incorporated into the sales contract, and therefore binding upon both the buyer and the seller once a bid is accepted.

Subpart C—Bids

BUYER ELIGIBILITY

§ 102–38.170 May we sell Federal personal property to anyone?

Generally, you may sell Federal personal property to anyone of legal age. However, certain persons or entities are debarred or suspended from purchasing Federal property. You must not enter into a contract with such a person or entity unless your agency head or designee responsible for the disposal action determines that there is a compelling reason for such an action.

§ 102–38.175 How do we find out if a person or entity has been suspended or debarred from doing business with the Government?

Refer to the List of Parties Excluded from Federal Procurement and Nonprocurement Programs to ensure you do not solicit from or award contracts to these persons or entities. The list is available through subscription from the U.S. Government Printing Office, or electronically on the Internet at *http://epls.arnet.gov.* For policies, procedures, and requirements for debarring/suspending a person or entity from the purchase of Federal personal property, follow the procedures in the Federal Acquisition Regulation (FAR) subpart 9.4 (48 CFR part 9, subpart 9.4).

[68 FR 51421, Aug. 26, 2003; 68 FR 53219, Sept. 9, 2003]

§ 102–38.180 May we sell Federal personal property to a Federal employee?

Yes, you may sell Federal personal property to any Federal employee whose agency does not prohibit their employees from purchasing such property. However, unless allowed by Federal or agency regulations, employees having nonpublic information regarding property offered for sale may not participate in that sale (see 5 CFR 2635.703). For purposes of this section, the term "Federal employee" also applies to an immediate member of the employee's household.

§ 102–38.185 May we sell Federal personal property to State or local governments?

Yes, you may sell Federal personal property to State or local governments. Additional guidelines on sales to State or local governments are contained in subpart G of this part.

ACCEPTANCE OF BIDS

§ 102–38.190 What is considered a responsive bid?

A responsive bid is a bid that complies with the terms and conditions of the sales offering, and satisfies the requirements as to the method and timeliness of the submission. Only responsive bids may be considered for award.

§ 102–38.195 Must bidders use authorized bid forms?

No, bidders do not have to use authorized bid forms; however if a bidder uses his/her own bid form to submit a bid, the bid may be considered only if—

(a) The bidder accepts all the terms and conditions of the offer to sell; and

(b) Award of the bid would result in a binding contract.

§ 102–38.200 Who may accept bids?

Authorized agency representatives may accept bids for your agency. These individuals should meet your agency's requirements for approval of Government contracts.

§ 102–38.205 Must we accept all bids?

No, the Government reserves the right to accept or reject any or all bids. You may reject any or all bids when such action is advantageous to the Government, or when it is in the public interest to do so.

§ 102–38.210 What happens when bids have been rejected?

You may re-offer items for which all bids have been rejected at the same sale, if possible, or another sale.

§ 102–38.215 When may we disclose the bid results to the public?

You may disclose bid results to the public after the sales award of any item or lot of property. On occasions when there is open bidding, usually at a spot bid sale or auction, all bids are disclosed as they are submitted. No information other than names may be disclosed regarding the bidder(s).

§ 102–38.220 What must we do when the highest bids received have the same bid amount?

When the highest bids received have the same bid amount, you must consider other factors of the sale (e.g., timely removal of the property, terms of payment, etc.) that would make one offer more advantageous to the Government. However, if you are unable to make a determination based on available information, and the Government has an acceptable offer, you may re-offer the property for sale, or you may utilize random tiebreakers to avoid the expense of reselling the property.

§ 102–38.225 What are the additional requirements in the bid process?

All sales except fixed price sales must contain a certification of independent price determination. If there is suspicion of false certification or an indication of collusion, you must refer the matter to the Department of Justice or your agency's Office of the Inspector General.

BID DEPOSITS

§ 102–38.230 Is a bid deposit required to buy personal property?

No, a bid deposit is not required to buy personal property. However, should you require a bid deposit to protect the Government's interest, a deposit of 20 percent of the total amount of the bid is generally considered reasonable.

§ 102–38.235 What types of payment may we accept as bid deposits?

In addition to the acceptable types of payments in § 102–38.290, you may also accept a deposit bond. A deposit bond may be used in lieu of cash or other acceptable form of deposit when permitted by the offer to sell, such as the Standard Form (SF) 150, Deposit Bond—Individual Invitation, Sale of Government Personal Property, SF 151, Deposit Bond—Annual, Sale of Government Personal Property, and SF 28, Affidavit of Individual Surety. For information on how to obtain these forms, see § 102–2.135 of subchapter A.

§ 102–38.240 What happens to the deposit bond if the bidder defaults or wants to withdraw his/her bid?

(a) When a bid deposit is secured by a deposit bond and the bidder defaults, you must issue a notice of default to the bidder and the surety company.

(b) When a bid deposit is secured by a deposit bond and the bidder wants to withdraw his/her bid, you should return the deposit bond to the bidder.

LATE BIDS

§ 102–38.245 Do we consider late bids for award?

Consider late bids for award only when the bids were delivered timely to the address specified and your agency caused the delay in delivering the bids to the official designated to accept the bids.

§ 102–38.250 How do we handle late bids that are not considered?

Late bids that are not considered must be returned to the bidder promptly. You must not disclose information contained in returned bids.

MODIFICATION OR WITHDRAWAL OF BIDS

§ 102–38.255 May we allow a bidder to modify or withdraw a bid?

(a) Yes, a bidder may modify or withdraw a bid prior to the start of the sale or the time set for the opening of the bids. After the start of the sale, or the time set for opening the bids, the bidder will not be allowed to withdraw his/her bid.

(b) You may consider late modifications to an otherwise successful bid at any time, but only when it makes the terms of the bid more favorable to the Government.

MISTAKES IN BIDS

§ 102–38.260 Who makes the administrative determinations regarding mistakes in bids?

The administrative procedures for handling mistakes in bids are contained in FAR 14.407, Mistakes in Bids (48 CFR 14.407). Your agency head, or his/her designee, may delegate the authority to make administrative decisions regarding mistakes in bids to a central authority, or a limited number of authorities in your agency, who must not re-delegate this authority.

§ 102–38.265 Must we keep records on administrative determinations?

Yes, you must—

(a) Maintain records of all administrative determinations made, to include the pertinent facts and the action taken in each case. A copy of the determination must be attached to its corresponding contract; and

(b) Provide a signed copy of any related determination with the copy of the contract you file with the Comptroller General when requested.

§ 102–38.270 May a bidder protest the determinations made on sales of personal property?

Yes, protests regarding the validity or the determinations made on the sale of personal property may be submitted to the Comptroller General.

Subpart D—Completion of Sale

AWARDS

§ 102–38.275 To whom do we award the sales contract?

You must award the sales contract to the bidder with the highest responsive bid, unless a determination is made to reject the bid under § 102–38.205.

§ 102–38.280 What happens when there is no award?

When there is no award made, you may sell the personal property at another sale, or you may abandon or destroy it pursuant to § 102–36.305 of this subchapter B.

TRANSFER OF TITLE

§ 102–38.285 How do we transfer title from the Government to the buyer for personal property sold?

(a) Generally, no specific form or format is designated for transferring title from the Government to the buyer for personal property sold. For internal control and accountability, you must execute a bill of sale or another document as evidence of transfer of title or any other interest in Government personal property. You must also ensure that the buyer submits any additional certifications to comply with specific conditions and restrictions of the sale.

(b) For sales of vehicles, you must issue to the purchaser a Standard Form (SF) 97, the United States Government Certificate to Obtain Title to a Vehicle, or a SF 97A, the United States Government Certificate to Obtain a Non-Repairable or Salvage Certificate, as appropriate, as evidence of transfer of title. For information on how to obtain these forms, see § 102–2.135 of this chapter.

PAYMENTS

§ 102–38.290 What types of payment may we accept?

You must adopt a payment policy that protects the Government against fraud. Acceptable payments include, but are not limited to, the following:

(a) U.S. currency or any form of credit instrument made payable on demand in U.S. currency, e.g., cashier's check, money order. Promissory notes and postdated credit instruments are not acceptable.

(b) Irrevocable commercial letters of credit issued by a United States bank payable to the Treasurer of the United States or to the Government agency conducting the sale.

(c) Credit or debit cards.

DISPOSITION OF PROCEEDS

§ 102–38.295 May we retain sales proceeds?

(a) You may retain that portion of the sales proceeds, in accordance with your agreement with the holding agency, equal to your direct costs and reasonably related indirect costs (including your share of the Governmentwide costs to support the eFAS Internet portal and Governmentwide reporting requirements) incurred in selling personal property.

(b) A holding agency may retain that portion of the sales proceeds equal to its costs of care and handling directly related to the sale of personal property by the SC (e.g., shipment to the SC, storage pending sale, and inspection by prospective buyers).

(c) After accounting for amounts retained under paragraphs (a) and (b) of this section, as applicable, a holding agency may retain the balance of proceeds from the sale of its agency's personal property when—

(1) It has the statutory authority to retain all proceeds from sales of personal property;

(2) The property sold was acquired with non-appropriated funds as defined in § 102–36.40 of this subchapter B;

(3) The property sold was surplus Government property that was in the custody of a contractor or subcontractor, and the contract or subcontract provisions authorize the proceeds of sale to be credited to the price or cost of the contract or subcontract;

(4) The property was sold to obtain replacement property under the exchange/sale authority pursuant to part 102–39 of this subchapter B; or

(5) The property sold was related to waste prevention and recycling programs, under the authority of Section 607 of Public Law 107–67 (Omnibus Consolidated and Emergency Supplemental Appropriations Act, 1999, Pub. L. 107–67, 115 Stat. 514). Consult your General Counsel or Chief Financial Officer for guidance on use of this authority.

[73 FR 20803, Apr. 17, 2008]

§ 102–38.300 What happens to sales proceeds that neither we nor the holding agency are authorized to retain, or that are unused?

Any sales proceeds that are not retained pursuant to the authorities in § 102–38.295 must be deposited as miscellaneous receipts in the U.S. Treasury.

DISPUTES

§ 102–38.305 How do we handle disputes involved in the sale of Federal personal property?

First contact your Office of General Counsel. Further guidance can be found in the Contract Disputes Act of 1978, as amended (41 U.S.C. 601–613), and the Federal Acquisition Regulation (FAR) at 48 CFR part 33.

§ 102–38.310 Are we required to use the Disputes clause in the sale of personal property?

Yes, you must ensure the Disputes clause contained in Federal Acquisition Regulation (FAR) 52.233–1 (48 CFR part 52) is included in all offers to sell and contracts for the sale of personal property.

§ 102–38.315 Are we required to use Alternative Disputes Resolution for sales contracts?

No, you are not required to use Alternative Disputes Resolution (ADR) for sales contracts. However, you are encouraged to use ADR procedures in accordance with the authority and the requirements of the Alternative Disputes Resolution Act of 1998 (28 U.S.C. 651–658).

Subpart E—Other Governing Statutes

§ 102–38.320 Are there other statutory requirements governing the sale of Federal personal property?

Yes, in addition to Title 40 of the U.S. Code the sale of Federal personal property is governed by other statutory requirements, such as the Debt Collection Improvement Act of 1996 (Public Law 104–134, sec. 31001, 110 Stat. 1321–358) and antitrust requirements that are discussed in § 102–38.325.

ANTITRUST REQUIREMENTS

§ 102–38.325 What are the requirements pertaining to antitrust laws?

When the sale of personal property has an estimated fair market value of $3 million or more or if the sale involves a patent, process, technique, or invention, you must notify the Attorney General of the Department of Justice (DOJ) and get DOJ's opinion as to whether the sale would give the buyer an unfair advantage in the marketplace and violate any antitrust laws. Include in the notification the description and location of the property, method of sale and proposed selling price, and information on the proposed purchaser and intended use of the property. You must not complete the sale until you have received confirmation from the Attorney General that the proposed transaction would not violate any antitrust laws.

[68 FR 51421, Aug. 26, 2003; 68 FR 53219, Sept. 9, 2003]

Subpart F—Reporting Requirements

§102–38.330 Are there any reports that we must submit to the General Services Administration?

Yes, there are two sales reports you must submit to the General Services Administration (GSA), Personal Property Management Policy Division (MTP), 1800 F Street, NW., Washington, DC 20405—

(a) *Negotiated sales report.* Within 60 calendar days after the close of each fiscal year, you must provide GSA with a listing and description of all negotiated sales with an estimated fair market value in excess of $5,000 (see §102–38.115). For each negotiated sale that meets this criterion, provide the following:

(1) Description of the property (including quantity and condition).

(2) Acquisition cost and date (if not known, estimate and so indicate).

(3) Estimated fair market value (including date of estimate and name of estimator).

(4) Name and address of purchaser.

(5) Date of sale.

(6) Gross and net sales proceeds.

(7) Justification for conducting a negotiated sale.

(b) *Exchange/sale report.* Within 90 calendar days after the close of each fiscal year, you must provide a summary report to GSA of transactions conducted under the exchange/sale authority under part 102–39 of this subchapter B (see §102–39.75).

§102–38.335 Is there any additional personal property sales information that we must submit to the General Services Administration?

Yes, you must report to the General Services Administration's (GSA's) Asset Disposition Management System (ADMS), once that capability is established, any sales information that GSA deems necessary.

Subpart G—Provisions for State and Local Governments

§102–38.340 How may we sell personal property to State and local governments?

You may sell Government personal property to State and local governments through—

(a) Competitive sale to the public;

(b) Negotiated sale, through the appropriate State Agency for Surplus Property (SASP); or

(c) Negotiated sale at fixed price (fixed price sale), through the appropriate SASP. (This method of sale can be used prior to a competitive sale to the public, if desired.)

§102–38.345 Do we have to withdraw personal property advertised for public sale if a State Agency for Surplus Property wants to buy it?

No, you are not required to withdraw the item from public sale if the property has been advertised.

§102–38.350 Are there special provisions for State and local governments regarding negotiated sales?

Yes, you must waive the requirement for bid deposits and payment prior to removal of the property. However, payment must be made within 30 calendar days after purchase. If payment is not made within 30 days, you may charge simple interest at the rate established by the Secretary of the Treasury as provided in section 12 of the Contract Disputes Act of 1978 (41 U.S.C. 611), from the date of written demand for payment.

§ 102–38.355 Do the regulations of this part apply to State Agencies for Surplus Property (SASPs) when conducting sales?

Yes, State Agencies for Surplus Property (SASPs) must follow the regulations in this part when conducting sales on behalf of the General Services Administration of Government personal property in their custody.

Subpart H—Implementation of the Federal Asset Sales Program

Source: 73 FR 20803, Apr. 17, 2008, unless otherwise noted.

§ 102–38.360 What must an executive agency do to implement the eFAS program?

(a) An executive agency must review the effectiveness of all sales solutions, and compare them to the effectiveness (e.g., cost, level of service, and value added services) of the eFAS SCs. Agencies should give full consideration to sales solutions utilizing private sector entities, including small businesses, that are more effective than the solutions provided by any eFAS-approved SC. If the agency decides that there are more effective sales solutions than those solutions offered by the eFAS SCs, the agency must request a waiver from the milestones using the procedures and forms provided by the eFAS Planning Office. Waivers will be approved by the eFAS Planning Office upon presentation of a business case showing that complying with an eFAS milestone is either impracticable or inefficient. Waiver approval will be coordinated with GSA's Office of Travel, Transportation, and Asset Management. Contact the eFAS Planning Office at *FASPlanningOffice@gsa.gov* to obtain these procedures and forms.

(b) An approved waiver for meeting one of the eFAS milestones does not automatically waive all milestone requirements. For example, if an agency receives a waiver to the migration milestone, the agency must still (1) post asset information on the eFAS Web site and (2) provide post-sales data to the eFAS Planning Office in accordance with the content and format requirements developed by the eFAS ESC, unless waivers to these milestones are also requested and approved. Waivers to the eFAS milestones will not be permanent. Upon expiration of the waiver to the migration milestone, an agency must either migrate to an approved SC, or serve as a fully functioning SC, as soon as practicable. See the definition of a "Sales Center" at § 102–38.35 for an overview of how agency sales solutions become SCs.

(c) An agency which receives a waiver from the eFAS milestones must comply with subparts A through G of this part as if it were an SC.

(d) An executive agency must comply with all eFAS milestones approved by OMB including those regarding the completion of an agency-wide sales migration plan, the reporting of pre- and post-sales data, and the migration to approved SCs unless a waiver has been submitted by the agency and approved by the eFAS Planning Office. The eFAS milestones are available for viewing at *http://www.gsa.gov/govsalesmilestones*.

§ 102–38.365 Is a holding agency required to report property in "scrap" condition to its selected SC?

No. Property which has no value except for its basic material content (scrap material) may be disposed of by the holding agency by sale or as otherwise provided in § 102–38.70. However, the holding agency should consult the SC(s) selected by the holding agency as to the feasibility of selling the scrap material. Agencies selling scrap property under authority of this subpart are still required to report sales metrics in accordance with eFAS ESC-approved format and content.

§ 102–38.370 What does a holding agency do with property which cannot be sold by its SC?

All reasonable efforts must be afforded the SC to sell the property. If the property remains unsold after the time frame agreed to between the SC and the holding agency, the holding agency may dispose of the property by sale or as otherwise provided in § 102–38.70. The lack of public interest in buying the property is evidence that the sales proceeds would be minimal.

Agencies selling property under authority of this subpart are still required to report sales metrics in accordance with eFAS ESC-approved format and content.

PART 102–39—REPLACEMENT OF PERSONAL PROPERTY PURSUANT TO THE EXCHANGE/SALE AUTHORITY

Subpart A—General

AUTHORITY: 40 U.S.C. 121(c); 40 U.S.C. 503.

SOURCE: 66 FR 48614, Sept. 21, 2001, unless otherwise noted.

Subpart A—General

§ 102–39.5 What is the exchange/sale authority?

The exchange/sale authority is a statutory provision, (40 U.S.C. 503), which states in part: "In acquiring personal property, an executive agency may exchange or sell similar items and may apply the exchange allowance or proceeds of sale in whole or in part payment for the property acquired."

[73 FR 50880, Aug. 29, 2008]

§ 102–39.10 What does this part cover?

This part covers the exchange/sale authority, and applies to all personal property owned by executive agencies worldwide. For the exchange/sale of aircraft parts and hazardous materials, you must meet the requirements in this part and in parts 101–33 and 101–42 of this title.

[66 FR 48614, Sept. 21, 2001, as amended at 69 FR 11539, Mar. 11, 2004]

§ 102–39.15 How are the terms "I" and "you" used in this part?

Use of pronouns "I" and "you" throughout this part refer to executive agencies.

[66 FR 48614, Sept. 21, 2001. Redesignated at 73 FR 50880, Aug. 29, 2008]

§ 102–39.20 What definitions apply to this part?

The following definitions apply to this part:

Acquire means to procure or otherwise obtain personal property, including by lease (sometimes known as rent).

Combat material means arms, ammunition, and implements of war listed in the U.S. munitions list (22 CFR part 121).

Excess property means any personal property under the control of any Federal agency that is no longer required for that agency's needs or responsibilities, as determined by the agency head or designee.

Exchange means to replace personal property by trade or trade-in with the supplier of the replacement property.

Exchange/sale means to exchange or sell non-excess, non-surplus personal property and apply the exchange allowance or proceeds of sale in whole or in part payment for the acquisition of similar property.

Executive agency means any executive department or independent establishment in the executive branch of the Government, including any wholly owned Government corporation.

Federal agency means any executive agency or any establishment in the legislative or judicial branch of the Government (except the Senate, the House of Representatives, and the Architect of the Capitol and any activities under his/her direction).

Historic item means property having added value for display purposes because its historical significance is greater than its fair market value for continued use. Items that are commonly available and remain in use for their intended purpose, such as military aircraft still in use by active or reserve units, are not historic items.

Replacement means the process of acquiring personal property to be used in place of personal property that is still needed but:

(1) No longer adequately performs the tasks for which it is used; or

(2) Does not meet the agency's need as well as the personal property to be acquired.

Service Life Extension Program (SLEP) means the modification of a personal property item undertaken to extend the life of the item beyond that which was previously planned. SLEPs extend capital asset life by retrofit, major modification, remanufacturing, betterment, or enhancement.

Similar means the acquired item(s) and replaced item(s):

(1) Are identical; or

(2) Fall within a single Federal Supply Classification (FSC) Group of property (includes any and all forms of property within a single FSC Group); or

(3) Are parts or containers for similar end items; or

(4) Are designed or constructed for the same purpose (includes any and all forms of property regardless of the FSC Group to which they are assigned).

Surplus property means excess personal property not required for the needs of any Federal agency, as determined by GSA under part 102–37 of this chapter.

[66 FR 48614, Sept. 21, 2001, as amended at 73 FR 50880, Aug. 29, 2008]

§ 102–39.25 Which exchange/sale provisions are subject to deviation?

All of the provisions in this part are subject to deviation (upon presentation of adequate justification) except those mandated by statute. See the link on "Exchange/Sale" at *www.gsa.gov/personalpropertypolicy* for additional information on requesting deviations from this part.

[73 FR 50880, Aug. 29, 2008]

§ 102–39.30 How do I request a deviation from this part?

See part 102–2 of this chapter (41 CFR part 102–2) to request a deviation from the requirements of this part.

[73 FR 50880, Aug. 29, 2008]

Subpart B—Exchange/Sale Considerations

§ 102–39.35 When should I consider using the exchange/sale authority?

You should consider using the exchange/sale authority when replacing personal property.

[73 FR 50880, Aug. 29, 2008]

§ 102–39.40 Why should I consider using the exchange/sale authority?

You should consider using the exchange/sale authority to reduce the cost of replacement personal property. When you have personal property that is wearing out or obsolete and must be replaced, you should consider either exchanging or selling that property and using the exchange allowance or sales proceeds to offset the cost of the replacement personal property. Conversely, if you choose not to replace the property using the exchange/sale authority, you may declare it as excess and dispose of it through the normal disposal process as addressed in part 102–36 of this chapter. Keep in mind, however, that any net proceeds from the eventual sale of that property as surplus generally must be forwarded to the miscellaneous receipts account at the United States Treasury and thus would not be available to you. You may use the exchange/sale authority in the acquisition of personal property even if the acquisition is under a services contract, as long as the property acquired under the services contract is similar to the property exchanged or sold (e.g., for a SLEP, exchange allowances or sales proceeds would be available for replacement of similar items, but not for services).

[73 FR 50880, Aug. 29, 2008]

§ 102–39.45 When should I not use the exchange/sale authority?

You should not use the exchange/sale authority if the exchange allowance or estimated sales proceeds for the property will be unreasonably low. You must either abandon or destroy such property, or declare the property excess, in accordance with part 102–36 of this chapter. Further, you must not use the exchange/sale authority if the transaction(s) would violate any other applicable statute or regulation.

[66 FR 48614, Sept. 21, 2001, as amended at 69 FR 11539, Mar. 11, 2004. Redesignated at 73 FR 50880, Aug. 29, 2008]

§ 102–39.50 How do I determine whether to do an exchange or a sale?

You must determine whether an exchange or sale will provide the greater return for the Government. When estimating the return under each method, consider all related administrative and overhead costs.

[66 FR 48614, Sept. 21, 2001. Redesignated at 73 FR 50880, Aug. 29, 2008]

§ 102–39.55 When should I offer property I am exchanging or selling under the exchange/sale authority to other Federal agencies or State Agencies for Surplus Property (SASP)?

If you have property to replace which is eligible for exchange/sale, you should first, to the maximum extent practicable, solicit:

(a) Federal agencies known to use or distribute such property. If a Federal agency is interested in acquiring and paying for the property, you should arrange for a reimbursable transfer. Reimbursable transfers may also be conducted with the Senate, the House of Representatives, the Architect of the Capitol and any activities under the Architect's direction, the District of Columbia, and mixed-ownership Government corporations. When conducting a reimbursable transfer, you must:

(1) Do so under terms mutually agreeable to you and the recipient.

(2) Not require reimbursement of an amount greater than the estimated fair market value of the transferred property.

(3) Apply the transfer proceeds in whole or part payment for property acquired to replace the transferred property; and

(b) State Agencies for Surplus Property (SASPs) known to have an interest in acquiring such property. If a SASP is interested in acquiring the property, you should consider selling it to the SASP by negotiated sale at fixed price under the conditions specified at § 102–38.125 of this title. The sales proceeds must be applied in whole or part payment for property acquired to replace the transferred property.

[66 FR 48614, Sept. 21, 2001, as amended at 69 FR 11539, Mar. 11, 2004. Redesignated at 73 FR 50880, Aug. 29, 2008]

§ 102–39.60 What restrictions and prohibitions apply to the exchange/sale of personal property?

Unless a deviation is requested of and approved by GSA as addressed in part 102–2 of this chapter and the provisions of §§ 102–39.25 and 102–39.30, you must not use the exchange/sale authority for:

(a) The following FSC groups of personal property:

10 Weapons.

11 Nuclear ordnance.

42 Firefighting, rescue, and safety equipment.

44 Nuclear reactors (FSC Class 4470 only).

51 Hand tools.

54 Prefabricated structure and scaffolding (FSC Class 5410 Prefabricated and Portable Buildings, FSC Class 5411 Rigid Wall Shelters, and FSC Class 5419 Collective Modular Support System only).

68 Chemicals and chemical products, except medicinal chemicals.

84 Clothing, individual equipment, and insignia.

NOTE TO § 102–39.60(a): Under no circumstances will deviations be granted for FSC Class 1005, Guns through 30mm. Deviations are not required for Department of Defense (DoD) property in FSC Groups 10 (for classes other than FSC Class 1005), 12 and 14 for which the applicable DoD demilitarization requirements, and any other applicable regulations and statutes are met.

(b) Materials in the National Defense Stockpile (50 U.S.C. 98–98h) or the Defense Production Act inventory (50 U.S.C. App. 2093).

(c) Nuclear Regulatory Commission-controlled materials unless you meet the requirements of § 101–42.1102–4 of this title.

(d) Controlled substances, unless you meet the requirements of § 101–42.1102–3 of this title.

(e) Property with a condition code of scrap, as defined at FMR 102–36.40, except:

(1) Property that had utility and value at the point in time when a determination was made to use the exchange/sale authority;

(2) Property that was otherwise eligible for exchange/sale, but was coded as scrap due to damage (e.g., accident or natural disaster); or

(3) Scrap gold for fine gold.

(f) Property that was originally acquired as excess or forfeited property or from another source other than new procurement, unless such property has been in official use by the acquiring agency for at least 1 year. You may exchange or sell forfeited property in official use for less than 1 year if the head of your agency determines that a continuing valid requirement exists, but the specific item in use no longer meets that requirement, and that exchange or sale meets all other requirements of this part.

(g) Property that is dangerous to public health or safety without first rendering such property innocuous or providing for adequate safeguards as part of the exchange/sale;

(h) Combat material without demilitarizing it or obtaining a demilitarization waiver or other necessary clearances from the Department of Defense Demilitarization Office.

(i) Flight Safety Critical Aircraft Parts (FSCAP) and Critical Safety Items (CSI) unless you meet the provisions of § 102–33.370 of this title.

(j) Acquisition of unauthorized replacement property.

(k) Acquisition of replacement property that violates any:

(1) Restriction on procurement of a commodity or commodities;

(2) Replacement policy or standard prescribed by the President, the Congress, or the Administrator of General Services; or

(3) Contractual obligation.

(1) Vessels subject to 40 U.S.C. 548.

(m) Aircraft and aircraft parts, unless there is full compliance with all exchange/sale provisions in part 102–33 of this chapter (41 CFR part 102–33).

[66 FR 48614, Sept. 21, 2001; 66 FR 51095, Oct. 5, 2001, as amended at 69 FR 11539, Mar. 11, 2004; 71 FR 20900, Apr. 24, 2006. Redesignated at 73 FR 50880, Aug. 29, 2008; 75 FR 24820, May 6, 2010; 76 FR 67372, Nov. 1, 2011]

§ 102–39.65 What conditions apply to the exchange/sale of personal property?

You may use the exchange/sale authority only if you meet all of the following conditions:

(a) The property exchanged or sold is similar to the property acquired;

(b) The property exchanged or sold is not excess or surplus and you have a continuing need for similar property;

(c) The property exchanged or sold was not acquired for the principal purpose of exchange or sale;

(d) When replacing personal property, the exchange allowance or sales proceeds from the disposition of that property may only be used to offset the cost of the replacement property, not services; and

(e) Except for transactions involving books and periodicals in your libraries, you document the basic facts associated with each exchange/sale transaction. At a minimum, the documentation must include:

(1) The FSC Group of the items exchanged or sold, and the items acquired;

(2) The number of items exchanged or sold, and the number of items acquired;

(3) The acquisition cost and exchange allowance or net sales proceeds of the items exchanged or sold, and the acquisition cost of the items acquired;

(4) The date of the transaction(s);

(5) The parties involved; and

(6) A statement that the transactions comply with the requirements of this part 102–39.

NOTE TO § 102–39.65: In acquiring items for historical preservation or display at Federal museums, you may exchange historic items in the museum property account without regard to the FSC group, provided the exchange transaction is documented and certified by the head of your agency to be in the best interests of the Government and all other provisions of this part are met. The documentation must contain a determination that the item exchanged and the item acquired are historic items.

[73 FR 50881, Aug. 29, 2008]

Subpart C—Exchange/Sale Methods and Reports

§ 102–39.70 What are the exchange methods?

Exchange of property may be accomplished by either of the following methods:

(a) The supplier (e.g., a Government agency, commercial or private organization, or an individual) delivers the replacement property to one of your organizational units and removes the property being replaced from that same organizational unit.

(b) The supplier delivers the replacement property to one of your organizational units and removes the property being replaced from a different organizational unit.

[66 FR 48614, Sept. 21, 2001. Redesignated at 73 FR 50880, Aug. 29, 2008]

§ 102–39.75 What are the sales methods?

(a) You must use the methods, terms, and conditions of sale, and the forms prescribed in part 102–38 of this title, in the sale of property being replaced, except for the provisions of §§ 102–38.100 through 102–38.115 of this title regarding negotiated sales. Section 3709, Revised Statutes (41 U.S.C. 5), specifies the following conditions under which property being replaced can be sold by negotiation, subject to obtaining such competition as is feasible:

(1) The reasonable value involved in the contract does not exceed $500; or

(2) Otherwise authorized by law.

(b) You may sell property being replaced by negotiation at fixed prices in accordance with the provisions of § 102–38.120 and 102–38.125 of this title.

[66 FR 48614, Sept. 21, 2001, as amended at 69 FR 11539, Mar. 11, 2004. Redesignated at 73 FR 50880, Aug. 29, 2008]

§ 102–39.80 What are the accounting requirements for exchange allowances or proceeds of sale?

You must account for exchange allowances or proceeds of sale in accordance with the general finance and accounting rules applicable to you. Except as otherwise authorized by law, all exchange allowances or proceeds of sale under this part will be available during the fiscal year in which the property was exchanged or sold and for one fiscal year thereafter for the purchase of replacement property. Any proceeds of sale not applied to replacement purchases during this time must be deposited in the United States Treasury as miscellaneous receipts.

[73 FR 50881, Aug. 29, 2008, as amended at 75 FR 24820, May 6, 2010]

§ 102–39.85 What information am I required to report?

(a) You must submit, within 90 calendar days after the close of each fiscal year, a summary report in a format of your choice on the exchange/sale transactions made under this part during the fiscal year (except for transactions involving books and periodicals in your libraries). The report must include:

(1) A list by Federal Supply Classification Group of property sold under this part showing the:

(i) Number of items sold;

(ii) Acquisition cost; and

(iii) Net proceeds.

(2) A list by Federal Supply Classification Group of property exchanged under this part showing the:

(i) Number of items exchanged;

(ii) Acquisition cost; and

(iii) Exchange allowance.

(b) Submit your report electronically or by mail to the General Services Administration, Office of Travel, Transportation and Asset Management (MT), 1800 F Street, NW., Washington, DC 20405.

(c) Report control number: 1528–GSA–AN.

(d) If you make no transactions under this part during a fiscal year, you must submit a report stating that no transactions occurred.

[66 FR 48614, Sept. 21, 2001, as amended at 71 FR 20900, Apr. 24, 2006. Redesignated at 73 FR 50880, Aug. 29, 2008]

PART 102–40—UTILIZATION AND DISPOSITION OF PERSONAL PROPERTY WITH SPECIAL HANDLING REQUIREMENTS

Subpart A—General Provisions

Subpart B—Responsibilities

Subpart C—Transfer and Donation of Personal Property With Special Handling Requirements

Subpart D—Sale of Personal Property With Special Handling Requirements

Subpart E—Categories of Personal Property With Special Handling Requirements

AUTHORITY: 40 U.S.C. 121(c).

SOURCE: 80 FR 7353, Feb. 10, 2015, unless otherwise noted.

Subpart A—General Provisions

§ 102–40.5   What does this part cover?

This part provides guidance regarding the utilization, transfer, donation, sale, and other disposal of Government personal property with special handling requirements (*i.e.,* hazardous materials, dangerous property, etc.) located in the United States, the District of Columbia, the U.S. Virgin Islands, American Samoa, Guam, Puerto Rico, the Northern Mariana Islands, Federated States of Micronesia, the Marshall Islands, and Palau. For guidance regarding the disposal of personal property located outside of these areas, see §§ 102–36.380 through 102–36.400 of this subchapter; however, the disposal of personal property located outside of these areas should conform to the provisions in this part, whenever feasible, in the interest of promoting safety, security, and environmental stewardship.

§ 102–40.10   What is the governing authority for this part?

40 U.S.C. 121(c) authorizes the Administrator of General Services to prescribe regulations necessary to perform functions under this part.

§ 102–40.15   Who must comply with the provisions in this part?

All executive agencies must comply with the provisions of this part unless authorized by specific, separate statutory authority to do otherwise. Also, pursuant to 40 U.S.C. 549(b)(1), state agencies for surplus property (SASPs) must comply with the provisions of this part related to the donation of surplus property with special handling requirements. Legislative and judicial agencies are encouraged to follow these provisions.

§ 102–40.20   To whom do "we," "you," and their variants refer?

The pronouns "we," "you," and their variants throughout this part refer to the executive agency, or other entity using these regulations, unless otherwise indicated.

§ 102–40.25   How do we request a deviation from these requirements and who can approve it?

See §§ 102–2.60 through 102–2.110 of this chapter to request a deviation from the requirements of this part.

DEFINITIONS

§ 102–40.30   What definitions apply to this part?

The following definitions apply to this part:

Acid-contaminated property means property that may cause burns or toxicosis when improperly handled due to acid residues adhering to or trapped within the material.

Ammunition as defined in 18 U.S.C. 921(a)(17), means ammunition or cartridge cases, primers, bullets, or propellant powder designed for use in any firearm.

Ammunition components means the individual parts of ammunition, including cartridge cases, primers, bullets/projectiles, and propellant powder.

Biologicals means hazardous materials associated with the products and operations of applied biology and/or biochemistry, especially serums, vaccines, etc., produced from microorganisms.

Certified electronic product means any electronic product which bears the manufacturer's certification label or tag (21 CFR 1010.2) indicating that the product meets applicable radiation safety performance standards prescribed by the Food and Drug Administration (FDA) under 21 CFR part 1020.

Commerce Control List Item (CCLI) means property identified on the Commerce Control List (15 CFR part 774, supp. 1) subject to export controls under the Export Administration Act of 1979, as amended (50 App. U.S.C. 2401–2420) and implemented by the Export Administration Regulations (15 CFR part 730). Items may be placed on the list for reasons including, but not limited to, technology transfer, scarcity of materials, crime control, and national security.

Controlled substances means—

(1) Any narcotic, depressant, stimulant, or hallucinogenic drug, or any other drug or substance included in Schedules I, II, III, IV, or V of section 202 of the Controlled Substances Act (21 U.S.C. 812), except exempt chemical preparations and mixtures and excluded substances contained in 21 CFR part 1308; or

(2) Any other drug or substance that the Attorney General determines to be subject to control under Subchapter I of the Controlled Substances Act (21 U.S.C. 801, *et seq.*); or

(3) Any other drug or substance that by international treaty, convention, or protocol is to be controlled by the United States.

Demilitarization means, as defined by the Department of Defense (DOD) in the Defense Material Disposition Manual, DOD 4160.21–M, to be the act of destroying the military offensive or defensive advantages inherent in certain types of equipment or material. The term includes mutilation, dumping at sea, scrapping, melting, burning, or alteration designed to prevent the further use of this equipment and material for its originally intended military or lethal purpose and applies equally to material in unserviceable or serviceable condition that has been screened through an Inventory Control Point and declared excess or foreign excess.

Electronic Product means any item powered by electricity that has logic circuitry enabling the item to perform its intended function.

Explosive-contaminated property means property that may ignite or explode when exposed to shock, flame, sparks, or other high temperature sources due to residual explosive material in joints, angles, cracks, or around bolts.

Extremely hazardous material means property hazardous to the extent that it generally requires special handling such as licensing and training of handlers, protective clothing, and special containers and storage. Because of its extreme flammability, toxicity, corrosivity or other perilous qualities, it could constitute an immediate danger or threat to life and property and which usually have specialized uses under controlled conditions. It is also material which have been determined by the holding agency to endanger public health and safety or the environment if released to the general public.

Firearm, as defined in 18 U.S.C. 921(a)(3), means:

(1) Any weapon (including a starter gun) which will or is designed to or may readily be converted to expel a projectile by the action of an explosive;

(2) The frame or receiver of any such weapon;

(3) Any firearm muffler or firearm silencer; or

(4) Any destructive device. Such term does not include an antique firearm.

Hazardous material means property that is deemed a *hazardous material*, chemical substance or mixture, or hazardous waste under the Federal *hazardous materials* transportation law (49 U.S.C. 5101, *et seq.*), the Resource Conservation and Recovery Act (RCRA) (42 U.S.C. 6901, *et seq.*), or the Toxic Substances Control Act (TSCA) (15 U.S.C. 2601, *et seq.*). Generally, *hazardous materials* have one or more of the following characteristics:

(1) Are carcinogens (according to Occupational Safety and Health Administration (OSHA) regulations at 29 CFR part 1910), toxic or highly toxic agents, reproductive toxins, irritants, corrosives, hepatotoxins, nephrotoxins, neurotoxins, agents that act on the hematopoietic system, and agents that damage the lungs, skin, eyes, or mucous membranes;

(2) Are combustible liquids, compressed gases, explosives, flammable

liquids, flammable solids, organic per-oxides, oxidizers, pyrophorics, unstable (reactive) or water-reactive;

(3) Are radioactive to the extent it requires special handling;

(4) Identify hazards on associated SDS, MSDS, or HMIS documentation;

(5) Possess special characteristics which, in the opinion of the holding agency, could be hazardous to health, safety, or the environment if improperly handled, stored, transported, disposed of, or otherwise improperly used.

(6) Materials that, in the course of normal handling, use or storage, may produce or release dusts, gases, fumes, vapors, mists or smoke having any of the above characteristics.

Hazardous waste means those materials or substances, the handling and disposal of which are governed by 40 CFR part 261. Hazardous materials generally become *hazardous wastes* when they are no longer suitable for their intended or valid alternate purpose, or for resource recovery. Some solid (non-hazardous) wastes are predetermined *hazardous wastes* upon generation (40 CFR part 261, subpart D); some are determined *hazardous wastes* when they exhibit ignitability, corrosivity, reactivity, or extraction procedure toxicity. Hazardous materials having an expired shelf life should be reclassified as *hazardous waste* if required by Federal and/or state environmental laws or regulations. Before reclassification, the shelf life may be extended if supported by results of tests and recertification performed by authorized personnel in accordance with applicable regulations.

Lead-containing paint means paint or other similar surface coating material containing lead or lead compounds in excess of 0.06 percent of the weight of the total nonvolatile content of the paint or the weight of the dried paint film.

Medical device means any health-care product that does not achieve its principal intended purposes by chemical action in or on the body or by being metabolized. *Medical devices* are categorized in the Federal Food, Drug, and Cosmetic Act (21 U.S.C. 301, *et seq.*). Potential hazards of these devices include chemical and heavy metal hazards, and biohazards.

Munitions List Item (MLI) means property and related technical data designated as defense articles and defense services pursuant to sections 2778 and 2794(7) of the Arms Export Control Act (22 U.S.C. 2778 and 2794(7)).

Noncertified Electronic Product means any electronic product for which there is an applicable radiation safety performance standard prescribed or hereafter prescribed by the FDA under 21 CFR part 1020, and which the manufacturer has not certified as meeting such standard. The non-certification may be due to either:

(1) Manufacture of the product before the effective date of the standard; or

(2) The product was exempted from the applicable standard and is so labeled.

Nuclear Regulatory Commission-Controlled Material means material subject to the controls of the Nuclear Regulatory Commission (NRC) pursuant to the Energy Reorganization Act of 1974. The materials are defined as follows:

(1) *Byproduct material.* Any radioactive material (except special nuclear material) yielded in or made radioactive by exposure to the radiation, incident to the process of producing or utilizing special nuclear material. (See 10 CFR part 30).

(2) *Source material.* Uranium or thorium, or any combination thereof, in any physical or chemical form or ores which contain by weight, one-twentieth of one percent (0.05%) or more of uranium, thorium, or any combination thereof. Source material does not include special nuclear material. (See 10 CFR part 40).

(3) *Special nuclear material.* Plutonium, uranium 233, uranium enriched in the isotope 233 or in the isotope 235, any other materials which the NRC, pursuant to the Atomic Energy Act of 1954 (42 U.S.C. 2011, *et seq.*), including any amendments thereto, determined to be special nuclear material, or any material artificially enriched by any of the foregoing, but does not include source material. (See 10 CFR part 70).

Perishable means an item subject to rapid deterioration, spoilage or death, when removed from special storage conditions or care, such as fresh food, animals, and plants.

Precious metal means gold, silver, and platinum group metals (platinum, palladium, iridium, rhodium, osmium, and ruthenium).

Radiation Safety Performance Standards. Certain electronic items or components emitting hazardous electronic radiation are subject to performance standards (21 CFR part 1020). You must follow FDA policies related to acquisition, use, and disposal of items identified by the FDA or other authority for which performance standards are established. See 21 CFR 1000.15 for examples of electronic items that are required to follow *radiation safety performance standards.* Several types of electronic radiation (and examples of items that may emit that type of radiation) include: ionizing electromagnetic radiation (television receivers); ultraviolet electromagnetic radiation (tanning and therapeutic lamps); infrared and microwave electromagnetic radiation (certain alarm systems); and, laser emissions (certain cauterizing, burning, and welding devices).

Reagent means any hazardous material used to detect or measure another substance or to convert one substance into another by means of the reactions it causes.

Safety Data Sheet (SDS) means the documentation, as required by 29 CFR 1910.1200, identifying the potential hazards associated with the specific category of product or property. Sources of SDS information may be the manufacturer, distributor, or the procuring agency. Related documentation, such as a Material Safety Data Sheet (MSDS) may also provide information on hazards associated with assets handled under this part.

Universal Waste(s) mean(s) any of the following hazardous waste that is/are managed under the universal waste requirements of 40 CFR part 273:

(1) Batteries as described in 40 CFR 273.2;

(2) Pesticides as described in 40 CFR 273.3;

(3) Mercury-containing equipment (including thermostats) as described in 40 CFR 273.4 and as defined at 40 CFR 273.9; and

(4) Light bulbs containing mercury (such as fluorescent bulbs) as described in 40 CFR 273.5.

Subpart B—Responsibilities

§ 102–40.35 What types of personal property require special handling?

Personal property requiring special handling includes property containing hazardous materials or property which exhibits dangerous characteristics such that improper use, storage, transportation or disposal may lead to potential safety, health, environmental, economic, or national security risks. In many situations, the use, storage, transportation or disposal of these items is governed by Federal, state, and local laws. Personal property requiring special handling may also include animals and plants which may perish if not handled appropriately, as well as perishable products that may lose their utility if not handled appropriately.

§ 102–40.40 What are our responsibilities concerning personal property requiring special handling?

You are responsible for—

(a) Identifying and accounting for property with special handling requirements;

(b) Complying with applicable Federal, state, and local laws and regulations concerning the handling, storage, labeling, use, and final disposition of such property;

(c) Ensuring adequate storage and safeguarding of such property, *e.g.,* secured or limited access storage areas, warning signs, and protective clothing and equipment; and

(d) Transporting materials requiring special handling in accordance with Department of Transportation (DOT), EPA, state and local regulations.

§ 102–40.45 What must we do when we have identified personal property with special handling requirements?

You must properly mark, tag, or label personal property with special handling requirements in accordance with applicable Federal law, including the Occupational Safety and Health Administration requirements (29 CFR

1910.1200), regarding the actual or potential hazard associated with the property, and ensure that such information is maintained and perpetuated in the official agency property records. Labeling requirements for substances that are excluded from the requirements of 29 CFR 1910.1200 are found in the references listed in 29 CFR 1910.1200(b)(5) and (6).

§102–40.50 What must we do when we no longer need personal property with special handling requirements?

Except for the items listed in §102–40.55, you must report excess personal property with special handling requirements that you no longer need to GSA for Federal and donation screening (see §102–36.215 of this subchapter for how to report excess personal property to GSA). The report to GSA must clearly identify property requiring special handling, and all related hazards, precautions, and handling requirements related to this property. You must dispose of property not required to be reported to GSA in accordance with applicable Federal, state, and local laws and regulations, and your agency procedures. See §102–40.125 for policy regarding disposal of property requiring special handling by abandonment or destruction. Disposal must be accomplished so as to preserve as much as possible, any civilian utility or commercial value of the property.

§102–40.55 Do we report all excess personal property with special handling requirements to GSA?

No. Because of their characteristics, certain items are not subject to the usual disposal procedures. You are not required to report to GSA excess personal property with special handling requirements in any of the following categories listed below.

(a) *Extremely hazardous personal property.* You must dispose of extremely hazardous personal property not reported to GSA in accordance with applicable demilitarization requirements, EPA regulations, state and local laws or regulations, and other Federal laws, regulations or guidelines. However, if time and circumstances permit, this material may be reported to GSA to optimize use of this already-acquired material. When an item that is determined to be extremely hazardous property becomes excess, the holding agency should notify the appropriate GSA regional personal property office, which will determine if the property should be reported using Report of Excess Personal Property, Standard Form (SF) 120 or another method. At a minimum, you must identify the item, and describe the actual or potential hazard(s) associated with the handling, storage, or use of the item(s). This GSA regional office will determine the utilization, donation, sales or other disposal requirements, and provide appropriate guidance to the holding agency.

(b) *Hazardous wastes.* You must dispose of hazardous wastes not reported to GSA in accordance with applicable demilitarization requirements, EPA regulations, state and local laws or regulations, and other Federal laws, regulations or guidelines.

(c) *Perishables.* You may dispose of perishables with no further utility by abandonment or destruction when it is not detrimental to public health or safety (see the abandonment/destruction provisions in §102–40.125 and in part 102–36 of this subchapter). Although there is no requirement to report perishables to GSA if their spoilage is imminent (see §102–36.220), perishables that have a longer time before spoilage and are clearly able to be used may be reported to GSA in accordance with part 102–36. When reporting perishables to GSA, you should annotate the Report for Excess Personal Property, SF 120 or electronic reporting form to show whether there is a specific expiration date for the perishable item and whether such date is an original or extended date.

(d) *EPA research and cleanup materials.* The EPA, under its independent authority, may transfer accountability for hazardous materials deemed by EPA to be research materials to Federal, state, and local agencies, research institutions, or commercial businesses to conduct research or to clean-up a contaminated site.

§102–40.60 May we reassign hazardous materials?

Yes, when hazardous materials are reassigned within an executive agency, information on the actual or potential hazard must be included in the documentation effecting the reassignment, and the recipient organization must perpetuate in the inventory or control records visibility of the nature of the actual or potential hazard.

§ 102–40.65 Who is responsible for the custody of hazardous materials and property requiring special handling?

The holding agency is responsible for the custody of hazardous materials and property requiring special handling. Custody of these items may be transferred in whole or in part to another Federal agency with that receiving agency's consent.

§ 102–40.70 Who is responsible for the care and handling of hazardous materials and property requiring special handling?

(a) The holding agency is responsible for the care and handling of hazardous materials and property requiring special handling until the time the property has:

(1) Completed the disposal process; and

(2) Been transferred, donated, sold or destroyed, as authorized by this part. The nature of this material may require extra precautions, processes or equipment, thereby increasing the cost of care and handling. The costs associated with performing care and handling may be charged to the Federal agency or donation recipient in accordance with § 102–40.95.

(b) When transferring personal property to another federal agency, failure to disclose hazards or special handling requirements may result in the transferring agency being liable for additional costs incurred by the recipient agency, when authorized by applicable law and policy.

Subpart C—Transfer and Donation of Personal Property With Special Handling Requirements

§ 102–40.75 What must we do when reporting excess personal property with special handling requirements?

You must include with your report of excess personal property a complete description of the characteristics of the property, use or disposal restrictions, and the actual or potential hazard(s) associated with the use, handling, or storage of the item. You should include a Safety Data Sheet (SDS), Material Safety Data Sheet (MSDS), or Hazardous Material Information System (HMIS) record (or equivalent) if available. The physical item which requires special handling must also be marked so as to identify its special characteristic(s).

§ 102–40.80 Is personal property requiring special handling available for transfer or donation?

Generally, yes, with the exceptions contained in this part, personal property requiring special handling is available for transfer or donation in accordance with parts 102–36 and 102–37 of this subchapter, respectively. Surplus personal property identified as hazardous material not required for transfer as excess personal property to Federal agencies should normally be made available for donation. However, state agencies should not acquire hazardous materials without first ensuring that there are known eligible donees for such property. Moreover, all transfer and donation documents must include a complete description of the actual or potential hazard(s) associated with the handling, storage, use, or disposal of the item. Also, any continuing restrictions or instructions must be clearly identified on these documents.

§ 102–40.85 Is donee certification required for the donation of personal property requiring special handling?

Yes, the transfer document must contain a full description of the actual or potential hazard(s) and restriction(s) associated with the handling, storage, use, transportation or disposal of the item. GSA will not approve a donation to a State Agency for Surplus Property (SASP) unless an eligible donee has been identified. This subpart does not prohibit a SASP from bringing an item requiring special handling into its warehouse or other place of storage, provided that this storage is of a temporary nature, that the storage arrangement is agreeable to all parties involved in the donation, and that the storage location has the necessary facilities, gear, and trained personnel to handle, store, protect, and transport the property. In addition, the following certification (or an equivalent) must be signed by the donee:

I (We), the undersigned, hereby certify that the donee has knowledge and understanding of the nature of the property hereby donated which requires special handling, and will comply with all applicable Federal, state, and local laws, ordinances, and regulations with respect to the care, handling, storage, shipment, and disposal of the property. The donee agrees and certifies that the United States shall not be liable for personal injuries to, disabilities of, or death of the donee or the donee's employees, or any other person arising from or incident to the donation of the property, its use, or its final disposition. Additionally, the donee agrees and certifies to hold the United States harmless from and shall indemnify the United States against any or all debts, liabilities, judgments, costs, demands, suits, actions, or claims of any nature arising from or incident to the donation of the property, its use, or final disposition.

_____
Name and title of Donee (print or type)

_____
Signature of Donee

§ 102–40.90 Must we establish additional requirements for the inspection of personal property with special handling requirements?

Yes, you are responsible for establishing appropriate safeguards and providing instructions for personal protection to screeners who are inspecting property with special handling requirements. Also, it is the responsibility of the state agency and/or donee to comply with DOT regulations (49 CFR parts 171 through 177) when transporting hazardous material. Any costs incident to repacking or recontainment will be borne by the state agency and/or donee. Also, state agencies and/or donees will

comply with EPA's Resource Conservation and Recovery Act (40 CFR parts 261 through 265) including its application to transporters, storers, users, and permitting of hazardous wastes.

§ 102–40.95 Who pays for the costs incident to the transfer of personal property with special handling requirements?

You may charge the Federal agency or the SASP any costs you incur in packing, preparing for shipment, and transporting property with special handling requirements (see parts 102–36 and 102–37 of this subchapter).

Subpart D—Sale of Personal Property With Special Handling Requirements

§ 102–40.100 May we sell personal property with special handling requirements?

Generally, yes, you may sell personal property with special handling requirements through an authorized Sales Center, provided that the property has been reported in accordance with subpart B and C of this part, when you:

(a) Comply with applicable Federal, state, and local laws and regulations, including part 102–38 of this subchapter; and

(b) Follow applicable precautions including but not limited to proper packaging of the property, labeling with appropriate warning signs, and allowing for inspection of the property with proper safeguards.

§ 102–40.105 May we use any sales method to sell personal property that requires special handling?

Yes, unless specifically restricted as to sales methods by provisions in subpart E of this part, you may use any of the sales methods provided in part 102–38 of this subchapter, but you must:

(a) Advertise and conduct sales of such property separately from other sales;

(b) Store and display such property in a safe and controlled manner as required by applicable statutes and/or regulations;

(c) Indicate if the property is being sold only for scrap, and/or if there are any use requirements or restrictions;

(d) Comply with the requirements of other Federal, state, and local laws and regulations; and

(e) Conduct the sale through an agency authorized to sell Federal property in accordance with part 102–38 of this subchapter.

§ 102–40.110 What must we include in the sales terms and conditions when selling personal property with special handling requirements?

In addition to the recommended sales terms and conditions contained in part 102–38 of this subchapter, when selling personal property with special handling requirements you must include the following in the sales terms and conditions:

(a) A full description of the actual or potential hazard(s) associated with handling, storage, or use of the item, as well as any use requirements, restrictions, or limitations;

(b) An SDS, MSDS, or HMIS when available;

(c) A certification, executed by a duly authorized agency official, that the item is appropriately labeled and packaged in accordance with applicable regulatory and statutory requirements;

(d) Any additional requirements the purchaser must comply with prior to removal, *e.g.*, demilitarization on-site;

(e) The necessary steps the purchaser must take in the handling and transportation of the property when the property is sold; and

(f) A statement that it is the purchaser's responsibility to comply with all applicable Federal, state, local, and export laws and regulations to ensure the proper registration, licensing, possession, transportation, and subsequent use, resale or disposal of the property. You must use the following certification (or an equivalent certification) when offering for sale an item requiring special handling. Failure to sign the certification may result in the bid being rejected as nonresponsive:

The undersigned bidder hereby certifies that if awarded a contract under this invitation for bids, the bidder will comply with all applicable Federal, state, and local laws, ordinances, and regulations with respect to the care, handling, storage, shipment, resale, export, or other use of the material hereby purchased. The bidder will hold the United States harmless from and indemnify the United States against any or all debts, liabilities, judgments, costs, demands, suits, actions, or other claims of any nature arising from or incident to the handling, use, storage, shipment, resale, export, or other disposition of the items purchased.

Name of bidder (print or type)

Signature of bidder

§ 102–40.115 Are certifications required from the purchaser when selling personal property with special handling requirements?

Yes, in addition to receiving a certification that the purchaser will comply with all Federal, state, and local laws and regulations with respect to the care, handling, storage, shipment, and disposal of personal property with special handling requirements (see certification at § 102–40.110), you must obtain from the purchaser a certification that the purchaser will comply with any additional requirements associated with the property, such as demilitarization, export controls on CCLI, or mutilation requirements for flight safety critical aircraft parts. These additional requirements may be imposed by any law, regulation, or policy.

§ 102–40.120 What precautions must we take during the sales process for personal property requiring special handling?

(a) It is your responsibility to prepare items with special handling requirements for sale, provide all necessary information to ensure that prospective bidders are informed of hazards and special processing requirements, and identify precautions that bidders should take to protect themselves while inspecting, packing or moving items with special handling requirements. You must make any safety gear or equipment needed during the sales process available to prospective bidders and others involved in the inspection, packing or moving of these items.

(b) Unless authorized by the appropriate GSA regional office, you must not sell extremely hazardous property unless the property is rendered innocuous or adequate safeguards are provided. Such property must be rendered innocuous in a manner so as to preserve the utility or commercial value of the property.

§ 102–40.125 May we dispose of personal property requiring special handling by abandonment or destruction?

Yes, you may dispose of personal property requiring special handling by abandonment or destruction. However, in addition to the requirements for the abandonment or destruction of property in §§ 102–36.305 through 102–36.330 of this subchapter, you must also satisfy applicable Federal, state, and local waste disposal and air and water pollution control standards, laws, and regulations. You must ensure that such property, including empty hazardous material containers, not be abandoned until made safe, demilitarized, reduced to scrap, or otherwise made innocuous. You should also preserve, as much as possible, any civilian utility or commercial value of the property (see § 102–40.50.) National security classified items must be declassified or destroyed in accordance with holding agency regulations.

Subpart E—Categories of Personal Property With Special Handling Requirements

§ 102–40.130 What categories of personal property require special handling?

Many categories of personal property have special handling requirements in compliance with applicable Federal, state, and local regulations and ordinances for their handling, transportation, storage, disposal and use. See appendix A to this part for a listing of Federal Supply Classifications (FSCs) containing predominately hazardous items and appendix B to this part for a listing of FSCs containing a significant number of hazardous items. See §§ 102–40.130 through 102–40.235 for special handling instructions for some categories of property for which Federal property managers are likely to have responsibility.

§ 102–40.135 How do we manage acid-contaminated and explosive-contaminated property?

(a) Acid-contaminated or explosive-contaminated property is considered extremely hazardous property and is not reported to GSA for subsequent transfer or donation. However, you should notify GSA of this property in accordance with § 102–40.55. If the property is not transferred or donated, you may dispose of such property by sale, in accordance with subpart D of this part and with the condition that the purchaser sufficiently decontaminates the property to the degree that it is no longer extremely hazardous. Also, such property must be properly labeled in accordance with § 102–40.45 and should not be abandoned. When destroyed, such destruction should be accomplished under § 102–40.125.

(b) When selling acid or explosive contaminated property, the sales terms and sales documentation must both include the following certification, or an equivalent certification, which must be signed by the successful bidder.

It is hereby certified that the undersigned purchaser will comply with all the applicable Federal, state, and local laws, ordinances and regulations with respect to the care, handling, storage, and shipment, resale, export, and other use of the materials, hereby purchased, and that he/she is a user of, or dealer in, said materials. This certification is made in accordance with and subject to the penalties of Title 18, Section 1001, the United States Code, Crime and Criminal Procedures.

_____
Name of purchaser (print or type)

_____
Signature of purchaser

§ 102–40.140 How do we handle all-terrain vehicles (ATVs)?

(a) Three-wheeled and four-wheeled all-terrain vehicles (ATVs) can be exchanged with a dealer under the provisions of part 102–39 of this subchapter. Three-wheeled ATVs not exchanged must be mutilated in a manner to prevent operational use and may be sold only as salvage or scrap. Four-wheeled ATVs not exchanged may be offered for transfer and donation only when documented in accordance with §§ 102–40.75 and 102–40.80. In addition, any transfer or donation documentation for four-wheeled ATVs must require the recipient to acknowledge that the recipient will follow regulations and guidelines published by the Consumer Product Safety Commission related to these items, including age recommendations, restrictions on usage, and operator training. Four-wheeled ATVs not exchanged, transferred, or donated may be offered for sale as either salvage or scrap only after they have been mutilated in a manner to prevent operational use. Four-wheeled ATVs must not be released to the public after donee use, nor may they be released to the public after Federal use if the ATVs are not donated.

(b) A donation transfer document must contain a full description of the actual or potential hazard(s) and restriction(s) associated with the handling, storage, use, transportation or disposal of the item. In addition, the following certification (or an equivalent) must be signed by the donee:

I (We), the undersigned, hereby certify that the donee has knowledge and understanding of the nature of the property hereby donated which requires special handling, and will comply with all applicable Federal, state, and local laws, ordinances, and regulations with respect to the care, handling, storage, shipment, and disposal of the property. The donee agrees and certifies that the United States shall not be liable for personal injuries to, disabilities of, or death of the donee or the donee's employees, or any other person arising from or incident to the donation of the property, its use, or its final disposition. Additionally, the donee agrees and certifies to hold the United States harmless from and shall indemnify the United States against any or all debts, liabilities, judgments, costs, demands, suits, actions, or claims of any nature arising from or incident to the donation of the property, its use, or final disposition.

_____
Name and title of Donee (print or type)

_____
Signature of Donee

§ 102–40.145 How do we handle ammunition and ammunition components?

(a) Report usable ammunition to GSA for possible transfer to a Federal agency. You must not donate surplus ammunition, but you may donate surplus ammunition components to eligible donation recipients. You may sell non-expended ammunition and ammunition components (expended and non-expended) only to companies licensed to perform manufacturing/remanufacturing processes under the provisions of 18 U.S.C. 923 or other Federal law or regulation or to companies allowed to purchase ammunition components under local and state laws. If the ammunition is regulated pursuant to the National Firearms Act (NFA) or any other Federal regulation, then the ammunition can only be disposed of in accordance with applicable regulation. Ammunition greater than .50 caliber can, in some instances, be regulated under the NFA. You must follow any demilitarization requirements. When selling ammunition and ammunition components, the sales terms and sales documentation must both include the following certification, or an equivalent certification, which must be signed by the successful bidder:

Item No. ___contains ammunition or ammunition components offered for sale in this invitation. The undersigned certifies that he/she will comply with all applicable local, state, and Federal laws and regulations concerning ammunition or ammunition components.

If the item being sold is scrap ammunition, the undersigned certifies that he/she is licensed to perform manufacturing/remanufacturing under the provisions of 18 U.S.C. 923 or other Federal law or regulation.

If the item being sold is a scrap ammunition component, the undersigned certifies that these scrap ammunition components will not be used for the original manufactured purpose.

_____
License issuing authority and license number

_____
Name of bidder (print or type)

_____
Signature of bidder

(b) In addition to sales as described in paragraph (a) of this section, expended ammunition cartridge cases may also be transferred or donated when the recipient certifies that the spent brass will be reloaded and used only for law enforcement purposes. If there is no Federal or state donation interest in the cases, and a sale of the scrap is not feasible, cartridge cases may be disposed of using abandonment or destruction procedures under § 102–40.125. The recipient must certify that the expended cartridge cases will not be used for the original manufactured purpose.

(c) The transportation of primers or propellant powder is governed by 49 CFR parts 171 through 180.

§ 102–40.150 How do we handle animals and plants?

(a) Whenever possible, you should report live animals and plants to GSA for transfer, donation or sale. They are, however, considered perishables and may be disposed of by abandonment or destruction procedures in accordance with the authority contained in § 102–40.125. Abandonment or destruction procedures may be used for animals other than those specifically addressed below, where warranted for humane purposes.

(b) Unfit horses and mules may be humanely euthanized or put out to pasture in accordance with 40 U.S.C. 1308 and agency policies. Transfers of unfit horses or mules to Federal agencies must be conducted in accordance with part 102–36 of this subchapter. In the event that a transfer of these animals can be made to a humane organization, the transfer may be conducted under procedures contained in part 102–37 of this subchapter.

(c) Under 40 U.S.C. 555, you may transfer canines formerly used in the performance of law enforcement duties to an individual experienced in handling canines in the performance of those duties, in accordance with agency policy and procedures. For example, the "individual" may be the current handler of that canine or a previous handler.

§ 102–40.155 How do we handle asbestos?

(a) Items with asbestos content must be handled in accordance with the EPA regulations found at 40 CFR part 61, subpart M. Further information on laws and regulations related to asbestos may be found at *www.epa.gov/asbestos*.

(b) Report to GSA excess personal property containing nonfriable asbestos, as defined in 40 CFR 61.141, for subsequent transfer, donation or sale in accordance with parts 102–36 through 102–38 of this subchapter. Nonfriable asbestos materials cannot:

(1) When dry, be crumbled, pulverized, or reduced to powder by hand pressure; or

(2) Contain asbestos which is bonded or otherwise rendered unavailable for release into the atmosphere through normal usage. All disposal documentation related to personal property containing nonfriable asbestos, such as exchange/sale, reporting, transfer, donation, and sales documents, must include a warning statement that the item may contain asbestos and must not be cut, crushed, sanded, disassembled or otherwise altered. The property must also be labeled or marked with such warning statements.

(c) You must use a warning such as the following on the documentation reporting or requesting the exchange/sale, transfer, donation or sale of an item containing asbestos:

WARNING

This property contains asbestos. Inhaling asbestos fibers may cause cancer. Do not release fibers by cutting, crushing, sanding, disassembling, or otherwise altering this property. End users and new owners, if transferred, should be warned. OSHA standards for personnel protection are codified at 29 CFR 1910.1001. EPA disposal standards are codified at 40 CFR part 61. State and local authorities may have additional restrictions on the disposal of items containing asbestos.

(d) Property containing asbestos should be labeled with a warning such as the following:

WARNING

This property contains asbestos. Inhaling asbestos fibers may cause cancer. Do not release fibers by cutting, crushing, sanding, disassembling, or otherwise altering this property.

(e) Nonfriable asbestos that is not transferred, donated, or sold may be abandoned as provided in § 102–40.125 and part 102–36 of this subchapter. If destroyed by burial, items containing friable or nonfriable asbestos must be disposed of by burial at a site that meets the requirements of 40 CFR 61.154.

(f) Friable asbestos materials that contain more than one percent asbestos by weight and can, by hand pressure, be crumbled, pulverized, or reduced to powder, thus allowing for potential release of asbestos fibers into the air. Property containing friable asbestos normally is not to be transferred, donated or sold. Notwithstanding these provisions, holding agencies, on a case-by-case basis, may request approval from GSA Central Office, with consultation from the EPA, to transfer, donate or sell such property if in the judgment of the holding agency, special circumstances warrant such action.

(g) Excess personal property known to contain friable asbestos shall neither be reported to GSA nor transferred among Federal agencies excepted as noted in paragraph (f) of this section.

(h) Surplus property containing friable asbestos is to be neither donated nor sold. Such property is disposed of under paragraph (i) of this section.

(i) Excess and surplus property containing friable asbestos is to be disposed of by burial in a site that meets the EPA requirements of 40 CFR 61.156. Holding agencies should contact the nearest office of the EPA for assistance with regard to the disposal of materials containing asbestos, with the exception of DOD, who should contact the Defense Logistics Agency (DLA).

§ 102–40.160 How do we handle controlled substances?

(a) You are not required to report excess controlled substances to GSA, but you should make reasonable efforts to transfer them to Federal agencies in accordance with Drug Enforcement Administration (DEA) regulations (21 CFR part 1307). The recipient agency must certify that it is authorized to procure the particular controlled substance and provide the registration number on the Certificate of Registration, issued by the DEA. See the transfer procedures in FMR part 102–36 (41 CFR part 102–36).

(b) You must not donate controlled substances.

(c) In accordance with sales procedures specified in part 102–38 of this subchapter, and under the conditions specified in this paragraph, you may sell controlled substances by sealed bid only, to bidders who have registered with the DEA to manufacture, distribute, or dispense of the particular controlled substance. As a condition of sale, the bidder must submit verification of DEA registration. Prior to finalizing the sale, you must obtain confirmation from the DEA of the bidder's status as a registered manufacturer, distributor or dispenser of controlled substances.

(1) The invitation for bids for controlled substances must list only controlled substances and must only be distributed to bidders who are registered with the DEA, Department of Justice, to manufacture, distribute or dispense of the controlled substances being sold. In addition, the following statement, or an equivalent statement, must be included in the sales terms and conditions when selling controlled substances:

The bidder shall complete, sign, and return with his/her bid, the certificate as contained in this invitation. No award will be made or sale consummated until after this agency has obtained from the Drug Enforcement Administration, Department of Justice, verification that the bidder is registered to manufacture, distribute, or dispense those controlled substances which are the subject of the award.

(2) The following certification, or an equivalent certification, must be made a part of the invitation for bids and contract to be completed and signed by the bidder and returned with the bid. Failure to sign the certification may result in the bid being rejected as non-responsive:

The undersigned bidder certifies that he/she is Registered with the Drug Enforcement Administration, Department of Justice, as a manufacturer, distributor, or dispenser of the controlled substances for which a bid is submitted and the registration number is:

_____.
 This certification is made in accordance with and subject to the penalties of Title 18, Section 1001, United States Code, Crime and Criminal procedures.

_____
Name of bidder (print or type)

_____
Signature of bidder

_____

Address of bidder (print or type)

_____

City, State, Zip code

(d) As a condition precedent to making an award for the sale of surplus controlled substances, holding agencies should follow procedures provided by the DEA in 21 CFR part 1310.

(e) You must not abandon controlled substances. You must destroy controlled substances in such a manner as to ensure total destruction to preclude any further use, and ensure such destruction is in compliance with DEA regulations, 21 CFR part 1307, or other procedures approved by DEA, and coordinate with local air and water pollution control authorities when required. Destruction must be witnessed and certified by two employees of your agency, unless DEA directs otherwise. The following certification, or an equivalent certification, must be used to document the destruction of controlled substances:

We, the undersigned, have witnessed the destruction of the (controlled substance(s)) described herein and in the manner of destruction and on the date stated herein:

Certification of destruction of: _____

_____
Manner in which destruction was performed

_____
Date

_____
Witness

_____
Date

_____
Witness

_____
Date

§ 102–40.165 How do we handle drugs, biologicals, and reagents other than controlled substances?

(a) Drugs, biologicals, and reagents other than controlled substances may be transferred to another Federal agency for official purposes under procedures specified in part 102–36 of this subchapter. For donation of drugs, biologicals, or reagents other than controlled substances, follow the procedures in part 102–37 of this subchapter, and paragraph (c) of this section.

(b) Drugs, biologicals, and reagents other than controlled substances must be clearly identified when they are unfit for human use. As a general rule, you must destroy drugs, biologicals, and reagents unfit for human use, with destruction performed by an agency employee and witnessed and certified by two additional representatives of your agency. Similarly, destruction of this property held by a SASP or donee must be destroyed by a SASP employee and witnessed by two additional SASP employees. Destruction shall be coordinated with local air and water pollution control authorities, when required. However, you may report such property to GSA for subsequent transfer or donation for the purpose of animal experimental use when the property is unfit due to expired shelf life. The following certification, or an equivalent certification, must be used and retained by the Federal agency or SASP to document the destruction of drugs, biologicals, and reagents:

We, the undersigned, have witnessed the destruction of the (drugs, biologicals, and reagents) described in the foregoing certification in the manner of destruction and on the date stated herein:

Certification of destruction of: _____

_____
Manner in which destruction was performed

_____
Date

_____
Witness

_____
Date

_____
Witness

_____
Date

(c) When donating drugs, biologicals, or reagents other than controlled substances, the SASP shall obtain a certification from the donee indicating that the items donated will be safeguarded, dispensed, and administered under competent supervision and in accordance with Federal, state, and local laws and regulations. Surplus drugs, biologicals, and reagents requested for donation by state agencies will not be transported by the state agency or stored in its warehouse prior to distribution to donees. Arrangements will be made by the state agency for the donee to make direct pickup at the holding agency after approval by GSA and after notification by the holding agency that the property is ready for pickup. Additionally, Transfer Order Surplus Personal Property, SF 123 from a state agency requesting surplus drugs, biologicals, and reagents for donation will not be processed or approved by GSA until it has been determined by the GSA donation representative that the specific donee is legally licensed to administer, dispense, store, or distribute such property. A copy of the donee's license, registration, or other legal authorization to administer, dispense, store, or distribute such property should be attached and made a part of the SF 123. The administration or use of drugs, biologicals, and reagents must be in compliance with the Federal Food, Drug, and Cosmetic Act, as amended (21 U.S.C. 301, *et seq.*).

(d) The sale of any unexpired drugs, biologicals, or reagents must be in accordance with rules published by the Food and Drug Administration (FDA). You may sell drugs, biologicals, and reagents other than controlled substances, only to those entities legally qualified to engage in the sale, manufacture or distribution of such items and a certification or evidence of licensing must accompany the bids. An entity is legally qualified when a Federal agency (*e.g.*, the Department of Health and Human Services, the DEA, or the Department of Agriculture) or state agency having legal or regulatory oversight over that commodity has approved the entity to engage in the designated activity.

(1) When selling drugs, biologicals, and reagents other than controlled substances, the following condition of sale (or an equivalent condition of sale) must be used:

The bidder shall complete, sign, and return with his/her bid the certification as contained in this invitation. No award will be made or sale consummated until after this agency has determined that the bidder is legally licensed to engage in the manufacture, sale, or distribution of drugs.

(2) The following certification, or an equivalent certification, must be made

a part of the invitation for bids (and contract), to be completed and signed by the bidder, and returned with the bid with a copy of his/her license. Failure to sign the certification may result in the bid being rejected as nonresponsive.

The undersigned bidder certifies that he/she is legally licensed to engage in the manufacture, sale, or distribution of drugs, and proof of his/her license to deal in such materials is furnished with this bid. This certification is made in accordance with and subject to the penalties of Title 18, Section 1001, United States Code, Crime and Criminal procedures.

_____
Name of bidder (print or type)

_____
Signature of bidder

_____
Address of bidder (print or type)

_____
City, State, Zip code

§ 102–40.170 How do we handle electronic products?

(a) Additional guidance regarding the disposal and reporting of Federal electronic products is found under FMR part 102–36 (41 CFR part 102–36).

(b) Excess electronic products, certified and noncertified, meeting radiation safety performance standards or electronic products which are not required to meet such performance standards must be reported to GSA for transfer to Federal agencies in accordance with part 102–36 of this subchapter and may be donated or sold in accordance with parts 102–37 and 102–38 of this subchapter, respectively.

(c) Excess electronic products NOT meeting radiation safety performance standards must be reported to GSA for transfer to Federal agencies in accordance with FMR part 102–36 (41 CFR part 102–36) and may be donated or sold in accordance with parts 102–37 and 102–38 of this subchapter, respectively. The report to GSA, and any subsequent transfer, donation, or sales documents, must include a statement that the items are not in compliance with applicable radiation safety performance standards and specify the standard which is not being met. Additionally, the recipient must acknowledge that they are aware of the potential danger in handling or using such items.

(d) Donation documentation for items not meeting radiation safety performance standards must contain the following certification, or an equivalent certification, signed by the donee before release:

I (We), the undersigned, hereby certify that the donee has knowledge and understanding of the potential danger in using the product without a radiation test to determine the acceptability for use and/or modification to bring it into compliance with the radiation safety performance standards prescribed for the item under 21 CFR parts 1010 through 1050, and agrees to accept the item from the holding agency for donation under those conditions. The undersigned further agrees that the Government shall not be liable for personal injuries to, disabilities of, or death of the donee or the donee's employees, or any other person arising from or incident to the donation of the item, its use, or its final disposition. The undersigned also agrees to hold the Government harmless from any or all debts, liabilities, judgments, costs, demands, suits, actions, or claims of any nature arising from or incident to the donation of the item, its use, or its final disposition.

_____
Name of Donee (print or type)

_____
Signature of Donee

(e) Sales documents listing electronic products not meeting safety performance standards must also clearly warn purchasers that the items may not be in compliance with FDA radiation safety performance standards prescribed pursuant to 21 CFR parts 1010 through 1050 and that the purchaser assumes all risks associated with the use or resale of the items. The following type of warning will be placed on the sales documentation:

WARNING

Purchasers are warned that the item purchased herewith may not be in compliance with Food and Drug Administration radiation safety performance standards prescribed pursuant to 21 CFR parts 1010 through 1050, and use may result in personal injury unless modified. The purchaser agrees that the United States shall not be liable for personal injuries to, disabilities of, or death of the purchaser, the purchaser's employees, or to any other persons arising from or incident to the purchase of this item, its use, or disposition. The purchaser shall hold the United States harmless from and shall in-

demnify the United States against any or all debts, liabilities, judgments, costs, demands, suits, actions, or claims of any nature arising from or incident to the purchase, use or resale of this item. The purchaser agrees to notify any subsequent purchaser of this property of the potential for personal injury in using this item without a radiation survey to determine the acceptability for use and/or modification to bring it into compliance with the radiation safety performance standards prescribed for the item under 21 CFR parts 1010 through 1050, unless authorized by 21 CFR 1002.4 to have the dealer or distributor hold and preserve.

(f) You must dispose of all electronic products in accordance with all Federal and state laws, including the Solid Waste Disposal Act (42 U.S.C. 6901, _et seq._) and Executive Order 13423, Strengthening Federal Environmental, Energy, and Transportation Management. You should also be aware of the prohibitions and liabilities contained in 42 U.S.C. 9607.

(g) When donating or selling electronic products, the sales terms and sales documentation, or donation document, must include the following certification, or an equivalent certification, which must be signed by the donee or successful bidder:

It is hereby certified that the undersigned purchaser or donee will comply with all the applicable Federal, state, and local laws, ordinances and regulations with respect to the care, handling, storage, disposal, and shipment, resale, export, or other use of the electronic products, hereby purchased or donated, and that he/she is a user of, or dealer in, said products. This certification is made in accordance with and subject to the penalties of Title 18, Section 1001, the United States Code, Crime and Criminal Procedures.

When recycling electronic products, purchaser or donee should use any national standards, best management practices, or existing certification programs for recyclers in addition to Federal, state, and local laws, ordinances and regulations. In the absence of national standards, best management practices, or a national certification program for recyclers, the purchaser/donee should use "EPA's Guidelines for Materials Management" found at _http://www.epa.gov/epawaste/index.htm_

_____
Name of purchaser or donee (print or type)

_____
Signature of purchaser or donee

(h) Additionally, noncertified and certified electronic products must be abandoned under the provisions of §102–40.125.

§ 102–40.175　How do we handle firearms?

(a) You must submit reports and transfer documents on excess firearms to GSA (8QSC), Denver, CO 80225–0506. GSA will approve transfers of firearms only to those Federal agencies authorized to acquire firearms for official use, and may require additional written justification from the requesting agency.

(b) GSA may donate only surplus hand guns, rifles, shotguns, and individual light automatic weapons previously used by the Federal Government, with less than .50 caliber in Federal Supply Classification (FSC) 1005, and rifle and shoulder fired grenade launchers in FSC 1010, with a disposal condition code of 4 or better (see condition codes in §102–36.240 of this subchapter). Only eligible law enforcement entities whose primary function is the enforcement of applicable Federal, state, and/or local laws, and whose compensated law enforcement officers have powers to apprehend and arrest, may obtain these donated firearms for law enforcement purposes.

(c)(1) For purposes of donation under paragraph (b) of this section, each Transfer Order Surplus Personal Property SF 123 must be accompanied by a conditional transfer document, signed by both the intended donee agency and the SASP, which includes the special terms, conditions, restrictions, and other forms or information required for the transfer of the donated firearms. Restrictions on donated firearms are perpetual and may not be amended by the SASP without prior written approval from GSA. Donated firearms must be released or shipped directly from the Federal donor agency to the designated donee.

(2) If the firearms to be donated are subject to the National Firearms Act, 26 U.S.C. Chapter 53, (e.g., machineguns, silencers, short-barrel rifles, short-barrel shotguns, firearms over .50 caliber or with a bore diameter of more than ½ inch, and destructive devices) the SF 123 must be accompanied by an ATF Form 10, Application for Registration of Firearms Acquired by Certain Governmental Entities, completed by

the donee agency as specified in 27 CFR 479.104. Upon approval of the donation by the SASP, the Form 10 shall be forwarded in accordance with the form's instructions. The Chief, National Firearms Act Branch, shall notify the donee agency of ATF registration of the donated firearms by returning the approved Form 10 to the donee agency. The donee agency shall provide a copy of the approved Form 10 to the SASP who shall retain a copy of the approved Form 10 and attach it to the SF 123. Firearms shall not be released for shipment until the ATF Form 10 has been approved by the ATF and a copy provided to the SASP. The registration of any firearms on ATF Form 10 is for official use only and subsequent transfers will be approved only to other Governmental entities for official use and in accordance with paragraph (e)(2) of this section. If you have questions concerning whether particular firearms are subject to the National Firearms Act, contact the Firearms Technology Industry Services Branch, ATF, at (304) 616–4300 or FIRE_TECH@atf.gov.

(d) When authorized by circumstances described in paragraphs (e), (f), (g), or (i) of this section, the destruction of firearms must be performed by an entity authorized by your agency head or designee. The destruction must be witnessed by two additional agency employees authorized by the agency head or designee.

(e)(1) When the approved donee agency no longer needs the donated firearms, the donee agency must notify the SASP. The SASP may, with GSA approval and in accordance with paragraph (e)(2) of this section, reassign firearms to another donee agency within the state or to a donee agency in another state through the appropriate SASP. In such a case, transfer of the firearms must be between eligible donee agencies only. No SASP is eligible to take custody of the firearms. If the firearms are not sought for reassignment, the donee agency and a representative from the SASP, or designee, must witness destruction of the firearms and complete and sign a certificate of destruction, which will be maintained by the SASP. If firearms subject to the National Firearms Act are destroyed, the SASP shall notify the Chief, National Firearms Act Branch, ATF, so the destruction can be noted in the National Firearms Registration and Transfer Record.

(2) If the firearms sought for reassignment are subject to the National Firearms Act, the firearms must be transferred in accordance with 27 CFR 479.90. This regulation requires that the donor agency submit an ATF Form 5, Application for Tax Exempt Transfer and Registration of Firearm, which must be approved prior to transfer of the firearms. Donor agencies wishing to reassign firearms subject to the National Firearms Act shall submit a completed ATF Form 5 to the SASP along with the request to reassign the firearms to another donee agency. The SASP shall forward the ATF Form 5 to the Chief, National Firearms Act Branch. If transfer is approved by the ATF, the donor agency will receive a copy of the Form 5, with approval noted thereon, from the Chief, National Firearms Act Branch, ATF. The donor agency shall provide a copy of the approved Form 5 to the SASP at which time the reassignment shall be approved.

(f) You must not abandon firearms. You must destroy unneeded firearms by crushing, cutting, breaking, or deforming each firearm in a manner to ensure that each firearm is rendered completely inoperative and incapable of being made operable for any purpose except the recovery of basic material content. Destruction of firearms must be performed as stated in paragraphs (d) and (e) of this section.

(g) You must not dispose of functional or repairable firearms under an exchange/sale transaction or by sale. Surplus firearms may be sold only for scrap after total destruction as described in paragraph (f) of this section to ensure that the firearms are rendered completely inoperative and to preclude their being made operative. Such sale shall be conducted under part 102–38 of this subchapter.

(h)(1) Except as provided in paragraph (h)(2) of this section, firearms received as foreign gifts may be offered for transfer to Federal agencies or sold to the gift recipient in accordance with part 102–42 of this subchapter. If sold to the gift recipient, a certification

signed by the gift recipient certifying compliance with all Federal, state, and local laws regarding purchase and possession of firearms must be received by the gift recipient's agency and the agency conducting the sale prior to the sale and release of such firearm to the gift recipient.

(2) Firearms subject to the National Firearms Act, 26 U.S.C. Chapter 53 that are received as foreign gifts cannot be lawfully transferred to an individual gift recipient. These firearms must remain the property of the United States or may be transferred to a donee agency in accordance with paragraphs (b) and (c) of this section. In addition, all firearms must also be transferred, shipped, received, and possessed in accordance with the Gun Control Act of 1968. Persons having questions concerning compliance with the Gun Control Act should contact the nearest ATF field office.

(i) Firearms that are forfeited, voluntarily abandoned, or unclaimed as described in 40 U.S.C. 1306 and 40 U.S.C. 552, must be reported to GSA for disposal in accordance with § 102–41.195 of this subchapter. GSA will direct the disposition of these firearms under this section.

§ 102–40.180 How do we handle hazardous materials?

(a) You may use any of the following methods for the identification of hazardous materials:

(1) As part of the process under current acquisition standards, manufacturers must provide SDSs or similar documentation to identify potential hazards. SDSs are also prescribed by OSHA under 29 CFR part 1910.

(2) An automated database maintained by GSA Federal Acquisition Service contains MSDSs for all GSA-procured hazardous materials. To request an MSDS, you may send an email to *MSDS@gsa.gov*, or call, Toll Free: 866–588–7659, DSN: 465–5097, or Commercial: 816–926–5097.

(3) A collection of hazard-related information in DOD's HMIS provides transportation and disposal information.

(4) Appendix A to this part contains a list of the Federal Supply Classes

179

(FSC) of property that are composed predominantly of hazardous items.

(5) When information is not available under paragraphs (a)(1), (2), (3), or (4) of this section, contact the manufacturer, the procuring agency, or your technical staff for assistance in obtaining the SDS, MSDS, or HMIS information.

(b) You must verify items with an expired shelf life or reclassify them as hazardous wastes when required by Federal, state, or local environmental laws or regulations. If the item has been determined hazardous, the owning Federal agency must document the accountable inventory record accordingly. If the item has not been appropriately labeled by the manufacturer or distributor, the owning agency must appropriately label, mark, or tag the item in accordance with OSHA requirements (29 CFR 1919.1200) regarding the actual potential hazard associated with the handling, storage, or use of the item.

(c) For transportation of hazardous materials, see 49 CFR parts 171 through 180.

(d) For disposal of hazardous materials, see §§ 102–40.35 through 102–40.125.

(e) Unless authorized by GSA, extremely hazardous property may not be sold unless it is rendered innocuous, mutilated or otherwise made safe. You should, however, render such property innocuous in a manner so as to preserve the maximum utility or commercial value of the property when possible.

§ 102–40.185 How do we handle lead-containing paints and items bearing lead-containing paint?

(a) You may transfer, donate or sell such items in compliance with restrictions and requirements found in the Consumer Product Safety Commission regulations set forth in 16 CFR part 1303. The transfer, donation or sales documents must clearly describe these leaded items and why they require special handling, and identify the danger inherent in the use or disposal of such paint and items bearing lead-containing paint. You must not abandon such items or their containers. You must destroy them in a way that will prohibit future acquisition and use, and in a manner authorized by law and

regulation. Any removal (stripping) of lead paint incident to disposal must be accomplished in conformance with Federal regulations and industry guidelines such as those promulgated by the EPA (*http://www.epa.gov*) or OSHA (*http://www.osha.gov*).

(b) If disposal of the items described in paragraph (a) of this section is allowable, the following must be placed on the items:

(1) The following warning:

WARNING

Contains Lead. Dried Film of This Paint May be Harmful if Eaten or Chewed.

(2) The following additional statement or its practical equivalent on their labels:

Do not apply on toys and other children's articles, furniture or interior surfaces of any dwelling or facility which may be occupied or used by children. Do not apply on exterior surfaces of dwelling units, such as window sills, porches, stairs or railings, to which children may be commonly exposed.

KEEP OUT OF REACH OF CHILDREN

(c) Donation documentation (including the SF 123) must contain the following certification, or an equivalent certification:

The property requested herein shall be used only as specified in 16 CFR part 1303 and in no case shall be in contact with children. I, the undersigned, agree the United States shall not be liable for personal injuries to, disabilities of or death of the donee's employees, or any other person arising from or incident to the donation of this property, its use or its final disposition; and to hold the United States harmless from, and shall indemnify the United States against, any or all debts, liabilities, judgments, costs, demands, suits, actions or claims of any nature arising from or incident to the donation of this property, its use or its final disposition.

_____
Name of donee (print or type)

_____
Signature of donee

(d) When selling lead-containing paint or items bearing lead-containing paint, the sales terms and sales documentation must include this certification, or an equivalent certification. Failure to sign the certification where it appears as a sales term may result in the bid being rejected as nonresponsive:

I, the undersigned, certify that I have read and fully comprehend the aforementioned terms and conditions of this sale. I shall comply with the applicable Consumer Product Safety Commission regulations set forth in 16 CFR part 1303 if I am the successful bidder. I further agree the United States shall not be liable for personal injuries to, disabilities of, or death of any persons arising from or incident to the sale of this property, its uses or its final disposition; and to hold the United States harmless from, and shall indemnify the United States against, any or all debts, liabilities, judgments, costs, demands, suits, actions, or claims of any nature arising from or incident to the sale of this property, its use, or its final disposition.

Name of bidder (print or type)

Signature of bidder

§ 102–40.190 How do we handle medical devices?

(a) Medical devices are subject to the laws and regulations administered by FDA. Provisions of the governing statute, the Federal Food, Drug, and Cosmetic Act, appear in 21 U.S.C. 301, *et seq.* FDA regulations covering medical devices are found in 21 CFR chapter I, subpart H. The Act prohibits the movement in interstate commerce of medical devices that are adulterated or misbranded (21 U.S.C. 331). The Act authorizes FDA to initiate civil proceedings to seize or enjoin the distribution of such items (21 U.S.C. 334), and to report any violations to a U.S. Attorney for prosecution, after such individual is given notice and a hearing (21 U.S.C. 335).

(b) Prescription devices are subject to additional Federal, state, local, and other applicable laws. Federal law requires that prescription devices be in the possession of either: Persons lawfully engaged in the manufacture, transportation, storage, or wholesale or retail distribution of such device; or, practitioners licensed by their states. Federal law also requires that prescription devices be sold only to, or on the prescription or order of, a licensed practitioner for use in the course of his or her professional practice, and that the devices are labeled in a specific manner.

(c) Non-Federal recipients must certify in writing that such property will be used, resold or transported in conformance with FDA regulations. Any proposed destruction of medical equipment must be coordinated with local health and sanitation officials.

§ 102–40.195 How do we handle Munitions List Items (MLIs)?

(a) Munitions List Items (MLIs) are listed in 22 CFR part 121. A system of demilitarization codes identifies the extent of alteration or destruction necessary when transferring or selling MLIs. The appropriate code is normally assigned to items when they enter the supply system of the Department of Defense (DOD) or a civilian agency. Refer to DOD 4160.21–M–1 (Change No. 1) for a complete description of the DOD program and the requirements to be followed for property owned, procured by or under the control of DOD. The DOD manual is available from the Defense Logistics Agency, 8725 John J. Kingman Road, Fort Belvoir, VA 22060. If your agency uses another system of identifying items requiring demilitarization, you must provide a detailed description of that system to the General Services Administration, Mail Code MA, 1800 F Street NW., Washington, DC 20405, Attn: Director, Personal Property Policy.

(b) When disposing of MLIs, you must perpetuate these demilitarization codes; alert those to whom you are transferring or selling property that the item may require demilitarization; and perform any required demilitarization, or provide any documentation or certifications in accordance with the DOD demilitarization manual, DOD 4160.21–M–1 (Change No. 1), or other agency policy manual if the MLIs are not governed by the DOD demilitarization manual.

(c) Disposal of MLIs will follow the provisions of parts 102–36, 102–37, and 102–38 of this subchapter unless different disposal procedures are required by law or your agency regulation issued in support of 22 U.S.C. 2778.

§ 102–40.200 How do we handle Commerce Control List Items (CCLIs)?

(a) CCLIs are subject to the controls of 15 CFR parts 738 and 774. Export licenses are required for transfer of items to the countries listed in 15 CFR part 738, supp. 1. CCLIs may also be identified by the demilitarization code assigned to the item in the DOD supply system.

(b) When disposing of CCLIs, you must notify the recipient that the item may be subject to Department of Commerce export licensing requirements when transported out of the U.S., for reasons of national security, crime control, technology transfer, and scarcity of materials. Furthermore:

(1) The recipient must be informed that this notification must pass to all subsequent recipients of the item.

(2) When being sold, completed end-use certificates are required of all bidders. An end-use certificate is a statement signed by a prospective recipient indicating the intended designation and disposition of CCLIs to be acquired, and acknowledging U.S. export licensing requirements.

(3) All disposal activity must conform to the requirements of 15 CFR, chapter VII, subchapter C.

§ 102–40.205 How do we handle national stockpile material?

In accordance with 40 U.S.C. 113(e)(6), materials acquired for the national stockpile, the supplemental stockpile, or materials or equipment acquired under section 303 of the Defense Production Act of 1950, as amended (50 App. U.S.C. 2093), are not covered by the Federal Management Regulation. The disposal of these assets is governed by 50 U.S.C. 98d, 98e, and 98f.

§ 102–40.210 How do we handle Nuclear Regulatory Commission-controlled materials?

The Nuclear Regulatory Commission (NRC) has exclusive control over licensing, use, transfer, and disposition of NRC-controlled materials. Direct all inquiries to the U.S. Nuclear Regulatory Commission, Washington, DC 20555.

§ 102–40.215 How do we handle ozone depleting substances (ODSs)?

Handle ODSs in accordance with Federal and state laws and regulations. Prior to disposal of ODSs removed or reclaimed from facilities or equipment, including disposal as part of a contract, trade or donation, coordinate with the Defense Ozone Depleting Sub-

stances Reserve Program Office to determine if the recovered ODS is a critical requirement for DOD missions. Direct inquiries to the Defense Ozone Depleting Substances Reserve Program Office, Defense Supply Center, Richmond, Virginia; email: *DSCR.ODSReserve@dla.mil;* phone: (804) 279–3064. Additional guidance is available from EPA at: *http://www.epa.gov/ozone/title6/608/608fact.html#overview.*

§ 102–40.220 How do we handle polychlorinated biphenyls (PCBs)?

(a) In accordance with EPA regulations (40 CFR 761.1 and 761.3), property defined by EPA as excluded polychlorinated biphenyl (PCB) products may be transferred, donated or sold in accordance with parts 102–36, 102–37, or 102–38 of this subchapter. For additional guidance on PCB classifications and other Federal restrictions, contact: Director, National Program Chemicals Division (NPCD), (7404), Office of Pollution Prevention and Toxics, 1200 Pennsylvania Avenue NW., Washington, DC or visit the EPA's Web site at: *http://www.epa.gov/waste/hazard/tsd/pcbs/index.htm.* You should also contact state regulatory agencies since some states regulate at a stricter level than the Federal Government.

(b) Property defined by the EPA in 40 CFR 761.3 as either a PCB item or PCB must be labeled or marked with a warning statement that the item contains PCB and must be handled and disposed of in accordance with EPA regulations (40 CFR part 761), DOT regulations (49 CFR parts 171 through 180), and applicable state laws.

(1) PCB items and PCBs may be transferred or donated, provided:

(i) The items are intact, non-leaking, and totally enclosed.

(ii) All transfers orders or transfer documents must cite the specific provision in 40 CFR part 761 that permits continued use of the item, and contains a certification that the property has been inspected by the transferee and complies with all the use, inspection, labeling, and other provisions of 40 CFR part 761.

(iii) The recipient must annotate its property accountability records to reflect the nature and extent of the PCB content and must provide the specific authorization covering the use of this item from 40 CFR part 761. If tests are conducted to ascertain the nature and extent of PCB contamination, the recipient must furnish the GSA regional office with a copy of the test results. This information will be perpetuated on any notification or release document when the agency disposes of the property.

(iv) If PCBs or PCB items are donated to service educational activities or to public airports, the Department of Defense and the Federal Aviation Administration, respectively, must obtain the warning and certification as described in paragraph (e) of this section.

(v) The recipient certifies to you that the item will be handled and disposed of in accordance with EPA regulation 40 CFR part 761, DOT regulations 49 CFR parts 171 through 180, and other applicable Federal and state laws.

(2) PCB and PCB items not transferred or donated must be destroyed or otherwise disposed of under EPA regulations and applicable state laws. You must not sell any PCB or PCB item unless 40 CFR part 761 authorizes the sale and continued use of the specific item.

(c) You must not transfer, donate, or sell items with an unknown level of concentrations of PCBs.

(d) Property containing PCBs and PCB items should be labeled with a warning such as the following:

Caution—This item contains PCBs (polychlorinated biphenyls), a toxic environmental contaminant requiring special handling and disposal in accordance with the U.S. Environmental Protection Agency regulations (40 CFR part 761), applicable state laws, and 41 CFR 102–40.215. For proper disposal information, contact the nearest EPA office. For transportation requirements, see 49 CFR parts 171 through 180.

(e) The SASP must have the following certification, or an equivalent certification, on all transfer paperwork where PCBs are involved.

WARNING AND CERTIFICATION

The undersigned donee is aware that the item(s) listed as containing polychlorinated biphenyls (PCBs), a toxic environmental contaminant, require(s) special handling and disposal in accordance with U.S. Environmental Protection Agency regulation (40 CFR part 761) and U.S. Department of Transportation regulations codified in 49 CFR parts 171 through 180. The donee certifies that this item (or these items) will be handled and disposed of in accordance with applicable Federal statutes and regulations and applicable state laws. This certification is made in accordance with and subject to the penalties of Title 18, Section 1001, the United States Code, Crime and Criminal Procedures.

_____
Name and title of donee (print or type)

_____
Signature of donee

§ 102–40.225 How do we handle precious metals?

(a) You must identify activities in your organization that generate precious metals; recover precious metals created from work processes, such as photographic film developing, and identify equipment or materials containing recoverable precious metals; and adequately control precious metals in your custody. Federal civil agencies may participate in the DOD Precious Metal Recovery Program (PMRP) in accordance with this subpart, and have an Inter-Agency Service Agreement (ISA) in effect between the Defense Logistics Agency (DLA) and individual Federal civil agencies. You may acquire recovered fine precious metals as Government Furnished Material or for other authorized uses by submitting a request to the Commander, Defense Supply Center, Philadelphia (DSCP), 700 Robbins Avenue, Philadelphia, Pennsylvania 19111–5096.

(b) Precious metals will be sold in accordance with this subpart and part 102–38 of this subchapter.

(c) Sales of precious metals will be processed as follows:

(1) Require a bid deposit appropriate to the circumstances of the sale;

(2) Certify all forms of bid deposit and payments; and

(3) Include in the invitation for bids only precious and semiprecious materials as may be available for sale at that time.

(d) Each agency generating scrap precious metals and also having a continuing need for fine precious metals may arrange for the acceptance of scrap precious metals for fine precious metals with a private contractor or the DLA.

§ 102–40.230 How do we handle universal waste(s) (UWs)?

When disposing of universal waste, follow the instructions on the Web sites below, which contain descriptions of the commodities addressed, as well as the handling and disposal requirements from the relevant sections of 40 CFR part 273:

(a) *Batteries. http://www.epa.gov/hazard/wastetypes/universal/batteries.htm;*

(b) *Pesticides. http://www.epa.gov/epawaste/hazard/wastetypes/universal/pesticides.htm;*

(c) *Mercury-containing equipment. http://www.epa.gov/epawaste/hazard/wastetypes/universal/mce.htm;* and

(d) *Mercury-containing light bulbs (such as fluorescent bulbs). http://www.epa.gov/osw/hazard/wastetypes/universal/lamps/index.htm.*

§ 102–40.235 How do we handle motor vehicles not suitable for highway use?

Refer to subpart H of part 102–34 of this subchapter for the general policies regarding disposal of motor vehicles. Some Government-owned motor vehicles might receive such extensive damage as a result of an accident, event or other activity, that they are no longer suitable for utilization, donation, or sale for highway use. Such vehicles may only be donated or sold for salvage or scrap. Prior to disposal of damaged motor vehicles, you must evaluate known damage to determine their suitability for continued highway use. When a determination is made that a vehicle is unfit for continued highway use, you must include such information in the property record and subsequent reports. When selling such vehicles, provide an appropriate warning statement in the solicitation regarding vehicle condition that the vehicle cannot be titled for highway use. See § 102–34.305 of this subchapter (note to § 102–34.305(a)(2)) if the vehicle is not designed or not legal for operation on highways.

APPENDIX A TO PART 102–40—FEDERAL SUPPLY CLASSES (FSC) COMPOSED PREDOMINANTLY OF HAZARDOUS ITEMS

FSC	Nomenclature
6810	Chemicals.
6820	Dyes.
6830	Gases: Compressed & liquefied.
6840	Pest control agents & disinfectants.
6850	Misc. chemical specialties.
7930	Cleaning & polishing compounds & preparations.
8010	Paints, dopes, varnishes, & related products.
8030	Preservative & sealing compounds.
8040	Adhesives.
9110	Fuels, solid.
9130	Liquid propellants & fuels, petroleum base.
9135	Liquid propellant fuels & oxidizers, chemical base.
9140	Fuel oils.
9150	Oils & greases: cutting, lubricating, & hydraulic.
9160	Misc. waxes, oils, & fats.

APPENDIX B TO PART 102–40—FEDERAL SUPPLY CLASSES AND GROUPS WHICH CONTAIN A SIGNIFICANT NUMBER OF HAZARDOUS ITEMS

NOTE: If an item is determined to be hazardous material as defined in § 102–40.30, a Material Safety Data Sheet (or equivalent) should accompany the item even though the Federal Supply Class or Group is not listed in this table.

Federal supply class/group	Title	Examples of hazardous materials requiring identification
1370	Pyrotechnics	Warning fuse, fire starter.
1375	Demolition materials	Explosive device.
2520	Vehicular power transmission components.	Items containing asbestos.
2530	Vehicular brake, steering, axle, wheel, and track components.	Items containing asbestos.

Federal supply class/ group	Title	Examples of hazardous materials requiring identification
2540 ....,...........	Vehicular furniture and accessories	Items containing asbestos.
2640	Tire rebuilding and tire and tube repair materials.	Items containing flammable or toxic compounds.
Group 28	Engines, turbines, and components	Engine valves containing metallic sodium.
Group 29	Engine accessories	Engine valves containing metallic sodium.
Group 30	Mechanical power transmission equipment.	Equipment containing hazardous hydraulic fluid, including PCBs.
Group 34	Metalworking machinery	Equipment containing hazardous hydraulic fluids, including PCBs.
3433	Gas welding, heat cutting, and metalizing equipment.	Compressed gases.
3439	Miscellaneous welding, soldering, and brazing supplies and accessories.	Hazardous items such as cleaners, acids, flux, and supplies that contain or produce hazardous fumes.
3610	Printing, duplication, and bookbinding equipment.	Flammable or toxic lithographic solutions.
3655	Gas generating and dispensing systems, fixed or mobile.	Items that produce hazardous fumes.
3680	Foundry machinery, related equipment and supplies.	Flammable or toxic casting compounds.
4240	Safety and rescue equipment	Items which involve oxygen, compressed gases, or contain emitting charges.
5610	Mineral construction materials, bulk	Hazardous items such as cutback asphalt, deck and floor covering, deck and surface underlay compound, sealing compound, flight deck compound.
5660	Wallboard, building paper, and thermal insulation materials.	Asbestos cloth which has loose fibers or particles that may become airborne and materials containing formaldehyde.
5820	Radio and television communication equipment, except airborne.	Circuit cooler items that contain gases that are regarded as hazardous to the earth's ozone layer.
5835	Sound recording and reproducing equipment.	Recording tape cleaners that contain hazardous cleaning fluids.
5910	Capacitors	Items that contain polychlorinated biphenyls (PCBs) or sulfuric acid.
5915	Filters and networks	Items that contain polychlorinated biphenyls (PCBs).
5920	Fuses and lighting arresters	Items containing radioactive material.
5925	Circuit breakers	Items containing radioactive material.
5930	Switches	Items containing radioactive material.
5935	Connectors, electrical	Kits that contain flammable chemicals.
5950	Coils and transformers	Items containing polychlorinated biphenyls (PCBs).
5960	Electron tubes and associated hardware	Tubes that contain radioactive isotopes and require warning labels and magnetron tubes, which require special precautions when being prepared for air shipment.
5965	Headsets, handsets, microphones, and speakers.	Items containing magnetic material.
5970	Electrical insulators and insulating materials.	Items containing flammable solvents.
5975	Electrical hardware and supplies	Items containing asbestos.
5985	Antennas, waveguides, and related equipment.	Kits that contain flammable chemicals.
5999	Miscellaneous electrical and oxide electronic components.	Contact plates that contain beryllium.
Group 61	Electric wire and power and distribution equipment.	Power factor capacitors containing PCBs.
6120	Transformers: Distribution and power station.	Transformers containing PCBs.
6135	Batteries, primary	Lead-acid, lithium, and mercury batteries and alkaline (with electrolyte).
6140	Batteries, secondary	Items that are wet or moist containing corrosive or other hazardous compounds.
6145	Wire and cable, electrical	Insulated wire containing asbestos.
6220	Electric vehicular lights and fixtures	Items that contain mercury.
6230	Electric portable and hand lighting equipment.	Items that contain wet batteries.
6240	Electric lamps	Items that contain mercury.
6260	Nonelectrical lighting fixtures	Items that contain mercury.
6350	Miscellaneous signal and security detection systems.	Items that contain wet batteries or radioactive material.
6505	Drugs, biologicals, and official reagents	Hazardous items as defined in Sec. 102–40.30.
6508	Medicated cosmetics and toiletries	Hazardous items as defined in Sec. 102–40.30, subject to DOT Hazardous Materials Regulations.
6510	Surgical dressing materials	Items containing flammable solvents.
6520	Dental instruments, equipment, and supplies.	Items containing flammable solvents, mercury or asbestos.

185

Federal supply class/group	Title	Examples of hazardous materials requiring identification
6525	X-ray equipment and supplies: medical, dental, veterinary.	Items containing hazardous chemicals, solvents, .
6625	Electrical and electronic properties measuring and testing instruments.	Items containing radioactive materials.
6640	Laboratory equipment and supplies	Items containing flammable compounds, mercury or asbestos.
6685	Pressure, temperature, and humidity measuring and controlling instruments.	Items containing mercury or compressed gases.
6740	Photographic	Items containing radioactive compounds.
6750	Photographic supplies	Items containing hazardous chemicals, solvents, thinners, and cements.
6780	Photographic sets, kits, and outfits	Items containing hazardous chemicals, solvents, thinners, and cements.
7360	Sets, kits, and outfits; food preparation and serving.	Items containing compressed gases such as fire extinguishers.
7510	Office supplies	Hazardous items, such as thinners, cleaning fluids, flammable inks, and varnishes.
8405	Outerwear, men's	Maintenance kits containing flammable solvents.
8410	Outerwear, women's	Maintenance kits containing flammable solvents.
8415	Clothing, special purpose	Maintenance kits containing flammable solvents.
8465	Individual equipment	Maintenance kits containing flammable solvents.
8510	Perfumes, toilet preparations, and powders.	Shipping containers and pressurized containers with flammable or nonflammable propellants.
8520	Toilet soap, shaving preparations, and dentifrices.	Shipping containers and pressurized containers with flammable or nonflammable propellants.
8720	Fertilizers	Items containing weed and pest control or other harmful ingredients or because of their composition, are hazardous.
9390	Miscellaneous fabricated nonmetallic materials.	Items containing flammable solvents or asbestos.
9920	Smokers' articles and matches	Lighter fuel and matches only.
9930	Memorials; cemeteries and mortuary equipment and supplies.	Items containing formaldehyde or its solutions.

PART 102–41—DISPOSITION OF SEIZED, FORFEITED, VOLUNTARILY ABANDONED, AND UNCLAIMED PERSONAL PROPERTY

Subpart A—General Provisions

Sec.

Subpart B—Seized or Forfeited Personal Property

Subpart C—Voluntarily Abandoned Personal Property

AUTHORITY: 40 U.S.C. 121(c).

SOURCE: 71 FR 41370, July 21, 2006, unless otherwise noted.

Subpart A—General Provisions

§ 102–41.5 What does this part cover?

(a) This part covers the disposition of seized, forfeited, voluntarily abandoned, and unclaimed personal property under the custody of any Federal agency located in the United States, the U.S. Virgin Islands, American Samoa, Guam, the Commonwealth of Puerto Rico, the Northern Mariana Islands, the Federated States of Micronesia, the Marshall Islands, and Palau. Disposition of such personal property located elsewhere must be in accordance with holding agency regulations. Please see § 102–36.380 of this subchapter B regarding the disposal of foreign excess. The General Services Administration (GSA) does not normally accept responsibility for disposal of property located outside the United States and its territories. Additional guidance on disposition of seized, forfeited, voluntarily abandoned, and unclaimed personal property that requires special handling (e.g., firearms, hazardous materials) is contained in part 101–42 of this title. Additional guidance on the disposition of firearms (as scrap only), distilled spirits, wine, beer, and drug paraphernalia is provided in subpart E of this part.

(b) These regulations do not include disposal of seized, forfeited, voluntarily abandoned, and unclaimed personal property covered under authorities outside of the following statutes:

(1) 40 U.S.C. 552, Abandoned or Unclaimed Property on Government Premises.

(2) 40 U.S.C. 1306, Disposition of Abandoned or Forfeited Property.

(3) 26 U.S.C. 5688, Forfeited Distilled Spirits, Wines, and Beer.

(4) 26 U.S.C. 5872, Forfeited Firearms.

(5) 21 U.S.C. 863, Drug Paraphernalia.

§ 102–41.10 To whom do "we", "you", and their variants refer?

Use of pronouns "we", "you", and their variants throughout this part refer to the agency having custody of the personal property.

§ 102–41.15 How do we request a deviation from these requirements and who can approve it?

See §§ 102–2.60 through 102–2.110 of this chapter to request a deviation from the requirements of this part.

DEFINITIONS

§ 102–41.20 What definitions apply to this part?

The following definitions apply to this part:

Beer means an alcoholic beverage made from malted cereal grain, flavored with hops, and brewed by slow fermentation.

Distilled spirits, as defined in the Federal Alcohol Administration Act (27 U.S.C. 211), means ethyl alcohol; hydrated oxide of ethyl; or spirits of wine, whiskey, rum, brandy, gin, and other distilled spirits, including all dilutions and mixtures thereof, for non-industrial use.

Drug paraphernalia means any equipment, product, or material primarily intended or designed for use in manufacturing, compounding, converting, concealing, processing, preparing, or introducing into the human body a controlled substance in violation of the Controlled Substances Act (see 21 U.S.C. 863). It includes items primarily for use in injecting, ingesting, inhaling, or otherwise introducing marijuana, cocaine, hashish, hashish oil, PCP, or amphetamines into the human body.

Eleemosynary institution means any nonprofit health or medical institution that is organized and operated for charitable purposes.

Firearms means any weapon, silencer, or destructive device designed to, or readily convertible to, expel a projectile by the action of an explosive, as defined in the Internal Revenue Code (26 U.S.C. 5845). Excludes antique firearms as defined in 26 U.S.C. 5845(g).

Forfeited property means personal property that the Government has acquired ownership of through a summary process or court order pursuant to any law of the United States.

Seized property means personal property that has been confiscated by a Federal agency, and whose care and handling will be the responsibility of the agency until final ownership is determined by the judicial process.

Unclaimed property means personal property unknowingly abandoned and found on premises owned or leased by the Government, i.e., lost and found property.

Voluntarily abandoned property means personal property abandoned to any Federal agency in a way that immediately vests title to the property in the Government. There must be written or circumstantial evidence that the property was intentionally and voluntarily abandoned. This evidence should be clear that the property was not simply lost by the owner.

Wine means the fermented juice of a plant product, as defined in 27 U.S.C. 211.

RESPONSIBILITY

§ 102–41.25 Who retains custody and is responsible for the reporting, care, and handling of property covered by this part?

You, the holding agency, normally retain physical custody of the property and are responsible for its care and handling pending final disposition. With the exception of property listed in § 102–41.35, you must report promptly to the GSA forfeited, voluntarily abandoned, or unclaimed personal property not being retained for official use and seized property on which proceedings for forfeiture by court decree are being started or have begun. In general, the procedures for reporting such property parallel those for reporting excess personal property under part 102–36 of this subchapter B.

§ 102–41.30 What is GSA's role in the disposition of property covered by this part?

(a) *Seized property subject to court proceedings for forfeiture.* (1) If the seizing agency files a request for the property for its official use, the GSA Region 3/National Capital Region will apply to the court for an order to turn the property over to the agency should forfeiture be decreed. If no such request has been filed, GSA will determine whether retention of the property for Federal official use is in the Government's best interest, and, if so, will apply to the court to order delivery of the property to—

(i) Any other Federal agency that requests it; or

(ii) The seizing agency to be retained for a reasonable time in case the property may later become necessary to any agency for official use.

(2) In the event that the property is not ordered by competent authority to be forfeited to the United States, it may be returned to the claimant.

(b) *Forfeited, voluntarily abandoned, or unclaimed property.* When forfeited, voluntarily abandoned, or unclaimed property is reported to GSA for disposal, GSA will direct its disposition by—

(1) Transfer to another Federal agency;

(2) Donation to an eligible recipient, if the property is not needed by a Federal agency and there are no requirements for reimbursement to satisfy the claims of owners, lien holders, or other lawful claimants;

(3) Sale; or

(4) Abandonment and destruction in accordance with § 102–36.305 of this subchapter B.

§ 102–41.35 Do we report to GSA all seized personal property subject to judicial forfeiture as well as forfeited, voluntarily abandoned, or unclaimed personal property not retained for official use?

Yes, send GSA reports of excess (see § 102–36.125 of this subchapter B) for all seized personal property subject to judicial forfeiture as well as forfeited, voluntarily abandoned, or unclaimed personal property not required for official use, except the following, whose disposition is covered under other statutes and authorities:

(a) Forfeited firearms or munitions of war seized by the Department of Commerce and transferred to the Department of Defense (DOD) pursuant to 22 U.S.C. 401.

(b) Forfeited firearms directly transferable to DOD by law.

(c) Seeds, plants, or misbranded packages seized by the Department of Agriculture.

(d) Game animals and equipment (other than vessels, including cargo) seized by the Department of the Interior.

(e) Files of papers and undeliverable mail in the custody of the United States Postal Service.

(f) Articles in the custody of the Department of Commerce Patent and Trademark Office that are in violation of laws governing trademarks or patents.

(g) Unclaimed and voluntarily abandoned personal property subject to laws and regulations of the U.S. Customs and Border Protection, Department of Homeland Security.

(h) Property seized in payment of or as security for debts arising under the internal revenue laws.

(i) Lost, abandoned, or unclaimed personal property the Coast Guard or the military services are authorized to dispose of under 10 U.S.C. 2575.

(j) Property of deceased veterans left on a Government facility subject to 38 U.S.C. 8501.

(k) Controlled substances reportable to the Drug Enforcement Administration, Department of Justice, Washington, DC 20537.

(l) Forfeited, condemned, or voluntarily abandoned tobacco, snuff, cigars, or cigarettes which, if offered for sale, will not bring a price equal to the internal revenue tax due and payable thereon; and which is subject to destruction or delivery without payment of any tax to any hospital maintained by the Federal Government for the use of present or former members of the military.

(m) Property determined appropriate for abandonment/destruction (see § 102–36.305 of this subchapter B).

(n) Personal property where handling and disposal is governed by specific legislative authority notwithstanding Title 40 of the United States Code.

Subpart B—Seized or Forfeited Personal Property

§ 102–41.40 How is personal property forfeited?

Personal property that has been seized by a Federal agency may be forfeited through court decree (judicial forfeiture) or administratively forfeited if the agency has specific authority without going through the courts.

§ 102–41.45 May we place seized personal property into official use before the forfeiture process is completed?

No, property under seizure and pending forfeiture cannot be placed into official use until a final determination is made to vest title in the Government.

§ 102–41.50 May we retain forfeited personal property for official use?

Yes, you may retain for official use personal property forfeited to your agency, except for property you are required by law to sell. Retention of large sedans and limousines for official use is only authorized under the provisions of part 102–34 of this subchapter B. Except for the items noted in § 102–41.35, report to GSA all forfeited personal property not being retained for official use.

§ 102–41.55 Where do we send the reports for seized or forfeited personal property?

(a) Except for the items noted in paragraph (b) of this section, report seized or forfeited personal property not retained for official use to the General Services Administration, Property Management Branch (3FPD), Washington, DC 20407.

(b) Report aircraft, firearms, and vessels to the regional GSA Property Management Branch office specified in § 102–36.125 of this subchapter B.

§ 102–41.60 Are there special requirements in reporting seized or forfeited personal property to GSA?

Yes, in addition to the information required in § 102–36.235 of this subchapter B for reporting excess, you must indicate—

(a) Whether the property—

(1) Was forfeited in a judicial proceeding or administratively (without going through a court);

(2) Is subject to pending court proceedings for forfeiture, and, if so, the name of the defendant, the place and judicial district of the court from which the decree will be issued, and whether you wish to retain the property for official use;

(b) The report or case number under which the property is listed; and

(c) The existence or probability of a lien, or other accrued or accruing charges, and the amount involved.

§ 102–41.65 What happens to forfeited personal property that is transferred or retained for official use?

Except for drug paraphernalia (see §§ 102–41.210 through 102–41.235), forfeited personal property retained for official use or transferred to another Federal agency under this subpart loses its identity as forfeited property. When no longer required for official use, you must report it to GSA as excess for disposal in accordance with part 102–36 of this subchapter B. You must follow the additional provisions of subpart E of this part and part 101–42 of Chapter 101, Federal Property Management Regulations in this title when disposing of firearms, distilled spirits, wine, beer, and drug paraphernalia.

§ 102–41.70 Are transfers of forfeited personal property reimbursable?

Recipient agencies do not pay for the property. However, you may charge the recipient agency all costs you incurred in storing, packing, loading, preparing for shipment, and transporting the property. If there are commercial charges incident to forfeiture prior to the transfer, the recipient agency must pay these charges when billed by the commercial organization. Any payment due to lien holders or other lawful claimants under a judicial forfeiture must be made in accordance with provisions of the court decree.

§ 102–41.75 May we retain the proceeds from the sale of forfeited personal property?

No, you must deposit the sales proceeds in the U.S. Treasury as miscellaneous receipts, unless otherwise directed by court decree or specifically authorized by statute.

Subpart C—Voluntarily Abandoned Personal Property

§ 102–41.80 When is personal property voluntarily abandoned?

Personal property is voluntarily abandoned when the owner of the property intentionally and voluntarily gives up title to such property and title vests in the Government. The receiving agency ordinarily documents receipt of the property to evidence its voluntary relinquishment. Evidence of the voluntary abandonment may be circumstantial.

§ 102–41.85 What choices do I have for retaining or disposing of voluntarily abandoned personal property?

You may either retain or dispose of voluntarily abandoned personal property based on the following circumstances:

(a) If your agency has a need for the property, you may retain it for official use, except for large sedans and limousines which may only be retained for official use as authorized under part 102–34 of this subchapter B. See § 102–41.90 for how retained property must be handled.

(b) If your agency doesn't need the property, you should determine whether it may be abandoned or destroyed in accordance with the provisions at FMR 102–36.305 through 102–36.330. Furthermore, in addition to the circumstances when property may be abandoned or destroyed without public notice at

FMR 102–36.330, voluntarily abandoned property may also be abandoned or destroyed without public notice when the estimated resale value of the property is less than $500.

(c) If the property is not retained for official use or abandoned or destroyed, you must report it to GSA as excess in accordance with § 102–41.95.

§ 102–41.90 What happens to voluntarily abandoned personal property retained for official use?

Voluntarily abandoned personal property retained for official use or transferred to another Federal agency under this subpart loses its identity as voluntarily abandoned property. When no longer required for official use, you must report it to GSA as excess, or abandon/destroy the property, in accordance with part 102–36 of this subchapter B.

§ 102–41.95 Where do we send the reports for voluntarily abandoned personal property?

Except for aircraft, firearms, and vessels, report voluntarily abandoned personal property to the regional GSA Property Management Branch office for the region in which the property is located. Report aircraft, firearms, and vessels to the regional GSA Property Management Branch office specified in § 102–36.125 of this subchapter B.

§ 102–41.100 What information do we provide when reporting voluntarily abandoned personal property to GSA?

When reporting voluntarily abandoned personal property to GSA, you must provide a description and location of the property, and annotate that the property was voluntarily abandoned.

§ 102–41.105 What happens to voluntarily abandoned personal property when reported to GSA?

Voluntarily abandoned personal property reported to GSA will be made available for transfer, donation, sale, or abandonment/destruction in accordance with parts 102–36, 102–37, 102–38, and §§ 102–36.305 through 102–36.330 of this subchapter B, respectively. You must follow the additional provisions of §§ 102–41.190 through 102–41.235 and part 101–42 of Chapter 101, Federal Property Management Regulations in this title when disposing of firearms and other property requiring special handling.

§ 102–41.110 Are transfers of voluntarily abandoned personal property reimbursable?

No, all transfers of voluntarily abandoned personal property will be without reimbursement. However, you may charge the recipient agency all costs you incurred in storing, packing, loading, preparing for shipment, and transporting the property.

§ 102–41.115 May we retain the proceeds received from the sale of voluntarily abandoned personal property?

No, you must deposit the sales proceeds in the U.S. Treasury as miscellaneous receipts unless your agency has specific statutory authority to do otherwise.

Subpart D—Unclaimed Personal Property

§ 102–41.120 How long must we hold unclaimed personal property before disposition?

You must generally hold unclaimed personal property for 30 calendar days from the date it was found. Unless the previous owner files a claim, title to the property vests in the Government after 30 days, and you may retain or dispose of the property in accordance with this part. However, see the following sections for handling of unclaimed personal property under specific circumstances.

§ 102–41.125 What choices do I have for retaining or disposing of unclaimed personal property?

You may either retain or dispose of unclaimed abandoned personal property based on the following circumstances:

(a) If your agency has a need for the property, you may retain it for official use if you have held the unclaimed property for 30 calendar days and the former owner has not filed a claim. After 30 days, title vests in the Government and you may retain the un-

claimed property for official use. Large sedans and limousines which may only be retained for official use as authorized under part 102–34 of this subchapter B. See § 102–41.130 for how retained property must be handled.

(b) If your agency doesn't need the property, you should determine whether it may be immediately abandoned or destroyed in accordance with the provisions at FMR 102–36.305 through 102–36.330. You are not required to hold unclaimed property for 30 days, if you decide to abandon or destroy it. Title to the property immediately vests in the Government in these circumstances. In addition to the circumstances when property may be abandoned or destroyed without public notice at FMR 102–36.330, unclaimed personal property may also be abandoned or destroyed without public notice when the estimated resale value of the property is less than $500. See § 102–41.135 for procedures to be followed if a claim is filed.

(c) If the property is not retained for official use or abandoned or destroyed, you must report it to GSA as excess in accordance with § 102–41.140.

§ 102–41.130 What must we do when we retain unclaimed personal property for official use?

(a) You must maintain records of unclaimed personal property retained for official use for 3 years after title vests in the Government to permit identification of the property should the former owner file a claim for the property. You must also deposit funds received from disposal of such property in a special account to cover any valid claim filed within this 3-year period.

(b) When you no longer need the unclaimed property which you have placed in official use, report it as excess in the same manner as other excess property under part 102–36 of this subchapter B.

§ 102–41.135 How much reimbursement do we pay the former owner when he or she files a claim for unclaimed personal property that we no longer have?

If the property was sold, reimbursement of the property to the former owner must not exceed any proceeds from the disposal of such property, less the costs of the Government's care and handling of the property. If the property was abandoned or destroyed in accordance with § 102–41.125, or otherwise used or transferred, reimbursement of the property to the former owner must not exceed the estimated resale value of the property at the time of the vesting of the property with the Government, less costs incident to the care and handling of the property, as determined by the General Services Administration, Office of Travel, Transportation, and Asset Management (MT), Washington DC, 20405.

§ 102–41.140 When do we report to GSA unclaimed personal property not retained for official use?

After you have held the property for 30 calendar days and no one has filed a claim for it, the title to the property vests in the Government. If you decide not to retain the property for official use, report it as excess to GSA in accordance with part 102–36 of this subchapter B.

§ 102–41.145 Where do we send the reports for unclaimed personal property?

Except for the items noted in § 102–36.125 of this subchapter B, report unclaimed personal property to the regional GSA Property Management Branch office for the region in which the property is located.

§ 102–41.150 What special information do we provide on reports of unclaimed personal property?

On reports of unclaimed personal property, you must provide the report or case number assigned by your agency, property description and location, and indicate the property as unclaimed and the estimated fair market value.

§ 102–41.155 Is unclaimed personal property available for transfer to another Federal agency?

Yes, unclaimed personal property is available for transfer to another Federal agency, but only after 30 calendar days from the date of finding such property and no claim has been filed by the former owner, and with fair market value reimbursement from the recipient agency. The transferred property then loses its identity as unclaimed property and becomes property of the Government, and when no longer needed it must be reported excess in accordance with part 102–36 of this subchapter B.

§ 102–41.160 May we retain the reimbursement from transfers of unclaimed personal property?

No, you must deposit the reimbursement from transfers of unclaimed personal property in a special account for a period of 3 years pending a claim from the former owner. After 3 years, you must deposit these funds into miscellaneous receipts of the U.S. Treasury unless your agency has statutory authority to do otherwise.

§ 102–41.165 May we require reimbursement for the costs incurred in the transfer of unclaimed personal property?

Yes, you may require reimbursement from the recipient agency of any direct costs you incur in the transfer of the unclaimed property (e.g., storage, packing, preparation for shipping, loading, and transportation).

§ 102–41.170 Is unclaimed personal property available for donation?

No, unclaimed personal property is not available for donation because reimbursement at fair market value is required.

§ 102–41.175 May we sell unclaimed personal property?

Yes, you may sell unclaimed personal property after title vests in the Government (as provided for in § 102–41.120) and when there is no Federal interest. You may sell unclaimed personal property subject to the same terms and conditions as applicable to surplus personal property and in accordance with part 102–38 of this subchapter B.

§ 102–41.180 May we retain the proceeds from the sale of unclaimed personal property?

No, you must deposit proceeds from the sale of unclaimed personal property in a special account to be maintained for a period of 3 years pending a possible claim by the former owner. After the 3-year period, you must deposit the funds in the U.S. Treasury as miscellaneous receipts or in such other agency accounts when specifically authorized by statute.

Subpart E—Personal Property Requiring Special Handling

§ 102–41.185 Are there certain types of forfeited, voluntarily abandoned, or unclaimed property that must be handled differently than other property addressed in this part?

Yes, you must comply with the additional provisions in this subpart when disposing of the types of property listed here.

FIREARMS

§ 102–41.190 May we retain forfeited, voluntarily abandoned, or unclaimed firearms for official use?

Generally, no; you may retain forfeited, voluntarily abandoned, or unclaimed firearms only when you are statutorily authorized to use firearms for official purposes.

§ 102–41.195 How do we dispose of forfeited, voluntarily abandoned, or unclaimed firearms not retained for official use?

Report forfeited, voluntarily abandoned, or unclaimed firearms not retained for official use to the General Services Administration, Property Management Branch (7FP–8), Denver, CO 80225–0506 for disposal in accordance with § 101–42.1102–10 of the Federal Property Management Regulations in this title.

§ 102–41.200 Are there special disposal provisions for firearms that are seized and forfeited for a violation of the National Firearms Act?

Yes, firearms seized and forfeited for a violation of the National Firearms Act (26 U.S.C. 5801—5872) are subject to the disposal provisions of 26 U.S.C. 5872(b). When there is no contrary judgment or action under such forfeiture, GSA will direct the disposition of the firearms. GSA may—

(a) Authorize retention for official use by the Treasury Department;

(b) Transfer to an executive agency for use by it; or

(c) Order the firearms destroyed.

FORFEITED DISTILLED SPIRITS, WINE, AND BEER

§ 102–41.205 Do we report all forfeited distilled spirits, wine, and beer to GSA for disposal?

(a) Yes, except do not report distilled spirits, wine, and beer not fit for human consumption or for medicinal, scientific, or mechanical purposes. When reporting, indicate quantities and kinds, proof rating, and condition for shipping. GSA (3FPD) may transfer such property to another Federal agency for official purposes, or donate it to eligible eleemosynary institutions for medicinal purposes only.

(b) Forfeited distilled spirits, wine, and beer that are not retained for official use by the seizing agency or transferred or donated to eligible recipients by GSA must be destroyed. You must document the destruction with a record of the time and location, property description, and quantities destroyed.

DRUG PARAPHERNALIA

§ 102–41.210 What are some examples of drug paraphernalia?

Some examples of drug paraphernalia are—

(a) Metal, wooden, acrylic, glass, stone, plastic or ceramic pipes with or without screens, permanent screens, hashish heads, or punctured metal bowls;

(b) Water pipes;

(c) Carburetion tubes and devices;

(d) Smoking and carburetion masks;

(e) Roach clips (objects used to hold burning material, such as a marijuana cigarette, that has become too small or too short to be held in the hand);

(f) Miniature spoons with level capacities of one-tenth cubic centimeter or less;

(g) Chamber pipes;

(h) Carburetor pipes;

(i) Electric pipes;

(j) Air-driven pipes;

(k) Chillums;

(l) Bongs;

(m) Ice pipes or chillers;

(n) Wired cigarette papers; or

(o) Cocaine freebase kits.

§ 102–41.215 Do we report to GSA all forfeited, voluntarily abandoned, or unclaimed drug paraphernalia not required for official use?

No, only report drug paraphernalia that has been seized and forfeited for a violation of 21 U.S.C. 863. Unless statutorily authorized to do otherwise, destroy all other forfeited, voluntarily abandoned, or unclaimed drug paraphernalia. You must ensure the destruction is performed in the presence of two witnesses (employees of your agency), and retain in your records a signed certification of destruction.

§ 102–41.220 Is drug paraphernalia forfeited under 21 U.S.C. 863 available for transfer to other Federal agencies or donation through a State Agency for Surplus Property (SASP)?

Yes, but GSA will only transfer or donate forfeited drug paraphernalia for law enforcement or educational purposes and only for use by Federal, State, or local authorities. Federal or State Agencies for Surplus Property (SASP) requests for such items must be processed through the General Services Administration, Property Management Branch (3FPD), Washington, DC 20407. The recipient must certify on the transfer document that the drug paraphernalia will be used for law enforcement or educational purposes only.

§ 102–41.225 Are there special provisions to reporting and transferring drug paraphernalia forfeited under 21 U.S.C. 863?

Yes, you must ensure that such drug paraphernalia does not lose its identity as forfeited property. Reports of excess and transfer documents for such drug paraphernalia must include the annotation that the property was seized and forfeited under 21 U.S.C. 863.

§ 102–41.230 May SASPs pick up or store donated drug paraphernalia in their distribution centers?

No, you must release donated drug paraphernalia directly to the donee as designated on the transfer document.

§ 102–41.235 May we sell forfeited drug paraphernalia?

No, you must destroy any forfeited drug paraphernalia not needed for transfer or donation and document the destruction as specified in § 102–41.215.

PART 102–42—UTILIZATION, DONATION, AND DISPOSAL OF FOREIGN GIFTS AND DECORATIONS

Subpart A—General Provisions

Sec.
102–42.5　What does this part cover?

DEFINITIONS

102–42.10　What definitions apply to this part?

CARE, HANDLING AND DISPOSITION

102–42.15　Under what circumstances may an employee retain a foreign gift or decoration?
102–42.20　What is the typical disposition process for gifts and decorations that employees are not authorized to retain?
102–42.25　Who retains custody of gifts and decorations pending disposal?
102–42.30　Who is responsible for the security, care and handling, and delivery of gifts and decorations to GSA, and all costs associated with such functions?
102–42.35　Can the employing agency be reimbursed for transfers of gifts and decorations?

APPRAISALS

102–42.40　When is a commercial necessary?
102–42.45　What is my agency's responsibility for establishing procedures for obtaining an appraisal?
102–42.50　What types of appraisals may my agency consider?
102–42.55　What does the employing agency do with the appraisal?

SPECIAL DISPOSALS

102–42.60　Who is responsible for gifts and decorations received by Senators and Senate employees?
102–42.65　What happens if the Commission on Art and Antiquities does not dispose of a gift or decoration?
102–42.70　Who handles gifts and decorations received by the President or Vice President or a member of their family?
102–42.75　How are gifts containing hazardous materials handled?

Subpart B—Utilization of Foreign Gifts and Decorations

102–42.80　To whom do "we", "you", and their variants refer?
102–42.85　What gifts or decorations must we report to GSA?

AUTHORITY: 40 U.S.C. 121(c); sec. 515, 5 U.S.C. 7342 (91 Stat. 862).

SOURCE: 65 FR 45539, July 24, 2000, unless otherwise noted.

Subpart A—General Provisions

§ 102–42.5   What does this part cover?

This part covers the acceptance and disposition of gifts of more than minimal value and decorations from foreign governments under 5 U.S.C. 7342. If you receive gifts other than from a foreign government, you should refer to § 102–36.405 of this subchapter B.

[71 FR 28778, May 18, 2006]

DEFINITIONS

§ 102–42.10   What definitions apply to this part?

The following definitions apply to this part:

Decoration means an order, device, medal, badge, insignia, emblem, or award offered by or received from a foreign government.

Employee means:

(1) An employee as defined by 5 U.S.C. 2105 and an officer or employee of the United States Postal Service or of the Postal Rate Commission;

(2) An expert or consultant who is under contract under 5 U.S.C. 3109 with the United States or any agency, department, or establishment thereof, including, in the case of an organization performing services under that section, any individual involved in the performance of such services;

(3) An individual employed by or occupying an office or position in the government of a territory or possession of the United States or the government of the District of Columbia;

(4) A member of a uniformed service as specified in 10 U.S.C 101;

(5) The President and the Vice President;

(6) A Member of Congress as defined by 5 U.S.C. 2106 (except the Vice President) and any Delegate to the Congress; and

(7) The spouse of an individual described in paragraphs (1) through (6) of this definition of *employee* (unless this individual and his or her spouse are separated) or a dependent (within the meaning of section 152 of the Internal Revenue Code of 1986 (26 U.S.C. 152)) of this individual, other than a spouse or dependent who is an employee under paragraphs (1) through (6) of this definition of *employee.*

Employing agency means:

(1) The department, agency, office, or other entity in which an employee is employed, for other legislative branch employees and for all executive branch employees;

(2) The Committee on Standards of Official Conduct of the House of Representatives, for Members and employees of the House of Representatives, except that those responsibilities specified in 5 U.S.C. 7342(c)(2)(A), (e)(1), and (g)(2)(B) must be carried out by the Clerk of the House;

(3) The Select Committee on Ethics of the Senate, for Senators and employees of the Senate, except that

those responsibilities (other than responsibilities involving approval of the employing agency) specified in 5 U.S.C. 7342(c)(2), (d), and (g)(2)(B) must be carried out by the Secretary of the Senate; and

(4) The Administrative Offices of the United States Courts, for judges and judicial branch employees.

Foreign government means:

(1) Any unit of foreign government, including any national, State, local, and municipal government and their foreign equivalents;

(2) Any international or multinational organization whose membership is composed of any unit of a foreign government; and

(3) Any agent or representative of any such foreign government unit or organization while acting as such.

Gift means a monetary or non-monetary present (other than a decoration) offered by or received from a foreign government. A monetary gift includes anything that may commonly be used in a financial transaction, such as cash or currency, checks, money orders, bonds, shares of stock, and other securities and negotiable financial instruments.

Minimal value means a retail value in the United States at the time of acceptance that is at or below the dollar value established by GSA and published in a Federal Management Regulation (FMR) Bulletin at *www.gsa.gov/ personalpropertypolicy*.

(1) GSA will adjust the definition of minimal value every three years, in consultation with the Secretary of State, to reflect changes in the Consumer Price Index for the immediately preceding 3-year period.

(2) An employing agency may, by regulation, specify a lower value than this Government-wide value for its agency employees.

Spouse means any individual who is lawfully married (unless legally separated), including an individual married to a person of the same sex who was legally married in a state or other jurisdiction (including a foreign country), that recognizes such marriages, regardless of whether or not the individual's state of residency recognizes such marriages. The term *spouse* does not include individuals in a formal relationship recognized by a state, which is other than lawful marriage; it also does not include individuals in a marriage in a jurisdiction outside the United States that is not recognized as a lawful marriage under United States law.

[65 FR 45539, July 24, 2000, as amended at 68 FR 56496, Sept. 4, 2002; 70 FR 2318, Jan. 12, 2005; 71 FR 28778, May 18, 2006; 73 FR 7475, Feb. 8, 2008; 76 FR 30551, May 26, 2011; 79 FR 18477, Apr. 2, 2014; 80 FR 21190, Apr. 17, 2015]

CARE, HANDLING AND DISPOSITION

§ 102–42.15 Under what circumstances may an employee retain a foreign gift or decoration?

Employees, with the approval of their employing agencies, may accept and retain:

(a) Gifts of minimal value received as souvenirs or marks of courtesy. When a gift of more than minimal value is accepted, the gift becomes the property of the U.S. Government, not the employee, and must be reported.

(b) Decorations that have been offered or awarded for outstanding or unusually meritorious performance. If the employing agency disapproves retention of the decoration by the employee, the decoration becomes the property of the U.S. Government.

§ 102–42.20 What is the typical disposition process for gifts and decorations that employees are not authorized to retain?

(a) *Non-monetary gifts or decorations.* When an employee receives a non-monetary gift above the minimal value or a decoration that he/she is not authorized to retain:

(1) The employee must report the gift or decoration to his/her employing agency within 60 days after accepting it.

(2) The employing agency determines if it will keep the gift or decoration for official use.

(3) If it does not return the gift or decoration to the donor or keep it for official use, the employing agency reports it as excess personal property to GSA for Federal utilization screening under § 102–42.95.

(4) If GSA does not transfer the gift or decoration during Federal utilization screening, the employee may purchase the gift or decoration (see § 102–42.140).

(5) If the employee declines to purchase the gift or decoration, and there is no Federal requirement for either, GSA may offer it for donation through State Agencies for Surplus Property (SASP) under part 102–37 of this subchapter B.

(6) If no SASP requests the gift or decoration for donation, GSA may offer it for public sale, with the approval of the Secretary of State, or will authorize the destruction of the gift or decoration under part 102–38 of this subchapter B.

(b) *Monetary gifts.* When an employee receives a monetary gift above the minimal value:

(1) The employee must report the gift to his/her employing agency within 60 days after accepting it.

(2) The employing agency must:

(i) Report a monetary gift with possible historic or numismatic (i.e., collectible) value to GSA; or

(ii) Deposit a monetary gift that has no historic or numismatic value with the Department of the Treasury.

[65 FR 45539, July 24, 2000, as amended at 71 FR 28778, May 18, 2006]

§ 102–42.25 Who retains custody of gifts and decorations pending disposal?

(a) The employing agency retains custody of gifts and decorations that employees have expressed an interest in purchasing.

(b) GSA will accept physical custody of gifts above the minimal value, which employees decline to purchase, or decorations that are not retained for official use or returned to donors.

NOTE TO § 102–42.25(b): GSA will not accept physical custody of foreign gifts of firearms. Firearms reported by the agency as excess must be disposed of in accordance with part 101–42 of this title.

§ 102–42.30 Who is responsible for the security, care and handling, and delivery of gifts and decorations to GSA, and all costs associated with such functions?

The employing agency is responsible for the security, care and handling, and delivery of gifts and decorations to GSA, and all costs associated with such functions.

§ 102–42.35 Can the employing agency be reimbursed for transfers of gifts and decorations?

No, all transfers of gifts and decorations to Federal agencies or donation through SASPs will be without reimbursement. However, the employing agency may require the receiving agency to pay all or part of the direct costs incurred by the employing agency in packing, preparation for shipment, loading, and transportation.

APPRAISALS

§ 102–42.40 When is an appraisal necessary?

An appraisal is necessary when—

(a) An employee indicates an interest in purchasing a gift or decoration. In this situation, the appraisal must be obtained before the gift or decoration is reported to GSA for screening (see 102–42.20); or

(b) GSA requires the employing agency to obtain an appraisal of a gift or decoration that the agency has retained for official use and no longer needs before accepting the agency's report of the item as excess personal property; or

(c) The policy of one's own agency requires it, pursuant to 5 U.S.C. 7342(g).

NOTE TO § 102–42.40 PARAGRAPHS (a) AND (b): Refer to § 102–42.50 for how appraisals under these two situations are handled.

[74 FR 2396, Jan. 15, 2009]

§ 102–42.45 What is my agency's responsibility for establishing procedures for obtaining an appraisal?

The employing agency is responsible for establishing its own procedure for obtaining an appraisal that represents the value of the gift in the United States. This applies to all gifts, even when the recipient wishes to retain and/or purchase the gift. Appraisals are required for gifts that are personalized (e.g., Books signed by the author, Gifts personally labeled).

[74 FR 2396, Jan. 15, 2009]

§ 102–42.50 What types of appraisals may my agency consider?

Your agency may allow—

(a) Written commercial appraisals conducted by an appraisal firm or trade organization; and

(b) Retail value appraisals where the value of the gift may be ascertained by reviewing current and reliable non-discounted retail catalogs, retail price lists, or retail Web site valuations.

[74 FR 2396, Jan. 15, 2009]

§ 102–42.55 What does the employing agency do with the appraisal?

When an appraisal is necessary under § 102–42.40, the employing agency must include the appraisal with the Standard Form (SF) 120, Report of Excess Personal Property, and send it to GSA in accordance with the requirements of § 102–42.95. By attaching the appraisal, the employing agency is certifying that the value cited is the retail value/appraised value of the item in the United States in U.S. dollars on the date set forth on the appraisal.

[74 FR 2396, Jan. 15, 2009]

SPECIAL DISPOSALS

§ 102–42.60 Who is responsible for gifts and decorations received by Senators and Senate employees?

Gifts and decorations received by Senators and Senate employees are deposited with the Secretary of the Senate for disposal by the Commission on Art and Antiquities of the United States Senate under 5 U.S.C. 7342(e)(2). GSA is responsible for disposing of gifts or decorations received by Members and employees of the House of Representatives.

§ 102–42.65 What happens if the Commission on Art and Antiquities does not dispose of a gift or decoration?

If the Commission on Art and Antiquities does not dispose of a gift or decoration, then it must be reported to GSA for disposal. If GSA does not dispose of a gift or decoration within one

year of the Commission's reporting, the Commission may:

(a) Request that GSA return the gift or decoration and dispose of it itself; or

(b) Continue to allow GSA to dispose of the gift or decoration in accordance with this part.

§ 102–42.70 Who handles gifts and decorations received by the President or Vice President or a member of their family?

The National Archives and Records Administration normally handles gifts and decorations received by the President and Vice President or a member of the President's or Vice President's family.

[71 FR 28778, May 18, 2006]

§ 102–42.75 How are gifts containing hazardous materials handled?

Gifts containing hazardous materials are handled in accordance with the requirements and provisions of this part and part 101–42 of this title.

Subpart B—Utilization of Foreign Gifts and Decorations

§ 102–42.80 To whom do "we", "you", and their variants refer?

Use of pronouns "we", "you", and their variants throughout this subpart refers to the employing agency.

§ 102–42.85 What gifts or decorations must we report to GSA?

You must report to GSA gifts of more than minimal value, except for monetary gifts that have no historic or numismatic value (see § 102–42.20), or decorations the employee is not authorized to retain that are:

(a) Not being retained for official use or have not been returned to the donor; or

(b) Received by a Senator or a Senate employee and not disposed of by the Commission on Art and Antiquities of the United States Senate.

§ 102–42.90 What is the requirement for reporting gifts or decorations that were retained for official use but are no longer needed?

Non-monetary gifts or decorations that were retained for official use must be reported to GSA as excess property within 30 days after termination of the official use.

§ 102–42.95 How do we report gifts and decorations as excess personal property?

You must complete a Standard Form (SF) 120, Report of Excess Personal Property, and send it to the General Services Administration, Utilization and Donation Program Division (QSCA), Washington, DC 20406. Conspicuously mark the SF 120, "FOREIGN GIFTS AND/OR DECORATIONS", and include the following information:

Entry	Description
(a) Identity of Employee.	Give the name and position of the employee.
(b) Description of Item	Give a full description of the gift or decoration, including the title of the decoration.
(c) Identity of Foreign Government.	Give the identity of the foreign government (if known) and the name and position of the individual who presented the gift or decoration.
(d) Date of Acceptance	Give the date the gift or decoration was accepted by the employee.
(e) Appraised Value	Give the appraised value in United States dollars of the gift or decoration, including the cost of the appraisal. (The employing agency must obtain a commercial appraisal before the gift is offered for sale to the employee.)
(f) Current Location of Item.	Give the current location of the gift or decoration.
(g) Employing Agency Contact Person.	Give the name, address, and telephone number of the accountable official in the employing agency.
(h) Purchase Interest or Donation Recommendation.	Indicate whether the employee wants to buy the gift, or whether the employee wants the gift or decoration donated to an eligible donee through GSA's surplus donation program. Document this interest in a letter outlining any special significance of the gift or decoration to the proposed donee. Also provide the mailing address and telephone number of both the employee and the proposed donee.
(i) Administration	Give the Administration in which the gift or decoration was received (for example, Clinton Administration).
(j) Multiple Items	Identify each gift or decoration as a separate line item. Report multiple gift items that make up a set (for example, a tea set, a necklace and matching earrings) as a single line item.

[65 FR 45539, July 24, 2000, as amended at 74 FR 2396, Jan. 15, 2009]

§ 102–42.100 How can we obtain an excess gift or decoration from another agency?

To obtain an excess gift or decoration from another agency, you would complete a Standard Form (SF) 122, Transfer Order Excess Personal Property, or any other transfer order form approved by GSA, for the desired item(s) and submit the form to the General Services Administration, Property Management Division (FBP), Washington, DC 20406.

§ 102–42.105 What special information must be included on the SF 122?

Conspicuously mark the SF 122, "FOREIGN GIFTS AND/OR DECORATIONS", and include all information furnished by the employing agency as specified in § 102–42.95. Also, include on the form the following statement: "At such time as these items are no longer required, they will be reported to the

General Services Administration, Property Management Division (FBP), Washington, DC 20406, and will be identified as foreign gift items and cross-referenced to this transfer order number.''

§ 102–42.110 How must we justify a transfer request?

You may only request excess gifts and decorations for public display or other bona fide agency use and not for the personal benefit of any individual. GSA may require that transfer orders be supported by justifications for the intended display or official use of requested gifts and decorations. Jewelry and watches that are transferred for official display must be displayed with adequate provisions for security.

§ 102–42.115 What must we do when the transferred gifts and decorations are no longer required for official use?

When transferred gifts and decorations are no longer required for official use, report these gifts and decorations to the GSA as excess property on a SF 120, including the original transfer order number or a copy of the original transfer order.

Subpart C—Donation of Foreign Gifts and Decorations

§ 102–42.120 When may gifts or decorations be donated to State agencies?

If there is no Federal requirement for the gifts or decorations, and if gifts were not sold to the employee, GSA may make the gifts or decorations available for donation to State agencies under this subpart and part 102–37 of this subchapter B.

[65 FR 45539, July 24, 2000, as amended at 71 FR 28778, May 18, 2006]

§ 102–42.125 How is donation of gifts or decorations accomplished?

The State Agencies for Surplus Property (SASP) must initiate the process on behalf of a prospective donee (e.g., units of State or local governments and eligible non-profit organizations) by:

(a) Completing a Standard Form (SF) 123, Transfer Order Surplus Personal Property, and submitting it to General Services Administration, Property Management Division (FBP), Washington, DC 20406. Conspicuously mark the SF 123 with the words, "FOREIGN GIFTS AND/OR DECORATIONS.''

(b) Attaching an original and two copies of a letter of intent to each SF 123 submitted to GSA. An authorized representative of the proposed donee must sign and date the letter, setting forth a detailed plan for use of the property. The letter of intent must provide the following information:

(1) Identifying the donee applicant, including its legal name and complete address, its status as a public agency or as an eligible nonprofit tax-exempt activity, and the name, title, and telephone number of its authorized representative;

(2) A description of the gift or decoration requested, including the gift's commercially appraised value or estimated fair market value if no commercial appraisal was performed; and

(3) Details on the planned use of the gift or decoration, including where and how it will be used and how it will be safeguarded.

§ 102–42.130 Are there special requirements for the donation of gifts and decorations?

Yes, GSA imposes special handling and use limitations on the donation of gifts and decorations. The SASP distribution document must contain or incorporate by reference the following:

(a) The donee must display or use the gift or decoration in accordance with its GSA-approved letter of intent.

(b) There must be a period of restriction which will expire after the gift or decoration has been used for the purpose stated in the letter of intent for a period of 10 years, except that GSA may restrict the use of the gift or decoration for such other period when the inherent character of the property justifies such action.

(c) The donee must allow the right of access to the donee's premises at reasonable times for inspection of the gift or decoration by duly authorized representatives of the SASP or the U.S. Government.

(d) During the period of restriction, the donee must not:

(1) Sell, trade, lease, lend, bail, encumber, cannibalize or dismantle for parts, or otherwise dispose of the property;

(2) Remove it permanently for use outside the State;

(3) Transfer title to the gift or decoration directly or indirectly; or

(4) Do or allow anything to be done that would contribute to the gift or decoration being seized, attached, lost, stolen, damaged, or destroyed.

(e) If the gift or decoration is no longer suitable, usable, or needed by the donee for the stated purpose of donation during the period of restriction, the donee must promptly notify the General Services Administration, Property Management Division (FBP), Washington, DC 20406, through the SASP, and upon demand by GSA, title and right to possession of the gift or decoration reverts to the U.S. Government. In this event, the donee must comply with transfer or disposition instructions furnished by GSA through the SASP, and pay the costs of transportation, handling, and reasonable insurance during transportation.

(f) The donee must comply with all additional conditions covering the handling and use of any gift or decoration imposed by GSA.

(g) If the donee fails to comply with the conditions or limitations during the period of restriction, the SASP may demand return of the gift or decoration and, upon such demand, title and right to possession of the gift or decoration reverts to the U.S. Government. In this event, the donee must return the gift or decoration in accordance with instructions furnished by the SASP, with costs of transportation, handling, and reasonable insurance during transportation to be paid by the donee or as directed by the SASP.

(h) If the gift or decoration is lost, stolen, or cannot legally be recovered or returned for any other reason, the donee must pay to the U.S. Government the fair market value of the gift or decoration at the time of its loss, theft, or at the time that it became unrecoverable as determined by GSA. If the gift or decoration is damaged or destroyed, the SASP may require the donee to:

(1) Return the item and pay the difference between its former fair market value and its current fair market value; or

(2) Pay the fair market value, as determined by GSA, of the item had it not been damaged or destroyed.

Subpart D—Sale or Destruction of Foreign Gifts and Decorations

§ 102–42.135 Whose approval must be obtained before a foreign gift or decoration is offered for public sale?

The Secretary of State or the Secretary's designee must approve any sale of foreign gifts or decorations (except sale of foreign gifts to the employee, that is approved in this part).

§ 102–42.140 How is a sale of a foreign gift or decoration to an employee conducted?

Foreign gifts and decorations must be offered first through negotiated sales to the employee who has indicated an interest in purchasing the item. The sale price must be the commercially appraised value of the gift. Sales must be conducted and documented in accordance with part 102–38 of this subchapter B.

[68 FR 56496, Sept. 4, 2003, as amended at 71 FR 28778, May 18, 2006]

§ 102–42.145 When is public sale of a foreign gift or decoration authorized?

A public sale is authorized if a foreign gift or decoration:

(a) Survives Federal utilization screening;

(b) Is not purchased by the employee;

(c) Survives donation screening; and

(d) Is approved by the Secretary of State or designee.

§ 102–42.150 What happens to proceeds from sales?

The proceeds from the sale of foreign gifts or decorations must be deposited in the Treasury as miscellaneous receipts, unless otherwise authorized.

§ 102–42.155 Can foreign gifts or decorations be destroyed?

Yes, foreign gifts or decorations that are not sold under this part may be destroyed and disposed of as scrap or for their material content under part 102–38 of this subchapter B.

[65 FR 45539, July 24, 2000, as amended at 71 FR 28778, May 18, 2006]

SUBCHAPTER C—REAL PROPERTY

PART 102–71—GENERAL

AUTHORITY: 40 U.S.C. 121(c).

SOURCE: 70 FR 67786, Nov. 8, 2005, unless otherwise noted.

§ 102–71.5 What is the scope and philosophy of the General Services Administration's (GSA) real property policies?

GSA's real property policies contained in this part and parts 102–72 through 102–82 of this chapter apply to Federal agencies, including GSA's Public Buildings Service (PBS), operating under, or subject to, the authorities of the Administrator of General Services. These policies cover the acquisition, management, utilization, and disposal of real property by Federal agencies that initiate and have decision-making authority over actions for real property services. The detailed guidance implementing these policies is contained in separate customer service guides.

§ 102–71.10 How are these policies organized?

GSA has divided its real property policies into the following functional areas:

(a) Delegation of authority.
(b) Real estate acquisition.
(c) Facility management.
(d) Real property disposal.
(e) Design and construction.
(f) Art-in-architecture.
(g) Historic preservation.
(h) Assignment and utilization of space.
(i) Safety and environmental management.
(j) Security.
(k) Utility services.
(l) Location of space.

§ 102–71.15 [Reserved]

§ 102–71.20 What definitions apply to GSA's real property policies?

The following definitions apply to GSA's real property policies:

Airport means any area of land or water that is used, or intended for use, for the landing and takeoff of aircraft, and any appurtenant areas that are used, or intended for use, for airport buildings or other airport facilities or rights-of-way, together with all airport buildings and facilities located thereon.

Alteration means remodeling, improving, extending, or making other changes to a facility, exclusive of maintenance repairs that are preventive in nature. The term includes planning, engineering, architectural work, and other similar actions.

Carpool means a group of two or more people regularly using a motor vehicle for transportation to and from work on a continuing basis.

Commercial activities, within the meaning of subpart D, part 102–74 of this chapter, are activities undertaken for the primary purpose of producing a profit for the benefit of an individual or organization organized for profit. (Activities where commercial aspects are incidental to the primary purpose of expression of ideas or advocacy of causes are not commercial activities for purposes of this part.)

Cultural activities include, but are not limited to, films, dramatics, dances, musical presentations, and fine art exhibits, whether or not these activities are intended to make a profit.

Decontamination means the complete removal or destruction by flashing of explosive powders; the neutralizing and cleaning-out of acid and corrosive materials; the removal, destruction, or neutralizing of toxic, hazardous or infectious substances; and the complete removal and destruction by burning or detonation of live ammunition from contaminated areas and buildings.

Designated Official is the highest ranking official of the primary occupant agency of a Federal facility, or, alternatively, a designee selected by mutual agreement of occupant agency officials.

Disabled employee means an employee who has a severe, permanent impairment that for all practical purposes precludes the use of public transportation, or an employee who is unable to operate a car as a result of permanent impairment who is driven to work by another. Priority may require certification by an agency medical unit, including the Department of Veterans Affairs or the Public Health Service.

Disposal agency means the Executive agency designated by the Administrator of General Services to dispose of surplus real or personal property.

Educational activities mean activities such as (but not limited to) the operation of schools, libraries, day care centers, laboratories, and lecture or demonstration facilities.

Emergency includes bombings and bomb threats, civil disturbances, fires, explosions, electrical failures, loss of water pressure, chemical and gas leaks, medical emergencies, hurricanes, tornadoes, floods, and earthquakes. The term does not apply to civil defense matters such as potential or actual enemy attacks that are addressed by the U.S. Department of Homeland Security.

Executive means a Government employee with management responsibilities who, in the judgment of the employing agency head or his/her designee, requires preferential assignment of parking privileges.

Executive agency means an Executive department specified in section 101 of title 5; a military department specified in section 102 of such title; an independent establishment as defined in section 104(1) of such title; and a wholly owned Government corporation fully subject to the provisions of chapter 91 of title 31.

Federal agency means any Executive agency or any establishment in the legislative or judicial branch of the Government (except the Senate, the House of Representatives, and the Architect of the Capitol and any activities under his or her direction).

Federal agency buildings manager means the buildings manager employed by GSA or a Federal agency that has been delegated real property management and operation authority from GSA.

Federal Government real property services provider means any Federal Government entity operating under, or subject to, the authorities of the Administrator of General Services that provides real property services to Federal agencies. This definition also includes private sector firms under contract with Federal agencies that deliver real property services to Federal agencies. This definition excludes any entity operating under, or subject to, authorities other than those of the Administrator of General Services.

Flame-resistant means meeting performance standards as described by the National Fire Protection Association (NFPA Standard No. 701). Fabrics labeled with the Underwriters Laboratories Inc., classification marking for flammability are deemed to be flame resistant for purposes of this part.

Foot-candle is the illumination on a surface one square foot in area on which there is a uniformly distributed flux of one lumen, or the illuminance produced on a surface all points of which are at a distance of one foot from a directionally uniform point source of one candela.

GSA means the U.S. General Services Administration, acting by or through the Administrator of General Services, or a designated official to whom functions under this part have been delegated by the Administrator of General Services.

Highest and best use means the most likely use to which a property can be put, which will produce the highest monetary return from the property, promote its maximum value, or serve a public or institutional purpose. The highest and best use determination must be based on the property's economic potential, qualitative values (social and environmental) inherent in the property itself, and other utilization factors controlling or directly affecting land use (e.g., zoning, physical characteristics, private and public uses in the vicinity, neighboring improvements, utility services, access, roads, location, and environmental and historical considerations). Projected highest and best use should not be remote, speculative, or conjectural.

Indefinite quantity contract (commonly referred to as *term contract*) provides for the furnishing of an indefinite quantity, within stated limits, of specific property or services during a specified contract period, with deliveries to be scheduled by the timely placement of orders with the contractor by activities designated either specifically or by class.

Industrial property means any real property and related personal property that has been used or that is suitable to be used for manufacturing, fabricating, or processing of products; mining operations; construction or repair of ships and other waterborne carriers; power transmission facilities; railroad facilities; and pipeline facilities for transporting petroleum or gas.

Landholding agency means the Federal agency that has accountability for the property involved. For the purposes of this definition, accountability means that the Federal agency reports the real property on its financial statements and inventory records.

Landing area means any land or combination of water and land, together with improvements thereon and necessary operational equipment used in connection therewith, which is used for landing, takeoff, and parking of aircraft. The term includes, but is not limited to, runways, strips, taxiways, and parking aprons.

Life cycle cost is the total cost of owning, operating, and maintaining a building over its useful life, including its fuel and energy costs, determined on the basis of a systematic evaluation and comparison of alternative building systems; except that in the case of leased buildings, the life cycle cost shall be calculated over the effective remaining term of the lease.

Limited combustible means rigid materials or assemblies that have fire hazard ratings not exceeding 25 for flame spread and 150 for smoke development when tested in accordance with the American Society for Testing and Materials, Test E 84, Surface Burning Characteristics of Building Materials.

Maintenance, for the purposes of part 102–75, entitled "Real Property Disposal," of this chapter, means the upkeep of property only to the extent necessary to offset serious deterioration; also such operation of utilities, including water supply and sewerage systems, heating, plumbing, and air-conditioning equipment, as may be necessary for fire protection, the needs of interim tenants, and personnel employed at the site, and the requirements for preserving certain types of equipment. For the purposes of part 102–74, entitled "Facility Management," of this chapter, maintenance means preservation by inspection, adjustment, lubrication, cleaning, and the making of minor repairs. *Ordinary maintenance* means routine recurring work that is incidental to everyday operations; *preventive maintenance* means work programmed at scheduled intervals.

Management means the safeguarding of the Government's interest in property, in an efficient and economical manner consistent with the best business practices.

Nationally recognized standards encompasses any standard or modification thereof that—

(1) Has been adopted and promulgated by a nationally recognized standards-producing organization under procedures whereby those interested and affected by it have reached substantial agreement on its adoption; or

(2) Was formulated through consultation by appropriate Federal agencies in a manner that afforded an opportunity for diverse views to be considered.

No commercial value means real property, including related personal property, which has no reasonable prospect of producing any disposal revenues.

Nonprofit organization means an organization identified in 26 U.S.C. 501(c).

Normally furnished commercially means consistent with the level of services provided by a commercial building operator for space of comparable quality and housing tenants with comparable requirements. Service levels are based on the effort required to service space for a five-day week, one eight-hour shift schedule.

Occupancy Emergency Organization means the emergency response organization comprised of employees of Federal agencies designated to perform the requirements established by the Occupant Emergency Plan.

Occupant agency means an organization that is assigned space in a facility under GSA's custody and control.

Occupant Emergency Plan means procedures developed to protect life and property in a specific federally occupied space under stipulated emergency conditions.

Occupant Emergency Program means a short-term emergency response program. It establishes procedures for safeguarding lives and property during emergencies in particular facilities.

Postal vehicle means a Government-owned vehicle used for the transportation of mail, or a privately owned vehicle used under contract with the U.S. Postal Service for the transportation of mail.

Protection means the provisions of adequate measures for prevention and extinguishment of fires, special inspections to determine and eliminate fire and other hazards, and necessary guards to protect property against thievery, vandalism, and unauthorized entry.

Public area means any area of a building under the control and custody of GSA that is ordinarily open to members of the public, including lobbies, courtyards, auditoriums, meeting rooms, and other such areas not assigned to a lessee or occupant agency.

Public body means any State of the United States, the District of Columbia, the Commonwealth of Puerto Rico, the Virgin Islands, or any political subdivision, agency, or instrumentality of the foregoing.

Public building means:

(1) Any building that is suitable for office and/or storage space for the use of one or more Federal agencies or mixed-ownership corporations, such as Federal office buildings, post offices, customhouses, courthouses, border inspection facilities, warehouses, and any such building designated by the President. It also includes buildings of this sort that are acquired by the Federal Government under the Administrator's installment-purchase, lease-purchase, and purchase-contract authorities.

(2) Public building does not include buildings:

(i) On the public domain.

(ii) In foreign countries.

(iii) On Indian and native Eskimo properties held in trust by the United States.

(iv) On lands used in connection with Federal programs for agricultural, recreational, and conservation purposes.

(v) On or used in connection with river, harbor, flood control, reclamation or power projects, or for chemical manufacturing or development projects, or for nuclear production, research, or development projects.

(vi) On or used in connection with housing and residential projects.

(vii) On military installations.

(viii) On Department of Veterans Affairs installations used for hospital or domiciliary purposes.

(ix) Excluded by the President.

Real property means:

(1) Any interest in land, together with the improvements, structures, and fixtures located thereon (including prefabricated movable structures, such as Butler-type storage warehouses and Quonset huts, and house trailers with or without undercarriages), and appurtenances thereto, under the control of any Federal agency, except—

(i) The public domain;

(ii) Lands reserved or dedicated for national forest or national park purposes;

(iii) Minerals in lands or portions of lands withdrawn or reserved from the public domain that the Secretary of the Interior determines are suitable for disposition under the public land mining and mineral leasing laws;

(iv) Lands withdrawn or reserved from the public domain but not including lands or portions of lands so withdrawn or reserved that the Secretary of the Interior, with the concurrence of the Administrator of General Services, determines are not suitable for return to the public domain for disposition under the general public land laws because such lands are substantially changed in character by improvements or otherwise; and

(v) Crops when designated by such agency for disposition by severance and removal from the land.

(2) Improvements of any kind, structures, and fixtures under the control of any Federal agency when designated by such agency for disposition without the underlying land (including such as may be located on the public domain, on lands withdrawn or reserved from the public domain, on lands reserved or dedicated for national forest or national park purposes, or on lands that are not owned by the United States) excluding, however, prefabricated movable structures, such as Butler-type storage warehouses and Quonset huts, and house trailers (with or without undercarriages).

(3) Standing timber and embedded gravel, sand, or stone under the control of any Federal agency, whether designated by such agency for disposition with the land or by severance and removal from the land, excluding timber felled, and gravel, sand, or stone excavated by or for the Government prior to disposition.

Recognized labor organization means a labor organization recognized under title VII of the Civil Service Reform Act of 1978 (Pub. L. 95–454), as amended, governing labor-management relations.

Recreational activities include, but are not limited to, the operations of gymnasiums and related facilities.

Regional Officer, within the meaning of part 102–74, subpart D of this chapter, means the Federal official designated to supervise the implementation of the occasional use provisions of 40 U.S.C. 581(h)(2). The Federal official may be an employee of GSA or a Federal agency that has delegated authority from GSA to supervise the implementation of the occasional use provisions of 40 U.S.C. 581(h)(2).

Related personal property means any personal property—

(1) That is an integral part of real property or is related to, designed for, or specially adapted to the functional or productive capacity of the real property and the removal of which would significantly diminish the economic value of the real property (normally common use items, including but not limited to general-purpose furniture, utensils, office machines, office sup-

plies, or general-purpose vehicles, are not considered to be related personal property); or

(2) That is determined by the Administrator of General Services to be related to the real property.

Repairs means those additions or changes that are necessary for the protection and maintenance of property to deter or prevent excessive or rapid deterioration or obsolescence, and to restore property damaged by storm, flood, fire, accident, or earthquake.

Ridesharing means the sharing of the commute to and from work by two or more people, on a continuing basis, regardless of their relationship to each other, in any mode of transportation, including, but not limited to, carpools, vanpools, buspools, and mass transit.

State means the fifty States, political subdivisions thereof, the District of Columbia, the Commonwealths of Puerto Rico and Guam, and the territories and possessions of the United States.

Unit price agreement provides for the furnishing of an indefinite quantity, within stated limits, of specific property or services at a specified price, during a specified contract period, with deliveries to be scheduled by the timely placement of orders upon the lessor by activities designated either specifically or by class.

Unusual hours means work hours that are frequently required to be varied and do not coincide with any regular work schedule. This category includes time worked by individuals who regularly or frequently work significantly more than 8 hours per day. Unusual hours does not include time worked by shift workers, by those on alternate work schedules, and by those granted exceptions to the normal work schedule (e.g., flex-time).

Upon approval from GSA means when an agency either has a delegation of authority document from the Administrator of General Services or written approval from the Administrator or his/her designee before proceeding with a specified action.

Vanpool means a group of at least 8 persons using a passenger van or a commuter bus designed to carry 10 or more passengers. Such a vehicle must be used for transportation to and from work in a single daily round trip.

Zonal allocations means the allocation of parking spaces on the basis of zones established by GSA in conjunction with occupant agencies. In metropolitan areas where this method is used, all agencies located in a designated zone will compete for available parking in accordance with instructions issued by GSA. In establishing this procedure, GSA will consult with all affected agencies.

§ 102–71.25 Who must comply with GSA's real property policies?

Federal agencies operating under, or subject to, the authorities of the Administrator of General Services must comply with these policies.

§ 102–71.30 How must these real property policies be implemented?

Each Federal Government real property services provider must provide services that are in accord with the policies presented in parts 102–71 through 102–82 of this chapter. Also, Federal agencies must make the provisions of any contract with private sector real property services providers conform to the policies in parts 102–71 through 102–82 of this chapter.

§ 102–71.35 Are agencies allowed to deviate from GSA's real property policies?

Yes, see §§ 102–2.60 through 102–2.110 of this chapter to request a deviation from the requirements of these real property policies.

PART 102–72—DELEGATION OF AUTHORITY

Subpart A—General Provisions

Subpart B—Delegation of Authority

AUTHORITY: 40 U.S.C. 121(c), (d) and (e).

SOURCE: 70 FR 67789, Nov. 8, 2005, unless otherwise noted.

Subpart A—General Provisions

§ 102-72.5 What is the scope of this part?

The real property policies contained in this part apply to Federal agencies, including GSA's Public Buildings Service (PBS), operating under, or subject to, the authorities of the Administrator of General Services.

§ 102-72.10 What basic policy governs delegation of authority to Federal agencies?

The Administrator of General Services may delegate and may authorize successive redelegations of the real property authority vested in the Administrator to any Federal agency.

Subpart B—Delegation of Authority

§ 102-72.15 What criteria must a delegation meet?

Delegations must be in the Government's best interest, which means that GSA must evaluate such factors as whether a delegation would be cost effective for the Government in the delivery of space.

§ 102-72.20 Are there limitations on this delegation of authority?

Federal agencies must exercise delegated real property authority and functions according to the parameters described in each delegation of authority document, and Federal agencies may only exercise the authority of the Administrator that is specifically provided within the delegation of authority document.

§ 102-72.25 What are the different types of delegations of authority?

The basic types of GSA Delegations of Authority are—

(a) Delegation of Leasing Authority;

(b) Delegation of Real Property Management and Operation Authority;

(c) Delegation of Individual Repair and Alteration Project Authority;

(d) Delegation of Lease Management Authority (Contracting Office Representative Authority);

(e) Delegation of Administrative Contracting Officer (ACO) Authority;

(f) Delegation of Real Property Disposal Authority;

(g) Security Delegation of Authority; and

(h) Utility Services Delegation of Authority.

§ 102-72.30 What are the different types of delegations related to real estate leasing?

Delegations related to real estate leasing include the following:

(a) Categorical space delegations and agency special purpose space delegations (see § 102-73.140 of this title).

(b) The Administrator of General Services has issued a standing delegation of authority (under a program known as "Can't Beat GSA Leasing") to the heads of all Federal agencies to accomplish all functions relating to leasing of up to 19,999 rentable square feet of general purpose space for terms of up to 20 years and below prospectus level requirements, regardless of geographic location. This delegation includes some conditions Federal agencies must meet when conducting the procurement themselves, such as training in lease contracting and reporting data to GSA.

(c) An ACO delegation, in addition to lease management authority, provides Federal agencies with limited contracting officer authority to perform such duties as paying and withholding lessor rent and modifying lease provisions that do not change the lease term length or the amount of space under lease.

[70 FR 67789, Nov. 8, 2005, as amended at 73 FR 2167, Jan. 14, 2008]

§ 102-72.35 What are the requirements for obtaining an Administrative Contracting Officer (ACO) delegation from GSA?

When Federal agencies do not exercise the delegation of authority for general purpose space mentioned in § 102-72.30(b) of this part, GSA may consider granting an ACO delegation when Federal agencies—

(a) Occupy at least 90 percent of the building's GSA-controlled space, or Federal agencies have the written concurrence of 100 percent of rent-paying occupants covered under the lease; and

(b) Have the technical capability to perform the leasing function.

§ 102–72.40 What are facility management delegations?

Facility management delegations give Executive agencies authority to operate and manage buildings day to day, to perform individual repair and alteration projects, and manage real property leases.

§ 102–72.45 What are the different types of delegations related to facility management?

The principal types of delegations involved in the management of facilities are—

(a) Real property management and operation authority;

(b) Individual repair and alteration project authority; and

(c) Lease management authority (contracting officer representative authority).

§ 102–72.50 What are Executive agencies' responsibilities under a delegation of real property management and operation authority from GSA?

With this delegation, Executive agencies have the authority to operate and manage buildings day to day. Delegated functions may include building operations, maintenance, recurring repairs, minor alterations, historic preservation, concessions, and energy management of specified buildings subject to the conditions in the delegation document.

§ 102–72.55 What are the requirements for obtaining a delegation of real property management and operation authority from GSA?

An Executive agency may be delegated real property management and operation authority when it—

(a) Occupies at least 90 percent of the space in the Government-controlled facility, or has the concurrence of 100 percent of the rent-paying occupants to perform these functions; and

(b) Demonstrates that it can perform the delegated real property management and operation responsibilities.

§ 102–72.60 What are Executive agencies' responsibilities under a delegation of individual repair and alteration project authority from GSA?

With this delegation of authority, Executive agencies have the responsibility to perform individual repair and alterations projects. Executive agencies are delegated repair and alterations authority for reimbursable space alteration projects up to the simplified acquisition threshold, as specified in the GSA Customer Guide to Real Property.

§ 102–72.65 What are the requirements for obtaining a delegation of individual repair and alteration project authority from GSA?

Executive agencies may be delegated repair and alterations authority for other individual alteration projects when they demonstrate the ability to perform the delegated repair and alterations responsibilities and when such a delegation promotes efficiency and economy.

§ 102–72.66 Do Executive agencies have a delegation of authority to perform ancillary repair and alteration projects in federally owned buildings under the jurisdiction, custody or control of GSA?

Yes. Executive agencies, as defined in § 102–71.20, are hereby delegated the authority to perform ancillary repair and alteration work in federally owned buildings under the jurisdiction, custody or control of GSA in accordance with the terms, conditions and limitations set forth in §§ 102–72.67 through 102–72.69.

[74 FR 12273, Mar. 24, 2009]

§ 102–72.67 What work is covered under an ancillary repair and alteration delegation?

(a) For purposes of this delegation, ancillary repair and alteration projects are those—

(1) Where an Executive agency has placed an order from a vendor under a GSA Multiple Award Schedule and ancillary repair and alteration services

also are available from that same vendor as a Special Item Number (SIN);

(2) Where the ancillary repair and alteration work to be performed is associated solely with the repair, alteration, delivery, or installation of products or services also purchased under the same GSA Multiple Award Schedule;

(3) That are routine and non-complex in nature, such as routine painting or carpeting, simple hanging of drywall, basic electrical or plumbing work, landscaping, and similar non-complex services; and

(4) That are necessary to be performed to use, execute or implement successfully the products or services purchased from the GSA Multiple Award Schedule.

(b) Ancillary repair and alteration projects do not include—

(1) Major or new construction of buildings, roads, parking lots, and other facilities;

(2) Complex repair and alteration of entire facilities or significant portions of facilities; or

(3) Architectural and engineering services procured pursuant to 40 U.S.C. 1101–1104.

[74 FR 12273, Mar. 24, 2009]

§ 102–72.68 What preconditions must be satisfied before an Executive agency may exercise the delegated authority to perform an individual ancillary repair and alteration project?

The preconditions that must be satisfied before an Executive agency may perform ancillary repair and alteration work are as follows:

(a) The ordering agency must order both the products or services and the ancillary repair and alteration services under the same GSA Multiple Award Schedule from the same vendor;

(b) The value of the ancillary repair and alteration work must be less than or equal to $100,000 (for work estimated to exceed $100,000, the Executive agency must contact the GSA Assistant Regional Administrator, Public Buildings Service, in the region where the work is to be performed to request a specific delegation);

(c) All terms and conditions applicable to the acquisition of ancillary repair and alteration work as required by the GSA Multiple Award Schedule ordering procedures must be satisfied;

(d) The ancillary repair and alteration work must not be in a facility leased by GSA or in any other leased facility acquired under a lease delegation from GSA; and

(e) As soon as reasonably practicable, the Executive agency must provide the building manager with a detailed scope of work, including cost estimates, and schedule for the project, and such other information as may be reasonably requested by the building manager, so the building manager can determine whether or not the proposed work is reasonably expected to have an adverse effect on the operation and management of the building, the building's structural, mechanical, electrical, plumbing, or heating and air conditioning systems, the building's aesthetic or historic features, or the space or property of any other tenant in the building. The Executive agency must obtain written approval from the building manager prior to placing an order for any ancillary repair and alteration work.

[74 FR 12273, Mar. 24, 2009]

§ 102–72.69 What additional terms and conditions apply to an Executive agencies' delegation of ancillary repair and alteration authority?

(a) Before commencing any ancillary repair and alteration work, the Executive agency shall deliver, or cause its contractor to deliver, to the building manager evidence that the contractor has obtained at least $5,000,000 comprehensive general public liability and property damage insurance policies to cover claims arising from or relating to the contractor's operations that cause damage to persons or property; such insurance shall name the United States as an additional insured.

(b) The Executive agency shall agree that GSA has no responsibility or liability, either directly or indirectly, for any contractual claims or disputes that arise out of or relate to the performance of ancillary repair and alteration work, except to the extent such claim or dispute arises out of or relates to the wrongful acts or negligence of GSA's agents or employees.

(c) The Executive agency shall agree to administer and defend any claims and actions, and shall be responsible for the payment of any judgments rendered or settlements agreed to, in connection with contract claims or other causes of action arising out of or relating to the performance of the ancillary repair and alteration work.

(d) For buildings under GSA's custody and control, GSA shall have the right, but not the obligation, to review the work from time to time to ascertain that it is being performed in accordance with the approved project requirements, schedules, plans, drawings, specifications, and other related construction documents. The Executive agency shall promptly correct, or cause to be corrected, any non-conforming work or property damage identified by GSA, including damage to the space or property of any other tenant in the building, at no cost or expense to GSA.

(e) The Executive agency shall remain liable and financially responsible to GSA for any and all personal or property damage caused, in whole or in part, by the acts or omissions of the Executive agency, its employees, agents, and contractors.

(f) If the cost or expense to GSA to operate the facility is increased as a result of the ancillary repair and alteration project, the Executive agency shall be responsible for any such costs or expenses.

(g) Disputes between the Executive agency and GSA arising out of the ancillary repair and alteration work will, to the maximum extent practicable, be resolved informally at the working level. In the event a dispute cannot be resolved informally, the matter shall be referred to GSA's Public Buildings Service. The Executive agency agrees that, in the event GSA's Public Buildings Service and the Executive agency fail to resolve the dispute, they shall refer it for resolution to the Administrator of General Services, whose decision shall be binding.

[74 FR 12273, Mar. 24, 2009]

§ 102–72.70 What are Executive agencies' responsibilities under a delegation of lease management authority (contracting officer representative authority) from GSA?

When an Executive agency does not exercise the delegation of authority mentioned in § 102–72.30(b) to lease general purpose space itself, it may be delegated, upon request, lease management authority to manage the administration of one or more lease contracts awarded by GSA.

§ 102–72.75 What are the requirements for obtaining a delegation of lease management authority (contracting officer representative authority) from GSA?

An Executive agency may be delegated lease management authority when it—

(a) Occupies at least 90 percent of the building's GSA-controlled space or has the written concurrence of 100 percent of rent-paying occupants covered under the lease to perform this function; and

(b) Demonstrates the ability to perform the delegated lease management responsibilities.

§ 102–72.80 What are Executive agencies' responsibilities under a disposal of real property delegation of authority from GSA?

With this delegation, Executive agencies have the authority to utilize and dispose of excess or surplus real and related personal property and to grant approvals and make determinations, subject to the conditions in the delegation document.

§ 102–72.85 What are the requirements for obtaining a disposal of real property delegation of authority from GSA?

While disposal delegations to Executive agencies are infrequent, GSA may delegate authority to them based on situations involving certain low-value properties and when they can demonstrate that they have the technical expertise to perform the disposition functions. GSA may grant special delegations of authority to Executive agencies for the utilization and disposal of certain real property through the procedures set forth in part 102–75, subpart F of this chapter.

§ 102–72.90 What are Executive agencies' responsibilities under a security delegation of authority from GSA?

Law enforcement and related security functions were transferred to the Department of Homeland Security upon its establishment in 2002. The Homeland Security Act authorizes the Secretary of Homeland Security, in consultation with the Administrator of General Services, to issue regulations necessary for the protection and administration of property owned or occupied by the Federal Government and persons on the property. Notwithstanding the foregoing, GSA retained all powers, functions and authorities necessary for the operation, maintenance, and protection of buildings and grounds owned and occupied by the Federal Government and under the jurisdiction, custody, or control of GSA.

§ 102–72.95 What are the requirements for obtaining a security delegation of authority from GSA?

An Executive agency may request a security delegation from GSA by submitting a written request with the detailed basis for the requested delegation to the Assistant Regional Administrator, PBS, in the region where the building is located. A request for multiple buildings in multiple regions should be directed to the Commissioner of PBS. The delegation may be granted where the requesting agency demonstrates a compelling need for the delegated authority and the delegation is not inconsistent with the authorities of any other law enforcement agency.

§ 102–72.100 What are Executive agencies' responsibilities under a utility service delegation of authority from GSA?

With this delegation, Executive agencies have the authority to negotiate and execute utility services contracts for periods over one year but not exceeding ten years for their use and benefit. Agencies also have the authority to intervene in utility rate proceedings to represent the consumer interests of the Federal Government, if so provided in the delegation of authority.

§ 102–72.105 What are the requirements for obtaining a utility services delegation of authority from GSA?

Executive agencies may be delegated utility services authority when they have the technical expertise and adequate staffing.

PART 102–73—REAL ESTATE ACQUISITION

Subpart A—General Provisions

Subpart C—Acquisition by Purchase or Condemnation

BUILDINGS

AUTHORITY: 40 U.S.C. 121(c); Sec. 3(c), Reorganization Plan No. 18 of 1950 (40 U.S.C. 301 note); Sec. 1–201(b), E.O. 12072, 43 FR 36869, 3 CFR, 1978 Comp., p. 213.

SOURCE: 70 FR 67791, Nov. 8, 2005, unless otherwise noted.

Subpart A—General Provisions

§ 102–73.5　What is the scope of this part?

The real property policies contained in this part apply to Federal agencies, including GSA's Public Buildings Service (PBS), operating under, or subject to, the authorities of the Administrator of General Services.

§ 102–73.10　What is the basic real estate acquisition policy?

When seeking to acquire space, Federal agencies should first seek space in Government-owned and Government-leased buildings. If suitable Government-controlled space is unavailable, Federal agencies must acquire real estate and related services in an efficient and cost effective manner.

§ 102–73.15　What real estate acquisition and related services may Federal agencies provide?

Federal agencies, upon approval from GSA, may provide real estate acquisition and related services, including leasing (with or without purchase options), building and/or site purchase, condemnation, and relocation assistance. For information on the design and construction of Federal facilities, see part 102–76 of this chapter.

UNITED STATES POSTAL SERVICE-CONTROLLED SPACE

§ 102–73.20　Are Federal agencies required to give priority consideration to space in buildings under the custody and control of the United States Postal Service in fulfilling Federal agency space needs?

Yes, after considering the availability of GSA-controlled space and determining that no such space is available to meet its needs, Federal agencies must extend priority consideration to available space in buildings under the custody and control of the United States Postal Service (USPS) in fulfilling Federal agency space needs, as specified in the "Agreement Between General Services Administration and the United States Postal Service Covering Real and Personal Property Relationships and Associated Services," dated July 1985.

LOCATING FEDERAL FACILITIES

§102–73.25 What policies must Executive agencies comply with in locating Federal facilities?

Executive agencies must comply with the location policies in this part and part 102–83 of this chapter.

HISTORIC PRESERVATION

§102–73.30 What historic preservation provisions must Federal agencies comply with prior to acquiring, constructing, or leasing space?

Prior to acquiring, constructing, or leasing space, Federal agencies must comply with the provisions of section 110(a) of the National Historic Preservation Act of 1966, as amended (16 U.S.C. 470h–2(a)), regarding the use of historic properties. Federal agencies can find guidance on protecting, enhancing, and preserving historic and cultural property in part 102–78 of this chapter.

PROSPECTUS REQUIREMENTS

§102–73.35 Is a prospectus required for all acquisition, construction, or alteration projects?

No, a prospectus is not required if the dollar value of a project does not exceed the prospectus threshold. 40 U.S.C. 3307 establishes a prospectus threshold, applicable to Federal agencies operating under, or subject to, the authorities of the Administrator of General Services, for the construction, alteration, purchase, and acquisition of any building to be used as a public building, and establishes a prospectus threshold to lease any space for use for public purposes. The current prospectus threshold value for each fiscal year can be accessed by entering GSA's Web site at *http://www.gsa.gov* and then inserting "prospectus thresholds" in the search mechanism in the upper right-hand corner of the page.

§102–73.40 What happens if the dollar value of the project exceeds the prospectus threshold?

Projects require approval by the Senate and the House of Representatives if the dollar value of a project exceeds the prospectus threshold. To obtain this approval, the Administrator of General Services will transmit the proposed prospectuses to Congress for consideration by the Senate and the House of Representatives. Furthermore, as indicated in §102–72.30(b), the general purpose lease delegation authority is restricted to below the prospectus threshold, and therefore, GSA must conduct all lease acquisitions over the threshold.

Subpart B—Acquisition by Lease

§102–73.45 When may Federal agencies consider leases of privately owned land and buildings to satisfy their space needs?

Federal agencies may consider leases of privately owned land and buildings only when needs cannot be met satisfactorily in Government-controlled space and one or more of the following conditions exist:

(a) Leasing is more advantageous to the Government than constructing a new building, or more advantageous than altering an existing Federal building.

(b) New construction or alteration is unwarranted because demand for space in the community is insufficient, or is indefinite in scope or duration.

(c) Federal agencies cannot provide for the completion of a new building within a reasonable time.

§102–73.50 Are Federal agencies that possess independent statutory authority to acquire leased space subject to requirements of this part?

No, Federal agencies possessing independent statutory authority to acquire leased space are not subject to GSA authority and, therefore, may not be subject to the requirements of this part. However, lease prospectus approval requirements of 40 U.S.C. Section 3307 may still apply appropriations to lease of space for public purposes under an agency's independent leasing authority.

§102–73.55 On what basis must Federal agencies acquire leases?

Federal agencies must acquire leases on the most favorable basis to the Federal Government, with due consideration to maintenance and operational efficiency, and at charges consistent with prevailing market rates for comparable facilities in the community.

§ 102–73.60 With whom may Federal agencies enter into lease agreements?

Federal agencies, upon approval from GSA, may enter into lease agreements with any person, partnership, corporation, or other public or private entity, provided that such lease agreements do not bind the Government for periods in excess of twenty years (40 U.S.C. 585(a)). Federal agencies may not enter into lease agreements with persons who are barred from contracting with the Federal Government (e.g., Members of Congress or debarred or suspended contractors).

§ 102–73.65 Are there any limitations on leasing certain types of space?

Yes, the limitations on leasing certain types of space are as follows:

(a) In general, Federal agencies may not lease any space to accommodate computer and telecommunications operations; secure or sensitive activities related to the national defense or security; or a permanent courtroom, judicial chamber, or administrative office for any United States court, if the average annual net rental cost of leasing such space would exceed the prospectus threshold (40 U.S.C. 3307(f)(1)).

(b) However, Federal agencies may lease such space if the Administrator of General Services first determines that leasing such space is necessary to meet requirements that cannot be met in public buildings, and then submits such determination to the Committee on Environment and Public Works of the Senate and the Committee on Transportation and Infrastructure of the House of Representatives in accordance with 40 U.S.C. 3307(f)(2).

§ 102–73.70 Are Executive agencies required to acquire leased space by negotiation?

Yes, Executive agencies must acquire leased space by negotiation, except where the sealed bid procedure is required by the Competition in Contracting Act, as amended (CICA) (41 U.S.C. 253(a)).

§ 102–73.75 What functions must Federal agencies perform with regard to leasing building space?

Federal agencies, upon approval from GSA, must perform all functions of leasing building space, and land incidental thereto, for their use except as provided in this subpart.

§ 102–73.80 Who is authorized to contact lessor, offerors, or potential offerors concerning space leased or to be leased?

No one, except the Contracting Officer or his or her designee, may contact lessors, offerors, or potential offerors concerning space leased or to be leased for the purpose of making oral or written representation or commitments or agreements with respect to the terms of occupancy of particular space, tenant improvements, alterations and repairs, or payment for overtime services.

§ 102–73.85 Can agencies with independent statutory authority to lease space have GSA perform the leasing functions?

Yes, upon request, GSA may perform, on a reimbursable basis, all functions of leasing building space, and land incidental thereto, for Federal agencies possessing independent statutory authority to lease space. However, GSA reserves the right to accept or reject reimbursable leasing service requests on a case-by-case basis.

§ 102–73.90 What contingent fee policy must Federal agencies apply to the acquisition of real property by lease?

Federal agencies must apply the contingent fee policies in 48 CFR 3.4 to all negotiated and sealed bid contracts for the acquisition of real property by lease. Federal agencies must appropriately adapt the representations and covenants required by that subpart for use in leases of real property for Government use.

§ 102–73.95 How are Federal agencies required to assist GSA?

The heads of Federal agencies must—

(a) Cooperate with and assist the Administrator of General Services in carrying out his responsibilities respecting office buildings and space;

(b) Take measures to give GSA early notice of new or changing space requirements;

(c) Seek to economize their requirements for space; and

(d) Continuously review their needs for space in and near the District of Columbia, taking into account the feasibility of decentralizing services or activities that can be carried on elsewhere without excessive costs or significant loss of efficiency.

COMPETITION IN CONTRACTING ACT OF 1984

§ 102–73.100 Is the Competition in Contracting Act of 1984, as amended (CICA), applicable to lease acquisition?

Yes, Executive agencies must obtain full and open competition among suitable locations meeting minimum Government requirements, except as otherwise provided by CICA, 41 U.S.C. 253.

NATIONAL ENVIRONMENTAL POLICY ACT OF 1969 (NEPA)

§ 102–73.105 What policies must Federal agencies follow to implement the requirements of NEPA when acquiring real property by lease?

Federal agencies must follow the NEPA policies identified in §§ 102–76.40 and 102–76.45 of this chapter.

LEASE CONSTRUCTION

§ 102–73.110 What rules must Executive agencies follow when acquiring leasehold interests in buildings constructed for Federal Government use?

When acquiring leasehold interests in buildings to be constructed for Federal Government use, Executive agencies must—

(a) Establish detailed building specifications before agreeing to a contract that will result in the construction of a building;

(b) Use competitive procedures;

(c) Inspect every building during construction to ensure that the building complies with the Government's specifications;

(d) Evaluate every building after completion of construction to determine that the building complies with the Government's specifications; and

(e) Ensure that any contract that will result in the construction of a building contains provisions permitting the Government to reduce the rent during any period when the building does not comply with the Government's specifications.

PRICE PREFERENCE FOR HISTORIC PROPERTIES

§ 102–73.115 Must Federal agencies offer a price preference to space in historic properties when acquiring leased space?

Yes, Federal agencies must give a price preference to space in historic properties when acquiring leased space using either the lowest price technically acceptable or the best value tradeoff source selection processes.

§ 102–73.120 How much of a price preference must Federal agencies give when acquiring leased space using the lowest price technically acceptable source selection process?

Federal agencies must give a price evaluation preference to space in historic properties as follows:

(a) First to suitable historic properties within historic districts, a 10 percent price preference.

(b) If no suitable historic property within an historic district is offered, or the 10 percent preference does not result in such property being the lowest price technically acceptable offer, the Government will give a 2.5 percent price preference to suitable non-historic developed or undeveloped sites within historic districts.

(c) If no suitable non-historic developed or undeveloped site within an historic district is offered, or the 2.5 percent preference does not result in such property being the lowest price technically acceptable offer, the Government will give a 10 percent price preference to suitable historic properties outside of historic districts.

(d) Finally, if no suitable historic property outside of historic districts is offered, no historic price preference will be given to any property offered.

§ 102–73.125 How much of a price preference must Federal agencies give when acquiring leased space using the best value tradeoff source selection process?

When award will be based on the best value tradeoff source selection process, which permits tradeoffs among price and non-price factors, the Government will give a price evaluation preference to historic properties as follows:

(a) First to suitable historic properties within historic districts, a 10 percent price preference.

(b) If no suitable historic property within an historic district is offered or remains in the competition, the Government will give a 2.5 percent price preference to suitable non-historic developed or undeveloped sites within historic districts.

(c) If no suitable non-historic developed or undeveloped site within an historic district is offered or remains in the competition, the Government will give a 10 percent price preference to suitable historic properties outside of historic districts.

(d) Finally, if no suitable historic property outside of historic districts is offered, no historic price preference will be given to any property offered.

LEASES WITH PURCHASE OPTIONS

§ 102–73.130 When may Federal agencies consider acquiring leases with purchase options?

Agencies may consider leasing with a purchase option at or below fair market value, consistent with the lease-purchase scoring rules, when one or more of the following conditions exist:

(a) The purchase option offers economic and other advantages to the Government and is consistent with the Government's goals.

(b) The Government is the sole or major tenant of the building, and has a long-term need for the property.

(c) Leasing with a purchase option is otherwise in the best interest of the Government.

SCORING RULES

§ 102–73.135 What scoring rules must Federal agencies follow when considering leases and leases with purchase options?

All Federal agencies must follow the budget scorekeeping rules for leases, capital leases, and lease-purchases identified in appendices A and B of OMB Circular A–11. (For availability, see 5 CFR 1310.3.)

DELEGATIONS OF LEASING AUTHORITY

§ 102–73.140 When may agencies that do not possess independent leasing authority lease space?

Federal agencies may perform for themselves all functions necessary to acquire leased space in buildings and land incidental thereto when—

(a) The authority may be delegated (see § 102–72.30) on the different types of delegations related to real estate leasing);

(b) The space may be leased for no rental, or for a nominal consideration of $1 per annum, and is limited to terms not to exceed 1 year;

(c) Authority has been requested by an Executive agency and a specific delegation has been granted by the Administrator of General Services;

(d) A categorical delegation has been granted by the Administrator of General Services for space to accommodate particular types of agency activities, such as military recruiting offices or space for certain county level agricultural activities (see § 102–73.155 for a listing of categorical delegations); or

(e) The required space is found by the Administrator of General Services to be wholly or predominantly utilized for the special purposes of the agency to occupy such space and is not generally suitable for use by other agencies. Federal agencies must obtain prior approval from the GSA regional office having jurisdiction for the proposed leasing action, before initiating a leasing action involving 2,500 or more square feet of such special purpose space. GSA's approval must be based upon a finding that there is no vacant Government-owned or leased space available that will meet the agency's requirements. Agency special purpose space delegations can be found in §§ 102–73.170 through 102–73.225.

CATEGORICAL SPACE DELEGATIONS

§ 102–73.145 What is a categorical space delegation?

A categorical space delegation is a standing delegation of authority from the Administrator of General Services to a Federal agency to acquire a type of space identified in § 102–73.155, subject to limitations in this part.

§ 102–73.150 What is the policy for categorical space delegations?

Subject to the limitations cited in §§ 102–73.230 through 102–73.240, all Federal agencies are authorized to acquire the types of space listed in § 102–73.155 and, except where otherwise noted, may lease space for terms, including all options, of up to 20 years.

§ 102–73.155 What types of space can Federal agencies acquire with a categorical space delegation?

Federal agencies can use categorical space delegations to acquire—

(a) Space to house antennas, repeaters, or transmission equipment;

(b) Depots, including, but not limited to, stockpiling depots and torpedo net depots;

(c) Docks, piers, and mooring facilities (including closed storage space required in combination with such facilities);

(d) Fumigation areas;

(e) Garage space (may be leased only on a fiscal year basis);

(f) Greenhouses;

(g) Hangars and other airport operating facilities including, but not limited to, flight preparation space, aircraft storage areas, and repair shops;

(h) Hospitals, including medical clinics;

(i) Housing (temporary), including hotels (does not include quarters obtained pursuant to temporary duty travel or employee relocation);

(j) Laundries;

(k) Quarantine facilities for plants, birds, and other animals;

(l) Ranger stations, i.e., facilities that typically include small offices staffed by one or more uniformed employees, and may include sleeping/family quarters, parking areas, garages, and storage space. Office space within ranger stations is minimal and does not comprise a majority of the space. (May also be referred to as guard stations, information centers, or kiosks);

(m) Recruiting space for the armed forces (lease terms, including all options, limited to 5 years);

(n) Schools directly related to the special purpose function(s) of an agency;

(o) Specialized storage/depot facilities, such as cold storage; self-storage units; and lumber, oil, gasoline, shipbuilding materials, and pesticide materials/equipment storage (general purpose warehouse type storage facilities not included); and

(p) Space for short-term use (such as conferences and meetings, judicial proceedings, and emergency situations).

SPECIAL PURPOSE SPACE DELEGATIONS

§ 102–73.160 What is an agency special purpose space delegation?

An agency special purpose space delegation is a standing delegation of authority from the Administrator of General Services to specific Federal agencies to lease their own special purpose space (identified in §§ 102–73.170 through 102–73.225), subject to limitations in this part.

§ 102–73.165 What is the policy for agency special purpose space delegations?

Subject to the limitations on annual rental amounts, lease terms, and leases on parking spaces cited in §§ 102–73.230 through 102–73.240, the agencies listed below are authorized to acquire special purpose space associated with that agency and, except where otherwise noted, may lease such space for terms, including all options, of up to 20 years. The agencies and types of space subject to special purpose space delegations are specified in §§ 102–73.170 through 102–73.225.

§ 102–73.170 What types of special purpose space may the Department of Agriculture lease?

The Department of Agriculture is delegated the authority to lease the following types of special purpose space:

(a) Cotton classing laboratories (lease terms, including all options, limited to 5 years).

(b) Land (if unimproved, may be leased only on a fiscal year basis).

(c) Miscellaneous storage by cubic foot or weight basis.

(d) Office space when required to be located in or adjacent to stockyards, produce markets, produce terminals, airports, and other ports (lease terms, including all options, limited to 5 years).

(e) Space for agricultural commodities stored in licensed warehouses and utilized under warehouse contracts.

(f) Space utilized in cooperation with State and local governments or their instrumentalities (extension services) where the cooperating State or local government occupies a portion of the space and pays a portion of the rent.

§ 102–73.175 What types of special purpose space may the Department of Commerce lease?

The Department of Commerce is delegated authority to lease the following types of special purpose space:

(a) Space required by the Census Bureau in connection with conducting the decennial census (lease terms, including all options, limited to 5 years).

(b) Laboratories for testing materials, classified or ordnance devices, calibration of instruments, and atmospheric and oceanic research (lease terms, including all options, limited to 5 years).

(c) Maritime training stations.

(d) Radio stations.

(e) Land (if unimproved, may be leased only on a fiscal year basis).

(f) National Weather Service meteorological facilities.

§ 102–73.180 What types of special purpose space may the Department of Defense lease?

The Department of Defense is delegated authority to lease the following types of special purpose space:

(a) Air Force—Civil Air Patrol Liaison Offices and land incidental thereto when required for use incidental to, in conjunction with, and in close proximity to airports, including aircraft and warning stations (if unimproved, land may be leased only on a fiscal

year basis; for space, lease terms, including all options, limited to 5 years).

(b) Armories.

(c) Film library in the vicinity of Washington, DC.

(d) Mess halls.

(e) Ports of embarkation and debarkation.

(f) Post exchanges.

(g) Postal Concentration Center, Long Island City, NY.

(h) Recreation centers.

(i) Reserve training space.

(j) Service clubs.

(k) Testing laboratories (lease terms, including all options, limited to 5 years).

§ 102–73.185 What types of special purpose space may the Department of Energy lease?

The Department of Energy, as the successor to the Atomic Energy Commission, is delegated authority to lease facilities housing the special purpose or special location activities of the old Atomic Energy Commission.

§ 102–73.190 What types of special purpose space may the Federal Communications Commission lease?

The Federal Communications Commission is delegated authority to lease monitoring station sites.

§ 102–73.195 What types of special purpose space may the Department of Health and Human Services lease?

The Department of Health and Human Services is delegated authority to lease laboratories (lease terms, including all options, limited to 5 years).

§ 102–73.196 What types of special purpose space may the Department of Homeland Security lease?

The Department of Homeland Security is delegated authority to lease whatever space its organizational units or components had authority to lease prior to the creation of the Department of Homeland Security, including—

(a) Border patrol offices similar in character and utilization to police stations, involving the handling of prisoners, firearms, and motor vehicles, regardless of location (lease terms, including all options limited to 5 years);

(b) Space for the U.S. Coast Guard oceanic unit, Woods Hole, MA; and

(c) Space for the U.S. Coast Guard port security activities.

§102–73.200 What types of special purpose space may the Department of the Interior lease?

The Department of the Interior is delegated authority to lease the following types of special purpose space:

(a) Space in buildings and land incidental thereto used by field crews of the Bureau of Reclamation, Bureau of Land Management, and the Geological Survey in areas where no other Government agencies are quartered (unimproved land may be leased only on a fiscal year basis).

(b) National Parks/Monuments Visitors Centers consisting primarily of special purpose space (e.g., visitor reception, information, and rest room facilities) and not general office or administrative space.

§102–73.205 What types of special purpose space may the Department of Justice lease?

The Department of the Justice is delegated authority to lease the following types of special purpose space:

(a) U.S. marshals office in any Alaska location (lease terms, including all options, limited to 5 years).

(b) Space used for storage and maintenance of surveillance vehicles and seized property (lease terms, including all options, limited to 5 years).

(c) Space used for review and custody of records and other evidentiary materials (lease terms, including all options, limited to 5 years).

(d) Space used for trial preparation where space is not available in Federal buildings, Federal courthouses, USPS facilities, or GSA-leased buildings (lease terms limited to not more than 1 year).

§102–73.210 What types of special purpose space may the Office of Thrift Supervision lease?

The Office of Thrift Supervision is delegated authority to lease space for field offices of Examining Divisions required to be located within Office of Thrift Supervision buildings or immediately adjoining or adjacent to such buildings (lease terms, including all options, limited to 5 years).

§102–73.215 What types of special purpose space may the Department of Transportation lease?

The Department of Transportation is delegated authority to lease the following types of special purpose space (or real property):

(a) Land for the Federal Aviation Administration (FAA) at airports (unimproved land may be leased only on a fiscal year basis).

(b) General purpose office space not exceeding 10,000 square feet for the FAA at airports in buildings under the jurisdiction of public or private airport authorities (lease terms, including all options, limited to 5 years).

§102–73.220 What types of special purpose space may the Department of the Treasury lease?

The Department of the Treasury is delegated authority to lease the following types of special purpose space:

(a) Space and land incidental thereto for the use of the Comptroller of the Currency, as well as the operation, maintenance and custody thereof (if unimproved, land may be leased only on a fiscal year basis; lease term for space, including all options, limited to 5 years).

(b) Aerostat radar facilities necessary for U.S. Custom Service mission activities.

§102–73.225 What types of special purpose space may the Department of Veterans Affairs lease?

The Department of Veterans Affairs is delegated authority to lease the following types of special purpose space:

(a) Guidance and training centers located at schools and colleges.

(b) Space used for veterans hospitals, including outpatient and medical-related clinics, such as drug, mental health, and alcohol.

LIMITATIONS ON THE USE OF DELEGATED AUTHORITY

§102–73.230 When must Federal agencies submit a prospectus to lease real property?

In accordance with 40 U.S.C. 3307, Federal agencies must submit a prospectus to the Administrator of General Services for leases involving a net annual rental, excluding services and utilities, in excess of the prospectus threshold provided in 40 U.S.C. 3307. Agencies must be aware that prospectus thresholds are indexed and change each year.

§ 102–73.235 What is the maximum lease term that a Federal agency may agree to when it has been delegated lease acquisition authority from GSA?

Pursuant to GSA's authority to enter into lease agreements contained in 40 U.S.C. 585(a)(2), agencies delegated the authorities outlined herein may enter into leases for the term specified in the delegation. In those cases where agency special purposes space delegations include the authority to acquire unimproved land, the land may be leased only on a fiscal year basis.

§ 102–73.240 What policy must Federal agencies follow to acquire official parking spaces?

Federal agencies that need parking must utilize available Government-owned or leased facilities. Federal agencies must make inquiries regarding availability of such Government-controlled space to GSA regional offices and document such inquiries. If no suitable Government-controlled facilities are available, an agency may use its own procurement authority to acquire parking by service contract.

Subpart C—Acquisition by Purchase or Condemnation

BUILDINGS

§ 102–73.245 When may Federal agencies consider purchase of buildings?

A Federal agency may consider purchase of buildings on a case-by-case basis if it has landholding authority and when one or more of the following conditions exist:

(a) It is economically more beneficial to own and manage the property.

(b) There is a long-term need for the property.

(c) The property is an existing building, or a building nearing completion, that can be purchased and occupied within a reasonable time.

(d) When otherwise in the best interests of the Government.

§ 102–73.250 Are agencies required to adhere to the policies for locating Federal facilities when purchasing buildings?

Yes, when purchasing buildings, agencies must comply with the location policies in this part and part 102–83 of this chapter.

§ 102–73.255 What factors must Executive agencies consider when purchasing sites?

Agencies must locate proposed Federal buildings on sites that are most advantageous to the United States. Executive agencies must consider factors such as whether the site will contribute to economy and efficiency in the construction, maintenance, and operation of the individual building, and how the proposed site relates to the Government's total space needs in the community. Prior to acquiring, constructing, or leasing buildings (or sites for such buildings), Federal agencies must use, to the maximum extent feasible, historic properties available to the agency. In site selections, Executive agencies must consider Executive Order 12072 (August 16, 1978, 43 FR 36869) and Executive Order 13006 (40 U.S.C. 3306 note). In addition, Executive agencies must consider all of the following:

(a) Maximum utilization of Government-owned land (including excess land) whenever it is adequate, economically adaptable to requirements and properly located, where such use is consistent with the provisions of part 102–75, subpart B, of this chapter.

(b) A site adjacent to or in the proximity of an existing Federal building that is well located and is to be retained for long-term occupancy.

(c) The environmental condition of proposed sites prior to purchase. The sites must be free from contamination, unless it is otherwise determined to be in the best interests of the Government to purchase a contaminated site (e.g., reuse of a site under an established "Brownfields" program).

(d) Purchase options to secure the future availability of a site.

(e) All applicable location policies in this part and part 102–83 of this chapter.

LAND

§ 102-73.260 What land acquisition policy must Federal agencies follow?

Federal agencies must follow the land acquisition policy in the Uniform Relocation Assistance and Real Property Acquisition Policies Act, as amended, 42 U.S.C. 4651–4655, which—

(a) Encourages and expedites the acquisition of real property by agreements with owners;

(b) Avoids litigation, including condemnation actions, where possible and relieves congestion in the courts;

(c) Provides for consistent treatment of owners; and

(d) Promotes public confidence in Federal land acquisition practices.

§ 102-73.265 What actions must Federal agencies take to facilitate land acquisition?

To facilitate land acquisition, Federal agencies must, among other things—

(a) Appraise the real property before starting negotiations and give the owner (or the owner's representative) the opportunity to accompany the appraiser during the inspection;

(b) Establish an amount estimated to be the just compensation before starting negotiations and promptly offer to acquire the property for this full amount;

(c) Try to negotiate with owners on the price;

(d) Pay the agreed purchase price to the property owner, or in the case of a condemnation, deposit payment in the registry of the court, for the benefit of the owner, before requiring the owner to surrender the property; and

(e) Provide property owners (and occupants) at least 90 days' notice of displacement before requiring anyone to move. If a Federal agency permits the owner to keep possession for a short time after acquiring the owner's property, Federal agencies must not charge rent in excess of the property's fair rental value to a short-term occupier.

JUST COMPENSATION

§ 102-73.270 Are Federal agencies required to provide the owner with a written statement of the amount established as just compensation?

Yes, Federal agencies must provide the owner with a written statement of this amount and summarize the basis for it. When it is appropriate, Federal agencies must separately state the just compensation for the property to be acquired and damages to the remaining real property.

§ 102-73.275 What specific information must be included in the summary statement for the owner that explains the basis for just compensation?

The summary statement must—

(a) Identify the real property and the estate or interest the Federal agency is acquiring;

(b) Identify the buildings, structures, and other improvements the Federal agency considers part of the real property for which just compensation is being offered;

(c) State that the Federal agency based the estimate of just compensation on the Government's estimate of the property's fair market value. If only part of a property or less than a full interest is being acquired, Federal agencies must explain how they determined the just compensation for it; and

(d) State that the Government's estimate of just compensation is at least as much as the property's approved appraisal value.

§ 102-73.280 Where can Federal agencies find guidance on how to appraise the value of properties being acquired by the Federal Government?

The Interagency Land Acquisition Conference has developed, promulgated, and adopted the Uniform Appraisal Standards for Federal Land Acquisitions, sometimes referred to as the "Yellow Book." The Interagency Land Acquisition Conference, established on November 27, 1968, by invitation of the Attorney General, is a voluntary organization composed of the many Federal agencies engaged in the acquisition of real estate for public uses. The "Yellow Book" is published by the Appraisal Institute in cooperation with the U.S. Department of Justice and is available in hard copy or on the Department of Justice's internet Web site at *http://www.usdoj.gov/enrd/land-ack/*.

§ 102–73.285　[Reserved]

§ 102–73.290　Are there any prohibitions when a Federal agency pays "just compensation" to a tenant?

Yes, Federal agencies must not—

(a) Duplicate any payment to the tenant otherwise authorized by law; and

(b) Pay a tenant unless the landowner disclaims all interests in the tenant's improvements. In consideration for any such payment, the tenant must assign, transfer, and release to the Federal agency all of its right, title, and interest in the improvements. The tenant may reject such payment under this subpart and obtain payment for its property interests according to other sections of applicable law.

EXPENSES INCIDENTAL TO PROPERTY TRANSFER

§ 102–73.295　What property transfer expenses must Federal agencies cover when acquiring real property?

Federal agencies must—

(a) Reimburse property owners for all reasonable expenses actually incurred for recording fees, transfer taxes, documentary stamps, evidence of title, boundary surveys, legal descriptions of the real property, and similar expenses needed to convey the property to the Federal Government;

(b) Reimburse property owners for all reasonable expenses actually incurred for penalty costs and other charges to prepay any existing, recorded mortgage that a property owner entered into in good faith and that encumbers the real property;

(c) Reimburse property owners for all reasonable expenses actually incurred for the prorated part of any prepaid real property taxes that cover the period after the Federal Government gets title to the property or effective possession of it, whichever is earlier; and

(d) Whenever possible, directly pay the costs identified in this section, so property owners will not have to pay them and then seek reimbursement from the Government.

LITIGATION EXPENSES

§ 102–73.300　Are Federal agencies required to pay for litigation expenses incurred by a property owner because of a condemnation proceeding?

Federal agencies must pay reasonable expenses for attorneys, appraisals, and engineering fees that a property owner incurs because of a condemnation proceeding, if any of the following are true:

(a) The court's final judgment is that the Federal agency cannot acquire the real property by condemnation.

(b) The Federal agency abandons the condemnation proceeding other than under an agreed-on settlement.

(c) The court renders a judgment in the property owner's favor in an inverse condemnation proceeding or the Federal agency agrees to settle such proceeding.

RELOCATION ASSISTANCE POLICY

§ 102–73.305　What relocation assistance policy must Federal agencies follow?

Federal agencies, upon approval from GSA, must provide appropriate relocation assistance under the Uniform Relocation Assistance and Real Property Acquisition Policies Act, as amended, 42 U.S.C. 4651–4655, to eligible owners and tenants of property purchased for use by Federal agencies in accordance with the implementing regulations found in 49 CFR part 24. Appropriate relocation assistance means that the Federal agency must pay the displaced person for actual—

(a) Reasonable moving expenses (in moving himself, his family, and business);

(b) Direct losses of tangible personal property as a result of moving or discontinuing a business;

(c) Reasonable expenses in searching for a replacement business or farm; and

(d) Reasonable expenses necessary to reestablish a displaced farm, nonprofit organization, or small business at its new site, but not to exceed $10,000.

PART 102–74—FACILITY MANAGEMENT

Subpart A—General Provisions

102–74.550 What items are permittees responsible for furnishing?

CONDUCT

102–74.555 What rules of conduct must all permittees observe while on Federal property?

NON-AFFILIATION WITH THE GOVERNMENT

102–74.560 May Federal agencies advise the public of the presence of any permittees and their non-affiliation with the Federal Government?

Subpart E—Installing, Repairing, and Replacing Sidewalks

102–74.565 What is the scope of this subpart?
102–74.570 Are State and local governments required to fund the cost of installing, repairing, and replacing sidewalks?
102–74.575 How do Federal agencies arrange for work on sidewalks?
102–74.580 Who decides when to replace a sidewalk?

Subpart F—Telework

102–74.585 What Federal facility telework policy must Executive agencies follow?
102–74.590 What steps must agencies take to implement these laws and policies?
102–74.595 How can agencies obtain guidance, assistance, and oversight regarding alternative workplace arrangements from GSA?
102–74.600 Should Federal agencies utilize telework centers?
APPENDIX TO PART 102–74—RULES AND REGULATIONS GOVERNING CONDUCT ON FEDERAL PROPERTY

AUTHORITY: 40 U.S.C. 121(c); Executive Order 12191, 45 FR 7997, 3 CFR, 1980 Comp., p 138.

SOURCE: 70 FR 67798, Nov. 8, 2005, unless otherwise noted.

Subpart A—General Provisions

§ 102–74.5 What is the scope of this part?

The real property policies contained in this part apply to Federal agencies, including the GSA's Public Buildings Service (PBS), operating under, or subject to, the authorities of the Administrator of General Services.

§ 102–74.10 What is the basic facility management policy?

Executive agencies must manage, operate and maintain Government-owned and leased buildings in a manner that provides for quality space and services consistent with their operational needs and accomplishes overall Government objectives. The management, operation and maintenance of buildings and building systems must—

(a) Be cost effective and energy efficient;

(b) Be adequate to meet the agencies' missions;

(c) Meet nationally recognized standards; and

(d) Be at an appropriate level to maintain and preserve the physical plant assets, consistent with available funding.

Subpart B—Facility Management

§ 102–74.15 What are the facility management responsibilities of occupant agencies?

Occupants of facilities under the custody and control of Federal agencies must—

(a) Cooperate to the fullest extent with all pertinent facility procedures and regulations;

(b) Promptly report all crimes and suspicious circumstances occurring on Federally controlled property first to the regional Federal Protective Service, and as appropriate, the local responding law enforcement authority;

(c) Provide training to employees regarding protection and responses to emergency situations; and

(d) Make recommendations for improving the effectiveness of protection in Federal facilities.

OCCUPANCY SERVICES

§ 102–74.20 What are occupancy services?

Occupancy services are—

(a) Building services (see § 102–74.35);

(b) Concession services (see § 102–74.40); and

(c) Conservation programs (see § 102–74.100).

§ 102–74.25 What responsibilities do Executive agencies have regarding occupancy services?

Executive agencies, upon approval from GSA, must manage, administer and enforce the requirements of agreements (such as Memoranda of Understanding) and contracts that provide for the delivery of occupancy services.

§ 102–74.30 What standard in providing occupancy services must Executive agencies follow?

Executive agencies must provide occupancy services that substantially conform to nationally recognized standards. As needed, Executive agencies may adopt other standards for buildings and services in Federally controlled facilities to conform to statutory requirements and to implement cost-reduction efforts.

§ 102–74.35 What building services must Executive agencies provide?

Executive agencies, upon approval from GSA, must provide—

(a) Building services such as custodial, solid waste management (including recycling), heating and cooling, landscaping and grounds maintenance, tenant alterations, minor repairs, building maintenance, integrated pest management, signage, parking, and snow removal, at appropriate levels to support Federal agency missions; and

(b) Arrangements for raising and lowering the United States flags at appropriate times. In addition, agencies must display P.O.W. and M.I.A. flags at locations specified in 36 U.S.C. 902 on P.O.W./M.I.A. flag display days.

CONCESSION SERVICES

§ 102–74.40 What are concession services?

Concession services are any food or snack services provided by a Randolph-Sheppard Act vendor, commercial contractor or nonprofit organization (see definition in § 102–71.20 of this chapter), in vending facilities such as—

(a) Vending machines;

(b) Sundry facilities;

(c) Prepackaged facilities;

(d) Snack bars; and

(e) Cafeterias.

§ 102–74.45 When must Federal agencies provide concession services?

Federal agencies, upon approval from GSA, must provide concession services where building population supports such services and when the availability of existing commercial services is insufficient to meet Federal agency needs. Prior to establishing concessions, Federal agencies must ensure that—

(a) The proposed concession will be established and operated in conformance with applicable policies, safety, health and sanitation codes, laws, regulations, etc., and will not contravene the terms of any lease or other contractual arrangement; and

(b) Sufficient funds are legally available to cover all costs for which the Government may be responsible.

§ 102–74.50 Are Federal agencies required to give blind vendors priority in operating vending facilities?

With certain exceptions, the Randolph-Sheppard Act (20 U.S.C. 107 *et seq.*) requires that blind persons licensed by a State licensing agency under the provisions of the Randolph-Sheppard Act be authorized to operate vending facilities on Federal property, including leased buildings. The Department of Education (ED) is responsible for the administration of the Randolph-Sheppard Act as set forth at 34 CFR part 395. The ED designates individual State licensing agencies with program administration responsibility. The Randolph-Sheppard Act and its implementing regulations require that Federal property managers give priority to and notify the State licensing agencies in writing of any opportunity.

§ 102–74.55 Are vending facilities authorized under the Randolph-Sheppard Act operated by permit or contract?

Vending facilities are authorized by permit. As set forth in 34 CFR part 395, the Federal property manager approves and signs State licensing agency permits that authorize States to license blind vendors to operate vending facilities (including vending machines) on Federal property.

§ 102–74.60 Are Federal agencies required to give blind vendors priority in operating cafeterias?

Yes. Federal agencies are required to give Randolph-Sheppard vendors priority in the operation of cafeterias when the State licensing agency is in the competitive range as set forth at 34 CFR part 395.

§ 102–74.65 Are cafeterias authorized under the Randolph-Sheppard Act operated by permit or contract?

They are operated by contract. As set forth at 34 CFR part 395, the Federal property manager contracts with the State licensing agency to license blind vendors to operate cafeterias on Federal property.

§ 102–74.70 Are commercial vendors and nonprofit organizations required to operate vending facilities by permit or contractual arrangement?

Commercial vendors and nonprofit organizations must operate vending facilities, including cafeterias, under a contractual arrangement with Federal agencies.

§ 102–74.75 May Federal agencies sell tobacco products in vending machines in Government-owned and leased space?

No. Section 636 of Public Law 104–52 prohibits the sale of tobacco products in vending machines in Government-owned and leased space. The Administrator of GSA or the head of an Agency may designate areas not subject to the prohibition, if minors are prohibited and reports are made to the appropriate committees of Congress.

§§ 102–74.80—102–74.95 [Reserved]

CONSERVATION PROGRAMS

§ 102–74.100 What are conservation programs?

Conservation programs are programs that improve energy and water efficiency and promote the use of solar and other renewable energy. These programs must promote and maintain an effective source reduction activity (reducing consumption of resources such as energy, water, and paper), resource recovery activity (obtaining materials from the waste stream that can be recycled into new products), and reuse activity (reusing same product before disposition, such as reusing unneeded memos for scratch paper).

ASSET SERVICES

§ 102–74.105 What are asset services?

Asset services include repairs (other than those minor repairs identified in § 102–74.35(a)), alterations and modernizations for real property assets. Typically, these are the types of repairs and alterations necessary to preserve or enhance the value of the real property asset.

§ 102–74.110 What asset services must Executive agencies provide?

Executive agencies, upon approval from GSA, must provide asset services such as repairs (in addition to those minor repairs identified in § 102–74.35(a)), alterations, and modernizations for real property assets. For repairs and alterations projects for which the estimated cost exceeds the prospectus threshold, Federal agencies must follow the prospectus submission and approval policy identified in this part and part 102–73 of this chapter.

§ 102–74.115 What standard in providing asset services must Executive agencies follow?

Executive agencies must provide asset services that maintain continuity of Government operations, continue efficient building operations, extend the useful life of buildings and related building systems, and provide a quality workplace environment that enhances employee productivity.

§ 102–74.120 Is a prospectus required to be submitted before emergency alterations can be performed?

No. A prospectus does not need to be submitted before emergency alterations are performed, but GSA must submit a prospectus as soon as possible after the emergency. Federal agencies must immediately alter a building if the alteration protects people, buildings, or equipment, saves lives, and/or avoids further property damage. Federal agencies can take these actions in an emergency before GSA submits a prospectus on the alterations to the Senate Committee on Environment and Public Works and the House Committee on Transportation and Infrastructure.

§102–74.125 **Are prospectuses required for reimbursable alteration projects?**

A project that is to be financed in whole or in part from funds appropriated to the requesting agency may be performed without a prospectus if—

(a) Payment is made from agency appropriations that are not subject to 40 U.S.C. 3307; and

(b) GSA's portion of the cost, if any, does not exceed the prospectus threshold.

§102–74.130 **When a prospectus is required, can GSA prepare a prospectus for a reimbursable alteration project?**

Yes, if requested by a Federal agency, GSA will prepare a prospectus for a reimbursable alteration project.

§102–74.135 **Who selects construction and alteration projects that are to be performed?**

The Administrator of General Services selects construction and alteration projects to be performed.

§102–74.140 **On what basis does the Administrator select construction and alteration projects?**

The Administrator selects projects based on a continuing investigation and survey of the public building needs of the Federal Government. These projects must be equitably distributed throughout the United States, with due consideration given to each project's comparative urgency.

§102–74.145 **What information must a Federal agency submit to GSA after the agency has identified a need for construction or alteration of a public building?**

Federal agencies identifying a need for construction or alteration of a public building must provide information, such as a description of the work, location, estimated maximum cost, and justification to the Administrator of General Services.

§102–74.150 **Who submits prospectuses for the construction or alteration of public buildings to the Congressional committees?**

The Administrator of General Services must submit prospectuses for public building construction or alteration projects to the Senate Committee on Environment and Public Works and the House Committee on Transportation and Infrastructure for approval.

ENERGY CONSERVATION

§102–74.155 **What energy conservation policy must Federal agencies follow in the management of facilities?**

Federal agencies must—

(a) Comply with the energy conservation guidelines in 10 CFR part 436 (Federal Energy Management and Planning Programs); and

(b) Observe the energy conservation policies cited in this part.

§102–74.160 **What actions must Federal agencies take to promote energy conservation?**

Federal agencies must—

(a) Turn off lights and equipment when not needed;

(b) Not block or impede ventilation; and

(c) Keep windows and other building accesses closed during the heating and cooling seasons.

§102–74.165 **What energy standards must Federal agencies follow for existing facilities?**

Existing Federal facilities must meet the energy standards prescribed by the American Society of Heating, Refrigerating, and Air Conditioning Engineers and the Illuminating Engineering Society of North American in ASHRAE/IES Standard 90A–1980, as amended by the Department of Energy. Federal agencies must apply these energy standards where they can be achieved through life cycle, cost effective actions.

§102–74.170 **May exceptions to the energy conservation policies in this subpart be granted?**

Yes, the Federal agency buildings manager may grant exceptions to the foregoing policies in this subpart to enable agencies to accomplish their missions more effectively and efficiently.

§ 102–74.175 Are Government-leased buildings required to conform with the policies in this subpart?

Yes, all new lease contracts must be in conformance with the policies prescribed in this subpart. Federal agencies must administer existing lease contracts in accordance with these policies to the maximum extent feasible.

§ 102–74.180 What illumination levels must Federal agencies maintain on Federal facilities?

Except where special circumstances exist, Federal agencies must maintain illumination levels at—

(a) 50 foot-candles at work station surfaces, measured at a height of 30 inches above floor level, during working hours (for visually difficult or critical tasks, additional lighting may be authorized by the Federal agency buildings manager);

(b) 30 foot-candles in work areas during working hours, measured at 30 inches above floor level;

(c) 10 foot-candles, but not less than 1 foot-candle, in non-work areas, during working hours (normally this will require levels of 5 foot-candles at elevator boarding areas, minimum of 1 foot-candle at the middle of corridors and stairwells as measured at the walking surface, 1 foot-candle at the middle of corridors and stairwells as measured at the walking surface, and 10 foot-candles in storage areas); and

(d) Levels essential for safety and security purposes, including exit signs and exterior lights.

§ 102–74.185 What heating and cooling policy must Federal agencies follow in Federal facilities?

Within the limitations of the building systems, Federal agencies must—

(a) Operate heating and cooling systems in the most overall energy efficient and economical manner;

(b) Maintain temperatures to maximize customer satisfaction by conforming to local commercial equivalent temperature levels and operating practices;

(c) Set heating temperatures no higher than 55 degrees Fahrenheit during non-working hours;

(d) Not provide air-conditioning during non-working hours, except as necessary to return space temperatures to a suitable level for the beginning of working hours;

(e) Not permit reheating, humidification and simultaneous heating and cooling; and

(f) Operate building systems as necessary during extreme weather conditions to protect the physical condition of the building.

§ 102–74.190 Are portable heaters, fans and other such devices allowed in Government-controlled facilities?

Federal agencies are prohibited from operating portable heaters, fans, and other such devices in Government-controlled facilities unless authorized by the Federal agency buildings manager.

§ 102–74.195 What ventilation policy must Federal agencies follow?

During working hours in periods of heating and cooling, Federal agencies must provide ventilation in accordance with ASHRAE Standard 62, Ventilation for Acceptable Indoor Air Quality, where physically practical. Where not physically practical, Federal agencies must provide the maximum allowable amount of ventilation during periods of heating and cooling and pursue opportunities to increase ventilation up to current standards. ASHRAE Standard 62 is available from ASHRAE Publications Sales, 1791 Tullie Circle NE, Atlanta, GA 30329–2305.

§ 102–74.200 What information are Federal agencies required to report to the Department of Energy (DOE)?

Federal agencies, upon approval of GSA, must report to the DOE the energy consumption in buildings, facilities, vehicles, and equipment within 45 calendar days after the end of each quarter as specified in the DOE Federal Energy Usage Report DOE F 6200.2 Instructions.

RIDESHARING

§ 102–74.205 What Federal facility ridesharing policy must Executive agencies follow?

(a) In accordance with Executive Order 12191, "Federal Facility Ridesharing Program" (3 CFR, 1980 Comp.,

p. 138), Executive agencies must actively promote the use of ridesharing (carpools, vanpools, privately leased buses, public transportation, and other multi-occupancy modes of travel) by personnel working at Federal facilities to conserve energy, reduce congestion, improve air quality, and provide an economical way for Federal employees to commute to work.

(b) In accordance with the Federal Employees Clean Air Incentives Act (Public Law 103–172), the Federal Government is required to take steps to improve the air quality, and to reduce traffic congestion by providing for the establishment of programs that encourage Federal employees to commute to work by means other than single-occupancy motor vehicles.

(c) In accordance with the Transportation Equity Act for the 21st Century (Public Law 105–178), employers, including the Federal Government, are to offer employees transportation fringe benefits.

§ 102–74.210 What steps must Executive agencies take to promote ridesharing at Federal facilities?

(a) Under Executive Order 12191, "Federal Facility Ridesharing Program," agencies shall—

(1) Establish an annual ridesharing goal for each facility; and

(2) Cooperate with State and local ridesharing agencies where such agencies exist.

(b) Under the Federal Employees Clean Air Incentives Act (Public Law 103–172), agencies shall—

(1) Issue transit passes or similar vouchers to exchange for transit passes;

(2) Furnish space, facilities, and services to bicyclists;

(3) Provide non-monetary incentives as provided by other provisions of law or other authority; and

(4) Submit biennially to GSA (as directed in House of Representatives Report 103–356, dated November 10, 1993) a report that covers—

(i) Agency programs offered under Public law 103–172;

(ii) Description of each program;

(iii) Extent of employee participation in, and costs to the Government associated with, each program;

(iv) Assessment of environmental or other benefits realized from these programs; and

(v) Other matters that may be appropriate under Public Law 103–172.

(c) In accordance with the Transportation Equity Act for the 21st Century, agencies may (in lieu of or in combination with other commuter benefits) provide fringe benefits to qualified commuters, at no cost, by giving them a monthly pretax payroll deduction to support and encourage the use of mass transportation systems.

§§ 102–74.215—102–74.225 [Reserved]

OCCUPANT EMERGENCY PROGRAM

§ 102–74.230 Who is responsible for establishing an occupant emergency program?

The Designated Official (as defined in § 102–71.20 of this chapter) is responsible for developing, implementing and maintaining an Occupant Emergency Plan (as defined in § 102–71.20 of this chapter). The Designated Official's responsibilities include establishing, staffing and training an Occupant Emergency Organization with agency employees. Federal agencies, upon approval from GSA, must assist in the establishment and maintenance of such plans and organizations.

§ 102–74.235 Are occupant agencies required to cooperate with the Designated Official in the implementation of the emergency plans and the staffing of the emergency organization?

Yes, all occupant agencies of a facility must fully cooperate with the Designated Official in the implementation of the emergency plans and the staffing of the emergency organization.

§ 102–74.240 What are Federal agencies' occupant emergency responsibilities?

Federal agencies, upon approval from GSA, must—

(a) Provide emergency program policy guidance;

(b) Review plans and organizations annually;

(c) Assist in training of personnel;

(d) Otherwise provide for the proper administration of Occupant Emergency

Programs (as defined in § 102–71.20 of this chapter);

(e) Solicit the assistance of the lessor in the establishment and implementation of plans in leased space; and

(f) Assist the Occupant Emergency Organization (as defined in § 102–71.20 of this chapter) by providing technical personnel qualified in the operation of utility systems and protective equipment.

§ 102–74.245 Who makes the decision to activate the Occupant Emergency Organization?

The decision to activate the Occupant Emergency Organization must be made by the Designated Official, or by the designated alternate official. After normal duty hours, the senior Federal official present must represent the Designated Official or his/her alternates and must initiate action to cope with emergencies in accordance with the plans.

§ 102–74.250 What information must the Designated Official use to make a decision to activate the Occupant Emergency Organization?

The Designated Official must make a decision to activate the Occupant Emergency Organization based upon the best available information, including—

(a) An understanding of local tensions;

(b) The sensitivity of target agency(ies);

(c) Previous experience with similar situations;

(d) Advice from the Federal agency buildings manager;

(e) Advice from the appropriate Federal law enforcement official; and

(f) Advice from Federal, State, and local law enforcement agencies.

§ 102–74.255 How must occupant evacuation or relocation be accomplished when there is immediate danger to persons or property, such as fire, explosion or the discovery of an explosive device (not including a bomb threat)?

The Designated Official must initiate action to evacuate or relocate occupants in accordance with the plan by sounding the fire alarm system or by other appropriate means when there is immediate danger to persons or property, such as fire, explosion or the discovery of an explosive device (not including a bomb threat).

§ 102–74.260 What action must the Designated Official initiate when there is advance notice of an emergency?

The Designated Official must initiate appropriate action according to the plan when there is advance notice of an emergency.

PARKING FACILITIES

§ 102–74.265 Who must provide for the regulation and policing of parking facilities?

Federal agencies, upon approval from GSA, must provide for any necessary regulation and policing of parking facilities, which may include—

(a) The issuance of traffic rules and regulations;

(b) The installation of signs and markings for traffic control (Signs and markings must conform with the Manual on Uniform Traffic Control Devices published by the Department of Transportation);

(c) The issuance of citations for parking violations; and

(d) The immobilization or removal of illegally parked vehicles.

§ 102–74.270 Are vehicles required to display parking permits in parking facilities?

When the use of parking space is controlled as in § 102–74.265, all privately owned vehicles other than those authorized to use designated visitor or service areas must display a parking permit. This requirement may be waived in parking facilities where the number of available spaces regularly exceeds the demand for such spaces.

§ 102–74.275 May Federal agencies authorize lessors or parking management contractors to manage, regulate and police parking facilities?

Yes, Federal agencies, upon approval from GSA, may authorize lessors or parking management contractors to manage, regulate and police parking facilities.

§ 102–74.280 Are privately owned vehicles converted for propane carburetion permitted in underground parking facilities?

Federal agencies must not permit privately owned vehicles converted for propane carburetion to enter underground parking facilities unless the owner provides to the occupant agency and the Federal agency buildings manager the installer's certification that the installation methods and equipment comply with National Fire Protection Association (NFPA) Standard No. 58.

§ 102–74.285 How must Federal agencies assign priority to parking spaces in controlled areas?

Federal agencies must reserve official parking spaces, in the following order of priority, for—

(a) Official postal vehicles at buildings containing the U.S. Postal Service's mailing operations;

(b) Federally owned vehicles used to apprehend criminals, fight fires and handle other emergencies;

(c) Private vehicles owned by Members of Congress (but not their staffs);

(d) Private vehicles owned by Federal judges (appointed under Article III of the Constitution), which may be parked in those spaces assigned for the use of the Court, with priority for them set by the Administrative Office of the U.S. Courts;

(e) Other Federally owned and leased vehicles, including those in motor pools or assigned for general use;

(f) Service vehicles, vehicles used in child care center operations, and vehicles of patrons and visitors (Federal agencies must allocate parking for disabled visitors whenever an agency's mission requires visitor parking); and

(g) Private vehicles owned by employees, using spaces not needed for official business.

However, in major metropolitan areas, Federal agencies may determine that allocations by zone would make parking more efficient or equitable, taking into account the priority for official parking set forth in this section.

§ 102–74.290 May Federal agencies allow employees to use parking spaces not required for official needs?

Yes, Federal agencies may allow employees to use parking spaces not required for official needs.

§ 102–74.295 Who determines the number of employee parking spaces for each facility?

The Federal agency buildings manager must determine the total number of spaces available for employee parking. Typically, Federal agencies must make a separate determination for each parking facility. However, in major metropolitan areas, Federal agencies may determine that allocations by zone would make parking more efficient or more equitably available.

§ 102–74.300 How must space available for employee parking be allocated among occupant agencies?

The Federal agency buildings manager must allocate space available for employee parking among occupant agencies on an equitable basis, such as by allocating such parking in proportion to each agency's share of building space, office space or total employee population, as appropriate. In certain cases, Federal agencies may allow a third party, such as a board composed of representatives of agencies sharing space, to determine proper parking allocations among the occupant agencies.

§ 102–74.305 How must Federal agencies assign available parking spaces to their employees?

Federal agencies must assign available parking spaces to their employees using the following order of priority:

(a) Severely disabled employees (see definition in §102–71.20 of this chapter).

(b) Executive personnel and persons who work unusual hours.

(c) Vanpool/carpool vehicles.

(d) Privately owned vehicles of occupant agency employees that are regularly used for Government business at least 12 days per month and that qualify for reimbursement of mileage and travel expenses under Government travel regulations.

(e) Other privately owned vehicles of employees, on a space-available basis. (In locations where parking allocations are made on a zonal basis, GSA and affected agencies may cooperate to issue additional rules, as appropriate.)

§ 102-74.310 What measures must Federal agencies take to improve the utilization of parking facilities?

Federal agencies must take all feasible measures to improve the utilization of parking facilities, including—

(a) The conducting of surveys and studies;

(b) The periodic review of parking space allocations;

(c) The dissemination of parking information to occupant agencies;

(d) The implementation of parking incentives that promote ridesharing;

(e) The use of stack parking practices, where appropriate; and

(f) The employment of parking management contractors and concessionaires, where appropriate.

SMOKING

§ 102-74.315 What is the smoking policy for interior space in Federal facilities?

Pursuant to Executive Order 13058, "Protecting Federal Employees and the Public From Exposure to Tobacco Smoke in the Federal Workplace" (3 CFR, 1997 Comp., p. 216), it is the policy of the executive branch to establish a smoke-free environment for Federal employees and members of the public visiting or using Federal facilities. The smoking of tobacco products is prohibited in all interior space owned, rented or leased by the executive branch of the Federal Government.

[73 FR 77518, Dec. 19, 2008]

§ 102-74.320 Are there any exceptions to the smoking policy for interior space in Federal facilities?

Yes, the smoking policy does not apply in—

(a) Any residential accommodation for persons voluntarily or involuntarily residing, on a temporary or long-term basis, in a building owned, leased or rented by the Federal Government;

(b) Portions of Federally owned buildings leased, rented or otherwise

provided in their entirety to non-Federal parties;

(c) Places of employment in the private sector or in other non-Federal Governmental units that serve as the permanent or intermittent duty station of one or more Federal employees; and

(d) Instances where an agency head establishes limited and narrow exceptions that are necessary to accomplish agency missions. Such exceptions must be in writing, approved by the agency head and, to the fullest extent possible, provide protection of nonsmokers from exposure to environmental tobacco smoke. Authority to establish such exceptions may not be delegated.

[73 FR 77518, Dec. 19, 2008]

§ 102-74.325 Are designated smoking areas authorized in interior space?

No, unless specifically established by an agency head as provided by § 102-74.320(d). A previous exception for designated smoking areas is being eliminated. All designated interior smoking areas will be closed effective June 19, 2009. This six-month phase-in period is designed to establish a fixed but reasonable time for implementing this policy change. This phase-in period will provide agencies with time to comply with their obligations under the Federal Service Labor-Management Relations Act, as amended, 5 U.S.C. Ch. 71, Labor-Management Relations, in those circumstances where there is an exclusive union representative for the employees.

[73 FR 77518, Dec. 19, 2008]

§ 102-74.330 What smoking restrictions apply to outside areas under Executive branch control?

Effective June 19, 2009, smoking is prohibited in courtyards and within twenty-five (25) feet of doorways and air intake ducts on outdoor space under the jurisdiction, custody or control of GSA. This six-month phase-in period is designed to establish a fixed but reasonable time for implementing this policy change. This phase-in period will provide agencies with time to comply with their obligations under the Federal Service Labor-Management Relations Act, as amended, 5

U.S.C. Ch. 71, Labor-Management Relations, in those circumstances where there is an exclusive union representative for the employees.

[73 FR 77518, Dec. 19, 2008]

§ 102–74.335 Who is responsible for furnishing and installing signs concerning smoking restrictions in the building, and in and around building entrance doorways and air intake ducts?

Federal agency building managers are responsible for furnishing and installing suitable, uniform signs in the building, and in and around building entrance doorways and air intake ducts, reading "No Smoking," "No Smoking Except in Designated Areas," "No Smoking Within 25 Feet of Doorway," or "No Smoking Within 25 Feet of Air Duct," as applicable.

[73 FR 77518, Dec. 19, 2008]

§ 102–74.340 Who is responsible for monitoring and controlling areas designated for smoking by an agency head and for identifying those areas with proper signage?

Agency heads are responsible for monitoring and controlling areas designated by them under § 102–74.320(d) for smoking and identifying these areas with proper signage. Suitable, uniform signs reading "Designated Smoking Area" must be furnished and installed by the occupant agency.

[73 FR 77518, Dec. 19, 2008]

§ 102–74.345 Does the smoking policy in this part apply to the judicial branch?

This smoking policy applies to the judicial branch when it occupies space in buildings controlled by the executive branch. Furthermore, the Federal Chief Judge in a local jurisdiction may be deemed to be comparable to an agency head and may establish exceptions for Federal jurors and others as provided in § 102–74.320(d).

[73 FR 77518, Dec. 19, 2008]

§ 102–74.350 Are agencies required to meet their obligations under the Federal Service Labor-Management Relations Act where there is an exclusive representative for the employees prior to implementing this smoking policy?

Yes. Where there is an exclusive representative for the employees, Federal agencies must meet their obligations under the Federal Service Labor-Management Relations Act, 5 U.S.C. Ch. 71, Labor-Management Relations, prior to implementing this section. In all other cases, agencies may consult directly with employees.

[73 FR 77518, Dec. 19, 2008]

§ 102–74.351 If a state or local government has a smoke-free ordinance that is more strict than the smoking policy for Federal facilities, does the state or local law or Federal policy control?

The answer depends on whether the facility is Federally owned or privately owned. If the facility is Federally owned, then Federal preemption principles apply and the Federal policy controls. If the facility is privately owned, then Federal tenants are subject to the provisions of the state or local ordinance, even in the Federally leased space, if the state or local restrictions are more stringent than the Federal policy.

[73 FR 77518, Dec. 19, 2008]

ACCIDENT AND FIRE PREVENTION

§ 102–74.355 With what accident and fire prevention standards must Federal facilities comply?

To the maximum extent feasible, Federal agencies must manage facilities in accordance with the accident and fire prevention requirements identified in § 102–80.80 of this chapter.

§ 102–74.360 What are the specific accident and fire prevention responsibilities of occupant agencies?

Each occupant agency must—
(a) Participate in at least one fire drill per year;
(b) Maintain a neat and orderly facility to minimize the risk of accidental injuries and fires;

(c) Keep all exits, accesses to exits and accesses to emergency equipment clear at all times;

(d) Not bring hazardous, explosive or combustible materials into buildings unless authorized by appropriate agency officials and by GSA and unless protective arrangements determined necessary by GSA have been provided;

(e) Use only draperies, curtains or other hanging materials that are made of non-combustible or flame-resistant fabric;

(f) Use only freestanding partitions and space dividers that are limited combustible, and fabric coverings that are flame resistant;

(g) Cooperate with GSA to develop and maintain fire prevention programs that provide the maximum safety for the occupants;

(h) Train employees to use protective equipment and educate employees to take appropriate fire safety precautions in their work;

(i) Keep facilities in the safest condition practicable, and conduct periodic inspections in accordance with Executive Order 12196 and 29 CFR part 1960;

(j) Immediately report accidents involving personal injury or property damage, which result from building system or maintenance deficiencies, to the Federal agency building manager; and

(k) Appoint a safety, health and fire protection liaison to represent the occupant agency with GSA.

Subpart C—Conduct on Federal Property

APPLICABILITY

§ 102–74.365 To whom does this subpart apply?

The rules in this subpart apply to all property under the authority of GSA and to all persons entering in or on such property. Each occupant agency shall be responsible for the observance of these rules and regulations. Federal agencies must post the notice in the Appendix to this part at each public entrance to each Federal facility.

INSPECTION

§ 102–74.370 What items are subject to inspection by Federal agencies?

Federal agencies may, at their discretion, inspect packages, briefcases and other containers in the immediate possession of visitors, employees or other persons arriving on, working at, visiting, or departing from Federal property. Federal agencies may conduct a full search of a person and the vehicle the person is driving or occupying upon his or her arrest.

ADMISSION TO PROPERTY

§ 102–74.375 What is the policy on admitting persons to Government property?

Federal agencies must—

(a) Except as otherwise permitted, close property to the public during other than normal working hours. In those instances where a Federal agency has approved the after-normal-working-hours use of buildings or portions thereof for activities authorized by subpart D of this part, Federal agencies must not close the property (or affected portions thereof) to the public;

(b) Close property to the public during working hours only when situations require this action to provide for the orderly conduct of Government business. The designated official under the Occupant Emergency Program may make such decision only after consultation with the buildings manager and the highest ranking representative of the law enforcement organization responsible for protection of the property or the area. The designated official is defined in § 102–71.20 of this chapter as the highest ranking official of the primary occupant agency, or the alternate highest ranking official or designee selected by mutual agreement by other occupant agency officials; and

(c) When property or a portion thereof is closed to the public, restrict admission to the property, or the affected portion, to authorized persons who must register upon entry to the property and must, when requested, display Government or other identifying credentials to Federal police officers or other authorized individuals when entering, leaving or while on the property. Failure to comply with any of the applicable provisions is a violation of these regulations.

PRESERVATION OF PROPERTY

§ 102–74.380 What is the policy concerning the preservation of property?

All persons entering in or on Federal property are prohibited from—

(a) Improperly disposing of rubbish on property;

(b) Willfully destroying or damaging property;

(c) Stealing property;

(d) Creating any hazard on property to persons or things; or

(e) Throwing articles of any kind from or at a building or climbing upon statues, fountains or any part of the building.

CONFORMITY WITH SIGNS AND DIRECTIONS

§ 102–74.385 What is the policy concerning conformity with official signs and directions?

Persons in and on property must at all times comply with official signs of a prohibitory, regulatory or directory nature and with the lawful direction of Federal police officers and other authorized individuals.

DISTURBANCES

§ 102–74.390 What is the policy concerning disturbances?

All persons entering in or on Federal property are prohibited from loitering, exhibiting disorderly conduct or exhibiting other conduct on property that—

(a) Creates loud or unusual noise or a nuisance;

(b) Unreasonably obstructs the usual use of entrances, foyers, lobbies, corridors, offices, elevators, stairways, or parking lots;

(c) Otherwise impedes or disrupts the performance of official duties by Government employees; or

(d) Prevents the general public from obtaining the administrative services provided on the property in a timely manner.

GAMBLING

§ 102–74.395 What is the policy concerning gambling?

(a) Except for the vending or exchange of chances by licensed blind operators of vending facilities for any lottery set forth in a State law and authorized by section 2(a)(5) of the Randolph-Sheppard Act (20 U.S.C. 107 *et seq.*), all persons entering in or on Federal property are prohibited from—

(1) Participating in games for money or other personal property;

(2) Operating gambling devices;

(3) Conducting a lottery or pool; or

(4) Selling or purchasing numbers tickets.

(b) This provision is not intended to prohibit prize drawings for personal property at otherwise permitted functions on Federal property, provided that the game or drawing does not constitute gambling per se. Gambling per se means a game of chance where the participant risks something of value for the chance to gain or win a prize.

NARCOTICS AND OTHER DRUGS

§ 102–74.400 What is the policy concerning the possession and use of narcotics and other drugs?

Except in cases where the drug is being used as prescribed for a patient by a licensed physician, all persons entering in or on Federal property are prohibited from—

(a) Being under the influence, using or possessing any narcotic drugs, hallucinogens, marijuana, barbiturates, or amphetamines; or

(b) Operating a motor vehicle on the property while under the influence of alcoholic beverages, narcotic drugs, hallucinogens, marijuana, barbiturates, or amphetamines.

ALCOHOLIC BEVERAGES

§ 102–74.405 What is the policy concerning the use of alcoholic beverages?

Except where the head of the responsible agency or his or her designee has granted an exemption in writing for the appropriate official use of alcoholic beverages, all persons entering in or on Federal property are prohibited from being under the influence or using alcoholic beverages. The head of the responsible agency or his or her designee must provide a copy of all exemptions granted to the buildings manager and the highest ranking representative of the law enforcement organization, or other authorized officials, responsible for the security of the property.

SOLICITING, VENDING AND DEBT
COLLECTION

§ 102–74.410 What is the policy concerning soliciting, vending and debt collection?

All persons entering in or on Federal property are prohibited from soliciting alms (including money and non-monetary items) or commercial or political donations, vending merchandise of all kinds, displaying or distributing commercial advertising, or collecting private debts, except for—

(a) National or local drives for funds for welfare, health or other purposes as authorized by 5 CFR part 950, entitled "Solicitation Of Federal Civilian And Uniformed Service Personnel For Contributions To Private Voluntary Organizations," and sponsored or approved by the occupant agencies;

(b) Concessions or personal notices posted by employees on authorized bulletin boards;

(c) Solicitation of labor organization membership or dues authorized by occupant agencies under the Civil Service Reform Act of 1978 (Pub. L. 95–454);

(d) Lessee, or its agents and employees, with respect to space leased for commercial, cultural, educational, or recreational use under 40 U.S.C. 581(h). Public areas of GSA-controlled property may be used for other activities in accordance with subpart D of this part;

(e) Collection of non-monetary items that are sponsored or approved by the occupant agencies; and

(f) Commercial activities sponsored by recognized Federal employee associations and on-site child care centers.

POSTING AND DISTRIBUTING MATERIALS

§ 102–74.415 What is the policy for posting and distributing materials?

All persons entering in or on Federal property are prohibited from—

(a) Distributing free samples of tobacco products in or around Federal buildings, as mandated by Section 636 of Public Law 104–52;

(b) Posting or affixing materials, such as pamphlets, handbills, or flyers, on bulletin boards or elsewhere on GSA-controlled property, except as authorized in § 102–74.410, or when these displays are conducted as part of authorized Government activities; and

(c) Distributing materials, such as pamphlets, handbills or flyers, unless conducted as part of authorized Government activities. This prohibition does not apply to public areas of the property as defined in § 102–71.20 of this chapter. However, any person or organization proposing to distribute materials in a public area under this section must first obtain a permit from the building manager as specified in subpart D of this part. Any such person or organization must distribute materials only in accordance with the provisions of subpart D of this part. Failure to comply with those provisions is a violation of these regulations.

PHOTOGRAPHS FOR NEWS, ADVERTISING
OR COMMERCIAL PURPOSES

§ 102–74.420 What is the policy concerning photographs for news, advertising or commercial purposes?

Except where security regulations, rules, orders, or directives apply or a Federal court order or rule prohibits it, persons entering in or on Federal property may take photographs of—

(a) Space occupied by a tenant agency for non-commercial purposes only with the permission of the occupying agency concerned;

(b) Space occupied by a tenant agency for commercial purposes only with written permission of an authorized official of the occupying agency concerned; and

(c) Building entrances, lobbies, foyers, corridors, or auditoriums for news purposes.

DOGS AND OTHER ANIMALS

§ 102–74.425 What is the policy concerning dogs and other animals on Federal property?

No person may bring dogs or other animals on Federal property for other than official purposes. However, a disabled person may bring a seeing-eye dog, a guide dog, or other animal assisting or being trained to assist that individual.

BREASTFEEDING

§ 102–74.426 May a woman breastfeed her child in a Federal building or on Federal property?

Yes. Public Law 108–199, Section 629, Division F, Title VI (January 23, 2004), provides that a woman may breastfeed her child at any location in a Federal building or on Federal property, if the woman and her child are otherwise authorized to be present at the location.

VEHICULAR AND PEDESTRIAN TRAFFIC

§ 102–74.430 What is the policy concerning vehicular and pedestrian traffic on Federal property?

All vehicle drivers entering or while on Federal property—

(a) Must drive in a careful and safe manner at all times;

(b) Must comply with the signals and directions of Federal police officers or other authorized individuals;

(c) Must comply with all posted traffic signs;

(d) Must comply with any additional posted traffic directives approved by the GSA Regional Administrator, which will have the same force and effect as these regulations;

(e) Are prohibited from blocking entrances, driveways, walks, loading platforms, or fire hydrants; and

(f) Are prohibited from parking on Federal property without a permit. Parking without authority, parking in unauthorized locations or in locations reserved for other persons, or parking contrary to the direction of posted signs is prohibited. Vehicles parked in violation, where warning signs are posted, are subject to removal at the owner's risk and expense. Federal agencies may take as proof that a motor vehicle was parked in violation of these regulations or directives as prima facie evidence that the registered owner was responsible for the violation.

EXPLOSIVES

§ 102–74.435 What is the policy concerning explosives on Federal property?

No person entering or while on Federal property may carry or possess explosives, or items intended to be used to fabricate an explosive or incendiary device, either openly or concealed, except for official purposes.

WEAPONS

§ 102–74.440 What is the policy concerning weapons on Federal property?

Federal law prohibits the possession of firearms or other dangerous weapons in Federal facilities and Federal court facilities by all persons not specifically authorized by 18 U.S.C. 930. Violators will be subject to fine and/or imprisonment for periods up to five (5) years.

NONDISCRIMINATION

§ 102–74.445 What is the policy concerning discrimination on Federal property?

Federal agencies must not discriminate by segregation or otherwise against any person or persons because of race, creed, religion, age, sex, color, disability, or national origin in furnishing or by refusing to furnish to such person or persons the use of any facility of a public nature, including all services, privileges, accommodations, and activities provided on the property.

PENALTIES

§ 102–74.450 What are the penalties for violating any rule or regulation in this subpart?

A person found guilty of violating any rule or regulation in this subpart while on any property under the charge and control of GSA shall be fined under title 18 of the United States Code, imprisoned for not more than 30 days, or both.

IMPACT ON OTHER LAWS OR
REGULATIONS

§ 102–74.455 What impact do the rules and regulations in this subpart have on other laws or regulations?

No rule or regulation in this subpart may be construed to nullify any other Federal laws or regulations or any State and local laws and regulations applicable to any area in which the property is situated (40 U.S.C. 121 (c)).

Subpart D—Occasional Use of Public Buildings

§ 102–74.460 What is the scope of this subpart?

This subpart establishes rules and regulations for the occasional use of public areas of public buildings for cultural, educational and recreational activities as provided by 40 U.S.C. 581(h)(2).

APPLICATION FOR PERMIT

§ 102–74.465 Is a person or organization that wishes to use a public area required to apply for a permit from a Federal agency?

Yes, any person or organization wishing to use a public area must file an application for a permit from the Federal agency buildings manager.

§ 102–74.470 What information must persons or organizations submit so that Federal agencies may consider their application for a permit?

Applicants must submit the following information:

(a) Their full names, mailing addresses, and telephone numbers.

(b) The organization sponsoring the proposed activity.

(c) The individual(s) responsible for supervising the activity.

(d) Documentation showing that the applicant has authority to represent the sponsoring organization.

(e) A description of the proposed activity, including the dates and times during which it is to be conducted and the number of persons to be involved.

§ 102–74.475 If an applicant proposes to use a public area to solicit funds, is the applicant required to make a certification?

Yes, if an applicant proposes to use a public area to solicit funds, the applicant must certify, in writing, that—

(a) The applicant is a representative of and will be soliciting funds for the sole benefit of a religion or religious group; or

(b) The applicant's organization has received an official ruling of tax-exempt status from the Internal Revenue Service under 26 U.S.C. 501; or, alternatively, that an application for such a ruling is still pending.

PERMITS

§ 102–74.480 How many days does a Federal agency have to issue a permit following receipt of a completed application?

Federal agencies must issue permits within 10 working days following the receipt of the completed applications, unless the permit is disapproved in accordance with § 102–74.500.

§ 102–74.485 Is there any limitation on the length of time of a permit?

Yes, a permit may not be issued for a period of time in excess of 30 calendar days, unless specifically approved by the Regional Officer (as defined in § 102–71.20 of this chapter). After the expiration of a permit, Federal agencies may issue a new permit upon submission of a new application. In such a case, applicants may incorporate by reference all required information filed with the prior application.

§ 102–74.490 What if more than one permit is requested for the same area and time?

Federal agencies will issue permits on a first-come, first-served, basis when more than one permit is requested for the same area and times.

§ 102–74.495 If a permit involves demonstrations or activities that may lead to civil disturbances, what action must a Federal agency take before approving such a permit application?

Before approving a permit application, Federal agencies must coordinate with their law enforcement organization if a permit involves demonstrations or activities that may lead to civil disturbances.

DISAPPROVAL OF APPLICATIONS OR CANCELLATION OF PERMITS

§ 102–74.500 Can Federal agencies disapprove permit applications or cancel issued permits?

Yes, Federal agencies may disapprove any permit application or cancel an issued permit if—

(a) The applicant has failed to submit all information required under §§ 102–74.470 and 102–74.475, or has falsified such information;

(b) The proposed use is a commercial activity as defined in § 102–71.20 of this chapter;

(c) The proposed use interferes with access to the public area, disrupts official Government business, interferes with approved uses of the property by tenants or by the public, or damages any property;

(d) The proposed use is intended to influence or impede any pending judicial proceeding;

(e) The proposed use is obscene within the meaning of obscenity as defined in 18 U.S.C. 1461–65; or

(f) The proposed use violates the prohibition against political solicitations in 18 U.S.C. 607.

§ 102–74.505 What action must Federal agencies take after disapproving an application or canceling an issued permit?

Upon disapproving an application or canceling a permit, Federal agencies must promptly—

(a) Notify the applicant or permittee of the reasons for the action; and

(b) Inform the applicant or permittee of his/her appeal rights under § 102–74.510.

APPEALS

§ 102–74.510 How may the disapproval of a permit application or cancellation of an issued permit be appealed?

A person or organization may appeal the disapproval of an application or cancellation of an issued permit by notifying the Regional Officer (as defined in § 102–71.20 of this chapter), in writing, of the intent to appeal within 5 calendar days of the notification of disapproval or cancellation.

§ 102–74.515 Will the affected person or organization and the Federal agency buildings manager have an opportunity to state their positions on the issues?

Yes, during the appeal process, the affected person or organization and the Federal agency buildings manager will have an opportunity to state their positions on the issues, both verbally and in writing.

§ 102–74.520 How much time does the Regional Officer have to affirm or reverse the Federal agency buildings manager's decision after receiving the notification of appeal from the affected person or organization?

The Regional Officer must affirm or reverse the Federal agency buildings manager's decision, based on the information submitted, within 10 calendar days of the date on which the Regional Officer received notification of the appeal. If the decision is not rendered within 10 days, the application will be considered to be approved or the permit validly issued. The Regional Officer will promptly notify the applicant or permittee and the buildings manager of the decision and the reasons therefor.

SCHEDULE OF USE

§ 102–74.525 May Federal agencies reserve time periods for the use of public areas for official Government business or for maintenance, repair and construction?

Yes, Federal agencies may reserve certain time periods for use of public areas—

(a) For official Government business; or

(b) For maintenance, repair, and construction.

HOURS OF USE

§ 102–74.530 When may public areas be used?

Permittees may use public areas during or after regular working hours of Federal agencies, provided that such uses will not interfere with Government business. When public areas are used by permittees after normal working hours, Federal agencies must lock, barricade or identify by signs, as appropriate, all adjacent areas not approved for such use to restrict permittees' activities to approved areas.

SERVICES AND COSTS

§ 102–74.535　What items may Federal agencies provide to permittees free of charge?

Federal agencies may provide to permittees at no cost—

(a) Space; and

(b) Services normally provided at the building in question during normal hours of building operation, such as security, cleaning, heating, ventilation, and air-conditioning. The Regional Officer must approve an applicant's request to provide its own services, such as security and cleaning, prior to permit approval.

§ 102–74.540　What are the items for which permittees must reimburse Federal agencies?

Permittees must reimburse Federal agencies for services over and above those normally provided during normal business hours. Federal agencies may provide the services free of charge if the cost is insignificant and if it is in the public interest.

§ 102–74.545　May permittees make alterations to the public areas?

Permittees must not make alterations to public areas, except with the prior written approval of the Federal agency buildings manager. Federal agencies must not approve such alterations unless the Federal agency determines that the proposed alterations to a building should be made to encourage and aid in the proposed use. Permittees making alterations must ensure the safety of users and prevent damage to property.

§ 102–74.550　What items are permittees responsible for furnishing?

Permittees are responsible for furnishing items such as tickets, audiovisual equipment, and other items that are necessary for the proposed use.

CONDUCT

§ 102–74.555　What rules of conduct must all permittees observe while on Federal property?

Permittees are subject to all rules and regulations governing conduct on Federal property as set forth in subpart C of this part. In addition, a permittee must—

(a) Not misrepresent his or her identity to the public;

(b) Not conduct any activities in a misleading or fraudulent manner;

(c) Not discriminate on the basis of race, creed, religion, age, color, disability, sex, or national origin in conducting activities;

(d) Not distribute any item, nor post or otherwise affix any item, for which prior written approval under § 102–74.415 has not been obtained;

(e) Not leave leaflets or other materials unattended on the property;

(f) Not engage in activities that would interfere with the preferences afforded blind licensees under the Randolph-Sheppard Act (20 U.S.C. 107); and

(g) Display identification badges while on Federal property, if engaging in the solicitation of funds as authorized by § 102–74.475. Each badge must indicate the permittee's name, address, telephone number, and organization.

NON-AFFILIATION WITH THE GOVERNMENT

§ 102–74.560　May Federal agencies advise the public of the presence of any permittees and their non-affiliation with the Federal Government?

Yes, Federal agencies reserve the right to advise the public through signs or announcements of the presence of any permittees and of their non-affiliation with the Federal Government.

Subpart E—Installing, Repairing, and Replacing Sidewalks

§ 102–74.565　What is the scope of this subpart?

In accordance with 40 U.S.C. 589, Federal agencies must comply with the real property policies in this subpart governing the installation, repair and replacement of sidewalks around buildings, installations, properties, or grounds under the control of Executive agencies and owned by the United States.

§102–74.570 Are State and local governments required to fund the cost of installing, repairing, and replacing sidewalks?

No, the Federal Government must fund the cost of installing, repairing, and replacing sidewalks. Funds appropriated to the agency for installation, repair, and maintenance, generally, must be available for expenditure to accomplish the purposes of this subpart.

§102–74.575 How do Federal agencies arrange for work on sidewalks?

Upon approval from GSA, Federal agencies may—

(a) Authorize the appropriate State or local government to install, repair and replace sidewalks, or arrange for this work, and reimburse them for this work; or

(b) Contract or otherwise arrange and pay directly for installing, repairing and/or replacing sidewalks.

§102–74.580 Who decides when to replace a sidewalk?

Federal agencies, giving due consideration to State and local standards and specifications for sidewalks, decide when to install, repair or replace a sidewalk. However, Federal agencies may prescribe other standards and specifications for sidewalks whenever necessary to achieve architectural harmony and maintain facility security.

Subpart F—Telework

§102–74.585 What Federal facility telework policy must Executive agencies follow?

Executive agencies must follow these telework policies:

(a) In accordance with Section 359 of Public Law 106–346, each Executive agency must establish a policy under which eligible employees of the agency may participate in telecommuting to the maximum extent possible without diminished employee performance. Public 106–346 became effective on October 23, 2000, and required the Director of the Office of Personnel Management

(OPM) to ensure the application and implementation of Section 359 to 25 percent of the Federal workforce by April 2001, and to an additional 25 percent of such workforce each year thereafter. Thus, the law provides that its requirements must be applied to 100 percent of the Federal workforce by April 2004.

(b) In accordance with 40 U.S.C. 587, when considering whether to acquire any space, quarters, buildings, or other facilities for use by employees of any Executive agency, the head of that agency shall consider whether the need for the facilities can be met using alternative workplace arrangements.

§102–74.590 What steps must agencies take to implement these laws and policies?

(a) As interpreted by OPM Memorandum to agencies (February 9, 2001), Public Law 106–346 instructs Federal agencies to—

(1) Review telework barriers, act to remove them, and increase actual participation;

(2) Establish eligibility criteria; and

(3) Subject to any applicable agency policies or bargaining obligations, allow employees who meet the criteria and want to participate the opportunity if they are satisfactory performers.

(b) 40 U.S.C. 587 requires agencies considering the acquisition of facilities for use by Federal employees to consider whether the facility need can be met using alternative workplace arrangements, such as telecommuting, hoteling, virtual offices, and other distributive work arrangements. If the agency needs assistance in this investigation and/or subsequent application of alternative workplace arrangements, GSA will provide guidance, assistance, and oversight, as needed, regarding establishment and operation of alternative workplace arrangements.

(c) Agencies evaluating alternative workplace arrangements should also make these evaluations in coordination with Integrated Workplace policies and strategies. See §102–79.110.

§ 102–74.595 How can agencies obtain guidance, assistance, and oversight regarding alternative workplace arrangements from GSA?

Agencies may request assistance from the GSA/PBS regional office responsible for providing space in the geographic area under consideration.

§ 102–74.600 Should Federal agencies utilize telework centers?

Yes. In accordance with Public Law 107–217 (August 21, 2002), each of the following departments and agencies, in each fiscal year, must make at least $50,000 available from amounts provided for salaries and expenses for carrying out a flexiplace work telecommuting program (i.e., to pay telework center program user fees):

(a) Department of Agriculture.

(b) Department of Commerce.

(c) Department of Defense.

(d) Department of Education.

(e) Department of Energy.

(f) Department of Health and Human Services.

(g) Department of Housing and Urban Development.

(h) Department of the Interior.

(i) Department of Justice.

(j) Department of Labor.

(k) Department of State.

(l) Department of Transportation.

(m) Department of the Treasury.

(n) Department of Veterans Affairs.

(o) Environmental Protection Agency.

(p) General Services Administration.

(q) Office of Personnel Management.

(r) Small Business Administration.

(s) Social Security Administration.

(t) United States Postal Service.

APPENDIX TO PART 102–74—RULES AND REGULATIONS GOVERNING CONDUCT ON FEDERAL PROPERTY

FEDERAL MANAGEMENT REGULATIONS

TITLE 41, CODE OF FEDERAL REGULATIONS, PART 102–74, SUBPART C

Applicability (41 CFR 102–74.365). The rules in this subpart apply to all property under the authority of the U.S. General Services Administration and to all persons entering in or on such property. Each occupant agency shall be responsible for the observance of these rules and regulations. Federal agencies must post the notice in the Appendix to part 102–74 at each public entrance to each Federal facility.

Inspection (41 CFR 102–74.370). Federal agencies may, at their discretion, inspect packages, briefcases and other containers in the immediate possession of visitors, employees or other persons arriving on, working at, visiting, or departing from Federal property. Federal agencies may conduct a full search of a person and the vehicle the person is driving or occupying upon his or her arrest.

Admission to Property (41 CFR 102–74.375). Federal agencies must—

(a) Except as otherwise permitted, close property to the public during other than normal working hours. In those instances where a Federal agency has approved the after-normal-working-hours use of buildings or portions thereof for activities authorized by subpart D of this part, Federal agencies must not close the property (or affected portions thereof) to the public;

(b) Close property to the public during working hours only when situations require this action to provide for the orderly conduct of Government business. The designated official under the Occupant Emergency Program may make such decision only after consultation with the buildings manager and the highest ranking representative of the law enforcement organization responsible for protection of the property or the area. The designated official is defined in § 102–71.20 of this chapter as the highest ranking official of the primary occupant agency, or the alternate highest ranking official or designee selected by mutual agreement by other occupant agency officials; and

(c) When property or a portion thereof is closed to the public, restrict admission to the property, or the affected portion, to authorized persons who must register upon entry to the property and must, when requested, display Government or other identifying credentials to Federal police officers or other authorized individuals when entering, leaving or while on the property. Failure to comply with any of the applicable provisions is a violation of these regulations.

Preservation of Property (41 CFR 102–74.380). All persons entering in or on Federal property are prohibited from—

(a) Improperly disposing of rubbish on property;

(b) Willfully destroying or damaging property;

(c) Stealing property;

(d) Creating any hazard on property to persons or things; and

(e) Throwing articles of any kind from or at a building or the climbing upon statues, fountains or any part of the building.

Conformity with Signs and Directions (41 CFR 102–74.385). Persons in and on property must at all times comply with official signs of a prohibitory, regulatory or directory nature and with the lawful direction of Federal police officers and other authorized individuals.

Disturbances (41 CFR 102–74.390). All persons entering in or on Federal property are prohibited from loitering, exhibiting disorderly conduct or exhibiting other conduct on property that—

(a) Creates loud or unusual noise or a nuisance;

(b) Unreasonably obstructs the usual use of entrances, foyers, lobbies, corridors, offices, elevators, stairways, or parking lots;

(c) Otherwise impedes or disrupts the performance of official duties by Government employees; or

(d) Prevents the general public from obtaining the administrative services provided on the property in a timely manner.

Gambling (41 CFR 102–74.395). Except for the vending or exchange of chances by licensed blind operators of vending facilities for any lottery set forth in a State law and authorized by section 2(a)(5) of the Randolph-Sheppard Act (20 U.S.C. 107 *et seq.*), all persons entering in or on Federal property are prohibited from—

(a) Participating in games for money or other personal property;

(b) Operating gambling devices;

(c) Conducting a lottery or pool; or

(d) Selling or purchasing numbers tickets.

Narcotics and Other Drugs (41 CFR 102–74.400). Except in cases where the drug is being used as prescribed for a patient by a licensed physician, all persons entering in or on Federal property are prohibited from—

(a) Being under the influence, using or possessing any narcotic drugs, hallucinogens, marijuana, barbiturates, or amphetamines; or

(b) Operating a motor vehicle on the property while under the influence of alcoholic beverages, narcotic drugs, hallucinogens, marijuana, barbiturates, or amphetamines.

Alcoholic Beverages (41 CFR 102–74.405). Except where the head of the responsible agency or his or her designee has granted an exemption in writing for the appropriate official use of alcoholic beverages, all persons entering in or on Federal property are prohibited from being under the influence or using alcoholic beverages. The head of the responsible agency or his or her designee must provide a copy of all exemptions granted to the buildings manager and the highest ranking representative of the law enforcement organization, or other authorized officials, responsible for the security of the property.

Soliciting, Vending and Debt Collection (41 CFR 102–74.410). All persons entering in or on Federal property are prohibited from soliciting alms (including money and non-monetary items) or commercial or political donations; vending merchandise of all kinds; displaying or distributing commercial advertising, or collecting private debts, except for—

(a) National or local drives for funds for welfare, health or other purposes as authorized by 5 CFR part 950, entitled "Solicitation of Federal Civilian And Uniformed Service Personnel For Contributions To Private Voluntary Organizations," and sponsored or approved by the occupant agencies;

(b) Concessions or personal notices posted by employees on authorized bulletin boards;

(c) Solicitation of labor organization membership or dues authorized by occupant agencies under the Civil Service Reform Act of 1978 (Public Law 95–454);

(d) Lessee, or its agents and employees, with respect to space leased for commercial, cultural, educational, or recreational use under the Public Buildings Cooperative Use Act of 1976 (40 U.S.C. 581(h)). Public areas of GSA-controlled property may be used for other activities in accordance with subpart D of this part;

(e) Collection of non-monetary items that are sponsored or approved by the occupant agencies; and

(f) Commercial activities sponsored by recognized Federal employee associations and on-site child care centers.

Posting and Distributing Materials (41 CFR 102–74.415). All persons entering in or on Federal property are prohibited from—

(a) Distributing free samples of tobacco products in or around Federal buildings, under Public Law 104–52, Section 636;

(b) Posting or affixing materials, such as pamphlets, handbills, or flyers, on bulletin boards or elsewhere on GSA-controlled property, except as authorized in § 102–74.410, or when these displays are conducted as part of authorized Government activities; and

(c) Distributing materials, such as pamphlets, handbills, or flyers, unless conducted as part of authorized Government activities. This prohibition does not apply to public areas of the property as defined in § 102–71.20 of this chapter. However, any person or organization proposing to distribute materials in a public area under this section must first obtain a permit from the building manager as specified in subpart D of this part. Any such person or organization must distribute materials only in accordance with the provisions of subpart D of this part. Failure to comply with those provisions is a violation of these regulations.

Photographs for News, Advertising, or Commercial Purposes (41 CFR 102–74.420). Except where security regulations, rules, orders, or directives apply or a Federal court order or rule prohibits it, persons entering in or on Federal property may take photographs of—

(a) Space occupied by a tenant agency for non-commercial purposes only with the permission of the occupying agency concerned;

(b) Space occupied by a tenant agency for commercial purposes only with written permission of an authorized official of the occupying agency concerned; and

(c) Building entrances, lobbies, foyers, corridors, or auditoriums for news purposes.

Dogs and Other Animals (41 CFR 102–74.425). No person may bring dogs or other animals on Federal property for other than official purposes. However, a disabled person may bring a seeing-eye dog, a guide dog, or other animal assisting or being trained to assist that individual.

Breastfeeding (41 CFR 102–74.426). Public Law 108–199, Section 629, Division F, Title VI (January 23, 2004), provides that a woman may breastfeed her child at any location in a Federal building or on Federal property, if the woman and her child are otherwise authorized to be present at the location.

Vehicular and Pedestrian Traffic (41 CFR 102–74.430). All vehicle drivers entering or while on Federal property—

(a) Must drive in a careful and safe manner at all times;

(b) Must comply with the signals and directions of Federal police officers or other authorized individuals;

(c) Must comply with all posted traffic signs;

(d) Must comply with any additional posted traffic directives approved by the GSA Regional Administrator, which will have the same force and effect as these regulations;

(e) Are prohibited from blocking entrances, driveways, walks, loading platforms, or fire hydrants; and

(f) Are prohibited from parking on Federal property without a permit. Parking without authority, parking in unauthorized locations or in locations reserved for other persons, or parking contrary to the direction of posted signs is prohibited. Vehicles parked in violation, where warning signs are posted, are subject to removal at the owner's risk and expense. Federal agencies may take as proof that a motor vehicle was parked in violation of these regulations or directives as prima facie evidence that the registered owner was responsible for the violation.

Explosives (41 CFR 102–74.435). No person entering or while on property may carry or possess explosives, or items intended to be used to fabricate an explosive or incendiary device, either openly or concealed, except for official purposes.

Weapons (41 CFR 102–74.440). Federal law prohibits the possession of firearms or other dangerous weapons in Federal facilities and Federal court facilities by all persons not specifically authorized by Title 18, United States Code, Section 930. Violators will be subject to fine and/or imprisonment for periods up to five (5) years.

Nondiscrimination (41 CFR 102–74.445). Federal agencies must not discriminate by segregation or otherwise against any person or persons because of race, creed, religion, age, sex, color, disability, or national origin in furnishing or by refusing to furnish to such person or persons the use of any facility of a public nature, including all services, privileges, accommodations, and activities provided on the property.

Penalties (41 CFR 102–74.450). A person found guilty of violating any rule or regulation in subpart C of this part while on any property under the charge and control of the U.S. General Services Administration shall be fined under title 18 of the United States Code, imprisoned for not more than 30 days, or both.

Impact on Other Laws or Regulations (41 CFR 102–74.455). No rule or regulation in this subpart may be construed to nullify any other Federal laws or regulations or any State and local laws and regulations applicable to any area in which the property is situated (40 U.S.C. 121 (c)).

WARNING—WEAPONS PROHIBITED

Federal law prohibits the possession of firearms or other dangerous weapons in Federal facilities and Federal court facilities by all persons not specifically authorized by Title 18, United States Code, Section 930. Violators will be subject to fine and/or imprisonment for periods up to five (5) years.

PART 102–75—REAL PROPERTY DISPOSAL

Subpart A—General Provisions

Sec.
102–75.5 What is the scope of this part?
102–75.10 What basic real property disposal policy governs disposal agencies?

REAL PROPERTY DISPOSAL SERVICES

102–75.15 What real property disposal services must disposal agencies provide under a delegation of authority from GSA?
102–75.20 How can Federal agencies with independent disposal authority obtain related disposal services?

Subpart B—Utilization of Excess Real Property

102–75.25 What are landholding agencies' responsibilities concerning the utilization of excess property?
102–75.30 What are disposal agencies' responsibilities concerning the utilization of excess property?
102–75.35 [Reserved]

STANDARDS

102–75.40 What are the standards that each Executive agency must use to identify unneeded Federal real property?

102–75.345 What is different about the statements in the offer to purchase and conveyance document if the sale is to a potentially responsible party with respect to the hazardous substance activity?

PUBLIC BENEFIT CONVEYANCES

102–75.350 What are disposal agencies' responsibilities concerning public benefit conveyances?

102–75.351 May the disposal agency waive screening for public benefit conveyances?

102–75.355 What clause must be in the offer to purchase and the conveyance documents for public benefit conveyances?

102–75.360 What wording must be in the non-discrimination clause that is required in the offer to purchase and the conveyance document?

POWER TRANSMISSION LINES

102–75.365 Do disposal agencies have to notify State entities and Government agencies that a surplus power transmission line and right-of-way is available?

102–75.370 May a State, or any political subdivision thereof, certify to a disposal agency that it needs a surplus power transmission line and the right-of-way acquired for its construction to meet the requirements of a public or cooperative power project?

102–75.375 What happens once a State, or political subdivision, certifies that it needs a surplus power transmission line and the right-of-way acquired for its construction to meet the requirements of a public or cooperative power project?

102–75.380 May power transmission lines and rights-of-way be disposed of in other ways?

PROPERTY FOR PUBLIC AIRPORTS

102–75.385 Do disposal agencies have the responsibility to notify eligible public agencies that airport property has been determined to be surplus?

102–75.390 What does the term "surplus airport property" mean?

102–75.395 May surplus airport property be conveyed or disposed of to a State, political subdivision, municipality, or tax-supported institution for a public airport?

102–75.400 Is industrial property located on an airport also considered to be "airport property"?

102–75.405 What responsibilities does the Federal Aviation Administration (FAA) have after receiving a copy of the notice (and a copy of the Report of Excess Real Property (Standard Form 118)) given to eligible public agencies that there is surplus airport property?

102–75.410 What action must the disposal agency take after an eligible public agency has submitted a plan of use and application to acquire property for a public airport?

102–75.415 What happens after the disposal agency receives the FAA's recommendation for disposal of the property for a public airport?

102–75.420 What happens if the FAA informs the disposal agency that it does not recommend disposal of the property for a public airport?

102–75.425 Who has sole responsibility for enforcing compliance with the terms and conditions of disposal for property disposed of for use as a public airport?

102–75.430 What happens if property conveyed for use as a public airport is revested in the United States?

102–75.435 Does the Airport and Airway Development Act of 1970, as amended (Airport Act of 1970) apply to the transfer of airports to State and local agencies?

PROPERTY FOR USE AS HISTORIC MONUMENTS

102–75.440 Who must disposal agencies notify that surplus property is available for historic monument use?

102–75.445 Who can convey surplus real and related personal property for historic monument use?

102–75.450 What type of property is suitable or desirable for use as a historic monument?

102–75.455 May historic monuments be used for revenue-producing activities?

102–75.460 What information must disposal agencies furnish eligible public agencies?

102–75.465 What information must eligible public agencies interested in acquiring real property for use as a historic monument submit to the appropriate regional or field offices of the National Park Service (NPS) of the Department of the Interior (DOI)?

102–75.470 What action must NPS take after an eligible public agency has submitted an application for conveyance of surplus property for use as a historic monument?

102–75.475 What happens after the disposal agency receives the Secretary of the Interior's determination for disposal of the surplus property for a historic monument and compatible revenue-producing activities?

102–75.480 Who has the responsibility for enforcing compliance with the terms and conditions of disposal for surplus property conveyed for use as a historic monument?

102–75.485 What happens if property that was conveyed for use as a historic monument is revested in the United States?

Subpart I—Screening Excess Federal Real Property

AUTHORITY: 40 U.S.C. 121(c), 521–523, 541–559; E.O. 12512, 50 FR 18453, 3 CFR, 1985 Comp., p. 340.

SOURCE: 70 FR 67811, Nov. 8, 2005, unless otherwise noted.

Subpart A—General Provisions

§ 102–75.5 What is the scope of this part?

The real property policies contained in this part apply to Federal agencies, including GSA's Public Buildings Service (PBS), operating under, or subject to, the authorities of the Administrator of General Services. Federal agencies with authority to dispose of real property under Subchapter III of Chapter 5 of Title 40 of the United States Code will be referred to as "disposal agencies" in this part. Except in rare instances where GSA delegates disposal authority to a Federal agency, the "disposal agency" as used in this part refers to GSA.

§ 102–75.10 What basic real property disposal policy governs disposal agencies?

Disposal agencies must provide, in a timely, efficient, and cost effective manner, the full range of real estate services necessary to support their real property utilization and disposal needs. Landholding agencies must survey the real property under their custody or control to identify property that is not utilized, underutilized, or not being put to optimum use. Disposal agencies must have adequate procedures in place to promote the effective utilization and disposal of such real property.

REAL PROPERTY DISPOSAL SERVICES

§ 102–75.15 What real property disposal services must agencies provide under a delegation of authority from GSA?

Disposal agencies must provide real property disposal services for real property assets under their custody and control, such as the utilization of excess property, surveys, and the disposal of surplus property, which includes public benefit conveyances, negotiated sales, public sales, related disposal services, and appraisals.

§ 102–75.20 How can Federal agencies with independent disposal authority obtain related disposal services?

Federal agencies with independent disposal authority are encouraged to obtain utilization, disposal, and related services from those agencies with expertise in real property disposal, such as GSA, as allowed by 31 U.S.C. 1535 (the Economy Act), so that they can remain focused on their core mission.

Subpart B—Utilization of Excess Real Property

§ 102–75.25 What are landholding agencies' responsibilities concerning the utilization of excess property?

Landholding agencies' responsibilities concerning the utilization of excess property are to—

(a) Achieve maximum use of their real property, in terms of economy and efficiency, to minimize expenditures for the purchase of real property;

(b) Increase the identification and reporting of their excess real property; and

(c) Fulfill its needs for real property, so far as practicable, by utilization of real property determined excess by other agencies, pursuant to the provision of this part, before it purchases non-Federal real property.

§ 102–75.30 What are disposal agencies' responsibilities concerning the utilization of excess property?

Disposal agencies' responsibilities concerning the utilization of excess property are to—

(a) Provide for the transfer of excess real property among Federal agencies, to mixed-ownership Government corporations, and to the municipal government of the District of Columbia; and

(b) Resolve conflicting requests for transferring real property that the involved agencies cannot resolve.

§ 102–75.35 [Reserved]

STANDARDS

§ 102–75.40 What are the standards that each Executive agency must use to identify unneeded Federal real property?

Each Executive agency must identify unneeded Federal property using the following standards:

(a) Not utilized.

(b) Underutilized.

(c) Not being put to optimum use.

§ 102–75.45 What does the term "Not utilized" mean?

Not utilized means an entire property or portion thereof, with or without improvements, not occupied for current program purposes of the ac-

countable Executive agency, or occupied in caretaker status only.

§ 102–75.50 What does the term "Underutilized" mean?

Underutilized means an entire property or portion thereof, with or without improvements, which is used—

(a) Irregularly or intermittently by the accountable Executive agency for current program purposes of that agency; or

(b) For current program purposes that can be satisfied with only a portion of the property.

§ 102–75.55 What does the term "Not being put to optimum use" mean?

Not being put to optimum use means an entire property or portion thereof, with or without improvements, which—

(a) Even though used for current program purposes, the nature, value, or location of the property is such that it could be utilized for a different and significantly higher and better purpose; or

(b) The costs of occupying are substantially higher than other suitable properties that could be made available through transfer, purchase, or lease with total net savings to the Government, after considering property values, costs of moving, occupancy, operational efficiency, environmental effects, regional planning, and employee morale.

GUIDELINES

§ 102–75.60 What are landholding agencies' responsibilities concerning real property surveys?

A landholding agency's responsibilities concerning real property utilization surveys are to—

(a) Survey real property under its control (i.e., property reported on its financial statements) at least annually to identify property that is not utilized, underutilized, or not being put to optimum use. When other needs for the property are identified or recognized, the agency must determine whether continuation of the current use or another use would better serve the public interest, considering both the Federal agency's needs and the property's location. In conducting annual reviews of their property holdings, the GSA Customer Guide to Real Property Disposal can provide guidelines for Executive agencies to consider in identifying unneeded Federal real property;

(b) Maintain its inventory of real property at the absolute minimum consistent with economical and efficient conduct of the affairs of the agency; and

(c) Promptly report to GSA real property that it has determined to be excess.

§ 102–75.65 Why is it important for Executive agencies to notify the disposal agency of its real property needs?

It is important that each Executive agency notify the disposal agency of its real property needs to determine whether the excess or surplus property of another agency is available that would meet its need and prevent the unnecessary purchase or lease of real property.

§ 102–75.70 Are there any exceptions to this notification policy?

Yes, Executive agencies are not required to notify the disposal agency when an agency's proposed acquisition of real property is dictated by such factors as exact geographical location, topography, engineering, or similar characteristics that limit the possible use of other available property. For example, Executive agencies are not required to notify disposal agencies concerning the acquisition of real property for a dam site, reservoir area, or the construction of a generating plant or a substation, since specific lands are needed, which limit the possible use of other available property. Therefore, no useful purpose would be served by notifying the disposal agency.

§ 102–75.75 What is the most important consideration in evaluating a proposed transfer of excess real property?

In every case of a proposed transfer of excess real property, the most important consideration is the validity and appropriateness of the requirement upon which the proposal is based. Also, a proposed transfer must not establish a new program that has never been reflected in any previous budget submission or congressional action. Additionally, a proposed transfer must not substantially increase the level of an agency's existing programs beyond that which has been contemplated in the President's budget or by the Congress.

(Note: See Subpart I—Screening of Excess Federal Real Property (§§ 102–75.1220 through 102–75.1290) for information on screening and transfer requests.)

§ 102–75.80 What are an Executive agency's responsibilities before requesting a transfer of excess real property?

Before requesting a transfer of excess real property, an Executive agency must—

(a) Screen its own property holdings to determine whether the new requirement can be met through improved utilization of existing real property; however, the utilization must be for purposes that are consistent with the highest and best use of the property under consideration;

(b) Review all real property under its accountability that has been permitted or outleased and terminate the permit or lease for any property, or portion thereof, suitable for the proposed need, if termination is not prohibited by the terms of the permit or lease;

(c) Utilize property that is or can be made available under § 102–75.80(a) or (b) for the proposed need in lieu of requesting a transfer of excess real property and reassign the property, when appropriate;

(d) Confirm that the appraised fair market value of the excess real property proposed for transfer will not substantially exceed the probable purchase price of other real property that would be suitable for the intended purpose;

(e) Limit the size and quantity of excess real property to be transferred to the actual requirements and separate, if possible, other portions of the excess installation for possible disposal to other agencies or to the public; and

(f) Consider the design, layout, geographic location, age, state of repair, and expected maintenance costs of excess real property proposed for transfer; agencies must be able to demonstrate that the transfer will be more economical over a sustained period of time than the acquisition of a new facility specifically planned for the purpose.

§ 102–75.85 Can disposal agencies transfer excess real property to agencies for programs that appear to be scheduled for substantial curtailment or termination?

Yes, but only on a temporary basis with the condition that the property will be released for further Federal utilization or disposal as surplus property at an agreed upon time when the transfer is arranged.

§ 102–75.90 How is excess real property needed for office, storage, and related purposes normally transferred to the requesting agency?

GSA may temporarily assign or direct the use of such excess real property to the requesting agency. See § 102–75.240.

§ 102–75.95 Can Federal agencies that normally do not require real property (other than for office, storage, and related purposes) or that may not have statutory authority to acquire such property, obtain the use of excess real property?

Yes, GSA can authorize the use of excess real property for an approved program. See § 102–75.240.

LAND WITHDRAWN OR RESERVED FROM THE PUBLIC DOMAIN

§ 102–75.100 When an agency holds land withdrawn or reserved from the public domain and determines that it no longer needs this land, what must it do?

An agency holding unneeded land withdrawn or reserved from the public domain must submit to the appropriate GSA Regional Office a Report of Excess Real Property (Standard Form 118), with appropriate Schedules A, B, and C, only when—

(a) It has filed a notice of intention to relinquish with the Department of the Interior (43 CFR part 2372 *et seq.*) and sent a copy of the notice to the appropriate GSA Regional Office;

(b) The Department of the Interior has notified the agency that the Secretary of the Interior has determined that the lands are not suitable for return to the public domain for disposition under the general public land laws because the lands are substantially changed in character by improvements or otherwise; and

(c) The Department of the Interior provides a report identifying whether or not any other agency claims primary, joint, or secondary jurisdiction over the lands and whether its records show that the lands are encumbered by rights or privileges under the public land laws.

§ 102–75.105 What responsibility does the Department of the Interior have if it determines that minerals in the land are unsuitable for disposition under the public land mining and mineral leasing laws?

In such cases, the Department of the Interior must—

(a) Notify the appropriate GSA Regional Office of such a determination; and

(b) Authorize the landholding agency to identify in the Standard Form 118 any minerals in the land that the Department of the Interior determines to be unsuitable for disposition under the public land mining and mineral leasing laws.

TRANSFERS UNDER OTHER LAWS

§ 102–75.110 Can transfers of real property be made under authority of laws other than those codified in Title 40 of the United States Code?

Yes, the provisions of this section shall not apply to transfers of real property authorized to be made by 40 U.S.C. 113(e) or by any special statute that directs or requires an Executive agency to transfer or convey specifically described real property in accordance with the provisions of that statute. Transfers of real property must be made only under the authority of Title 40 of the United States Code, unless the independent authority granted to such agency specifically exempts the authority from the requirements of Title 40.

REPORTING OF EXCESS REAL PROPERTY

§ 102–75.115 Must reports of excess real property and related personal property be prepared on specific forms?

Yes, landholding agencies must prepare reports of excess real property and related personal property on—

(a) Standard Form 118, Report of Excess Real Property, and accompanying Standard Form 118a, Buildings Structures, Utilities, and Miscellaneous Facilities, Schedule A;

(b) Standard Form 118b, Land, Schedule B; and

(c) Standard Form 118c, Related Personal Property, Schedule C.

§ 102–75.120 Is there any other information that needs to accompany (or be submitted with) the Report of Excess Real Property (Standard Form 118)?

Yes, in all cases where Government-owned land is reported excess, Executive agencies must include a title report, prepared or approved by a qualified employee of the landholding agency, documenting the Government's title to the property.

TITLE REPORT

§ 102–75.125 What information must agencies include in the title report?

When completing the title report, agencies must include—

(a) The description of the property;

(b) The date title vested in the United States;

(c) All exceptions, reservations, conditions, and restrictions, relating to the title;

(d) Detailed information concerning any action, thing, or circumstance that occurred from the date the United States acquired the property to the date of the report that in any way affected or may have affected the United States' right, title, or interest in and to the real property (including copies of legal comments or opinions discussing the manner in which and the extent to which such right, title, or interest may have been affected). In the absence of any such action, thing, or circumstance, a statement to that effect must be made a part of the report;

(e) The status of civil and criminal jurisdiction over the land that is peculiar to the property by reason of it being Government-owned land. In the absence of any special circumstances, a statement to that effect must be made a part of the report;

(f) Detailed information regarding any known flood hazards or flooding of the property, and, if the property is located in a flood-plain or on wetlands, a listing of restricted uses (along with the citations) identified in Federal, State, or local regulations as required by Executive Orders 11988 and 11990 of May 24, 1977;

(g) The specific identification and description of fixtures and related personal property that have possible historic or artistic value;

(h) The historical significance of the property and whether the property is listed, is eligible for, or has been nominated for listing in the National Register of Historic Places or is in proximity to a property listed in the National Register. If the landholding agency is aware of any effort by the public to have the property listed in the National Register, it must also include this information;

(i) A description of the type, location, and condition of asbestos incorporated in the construction, repair, or alteration of any building or improvement on the property (e.g., fire-proofing, pipe insulation, etc.) and a description of any asbestos control measures taken for the property. Agencies must also provide to GSA any available indication of costs and/or time necessary to remove all or any portion of the asbestos-containing materials. Agencies are not required to conduct any specific studies and/or tests to obtain this information. (The provisions of this subpart do not apply to asbestos on Federal property that is subject to section 120(h) of the Superfund Amendments and Reauthorization Act of 1986, Public Law 99–499);

(j) A statement indicating whether or not lead-based paint is present on the property. Additionally, if the property is target housing (all housing except housing for the elderly or persons with disabilities or any zero bedroom dwelling) constructed prior to 1978, provide a risk assessment and paint inspection report that details all lead-based paint hazards; and

(k) A statement ·indicating whether or not, during the time the property was owned by the United States, any hazardous substance activity, as defined by regulations issued by the U.S. Environmental Protection Agency (EPA) at 40 CFR part 373, took place on the property. Hazardous substance activity includes situations where any hazardous substance was stored for one year or more, known to have been released, or disposed of on the property. Agencies reporting such property must review the regulations issued by EPA at 40 CFR part 373 for details on the information required and must comply with these requirements. In addition, agencies reporting such property shall review and comply with the regulations for the utilization and disposal of hazardous materials and certain categories of property set forth at 41 CFR part 101–42.

§ 102–75.130 If hazardous substance activity took place on the property, what specific information must an agency include in the title report?

If hazardous substance activity took place on the property, the reporting agency must include information on the type and quantity of such hazardous substance and the time at which such storage, release, or disposal took place. The reporting agency must also advise the disposal agency if all remedial action necessary to protect human health and the environment with respect to any such hazardous substance activity was taken before the date the property was reported excess. If such action was not taken, the reporting agency must advise the disposal agency when such action will be completed or how the agency expects to comply with the Comprehensive Environmental Response, Compensation, and Liability Act (CERCLA) in the disposal. See §§ 102–75.340 and 102–75.345.

§ 102–75.135 If no hazardous substance activity took place on the property, what specific information must an agency include in the title report?

If no hazardous substance activity took place, the reporting agency must include the following statement:

The (reporting agency) has determined, in accordance with regulations issued by EPA at 40 CFR part 373, that there is no evidence indicating that hazardous substance activity took place on the property during the time the property was owned by the United States.

OTHER NECESSARY INFORMATION

§ 102–75.140 In addition to the title report, and all necessary environmental information and certifications, what information must an Executive agency transmit with the Report of Excess Real Property (Standard Form 118)?

Executive agencies must provide—

(a) A legible, reproducible copy of all instruments in possession of the agency that affect the United States' right, title, or interest in the property reported or the use and operation of such property (including agreements covering and licenses to use, any patents, processes, techniques, or inventions). If it is impracticable to transmit the abstracts of title and related title evidence, agencies must provide the name and address of the custodian of such documents in the title report referred to in § 102–75.120;

(b) Any appraisal reports indicating or providing the fair market value or the fair annual rental of the property, if requested by the disposal agency; and

(c) A certification by a responsible person that the property does or does not contain polychlorinated biphenyl (PCB) transformers or other equipment regulated by EPA under 40 CFR part 761, if requested by the disposal agency. If the property does contain any equipment subject to EPA regulation under 40 CFR part 761, the certification must include the landholding agency's assurance that each piece of equipment is now and will continue to be in compliance with the EPA regulations until disposal of the property.

EXAMINATION FOR ACCEPTABILITY

§ 102–75.145 Is GSA required to review each report of excess?

Yes, GSA must review each report of excess to ascertain whether the report was prepared according to the provisions of this part. GSA must notify the landholding agency, in writing, whether the report is acceptable or other information is needed within 15 calendar days after receipt of the report.

§ 102–75.150 What happens when GSA determines that the report of excess is adequate?

When GSA determines that a report is adequate, GSA will accept the report and inform the landholding agency of the acceptance date. However, the landholding agency must, upon request, promptly furnish any additional information or documents relating to the property required by GSA to accomplish a transfer or a disposal.

§ 102–75.155 What happens if GSA determines that the report of excess is insufficient?

Where GSA determines that a report is insufficient, GSA will return the report and inform the landholding agency of the facts and circumstances that make the report insufficient. The landholding agency must promptly take appropriate action to submit an acceptable report to GSA. If the landholding agency is unable to submit an acceptable report, the property will no longer be considered as excess property and the disposal agency will cease activity for the disposal of the property. However, GSA may accept the report of excess on a conditional basis and identify what deficiencies in the report must be corrected in order for the report to gain full acceptance.

DESIGNATION AS PERSONAL PROPERTY

§ 102–75.160 Should prefabricated movable structures be designated real or personal property for disposition purposes?

Prefabricated movable structures such as Butler-type storage warehouses, Quonset huts, and house trailers (with or without undercarriages) reported to GSA along with the land on which they are located may, at GSA's discretion, be designated for disposition as personal property for off-site use or as real property for disposal with the land.

§ 102–75.165 Should related personal property be designated real or personal property for disposition purposes?

Related personal property may, at the disposal agency's discretion, be designated as personal property for disposal purposes. However, for fine artwork and sculptures, GSA's policy is that artwork specifically created for a Federal building is considered as a fixture of the building. This also applies to sculptures created for a Federal building or a public park. Disposal agencies must follow the policies and guidance for disposal of artwork and sculptures developed by the GSA Office of the Chief Architect, Center for Design Excellence and the Arts, and the Bulletin dated March 26, 1934, entitled "Legal Title to Works Produced under the Public Works of Art Project."

§ 102–75.170 What happens to the related personal property in a structure scheduled for demolition?

When a structure is to be demolished, any fixtures or related personal property therein may, at the disposal agency's discretion, be designated for disposition as personal property where a ready disposition can be made of these items. As indicated in § 102–75.165, particular consideration should be given to designating items having possible historical or artistic value as personal property.

TRANSFERS

§ 102–75.175 What are GSA's responsibilities regarding transfer requests?

Before property can be transferred among Federal agencies, to mixed-ownership Government corporations, and to the municipal government of the District of Columbia, GSA must determine that—

(a) The transfer is in the best interest of the Government;

(b) The requesting agency is the appropriate agency to hold the property; and

(c) The proposed land use will maximize use of the real property, in terms of economy and efficiency, to minimize expenditures for the purchase of real property.

(Note: See Subpart I—Screening of Excess Federal Real Property (§§ 102–75.1220 through 102–75.1290) for information on screening and transfer requests.)

§ 102–75.180 May landholding agencies transfer excess real property without notifying GSA?

Landholding agencies may, without notifying GSA, transfer excess real property that they use, occupy, or control under a lease, permit, license, easement, or similar instrument when—

(a) The lease or other instrument is subject to termination by the grantor or owner of the premises within nine months;

(b) The remaining term of the lease or other instrument, including renewal rights, will provide for less than nine months of use and occupancy; or

(c) The lease or other instrument provides for use and occupancy of space for office, storage, and related facilities, which does not exceed a total of 2,500 square feet.

§ 102–75.185 In those instances where landholding agencies may transfer excess real property without notifying GSA, which policies must they follow?

In those instances, landholding agencies must transfer property following the policies in this subpart.

§ 102–75.190 What amount must the transferee agency pay for the transfer of excess real property?

The transferee agency must pay an amount equal to the property's fair market value (determined by the Administrator)—

(a) Where the transferor agency has requested the net proceeds of the transfer pursuant to 40 U.S.C. 574; or

(b) Where either the transferor or transferee agency (or organizational unit affected) is subject to the Government Corporation Control Act (31 U.S.C. 841), is a mixed-ownership Government corporation, or the municipal government of the District of Columbia.

§ 102–75.195 If the transferor agency is a wholly owned Government corporation, what amount must the transferee agency pay?

As may be agreed upon by GSA and the corporation, the transferee agency must pay an amount equal to—

(a) The estimated fair market value of the property; or

(b) The corporation's book value of the property.

§ 102–75.200 What amount must the transferee agency pay if property is being transferred for the purpose of upgrading the transferee agency's facilities?

Where the transfer is for the purpose of upgrading facilities (i.e., for the purpose of replacing other property of the transferee agency, which because of the location, nature, or condition thereof, is less efficient for use), the transferee must pay an amount equal to the difference between the fair market value of the property to be replaced and the fair market value of the property requested, as determined by the Administrator.

§ 102–75.205 Are transfers ever made without reimbursement by the transferee agency?

Transfers may be made without reimbursement by the transferee agency only if—

(a) Congress has specifically authorized the transfer without reimbursement, or

(b) The Administrator, with the approval of the Director of the Office of Management and Budget (OMB), has approved a request for an exception from the 100 percent reimbursement requirement.

§ 102–75.210 What must a transferee agency include in its request for an exception from the 100 percent reimbursement requirement?

The request must include an explanation of how granting the exception would further essential agency program objectives and at the same time be consistent with Executive Order 12512, Federal Real Property Management, dated April 29, 1985. The transferee agency must attach the explanation to the Request for Transfer of Excess Real and Related Personal

Property (GSA Form 1334) prior to submitting the form to GSA. The unavailability of funds alone is not sufficient to justify an exception.

§ 102–75.215 Who must endorse requests for exception to the 100 percent reimbursement requirement?

Agency heads must endorse requests for exceptions to the 100 percent reimbursement requirement.

§ 102–75.220 Where should an agency send a request for exception to the 100 percent reimbursement requirement?

Agencies must submit all requests for exception from the 100 percent reimbursement requirement to the appropriate GSA regional property disposal office.

§ 102–75.225 Who must review and approve a request for exception from the 100 percent reimbursement requirement?

The Administrator must review all requests for exception from the 100 percent reimbursement requirement. If the Administrator approves the request, it is then submitted to OMB for final concurrence. If OMB approves the request, then GSA may complete the transfer.

§ 102–75.230 Who is responsible for property protection and maintenance costs while the request for exception is being reviewed?

The agency requesting the property will assume responsibility for protection and maintenance costs not more than 40 days from the date of the Administrator's letter to OMB requesting concurrence for an exception to the 100 percent reimbursement requirement. If the request is denied, the requesting agency may pay the fair market value for the property or withdraw its request. If the request is withdrawn, responsibility for protection and maintenance cost will return to the landholding agency at that time.

§ 102–75.235 May disposal agencies transfer excess property to the Senate, the House of Representatives, and the Architect of the Capitol?

Yes, disposal agencies may transfer excess property to the Senate, the House of Representatives, and the Architect of the Capitol and any activities under his or her direction, pursuant to the provisions of 40 U.S.C. 113(d). The amount of reimbursement for such transfer must be the same as would be required for a transfer of excess property to an Executive agency under similar circumstances.

TEMPORARY UTILIZATION

§ 102–75.240 May excess real property be temporarily assigned/reassigned?

Yes, whenever GSA determines that it is more advantageous to assign property temporarily rather than permanently, it may do so. If the space is for office, storage, or related facilities, GSA will determine the length of the assignment/reassignment. Agencies are required to reimburse the landholding agency (or GSA, if GSA has become responsible for seeking an appropriation for protection and maintenance expenses) (see § 102–75.970) for protection and maintenance expenses. GSA may also temporarily assign/reassign excess real property for uses other than storage, office or related facilities. In such cases, the agency receiving the temporary assignment may be required to pay a rental or users charge based upon the fair market value of the property, as determined by GSA. If the property will be required by the agency for a period of more than 1 year, it may be transferred on a conditional basis, with an understanding that the property will be reported excess at an agreed upon time (see § 102–75.85). The requesting agency is responsible for protection and maintenance expenses.

NON-FEDERAL INTERIM USE OF EXCESS PROPERTY

§ 102–75.245 When can landholding agencies grant rights for non-Federal interim use of excess property reported to GSA?

Landholding agencies, upon approval from GSA, may grant rights for non-Federal interim use of excess property reported to GSA, when it is determined that such excess property is not required for the needs of any Federal agency and when the interim use will not impair the ability to dispose of the property.

Subpart C—Surplus Real Property Disposal

§ 102–75.250 What general policy must the disposal agency follow concerning the disposal of surplus property?

The disposal agency must dispose of surplus real property—

(a) In the most economical manner consistent with the best interests of the Government; and

(b) Ordinarily for cash, consistent with the best interests of the Government.

§ 102–75.255 What are disposal agencies' specific responsibilities concerning the disposal of surplus property?

The disposal agency must determine that there is no further Federal need or requirement for the excess real property and the property is surplus to the needs of the Federal Government. After reaching this determination, the disposal agency must expeditiously make the surplus property available for acquisition by State and local governmental units and non-profit institutions (see § 102–75.350) or for sale by public advertising, negotiation, or other disposal action. The disposal agency must consider the availability of real property for public purposes on a case-by-case basis, based on highest and best use and estimated fair market value. Where hazardous substance activity is identified, see §§ 102–75.340 and 102–75.345 for required information that the disposal agency must incorporate into the offer to purchase and conveyance document.

§ 102–75.260 When may the disposal agency dispose of surplus real property by exchange for privately owned property?

The disposal agency may dispose of surplus real property by exchange for privately owned property for property management considerations such as boundary realignment or for providing access. The disposal agency may also dispose of surplus real property by exchange for privately owned property where authorized by law, when the requesting Federal agency receives approval from the Office of Management and Budget and the appropriate oversight committees, and where the transaction offers substantial economic or unique program advantages not otherwise obtainable by any other acquisition method.

§ 102–75.265 Are conveyance documents required to identify all agreements and representations concerning property restrictions and conditions?

Yes, conveyance documents must identify all agreements and representations concerning restrictions and conditions affecting the property's future use, maintenance, or transfer.

APPLICABILITY OF ANTITRUST LAWS

§ 102–75.270 Must antitrust laws be considered when disposing of property?

Yes, antitrust laws must be considered in any case in which there is contemplated a disposal to any private interest of—

(a) Real and related personal property that has an estimated fair market value of $3 million or more; or

(b) Patents, processes, techniques, or inventions, irrespective of cost.

§ 102–75.275 Who determines whether the proposed disposal would create or maintain a situation inconsistent with antitrust laws?

The Attorney General determines whether the proposed disposal would create or maintain a situation inconsistent with antitrust laws.

§ 102–75.280 What information concerning a proposed disposal must a disposal agency provide to the Attorney General to determine the applicability of antitrust laws?

The disposal agency must promptly provide the Attorney General with notice of any such proposed disposal and the probable terms or conditions, as required by 40 U.S.C. 559. If notice is given by any disposal agency other than GSA, a copy of the notice must also be provided simultaneously to the GSA Regional Office in which the property is located. Upon request, a disposal agency must furnish information

268

that the Attorney General believes to be necessary in determining whether the proposed disposition or any other disposition of surplus real property violates or would violate any of the antitrust laws.

§ 102–75.285 Can a disposal agency dispose of real property to a private interest specified in § 102–75.270 before advice is received from the Attorney General?

No, advice from the Attorney General must be received before disposing of real property.

DISPOSALS UNDER OTHER LAWS

§ 102–75.290 Can disposals of real property be made under authority of laws other than Chapter 5 of Subtitle I of Title 40 of the United States Code?

Except for disposals specifically authorized by special legislation, disposals of real property must be made only under the authority of Chapter 5 of Subtitle I of Title 40 of the United States Code. However, the Administrator of General Services can evaluate, on a case-by-case basis, the disposal provisions of any other law to determine consistency with the authority conferred by Title 40. The provisions of this section do not apply to disposals of real property authorized to be made by 40 U.S.C. 113 or by any special statute that directs or requires an Executive agency named in the law to transfer or convey specifically described real property in accordance with the provisions of that statute.

CREDIT DISPOSALS

§ 102–75.295 What is the policy on extending credit in connection with the disposal of surplus property?

The disposal agency—

(a) May extend credit in connection with any disposal of surplus property when it determines that credit terms are necessary to avoid reducing the salability of the property and potential obtainable price and, when below market rates are extended, confer with the Office of Management and Budget to determine if the Federal Credit Reform Act of 1990 is applicable to the transaction;

(b) Must administer and manage the credit disposal and any related security;

(c) May enforce, adjust, or settle any right of the Government with respect to extending credit in a manner and with terms that are in the best interests of the Government; and

(d) Must include provisions in the conveyance documents that obligate the purchaser, where a sale is made upon credit, to obtain the disposal agency's prior written approval before reselling or leasing the property. The purchaser's credit obligations to the United States must be fulfilled before the disposal agency may approve the resale of the property.

DESIGNATION OF DISPOSAL AGENCIES

§ 102–75.296 When may a landholding agency other than GSA be the disposal agency for real and related personal property?

A landholding agency may be the disposal agency for real and related personal property when—

(a) The agency has statutory authority to dispose of real and related personal property;

(b) The agency has delegated authority from GSA to dispose of real and related personal property; or

(c) The agency is disposing of—

(1) Leases, licenses, permits, easements, and other similar real estate interests held by agencies in non-Government-owned real property;

(2) Government-owned improvements, including fixtures, structures, and other improvements of any kind as long as the underlying land is not being disposed; or

(3) Standing timber, embedded gravel, sand, stone, and underground water, without the underlying land.

§ 102–75.297 Are there any exceptions to when landholding agencies can serve as the disposal agency?

Yes, landholding agencies may not serve as the disposal agency when—

(a) Either the landholding agency or GSA determines that the Government's best interests are served by disposing of leases, licenses, permits, easements and similar real estate interests together with other property owned or controlled by the Government that has been or will be reported to GSA, or

(b) Government-owned machinery and equipment being used by a contractor-operator will be sold to a contractor-operator.

§ 102–75.298 Can agencies request that GSA be the disposal agency for real property and real property interests described in § 102–75.296?

Yes. If requested, GSA, at its discretion, may be the disposal agency for such real property and real property interests.

§ 102–75.299 What are landholding agencies' responsibilities if GSA conducts the disposal?

Landholding agencies are and remain responsible for all rental/lease payments until the lease expires or is terminated. Landholding agencies are responsible for paying any restoration or other direct costs incurred by the Government associated with termination of a lease, and for paying any demolition and removal costs not offset by the sale of the property. (See also § 102–75.965.)

APPRAISAL

§ 102–75.300 Are appraisals required for all real property disposal transactions?

Generally, yes, appraisals are required for all real property disposal transactions, except when—

(a) An appraisal will serve no useful purpose (e.g., legislation authorizes conveyance without monetary consideration or at a fixed price). This exception does not apply to negotiated sales to public agencies intending to use the property for a public purpose not covered by any of the special disposal provisions in subpart C of this part; or

(b) The estimated fair market value of property to be offered on a competitive sale basis does not exceed $300,000.

§ 102–75.305 What type of appraisal value must be obtained for real property disposal transactions?

For all real property transactions requiring appraisals, agencies must obtain, as appropriate, an appraisal of either the fair market value or the fair annual rental value of the property available for disposal.

§ 102–75.310 Who must agencies use to appraise the real property?

Agencies must use only experienced and qualified real estate appraisers familiar with the types of property to be appraised when conducting the appraisal. When an appraisal is required for negotiation purposes, the same standard applies. However, agencies may authorize other methods of obtaining an estimate of the fair market value or the fair annual rental when the cost of obtaining that data from a contract appraiser would be out of proportion to the expected recoverable value of the property.

§ 102–75.315 Are appraisers authorized to consider the effect of historic covenants on the fair market value?

Yes, appraisers are authorized to consider the effect of historic covenants on the fair market value, if the property is in or eligible for listing in the National Register of Historic Places.

§ 102–75.320 Does appraisal information need to be kept confidential?

Yes, appraisals, appraisal reports, appraisal analyses, and other predecisional appraisal documents are confidential and can only be used by authorized Government personnel who can substantiate the need to know this information. Appraisal information must not be divulged prior to the delivery and acceptance of the deed. Any persons engaged to collect or evaluate appraisal information must certify that—

(a) They have no direct or indirect interest in the property; and

(b) The report was prepared and submitted without bias or influence.

INSPECTION

§ 102–75.325 What responsibility does the landholding agency have to provide persons the opportunity to inspect available surplus property?

Landholding agencies should provide all persons interested in acquiring available surplus property with the opportunity to make a complete inspection of the property, including any available inventory records, plans, specifications, and engineering reports that relate to the property. These inspections are subject to any necessary national security restrictions and are subject to the disposal agency's rules. (See §§ 102–75.335 and 102–75.985.)

SUBMISSION OF OFFERS TO PURCHASE OR LEASE

§ 102–75.330 **What form must all offers to purchase or lease be in?**

All offers to purchase or lease must be in writing, accompanied by any required earnest money deposit, using the form prescribed by the disposal agency. In addition to the financial terms upon which the offer is predicated, the offer must set forth the willingness of the offeror to abide by the terms, conditions, reservations, and restrictions upon which the property is offered, and must contain such other information as the disposal agency may request.

PROVISIONS RELATING TO ASBESTOS

§ 102–75.335 **Where asbestos is identified, what information must the disposal agency incorporate into the offer to purchase and the conveyance document?**

Where the existence of asbestos on the property has been brought to the attention of the disposal agency by the Report of Excess Real Property (Standard Form 118) information provided (see § 102–75.125), the disposal agency must incorporate this information (less any cost or time estimates to remove the asbestos-containing materials) into any offer to purchase and conveyance document and include the following wording:

Notice of the Presence of Asbestos—Warning!

(a) The Purchaser is warned that the property offered for sale contains asbestos-containing materials. Unprotected or unregulated exposures to asbestos in product manufacturing, shipyard, and building construction workplaces have been associated with asbestos-related diseases. Both the U.S. Occupational Safety and Health Administration (OSHA) and the U.S. Environmental Protection Agency (EPA) regulate asbestos because of the potential hazards associated with exposure to airborne asbestos fibers. Both OSHA and EPA have determined that such exposure increases the risk of asbestos-related diseases, which include certain cancers and which can result in disability or death.

(b) Bidders (offerors) are invited, urged and cautioned to inspect the property to be sold prior to submitting a bid (offer). More particularly, bidders (offerors) are invited, urged and cautioned to inspect the property as to its asbestos content and condition and any hazardous or environmental conditions relating thereto. The disposal agency will assist bidders (offerors) in obtaining any authorization(s) that may be required in order to carry out any such inspection(s). Bidders (offerors) shall be deemed to have relied solely on their own judgment in assessing the overall condition of all or any portion of the property including, without limitation, any asbestos hazards or concerns.

(c) No warranties either express or implied are given with regard to the condition of the property including, without limitation, whether the property does or does not contain asbestos or is or is not safe for a particular purpose. The failure of any bidder (offeror) to inspect, or to be fully informed as to the condition of all or any portion of the property offered, will not constitute grounds for any claim or demand for adjustment or withdrawal of a bid or offer after its opening or tender.

(d) The description of the property set forth in the Invitation for Bids (Offer to Purchase) and any other information provided therein with respect to said property is based on the best information available to the disposal agency and is believed to be correct, but an error or omission, including, but not limited to, the omission of any information available to the agency having custody over the property and/or any other Federal agency, shall not constitute grounds or reason for nonperformance of the contract of sale, or any claim by the Purchaser against the Government including, without limitation, any claim for allowance, refund, or deduction from the purchase price.

(e) The Government assumes no liability for damages for personal injury, illness, disability, or death, to the Purchaser, or to the Purchaser's successors, assigns, employees, invitees, or any other person subject to Purchaser's control or direction, or to any other person, including members of the general public, arising from or incident to the purchase, transportation, removal, handling, use, disposition, or other activity causing or leading to contact of any kind whatsoever with asbestos on the property that is the subject of this sale, whether the Purchaser, its successors or assigns has or have properly warned or failed properly to warn the individual(s) injured.

(f) The Purchaser further agrees that, in its use and occupancy of the property, it will comply with all Federal, State, and local laws relating to asbestos.

PROVISIONS RELATING TO HAZARDOUS
SUBSTANCE ACTIVITY

§ 102–75.340 Where hazardous substance activity has been identified on property proposed for disposal, what information must the disposal agency incorporate into the offer to purchase and the conveyance document?

Where the existence of hazardous substance activity has been brought to the attention of the disposal agency by the Report of Excess Real Property (Standard Form 118) information provided (see §§ 102–75.125 and 102–75.130), the disposal agency must incorporate this information into any offer to purchase and conveyance document. In any offer to purchase and conveyance document, disposal agencies, generally, must also address the following (specific recommended language that addresses the following issues can be found in the GSA Customer Guide to Real Property Disposal):

(a) Notice of all hazardous substance activity identified as a result of a complete search of agency records by the landholding agency.

(b) A statement, certified by a responsible landholding agency official in the Report of Excess Real Property, that all remedial actions necessary to protect human health and the environment with regard to such hazardous substance activity have been taken (this is not required in the offer to purchase or conveyance document in the case of a transfer of property under the authority of section 120(h)(3)(C) of CERCLA, or the Early Transfer Authority, or a conveyance to a "potentially responsible party", as defined by CERCLA (see 102–75.345)).

(c) A commitment, on behalf of the United States, to return to correct any hazardous condition discovered after the conveyance that results from hazardous substance activity prior to the date of conveyance.

(d) A reservation by the United States of a right of access in order to accomplish any further remedial actions required in the future.

§ 102–75.345 What is different about the statements in the offer to purchase and conveyance document if the sale is to a potentially responsible party with respect to the hazardous substance activity?

In the case where the purchaser or grantee is a potentially responsible party (PRP) with respect to hazardous substance activity on the property under consideration, the United States is no longer under a general obligation to certify that the property has been successfully remediated, or to commit to return to the property to address contamination that is discovered in the future. Therefore, the statements of responsibility and commitments on behalf of the United States referenced in § 102–75.340 should not be used. Instead, language should be included in the offer to purchase and conveyance document that is consistent with any agreement that has been reached between the landholding agency and the PRP with regard to prior hazardous substance activity.

PUBLIC BENEFIT CONVEYANCES

§ 102–75.350 What are disposal agencies' responsibilities concerning public benefit conveyances?

Based on a highest and best use analysis, disposal agencies may make surplus real property available to State and local governments and certain nonprofit institutions or organizations at up to 100 percent public benefit discount for public benefit purposes. Some examples of such purposes are education, health, park and recreation, the homeless, historic monuments, public airports, highways, correctional facilities, ports, and wildlife conservation. The implementing regulations for these conveyances are found in this subpart.

§ 102–75.351 May the disposal agency waive screening for public benefit conveyances?

All properties, consistent with the highest and best use analysis, will normally be screened for public benefit uses. However, the disposal agency may waive public benefit screening, with the exception of the mandatory McKinney-Vento homeless screening, for specific property disposal considerations, e.g., when a property has been reported excess for exchange purposes.

§ 102–75.355 What clause must be in the offer to purchase and the conveyance documents for public benefit conveyances?

Executive agencies must include in the offer to purchase and conveyance documents the non-discrimination clause in § 102–75.360 for public benefit conveyances.

§ 102–75.360 What wording must be in the non-discrimination clause that is required in the offer to purchase and in the conveyance document?

The wording of the non-discrimination clause must be as follows:

The Grantee covenants for itself, its heirs, successors, and assigns and every successor in interest to the property hereby conveyed, or any part thereof, that the said Grantee and such heirs, successors, and assigns shall not discriminate upon the basis of race, creed, color, religion, sex, disability, age, or national origin in the use, occupancy, sale, or lease of the property, or in their employment practices conducted thereon. This covenant shall not apply, however, to the lease or rental of a room or rooms within a family dwelling unit; nor shall it apply with respect to religion to premises used primarily for religious purposes. The United States of America shall be deemed a beneficiary of this covenant without regard to whether it remains the owner of any land or interest therein in the locality of the property hereby conveyed and shall have the sole right to enforce this covenant in any court of competent jurisdiction.

POWER TRANSMISSION LINES

§ 102–75.365 Do disposal agencies have to notify State entities and Government agencies that a surplus power transmission line and right-of-way is available?

Yes, disposal agencies must notify State entities and Government agencies of the availability of a surplus power transmission line and right-of-way.

§ 102–75.370 May a State, or any political subdivision thereof, certify to a disposal agency that it needs a surplus power transmission line and the right-of-way acquired for its construction to meet the requirements of a public or cooperative power project?

Yes, section 13(d) of the Surplus Property Act of 1944 (50 U.S.C. App. 1622(d)) allows any State or political subdivision, or any State or Government agency or instrumentality to certify to the disposal agency that a surplus power transmission line and the right-of-way acquired for its construction is needed to meet the requirements of a public or cooperative power project.

§ 102–75.375 What happens once a State, or political subdivision, certifies that it needs a surplus power transmission line and the right-of-way acquired for its construction to meet the requirements of a public or cooperative power project?

Generally, once a State or political subdivision certifies that it needs a surplus power transmission line and the right-of-way, the disposal agency may sell the property to the state, or political subdivision thereof, at the fair market value. However, if a sale of a surplus transmission line cannot be accomplished because of the price to be charged, or other reasons, and the certification by the State or political subdivision is not withdrawn, the disposal agency must report the facts involved to the Administrator of General Services, to determine what further action will or should be taken to dispose of the property.

§ 102–75.380 May power transmission lines and rights-of-way be disposed of in other ways?

Yes, power transmission lines and rights-of-way not disposed of by sale for fair market value may be disposed of following other applicable provisions of this part, including, if appropriate, reclassification by the disposal agency.

273

PROPERTY FOR PUBLIC AIRPORTS

§ 102–75.385 Do disposal agencies have the responsibility to notify eligible public agencies that airport property has been determined to be surplus?

Yes, the disposal agency must notify eligible public agencies that property currently used as or suitable for use as a public airport under the Surplus Property Act of 1944, as amended, has been determined to be surplus. A copy of the landholding agency's Report of Excess Real Property (Standard Form 118, with accompanying schedules) must be transmitted with the copy of the surplus property notice sent to the appropriate regional office of the Federal Aviation Administration (FAA). The FAA must furnish an application form and instructions for the preparation of an application to eligible public agencies upon request.

§ 102–75.390 What does the term "surplus airport property" mean?

For the purposes of this part, surplus airport property is any surplus real property including improvements and personal property included as a part of the operating unit that the Administrator of FAA deems is—

(a) Essential, suitable, or desirable for the development, improvement, operation, or maintenance of a public airport, as defined in the Federal Airport Act, as amended (49 U.S.C. 1101); or

(b) Reasonably necessary to fulfill the immediate and foreseeable future requirements of the grantee for the development, improvement, operation, or maintenance of a public airport, including property needed to develop sources of revenue from non-aviation businesses at a public airport. Approval for non-aviation revenue-producing areas may only be given for such areas as are anticipated to generate net proceeds that do not exceed expected deficits for operation of the aviation area applied for at the airport.

§ 102–75.395 May surplus airport property be conveyed or disposed of to a State, political subdivision, municipality, or tax-supported institution for a public airport?

Yes, section 13(g) of the Surplus Property Act of 1944 (49 U.S.C. § 47151)

authorizes the disposal agency to convey or dispose of surplus airport property to a State, political subdivision, municipality, or tax-supported institution for use as a public airport.

§ 102–75.400 Is industrial property located on an airport also considered to be "airport property"?

No, if the Administrator of General Services determines that a property's highest and best use is industrial, then the property must be classified as such for disposal without regard to the public benefit conveyance provisions of this subpart.

§ 102–75.405 What responsibilities does the Federal Aviation Administration (FAA) have after receiving a copy of the notice (and a copy of the Report of Excess Real Property (Standard Form 118)) given to eligible public agencies that there is surplus airport property?

As soon as possible after receiving the copy of the surplus notice, the FAA must inform the disposal agency of its determination. Then, the FAA must provide assistance to any eligible public agency known to have a need for the property for a public airport, so that the public agency may develop a comprehensive and coordinated plan of use and procurement for the property.

§ 102–75.410 What action must the disposal agency take after an eligible public agency has submitted a plan of use and application to acquire property for a public airport?

After an eligible public agency submits a plan of use and application, the disposal agency must transmit two copies of the plan and two copies of the application to the appropriate FAA regional office. The FAA must promptly submit a recommendation to the disposal agency for disposal of the property for a public airport or must inform the disposal agency that no such recommendation will be submitted.

§ 102–75.415 What happens after the disposal agency receives the FAA's recommendation for disposal of the property for a public airport?

The head of the disposal agency, or his or her designee, may convey property approved by the FAA for use as a public airport to the eligible public agency, subject to the provisions of the Surplus Property Act of 1944, as amended.

§ 102–75.420 What happens if the FAA informs the disposal agency that it does not recommend disposal of the property for a public airport?

Any airport property that the FAA does not recommend for disposal as a public airport must be disposed of in accordance with other applicable provisions of this part. However, the disposal agency must first notify the landholding agency of its inability to dispose of the property for use as a public airport. In addition, the disposal agency must allow the landholding agency 30 days to withdraw the property from surplus or to waive any future interest in the property for public airport use.

§ 102–75.425 Who has sole responsibility for enforcing compliance with the terms and conditions of disposal for property disposed of for use as a public airport?

The Administrator of the FAA has the sole responsibility for enforcing compliance with the terms and conditions of disposals to be used as a public airport. The FAA is also responsible for reforming, correcting, or amending any disposal instruments; granting releases; and any action necessary for recapturing the property, using the provisions of 49 U.S.C. 47101 *et seq.*

§ 102–75.430 What happens if property conveyed for use as a public airport is revested in the United States?

If property that was conveyed for use as a public airport is revested in the United States for noncompliance with the terms of the disposal, or other cause, the Administrator of the FAA must be accountable for the property and must report the property to GSA as excess property following the provisions of this part.

§ 102–75.435 Does the Airport and Airway Development Act of 1970, as amended (Airport Act of 1970), apply to the transfer of airports to State and local agencies?

No, the Airport and Airway Development Act of 1970, as amended (49 U.S.C. 47101–47131) (Airport Act of 1970), does not apply to the transfer of airports to State and local agencies. The transfer of airports to State and local agencies may be made only under section 13(g) of the Surplus Property Act of 1944 (49 U.S.C. 47151–47153). Only property that the landholding agency determines cannot be reported excess to GSA for disposal under Title 40, but nevertheless may be made available for use by a State or local public body as a public airport without being inconsistent with the Federal program of the landholding agency, may be conveyed under the Airport Act of 1970. In the latter instance, the Airport Act of 1970 may be used to transfer non-excess land for airport development purposes provided it does not constitute an entire airport. An entire, existing and established airport can only be disposed of to a State or eligible local government under section 13(g) of the Surplus Property Act of 1944.

PROPERTY FOR USE AS HISTORIC MONUMENTS

§ 102–75.440 Who must disposal agencies notify that surplus property is available for historic monument use?

Disposal agencies must notify State and area wide clearinghouses and eligible public agencies that property that may be conveyed for use as a historic monument has been determined to be surplus. A copy of the landholding agency's Report of Excess Real Property (Standard Form 118) with accompanying schedules must be transmitted with the copy of each notice that is sent to the appropriate regional or field offices of the National Park Service (NPS) of the Department of the Interior (DOI).

§ 102–75.445 Who can convey surplus real and related personal property for historic monument use?

A disposal agency may convey surplus real and related personal property for use as a historic monument, without monetary consideration, to any State, political subdivision, instrumentality thereof, or municipality, for the benefit of the public, provided the Secretary of the Interior has determined that the property is suitable and desirable for such use.

§ 102–75.450 What type of property is suitable or desirable for use as a historic monument?

Only property conforming with the recommendation of the Advisory Board on National Parks, Historic Sites, Buildings, and Monuments shall be determined to be suitable or desirable for use as a historic monument.

§ 102–75.455 May historic monuments be used for revenue-producing activities?

The disposal agency may authorize the use of historic monuments conveyed under 40 U.S.C. 550(h) or the Surplus Property Act of 1944, as amended, for revenue-producing activities, if the Secretary of the Interior—

(a) Determines that the activities, described in the applicant's proposed program of use, are compatible with the use of the property for historic monument purposes;

(b) Approves the grantee's plan for repair, rehabilitation, restoration, and maintenance of the property;

(c) Approves the grantee's plan for financing the repair, rehabilitation, restoration, and maintenance of the property. DOI must not approve the plan unless it provides that all income in excess of costs of repair, rehabilitation, restoration, maintenance, and a specified reasonable profit or payment that may accrue to a lessor, sublessor, or developer in connection with the management, operation, or development of the property for revenue producing activities, is used by the grantee, lessor, sublessor, or developer, only for public historic preservation, park, or recreational purposes; and

(d) Examines and approves the grantee's accounting and financial procedures for recording and reporting on revenue-producing activities.

§ 102–75.460 What information must disposal agencies furnish eligible public agencies?

Upon request, the disposal agency must furnish eligible public agencies with adequate preliminary property information and, with the landholding agency's cooperation, provide assistance to enable public agencies to obtain adequate property information.

§ 102–75.465 What information must eligible public agencies interested in acquiring real property for use as a historic monument submit to the appropriate regional or field offices of the National Park Service (NPS) of the Department of the Interior (DOI)?

Eligible public agencies must submit the original and two copies of the completed application to acquire real property for use as a historic monument to the appropriate regional or field offices of NPS, which will forward one copy of the application to the appropriate regional office of the disposal agency.

§ 102–75.470 What action must NPS take after an eligible public agency has submitted an application for conveyance of surplus property for use as a historic monument?

NPS must promptly—

(a) Submit the Secretary of the Interior's determination to the disposal agency; or

(b) Inform the disposal agency that no such recommendation will be submitted.

§ 102–75.475 What happens after the disposal agency receives the Secretary of the Interior's determination for disposal of the surplus property for a historic monument and compatible revenue-producing activities?

The head of the disposal agency or his or her designee may convey to an eligible public agency surplus property determined by the Secretary of the Interior to be suitable and desirable for use as a historic monument for the benefit of the public and for compatible revenue-producing activities subject to the provisions of 40 U.S.C. 550(h).

§ 102–75.480 Who has the responsibility for enforcing compliance with the terms and conditions of disposal for surplus property conveyed for use as a historic monument?

The Secretary of the Interior has the responsibility for enforcing compliance with the terms and conditions of such a disposal. DOI is also responsible for reforming, correcting, or amending any disposal instrument; granting releases; and any action necessary for recapturing the property using the provisions of 40 U.S.C. 550(b). The actions are subject to the approval of the head of the disposal agency.

§102–75.485 What happens if property that was conveyed for use as a historic monument is revested in the United States?

In such a case, DOI must notify the appropriate GSA Public Buildings Service (PBS) Regional Office immediately by letter when title to the historic property is to be revested in the United States for noncompliance with the terms and conditions of disposal or for other cause. The notification must cite the legal and administrative actions that DOI must take to obtain full title and possession of the property. In addition, it must include an adequate description of the property, including any improvements constructed since the original conveyance to the grantee. After receiving a statement from DOI that title to the property is proposed for revesting, GSA will review the statement and determine if title should be revested. If GSA, in consultation with DOI, determines that the property should be revested, DOI must submit a Report of Excess Real Property, Standard Form 118 to GSA. GSA will review and act upon the Standard Form 118, if acceptable. However, the grantee must provide protection and maintenance of the property until the title reverts to the Federal Government, including the period of the notice of intent to revert. Such protection and maintenance must, at a minimum, conform to the standards prescribed in the GSA Customer Guide to Real Property Disposal.

PROPERTY FOR EDUCATIONAL AND PUBLIC HEALTH PURPOSES

§102–75.490 Who must notify eligible public agencies that surplus real property for educational and public health purposes is available?

The disposal agency must notify eligible public agencies that surplus property is available for educational and/or public health purposes. The notice must require that any plans for an educational or public health use, resulting from the development of the comprehensive and coordinated plan of use and procurement for the property, must be coordinated with the Department of Education (ED) or the Department of Health and Human Services (HHS), as appropriate. The notice must also let eligible public agencies know where to obtain the applications, instructions for preparing them, and where to submit the application. The requirement for educational or public health use of the property by an eligible public agency is contingent upon the disposal agency's approval, under §102–75.515, of a recommendation for assignment of Federal surplus real property received from ED or HHS. Further, any subsequent transfer is subject to the approval of the head of the disposal agency as stipulated under 40 U.S.C. 550(c) or (d) and referenced in §102–75.535.

§102–75.495 May the Department of Education (ED) or the Department of Health and Human Services (HHS) notify nonprofit organizations that surplus real property and related personal property is available for educational and public health purposes?

Yes, ED or HHS may notify eligible non-profit institutions that such property has been determined to be surplus. Notices to eligible non-profit institutions must require eligible non-profit institutions to coordinate any request for educational or public health use of the property with the appropriate public agency responsible for developing and submitting a comprehensive and coordinated plan of use and procurement for the property.

§102–75.500 Which Federal agencies may the head of the disposal agency (or his or her designee) assign for disposal surplus real property to be used for educational and public health purposes?

The head of the disposal agency or his designee may—

(a) Assign to the Secretary of ED for disposal under 40 U.S.C. 550(c) surplus real property, including buildings, fixtures, and equipment, as recommended by the Secretary as being needed for school, classroom, or other educational use; or

(b) Assign to the Secretary of HHS for disposal under 40 U.S.C. 550 (d) such surplus real property, including buildings, fixtures, and equipment situated thereon, as recommended by the Secretary as being needed for use in the protection of public health, including research.

§ 102–75.505 **Is the request for educational or public health use of a property by an eligible nonprofit institution contingent upon the disposal agency's approval?**

Yes, eligible non-profit organizations will only receive surplus real property for an educational or public health use if the disposal agency approves or grants the assignment request from either ED or HHS. The disposal agency will also consider other uses for available surplus real property, taking into account the highest and best use determination. Any subsequent transfer is subject to the approval of the head of the disposal agency as stipulated under 40 U.S.C. 550(c) or (d) and referenced in this part.

§ 102–75.510 **When must the Department of Education and the Department of Health and Human Services notify the disposal agency that an eligible applicant is interested in acquiring the property?**

ED and HHS must notify the disposal agency if it has an eligible applicant interested in acquiring the property within 30 calendar days after the date of the surplus notice. Then, after the 30-day period expires, ED or HHS has 30 calendar days to review and approve an application and request assignment of the property, or inform the disposal agency that no assignment request will be forthcoming.

§ 102–75.515 **What action must the disposal agency take after an eligible public agency has submitted a plan of use for property for an educational or public health requirement?**

When an eligible public agency submits a plan of use for property for an educational or public health requirement, the disposal agency must transmit two copies of the plan to the regional office of ED or HHS, as appropriate. The ED or HHS must submit to the disposal agency, within 30 calendar days after the date the plan is transmitted, a recommendation for assignment of the property to the Secretary

of ED or HHS, as appropriate, or must inform the disposal agency, within the 30–calendar day period, that a recommendation will not be made for assignment of the property to ED or HHS. If, after considering other uses for the property, the disposal agency approves the assignment recommendation from ED or HHS, it must assign the property by letter or other document to the Secretary of ED or HHS, as appropriate. The disposal agency must furnish to the landholding agency a copy of the assignment, unless the landholding agency is also the disposal agency. If the recommendation is disapproved, the disposal agency must likewise notify the appropriate Department.

§ 102–75.520 **What must the Department of Education or the Department of Health and Human Services address in the assignment recommendation that is submitted to the disposal agency?**

Any assignment recommendation that ED or HHS submits to the disposal agency must provide complete information concerning the educational or public health use, including—

(a) Identification of the property;

(b) The name of the applicant and the size and nature of its program;

(c) The specific use planned;

(d) The intended public benefit allowance;

(e) The estimate of the value upon which such proposed allowance is based; and

(f) An explanation if the acreage or value of the property exceeds the standards established by the Secretary.

§ 102–75.525 **What responsibilities do landholding agencies have concerning properties to be used for educational and public health purposes?**

Landholding agencies must cooperate to the fullest extent possible with representatives of ED or HHS in their inspection of such property and in furnishing information relating to the property.

§ 102–75.530 What happens if the Department of Education or the Department of Health and Human Services does not approve any applications for conveyance of the property for educational or public health purposes?

In the absence of an approved application from ED or HHS to convey the property for educational or public health purposes, which must be received within the 30 calendar day time limit, the disposal agency will proceed with other disposal actions.

§ 102–75.535 What responsibilities does the Department of Education or the Department of Health and Human Services have after receiving the disposal agency's assignment letter?

After receiving the disposal agency's assignment letter, ED or HHS must furnish the disposal agency with a Notice of Proposed Transfer within 30 calendar days. If the disposal agency approves the proposed transfer within 30 days of receiving the Notice of Proposed Transfer, ED or HHS may prepare the transfer documents and proceed with the transfer. ED or HHS must take all necessary actions to accomplish the transfer within 15–calendar days beginning when the disposal agency approves the transfer. ED or HHS must furnish the disposal agency two conformed copies of deeds, leases or other instruments conveying the property under 40 U.S.C. 550(c) or (d) and all related documents containing restrictions or conditions regulating the future use, maintenance or transfer of the property.

§ 102–75.540 Who is responsible for enforcing compliance with the terms and conditions of the transfer for educational or public health purposes?

ED or HHS, as appropriate, is responsible for enforcing compliance with the terms and conditions of transfer. ED or HHS is also responsible for reforming, correcting, or amending any transfer instruments; granting releases; and for taking any necessary actions for recapturing the property using or following the provisions of 40 U.S.C. 550(b). These actions are subject to the approval of the head of the disposal agency. ED or HHS must notify the disposal agency of its intent to take any actions to recapture the property. The notice must identify the property affected, describe in detail the proposed action, and state the reasons for the proposed action.

§ 102–75.545 What happens if property that was transferred to meet an educational or public health requirement is revested in the United States for noncompliance with the terms of sale, or other cause?

In each case of repossession under a terminated lease or reversion of title for noncompliance with the terms or conditions of sale or other cause, ED or HHS must, prior to repossession or reversion of title, provide the appropriate GSA regional property disposal office with an accurate description of the real and related personal property involved using the Report of Excess Real Property (Standard Form 118), and the appropriate schedules. After receiving a statement from ED or HHS that the property is proposed for revesting, GSA will review the statement and determine if title should be revested. If GSA, in conjunction with ED or HHS, determines that the property should be revested, ED or HHS must submit a Standard Form 118 to GSA. GSA will review and act upon the Standard Form 118, if acceptable. However, the grantee must provide protection and maintenance for the property until the title reverts to the Federal Government, including the period of any notice of intent to revert. Such protection and maintenance must, at a minimum, conform to the standards prescribed in the GSA Customer Guide to Real Property Disposal.

PROPERTY FOR PROVIDING SELF-HELP HOUSING OR HOUSING ASSISTANCE

§ 102–75.550 What does "self-help housing or housing assistance" mean?

Property for self-help housing or housing assistance (which is separate from the program under Title V of the McKinney-Vento Homeless Assistance Act covered in subpart H of this part) is property for low-income housing opportunities through the construction, rehabilitation, or refurbishment of housing, under terms that require that—

(a) Any individual or family receiving housing or housing assistance must contribute a significant amount of labor toward the construction, rehabilitation, or refurbishment; and

(b) Dwellings constructed, rehabilitated, or refurbished must be quality dwellings that comply with local building and safety codes and standards and must be available at prices below prevailing market prices.

§ 102–75.555 **Which Federal agency receives the property assigned for self-help housing or housing assistance for low-income individuals or families?**

The head of the disposal agency, or designee, may assign, at his/her discretion, surplus real property, including buildings, fixtures, and equipment to the Secretary of the Department of Housing and Urban Development (HUD).

§ 102–75.560 **Who notifies eligible public agencies that real property to be used for self-help housing or housing assistance purposes is available?**

The disposal agency must notify eligible public agencies that surplus property is available. The notice must require that any plans for self-help housing or housing assistance use resulting from the development of the comprehensive and coordinated plan of use and procurement for the property must be coordinated with HUD. Eligible public agencies may obtain an application form and instructions for preparing and submitting the application from HUD.

§ 102–75.565 **Is the requirement for self-help housing or housing assistance use of the property by an eligible public agency or non-profit organization contingent upon the disposal agency's approval of an assignment recommendation from the Department of Housing and Urban Development (HUD)?**

Yes, the requirement for self-help housing or housing assistance use of the property by an eligible public agency or nonprofit organization is contingent upon the disposal agency's approval under § 102–75.585 of HUD's assignment recommendation/request. Any subsequent transfer is subject to

the approval of the head of the disposal agency as stipulated under 40 U.S.C. 550(f) and referenced in § 102–75.605.

§ 102–75.570 **What happens if the disposal agency does not approve the assignment recommendation?**

If the recommendation is not approved, the disposal agency must also notify the Secretary of HUD and then may proceed with other disposal action.

§ 102–75.575 **Who notifies non-profit organizations that surplus real property and related personal property to be used for self-help housing or housing assistance purposes is available?**

HUD notifies eligible non-profit organizations, following guidance in the GSA Customer Guide to Real Property Disposal. Such notices must require eligible nonprofit organizations to—

(a) Coordinate any requirement for self-help housing or housing assistance use of the property with the appropriate public agency; and

(b) Declare to the disposal agency an intent to develop and submit a comprehensive and coordinated plan of use and procurement for the property.

§ 102–75.580 **When must HUD notify the disposal agency that an eligible applicant is interested in acquiring the property?**

HUD must notify the disposal agency within 30 calendar days after the date of the surplus notice. Then, after the 30-day period expires, HUD has 30 calendar days to review and approve an application and request assignment or inform the disposal agency that no assignment request is forthcoming.

§ 102–75.585 **What action must the disposal agency take after an eligible public agency has submitted a plan of use for property for a self-help housing or housing assistance requirement?**

When an eligible public agency submits a plan of use for property for a self-help housing or housing assistance requirement, the disposal agency must transmit two copies of the plan to the appropriate HUD regional office. HUD must submit to the disposal agency, within 30 calendar days after the date the plan is transmitted, a recommendation for assignment of the property to the Secretary of HUD, or must inform the disposal agency, within the 30–calendar day period, that a recommendation will not be made for assignment of the property to HUD. If, after considering other uses for the property, the disposal agency approves the assignment recommendation from HUD, it must assign the property by letter or other document to the Secretary of HUD. The disposal agency must furnish to the landholding agency a copy of the assignment, unless the landholding agency is also the disposal agency. If the disposal agency disapproves the recommendation, the disposal agency must likewise notify the Secretary of HUD.

§ 102–75.590 What does the assignment recommendation contain?

Any assignment recommendation that HUD submits to the disposal agency must set forth complete information concerning the self-help housing or housing assistance use, including—

(a) Identification of the property;

(b) Name of the applicant and the size and nature of its program;

(c) Specific use planned;

(d) Intended public benefit allowance;

(e) Estimate of the value upon which such proposed allowance is based; and

(f) An explanation, if the acreage or value of the property exceeds the standards established by the Secretary.

§ 102–75.595 What responsibilities do landholding agencies have concerning properties to be used for self-help housing or housing assistance use?

Landholding agencies must cooperate to the fullest extent possible with HUD representatives in their inspection of such property and in furnishing information relating to such property.

§ 102–75.600 What happens if HUD does not approve any applications for self-help housing or housing assistance use?

In the absence of an approved application from HUD for self-help housing or housing assistance use, which must be received within the 30–calendar day time limit specified therein, the dis-posal agency must proceed with other disposal action.

§ 102–75.605 What responsibilities does HUD have after receiving the disposal agency's assignment letter?

After receiving the disposal agency's assignment letter, HUD must furnish the disposal agency with a Notice of Proposed Transfer within 30 calendar days. If the disposal agency approves the proposed transfer within 30 calendar days of receiving the Notice of Proposed Transfer, HUD may prepare the transfer documents and proceed with the transfer. HUD must take all necessary actions to accomplish the transfer within 15 calendar days beginning when the disposal agency approves the transfer. HUD must furnish the disposal agency two conformed copies of deeds, leases or other instruments conveying the property under 40 U.S.C. 550(f) and all related documents containing restrictions or conditions regulating the future use, maintenance or transfer of the property.

§ 102–75.610 Who is responsible for enforcing compliance with the terms and conditions of the transfer of the property for self-help housing or housing assistance use?

HUD is responsible for enforcing compliance with the terms and conditions of transfer. HUD is also responsible for reforming, correcting, or amending any transfer instrument; granting releases; and for taking any necessary actions for recapturing the property using the provisions of 40 U.S.C. 550(b). These actions are subject to the approval of the head of the disposal agency. HUD must notify the head of the disposal agency of its intent to take action to recapture the property. The notice must identify the property affected, describe in detail the proposed action, and state the reasons for the proposed action.

§ 102–75.615 Who is responsible for enforcing compliance with the terms and conditions of property transferred under section 414(a) of the 1969 HUD Act?

HUD maintains responsibility for properties previously conveyed under section 414(a) of the 1969 HUD Act. Property transferred to an entity other than a public body and used for any purpose other than that for which it was sold or leased within a 30-year period must revert to the United States. If the property was leased, then the lease terminates. The appropriate Secretary (HUD or Department of Agriculture) and the Administrator of GSA can approve the new use of the property after the first 20 years of the original 30-year period has expired.

§ 102–75.620 What happens if property that was transferred to meet a self-help housing or housing assistance use requirement is found to be in noncompliance with the terms of sale?

In each case of repossession under a terminated lease or reversion of title for noncompliance with the terms or conditions of sale or other cause, HUD (or USDA for property conveyed through the former Farmers Home Administration program under section 414(a) of the 1969 HUD Act) must, prior to repossession or reversion of title, provide the appropriate GSA regional office with an accurate description of the real and related personal property involved using the Report of Excess Real Property (Standard Form 118), and the appropriate schedules. After receiving a statement from HUD (or USDA) that title to the property is proposed for revesting, GSA will review the statement and determine if title should be revested. If GSA, in conjunction with HUD (or USDA), determines that the property should be revested, HUD (or USDA) must submit a Standard Form 118 to GSA. GSA will review and act upon the Standard Form 118, if acceptable. However, the grantee must provide protection and maintenance for the property until the title reverts to the Federal Government, including the period of any notice of intent to revert. Such protection and maintenance must, at a minimum, conform to the standards prescribed in the GSA Customer Guide to Real Property Disposal.

PROPERTY FOR USE AS PUBLIC PARK OR RECREATION AREAS

§ 102–75.625 Which Federal agency is assigned surplus real property for public park or recreation purposes?

The head of the disposal agency or his or her designee is authorized to assign to the Secretary of the Interior for disposal under 40 U.S.C. 550(e), surplus real property, including buildings, fixtures, and equipment as recommended by the Secretary as being needed for use as a public park or recreation area for conveyance to a State, political subdivision, instrumentalities, or municipality.

§ 102–75.630 Who must disposal agencies notify that real property for public park or recreation purposes is available?

The disposal agency must notify established State, regional, or metropolitan clearinghouses and eligible public agencies that surplus property is available for use as a public park or recreation area. The disposal agency must transmit the landholding agency's Report of Excess Real Property (Standard Form 118, with accompanying schedules) with the copy of each notice sent to a regional or field office of the National Park Service (NPS) of the Department of the Interior (DOI).

§ 102–75.635 What information must the Department of the Interior (DOI) furnish eligible public agencies?

Upon request, DOI must furnish eligible public agencies with an application form to acquire property for permanent use as a public park or recreation area and preparation instructions for the application.

§ 102–75.640 When must DOI notify the disposal agency that an eligible applicant is interested in acquiring the property?

DOI must notify the disposal agency if it has an eligible applicant interested in acquiring the property within 30 calendar days from the date of the surplus notice.

§ 102–75.645 What responsibilities do landholding agencies have concerning properties to be used for public park or recreation purposes?

Landholding agencies must cooperate to the fullest extent possible with DOI representatives in their inspection of the property and in furnishing information relating to the property.

§ 102–75.650 When must DOI request assignment of the property?

Within 30 calendar days after the expiration of the 30–calendar day period specified in § 102–75.640, DOI must submit to the disposal agency an assignment recommendation along with a copy of the application or inform the disposal agency that a recommendation will not be made for assignment of the property.

§ 102–75.655 What does the assignment recommendation contain?

Any recommendation submitted by DOI must provide complete information concerning the plans for use of the property as a public park or recreation area, including—

(a) Identification of the property;

(b) The name of the applicant;

(c) The specific use planned; and

(d) The intended public benefit allowance.

§ 102–75.660 What happens if DOI does not approve any applications or does not submit an assignment recommendation?

If DOI does not approve any applications or does not submit an assignment recommendation to convey the property for public park or recreation purposes, the disposal agency must proceed with other disposal action.

§ 102–75.665 What happens after the disposal agency receives the assignment recommendation from DOI?

If, after considering other uses for the property, the disposal agency approves the assignment recommendation from DOI, it must assign the property by letter or other document to the Secretary of the Interior. The disposal agency must furnish to the landholding agency a copy of the assignment, unless the landholding agency is also the disposal agency. If the recommendation is disapproved, the disposal agency must likewise notify the Secretary.

§ 102–75.670 What responsibilities does DOI have after receiving the disposal agency's assignment letter?

After receiving the disposal agency's assignment letter, the Secretary of the Interior must provide the disposal agency with a Notice of Proposed Transfer within 30 calendar days. If the disposal agency approves the proposed transfer within 30 calendar days, the Secretary may proceed with the transfer. DOI must take all necessary actions to accomplish the transfer within 15 calendar days after the expiration of the 30–calendar day period provided for the disposal agency to consider the notice. DOI may place the applicant in possession of the property as soon as practicable to minimize the Government's expense of protection and maintenance of the property. As of the date the applicant takes possession of the property, or the date it is conveyed, whichever occurs first, the applicant must assume responsibility for care and handling and all risks of loss or damage to the property, and has all obligations and liabilities of ownership. DOI must furnish the disposal agency two conformed copies of deeds, leases, or other instruments conveying property under 40 U.S.C. 550(e) and related documents containing reservations, restrictions, or conditions regulating the future use, maintenance or transfer of the property.

§ 102–75.675 What responsibilities does the grantee or recipient of the property have in accomplishing or completing the transfer?

Where appropriate, the disposal agency may make the assignment subject to DOI requiring the grantee or recipient to bear the cost of any out-of-pocket expenses necessary to accomplish the transfer, such as for surveys, fencing, security of the remaining property, or otherwise.

§ 102–75.680 What information must be included in the deed of conveyance of any surplus property transferred for public park or recreation purposes?

The deed of conveyance of any surplus real property transferred for public park and recreation purposes under 40 U.S.C. 550(e) must require that the property be used and maintained for the purpose for which it was conveyed in perpetuity. In the event that the property ceases to be used or maintained for that purpose, all or any portion of such property will in its existing condition, at the option of the United States, revert to the United States. The deed of conveyance may contain additional terms, reservations, restrictions, and conditions determined by the Secretary of the Interior to be necessary to safeguard the interests of the United States.

§ 102–75.685 Who is responsible for enforcing compliance with the terms and conditions of the transfer of property used for public park or recreation purposes?

The Secretary of the Interior is responsible for enforcing compliance with the terms and conditions of transfer. The Secretary of the Interior is also responsible for reforming, correcting, or amending any transfer instrument; granting releases; and for recapturing any property following the provisions of 40 U.S.C. 550(b). These actions are subject to the approval of the head of the disposal agency. DOI must notify the head of the disposal agency of its intent to take or recapture the property. The notice must identify the property affected and describe in detail the proposed action, including the reasons for the proposed action.

§ 102–75.690 What happens if property that was transferred for use as a public park or recreation area is revested in the United States by reason of noncompliance with the terms or conditions of disposal, or for other cause?

DOI must notify the appropriate GSA regional office immediately by letter when title to property transferred for use as a public park or recreation area is to be revested in the United States for noncompliance with the terms or conditions of disposal or for other cause. The notification must cite the legal and administrative actions that DOI must take to obtain full title and possession of the property. In addition, it must include an adequate description of the property, using the Report of Excess Real Property (Standard Form 118) and the appropriate schedules. After receiving notice from DOI that title to the property is proposed for revesting, GSA will review the statement and determine if title should be revested. If GSA, in consultation with DOI, determines that the property should be revested, DOI must submit a Standard Form 118 to GSA. GSA will review and act upon the Standard Form 118, if acceptable. However, the grantee must provide protection and maintenance for the property until the title reverts to the Federal Government, including the period of any notice of intent to revert. Such protection and maintenance must, at a minimum, conform to the standards prescribed in the GSA Customer Guide to Real Property Disposal.

PROPERTY FOR DISPLACED PERSONS

§ 102–75.695 Who can receive surplus real property for the purpose of providing replacement housing for persons who are to be displaced by Federal or Federally assisted projects?

Section 218 of the Uniform Relocation Assistance and Real Property Acquisition Policies Act of 1970, as amended, 42 U.S.C. 4638 (the Relocation Act), authorizes the disposal agency to transfer surplus real property to a State agency to provide replacement housing under title II of the Relocation Act for persons who are or will be displaced by Federal or Federally assisted projects.

§ 102–75.700 Which Federal agencies may solicit applications from eligible State agencies interested in acquiring the property to provide replacement housing for persons being displaced by Federal or Federally assisted projects?

After receiving the surplus notice, any Federal agency needing property for replacement housing for displaced persons may solicit applications from eligible State agencies.

§ 102–75.705 When must the Federal agency notify the disposal agency that an eligible State agency is interested in acquiring the property under section 218?

Federal agencies must notify the disposal agency within 30 calendar days after the date of the surplus notice, if an eligible State agency is interested in acquiring the property under section 218 of the Relocation Act.

§ 102–75.710 What responsibilities do landholding and disposal agencies have concerning properties used for providing replacement housing for persons who will be displaced by Federal or Federally assisted projects?

Both landholding and disposal agencies must cooperate, to the fullest extent possible, with Federal and State agency representatives in their inspection of the property and in furnishing information relating to the property.

§ 102–75.715 When can a Federal agency request transfer of the property to the selected State agency?

Federal agencies must advise the disposal agency and request transfer of the property to the selected State agency within 30 calendar days after the expiration of the 30–calendar day period specified in § 102–75.705.

§ 102–75.720 Is there a specific or preferred format for the transfer request and who should receive it?

Any request submitted by a Federal agency must be in the form of a letter addressed to the appropriate GSA Public Buildings Service (PBS) regional property disposal office.

§ 102–75.725 What does the transfer request contain?

Any transfer request must include—

(a) Identification of the property by name, location, and control number;

(b) The name and address of the specific State agency and a copy of the State agency's application or proposal;

(c) A certification by the appropriate Federal agency official that the property is required to house displaced persons authorized by section 218; that all

other options authorized under title II of the Relocation Act have been explored and replacement housing cannot be found or made available through those channels; and that the Federal or Federally assisted project cannot be accomplished unless the property is made available for replacement housing;

(d) Any special terms and conditions that the Federal agency deems necessary to include in conveyance instruments to ensure that the property is used for the intended purpose;

(e) The name and proposed location of the Federal or Federally assisted project that is creating the requirement;

(f) Purpose of the project;

(g) Citation of enabling legislation or authorization for the project, when appropriate;

(h) A detailed outline of steps taken to obtain replacement housing for displaced persons as authorized under title II of the Relocation Act; and

(i) Details of the arrangements that have been made to construct replacement housing on the surplus property and to ensure that displaced persons will be provided housing in the development.

§ 102–75.730 What happens if a Federal agency does not submit a transfer request to the disposal agency for property to be used for replacement housing for persons who will be displaced by Federal or Federally assisted projects?

If the disposal agency does not receive a request for assignment or transfer of the property under § 102–75.715, then the disposal agency must proceed with other appropriate disposal actions.

§ 102–75.735 What happens after the disposal agency receives the transfer request from the Federal agency?

If, after considering other uses for the property, the disposal agency determines that the property should be made available for replacement housing under section 218, it must transfer the property to the designated State agency on such terms and conditions as will protect the United States' interests, including the payment or the agreement to pay to the United States all amounts received by the State agency from any sale, lease, or other disposition of the property for such housing. The sale, lease, or other disposition of the property by the State agency must be at the fair market value as approved by the disposal agency, unless a compelling justification is offered for disposal of the property at less than fair market value. Disposal of the property at less than fair market value must also be approved by the disposal agency.

§ 102–75.740 Does the State agency have any responsibilities in helping to accomplish the transfer of the property?

Yes, the State agency is required to bear the costs of any out-of-pocket expenses necessary to accomplish the transfer, such as costs of surveys, fencing, or security of the remaining property.

§ 102–75.745 What happens if the property transfer request is not approved by the disposal agency?

If the request is not approved, the disposal agency must notify the Federal agency requesting the transfer. The disposal agency must furnish a copy of the notice of disapproval to the landholding agency.

PROPERTY FOR CORRECTIONAL FACILITY, LAW ENFORCEMENT, OR EMERGENCY MANAGEMENT RESPONSE PURPOSES

§ 102–75.750 Who is eligible to receive surplus real and related personal property for correctional facility, law enforcement, or emergency management response purposes?

Under 40 U.S.C. 553, the head of the disposal agency or designee may, in his or her discretion, convey, without monetary consideration, to any State, or to those governmental bodies named in the section; or to any political subdivision or instrumentality, surplus real and related personal property for—

(a) Correctional facility purposes, if the Attorney General has determined that the property is required for such purposes and has approved an appropriate program or project for the care or rehabilitation of criminal offenders;

(b) Law enforcement purposes, if the Attorney General has determined that the property is required for such purposes; or

(c) Emergency management response purposes, including fire and rescue services, if the Director of the Federal Emergency Management Agency (FEMA) has determined that the property is required for such purposes.

§ 102–75.755 Which Federal agencies must the disposal agency notify concerning the availability of surplus properties for correctional facility, law enforcement, or emergency management response purposes?

The disposal agency must provide prompt notification to the Office of Justice Programs (OJP), Department of Justice (DOJ), and FEMA that surplus property is available. The disposal agency's notice or notification must include a copy of the landholding agency's Report of Excess Real Property (Standard Form 118), with accompanying schedules.

§ 102–75.760 Who must the Office of Justice Programs (OJP) and the Federal Emergency Management Agency (FEMA) notify that surplus real property is available for correctional facility, law enforcement, or emergency management response purposes?

OJP or FEMA must send notices of availability to the appropriate State and local public agencies. The notices must state that OJP or FEMA, as appropriate, must coordinate and approve any planning involved in developing a comprehensive and coordinated plan of use and procurement for the property for correctional facility, law enforcement, or emergency management response use. The notice must also state that public agencies may obtain application forms and preparation instructions from OJP or FEMA.

§ 102–75.765 What does the term "law enforcement" mean?

The OJP defines "law enforcement" as "any activity involving the control or reduction of crime and juvenile delinquency, or enforcement of the criminal law, including investigative activities such as laboratory functions as well as training.''

§ 102–75.770 Is the disposal agency required to approve a determination by the Department of Justice (DOJ) that identifies surplus property for correctional facility use or for law enforcement use?

Yes, the disposal agency must approve a determination, under § 102–75.795, by DOJ that identifies surplus property required for correctional facility use or for law enforcement use before an eligible public agency can obtain such property for correctional facility or law enforcement use.

§ 102–75.775 Is the disposal agency required to approve a determination by FEMA that identifies surplus property for emergency management response use?

Yes, the disposal agency must approve a determination, under § 102–75.795, by FEMA that identifies surplus property required for emergency management response use before an eligible public agency can obtain such property for emergency management response use.

§ 102–75.780 When must DOJ or FEMA notify the disposal agency that an eligible applicant is interested in acquiring the property?

OJP or FEMA must notify the disposal agency within 30 calendar days after the date of the surplus notice, if there is an eligible applicant interested in acquiring the property. After that 30–calendar day period expires, OJP or FEMA then has another 30 days to review and approve an appropriate program and notify the disposal agency of the need for the property. If no application is approved, then OJP or FEMA must notify the disposal agency that there is no requirement for the property within the 30–calendar day period allotted for review and approval.

§ 102–75.785 What specifically must DOJ or FEMA address in the assignment request or recommendation that is submitted to the disposal agency?

Any determination that DOJ or FEMA submits to the disposal agency must provide complete information concerning the correctional facility, law enforcement, or emergency management response use, including—

(a) Identification of the property;

(b) Certification that the property is required for correctional facility, law enforcement, or emergency management response use;

(c) A copy of the approved application that defines the proposed plan of use; and

(d) The environmental impact of the proposed correctional facility, law enforcement, or emergency management response use.

§ 102–75.790 What responsibilities do landholding agencies and disposal agencies have concerning properties to be used for correctional facility, law enforcement, or emergency management response purposes?

Both landholding and disposal agencies must cooperate to the fullest extent possible with Federal and State agency representatives in their inspection of such property and in furnishing information relating to the property.

§ 102–75.795 What happens after the disposal agency receives the assignment request by DOJ or FEMA?

If, after considering other uses for the property, the disposal agency approves the assignment request by DOJ or FEMA, the disposal agency must convey the property to the appropriate grantee. The disposal agency must proceed with other disposal action if it does not approve the assignment request, if DOJ or FEMA does not submit an assignment request, or if the disposal agency does not receive the determination within the 30 calendar days specified in § 102–75.780. The disposal agency must notify OJP or FEMA 15 days prior to any announcement of a determination to either approve or disapprove an application for correctional, law enforcement, or emergency management response purposes and must furnish to OJP or FEMA a copy of the conveyance documents.

§ 102–75.800 What information must be included in the deed of conveyance?

The deed of conveyance of any surplus real property transferred under the provisions of 40 U.S.C. 553 must provide that all property be used and maintained for the purpose for which it was conveyed in perpetuity. If the property ceases to be used or maintained for that purpose, all or any portion of the property must, at the option of the United States, revert to the United States in its existing condition. The deed of conveyance may contain additional terms, reservations, restrictions, and conditions the Administrator of General Services determines to be necessary to safeguard the United States' interests.

§ 102–75.805 Who is responsible for enforcing compliance with the terms and conditions of the transfer of the property used for correctional facility, law enforcement, or emergency management response purposes?

The Administrator of General Services is responsible for enforcing compliance with the terms and conditions of disposals of property to be used for correctional facility, law enforcement, or emergency management response purposes. GSA is also responsible for reforming, correcting, or amending any disposal instrument; granting releases; and any action necessary for recapturing the property following the provisions of 40 U.S.C. 553(e).

§ 102–75.810 What responsibilities do OJP or FEMA have if they discover any information indicating a change in use of a transferred property?

Upon discovery of any information indicating a change in use, OJP or FEMA must—

(a) Notify GSA; and

(b) Upon request, make a redetermination of continued appropriateness of the use of a transferred property.

§ 102–75.815 What happens if property conveyed for correctional facility, law enforcement, or emergency management response purposes is found to be in noncompliance with the terms of the conveyance documents?

OJP or FEMA must, prior to the repossession, provide the appropriate GSA regional property disposal office with an accurate description of the real and related personal property involved. OJP or FEMA must use the Report of Excess Real Property (Standard Form 118), and the appropriate schedules for this purpose. After receiving a statement from OJP or FEMA that the title to the property is proposed for revesting, GSA will review the statement and determine if title should be revested. If GSA, in consultation with OJP or FEMA, determines that the property should be revested, OJP or FEMA must submit a Standard Form 118 to GSA. GSA will review and act upon the Standard Form 118, if acceptable. However, the grantee must provide protection and maintenance for the property until the title reverts to the Federal Government, including the period following any notice of intent to revert. Such protection and maintenance must, at a minimum, conform to the standards prescribed in the GSA Customer Guide to Real Property Disposal.

PROPERTY FOR PORT FACILITY USE

§ 102–75.820 Which Federal agency is eligible to receive surplus real and related personal property for the development or operation of a port facility?

Under 40 U.S.C. 554, the Administrator of General Services, the Secretary of the Department of Defense (in the case of property located at a military installation closed or realigned pursuant to a base closure law), or their designee, may assign to the Secretary of the Department of Transportation (DOT) for conveyance, without monetary consideration, to any State, or to governmental bodies, any political subdivision, municipality, or instrumentality, surplus real and related personal property, including buildings, fixtures, and equipment situated on the property, that DOT recommends as being needed for the development or operation of a port facility.

§ 102–75.825 Who must the disposal agency notify when surplus real and related personal property is available for port facility use?

The disposal agency must notify established State, regional or metropolitan clearinghouses and eligible public agencies that surplus real property is available for the development or operation of a port facility. The disposal agency must transmit a copy of the notice to DOT and a copy of the landholding agency's Report of Excess Real Property (Standard Form 118 and supporting schedules).

§ 102–75.830 What does the surplus notice contain?

Surplus notices to eligible public agencies must state—

(a) That public agencies must coordinate any planning involved in the development of the comprehensive and coordinated plan of use and procurement of property, with DOT, the Secretary of Labor, and the Secretary of Commerce;

(b) That any party interested in acquiring the property for use as a port facility must contact the Department of Transportation, Maritime Administration, for the application and instructions;

(c) That the disposal agency must approve a recommendation from DOT before it can assign the property to DOT (see § 102–75.905); and

(d) That any subsequent conveyance is subject to the approval of the head of the disposal agency as stipulated under 40 U.S.C. 554 and referenced in § 102–75.865.

§ 102–75.835 When must DOT notify the disposal agency that an eligible applicant is interested in acquiring the property?

DOT must notify the disposal agency within 30 calendar days after the date of the surplus notice if there is an eligible applicant interested in acquiring the property. After that 30–calendar day period expires, DOT then has another 30 calendar days to review and approve applications and notify the disposal agency of the need for the property. If no application is approved, then DOT must notify the disposal agency that there is no requirement for the property within the same 30–calendar day period allotted for review and approval.

§ 102–75.840 What action must the disposal agency take after an eligible public agency has submitted a plan of use for and an application to acquire a port facility property?

Whenever an eligible public agency has submitted a plan of use for a port facility requirement, the disposal agency must transmit two copies of the plan to DOT. DOT must either submit to the disposal agency, within 30 calendar days after the date the plan is transmitted, a recommendation for assignment of the property to DOT, or inform the disposal agency, within the 30–calendar day period, that a recommendation will not be made for assignment of the property to DOT.

§ 102–75.845 What must DOT address in the assignment recommendation submitted to the disposal agency?

Any assignment recommendation that DOT submits to the disposal agency must provide complete information concerning the contemplated port facility use, including—

(a) An identification of the property;

(b) An identification of the applicant;

(c) A copy of the approved application, which defines the proposed plan of use of the property;

(d) A statement that DOT's determination (that the property is located in an area of serious economic disruption) was made in consultation with the Secretary of Labor;

(e) A statement that DOT approved the economic development plan, associated with the plan of use of the property, in consultation with the Secretary of Commerce; and

(f) A copy of the explanatory statement, required under 40 U.S.C. 554(c)(2)(C).

§ 102–75.850 What responsibilities do landholding agencies have concerning properties to be used in the development or operation of a port facility?

Landholding agencies must cooperate to the fullest extent possible with DOT representatives and the Secretary of

Commerce in their inspection of such property, and with the Secretary of Labor in affirming that the property is in an area of serious economic disruption, and in furnishing any information relating to such property.

§ 102–75.855 What happens if DOT does not submit an assignment recommendation?

If DOT does not submit an assignment recommendation or if it is not received within 30 calendar days, the disposal agency must proceed with other disposal action.

§ 102–75.860 What happens after the disposal agency receives the assignment recommendation from DOT?

If, after considering other uses for the property, the disposal agency approves the assignment recommendation from DOT, the disposal agency must assign the property by letter or other document to DOT. If the disposal agency disapproves the recommendation, the disposal agency must likewise notify DOT. The disposal agency must furnish to the landholding agency a copy of the assignment, unless the landholding agency is also the disposal agency.

§ 102–75.865 What responsibilities does DOT have after receiving the disposal agency's assignment letter?

After receiving the assignment letter from the disposal agency, DOT must provide the disposal agency with a Notice of Proposed Transfer within 30 calendar days after the date of the assignment letter. If the disposal agency approves the proposed transfer within 30 calendar days of the receipt of the Notice of Proposed Transfer, DOT may prepare the conveyance documents and proceed with the conveyance. DOT must take all necessary actions to accomplish the conveyance within 15 calendar days after the expiration of the 30–calendar day period provided for the disposal agency to consider the notice. DOT must furnish the disposal agency two conformed copies of the instruments conveying property and all related documents containing restrictions or conditions regulating the future use, maintenance, or transfer of the property.

§ 102–75.870 Who is responsible for enforcing compliance with the terms and conditions of the port facility conveyance?

DOT is responsible for enforcing compliance with the terms and conditions of conveyance, including reforming, correcting, or amending any instrument of conveyance; granting releases; and taking any necessary actions to recapture the property following the provisions of 40 U.S.C. 554(f). Any of these actions are subject to the approval of the head of the disposal agency. DOT must notify the head of the disposal agency of its intent to take any proposed action, identify the property affected, and describe in detail the proposed action, including the reasons for the proposed action.

§ 102–75.875 What happens in the case of repossession by the United States under a reversion of title for non-compliance with the terms or conditions of conveyance?

In each case of a repossession by the United States, DOT must, at or prior to reversion of title, provide the appropriate GSA regional property disposal office, with a Report of Excess Real Property (Standard Form 118) and accompanying schedules. After receiving a statement from DOT that title to the property is proposed for revesting, GSA will review the statement and determine if title should be revested. If GSA, in consultation with DOT, determines that the property should be revested, DOT must submit a Standard Form 118 to GSA. GSA will review and act upon the Standard Form 118, if acceptable. However, the grantee must provide protection and maintenance for the property until the title reverts to the Federal Government, including the period following the notice of intent to revert. Such protection and maintenance must, at a minimum, conform to the standards prescribed in the GSA Customer Guide to Real Property Disposal.

NEGOTIATED SALES

§ 102–75.880 When may Executive agencies conduct negotiated sales?

Executive agencies may conduct negotiated sales only when—

(a) The estimated fair market value of the property does not exceed $15,000;

(b) Bid prices after advertising are unreasonable (for all or part of the property) or were not independently arrived at in open competition;

(c) The character or condition of the property or unusual circumstances make it impractical to advertise for competitive bids and the fair market value of the property and other satisfactory terms of disposal are obtainable by negotiation;

(d) The disposals will be to States, the Commonwealth of Puerto Rico, possessions, political subdivisions, or tax-supported agencies therein, and the estimated fair market value of the property and other satisfactory terms of disposal are obtainable by negotiation. Negotiated sales to public bodies can only be conducted if a public benefit, which would not be realized from a competitive sale, will result from the negotiated sale; or

(e) Negotiation is otherwise authorized by Chapter 5 of Subtitle I of Title 40 of the United States Code or other law, such as disposals of power transmission lines for public or cooperative power projects.

§102–75.885 What are the disposal agency's responsibilities concerning negotiated sales?

The disposal agency must—

(a) Obtain such competition as is feasible in all negotiations of disposals and contracts for disposal of surplus property; and

(b) Prepare and transmit an explanatory statement if the fair market value of the property exceeds $100,000, identifying the circumstances of each disposal by negotiation for any real property specified in 40 U.S.C. 545(e), to the appropriate committees of the Congress in advance of such disposal.

§102–75.890 What clause must be in the offer to purchase and conveyance documents for negotiated sales to public agencies?

Disposal agencies must include in the offer to purchase and conveyance documents an excess profits clause, which usually runs for 3 years, to eliminate the potential for windfall profits to public agencies. This clause states that, if the purchaser should sell or enter into agreements to sell the property within 3 years from the date of title transfer by the Federal Government, all proceeds in excess of the purchaser's costs will be remitted to the Federal Government.

§102–75.895 What wording must generally be in the excess profits clause that is required in the offer to purchase and in the conveyance document?

The wording of the excess profits clause should generally be as follows:

Excess Profits Covenant for Negotiated Sales to Public Bodies

(a) This covenant shall run with the land for a period of 3 years from the date of conveyance. With respect to the property described in this deed, if at any time within a 3-year period from the date of transfer of title by the Grantor, the Grantee, or its successors or assigns, shall sell or enter into agreements to sell the property, either in a single transaction or in a series of transactions, it is covenanted and agreed that all proceeds received or to be received in excess of the Grantee's or a subsequent seller's actual allowable costs will be remitted to the Grantor. In the event of a sale of less than the entire property, actual allowable costs will be apportioned to the property based on a fair and reasonable determination by the Grantor.

(b) For purposes of this covenant, the Grantee's or a subsequent seller's allowable costs shall include the following:

(1) The purchase price of the real property.

(2) The direct costs actually incurred and paid for improvements that serve only the property, including road construction, storm and sanitary sewer construction, other public facilities or utility construction, building rehabilitation and demolition, landscaping, grading, and other site or public improvements.

(3) The direct costs actually incurred and paid for design and engineering services with respect to the improvements described in (b)(2) of this section.

(4) The finance charges actually incurred and paid in conjunction with loans obtained to meet any of the allowable costs enumerated above.

(c) None of the allowable costs described in paragraph (b) of this section will be deductible if defrayed by Federal grants or if used as matching funds to secure Federal grants.

(d) To verify compliance with the terms and conditions of this covenant, the Grantee, or its successors or assigns, shall submit an annual report for each of the subsequent 3 years to the Grantor on the anniversary date of this deed. Each report will identify the property involved in this transaction and will contain such of the following items of information as are applicable at the time of submission:

(1) A statement indicating whether or not a resale has been made.

(2) A description of each portion of the property that has been resold.

(3) The sale price of each such resold portion.

(4) The identity of each purchaser.

(5) The proposed land use.

(6) An enumeration of any allowable costs incurred and paid that would offset any realized profit.

(e) The Grantor may monitor the property and inspect records related thereto to ensure compliance with the terms and conditions of this covenant and may take any actions that it deems reasonable and prudent to recover any excess profits realized through the resale of the property.

§ 102–75.900 What is a negotiated sale for economic development purposes?

A negotiated sale for economic development purposes means that the public body purchasing the property will develop or make substantial improvements to the property with the intention of reselling or leasing the property in parcels to users to advance the community's economic benefit. This type of negotiated sale is acceptable where the expected public benefits to the community are greater than the anticipated proceeds derived from a competitive public sale.

EXPLANATORY STATEMENTS FOR NEGOTIATED SALES

§ 102–75.905 When must the disposal agency prepare an explanatory statement?

The disposal agency must prepare an explanatory statement of the circumstances of each of the following proposed disposals by negotiation:

(a) Any real property that has an estimated fair market value in excess of $100,000, except that any real property disposed of by lease or exchange is subject only to paragraphs (b) through (d) of this section.

(b) Any real property disposed of by lease for a term of 5 years or less, if the estimated fair annual rent is in excess of $100,000 for any of such years.

(c) Any real property disposed of by lease for a term of more than 5 years, if the total estimated rent over the term of the lease is in excess of $100,000.

(d) Any real property or real and related personal property disposed of by exchange, regardless of value, or any property disposed in which any part of the consideration is real property.

§ 102–75.910 Are there any exceptions to this policy of preparing explanatory statements?

Yes, the disposal agency is not required to prepare an explanatory statement for property authorized to be disposed of without advertising by any provision of law other than 40 U.S.C. 545.

§ 102–75.915 Do disposal agencies need to retain a copy of the explanatory statement?

Yes, disposal agencies must retain a copy of the explanatory statement in their files.

§ 102–75.920 Where is the explanatory statement sent?

Disposal agencies must submit each explanatory statement to the Administrator of General Services for review and transmittal by letter from the Administrator of General Services to the Senate Committee on Governmental Affairs and the House Committee on Government Reform and any other appropriate committees of the Senate and House of Representatives. Disposal agencies must include in the submission to the Administrator of General Services any supporting data that may be relevant and necessary for evaluating the proposed action.

§ 102–75.925 Is GSA required to furnish the disposal agency with the explanatory statement's transmittal letter sent to Congress?

Yes, GSA must furnish copies of its transmittal letters to the committees of the Congress (see § 102–75.920) to the disposal agency.

§ 102–75.930 What happens if there is no objection by an appropriate committee or subcommittee of Congress concerning the proposed negotiated sale?

If there is no objection, the disposal agency may consummate the sale on or after 35 days from the date the Administrator of General Services transmitted the explanatory statement to the committees. If there is an objection, the disposal agency must resolve objections with the appropriate Congressional committee or subcommittee before consummating the sale.

PUBLIC SALES

§ 102–75.935 What are disposal agencies' responsibilities concerning public sales?

Disposal agencies must make available by competitive public sale any surplus property that is not disposed of by public benefit discount conveyance or by negotiated sale. Awards must be made to the responsible bidder whose bid will be most advantageous to the Government, price and other factors considered.

DISPOSING OF EASEMENTS

§ 102–75.936 When can an agency dispose of an easement?

When the use, occupancy or control of an easement is no longer needed, agencies may release the easement to the owner of the land subject to the easement (servient estate).

§ 102–75.937 Can an easement be released or disposed of at no cost?

Yes. However, agencies must consider the Government's cost of acquiring the easement and other factors when determining if the easement will be disposed of with or without monetary or other consideration. If the easement was acquired at substantial consideration, agencies must—

(a) Determine the easement's fair market value (estimate the fair market value of the fee land without the easement and with the easement then compute the difference or compute the damage the easement caused to the fee land); and

(b) Negotiate the highest obtainable price with the owner of the servient estate to release the easement.

§ 102–75.938 May the easement and the land that benefited from the easement (dominant estate) be disposed of separately?

Yes. If the easement is no longer needed in connection with the dominant estate, it may be disposed of separately to the owner of the servient estate. However, if the dominant estate is also surplus, the easement should be disposed of with the dominant estate.

GRANTING EASEMENTS

§ 102–75.939 When can agencies grant easements?

Agencies may grant easements in, on, or over Government-owned real property upon determining that the easement will not adversely impact the Government's interests.

§ 102–75.940 Can agencies grant easements at no cost?

Yes. Easements may be granted with or without monetary or other consideration, including any interest in real property.

§ 102–75.941 Does an agency retain responsibility for the easement?

Agencies may relinquish legislative jurisdiction as deemed necessary and desirable to the State where the real property containing the easement is located.

§ 102–75.942 What must agencies consider when granting easements?

Agencies must—

(a) Determine the easement's fair market value; and

(b) Determine the remaining property's reduced or enhanced value because of the easement.

§ 102–75.943 What happens if granting an easement will reduce the value of the property?

If the easement will reduce the property's value, agencies must grant the easement for the amount by which the property's fair market value is decreased unless the agency determines that the Government's best interests are served by granting the easement at either reduced or without monetary or other consideration.

Non-Federal Interim Use of Surplus Property

§ 102-75.944 **Can landholding agencies outlease surplus real property for non-Federal interim use?**

Yes, landholding agencies who possess independent authority to outlease property may allow organizations to use surplus real property awaiting disposal using either a lease or permit, only when—

(a) The lease or permit does not exceed one year and is revocable with not more than a 30-day notice by the disposal agency;

(b) The use and occupancy will not interfere with, delay, or impede the disposal of the property; and

(c) The agency executing the agreement is responsible for the servicing of such property.

Subpart D—Management of Excess and Surplus Real Property

§ 102-75.945 **What is GSA's policy concerning the physical care, handling, protection, and maintenance of excess and surplus real property and related personal property?**

GSA's policy is to—

(a) Manage excess and surplus real property, including related personal property, by providing only those minimum services necessary to preserve the Government's interest and realizable value of the property considered;

(b) Place excess and surplus real property in productive use through interim utilization, provided, that such temporary use and occupancy do not interfere with, delay, or impede its transfer to a Federal agency or disposal; and

(c) Render safe or destroy aspects of excess and surplus real property that are dangerous to the public health or safety.

Taxes and Other Obligations

§ 102-75.950 **Who has the responsibility for paying property-related obligations pending transfer or disposal of the property?**

Except as otherwise provided in § 102-75.230, the landholding agency is still responsible for any and all operational costs and expenses or other property-related obligations pending transfer or disposal of the property.

Decontamination

§ 102-75.955 **Who is responsible for decontaminating excess and surplus real property?**

The landholding agency is responsible for all expenses to the Government and for the supervision of the decontamination of excess and surplus real property that has been contaminated with hazardous materials of any sort. Extreme care must be exercised in the decontamination, management, and disposal of contaminated property in order to prevent such properties from becoming a hazard to the general public. The landholding agency must inform the disposal agency of any and all hazards involved relative to such property to protect the general public from hazards and to limit the Government's liability resulting from disposal or mishandling of hazardous materials.

Improvements or Alterations

§ 102-75.960 **May landholding agencies make improvements or alterations to excess or surplus property in those cases where disposal is otherwise not feasible?**

Yes, landholding agencies may make improvements or alterations that involve rehabilitation, reconditioning, conversion, completion, additions, and replacements in excess or surplus structures, utilities, installations, and land improvements, in those cases where disposal cannot be accomplished without such improvements or alterations. However, agencies must not enter into commitments concerning improvements or alterations without GSA's prior approval.

Protection and Maintenance

§ 102-75.965 **Who must perform the protection and maintenance of excess and surplus real property pending transfer to another Federal agency or disposal?**

The landholding agency remains responsible and accountable for excess and surplus real property, including related personal property, and must perform the protection and maintenance of such property pending transfer to another Federal agency or disposal. Guidelines for protection and maintenance of excess and surplus real property are in the GSA Customer Guide to Real Property Disposal. The landholding agency is responsible for complying with the requirements of the National Oil and Hazardous Substances Pollution Contingency Plan and initiating or cooperating with others in the actions prescribed for the prevention, containment, or remedy of hazardous conditions.

§ 102–75.970 How long is the landholding agency responsible for the expense of protection and maintenance of excess and surplus real property pending its transfer or disposal?

Generally, the landholding agency is responsible for the cost of protection and maintenance of excess or surplus property until the property is transferred or disposed, but not more than 15 months. However, the landholding agency is responsible for providing and funding protection and maintenance during any delay beyond that 15 month period, if the landholding agency—

(a) Requests deferral of the disposal beyond the 15 month period;

(b) Continues to occupy the property beyond the 15 month period to the detriment of orderly disposal; or

(c) Otherwise takes actions that result in a delay in the disposition beyond the 15 months.

§ 102–75.975 What happens if the property is not conveyed or disposed of during this time frame?

If the property is not transferred to a Federal agency or disposed of during the 15-month period mentioned in § 102–75.970, then the disposal agency must pay or reimburse the landholding agency for protection and maintenance expenses incurred from the expiration date of said time period to final disposal, unless—

(a) There is no written agreement between the landholding agency and the disposal agency specifying the maximum amount of protection and maintenance expenses for which the disposal agency is responsible;

(b) The disposal agency's appropriation, as authorized by Congress, does not contain a provision to allow for payment and/or reimbursement of protection and maintenance expenses; or

(c) The delay is caused by an Executive agency's request for an exception from the 100 percent reimbursement requirement specified in § 102–75.205. In this latter case, the requesting agency becomes responsible for protection and maintenance expenses incurred because of the delay.

§ 102–75.980 Who is responsible for protection and maintenance expenses if there is no written agreement or no Congressional appropriation to the disposal agency?

If there is no written agreement (between the landholding agency and the disposal agency) or no Congressional appropriation to the disposal agency, the landholding agency is responsible for all protection and maintenance expenses, without any right of contribution or reimbursement from the disposal agency.

ASSISTANCE IN DISPOSITION

§ 102–75.985 Is the landholding agency required to assist the disposal agency in the disposition process?

Yes, the landholding agency must cooperate with the disposal agency in showing the property to prospective transferees or purchasers. Unless extraordinary expenses are incurred in showing the property, the landholding agency must absorb the entire cost of such actions.

Subpart E—Abandonment, Destruction, or Donation to Public Bodies

§ 102–75.990 May Federal agencies abandon, destroy, or donate to public bodies real property?

Yes, subject to the restrictions in this subpart, any Federal agency having control of real property that has no commercial value or for which the estimated cost of continued care and handling exceeds the estimated proceeds from its sale, may—

(a) Abandon or destroy Government-owned improvements and related personal property located on privately-owned land;

(b) Destroy Government-owned improvements and related personal property located on Government-owned land (abandonment of such property is not authorized); or

(c) Donate to public bodies any Government-owned real property (land and/or improvements and related personal property), or interests therein.

DANGEROUS PROPERTY

§ 102–75.995 May Federal agencies dispose of dangerous property?

No, property that is dangerous to public health or safety must be made harmless or have adequate safeguards in place before it can be abandoned, destroyed, or donated to public bodies.

DETERMINATIONS

§ 102–75.1000 How is the decision made to abandon, destroy, or donate property?

No property shall be abandoned, destroyed, or donated by a Federal agency under § 102–75.990, unless a duly authorized official of that agency determines, in writing, that—

(a) The property has no commercial value; or

(b) The estimated cost of its continued care and handling exceeds the estimated proceeds from its sale.

§ 102–75.1005 Who can make the determination within the Federal agency on whether a property can be abandoned, destroyed, or donated?

Only a duly authorized official of that agency not directly accountable for the subject property can make the determination.

§ 102–75.1010 When is a reviewing authority required to approve the determination concerning a property that is to be abandoned, destroyed, or donated?

A reviewing authority must approve determinations made under § 102–75.1000 before any such disposal, whenever all the property proposed to be disposed of by a Federal agency has a current estimated fair market value of more than $50,000.

RESTRICTIONS

§ 102–75.1015 Are there any restrictions on Federal agencies concerning property donations to public bodies?

Yes, Federal agencies must obtain prior concurrence of GSA before donating to public bodies—

(a) Improvements on land or related personal property having a current estimated fair market value in excess of $250,000; and

(b) Land, regardless of cost.

DISPOSAL COSTS

§ 102–75.1020 Are public bodies ever required to pay the disposal costs associated with donated property?

Yes, any public body receiving donated improvements on land or related personal property must pay the disposal costs associated with the donation, such as dismantling, removal, and the cleaning up of the premises.

ABANDONMENT AND DESTRUCTION

§ 102–75.1025 When can a Federal agency abandon or destroy improvements on land or related personal property in lieu of donating it to a public body?

A Federal agency may not abandon or destroy improvements on land or related personal property unless a duly authorized official of that agency finds, in writing, that donating the property is not feasible. This written finding is in addition to the determination prescribed in §§ 102–75.1000, 102–75.1005, and 102–75.1010. If donating the property becomes feasible at any time prior to actually abandoning or destroying the property, the Federal agency must donate it.

§ 102–75.1030 May Federal agencies abandon or destroy property in any manner they decide?

No, Federal agencies may not abandon or destroy property in a manner that is detrimental or dangerous to public health or safety or that will infringe on the rights of other persons.

§ 102–75.1035 Are there any restrictions on Federal agencies concerning the abandonment or destruction of improvements on land or related personal property?

Yes, GSA must concur in an agency's abandonment or destruction of improvements on land or related personal property prior to abandoning or destroying such improvements on land or related personal property—

(a) That are of permanent type construction; or

(b) The retention of which would enhance the value of the underlying land, if it were to be made available for sale or lease.

§ 102–75.1040 May Federal agencies abandon or destroy improvements on land or related personal property before public notice is given of such proposed abandonment or destruction?

Except as provided in § 102–75.1045, a Federal agency must not abandon or destroy improvements on land or related personal property until after it has given public notice of the proposed abandonment or destruction. This notice must be given in the area in which the property is located, must contain a general description of the property to be abandoned or destroyed, and must include an offering of the property for sale. A copy of the notice must be given to the GSA regional property disposal office for the region in which the property is located.

§ 102–75.1045 Are there exceptions to the policy that requires public notice be given before Federal agencies abandon or destroy improvements on land or related personal property?

Yes, property can be abandoned or destroyed without public notice if—

(a) Its value is so low or the cost of its care and handling so great that retaining the property to post public notice is clearly not economical;

(b) Health, safety, or security considerations require its immediate abandonment or destruction; or

(c) The assigned mission of the agency might be jeopardized by the delay, and a duly authorized Federal agency official finds in writing, with respect to paragraph (a), (b), or (c) of this section,

and a reviewing authority approves this finding. The finding must be in addition to the determinations prescribed in §§ 102–75.1000, 102–75.1005, 102–75.1010, and 102–75.1025.

§ 102–75.1050 Is there any property for which this subpart does not apply?

Yes, this subpart does not apply to surplus property assigned for disposal to educational or public health institutions pursuant to 40 U.S.C. 550(c) or (d).

Subpart F—Delegations

DELEGATION TO THE DEPARTMENT OF DEFENSE (DoD)

§ 102–75.1055 What is the policy governing delegations of real property disposal authority to the Secretary of Defense?

GSA delegates to the Secretary of Defense the authority to determine that Federal agencies do not need Department of Defense controlled excess real property and related personal property having a total estimated fair market value, including all the component units of the property, of less than $50,000; and to dispose of the property by means deemed most advantageous to the United States.

§ 102–75.1060 What must the Secretary of Defense do before determining that DoD-controlled excess real property and related personal property is not required for the needs of any Federal agency and prior to disposal?

The Secretary must conduct a Federal screening to determine that there is no further Federal need or requirement for the property.

§ 102–75.1065 When using a delegation of real property disposal authority under this subpart, is DoD required to report excess property to GSA?

No, although the authority in this delegation must be used following the provisions of Chapter 5 of Subtitle I of Title 40 of the United States Code and its implementing regulations.

§ 102-75.1070 Can this delegation of authority to the Secretary of Defense be redelegated?

Yes, the Secretary of Defense may redelegate the authority delegated in § 102-75.1055 to any officer or employee of the Department of Defense.

DELEGATION TO THE DEPARTMENT OF AGRICULTURE (USDA)

§ 102-75.1075 What is the policy governing delegations of real property disposal authority to the Secretary of Agriculture?

GSA delegates authority to the Secretary of Agriculture to determine that Federal agencies do not need USDA-controlled excess real property and related personal property having a total estimated fair market value, including all the component units of the property, of less than $50,000; and to dispose of the property by means deemed most advantageous to the United States.

§ 102-75.1080 What must the Secretary of Agriculture do before determining that USDA-controlled excess real property and related personal property is not required for the needs of any Federal agency and prior to disposal?

The Secretary must conduct a Federal screening to determine that there is no further Federal need or requirement for the property.

§ 102-75.1085 When using a delegation of real property disposal authority under this subpart, is USDA required to report excess property to GSA?

No, although the authority in this delegation must be used following the provisions of Chapter 5 of Subtitle I of Title 40 of the United States Code and its implementing regulations.

§ 102-75.1090 Can this delegation of authority to the Secretary of Agriculture be redelegated?

Yes, the Secretary of Agriculture may redelegate authority delegated in § 102-75.1075 to any officer or employee of the Department of Agriculture.

DELEGATION TO THE DEPARTMENT OF THE INTERIOR

§ 102-75.1095 What is the policy governing delegations of authority to the Secretary of the Interior?

GSA delegates authority to the Secretary of the Interior to—

(a) Maintain custody, control, and accountability for mineral resources in, on, or under Federal real property that the Administrator or his designee occasionally designates as currently utilized, excess, or surplus to the Government's needs;

(b) Dispose of mineral resources by lease and to administer those leases that are made; and

(c) Determine that Federal agencies do not need Department of the Interior controlled excess real property and related personal property with an estimated fair market value, including all components of the property, of less than $50,000; and to dispose of the property by means most advantageous to the United States.

§ 102-75.1100 Can this delegation of authority to the Secretary of the Interior be redelegated?

Yes, the Secretary of the Interior may redelegate this authority to any officer, official, or employee of the Department of the Interior.

§ 102-75.1105 What other responsibilities does the Secretary of the Interior have under this delegation of authority?

Under this authority, the Secretary of the Interior is responsible for—

(a) Maintaining proper inventory records, as head of the landholding agency;

(b) Monitoring the minerals as necessary, as head of the landholding agency, to prevent unauthorized mining or removal of the minerals;

(c) Securing any appraisals deemed necessary by the Secretary;

(d) Coordinating with all surface landowners, Federal or otherwise, to prevent unnecessary interference with the surface use;

(e) Restoring damaged or disturbed lands after removal of the mineral deposits;

(f) Notifying the Administrator of General Services when the disposal of all marketable mineral deposits is complete;

(g) Complying with the applicable environmental laws and regulations, including the National Environmental Policy Act of 1969, as amended (42 U.S.C. 4321 *et seq.*); and the implementing regulations issued by the Council on Environmental Quality (40 CFR part 1500); section 106 of the National Historic Preservation Act of 1966, as amended (16 U.S.C. 470f); and the Coastal Zone Management Act of 1972 (16 U.S.C. 1451 *et seq.*) and the Department of Commerce implementing regulations (15 CFR parts 923 and 930);

(h) Forwarding promptly to the Administrator of General Services copies of any agreements executed under this authority; and

(i) Providing the Administrator of General Services with an annual accounting of the proceeds received from leases executed under this authority.

NATIVE AMERICAN-RELATED
DELEGATIONS

§ 102–75.1110 What is the policy governing delegations of authority to the Secretary of the Interior, the Secretary of Health and Human Services, and the Secretary of Education for property used in the administration of any Native American-related functions?

GSA delegates authority to the Secretary of the Interior, the Secretary of Health and Human Services, and the Secretary of Education to transfer and to retransfer to each other, upon request, any of the property of each agency that is being used and will continue to be used in the administration of any functions relating to the Native Americans. The term property, as used in this delegation, includes real property and such personal property as the Secretary making the transfer or retransfer determines to be related personal property. The Departments must exercise the authority conferred in this section following applicable GSA regulations issued pursuant to the provisions of Chapter 5 of Subtitle I of Title 40 of the United States Code.

§ 102–75.1115 Are there any limitations or restrictions on this delegation of authority?

This authority must be used only in connection with property that the appropriate Secretary determines—

(a) Comprises a functional unit;

(b) Is located within the United States; and

(c) Has an acquisition cost of $100,000 or less, provided that the transfer or retransfer does not include property situated in any area that is recognized as an urban area or place as identified by the most recent decennial census.

§ 102–75.1120 Does the property have to be Federally screened?

No, screening is not required because it would accomplish no useful purpose, since the property subject to transfer or retransfer will continue to be used in the administration of any functions relating to Native Americans.

§ 102–75.1125 Can the transfer/retransfer under this delegation be at no cost or without consideration?

Yes, transfers/retransfers under this delegation can be at no cost or without consideration, except—

(a) Where funds programmed and appropriated for acquisition of the property are available to the Secretary requesting the transfer or retransfer; or

(b) Whenever reimbursement at fair market value is required by subpart B of this part (entitled "Utilization of Excess Real Property").

§ 102–75.1130 What action must the Secretary requesting the transfer take where funds were not programmed and appropriated for acquisition of the property?

The Secretary requesting the transfer or retransfer must certify in writing that no funds are available to acquire the property. The Secretary transferring or retransferring the property may make any determination necessary that would otherwise be made by GSA to carry out the authority contained in this delegation.

§ 102–75.1135 May this delegation of authority to the Secretary of the Interior, the Secretary of Health and Human Services, and the Secretary of Education be redelegated?

Yes, the Secretary of the Interior, the Secretary of Health and Human Services, and the Secretary of Education may redelegate any of the authority contained in this delegation to any officers or employees of their respective departments.

Subpart G—Conditional Gifts of Real Property to Further the Defense Effort

§ 102–75.1140 What is the policy governing the acceptance or rejection of a conditional gift of real property for a particular defense purpose?

Any Federal agency receiving an offer of a conditional gift of real property for a particular defense purpose within the purview of Chapter 582–Public Law 537 (July 27, 1954) must notify the appropriate GSA regional property disposal office and must submit to GSA a recommendation indicating whether the Government should accept or reject the gift. Nothing in this subpart shall be construed as applicable to the acceptance of gifts under the provisions of other laws. Following receipt of such notification and recommendation, GSA must—

(a) Consult with the interested agencies before it may accept or reject such conditional gifts of real property on behalf of the United States or before it transfers such conditional gifts of real property to an agency; and

(b) Advise the donor and the agencies concerned of the action taken with respect to acceptance or rejection of the conditional gift and of its final disposition.

§ 102–75.1145 What action must the Federal agency receiving an offer of a conditional gift take?

Prior to notifying the appropriate GSA regional property disposal office, the receiving Federal agency must acknowledge receipt of the offer in writing and advise the donor that the offer will be referred to the appropriate GSA regional property disposal office. The receiving agency must not indicate acceptance or rejection of the gift on behalf of the United States at this time. The receiving agency must provide a copy of the acknowledgment with the notification and recommendation to the GSA regional property disposal office.

§ 102–75.1150 What happens to the gift if GSA determines it to be acceptable?

When GSA determines that the gift is acceptable and can be accepted and used in the form in which it was offered, GSA must designate an agency and transfer the gift without reimbursement to this agency to use as the donor intended.

§ 102–75.1155 May an acceptable gift of property be converted to money?

GSA can determine whether or not a gift of property can and should be converted to money. After conversion, GSA must deposit the funds with the Treasury Department for transfer to an appropriate account that will best effectuate the intent of the donor, in accordance with Treasury Department procedures.

Subpart H—Use of Federal Real Property to Assist the Homeless

DEFINITIONS

§ 102–75.1160 What definitions apply to this subpart?

Applicant means any representative of the homeless that has submitted an application to the Department of Health and Human Services to obtain use of a particular suitable property to assist the homeless.

Checklist or property checklist means the form developed by HUD for use by landholding agencies to report the information to be used by HUD in making determinations of suitability.

Classification means a property's designation as unutilized, underutilized, excess, or surplus.

Day means one calendar day, including weekends and holidays.

Eligible organization means a State, unit of local government, or a private, non-profit organization that provides assistance to the homeless, and that is authorized by its charter or by State law to enter into an agreement with the Federal Government for use of real property for the purposes of this subpart. Representatives of the homeless interested in receiving a deed for a particular piece of surplus Federal property must be section 501(c)(3) tax exempt.

Excess property means any property under the control of any Executive agency that is not required for the agency's needs or the discharge of its responsibilities, as determined by the head of the agency pursuant to 40 U.S.C. 524.

GSA means the United States General Services Administration.

HHS means the United States Department of Health and Human Services.

Homeless means—

(1) An individual or family that lacks a fixed, regular, and adequate nighttime residence; or

(2) An individual or family that has a primary nighttime residence that is—

(i) A supervised publicly or privately operated shelter designed to provide temporary living accommodations (including welfare hotels, congregate shelters, and transitional housing for the mentally ill);

(ii) An institution that provides a temporary residence for individuals intended to be institutionalized; or

(iii) A public or private place not designed for, or ordinarily used as, a regular sleeping accommodation for human beings. This term does not include any individual imprisoned or otherwise detained under an Act of Congress or a State law.

HUD means the United States Department of Housing and Urban Development.

ICH means the Interagency Council on the Homeless.

Landholding agency means a Federal department or agency with statutory authority to control real property.

Lease means an agreement between either HHS for surplus property, or landholding agencies in the case of non-excess properties or properties subject to the Base Closure and Realignment Act (Pub. L. 100–526, 10 U.S.C. 2687), and the applicant, giving rise to the relationship of lessor and lessee for the use of Federal real property for a term of at least one year under the conditions set forth in the lease document.

Non-profit organization means an organization, no part of the net earnings of which inures to the benefit of any member, founder, contributor, or individual; that has a voluntary board; that has an accounting system or has designated an entity that will maintain a functioning accounting system for the organization in accordance with generally accepted accounting procedures; and that practices non-discrimination in the provision of assistance.

Permit means a license granted by a landholding agency to use unutilized or underutilized property for a specific amount of time under terms and conditions determined by the landholding agency.

Property means real property consisting of vacant land or buildings, or a portion thereof, that is excess, surplus, or designated as unutilized or underutilized in surveys by the heads of landholding agencies conducted pursuant to 40 U.S.C. 524.

Regional Homeless Coordinator means a regional coordinator of the Interagency Council on the Homeless.

Representative of the Homeless means a State or local government agency, or private non-profit organization that provides, or proposes to provide, services to the homeless.

Screen means the process by which GSA surveys Federal agencies, or State, local and non-profit entities, to determine if any such entity has an interest in using excess Federal property to carry out a particular agency mission or a specific public use.

State Homeless Coordinator means a State contact person designated by a State to receive and disseminate information and communications received from the Interagency Council on the Homeless in accordance with the McKinney-Vento Homeless Assistance Act of 1987, as amended (42 U.S.C. 11320).

Suitable property means that HUD has determined that a particular property satisfies the criteria listed in § 102–75.1185.

Surplus property means any excess real property not required by any Federal landholding agency for its needs or the discharge of its responsibilities, as determined by the Administrator of GSA.

Underutilized means an entire property or portion thereof, with or without improvements, which is used only at irregular periods or intermittently by the accountable landholding agency for current program purposes of that agency, or which is used for current program purposes that can be satisfied with only a portion of the property.

Unsuitable property means that HUD has determined that a particular property does not satisfy the criteria in § 102–75.1185.

Unutilized property means an entire property or portion thereof, with or without improvements, not occupied for current program purposes for the accountable Executive agency or occupied in caretaker status only.

APPLICABILITY

§ 102–75.1165 **What is the applicability of this subpart?**

(a) This part applies to Federal real property that has been designated by Federal landholding agencies as unutilized, underutilized, excess, or surplus, and is, therefore, subject to the provisions of title V of the McKinney-Vento Homeless Assistance Act, as amended (42 U.S.C. 11411).

(b) The following categories of properties are not subject to this subpart (regardless of whether they may be unutilized or underutilized):

(1) Machinery and equipment.

(2) Government-owned, contractor-operated machinery, equipment, land, and other facilities reported excess for sale only to the using contractor and subject to a continuing military requirement.

(3) Properties subject to special legislation directing a particular action.

(4) Properties subject to a court order.

(5) Property not subject to survey requirements of Executive Order 12512 (April 29, 1985).

(6) Mineral rights interests.

(7) Air Space interests.

(8) Indian Reservation land subject to 40 U.S.C. 523.

(9) Property interests subject to reversion.

(10) Easements.

(11) Property purchased in whole or in part with Federal funds, if title to the property is not held by a Federal landholding agency as defined in this part.

COLLECTING THE INFORMATION

§ 102–75.1170 **How will information be collected?**

(a) *Canvass of landholding agencies.* On a quarterly basis, HUD will canvass landholding agencies to collect information about property described as unutilized, underutilized, excess, or surplus in surveys conducted by the agencies under 40 U.S.C. 524, Executive Order 12512, and subpart H of this part. Each canvass will collect information on properties not previously reported and about property reported previously the status or classification of which has changed or for which any of the information reported on the property checklist has changed.

(1) HUD will request descriptive information on properties sufficient to make a reasonable determination, under the criteria described below, of the suitability of a property for use as a facility to assist the homeless.

(2) HUD will direct landholding agencies to respond to requests for information within 25 days of receipt of such requests.

(b) *Agency annual report.* By December 31 of each year, each landholding agency must notify HUD regarding the current availability status and classification of each property controlled by the agency that—

(1) Was included in a list of suitable properties published that year by HUD; and

(2) Remains available for application for use to assist the homeless, or has become available for application during that year.

(c) *GSA inventory.* HUD will collect information, in the same manner as described in paragraph (a) of this section, from GSA regarding property that is in GSA's current inventory of excess or surplus property.

(d) *Change in status.* If the information provided on the property checklist changes subsequent to HUD's determination of suitability, and the property remains unutilized, underutilized, excess or surplus, the landholding agency must submit a revised property checklist in response to the next quarterly canvass. HUD will make a new determination of suitability and, if it differs from the previous determination, republish the property information in the FEDERAL REGISTER. For example, property determined unsuitable for national security concerns may no longer be subject to security restrictions, or property determined suitable may subsequently be found to be contaminated.

SUITABILITY DETERMINATION

§ 102–75.1175 Who issues the suitability determination?

(a) *Suitability determination.* Within 30 days after the receipt of information from landholding agencies regarding properties that were reported pursuant to the canvass described in § 102–75.1170(a), HUD will determine, under criteria set forth in § 102–75.1185, which properties are suitable for use as facilities to assist the homeless and report its determination to the landholding agency. Properties that are under lease, contract, license, or agreement by which a Federal agency retains a real property interest or which are scheduled to become unutilized or underutilized will be reviewed for suitability no earlier than six months prior to the expected date when the property will become unutilized or underutilized, except that properties subject to the Base Closure and Realignment Act may be reviewed up to eighteen months prior to the expected date when the property will become unutilized or underutilized.

(b) *Scope of suitability.* HUD will determine the suitability of a property for use as a facility to assist the homeless without regard to any particular use.

(c) *Environmental information.* HUD will evaluate the environmental information contained in property checklists forwarded to HUD by the landholding agencies solely for the purpose of determining suitability of properties under the criteria in § 102–75.1185.

(d) *Written record of suitability determination.* HUD will assign an identification number to each property reviewed for suitability. HUD will maintain a written public record of the following:

(1) The suitability determination for a particular piece of property, and the reasons for that determination; and

(2) The landholding agency's response to the determination pursuant to the requirements of § 102–75.1190(a).

(e) *Property determined unsuitable.* Property that is reviewed by HUD under this section and that is determined unsuitable for use to assist the homeless may not be made available for any other purpose for 20 days after publication in the FEDERAL REGISTER of a notice of unsuitability to allow for review of the determination at the request of a representative of the homeless.

(f) *Procedures for appealing unsuitability determinations.* (1) To request review of a determination of unsuitability, a representative of the homeless must contact HUD within 20 days of publication of notice in the FEDERAL REGISTER that a property is unsuitable. Requests may be submitted to HUD in writing or by calling 1–800–927–7588 (Toll Free). Written requests must be received no later than 20 days after notice of unsuitability is published in the FEDERAL REGISTER.

(2) Requests for review of a determination of unsuitability may be made only by representatives of the homeless, as defined in § 102–75.1160.

(3) The request for review must specify the grounds on which it is based, i.e., that HUD has improperly applied the criteria or that HUD has relied on incorrect or incomplete information in making the determination (e.g., that property is in a floodplain but not in a floodway).

(4) Upon receipt of a request to review a determination of unsuitability, HUD will notify the landholding agency that such a request has been made, request that the agency respond with any information pertinent to the review, and advise the agency that it should refrain from initiating disposal procedures until HUD has completed its reconsideration regarding unsuitability.

(i) HUD will act on all requests for review within 30 days of receipt of the landholding agency's response and will notify the representative of the homeless and the landholding agency in writing of its decision.

(ii) If a property is determined suitable as a result of the review, HUD will request the landholding agency's determination of availability pursuant to § 102–75.1190(a), upon receipt of which HUD will promptly publish the determination in the FEDERAL REGISTER. If the determination of unsuitability stands, HUD will inform the representative of the homeless of its decision.

REAL PROPERTY REPORTED EXCESS TO GSA

§ 102–75.1180 For the purposes of this subpart, what is the policy concerning real property reported excess to GSA?

(a) Each landholding agency must submit a report to GSA of properties it determines excess. Each landholding agency must also provide a copy of HUD's suitability determination, if any, including HUD's identification number for the property.

(b) If a landholding agency reports a property to GSA that has been reviewed by HUD for homeless assistance suitability and HUD determined the property suitable, GSA will screen the property pursuant to § 102–75.1180(g) and will advise HUD of the availability of the property for use by the homeless as provided in § 102–75.1180(e). In lieu of the above, GSA may submit a new checklist to HUD and follow the procedures in § 102–75.1180(c) through § 102–75.1180(g).

(c) If a landholding agency reports a property to GSA that has not been reviewed by HUD for homeless assistance suitability, GSA will complete a property checklist, based on information provided by the landholding agency, and will forward this checklist to HUD for a suitability determination. This checklist will reflect any change in classification, i.e., from unutilized or underutilized to excess.

(d) Within 30 days after GSA's submission, HUD will advise GSA of the suitability determination.

(e) When GSA receives a letter from HUD listing suitable excess properties in GSA's inventory, GSA will transmit to HUD within 45 days a response that includes the following for each identified property:

(1) A statement that there is no other compelling Federal need for the property and, therefore, the property will be determined surplus; or

(2) A statement that there is further and compelling Federal need for the property (including a full explanation of such need) and that, therefore, the property is not presently available for use to assist the homeless.

(f) When an excess property is determined suitable and available and notice is published in the FEDERAL REGISTER, GSA will concurrently notify HHS, HUD, State and local government units, known homeless assistance providers that have expressed interest in the particular property, and other organizations, as appropriate, concerning suitable properties.

(g) Upon submission of a Report of Excess to GSA, GSA may screen the property for Federal use. In addition, GSA may screen State and local governmental units and eligible non-profit organizations to determine interest in the property in accordance with current regulations. (See GSA Customer Guide to Real Property Disposal.)

(h) The landholding agency will retain custody and accountability and will protect and maintain any property that is reported excess to GSA as provided in § 102–75.965.

SUITABILITY CRITERIA

§ 102–75.1185 What are suitability criteria?

(a) All properties, buildings, and land will be determined suitable unless a property's characteristics include one or more of the following conditions:

(1) *National security concerns.* A property located in an area to which the general public is denied access in the interest of national security (e.g., where a special pass or security clearance is a condition of entry to the property) will be determined unsuitable. Where alternative access can be provided for the public without compromising national security, the property will not be determined unsuitable on this basis.

(2) *Property containing flammable or explosive materials.* A property located within 2,000 feet of an industrial, commercial, or Federal facility handling flammable or explosive material (excluding underground storage) will be determined unsuitable. Above ground containers with a capacity of 100 gallons or less, or larger containers that provide the heating or power source for the property, and that meet local safety, operation, and permitting standards, will not affect whether a particular property is determined suitable or unsuitable. Underground storage, gasoline stations, and tank trucks are not included in this category, and their presence will not be the basis of an unsuitability determination unless there is evidence of a threat to personal safety as provided in paragraph (a)(5) of this section.

(3) *Runway clear zone and military airfield clear zone.* A property located within an airport runway clear zone or military airfield clear zone will be determined unsuitable.

(4) *Floodway.* A property located in the floodway of a 100-year floodplain will be determined unsuitable. If the floodway has been contained or corrected, or if only an incidental portion of the property not affecting the use of the remainder of the property is in the floodway, the property will not be determined unsuitable.

(5) *Documented deficiencies.* A property with a documented and extensive condition(s) that represents a clear threat to personal physical safety will be determined unsuitable. Such conditions may include, but are not limited to, contamination, structural damage, extensive deterioration, friable asbestos, PCBs, natural hazardous substances such as radon, periodic flooding, sinkholes, or earth slides.

(6) *Inaccessible.* A property that is inaccessible will be determined unsuitable. An inaccessible property is one that is not accessible by road (including property on small off-shore islands) or is land locked (e.g., can be reached only by crossing private property and there is no established right or means of entry).

(b) [Reserved]

DETERMINATION OF AVAILABILITY

§ 102–75.1190 What is the policy concerning determination of availability statements?

(a) Within 45 days after receipt of a letter from HUD pursuant to § 102–75.1170(a), each landholding agency must transmit to HUD a statement of one of the following:

(1) In the case of unutilized or underutilized property—

(i) An intention to declare the property excess;

(ii) An intention to make the property available for use to assist the homeless; or

(iii) The reasons why the property cannot be declared excess or made available for use to assist the homeless. The reasons given must be different than those listed as suitability criteria in § 102–75.1185.

(2) In the case of excess property that had previously been reported to GSA—

(i) A statement that there is no compelling Federal need for the property and that, therefore, the property will be determined surplus; or

(ii) A statement that there is a further and compelling Federal need for the property (including a full explanation of such need) and that, therefore, the property is not presently available for use to assist the homeless.

(b) [Reserved]

PUBLIC NOTICE OF DETERMINATION

§ 102–75.1195 What is the policy concerning making public the notice of determination?

(a) No later than 15 days after the last 45 day period has elapsed for receiving responses from the landholding agencies regarding availability, HUD will publish in the FEDERAL REGISTER a list of all properties reviewed, including a description of the property, its address, and classification. The following designations will be made:

(1) Properties that are suitable and available.

(2) Properties that are suitable and unavailable.

(3) Properties that are suitable and to be declared excess.

(4) Properties that are unsuitable.

(b) Information about specific properties can be obtained by contacting HUD at the following toll free number: 1–800–927–7588.

(c) HUD will transmit to the ICH a copy of the list of all properties published in the FEDERAL REGISTER. The ICH will immediately distribute to all state and regional homeless coordinators area-relevant portions of the list. The ICH will encourage the state and regional homeless coordinators to disseminate this information widely.

(d) No later than February 15 of each year, HUD will publish in the FEDERAL REGISTER a list of all properties reported pursuant to § 102–75.1170(b).

(e) HUD will publish an annual list of properties determined suitable, but that agencies reported unavailable, including the reasons such properties are not available.

(f) Copies of the lists published in the FEDERAL REGISTER will be available for review by the public in the HUD headquarters building library (room 8141); area-relevant portions of the lists will be available in the HUD regional offices and in major field offices.

APPLICATION PROCESS

§ 102–75.1200 How may representatives of the homeless apply for the use of properties to assist the homeless?

(a) *Holding period.* (1) Properties published as available for application for use to assist the homeless shall not be available for any other purpose for a period of 60 days beginning on the date of publication. Any representative of the homeless interested in any underutilized, unutilized, excess or surplus Federal property for use as a facility to assist the homeless must send to HHS a written expression of interest in that property within 60 days after the property has been published in the FEDERAL REGISTER.

(2) If a written expression of interest to apply for suitable property for use to assist the homeless is received by HHS within the 60-day holding period, such property may not be made available for any other purpose until the date HHS or the appropriate landholding agency has completed action on the application submitted pursuant to that expression of interest.

(3) The expression of interest should identify the specific property, briefly describe the proposed use, the name of the organization, and indicate whether it is a public body or a private, non-profit organization. The expression of interest must be sent to the Division of Health Facilities Planning (DHFP) of the Department of Health and Human Services at the following address: Director, Division of Health Facilities Planning, Public Health Service, Room 17A–10, Parklawn Building, 5600 Fishers Lane, Rockville, Maryland 20857. HHS will notify the landholding agency (for unutilized and underutilized properties) or GSA (for excess and surplus properties) when an expression of interest has been received for a particular property.

(4) An expression of interest may be sent to HHS any time after the 60-day holding period has expired. In such a case, an application submitted pursuant to this expression of interest may be approved for use by the homeless if—

(i) No application or written expression of interest has been made under any law for use of the property for any purpose; and

(ii) In the case of excess or surplus property, GSA has not received a bona fide offer to purchase that property or advertised for the sale of the property by public auction.

(b) *Application requirements.* Upon receipt of an expression of interest, DHFP will send an application packet to the interested entity. The application packet requires the applicant to provide certain information, including the following:

(1) *Description of the applicant organization.* The applicant must document that it satisfies the definition of a "representative of the homeless," as specified in § 102–75.1160. The applicant must document its authority to hold real property. Private, non-profit organizations applying for deeds must document that they are section 501(c)(3) tax-exempt.

(2) *Description of the property desired.* The applicant must describe the property desired and indicate that any modifications made to the property will conform to local use restrictions,

except for, in the case of leasing the property, local zoning regulations.

(3) *Description of the proposed program.* The applicant must fully describe the proposed program and demonstrate how the program will address the needs of the homeless population to be assisted. The applicant must fully describe what modifications will be made to the property before the program becomes operational.

(4) *Ability to finance and operate the proposed program.* The applicant must specifically describe all anticipated costs and sources of funding for the proposed program. The applicant must indicate that it can assume care, custody, and maintenance of the property and that it has the necessary funds or the ability to obtain such funds to carry out the approved program of use for the property.

(5) *Compliance with non-discrimination requirements.* Each applicant and lessee under this part must certify in writing that it will comply with the requirements of the Fair Housing Act (42 U.S.C. 3601–3619) and implementing regulations; and as applicable, Executive Order 11063 (Equal Opportunity in Housing) and implementing regulations; Title VI of the Civil Rights Act of 1964 (42 U.S.C. 2000d to d–4) (Nondiscrimination in Federally-Assisted Programs) and implementing regulations; the prohibitions against discrimination on the basis of age under the Age Discrimination Act of 1975 (42 U.S.C. 6101–6107) and implementing regulations; and the prohibitions against otherwise qualified individuals with handicaps under section 504 of the Rehabilitation Act of 1973 (29 U.S.C. 794) and implementing regulations. The applicant must state that it will not discriminate on the basis of race, color, national origin, religion, sex, age, familial status, or disability in the use of the property, and will maintain the required records to demonstrate compliance with Federal laws.

(6) *Insurance.* The applicant must certify that it will insure the property against loss, damage, or destruction in accordance with the requirements of 45 CFR §12.9.

(7) *Historic preservation.* Where applicable, the applicant must provide information that will enable HHS to comply with Federal historic preservation requirements.

(8) *Environmental information.* The applicant must provide sufficient information to allow HHS to analyze the potential impact of the applicant's proposal on the environment, in accordance with the instructions provided with the application packet. HHS will assist applicants in obtaining any pertinent environmental information in the possession of HUD, GSA, or the landholding agency.

(9) *Local government notification.* The applicant must indicate that it has informed, in writing, the applicable unit of general local government responsible for providing sewer, water, police, and fire services of its proposed program.

(10) *Zoning and local use restrictions.* The applicant must indicate that it will comply with all local use restrictions, including local building code requirements. Any applicant applying for a lease or permit for a particular property is not required to comply with local zoning requirements. Any applicant applying for a deed of a particular property, pursuant to §102–75.1200(b)(3), must comply with local zoning requirements, as specified in 45 CFR part 12.

(c) *Scope of evaluations.* Due to the short time frame imposed for evaluating applications, HHS' evaluation will, generally, be limited to the information contained in the application.

(d) *Deadline.* Completed applications must be received by DHFP, at the above address, within 90 days after an expression of interest is received from a particular applicant for that property. Upon written request from the applicant, HHS may grant extensions, provided that the appropriate landholding agency concurs with the extension. Because each applicant will have a different deadline based on the date the applicant submitted an expression of interest, applicants should contact the individual landholding agency to confirm that a particular property remains available prior to submitting an application.

(e) *Evaluations.* (1) Upon receipt of an application, HHS will review it for completeness and, if incomplete, may return it or ask the applicant to furnish any missing or additional required information prior to final evaluation of the application.

(2) HHS will evaluate each completed application within 25 days of receipt and will promptly advise the applicant of its decision. Applications are evaluated on a first-come, first-serve basis. HHS will notify all organizations that have submitted expressions of interest for a particular property regarding whether the first application received for that property has been approved or disapproved. All applications will be reviewed on the basis of the following elements, which are listed in descending order of priority, except that paragraphs (e)(2)(iv) and (e)(2)(v) of this section are of equal importance:

(i) *Services offered.* The extent and range of proposed services, such as meals, shelter, job training, and counseling.

(ii) *Need.* The demand for the program and the degree to which the available property will be fully utilized.

(iii) *Implementation time.* The amount of time necessary for the proposed program to become operational.

(iv) *Experience.* Demonstrated prior success in operating similar programs and recommendations attesting to that fact by Federal, State, and local authorities.

(v) *Financial ability.* The adequacy of funding that will likely be available to run the program fully and properly and to operate the facility.

(3) Additional evaluation factors may be added as deemed necessary by HHS. If additional factors are added, the application packet will be revised to include a description of these additional factors.

(4) If HHS receives one or more competing applications for a property within 5 days of the first application, HHS will evaluate all completed applications simultaneously. HHS will rank approved applications based on the elements listed in § 102–75.1200(e)(2) and notify the landholding agency, or GSA, as appropriate, of the relative ranks.

§ 102–75.1205 What action must be taken on approved applications?

(a) *Unutilized and underutilized properties.* (1) When HHS approves an application, it will so notify the applicant and forward a copy of the application to the landholding agency. The landholding agency will execute the lease, or permit document, as appropriate, in consultation with the applicant.

(2) The landholding agency maintains the discretion to decide the following:

(i) The length of time the property will be available. (Leases and permits will be for a period of at least one year, unless the applicant requests a shorter term.)

(ii) Whether to grant use of the property pursuant to a lease or permit.

(iii) The terms and conditions of the lease or permit document.

(b) *Excess and surplus properties.* (1) When HHS approves an application, it will so notify the applicant and request that GSA assign the property to HHS for leasing. Upon receipt of the assignment, HHS will execute a lease in accordance with the procedures and requirements set out in 45 CFR part 12. In accordance with § 102–75.965, custody and accountability of the property will remain throughout the lease term with the agency that initially reported the property as excess.

(2) Prior to assignment to HHS, GSA may consider other Federal uses and other important national needs; however, in deciding the disposition of surplus real property, GSA will generally give priority of consideration to uses to assist the homeless. GSA may consider any competing request for the property made under 40 U.S.C. 550 (education, health, public park or recreation, and historic monument uses) that is so meritorious and compelling that it outweighs the needs of the homeless, and HHS may likewise consider any competing request made under 40 U.S.C. 550(c) or (d) (education and health uses).

(3) Whenever GSA or HHS decides in favor of a competing request over a request for property for homeless assistance use as provided in paragraph (b)(2) of this section, the agency making the

decision will transmit to the appropriate committees of the Congress an explanatory statement that details the need satisfied by conveyance of the surplus property, and the reasons for determining that such need was so meritorious and compelling as to outweigh the needs of the homeless.

(4) *Deeds.* Surplus property may be conveyed to representatives of the homeless pursuant to 40 U.S.C. 550, and section 501(f) of the McKinney-Vento Homeless Assistance Act, as amended, 42 U.S.C. 11411. Representatives of the homeless must complete the application packet pursuant to the requirements of §102–75.1200 and in accordance with the requirements of 45 CFR part 12.

(c) *Completion of lease term and reversion of title.* Lessees and grantees will be responsible for the protection and maintenance of the property during the time that they possess the property. Upon termination of the lease term or reversion of title to the Federal Government, the lessee or grantee will be responsible for removing any improvements made to the property and will be responsible for restoration of the property. If such improvements are not removed, they will become the property of the Federal Government. GSA or the landholding agency, as appropriate, will assume responsibility for protection and maintenance of a property when the lease terminates or title reverts.

UNSUITABLE PROPERTIES

§102–75.1210 What action must be taken on properties determined unsuitable for homeless assistance?

The landholding agency will defer, for 20 days after the date that notice of a property is published in the FEDERAL REGISTER, action to dispose of properties determined unsuitable for homeless assistance. HUD will inform landholding agencies or GSA, if a representative of the homeless files an appeal of unsuitability pursuant to §102–75.1175(f)(4). HUD will advise the agency that it should refrain from initiating disposal procedures until HUD has completed its reconsideration process regarding unsuitability. Thereafter, or if no appeal has been filed after 20 days, GSA or the appropriate land-

holding agency may proceed with disposal action in accordance with applicable law.

NO APPLICATIONS APPROVED

§102–75.1215 What action must be taken if there is no expression of interest?

(a) At the end of the 60-day holding period described in §102–75.1200(a), HHS will notify GSA, or the landholding agency, as appropriate, if an expression of interest has been received for a particular property. Where there is no expression of interest, GSA or the landholding agency, as appropriate, will proceed with disposal in accordance with applicable law.

(b) Upon advice from HHS that all applications have been disapproved, or if no completed applications or requests for extensions have been received by HHS within 90 days from the date of the last expression of interest, disposal may proceed in accordance with applicable law.

Subpart I—Screening of Federal Real Property

§102–75.1220 How do landholding agencies find out if excess Federal real property is available?

If agencies report excess real and related personal property to GSA, GSA conducts a "Federal screening" for the property. Federal screening consists of developing a "Notice of Availability" and circulating the "Notice" among all Federal landholding agencies for a maximum of 30 days.

§102–75.1225 What details are provided in the "Notice of Availability"?

The "Notice of Availability" describes the physical characteristics of the property; it also provides information on location, hazards or restrictions, contact information, and a date by which an interested Federal agency must respond in writing to indicate a definite or potential need for the property.

§ 102–75.1230   How long does an agency have to indicate its interest in the property?

Generally, agencies have 30 days to express written interest in the property. However, sometimes GSA has cause to conduct an expedited screening of the real property and the time allotted for responding is less than 30 days. The Notice of Availability always contains a "respond by" date.

§ 102–75.1235   Where should an agency send its written response to the "Notice of Availability"?

Look for the contact information provided in the Notice of Availability. Most likely, an agency will be directed to contact one of GSA's regional offices.

§ 102–75.1240   Who, from the interested landholding agency, should submit the written response to GSA's "Notice of Availability"?

An authorized official of the landholding agency must sign the written response to the Notice of Availability. An "authorized official" is one who is responsible for acquisition and/or disposal decisions (e.g., head of the agency or official designee).

§ 102–75.1245   What happens after the landholding agency properly responds to a "Notice of Availability"?

The landholding agency has 60 days (from the expiration date of the "Notice of Availability") to submit a formal transfer request for the property. Absent a formal request for transfer within the prescribed 60 days, GSA may, at its discretion, pursue other disposal options.

§ 102–75.1250   What if the agency is not quite sure it wants the property and needs more time to decide?

If the written response to the "Notice of Availability" indicates a potential need, then the agency has an additional 30 days (from the expiration date of the "Notice of Availability") to determine whether or not its has a definite requirement for the property, and then 60 days to submit a transfer request.

§ 102–75.1255   What happens when more than one agency has a valid interest in the property?

GSA will attempt to facilitate an equitable solution between the agencies involved. However, the Administrator has final decision making authority in determining which requirement aligns with the Federal Government's best interests.

§ 102–75.1260   Does GSA conduct Federal screening on every property reported as excess real property?

No. GSA may waive the Federal screening for excess real property when it determines that doing so is in the best interest of the Federal Government.

Below is a sample list of some of the factors GSA may consider when making the decision to waive Federal screening. This list is a representative sample and is not all-inclusive:

(a) There is a known Federal need;

(b) The property is located within the boundaries of tribal lands;

(c) The property has known disposal limitations precluding further Federal use (e.g., title and/or utilization restrictions; reported excess specifically for participation in the Relocation Program; reported excess for transfer to the current operating contractor who will continue production according to the terms of the disposal documents; directed for disposal by law or special legislation);

(d) The property will be transferred to a "potentially responsible party" (PRP) that stored, released, or disposed of hazardous substances at the Government-owned facility;

(e) The property is an easement;

(f) The excess property is actually a leasehold interest where there are Government-owned improvements with substantial value and cannot be easily removed;

(g) Government-owned improvements on Government-owned land, where the land is neither excess nor expected to become excess; or

(h) Screening for public benefit uses, except for the McKinney-Vento homeless screening, for specific property disposal considerations (see § 102–75.351).

§ 102-75.1265 Are extensions granted to the Federal screening and response timeframes?

Generally, no. GSA believes the timeframes are sufficient for agencies to make a decision and respond. Requests for extensions must be strongly justified and approved by the appropriate GSA Regional Administrator. For example, agencies may request an extension of time to submit their formal transfer request if they are not promptly provided GSA's estimate of FMV after submission of the initial expression of interest. Agencies requesting extensions must also submit an agreement accepting responsibility for providing and funding protection and maintenance for the requested property during the period of the extension until the property is transferred to the requesting agency or the requesting agency notifies GSA that it is no longer interested in the property. This assumption of protection and maintenance responsibility also applies to extensions associated with a requesting agency's request for an exception from the 100 percent reimbursement requirement (see § 102-75.205).

§ 102-75.1270 How does an agency request a transfer of Federal real property?

Agencies must use GSA Form 1334, Request for Transfer of Excess Real and Related Personal Property.

§ 102-75.1275 Does a requesting agency have to pay for excess real property?

Yes. GSA is required by law to obtain full fair market value (as determined by the Administrator) for all real property (see § 102-75.190), except when a transfer without reimbursement has been authorized (see § 102-75.205). GSA, upon receipt of a valid expression of interest, will promptly provide each interested landholding agency with an estimate of fair market value for the property. GSA may transfer property without reimbursement, if directed to do so by law or special legislation and for the following purposes:

(a) Migratory Bird Management under Pub. L. 80-537, as amended by Pub. L. 92-432.

(b) Wildlife Conservation under Pub. L. 80-537.

(c) Federal Correctional facilities.

(d) Joint Surveillance System.

§ 102-75.1280 What happens if the property has already been declared surplus and an agency discovers a need for it?

GSA can redesignate surplus property as excess property, if the agency requests the property for use in direct support of its mission and GSA is satisfied that this transfer would be in the best interests of the Federal Government.

§ 102-75.1285 How does GSA transfer excess real property to the requesting agency?

GSA transfers the property via letter assigning "custody and accountability" for the property to the requesting agency. Title to the property is held in the name of the United States; however, the requesting agency becomes the landholding agency and is responsible for providing and funding protection and maintenance for the property.

§ 102-75.1290 What happens if the landholding agency requesting the property does not promptly accept custody and accountability?

(a) The requesting agency must assume protection and maintenance responsibilities for the property within 30 days of the date of the letter assigning custody and accountability for the property.

(b) After notifying the requesting agency, GSA may, at its discretion, pursue other disposal options.

PART 102-76—DESIGN AND CONSTRUCTION

Subpart A—General Provisions

Subpart B—Design and Construction

102–76.20 What issues must Federal agencies consider in providing site planning and landscape design services?
102–76.25 What standards must Federal agencies meet in providing architectural and interior design services?
102–76.30 What seismic safety standards must Federal agencies follow in the design and construction of Federal facilities?

NATIONAL ENVIRONMENTAL POLICY ACT OF 1969

102–76.35 What is the purpose of the National Environmental Policy Act of 1969, as amended (NEPA)?
102–76.40 To which real property actions does NEPA apply?
102–76.45 What procedures must Federal agencies follow to implement the requirements of NEPA?

SUSTAINABLE DEVELOPMENT

102–76.50 What is sustainable development?
102–76.55 What sustainable development principles must Federal agencies apply to the siting, design, and construction of new facilities?

Subpart C—Architectural Barriers Act

102–76.60 To which facilities does the Architectural Barriers Act Apply?
102–76.65 What standards must facilities subject to the Architectural Barriers Act meet?
102–76.70 When are the costs of alterations to provide an accessible path of travel to an altered area containing a primary function disproportionate to the costs of the overall alterations for facilities subject to the standards in § 102–76.65(a)?
102–76.75 What costs are included in the costs of alterations to provide an accessible path of travel to an altered area containing a primary function for facilities subject to the standards in § 102–76.65(a)?
102–76.80 What is required if the costs of alterations to provide an accessible path of travel to an altered area containing a primary function are disproportionate to the costs of the overall alterations for facilities subject to the standards in § 102–76.65(a)?
102–76.85 What is a primary function area for purposes of providing an accessible route in leased facilities subject to the standards in § 102–76.65(a)?
102–76.90 Who has the authority to waive or modify the standards in § 102–76.65(a)?
102–76.95 What recordkeeping responsibilities do Federal agencies have?

AUTHORITY: 40 U.S.C. 121(c) (in furtherance of the Administrator's authorities under 40 U.S.C. 3301–3315 and elsewhere as included under 40 U.S.C. 581 and 583); 42 U.S.C. 4152; E.O. 12411, 48 FR 13391, 3 CFR, 1983 Comp., p. 155; E.O. 12512, 50 FR 18453, 3 CFR, 1985 Comp., p. 340.

SOURCE: 70 FR 67845, Nov. 8, 2005, unless otherwise noted.

Subpart A—General Provisions

§ 102–76.5 What is the scope of this part?

The real property policies contained in this part apply to Federal agencies, including GSA's Public Buildings Service (PBS), operating under, or subject to, the authorities of the Administrator of General Services. The accessibility standards in subpart C of this part apply to Federal agencies and other entities whose facilities are subject to the Architectural Barriers Act.

[70 FR 67845, Nov. 8, 2005, as amended at 72 FR 5943, Feb. 8, 2007]

§ 102–76.10 What basic design and construction policy governs Federal agencies?

Federal agencies, upon approval from GSA, are bound by the following basic design and construction policies:

(a) Provide the highest quality services for designing and constructing new Federal facilities and for repairing and altering existing Federal facilities. These services must be timely, efficient, and cost effective.

(b) Use a distinguished architectural style and form in Federal facilities that reflects the dignity, enterprise, vigor and stability of the Federal Government.

(c) Follow nationally recognized model building codes and other applicable nationally recognized codes that govern Federal construction to the maximum extent feasible and consider local building code requirements. (See 40 U.S.C. 3310 and 3312.)

(d) Design Federal buildings to have a long life expectancy and accommodate periodic changes due to renovations.

(e) Make buildings cost effective, energy efficient, and accessible to and usable by the physically disabled.

(f) Provide for building service equipment that is accessible for maintenance, repair, or replacement without significantly disturbing occupied space.

(g) Consider ease of operation when selecting mechanical and electrical equipment.

(h) Agencies must follow the prospectus submission and approval policy identified in §§ 102–73.35 and 102–73.40 of this chapter.

Subpart B—Design and Construction

§ 102–76.15 What are design and construction services?

Design and construction services are—

(a) Site planning and landscape design;

(b) Architectural and interior design; and

(c) Engineering systems design.

§ 102–76.20 What issues must Federal agencies consider in providing site planning and landscape design services?

In providing site planning and design services, Federal agencies must—

(a) Make the site planning and landscape design a direct extension of the building design;

(b) Make a positive contribution to the surrounding landscape;

(c) Consider requirements (other than procedural requirements) of local zoning laws and laws relating to setbacks, height, historic preservation, and aesthetic qualities of a building;

(d) Identify areas for future building expansion in the architectural and site design concept for all buildings where an expansion need is identified to exist;

(e) Create a landscape design that is a pleasant, dynamic experience for occupants and visitors to Federal facilities and, where appropriate, encourage public access to and stimulate pedestrian traffic around the facilities. Coordinate the landscape design with the architectural characteristics of the building;

(f) Comply with the requirements of the National Environmental Policy Act of 1969, as amended, 42 U.S.C. 4321 *et seq.*, and the National Historic Preservation Act of 1966, as amended, 16 U.S.C. 470 *et seq.*, for each project; and

(g) Consider the vulnerability of the facility as well as the security needs of the occupying agencies, consistent with the Interagency Security Committee standards and guidelines.

§ 102–76.25 What standards must Federal agencies meet in providing architectural and interior design services?

Federal agencies must design distinctive and high quality Federal facilities that meet all of the following standards:

(a) Reflect the local architecture in buildings through the use of building form, materials, colors, or detail. Express a quality of permanence in the building interior similar to the building exterior.

(b) Provide individuals with disabilities ready access to, and use of, the facilities in accordance with the standards in § 102–76.65.

(c) Use metric specifications in construction where the metric system is the accepted industry standard, and to the extent that such usage is economically feasible and practical.

(d) Provide for the design of security systems to protect Federal workers and visitors and to safeguard facilities against criminal activity and/or terrorist activity. Security design must support the continuity of Government operations during civil disturbances, natural disasters and other emergency situations.

(e) Design and construct facilities that meet or exceed the energy performance standards applicable to Federal buildings in 10 CFR part 435.

§ 102–76.30 What seismic safety standards must Federal agencies follow in the design and construction of Federal facilities?

Federal agencies must follow the seismic safety standards identified in § 102–80.45 of this chapter.

NATIONAL ENVIRONMENTAL POLICY ACT OF 1969

§ 102–76.35 What is the purpose of the National Environmental Policy Act of 1969, as amended (NEPA)?

The purpose of NEPA is to—

(a) Declare a national policy which will encourage productive and enjoyable harmony between man and his environment;

(b) Promote efforts which will prevent or eliminate damage to the environment and biosphere and stimulate the health and welfare of man;

(c) Enrich the understanding of the ecological systems and natural resources important to the Nation; and

(d) Establish a Council on Environmental Quality (CEQ).

§ 102–76.40 To which real property actions does NEPA apply?

NEPA applies to actions that may have an impact on the quality of the human environment, including leasing, acquiring, developing, managing and disposing of real property.

§ 102–76.45 What procedures must Federal agencies follow to implement the requirements of NEPA?

Federal agencies must follow the procedures identified in the Council on Environmental Quality's NEPA implementing regulations, 40 CFR 1500–1508. In addition, Federal agencies must follow the standards that they have promulgated to implement CEQ's regulations.

SUSTAINABLE DEVELOPMENT

§ 102–76.50 What is sustainable development?

Sustainable development means integrating the decision-making process across the organization, so that every decision is made to promote the greatest long-term benefits. It means eliminating the concept of waste and building on natural processes and energy flows and cycles; and recognizing the interrelationship of our actions with the natural world.

§ 102–76.55 What sustainable development principles must Federal agencies apply to the siting, design, and construction of new facilities?

In keeping with the objectives of Executive Order 13123, "Greening of the Government Through Efficient Energy Management," and Executive Order 13101, "Greening of the Government Through Waste Prevention, Recycling, and Federal Acquisition," Federal agencies must apply sustainable development principles to the siting, design, and construction of new facilities, which include—

(a) Optimizing site potential;

(b) Minimizing non-renewable energy consumption;

(c) Using environmentally preferable products;

(d) Protecting and conserving water;

(e) Enhancing indoor environmental quality; and

(f) Optimizing operational and maintenance practices.

Subpart C—Architectural Barriers Act

§ 102–76.60 To which facilities does the Architectural Barriers Act apply?

(a) The Architectural Barriers Act applies to any facility that is intended for use by the public or that may result in the employment or residence therein of individuals with disabilities, which is to be—

(1) Constructed or altered by, or on behalf of, the United States;

(2) Leased in whole or in part by the United States;

(3) Financed in whole or in part by a grant or loan made by the United States, if the building or facility is subject to standards for design, construction, or alteration issued under the authority of the law authorizing such a grant or loan; or

(4) Constructed under the authority of the National Capital Transportation Act of 1960, the National Capital Transportation Act of 1965, or Title III of the Washington Metropolitan Area Transit Regulation Compact.

(b) The Architectural Barriers Act does not apply to any privately owned residential facility unless leased by the Government for subsidized housing programs, and any facility on a military reservation designed and constructed primarily for use by able bodied military personnel.

§ 102–76.65 What standards must facilities subject to the Architectural Barriers Act meet?

(a) GSA adopts Appendices C and D to 36 CFR part 1191 (ABA Chapters 1 and 2, and Chapters 3 through 10) as the

Architectural Barriers Act Accessibility Standard (ABAAS). Facilities subject to the Architectural Barriers Act (other than facilities described in paragraphs (b) and (c) of this section) must comply with ABAAS as set forth below:

(1) For construction or alteration of facilities subject to the Architectural Barriers Act (other than Federal lease-construction and other lease actions described in paragraphs (a)(2) and (3), respectively, of this section), compliance with ABAAS is required if the construction or alteration commenced after May 8, 2006. If the construction or alteration of such a facility commenced on or before May 8, 2006, compliance with the Uniform Federal Accessibility Standards (UFAS) is required.

(2) For Federal lease-construction actions subject to the Architectural Barriers Act, where the Government expressly requires new construction to meet its needs, compliance with ABAAS is required for all such leases awarded on or after June 30, 2006. UFAS compliance is required for all such leases awarded before June 30, 2006.

(3) For all other lease actions subject to the Architectural Barriers Act (other than those described in paragraph (a)(2) of this section), compliance with ABAAS is required for all such leases awarded pursuant to solicitations issued after February 6, 2007. UFAS compliance is required for all such leases awarded pursuant to solicitations issued on or before February 6, 2007.

(b) Residential facilities subject to the Architectural Barriers Act must meet the standards prescribed by the Department of Housing and Urban Development.

(c) Department of Defense and United States Postal Service facilities subject to the Architectural Barriers Act must meet the standards prescribed by those agencies.

[70 FR 67845, Nov. 8, 2005, as amended at 71 FR 52499, Sept. 6, 2006; 72 FR 5943, Feb. 8, 2007]

§ 102–76.70 When are the costs of alterations to provide an accessible path of travel to an altered area containing a primary function disproportionate to the costs of the overall alterations for facilities subject to the standards in § 102–76.65(a)?

For facilities subject to the standards in § 102–76.65(a), the costs of alterations to provide an accessible path of travel to an altered area containing a primary function are disproportionate to the costs of the overall alterations when they exceed 20 percent of the costs of the alterations to the primary function area. If a series of small alterations are made to areas containing a primary function and the costs of any of the alterations considered individually would not result in providing an accessible path of travel to the altered areas, the total costs of the alterations made within the three year period after the initial alteration must be considered when determining whether the costs of alterations to provide an accessible path of travel to the altered areas are disproportionate. Facilities for which new leases are entered into must comply with F202.6 of the Architectural Barriers Act Accessibility Standard without regard to whether the costs of alterations to comply with F202.6 are disproportionate to the costs of the overall alterations.

§ 102–76.75 What costs are included in the costs of alterations to provide an accessible path of travel to an altered area containing a primary function for facilities subject to the standards in § 102–76.65(a)?

For facilities subject to the standards in § 102–76.65(a), the costs of alterations to provide an accessible path of travel to an altered area containing a primary function include the costs associated with—

(a) Providing an accessible route to connect the altered area and site arrival points, including but not limited to interior and exterior ramps, elevators and lifts, and curb ramps;

(b) Making entrances serving the altered area accessible, including but not limited to widening doorways and installing accessible hardware;

(c) Making restrooms serving the altered area accessible, including, but not limited to, enlarging toilet stalls, installing grab bars and accessible faucet controls, and insulating pipes under lavatories;

(d) Making public telephones serving the altered area accessible, including, but not limited to, placing telephones at an accessible height, and installing amplification devices and TTYs;

(e) Making drinking fountains serving the altered area accessible; and

(f) Making parking spaces serving the altered area accessible.

§ 102–76.80 What is required if the costs of alterations to provide an accessible path of travel to an altered area containing a primary function are disproportionate to the costs of the overall alterations for facilities subject to the standards in § 102–76.65(a)?

For facilities subject to the standards in § 102–76.65(a), if the costs of alterations to provide an accessible path of travel to an altered area containing a primary function are disproportionate to the costs of the overall alterations, the path of travel must be made accessible to the extent possible without exceeding 20 percent of the costs of the alterations to the primary function area. Priority should be given to those elements that will provide the greatest access in the following order:

(a) An accessible route and an accessible entrance;

(b) At least one accessible restroom for each sex or a single unisex restroom;

(c) Accessible telephones;

(d) Accessible drinking fountains; and

(e) Accessible parking spaces.

§ 102–76.85 What is a primary function area for purposes of providing an accessible route in leased facilities subject to the standards in § 102–76.65(a)?

For purposes of providing an accessible route in leased facilities subject to the standards in § 102–76.65(a), a primary function area is an area that contains a major activity for which the leased facility is intended. Primary function areas include areas where services are provided to customers or the public, and offices and other work areas in which the activities of the

Federal agency using the leased facility are carried out.

§ 102–76.90 Who has the authority to waive or modify the standards in § 102–76.65(a)?

The Administrator of General Services has the authority to waive or modify the standards in § 102–76.65(a) on a case-by-case basis if the agency head or GSA department head submits a request for waiver or modification and the Administrator determines that the waiver or modification is clearly necessary.

§ 102–76.95 What recordkeeping responsibilities do Federal agencies have?

(a) The head of each Federal agency must ensure that documentation is maintained on each contract, grant or loan for the design, construction or alteration of a facility and on each lease for a facility subject to the standards in § 102–76.65(a) containing one of the following statements:

(1) The standards have been or will be incorporated in the design, the construction or the alteration.

(2) The grant or loan has been or will be made subject to a requirement that the standards will be incorporated in the design, the construction or the alteration.

(3) The leased facility meets the standards, or has been or will be altered to meet the standards.

(4) The standards have been waived or modified by the Administrator of General Services, and a copy of the waiver or modification is included with the statement.

(b) If a determination is made that a facility is not subject to the standards in § 102–76.65(a) because the Architectural Barriers Act does not apply to the facility, the head of the Federal agency must ensure that documentation is maintained to justify the determination.

PART 102–77—ART-IN-ARCHITECTURE

Subpart A—General Provisions

Sec.
102–77.5 What is the scope of this part?

AUTHORITY: 40 U.S.C. 121 and 3306.

SOURCE: 70 FR 67847, Nov. 8, 2005, unless otherwise noted.

Subpart A—General Provisions

§ 102–77.5 What is the scope of this part?

The real property policies contained in this part apply to Federal agencies, including GSA's Public Buildings Service (PBS), operating under, or subject to, the authorities of the Administrator of General Services.

§ 102–77.10 What basic Art-in-Architecture policy governs Federal agencies?

Federal agencies must incorporate fine arts as an integral part of the total building concept when designing new Federal buildings, and when making substantial repairs and alterations to existing Federal buildings, as appropriate. The selected fine arts, including painting, sculpture, and artistic work in other media, must reflect the national cultural heritage and emphasize the work of living American artists.

Subpart B—Art-in-Architecture

§ 102–77.15 Who funds the Art-in-Architecture efforts?

To the extent not prohibited by law, Federal agencies must fund the Art-in-Architecture efforts by allocating a portion of the estimated cost of constructing or purchasing new Federal buildings, or of completing major repairs and alterations of existing buildings. Funding for qualifying projects, including new construction, building purchases, other building acquisition, or prospectus-level repair and alteration projects, must be in a range determined by the Administrator of General Services.

§ 102–77.20 With whom should Federal agencies collaborate with when commissioning and selecting art for Federal buildings?

To the maximum extent practicable, Federal agencies should seek the support and involvement of local citizens in selecting appropriate artwork. Federal agencies should collaborate with the artist and community to produce works of art that reflect the cultural, intellectual, and historic interests and values of a community. In addition, Federal agencies should work collaboratively with the architect of the building and art professionals, when commissioning and selecting art for Federal buildings. Federal agencies should commission artwork that is diverse in style and media.

§ 102–77.25 Do Federal agencies have responsibilities to provide national visibility for Art-in-Architecture?

Yes, Federal agencies should provide Art-in-Architecture that receives appropriate national and local visibility to facilitate participation by a large and diverse group of artists representing a wide variety of types of artwork.

PART 102–78—HISTORIC PRESERVATION

Subpart A—General Provisions

AUTHORITY: 16 U.S.C. 470h–2; 40 U.S.C. 121(c)
and 581.

SOURCE: 70 FR 67848, Nov. 8, 2005, unless
otherwise noted.

Subpart A—General Provisions

§ 102–78.5 What is the scope of this part?

The real property policies contained
in this part apply to Federal agencies,
including GSA's Public Buildings Service (PBS), operating under, or subject
to, the authorities of the Administrator of General Services. The policies
in this part are in furtherance of GSA's
preservation program under section 110
of the National Historic Preservation
Act of 1966, as amended (16 U.S.C. 470)
and apply to properties under the jurisdiction or control of the Administrator
and to any Federal agencies operating,
maintaining or protecting such properties under a delegation of authority
from the Administrator.

§ 102–78.10 What basic historic preser-vation policy governs Federal agen-cies?

To protect, enhance and preserve historic and cultural property under their
control, Federal agencies must consider the effects of their undertakings
on historic and cultural properties and
give the Advisory Council on Historic
Preservation (Advisory Council), the
State Historic Preservation Officer
(SHPO), and other consulting parties a
reasonable opportunity to comment regarding the proposed undertakings.

Subpart B—Historic Preservation

§ 102–78.15 What are historic prop-erties?

Historic properties are those that are
included in, or eligible for inclusion in,
the National Register of Historic
Places (National Register) as more specifically defined at 36 CFR 800.16.

§ 102–78.20 Are Federal agencies re-quired to identify historic prop-erties?

Yes, Federal agencies must identify
all National Register or National Register-eligible historic properties under
their control. In addition, Federal
agencies must apply National Register
Criteria (36 CFR part 63) to properties
that have not been previously evaluated for National Register eligibility
and that may be affected by the undertakings of Federally sponsored activities.

§ 102–78.25 What is an undertaking?

The term undertaking means a
project, activity, or program funded in
whole or in part under the direct or indirect jurisdiction of a Federal agency,
including those—
(a) Carried out by or on behalf of the
agency;
(b) Carried out with Federal financial
assistance; or
(c) Requiring a Federal permit, license, or approval.

§ 102–78.30 Who are consulting par-ties?

As more particularly described in 36
CFR 800.2(c), consulting parties are
those parties having consultative roles
in the Section 106 process (i.e., Section
106 of the National Historic Preservation Act), which requires Federal agencies to take into account the effects of
their undertakings on historic properties and afford the Council a reasonable opportunity to comment on such
undertakings. Specifically, consulting
parties include the State Historic Preservation Officer; the Tribal Historic
Preservation Officer; Indian tribes and
Native Hawaiian organizations; representatives of local governments; applicants for Federal assistance, permits, licenses, and other approvals;
other individuals and organizations

with a demonstrated interest in the undertaking; and the Advisory Council (if it elects to participate in the consultation).

§ 102–78.35 Are Federal agencies required to involve consulting parties in their historic preservation activities?

Yes, Federal agencies must solicit information from consulting parties to carry out their responsibilities under historic and cultural preservation laws and regulations. Federal agencies must invite the participation of consulting parties through their normal public notification processes.

§ 102–78.40 What responsibilities do Federal agencies have when an undertaking adversely affects a historic or cultural property?

Federal agencies must not perform an undertaking that could alter, destroy, or modify an historic or cultural property until they have consulted with the SHPO and the Advisory Council. Federal agencies must minimize all adverse impacts of their undertakings on historic or cultural properties to the extent that it is feasible and prudent to do so. Federal agencies must follow the specific guidance on the protection of historic and cultural properties in 36 CFR part 800.

§ 102–78.45 What are Federal agencies' responsibilities concerning nomination of properties to the National Register?

Federal agencies must nominate to the National Register all properties under their control determined eligible for inclusion in the National Register.

§ 102–78.50 What historic preservation services must Federal agencies provide?

Federal agencies must provide the following historic preservation services:

(a) Prepare a Historic Building Preservation Plan for each National Register or National Register-eligible property under their control. When approved by consulting parties, such plans become a binding management plan for the property.

(b) Investigate for historic and cultural factors all proposed sites for direct and leased construction.

§ 102–78.55 For which properties must Federal agencies assume historic preservation responsibilities?

Federal agencies must assume historic preservation responsibilities for real property assets under their custody and control. Federal agencies occupying space in buildings under the custody and control of other Federal agencies must obtain approval from the agency having custody and control of the building.

§ 102–78.60 When leasing space, are Federal agencies able to give preference to space in historic properties or districts?

Yes, Executive Order 13006 requires Federal agencies that have a mission requirement to locate in an urban area to give first consideration to space in historic buildings and districts inside central business areas. Agencies may give a price preference of up to 10 percent to space in historic buildings and districts, in accordance with §§ 102–73.120 and 102–73.125 of this chapter.

§ 102–78.65 What are Federal agencies' historic preservation responsibilities when disposing of real property under their control?

Federal agencies must—

(a) To the extent practicable, establish and implement alternatives for historic properties, including adaptive use, that are not needed for current or projected agency purposes. Agencies are required to get the Secretary of the Interior's approval of the plans of transferees of surplus Federally-owned historic properties; and

(b) Review all proposed excess actions to identify any properties listed in or eligible for listing in the National Register. Federal agencies must not perform disposal actions that could result in the alteration, destruction, or modification of an historic or cultural property until Federal agencies have consulted with the SHPO and the Advisory Council.

§ 102–78.70 What are an agency's historic preservation responsibilities when disposing of another Federal agency's real property?

Federal agencies must not accept property declared excess by another Federal agency nor act as an agent for transfer or sale of such properties until the holding agency provides evidence that the Federal agency has met its National Historic Preservation Act responsibilities.

PART 102–79—ASSIGNMENT AND UTILIZATION OF SPACE

Subpart A—General Provisions

Subpart B—Assignment and Utilization of Space

AUTHORITY: 40 U.S.C. 121(c); E.O. 12411, 48 FR 13391, 3 CFR, 1983 Comp., p. 155; and E.O. 12512, 50 FR 18453, 3 CFR, 1985 Comp., p. 340.

SOURCE: 70 FR 67849, Nov. 8, 2005, unless otherwise noted.

Subpart A—General Provisions

§ 102–79.5 What is the scope of this part?

The real property policies contained in this part apply to Federal agencies, including GSA's Public Buildings Service (PBS), operating under, or subject to, the authorities of the Administrator of General Services.

§ 102–79.10 What basic assignment and utilization of space policy governs an Executive agency?

Executive agencies must provide a quality workplace environment that supports program operations, preserves the value of real property assets, meets the needs of the occupant agencies, and provides child care and physical fitness facilities in the workplace when adequately justified. An Executive agency must promote maximum utilization of Federal workspace, consistent with mission requirements, to maximize its value to the Government.

Subpart B—Assignment and Utilization of Space

§ 102–79.15 What objectives must an Executive agency strive to meet in providing assignment and utilization of space services?

Executive agencies must provide assignment and utilization services that will maximize the value of Federal real property resources and improve the productivity of the workers housed therein.

ASSIGNMENT OF SPACE

§ 102–79.20 What standard must Executive agencies promote when assigning space?

Executive agencies must promote the optimum use of space for each assignment at an economical cost to the Government, provide quality workspace that is delivered and occupied in a timely manner, and assign space based on mission requirements.

CHILD CARE

§ 102–79.25 May Federal agencies allot space in Federal buildings for the provision of child care services?

Yes, in accordance with 40 U.S.C. 590, Federal agencies can allot space in Federal buildings to individuals or entities who will provide child care services to Federal employees if such—

(a) Space is available;

(b) Agency determines that such space will be used to provide child care services to children of whom at least 50 percent have one parent or guardian who is a Federal Government employee; and

(c) Agency determines that such individual or entity will give priority for available child care services in such space to Federal employees.

FITNESS CENTERS

§ 102–79.30 May Federal agencies allot space in Federal buildings for establishing fitness centers?

Yes, in accordance with 5 U.S.C. 7901, Federal agencies can allot space in Federal buildings for establishing fitness programs.

§ 102–79.35 What elements must Federal agencies address in their planning effort for establishing fitness programs?

Federal agencies must address the following elements in their planning effort for establishing fitness programs:

(a) A survey indicating employee interest in the program.

(b) A three-to five-year implementation plan demonstrating long-term commitment to physical fitness/health for employees.

(c) A health related orientation, including screening procedures, individualized exercise programs, identification of high-risk individuals, and appropriate follow-up activities.

(d) Identification of a person skilled in prescribing exercise to direct the fitness program.

(e) An approach that will consider key health behavior related to degenerative disease, including smoking and nutrition.

(f) A modest facility that includes only the essentials necessary to conduct a program involving cardiovascular and muscular endurance, strength activities, and flexibility.

(g) Provision for equal opportunities for men and women, and all employees, regardless of grade level.

FEDERAL CREDIT UNIONS

§ 102–79.40 Can Federal agencies allot space in Federal buildings to Federal credit unions?

Yes, in accordance with 12 U.S.C. 1770, Federal agencies may allot space in Federal buildings to Federal credit unions without charge for rent or services if—

(a) At least 95 percent of the membership of the credit union to be served by the allotment of space is composed of persons who either are presently Federal employees or were Federal employees at the time of admission into the credit union, and members of their families; and

(b) Space is available.

§ 102–79.45 What type of services may Federal agencies provide without charge to Federal credit unions?

Federal agencies may provide without charge to Federal credit union services such as—

(a) Lighting;

(b) Heating and cooling;

(c) Electricity;

(d) Office furniture;

(e) Office machines and equipment;

(f) Telephone service (including installation of lines and equipment and other expenses associated with telephone service); and

(g) Security systems (including installation and other expenses associated with security systems).

UTILIZATION OF SPACE

§ 102–79.50 What standard must Executive agencies promote in their utilization of space?

Executive agencies, when acquiring or utilizing Federally owned or leased space under Title 40 of the United States Code, must promote efficient utilization of space. Where there is no Federal agency space need, Executive agencies must make every effort to maximize the productive use of vacant space through the issuance of permits, licenses or leases to non-Federal entities to the extent authorized by law. (For vacant property determined excess to agency needs, refer to part 102–75, Real Property Disposal.)

§ 102–79.55 Is there a general hierarchy of consideration that agencies must follow in their utilization of space?

Yes, Federal agencies must—

(a) First utilize space in Government-owned and Government-leased buildings; and

(b) If there is no suitable space in Government-owned and Government-leased buildings, utilize space in buildings under the custody and control of the U.S. Postal Service; and

(c) If there is no suitable space in buildings under the custody and control of the U.S. Postal Service, agencies may acquire real estate by lease, purchase, or construction, as specified in part 102–73 of this chapter.

§ 102–79.60 Are agencies required to use historic properties available to the agency?

Yes, Federal agencies must assume responsibility for the preservation of the historic properties they own or control. Prior to acquiring, constructing or leasing buildings, agencies must use, to the maximum extent feasible, historic properties already owned or leased by the agency (16 U.S.C. 470h–2).

OUTLEASING

§ 102–79.65 May Executive agencies outlease space on major public access levels, courtyards and rooftops of public buildings?

Yes. Authority to execute such outleases may be delegated by the Administrator based on authorities provided by the Public Buildings Cooperative Use Act (40 U.S.C. § 581(h)), the proceeds of which are to be deposited into GSA's Federal Buildings Fund. Using such authority, Executive agencies, upon approval from GSA, may—

(a) Enter into leases of space on major public access levels, courtyards and rooftops of any public building with persons, firms, or organizations engaged in commercial, cultural, educational, or recreational activities (as defined in 40 U.S.C. 3306);

(b) Establish rental rates for such leased space equivalent to the prevailing commercial rate for comparable space devoted to a similar purpose in the vicinity of the building; and

(c) Use leases that contain terms and conditions that the Administrator deems necessary to promote competition and protect the public interest.

SITING ANTENNAS ON FEDERAL PROPERTY

§ 102–79.70 May Executive agencies assess fees against other Executive agencies for antenna placements and supporting services?

Yes. Executive agencies, upon approval from GSA, may assess fees for placement of antennas and supporting services against other agencies (that own these antennas) under 40 U.S.C. 586(c) and 40 U.S.C. 121(e). Unless a differing rate has been approved by the Administrator, such fees or charges must approximate commercial charges for comparable space and services (i.e., market rates). The proceeds from such charges or fees must be credited to the appropriation or fund initially charged for providing the space or services. Any amounts in excess of actual operating and maintenance costs must be credited to miscellaneous receipts unless otherwise provided by law. The charges or fees assessed by the Administrator for the placement of antennas and supporting services in GSA-controlled space are generally credited to GSA's Federal Buildings Fund.

§ 102–79.75 May Executive agencies assess fees for antenna placements against public service organizations for antenna site outleases on major pedestrian access levels, courtyards, and rooftops of public buildings?

Yes. Executive agencies in GSA-controlled space, upon approval from GSA, may assess fees for antenna placements against public service organizations under 40 U.S.C. 581(h) and 40 U.S.C. 121(e). Such fees or rental rates must be equivalent to the prevailing commercial rate for comparable space devoted to commercial antenna place-

ments in the vicinity of the public building and the proceeds from such charges or fees must be credited to GSA's Federal Buildings Fund.

§ 102–79.80 May Executive agencies assess fees for antenna placements against telecommunication service providers for antenna site outleases on major pedestrian access levels, courtyards, and rooftops of public buildings?

Yes. GSA, or other Executive agencies, upon approval from GSA, may charge fees based on market value to telecommunication service providers for antenna placements in public buildings. Market value should be equivalent to the prevailing commercial rate for comparable space for commercial antenna placements in the vicinity of the public building. Such fees must be credited to GSA's Federal Buildings Fund.

§ 102–79.85 What policy must Executive agencies follow concerning the placement of commercial antennas on Federal property?

Executive agencies will make antenna sites available on a fair, reasonable, and nondiscriminatory basis. Collocation of antennas should be encouraged where there are multiple antenna siting requests for the same location. In cases where this is not feasible and space availability precludes accommodating all antenna siting applicants, competitive procedures may be used. This should be done in accordance with applicable Federal, State and local laws and regulations, and consistent with national security concerns. In making antenna sites available, agencies must avoid electromagnetic intermodulations and interferences. To the maximum extent practicable, when placing antennas for the provision of telecommunication services to the Federal Government, agencies should use redundant and physically separate entry points into the building and physically diverse local network facilities in accordance with guidance issued by the Office of Management and Budget.

§ 102–79.90 What criteria must Executive agencies consider when evaluating antenna siting requests?

When evaluating antenna siting requests, Executive agencies must consider issues such as—

(a) Public health and safety with respect to the antenna installation and maintenance;

(b) Aesthetics;

(c) Effects on historic districts, sites, buildings, monuments, structures, or other objects pursuant to the National Historic Preservation Act of 1966, as amended, and implementing regulations;

(d) Protection of natural and cultural resources (e.g., National Parks and Wilderness areas, National Wildlife Refuge systems);

(e) Compliance with the appropriate level of review and documentation as necessary under the National Environmental Policy Act of 1969, as amended, and implementing regulations of each Federal department and agency responsible for the antenna siting project, and the Federal Aviation Administration, the National Telecommunications and Information Administration, and other relevant departments and agencies;

(f) Compliance with the Federal Communications Commission's (FCC) guidelines for radiofrequency exposure, ET Docket No. 93–62, entitled "Guidelines for Evaluating the Environmental Effects of Radiofrequency Radiation," issued August 1, 1996, and any other order on reconsideration relating to radiofrequency guidelines and their enforcement. These are updated guidelines for meeting health concerns that reflect the latest scientific knowledge in this area, and are supported by Federal health and safety agencies such as the Environmental Protection Agency and the Food and Drug Administration; and

(g) Any requirements of the Federal agency managing the facility, FCC, Federal Aviation Administration, National Telecommunications and Information Administration, and other relevant departments and agencies. To the maximum extent practicable, when placing antennas for the provision of telecommunication services to the Federal Government, agencies should use redundant and physically separate entry points into the building and physically diverse local network facilities in accordance with guidance issued by the Office of Management and Budget. In addition, the National Capital Planning Commission should be consulted for siting requests within the Washington, D.C. metropolitan area.

§ 102–79.95 Who is responsible for the costs associated with providing access to antenna sites?

The telecommunications service provider is responsible for any reasonable costs to Federal agencies associated with providing access to antenna sites, including obtaining appropriate clearance of provider personnel for access to buildings or land deemed to be security sensitive as is done with service contractor personnel. OMB Circular A–25, entitled "User Charges," revised July 8, 1993, provides guidelines that agencies should use to assess fees for Government services and for the sale or use of Government property or resources. For antenna sites on non-GSA property, see also the Department of Commerce Report on "Improving Rights-of-Way Management Across Federal Lands: A Roadmap for Greater Broadband Deployment" (April 2004) beginning at page 26. Under 40 U.S.C. 1314, GSA is covered in granting easements and permits to support the installation of antennas and cabling across raw land in support of constructing new and improving existing telecommunication infrastructures provided that such installation does not negatively impact on the Government.

§ 102–79.100 What must Federal agencies do with antenna siting fees that they collect?

The account into which an antenna siting fee is to be deposited depends on the authority under which the antenna site is made available and the fee assessed. For GSA-controlled property outleased under 40 U.S.C. 581(h) or section 412 of Division H of public law 108–447, the fee is to be deposited into GSA's Federal Building Fund. For surplus property outleased under 40 U.S.C. 543, the fee is to be deposited in accordance with the provisions of Subchapter

IV of Chapter 5 of Subtitle I of Title 40 of the United States Code. For siting fees collected under other statutory authorities, the fees might be deposited into miscellaneous receipts, an account of the landholding agency, or as otherwise provided by law. Federal agencies should consult with their agency's legal advisors before depositing antenna proceed from sites on agency-controlled Federal property.

INTEGRATED WORKPLACE

§ 102–79.105 What is the Integrated Workplace?

The Integrated Workplace, developed by the GSA Office of Governmentwide Policy, is a comprehensive, multidisciplinary approach to developing workspace and work strategies that best support an organization's strategic business goals and work processes, and have the flexibility to accommodate the changing needs of the occupants and the organization. Integrated Workplace concepts support the objectives of Executive Order 13327, "Federal Real Property Asset Management," which calls for the enhancement of Federal agency productivity through an improved working environment.

§ 102–79.110 What Integrated Workplace policy must Federal agencies strive to promote?

Federal agencies must strive to design work places that—

(a) Are developed using sustainable development concepts (see § 102–76.55);

(b) Align with the organization's mission and strategic plan;

(c) Serve the needs and work practices of the occupants;

(d) Can be quickly and inexpensively adjusted by the user to maximize his or her productivity and satisfaction;

(e) Are comfortable, efficient, and technologically advanced and allow people to accomplish their work in the most efficient way;

(f) Meet the office's needs and can justify its cost through the benefits gained;

(g) Are developed with an integrated building systems approach;

(h) Are based on a life cycle cost analysis that considers both facility and human capital costs over a substantial time period; and

(i) Support alternative workplace arrangements, including telecommuting, hoteling, virtual offices, and other distributive work arrangements (see part 102–74, subpart F—Telework).

§ 102–79.111 Where may Executive agencies find additional information on Integrated Workplace concepts?

The GSA Office of Governmentwide Policy provides additional guidance in its publication entitled "Innovative Workplace Strategies."

PUBLIC ACCESS DEFIBRILLATION PROGRAMS

§ 102–79.115 What guidelines must an agency follow if it elects to establish a public access defibrillation program in a Federal facility?

Federal agencies electing to establish a public access defibrillation program in a Federal facility must follow the guidelines, entitled "Guidelines for Public Access Defibrillation Programs in Federal Facilities," which can be obtained from the Office of Governmentwide Policy, Office of Real Property (MP), General Services Administration, 1800 F Street, NW, Washington, DC 20405.

PART 102–80—SAFETY AND ENVIRONMENTAL MANAGEMENT

Subpart A—General Provisions

Sec.
102–80.5 What is the scope of this part?
102–80.10 What are the basic safety and environmental management policies for real property?

Subpart B—Safety and Environmental Management

ASBESTOS

102–80.15 What are Federal agencies' responsibilities concerning the assessment and management of asbestos?

RADON

102–80.20 What are Federal agencies' responsibilities concerning the abatement of radon?

INDOOR AIR QUALITY

102–80.25 What are Federal agencies' responsibilities concerning the management of indoor air quality?

LEAD

102–80.30 What are Federal agencies' responsibilities concerning lead?

HAZARDOUS MATERIALS AND WASTES

102–80.35 What are Federal agencies' responsibilities concerning the monitoring of hazardous materials and wastes?

UNDERGROUND STORAGE TANKS

102–80.40 What are Federal agencies' responsibilities concerning the management of underground storage tanks?

SEISMIC SAFETY

102–80.45 What are Federal agencies' responsibilities concerning seismic safety in Federal facilities?

RISKS AND RISK REDUCTION STRATEGIES

102–80.50 Are Federal agencies responsible for identifying/estimating risks and for appropriate risk reduction strategies?
102–80.55 Are Federal agencies responsible for managing the execution of risk reduction projects?

FACILITY ASSESSMENTS

102–80.60 Are Federal agencies responsible for performing facility assessments?

INCIDENT INVESTIGATION

102–80.65 What are Federal agencies' responsibilities concerning the investigation of incidents, such as fires, accidents, injuries, and environmental incidents?

RESPONSIBILITY FOR INFORMING TENANTS

102–80.70 Are Federal agencies responsible for informing their tenants of the condition and management of their facility safety and environment?

ASSESSMENT OF ENVIRONMENTAL ISSUES

102–80.75 Who assesses environmental issues in Federal construction and lease construction projects?

Subpart C—Accident and Fire Prevention

102–80.80 With what general accident and fire prevention policy must Federal agencies comply?

STATE AND LOCAL CODES

102–80.85 Are Federally owned and leased buildings exempt from State and local code requirements in fire protection?

FIRE ADMINISTRATION AUTHORIZATION ACT OF 1992

102–80.90 Is the Fire Administration Authorization Act of 1992 (Pub. L. 102–522) relevant to fire protection engineering?

102–80.95 Is the Fire Administration Authorization Act of 1992 applicable to all Federal agencies?

AUTOMATIC SPRINKLER SYSTEMS

102–80.100 What performance objective should an automatic sprinkler system be capable of meeting?

EQUIVALENT LEVEL OF SAFETY ANALYSIS

102–80.105 What information must be included in an equivalent level of safety analysis?
102–80.110 What must an equivalent level of safety analysis indicate?
102–80.115 Is there more than one option for establishing that an equivalent level of safety exists?
102–80.120 What analytical and empirical tools should be used to support the life safety equivalency evaluation?
102–80.125 Who has the responsibility for determining the acceptability of each equivalent level of safety analysis?
102–80.130 Who must perform the equivalent level of safety analysis?
102–80.135 Who is a qualified fire protection engineer?

ROOM OF ORIGIN

102–80.140 What is meant by "room of origin"?

FLASHOVER

102–80.145 What is meant by "flashover"?

REASONABLE WORST CASE FIRE SCENARIO

102–80.150 What is meant by "reasonable worst case fire scenario"?

AUTHORITY: 40 U.S.C. 121(c) and 581–593.

SOURCE: 70 FR 67852, Nov. 8, 2005, unless otherwise noted.

Subpart A—General Provisions

§ 102–80.5 What is the scope of this part?

The real property policies contained in this part apply to Federal agencies, including GSA's Public Buildings Service (PBS), operating under, or subject to, the authorities of the Administrator of General Services. The responsibilities for safety and environmental management under this part are intended to apply to GSA or those Federal agencies operating in GSA space pursuant to a GSA delegation of authority.

§102–80.10 What are the basic safety and environmental management policies for real property?

The basic safety and environmental management policies for real property are that Federal agencies must—

(a) Provide for a safe and healthful work environment for Federal employees and the visiting public;

(b) Protect Federal real and personal property;

(c) Promote mission continuity;

(d) Provide reasonable safeguards for emergency forces if an incident occurs;

(e) Assess risk;

(f) Make decision makers aware of risks; and

(g) Act promptly and appropriately in response to risk.

Subpart B—Safety and Environmental Management

ASBESTOS

§102–80.15 What are Federal agencies' responsibilities concerning the assessment and management of asbestos?

Federal agencies have the following responsibilities concerning the assessment and management of asbestos:

(a) Inspect and assess buildings for the presence and condition of asbestos-containing materials. Space to be leased must be free of all asbestos containing materials, except undamaged asbestos flooring in the space or undamaged boiler or pipe insulation outside the space, in which case an asbestos management program conforming to U.S. Environmental Protection Agency (EPA) guidance must be implemented.

(b) Manage in-place asbestos that is in good condition and not likely to be disturbed.

(c) Abate damaged asbestos and asbestos likely to be disturbed. Federal agencies must perform a pre-alteration asbestos assessment for activities that may disturb asbestos.

(d) Not use asbestos in new construction, renovation/modernization or repair of their owned or leased space. Unless approved by GSA, Federal agencies must not obtain space with asbestos through purchase, exchange, transfer, or lease, except as identified in paragraph (a) of this section.

(e) Communicate all written and oral asbestos information about the leased space to tenants.

RADON

§102–80.20 What are Federal agencies' responsibilities concerning the abatement of radon?

Federal agencies have the following responsibilities concerning the abatement of radon in space when radon levels exceed current EPA standards:

(a) Retest abated areas and make lessors retest, as required, abated areas to adhere to EPA standards.

(b) Test non-public water sources (in remote areas for projects such as border stations) for radon according to EPA guidance. Radon levels that exceed current applicable EPA standards must be mitigated. Federal agencies must retest, as required, to adhere to EPA standards.

INDOOR AIR QUALITY

§102–80.25 What are Federal agencies' responsibilities concerning the management of indoor air quality?

Federal agencies must assess indoor air quality of buildings as part of their safety and environmental facility assessments. Federal agencies must respond to tenant complaints on air quality and take appropriate corrective action where air quality does not meet applicable standards.

LEAD

§102–80.30 What are Federal agencies' responsibilities concerning lead?

Federal agencies have the following responsibilities concerning lead in buildings:

(a) Test space for lead-based paint in renovation projects that require sanding, welding or scraping painted surfaces.

(b) Not remove lead based paint from surfaces in good condition.

(c) Test all painted surfaces for lead in proposed or existing child care centers.

(d) Abate lead-based paint found in accordance with U.S. Department of Housing and Urban Development (HUD)

Lead-Based Paint Guidelines, available by writing to HUD USER, P.O. Box 6091, Rockville, MD 20850.

(e) Test potable water for lead in all drinking water outlets.

(f) Take corrective action when lead levels exceed the HUD Guidelines.

HAZARDOUS MATERIALS AND WASTES

§ 102–80.35 What are Federal agencies' responsibilities concerning the monitoring of hazardous materials and wastes?

Federal agencies' responsibilities concerning the monitoring of hazardous materials and wastes are as follows:

(a) Monitor the transport, use, and disposition of hazardous materials and waste in buildings to provide for compliance with GSA, Occupational Safety and Health Administration (OSHA), Department of Transportation, EPA, and applicable State and local requirements. In addition to those operating in GSA space pursuant to a delegation of authority, tenants in GSA space must comply with these requirements.

(b) In leased space, include in all agreements with the lessor requirements that hazardous materials stored in leased space are kept and maintained according to applicable Federal, State, and local environmental regulations.

UNDERGROUND STORAGE TANKS

§ 102–80.40 What are Federal agencies' responsibilities concerning the management of underground storage tanks?

Federal agencies have the following responsibilities concerning the management of underground storage tanks in real property:

(a) Register, manage and close underground storage tanks, including heating oil and fuel oil tanks, in accordance with GSA, EPA, and applicable State and local requirements.

(b) Require the party responsible for tanks they use but do not own to follow these requirements and to be responsible for the cost of compliance.

SEISMIC SAFETY

§ 102–80.45 What are Federal agencies' responsibilities concerning seismic safety in Federal facilities?

Federal agencies must follow the standards issued by the Interagency Committee on Seismic Safety in Construction (ICSSC) as the minimum level acceptable for use by Federal agencies in assessing the seismic safety of their owned and leased buildings and in mitigating unacceptable seismic risks in those buildings.

RISKS AND RISK REDUCTION STRATEGIES

§ 102–80.50 Are Federal agencies responsible for identifying/estimating risks and for appropriate risk reduction strategies?

Yes, Federal agencies must identify and estimate safety and environmental management risks and appropriate risk reduction strategies for buildings. Federal agencies occupying as well as operating buildings must identify any safety and environmental management risks and report or correct the situation, as appropriate. Federal agencies must use the applicable national codes and standards as a guide for their building operations.

§ 102–80.55 Are Federal agencies responsible for managing the execution of risk reduction projects?

Yes, Federal agencies must manage the execution of risk reduction projects in buildings they operate. Federal agencies must identify and take appropriate action to eliminate hazards and regulatory noncompliance.

FACILITY ASSESSMENTS

§ 102–80.60 Are Federal agencies responsible for performing facility assessments?

Yes, Federal agencies must evaluate facilities to comply with GSA's safety and environmental program and applicable Federal, State and local environmental laws and regulations. Federal agencies should conduct these evaluations in accordance with schedules that are compatible with repair and alteration and leasing operations.

INCIDENT INVESTIGATION

§102–80.65 What are Federal agencies' responsibilities concerning the investigation of incidents, such as fires, accidents, injuries, and environmental incidents?

Federal agencies have the following responsibilities concerning the investigation of incidents, such as fires, accidents, injuries, and environmental incidents in buildings they operate:

(a) Investigate all incidents regardless of severity.

(b) Form Boards of Investigation for incidents resulting in serious injury, death, or significant property losses.

RESPONSIBILITY FOR INFORMING TENANTS

§102–80.70 Are Federal agencies responsible for informing their tenants of the condition and management of their facility safety and environment?

Yes, Federal agencies must inform their tenants of the condition and management of their facility safety and environment. Agencies operating GSA buildings must report any significant facility safety or environmental concerns to GSA.

ASSESSMENT OF ENVIRONMENTAL ISSUES

§102–80.75 Who assesses environmental issues in Federal construction and lease construction projects?

Federal agencies must assess required environmental issues throughout planning and project development so that the environmental impacts of a project are considered during the decision making process.

Subpart C—Accident and Fire Prevention

§102–80.80 With what general accident and fire prevention policy must Federal agencies comply?

Federal agencies must—

(a) Comply with the occupational safety and health standards established in the Occupational Safety and Health Act of 1970 (Pub. L. 91–596); Executive Order 12196; 29 CFR part 1960; and applicable safety and environmental management criteria identified in this part;

(b) Not expose occupants and visitors to unnecessary risks;

(c) Provide safeguards that minimize personal harm, property damage, and impairment of Governmental operations, and that allow emergency forces to accomplish their missions effectively;

(d) Follow accepted fire prevention practices in operating and managing buildings;

(e) To the maximum extent feasible, comply with one of the nationally recognized model building codes and with other nationally-recognized codes in their construction or alteration of each building in accordance with 40 U.S.C. 3312; and

(f) Use the applicable national codes and standards as a guide for their building operations.

STATE AND LOCAL CODES

§102–80.85 Are Federally owned and leased buildings exempt from State and local code requirements in fire protection?

Federally owned buildings are generally exempt from State and local code requirements in fire protection; however, in accordance with 40 U.S.C. 3312, each building constructed or altered by a Federal agency must be constructed or altered, to the maximum extent feasible, in compliance with one of the nationally recognized model building codes and with other nationally recognized codes. Leased buildings are subject to local code requirements and inspection.

FIRE ADMINISTRATION AUTHORIZATION ACT OF 1992

§102–80.90 Is the Fire Administration Authorization Act of 1992 (Public Law 102–522) relevant to fire protection engineering?

Yes, the Fire Administration Authorization Act of 1992 (Pub. L. 102–522) requires sprinklers or an equivalent level of safety in certain types of Federal employee office buildings, Federal employee housing units, and Federally assisted housing units (15 U.S.C. 2227).

§ 102–80.95 Is the Fire Administration Authorization Act of 1992 applicable to all Federal agencies?

Yes, the Fire Administration Authorization Act applies to all Federal agencies and all Federally owned and leased buildings in the United States.

AUTOMATIC SPRINKLER SYSTEMS

§ 102–80.100 What performance objective should an automatic sprinkler system be capable of meeting?

The performance objective of the automatic sprinkler system is that it must be capable of protecting human lives. Sprinklers should be capable of controlling the spread of fire and its effects beyond the room of origin. A functioning sprinkler system should activate prior to the onset of flashover.

EQUIVALENT LEVEL OF SAFETY ANALYSIS

§ 102–80.105 What information must be included in an equivalent level of safety analysis?

The equivalent level of life safety evaluation is to be performed by a qualified fire protection engineer. The analysis should include a narrative discussion of the features of the building structure, function, operational support systems and occupant activities that impact fire protection and life safety. Each analysis should describe potential reasonable worst case fire scenarios and their impact on the building occupants and structure. Specific issues that must be addressed include rate of fire growth, type and location of fuel items, space layout, building construction, openings and ventilation, suppression capability, detection time, occupant notification, occupant reaction time, occupant mobility, and means of egress.

§ 102–80.110 What must an equivalent level of safety analysis indicate?

To be acceptable, the analysis must indicate that the existing and/or proposed safety systems in the building provide a period of time equal to or greater than the amount of time available for escape in a similar building complying with the Fire Administration Authorization Act. In conducting these analyses, the capability, ade-

quacy, and reliability of all building systems impacting fire growth, occupant knowledge of the fire, and time required to reach a safety area will have to be examined. In particular, the impact of sprinklers on the development of hazardous conditions in the area of interest will have to be assessed.

§ 102–80.115 Is there more than one option for establishing that an equivalent level of safety exists?

Yes, the following are three options for establishing that an equivalent level of safety exists:

(a) In the first option, the margin of safety provided by various alternatives is compared to that obtained for a code complying building with complete sprinkler protection. The margin of safety is the difference between the available safe egress time and the required safe egress time. Available safe egress time is the time available for evacuation of occupants to an area of safety prior to the onset of untenable conditions in occupied areas or the egress pathways. The required safe egress time is the time required by occupants to move from their positions at the start of the fire to areas of safety. Available safe egress times would be developed based on analysis of a number of assumed reasonable worst case fire scenarios including assessment of a code complying fully sprinklered building. Additional analysis would be used to determine the expected required safe egress times for the various scenarios. If the margin of safety plus an appropriate safety factor is greater for an alternative than for the fully sprinklered building, then the alternative should provide an equivalent level of safety.

(b) A second alternative is applicable for typical office and residential scenarios. In these situations, complete sprinkler protection can be expected to prevent flashover in the room of fire origin, limit fire size to no more than 1 megawatt (950 Btu/sec), and prevent flames from leaving the room of origin. The times required for each of these conditions to occur in the area of interest must be determined. The shortest of these three times would become the time available for escape. The difference between the minimum time available for escape and the time required for evacuation of building occupants would be the target margin of safety. Various alternative protection strategies would have to be evaluated to determine their impact on the times at which hazardous conditions developed in the spaces of interest and the times required for egress. If a combination of fire protection systems provides a margin of safety equal to or greater than the target margin of safety, then the combination could be judged to provide an equivalent level of safety.

(c) As a third option, other technical analysis procedures, as approved by the responsible agency head, can be used to show equivalency.

§ 102–80.120 What analytical and empirical tools should be used to support the life safety equivalency evaluation?

Analytical and empirical tools, including fire models and grading schedules such as the Fire Safety Evaluation System (Alternative Approaches to Life Safety, NEPA 101A) should be used to support the life safety equivalency evaluation. If fire modeling is used as part of an analysis, an assessment of the predictive capabilities of the fire models must be included. This assessment should be conducted in accordance with the American Society for Testing and Materials Standard Guide for Evaluating the Predictive Capability of Fire Models (ASTM E 1355).

§ 102–80.125 Who has the responsibility for determining the acceptability of each equivalent level of safety analysis?

The head of the agency responsible for physical improvements in the facility or providing Federal assistance or a designated representative will determine the acceptability of each equivalent level of safety analysis. The determination of acceptability must include a review of the fire protection engineer's qualifications, the appropriateness of the fire scenarios for the facility, and the reasonableness of the assumed maximum probable loss. Agencies should maintain a record of each accepted equivalent level of safety analysis and provide copies to fire departments or other local authorities for use in developing pre-fire plans.

§ 102–80.130 Who must perform the equivalent level of safety analysis?

A qualified fire protection engineer must perform the equivalent level of safety analysis.

§ 102–80.135 Who is a qualified fire protection engineer?

A qualified fire protection engineer is defined as an individual with a thorough knowledge and understanding of the principles of physics and chemistry governing fire growth, spread, and suppression, meeting one of the following criteria:

(a) An engineer having an undergraduate or graduate degree from a college or university offering a course of study in fire protection or fire safety engineering, plus a minimum of 4 years work experience in fire protection engineering.

(b) A professional engineer (P.E. or similar designation) registered in Fire Protection Engineering.

(c) A professional engineer (P.E. or similar designation) registered in a related engineering discipline and holding Member grade status in the International Society of Fire Protection Engineers.

ROOM OF ORIGIN

§ 102–80.140 What is meant by "room of origin"?

Room of origin means an area of a building where a fire can be expected to start. Typically, the size of the area will be determined by the walls, floor, and ceiling surrounding the space. However, this could lead to unacceptably large areas in the case of open plan office space or similar arrangements. Therefore, the maximum allowable fire area should be limited to 200 m2 (2000 ft2), including intervening spaces. In the case of residential units, an entire apartment occupied by one tenant could be considered as the room of origin to the extent it did not exceed the 200 m2 (2000 ft2) limitation.

FLASHOVER

§ 102–80.145 What is meant by "flashover"?

Flashover means fire conditions in a confined area where the upper gas layer temperature reaches 600 °C (1100 °F) and the heat flux at floor level exceeds 20 kW/m2 (1.8 Btu/ft2/sec).

REASONABLE WORST CASE FIRE SCENARIO

§ 102–80.150 What is meant by "reasonable worst case fire scenario"?

Reasonable worst case fire scenario means a combination of an ignition source, fuel items, and a building location likely to produce a fire that would have a significant adverse impact on the building and its occupants. The development of reasonable worst case scenarios must include consideration of types and forms of fuels present (e.g., furniture, trash, paper, chemicals), potential fire ignition locations (e.g., bedroom, office, closet, corridor), occupant capabilities (e.g., awake, intoxicated, mentally or physically impaired), numbers of occupants, detection and suppression system adequacy and reliability, and fire department capabilities. A quantitative analysis of the probability of occurrence of each scenario and combination of events will be necessary.

PART 102–81—SECURITY

Subpart A—General Provisions

Sec.
102–81.5 What is the scope of this part?
102–81.10 What basic security policy governs Federal agencies?

Subpart B—Security

102–81.15 Who is responsible for upgrading and maintaining security standards in each existing Federally owned and leased facility?
102–81.20 Are the security standards for new Federally owned and leased facilities the same as the standards for existing Federally owned and leased facilities?
102–81.25 Do the Interagency Security Committee Security Design Criteria apply to all new Federally owned and leased facilities?
102–81.30 What information must job applicants at child care centers reveal?

AUTHORITY: 40 U.S.C. 121(c), 581–593, and 1315.

SOURCE: 70 FR 67856, Nov. 8, 2005, unless otherwise noted.

Subpart A—General Provisions

§ 102–81.5 What is the scope of this part?

The real property policies contained in this part apply to Federal agencies, including GSA's Public Buildings Service (PBS), operating under, or subject to, the authorities of the Administrator of General Services.

§ 102–81.10 What basic security policy governs Federal agencies?

Federal agencies on Federal property under the charge and control of the Administrator and having a security delegation of authority from the Secretary of the Department of Homeland Security must provide for the security and protection of the real estate they occupy, including the protection of persons within the property.

Subpart B—Security

§ 102–81.15 Who is responsible for upgrading and maintaining security standards in each existing Federally owned and leased facility?

In a June 28, 1995, Presidential Policy Memorandum for Executive Departments and Agencies, entitled "Upgrading Security at Federal Facilities" (see the Weekly Compilation of Presidential Documents, vol. 31, p. 1148), the President directed that Executive agencies must, where feasible, upgrade and maintain security in facilities they own or lease under their own authority to the minimum standards specified in the Department of Justice's June 28, 1995, study entitled "Vulnerability Assessment of Federal Facilities." The study may be obtained by writing to the Superintendent of Documents, P.O. Box 371954, Pittsburgh, PA 15250–7954.

§ 102–81.20 Are the security standards for new Federally owned and leased facilities the same as the standards for existing Federally owned and leased facilities?

No, the minimum standards specified in the Department of Justice's June 28,

1995, study entitled "Vulnerability Assessment of Federal Facilities" identifies the minimum-security standards that agencies must adhere to for all existing owned and leased Federal facilities. As specified in § 102–81.25, new Federally owned and leased facilities must be designed to meet the standards identified in the document entitled "Interagency Security Committee Security Design Criteria for New Federal Office Buildings and Major Modernization Projects," dated May 28, 2001. The security design criteria for new facilities takes into consideration technology developments, new cost consideration, the experience of practitioners applying the criteria, and the need to balance security requirements with public building environments that remain lively, open, and accessible.

§ 102–81.25 Do the Interagency Security Committee Security Design Criteria apply to all new Federally owned and leased facilities?

No, the Interagency Security Committee Security Design Criteria—

(a) Apply to new construction of general purpose office buildings and new or lease-construction of courthouses occupied by Federal employees in the United States and not under the jurisdiction and/or control of the Department of Defense. The criteria also apply to lease-construction projects being submitted to Congress for appropriations or authorization. Where prudent and appropriate, the criteria apply to major modernization projects; and

(b) Do not apply to airports, prisons, hospitals, clinics, and ports of entry, or to unique facilities such as those classified by the Department of Justice Vulnerability Assessment Study as Level V. Nor will the criteria overrule existing Federal laws and statutes, and other agency standards that have been developed for special facilities, such as border stations and child care centers.

§ 102–81.30 What information must job applicants at child care centers reveal?

Anyone who applies for employment (including volunteer positions) at a child care facility, located on Federally controlled property (including Federally leased property), must reveal any arrests and convictions on the job application. Employment at a child care facility means any position that involves work with minor children, such as a teacher, daycare worker, or school administrator.

PART 102–82—UTILITY SERVICES

Subpart A—General Provisions

Sec.
102–82.5 What is the scope of this part?
102–82.10 What basic utility services policy govern Executive agencies?

Subpart B—Utility Services

102–82.15 What utility services must Executive agencies provide?
102–82.20 What are Executive agencies' rate intervention responsibilities?
102–82.25 What are Executive agencies' responsibilities concerning the procurement of utility services?

AUTHORITY: 40 U.S.C. 121(c) and 501.

SOURCE: 70 FR 67856, Nov. 8, 2005, unless otherwise noted.

Subpart A—General Provisions

§ 102–82.5 What is the scope of this part?

The real property policies contained in this part apply to Federal agencies, including GSA's Public Buildings Service (PBS), operating under, or subject to, the authorities of the Administrator of General Services.

§ 102–82.10 What basic utility services policy govern Executive agencies?

Executive agencies procuring, managing or supplying utility services under Title 40 of the United States Code must provide or procure services that promote economy and efficiency with due regard to the mission responsibilities of the agencies concerned.

Subpart B—Utility Services

§ 102–82.15 What utility services must Executive agencies provide?

Executive agencies must negotiate with public utilities to procure utility services and, where appropriate, provide rate intervention services in proceedings (see §§ 102–72.100 and 102–72.105

of this chapter) before Federal and State utility regulatory bodies.

§ 102–82.20 What are Executive agencies' rate intervention responsibilities?

Where the consumer interests of the Federal Government will be significantly affected and upon receiving a delegation of authority from GSA, Executive agencies must provide representation in proceedings involving utility services before Federal and State regulatory bodies. Specifically, these responsibilities include instituting formal or informal action before Federal and State regulatory bodies to contest the level, structure, or applicability of rates or service terms of utility suppliers. The Secretary of Defense is independently authorized to take such actions without a delegation from GSA, when the Secretary determines such actions to be in the best interests of national security.

§ 102–82.25 What are Executive agencies' responsibilities concerning the procurement of utility services?

Executive agencies, operating under a utility services delegation from GSA, or the Secretary of Defense, when the Secretary determines it to be in the best interests of national security, must provide for the procurement of utility services (such as commodities and utility rebate programs), as required, and must procure from sources of supply that are the most advantageous to the Federal Government in terms of economy, efficiency, reliability, or quality of service. Executive agencies, upon receiving a delegation of authority from GSA, may enter into contracts for utility services for periods not exceeding ten years (40 U.S.C. 501(b)(1)(B)).

PART 102–83—LOCATION OF SPACE

Subpart A—General Provisions

Subpart B—Location of Space

AUTHORITY: 40 U.S.C. 121(c); E.O. 12072; and E.O. 13006.

SOURCE: 70 FR 67857, Nov. 8, 2005, unless otherwise noted.

Subpart A—General Provisions

§ 102–83.5 What is the scope of this part?

The real property policies contained in this part apply to Federal agencies, including GSA's Public Buildings Service (PBS), operating under, or subject to, the authorities of the Administrator of General Services.

§ 102–83.10 What basic location of space policy governs an Executive agency?

Each Executive agency is responsible for identifying its geographic service area and the delineated area within which it wishes to locate specific activities, consistent with its mission and program requirements, and in accordance with all applicable statutes, regulations and policies.

§ 102–83.15 Is there a general hierarchy of consideration that agencies must follow in their utilization of space?

Yes, Federal agencies must follow the hierarchy of consideration identified in § 102–79.55 of this chapter.

Subpart B—Location of Space

DELINEATED AREA

§ 102–83.20 What is a delineated area?

Delineated area means the specific boundaries within which space will be obtained to satisfy an agency space requirement.

§ 102–83.25 Who is responsible for identifying the delineated area within which a Federal agency wishes to locate specific activities?

Each Federal agency is responsible for identifying the delineated area within which it wishes to locate specific activities, consistent with its mission and program requirements, and in accordance with all applicable laws, regulations, and Executive Orders.

§ 102–83.30 In addition to its mission and program requirements, are there any other issues that Federal agencies must consider in identifying the delineated area?

Yes, Federal agencies must also consider real estate, labor, and other operational costs and applicable local incentives, when identifying the delineated area.

§ 102–83.35 Are Executive agencies required to consider whether the central business area will provide for adequate competition when acquiring leased space?

In accordance with the Competition in Contracting Act of 1984, as amended (41 U.S.C. 253(a)), Executive agencies must consider whether restricting the delineated area for obtaining leased space to the central business area (CBA) will provide for adequate competition when acquiring leased space. Where an Executive agency determines that the delineated area must be expanded beyond the CBA to provide adequate competition, the agency may expand the delineated area in consultation with local officials. Executive agencies must continue to include the CBA in such expanded areas.

§ 102–83.40 Who must approve the final delineated area?

Federal agencies conducting the procurement must approve the final delineated area for site acquisitions and lease actions and must confirm that the final delineated area complies with the requirements of all applicable laws, regulations, and Executive Orders.

§ 102–83.45 Where may Executive agencies find guidance on appealing GSA's decisions and recommendations concerning delineated areas?

GSA's PBS provides guidance in its Customer Guide to Real Property on the process for appealing GSA's decisions and recommendations concerning delineated areas.

RURAL AREAS

§ 102–83.50 What is the Rural Development Act of 1972?

The Rural Development Act of 1972, as amended (7 U.S.C. 2204b–1), directs Federal agencies to develop policies and procedures to give first priority to the location of new offices and other Federal facilities in rural areas. The intent of the Rural Development Act is to revitalize and develop rural areas and to help foster a balance between rural and urban America.

§ 102–83.55 What is a rural area?

As defined in 7 U.S.C. 1991(a)(13)(A), rural area means any area other than—

(a) A city or town that has a population of greater than 50,000 inhabitants; and

(b) The urbanized area contiguous and adjacent to such a city or town.

§ 102–83.60 What is an urbanized area?

An urbanized area is a statistical geographic area defined by the Census Bureau, consisting of a central place(s) and adjacent densely settled territory that together contain at least 50,000 people, generally with an overall population density of at least 1,000 people per square mile.

§ 102–83.65 Are Executive agencies required to give first priority to the location of new offices and other facilities in rural areas?

Yes, Executive agencies must give first priority to the location of new offices and other facilities in rural areas in accordance with the Rural Development Act (7 U.S.C. 2204b–1), unless their mission or program requirements call for locations in an urban area. First priority to the location of new offices and other facilities in rural areas must be given in accordance with the

hierarchy specified in § 102–79.55 of this chapter.

URBAN AREAS

§ 102–83.70 What is Executive Order 12072?

Executive Order 12072, entitled "Federal Space Management," requires all Executive agencies that have a mission requirement to locate in an urban area to give first consideration to locating Federal facilities in central business areas, and/or adjacent areas of similar character, to use them to make downtowns attractive places to work, conserve existing resources, and encourage redevelopment. It also directs Executive agencies to consider opportunities for locating cultural, educational, recreational, or commercial activities within the proposed facility.

§ 102–83.75 What is Executive Order 13006?

Executive Order 13006, entitled "Locating Federal Facilities on Historic Properties in Our Nation's Central Cities," requires all Executive agencies that have a mission requirement to locate in an urban area to give first consideration to locating Federal facilities in historic buildings and districts within central business areas. It also directs Executive agencies to remove regulatory barriers, review their policies, and build new partnerships with the goal of enhancing participation in the National Historic Preservation program.

§ 102–83.80 What is an urban area?

Urban area means any metropolitan area (MA) as defined by the Office of Management and Budget (OMB) in OMB Bulletin No. 99–04, or succeeding OMB Bulletin, that does not meet the definition of rural area in § 102–83.55.

§ 102–83.85 What is a central business area?

Central business area (CBA) means the centralized community business area and adjacent areas of similar character, including other specific areas that may be recommended by local officials in accordance with Executive Order 12072. The CBAs are designated by local government and not by Federal agencies.

§ 102–83.90 Do Executive Orders 12072 and 13006 apply to rural areas?

No, Executive Orders 12072 and 13006 only apply to agencies looking for space in urban areas.

§ 102–83.95 After an agency has identified that its geographic service area and delineated area are in an urban area, what is the next step for an agency?

After an agency identifies its geographic service area and delineated area within which it wishes to locate specific activities are in an urban area (i.e., determined that the agency's mission requirements dictate a need to locate its facility in an urban area), Federal agencies must seek space in historic properties already under agency control, in accordance with section 110 of the National Historic Preservation Act. The National Historic Preservation Act provides that prior to purchasing, constructing or leasing new space, Federal agencies must—

(a) Consider agency-controlled historic properties within historic districts inside CBAs when locating Federal operations, in accordance with Executive Order 13006 (which, by reference, also incorporates the requirements in Executive Order 12072 and the Rural Development Act of 1972);

(b) Then consider agency-controlled developed or undeveloped sites within historic districts, if no suitable agency-controlled historic property specified in paragraph (a) of this section is available;

(c) Then consider agency-controlled historic properties outside of historic districts, if no suitable agency-controlled site exists within a historic district as specified in paragraph (b) of this section;

(d) Then consider non-historic agency-controlled properties, if no suitable agency-controlled historic properties outside of historic districts exist as specified in paragraph (c) of this section;

(e) Then consider historic properties under the custody and control of the U.S. Postal Service, if there is no available space in non-historic agency-controlled properties specified in paragraph (d) of this section.

(f) Then consider non-historic properties under the custody and control of the U.S. Postal Service, if there is no available space in historic properties under the custody and control of the U.S. Postal Service specified in paragraph (e) of this section.

§ 102–83.100 Why must agencies consider available space in properties under the custody and control of the U.S. Postal Service?

See § 102–73.20 of this chapter.

§ 102–83.105 What happens if there is no available space in non-historic buildings under the custody and control of the U.S. Postal Service?

If no suitable space in non-historic buildings under the custody and control of the U.S. Postal Service is available, agencies may then acquire real estate by purchase, lease, or construction, in accordance with FMR part 102–73.

§ 102–83.110 When an agency's mission and program requirements call for the location in an urban area, are Executive agencies required to give first consideration to central business areas?

Yes, if an agency has a specific location need to be in an urban area, then Executive Orders 12072 and 13006 require that agencies should give first consideration to locating in a historic building in a historic district in the CBA of a central city of the appropriate metropolitan area. If no such space is available, agencies must give consideration to locating in a non-historic building in a historic district in the CBA of a central city of the appropriate metropolitan area. If no such space is available, agencies must give consideration to locating in a historic building outside of a historic district in the CBA of a central city of the appropriate metropolitan area. If no such space is available, agencies should give consideration to locating in a non-historic building outside of a historic district in the CBA of a central city of the appropriate metropolitan area.

§ 102–83.115   What is a central city?

Central cities are those central cities defined by OMB in OMB Bulletin No. 99–04, or succeeding OMB Bulletin.

§ 102–83.120   What happens if an agency has a need to be in a specific urban area that is not a central city in a metropolitan area?

If an agency has a need to be in a specific urban area that is not a central city in a metropolitan area, then the agency must give first consideration to locating in a historic building in a historic district in the CBA of the appropriate metropolitan area. If no such space is available, agencies must give consideration to locating in a non-historic building in a historic district in the CBA of the appropriate metropolitan area. If no such space is available, agencies must give consideration to locating in a historic building outside of a historic district in the CBA of the appropriate metropolitan area. If no such space is available, agencies should give consideration to locating in a non-historic building outside of a historic district in the CBA of the appropriate metropolitan area.

PREFERENCE TO HISTORIC PROPERTIES

§ 102–83.125   Are Executive agencies required to give preference to historic properties when acquiring leased space?

Yes, Federal agencies must give a price preference when acquiring space using either the lowest price technically acceptable or the best value tradeoff source selection process. See part 102–73 of this chapter for additional guidance.

APPLICATION OF SOCIOECONOMIC
CONSIDERATIONS

§ 102–83.130   When must agencies consider the impact of location decisions on low- and moderate-income employees?

Federal agencies proposing locations for Federal construction or major lease actions involving the relocation of a major work force must consider the impact on employees with low and moderate incomes.

§ 102–83.135   With whom must agencies consult in determining the availability of low- and moderate-income housing?

Federal agencies must consult with the U.S. Department of Housing and Urban Development (HUD) in accordance with the Memorandum of Understanding (MOU) between HUD and GSA. The text of the HUD-GSA MOU is located in the appendix to this part.

APPENDIX TO PART 102–83—MEMO-
RANDUM OF UNDERSTANDING BE-
TWEEN THE DEPARTMENT OF HOUS-
ING AND URBAN DEVELOPMENT AND
THE GENERAL SERVICES ADMINIS-
TRATION CONCERNING LOW- AND
MODERATE-INCOME HOUSING

Purpose. The purpose of the memorandum of understanding is to provide an effective, systematic arrangement under which the Federal Government, acting through HUD and GSA, will fulfill its responsibilities under law, and as a major employer, in accordance with the concepts of good management, to assure for its employees the availability of low- and moderate-income housing without discrimination because of race, color, religion, or national origin, and to consider the need for development and redevelopment of areas and the development of new communities and the impact on improving social and economic conditions in the area, whenever Federal Government facilities locate or relocate at new sites, and to use its resources and authority to aid in the achievement of these objectives.

1. Title VIII of the Civil Rights Act of 1968 (42 U.S.C. 3601) states, in section 801, that "It is the policy of the United States to provide, within constitutional limitations, for fair housing throughout the United States." Section 808(a) places the authority and responsibility for administering the Act in the Secretary of Housing and Urban Development. Section 808(d) requires all Executive departments and agencies to administer their programs and activities relating to housing and urban development in a manner affirmatively to further the purposes of title VIII (fair housing) and to cooperate with the Secretary to further such purposes. Section 808(e)(5) provides that the Secretary of HUD shall administer the programs and activities relating to housing and urban development in a manner affirmatively to further the policies of title VIII.

2. Section 2 of the Housing Act of 1949 (42 U.S.C. 1441) declares the national policy of "* * * the realization as soon as feasible of the goal of a decent home and a suitable living environment for every American family

* * *." This goal was reaffirmed in the Housing and Urban Development Act of 1968 (sections 2 and 1601; 12 U.S.C. 1701t and 42 U.S.C. 1441a).

3. By virtue of the Public Buildings Act of 1959, as amended; the Federal Property and Administrative Services Act of 1949, as amended; and Reorganization Plan No. 18 of 1950, the Administrator of General Services is given certain authority and responsibility in connection with planning, developing, and constructing Government-owned public buildings for housing Federal agencies, and for acquiring leased space for Federal agency use.

4. Executive Order 11512, February 27, 1970, sets forth the policies by which the Administrator of General Services and the heads of Executive agencies will be guided in the acquisition of both federally owned and leased office buildings and space.

5. While Executive Order No. 11512 provides that material consideration will be given to the efficient performance of the missions and programs of the Executive agencies and the nature and functions of the facilities involved, there are six other guidelines set forth, including:

• The need for development and redevelopment of areas and the development of new communities, and the impact a selection will have on improving social and economic conditions in the area; and

• The availability of adequate low- and moderate-income housing, adequate access from other areas of the urban center, and adequacy of parking.

6. General Services Administration (GSA) recognizes its responsibility, in all its determinations with respect to the construction of Federal buildings and the acquisition of leased space, to consider to the maximum possible extent the availability of low- and moderate-income housing without discrimination because of race, color, religion, or national origin, in accordance with its duty affirmatively to further the purposes of title VIII of the Civil Rights Act of 1968 and with the authorities referred to in paragraph 2 above, and the guidelines referred to in paragraph 5 above, and consistent with the authorities cited in paragraphs 3 and 4 above. In connection with the foregoing statement, it is recognized that all the guidelines must be considered in each case, with the ultimate decision to be made by the Administrator of General Services upon his determination that such decision will improve the management and administration of governmental activities and services, and will foster the programs and policies of the Federal Government.

7. In addition to its fair housing responsibilities, the responsibilities of HUD include assisting in the development of the Nation's housing supply through programs of mortgage insurance, home ownership and rental housing assistance, rent supplements, below market interest rates, and low-rent public housing. Additional HUD program responsibilities which relate or impinge upon housing and community development include comprehensive planning assistance, metropolitan area planning coordination, new communities, relocation, urban renewal, model cities, rehabilitation loans and grants, neighborhood facilities grants, water and sewer grants, open space, public facilities loans, Operation BREAKTHROUGH, code enforcement, workable programs, and others.

8. In view of its responsibilities described in paragraphs 1 and 7 above, HUD possesses the necessary expertise to investigate, determine, and report to GSA on the availability of low- and moderate-income housing on a nondiscriminatory basis and to make findings as to such availability with respect to proposed locations for a federally-constructed building or leased space which would be consistent with such reports. HUD also possesses the necessary expertise to advise GSA and other Federal agencies with respect to actions which would increase the availability of low- and moderate-income housing on a nondiscriminatory basis, once a site has been selected for a federally-constructed building or a lease executed for space, as well as to assist in increasing the availability of such housing through its own programs such as those described in paragraph 7 above.

9. HUD and GSA agree that:

(a) GSA will pursue the achievement of low- and moderate-income housing objectives and fair housing objectives, in accordance with its responsibilities recognized in paragraph 6 above, in all determinations, tentative and final, with respect to the location of both federally constructed buildings and leased buildings and space, and will make all reasonable efforts to make this policy known to all persons, organizations, agencies and others concerned with federally owned and leased buildings and space in a manner which will aid in achieving such objectives.

(b) In view of the importance to the achievement of the objectives of this memorandum of agreement of the initial selection of a city or delineation of a general area for location of public buildings or leased space, GSA will provide the earliest possible notice to HUD of information with respect to such decisions so that HUD can carry out its responsibilities under this memorandum of agreement as effectively as possible.

(c) *Government-owned Public Buildings Projects.* (1) In the planning for each new public buildings project under the Public Buildings Act of 1959, during the survey preliminary to the preparation and submission of a project development report, representatives of the regional office of GSA in which the project is proposed will consult with, and receive advice from, the regional office of HUD, and local planning and housing authorities concerning the present and planned availability of low- and moderate-income housing on a nondiscriminatory basis in the area where the project is to be located. Such advice will constitute the principal basis for GSA's consideration of the availability of such housing in accordance with paragraphs 6 and 9(a). A copy of the prospectus for each project which is authorized by the Committees on Public Works of the Congress in accordance with the requirements of section 7(a) of the Public Buildings Act of 1959, will be provided to HUD.

(2) When a site investigation for an authorized public buildings project is conducted by regional representatives of GSA to identify a site on which the public building will be constructed, a representative from the regional office of HUD will participate in the site investigation for the purposes of providing a report on the availability of low- and moderate-income housing on a nondiscriminatory basis in the area of the investigation. Such report will constitute the principal basis for GSA's consideration of the availability of such housing in accordance with paragraphs 6 and 9(a).

(d) Major lease actions having a significant socioeconomic impact on a community: At the time GSA and the agencies who will occupy the space have tentatively delineated the general area in which the leased space must be located in order that the agencies may effectively perform their missions and programs, the regional representative of HUD will be consulted by the regional representative of GSA who is responsible for the leasing action to obtain advice from HUD concerning the availability of low- and moderate-income housing on a nondiscriminatory basis to the delineated area. Such advice will constitute the principal basis for GSA's consideration of the availability of such housing in accordance with paragraphs 6 and 9(a). Copies of lease-construction prospectuses approved by the Committees on Public Works of the Congress in conformity with the provisions of the Independent Offices and Department of Housing and Urban Development appropriation acts, will be provided to HUD.

(e) GSA and HUD will each issue internal operating procedures to implement this memorandum of understanding within a reasonable time after its execution. These procedures shall recognize the right of HUD, in the event of a disagreement between HUD and GSA representatives at the area or regional level, to bring such disagreement to the attention of GSA officials at headquarters in sufficient time to assure full consideration of HUD's views, prior to the making of a determination by GSA.

(f) In the event a decision is made by GSA as to the location of a federally constructed building or leased space, and HUD has made findings, expressed in the advice given or a report made to GSA, that the availability to such location of low- and moderate-income housing on a nondiscriminatory basis is inadequate, the GSA shall provide the DHUD with a written explanation why the location was selected.

(g) Whenever the advice or report provided by HUD in accordance with paragraph 9(c)(1), 9(c)(2), or 9(d) with respect to an area or site indicates that the supply of low-and moderate-income housing on a nondiscriminatory basis is inadequate to meet the needs of the personnel of the agency involved, GSA and HUD will develop an affirmative action plan designed to insure that an adequate supply of such housing will be available before the building or space is to be occupied or within a period of 6 months thereafter. The plan should provide for commitments from the community involved to initiate and carry out all feasible efforts to obtain a sufficient quantity of low- and moderate-income housing available to the agency's personnel on a nondiscriminatory basis with adequate access to the location of the building or space. It should include commitments by the local officials having the authority to remove obstacles to the provision of such housing, when such obstacles exist, and to take effective steps to assure its provision. The plan should also set forth the steps proposed by the agency to develop and implement a counseling and referral service to seek out and assist its personnel to obtain such housing. As part of any plan during, as well as after its development, HUD agrees to give priority consideration to applications for assistance under its housing programs for the housing proposed to be provided in accordance with the plan.

10. This memorandum will be reviewed at the end of one year, and modified to incorporate any provision necessary to improve its effectiveness in light of actual experience.

PART 102–84 [RESERVED]

PART 102–85—PRICING POLICY FOR OCCUPANCY IN GSA SPACE

Subpart A—Pricing Policy—General

Sec.
102–85.5　By what authority is the pricing policy in this part prescribed?
102–85.10　What is the scope of this part?
102–85.15　What are the basic policies for charging Rent for space and services?
102–85.20　What does an Occupancy Agreement (OA) do?

AUTHORITY: 40 U.S.C. 486(c).

SOURCE: 66 FR 23169, May 8, 2001, unless otherwise noted.

Subpart A—Pricing Policy— General

§ 102–85.5 By what authority is the pricing policy in this part prescribed?

(a) General authority is granted in the Federal Property and Administrative Services Act of 1949, as amended, Sec. 205(c) and 210(j), 63 Stat. 390 and 86 Stat. 219; (40 U.S.C. 486(c) and 40 U.S.C. 490(j), respectively).

(b) This part implements the applicable provisions of Federal law, including, but not limited to, the:

(1) Federal Property and Administrative Services Act of 1949, 63 Stat. 377, as amended;

(2) Act of July 1, 1898 (40 U.S.C. 285);

(3) Act of April 28, 1902 (40 U.S.C. 19);

(4) Act of August 27, 1935 (40 U.S.C. 304c);

(5) Public Buildings Act of 1959, as amended (40 U.S.C. 601–619);

(6) Public Buildings Amendments of 1972, Pub. L. 92–313, (86 Stat. 219);

(7) Rural Development Act of 1972, Pub. L. 92–419, (86 Stat. 674);

(8) Reorganization Plan No. 18 of 1950 (40 U.S.C. 490 note);

(9) Title VIII of the Civil Rights Act of 1968 (42 U.S.C. 3601 *et seq.*);

(10) National Environmental Policy Act of 1969, as amended (42 U.S.C. 4321 *et seq.*);

(11) Intergovernmental Cooperation Act of 1968 and the Federal Urban Land Use Act (42 U.S.C. 4201–4244; 40 U.S.C. 531–535);

(12) Public Buildings Cooperative Use Act of 1976, as amended (40 U.S.C. 490(a)(16)–(19), 601a and 612a);

(13) Public Buildings Amendments of 1988, Pub. L. 100–678, (102 Stat. 4049);

(14) National Historic Preservation Act of 1966 as amended (16 U.S.C. 461 *et seq.*);

(15) Executive Order 12072 of August 16, 1978 (43 FR 36869);

(16) Executive Order 12411 of March 29, 1983 (48 FR 13391);

(17) Executive Order 12512 of April 29, 1985 (50 FR 18453);

(18) Executive Order 13005 of May 21, 1996 (61 FR 26069); and

(19) Executive Order 13006 of May 21, 1996 (61 FR 26071).

§ 102–85.10 What is the scope of this part?

(a) This part describes GSA policy and principles for the assignment and occupancy of space under its control and the rights and obligations of GSA and the customer agencies that request or occupy such space pursuant to GSA Occupancy Agreements (OA).

(b) Space managed by agencies under delegation of authority from GSA is subject to the provisions of this part.

(c) This part is not applicable to:

(1) Licenses, permits or leases with non-Federal entities under the Public Buildings Cooperative Use Act (40 U.S.C. 490(a)(16–19)); or

(2) The disposal of surplus lease space under section 210(h)(2) of the Federal Property and Administrative Services Act of 1949, as amended (40 U.S.C. 490(h)(2)).

§ 102–85.15 What are the basic policies for charging Rent for space and services?

(a) GSA will charge for space and services furnished by GSA (unless otherwise exempted by the Administrator of General Services) a Rent charge which will approximate commercial charges for comparable space and services. Rent for all assignments for GSA-controlled space will be priced according to the principles of the pricing policy in this part. These principles are reflected in the following elements of GSA Rent charges:

(1) "Shell" Rent based on approximate commercial charges for comparable space and services for Federally owned space (accomplished using appraisal procedures);

(2) Rent based on actual cost of the lease, including the costs (if any) of services not provided by the lessor, plus a GSA fee;

(3) Amortization of any tenant improvement allowance used;

(4) Any applicable real estate taxes, operating costs, parking, security and joint use fees; and

(5) For certain projects involving new construction or major renovation of Federally-owned buildings, a return on investment pricing approach if an appraisal-determined rental value does not provide a minimum return (OMB discount rate for calculating the present value of yearly costs plus 2%) on the cost of the prospective capital investment. Each specific use of Return on Investment (ROI) pricing must be approved by OMB and duly recorded in an Occupancy Agreement (OA) with the customer agency. Once the ROI methodology is employed to establish Rent for a capital investment, the ROI method must be retained for the duration of the OA term.

(b) Special services not included in the standard levels of service may be provided by GSA on a reimbursable basis. GSA may also furnish alterations on a reimbursable basis in buildings where GSA is responsible for alterations only.

(c) The financial terms and conditions under which GSA assigns, and a customer agency occupies, each block of GSA-controlled space, shall be documented in a written OA.

§102–85.20 What does an Occupancy Agreement (OA) do?

An OA defines GSA's relationship with each customer agency and:

(a) Establishes specific financial terms, provisions, rights, and obligations of GSA and its customer for each space assignment;

(b) Minimizes exposure to future unknown costs for both GSA and customer agencies;

(c) Stabilizes Rent payments to the extent reasonable and desired by customers; and

(d) Allows tailoring of space and related services to meet customer agency needs.

§102–85.25 What is the basic principle governing OAs?

The basic principle governing OAs is to adopt the private sector practice of capturing in a written document the business terms to which GSA and a customer agency agree concerning individual space assignments.

§102–85.30 Are there special rules for certain Federal customers?

Yes, in lieu of OAs, GSA is able to enter into agreements with customer agencies that reflect the parties particular needs. For example, the space and services provided to the U.S. House of Representatives and the U.S. Senate are governed by existing memoranda of agreement (MOA). When there are conflicts between the provisions of this part and MOAs, the MOAs prevail.

§102–85.35 What definitions apply to this part?

The following definitions apply to this part:

Accept space or *acceptance of space* means a commitment from an agency to occupy specified GSA-controlled space.

Agency-controlled and/or operated space means:

(1) Space that is owned, leased, or otherwise controlled or operated by Federal agencies under any authority other than the Federal Property and Administrative Services Act of 1949, as amended; and

(2) it also includes agency-acquired space for which acquisition authority has been delegated or otherwise granted to the agency by GSA. It does not include space covered by an OA.

Assign or *assignment* is defined in the definition for space assignment.

Building shell means the complete enveloping structure, the base-building systems, and the finished common areas (building common and floor common) of a building that bound the tenant areas.

Customer agency means any department, agency, or independent establishment in the Federal Government, including any wholly-owned corporation; any executive agency or any establishment in the legislative or judicial branch of the Government (except the Senate, the House of Representatives, and the Architect of the Capitol, and any activities under his direction).

Emergency relocation is a customer move that results from an extraordinary event such as a fire, natural disaster, or immediate threat to the health and safety of occupants that renders a current space assignment unusable and requires that it be vacated, permanently or temporarily.

Federal Buildings Fund means the fund into which Rent charges and other revenues are deposited, and collections cited in section 210(j) of the Federal Property and Administrative Services Act of 1949, as amended (U.S.C. 490(j)), and from which monies are available for expenditures for real property management and related activities in such amounts as are specified in annual appropriations acts without regard to fiscal year limitations.

Federally controlled space means workspace for which the United States Government has a right of occupancy by ownership, by lease, or by any other means, such as by contract, barter, license, easement, permit, requisition, or condemnation. Such workspace excludes space owned or leased by private sector entities performing work on Government contracts.

Federally owned space means space, the title to which is vested in the United States Government or which will vest automatically according to an existing agreement.

Forced move means the involuntary physical relocation, from one space assignment to another, of a customer agency housed in GSA-controlled space initiated by another customer agency or by GSA, before the expiration of a lease or an OA term. (See also the definition of GSA-initiated move.)

General use space means all types of space other than "warehouse," "parking," or "unique" space, as defined elsewhere in this part. Examples of general use space are:

(1) Office and office-related space such as file areas, libraries, meeting rooms, computer rooms, mail rooms, training and conference, automated data processing operations, courtrooms, and judicial chambers; and

(2) Storage space that contains different quality and finishes from general use space, but that is within a building where predominantly general use space is located.

GSA-controlled space means Federally controlled space under the custody or control of GSA. It includes space for which GSA has delegated operational, maintenance, or protection authority to the customer agency.

GSA-delegated space (or GSA delegated building) means GSA-controlled space for which GSA has delegated operational, maintenance or protection authority to the customer agency.

GSA-initiated move means any relocation action in GSA-controlled space that:

(1) Is involuntary to the customer agency and required to be effective prior to the expiration of an effective OA, or in the case of leased space, prior to the expiration of the lease; or

(2) Is an emergency relocation initiated by GSA.

Initial space alteration (ISA). See definition of "tenant improvement."

Initial space layout means the specific placement of workstations, furniture and equipment within new space assignments.

Inventory means a summary or itemized list of the real property, and associated descriptive information, that is under the control of a Federal agency.

Joint-use space means common space within a Federally controlled facility, not specifically assigned to any one agency, and available for use by multiple agencies, such as cafeterias, auditoriums, conference rooms, credit unions, visitor parking spaces, snack bars, certain wellness/physical fitness facilities, and child care centers.

Leased space means space for which the United States Government has a right of use and occupancy by virtue of having acquired a leasehold interest.

Non-cancelable space means space that, due to its layout, design, location, or other characteristics, is unlikely to be needed by another GSA customer agency. Typical conditions that might cause space to be defined as non-cancelable are:

(1) Special space construction features;

(2) Lack of any realistic Federal need for the space other than by the requesting agency; and

(3) Remote location or unusual term (short or long) desired by the agency.

Occupancy Agreement (OA) means a written agreement descriptive of the financial terms and conditions under which GSA assigns, and a customer agency occupies, the GSA-controlled space identified therein.

Parking or *parking space* means surface land, structures, or areas within structures designed and designated for the purpose of parking vehicles.

Personnel means the peak number of persons to be housed during a single shift, regardless of how many workstations are provided for them. In addition to permanent employees of the agency, personnel includes temporaries, part-time, seasonal, and contractual employees, budgeted vacancies, and employees of other agencies and organizations who are housed in a space assignment.

Portfolio leases mean long term or "master" leases, usually negotiated to house several agencies whose individual term requirements differ from the terms of the underlying GSA lease with the lessor, and from each other. These may also be leases housing single agencies, but which entail for GSA responsibilities (burdens and benefits) which mimic an ownership position, or equity rights, even though no equity interest or ownership liability exists. An example of the latter would be long term renewal options on a lease which, in order to enjoy, involve substantial capital outlays by GSA to improve the building infrastructure. In both these cases, GSA is assuming risks or capital expenditures outside of the conventions of single transactions or occupancies. Accordingly, for a portfolio lease, it is not appropriate merely to pass through to the customer agency(ies) the rental rate of the underlying GSA lease. Portfolio leases are treated for pricing purposes as owned space, with Rent set by appraisal.

Predominant use means the use to which the greatest portion of a location is put. Predominant use is determined by the Public Buildings Service (PBS), GSA, and will typically result in the designation of a location as one of four types of space—General Use, Warehouse, Unique, or Parking—even though some smaller portions of the space may be used for one or more of the other types of uses.

Rent means the amounts charged by GSA for space and related services to the customer agencies with tenancy in GSA-controlled space. The word "Rent" is capitalized to differentiate it from the contract "rent" that GSA pays lessors.

Rentable square footage means the amount of space as defined in "Building Owners and Managers Association (BOMA)/American National Standards Institute (ANSI) Standard Z65.1–1996." The BOMA/ANSI standard also defines "gross," "office area," "floor common," and "building common" areas. Any references to these terms in this part refer to the BOMA/ANSI standard definitions. This standard has been adopted in accordance with GSA's interest in conforming its practices to nationally recognized industry standards to the extent possible.

NOTE TO THE DEFINITION OF RENTABLE SQUARE FOOTAGE: *Rentable square footage* generally includes square footage of areas occupied by customers plus a prorated share of floor common areas such as elevator lobbies, building corridors, public restrooms, utility closets, and machine rooms. Rentable square footage also includes a prorated share of building common areas located throughout the building. Examples of building common space include ground floor entrance lobby, enclosed atrium, loading dock, and mail room.

Request for space or *space request* means a written or electronically submitted document or an oral request, within which an agency's space needs are summarized. A request for space is requisite for development of an OA. Thus, it must be submitted to GSA by a duly authorized official of the customer agency, and it must be accompanied by documentation of the customer agency's ability to fund payment of required Rent charges.

Return on Investment (ROI) pricing is one possible methodology used to establish a Rent rate for certain owned space. Typically, ROI pricing is a Rent rate that ensures GSA a reasonable return on its cost to acquire and improve the asset. ROI pricing may be used where no other comparable commercial space is available or no other appraisal method would be appropriate. It may also be used in cases in which an appraisal-based rental rate will not meet GSA's minimum return requirements for the planned level of investment.

Security fees mean Rent charges for building services provided by GSA's Federal Protective Service. Security fees are comprised of basic and building specific charges.

(a) A basic security fee is assessed in all PBS-controlled properties where the Federal Protective Service (FPS) provides security services. The rate is set annually on a per-square-foot basis. The charge includes the following services:

(1) General law enforcement on PBS-controlled property;

(2) Physical security assessments;

(3) Crime prevention and awareness training;

(4) Advice and assistance to building security committees;

(5) Intelligence sharing program;

(6) Criminal investigation;

(7) Assistance and coordination in Occupancy Emergency Plan development;

(8) Coordination of mobilization and response to terrorist threat or civil disturbance;

(9) Program administration for security guard contracts; and

(10) Megacenter operations for monitoring building perimeter alarms and

dispatching appropriate law enforcement response.

(b) The building specific security charge is comprised of two elements: Operating expenses and amortized capital costs. Building specific charges, whether operating expenses or capital costs, are distributed overall federal users by building or facility in direct proportion to each customer agency's percentage of federal occupancy. As with joint use charges, the distribution of building-specific charges among customer agencies is not re-adjusted for vacancy.

Space means a defined area within a building and/or parcel of land. (Personal property and furniture are not included.)

Space allocation standard (SAS) means a standard agreed upon by GSA and a customer agency, written in terms that permit nationwide or regional application, that is used as a basis for establishing that agency's space requirements. An SAS may describe special GSA and customer agency funding responsibilities, although such responsibilities will be covered in OAs for space assignments. An SAS may also be developed between GSA and customer agencies on a regional level to standardize or simplify transactions, provided that the terms of a regional SAS are consistent with the terms of that agency's national SAS and the terms of this part.

Space assignment or *assignments* means a transaction between GSA and a customer agency that results in a customer agency's right to occupy certain GSA-controlled space, usually in return for customer agency payment(s) to GSA for use of the space. Space assignment rights, obligations, and responsibilities not covered in this part, or in the customer guides, are formalized in an OA.

Space planning means the process of using recognized professional techniques of planning, layout and interior design to determine the best internal location and the most efficient configuration for satisfying agency space needs.

Space program of requirements means a summary statement of an agency's space needs. These requirements will generally include information about lo-

cation, square footage, construction requirements, and duration of the agency's space need. They may be identified in any format mutually agreeable to GSA and the agency.

Special space means space which has unusual architectural/construction features, requires the installation of special equipment, or requires disproportionately high or low costs to construct, maintain and/or operate as compared to office or storage space. Special space generally refers to space which has construction features, finishes, services, utilities, or other additional costs beyond those specified in the customer general allowance (e.g., courtrooms, laboratories).

Standard level of service. See § 102–85.165 for the definition of standard level of service.

Telecommunications means electronic processing of information, either voice or data or both, over a wide variety of media, (e.g., copper wire, microwave, fiber optics, radio frequencies), between individuals or offices within a building (e.g., local area networks), between buildings, and between cities.

Tenant improvement (TI) means a finished component of an interior block of space. Tenant improvements represent additions to or alterations of the building shell that adapt the workspace to the specific uses of the customer. If made at initial occupancy, the TIs are known as initial space alterations or ISAs.

Tenant improvement (TI) allowance means the dollar amount, including design, labor, materials, contractor costs (if contractors are used), management, and inspection, that GSA will spend to construct, alter, and finish space for customer occupancy (excluding personal property and furniture, which are customer agency responsibilities) at initial occupancy. The dollar amounts for the allowances are different for each agency and bureau to accommodate agencies' different mission needs. The dollar amounts also may vary by locations reflecting different costs in different markets. The PBS bill will only reflect the actual amount the customers spend, not the allowance. The amount of the TI allowance is determined by GSA. Agencies can request that GSA revise the TI allowance amount by project or categorically for an entire bureau. The cost of replacement of tenant improvements is borne by the customer agency. ⋅

Unique space means space for which there is no commercial market comparable (e.g., border stations).

Warehouse or *warehouse space* means space contained in a structure primarily intended for the housing of files, records, equipment, or other personal property, and is not primarily intended for housing personnel and office operations. Warehouse space generally is designed and constructed to lower specifications than office buildings, with features such as exposed ceilings, unfinished perimeter and few dividing partitions. Warehouse space also is usually heated to a lesser degree but not air-conditioned, and is cleaned to lesser standards than office space.

Workspace means Federally controlled space in buildings and structures (permanent, semi-permanent, or temporary) that provides an acceptable environment for the performance of agency mission requirements by employees or by other persons occupying it.

§ 102–85.40 What are the major components of the pricing policy?

The major components of the pricing policy are:

(a) An OA between a customer agency and GSA;

(b) Tenant improvement allowance; and

(c) The establishment of Rent the agency pays to GSA based on the OA for:

(1) Leased space, a pass-through to the customer agency of the underlying GSA lease contract costs, and a PBS fee; or

(2) GSA-owned space, Rent determined by appraisal.

Subpart B—Occupancy Agreement

§ 102–85.45 When is an Occupancy Agreement required?

An Occupancy Agreement (OA) is required for each customer agency's space assignment. The OA must be agreed to by GSA and the customer agency prior to GSA's commitment of funds for occupancy and formal assignment of space.

§ 102–85.50 When does availability of funding have to be certified?

The customer agency must sign an OA prior to GSA's making any major contractual commitments associated with the space request. Typically, this should occur at the earliest possible opportunity-i.e., when funds become available. However, in no event shall certification occur later than just prior to the award of the contract to a design architect in the case of Federal construction or renovation in Federally owned space or prior to the award of a lease. This serves as a customer agency's funding commitment unless certification is provided on another document.

§ 102–85.55 What are the terms and conditions included in an OA?

The terms and conditions are modeled after commercial practice. They are intended to reflect a full mutual understanding of the financial terms and agreement of the parties. The OA describes the actual space and services to be provided and all associated actual costs to the customer during the term of occupancy. The OA does not include any general provisions or terms contained in this part. OAs typically describe the following, depending on whether the space is leased or Federally owned:

(a) Assigned square footage;

(b) Shell Rent and term of occupancy;

(c) Amortized amount of customer allowance used;

(d) Operating costs and escalations;

(e) One time charges; e.g., lump sum payments by the customer;

(f) Real estate tax and escalations;

(g) Parking and escalations;

(h) Additional/reduced services;

(i) Security services and associated Rent;

(j) Joint use space and associated Rent;

(k) PBS fee;

(l) Customer rights and provisions for occupancy after OA expiration;

(m) Cancellation provisions if different from this part or the customer service guides;

(n) Any special circumstances associated with the occupancy, such as environmental responsibilities, unusual use restrictions, or agreements with local authorities;

(o) Emergency relocations;

(p) Clauses specific to the agreement;

(q) Other Rent, e.g., charges for antenna sites, land;

(r) Agency standard clauses; and

(s) General clauses defining the obligations of both parties.

§ 102–85.60 Who can execute an OA?

Authorized GSA and customer agency officials who can commit or obligate the funds of their respective agencies can execute an OA. Higher level signatories may be appropriate from both agencies for space assignments in owned or leased space, that are unusual in size, location, duration, public interest, or other factors. Each agency decides its appropriate signatory level.

§ 102–85.65 How does an OA obligate the customer agency?

An OA obligates the executing customer agency to fund the current-year Rent obligation owed GSA, as well as to reimburse GSA for any other *bona fide* obligations that GSA may have incurred on behalf of the customer agency. Although the OA is an interagency agreement, memorializing the understanding of GSA and its customer agency, the OA may not be construed as obligating future year customer agency funds until they are legally available. A multi-year OA commitment assumes the customer agency will seek the necessary funding through budget and appropriations processes.

§ 102–85.70 Are the standard OA terms appropriate for non-cancelable space?

Yes, most of the standard terms apply; however, the right to cancel upon a 4-month (120 day) notice is not available. See § 102–85.35 for the definition of non-cancelable space.

§ 102–85.75 When can space assignments be terminated?

(a) Customer agencies can terminate any space assignments, except those designated as non-cancelable, with the following stipulations:

(1) The agency must give GSA written notice at least four months prior to termination.

(2) The agency is responsible for reimbursing GSA for the unpaid balance of the cost of tenant improvements, generally prior to GSA releasing the agency from the space assignment. In the event the customer agency received a rent concession (e.g., free rent) at the inception of the assignment as part of the consideration for the entire lease term, then the amount of the concession applicable to the remaining term must be repaid to GSA.

(3) If the space to be vacated is ready for occupancy by another customer and marketable, GSA accepts the termination of assignment.

(4) If the agency has vacated all of the space and removed all personal property and equipment from the space by the cancellation date in the written notice, the agency will be released effective that date from further Rent payments.

(5) An agency may terminate a GSA space assignment with less than a four-month advance written notice to GSA, if:

(i) Either GSA or the terminating agency has identified another agency customer for the assigned space and that substitute agency wants and is able to fully assume the Rent payments due from the terminating agency; and

(ii) The terminating agency continues to pay Rent until the new agency starts paying Rent.

(b) GSA can terminate space assignments according to GSA regulations for emergency or forced moves.

(c) OAs terminate automatically at expiration.

§ 102–85.80 Who is financially responsible for expenses resulting from tenant non-performance?

The customer agencies are financially responsible for expenses incurred by the Government as a result of any failure on their part to fulfill a commitment outlined in an OA or other written agreements in advance of, or in addition to, the OA. Customer agencies are also financially responsible for revised design costs and any additional costs resulting from changes to space requirements or space layouts made by the agency after a lease, alteration, design, or construction contract has been awarded by GSA.

§102–85.85 What if a customer agency participates in a consolidation?

If an agency agrees to participate in a consolidation upon expiration of an OA, the relocation expenses will be addressed in the new OA negotiated by GSA and the customer agency. The customer agency generally pays such costs.

Subpart C—Tenant Improvement Allowance

§102–85.90 What is a tenant improvement allowance?

A tenant improvement (TI) allowance enables the customer agency to design, configure and build out space to support its program operations. It is based on local market construction costs and the specific bureau's historical use of space. (See also the definition at §102–85.35.)

§102–85.95 Who pays for the TI allowance?

The customer agency pays for the amount of the tenant improvement allowance actually used.

§102–85.100 How does a customer agency pay for tenant improvements?

To pay for the installation of tenant improvements, the customer agency may spend an amount not to exceed the tenant allowance. The amount spent by the customer agency for TIs is amortized over a period of time specified in the OA, not to exceed the useful life of the improvements. This amortization payment is in addition to the shell rent and services.

§102–85.105 How does an agency pay for customer alterations that exceed the TI allowance?

Amounts exceeding the TI allowance are paid in a one-time lump sum and are not amortized over the term of the occupancy. The agency certifies lump sum funds are available prior to GSA proceeding with the work.

§102–85.110 Can the allowance amount be changed?

The GSA schedule of allowances for new assignments is adjusted annually for design and construction cost changes. As the need arises, GSA may adjust an agency or bureau's TI allowance. GSA may also adjust a TI allowance for a specific project, if conditions warrant. This decision is solely GSA's. In addition, the customer agency may waive any part or all of its customization allowance in the case of a new space assignment. In the case of backfill space (also known as relet space), the customer agency can also waive any part or all of the tenant general allowance, if the customer agency will use the existing tenant improvements, with or without modifications.

Subpart D—Rent Charges

§102–85.115 How is the Rent determined?

Unless an exemption is granted under the authority of the Administrator of General Services, the Rent charged approximates commercial charges for comparable space and space-related services as follows:

(a) Generally, Rent for Federally owned space provided by GSA is based on market appraisals of fully serviced rental values for the predominant use to which space in a building is put; e.g., general use, warehouse use, and parking use. In cases where market appraisals are not practical; e.g., in cases involving unique space or when market comparables are not available, GSA may establish Rent on the basis of alternate commercial practices. See the discussion of alternate valuation methods in §102–85.125. Amortization of tenant improvements, parking fees, and security charges are calculated separately and added to the appraised shell Rent to establish the Rent charge. Customer agencies also pay for a pro rata share of joint use space.

(b) Generally, Rent for space leased by GSA is based on the actual cost of the lease, including the costs (if any) of services not provided by the lessor, plus a GSA fee, and security charges and parking (if not in the lease).

(1) The Rent is based on the terms and conditions of the OA, starting with the shell Rent.

(2) In addition to the shell Rent, the Rent includes amortization of TI allowances used, real estate taxes, operating costs, extra services, parking, GSA fee for its services, and charges for security, joint-use, and other applicable rental charges (e.g., antenna site, land, wareyard).

§ 102–85.120 What is shell Rent?

Shell Rent is that portion of GSA Rent charged for the building envelope and land. (See § 102–85.35 for the definition of building shell.)

§ 102–85.125 What alternate methods may be used to establish Rent in Federally-owned space?

Alternate methods of establishing Rent are based on private sector models. They include, but are not limited to:

(a) Return on investment (ROI) approach or a similar cost recovery method used when market comparables are not available and/or GSA must "build to suit" to fulfill customer agency requirements; e.g., border stations; and

(b) Rent schedules for the right to use rooftops and other floor areas not suitable for workspace; e.g., antenna sites and signage.

§ 102–85.130 How are exemptions from Rent granted?

Exemptions from Rent are rare. However, the Administrator of General Services may exempt any GSA customer from Rent after a determination that application of Rent would not be feasible or practical. Customer agency requests for exemptions must be addressed to the Administrator of General Services and submitted in accordance with GSA Order PBS 4210.1, "Rent Exemption Procedures," dated December 20, 1991, or in accordance with any superseding GSA order. A copy of the order may be obtained from the Office of Portfolio Management, General Services Administration, 1800 F Street, NW., Washington, DC 20405.

§ 102–85.135 What if space and services are provided by other executive agencies?

Any executive agency other than GSA providing space and services is authorized to charge the occupant for the space and services at rates approved by the Administrator of General Services and the Director of the Office of Management and Budget. If space and services are of the type provided by the Administrator of General Services, the executive agency providing the space and services must credit the monies derived from any fees or charges to the appropriation or fund initially charged for providing the space or services, as prescribed by Subsection 210(k) of the Federal Property and Administrative Services Act of 1949, as amended (40 U.S.C. 490(k)).

§ 102–85.140 How are changes in Rent reflected in OAs?

(a) If Rent changes in ways that are identified in the OA, then no change to the OA is required. Typically, OAs state that certain components of Rent are subject to annual escalation; e.g., operating expenses, real estate taxes, parking charges, the basic security charge, and building-specific security operating and amortized capital expenses which do not entail a change in service level. Also, in Federally-owned space, OAs state that the shell rent is re-marked to market every five years. In leased space, the OA will identify any programmed changes in the lease contract rent (such as pre-set increases or steps in the contract rent rate) that will translate into a change in the customer agency's Rent. Changes in Rent specified in OAs will serve as notice to agencies of future Rent changes for budgeting purposes. For a discussion of budgeting for Rent, see § 102–85.160.

(b) Changes to Rent other than those identified in paragraph (a) of this section typically require an amended OA. There are many events that might occasion a change in Rent, and an amended OA, such as:

(1) An agency expands or contracts at an existing location;

(2) PBS agrees to fund additional tenant improvements that are then amortized over the remaining OA term, or over an extended OA term;

(3) Upon physical re-measurement, the true square footage of the space assignment is found to be different from the square footage of record;

(4) The amount of joint use space in the building changes;

(5) The level of building-specific security services changes; or

(6) PBS undertakes new capital expenditures for new or enhanced security countermeasures.

§ 102–85.145 When are customer agencies responsible for Rent charges?

(a) When a customer agency occupies cancelable space, it is responsible for Rent charges until:

(1) The date of release specified in the OA, or until the date space is actually vacated, whichever occurs later; or

(2) Four months after having provided GSA written notice of release; or

(3) The date space is actually vacated, whenever occupancy extends beyond the date agreed upon under either paragraph (a)(1) or (2) of this section.

(b) When a customer agency releases non-cancelable space, it is responsible for all attributable Rent and other space charges until the OA expires. This responsibility is mitigated to the extent that GSA is able to assign the space to another user or dispose of it. (See § 102–85.65 How does an OA obligate the customer agency?)

(c) When a customer agency commits to occupy space in an OA or other binding document, but never occupies that space, that agency is responsible for:

(1) Non-cancelable space: Rent payments due for the space until the OA expires, unless GSA can mitigate; or

(2) All other space: Either GSA's space charges for 4 months plus the cost of tenant improvements or GSA's actual costs, whichever is less.

§ 102–85.150 How will Rent charges be reflected on the customer agency's Rent bill?

Rent charges are billed monthly, in arrears, based on an annual rate which is divided by 12. Billing commences the first month in which the agency occupies the space for more than half of the month, and ends in the last month the agency occupies the space.

§ 102–85.155 What does a customer agency do if it does not agree with a Rent bill?

(a) If a customer agency does not agree with the way GSA has determined its Rent obligation (e.g., the agency does not agree with GSA's space classification, appraised Rent, or the allocation of space), the agency may appeal its Rent bill to GSA.

(b) GSA will not increase or otherwise change Rent for any assignment, except as agreed in an OA, in the case of errors, or when the OA is amended. However, customer agencies may at any time request a regional review of the measurement, classification, service levels provided, or charges assessed that pertain to the space assignment without resorting to formal procedures. Such requests do not constitute appeals and should be directed to the appropriate GSA Regional Administrator.

(c) If a customer agency still wants to pursue a formal appeal of Rent charges, they may do so, but with the following limitations:

(1) Terms, including rates, to which the parties agree in an OA are not appealable;

(2) In leased space, the contract rent passed through from the underlying lease cannot be appealed;

(3) In GSA-owned space, when the fully-serviced shell Rent is established through appraisal, the appraised rate must exceed comparable commercial square foot rates by 20 percent. When shell Rent in owned space is established on the basis of ROI at the inception of an OA, and the customer agency executes the OA, then the ROI rate cannot later be appealed. Other components of Rent that are established on the basis of actual cost—eg., amortization of TIs and building specific security charges—also cannot be appealed.

(4) Additionally, the customer agency is required to compare its assigned space with other space in the surrounding community that:

(i) Is available in similar size block of space in a comparable location;

(ii) Is comparable in quality to the space provided by GSA;

(iii) Provides similar service levels as part of the charges;

(iv) Contains similar contractual terms, conditions, and escalations clauses; and

(v) Represents a lease transaction completed at a similar point in time.

(5) Data from at least three comparable locations will be necessary to demonstrate a market trend sufficient to warrant revising an appraised Rent charge.

(d) A customer agency filing an appeal for a particular location or building must develop documentation supporting the appeal and file the appeal with the appropriate Regional Administrator. The GSA regional office will verify all pertinent information and documentation supporting the appeal. The GSA Regional Administrator will accept or deny the appeal and will notify the appealing agency of his or her ruling.

(e) A further appeal may be filed by the customer agency's headquarters level officials with the Commissioner, Public Buildings Service, if equitable resolution has not been obtained from the initial appeal. A head of a customer agency may further appeal to the Administrator of the General Services. Documentation of the procedures followed for prior resolution must accompany an appeal to the Administrator. Decisions made by the Administrator are final.

(f) Adjustments of Rent resulting from reviews and appeals will be effective in the month that the agency submitted a properly documented appeal. Adjustments in Rent made under this section remain in effect for the remainder of the 5-year period in which the charges cited in the OA were applicable.

§ 102–85.160 How does a customer agency know how much to budget for Rent?

GSA normally provides customer agencies an estimate of Rent increases approximately 2 months prior to the agencies' Office of Management and Budget (OMB) submission for the fiscal year in which GSA will charge Rent. This gives the affected customer agencies an opportunity to budget for an increase or decrease. However, GSA must obtain the concurrence of OMB for such changes prior to notifying customer agencies. In the event GSA is unable to provide timely notice of a future Rent increase, customer agencies are nonetheless obligated to pay the increased Rent amount. For existing assignments in owned buildings, GSA charges for fully serviced shell Rent, in aggregate, shall not exceed the bureau level budget estimates provided to the customer agencies annually. This provision does not apply to:

(a) New assignments;

(b) Changes in current assignments;

(c) Leased space;

(d) New tenant improvement amortization;

(e) Building specific security costs; and

(f) New amortization of capital expenditures under ROI pricing due to changes in scope of proposed projects or repair and/or replacement of building components

Subpart E—Standard Levels of Service

§ 102–85.165 What are standard levels of service?

(a) The standard levels of service covered by GSA Rent are comparable to those furnished in commercial practice. They are based on the effort required to service the customer agency's space for a 5-day week (Monday to Friday), one-shift regular work schedule. GSA will provide adequate building startup services, before the beginning of the customer's regular one-shift work schedule, and shutdown services after the end of this schedule.

(b) Without additional charge, GSA customers may use their assigned space and supporting automatic elevator systems, lights and small office and business machines including personal computers on an incidental basis, unless specified otherwise in the OA.

§ 102–85.170 Can flexitime and other alternative work schedules cost the customer agency more?

Yes, GSA customers who extend their regular work schedule by a system of flexible hours shall reimburse GSA for its approximate cost of the additional services required.

§ 102–85.175 Are the standard level services for cleaning, mechanical operation, and maintenance identified in an OA?

Unless specified otherwise in the OA, standard level services for cleaning, mechanical operation, and maintenance shall be provided in accordance with the GSA standard level of services as defined in § 102–85.165, and in the PBS Customer Guide to Real Property. A copy of the guide may be obtained from the General Services Administration, Office of Business Performance (PX), 1800 F Street, NW., Washington, DC 20405.

§ 102–85.180 Can there be other standard services?

GSA may provide additional services to its customers at the levels and times deemed by the Administrator of General Services to be necessary for efficient operations and proper servicing of space under the assignment responsibility of GSA.

§ 102–85.185 Can space be exempted from the standard levels of service

Yes, customer agencies may be excused from paying for standard service levels for space assignments when:

(a) In GSA-delegated space, the customer agency provides for these services itself and thus pays Rent minus charges for these services; or

(b) In rare instances, standard service levels may be waived by the Administrator of General Services in instances where charging for such standard services would not be feasible or practical, e.g., in assignments of limited square footage or functional use.

§ 102–85.190 Can GSA Rent be adjusted when standard levels of service are performed by other customer agencies?

Customer agencies that arrange and pay separately for the costs of standard level services normally covered by GSA Rent will receive a Rent credit or other type of reimbursement by GSA for the amount GSA would have charged for such services. The type of reimbursement is at GSA's discretion. The reimbursement is limited to the amount included for the services in GSA Rent. Approval to perform or contract for

such services must be obtained in advance by the customer agency from the appropriate GSA regional office.

Subpart F—Special Services

§ 102–85.195 Does GSA provide special services?

Yes, GSA provides special services on a cost-reimbursable basis:

(a) In GSA-controlled space, GSA may provide for special services that cannot be separated from the building or space costs (inseparable services, such as utilities, which are not individually metered). GSA's estimate of the special service cost is the basis for the bill amount. The bill amount for separable special services is either based on a previously agreed upon fixed price or the actual cost, including a fee for GSA's services.

(b) GSA can also provide special services to other Federal agencies in agency-controlled and operated space on a cost-reimbursable basis.

Subpart G—Continued Occupancy, Relocation and Forced Moves

§ 102–85.200 Can customer agencies continue occupancy of space or must they relocate at the end of an OA?

The answer is contingent upon whether the customer agency is in Federally owned or leased space.

(a) Unless stated otherwise in the OA, a customer agency within a GSA controlled, Federally owned building has automatic occupancy rights at the end of the OA term for occupied space. However, a new OA must be negotiated.

(b) In leased space, the OA generally reflects the provisions of the underlying lease and will specify whether or not renewal options are available. If the OA does not include a renewal option, customer agencies should assume relocation would be necessary upon OA expiration, and budget for it. Further, renewal options are not, in themselves, a guarantee of continued occupancy at that location. In some cases, the renewal rate is substantially above market or the option was not part of the initial price evaluation for the occupancy. In such cases, GSA may be required to run a competition for the replacement lease, and a relocation may ensue. Nonetheless, it is also possible that GSA may execute a succeeding lease with the incumbent lessor, in which case there is no move.

(c) GSA and customer agencies should initiate discussions at least 18–20 months in advance of OA expiration to address an action for the replacement or continued occupancy of the existing space assignment. This allows both agencies time to budget for the work and the cost.

§ 102–85.205　What happens if a customer agency continues occupancy after the expiration of an OA?

A mutual goal of GSA and its customers is to have current OAs in place for all space assignments. However, provisions are necessary to cover the GSA and customer relationship if an OA expires prior to execution of a mutually desired succeeding agreement. Because the risks, liabilities, and consequences of a customer's continued occupancy depend on whether the assigned space is leased or Federally owned, different provisions in the following table apply:

HOLDOVER TENANCY—CUSTOMER AGENCY RESPONSIBILITIES IN THE EVENT OF TENANT DELAY IN VACATING SPACE

In leased space	In federally owned space
To pay those costs associated with lease contract, GSA fee, and damages/claims, arising from changes in GSA contract costs which are caused by the tenant's delay.	To pay Rent as determined by GSA's pricing policy, as described in this part, and those added costs to GSA (claims, damages, changes, etc.) resulting from the tenant-caused delay.

§ 102–85.210　What if a customer agency has to relocate?

If the agency or GSA determines relocation is necessary at the expiration of an OA for either Federally owned or leased space, the customer agency is responsible for all costs associated with relocation at that time.

§ 102–85.215　What if another customer agency forces a GSA customer to move?

If a GSA customer agency, or GSA, forces the relocation of another GSA customer agency prior to the expiration of the customer's OA, the "forcing" agency is responsible:

(a) For all reasonable costs associated with the relocation of the agency being "forced" to move, including architectural-engineering design, move coordination and physical relocation, telecommunications and ADP equipment relocation and installation;

(b) To GSA for all of the relocated agency's unpaid tenant improvements, if any; and

(c) To the customer agency for the undepreciated amount of any lump sum payment that was already made by the agency for alterations.

§ 102–85.220　Can a customer agency forced to relocate waive the reimbursements?

Yes, a customer agency forced to relocate can waive some or all of the reimbursements from the forcing agency that are prescribed in § 102–85.215. However, a relocated customer agency cannot waive the requirement for the forcing customer agency to reimburse GSA for unpaid tenant improvements. If GSA is the "forcing" agency, it is responsible for the same costs as any other forcing customer agency.

§ 102–85.225　What are the funding responsibilities for relocations resulting from emergencies?

(a) In emergencies, swift remedies, including the possible relocation of a customer agency to alternate space, are required. The remedies may include requests for funding authorizations from OMB and Congress. GSA may serve as the central coordinator of such remedies.

(b) Funding responsibility will vary by situation. If a customer agency is only temporarily displaced from its space, GSA typically covers the cost of temporary set-up in a provisional location. If the agency is obliged to relocate permanently, an OA will be prepared which will address all terms of the occupancy. In such cases, new tenant improvements will be constructed

which can be amortized over the life of
a new occupancy term, and a new Rent
rate will be developed.

PARTS 102–86–102–115 [RESERVED]

SUBCHAPTER D—TRANSPORTATION

PART 102–116—GENERAL [RESERVED]

PART 102–117—TRANSPORTATION MANAGEMENT

Subpart A—General

Subpart B—Acquiring Transportation or Related Services

Subpart C—Business Rules To Consider Before Shipping Freight or Household Goods

Subpart D—Restrictions That Affect International Transportation of Freight and Household Goods

Subpart E—Shipping Freight

Subpart F—Shipping Hazardous Material (HAZMAT)

AUTHORITY: 31 U.S.C. 3726; 40 U.S.C. 121(c); 40 U.S.C. 501, et seq.; 46 U.S.C. 55305; 49 U.S.C. 40118.

SOURCE: 65 FR 60061, Oct. 6, 2000, unless otherwise noted.

Subpart A—General

§ 102–117.5 What is transportation management?

Transportation management is agency oversight of the physical movement of commodities, household goods (HHG) and other freight from one location to another by a transportation service provider (TSP).

§ 102–117.10 What is the scope of this part?

This part addresses shipping freight and household goods worldwide. Freight is property or goods transported as cargo. Household goods are not Government property, but are employees' personal property entrusted to the Government for shipment.

§ 102–117.15 To whom does this part apply?

This part applies to all agencies and wholly-owned Government corporations as defined in 5 U.S.C. 101, *et seq.* and 31 U.S.C. 9101(3), except as otherwise expressly provided.

[79 FR 33476, June 11, 2014]

§ 102–117.20 Are any agencies exempt from this part?

(a) The Department of Defense is exempted from this part by an agreement under the Federal Property and Administrative Services Act of 1949, as amended (40 U.S.C. 481 *et seq.*), except for the rules to debar or suspend a TSP under the Federal Acquisition Regulation (48 CFR part 9, subpart 9.4).

(b) Subpart D of this part, covering household goods, does not apply to the uniformed service members, under Title 37 of the United States Code, "Pay and Allowances of the Uniformed Services," including the uniformed service members serving in civilian agencies such as the U.S. Coast Guard, National Oceanic and Atmospheric Administration and the Public Health Service.

§ 102–117.25 What definitions apply to this part?

The following definitions apply to this part:

Accessorial charges means charges that are applied to the base tariff rate or base contract of carriage rate. Examples of accessorial charges are:

(1) Bunkers, destination/delivery, container surcharges, and currency exchange for international shipments.

(2) Inside delivery, redelivery, re-consignment, and demurrage or detention for freight.

(3) Packing, unpacking, appliance servicing, blocking and bracing, and special handling for household goods.

Agency means a department, agency, and independent establishment in the executive branch of the Government as defined in 5 U.S.C. 101 *et seq.*, and a wholly-owned Government corporation as defined in 31 U.S.C. 9101(3).

Bill of lading (BOL), sometimes referred to as a commercial bill of lading, but includes a Government bill of lading (GBL), means the document used as a receipt of goods, a contract of carriage, and documentary evidence of title.

Cargo preference is the legal requirement for all, or a portion of all, ocean-borne cargo to be transported on U.S. flag vessels.

Commuted rate system is the system under which an agency may allow its employees to make their own household goods shipping arrangements, and apply for reimbursement.

Consignee is the person or agent to whom freight or household goods are delivered.

Consignor, also referred to as the shipper, is the person or firm that ships freight or household goods to a consignee.

Contract of carriage is a contract between the TSP and the agency to transport freight or household goods.

Debarment is an action to exclude a TSP, for a period of time, from providing services under a rate tender or any contract under the Federal Acquisition Regulation (48 CFR part 9, subpart 9.406).

Declared value means the actual value of cargo as declared by the agency for reimbursement purposes or to establish duties, taxes, or other customs fees. The *declared value* is the maximum amount that could be recovered by the agency in the event of loss or damage for the shipments of freight and household goods, unless the declared value exceeds the carrier's released value (see "Released value"). The statement of declared value must be shown on any applicable tariff, tender, contract, bill of lading, or other document covering the shipment.

Demurrage is the penalty charge to an agency for delaying the agreed time to load or unload shipments by rail or ocean TSPs.

Detention is the penalty charge to an agency for delaying the agreed time to load or unload shipments by truck TSPs. It is also a penalty charge in some ocean shipping contracts of carriage that take effect after the demurrage time ends.

Electronic commerce is an electronic technique for carrying out business transactions (ordering and paying for goods and services), including electronic mail or messaging, Internet technology, electronic bulletin boards, charge cards, electronic funds transfers, and electronic data interchange.

Foreign flag vessel is any vessel of foreign registry including vessels owned by U.S. citizens but registered in a foreign country.

Freight is property or goods transported as cargo.

Government bill of lading (GBL) means the transportation document used as a receipt of goods, evidence of title, and a contract of carriage for Government international shipments (see Bill of Lading (BOL) definition).

Governmentwide Transportation Policy Council (GTPC) is an interagency forum to help GSA formulate policy. It provides agencies managing transportation programs a forum to exchange information and ideas to solve common problems. For further information on this council, see web site: *http://www.policyworks.gov/transportation.*

Hazardous material (HAZMAT) is a substance or material the Secretary of Transportation determines to be an unreasonable risk to health, safety, and property when transported in commerce, and labels as hazardous under section 5103 of the Federal Hazardous Materials Transportation Law (49 U.S.C. 5103 *et seq.*). When transported internationally hazardous material may be classified as "Dangerous Goods." All such freight must be marked in accordance with applicable regulations and the carrier must be notified in advance.

Household goods (HHG) are the personal effects of Government employees and their dependents.

Line-Haul is the movement of freight between cities excluding pickup and delivery service.

Mode is a method of transportation, such as rail, motor, air, water, or pipeline.

Rate schedule is a list of freight rates, taxes, and charges assessed against non-household goods cargo.

Rate tender is an offer a TSP sends to an agency, containing service rates and charges.

Receipt is a written or electronic acknowledgment by the consignee or TSP as to when and where a shipment was received.

Released value means an assigned value of the cargo for reimbursement purposes that is not necessarily the actual value of the cargo. Released value may be more or less than the actual value of the cargo; however, in the event of loss or damage to the shipment, if the released value exceeds the actual value, reimbursement would be the lesser of the two values. When the released value is agreed upon as the basis of reimbursement and the actual value exceeds the released value, the released value is the maximum amount that could be recovered by the agency in the event of loss or damage to the shipments of freight or household goods. When negotiating for rates and the released value is proposed to be less than the actual value of the cargo, the TSP should offer a rate lower than other rates for shipping cargo at full value. The statement of released value may be shown in any applicable tariff, tender, contract, transportation document or other documents covering the shipment.

Reparation is a payment to or from an agency to correct an improper transportation billing involving a TSP. Improper routing, overcharges or duplicate payments may cause such improper billing. This is different from a payment to settle a claim for loss and damage.

Suspension is an action taken by an agency to disqualify a TSP from receiving orders for certain services under a contract or rate tender (48 CFR part 9, subpart 9.407).

Third Party Logistics (3PL) is an entity that provides multiple logistics services for use by customers. Among the transportation services that 3PLs generally provide are integration transportation, warehousing, cross-docking, inventory management, packaging, and freight forwarding.

Transportation document (TD) means any executed document for transportation service, such as a bill of lading, a tariff, a tender, a contract, a Government Transportation Request (GTR), invoices, paid invoices, any transportation bills, or other equivalent documents, including electronic documents.

Transportation Officer (TO) is a person authorized, in accordance with this part, to select transportation service providers using rate tenders. Duties may include, but are not limited to, selecting Third Party Logistics (3PL) or Transportation Service Providers (TSP), and issuing bills of lading.

Transportation Officer Warrant is an agency-issued document that authorizes a Transportation Officer (TO) to procure transportation services using rate tenders, which may include, but are not limited to, selecting Third Party Logistics (3PL) or Transportation Service Providers (TSP), issuing bills of lading, and otherwise performing the duties of a TO.

Transportation service provider (TSP) means any party, person, agent, or carrier that provides freight, household goods, or passenger transportation or related services to an agency.

U.S. flag air carrier is an air carrier holding a certificate issued by the United States under 49 U.S.C. 41102 (49 U.S.C. 40118, 48 CFR part 47, subpart 47.4).

U.S. flag vessel is a commercial vessel, registered and operated under the laws of the U.S., owned and operated by U.S. citizens, and used in commercial trade of the United States.

[65 FR 60060, Oct. 6, 2000; 65 FR 81405, Dec. 26, 2000, as amended at 75 FR 51393, Aug. 20, 2010; 79 FR 55365, Sept. 16, 2014; 81 FR 65298, Sept. 22, 2016]

Subpart B—Acquiring Transportation or Related Services

§ 102–117.30 What choices do I have when acquiring transportation or related services?

When you acquire transportation or related services you may:

(a) Use the GSA tender of service;

(b) Use another agency's contract or rate tender with a TSP only if allowed by the terms of that agreement or if the Administrator of General Services delegates authority to another agency to enter an agreement available to other Executive agencies;

(c) Contract directly with a TSP using the acquisition procedures under the Federal Acquisition Regulation (FAR) (48 CFR chapter 1); or

(d) Negotiate a rate tender under a Federal transportation procurement statute, 49 U.S.C. 10721 or 13712.

§ 102–117.35 What are the advantages and disadvantages of using GSA's tender of service?

(a) It is an advantage to use GSA's tender of service when you want to:

(1) Use GSA's authority to negotiate on behalf of the Federal Government and take advantage of the lower rates and optimum service that result from a larger volume of business;

(2) Use a uniform tender of service;

(3) Obtain assistance with loss and damage claims; and

(4) Use GSA's Transportation management and operations expertise.

(b) It is a disadvantage to use GSA's tender of service when:

(1) You want an agreement that is binding for a longer term than the GSA tender of service;

(2) You have sufficient time to follow FAR contracting procedures and are in position to make volume or shipment commitments under a FAR contract;

(3) You do not want to pay for the GSA administrative service charge as a participant in the GSA rate tender programs; and

(4) Rates are not cost effective, as determined by the agency.

[65 FR 60061, Oct. 6, 2000, as amended at 75 FR 51393, Aug. 20, 2010]

§102–117.40 When is it advantageous for me to use another agency's contract or rate tender for transportation services?

It is advantageous to use another agency's contract or rate tender for transportation services when the contract or rate tender offers better or equal value than otherwise available to you.

§102–117.45 What other factors must I consider when using another agency's contract or rate tender?

When using another agency's contract or rate tender, you must:

(a) Assure that the contract or rate tender meets any special requirements unique to your agency;

(b) Pay any other charges imposed by the other agency for external use of their contract or rate tender;

(c) Ensure the terms of the other agency's contract or rate tender allow you to use it; and

(d) Ensure that the agency offering this service has the authority or a delegation of authority from GSA to offer such services to your agency.

[65 FR 60061, Oct. 6, 2000, as amended at 75 FR 51393, Aug. 20, 2010]

§102–117.50 What are the advantages and disadvantages of contracting directly with a TSP under the FAR?

(a) The FAR is an advantage to use when:

(1) You ship consistent volumes in consistent traffic lanes;

(2) You have sufficient time to follow FAR contracting procedures; and

(3) Your contract office is able to handle the requirement.

(b) The FAR may be a disadvantage when you:

(1) Cannot prepare and execute a FAR contract within your time frame;

(2) Have recurring shipments between designated places, but do not expect sufficient volume to obtain favorable rates; or

(3) Do not have the manpower to monitor quality control and administer a contract.

[65 FR 60061, Oct. 6, 2000, as amended at 75 FR 51393, Aug. 20, 2010]

§102–117.55 What are the advantages and disadvantages of using a rate tender?

(a) Using a rate tender is an advantage when you:

(1) Have a shipment that must be made within too short a time frame to identify or solicit for a suitable contract;

(2) Have shipments recurring between designated places, but do not expect sufficient volume to obtain favorable rates; or

(3) Are not in a position to make a definite volume and shipment commitment under a FAR contract.

(b) Using a rate tender may be a disadvantage when:

(1) You have sufficient time to use the FAR and this would achieve better results;

(2) You require transportation service for which no rate tender currently exists; or

(3) A TSP may revoke or terminate the tender on short notice.

[65 FR 60061, Oct. 6, 2000, as amended at 75 FR 51393, Aug. 20, 2010]

§102–117.60 What is the importance of terms and conditions in a rate tender or other transportation document?

Terms and conditions are important to protect the Government's interest and establish the performance and standards expected of the TSP. It is important to remember that terms and conditions are:

(a) Negotiated between the agency and the TSP before movement of any item; and

(b) Included in all contracts and rate tenders listing the services the TSP is offering to perform at the cost presented in the rate tender or other transportation document.

NOTE TO §102–117.60: You must reference the negotiated contract or rate tender on all transportation documents. For further information see §102–117.65.

§102–117.65 What terms and conditions must all rate tenders or contracts include?

All rate tenders and contracts must include, at a minimum, the following terms and conditions:

(a) Charges cannot be prepaid.

(b) Charges are not paid at time of delivery.

(c) Interest shall accrue from the voucher payment date on overcharges made and shall be paid at the same rate in effect on that date as published by the Secretary of the Treasury according to the Debt Collection Act of 1982, 31 U.S.C. 3717.

(d) To qualify for the rates specified in a rate tender filed under the provisions of the Federal transportation procurement statutes (49 U.S.C. 10721 or 13712), property must be shipped by or for the Government and the rate tender must indicate the Government is either the consignor or the consignee and include the following statement:

Transportation is for the (agency name) and the total charges paid to the transportation service provider by the consignor or consignee are for the benefit of the Government.

(e) When using a rate tender for transportation under a cost-reimbursable contract, include the following statement in the rate tender:

Transportation is for the (agency name), and the actual total transportation charges paid to the transportation service provider by the consignor or consignee are to be reimbursed by the Government pursuant to cost reimbursable contract (number). This may be confirmed by contacting the agency representative at (name, address and telephone number).

(f) Other terms and conditions that may be specific to your agency or the TSP such as specialized packaging requirements or HAZMAT. For further information see the "U.S. Government Freight Transportation Handbook," available by contacting:

General Services Administration, Office of Travel and Transportation Services, Transportation Audit Division (QMCA), 2200 Crystal Drive, Room 300, Arlington, VA 22202, http://www.gsa.gov/transaudits.

[65 FR 60061, Oct. 6, 2000, as amended at 75 FR 51393, Aug. 20, 2010]

§ 102-117.70 Where do I find more information on terms and conditions?

You may find more information about terms and conditions in part 102-118 of this chapter, or the "U.S. Government Freight Transportation Handbook" (see § 102-117.65(f)).

§ 102-117.75 How do I reference the rate tender on transportation documents?

To ensure proper reference of a rate tender on all shipments, you must show the applicable rate tender number and carrier identification on all transportation documents, such as, section 13712 quotation, "ABC Transportation Company, Tender Number * * *".

§ 102-117.80 How are rate tenders filed?

(a) The TSP must file an electronic rate tender with your agency. Details of what must be included when submitting electronic tenders is located in § 102-118.260(b) of this subchapter.

(b) You must send two copies of the rate tender to—General Services Administration, Federal Supply Service, Audit Division (FBA), 1800 F Street, NW., Washington, DC 20405, www.gsa.gov/transaudits.

[69 FR 57618, Sept. 24, 2004]

§ 102-117.85 What is the difference between a Government bill of lading (GBL) and a bill of lading?

(a) A Government bill of lading (GBL), Optional Forms 1103 or 1203, is a controlled document that conveys specific terms and conditions to protect the Government interest and serves as the contract of carriage.

(b) A GBL is used only for international shipments.

(c) A bill of lading, sometimes referred to as a commercial bill of lading, establishes the terms of contract between a shipper and TSP. It serves as a receipt of goods, a contract of carriage, and documentary evidence of title.

(d) Use a bill of lading for Government shipments if the specific terms and conditions of a GBL are included in any contract or rate tender (see § 102-117.65) and the bill of lading makes reference to that contract or rate tender (see § 102-117.75 and the "U.S. Government Freight Transportation Handbook").

[65 FR 60061, Oct. 6, 2000, as amended at 75 FR 51393, Aug. 20, 2010]

§ 102–117.90 May I use a U.S. Government bill of lading (GBL) to acquire freight, household goods or other related transportation services?

You may use the Government bill of lading (GBL) only for international shipments (including domestic offshore shipments).

[75 FR 31393, Aug. 20, 2010]

§ 102–117.95 What transportation documents must I use to acquire freight, household goods or other related transportation services?

(a) Bills of lading and purchase orders are the transportation documents you use to acquire freight, household goods shipments, and other transportation services. Terms and conditions in § 102–117.65 and the "U.S. Government Freight Transportation Handbook" are still required. For further information on payment methods, see part 102–118 of this chapter (41 CFR part 102–118).

(b) Government bills of lading (GBLs) are optional transportation documents for international shipments (including domestic offshore shipments).

[75 FR 31394, Aug. 20, 2010]

Subpart C—Business Rules To Consider Before Shipping Freight or Household Goods

§ 102–117.100 What business rules must I consider before acquiring transportation or related services?

When acquiring transportation or related services you must:

(a) Use the mode or individual transportation service provider (TSP) that provides the overall best value to the agency. For more information, see §§ 102–117.105 through 102–117.130;

(b) Demonstrate no preferential treatment to any TSP when arranging for transportation services except on international shipments. Preference on international shipments must be given to United States registered commercial vessels and aircraft;

(c) Ensure that small businesses receive equal opportunity to compete for all business they can perform to the maximum extent possible, consistent with the agency's interest (see 48 CFR part 19);

(d) Encourage minority-owned businesses and women-owned businesses, to compete for all business they can perform to the maximum extent possible, consistent with the agency's interest (see 48 CFR part 19);

(e) Review the need for insurance. Generally, the Government is self-insured; however, there are instances when the Government will purchase insurance coverage for Government property. An example may be cargo insurance for international air cargo shipments to cover losses over those allowed under the International Air Transport Association (IATA) or for ocean freight shipments; and

(f) Consider the added requirements on international transportation found in subpart D of this part.

§ 102–117.105 What does best value mean when routing a shipment?

Best value to your agency when routing a shipment means using the mode or individual TSP that provides satisfactory service with the best combination of service factors and price that meets the agency's requirements. A lower price may not be the best value if the service offered fails to meet the requirements of the shipment.

[75 FR 51394, Aug. 20, 2010]

§ 102–117.110 What is satisfactory service?

You should consider the following factors in assessing whether a TSP offers satisfactory service:

(a) Availability and suitability of the TSP's equipment;

(b) Adequacy of shipping and receiving facilities at origin and destination;

(c) Adequacy of pickup and/or delivery service;

(d) Availability of accessorial and special services;

(e) Estimated time in transit;

(f) Record of past performance of the TSP, including accuracy of billing and past performance record with Government agencies;

(g) Capability of warehouse equipment and storage space;

(h) Experience of company, management, and personnel to perform the requirements;

(i) The TSP's safety record; and

(j) The TSP's loss and damage record, including claims resolution.

[65 FR 60061, Oct. 6, 2000, as amended at 75 FR 51394, Aug. 20, 2010]

§ 102-117.115 How do I calculate total delivery costs?

You calculate total delivery costs for a shipment by considering all costs related to the shipping or receiving process, such as packing, blocking, bracing, drayage, loading and unloading, and transporting. Surcharges such as fuel, currency exchange, war risk insurance, and other surcharges should also be factored into the costs.

[75 FR 51394, Aug. 20, 2010]

§ 102-117.120 To what extent must I equally distribute orders for transportation and related services among TSPs?

You must assure that small businesses, socially or economically disadvantaged and women-owned TSPs have equal opportunity to provide the transportation or related services.

§ 102-117.125 How detailed must I describe property for shipment when communicating to a TSP?

You must describe property in enough detail for the TSP to determine the type of equipment or any special precautions necessary to move the shipment. Details might include weight, volume, measurements, routing, hazardous cargo, or special handling designations.

§ 102-117.130 Must I select TSPs who use alternative fuels?

No, but, whenever possible, you are encouraged to select TSPs that use alternative fuel vehicles and equipment, under policy in the Clean Air Act Amendments of 1990 (42 U.S.C. 7612) or the Energy Policy Act of 1992 (42 U.S.C. 13212).

Subpart D—Restrictions That Affect International Transportation of Freight and Household Goods

§ 102-117.135 What are the international transportation restrictions?

Several statutes mandate the use of U.S. flag carriers for international shipments, such as 49 U.S.C. 40118, commonly referred to as the "Fly America Act", and 46 U.S.C. 55305, the Cargo Preference Act of 1954, as amended. The principal restrictions are as follows:

(a) *Air cargo:* The use of foreign-flag air carriers when funded by the U.S. Government should be rare. International movement of cargo by air is subject to the Fly America Act, 49 U.S.C. 40118, which requires the use of U.S. flag air carrier service for all air cargo movements funded by the U.S. Government, including cargo shipped by contractors, grantees, and others at Government expense, except when one of the following exceptions applies:

(1) The transportation is provided under a bilateral or multilateral air transportation agreement to which the U.S. Government and the government of a foreign country are parties, and which the Department of Transportation has determined meets the requirements of the Fly America Act.

(i) Information on bilateral or multilateral air transport agreements impacting U.S. Government procured transportation can be accessed at *http://www.state.gov/e/eb/tra/ata/ index.htm;* and

(ii) If determined appropriate, GSA may periodically issue FMR Bulletins providing further guidance on bilateral or multilateral air transportation agreements impacting U.S. Government procured transportation. These bulletins may be accessed at *http:// www.gsa.gov/bulletins;*

(2) When the costs of transportation are reimbursed in full by a third party, such as a foreign government, an international agency, or other organization; or

(3) Use of a foreign air carrier is determined to be a matter of necessity by your agency, on a case-by-case basis, when:

(i) No U.S. flag air carrier can provide the specific air transportation needed;

(ii) No U.S. flag air carrier can meet the time requirements in cases of emergency;

(iii) There is a lack of or inadequate U.S. flag air carrier aircraft;

(iv) There is an unreasonable risk to safety when using a U.S. flag carrier aircraft (*e.g.*, terrorist threats). Written approval of the use of foreign air carrier service based on an unreasonable risk to safety must be approved by your agency on a case-by-case basis and must be supported by a travel advisory notice issued by the Federal Aviation Administration, Department of State, or the Transportation Security Administration; or

(v) No U.S. flag air carrier can accomplish the agency's mission.

(b) *Ocean cargo:* International movement of property by water is subject to the Cargo Preference Act of 1954, as amended, 46 U.S.C. 55305, and the implementing regulations found at 46 CFR part 381, which require the use of a U.S. flag carrier for 50% of the tonnage shipped by each Department or Agency when service is available. The Maritime Administration (MARAD) monitors agency compliance with these laws. All Departments or Agencies shipping Government-impelled cargo must comply with the provisions of 46 CFR 381.3. For further information contact MARAD, Tel: 1–800–996–2723, Email: *cargo.marad@dot.gov.* For further information on international ocean shipping, go to: *http://www.marad.dot.gov/cargopreference.*

[79 FR 33476, June 11, 2014]

§ 102–117.140 What is cargo preference?

Cargo preference is the statutory requirement that all, or a portion of all, ocean-borne cargo that moves internationally be transported on U.S. flag vessels. Deviations or waivers from the cargo preference laws must be approved by:

Department of Transportation, Maritime Administration, Office of Cargo Preference, 1200 New Jersey Ave., SE., Washington, DC

20590, *http://marad.dot.gov/.* Tel. 1–800–987–3524. E-mail: *cargo.marad@dot.gov.*

[65 FR 60060, Oct. 6, 2000; 65 FR 81405, Dec. 26, 2000, as amended at 75 FR 51394, Aug. 20, 2010]

§ 102–117.145 What are coastwise laws?

Coastwise laws refer to laws governing shipment of freight, household goods and passengers by water between points in the United States or its territories. The purpose of these laws is to assure reliable shipping service and the existence of a maritime capability in times of war or national emergency (see section 27 of the Merchant Marine Act of 1920, 46 App. U.S.C. 883, 19 CFR 4.80).

§ 102–117.150 What do I need to know about coastwise laws?

You need to know that:

(a) Goods transported entirely or partly by water between U.S. points, either directly or via a foreign port, must travel in U.S. flag vessels that have a coastwise endorsement;

(b) There are exceptions and limits for the U.S. Island territories and possessions in the Atlantic and Pacific Oceans (see § 102–117.155); and

(c) The Secretary of the Treasury is empowered to impose monetary penalties against agencies that violate the coastwise laws.

[65 FR 60061, Oct. 6, 2000, as amended at 75 FR 51394, Aug. 20, 2010]

§ 102–117.155 Where do I go for further information about coastwise laws?

You may refer to 46 App. U.S.C. 883, 19 CFR 4.80, DOT MARAD (800–987–3524 or *www.cargo.marad@dot.gov*), the U.S. Coast Guard or U.S. Customs Service for further information on exceptions to the coastwise laws.

[65 FR 60061, Oct. 6, 2000, as amended at 75 FR 51394, Aug. 20, 2010]

Subpart E—Shipping Freight

§ 102–117.160 What is freight?

Freight is property or goods transported as cargo.

§ 102–117.165 What shipping process must I use for freight?

Use the following shipping process for freight:

(a) For domestic shipments you must:

(1) Identify what you are shipping;

(2) Decide if the cargo is HAZMAT, classified, or sensitive that may require special handling or placards;

(3) Decide mode;

(4) Check for applicable contracts or rate tenders within your agency or other agencies, including GSA;

(5) Select the most efficient and economical TSP that gives the best value;

(6) Prepare shipping documents; and

(7) Schedule pickup, declare released value and ensure prompt delivery with a fully executed receipt, and oversee shipment.

(b) For international shipments you must follow all the domestic procedures and, in addition, comply with the cargo preference laws. For specific information, see subpart D of this part.

§ 102–117.170　What reference materials are available to ship freight?

(a) The following is a partial list of handbooks and guides available from GSA:

(1) U.S. Government Freight Transportation Handbook;

(2) Limited Authority to Use Commercial Forms and Procedures;

(3) Submission of Transportation Documents; and

(4) Things to be Aware of When Routing or Receiving Freight Shipments.

(b) For the list in paragraph (a) of the section and other reference materials, contact:

(1) General Services Administration, Federal Supply Service, Audit Division (FBA), 1800 F Street, NW. Washington, DC 20405, *www.gsa.gov/transaudits;* or

(2) General Services Administration, Federal Supply Service, 1500 Bannister Road, Kansas City, MO 64131, *http://www.kc.gsa.gov/fsstt.*

[65 FR 60060, Oct. 6, 2000; 65 FR 81405, Dec. 26, 2000, as amended at 69 FR 57618, Sept. 24, 2004]

§ 102–117.175　What factors do I consider to determine the mode of transportation?

Your shipping urgency and any special handling requirements determine which mode of transportation you select. Each mode has unique requirements for documentation, liability, size, weight and delivery time. HAZMAT, radioactive, and other specialized cargo may require special permits and may limit your choices.

§ 102–117.180　What transportation documents must I use to ship freight?

To ship freight:

(a) By land (domestic shipments), use a bill of lading;

(b) By land (international shipments), you may, but are not required to, use the optional GBL;

(c) By ocean, use an ocean bill of lading, when suitable, along with the GBL. You only need an ocean bill of lading for door-to-door movements; and

(d) By air, use a bill of lading.

[65 FR 60061, Oct. 6, 2000, as amended at 75 FR 51394, Aug. 20, 2010]

§ 102–117.185　Where must I send a copy of the transportation documents?

(a) You must forward an original copy of all transportation documents to:

General Services Administration
Federal Supply Service
Audit Division (FBA)
1800 F Street, NW.
Washington, DC 20405

(b) For all property shipments subject to the cargo preference laws (see § 102–117.140), a copy of the ocean carrier's bill of lading, showing all freight charges, must be sent to MARAD within 30 days of vessel loading.

§ 102–117.190　Where do I file a claim for loss or damage to property?

You must file a claim for loss or damage to property with the TSP.

§ 102–117.195　Are there time limits affecting filing of a claim?

Yes, several statutes limit the time for administrative or judicial action against a TSP. Refer to part 102–118 of this chapter for more information and the time limit tables.

Subpart F—Shipping Hazardous Material (HAZMAT)

§ 102–117.200   What is HAZMAT?

HAZMAT is a substance or material the Secretary of Transportation determines to be an unreasonable risk to health, safety and property when transported in commerce. Therefore, there are restrictions on transporting HAZMAT (49 U.S.C. 5103 *et seq.*).

§ 102–117.205   What are the restrictions for transporting HAZMAT?

Agencies that ship HAZMAT are subject to the Environmental Protection Agency and the Department of Transportation regulations, as well as applicable State and local government rules and regulations.

§ 102–117.210   Where can I get guidance on transporting HAZMAT?

The Secretary of Transportation prescribes regulations for the safe transportation of HAZMAT in intrastate, interstate, and foreign commerce in 49 CFR parts 171 through 180. The Environmental Protection Agency also prescribes regulations on transporting HAZMAT in 40 CFR parts 260 through 266. You may also call the HAZMAT information hotline at 1–800–467–4922 (Washington, DC area, call 202–366–4488).

Subpart G—Shipping Household Goods

§ 102–117.215   What are household goods (HHG)?

Household goods (HHG) are the personal effects of Government employees and their dependents.

§ 102–117.220   What choices do I have to ship HHG?

(a) You may choose to ship HHG by:

(1) Using the commuted rate system;

(2) GSA's Centralized Household Goods Traffic Management Program (CHAMP);

(3) Contracting directly with a TSP, (including a relocation company that offers transportation services) using the acquisition procedures under the Federal Acquisition Regulation (FAR) (see § 102–117.35);

(4) Using another agency's contract with a TSP (see §§ 102–117.40 and 102–117.45);

(5) Using a rate tender under the Federal transportation procurement statutes (49 U.S.C. 10721 or 13712) (see § 102–117.35).

(b) As an alternative to the choices in paragraph (a) of this section, you may request the Department of State to assist with shipments of HHG moving to, from, and between foreign countries or international shipments originating in the continental United States. The nearest U.S. Embassy or Consulate may assist with arrangements of movements originating abroad. For further information contact:

Department of State
Transportation Operations
2201 C Street, NW.
Washington, DC 20520

NOTE TO § 102–117–220: Agencies must use the commuted rate system for civilian employees who transfer between points inside the continental United States unless it is evident from the cost comparison that the Government will incur a savings ($100 or more) using another choice listed. The use of household goods rate tenders is not authorized when household goods are shipped under the commuted rate system.

[65 FR 60060, Oct. 6, 2000; 65 FR 81405, Dec. 26, 2000]

§ 102–117.225   What is the difference between a contract or a rate tender and a commuted rate system?

(a) Under a contract or a rate tender, the agency prepares the bill of lading and books the shipment. The agency is the shipper and pays the TSP the applicable charges. If loss or damage occurs, the agency may either file a claim on behalf of the employee directly with the TSP, or help the employee in filing a claim against the TSP.

(b) Under the commuted rate system an employee arranges for shipping HHG and is reimbursed by the agency for the resulting costs. Use this method only within the continental United States (not Hawaii or Alaska).

(c) Rate table information and the commuted rate schedule can be found at *www.gsa.gov/relocationpolicy* or the appropriate office designated in your agency.

[65 FR 60061, Oct. 6, 2000, as amended at 78 FR 75485, Dec. 12, 2013]

§ 102–117.230 Must I compare costs between a contract or a rate tender and the commuted rate system before choosing which method to use?

Yes, you must compare the cost between a contract or a rate tender, and the commuted rate system before you make a decision.

§ 102–117.235 How do I get a cost comparison?

(a) You may calculate a cost comparison internally according to 41 CFR 302–8.3.

(b) You may request GSA to perform the cost comparison if you participate in the CHAMP program by sending GSA the following information as far in advance as possible (preferably 30 calendar days):

(1) Name of employee;

(2) Origin city, county and State;

(3) Destination city, county, and State;

(4) Date of household goods pick up;

(5) Estimated weight of shipments;

(6) Number of days storage-in-transit (if applicable); and

(7) Other relevant data.

(c) For more information on cost comparisons contact:

General Services Administration
Federal Supply Service
1500 Bannister Road
Kansas City, MO 64131
http://www.kc.gsa.gov/fsstt

NOTE TO § 102–117.235(c): GSA may charge an administrative fee for agencies not participating in the CHAMP program.

§ 102–117.240 What is my agency's financial responsibility to an employee who chooses to move all or part of his/her HHG under the commuted rate system?

(a) Your agency is responsible for reimbursing the employee what it would cost the Government to ship the employee's HHG by the most cost-effective means available or the employee's actual moving expenses, whichever is less.

(b) The employee is liable for the additional cost when the cost of transpor-

tation arranged by the employee is more than what it would cost the Government.

NOTE TO § 102–117.240: For information on how to ship household goods, refer to the Federal Travel Regulation, 41 CFR part 302–7, Transportation and Temporary Storage of Household Goods and Professional Books, Papers, and Equipment (PBP&E).

[65 FR 60061, Oct. 6, 2000, as amended at 75 FR 51394, Aug. 20, 2010]

§ 102–117.245 What is my responsibility in providing guidance to an employee who wishes to use the commuted rate system?

You must counsel employees that they may be liable for all costs above the amount reimbursed by the agency if they select a TSP that charges more than provided under the Commuted Rate Schedule.

§ 102–117.250 What are my responsibilities after shipping the household goods?

(a) Each agency should develop an evaluation survey for the employee to complete following the move.

(b) Under the CHAMP program, you must counsel employees to fill out their portion of the GSA Form 3080, Household Goods Carrier Evaluation Report. This form reports the quality of the TSP's performance. After completing the appropriate sections of this form, the employee must send it to the bill of lading issuing officer who in turn will complete the form and forward it to:

General Services Administration
National Customer Service Center
1500 Bannister Rd.
Kansas City, MO 64131
http://www.kc.gsa.gov/fsstt

[65 FR 60060, Oct. 6, 2000; 65 FR 81405, Dec. 26, 2000]

§ 102–117.255 What actions may I take if the TSP's performance is not satisfactory?

If the TSP's performance is not satisfactory, you may place a TSP in temporary nonuse, suspended status, or debarred status. For more information on doing this, see subpart I of this part and the FAR (48 CFR 9.406–3 and 9.407–3).

§ 102–117.260 What are my responsibilities to employees regarding the TSP's liability for loss or damage claims?

Regarding the TSP's liability for loss or damage claims, you must:

(a) Advise employees on the limits of the TSP's liability for loss of and damage to their HHG so the employee may evaluate the need for added insurance;

(b) Inform the employee about the procedures to file claims for loss and damage to HHG with the TSP; and

(c) Counsel employees, who have a loss or damage to their HHG that exceeds the amount recovered from a TSP, on procedures for filing a claim against the Government for the difference. Agencies may compensate employees up to $40,000 on claims for loss and damage under 31 U.S.C. 3721, 3723 (41 CFR 302–8.2(f)).

§ 102–117.265 Are there time limits that affect filing a claim with a TSP for loss or damage?

Yes, several statutes limit the time for filing claims or taking other administrative or judicial action against a TSP. Refer to part 102–118 of this chapter for information on claims.

Subpart H—Performance Measures

§ 102–117.270 What are agency performance measures for transportation?

(a) Agency performance measures are indicators of how you are supporting your customers and doing your job. By tracking performance measures you can report specific accomplishments and your success in supporting the agency mission. The Government Performance and Results Act (GPRA) of 1993 (31 U.S.C. 1115) requires agencies to develop business plans and set up program performance measures.

(b) Examples of performance measurements in transportation would include how well you:

(1) Increase the use of electronic commerce;

(2) Adopt industry best practices and services to meet your agency requirements;

(3) Use TSPs with a track record of successful past performance or proven superior ability;

(4) Take advantage of competition in moving agency freight and household goods;

(5) Assure that delivery of freight and household goods is on time against measured criteria; and

(6) Create simplified procedures to be responsive and adaptive to the customer needs and concerns.

Subpart I—Transportation Service Provider (TSP) Performance

§ 102–117.275 What performance must I expect from a TSP?

You must expect the TSP to provide consistent and satisfactory service to meet your agency transportation needs.

§ 102–117.280 What aspects of the TSP's performance are important to measure?

Important TSP performance measures may include, but are not limited to the:

(a) TSP's percentage of on-time deliveries;

(b) Percentage of shipments that include overcharges or undercharges;

(c) Percentage of claims received in a given period;

(d) Percentage of returns received on-time;

(e) Percentage of shipments rejected;

(f) Percentage of billing improprieties;

(g) Average response time on tracing shipments;

(h) TSP's safety record (accidents, losses, damages or misdirected shipments) as a percentage of all shipments;

(i) TSP's driving record (accidents, traffic tickets and driving complaints) as a percentage of shipments; and

(j) Percentage of customer satisfaction reports on carrier performance.

§ 102–117.285 What are my choices if a TSP's performance is not satisfactory?

You may choose to place a TSP in temporary nonuse, suspension, or debarment if performance is unsatisfactory.

§ 102–117.290 What is the difference between temporary nonuse, suspension and debarment?

(a) Temporary nonuse is limited to your agency and initiated by the agency transportation officers for a period not to exceed 90 days for:

(1) Willful violations of the terms of the rate tender;

(2) Persistent or willful failure to meet requested packing and pickup service;

(3) Failure to meet required delivery dates;

(4) Violation of Department of Transportation (DOT) hazardous material regulations;

(5) Mishandling of freight, damaged or missing transportation seals, improper loading, blocking, packing or bracing of property;

(6) Improper routing of property;

(7) Subjecting your shipments to unlawful seizure or detention by failing to pay debts;

(8) Operating without legal authority;

(9) Failure to settle claims according to Government regulations; or

(10) Repeated failure to comply with regulations of DOT, Surface Transportation Board, State or local governments or other Government agencies.

(b) Suspension is disqualifying a TSP from receiving orders for certain services under a contract or rate tender pending an investigation or legal proceeding. A TSP may be suspended on adequate evidence of:

(1) Fraud or a criminal offense in connection with obtaining, attempting to obtain, or performing a contract for transportation;

(2) Violation of Federal or State antitrust statutes;

(3) Embezzlement, theft, forgery, bribery, falsification or destruction of records, making false statements, or receiving stolen property; and

(4) Any other offense indicating a lack of business integrity or business honesty that seriously and directly affects the present responsibility of the TSP as a transporter of the Government's property or the HHG of its employees relocated for the Government.

(c) Debarment means action taken to exclude a contractor from contracting with all Federal agencies. The seriousness of the TSP's acts or omissions and the mitigating factors must be considered in making any debarment decisions. A TSP may be debarred for the following reasons:

(1) Failure of a TSP to take the necessary corrective actions within the period of temporary nonuse; or

(2) Conviction of or civil judgment for any of the causes for suspension.

§ 102–117.295 Who makes the decisions on temporary nonuse, suspension and debarment?

(a) The transportation officer may place a TSP in temporary nonuse for a period not to exceed 90 days.

(b) The serious nature of suspension and debarment requires that these sanctions be imposed only in the public interest for the Government's protection and not for purposes of punishment. Only the agency head or his/her designee may suspend or debar a TSP.

§ 102–117.300 Do the decisions on temporary nonuse, suspension and debarment go beyond the agency?

(a) Temporary nonuse does not go beyond the agency.

(b) Decisions on suspended or debarred TSPs do go beyond the agency and are available to the general public on the Excluded Parties Lists System (EPLS) maintained by GSA at *http://www.epls.gov.*

[65 FR 60061, Oct. 6, 2000, as amended at 75 FR 51394, Aug. 20, 2010]

§ 102–117.305 Where do I go for information on the process for suspending or debarring a TSP?

Refer to the Federal Acquisition Regulation (48 CFR part 9, subpart 9.4) for policies and procedures governing suspension and debarment of a TSP.

§ 102–117.310 What records must I keep on temporary nonuse, suspension or debarment of a TSP?

(a) You must set up a program consistent with your agency's internal record retention procedures to document the placement of TSPs in a nonuse, suspended or debarred status.

(b) For temporary nonuse, your records must contain the following information:

(1) Name, address, and Standard Carrier Alpha Code and Taxpayer Identification Number of each TSP placed in temporary nonuse status;

(2) The duration of the temporary nonuse status;

(3) The cause for imposing temporary nonuse, and the facts showing the existence of such a cause;

(4) Information and arguments in opposition to the temporary nonuse period sent by the TSP or its representative; and

(5) The reviewing official's determination about keeping or removing temporary nonuse status.

(c) For suspended or debarred TSPs, your records must include the same information as paragraph (b) of this section and you must:

(1) Assure your agency does not award contracts to a suspended or debarred TSP; and

(2) Notify GSA (see § 102–117.315).

§ 102–117.315 Whom must I notify on suspension or debarment of a TSP?

Agencies must report electronically any suspension or debarment actions to the Excluded Parties List System: *http://www.epls.gov* in accordance with the provisions of 48 CFR 9.404(c).

[75 FR 51394, Aug. 20, 2010]

Subpart J—Representation Before Regulatory Body Proceedings

§ 102–117.320 What is a transportation regulatory body proceeding?

A transportation regulatory body proceeding is a hearing before a transportation governing entity, such as a State public utility commission, the Surface Transportation Board, or the Federal Maritime Commission. The proceeding may be at the Federal or State level depending on the activity regulated.

§ 102–117.325 May my agency appear on its own behalf before a transportation regulatory body proceeding?

Generally, no executive agency may appear on its own behalf in any proceeding before a transportation regulatory body, unless the Administrator of General Services delegates the authority to the agency. The statutory authority for the Administrator of

General Services to participate in regulatory proceedings on behalf of all Federal agencies is in section 201(a)(4) of the Federal Property and Administrative Services Act of 1949, as amended (40 U.S.C. 481(a)(4)).

§ 102–117.330 When, or under what circumstances, would GSA delegate authority to an agency to appear on its own behalf before a transportation regulatory body proceeding?

GSA will delegate authority when it does not have the expertise, or when it is outside of GSA's purview, to make a determination on an issue such as a protest of rates, routings or excessive charges.

§ 102–117.335 How does my agency ask for a delegation to represent itself in a regulatory body proceeding?

You must send your request for delegation with enough detail to explain the circumstances surrounding the need for delegation of authority for representation to:

General Services Administration
Office of Travel, Transportation and Asset Management (MT)
1800 F Street, NW.
Washington, DC 20405

[65 FR 60061, Oct. 6, 2000, as amended at 75 FR 51394, Aug. 20, 2010]

§ 102–117.340 What other types of assistance may GSA provide agencies in dealing with regulatory bodies?

(a) GSA has oversight of all public utilities used by the Federal Government including transportation. There are specific regulatory requirements a TSP must meet at the State level, such as the requirement to obtain a certificate of public convenience and necessity.

(b) GSA has a list of TSPs, which meet certain criteria regarding insurance and safety, approved by DOT. You must furnish GSA with an affidavit to determine if the TSP meets the basic qualification to protect the Government's interest. As an oversight mandate, GSA coordinates this function. For further information contact:

General Services Administration, Office of Travel and Transportation Services, Center for Transportation Management

(QMCC), 2200 Crystal Drive, Rm. #3042, Arlington, VA 20406.

[65 FR 60061, Oct. 6, 2000, as amended at 75 FR 51394, Aug. 20, 2010]

Subpart K—Transportation Reporting

SOURCE: 80 FR 57102, Sept. 22, 2015, unless otherwise noted.

§ 102–117.345 What is the Federal Interagency Transportation System (FITS)?

The Federal Interagency Transportation System (FITS) is a Web-based tool used to capture an agency's transaction level transportation data for freight and cargo, including household goods (HHG), procured either through contract or tender that is otherwise not currently reported by agencies to GSA in compliance with 31 U.S.C. 3726, as well as agency transportation management information.

§ 102–117.350 Do I have to report?

No; however all agencies are strongly encouraged to report for the preceding fiscal year through FITS by October 31.

§ 102–117.355 Why should I report?

(a) Reporting your agency's prior fiscal year transaction level transportation data for freight and cargo, including HHG, procured either through contract or tender, as well as your transportation management information will enable GSA to:

(1) Assess the magnitude and key characteristics of transportation within the Government (*e.g.*, how much agencies spend; what type of commodity is shipped; most used lanes, etc.); and

(2) Analyze and recommend changes to Governmentwide policies, standards, practices, and procedures to improve Government transportation management.

(b) Agencies that choose to report may identify opportunities within their organization to improve transportation management program performance as a result of the data analytics.

§ 102–117.356 What information should I report?

You should report your agency's prior fiscal year transaction level transportation data for freight and cargo, including HHG, and transportation management information. Transportation data that currently is otherwise provided to GSA in compliance with 31 U.S.C. 3726 is not requested. Transaction level transportation data submitted by agencies will remain confidential. Transportation management information should also be reported and should include related environmental information, agency points of contact, and transportation officer warrant and training data.

§ 102–117.360 How do I submit information to GSA through FITS?

GSA will post a Federal Management Regulation bulletin at *http://gsa.gov/ fmrbulletin*, which will detail the FITS submission process, including specific data requested, and provide information concerning available FITS training.

Subpart L—Governmentwide Transportation Policy Council (GTPC)

§ 102–117.361 What is the Governmentwide Transportation Policy Council (GTPC)?

The Office of Governmentwide Policy sponsors a Governmentwide Transportation Policy Council (GTPC) to help agencies establish, improve, and maintain effective transportation management policies, practices and procedures. The council:

(a) Collaborates with private and public stakeholders to develop valid performance measures and promote solutions that lead to effective results; and

(b) Provides assistance to your agency with the requirement to report your transportation activity to GSA (see § 102–117.345).

[65 FR 60061, Oct. 6, 2000, as amended at 75 FR 51395, Aug. 20, 2010. Redesignated at 80 FR 57102, Sept. 22, 2015]

§ 102–117.362 Where can I get more information about the GTPC?

For more information about the GTPC, contact:

General Services Administration
Office of Travel, Transportation and Asset Management (MT)
1800 F Street, NW.
Washington, DC 20405
http://www.policyworks.gov/transportation

[65 FR 60061, Oct. 6, 2000, as amended at 75 FR 51395, Aug. 20, 2010. Redesignated at 80 FR 57102, Sept. 22, 2015]

Subpart M—Recommendations for Authorization and Qualifications to Acquire Transportation Using a Rate Tender

SOURCE: 79 FR 55365, Sept. 16, 2014, unless otherwise noted.

§ 102–117.365 What are the responsibilities of a Transportation Officer?

A Transportation Officer's (TO) responsibilities may include:

(a) Negotiating rates;

(b) Signing bills of lading (BOL);

(c) Approving additional accessorial charges;

(d) Selecting and procuring services of a TSP;

(e) Selecting and procuring services of a 3PL;

(f) Serving as a transportation subject matter expert to a Contracting Officer (CO); and/or

(g) Other roles/responsibilities, such as serving as a certifying official for BOL or as a disbursement official.

§ 102–117.370 Should I have a Transportation Officer warrant to acquire transportation services using a rate tender?

Yes, it is recommended that you have a written document, such as a warrant, issued by the head of your agency or their designee, which expressly allows you to acquire transportation services for using approved non-Federal Acquisition Regulation (FAR) acquisition methods for specified transportation services, and states a dollar limit or range for the warrant authority.

§ 102–117.375 Are there instances where a Transportation Officer warrant is not necessary to acquire transportation services?

Yes, a Transportation Officer warrant is not necessary to:

(a) Ship packages through a contract under the GSA Schedules program, including any Blanket Purchase Agreement, as these are FAR-based contracts;

(b) Ship packages or other materials through any other FAR-based contract; or

(c) Send items through the United States Postal Service.

§ 102–117.380 What should be contained in a Transportation Officer warrant to acquire transportation services?

The warrant for authority to acquire transportation services for freight and cargo, including HHGs, issued by the agency head or their designee should:

(a) State that you have sufficient experience (any combination of Federal, public, and/or commercial) and/or training in transportation services, including any relevant acquisition or certifying officer training, that qualifies you to acquire the transportation services needed by your agency;

(b) List the maximum dollar limit, if any, and any other limits, such as the types of services that you may acquire;

(c) State your agency's necessary conditions to maintain the warrant; and

(d) Include an expiration date for the warrant, recommended not to exceed three years from the date of issuance.

§ 102–117.385 Is there a standard format for a Transportation Officer warrant?

No. GSA can provide your agency with a suggested format. Agencies could also model the Transportation Officer warrant after the Contracting Officer warrant, or they may establish their own format.

§ 102–117.390 What are the recommended Transportation Officer training and/or experience levels?

(a) The following are suggested agency transportation officer training and/or experience baselines:

(1) For a Basic (Level 1) Transportation Officer Warrant:

·(i) Twenty-four (24) hours of training in Federal transportation; or

(ii) Two (2) years of Federal, public, and/or commercial experience in acquiring transportation through rate tenders.

(2) For an Experienced (Level 2) Transportation Officer Warrant:

(i) Thirty-two (32) hours of training in transportation, including twenty (20) hours of training in Federal transportation; or

(ii) Three (3) years of Federal, public, and/or commercial experience in acquiring transportation through rate tenders.

(3) For a Senior (Level 3) Transportation Officer Warrant:

(i) Sixty (60) hours of training in transportation, including forty (40) hours of training in Federal transportation; or

(ii) Five (5) years of Federal, public, and/or commercial experience in acquiring transportation through rate tenders.

(b) GSA created an online eLearning Transportation Officer training site to provide a standard Governmentwide body of transportation knowledge available to all agencies. This Web-based eLearning site is available at *http://transportationofficer.golearnportal.org/*.

§ 102–117.395 Should I continue my training to maintain my warrant?

Yes, you should continue your training. Your agency will determine the continuing education that applies specifically to your warrant. It is recommended that at least twelve (12) hours of transportation training per year be completed in order to maintain a Transportation Officer warrant.

§ 102–117.400 How should my warrant be documented?

The head of your agency or their designee should state, in writing, that you have the recommended training and/or experience suggested by § 102–117.390. You should retain a copy of this Transportation Officer warrant. Agency heads or their designee(s) may amend, suspend, or terminate warrants in accordance with agency policies and/or procedures.

PART 102–118—TRANSPORTATION PAYMENT AND AUDIT

Subpart A—General

Introduction

Subpart C—Use of Government Billing Documents

Subpart D—Prepayment Audit of Transportation Services

AUTHORITY: 31 U.S.C. 3726; 40 U.S.C. 121(c); 40 U.S.C. 501, *et seq.;* 46 U.S.C. 55305; 49 U.S.C. 40118.

SOURCE: 65 FR 24569, Apr. 26, 2000, unless otherwise noted.

Subpart A—General

INTRODUCTION

§ 102–118.5 What is the purpose of this part?

The purpose of this part is to interpret statutes and other policies that assure that payment and payment mechanisms for agency transportation services are uniform and appropriate. This part communicates the policies clearly to agencies and transportation service providers (TSPs). (See § 102–118.35 for the definition of TSP.)

§ 102–118.10 What is a transportation audit?

A transportation audit is a thorough review and validation of transportation related documents and bills. The audit must examine the validity, propriety, and conformity of the charges or rates with tariffs, quotations, contracts, agreements, or tenders, as appropriate.

[81 FR 65298, Sept. 22, 2016]

§ 102–118.15 What is a transportation payment?

A transportation payment is a payment made by an agency to a TSP for the movement of goods, people or transportation related services.

[65 FR 24569, Apr. 26, 2000, as amended at 81 FR 65299, Sept. 22, 2016]

§ 102–118.20 Who is subject to this part?

This part applies to all agencies (including the Department of Defense (DoD)) and TSPs defined in § 102–118.35, and wholly-owned Government corporations as defined in 31 U.S.C. 101, *et seq.* and 31 U.S.C. 9101(3). Your agency is required to incorporate this part into its internal regulations.

[81 FR 65299, Sept. 22, 2016]

§ 102–118.25 What must my agency provide to GSA regarding its transportation policies?

As part of the evaluation of agencies' transportation program and postpayment audit, GSA may request to examine your agency's transportation prepayment audit program and policies to verify the performance of the prepayment audit. GSA Office of Government-wide Policy, Transportation Policy Division and GSA Transportation Audits Division may suggest revisions of agencies' audit program or policies.

[81 FR 65299, Sept. 22, 2016]

§ 102–118.30 Are Government-controlled corporations bound by this part?

This part does not apply to Government-controlled corporations and mixed-ownership Government corporations as defined in 31 U.S.C. 9101(1) and (2).

[81 FR 65299, Sept. 22, 2016]

DEFINITIONS

§ 102–118.35 What definitions apply to this part?

The following definitions apply to this part:

Agency means a department, agency, or instrumentality of the United States Government (31 U.S.C. 101).

Bill of lading (BOL), sometimes referred to as a commercial bill of lading, but includes a Government bill of lading (GBL), means the document used as a receipt of goods, a contract of carriage, and documentary evidence of title.

Cash means cash, personal checks, personal charge cards, and travelers checks. Cash may only be used to pay for transportation expenses in extremely limited cases where government payment mechanisms are not available or acceptable.

Claim means—

(1) Any demand by an agency upon a transportation service provider (TSP) for the payment of overcharges, ordinary debts, fines, penalties, administrative fees, special charges, and interest; or

(2) Any demand by the TSP for amounts not included in the original bill that the TSP believes an agency owes them. This includes amounts deducted or offset by an agency; amounts previously refunded by the TSP, which is believed to be owed; and any subsequent bills from the TSP resulting from a transaction that was prepayment or postpayment audited by the GSA Transportation Audits Division.

Document reference number (DRN) means the unique number on a bill of lading, Government Transportation Request (GTR), or transportation ticket used to track the movement of shipments and individuals.

EDI signature means a discrete authentication code which serves in place of a paper signature and binds parties to the terms and conditions of a contract in electronic communication.

Electronic commerce means electronic techniques for performing business transactions (ordering, billing, and paying for goods and services), including electronic mail or messaging, Internet technology, electronic bulletin boards, charge cards, electronic funds transfers, and electronic data interchange.

Electronic data interchange means electronic techniques for carrying out transportation transactions using electronic transmissions of the information between computers instead of paper documents. These electronic transmissions must use established and published formats and codes as authorized by the applicable Federal Information Processing Standards.

Electronic funds transfer means any transfer of funds, other than transactions initiated by cash, check, or similar paper instrument, that is initiated through an electronic terminal, telephone, computer, or magnetic tape, for the purpose of ordering, instructing, or authorizing a financial institution to debit or credit an account. The term includes Automated Clearinghouse transfers, Fed Wire transfers, and transfers made at automatic teller machines and point of sale terminals.

Government bill of lading (GBL) means the transportation document used as a receipt of goods, evidence of title, and a contract of carriage for Government international shipments (see Bill of lading (BOL) definition).

Government contractor-issued charge card means the charge card used by authorized individuals to pay for official travel and transportation related expenses for which the contractor bills the employee. This is different than a centrally billed account paying for official travel and transportation related expenses for which the agency is billed.

Government Transportation Request (GTR) (Optional Form 1169)—means a Government document used to procure passenger transportation services from a TSP. The document obligates the Government to pay for transportation services provided and is used when a Government contractor issued charge card is not.

Offset means something that serves to counterbalance or to compensate for something else. These are funds owed to a TSP that are not released by the agency but instead used to repay the agency for a debt incurred by the TSP.

Ordinary debt means an amount that a TSP owes an agency other than for the repayment of an overcharge. Ordinary debts include, but are not limited to, payments for transportation services ordered and not provided (including unused transportation tickets), duplicate payments, and amounts for which a TSP is liable because of loss and/or damage to property it transported.

Overcharge means those charges for transportation that exceed those applicable under the executed agreement for services such as bill of lading (including a GBL, contract, rate tender or a GTR).

Postpayment audit means an audit of transportation billing documents, and all related transportation documents after payment, to decide their validity, propriety, and conformity of rates with tariffs, quotations, agreements, contracts, or tenders. The audit process may also include subsequent adjustments and collection actions taken against a TSP by the Government (31 U.S.C. 3726).

Prepayment audit means an audit of transportation billing documents before payment to determine their validity, propriety, and conformity of rates with tariffs, quotations, agreements, contracts, or tenders (31 U.S.C. 3726).

Privately Owned Personal Property Government Bill of Lading, Optional Form 1203, means the agency transportation document used as a receipt of goods, evidence of title, and generally a contract of carriage. It is only available for the transportation of household goods. Use of this form is mandatory for Department of Defense, but optional for other agencies.

Rate authority means the document that establishes the legal charges for a transportation shipment. Charges included in a rate authority are those rates, fares, and charges for transportation and related services contained in tariffs, tenders, contracts, bills of lading, and other equivalent documents.

Reparation means a payment to or from an agency to correct an improper transportation billing as determined by a postpayment audit involving a TSP. Improper routing, overcharges, or duplicate payments may cause such improper billing. This is different from a payment to settle a claim for loss and damage.

Standard Carrier Alpha Code (SCAC) is a unique code, typically two to four characters, used to identify transportation companies.

Statement of difference means a statement issued by an agency or its designated audit contractor during a prepayment audit when they determine that a TSP has billed the agency for more than the proper amount for the services. This statement tells the TSP on the invoice, the amount allowed and the basis for the proper charges. The statement also cites the applicable rate references and other data relied on for support. The agency issues a separate statement of difference for each transportation transaction.

Statement of difference rebuttal means a document used by the agency to respond to a TSP's claim about an improper reduction made against the TSP's original bill by the paying agency.

Supplemental bill means the bill for services that the TSP submits to the agency for additional payment of the services provided.

Taxpayer identification number (TIN) means the number required by the Internal Revenue Service to be used by the TSP in reporting income tax or other returns. For a TSP, the TIN is an employer identification number.

Transportation means service involved in the physical movement (from one location to another) of people, household goods, and freight by a TSP or a Third Party Logistics (3PL) entity for an agency, as well as activities directly relating to or supporting that movement. These activities are defined in 49 U.S.C. 13102.

Transportation document (TD) means any executed document for transportation services, such as a bill of lading, a tariff, a tender, a contract, a GTR, invoices, paid invoices, any transportation bills, or other equivalent documents, including electronic documents.

Transportation service provider (TSP) means any party, person, agent, or carrier that provides freight, household goods, or passenger transportation or related services to an agency.

Virtual GBL (VGBL) means the use of a unique GBL number on a commercial document, which binds the TSP to the terms and conditions of a GBL.

NOTE TO § 102–118.35: 15 U.S.C. 96, *et seq.*, 49 U.S.C. 13102, *et seq.*, and 41 CFR Chapter 302 Federal Travel Regulation defines additional transportation terms not listed in this section.

[65 FR 24569, Apr. 26, 2000, as amended at 69 FR 57618, Sept. 24, 2004; 74 FR 30475, June 26, 2009; 81 FR 65299, Sept. 22, 2016]

Subpart B—Ordering and Paying for Transportation and Transportation Services

§ 102–118.40 How does my agency order transportation and transportation services?

Your agency orders:

(a) Transportation of freight and household goods and related transportation services (e.g., packaging, storage) with a Government contractor-issued charge card, purchase order (or electronic equivalent), or a Government bill of lading for international shipments (including domestic overseas shipments). In extremely limited cases, cash can be used where government payment mechanisms are not available or acceptable.

(b) Transportation of people through the purchase of transportation tickets with a Government issued charge card (or centrally billed travel account citation), Government issued individual travel charge card, personal charge card, cash (in accordance with Department of the Treasury regulations), or in limited prescribed situations, a Government Transportation Request

(GTR). See the "U.S. Government Passenger Transportation—Handbook," obtainable from:

General Services Administration
Transportation Audit Division (QMCA)
Crystal Plaza 4, Room 300

2200 Crystal Drive
Arlington, VA 22202
www.gsa.gov/transaudits

[65 FR 24569, Apr. 26, 2000, as amended at 66 FR 48812, Sept. 24, 2001; 69 FR 57618, Sept. 24, 2004; 74 FR 30475, June 26, 2009]

§ 102–118.45 How does a transportation service provider (TSP) bill my agency for transportation and transportation services?

The manner in which your agency orders transportation and transportation services determines the manner in which a TSP bills for service. This is shown in the following table:

TRANSPORTATION SERVICE PROVIDER BILLING

(a) Ordering method	(b) Billing method
(1)(i) Government issued agency charge card, ... (ii) Centrally billed travel account citation.	(1) Bill from charge card company (may be electronic).
(2)(i) Purchase order, ... (ii) Bill of lading, (iii) Government Bill of Lading, (iv) Government Transportation Request.	(2) Bill from TSP (may be electronic).
(3)(i) Contractor issued individual travel charge card (ii) Personal charge card, (iii) Personal cash.	(3) Voucher from employee (may be electronic).

§ 102–118.50 How does my agency pay for transportation services?

Your agency may pay for transportation services in three ways:

(a) *Electronic funds transfer (EFT) (31 U.S.C. 3332, et)*. Your agency is required by statute to make all payments by EFT unless your agency receives a waiver from the Department of the Treasury.

(b) *Check.* For those situations where EFT is not possible and the Department of the Treasury has issued a waiver, your agency may make payments by check.

(c) *Cash.* In very unusual circumstances and as a last option, your agency payments may be made in cash in accordance with Department of the Treasury regulations (31 CFR part 208).

§ 102–118.55 What administrative procedures must my agency establish for payment of freight, household goods, or other transportation services?

Your agency must establish administrative procedures which assure that the following conditions are met:

(a) The negotiated price is fair and reasonable;

(b) A document of agreement signifying acceptance of the arrangements with terms and conditions is filed with the participating agency by the TSP;

(c) The terms and conditions are included in all transportation agreements and referenced on all transportation documents (TDs);

(d) Bills are only paid to the TSP providing service under the bill of lading to your agency and may not be waived;

(e) All fees paid are accounted for in the aggregate delivery costs;

(f) All payments are subject to applicable statutory limitations;

(g) Procedures (such as an unique numbering system) are established to prevent and detect duplicate payments, properly account for expenditures and discrepancy notices;

(h) All transactions are verified with any indebtedness list. On charge card transactions, your agency must consult any indebtedness list if the charge card contract provisions allow for it; and

(i) Procedures are established to process any unused tickets.

§ 102–118.60　To what extent must my agency use electronic commerce?

Your agency must use electronic commerce in all areas of your transportation program. This includes the use of electronic systems and forms for ordering, receiving bills and paying for transportation and transportation services.

[69 FR 57618, Sept. 24, 2004]

§ 102–118.65　Can my agency receive electronic billing for payment of transportation services?

Yes, when mutually agreeable to the agency and the GSA Audit Division, your agency is encouraged to use electronic billing for the procurement and billing of transportation services.

§ 102–118.70　Must my agency make all payments via electronic funds transfer?

Yes, under 31 U.S.C. 3332, *et seq.*, your agency must make all payments for goods and services via EFT (this includes goods and services ordered using charge cards).

§ 102–118.75　What if my agency or the TSP does not have an account with a financial institution or approved payment agent?

Under 31 U.S.C. 3332, *et seq.*, your agency must obtain an account with a financial institution or approved payment agent in order to meet the statutory requirements to make all Federal payments via EFT unless your agency receives a waiver from the Department of the Treasury. To obtain a waiver, your agency must contact:

The Commissioner
Financial Management Service
Department of the Treasury
401 Fourteenth Street, SW.
Washington, DC 20227

http://www.fms.treas.gov/

§ 102–118.80　Who is responsible for keeping my agency's electronic commerce transportation billing records?

Your agency's internal financial regulations will identify responsibility for recordkeeping. In addition, the GSA Audit Division keeps a central repository of electronic transportation billing records for legal and auditing purposes. Therefore, your agency must forward all relevant electronic transportation billing documents to:

General Services Administration
Transportation Audit Division (QMCA)
Crystal Plaza 4, Room 300
2200 Crystal Drive
Arlington, VA 22202
www.gsa.gov/transaudits

[65 FR 24569, Apr. 26, 2000, as amended at 69 FR 57620, Sept. 24, 2004; 74 FR 30475, June 26, 2009]

§ 102–118.85　Can my agency use a Government contractor issued charge card to pay for transportation services?

Yes, your agency may use a Government contractor issued charge card to purchase transportation services if permitted under the charge card contract or task order. In these circumstances your agency will receive a bill for these services from the charge card company.

§ 102–118.90　If my agency orders transportation and/or transportation services with a Government contractor issued charge card or charge account citation, is this subject to prepayment audit?

Generally, no transportation or transportation services ordered with a Government contractor issued charge card or charge account citation can be prepayment audited because the bank or charge card contractor pays the TSP directly, before your agency receives a bill that can be audited from the charge card company. However, if your agency contracts with the charge card or charge account provider to provide for a prepayment audit, then, as long as your agency is not liable for paying the bank for improper charges (as determined by the prepayment audit verification process), a prepayment audit can be used. As with all prepayment audit programs, the charge card prepayment audit must be approved by the GSA Audit Division prior to implementation. If the charge card contract does not provide for a prepayment audit, your agency must submit the transportation line items on the charge card to the GSA Audit Division for a postpayment audit.

§102–118.91 May my agency authorize the use of cash?

Yes, in limited circumstances, a Government employee can use cash where government payment mechanisms are not available or acceptable.

[69 FR 57618, Sept. 24, 2004]

§102–118.92 How does my agency handle receipts, tickets or other records of cash payments?

Your agency must ensure that its employees keep the original receipts for transportation purchases over $75.00 made with cash. If it is impractical to furnish receipts in any instance as required by this subtitle, the failure to do so must be fully explained on the travel voucher. Mere inconvenience in the matter of taking receipts will not be considered. These receipts must be saved for a possible postpayment audit by the GSA Audit Division. If your agency requires the filing of paper receipts, then you must do so. For transportation purchases over $75.00, your agency must ensure that copies of all original papers are retained at your agency. Copies of tickets from a TSP must be sent to—General Services Administration, Transportation Audit Division (QMCA), Crystal Plaza 4, Room 300, 2200 Crystal Drive, Arlington, VA 22202, *www.gsa.gov/transaudits*.

[69 FR 57618, Sept. 24, 2004, as amended at 74 FR 30475, June 26, 2009]

§102–118.95 What forms can my agency use to pay transportation bills?

Your agency must use commercial payment practices and forms to the maximum extent possible; however, when viewed necessary by your agency, your agency may use the following Government forms to pay transportation bills:

(a) Standard Form (SF) 1113, Public Voucher for Transportation Charges, and SF 1113–A, Memorandum Copy;

(b) Optional Form (OF) 1103, Government Bill of Lading and OF 1103A Memorandum Copy (used for movement of things, both privately owned and Government property for official uses);

(c) OF 1169, Government Transportation Request (used to pay for tickets to move people); and

(d) OF 1203, Privately Owned Personal Property Government Bill of Lading, and OF 1203A, Memorandum Copy (used by the Department of Defense to move private property for official transfers).

NOTE TO §102–118.95: By March 31, 2002, your agency may no longer use the GBLs (OF 1103 and OF 1203) for domestic shipments. After September 30, 2000, your agency should minimize the use of GTRs (OF 1169).

[65 FR 24569, Apr. 26, 2000, as amended at 66 FR 48812, Sept. 24, 2001]

§102–118.100 What must my agency ensure is on each SF 1113?

Your agency must ensure during its prepayment audit of a TSP bill that the TSP filled out the Public Vouchers, SF 1113, completely including the taxpayer identification number (TIN), and standard carrier alpha code (SCAC). An SF 1113 must accompany all billings.

§102–118.105 Where can I find the rules governing the use of a Government Bill of Lading?

The "U.S. Government Freight Transportation—Handbook" contains information on how to prepare this GBL form. To get a copy of this handbook, you may write to: General Services Administration, Transportation Audit Division (QMCA), Crystal Plaza 4, Room 300, 2200 Crystal Drive, Arlington, VA 22202, *www.gsa.gov/transaudits*.

[65 FR 24569, Apr. 26, 2000, as amended at 69 FR 57620, Sept. 24, 2004; 74 FR 30475, June 26, 2009]

§102–118.110 Where can I find the rules governing the use of a Government Transportation Request?

The "U.S. Government Passenger Transportation—Handbook" contains information on how to prepare this

GTR form. To get a copy of this handbook, you may write to:

General Services Administration
Transportation Audit Division (QMCA)
Crystal Plaza 4, Room 300
2200 Crystal Drive
Arlington, VA 22202
www.gsa.gov/transaudits

[65 FR 24569, Apr. 26, 2000, as amended at 69 FR 57620, Sept. 24, 2004: 74 FR 30475, June 26, 2009]

§ 102–118.115 Must my agency use a GBL?

No, your agency is not required to use a GBL and must use commercial payment practices to the maximum extent possible. Effective March 31, 2002, your agency must phase out the use of the Optional Forms 1103 and 1203 for domestic shipments. After this date, your agency may use the GBL solely for international shipments.

[65 FR 24569, Apr. 26, 2000, as amended at 66 FR 48812, Sept. 24, 2001]

§ 102–118.120 Must my agency use a GTR?

No, your agency is not required to use a GTR. Your agency must adopt commercial practices and eliminate GTR use to the maximum extent possible.

§ 102–118.125 What if my agency uses a TD other than a GBL?

If your agency uses any other TD for shipping under its account, the requisite and the named safeguards must be in place (i.e., terms and conditions found herein and in the "U.S. Government Freight Transportation—Handbook," appropriate numbering, etc.).

§ 102–118.130 Must my agency use a GBL for express, courier, or small package shipments?

No, however, in using commercial forms all shipments must be subject to the terms and conditions set forth for use of a bill of lading for the Government. Any other non-conflicting applicable contracts or agreements between the TSP and an agency involving buying transportation services for Government traffic remain binding. This purchase does not require a SF 1113. When you are using GSA's schedule for small package express delivery, the terms

and conditions of that contract are binding.

§ 102–118.135 Where are the mandatory terms and conditions governing the use of bills of lading?

The mandatory terms and conditions governing the use of bills of lading are contained in this part and the "U.S. Government Freight Transportation Handbook."

§ 102–118.140 What are the major mandatory terms and conditions governing the use of GBLs and bills of lading?

The mandatory terms and conditions governing the use of GBLs and bills of lading are:

(a) Unless otherwise permitted by statute and approved by the agency, the TSP may not demand prepayment or collect charges from the consignee. The TSP, providing service under the bill of lading, must present a legible copy of the bill of lading or an original, properly certified GBL attached to Standard Form (SF) 1113, Public Voucher for Transportation Charges, to the paying office for payment;

(b) The shipment must be made at the restricted or limited valuation specified in the tariff or classification or limited contract, arrangement or exemption at or under which the lowest rate is available, unless indicated on the GBL or bill of lading. (This is commonly referred to as an alternation of rates);

(c) Receipt for the shipment is subject to the consignee's annotation of loss, damage, or shrinkage on the delivering TSP's documents and the consignee's copy of the same documents. If loss or damage is discovered after delivery or receipt of the shipment, the consignee must promptly notify the nearest office of the last delivering TSP and extend to the TSP the privilege of examining the shipment;

(d) The rules and conditions governing commercial shipments for the time period within which notice must be given to the TSP, or a claim must be filed, or suit must be instituted, shall not apply if the shipment is lost, damaged or undergoes shrinkage in transit. Only with the written concurrence of the Government official responsible for making the shipment is the deletion of this item considered to valid;

(e) Interest shall accrue from the voucher payment date on the overcharges made and shall be paid at the same rate in effect on that date as published by the Secretary of the Treasury pursuant to the Debt Collection Act of 1982 31 U.S.C. 3717); and

(f) Additional mandatory terms and conditions are in this part and the "U.S. Government Freight Transportation—Handbook."

[65 FR 24569, Apr. 26, 2000, as amended at 69 FR 57619, Sept. 24, 2004]

§ 102–118.145 Where are the mandatory terms and conditions governing the use of passenger transportation documents?

The mandatory terms and conditions governing the use of passenger transportation documents are contained in this part and the "U.S. Government Passenger Transportation—Handbook."

§ 102–118.150 What are the major mandatory terms and conditions governing the use of passenger transportation documents?

The mandatory terms and conditions governing the use of passenger transportation documents are:

(a) Government travel must be via the lowest cost available, that meets travel requirements; e.g., Government contract, fare, through, excursion, or reduced one way or round trip fare. This should be done by entering the term "lowest coach" on the Government travel document if the specific fare basis is not known;

(b) The U.S. Government is not responsible for charges exceeding those applicable to the type, class, or character authorized in transportation documents;

(c) The U.S. Government contractor-issued charge card must be used to the maximum extent possible to procure passenger transportation tickets. GTRs must be used minimally;

(d) Government passenger transportation documents must be in accordance with Federal Travel Regulation Chapters 300 and 301 (41 CFR chapters 300 and 301), and the "U.S. Government

Passenger Transportation—Handbook";

(e) Interest shall accrue from the voucher payment date on overcharges made hereunder and shall be paid at the same rate in effect on that date as published by the Secretary of the Treasury pursuant to the Debt Collection Act of 1982;

(f) The TSP must insert on the TD any known dates on which travel commenced;

(g) The issuing official or traveler, by signature, certifies that the requested transportation is for official business;

(h) The TSP must not honor any request containing erasures or alterations unless the TD contains the authentic, valid initials of the issuing official; and

(i) Additional mandatory terms and conditions are in this part and the "U. S. Government Passenger Transportation—Handbook."

§ 102–118.155 How does my agency handle supplemental billings from the TSP after payment of the original bill?

Your agency must process, review, and verify supplemental billings using the same procedures as on an original billing. If the TSP disputes the findings, your agency must attempt to resolve the disputed amount.

§ 102–118.160 Who is liable if my agency makes an overpayment on a transportation bill?

If the agency conducts prepayment audits of its transportation bills, agency transportation certifying and disbursing officers are liable for any overpayments made. If GSA has granted a waiver to the prepayment audit requirement and the agency performs a postpayment audit (31 U.S.C. 3528 and 31 U.S.C. 3322) neither the certifying nor disbursing officers are liable for the reasons listed in these two cited statutes.

§ 102–118.165 What must my agency do if it finds an error on a TSP bill?

Your agency must advise the TSP via statement of difference of any adjustment that you make either electronically or in writing within 7 days of receipt of the bill, as required by the Prompt Payment Act (31 U.S.C. 3901, *et* seq.). This notice must include the TSP's taxpayer identification number, standard carrier alpha code, bill number and document reference number, agency name, amount requested by the TSP, amount paid, payment voucher number, complete tender or tariff authority, the applicable rate authority and the complete fiscal authority including the appropriation.

§ 102–118.170 Will GSA continue to maintain a centralized numbering system for Government transportation documents?

Yes, GSA will maintain a numbering system for GBLs and GTRs. For commercial TDs, each agency must create a unique numbering system to account for and prevent duplicate numbers. The GSA Audit Division must approve this system. Write to:

General Services Administration
Transportation Audit Division (QMCA)
Crystal Plaza 4, Room 300
2200 Crystal Drive
Arlington, VA 22202
www.gsa.gov/transaudits

[65 FR 24569, Apr. 26, 2000, as amended at 69 FR 57620, Sept. 24, 2004; 74 FR 30475, June 26, 2009]

Subpart C—Use of Government Billing Documents

TERMS AND CONDITIONS GOVERNING ACCEPTANCE AND USE OF A GOVERNMENT BILL OF LADING (GBL) OR GOVERNMENT TRANSPORTATION REQUEST (GTR) (UNTIL FORM RETIREMENT)

§ 102–118.185 When buying freight transportation, must my agency reference the applicable contract or tender on the bill of lading (including a GBL)?

Yes, your agency must reference the applicable contract or tender when buying transportation on a bill of lading (including GBLs). However, the referenced information on a GBL or bill of lading does not limit an audit of charges.

§ 102–118.190 When buying passenger transportation must my agency reference the applicable contract?

Yes, when buying passenger transportation, your agency must reference the applicable contract on a GTR or passenger transportation document (e.g., ticket).

§ 102–118.195 What documents must a transportation service provider (TSP) send to receive payment for a transportation billing?

For shipments bought on a TD, the TSP must submit an original properly certified GBL, PPGBL, or bill of lading attached to an SF 1113, Public Voucher for Transportation Charges. The TSP must submit this package and all supporting documents to the agency paying office.

§ 102–118.200 Can a TSP demand advance payment for the transportation charges submitted on a bill of lading (including GBL)?

No, a TSP cannot demand advance payment for transportation charges submitted on a bill of lading (including GBL), unless authorized by law.

§ 102–118.205 May my agency pay a subcontractor or agent functioning as a warehouseman for the TSP providing service under the bill of lading?

No, your agency may only pay the TSP with whom it has a contract. The bill of lading will list the TSP with whom the Government has a contract.

§ 102–118.210 May my agency use bills of lading other than the GBL for a transportation shipment?

Yes, as long as the mandatory terms and conditions contained in this part (as also stated on a GBL) apply. The TSP must agree in writing to the mandatory terms and conditions (also found in the "U.S. Government Freight Transportation Handbook") contained in this part.

§ 102–118.215 May my agency pay a TSP any extra fees to pay for the preparation and use of the GBL or GTR?

No, your agency must not pay any additional charges for the preparation and use of the GBL or GTR. Your agency may not pay a TSP a higher rate than comparable under commercial procedures for transportation bought on a GBL or GTR.

§ 102–118.220 If a transportation debt is owed to my agency by a TSP because of loss or damage to property, does my agency report it to GSA?

No, if your agency has administratively determined that a TSP owes a debt resulting from loss or damage, follow your agency regulations.

§ 102–118.225 What constitutes final receipt of shipment?

Final receipt of the shipment occurs when the consignee or a TSP acting on behalf of the consignee with the agency's permission, fully signs and dates both the delivering TSP's documents and the consignee's copy of the same documents indicating delivery and/or explaining any delay, loss, damage, or shrinkage of shipment.

§ 102–118.230 What if my agency creates or eliminates a field office approved to prepare transportation documents?

Your agency must tell the GSA Audit Division whenever it approves a new or existing agency field office to prepare transportation documents or when an agency field office is no longer authorized to do so. This notice must show the name, field office location of the bureau or office, and the date on which your agency granted or canceled its authority to schedule payments for transportation service.

AGENCY RESPONSIBILITIES WHEN USING GOVERNMENT BILLS OF LADING (GBLs) OR GOVERNMENT TRANSPORTATION REQUESTS (GTRs)

§ 102–118.235 Must my agency keep physical control and accountability of the GBL and GTR forms or GBL and GTR numbers?

Yes, your agency is responsible for the physical control and accountability of the GBL and GTR stock and must have procedures in place and available for inspection by GSA. Your agency must consider these Government transportation documents to be the same as money.

§ 102–118.240 How does my agency get GBL and GTR forms?

Your agency can get GBL and GTR forms, in either blank or prenumbered formats, from:

General Services Administration
Federal Acquisition Service
Inventory Management Branch (QSDACDB-WS)
819 Taylor Street, Room 6A00
Fort Worth, TX 76102

[65 FR 24569, Apr. 26, 2000, as amended at 74 FR 30476, June 26, 2009]

§ 102–118.245 How does my agency get an assigned set of GBL or GTR numbers?

If your agency does not use prenumbered GBL and GTR forms, you may get an assigned set of numbers from:

General Services Administration
Federal Acquisition Service
Inventory Management Branch (QSDACDB-WS)
819 Taylor Street, Room 6A00
Fort Worth, TX 76102

[65 FR 24569, Apr. 26, 2000, as amended at 74 FR 30476, June 26, 2009]

§ 102–118.250 Who is accountable for the issuance and use of GBL and GTR forms?

Agencies and employees are responsible for the issuance and use of GBL and GTR forms and are accountable for their disposition.

§ 102–118.255 Are GBL and GTR forms numbered and used sequentially?

Yes, GBL and GTR forms are always sequentially numbered when printed and/or used. No other numbering of the forms, including additions or changes to the prefixes or additions of suffixes, is permitted.

QUOTATIONS, TENDERS OR CONTRACTS

§ 102–118.260 Must my agency send all quotations, tenders, or contracts with a TSP to GSA?

(a) Yes, your agency must send copies of each quotation, tender, or contract of special rates, fares, charges, or concessions with TSPs including those authorized by 49 U.S.C. 10721 and 13712, upon execution to—General Services Administration, Transportation Audit Division (QMCA), Crystal Plaza 4, Room 300, 2200 Crystal Drive, Arlington, VA 22202, *www.gsa.gov/transaudits*.

(b) Tenders must be submitted electronically, following the instructions provided by the requesting agency. The following information must be submitted with the tender:

(1) Issuing TSP, Bureau, Agency or Conference.

(2) Tender number.

(3) Standard Carrier Alpha Code (SCAC).

(4) TSP Tax Identification Number (TIN).

(5) Issue date.

(6) Effective date.

(7) Expiration date.

(8) Origin and destination.

(9) Freight Classification and/or commodity description (including origin and destination).

(10) Rate or charge for line haul rates.

(11) Minimum weights.

(12) Route(s).

(13) Accessorial services description(s) with rate or charge and governing publication.

(14) TSP operating authority.

(c) The TSP must include a statement that the TSP will adhere and agree to the following general terms and conditions. The services provided in this tender will be performed in accordance with applicable Federal, State and municipal laws and regulations, including Federal Management Regulation parts 102–117 and 102–118 (41 CFR parts 102–117 and 102–118), and the TSP(s) hold(s) the required operating authority to transport the commodity from, to, or between the places specified in the authorized certificates, permits or temporary operating authorities.

(d) The TSP shall bill the United States Government on Standard Form (SF) 1113, Public Voucher for Transportation Charges, appropriately completed and supported. The TSP(s) will send bills to the "Bill Charges To" address on the face of the bill of lading or agency-ordering document.

(e) The Optional Form (OF) 280, Uniform Tender of Rates and/or Charges for Transportation Services, includes all the provisions of paragraph (c) of this section and is another option to file a tender with the Government.

[69 FR 57619, Sept. 24, 2004, as amended at 74 FR 30475, June 26, 2009]

Subpart D—Prepayment Audit of Transportation Services

SOURCE: 81 FR 65300, Sept. 22, 2016, unless otherwise noted.

AGENCY REQUIREMENTS FOR A TRANSPORTATION PREPAYMENT AUDIT PROGRAM

§ 102–118.265 What is a prepayment audit?

Prepayment audit means a review of transportation documentation before payment to determine their validity, propriety, and conformity of rates with tariffs, quotations, agreements, contracts, or tenders. Prepayment auditing by your agency will detect and eliminate billing errors before payment (31 U.S.C. 3726).

§ 102–118.270 Must my agency establish a transportation prepayment audit program, and how is it funded?

(a) Yes, under 31 U.S.C. 3726, your agency is required to establish a transportation prepayment audit program. Your agency's Chief Financial Officer (CFO) must approve the prepayment audit program.

(b) Your agency must pay for the prepayment audit program from those funds appropriated for transportation services.

(1) Agencies are encouraged to consider using a GSA Transportation Audits Division approved third party electronic payment processor for transportation invoice processing, payment, and prepayment audit. These electronic payment processors are no cost to the agency and are fully compliant with GSA Transportation Audits Division prepayment audit requirements.

(2) Use of these third party payment processors generally means your agency will not have to provide any additional prepayment or postpayment documentation to GSA Transportation Audits Division.

§ 102–118.275 What must my agency consider when developing a transportation prepayment audit program?

(a) Your agency's transportation prepayment audit program must consider all of the methods that your agency uses to order and pay for passenger, household goods, and freight transportation to include Government contractor-issued charge cards (see § 102–118.35 for definition Government contractor-issued charge cards).

(b) Each method of ordering transportation and transportation services for passenger, household goods, and freight transportation may require a different kind of prepayment audit process. The manner in which your agency orders or procures transportation services determines how and by whom the bill for those services will be presented. Your agency should ensure that each TSP bill or employee travel voucher contains enough information for the prepayment audit to determine which contract or rate tender is used and that the type and quantity of any additional services are clearly delineated.

(c) The prepayment audit cannot be conducted by the same firm providing the transportation services for the agency. If a move manager is being utilized, the move manager may not have any affiliation with or financial interest in the transportation company providing the transportation services for which the prepayment audit is being conducted. Contracts with charge card companies that provide prepayment audit services are a valid option. The agency can choose to—

(1) Create an internal prepayment audit program;

(2) Contract directly with a prepayment audit service provider;

(3) Use the services of a prepayment audit contractor under GSA's multiple award schedule covering audit and financial management services (*SIN 520.10 Transportation Audits*); or

(4) Use a Third-Party Payment System or charge card company that includes prepayment audit functions, such as the GSA Center for Transportation Management's PayPort Express.

(d) An appeals process must be established for a TSP to appeal any reduction in the amount billed. It is recommended the agency establish an electronic appeal process that will direct TSP-filed appeals to an agency official for determination of the claim.

(e) A process to ensure that all agency transportation procurement and related documents including contracts and tenders are submitted electronically to GSA Transportation Audits Division.

(f) Use of GSA Transportation Audits Division's Prepayment Audit Program template is recommended (contact *Audit.Policy@gsa.gov* for a copy of the template). If the template is not used, provide the same information listed on the template to GSA Transportation Audits Division.

§ 102–118.280 Must all transportation payment records, whether they are electronic or paper, undergo a prepayment audit?

Yes, all transportation bills and payment records, whether they are electronic or paper, must undergo a prepayment audit with the following exceptions:

(a) Your agency's prepayment audit program uses a statistical sampling technique of the bills. If your agency chooses to use statistical sampling, all bills must be

(1) At or below the Comptroller General specified limit of $2,500.00 (31 U.S.C. 3521(b)); and

(2) In compliance with the U.S. Government Accountability Office Using Statistical Sampling (GAO/PEMD–10.1.6), Rev. 1992, Chapter 7 Random Selection Procedures obtainable from *http://www.gao.gov;* or

(b) The Administrator of General Services grants your agency a specific exemption from the prepayment audit requirement which may include bills determined to be below your agency's threshold, mode or modes of transportation, or for an agency or subagency.

§ 102–118.285 What must be included in an agency's transportation prepayment audit program?

The agency prepayment audit program must include—

(a) The agency's CFO approval of the transportation prepayment audit program with submission to GSA Transportation Audits Division;

(b) Compliance with the Prompt Payment Act (31 U.S.C. 3901, *et seq.*);

(c) Assurance that each TSP bill or employee travel voucher contains appropriate information for the prepayment audit to determine which contract or rate tender is used and that the type and quantity of any additional services are clearly delineated;

(d) Verification of all transportation bills against filed rates and charges before payment;

(e) A process to forward all transportation documentation (TD) monthly to the GSA Transportation Audits Division.

(1) GSA Transportation Audits Division can provide your agency a Prepayment Audit Program with a monthly reporting template upon request at *Audit.Policy@gsa.gov* (see § 102–118.35 for definition TD).

(2) In addition to the requirements for agencies to maintain transportation records, GSA will store paid transportation bills in accordance with the General Records Schedule 9, Travel and Transportation (36 CFR 1228.22). GSA will arrange for storage of any document requiring special handling, such as bankruptcy and court cases. These bills will be retained pursuant to 44 U.S.C. 3309 until claims have been settled;

(f) Establish procedures in which transportation bills not subject to prepayment audit, such as bills for unused tickets and charge card billings, are handled separately and are also forwarded monthly to the GSA Transportation Audits Division;

(g) A minimum dollar threshold for transportation bills subject to audit;

(h) A statement in a cost reimbursable contracts contract or rate tender that the contractor shall submit to the address and in the electronic format identified for prepayment audit, transportation documents which show that the United States will assume freight charges that were paid by the contractor. Cost reimbursable contractors shall only submit for audit bills of lading with freight shipment charges exceeding $100.00. Bills under $100.00 shall be retained on-site by the contractor and made available for on-site Government audits (Federal Acquisition Regulation (FAR) 52.247–67);

(i) Require your agency's paying office to offset, if directed by GSA's Transportation Audits Division, debts from amounts owed to the TSP within the 3 years (31 U.S.C. 3726(b));

(j) A process to ensure complete and accurate audits of all transportation bills and notification to the TSP of any adjustment within 7 calendar days of receipt of the bill;

(k) An appeals process as part of the approved prepayment audit program for a TSP to appeal any reduction in the amount billed. Refer to § 102–118.295 for details regarding the appeals process.

(l) Accurate notices and agency procedures for notifying the TSPs with a detailed description of the reasons for any full or partial rejection of the stated charges on the invoice. Refer to § 102–118.290 for notice requirements; and

(m) A unique agency numbering system to handle commercial paper and practices (see § 102–118.55 for information on administrative procedures your agency must establish).

AGENCY REQUIREMENTS WITH
TRANSPORTATION SERVICE PROVIDERS

§ 102–118.290 Must my agency notify the TSP of any adjustment to the TSP bill?

(a) Yes, your agency must notify the TSP of any adjustment to the TSP bill either electronically or in writing within seven calendar days of the agency receipt of the bill.

(b) This notice must include:

(1) TSP's bill number;

(2) Agency name;

(3) TSP's TIN;

(4) SCAC;

(5) DRN;

(6) Date invoice submitted;

(7) Amount billed;

(8) Date invoice was approved for payment;

(9) Date and amount agency paid;

(10) Payment location number and agency organization name;

(11) Payment voucher number;

(12) Complete contract, tender or tariff authority, including item or section number;

(13) Reason for the adjustment; and

(14) Complete information on the agency appeal process.

(c) A TSP must submit claims to the agency within three years under the guidelines established in subpart F, Claims and Appeals Procedures, of this part.

§ 102–118.295 Does my agency transportation prepayment audit program need to establish appeal procedures?

Yes, your agency must establish, in the approved prepayment audit program, an appeals process for a TSP to appeal any reduction in the amount billed. It is recommended the agency establish an electronic appeal process that will direct TSP-filed appeals to an agency official for determination of the claim. Your agency must complete the review of the appeal and inform the TSP of the agency determination within 30 calendar days of the receipt of the appeal, either electronically or in writing.

§ 102–118.300 What must my agency do if the TSP disputes the findings and my agency cannot resolve the dispute?

(a) If your agency is unable to resolve the disputed amount with the TSP, your agency must submit, within 30 calendar days, all relevant transportation documentation associated with the dispute, including a complete billing history and the appropriation or fund charged, to GSA Transportation Audits Division by email at *Audit.Policy@gsa.gov*, or by mail to: U.S. General Services Administration, 1800 F St. NW., 3rd Floor, Mail Hub 3400, Washington, DC 20405.

(b) The GSA Transportation Audits Division will review the appeal of an agency's final, full, or partial denial of a claim and issue a decision within 30 calendar days of receipt of appeal.

(c) A TSP must submit claims to the agency within three years under the guidelines established in subpart F of this part.

§ 102–118.305 What information must be on all transportation payment records that have completed my agency's prepayment audit?

(a) The following information must be annotated on all transportation payment records, electronically or on paper, that have completed your agency's prepayment audit and for submission to GSA Transportation Audits Division:

(1) The date the bill was received from a TSP;

(2) A TSP's invoice number;

(3) Your agency name;

(4) DRN;

(5) Amount billed;

(6) Date invoice was approved for payment;

(7) Date and amount agency paid;

(8) Payment location code number and office or organization name;

(9) Payment voucher number;

(10) Complete contract, tender or tariff authority, including item or section number;

(11) The TSP's TIN;

(12) The TSP's SCAC;

(13) The auditor's authorization code or initials; and

(14) A copy of any statement of difference and the date it was sent to the TSP.

(b) Your agency can find added guidance in the "U.S. Government Freight Transportation Handbook." This handbook is located at *www.gsa.gov/transaudits.*

§ 102–118.310 What does the GSA Transportation Audits Division consider when verifying an agency prepayment audit program?

GSA Transportation Audit Division bases verification of agency prepayment audit programs on objective cost-savings, paperwork reductions, current audit standards, and other positive improvements, as well as adherence to the guidelines listed in this part.

§ 102–118.315 How does my agency contact the GSA Transportation Audits Division?

Your agency may contact the GSA Transportation Audits Division at *Audit.Policy@gsa.gov.*

§ 102–118.320 What action should my agency take if the agency's transportation prepayment audit program changes?

(a) If your agency's transportation prepayment audit program changes in any way to include changes in prepayment auditors, your agency must submit the CFO-approved revised transportation prepayment audit program to GSA Transportation Audits Division via email at *Audit.Policy@gsa.gov,* Subject line: Agency PPA-Revised.

(b) If GSA determines the agency's approved plan is insufficient, GSA will contact the agency CFO to inform of the prepayment audit program deficiencies and request corrective action and resubmission to GSA Transportation Audits Division.

AGENCY CERTIFYING AND DISBURSING
OFFICERS

§ 102–118.325 Does establishing an agency Chief Financial Officer-approved transportation prepayment audit program change the responsibilities of the certifying officers?

No, in a prepayment audit program, the official certifying a transportation voucher is held liable for verifying transportation rates, freight classifications, and other information provided on a transportation billing instrument or transportation request undergoing a prepayment audit (31 U.S.C. 3528).

§ 102–118.330 Does a transportation prepayment audit waiver change any liabilities of the certifying officer?

Yes, a certifying official is not personally liable for verifying transportation rates, freight classifications, or other information provided on a bill of lading or passenger transportation request when the Administrator of General Services or designee waives the prepayment audit requirement and your agency uses postpayment audits.

§ 102–118.335 What relief from liability is available for the certifying official under a transportation postpayment audit?

The agency counsel relieves a certifying official from liability for transportation overpayments in cases where—

(a) Postpayment is the approved method of auditing;

(b) The overpayment occurred solely because the administrative review before payment did not verify transportation rates; and

(c) The overpayment was the result of using improper transportation rates or freight classifications or the failure to deduct the correct amount under a land grant law or agreement.

§ 102–118.340 Do the requirements of a transportation prepayment audit change the disbursing official's liability for overpayment?

No, the disbursing official has a liability for overpayments on all transportation bills subject to prepayment audit (31 U.S.C. 3322).

§ 102–118.345 Where does relief from transportation prepayment audit liability for certifying, accountable, and disbursing officers reside in my agency?

Your agency's counsel has the authority to relieve liability and give advance opinions on liability issues to certifying, accountable, and disbursing officers (31 U.S.C. 3527).

EXEMPTIONS AND SUSPENSIONS OF THE
MANDATORY TRANSPORTATION PRE-
PAYMENT AUDIT PROGRAM

§ 102–118.350 What agency has the authority to grant an exemption from the transportation prepayment audit requirement?

Only the Administrator of General Services or their designee has the authority to grant an exemption for a specific time period from the prepayment audit requirement. The Administrator may exempt bills, a particular mode or modes of transportation, or an agency or subagency from a prepayment audit and verification and in lieu thereof require a postpayment audit, based on cost effectiveness, public interest, or other factors the Administrator considers appropriate (31 U.S.C. 3726(a)(2)).

§ 102–118.355 How does my agency apply for an exemption from a transportation prepayment audit requirement?

Your agency must submit a request for an exemption from the requirement to perform transportation prepayment audits by email to *Audit.policy@gsa.gov,* Subject Line: Prepayment Audit Exemption Request. The agency exemption request must explain in detail why the request is submitted based on cost effectiveness, public interest, or other factors the Administrator considers appropriate, such as transportation modes, dollar thresholds, adversely affecting the agency's mission, or is not feasible (31 U.S.C. 3726(a)(2)).

§ 102–118.360 How long will GSA take to respond to an exemption request from a transportation prepayment audit requirement?

GSA will respond to the exemption from the transportation prepayment audit requirement request within 180 calendar days from the date of receipt.

§ 102–118.365 Can my agency renew an exemption from the transportation prepayment audit requirements?

It may be possible for your agency to be granted a prepayment audit exemption extension. Your agency must submit a request for the extension to GSA Transportation Audits Division at least six months in advance of the current exemption expiration.

§ 102–118.370 Are my agency's prepayment audited transportation documentation subject to periodic postpayment audit oversight from the GSA Transportation Audits Division?

Yes. All your agency's prepayment audited transportation documents are subject to the GSA Transportation Audits Division postpayment audit oversight. Upon request, GSA Transportation Audits Division will provide a report analyzing your agency's prepayment audit program.

§ 102–118.375 Can GSA suspend my agency's transportation prepayment audit program?

(a) Yes. The Director of the GSA Transportation Audits Division may suspend your agency's transportation prepayment audit program until the agency corrects their prepayment audit program deficiencies. This suspension may be in whole or in part. If GSA suspends your agency's transportation prepayment audit and GSA assumes responsibility for auditing an agencies prepayment audit program, the agency will reimburse GSA for the expense.

(b) This suspension determination is based on identification of a systematic or frequent failure of the agency's transportation prepayment audit program to—

(1) Conduct a prepayment audit of your agency's transportation bills; and/or

(2) Abide by the terms of the Prompt Payment Act (31 U.S.C. 3901, *et seq.*);

(3) Adjudicate TSP claims disputing prepayment audit positions of the agency regularly within 30 calendar days of receipt;

(4) Follow Comptroller General decisions, Civilian Board of Contract Appeals decisions, the Federal Management Regulation and GSA instructions or precedents about substantive and procedure matters; and/or

(5) Provide information and data or to cooperate with on-site inspections necessary to conduct a quality assurance review.

Subpart E—Postpayment Transportation Audits

SOURCE: 81 FR 65303, Sept. 22, 2016, unless otherwise noted.

§ 102–118.400 What is a transportation postpayment audit?

Postpayment audit means an audit of transportation billing documents after payment to decide their validity, propriety, and conformity of rates with tariffs, quotations, agreements, contracts, or tenders. The audit may also include subsequent adjustments and collection actions taken against a TSP by the Government (31 U.S.C. 3726).

§ 102–118.405 Who conducts a transportation postpayment audit?

The Administrator of General Services (GSA) has a congressionally mandated responsibility under 31 U.S.C. 3726 to perform oversight on transportation bills. The GSA Transportation Audits Division accomplishes this oversight by conducting postpayment audits of all agencies' transportation bills.

§ 102–118.410 If agencies perform the mandatory transportation prepayment audit, will this eliminate the requirement for a transportation postpayment audit conducted by GSA?

No, agency compliance to the mandatory transportation prepayment audit does not eliminate the requirement of the transportation postpayment audit conducted by GSA (31 U.S.C. 3726).

§ 102–118.415 Can the Administrator of General Services exempt the transportation postpayment audit requirement?

Yes. The Administrator of General Services or designee may exempt, for a specified time, an agency or subagency from the GSA transportation postpayment audit oversight requirements of this subpart. The Administrator can also exempt modes (31 U.S.C. 3726).

§ 102–118.420 Is my agency allowed to perform a postpayment audit on our transportation documents?

No. Your agency may not perform a transportation postpayment audit unless granted an exemption and specifically directed to do so by the Administrator in lieu of a prepayment audit. Whether such an exemption is granted or not, your agency must forward all transportation documents (TD) to GSA for postpayment audit (see § 102–118.35 for definition TD).

§ 102–118.425 Is my agency required to forward all transportation documents to GSA Transportation Audits Division, and what information must be on these documents?

(a) Yes, your agency must provide all TDs to GSA Transportation Audits Division (see § 102–118.35 for definition TD).

(b) The following information must be annotated on all TDs and bills that have completed your agency's prepayment audit for submission to GSA Transportation Audits Division:

(1) The date the bill was received from a TSP;

(2) A TSP's invoice number;

(3) Your agency name;

(4) A DRN;

(5) Amount billed;

(6) Date invoice was approved for payment;

(7) Payment date and amount agency paid;

(8) Payment location code number and office name;

(9) Payment voucher number;

(10) Complete contract, tender, or tariff authority, including item or section number;

(11) The TSP's TIN;

(12) The TSP's SCAC;

(13) The auditor's full name, email address, contact telephone number, and authorization code; and

(14) A copy of any statement of difference sent to the TSP.

(c) Your agency can find additional guidance in the "U.S. Government Freight Transportation Handbook." This handbook is located at *www.gsa.gov/transaudits*.

§ 102–118.430 What is the process the GSA Transportation Audits Division employs to conduct a postpayment audit?

The GSA Transportation Audits Division

(a) Audits select TSP bills after payment;

(b) Audits select TSP bills before payment as needed to protect the Government's interest;

(c) Examines, settles, and adjusts accounts involving payment for transportation and related services for the account of agencies;

(d) Adjudicates and settles transportation claims by and against agencies;

(e) Offsets an overcharge by any TSP from an amount subsequently found to be due that TSP;

(f) Issues a Notice of Overcharge stating that a TSP owes a debt to the agency. This notice states the amount paid and the basis for the proper charge for the document reference number (DRN), and cites applicable contract, tariff, or tender, along with other data relied on to support the overcharge; and

(g) Issues a GSA Notice of Indebtedness when a TSP owes an ordinary debt to an agency. This notice states the basis for the debt, the TSP's rights, interest, penalty, and other results of nonpayment. The debt is due immediately and is subject to interest charges, penalties, and administrative cost under 31 U.S.C. 3717.

§ 102–118.435 What are the transportation postpayment audit roles and responsibilities of the GSA Transportation Audits Division?

(a) The GSA Transportation Audits Division role is to perform the oversight responsibility of transportation prepayment and postpayment granted to the Administrator. The GSA Transportation Audits Division will—

(1) Examine and analyze transportation documents and payments to discover their validity, relevance and conformity with tariffs, quotations, contracts, agreements, or tenders and make adjustments to protect the interest of an agency;

(2) Examine, adjudicate, and settle transportation claims by and against the agency;

(3) Collect from TSPs by refund, setoff, offset, or other means, the amounts determined to be due the agency;

(4) Adjust, terminate, or suspend debts due on TSP overcharges;

(5) Prepare reports to the Attorney General of the United States with recommendations about the legal and technical bases available for use in prosecuting or defending suits by or against an agency and provide technical, fiscal, and factual data from relevant records;

(6) Provide transportation specialists and lawyers to serve as expert witnesses; assist in pretrial conferences; draft pleadings, orders, and briefs; and participate as requested in connection with transportation suits by or against an agency;

(7) Review agency policies, programs, and procedures to determine their adequacy and effectiveness in the audit of freight or passenger transportation payments, and review related fiscal and transportation practices;

(8) Furnish information on rates, fares, routes, and related technical data upon request;

(9) Inform an agency of irregular shipping routing practices, inadequate commodity descriptions, excessive transportation cost authorizations, and unsound principles employed in traffic and transportation management; and

(10) Confer with individual TSPs or related groups and associations presenting specific modes of transportation to resolve mutual problems concerning technical and accounting matters, and providing information on requirements.

(b) The Administrator of General Services may provide transportation audit and related technical assistance services, on a reimbursable basis, to any other agency. Such reimbursements may be credited to the appropriate revolving fund or appropriation from which the expenses were incurred (31 U.S.C. 3726(j)).

§ 102–118.440 Does my agency pay for a transportation postpayment audit conducted by the GSA Transportation Audits Division?

The GSA Transportation Audits Division does not charge agencies a fee for conducting the transportation postpayment audit. Transportation postpayment audits expenses are financed from overpayments collected from the TSP's bills previously paid by the agency and similar type of refunds. However, if a postpayment audit is conducted in lieu of a prepayment audit at the request of an agency, or if there are additional services required, GSA may charge the agency.

§ 102–118.445 How do I contact the GSA Transportation Audits Division?

You may contact the GSA Transportation Audits Division by email at *Audit.Policy@gsa.gov.*

Subpart F—Claims and Appeal Procedures

GENERAL AGENCY INFORMATION FOR ALL CLAIMS

§ 102–118.450 Can a TSP file a transportation claim against my agency?

Yes, a TSP may file a transportation claim against your agency under 31 U.S.C. 3726 for:

(a) Amounts owed but not included in the original billing;

(b) Amounts deducted or set off by an agency that are disputed by the TSP;

(c) Requests by a TSP for amounts previously refunded in error by that TSP; and/or

(d) Unpaid original bills requiring direct settlement by GSA, including those subject to doubt about the suitability of payment (mainly bankruptcy or fraud).

§ 102–118.455 What is the time limit for a TSP to file a transportation claim against my agency?

The time limits on a TSP transportation claim against the Government

differ by mode as shown in the following table:

TIME LIMITS ON ACTIONS TAKEN BY TSP

Mode	Freight charges	Statute
(a) Air Domestic	6 years	28 U.S.C. 2401, 2501.
(b) Air International	6 years	28 U.S.C. 2401, 2501.
(c) Freight Forwarders (subject to the IC Act).	3 years	49 U.S.C. 14705(f).
(d) Motor	3 years	49 U.S.C. 14705(f).

TIME LIMITS ON ACTIONS TAKEN BY TSP—
Continued

Mode	Freight charges	Statute
(e) Rail	3 years	49 U.S.C. 14705(f).
(f) Water (subject to the IC Act).	3 years	49 U.S.C. 14705(f).
(g) Water (not subject to the IC Act).	2 years	46 U.S.C. 745.
(h) TSPs exempt from regulation.	6 years	28 U.S.C. 2401, 2501.

§ 102–118.460 What is the time limit for my agency to file a court claim with a TSP for freight charges, reparations, and loss or damage to the property?

Statutory time limits vary depending on the mode and the service involved and may involve freight charges. The following tables list the time limits:

(A) TIME LIMITS ON ACTIONS TAKEN BY THE FEDERAL GOVERNMENT AGAINST TSPs

Mode	Freight charges	Reparations	Loss and damage
(1) Rail	3 years .... 49 U.S.C. 11705	3 years .... 49 U.S.C. 11705	6 years. 28 U.S.C. 2415.
(2) Motor	3 years .... 49 U.S.C. .... 14705(f)	3 years .... 49 U.S.C. .... 14705(f)	6 years. 28 U.S.C. 2415.
(3) Freight Forwarders subject to the IC Act.	3 years .... 49 U.S.C. .... 14705(f)	3 years .... 49 U.S.C. .... 14705(f)	6 years. 28 U.S.C. 2415.
(4) Water (subject to the IC Act).	3 years .... 49 U.S.C. .... 14705(f)	3 years .... 49 U.S.C. .... 14705(f)	6 years. 28 U.S.C. 2415.
(5) Water (not subject to the IC Act).	6 years 28 U.S.C. 2415	2 years 46 U.S.C. 821 ..	1 year. 46 U.S.C. 1303(6) (if subject to Carriage of Goods by Sear Act, 46 U.S.C. 1300–1315).
(6) Domestic Air	6 years .... 28 U.S.C. 2415		6 years. 28 U.S.C. 2415.
(7) International Air	6 years .... 28 U.S.C. 2415		2 years. 49 U.S.C. 40105.

(B) TIME LIMITS ON ACTIONS TAKEN BY THE FEDERAL GOVERNMENT AGAINST TSPs EXEMPT FROM REGULATION

Mode	Freight	Reparations	Loss and damage
(1) All	6 years .... 28 U.S.C. 2415		6 years. 28 U.S.C. 2415.

§ 102–118.465 Must my agency pay interest on a disputed amount claimed by a TSP?

No, interest penalties under the Prompt Payment Act, (31 U.S.C. 3901, *et seq.*), are not required when payment is delayed because of a dispute between an agency and a TSP.

§ 102–118.470 Are there statutory time limits for a TSP on filing an administrative claim with the GSA Audit Division?

Yes, an administrative claim must be received by the GSA Audit Division or its designee (the agency where the claim arose) within 3 years beginning the day after the latest of the following dates (except in time of war):

(a) Accrual of the cause of action;

(b) Payment of charges for the transportation involved;

(c) Subsequent refund for overpayment of those charges; or

(d) Deductions made to a TSP claim by the Government under 31 U.S.C. 3726.

§ 102–118.475 Does interest apply after certification of payment of claims?

Yes, interest under the Prompt Payment Act (31 U.S.C. 3901, *et seq.*) begins 30 days after certification for payment by GSA.

§ 102–118.480 How does my agency settle disputes with a TSP?

As a part of the prepayment audit program, your agency must have a plan to resolve disputes with a TSP. This program must allow a TSP to appeal payment decisions made by your agency.

§ 102–118.485 Is there a time limit for my agency to issue a decision on disputed claims?

Yes, your agency must issue a ruling on a disputed claim within 30 days of receipt of the claim.

§ 102–118.490 What if my agency fails to settle a dispute within 30 days?

(a) If your agency fails to settle a dispute within 30 days, the TSP may appeal to:

General Services Administration
Federal Supply Service
Audit Division (FBA)

Code: CC 1800 F Street, NW.
Washington, DC 20405
www.gsa.gov/transaudits

(b) If the TSP disagrees with the administrative settlement by the Audit Division, the TSP may appeal to the Civilian Board of Contract Appeals.

[65 FR 24569, Apr. 26, 2000, as amended at 69 FR 57620, Sept. 24, 2004; 78 FR 71529, Nov. 29, 2013]

§ 102–118.495 May my agency appeal a decision by the Civilian Board of Contract Appeals (CBCA)?

No, your agency may not appeal a decision made by the CBCA.

[65 FR 24569, Apr. 26, 2000, as amended at 74 FR 30476, June 26, 2009]

§ 102–118.500 How does my agency handle a voluntary refund submitted by a TSP?

(a) An agency must report all voluntary refunds to the GSA Audit Division (so that no Notice of Overcharge or financial offset occurs), unless other arrangements are made (e.g., charge card refunds, etc.). These reports must be addressed to:

General Services Administration
Federal Supply Service
Audit Division (FBA)
Code: CC
1800 F Street, NW.
Washington, DC 20405
www.gsa.gov/transaudits

(b) Once a Notice of Overcharge is issued by the GSA Audit Division, then any refund is no longer considered voluntary and the agency must forward the refund to the GSA Audit Division.

[65 FR 24569, Apr. 26, 2000, as amended at 69 FR 57620, Sept. 24, 2004]

§ 102–118.505 Must my agency send a voluntary refund to the Treasurer of the United States?

No, your agency may keep and use voluntary refunds submitted by a TSP, if the refund was made prior to a Notice of Overcharge issued by the GSA Audit Division.

§ 102–118.510 Can my agency revise or alter a GSA Form 7931, Certificate of Settlement?

Generally, no, an agency must not revise or alter amounts on a GSA Form 7931. The only change an agency can make to a GSA Form 7931 is to change the agency financial data to a correct cite. Any GSA Form 7931 that cannot be paid (e.g., an amount previously paid), must be immediately returned to the GSA Audit Division with an explanation.

§ 102–118.515 Does my agency have any recourse not to pay a Certificate of Settlement?

No, a Certificate of Settlement is the final administrative action.

§ 102–118.520 Who is responsible for determining the standards for collection, compromise, termination, or suspension of collection action on any outstanding debts to my agency?

Under the Federal Claims Collection Act of 1966, as amended (31 U.S.C. 3711, *et seq.*), the Comptroller General and the Attorney General have joint responsibility for issuing standards for your agency.

§ 102–118.525 What are my agency's responsibilities for verifying the correct amount of transportation charges?

Your agency's employees are responsible for diligently verifying the correct amount of transportation charges prior to payment (31 U.S.C. 3527).

§ 102–118.530 Will GSA instruct my agency's disbursing offices to offset unpaid TSP billings?

Yes, GSA will instruct one or more of your agency's disbursing offices to deduct the amount due from an unpaid TSP's bill. A 3-year limitation applies on the deduction of overcharges from amounts due a TSP (31 U.S.C. 3726) and a 10-year limitation applies on the deduction of ordinary debts (31 U.S.C. 3716).

§ 102–118.535 Are there principles governing my agency's TSP debt collection procedures?

Yes, the principles governing your agency collection procedures for reporting debts to the General Accounting Office (GAO) or the Department of Justice are found in 4 CFR parts 101 through 105 and in the GAO Policy and Procedures Manual for Guidance of Federal Agencies. The manual may be obtained by writing:

Superintendent of Documents
Government Printing Office
Washington, DC 20402
http://www.access.gpo.gov/

§ 102–118.540 Who has the authority to audit, settle accounts, and/or start collection action for all transportation services provided for my agency?

The Director of the GSA Audit Division has the authority and responsibility to audit and settle all transportation related accounts (31 U.S.C. 3726). The reason for this is that he or she has access to Governmentwide data on a TSP's payments and billings with the Government. Your agency has the responsibility to correctly pay individual transportation claims.

TRANSPORTATION SERVICE PROVIDER
(TSP) FILING REQUIREMENTS

§ 102–118.545 What information must a TSP claim include?

Transportation service provider (TSP) claims received by GSA or its designee must include one of the following:

(a) The signature of an individual or party legally entitled to receive payment for services on behalf of the TSP;

(b) The signature of the TSP's agent or attorney accompanied by a duly executed power of attorney or other documentary evidence of the agent's or attorney's right to act for the TSP; or

(c) An electronic signature, when mutually agreed upon.

§ 102–118.550 How does a TSP file an administrative claim using EDI or other electronic means?

The medium and precise format of data for an administrative claim filed electronically must be approved in advance by the GSA Audit Division. GSA will use an authenticating EDI signature to certify receipt of the claim. The data on the claim must contain proof of the delivery of goods, and an itemized bill reflecting the services provided, with the lowest charges available for service. The TSP must be able to locate, identify, and reproduce the records in readable form without loss of clarity.

§ 102–118.555 Can a TSP file a supplemental administrative claim?

Yes, a TSP may file a supplemental administrative claim. Each supplemental claim must cover charges relating to one paid transportation document.

§ 102–118.560 What is the required format that a TSP must use to file an administrative claim?

A TSP must bill for charges claimed on a SF 1113, Public Voucher for Transportation Charges, in the manner prescribed in the "U.S. Government Freight Transportation—Handbook" or the "U.S. Government Passenger Transportation—Handbook." To get a copy of these handbooks, you may write to:

General Services Administration
Transportation Audit Division (QMCA)
Crystal Plaza 4, Room 300
2200 Crystal Drive
Arlington, VA 22202
www.gsa.gov/transaudits

[65 FR 24569, Apr. 26, 2000, as amended at 69 FR 57620, Sept. 24, 2004; 74 FR 30475, June 26, 2009]

§ 102–118.565 What documentation is required when filing an administrative claim?

An administrative claim must be accompanied by the transportation document, payment record, reports and information available to GSA and/or to the agency involved and the written and documentary records submitted by the TSP. Oral presentations supplementing the written record are not acceptable.

TRANSPORTATION SERVICE PROVIDER (TSP) AND AGENCY APPEAL PROCEDURES FOR PREPAYMENT AUDITS

§ 102–118.570 If my agency denies the TSP's challenge to the statement of difference, may the TSP appeal?

Yes, the TSP may appeal if your agency denies its challenge to the statement of difference. However, the appeal must be handled at a higher level in your agency.

§ 102–118.575 If a TSP disagrees with the decision of my agency, can the TSP appeal?

Yes, the TSP may file a claim with the GSA Audit Division, which will review the TSP's appeal of your agency's final full or partial denial of a claim. The TSP may also appeal to the GSA Audit Division if your agency has not responded to a challenge within 30 days.

§ 102–118.580 May a TSP appeal a prepayment audit decision of the GSA Audit Division?

Yes, the TSP may appeal to the Civilian Board of Contract Appeals (CBCA) under guidelines established in this subpart F, or file a claim with the United States Court of Federal Claims. The TSP's request for review must be received by the CBCA in writing within 6 months (not including times of war) from the date the settlement action was taken or within the periods of limitation specified in 31 U.S.C. 3726, as amended, whichever is later. The TSP must address requests:

(a) By United States Postal Service to: Civilian Board of Contract Appeals (CBCA), 1800 F Street NW., Washington, DC 20405;

(b) In person or by courier to: Civilian Board of Contract Appeals, 6th floor, 1800 M Street NW., Washington, DC 20036;

(c) By facsimile (FAX) to: 202–606–0019; or

(d) By electronic mail to: *cbca.efile@cbca.gov.*

[78 FR 71529, Nov. 29, 2013]

§ 102–118.585 May a TSP appeal a prepayment audit decision of the CBCA?

No, a ruling by the CBCA is the final administrative remedy available and the TSP has no statutory right of appeal. This subpart governs administrative actions only and does not affect any of the TSP's rights. A TSP may still pursue a legal remedy through the courts.

[65 FR 24569, Apr. 26, 2000, as amended at 74 FR 30476, June 26, 2009]

§ 102–118.590 May my agency appeal a prepayment audit decision of the GSA Audit Division?

No, your agency may not appeal. A GSA Audit Division decision is administratively final for your agency.

§ 102–118.595 May my agency appeal a prepayment audit decision by the CBCA?

No, your agency may not appeal a prepayment audit decision. Your agency must follow the ruling of the CBCA.

[65 FR 24569, Apr. 26, 2000, as amended at 74 FR 30476, June 26, 2009]

TRANSPORTATION SERVICE PROVIDER (TSP) AND AGENCY APPEAL PROCEDURES FOR POSTPAYMENT AUDITS

§ 102–118.600 When a TSP disagrees with a Notice of Overcharge resulting from a postpayment audit, what are the appeal procedures?

A TSP who disagrees with the Notice of Overcharge may submit a written request for reconsideration to the GSA Audit Division at:

General Services Administration
Transportation Audit Division (QMCA)
Crystal Plaza 4, Room 300
2200 Crystal Drive
Arlington, VA 22202
www.gsa.gov/transaudits

[65 FR 24569, Apr. 26, 2000, as amended at 69 FR 57620, Sept. 24, 2004; 74 FR 30475, June 26, 2009]

§ 102–118.605 What if a TSP disagrees with the Notice of Indebtedness?

If a TSP disagrees with an ordinary debt, as shown on a Notice of Indebtedness, it may:

(a) Inspect and copy the agency's records related to the claim;

(b) Seek administrative review by the GSA Audit Division of the claim decision; and/or

(c) Enter a written agreement for the payment of the claims.

§ 102–118.610 Is a TSP notified when GSA allows a claim?

Yes, the GSA Audit Division will acknowledge each payable claim using GSA Form 7931, Certificate of Settlement. The certificate will give a complete explanation of any amount that is disallowed. GSA will forward the certificate to the agency whose funds are to be charged for processing and payment.

§ 102–118.615 Will GSA notify a TSP if they internally offset a payment?

Yes, the GSA Audit Division will inform the TSP if they internally offset a payment.

§ 102–118.620 How will a TSP know if the GSA Audit Division disallows a claim?

The GSA Audit Division will furnish a GSA Form 7932, Settlement Certificate, to the TSP explaining the disallowance.

§ 102–118.625 Can a TSP request a reconsideration of a settlement action by the GSA Audit Division?

Yes, a TSP desiring a reconsideration of a settlement action may request a review by the Administrator of General Services.

§ 102–118.630 How must a TSP refund amounts due to GSA?

(a) TSPs must promptly refund amounts due to GSA, preferably by EFT. If an EFT is not used, checks must be made payable to "General Services Administration", including the document reference number, TSP name, bill number(s), taxpayer identification number and standard carrier alpha code, then mailed to:

General Services Administration
P.O. Box 93746
Chicago, IL 60673

(b) If an EFT address is needed, please contact the GSA Audit Division at:

General Services Administration
Transportation Audit Division (QMCA)
Crystal Plaza 4, Room 300
2200 Crystal Drive
Arlington, VA 22202
www.gsa.gov/transaudits

NOTE TO § 102–118.630: Amounts collected by GSA are returned to the Treasurer of the United States (31 U.S.C. 3726).

[65 FR 24569, Apr. 26, 2000, as amended at 69 FR 57620, Sept. 24, 2004; 74 FR 30475, June 26, 2009]

§ 102–118.635 Can the Government charge interest on an amount due from a TSP?

Yes, the Government can charge interest on an amount due from a TSP. This procedure is provided for under the Debt Collection Act (31 U.S.C. 3717), the Federal Claims Collection Standards (4 CFR parts 101 through 105), and 41 CFR part 105–55.

§ 102–118.640 If a TSP fails to pay or to appeal an overcharge, what actions will GSA pursue to collect the debt?

GSA will pursue debt collection through one of the following methods:

(a) When an indebted TSP files a claim, GSA will apply all or any portion of the amount it determines to be due the TSP, to the outstanding balance owed by the TSP, under the Federal Claims Collection Standards (4 CFR parts 101 through 105) and 41 CFR part 105–55;

(b) When the action outlined in paragraph (a) of this section cannot be taken by GSA, GSA will instruct one or more Government disbursing offices to deduct the amount due to the agency from an unpaid TSP's bill. A 3-year limitation applies on the deduction of overcharges from amounts due a TSP (31 U.S.C. 3726) and a 10-year limitation applies on the deduction of ordinary debt (31 U.S.C. 3716);

(c) When collection cannot be accomplished through either of the procedures in paragraph (a) or (b) of this section, GSA normally sends two additional demand letters to the indebted TSP requesting payment of the amount due within a specified time. Lacking a satisfactory response, GSA may place a complete stop order against amounts otherwise payable to the indebted TSP by adding the name of that TSP to the Department of the Army "List of Contractors Indebted to the United States"; and/or

(d) When collection actions, as stated in paragraphs (a) through (c) of this section are unsuccessful, GSA may report the debt to the Department of Justice for collection, litigation, and related proceedings, as prescribed in 4 CFR parts 101 through 105.

§ 102–118.645 Can a TSP file an administrative claim on collection actions?

Yes, a TSP may file an administrative claim involving collection actions resulting from the transportation audit performed by the GSA directly with the GSA Audit Division. Any claims submitted to GSA will be considered "disputed claims" under section 4(b) of the Prompt Payment Act (31 U.S.C. 3901, *et seq.*). The TSP must file all other transportation claims with the agency out of whose activities they arose. If this is not feasible (e.g., where the responsible agency cannot be determined or is no longer in existence) claims may be sent to the GSA Audit Division for forwarding to the responsible agency or for direct settlement by the GSA Audit Division. Claims for GSA processing must be addressed to:

General Services Administration
Transportation Audit Division (QMCA)
Crystal Plaza 4, Room 300
2200 Crystal Drive
Arlington, VA 22202
www.gsa.gov/transaudits

[65 FR 24569, Apr. 26, 2000, as amended at 69 FR 57620, Sept. 24, 2004; 74 FR 30475, June 26, 2009]

§ 102–118.650 Can a TSP request a review of a settlement action by the Administrator of General Services?

Yes, a TSP desiring a review of a settlement action taken by the Administrator of General Services may request a review by the Civilian Board of Contract Appeals (CBCA) or file a claim with the United States Court of Federal Claims (28 U.S.C. 1491).

[65 FR 24569, Apr. 26, 2000, as amended at 74 FR 30476, June 26, 2009]

§ 102–118.655 Are there time limits on a TSP request for an administrative review by the Civilian Board of Contract Appeals (CBCA)?

Yes, the CBCA must receive a request for review from the TSP within six months (not including times of war) from the date the settlement action was taken or within the periods of limitation specified in 31 U.S.C. 3726, as amended, whichever is later. Address requests:

(a) By United States Postal Service to: Civilian Board of Contract Appeals

(CBCA), 1800 F Street NW., Washington, DC 20405;

(b) In person or by courier to: Civilian Board of Contract Appeals, 6th floor, 1800 M Street NW., Washington, DC 20036;

(c) By facsimile (FAX) to: 202–606–0019; or

(d) By electronic mail to: *cbca.efile@cbca.gov.*

[78 FR 71529, Nov. 29, 2013]

§ 102–118.660 **May a TSP appeal a postpayment audit decision of the CBCA?**

No, a ruling by the CBCA is the final administrative remedy and the TSP has no statutory right of appeal. This subpart governs administrative actions only and does not affect any rights of the TSPs. A TSP may still pursue a legal remedy through the courts.

[65 FR 24569, Apr. 26, 2000, as amended at 74 FR 30476, June 26, 2009]

§ 102–118.665 **May my agency appeal a postpayment audit decision by the CBCA?**

No, your agency may not appeal a postpayment audit decision and must follow the ruling of the CBCA.

[65 FR 24569, Apr. 26, 2000, as amended at 74 FR 30476, June 26, 2009]

TRANSPORTATION SERVICE PROVIDER (TSP) NON-PAYMENT OF A CLAIM

§ 102–118.670 **If a TSP cannot immediately pay a debt, can they make other arrangements for payment?**

Yes, if a TSP is unable to pay the debt promptly, the Director of the GSA Audit Division has the discretion to enter into alternative arrangements for payment.

§ 102–118.675 **What recourse does my agency have if a TSP does not pay a transportation debt?**

If a TSP does not pay a transportation debt, GSA may refer delinquent debts to consumer reporting agencies and Federal agencies including the Department of the Treasury and Department of Justice.

PARTS 102–119—102–140 [RESERVED]

SUBCHAPTER E—TRAVEL MANAGEMENT [RESERVED]

PART 102–141—GENERAL

[RESERVED]

PARTS 102–142—102–170 [RESERVED]

SUBCHAPTER F—TELECOMMUNICATIONS

PART 102–171—GENERAL
[RESERVED]

PART 102–172—TELECOMMUNICATIONS MANAGEMENT POLICY
[RESERVED]

PART 102–173—INTERNET GOV DOMAIN

Subpart A—General

AUTHORITY: 40 U.S.C. 486(c).

SOURCE: 68 FR 15090, Mar. 28, 2003, unless otherwise noted.

Subpart A—General

§ 102–173.5 What is Internet GOV Domain?

Internet GOV Domain refers to the Internet top-level domain "dot-gov" operated by the General Services Administration for the registration of U.S. government-related domain names. In general, these names reflect the organization names in the Federal Government and non-Federal government entities in the United States. These names are now being used to promote government services and increase the ease of finding these services.

§ 102–173.10 What is the authority or jurisdiction of the Internet GOV Domain?

Jurisdiction of the Internet GOV (dot-gov) domain was delegated to the General Services Administration in 1997 by the Federal Networking Council with guidance in the form of Internet Engineering Task Force (IETF) Informational RFC 2146, which can be obtained on the Internet at: *http://www.ietf.org/rfc/rfc2146.txt?number = 2146.*

§ 102–173.15 What is the scope of this part?

This part addresses the registration of second-level domain names used in the Internet GOV Domain. This registration process assures that the assigned domain names are unique worldwide.

§ 102–173.20 To whom does this part apply?

This part applies to Federal, State, and local governments, and Native Sovereign Nations. You do not need to register domain names with the General Services Administration if you will be using some other top-level domain registration, such as dot-us, dot-org, or dot-net.

§ 102–173.25 What definitions apply to this part?

The following definitions apply to this part:

Domain is a region of jurisdiction on the Internet for naming assignment. The General Services Administration (GSA) is responsible for registrations in the dot-gov domain.

Domain name is a name assigned to an Internet server. This is the name that you request from GSA. Typically, you would apply this name to a domain name server. A domain name locates the organization or other entity on the Internet. The dot gov part of the domain name reflects the purpose of the organization or entity. This part is called the Top-Level Domain name. The Second-Level Domain name to the left of the dot gov maps to a readable version of the Internet address. The Domain Name server has a registry of Internet Protocol (IP) address numbers that relate to the readable text name.

Domain name server is the computer that provides pointers from the domain name to the actual computers.

Dot-gov refers to domain names ending with a ".gov" suffix. The Internet GOV domain is another way of expressing the collection of dot-gov domain names.

Native Sovereign Nations (NSN) are federally recognized tribes.

Subpart B—Registration

§ 102–173.30   Who may register in the dot-gov domain?

Registration in the dot-gov domain is available to official governmental organizations in the United States including Federal, State, and local governments, and Native Sovereign Nations.

§ 102–173.35   Who authorizes domain names?

Domain names must be authorized by the Chief Information Officer (CIO) of the requesting or sponsoring governmental organization. For Federal departments and agencies, the General Services Administration (GSA) will accept authorization from the CIO of the department or agency. For independent Federal government agencies, boards, and commissions, GSA will accept authorization from the highest-ranking Information Technology Official. For State and local governments, GSA will accept authorization from appropriate State or local officials, see § 102–173.40.

For Native Sovereign Nations, GSA will only accept authorization from the Bureau of Indian Affairs, Department of the Interior. In most cases, GSA will not make determinations on the appropriateness of the selected domain names, but reserves the right to not assign domain names on a case-by-case basis. Non-Federal government domain names must follow the naming conventions described in §§ 102–173.50 through 102–173.65. For other government entities, CIO's may delegate this authority by notification to GSA.

§ 102–173.40   Who is my Chief Information Officer (CIO)?

Your Chief Information Officer (CIO) may vary according to the branch of government. For the Federal Government, the General Services Administration (GSA) recognizes the cabinet level CIOs listed at *http://www.cio.gov*. For States, GSA will accept authorization from the Office of the Governor or highest-ranking Information Technology (IT) official. Other officials include the Mayor (for city or town), County Commissioner (for counties) or highest ranking IT official. Native Sovereign Nations (NSN) must receive authorization from the Bureau of Indian Affairs. CIOs may delegate this authority by notification to GSA.

§ 102–173.45   Is there a registration charge for domain names?

The General Services Administration (GSA) reserves the right to charge for domain names in order to recover cost of operations. For current registration charges, please visit the GSA Web site at *http://www.nic.gov*. GSA does not currently charge a fee. GSA has the authority to employ a system of collection that includes a one-time setup fee for new registrations, which will not exceed $1000, depending on the level of assistance that may be provided by GSA, and a recurring annual charge that will not exceed $500 for all dot-gov domains. The fees are based on anticipated costs for operating the registration service.

§ 102–173.50 What is the naming convention for States?

(a) To register any second-level domain within dot-gov, State government entities must register the full State name or clearly indicate the State postal code within the name. Examples of acceptable names include virginia.gov, tennesseeanytime.gov, wa.gov, nmparks.gov, mysc.gov, emaryland.gov, and ne-taxes.gov. However—

(1) Use of the State postal code should not be embedded within a single word in a way that obscures the postal code. For example, Indiana (IN) should not register for win.gov, or independence.gov; and

(2) Where potential conflicts arise between postal codes and existing domain names, States are encouraged to register URL's that contain the full State name.

(b) There is no limit to the number of domain names for which a State may register.

(c) States are encouraged to make second-level domains available for third-level registration by local governments and State Government departments and programs. For example, the State of North Carolina could register NC.GOV as a second-level domain and develop a system of registration for their local governments. The State would be free to develop policy on how the local government should be registered under NC.GOV. One possibility might be to spell out the city, thus Raleigh.NC.gov could be a resulting domain name.

§ 102–173.55 What is the naming convention for Cities and Townships?

(a) To register any second-level domain within dot-gov, City (town) governments must register the domain name with the city (town) name or abbreviation, and clear reference to the State in which the city (town) is located. However—

(1) Use of the State postal code should not be embedded within a single word in a way that obscures the postal code; and

(2) Inclusion of the word city or town within the domain name is optional and may be used at the discretion of the local government.

(b)(1) The preferred format for city governments is to denote the State postal code after the city name, optionally separated by a dash. Examples of preferred domain names include—

(i) Chicago-il.gov;

(ii) Cityofcharleston-sc.gov;

(iii) Charleston-wv.gov;

(iv) Townofdumfries-va.gov; and

(v) Detroitmi.gov.

(2) GSA reserves the right to make exceptions to the naming conventions described in this subpart on a case-by-case basis in unique and compelling cases.

(c) If third-level domain naming is used, GSA reserves the right to offer exceptions to the third-level domain naming conventions described in this section on a case-by-case basis in unique and compelling cases.

§ 102–173.60 What is the naming convention for Counties or Parishes?

(a) To register any second-level domain within dot-gov, County or Parish governments must register the County's or Parish's name or abbreviation, the word "county" or "parish" (because many counties have the same name as cities within the same State), and a reference to the State in which the county or parish is located. However, the use of the State postal code should not be embedded within a single word in a way that obscures the postal code.

(b) The preferred format for county or parish governments is to denote the State postal code after the county or parish, optionally separated by a dash. Examples of preferred domain names include—

(1) Richmondcounty-ga.gov;

(2) Pwc-county-va.gov; and

(3) Countyofdorchestor-sc.gov.

(c) If third-level domain naming is available from the State government, counties or parishes are encouraged to register for a domain name under a State's registered second-level (e.g., richmondcounty.ga.gov).

§ 102–173.65 What is the naming convention for Native Sovereign Nations?

To register any second-level domain in dot-gov, Native Sovereign Nations (NSN) may register any second-level domain name provided that it contains the registering NSN name followed by a suffix of "-NSN.gov" (case insensitive).

§ 102–173.70 Where do I register my dot-gov domain name?

Registration is an online process at the General Services Administration's Web site at *http://www.nic.gov*. At the Network Information Site, you will find the instructions and online registration forms for registering your domain name. To register your domain name you will need to provide information such as your desired domain name, sponsoring organization, points of contact, and at least two name server addresses.

§ 102–173.75 How long does the process take?

The process can be completed within 48 hours if all information received is complete and accurate. Most requests take up to thirty (30) days because the registrar is waiting for Chief Information Officer (CIO) approval.

§ 102–173.80 How will I know if my request is approved?

A registration confirmation notice is sent within one business day after you register your domain name, informing you that your registration information was received. If all of your information is accurate and complete, a second notice will be sent to you within one business day, informing you that all of your information is in order. If you are ineligible, or if the information provided is incorrect or incomplete, your registration will be rejected and a notice will be sent to you stating the reason for rejection. Registration requests will be activated within two business days after receiving valid authorization from the appropriate Chief Information Officer (CIO). Once your do-

main name has been activated, a notice will be sent to you.

§ 102–173.85 How long will my application be held, pending approval by the Chief Information Officer (CIO)?

Registrations will be held in reserve status for sixty (60) days pending Chief Information Officer (CIO) authorization from your sponsoring organization.

§ 102–173.90 Are there any special restrictions on the use and registration of canonical, or category names like recreation.gov?

Yes, canonical names registration request must provide access coverage for the areas conveyed by the name. So the URL recreation.gov would not be approved for the state of Maryland, but the URL recreationMD.gov would be approved if it provides statewide coverage. The logic of the names adds value to the dot gov domain. GSA reserves the right deny use of canonical names that do not provide appropriate coverage and to arbitrate these issues.

§ 102–173.95 Are there any restrictions on the use of the dot-gov domain name?

The General Services Administration approves domain names for a specific term of time, generally two years unless otherwise stated, and under conditions of use. General conditions of registration are and are posted at the registration Web site at *http://www.nic.gov* and may be modified over time. Organizations that operate web sites that are not in compliance with the conditions of use may have their domain name terminated.

PARTS 102–174—102–190
[RESERVED]

SUBCHAPTER G—ADMINISTRATIVE PROGRAMS

PART 102–191—GENERAL [RESERVED]

PART 102–192—MAIL MANAGEMENT

AUTHORITY: 44 U.S.C. 2901–2904.

SOURCE: 79 FR 33478, June 11, 2014, unless otherwise noted.

Subpart A—Introduction to this Part

§ 102–192.5   What does this part cover?

This part prescribes policy and requirements for the effective, economical, and secure management of incoming, internal, and outgoing mail and materials in Federal agencies.

§ 102–192.10   What authority governs this part?

This part is governed by section 2 of Public Law 94–575, the Federal Records Management Amendments of 1976 (44 U.S.C. 2901–2904, as amended), that requires the Administrator of General Services to provide guidance and assistance to Federal agencies to ensure economical and effective records management and defines the processing of mail by Federal agencies as a records management activity.

§ 102–192.15   How are "I," "you," "me," "we," and "us" used in this part?

In this part, "I," "me," and "you" refer to the agency mail manager, a person working in a Federal mail operation, or the agency itself. Where the context does not make it entirely clear which is meant, the meaning is spelled out the first time a pronoun is used in the section. "We," "us," and "you" in the plural refer to your Federal agency.

§ 102–192.20 How are "must" and "should" used in this part?

In this part—

(a) "Must" identifies steps that Federal agencies are required to take; and

(b) "Should" identifies steps that the GSA recommends. In their internal policy statements, agencies may require steps that GSA recommends.

§ 102–192.25 Does this part apply to me?

Yes, this part applies to you if you work in mail management in a Federal agency, as defined in § 102–192.35.

§ 102–192.30 To what types of mail and materials does this part apply?

(a) This part applies to all materials that pass through a Federal mail center, including all incoming and outgoing materials. This includes:

(1) First Class Mail;

(2) Standard Mail;

(3) Periodicals;

(4) Package Services; and

(5) Express Mail.

(b) This part does not apply to shipments of parts or supplies from a material distribution center. A material distribution center is a warehouse that maintains and distributes an inventory of parts and supplies.

§ 102–192.35 What definitions apply to this part?

The following definitions apply to this part:

Accountable mail means any piece of mail for which a service provider and the mail center must maintain a record that shows where the mail piece is at any given time, and when and where it was delivered. Examples of *accountable mail* include United States Postal Service (USPS) registered mail and all expedited mail.

Agency mail manager means the person who manages the overall mail management program of a Federal agency.

Class of mail means one of the five categories of domestic mail as defined by the Mailing Standards of the USPS in the Domestic Mail Manual (DMM) located at *http://pe.usps.gov/*. These include:

(1) Express mail;

(2) First class (includes priority mail);

(3) Periodicals;

(4) Standard mail, bulk business mail; and

(5) Package services.

Commercial postage process means paying for postage using the United States Postal Service's Centralized Account Processing System or another payment approach used by the private sector.

Commingling means combining outgoing mail from one facility or agency with outgoing mail from at least one other source.

Consolidation means the process of combining into a container two or more pieces of mail directed to the same addressee or installation on the same day.

Consolidation of facilities means the process of combining more than one mail center into a central location. The decision to consolidate should be based on a cost analysis comparing the projected cost savings to the cost of implementation.

Expedited mail means mail designated for overnight and 2- or 3-day delivery by service providers. Examples of *expedited mail* include Dalsey, Hillblom, Lynn (DHL); Federal Express (FedEx); United Parcel Service (UPS); and United States Postal Service (USPS) express mail.

Federal agency or agency as defined in 44 U.S.C. 2901(14) means—

(1) An executive agency, which includes:

(i) Any executive department as defined in 5 U.S.C. 101;

(ii) Any wholly owned Government corporation as defined in 31 U.S.C. 9101;

(iii) Any independent establishment in the executive branch as defined in 5 U.S.C. 104; and

(2) Any establishment in the legislative or judicial branch of the Government, except the Supreme Court, the Senate, the U.S. House of Representatives, the Architect of the Capitol, and any activities under the direction of

the Architect of the Capitol. *Federal facility or facility* means any office building, installation, base, etc., where Federal agency employees work. This includes any facility where the Federal Government pays postage expenses even though few or no Federal employees are involved in processing the mail.

Incoming mail means any mail that comes into a facility delivered by any service provider, such as DHL, FedEx, UPS, and USPS.

Internal mail means mail generated within a Federal facility that is delivered within that facility or to a nearby facility of the same agency, so long as it is delivered by agency personnel.

Large agency means a Federal agency whose collective total payments to all mail service providers equals or exceeds $1 million per fiscal year.

Mail means that as described in § 102–192.30.

Mail center means an organization and/or place, within or associated with a Federal facility, where incoming and/or outgoing Federal mail and materials are processed.

Mail expenditures means direct expenses for postage, fees and services, and all other mail costs, meter fees, permit fees, etc. (*e.g.*, payments to service providers, mail center personnel costs, mail center overhead).

Mail piece design means creating and printing items to be mailed so that they can be processed efficiently and effectively by USPS automated mail processing equipment.

Official Mail means incoming or outgoing mail that is related to official business of the Federal Government.

Official Mail Accounting System (OMAS) means the USPS Government-specific system used to track postage.

Outgoing mail means mail generated within a Federal facility that is going outside that facility.

Personal mail means incoming or outgoing mail that is not related to official business of the Federal Government.

Postage means payment for delivery service that is affixed or imprinted to a mail piece usually in the form of a postage stamp, permit, imprint, or meter impression.

Presort means a mail preparation process used to receive a discounted

mail rate by sorting mail according to USPS standards.

Program level means a component, bureau, regional office, and/or a facility that generates outgoing mail.

Service provider means any agency or company that delivers materials and mail. Some examples of service providers are DHL, FedEx, UPS, USPS, courier services, the U.S. Department of Defense, the U.S. Department of State's Diplomatic Pouch and Mail Division, and other Federal agencies providing mail services.

Sustainability/Sustainable means to create and maintain conditions under which humans and nature can exist in productive harmony. *Sustainability* efforts seek to fulfill the social, economic, and environmental needs of present and future generations.

Telework means a flexible work arrangement under which an employee performs assigned duties and responsibilities, and other authorized activities, from an approved alternate location.

Unauthorized use of agency postage means the use of penalty or commercial mail stamps, meter impressions, or other postage indicia for personal or unofficial use.

Worksharing is one way of processing outgoing mail so that the mail qualifies for reduced postage rates (*e.g.*, presorting, bar coding, consolidating, commingling).

§ 102–192.40 Where can we obtain more information about the classes of mail?

You can learn more about mail classes in the Domestic Mail Manual (DMM). The DMM is available online at *http://pe.usps.gov*, or you can order a copy from: Superintendent of Documents, U.S. Government Printing Office, P.O. Box 979050, St. Louis, MO 63197–9000.

§ 102–192.45 How can we request a deviation from these requirements, and who can approve it?

See §§ 102–2.60 through 102–2.110 of this chapter to request a deviation from the requirements of this part. The Administrator of General Services and those to whom the Administrator has delegated such authority have the power to approve or deny a deviation.

Subpart B—Agency Requirements

FINANCIAL REQUIREMENTS FOR ALL AGENCIES

§ 102–192.50 What payment processes are we required to use?

(a) You must pay the USPS using one or more of the following:

(1) The U.S. Treasury Intergovernmental Payment and Collection Payment (IPAC) process associated with the Official Mail Accounting System (OMAS);

(2) The USPS Centralized Account Processing System (CAPS) associated with commercial payments; or

(3) Another Treasury approved means of paying the USPS.

(b) Payments made to service providers other than USPS must be made by U.S. Treasury payment methods such as automated clearing house-electronic funds transfer, or another Treasury approved means of paying the vendor.

§ 102–192.55 Why must we use these payment processes?

In accordance with 44 U.S.C. 2904, GSA is required to standardize and improve accountability with respect to records management, including Federal mail management.

§ 102–192.60 How do we implement these payment processes?

Guidance on implementing the Intragovernmental Payment and Collection System can be found at: *http://www.fms.treas.gov/ipac/index.html.*

§ 102–192.65 What features must our finance systems have to keep track of mail expenditures?

All agencies must have an accountable system for making postage payments; that is, a system that allocates postage expenses at the program level within the agency and makes program level managers accountable for obligating and tracking those expenses. The agency will have to determine the appropriate program level for this requirement because the level at which it is cost beneficial differs widely. The agency's finance systems should track all mail expenditures separately to the program level or below, and should—

(a) Show expenses for postage and all other mail expenditures, payments to service providers, etc., separate from all other administrative expenses;

(b) Allow mail centers to establish systems to charge their customers for mail expenditures; and

(c) Identify and charge the mail expenditures that are part of printing contracts down to the program level.

SECURITY REQUIREMENTS FOR ALL AGENCIES

§ 102–192.70 What security policies and plans must we have?

(a) Agencies must have a written mail security policy that applies throughout your agency.

(b) Agencies must have a written mail security plan for each facility that processes mail, regardless of the facility's mail volume.

(c) Agencies must have a security policy for employees receiving incoming and sending outgoing mail at an alternative worksite, such as a telework center.

(d) The scope and level of detail of each facility mail security plan should be commensurate with the size and responsibilities of each facility. For small facilities, agencies may use a general plan for similar locations. For larger locations, agencies must develop a plan that is specifically tailored to the threats and risks at your location. Agencies should determine which facilities they consider small and large for the purposes of this section, so long as the basic requirements for a security plan are met at every facility.

(e) All mail managers are required to annually report the status of their mail security plans to agency headquarters. At a minimum, these reports should assure that all mail security plans comply with the requirements of this part, including annual review by a subject matter expert and regular rehearsal of responses to various emergency situations by facility personnel.

(f) A security professional who has expertise in mail center security should review the agency's mail security plan and policies annually to include identification of any deficiencies. Review of facility mail security plans can be accomplished by subject matter experts such as agency security personnel. If these experts are not available within your agency, seek assistance from the U.S. Postal Inspection Service (*https:// postalinspectors.uspis.gov/*) or the Federal Protective Service (FPS) (*http:// www.dhs.gov/federal-protective-service*).

§ 102–192.75 Why must we have written security policies and plans?

All Federal mail programs must identify, prioritize, and coordinate the protection of all mail processing facilities in order to prevent, deter, and mitigate the effects of deliberate efforts to destroy, incapacitate, or exploit the mail center or the national mail infrastructure. Homeland Security Presidential Directive (HSPD 7) at *http://www.fas.org/irp/offdocs/nspd/hspd-7.html* requires all agencies to protect key resources from terrorist attacks. All Federal mail centers are identified as key resources under the Postal and Shipping Sector Plan. Further details on the plan can be found at the Department of Homeland Security's (DHS) Web site at *http://www.dhs.gov/*.

§ 102–192.80 How do we develop written security policies and plans?

Agency mail managers must coordinate with their agency security service and/or the FPS or the U.S. Postal Inspection Service to develop agency mail security policies and plans. The FPS has developed standards for building construction and management, including standards for mail centers. At a minimum, the agency mail security plan must address the following topics:

(a) Risk assessment;

(b) A plan to protect staff and all other occupants of agency facilities from hazards that might be delivered in the mail;

(c) Operating procedures;

(d) A plan to provide a visible mail screening operation;

(e) Training mail center personnel;

(f) Testing and rehearsing responses to various emergency situations by agency personnel;

(g) Managing threats;

(h) Communications plan;

(i) Occupant Emergency Plan;

(j) Continuity of Operations Plan; and

(k) Annual reviews of the agency's security plan.

REPORTING REQUIREMENTS

§ 102–192.85 Who must report to GSA annually?

Large agencies, as defined in § 102–192.35, must provide an annual Mail Management Report to GSA. If your agency is a cabinet level or independent agency, the agency mail manager must compile all offices or components and submit one report for the department or agency as a whole, for example, the U.S. Department of Defense or the U.S. Department of Health and Human Services.

§ 102–192.90 What must we include in our annual mail management report to GSA?

You must provide an agency-wide response to the GSA requested data elements. GSA will provide the list of data elements in a Federal Management Regulation (FMR) Bulletin. GSA coordinates all mail management related FMR bulletins with the Federal Mail Executive Council and updates them as necessary. FMR bulletins are available at: *http://www.gsa.gov/bulletins*.

§ 102–192.95 Why does GSA require annual mail management reports?

GSA requires annual agency mail management reports to—

(a) Ensure that Federal agencies have the policies, procedures, and data to manage their mail operations efficiently and effectively;

(b) Ensure that appropriate security measures are in place; and

(c) Allow GSA to fulfill its responsibilities under the Federal Records Act, especially with regard to sharing best practices, information on training, and promulgating standards, procedures, and guidelines.

§ 102–192.100 How do we submit our annual mail management report to GSA?

You must submit annual reports using the GSA web based Simplified Mail Accountability Reporting Tool (*SMART*). Training is available from GSA to agency mail managers and other authorized users on how to use the SMART data reporting system. Contact the Office of Government-wide Policy, Mail Management Policy office for access and training at *federal.mail@gsa.gov*.

§ 102–192.105 When must we submit our annual mail management report to GSA?

Beginning with FY 2015, the agency's annual mail management report is due on December 1, following the end of the fiscal year.

[80 FR 57103, Sept. 22, 2015]

PERFORMANCE MEASUREMENT
REQUIREMENTS FOR ALL AGENCIES

§ 102–192.110 At what levels in our agency must we have performance measures?

You must have performance measures for mail operations at the agency level and in all mail facilities and program levels.

§ 102–192.115 Why must we use performance measures?

Performance measures gauge the success of your mail management plans and processes by comparing performance over time and among organizations. Performance measures—

(a) Define goals and objectives;

(b) Enhance resource allocation; and

(c) Provide accountability.

AGENCY MAIL MANAGER REQUIREMENTS

§ 102–192.120 Must we have an agency mail manager?

Yes, every agency as defined in § 102–192.35, must have an agency mail manager.

§ 102–192.125 What is the appropriate managerial level for an agency mail manager?

The agency mail manager should be at a managerial level that enables him or her to speak for the agency on mail management as outlined in this part.

§ 102–192.130 What are your general responsibilities as an agency mail manager?

In addition to carrying out the responsibilities discussed above, you should—

(a) Establish written policies and procedures to provide timely and cost effective dispatch and delivery of mail and materials;

(b) Ensure agency-wide awareness and compliance with standards and operational procedures established by all service providers used by the agency;

(c) Set policies for expedited mail, mass mailings, mailing lists, and couriers;

(d) Implement cost savings through:

(1) Consolidating and presorting wherever practical, for example, internal and external mail, and consolidation of agency-wide mail operations and official mail facilities; and

(2) Reducing the volume of agency to agency mail whenever possible.

(e) Develop and direct agency programs and plans for proper and cost effective use of transportation, equipment, and supplies used for mail;

(f) Ensure that all facility and program level mail personnel receive appropriate training and certifications to successfully perform their assigned duties;

(g) Promote professional certification for mail managers and mail center employees;

(h) Ensure that expedited mail service providers are used only when authorized by the Private Express Statutes, 39 U.S.C. 601–606;

(i) Establish written policies and procedures to minimize incoming and outgoing personal mail;

(j) Provide guidance to agency representatives who develop correspondence or design mailing materials including Business Reply Mail, letterhead, and mail piece design;

(k) Represent the agency in its relations with service providers, other agency mail managers, and GSA's Office of Government-wide Policy;

(l) Ensure agency policy incorporates Federal hazardous materials requirements set forth in 49 CFR parts 100–185;

(m) Ensure agency sustainable activities become part of the mail program by incorporating strategies in accordance with *Executive Order 13514* of October 5, 2009, "Federal Leadership in Environmental, Energy, and Economic Performance". Section 8 describes the Agency Strategic Sustainability Performance Plan; and

(n) Ensure safety and security requirements specified in §§ 102–192.70 through 102–192.80 are fulfilled.

Subpart C—GSA's Responsibilities and Services

§ 102–192.135 What are GSA's responsibilities in mail management?

44 U.S.C. 2904(b) directs the Administrator of General Services to provide guidance and assistance to Federal agencies to ensure economical and efficient records management. 44 U.S.C. 2901(2) and (4)(C) define the processing of mail by Federal agencies as part of records management. In carrying out its responsibilities under the Act, GSA is required to—

(a) Develop standards, procedures, and guidelines;

(b) Conduct research to improve practices and programs;

(c) Collect and disseminate information on training programs, technological developments, etc;

(d) Establish one or more interagency committees (such as the Federal Mail Executive Council, and the Interagency Mail Policy Council) as necessary to provide an exchange of information among Federal agencies;

(e) Conduct studies, inspections, or surveys;

(f) Promote economy and efficiency in the selection and utilization of space, staff, equipment, and supplies; and

(g) In the event of an emergency, at the request of DHS, cooperate with DHS in communicating with agencies about mail related issues.

§ 102–192.140 What types of support does GSA offer to Federal agency mail management programs?

(a) GSA supports Federal agency mail management programs by—

(1) Assisting in the development of agency policy and guidance in mail management and mail operations;

(2) Identifying best business practices and sharing them with Federal agencies;

(3) Developing and providing access to a Government-wide management information system for mail;

(4) Helping agencies develop performance measures and management information systems for mail;

(5) Maintaining a current list of agency mail managers;

(6) Establishing, developing, and maintaining interagency mail committees;

(7) Maintaining liaison with the USPS and other service providers at the national level;

(8) Maintaining a publically accessible Web site for mail communications policy; and

(9) Serving as a point of contact for all Federal agencies on mail issues.

(b) For further information contact: U.S. General Services Administration, Office of Government-wide Policy (MA), 1800 F Street NW., Washington, DC 20504; telephone 202–501–1777, or email: *Federal.mail@gsa.gov.*

PART 102–193—CREATION, MAINTENANCE, AND USE OF RECORDS

AUTHORITY: 40 U.S.C. 486(c).

SOURCE: 66 FR 48358, Sept. 20, 2001, unless otherwise noted.

§ 102–193.5 What does this part cover?

This part prescribes policies and procedures related to the General Service Administration's (GSA) role to provide guidance on economic and effective records management for the creation, maintenance and use of Federal agencies' records. The National Archives and Records Administration Act of 1984 (the Act) (44 U.S.C. chapter 29) amended the records management statutes to divide records management responsibilities between GSA and the National Archives and Records Administration (NARA). Under the Act, GSA is responsible for economy and efficiency in records management and NARA is responsible for adequate documentation and records disposition. GSA regulations are codified in this part and NARA regulations are codified in 36 CFR chapter XII. The policies and procedures of this part apply to all records, regardless of medium (e.g., paper or electronic), unless otherwise noted.

§ 102–193.10 What are the goals of the Federal Records Management Program?

The statutory goals of the Federal Records Management Program are:

(a) Accurate and complete documentation of the policies and transactions of the Federal Government.

(b) Control of the quantity and quality of records produced by the Federal Government.

(c) Establishment and maintenance of management controls that prevent the creation of unnecessary records and promote effective and economical agency operations.

(d) Simplification of the activities, systems, and processes of records creation, maintenance, and use.

(e) Judicious preservation and disposal of records.

(f) Direction of continuing attention on records from initial creation to final disposition, with particular emphasis on the prevention of unnecessary Federal paperwork.

§ 102–193.15 What are the records management responsibilities of the Administrator of General Services (the Administrator), the Archivist of the United States (the Archivist), and the Heads of Federal agencies?

(a) The Administrator of General Services (the Administrator) provides guidance and assistance to Federal agencies to ensure economical and effective records management. Records management policies and guidance established by GSA are contained in this part and in parts 102–194 and 102–195 of this chapter, records management handbooks, and other publications issued by GSA.

(b) The Archivist of the United States (the Archivist) provides guidance and assistance to Federal agencies to ensure adequate and proper documentation of the policies and transactions of the Federal Government and to ensure proper records disposition. Records management policies and guidance established by the Archivist are contained in 36 CFR chapter XII and in bulletins and handbooks issued by the National Archives and Records Administration (NARA).

(c) The Heads of Federal agencies must comply with the policies and guidance provided by the Administrator and the Archivist.

§ 102–193.20 What are the specific agency responsibilities for records management?

You must follow both GSA regulations in this part and NARA regulations in 36 CFR chapter XII to carry out your records management responsibilities. To meet the requirements of this part, you must take the following actions to establish and maintain the agency's records management program:

(a) Assign specific responsibility to develop and implement agencywide records management programs to an office of the agency and to a qualified records manager.

(b) Follow the guidance contained in GSA handbooks and bulletins and comply with NARA regulations in 36 CFR chapter XII when establishing and implementing agency records management programs.

(c) Issue a directive establishing program objectives, responsibilities, authorities, standards, guidelines, and instructions for a records management program.

(d) Apply appropriate records management practices to all records, irrespective of the medium (e.g., paper, electronic, or other).

(e) Control the creation, maintenance, and use of agency records and the collection and dissemination of information to ensure that the agency:

(1) Does not accumulate unnecessary records while ensuring compliance with NARA regulations for adequate and proper documentation and records disposition in 36 CFR parts 1220 and 1228.

(2) Does not create forms and reports that collect information inefficiently or unnecessarily.

(3) Reviews all existing forms and reports (both those originated by the agency and those responded to by the agency but originated by another agency or branch of Government) periodically to determine if they can be improved or canceled.

(4) Maintains records economically and in a way that allows them to be retrieved quickly and reliably.

(5) Keeps mailing and copying costs to a minimum.

(f) Establish standard stationery formats and styles.

(g) Establish standards for correspondence to use in official agency communications, and necessary copies required, and their distribution and purpose.

§ 102–193.25 What type of records management business process improvements should my agency strive to achieve?

Your agency should strive to:

(a) Improve the quality, tone, clarity, and responsiveness of correspondence;

(b) Design forms that are easy to fill-in, read, transmit, process, and retrieve, and reduce forms reproduction costs;

(c) Provide agency managers with the means to convey written instructions to users and document agency policies and procedures through effective directives management;

(d) Provide agency personnel with the information needed in the right place, at the right time, and in a useful format;

(e) Eliminate unnecessary reports and design necessary reports for ease of use;

(f) Provide rapid handling and accurate delivery of mail at minimum cost; and

(g) Organize agency files in a logical order so that needed records can be found rapidly to conduct agency business, to ensure that records are complete, and to facilitate the identification and retention of permanent records and the prompt disposal of temporary records. Retention and disposal of records is governed by NARA regulations in 36 CFR chapter XII.

PART 102–194—STANDARD AND OPTIONAL FORMS MANAGEMENT PROGRAM

AUTHORITY: 40 U.S.C. 486(c).

SOURCE: 66 FR 48358, Sept. 20, 2001, unless otherwise noted.

§ 102–194.5 What is the Standard and Optional Forms Management Program?

The Standard and Optional Forms Management Program is a Governmentwide program that promotes economies and efficiencies through the development, maintenance and use of common forms. The General Services Administration (GSA) provides additional guidance on the Standard and Optional Forms Management Program through an external handbook called

Standard and Optional Forms Procedural Handbook. You may obtain a copy of the handbook from:

Standard and Optional Forms Management Office General Services Administration (Forms-XR)
1800 F Street, NW.; Room 7126
Washington, DC 20405–0002
(202) 501–0581
http://www.gsa.gov/forms

§ 102–194.10 What is a Standard form?

A Standard form is a fixed or sequential order of data elements, prescribed by a Federal agency through regulation, approved by GSA for mandatory use, and assigned a Standard form number. This criterion is the same whether the form resides on paper or purely electronic.

§ 102–194.15 What is an Optional form?

An Optional form is approved by GSA for nonmandatory Governmentwide use and is used by two or more agencies. This criteria is the same whether the form resides on paper or purely electronic.

§ 102–194.20 What is an electronic Standard or Optional form?

An electronic Standard or Optional form is an officially prescribed set of data residing in an electronic medium that is used to produce a mirror-like image or as near to a mirror-like image as the creation software will allow of the officially prescribed form.

§ 102–194.25 What is an automated Standard or Optional format?

An automated Standard or Optional format is an electronic version of the officially prescribed form containing the same data elements and used for the electronic transaction of information in lieu of using a Standard or Optional form.

§ 102–194.30 What role does my agency play in the Standard and Optional Forms Management Program?

Your agency head or designee's role is to:

(a) Designate an agency-level Standard and Optional Forms Liaison representative and alternate, and notify GSA, in writing, of their names, titles, mailing addresses, telephone numbers, fax numbers, and e-mail addresses within 30 days of the designation or redesignation.

(b) Promulgate Governmentwide Standard forms under the agency's statutory or regulatory authority in the FEDERAL REGISTER, and issue procedures on the mandatory use, revision, or cancellation of these forms.

(c) Ensure that the agency complies with the provisions of the Government Paperwork Elimination Act (GPEA) (Public Law 105–277, 112 Stat 2681), Section 508 of the Rehabilitation Act of 1973 (29 U.S.C. 74d), as amended, the Architectural and Transportation Barriers Compliance Board (Access Board) Standards (36 CFR part 1194), and OMB implementing guidance. In particular, agencies should allow the submission of Standard and Optional forms in an electronic/automated version unless the form is specifically exempted by § 102–194.40.

(d) Issue Governmentwide Optional forms when needed by two or more agencies and announce the availability, revision, or cancellation of these forms. Forms prescribed through a regulation for use by the Federal Government must be issued as a Standard form.

(e) Obtain GSA approval for each new, revised or canceled Standard and Optional form, 60 days prior to planned implementation. Certify that the forms comply with all applicable laws and regulations. Provide an electronic form unless exempted by § 102–194.40. Revised forms not approved by GSA will result in cancellation of the form.

(f) Provide GSA with both an electronic (unless exempted by § 102–194.40) and paper version of the official image of the Standard or Optional form prior to implementation.

(g) Obtain the prescribing agency's approval for exceptions to Standard and Optional forms, including electronic forms or automated formats prior to implementation.

(h) Review annually agency prescribed Standard and Optional forms, including exceptions, for improvement, consolidation, cancellation, or possible automation. The review must include approved electronic versions of the forms.

(i) Coordinate all health-care related Standard and Optional forms through GSA for the approval of the Inter-agency Committee on Medical Records (ICMR).

(j) Promote the use of electronic forms within the agency by following what the Government Paperwork Elimination Act (GPEA) prescribes and all guidance issued by the Office of Management and Budget and other responsible agencies. This guidance will promote the use of electronic transactions and electronic signatures.

(k) Notify GSA of the replacement of any Standard or Optional form by an automated format or electronic form, and its impact on the need to stock the paper form. GSA's approval is not necessary for this change, but a one-time notification should be made.

(l) Follow the specific instructions in the Standard and Optional Forms Procedural Handbook.

§ 102–194.35 Should I create electronic Standard or Optional forms?

Yes, you should create electronic Standard or Optional forms, especially when forms are used to collect information from the public. GSA will not approve a new or revision to a Standard or Optional form unless an electronic form is being made available. Only forms covered by § 102–194.40 are exempt from this requirement. Furthermore, you should to the extent possible, use electronic form products and services that are based on open standards. However, the use of proprietary products is permitted, provided that the end user is not required to purchase a specific product or subscription to use the electronic Standard or Optional form.

§ 102–194.40 For what Standard or Optional forms should an electronic version not be made available?

All forms should include an electronic version unless it is not practicable to do so. Areas where it may not be practicable include where the form has construction features for specialized use (e.g., labels), to prevent unauthorized use or could otherwise risk a security violation, (e.g., classification cover sheets), or require unusual production costs (e.g., specialized paper or envelopes). Such forms can be made available as an electronic form only if the originating agency approves an exception to do so. (See the Standard and Optional Forms Procedural Handbook for procedures and a list of these forms).

§ 102–194.45 Who should I contact about Standard and Optional forms?

For Standard and Optional forms, you should contact the:

Standard and Optional Forms Management Office General Services Administration (Forms-XR)
1800 F Street, NW.; Room 7126
Washington, DC 20405–0002
(202) 501–0581

PART 102–196—FEDERAL FACILITY RIDESHARING [RESERVED]

PARTS 102–197—102–199 [RESERVED]

SUBCHAPTERS H–Z [RESERVED]
CHAPTERS 103–104 [RESERVED]

CHAPTER 105—GENERAL SERVICES ADMINISTRATION

PART 105-1—INTRODUCTION

Sec.
105-1.000-50 Scope of part.

Subpart 105-1.1—Regulations System

AUTHORITY: Sec. 205(c), 63 Stat. 390; 40 U.S.C. 486(c).

SOURCE: 39 FR 25231, July 9, 1974, unless otherwise noted.

§ 105-1.000-50 Scope of part.

This part describes the method by which the General Services Administration (GSA) implements and supplements the Federal Property Management Regulations (FPMR) and implements certain regulations prescribed by other agencies. It contains procedures that implement and supplement part 101-1 of the FPMR.

Subpart 105-1.1—Regulations System

§ 105-1.100 Scope of subpart.

This subpart establishes the General Services Administration Property Management Regulations (GSPMR) and provides certain introductory material.

§ 105-1.101 General Services Administration Property Management Regulations.

The General Services Administration Property Management Regulations (GSPMR) include the GSA property management policies and procedures which, together with the Federal Property Management Regulations, certain regulations prescribed by other agencies, and various GSA orders govern the management of property and records and certain related activities of GSA. They may contain policies and procedures of interest to other agencies and the general public and are prescribed by the Administrator of General Services in this chapter 105.

§ 105-1.101-50 Exclusions.

(a) Certain GSA property management and related policies and procedures which come within the scope of this chapter 105 nevertheless may be excluded therefrom when there is justification. These exclusions may include the following categories:

(1) Subject matter that bears a security classification;

(2) Policies and procedures that are expected to be effective for a period of less than 6 months;

(3) Policies and procedures that are effective on an experimental basis for a reasonable period;

(4) Policies and procedures pertaining to other functions of GSA as well as property management functions and there is need to make the issuance available simultaneously to all GSA employees involved; and

(5) Where speed of issuance is essential, numerous changes are required in chapter, 105, and all necessary changes cannot be made promptly.

(b) Property management policies and procedures issued in other than the FPMR system format under paragraphs (a)(4) and (5) of this section, shall be codified into chapter 105 at the earliest practicable date, but in any event not later than 6 months from date of issuance.

§ 105-1.102 Relationship of GSPMR to FPMR.

(a) GSPMR implement and supplement the FPMR and implement certain other regulations. They are part of the General Services Administration Regulations System. Material published in the FPMR (which has Governmentwide applicability) becomes effective throughout GSA upon the effective date of the particular FPMR material. In general, the FPMR that are implemented and supplemented shall not be repeated, paraphrased, or otherwise restated in chapter 105.

(b) Implementing is the process of expanding upon the FPMR or other Government-wide regulations.

Supplementing is the process of prescribing material for which there is no counterpart in the Government-wide regulations.

(c) GSPMR may deviate from the regulations that are implemented when a deviation (see § 105–1.110) is authorized in and explicitly referenced to such regulations. Where chapter 105 contains no material implementing the FPMR, the FPMR shall govern.

§ 105–1.104 Publication of GSPMR.

(a) Most GSPMR are published in the FEDERAL REGISTER. This practice helps to ensure that interested business concerns, other agencies, and the public are apprised of GSA policies and procedures pertaining to property and records management and certain related activities.

(b) Most GSPMR are published in cumulative form in chapter 105 of title 41 of the Code of Federal Regulations. The FEDERAL REGISTER and title 41 of the Code of Federal Regulations may be purchased from the Superintendent of Documents, Government Printing Office, Washington, D.C. 20402.

§ 105–1.106 Applicability.

Chapter 105 applies to the management of property and records and to certain other programs and activities of GSA. Unless otherwise specified, chapter 105 applies to activities outside as well as within the United States.

§ 105–1.109 Numbering.

§ 105–1.109–50 General plan.

Chapter 105 is divided into parts, subparts, and further subdivisions as necessary.

§ 105–1.109–51 Arrangement.

(a) Parts 105–2 through 105–49 are used for GSPMR that implement regulations in the corresponding parts of chapter 101. This practice results in comparable grouping by subject area without establishment of subchapters.

(b) Parts 105–50 and above are used for GSPMR that supplement regulations in the FPMR and implement regulations of other agencies. Part numbers are assigned so as to accomplish a similar subject area grouping. Regulations on advisory committee manage-

ment are recodified as part 105–54 to place them in the appropriate subject area category. Regulations on standards of conduct remain in part 105–735 because the number 735 identifies regulations of the U.S. Civil Service Commission and various civil agencies on this subject.

§ 105–1.109–52 Cross-references.

(a) Within chapter 105, cross-references to the FPMR shall be made in the same manner as used within the FPMR. Illustrations of cross-references to the FPMR are:

(1) Part 101–3;

(2) Subpart 101–3.1;

(3) § 101–3.413–5.

(b) Within chapter 105, cross-references to parts, subparts, sections, and subsections of chapter 105 shall be made in a manner generally similar to that used in making cross-references to the FPMR. For example, this paragraph would be referenced as § 105–1.109–52(b).

§ 105–1.110 Deviation.

(a) In the interest of establishing and maintaining uniformity to the greatest extent feasible, deviations; i.e., the use of any policy or procedure in any manner that is inconsistent with a policy or procedure prescribed in the Federal Property Management Regulations, are prohibited unless such deviations have been requested from and approved by the Administrator of General Services or his authorized designee. Deviations may be authorized by the Administrator of General Services or his authorized designee when so doing will be in the best interest of the Government. Request for deviations shall clearly state the nature of the deviation and the reasons for such special action.

(b) Requests for deviations from the FPMR shall be sent to the General Services Administration for consideration in accordance with the following:

(1) For onetime (individual) deviations, requests shall be sent to the address provided in the applicable regulation. Lacking such direction, requests shall be sent to the Administrator of General Services, Washington, DC 20405.

(2) For class deviations, requests shall be sent to only the Administrator of General Services.

[55 FR 1673, Jan. 18, 1990]

§ 105–1.150 Citation.

(a) In formal documents, such as legal briefs, citations of chapter 105 material shall include a citation to title 41 of the Code of Federal Regulations or other titles as appropriate; e.g., 41 CFR 105–1.150.

(b) Any section of chapter 105, for purpose of brevity, may be informally identified as "GSPMR" followed by the section number. For example, this paragraph would be identified as "GSPMR 105–1.150(b)."

PART 105–8—ENFORCEMENT OF NONDISCRIMINATION ON THE BASIS OF HANDICAP IN PROGRAMS OR ACTIVITIES CONDUCTED BY GENERAL SERVICES ADMINISTRATION

AUTHORITY: 29 U.S.C. 794.

SOURCE: 56 FR 9871, Mar. 8, 1991, unless otherwise noted.

§ 105–8.101 Purpose.

The purpose of this part is to effectuate section 119 of the Rehabilitation, Comprehensive Services, and Developmental Disabilities Amendments of 1978, which amended section 504 of the Rehabilitation Act of 1973 to prohibit discrimination on the basis of handicap in programs or activities conducted by Executive agencies or the United States Postal Service.

§ 105–8.102 Application.

This part applies to all programs or activities conducted by the agency, except for programs or activities conducted outside the United States that do not involve individuals with handicaps in the United States.

§ 105–8.103 Definitions.

For purposes of this part, the term—

Agency means the General Services Administration (GSA), except when the context indicates otherwise.

Assistant Attorney General means the Assistant Attorney General, Civil Rights Division, United States Department of Justice.

Auxiliary aids means services or devices that enable persons with impaired sensory, manual, or speaking skills to have an equal opportunity to participate in and enjoy the benefits of programs or activities conducted by GSA. For example, auxiliary aids useful for persons with impaired vision include readers, Brailed materials, audio recordings, and other similar services and devices. Auxiliary aids useful for persons with impaired hearing include telephone handset amplifiers, telephones compatible with hearing aids, telecommunication devices for deaf persons (TDD's), interpreters, notetakers, written materials, and other similar services and devices.

Complete complaint means a written statement that contains the complainant's name and address and describes the agency's alleged discriminatory action in sufficient detail to inform the agency of the nature and date of the alleged violation of section 504. It shall be signed by the complainant or by someone authorized to do so on his or her behalf. Complaints filed on behalf of classes or third parties shall describe or identify (by name, if possible) the alleged victims of discrimination.

Facility means all or any portion of buildings, structures, equipment, roads, walks, parking lots, rolling stock or other conveyances, or other real or personal property.

Historic preservation program means programs conducted by the agency that have preservation of historic properties as a primary purpose.

Historic properties means those properties that are listed or eligible for listing in the National Register of Historic Places or properties designated as historic under a statute of the appropriate State or local government body.

Individual with handicaps means any person who has a physical or mental impairment that substantially limits one or more major life activities, has a record of such an impairment, or is regarded as having such an impairment. As used in this definition, the phrase:

(1) *Physical or mental impairment* includes—

(i) Any physiological disorder or condition, cosmetic disfigurement, or anatomical loss affecting one or more of the following body systems: Neurological musculoskeletal; special sense organs; respiratory, including speech organs; cardiovascular; reproductive; digestive; genitourinary; hemic and lymphatic; skin; and endocrine; or

(ii) Any mental or psychological disorder, such as mental retardation, organic brain syndrome, emotional or mental illness, and specific learning disabilities. The term ''Physical or mental impairment'' includes, but is not limited to, such diseases and conditions as orthopedic, visual, speech, and hearing impairments, cerebral palsy, epilepsy, muscular dystrophy, multiple sclerosis, cancer, heart disease, diabetes, mental retardation, emotional illness, and drug addiction and alcoholism.

(2) *Major life activities* includes functions such as caring for one's self, performing manual tasks, walking, seeing, hearing, speaking, breathing, learning, and working.

(3) *Has a record of such an impairment* means has a history of, or has been misclassified as having, a mental or physical impairment that substantially limits one or more major life activities.

(4) *Is regarded as having an impairment* means—

(i) Has a physical or mental impairment that does not substantially limit major life activities but is treated by the agency as constituting such a limitation;

(ii) Has a physical or mental impairment that substantially limits major life activities only as a result of the attitudes of others toward such impairment; or

(iii) Has none of the impairments defined in paragraph (a) of this definition but is treated by the agency as having such an impairment.

Official or Responsible Official means the Director of the Civil Rights Division of the General Services Administration or his or her designee.

Qualified individual with handicaps means—

(1) With respect to any agency program or activity under which a person is required to perform services or to achieve a level of accomplishment, an individual with handicaps who meets the essential eligibility requirements and who can achieve the purpose of the program or activity without modifications in the program or activity that the agency can demonstrate would result in a fundamental alteration in its nature;

(2) With respect to any other program or activity, an individual with handicaps who meets the essential eligibility requirements for participation

in, or receipt of benefits from, that program or activity; and

(3) *Qualified handicapped person* as that term is defined for purposes of employment in 29 CFR 1613.702(f), which is made applicable to this part by § 105–8.140.

Respondent means the organizational unit in which a complainant alleges that discrimination occurred.

Section 504 means section 504 of the Rehabilitation Act of 1973 (Pub. L. 93–112, 87 Stat. 394 (29 U.S.C. 794)), as amended by the Rehabilitation Act Amendments of 1974 (Pub. L. 93–516, 88 Stat. 1617); the Rehabilitation, Comprehensive Services, and Developmental Disabilities Amendments of 1978 (Pub. L. 95–602, 92 Stat. 2955); and the Rehabilitation Act Amendments of 1986 (Pub. L. 99–506, 100 Stat. 1810); the Civil Rights Restoration Act of 1987 (Pub. L. 100–259, 102 Stat. 28); and Handicapped Program Technical Amendments Act of 1988 (Pub. L. 100–630, 102 Stat. 3312). As used in this part, section 504 applies only to programs or activities conducted by the agency and not to federally assisted programs.

Substantial impairment means a significant loss of the integrity of finished materials, design quality, or special character resulting from a permanent alteration of historic properties.

§§ 105–8.104—105–8.109 [Reserved]

§ 105–8.110 Self-evaluation.

(a) The agency shall, by March 9, 1992, evaluate its current policies and practices, and the effects thereof, that do not or may not meet the requirements of this part, and, to the extent modification of any such policies and practices is required, the agency shall proceed to make the necessary modifications.

(b) The agency shall provide an opportunity to interested persons, including individuals with handicaps or organizations representing individuals with handicaps, to participate in the self-evaluation process by submitting comments (both oral and written).

(c) The agency shall, for at least three years following completion of the self-evaluation, maintain on file and make available for public inspection:

(1) A list of interested persons consulted;

(2) A description of the areas examined and any problems identified and;

(3) A description of any modifications made or to be made.

§ 105–8.111 Notice.

The agency shall make available to employees, applicants, participants, beneficiaries, and other interested persons such information regarding the provisions of this part and its applicability to the programs or activities conducted by the agency, and make such information available to them in such manner as the Administrator finds necessary to apprise such persons of the protections against discrimination assured them by section 504 and this part.

§§ 105–8.112—105–8.129 [Reserved]

§ 105–8.130 General prohibitions against discrimination.

(a) No qualified individual with handicaps shall, on the basis of handicap, be excluded from participation in, be denied the benefits of, or otherwise be subjected to discrimination under any program or activity conducted by the agency.

(1) The agency, in providing any aid, benefit, or service, may not, directly or through contractual, licensing, or other arrangements, on the basis of handicap—

(i) Deny a qualified individual with handicaps the opportunity to participate in or benefit from the aid, benefit, or service;

(ii) Afford a qualified individual with handicaps an opportunity to participate in or benefit from aid, benefit, or service that is not equal to that afforded others;

(iii) Provide a qualified individual with handicaps with an aid, benefit, or service that is not as effective in affording equal opportunity to obtain the same result, to gain the same benefit, or to reach the same level of achievement as that provided to others;

(iv) Provide different or separate aid, benefits, or services to individuals with handicaps or to any class of individuals with handicaps than is provided to others unless such action is necessary to provide qualified individuals with handicaps with aid, benefits, or services that are as effective as those provided to others;

(v) Deny a qualified individual with handicaps the opportunity to participate as a member of planning or advisory boards; or

(vi) Otherwise limit a qualified individual with handicaps in the enjoyment of any right, privilege, advantage, or opportunity enjoyed by others receiving the aid, benefit, or service.

(2) The agency may not deny a qualified individual with handicaps the opportunity to participate in programs or activities that are not separate or different, despite the existence of permissibly separate or different programs or activities.

(3) The agency may not, directly or through contractual or other arrangements, utilize criteria or methods of administration the purpose or effect of which would—

(i) Subject qualified individuals with handicaps to discrimination on the basis of handicap; or

(ii) Defeat or substantially impair accomplishment of the objectives of a program or activity with respect to individuals with handicaps.

(4) The agency may not, in determining the site or location of a facility, make selections the purpose or effect of which would—

(i) Exclude individuals with handicaps from, deny them the benefits of, or otherwise subject them to discrimination under any program or activity conducted by the agency; or

(ii) Defeat or substantially impair the accomplishment of the objectives of a program or activity with respect to individuals with handicaps.

(5) The agency, in the selection of procurement contractors, may not use criteria that subject qualified individuals with handicaps to discrimination on the basis of handicap.

(6) The agency may not administer a licensing or certification program in a manner that subjects qualified individuals with handicaps to discrimination on the basis of handicap, nor may the agency establish requirements for the programs or activities of licenses or certified entities that subject qualified individuals with handicaps to discrimi-

nation on the basis of handicap. However, the programs or activities of entities that are licensed or certified by the agency are not, themselves, covered by part.

(b) The exclusion of persons without handicaps from the benefits of a program limited by Federal statute or Executive order to individuals with handicaps or the exclusion of a specific class of individuals with handicaps from a program limited by Federal statute or Executive order to a different class of individuals with handicaps is not prohibited by this part.

(c) The agency shall administer programs and activities in the most integrated setting appropriate to the needs of qualified individuals with handicaps.

§§ 105–8.131—105–8.139 [Reserved]

§ 105–8.140 Employment.

No qualified individual with handicaps shall, on the basis of handicap, be subjected to discrimination in employment under any program or activity conducted by the agency. The definitions, requirements, and procedures of section 501 of the Rehabilitation Act of 1973 (29 U.S.C. 791), as established by the Equal Employment Opportunity Commission in 29 CFR part 1613, shall apply to employment in federally conducted programs or activities.

§§ 105–8.141—105–8.147 [Reserved]

§ 105–8.148 Consultation with the Architectural and Transportation Barriers Compliance Board.

GSA shall consult with the Architectural and Transportation Barriers Compliance Board (ATBCB) in carrying out its responsibilities under this part concerning architectural barriers in facilities that are subject to GSA control. GSA shall also consult with the ATBCB in providing technical assistance to other Federal agencies with respect to overcoming architectural barriers in facilities. The agency's Public Buildings Service shall implement this section.

§ 105–8.149 Program accessibility: Discrimination prohibited.

Except as otherwise provided in §§ 105–8.150 and 105–8.154, no qualified individual with handicaps shall, because the agency's facilities are inaccessible to or unusable by individuals with handicaps, be denied the benefits of, be excluded from participation in, or otherwise be subjected to discrimination under any program or activity conducted by the agency.

§ 105–8.150 Program accessibility: Existing facilities.

§ 105–8.150–1 General.

The agency shall operate each program or activity so that the program or activity, when viewed in its entirety, is readily accessible to and usable by individuals with handicaps. This section does not—

(a) Necessarily require the agency to make each of its existing facilities accessible to and usable by individuals with handicaps; or

(b) In the case of historic preservation programs, require the agency to take any action that would result in a substantial impairment of significant historic features of an historic property.

§ 105–8.150–2 Methods.

(a) *General.* The agency may comply with the requirements of § 105–8.150 through such means as redesign of equipment, reassignment of services to accessible buildings, assignment of aides to beneficiaries, home visits, delivery of services at alternate accessible sites, alteration of existing facilities and construction of new facilities, use of accessible rolling stock, or any other methods that result in making its programs or activities readily accessible to and usable by individuals with handicaps. The agency is not required to make structural changes in existing facilities where other methods are effective in achieving compliance with this section. The agency, in making alterations to existing buildings, shall meet accessibility requirements to the extent compelled by the Architectural Barriers Act of 1968, as amended (42 U.S.C. 4151–4157), and any regulations implementing it. In choosing among available methods for meeting the requirements of this section, the agency shall give priority to those methods that offer programs and activities to qualified individuals with handicaps in the most integrated setting appropriate.

(b) *Historic preservation programs.* In meeting the requirements of § 105–8.105–1 in historic preservation programs, the agency shall give priority to methods that provide physical access to individuals with handicaps. In cases where a physical alteration to a historic property is not required because of § 105–8.105–1(b) or § 105–8.154 alternative methods of achieving program accessibility include—

(1) Using audio-visual materials and devices to depict those portions of a historic property that cannot otherwise be made accessible;

(2) Assigning persons to guide individuals with handicaps into or through portions of historic properties that cannot otherwise be made accessible; or

(3) Adopting other innovative methods.

§ 105–8.150–3 Time period for compliance.

The agency shall comply with the obligations established under § 105–8.150 by May 7, 1991; except where structural changes in facilities are undertaken, such changes shall be made by March 8, 1994, but in any event as expeditiously as possible.

§ 105–8.150–4 Transition plan.

In the event that structural changes to facilities will be undertaken to achieve program accessibility, the agency shall develop, by March 9, 1992; the transition plan setting forth the steps necessary to complete such changes. The agency shall provide an opportunity to interested persons, including individuals with handicaps or organizations representing individuals with handicaps, to participate in the development of the transition plan by submitting comments (both oral and written). A copy of the transition plan shall be made available for public inspection. The plan shall, at a minimum—

(a) Identify physical obstacles in the facilities occupied by GSA that limit the accessibility of its programs or activities to individuals with handicaps;

(b) Describe in detail the methods that will be used to make the facilities accessible;

(c) Specify the schedule for taking the steps necessary to achieve compliance with § 105–8.150 and, if the time period of the transition plan is longer than one year, identify steps that will be taken during each year of the transition period; and

(d) Indicate the official responsible for implementation of the plan.

§ 105–8.151 Program accessibility: New construction and alterations.

Each building or part of a building that is constructed or altered by, on behalf of, of for the use of the agency shall be designed, constructed, or altered so as to be readily accessible to and usable by individuals with handicaps. The definitions, requirements, and standards of the Architectural Barriers Act (42 U.S.C. 4151–4157), as established in 41 CFR 101–19.600 to 101–19.607, apply to buildings covered by this section.

§ 105–8.152 Program accessibility: Assignment of space.

(a) When GSA assigns or reassigns space to an agency, it shall consult with the agency to ensure that the assignment or reassignment will not result in one or more of the agency's programs or activities being inaccessible to individuals with handicaps.

(b) Prior to the assignment or reassignment of space to an agency, GSA shall inform the agency of the accessibility, and/or the absence of accessibility features, of the space in which GSA intends to locate the agency. If the agency informs GSA that the use of the space will result in one or more of the agency's programs being inaccessible, GSA shall take one or more of the following actions to make the programs accessible:

(1) Arrange for alterations, improvements, and repairs to buildings and facilities;

(2) Locate and provide alternative space that will not result in one or more of the agency's programs being inaccessible; or

(3) Take any other actions that result in making this agency's programs accessible.

The responsibility for payment to make the physical changes in the space shall be assigned on a case-by-case basis as agreed to by GSA and the user agency, dependent on individual circumstances.

(c) GSA may not require the agency to accept space that results in one or more of the agency's programs being inaccessible.

§ 105–8.153 Program accessibility: Interagency cooperation.

§ 105–8.153–1 General.

GSA, upon request from an occupant agency engaged in the development of a transition plan under section 504, shall participate with the occupant agency in the development and implementation of the transition plan and shall provide information and guidance to the occupant agency. Upon request, GSA shall conduct space inspections to assist the agency in determining whether a current assignment of space results in one or more of the occupant agency's programs or activities being inaccessible. GSA shall provide the occupant agency with a written summary of significant findings and recommendations, together with data concerning programmed repairs and alterations planned by GSA and alterations that can be effected by the agency.

§ 105–8.153–2 Requests from occupant agencies.

(a) Upon receipt of an occupant agency's request for new space, additional space, relocation to accessible space, alterations, or other actions under GSA's control that are needed to ensure program accessibility in the requesting agency's program(s) as required by the agency's section 504 transition plan, GSA shall assist or advise the requesting agency in providing or arranging for the requested action within the timeframes specified in the requesting agency's transition plan.

(b) If the requested action cannot be completed within the time frame specified in an agency's transition plan, GSA shall so advise the requesting agency within 30 days of the request by submitting, after consultation with the agency, a revised schedule specifying the date by which the action shall be completed. If the delay in completing the action results in or continues the inaccessibility of the requesting agency's program, GSA and the agency shall, after consultation, take interim measures to make the agency's program accessible.

(c) If GSA determines that it is unable to take the requested action, GSA shall—

(1) Within 30 days, set forth in writing to the requesting agency the reasons for denying the agency's request, and

(2) Within 90 days, propose to the requesting agency other methods for making the agency's program accessible.

(d) Receipt of a copy of an occupant agency's transition plan under section 504 shall constitute notice to GSA of the requested actions in the transition plan and of the times frames which the actions are required to be completed.

§ 105–8.154 Program accessibility: Exceptions.

Sections 105–8.150, 105–8.152, and 105–8.153 do not require GSA to take any action that it can demonstrate would result in a fundamental alteration in the nature of a program or activity or in undue financial and administrative burdens. In those circumstances where GSA personnel believe that the proposed action would fundamentally alter the program or activity or would result in undue financial and administrative burdens, the agency has the burden of proving that compliance would result in such alteration or burdens. The decision that compliance would result in such alteration or burdens must be made by the Administrator or his or her designee after considering all resources available for use in the funding and operation of the conducted program or activity, and must be accompanied by a written statement of the reasons for reaching that conclusion. If an action would result in such an alteration or such burdens, the agency shall take any other action that would not result in such an alteration or such burdens but would nevertheless ensure that individuals with handicaps receive the benefits and services of the program or activity.

§§ 105–8.155—105–8.159 [Reserved]

§ 105–8.160 Communications.

(a) The agency shall take appropriate steps to ensure effective communication with applicants, participants, personnel of other Federal entities, and members of the public.

(1) The agency shall furnish appropriate auxiliary aids where necessary to afford an individual with handicaps an equal opportunity to participate in, and enjoy the benefits of, a program or activity conducted by the agency.

(i) In determining what type of auxiliary aid is necessary, the agency shall give primary consideration to the requests of the individual with handicaps.

(ii) The agency need not provide individually prescribed devices, readers for personal use or study, or other devices of a personal nature.

(2) Where the agency communicates with applicants and beneficiaries by telephone, telecommunication devices for deaf persons (TDD) or equally effective telecommunication systems shall be used to communicate with persons with impaired hearing.

(b) The agency shall ensure that interested persons, including persons with impaired vision or hearing, can obtain information as to the existence and location of accessible services, activities, and facilities.

(c) The agency shall provide signage at a primary entrance to each of its inaccessible facilities, directing users to a location at which they can obtain information about accessible facilities. The international symbol for accessibility shall be used at each primary entrance of an accessible facility.

(d) This section does not require the agency to take any action that it can demonstrate would result in a fundamental alteration in the nature of a program or activity or in undue financial and administrative burdens. In those circumstances where agency personnel believe that the proposed action would fundamentally alter the program or activity or would result in undue financial and administrative burdens, the agency has the burden of proving that compliance with § 150.8.160 would result in such alteration or burdens.

The decision that compliance would result in such alteration or burdens must be made by the Administrator or his or her designee after considering all agency resources available for use in the funding and operation of the conducted program or activity and must be accompanied by a written statement of the reasons for reaching that conclusion. If an action required to comply with § 105–8.160 would result in such an alteration or such burdnes, the agency shall take any other action that would not result in such an alteration or such burdens but would nevertheless ensure that, to the maximum extent possible, individuals with handicaps receive the benefits and services of the program or activity.

§§ 105–8.161—105–8.169 [Reserved]

§ 105–8.170 Compliance procedures.

§ 105–8.170–1 Applicability.

Except as provided in § 105–8.170–2, §§ 105–8.170 through 105–8.170–13 apply to all allegations of discrimination on the basis of handicap in programs or activities conducted by the agency.

§ 105–8.170–2 Employment complaints.

The agency shall process complaints alleging violations of section 504 with respect to employment according to the procedures established by the Equal Employment Opportunity Commission in 29 CFR part 1613 pursuant to section 501 of the Rehabilitation Act of 1973 (29 U.S.C. 791).

§ 105–8.170–3 Responsible Official.

The Responsible Official shall coordinate implementation of §§ 105–8.170 through 105–8.170–13.

§ 105–8.170–4 Filing a complaint.

(a) *Who may file a complaint.* Any person who believes that he or she has been subjected to discrimination prohibited by this part may by him or herself or by his or her authorized representative file a complaint with the Official. Any persons who believes that any specific class of persons has been subjected to discrimination prohibited by this part and who is a member of that class or the authorized representative of a member of that class may file a complaint with the Official.

(b) *Confidentiality.* The Official shall hold in confidence the identity of any person submitting a complaint, unless the person submits written authorization otherwise, and except to the extent necessary to carry out the purposes of this part, including the conduct of any investigation, hearing, or proceeding under this part.

(c) *When to file.* Complaints shall be filed within 180 days of the alleged act of discrimination. The Official may extend this time limit for good cause shown. For purposes of determining when a complaint is timely filed under this section, a complaint mailed to the agency shall be deemed filed on the date it is postmarked. Any other complaint shall be deemed filed on the date it is recevied by the agency.

(d) *How to file.* Complaints may be delivered or mailed to the Administrator, the Responsible Official, or other agency officials. Complaints should be sent to the Director of Civil Rights, Civil Rights Division (AKC), General Services Administration, 18th and F Streets, NW., Washington, DC 20405. If any agency official other than the Official receives a complaint, he or she shall forward the complaint to the Official immediately.

§ 105–8.170–5 Notification to the Architectural and Transportation Barriers Compliance Board.

The agency shall prepare and forward comprehensive quarterly reports to the Architectural and Transportation Barriers Compliance Board containing information regarding complaints received alleging that a building or facility that is subject to the Architectural Barriers Act of 1968, as amended (42 U.S.C. 4151–4157), is not readily accessible to and usable by individuals with handicaps. The agency shall not include in the report the identity of any complainant.

§ 105–8.170–6 Acceptance of complaint.

(a) The Official shall accept a complete complaint that is filed in accordance with § 105–8.170–4 and over which the agency has jurisdiction. The Official shall notify the complainant and the respondent of receipt and acceptance of the complaint.

(b) If the Official receives a complaint that is not complete, he or she shall notify the complainant within 30 days of receipt of the incomplete complaint that additional information is needed. If the complainant fails to complete the complaint within 30 days of receipt of this notice, the Official shall dismiss the complaint without prejudice.

(c) The Official may reject a complaint, or a position thereof, for any of the following reasons:

(1) It was not filed timely and the extension of the 180-day period as provided in § 105–8.170–4(c) is denied;

(2) It consists of an allegation identical to an allegation contained in a previous complaint filed on behalf of the same complainant(s) which is pending in the agency or which has been resolved or decided by the agency; or

(3) It is not within the purview of this part.

(d) If the Official receives a complaint over which the agency does not have jurisdiction, the Official shall promptly notify the complainant and shall make reasonable efforts to refer the complaint to the appropriate Government entity.

§ 105–8.170–7 Investigation/conciliation.

(a) Within 180 days of the receipt of a complete complaint, the Official shall complete the investigation of the complaint, attempt informal resolution, and if no informal resolution is achieved, issue a letter of findings. The 180-day time limit may be extended with the permission of the Assistant Attorney General. The investigation should include, where appropriate, a review of the practices and policies that led to the filing of the complaint, and other circumstances under which the possible noncompliance with this part occurred.

(b) The Official may require agency employees to cooperate in the investigation and attempted resolution of complaints. Employees who are required by the Official to participate in any investigation under this section shall do so as part of their official duties and during the course of regular duty hours.

(c) The Official shall furnish the complainant and the respondent a copy of the investigative report promptly after receiving it from the investigator and provide the complainant and the respondent with an opportunity for informal resolution of the complaint.

(d) If a complaint is resolved informally, the terms of the agreement shall be reduced to writing and signed by the complainant and respondent. The agreement shall be made part of the complaint file with a copy of the agreement provided to the complainant and the respondent. The written agreement may include a finding on the issue of discrimination and shall describe any corrective action to which the complainant and the respondent have agreed.

(e) The written agreement shall remain in effect until all corrective actions to which the complainant and the respondent have agreed upon have been completed. The complainant may reopen the complaint in the event that the agreement is not carried out.

§ 105–8.170–8 Letter of findings.

If an informal resolution of the complaint is not reached, the Official shall, within 180 days of receipt of the complete complaint, notify the complainant and the respondent of the results of the investigation in a letter sent by certified mail, return receipt requested. The letter shall contain, at a minimum, the following:

(a) Findings of fact and conclusions of law;

(b) A description of a remedy for each violation found;

(c) A notice of the right of the complainant and the respondent to appeal to the Special Counsel for Ethics and Civil Rights; and

(d) A notice of the right of the complainant and the respondent to request a hearing.

§ 105–8.170–9 Filing an appeal.

(a) Notice of appeal to the Special Counsel for Ethics and Civil Rights, with or without a request for hearing, shall be filed by the complainant or the respondent with the Responsible Official within 30 days of receipt of the letter of findings required by § 105–8.170–7.

(b) If a timely appeal without a request for hearing is filed by a party, any other party may file a written request for a hearing within the time limit specified in § 105–8.170–9(a) or within 10 days of the date on which the first timely appeal without a request for hearing was filed, whichever is later.

(c) If no party requests a hearing, the Responsible Official shall promptly transmit the notice of appeal and investigative record to the Special Counsel for Ethics and Civil Rights.

(d) If neither party files an appeal within the time prescribed in § 105–8.170–9(a) the Responsible Official shall certify, at the expiration of the time, that the letter of findings is the final agency decision on the complaint.

§ 105–8.170–10 Acceptance of appeals.

The Special Counsel shall accept and process any timely appeal. A party may appeal to the Deputy Administrator from a decision of the Special Counsel that an appeal is untimely. This appeal shall be filed within 15 days of receipt of the decision from the Special Counsel.

§ 105–8.170–11 Hearing.

(a) Upon a timely request for a hearing, the Special Counsel shall take the necessary action to obtain the services of an Administrative law judge (ALJ) to conduct the hearing. The ALJ shall issue a notice to all parties specifying the date, time, and place of the scheduled hearing. The hearing shall be commenced no earlier than 15 days after the notice is issued and no later than 60 days after the request for a hearing is filed, unless all parties agree to a different date, or there are other extenuating circumstances.

(b) The complainant and respondent shall be parties to the hearing. Any interested person or organization may petition to become a party or amicus curiae. The ALJ may, in his or her discretion, grant such a petition if, in his or her opinion, the petitioner has a legitimate interest in the proceedings and the participation will not unduly delay the outcome and may contribute materially to the proper disposition of the proceedings.

(c) The hearing, decision, and any administrative review thereof shall be conducted in conformity with 5 U.S.C. 554–557 (sections 5–8 of the Administrative Procedure Act). The ALJ shall have the duty to conduct a fair hearing, to take all necessary action to avoid delay, and to maintain order. He or she shall have all powers necessary to these ends, including (but not limited to) the power to—

(1) Arrange and change the date, time, and place of hearings and prehearing conferences and issue notices thereof;

(2) Hold conferences to settle, simplify, or determine the issue in a hearing, or to consider other matters that may aid in the expeditious disposition of the hearing;

(3) Require parties to state their position in writing with respect to the various issues in the hearing and to exchange such statements with all other parties;

(4) Examine witnesses and direct witnesses to testify;

(5) Receive, rule on, exclude, or limit evidence;

(6) Rule on procedural items pending before him or her; and

(7) Take any action permitted to the ALJ as authorized by this part, or by the provisions of the Administrative Procedure Act (5 U.S.C. 551–559).

(d) Technical rules of evidence shall not apply to hearings conducted pursuant to § 105–8.170–11, but rules or principles designed to assure production of credible evidence available and to subject testimony to cross-examination shall be applied by the ALJ whenever reasonably necessary. The ALJ may exclude irrelevant, immaterial, or unduly repetitious evidence. All documents and other evidence offered or taken for the record shall be open to examination by the parties and opportunity shall be given to refute facts and arguments advanced on either side of the issues. A transcript shall be made of the oral evidence except to the extent the substance thereof is stipulated for the record. All decisions shall be based upon the hearing record.

(e) The costs and expenses for the conduct of a hearing shall be allocated as follows:

(1) Persons employed by the agency shall, upon request to the agency by the ALJ, be made available to participate in the hearing and shall be on official duty status for this purpose. They shall not receive witness fees.

(2) Employees of other Federal agencies called to testify at a hearing shall, at the request of the ALJ and with the approval of the employing agency, be on official duty status during any period of absence from normal duties caused by their testimony, and shall not receive witness fees.

(3) The fees and expenses of other persons called to testify at a hearing shall be paid by the party requesting their appearance.

(4) The ALJ may require the agency to pay travel expenses necessary for the complainant to attend the hearing.

(5) The respondent shall pay the required expenses and charges for the ALJ and court reporter.

(6) All other expenses shall be paid by the party, the intervening party, or amicus curiae incurring them.

(f) The ALJ shall submit in writing recommended findings of fact, conclusions of law, and remedies to all parties and the Special Counsel for Ethics and Civil Rights within 30 days after receipt of the hearing transcripts, or within 30 days after the conclusion of the hearing if no transcript is made. This time limit may be extended with the permission of the Special Counsel.

(g) Within 15 days after receipt of the recommended decision of the ALJ any party may file exceptions to the decision with the Special Counsel. Thereafter, each party will have ten days to file reply exceptions with the Special Counsel.

§ 105–8.170–12 Decision.

(a) The Special Counsel shall make the decision of the agency based on information in the investigative record and, if a hearing is held, on the hearing record. The decision shall be made within 60 days of receipt of the transmittal of the notice of appeal and investitive record pursuant to § 105–8.170–9(c) or after the period for filing exceptions ends, which ever is applica-

ble. If the Special Counsel for Ethics and Civil Rights determines that he or she needs additional information from any party, he or she shall request the information and provide the other party or parties an opportunity to respond to that information. The Special Counsel shall have 60 days from receipt of the additional information to render the decision on the appeal. The Special Counsel shall transmit his or her decision by letter to the parties. The time limits established in this paragraph may be extended with the permission of the Assistant Attorney General. The decision shall set forth the findings, remedial action required, and reasons for the decision. If the decision is based on a hearing record, the Special Counsel shall consider the recommended decision of the ALJ and render a final decision based on the entire record. The Special Counsel may also remand the hearing record to the ALJ for a fuller development of the record.

(b) Any respondent required to take action under the terms of the decision of the agency shall do so promptly. The Official may require periodic compliance reports specifying—

(1) The manner in which compliance with the provisions of the decision has been achieved;

(2) The reasons any action required by the final decision has not yet been taken; and

(3) The steps being taken to ensure full compliance. The Official may retain responsibility for resolving disagreements that arise between the parties over interpretation fo the final agency decision or for specific adjudicatory decisions arising out of implementation.

§ 105–8.170–13 Delegation.

The agency may delegate its authority for conducting complaint investigations to other Federal agencies, except that the authority for making the final determination may not be delegated to another agency.

§ 105–8.171 Complaints against an occupant agency.

(a) Upon notification by an occupant agency that it has received a complete complaint alleging that the agency's program is inaccessible because existing facilities under GSA's control are not accessible and usable by individuals with handicaps, GSA shall be jointly responsible with the agency for resolving the complaint and shall participate in making findings of fact and conclusions of law in prescribing and implementing appropriate remedies for each violation found.

(b) GSA shall make reasonable efforts to follow the time frames for complaint resolution that go into effect under the notifying occupant agency's compliance procedures when it receives a complete complaint.

(c) Receipt of a copy of the complete complaint by GSA shall constitute notification to GSA for purposes of § 105-8.171(a).

PART 105–50—PROVISION OF SPECIAL OR TECHNICAL SERVICES TO STATE AND LOCAL UNITS OF GOVERNMENT

AUTHORITY: Sec. 205(c), 63 Stat. 390; 40 U.S.C. 486(c) and sec. 302, 82 Stat. 1102; 42 U.S.C. 4222.

SOURCE: 41 FR 21451, May 26, 1976, unless otherwise noted.

§ 105–50.000   Scope of part.

This part prescribes rules and procedures governing the provision of special or technical services to State and local units of government by GSA. This part also prescribes principles governing reimbursements for such services.

§ 105–50.001   Definitions.

The following definitions are established for terms used in this part.

§ 105–50.001–1   State.

State means any of the several States of the United States, the District of Columbia, Puerto Rico, any territory or possession of the United States, or any agency or instrumentality of a State, but does not include the governments of the political subdivisions of the State.

§ 105–50.001–2   Political subdivision or local government.

Political subdivision or *local government* means a local unit of government, including specifically a county, municipality, city, town, township, or a school or other special district created by or pursuant to State law.

§105–50.001–3 Unit of general local government.

Unit of general local government means any city, county, town, parish, village, or other general purpose political subdivision of a State.

§105–50.001–4 Special-purpose unit of local government.

Special-purpose unit of local government means any special district, public-purpose corporation, or other strictly limited-purpose political subdivision of a State, but shall not include a school district.

§105–50.001–5 Specialized or technical services.

Specialized or technical services means statistical and other studies and compilations, development projects, technical tests and evaluations, technical information, training activities, surveys, reports, documents, and any other similar service functions which any department or agency of the executive branch of the Federal Government is especially equipped and authorized by law to perform.

§105–50.001–6 GSA.

GSA means the General Services Administration.

Subpart 105–50.1—General Provisions

§105–50.101 Purpose.

(a) This part 105–50 implements the provisions of Title III of the Intergovernmental Cooperation Act of 1968 (82 Stat. 1102, 42 U.S.C. 4221–4225), the purpose of which is stated as follows:

It is the purpose of this title to encourage intergovernmental cooperation in the conduct of specialized or technical services and provision of facilities essential to the administration of State or local governmental activities, many of which are nationwide in scope and financed in part by Federal funds; to enable state and local governments to avoid unnecessary duplication of special service functions; and to authorize all departments and agencies of the executive branch of the Federal Government which do not have such authority to provide reimbursable specialized or technical services to State and local governments.

(b) This part is consistent with the rules and regulations promulgated by the Director, Office of Management and Budget, in the Office of Management and Budget Circular No. A–97, dated August 29, 1969, issued pursuant to section 302 of the cited Act (42 U.S.C. 4222).

§105–50.102 Applicability.

This part is applicable to all organizational elements of GSA insofar as the services authorized to be performed in subpart 105–50.2 fall within their designated functional areas.

§105–50.103 Policy.

It is the policy of GSA to cooperate to the maximum extent possible with State and local units of government in providing the specialized or technical services authorized within the limitations set forth in §105–50.104.

§105–50.104 Limitations.

The specialized or technical services provided under this part may be provided, in the discretion of the Administrator of General Services, only under the following conditions:

(a) Such services will be provided only to the States, political subdivisions thereof, and combinations or associations of such governments or their agencies and instrumentalities.

(b) Such services will be provided only upon the written request of a State or political subdivision thereof. Requests normally will be made by the chief executives of such entities and will be addressed to the General Services Administration as provided in §105–50.105.

(c) Such services will not be provided unless GSA is providing similar services for its own use under the policies set forth in the Office of Management and Budget Circular No. A–76 Revised, dated August 30, 1967, subject: Policies for acquiring commercial or industrial products and services for Government use. In addition, in accordance with the policies set forth in Circular No. A–76, the requesting entity must certify that such services cannot be procured reasonably and expeditiously through ordinary business channels.

(d) Such services will not be provided if they require any additions of staff or involve outlays for additional equipment or other facilities solely for the purpose of providing such services, except where the costs thereof are charged to the user of such services. Further, no staff additions may be made which impede the implementation of, or adherence to, the employment ceilings contained in the Office of Management and Budget allowance letters.

(e) Such services will be provided only upon payment or provision for reimbursement by the unit of government making the request of salaries and all other identifiable direct and indirect costs of performing such services. For cost determination purposes, GSA will be guided by the policies set forth in the Office of Management and Budget Circular No. A–25, dated September 23, 1959, subject: User charges.

§ 105–50.105   Coordination of requests.

(a) All inquiries of a general nature concerning services GSA can provide shall be addressed to the General Services Administration (BR), Washington, DC 20405. The Director of Management Services, Office of Administration, shall serve as the central coordinator for such inquiries and shall assign them to the appropriate organizational element of GSA for expeditious handling.

(b) Requests for specific services may be addressed directly to Heads of Services and Staff Offices and to Regional Administrators. Section 105–50.202 describes the specific services GSA can provide.

(c) If the proper GSA organizational element is not known to the State or local unit of government, the request shall be addressed as in paragraph (a) of this section to ensure appropriate handling.

§ 105–50.106   GSA response to requests.

(a) Direct response to each request shall be made by the Head of the applicable Service or Staff Office or Regional Administrator. He shall outline the service to be provided and the fee or reimbursement required. Any special conditions concerning time and priority, etc., shall be stated. Written acceptance by the authorized State or local governmental entity shall constitute a binding agreement.

(b) Heads of Services and Staff Offices and Regional Administrators shall maintain complete records and controls of services provided on a calendar year basis to facilitate accurate, annual reporting, as required in § 105–50.401.

Subpart 105–50.2—Services Available From General Services Administration

§ 105–50.201   Agencywide mission.

(a) In its role as a central property management agency, GSA constructs, leases, operates, and maintains office and other space: procures and distributes supplies; coordinates and provides for the economic and efficient purchase, lease, sharing, and maintenance of automatic data processing equipment by Federal agencies; manages stockpiles of materials maintained for use in national emergencies; transfers excess real and personal property among Federal agencies for further use; disposes of surplus real and personal property, by donation or otherwise, as well as materials excess to stockpile requirements; operates centralized data processing centers and telecommunications and motor pool systems; operates the National Archives and Presidential libraries; and provides a variety of records management services, including the operation of centers for storing and administering records, as well as other common services.

(b) Special or technical services may be provided by many organizational elements of GSA with respect to their functional areas, but the requesting State or local agency needs only to know that the service desired is related to one or more of the functional areas described above and direct its request as provided for under § 105–50.105. State and local units of government are also encouraged to consult the "Catalog of Federal Domestic Assistance" as a more complete guide to the many other Federal assistance programs available to them. The catalog, issued annually and updated periodically by the Office of Management and Budget, is available through the Superintendent of

Documents, Government Printing Office, Washington, DC 20402.

§ 105–50.202 Specific services.

Within the functional areas identified in § 105–50.201, GSA can provide the services hereinafter described.

§ 105–50.202–1 Copies of statistical or other studies.

This material includes a copy of any existing statistical or other studies and compilations, results of technical tests and evaluations, technical information, surveys, reports, and documents, and any such materials which may be developed or prepared in the future to meet the needs of the Federal Government or to carry out normal program responsibilities of GSA.

§ 105–50.202–2 Preparation of or assistance in the conduct of statistical or other studies.

(a) This service includes preparation of statistical or other studies and compilations, technical tests and evaluations, technical information, surveys, reports, and documents and assistance in the conduct of such activities and in the preparation of such materials, provided they are of a type similar to those which GSA is authorized by law to conduct or prepare and when resources are available.

(b) Specific areas in which GSA can conduct or participate in the conduct of studies include:

(1) Space management, including assignment and utilization;

(2) Supply management, including laboratory tests and evaluations;

(3) Management of motor vehicles;

(4) Archives and records management;

(5) Automatic data processing systems; and

(6) Telecommunications and teleprocessing systems and services.

§ 105–50.202–3 Training.

(a) This training consists of the type which GSA is authorized by law to conduct for Federal personnel and others or which is similar to such training.

(b) Descriptions of the specific training courses conducted by GSA are published annually in the Interagency Training Programs bulletin, copies of which are available from the U.S. Civil Service Commission, Washington, D.C. 20415.

§ 105–50.202–4 Technical assistance incident to Federal surplus personal property.

Technical assistance will be provided in the screening and selection of surplus personal property under existing laws, provided such aid primarily strengthens the ability of the recipient in developing its own capacity to prepare proposals.

§ 105–50.202–5 Data processing services.

GSA will develop ADP logistical feasibility studies, software, systems analyses, and programs. To the extent that data processing capabilities are available, GSA will also assist in securing data processing services on a temporary, short term basis from other Federal facilities or Federal Data Processing Centers.

§ 105–50.202–6 Communications services.

GSA will continue to make its bulk rate circuit ordering services available for use by State and local governments. Under a revised tariff effective December 12, 1971, GSA will bill the State and local governments for their share of the TEL PAK costs. Services provided prior to December 12, 1971, will be billed by the contractors under the former arrangements. In addition, certain activities, such as surplus property agencies which have frequent communications with Federal agencies, will be given access to the Federal Telecommunications System switchboards.

§ 105–50.202–7 Technical information and advice.

GSA will provide technical information, personnel management systems services, and technical advice on improving logistical and management services which GSA normally provides for itself or others under existing authorities.

Subpart 105–50.3—Principles Governing Reimbursements to GSA

§ 105–50.301   Established fees.

Where there is an established schedule of fees for services to other Government agencies or the public, the schedule shall be used as the basis for reimbursement for like services furnished to State and local governments.

§ 105–50.302   Special fee schedules.

Where there is no established schedule of fees for types of service which are ordinarily reimbursed on a fee basis, such schedules may be developed and promulgated in conjunction with the Office of Administration. The fees so established shall cover all direct costs, such as salaries of personnel involved plus personnel benefits, travel, and other related expenses and all indirect costs such as management, supervisory, and staff support expenses determined or estimated from the best available records in GSA. Periodically, fees shall be reviewed for adequacy of recovery and adjusted as necessary.

§ 105–50.303   Cost basis in lieu of fees.

Where the cost of services is to be recovered on other than a fee basis, upon receipt of a request from a State or local government for such services, a written reply shall be prepared by the service or staff office receiving the request stating the basis for reimbursement for the services to be performed. The proposal shall be based on an estimate of all direct costs, such as salaries of personnel involved plus personnel benefits, travel, and other related expenses and on such indirect costs as management, supervisory, and staff support expenses. An appropriate surcharge may be developed to recover these indirect costs. The terms thereof shall be concurred in by the Director of Administration. Acceptance in writing by the requester shall constitute a binding agreement between GSA and the requesting governmental unit.

§ 105–50.304   Services provided through revolving funds.

Where the service furnished is of the type which GSA is now billing through revolving funds, reimbursement shall be obtained from State and local governments on the same basis; i.e., the same pricing method, billing forms, and billing support shall be used.

§ 105–50.304a   Deposits.

Reimbursements to GSA for furnishing special or technical services to State and local units of government will be deposited to the credit of the appropriation from which the cost of providing such services has been paid or is to be charged if such reimbursements are authorized. Otherwise, the reimbursements will be credited to miscellaneous receipts in the U.S. Treasury (42 U.S.C. 4223).

§ 105–50.305   Exemptions.

(a) Single copies of existing reports covering studies and statistical compilations and other data or publications for which there is no established schedule of fees shall be furnished without charge unless significant expense is incurred in reproducing the material, in which instance the actual cost thereof shall be charged.

(b) GSA may, pursuant to section 302 of the Intergovernmental Personnel Act of 1970 (42 U.S.C. 4742), admit employees of State and local units of government to training programs established for professional, administrative, or technical personnel and may waive the requirement for reimbursement in whole or in part.

Subpart 105–50.4—Reports

§ 105–50.401   Reports submitted to the Congress.

(a) The Administrator of General Services will furnish annually to the respective Committees on Government Operations of the Senate and the House of Representatives a summary report on the scope of the services provided under Title III of the act and this part.

(b) Heads of Services and Staff Offices and all Regional Administrators shall furnish the Director of Management Services, OAD, by no later than January 15 of each year, the following information concerning services provided during the preceding calendar year to State and local units of government:

(1) A brief description of the services provided, including any other pertinent data;

(2) The State and/or local unit of government involved; and

(3) The cost of GSA to provide the service, including the amount of reimbursement, if any, made by the benefitting government.

(c) Reports Control Symbol LAW–27–OA is assigned to this report.

§ 105–50.402 Reports submitted to the Office of Management and Budget.

Copies of the foregoing reports will be submitted by the Administrator to the Office of Management and Budget not later than March 30 of each year.

PART 105–51—UNIFORM RELOCATION ASSISTANCE AND REAL PROPERTY ACQUISITION FOR FEDERAL AND FEDERALLY ASSISTED PROGRAMS

AUTHORITY: Sec. 213, Uniform Relocation Assistance and Real Property Acquisition Policies Act of 1970, Pub. L. 91–646, 84 Stat. 1894 (42 U.S.C. 4601) as amended by the Surface Transportation and Uniform Relocation Assistance Act of 1987, Title IV of Pub. L. 100–17, 101 Stat. 246–256 (42 U.S.C. 4601 note).

§ 105–51.001 Uniform relocation assistance and real property acquisition.

Regulations and procedures for complying with the Uniform Relocation Assistance and Real Property Acquisition Policies Act of 1970 (Pub. L. 91–646, 84 Stat. 1894, 42 U.S.C. 4601), as amended by the Surface Transportation and Uniform Relocation Assistance Act of 1987 (Title IV of Pub. L. 100–17, 101 Stat. 246–255, 42 U.S.C. 4601 note) are set forth in 49 CFR part 24.

[52 FR 48024, Dec. 17, 1987; 54 FR 8913, Mar. 2, 1989]

PART 105–53—STATEMENT OF ORGANIZATION AND FUNCTIONS

AUTHORITY: 5 U.S.C. 552(a)(1), Pub. L. 90–23, 81 Stat. 54 sec. (a)(1); 40 U.S.C. 486(c), Pub. L. 81–152, 63 Stat. 390, sec. 205(c).

SOURCE: 48 FR 25200, June 6, 1983, unless otherwise noted.

§ 105–53.100 Purpose.

This part is published in accordance with 5 U.S.C. 552 and is a general description of the General Services Administration.

Subpart A—General

§ 105–53.110 Creation and authority.

The General Services Administration was established by section 101 of the Federal Property and Administrative

Services Act of 1949 (63 Stat. 377), effective July 1, 1949. The act consolidated and transferred to the agency a variety of real and personal property and related functions fomerly assigned to various agencies. Subsequent laws and Executive orders assigned other related functions and programs.

§ 105-53.112 General statement of functions.

The General Services Administration, as a major policy maker, provides guidance and direction to Federal agencies in a number of management fields. GSA formulates and prescribes a variety of Governmentwide policies relating to procurement and contracting; real and personal property management; transportation, public transportation, public utilities and telecommunications management; automated data processing management; records management; the use and disposal of property; and the information security program. In addition to its policy role, GSA also provides a variety of basic services in the aforementioned areas to other Government agencies. A summary description of these services is presented by organizational component in subpart B.

[54 FR 26741, June 26, 1989]

§ 105-53.114 General statement of organization.

The General Services Administration is an independent agency in the executive branch of the Government. The work of the agency as a whole is directed by the Administrator of General Services, who is assisted by the Deputy Administrator. A summary description of each of GSA's major functions and organizational components is presented in subparts B and C.

§ 105-53.116 General regulations.

Regulations of the General Services Administration and its components are codified in the Code of Federal Regulations in title 1, chapters I and II; title 32, chapter XX; title 41, chapters 1, 5, 101, 105, and 201; and title 48, chapters 1 and 5. Titles 1, 32, 41, and 48 of the Code of Federal Regulations are available for review at most legal and depository libraries and at the General Services Administration Central Office and regional offices. Copies may be purchased from the Superintendent of Documents, Government Printing Office, Washington, DC 20402.

[49 FR 24995, June 19, 1984]

§ 105-53.118 Locations of material available for public inspection.

GSA maintains reading rooms containing materials available for public inspection and copying at the following locations:

(a) General Services Administration, 18th & F Streets, NW., Library (Room 1033), Washington, DC 20405. Telephone 202-535-7788.

(b) Business Service Center, General Services Administration, 10 Causeway Street, Boston, MA 02222. Telephone: 617-565-8100.

(c) Business Service Center, General Services Administration, 26 Federal Plaza, NY, NY 10278. Telephone: 212-264-1234.

(d) Business Service Center, General Services Administration, Seventh & D Streets, SW., Room 1050, Washington, DC 20407. Telephone: 202-472-1804.

(e) Business Service Center, General Services Administration, Ninth & Market Streets, Room 5151, Philadelphia, PA 19107. Telephone: 215-597-9613.

(f) Business Service Center, General Services Administration, Richard B. Russell Federal Building, U.S. Courthouse, 75 Spring Street, SW., Atlanta, GA 30303, Telephone: 404/331-5103.

(g) Business Service Center, General Services Administration, 230 South Dearborn Street, Chicago, IL 60604. Telephone: 312-353-5383.

(h) Business Service Center, General Services Administration, 1500 East Bannister Road, Kansas City, MO 64131. Telephone: 816-926-7203.

(i) Business Service Center, General Services Administration, 819 Taylor Street, Fort Worth, TX 76102. Telephone: 817-334-3284.

(j) Business Service Center, General Services Administration, Denver Federal Center, Denver, CO 80225. Telephone: 303-236-7408.

(k) Business Service Center, General Services Administration, 525 Market Street, San Francisco, CA 94105. Telephone: 415-974-9000.

(l) Business Service Center, General Services Administration, 300 North Los

Angeles Street, Room 3259, Los Angeles, CA 90012. Telephone: 213–688–3210.

(m) Business Service Center, General Services Administration, GSA Center, Auburn, WA 98001. Telephone: 206–931–7957.

[48 FR 25200, June 6, 1983, as amended at 49 FR 24995, June 19, 1984; 50 FR 26363, June 26, 1985; 51 FR 23229, June 26, 1986; 52 FR 23657, June 24, 1987; 53 FR 23761, June 24, 1988]

§ 105–53.120 Address and telephone numbers.

The Office of the Administrator; Office of Civil Rights; Office of Citizen Services and Innovative Technologies; Office of the Chief Information Officer; Office of Emergency Response and Recovery; Office of the Chief Financial Officer; Chief Administrative Services Officer; Office of Congressional and Intergovernmental Affairs; Office of Small Business Utilization; Office of General Counsel; Office of the Chief People Officer; Office of Communications and Marketing; Office of Governmentwide Policy; Public Buildings Service and the Office of Inspector General are located at 18th and F Streets NW., Washington, DC 20405. The Federal Acquisition Service is located at 2200 Crystal Drive Room 1000, Arlington, VA 22202–3713; however, the mailing address is Washington, DC 20406. The telephone number for the above addresses is 202–472–1082. The Civilian Board of Contract Appeals (CBCA) is located at 1800 M Street NW., 6th Floor, Washington, DC 20036; however, the CBCA mailing address is 1800 F Street NW., Washington, DC 20405. The CBCA telephone number is 202–606–8800. The addresses of the eleven regional offices are provided in § 105–53.151.

[78 FR 29246, May 20, 2013]

Subpart B—Central Offices

§ 105–53.130 Office of the Administrator.

The Administrator of General Services, appointed by the President with the advice and consent of the Senate, directs the execution of all programs assigned to the General Services Administration. The Deputy Administrator, who is appointed by the Admin-

istrator, assists in directing agency programs and coordinating activities related to the functions of the General Services Administration.

§ 105–53.130–1 [Reserved]

§ 105–53.130–2 Office of Ethics and Civil Rights.

The Office of Ethics and Civil Rights, headed by the Special Counsel for Ethics and Civil Rights, is responsible for developing, directing, and monitoring the agency's programs governing employee standards of ethical conduct, equal employment opportunity, and civil rights. It is the focal point for the agency's implementation of the Ethics in Government Act of 1978. The principal statutes covering the Civil Rights Program are Titles VI and VII of the Civil Rights Act of 1964, Title IX of the Educational Amendments Act of 1972, sections 501 and 504 of the Vocational Rehabilitation Act of 1973, the Age Discrimination in Employment Act of 1975, and the Equal Pay Act.

[53 FR 23761, June 24, 1988]

§ 105–53.130–3 Office of the Executive Secretariat.

The Office of the Executive Secretariat, headed by the Director of the Executive Secretariat, is responsible for policy coordination, correspondence control, and various administrative tasks in support of the Administrator and Deputy Administrator.

§ 105–53.130–4 Office of Small and Disadvantaged Business Utilization.

(a) *Creation and authority.* Public Law 95–507, October 14, 1978, an amendment to the Small Business Act and the Small Business Investment Act of 1958, established in each Federal agency having procurement authority the Office of Small and Disadvantaged Business Utilization. Each office is headed by a Director of Small and Disadvantaged Business Utilization. The Director is appointed by the head of the agency or department.

(b) *Functions.* The Director of Small and Disadvantaged Business Utilization is responsible for the implementation and execution of the functions and duties under Sections 8 and 15 of the Small Business Act to include the issuance of policy direction and guidance. The office provides information, assistance, and counseling to business concerns, including small businesses, small socially and economically disadvantaged persons, women-owned businesses, labor surplus area concerns, and workshops operated by the blind and other severely handicapped persons. The office also conducts outreach, liaison, source listings, and seminars for small and disadvantaged businesses and coordinates and promotes procurement programs and policies.

§ 105–53.131 Office of Inspector General.

(a) *Creation and authority.* Public Law 95–452, known as the Inspector General Act of 1978, consolidated existing audit and investigation functions and established an Office of Inspector General in 11 major domestic departments and agencies, including GSA. Each office is headed by an Inspector General appointed by the President with the advice and consent of the Senate.

(b) *Functions.* The Office of Inspector General is responsible for policy direction and conduct of audit, inspection, and investigation activities relating to programs and operations of GSA; and maintaining liaison with other law enforcement agencies, the Department of Justice, and United States Attorneys on all matters relating to the detection and prevention of fraud and abuse. The Inspector General reports semiannually to the Congress through the Administrator concerning fraud, abuses, other serious problems, and deficiencies of agency programs and operations; recommends corrective action; and reports on progress made in implementing these actions.

§ 105–53.132 Civilian Board of Contract Appeals.

(a) *Creation and authority.* The Civilian Board of Contract Appeals, headed by the Chairman, Civilian Board of Contract Appeals, was established on January 6, 2007, pursuant to section 847 of the National Defense Authorization Act for Fiscal Year 2006, Pub. L. 109–163, 119 Stat. 3391.

(b) *Functions.* The CBCA hears, considers, and decides contract disputes between Government contractors and Executive agencies (other than the U.S. Department of Defense, the U.S. Department of the Army, the U.S. Department of the Navy, the U.S. Department of the Air Force, the U.S. National Aeronautics and Space Administration, the U.S. Postal Service, the Postal Rate Commission, and the Tennessee Valley Authority) under the provisions of the Contract Disputes Act, 41 U.S.C. 7101–7109, and regulations and rules issued thereunder. The Board also conducts other proceedings as required or permitted under statutes or regulations. Such other proceedings include the resolution of disputes involving grants and contracts under the Indian Self-Determination and Education Assistance Act, 25 U.S.C. 450, *et seq.;* the resolution of disputes between insurance companies and the U.S. Department of Agriculture's Risk Management Agency (RMA) involving actions of the Federal Crop Insurance Corporation (FCIC) pursuant to the Federal Crop Insurance Act, 7 U.S.C. 1501, *et seq.;* requests by carriers or freight forwarders to review actions taken by the Audit Division of the U.S. General Services Administration's Office of Transportation and Property Management pursuant to 31 U.S.C. 3726(i)(1); claims by Federal civilian employees against the United States for reimbursement of expenses incurred while on official temporary duty travel, and expenses incurred in connection with relocation to a new duty station pursuant to 31 U.S.C. 3702; and requests of agency disbursing or certifying officials, or agency heads, on questions involving payment of travel or relocation expenses pursuant to section 204 of the U.S. General Accounting Office Act of 1996, Public Law 104–316.

(c) *Regulations.* Regulations pertaining to CBCA programs are published in 48 CFR Chapter 61. Information on availability of the regulations is provided in § 105–53.116.

[78 FR 29246, May 20, 2013]

§ 105–53.133 Information Security Oversight Office.

(a) *Creation and authority.* The Information Security Oversight Office (ISOO), headed by the Director of

ISOO, who is appointed by the Administrator with the approval of the President, was established by the Administrator on November 20, 1978, under the provisions of Executive Order 12065. Effective August 1, 1982, this authority is based upon Executive Order 12356, which superseded E.O. 12065.

(b) *Functions.* ISOO oversees and ensures, under the general policy direction of the National Security Council, Government-wide implementation of the information security program established by Executive order.

(c) *Regulations.* Regulations pertaining to ISOO Programs are published in 32 CFR chapter XX, part 2000 *et seq.*

§ 105–53.134 Office of Administration.

The Office of Administration, headed by the Associate Administrator for Administration, participates in the executive leadership of the agency; providing advice on the formulation of major policies and procedures, particularly those of a critical or controversial nature, to the Administrator and Deputy Administrator. The Office plans and administers programs in organization, productivity improvement, position management, training, staffing, position classification and pay administration, employee relations, workers' compensation, career development, GSA internal security, reporting requirements, regulations, internal directives, records correspondence procedures, Privacy and Freedom of Information Acts, printing and duplicating, mail, telecommunications, graphic design, cooperative administrative support, and support for congressional field offices. The office also serves as the central point of control for audit and inspection reports from the Inspector General and the Comptroller General of the United States; and manages the GSA internal controls evaluation, improvement, and reporting program. In addition, the office includes a secretariat to oversee Federal advisory committees.

[54 FR 26741, June 26, 1989]

§ 105–53.135 [Reserved]

§ 105–53.136 Office of Congressional Affairs.

The Office of Congressional Affairs, headed by the Associate Administrator for Congressional Affairs, is responsible for directing and coordinating the legislative and congressional activities of GSA.

[54 FR 26742, June 26, 1989]

§ 105–53.137 Office of Acquisition Policy.

(a) *Functions.* The Office of Acquisition Policy (OAP), headed by the Associate Administrator for Acquisition Policy, serves as the single focal point for GSA acquisition and contracting matters and is responsible for ensuring that the GSA procurement process is executed in compliance with all appropriate public laws and regulations and is based on sound business judgment. Also, OAP exercises Governmentwide acquisition responsibilities through its participation with the Department of Defense and the National Aeronautics and Space Administration in the development and publication of the Federal Acquisition Regulation.

(b) *Regulations.* Regulations pertaining to OAP programs are published in 48 CFR chapter 1, Federal Acquisition Regulation (FAR), and in 48 CFR chapter 5, General Services Acquisition Regulation (GSAR). Information on availability of the regulations is provided in § 105–53.116.

[52 FR 23657, June 24, 1987]

§ 105–53.138 Office of General Counsel.

Functions. The Office of General Counsel (OGC), headed by the General Counsel, is responsible for providing all legal services to the services, programs offices, staff offices, and regions of GSA with the exception of certain legal activities of the Office of Inspector General and legal activities of the Civilian Board of Contract Appeals; drafts legislation proposed by GSA;

furnishes legal advice required in connection with reports on legislation proposed by other agencies; provides liaison on legal matters with other Federal agencies; coordinates with the Department of Justice in litigation matters; and reviews and gives advice on matters of contract policy and contract operations.

[48 FR 25200, June 6, 1983, as amended at 78 FR 29247, May 20, 2013]

§ 105–53.139 Office of the Comptroller.

(a) *Functions.* The Office of the Comptroller, headed by the Comptroller, is responsible for centralized agencywide budget and accounting functions; overall allocation and administrative control of agencywide resources and financial management programs; planning, developing, and directing GSA's executive management information system; and overseeing implementation of OMB Circular A–76 agencywide.

(b) *Regulations.* Regulations pertaining to the Office of the Comptroller's programs are published in 41 CFR part 101–2. Information on availability of the regulations is provided in § 105–53.116.

[51 FR 23230, June 26, 1986, as amended at 53 FR 23762, June 24, 1988; 54 FR 26742, June 26, 1989]

§ 105–53.140 Office of Operations and Industry Relations.

The Office of Operations and Industry Relations, headed by the Associate Administrator for Operations and Industry Relations, is responsible for formulating GSA-wide policy that relates to regional operations, supervising GSA's Regional Administrators, and planning and coordinating GSA business and industry relations and customer liaison activities.

[54 FR 26742, June 26, 1989]

§ 105–53.141 Office of Policy Analysis.

The Office of Policy Analysis, headed by the Associate Administrator for Policy Analysis, is responsible for providing analytical support, independent, objective information concerning management policies and programs, and technical and analytical assistance in the areas of policy analysis and resource allocation to the Administrator, senior officials, and organizations in GSA.

[51 FR 23230, June 26, 1986]

§ 105–53.142 Office of Public Affairs.

The Office of Public Affairs, headed by the Associate Administrator for Public Affairs, is responsible for the planning, implementation, and coordination of GSA public information and public events and employee communication activities, and managing and operating the Consumer Information Center.

[51 FR 23230, June 26, 1986]

§ 105–53.143 Information Resources Management Service.

(a) *Creation and authority.* The Information Resources Management Service (IRMS), headed by the Commissioner, Information Resources Management Service, was established as the Office of Information Resources Management on August 17, 1982 and subsequently redesignated as IRMS on November 17, 1985, by the Administrator of General Services. The Information Resources Management Service was assigned responsibility for administering the Governmentwide information resources management program, including records management, and procurement, management, and use of automatic data processing and telecommunications resources.

(b) *Functions.* IRMS is responsible for directing and managing Governmentwide programs for the procurement and use of automatic data processing (ADP), office information systems, and telecommunications equipment and services; developing and coordinating Governmentwide plans, policies, procedures, regulations, and publications pertaining to ADP; telecommunications and records management activities; managing and operating the Information Technology Fund; managing and operating the Federal Telecommunications System (FTS); planning and directing programs for improving Federal records and information management practices Governmentwide; managing and operating the

Federal Information Centers; developing and overseeing GSA policy concerning automated information systems, equipment, and facilities; and providing policy and program direction for the GSA Emergency Preparedness and Disaster Support Programs.

(c) *Regulations.* Regulations pertaining to IRMS programs are published in 41 CFR chapter 201, Federal Information Resources Management Regulation (FIRMR), and 48 CFR chapters 1 and 5. Information on availability of the regulations is provided in §105–53.116.

[51 FR 23230, June 26, 1986, as amended at 52 FR 23657, June 24, 1987]

§105–53.144 Federal Property Resources Service.

(a) *Creation and authority.* The Federal Property Resources Service (FPRS), headed by the Commissioner, Federal Property Resources Service, was established on July 18, 1978, by the Administrator of General Services to carry out the utilization and disposal functions for real and related personal property.

(b) *Functions.* FPRS is responsible for utilization surveys of Federal real property holdings; the reuse of excess real property; and the disposal of surplus real property.

(c) *Regulations.* Regulations pertaining to FPRS programs are published in 41 CFR chapter 1, 41 CFR chapter 101, subchapter H, and 48 CFR chapter 1. Information on availability of the regulations is provided in §105–53.116

[54 FR 26742, June 26, 1989]

§105–53.145 Federal Supply Service.

(a) *Creation and authority.* The Federal Supply Service (FSS), headed by the Commissioner, FSS, was established on December 11, 1949, by the Administrator of General Services to supersede the Bureau of Federal Supply of the Department of the Treasury which was abolished by the Federal Property and Administrative Services Act of 1949. The Federal Supply Service has been known previously as the Office of Personal Property and the Office of Federal Supply and Services.

(b) *Functions.* FSS is responsible for determining supply requirements; procuring personal property and nonpersonal services; transferring excess (except ADP equipment) and donating and selling surplus personal property; managing GSA's Governmentwide transportation, traffic management, travel, fleet management, and employee relocation programs; auditing of transportation bills paid by the Government and subsequent settlement of claims; developing Federal standard purchase specifications and Commercial Item Descriptions; standardizing commodities purchased by the Federal Government; cataloging items of supply procured by civil agencies; and ensuring continuity of supply operations during defense emergency conditions.

(c) *Regulations.* Regulations pertaining to FSS programs are published in 41 CFR chapters 1 and 5; 41 CFR chapter 101, subchapters A, E, G, and H; and in 48 CFR chapters 1 and 5. Information on availability of the regulations is provided in §105–53.116.

[49 FR 24996, June 19, 1984, as amended at 51 FR 23230, June 26, 1986]

§105–53.146 [Reserved]

§105–53.147 Public Buildings Service.

(a) *Creation and authority.* The Public Buildings Service (PBS), headed by the Commissioner, Public Buildings Service, was established on December 11, 1949, by the Administrator of General Services to supersede the Public Buildings Administration, which was abolished by the Federal Property and Administrative Services Act of 1949.

(b) *Functions.* PBS is responsible for the design, construction, management, maintenance, operation, alteration, extension, remodeling, preservation, repair, improvement, protection, and control of buildings, both federally owned and leased, in which are provided housing accommodations for Government activities; the acquisition, utilization, custody, and accountability for GSA real property and related personal property; representing the consumer interests of the Federal executive agencies before Federal and State rate regulatory commissions and providing procurement support and contracting for public utilities (except telecommunications); the Safety and Environmental Management Program for GSA managed Government-owned and-leased facilities; providing for the protection and enhancement of the cultural environment for federally owned sites, structures, and objects of historical, architectural, or archaeological significance; ensuring that Federal work space is used more effectively and efficiently; providing leadership in the development and maintenance of needed property management information systems for the Government; and coordination of GSA activities towards improving the environment, as required by the National Environmental Policy Act of 1959.

(c) *Regulations.* Regulations pertaining to PBS programs are published in 41 CFR chapter 1, 41 CFR chapter 101, subchapters D and H; and in 48 CFR chapter 1. Information on availability of the regulations is provided in § 105–53.116.

[48 FR 25200, June 6, 1983, as amended at 49 FR 24996, June 19, 1984; 52 FR 23658, June 24, 1987]

Subpart C—Regional Offices

§ 105–53.150   Organization and functions.

Regional offices have been established in 11 cities throughout the United States. Each regional office is headed by a Regional Administrator who reports to the Associate Administrator for Operations and Industry Relations. The geographic composition of each region is shown in § 105–53.151.

[54 FR 26742, June 26, 1989]

§ 105–53.151   Geographic composition, addresses, and telephone numbers.

REGIONAL OFFICES—GENERAL SERVICES ADMINISTRATION

Region and Address

No. 1. (Comprising the States of Connecticut, Maine, Massachusetts, New Hampshire, Rhode Island, and Vermont); Boston FOB, 10 Causeway Street, Boston, MA 02222. Telephone: 617–565–5860.

No. 2. (Comprising the States of New Jersey and New York, the Commonwealth of Puerto Rico, and the Virgin Islands); 26 Federal Plaza, New York, NY 10278. Telephone: 212–264–2600.

No. 3. (Comprising the States of Maryland, Virginia (except those jurisdictions within the National Capital Region boundaries), West Virginia, Pennsylvania, and Delaware); Ninth and Market Streets, Philadelphia, PA 19107. Telephone 215–597–1237.

No. 4. (Comprising the States of Alabama, Florida, Georgia, Kentucky, Mississippi, North Carolina, South Carolina, and Tennessee); 75 Spring Street, SW., Atlanta, GA 30303. Telephone: 404–331–3200.

No. 5. (Comprising the States of Illinois, Indiana, Michigan, Minnesota, Ohio, and Wisconsin); 230 South Dearborn Street, Chicago, IL 60604. Telephone: 312–353–5395.

No. 6. (Comprising the States of Iowa, Kansas, Missouri, and Nebraska); 1500 East Bannister Road, Kansas City, MO 64131. Telephone: 816–926–7201.

No. 7. (Comprising the States of Arkansas, Louisiana, New Mexico, Oklahoma, and Texas); 819 Taylor Street, Fort Worth, TX 76102. Telephone: 817–334–2321.

No. 8. (Comprising the States of Colorado, Montana, North Dakota, South Dakota, Utah, and Wyoming); Building 41, Denver Federal Center, Denver, CO 80225. Telephone: 303–236–7329.

No. 9. (Comprising Guam and the States of Arizona, California, Hawaii, and Nevada); 525 Market Street, San Francisco, CA 94105. Telephone : 415–974–9147.

No. 10. (Comprising the States of Alaska, Idaho, Oregon, and Washington); GSA Center, Auburn, WA 98001. Telephone: 206–931–7000.

National Capital Region. (Comprising the District of Columbia; Counties of Montgomery and Prince Georges in Maryland; and the City of Alexandria and the Counties of Arlington, Fairfax, Loudoun, and Prince William in Virginia); Seventh and D Streets, SW., Washington, DC 20407. Telephone: 202–472–1100.

[51 FR 23231, June 26, 1986, as amended at 52 FR 23658, June 24, 1987; 53 FR 23762, June 24, 1988; 54 FR 26742, June 26, 1989]

PART 105–54—ADVISORY COMMITTEE MANAGEMENT

AUTHORITY: Pub. L. 92–463 dated October 6, 1972, as amended; and 5 U.S.C. 552.

SOURCE: 53 FR 40224, Oct. 14, 1988, unless otherwise noted.

§ 105–54.000 Scope of part.

This part sets forth policies and procedures in GSA regarding the establishment, operation, termination, and control of advisory committees for which GSA has responsibility. It implements the Federal Advisory Committee Act (Pub. L. 92–463), which authorizes a system governing the establishment and operation of advisory committees in the executive branch of the Federal Government, and Executive Order 11686 of October 7, 1972, which directs the heads of all executive departments and agencies to take appropriate action to ensure their ability to comply with the provisions of the Act.

Subpart 105–54.1—General Provisions

§ 105–54.101 Applicability.

This part 105–54 applies to all advisory committees for which GSA has responsibility. This part also applies to any committee that advises GSA officials even if the committee were not established for that purpose. This applicability, however, is limited to the period of the committee's use as an advisory body. This part does not apply to:

(a) An advisory committee exempted by an Act of Congress;

(b) A local civic group whose primary function is to render a public service in connection with a Federal program;

(c) A State or local committee, council, board, commission, or similar group established to advise or make recommendations to State or local officials or agencies;

(d) A meeting initiated by the President or one or more Federal official(s) for the purpose of obtaining advice or recommendations from one individual;

(e) A meeting with a group initiated by the President or one or more Federal official(s) for the sole purpose of exchanging facts or information;

(f) A meeting initiated by a group with the President or one or more Federal official(s) for the purpose of expressing the group's views, provided that the President or Federal official(s) does not use the group recurrently as a preferred source of advice or recommendations;

(g) A committee that is established to perform primarily operational as opposed to advisory functions. Operational functions are those specifically provided by law, such as making or implementing Government decisions or policy. An operational committee would be covered by the Act if it becomes primarily advisory in nature;

(h) A meeting initiated by a Federal official(s) with more than one individual for the purpose of obtaining the advice of individual attendees and not for the purpose of utilizing the group to obtain consensus advice or recommendations. However, such a group would be covered by the Act when an agency accepts the group's deliberations as a source of consensus advice or recommendations;

(i) A meeting of two or more advisory committee or subcommittee members convened solely to gather information or conduct research for a chartered advisory committee, to analyze relevant issues and facts, or to draft proposed position papers for deliberation by the advisory committee or a subcommittee of the advisory committee; and

(j) A committee composed wholly of full-time officers or employees of the Federal Government.

§ 105–54.102 Definitions.

(a) The term "advisory committee" means any committee, board, commission, council, conference, panel, task force, or other similar group or any subcommittee thereof that is:

(1) Established by statute,

(2) Established or utilized by the President, or

(3) Established or utilized by any agency official to obtain advice or recommendations that are within the scope of his/her responsibilies.

The term "advisory committee" excludes the Advisory Committee on Intergovernmental Relations and any committees composed wholly of full-time officers or employees of the Federal Government.

(b) "Presidential advisory committee" means any committee that advises the President. It may be established by the President or by the Congress, or may be used by the President to obtain advice or recommendations.

(c) "Independent Presidential advisory committee" means any Presidential advisory committee not assigned by the President, or the President's delegate, or by the Congress in law, to an agency for administrative and other support and for which the Administrator of General Services may provide administrative and other support on a reimbursable basis.

(d) "Committee member" means an individual who serves by appointment on a committee and has the full right and obligation to participate in the activities of the committee, including voting on committee recommendations.

(e) "Staff member" means any individual who serves in a support capacity to an advisory committee.

(f) "Secretariat" means the General Services Administration's Committee Management Secretariat. Established pursuant to the Federal Advisory Committee Act, it is responsible for all matters relating to advisory committees, and carries out the Administrator's responsibilities under the Act and Executive Order 12024.

(g) "Utilized" (or used), as stated in the definition of "advisory committee" above, refers to a situation in which a GSA official adopts a committee or other group composed in whole or in part of other than full-time Federal officers or employees with an established existence outside GSA as a preferred source from which to obtain advice or recommendations on a specific issue or policy within the scope of his/her responsibilities in the same manner as that official would obtain advice or recommendations from an established advisory committee.

§ 105–54.103 Policy.

The basic GSA policy on committee management is as follows:

(a) Advisory committees will be formed or used by GSA only when specifically authorized by law, or by the President, or specifically determined as a matter of formal record by the Administrator of General Services to be in the public interest in connection with the performance of duties imposed on GSA by law;

(b) Advisory committees will not be used to administer a function that is the assigned responsibility of a service or staff office;

(c) The assigned responsibility of a GSA official may not be delegated to any committee;

(d) No advisory committee may be used for functions that are not solely advisory unless specifically authorized by statute or Presidential directive. Making policy decisions and determining action to be taken with respect to any matter considered by an advisory committee is solely the responsibility of GSA; and

(e) In carrying out its responsibilities, GSA will consult with and obtain the advice of interested groups substantially affected by its programs. The use of advisory committees for this purpose is considered to be in the public interest and necessary for the proper performance by GSA of its assigned functions.

§ 105–54.104 Responsibilities.

(a) Responsibility for coordination and control of committee management in GSA is vested in the Associate Administrator for Administration, who serves as the GSA Committee Management Officer (CMO). This Officer carries out the functions prescribed in section 8(b) of the Federal Advisory Committee Act. In doing so, the Officer controls and supervises the establishment, procedures, and accomplishments of GSA-sponsored advisory committees. The Organization and Productivity Improvement Division, Office of Management Services, Office of Administration, provides staff resources and furnishes the Staff Contact Person (SCP) to the CMO.

(b) The Head of each Service and Staff Office and each Regional Administrator selects a Committee Management Officer (CMO) to coordinate and control committee management within the service, staff office, or regional office and to act as liaison to the GSA Committee Management Officer. The duties of the CMOs are as follows:

(1) Assemble and maintain the reports, records, and other papers of any GSA-sponsored committee during its existence (Arrangements may be made, however, for the Government chairperson or other GSA representative to retain custody of reports, records, and other papers to facilitate committee operations. After the committee is terminated, all committee records are disposed of following existing regulations.); and

(2) Under agency regulations in 41 CFR 105–60, carry out the provisions of 5 U.S.C. 552 with respect to the reports, records, and other papers of GSA-sponsored advisory committees.

Subpart 105–54.2—Establishment of Advisory Committees

§ 105–54.200 Scope of subpart.

This subpart prescribes the policy and procedures for establishing advisory committees within GSA.

§ 105–54.201 Proposals for establishing advisory committees.

(a) The Administrator approves the establishment of all GSA Federal Advisory Committees.

(b) When it is decided that it is necessary to establish a committee, the appropriate Head of the Service or Staff Office (HSSO) must consider functions of similar committees in GSA to ensure that no duplication of effort will occur.

(c) The HSSO proposes the establishment of a Central Office or regional advisory committee within the scope of assigned program responsibilities. In doing so, the HSSO assures that advisory committees are established only if they are essential to the conduct of agency business. Advisory committees are established only if there is a compelling need for the committees, the committees have a truly balanced membership, and the committees conduct their business as openly as possible under the law and their mandate. Each proposal is submitted to the GSA Committee Management Officer for review and coordination and includes:

(1) A letter addressed to the Committee Management Secretariat signed by the HSSO with information copies for the Administrator, Deputy Administrator, the Associate Administrator for Congressional and Industry Relations, and the Special Counsel for Ethics and Civil Rights, describing the nature and purpose of the proposed advisory committee; why it is essential to agency business and in the public interest; why its functions cannot be performed by an existing committee of GSA, by GSA, or other means such as a public hearing; and the plans to ensure balanced membership;

(2) A notice for publication in the FEDERAL REGISTER containing the Administrator's certification that creation of the advisory committee is in the public interest and describing the

nature and purpose of the committee; and

(3) A draft charter for review by the Committee Management Secretariat.

(d) Subcommittees that do not function independently of the full or parent advisory committee need not follow the requirements of paragraph (c) of this section. However, they are subject to all other requirements of the Federal Advisory Committee Act.

(e) The requirements of paragraphs (a) through (c) of this section apply to any subcommittee of a chartered committee, whether its members are drawn in whole or in part from the full or parent advisory committee, that functions independently of the parent advisory committee, such as by making recommendations directly to a GSA official rather than for consideration by the chartered advisory committee.

§ 105–54.202 Review and approval of proposals.

(a) The GSA Committee Management Officer reviews each proposal to make sure it conforms with GSA policies and procedures. The Officer sends the letter of justification, including the draft charter, to the Committee Management Secretariat. The Secretariat reviews the proposal and provides its views within 15 calendar days of receipt, if possible. The Administrator retains final authority for establishing a particular advisory committee.

(b) When the Secretariat notifies the Officer that establishing the committee conforms with the Federal Advisory Committee Act, the Officer obtains the Administrator's approval of the charter and the FEDERAL REGISTER notice. The Officer publishes the notice in the FEDERAL REGISTER at least 15 calendar days before the filing of the charter under § 105–54.203 with the standing committees of the Senate and the House of Representatives having legislative jurisdiction over GSA. The date of filing constitutes the date of establishment.

§ 105–54.203 Advisory committee charters.

No advisory committee may operate, meet, or take any action until the Administrator approves its charter and the Committee Management Officer sends a copy of it to the standing committees of the Senate and the House of Representatives having legislative jurisdiction over GSA.

§ 105–54.203–1 Preparation of charters.

Each committee charter contains the following information:

(a) The committee's official designation;

(b) The committee's objectives and the scope of its activities;

(c) The period of time necessary for the committee to carry out its purpose (if the committee is intended to function as a standing advisory committee, this should be made clear);

(d) The official to whom the committee reports, including the official's name, title, and organization;

(e) The agency and office responsible for providing the necessary support for the committee;

(f) A description of the duties for which the committee is responsible (if the duties are not solely advisory, the statutory or Presidential authority for additional duties shall be specified);

(g) The estimated annual operating costs in dollars and person-years for the committee;

(h) The estimated number and frequency of committee meetings;

(i) The committee's termination date, if it is less than 2 years from the date of its establishment; and

(j) The date the charter is filed. This date is inserted by the GSA Committee Management Officer after the Administrator approves the charter.

§ 105–54.203–2 Active charters file.

The GSA Committee Management Officer retains each original signed charter in a file of active charters.

§ 105–54.203–3 Submission to Library of Congress.

The GSA Committee Management Officer furnishes a copy of each charter to the Library of Congress when or shortly after copies are filed with the requisite committees of the Congress. Copies for the Library are addressed: Library of Congress, Exchange and Gift Division, Federal Documents Section, Federal Advisory Committee Desk, Washington, DC 20540.

§ 105–54.204 Advisory committee membership.

(a) Advisory committees that GSA establishes represent the points of view of the profession, industry, or other group to which it relates, taking into account the size, function, geographical location, affiliation, and other considerations affecting the character of a committee. To ensure balance, the agency considers for membership a cross-section of interested persons and groups with professional or personal qualifications or experience to contribute to the functions and tasks to be performed. This should be construed neither to limit the participation nor to compel the selection of any particular individual or group to obtain different points of view relevant to committee business. The Administrator designates members, alternates, and observers, as appropriate, of advisory committees. He/she designates a Federal officer or employee to chair or attend each meeting of each advisory committee. The Administrator also designates GSA employees to serve on advisory committees sponsored by other Government agencies. The HSSO or Regional Administrator submits nominations and letters of designation for the Administrator's signature to the GSA Committee Management Officer and to the Special Counsel for Ethics and Civil Rights for review and forwarding to the Administrator.

(b) Discrimination is prohibited on the basis of race, color, age, national origin, religion, sex, or mental and physical handicap in selecting advisory committee members.

(c) Nominees for membership must submit a Statement of Employment and Financial Interests (provided to the nominee by the HSSO or Regional Administrator) and may not be appointed until cleared by the Designated Agency Ethics Official.

Subpart 105–54.3—Advisory Committee Procedures

§ 105–54.300 Scope of subpart.

This subpart sets forth the procedures that will be followed in the operation of advisory committees within GSA.

§ 105–54.301 Meetings.

(a) Each GSA advisory committee meeting is open to the public unless the Administrator decides otherwise;

(b) Each meeting is held at a reasonable time and in a place reasonably accessible to the public;

(c) The meeting room size is sufficient to accommodate committee members, committee or GSA staff, and interested members of the public;

(d) Any private citizen is permitted to file a written statement with the advisory committee;

(e) Any private citizen is permitted to speak at the advisory committee meeting, at the chairperson's discretion;

(f) All persons attending committee meetings at which classified information will be considered are required to have an adequate security clearance;

(g) The Designated Federal Officer (who may be either full time or permanent part-time) for each advisory committee and its subcommittees does the following:

(1) Approves or calls the meetings of the advisory committee;

(2) Approves the meeting agenda, which lists the matters to be considered at the meeting and indicates whether any part of the meeting will be closed to the public under the Government in the Sunshine Act (5 U.S.C. 552b(c)). Ordinarily, copies of the agenda are distributed to committee members before the date of the meeting;

(3) Attends all meetings (no part of a meeting may proceed in the Designated Federal Officer's absence);

(4) Adjourns the meeting when he or she determines that adjournment is in the public interest; and

(5) Chairs the meeting when asked to do so.

(h) The Committee Chairperson makes sure that detailed minutes of each meeting are kept and certifies to their accuracy. The minutes include:

(1) Time, date, and place;

(2) A list of the following persons who were present:

(i) Advisory committee members and staff;

(ii) Agency employees; and

(iii) Private citizens who presented oral or written statements;

(3) The estimated number of private citizens present;

(4) An accurate description of each matter discussed and the resolution of the matter, if any; and

(5) Copies of each report or other document the committee received, issued, or approved.

(i) The responsible HSSO or the Regional Administrator publishes at least 15 calendar days before the meeting a notice in the FEDERAL REGISTER that includes:

(1) The name of the advisory committee as chartered;

(2) The time, date, place, and purpose of the meeting;

(3) A summary of the agenda; and

(4) A statement whether all or part of the meeting is open to the public of closed; and if closed, the reasons why, and citing the specific exemptions of the Government is the Sunshine Act (5 U.S.C. 552b) as the basis for closure;

(j) In exceptional circumstances and when approved by the General Counsel or designee, less than 15 calendar days notice may be given, provided the reasons for doing so are included in the committee meeting notice published in the FEDERAL REGISTER;

(k) Notices to be published in the FEDERAL REGISTER are submitted to the Federal Register Liaison Officer (CAID). At least five workdays are needed for printing of the notice;

(l) Meetings may also be announced by press release, direct mail, publication in trade and professional journals, or by notice to special interest and community groups affected by the Committee's deliberations. This procedure cannot be a substitute for FEDERAL REGISTER publication;

(m) The fact that a meeting may be closed to the public under the exemptions of the Government in the Sunshine Act does not relieve GSA of the requirement to publish a notice of it in the FEDERAL REGISTER. The Administrator may authorize an exception to this requirement for reasons of national security if the HSSO requests it at least 30 calendar days before the meeting, with the concurrence of the General Counsel of designee.

(n) An advisory committee meeting is not open to the public, nor is the attendance, appearance, or filing of statements by interested persons permitted, if the Administrator decides that the meeting is exempted under the Government in the Sunshine Act (5 U.S.C. 552b (c)) and there is sufficient reason to invoke the exemption. If only part of the meeting concerns exempted matters, only that part is closed. The HSSO or Regional Administrator submits any decisions concerning the closing of meetings in writing to the Administrator for approval at least 30 calendar days in advance of the meeting. These decisions clearly set forth the reasons for doing so, citing the specific exemptions used from the Government in the Sunshine Act in the meeting notice published in the FEDERAL REGISTER. They are made available to the public on request. The Administrator may waive the 30-day requirement when a lesser period of time is requested and adequately justified.

(o) If any meeting or portion of a meeting is closed to public attendance, the advisory committee issues a report at lease annually setting forth a summary of its activities and such related matters as would be informative to the public, consistent with the policy of 5 U.S.C. 552(b). Notice of the availability of the report and instructions on how to gain access to it are published in the FEDERAL REGISTER no later than 60 days after its completion. In addition, copies of the report are filed with the Library of Congress.

(p) The General Counsel reviews all requests to close meetings.

(q) The HSSO or Regional Administrator publishes the meeting notices in the FEDERAL REGISTER, including the reasons why all or part of the meeting is closed, citing the specified exemptions used from the Government in the Sunshine Act.

§ 105–54.302 Committee records and reports.

(a) Subject to the Freedom of Information Act (5 U.S.C. 552), the records, reports, transcripts, minutes, appendixes, working papers, drafts, studies, agenda, or other documents that were available to or prepared for or by a GSA advisory committee are available (until the committee ceases to exist) for public inspection and copying in the office of the Government Chairperson or Designated Federal Officer. Requests to inspect or copy these records are processed under 41 CFR 105–60.4. Except where prohibited by a contract entered into before January 5, 1973, copies of transcripts, if any, of committee meetings are made available by the Government chairperson or Designated Federal Officer to any person at the cost of duplication. After the committee's work ends, disposition of the committee documents and the release of information from them are made in accordance with Federal records, statutes, and regulations.

(b) Subject to 5 U.S.C. 552(b) and instructions of the Committee Management Secretariat, the Government chairperson or Designated Federal Officer files at least eight copies of each report an advisory committee makes, including any report on closed meetings with the Library of Congress at the time of its issuance. Where appropriate, the chairperson also files copies of background papers that consultants to the advisory committee prepare with the Library of Congress. The transmittal letter identifies the materials being furnished, with a copy of the transmittal provided to the GSA Committee Management Officer.

§ 105–54.303 Fiscal and administrative provisions.

(a) Each HSSO and each Regional Administrator ensures that under established GSA procedures, records are kept that fully disclose the disposition of funds at the disposal of an advisory committee and the nature and extent of the committee's activities.

(b) When GSA is assigned to provide administrative support for a Presidential advisory committee, the Agency Liaison Coordinator in the Office of the Deputy Regional Administrator, National Capital Region, as a part of its support, arranges with the Office of Finance, Office of the Comptroller, for maintaining all financial records.

(c) Unless otherwise provided in a Presidential order, statute, or other authority, the GSA service or staff office sponsoring an advisory committee provides support services for the committee.

(d) The guidelines in paragraph (e) through (l) of this section are established under section 7(d) of the Federal Advisory Committee Act, 86 Stat. 773. They apply to the pay of members, staff, and consultants of an advisory committee, except that nothing in this paragraph will affect a rate of pay or a limitation on a rate of pay that is established by statute or a rate of pay established under the General Schedule classification and pay system in Chapter 51 and Subchapter III of Chapter 53 of Title 5, U.S.C.

(e) The members of GSA advisory committee established pursuant to the Administrator's authority under section 205(g) of the Federal Property and Administrative Services Act of 1949, as amended (40 U.S.C. 486(g)), are not compensated, since, by law, members so appointed shall service without compensation. A person who (without regard to his or her service with an advisory committee) is a full-time Federal employee will normally receive compensation at the rate at which he or she would otherwise be compensated.

(f) When required by law, the pay of the members of GSA advisory committees will be fixed to the daily equivalent of a rate of the General Schedule in 5 U.S.C. 5332 unless the members are appointed as consultants and compensated as provided in paragraph (h) of this section. In determining an appropriate rate of pay for the members, GSA must give consideration to the significance, scope, and technical complexity of the matters with which the advisory committee is concerned and the qualifications required of the members of the advisory committee. GSA may not fix the pay of the members of an advisory committee at a rate higher than the daily equivalent of the maximum rate for a GS–15 under the General Schedule, unless a higher rate is mandated by statute, or the Administrator has personally determined that a higher rate of pay under the General Schedule is justified and necessary. Such a determination must be reviewed by the Administrator annually. Accordingly, the Administrator may not fix the pay of the members of an advisory committee at a rate of pay higher than the daily equivalent of a rate for a GSA 18, as provided in 5 U.S.C. 5332.

(g) The pay of each staff member of an advisory committee is fixed at a rate of the General Schedule, General Management Schedule, or Senior Executive Service pay rate in which the staff member's position would be placed (5 U.S.C. Chapter 51). GSA cannot fix the pay of a staff member higher than the daily equivalent of the maximum rate for GS–15 unless the Administrator decides that under the General Schedule, General Management Schedule, or Senior Executive Service classification system, the staff member's position should be higher than GS–15. The Administrator must review this decision annually.

(1) In establishing compensation rates, GSA must comply with applicable statutes, regulations, Executive Orders, and administrative guidelines.

(2) A staff member who is a Federal employee serves with the knowledge of the Designated Federal Officer and the approval of the employee's direct supervisor. A staff member who is a non-Federal employee is appointed under agency procedures, after consultation with the advisory committee.

(h) The pay of a consultant to an advisory committee will be fixed after giving consideration to the qualifications required of the consultant and the significance, scope, and technical complexity of the work. The rate of pay will not exceed the maximum rate of pay which the agency may pay experts and consultants under 5 U.S.C. 3109 and must be in accordance with any applicable statutes, regulations, Executive Orders, and administrative guidelines.

(i) Advisory committee and staff members, while performing their duties away from their homes or regular places of business, may be allowed travel expenses, including per diem instead of subsistence, as authorized by 5 U.S.C. 5703 for persons employed intermittently in the Government service.

(j) Members of an advisory committee and its staff who are blind or deaf or who otherwise qualify as handicapped persons (under section 501 of the Rehabilitation Act of 1973 (29 U.S.C. 794)), and who do not otherwise qualify for assistance under 5 U.S.C. 3102, as an employee of an agency (under section

3102(a)(1) of Title 5), may be provided the services of a personal assistant.

(k) Under this paragraph, GSA may accept the gratuitous services of a member, consultant, or staff member of an advisory committee who agrees in advance to serve without compensation.

(l) A person who immediately before his or her service with an advisory committee was a full-time Federal employee may receive compensation at the rate at which he or she was compensated as a Federal employee.

§ 105–54.304   Cost guidelines.

(a) The reporting and estimating of the costs of advisory committees include direct obligations for the following items:

(1) Pay compensation of committee members; consultants to the committee; all permanent, temporary, or part-time (GM, GS, WB, or other) positions which are a part of or support the committee; and all overtime related to committee functions (Compensation should reflect actual or estimated Federal person-years or parts thereof devoted to a committee's activities. It includes the compensation of Federal employees assigned to committees, on a reimbursable or nonreimbursable basis, from agencies or departments other than to which the committee reports.);

(2) Personnel benefits associated with the above compensation (13 percent of basic payroll);

(3) Travel costs (including per diem) of committee members; consultants; and all permanent, temporary, or part-time positions which are a part of or support the committee;

(4) Transportation of things, communications, and printing and reproduction;

(5) Rent for additional space acquired for committee use;

(6) Other services required by the committee, including data processing services, management studies and evaluations, contractual services, and reimbursable services; and

(7) Supplies, materials, and equipment acquired for committee use.

(b) The reporting and estimating of the cost of advisory committees does not include indirect or overhead costs;

e.g., the costs of the committee management system (committee management officers, etc.).

§ 105–54.305 Renewal of advisory committees.

(a) Each advisory committee being continued is renewed for successive 2-year periods beginning with the date when it was established according to the following, except for statutory advisory committees: (For renewal of statutory advisory committees, see paragraph (b) of this section.)

(1) Advisory committees are not renewed unless there is a compelling need for them, they have balanced membership, and they conduct their business as openly as possible under the law.

(2) The renewal of a committee requires that the responsible HSSO submit to the GSA Committee Management Officer the following:

(i) An updated charter with an explanation of the need for the renewal of the committee. The charter and explanation are furnished 60 calendar days before the 2-year anniversary date of the committee.);

(ii) A letter signed by the HSSO to the Director, Committee Management Secretariat, with information copies to the Administrator and the Deputy Administrator, setting forth:

(A) An explanation of why the committee is essential to the conduct of agency business and is in the public interest;

(B) GSA's plan to attain balanced membership of the committee; and

(C) An explanation of why the committee's functions cannot be performed by GSA, another existing GSA advisory committee, or other means such as a public hearing;

(iii) A notice for publication in the FEDERAL REGISTER describing the nature and purpose of the committee and containing a certification by the Administrator that renewing the advisory committee is in the public interest.

(3) On receiving the above documents, the GSA Committee Management Officer submits the renewal letter to the Committee Management Secretariat not more than 60 calendar days nor less than 30 days before the committee expires. Following receipt

of the Committee Management Secretariat's views on the committee renewal, the Officer obtains the Administrator's approval of the charter and the FEDERAL REGISTER notice. The Officer publishes notice of the renewal in the FEDERAL REGISTER and files copies of the updated charter. The 15-day notice requirement does not apply to committee renewals, notices of which may be published concurrently with the filing of the charter.

(b) Each statutory advisory committee is renewed by the filing of a renewal charter upon the expiration of each successive 2-year period following the date of enactment of the statute establishing the committee according to the following:

(1) The procedures in paragraph (a)(2) of this section apply to the renewal of a statutory committee except that neither prior consultation with the Committee Management Secretariat nor a FEDERAL REGISTER notice is required. Accordingly, the letter that paragraph a(2)(ii) requires is sent to the Administrator rather than the Committee Mangement Secretariat. Due to the nature of a committee the law established, the explanation of the need to continue the committee's existence is less extensive than the explanation for the continuation of a non-statutory committee; and

(2) The GSA Committee Management Officer provides the Committee Management Secretariat with a copy of the filed charter.

(c) An advisory committee required to file a new charter may not take any action other than preparing the charter between the date it is to be filed and the date it is actually filed.

§ 105–54.306 Amendment of advisory committee charters.

(a) A charter is amended when GSA decides that the existing charter no longer accurately reflects the objectives or functions of the committee. Changes may be minor, such as revising the name of the committee or modifying the estimated number or frequency of meetings, or they may be major dealing with the basic objectives or composition of the committee. The Administrator retains final authority for amending the charter of an advisory committee. Amending an existing advisory committee charter does not constitute renewal of the committee.

(b) To make a minor amendment, the Administrator approves the amended charter and has it filed according to § 105–54.203–1.

(c) To make a major amendment, the Committee Management Officer submits an amended charter and a letter to the Committee Management Secretariat, signed by the HSSO with the concurrence of the General Counsel or designee, requesting the Secretariat's views on the amended language, along with an explanation of the purpose of the changes and why they are necessary. The Secretariat reviews the proposed changes and notifies the Committee Management Officer of its views within 15 calendar days of receiving it, if possible. The Administrator has the charter filed according to § 105–54.203–1.

(d) Amending an existing charter does not constitute renewal of the committee.

§ 105–54.307 Termination of advisory committees.

(a) The sponsoring HSSO terminates an advisory committee that has fulfilled the purpose stated in its charter. The official takes action to rescind any existing orders relating to the committee and to notify committee members, the GSA Committee Management Officer, and the Committee Management Secretariat of the termination.

(b) Failing to continue an advisory committee by the 2-year anniversary date terminates the committee, unless its duration is provided for by law.

§ 105–54.308 Responsibilities of the Administrator.

The Administrator must ensure:

(a) Compliance with the Federal Advisory Committee Act and this chapter;

(b) Issuance of administrative guidelines and management controls that apply to all advisory committees established or used by the agency;

(c) Designation of a Committee Management Officer to carry out the functions specified in section 89(b) of the Federal Advisory Committee Act;

(d) Provision of a written determination stating the reasons for closing any advisory committee meeting to the public;

(e) A review, at least annually, of the need to continue each existing advisory committee, consistent with the public interest and the purpose and functions of each committee;

(f) The appointment of a Designated Federal Officer for each advisory committee and its subcommittee;

(g) The opportunity for reasonable public participation in advisory committee activities; and

(h) That the number of committee members is limited to the fewest necessary to accomplish committee objectives.

§ 105–54.309 Added responsibilities of service and staff office heads and regional administrators.

(a) No later than the first meeting of an advisory committee, submit to committee members, committee staff, consultants, and appropriate agency management personnel a written statement of the purpose, objectives, and expected accomplishments of the committee;

(b) Solicit in writing or in a formal meeting at least annually the views of committee members on the effectiveness, activities, and management of the committee, including recommendations for improvement. Review comments to determine whether improvements or corrective action is warranted. Retain recommendations until the committee is terminated or renewed.

(c) Involve key management personnel of the agency whose interests are affected by the committee in committee meetings, including reviewing reports and establishing agendas.

(d) Periodically, but not less than annually, review the level of committee staff suport to make sure that expenditures are justified by committee activity and benefit to the Government.

(e) Monitor the attendance and participation of committee members and consider replacing any member who misses a substantial number of scheduled meetings.

(f) Establish meeting dates and distribute agendas and other materials well in advance.

§ 105–54.310 Advisory committee duties of the GSA Committee Management Officer.

In addition to implementing the provisions of section 8(b) of the Federal Advisory Committee Act, the GSA Committee Management Officer carries out all responsibilities delegated by the Administrator. The Officer ensures that sections 10(b), 12(a), and 13 of the Act are implemented by GSA to provide for appropriate record keeping. Records include, but are not limited to:

(a) A set of approved charters and membership lists for each advisory committee;

(b) Copies of GSA's portion of the Annual Report of Federal Advisory Committees.

(c) Guidelines on committee management operations and procedures as maintained and updated; and

(d) Determinations to close advisory committee meetings.

§ 105–54.311 Complaint procedures.

(a) Any person whose request for access to an advisory committee document is denied may seek administrative review under 41 CFR 105–60, which implements the Freedom of Information Act. (See GSA Order, GSA regulations under the "Freedom of Information Act" (ADM 7900.3A).)

(b) Aggrieved individuals or organizations may file written complaints on matters not involving access to documents with the Deputy Administrator, General Services Administration, Washington, DC 20405. Complaints must be filed within 90 calendar days from the date the grievance arose. The Deputy Administrator promptly acts on each complaint and notifies the complainant in writing of the decision.

Subpart 105–54.4—Reports

§ 105–54.400 Scope of subpart.

This subpart sets forth the reports required by this part 105–54 and prescribes instructions for submission of the reports.

§ 105–54.401 Reports on GSA Federal Advisory Committees.

(a) The Committee Management Secretariat periodically issues reporting instructions and procedures. The GSA Committee Management Officer files a report each fiscal year providing program, financial, and membership information. The Secretariat uses the information in preparing recommendations and status reports on advisory committee matters and in assisting the President in preparing and submitting a fiscal year report to the Congress. Instructions for preparing GSA's submission are provided by the GSA Committee Management Officer.

(b) Reports on closed meetings are required as specified in § 105–54.301(o).

PART 105–55—COLLECTION OF CLAIMS OWED THE UNITED STATES

AUTHORITY: 5 U.S.C. 552–553; 31 U.S.C. 321, 3701, 3711, 3716, 3717, 3718, 3719, 3720B, 3720D; 31 CFR parts 900–904.

SOURCE: 68 FR 68741, Dec. 10, 2003, unless otherwise noted.

§ 105–55.001 Prescription of standards.

(a) The Secretary of the Treasury and the Attorney General of the United States issued regulations for collecting debts owed the United States under the authority contained in 31 U.S.C. 3711(d)(2). The regulations in this part prescribe standards for the General Services Administration (GSA) use in the administrative collection, offset, compromise, and the suspension or termination of collection activity for civil claims for money, funds, or property, as defined by 31 U.S.C. 3701(b), unless specific GSA statutes or regulations apply to such activities or, as provided for by Title 11 of the United States Code, when the claims involve bankruptcy. The regulations in this part also prescribe standards for referring debts to the Department of Justice for litigation. Additional guidance is contained in the Office of Management and Budget's Circular A–129 (Revised), "Policies for Federal Credit Programs and Non-Tax Receivables," the Department of the Treasury's "Managing Federal Receivables," and other publications concerning debt collection and debt management.

(b) GSA is not limited to the remedies contained in this part and will use all authorized remedies, including alternative dispute resolution and arbitration, to collect civil claims, to the extent such remedies are not inconsistent with the Federal Claims Collection Act, as amended, Chapter 37 of Title 31, United States Code; the Debt Collection Act of 1982, 5 U.S.C. 5514; the Debt Collection Improvement Act of 1996, 31 U.S.C. 3701 et seq., or other relevant statutes. The regulations in this part are not intended to impair GSA's common law rights to collect debts.

(c) Standards and policies regarding the classification of debt for accounting purposes (for example, write off of uncollectible debt) are contained in the Office of Management and Budget's Circular A–129 (Revised), "Policies for Federal Credit Programs and Non-Tax Receivables."

§ 105–55.002 Definitions.

(a) *Administrative offset,* as defined in 31 U.S.C. 3701(a)(1), means withholding funds payable by the United States (including funds payable by the United States on behalf of a State government) to, or held by the United States for, a person to satisfy a claim.

(b) *Compromise* means the reduction of a debt as provided in §§ 105–55.019 and 105–55.020.

(c) *Debt collection center* means the Department of the Treasury or other Government agency or division designated by the Secretary of the Treasury with authority to collect debts on behalf of creditor agencies in accordance with 31 U.S.C. 3711(g).

(d) *Debtor* means an individual, organization, association, corporation, partnership, or a State or local government indebted to the United States or a person or entity with legal responsibility for assuming the debtor's obligation.

(e) *Delinquent* or *past-due non-tax debt* means any non-tax debt that has not been paid by the date specified in GSA's initial written demand for payment or applicable agreement or instrument (including a post-delinquency payment agreement), unless other satisfactory payment arrangements have been made.

(f) For the purposes of the standards in this part, unless otherwise stated, the *term Administrator* refers to the *Administrator* of General Services or the Administrator's delegate.

(g) For the purposes of the standards in this part, the terms *claim* and *debt* are synonymous and interchangeable. They refer to an amount of money, funds, or property that has been determined by GSA to be due the United States from any person, organization, or entity, except another Federal agency, from sources which include loans insured or guaranteed by the United States and all other amounts due the United States from fees, leases, rents, royalties, services, sales of real or personal property, overpayments, penalties, damages, interest, fines and forfeitures and all other similar sources, including debt administered by a third party as an agent for the Federal Government. For the purposes of administrative offset under 31 U.S.C. 3716, the terms *claim* and *debt* include an amount of money, funds, or property owed by a person to a State (including past-due support being enforced by a State), the District of Columbia, American Samoa, Guam, the United States Virgin Islands, the Commonwealth of the Northern Mariana Islands, or the Commonwealth of Puerto Rico.

(h) For the purposes of the standards in this part, unless otherwise stated, the terms *GSA* and *Agency* are synonymous and interchangeable.

(i) For the purposes of the standards in this part, unless otherwise stated, *Secretary* means the Secretary of the Treasury or the Secretary's delegate.

(j) For the standards in this part, Federal agencies include agencies of the executive, legislative, and judicial branches of the Government, including Government corporations.

(k) *Hearing* means a review of the documentary evidence concerning the existence and/or amount of a debt, and/or the terms of a repayment schedule, provided such repayment schedule is established other than by a written agreement entered into pursuant to this part. If the hearing official determines the issues in dispute cannot be resolved solely by review of the written record, such as when the validity of the debt turns on the issue of credibility or veracity, an oral hearing may be provided.

(l) *Hearing official* means a Board Judge of the Civilian Board of Contract Appeals.

(m) In this part, words in the plural form shall include the singular and vice versa, and words signifying the masculine gender shall include the feminine and vice versa. The terms *includes* and *including* do not exclude matters not listed but do include matters that are in the same general class.

(n) *Reconsideration* means a request by the employee to have a secondary review by GSA of the existence and/or amount of the debt, and/or the proposed offset schedule.

(o) *Recoupment* is a special method for adjusting debts arising under the same transaction or occurrence. For example, obligations arising under the same contract generally are subject to recoupment.

(p) *Taxpayer identifying number* means the identifying number described under section 6109 of the Internal Revenue Code of 1986 (26 U.S.C. 6109). For an individual, the taxpayer identifying number is the individual's social security number.

(q) *Waiver* means the cancellation, remission, forgiveness, or non-recovery of a debt or debt-related charge as permitted or required by law.

[68 FR 68741, Dec. 10, 2003, as amended at 78 FR 29247, May 20, 2013]

§ 105–55.003 Antitrust, fraud, tax, interagency claims, and claims over $100,000 excluded.

(a) The standards in this part relating to compromise, suspension, and termination of collection activity do not apply to any debt based in whole or in part on conduct in violation of the antitrust laws or to any debt involving fraud, the presentation of a false claim, or misrepresentation on the part of the debtor or any party having an interest in the claim. The standards of this part relating to the administrative collection of claims do apply, but only to the extent authorized by the Department of Justice (DOJ) in a particular case. Upon identification of a claim based in whole or in part on conduct in violation of the antitrust laws or any claim involving fraud, the presentation of a false claim, or misrepresentation on the part of the debtor or any party having an interest in the claim, the General Services Administration (GSA) will promptly refer the case to the GSA Office of Inspector General (OIG). The OIG has the responsibility for investigating or referring the matter, where appropriate, to DOJ for action. At its discretion, DOJ may return the claim to GSA for further handling in accordance with the standards of this part.

(b) This part does not apply to tax debts.

(c) This part does not apply to claims between GSA and other Federal agencies.

(d) This part does not apply to claims over $100,000.

§ 105–55.004 Compromise, waiver, or disposition under other statutes not precluded.

Nothing in this part precludes the General Services Administration (GSA) disposition of any claim under statutes and implementing regulations other than subchapter II of chapter 37 of Title 31 of the United States Code (Claims of the United States Government) and the standards in this part. See, e.g., the Federal Medical Care Recovery Act, 42 U.S.C. 2651–2653, and applicable regulations, 28 CFR part 43. In such cases, the laws and regulations specifically applicable to claims collection activities of GSA generally take precedence.

§ 105–55.005 Form of payment.

Claims may be paid in the form of money or, when a contractual basis exists, the General Services Administration may demand the return of specific property or the performance of specific services.

§ 105–55.006 Subdivision of claims not authorized.

Debts will not be subdivided to avoid the monetary ceiling established by 31 U.S.C. 3711(a)(2). A debtor's liability arising from a particular transaction or contract shall be considered a single debt in determining whether the debt is one of less than $100,000 (excluding interest, penalties, and administrative costs) or such higher amount as the Attorney General shall from time to time prescribe for purposes of compromise, suspension or termination of collection activity.

§ 105–55.007 Required administrative proceedings.

The General Services Administration is not required to omit, foreclose, or duplicate administrative proceedings required by contract or other laws or regulations.

§ 105–55.008 No private rights created.

The standards in this part do not create any right or benefit, substantive or procedural, enforceable at law or in equity by a party against the United States, its agencies, its officers, or any other person, nor shall the failure of the General Services Administration to comply with any of the provisions of this part be available to any debtor as a defense.

§ 105–55.009 Aggressive agency collection activity.

(a) The General Services Administration (GSA) will aggressively collect all debts arising out of activities of, or referred or transferred for collection services to, GSA. Collection activities will be undertaken promptly, including letters, telephone calls, electronic mail (e-mail), and Internet inquiries, with follow-up action taken as necessary.

(b) Debts referred or transferred to Treasury, or Treasury-designated debt collection centers under the authority of 31 U.S.C. 3711(g), will be serviced, collected, or compromised, or the collection action will be suspended or terminated, in accordance with the statutory requirements and authorities applicable to the collection of such debts.

(c) GSA will cooperate with other agencies in their debt collection activities.

(d) GSA will consider referring debts that are less than 180 days delinquent to Treasury or to Treasury-designated "debt collection centers" to accomplish efficient, cost effective debt collection. Treasury is a debt collection center, is authorized to designate other Federal agencies as debt collection centers based on their performance in collecting delinquent debts, and may withdraw such designations. Referrals to debt collection centers shall be at the discretion of, and for a time period acceptable to, the Secretary. Referrals may be for servicing, collection, compromise, suspension, or termination of collection action.

(e) GSA will transfer to the Secretary any debt that has been delinquent for a period of 180 days or more so the Secretary may take appropriate action to collect the debt or terminate collection action. See 31 CFR 285.12

(Transfer of Debts to Treasury for Collection). This requirement does not apply to any debt that—

(1) Is in litigation or foreclosure;

(2) Will be disposed of under an approved asset sale program;

(3) Has been referred to a private collection contractor for a period of time acceptable to the Secretary;

(4) Is at a debt collection center for a period of time acceptable to the Secretary (see paragraph (d) of this section);

(5) Will be collected under internal offset procedures within three years after the debt first became delinquent;

(6) Is exempt from this requirement based on a determination by the Secretary that exemption for a certain class of debt is in the best interest of the United States. GSA may request the Secretary to exempt specific classes of debts;

(7) Is in bankruptcy (see § 105–55.010(h));

(8) Involves a deceased debtor;

(9) Is owed to GSA by a foreign government; or

(10) Is in an administrative appeals process, until the process is complete and the amount due is set.

(f) Agencies operating Treasury-designated debt collection centers are authorized to charge a fee for services rendered regarding referred or transferred debts. The fee may be paid out of amounts collected and will be added to the debt as an administrative cost (see § 105–55.016).

§ 105–55.010 Demand for payment.

(a) Written demand, as described in paragraph (b) of this section, will be made promptly upon a debtor of the United States in terms informing the debtor of the consequences of failing to cooperate with the General Services Administration (GSA) to resolve the debt. The specific content, timing, and number of demand letters (usually no more than three, thirty days apart) will depend upon the type and amount of the debt and the debtor's response, if any, to GSA's letters, telephone calls, electronic mail (e-mail) or Internet inquiries. In determining the timing of the demand letter(s), GSA will give due regard to the need to refer debts promptly to the Department of Justice

for litigation, in accordance with § 105–55.031. When necessary to protect the Government's interest (for example, to prevent the running of a statute of limitations), written demand may be preceded by other appropriate actions under this part, including immediate referral for litigation.

(b) Demand letters will inform the debtor—

(1) The basis and the amount of the indebtedness and the rights, if any, the debtor may have to seek review within GSA (see § 105–55.011(e));

(2) The applicable standards for imposing any interest, penalties, or administrative costs (see § 105–55.016);

(3) The date by which payment should be made to avoid late charges (i.e., interest, penalties, and administrative costs) and enforced collection, which generally will not be more than 30 days from the date the demand letter is mailed or hand-delivered; and

(4) The name, address, and phone number of a contact person or office within GSA.

(c) GSA will exercise care to ensure that demand letters are mailed or hand-delivered on the same day they are dated. For the purposes of written demand, notification by electronic mail (e-mail) and/or Internet delivery is considered a form of written demand notice. There is no prescribed format for demand letters. GSA will utilize demand letters and procedures that will lead to the earliest practicable determination of whether the debt can be resolved administratively or must be referred for litigation.

(d) GSA may include in demand letters such items as the willingness to discuss alternative methods of payment; Agency policies with respect to the use of credit bureaus, debt collection centers, and collection agencies; Agency remedies to enforce payment of the debt (including assessment of interest, administrative costs and penalties, administrative garnishment, the use of collection agencies, Federal salary offset, tax refund offset, administrative offset, and litigation); the requirement that any debt delinquent for more than

461

180 days will be transferred to the Department of the Treasury for collection; and, depending on applicable statutory authority, the debtor's entitlement to consideration of a waiver.

(e) GSA will respond promptly to communications from debtors, within 30 days whenever feasible, and will advise debtors who dispute debts to furnish available evidence to support their contentions.

(f) Prior to the initiation of the demand process or at any time during or after completion of the demand process, if GSA determines to pursue, or is required to pursue, offset, the procedures applicable to offset will be followed (see § 105–55.011). The availability of funds or money for debt satisfaction by offset and GSA's determination to pursue collection by offset will release the Agency from the necessity of further compliance with paragraphs (a), (b), (c), and (d) of this section.

(g) Prior to referring a debt for litigation, GSA will advise each person determined to be liable for the debt that, unless the debt can be collected administratively, litigation may be initiated. This notification will comply with Executive Order 12988 (3 CFR, 1996 Comp. pp. 157–163) and may be given as part of a demand letter under paragraph (b) of this section or in a separate document.

(h) When GSA learns a bankruptcy petition has been filed with respect to a debtor, before proceeding with further collection action, the Agency will ascertain the impact of the Bankruptcy Code on any pending or contemplated collection activities. Unless the Agency determines the automatic stay imposed at the time of filing pursuant to 11 U.S.C. 362 has been lifted or is no longer in effect, in most cases collection activity against the debtor will stop immediately.

(1) A proof of claim will be filed in most cases with the bankruptcy court or the Trustee. GSA will refer to the provisions of 11 U.S.C. 106 relating to the consequences on sovereign immunity of filing a proof of claim.

(2) If GSA is a secured creditor, it may seek relief from the automatic stay regarding its security, subject to the provisions and requirements of 11 U.S.C. 362.

(3) Offset is stayed in most cases by the automatic stay. However, GSA will determine whether its payments to the debtor and payments of other agencies available for offset may be frozen by the Agency until relief from the automatic stay can be obtained from the bankruptcy court. GSA also will determine whether recoupment is available.

§ 105–55.011 Collection by administrative offset.

(a) *Scope.* (1) The term "administrative offset" has the meaning provided in 31 U.S.C. 3701(a)(1).

(2) This section does not apply to—

(i) Debts arising under the Social Security Act, except as provided in 42 U.S.C. 404;

(ii) Payments made under the Social Security Act, except as provided for in 31 U.S.C. 3716(c) (see 31 CFR 285.4, Federal Benefit Offset);

(iii) Debts arising under, or payments made under, the Internal Revenue Code (see 31 CFR 285.2, Tax Refund Offset) or the tariff laws of the United States;

(iv) Offsets against Federal salaries to the extent these standards are inconsistent with regulations published to implement such offsets under 5 U.S.C. 5514 and 31 U.S.C. 3716 (see 5 CFR part 550, subpart K, and 31 CFR 285.7, Federal Salary Offset);

(v) Offsets under 31 U.S.C. 3728 against a judgment obtained by a debtor against the United States;

(vi) Offsets or recoupments under common law, State law, or Federal statutes specifically prohibiting offsets or recoupments of particular types of debts; or

(vii) Offsets in the course of judicial proceedings, including bankruptcy.

(3) Unless otherwise provided for by contract or law, debts or payments that are not subject to administrative offset under 31 U.S.C. 3716 may be collected by administrative offset under the common law or other applicable statutory authority.

(4) Unless otherwise provided by law, administrative offset of payments under the authority of 31 U.S.C. 3716 to collect a debt may not be conducted more than 10 years after the General Services Administration's (GSA's) right to collect the debt first accrued, unless facts material to GSA's right to

collect the debt were not known and could not reasonably have been known by the official or officials of GSA who were charged with the responsibility to discover and collect such debts. This limitation does not apply to debts reduced to a judgment.

(5) In bankruptcy cases, GSA will ascertain the impact of the Bankruptcy Code, particularly 11 U.S.C. 106, 362, and 553, on pending or contemplated collections by offset.

(b) *Mandatory centralized administrative offset.* (1) GSA is required to refer past due, legally enforceable non-tax debts that are over 180 days delinquent to the Secretary for collection by centralized administrative offset. Debts that are less than 180 days delinquent also may be referred to the Secretary for this purpose. See paragraph (b)(5) of this section for debt certification requirements.

(2) The names and taxpayer identifying numbers (TINs) of debtors who owe debts referred to the Secretary as described in paragraph (b)(1) of this section will be compared to the names and TINs on payments to be made by Federal disbursing officials. Federal disbursing officials include disbursing officials of the Department of the Treasury, the Department of Defense, the United States Postal Service, other Government corporations, and disbursing officials of the United States designated by the Secretary. When the name and TIN of a debtor match the name and TIN of a payee and all other requirements for offset have been met, the payment will be offset to satisfy the debt.

(3) Federal disbursing officials will notify the debtor/payee in writing that an offset has occurred to satisfy, in part or in full, a past due, legally enforceable delinquent debt. The notice will include a description of the type and amount of the payment from which the offset was taken, the amount of offset that was taken, the identity of GSA as the creditor agency requesting the offset, and a contact point within GSA who will respond to questions regarding the offset.

(4)(i) Offsets may be initiated only after the debtor—

(A) Has been sent written notice of the type and amount of the debt, the intention of GSA to use administrative offset to collect the debt, and an explanation of the debtor's rights under 31 U.S.C. 3716(c)(7); and

(B) The debtor has been given—

(1) The opportunity to inspect and copy Agency records related to the debt;

(2) The opportunity for a review within GSA of the determination of indebtedness (see paragraph (e) of this section); and

(3) The opportunity to make a written agreement to repay the debt.

(ii) The procedures set forth in paragraph (b)(4)(i) of this section may be omitted when—

(A) The offset is in the nature of a recoupment;

(B) The debt arises under a contract as set forth in *Cecile Industries, Inc.* v. *Cheney,* 995 F.2d 1052 (Fed. Cir. 1993) (notice and other procedural protections set forth in 31 U.S.C. 3716(a) do not supplant or restrict established procedures for contractual offsets accommodated by the Contracts Disputes Act); or

(C) In the case of non-centralized administrative offsets conducted under paragraph (c) of this section, GSA first learns of the existence of the amount owed by the debtor when there is insufficient time before payment would be made to the debtor/payee to allow for prior notice and an opportunity for review. When prior notice and an opportunity for review are omitted, GSA will give the debtor such notice and an opportunity for review as soon as practicable and will promptly refund any money ultimately found not to have been owed to the Government.

(iii) When GSA previously has given a debtor any of the required notice and review opportunities with respect to a particular debt (see, e.g., §105–55.010), the Agency need not duplicate such notice and review opportunities before administrative offset may be initiated.

(5) When referring delinquent debts to the Secretary, GSA will certify, in a form acceptable to the Secretary, that—

(i) The debt(s) is (are) past due and legally enforceable; and

(ii) GSA has complied with all due process requirements under 31 U.S.C. 3716(a) and Agency regulations.

(6) Payments that are prohibited by law from being offset are exempt from centralized administrative offset. The Secretary shall exempt payments under means-tested programs from centralized administrative offset when requested in writing by the Administrator. Also, the Secretary may exempt other classes of payments from centralized offset upon the written request of the Administrator.

(7) Benefit payments made under the Social Security Act (42 U.S.C. 301 et seq.), part B of the Black Lung Benefits Act (30 U.S.C. 921 et seq.), and any law administered by the Railroad Retirement Board (other than tier 2 benefits), may be offset only in accordance with Treasury regulations, issued in consultation with the Social Security Administration, the Railroad Retirement Board, and the Office of Management and Budget. See 31 CFR 285.4.

(8) In accordance with 31 U.S.C. 3716(f), the Secretary may waive the provisions of the Computer Matching and Privacy Protection Act of 1988 concerning matching agreements and post-match notification and verification (5 U.S.C. 552a(o) and (p)) for centralized administrative offset upon receipt of a certification from GSA that the due process requirements enumerated in 31 U.S.C. 3716(a) have been met. The certification of a debt in accordance with paragraph (b)(5) of this section will satisfy this requirement. If such a waiver is granted, only the Data Integrity Board of the Department of the Treasury is required to oversee any matching activities, in accordance with 31 U.S.C. 3716(g). This waiver authority does not apply to offsets conducted under paragraphs (c) and (d) of this section.

(c) *Non-centralized administrative offset.* (1) Generally, non-centralized administrative offsets are ad hoc case-by-case offsets that GSA conducts, at the Agency's discretion, internally or in cooperation with another agency certifying or authorizing payments to the debtor. Unless otherwise prohibited by law, when centralized administrative offset is not available or appropriate, past due, legally enforceable non-tax delinquent debts may be collected through non-centralized administrative offset. In these cases, GSA may make a request directly to a payment authorizing agency to offset a payment due a debtor to collect a delinquent debt. For example, it may be appropriate for GSA to request the Office of Personnel Management (OPM) offset a Federal employee's lump sum payment upon leaving Government service to satisfy an unpaid advance.

(2) Such offsets will occur only after—

(i) The debtor has been provided due process as set forth in paragraph (b)(4) of this section; and

(ii) The payment authorizing agency has received written certification from GSA that the debtor owes the past due, legally enforceable delinquent debt in the amount stated, and that GSA has fully complied with its regulations concerning administrative offset.

(3) Payment authorizing agencies will comply with offset requests by GSA to collect debts owed to the United States, unless the offset would not be in the best interests of the United States with respect to the program of the payment authorizing agency, or would otherwise be contrary to law.

(4) When collecting multiple debts by non-centralized administrative offset, GSA will apply the recovered amounts to those debts in accordance with the best interests of the United States, as determined by the facts and circumstances of the particular case, particularly the applicable statute of limitations.

(d) *Requests to OPM to offset a debtor's anticipated or future benefit payments under the Civil Service Retirement and Disability Fund.* Upon providing OPM written certification that a debtor has been afforded the procedures provided in paragraph (b)(4) of this section, GSA may request OPM to offset a debtor's anticipated or future benefit payments under the Civil Service Retirement and Disability Fund (Fund) in accordance with regulations codified at 5 CFR 831.1801 through 831.1808. Upon receipt of such a request, OPM will identify and "flag" a debtor's account in anticipation of the time when the debtor requests, or becomes eligible to receive, payments from the Fund. This will satisfy any requirement that offset be initiated prior to the expiration of the time limitations referenced in paragraph (a)(4) of this section.

(e) *Review requirements.* (1) A debtor may seek review of a debt by sending a signed and dated petition for review to the official named in the demand letter. A copy of the petition must also be sent to the Civilian Board of Contract Appeals (CBCA) at 1800 F Street NW., Washington, DC 20405.

(2) For purposes of this section, whenever GSA is required to afford a debtor a review within the Agency, the hearing official will provide the debtor with a reasonable opportunity for an oral hearing when the debtor requests reconsideration of the debt and the hearing official determines that the question of the indebtedness cannot be resolved by review of the documentary evidence; for example, when the validity of the debt turns on an issue of credibility or veracity.

(3) Witnesses will be asked to testify under oath or affirmation, and a written transcript of the hearing will be kept and made available to either party in the event of an appeal under the Administrative Procedure Act, 5 U.S.C. 701–706. Arrangements for the taking of the transcript will be made by the hearing official, and all charges associated with the taking of the transcript will be the responsibility of GSA.

(4) In those cases when an oral hearing is not required by this section, the hearing official will accord the debtor a "paper hearing," that is, a determination of the request for reconsideration based upon a review of the written record.

(5) Hearings will be conducted by a Board Judge of the CBCA. GSA must provide proof that a valid non-tax debt exists, and the debtor must provide evidence that no debt exists or that the amount of the debt is incorrect.

(6) If an oral hearing is provided, the debtor may choose to have it conducted in the hearing official's office located at 1800 M Street NW., 6th Floor, Washington, DC 20036, at another location designated by the hearing official, or may choose a hearing by telephone. All personal and travel expenses incurred by the debtor in connection with an in-person hearing will be borne by the debtor. All telephonic charges incurred during a hearing will be the responsibility of GSA.

(7) If the debtor is an employee of GSA, the employee may represent himself or herself or may be represented by another person of his or her choice at the hearing. GSA will not compensate the employee for representation expenses, including hourly fees for attorneys, travel expenses, and costs for reproducing documents.

(8) A written decision will be issued by the hearing official no later than 60 days from the date the petition for review is received by GSA. The decision will state the—

(i) Facts supporting the nature and origin of the debt;

(ii) Hearing officials analysis, findings, and conclusions as to the debtor's and/or GSA's grounds;

(iii) Amount and validity of the debt; and

(iv) Repayment schedule, if applicable.

(9) The hearing official's decision will be the final Agency action for the purposes of judicial review under the Administrative Procedure Act (5 U.S.C. 701 *et seq.*).

(f) *Waiver requirements.* (1) Under certain circumstances, a waiver of a claim against an employee of GSA arising out of an erroneous payment of pay, allowances, travel, transportation, or relocation expenses and allowances may be granted in whole or in part.

(2) GSA procedures for waiving a claim of erroneous payment of pay and allowances can be found in GSA Order CFO 4200.1, "Waiver of Claims for Overpayment of Pay and Allowances".

(3) GSA will follow the procedures of 5 U.S.C. 5584 when considering a request for waiver of erroneous payment of travel, transportation, or relocation expenses and allowances.

[68 FR 68741, Dec. 10, 2003, as amended at 78 FR 29247, May 20, 2013]

§ 105–55.012 Contracting with private collection contractors and with entities that locate and recover unclaimed assets.

(a) Subject to the provisions of paragraph (b) of this section, the General Services Administration (GSA) may contract with private collection contractors, as defined in 31 U.S.C. 3701(f), to recover delinquent debts provided that—

(1) GSA retain the authority to resolve disputes, compromise debts, suspend or terminate collection activity, and refer debts for litigation;

(2) The private collection contractor is not allowed to offer the debtor, as an incentive for payment, the opportunity to pay the debt less the private collection contractor's fee unless GSA has granted such authority prior to the offer;

(3) The contract provides that the private collection contractor is subject to the Privacy Act of 1974 to the extent specified in 5 U.S.C. 552a(m), and to applicable Federal and state laws and regulations pertaining to debt collection practices, including but not limited to the Fair Debt Collection Practices Act, 15 U.S.C. 1692; and

(4) The private collection contractor is required to account for all amounts collected.

(b) GSA will use Governmentwide debt collection contracts to obtain debt collection services provided by private collection contractors. However, GSA may refer debts to private collection contractors pursuant to a contract between the Agency and the private collection contractor only if such debts are not subject to the requirement to transfer debts to Treasury for debt collection. See 31 U.S.C. 3711(g); 31 CFR 285.12(e).

(c) GSA may fund private collection contractor contracts in accordance with 31 U.S.C. 3718(b), or as otherwise permitted by law.

(d) GSA may enter into contracts for locating and recovering assets of the United States, such as unclaimed assets.

(e) GSA may enter into contracts for debtor asset and income search reports. In accordance with 31 U.S.C. 3718(b), such contracts may provide that the fee a contractor charges the Agency for such services may be payable from the amounts recovered, unless otherwise prohibited by statute.

§ 105–55.013 Suspension or revocation of eligibility for loans and loan guaranties, licenses, permits, or privileges.

(a) Unless waived by the Administrator, the General Services Administration (GSA) will not extend financial assistance in the form of a loan, loan guarantee, or loan insurance to any person delinquent on a non-tax debt owed to a Federal agency. This prohibition does not apply to disaster loans. The authority to waive the application of this section may be delegated to the Chief Financial Officer and re-delegated only to the Deputy Chief Financial Officer of GSA. GSA may extend credit after the delinquency has been resolved. The Secretary may exempt classes of debts from this prohibition and has prescribed standards defining when a "delinquency" is "resolved" for purposes of this prohibition. See 31 CFR 285.13.

(b) In non-bankruptcy cases, GSA, when seeking the collection of statutory penalties, forfeitures, or other types of claims, will consider the suspension or revocation of licenses, permits, or other privileges for any inexcusable or willful failure of a debtor to pay such a debt in accordance with GSA regulations or governing procedures. The debtor will be advised in GSA's written demand for payment of the Agency's ability to suspend or revoke licenses, permits, or privileges. If GSA makes, guarantees, insures, acquires, or participates in loans, the Agency will consider suspending or disqualifying any lender, contractor, or broker from doing further business with the Agency or engaging in programs sponsored by the Agency if such lender, contractor, or broker fails to pay its debts to the Government within a reasonable time or if such lender, contractor, or broker has been suspended, debarred, or disqualified from participation in a program or activity by another Federal agency. The failure of any surety to honor its obligations in accordance with 31 U.S.C. 9305 will be reported to the Treasury. The Treasury will forward notification to all interested agencies that a surety's certificate of authority to do business with the Government has been revoked by the Treasury.

(c) The suspension or revocation of licenses, permits, or privileges also may extend to GSA programs or activities administered by the states on behalf of GSA, to the extent they affect GSA's ability to collect money or funds owed by debtors.

(d) In bankruptcy cases, before advising the debtor of GSA's intention to suspend or revoke licenses, permits, or privileges, the Agency will ascertain the impact of the Bankruptcy Code, particularly 11 U.S.C. 362 and 525, which may restrict such action.

§ 105–55.014 Liquidation of collateral.

(a) The General Services Administration (GSA) will liquidate security or collateral through the exercise of a power of sale in the security instrument or a non-judicial foreclosure, and apply the proceeds to the applicable debt(s), if the debtor fails to pay the debt(s) within a reasonable time after demand and if such action is in the best interest of the United States. Collection from other sources, including liquidation of security or collateral, is not a prerequisite to requiring payment by a surety, insurer, or guarantor unless such action is expressly required by statute or contract.

(b) When GSA learns a bankruptcy petition has been filed with respect to a debtor, the Agency will ascertain the impact of the Bankruptcy Code, including, but not limited to, 11 U.S.C. 362, to determine the applicability of the automatic stay and the procedures for obtaining relief from such stay prior to proceeding under paragraph (a) of this section.

§ 105–55.015 Collection in installments.

(a) Whenever feasible, the General Services Administration (GSA) will collect the total amount of a debt in one lump sum. If a debtor is financially unable to pay a debt in one lump sum, GSA may accept payment in regular installments. GSA may obtain financial statements from debtors who represent they are unable to pay in one lump sum and independently verify such representations whenever possible (see § 105–55.020(g)). When GSA agrees to accept payments in regular installments, a legally enforceable written agreement from the debtor will be ob-

tained specifying all of the terms of the arrangement and containing a provision accelerating the debt in the event of default. If the debtor's financial statement discloses the ownership of assets which are free and clear of liens or security interests, or assets in which the debtor owns an equity, the debtor may be asked to secure the payment of an installment note by executing a Security Agreement and Financing Statement transferring to the United States a security interest in the asset until the debt is paid.

(b) The size and frequency of installment payments will bear a reasonable relation to the size of the debt and the debtor's ability to pay. The installment payments will be sufficient in size and frequency to liquidate the debt in three years or less, unless circumstances warrant a longer period.

(c) Security for deferred payments may be obtained in appropriate cases. GSA may accept installment payments notwithstanding the refusal of the debtor to execute a written agreement or to give security, at the Agency's option.

§ 105–55.016 Interest, penalties, and administrative costs.

(a) Except as provided in paragraphs (g), (h), and (i) of this section, the General Services Administration (GSA) will charge interest, penalties, and administrative costs on debts owed to the United States pursuant to 31 U.S.C. 3717. GSA will send by U.S. mail, overnight delivery service, or hand-delivery a written notice to the debtor, at the debtor's most recent address available to the Agency, explaining the Agency's requirements concerning these charges, except where these requirements are included in a contractual or repayment agreement. These charges will continue to accrue until the debt is paid in full or otherwise resolved through compromise, termination, or waiver of the charges.

(b) GSA will charge interest on debts owed the United States as follows:

(1) Interest will accrue from the date of delinquency, or as otherwise provided by law.

(2) Unless otherwise established in a contract, repayment agreement, or by statute, the rate of interest charged

will be the rate established annually by the Secretary in accordance with 31 U.S.C. 3717(a)(1). Pursuant to 31 U.S.C. 3717, GSA may charge a higher rate of interest if it is reasonably determined that a higher rate is necessary to protect the rights of the United States. GSA will document the reason(s) for a determination that the higher rate is necessary.

(3) The rate of interest, as initially charged, will remain fixed for the duration of the indebtedness. When a debtor defaults on a repayment agreement and seeks to enter into a new agreement, GSA may require payment of interest at a new rate that reflects the Current Value of Funds Rate (CVFR) at the time the new agreement is executed. Interest will not be compounded, that is, interest will not be charged on interest, penalties, or administrative costs required by this section. If a debtor defaults on a previous repayment agreement, charges that accrued but were not collected under the defaulted agreement will be added to the principal under the new repayment agreement.

(c) GSA will assess administrative costs incurred for processing and handling delinquent debts. The calculation of administrative costs will be based on actual costs incurred or upon estimated costs as determined by the Agency.

(d) Unless otherwise established in a contract, repayment agreement, or by statute, GSA will charge a penalty, pursuant to 31 U.S.C. 3717(e)(2), not to exceed six percent a year on the amount due on a debt that is delinquent for more than 90 days. This charge will accrue from the date of delinquency.

(e) GSA may increase an "administrative debt" by the cost of living adjustment in lieu of charging interest and penalties under this section. "Administrative debt" includes, but is not limited to, a debt based on fines, penalties, and overpayments, but does not include a debt based on the extension of Government credit, such as those arising from loans and loan guaranties. The cost of living adjustment is the percentage by which the Consumer Price Index for the month of June of the calendar year preceding the adjust-

ment exceeds the Consumer Price Index for the month of June of the calendar year in which the debt was determined or last adjusted. Increases to administrative debts will be computed annually. GSA will use this alternative only when there is a legitimate reason to do so, such as when calculating interest and penalties on a debt would be extremely difficult because of the age of the debt.

(f) When a debt is paid in partial or installment payments, amounts received by GSA will be applied first to outstanding penalties, second to administrative charges, third to interest, and last to principal.

(g) GSA will waive the collection of interest, penalty and administrative charges imposed pursuant to this section on the portion of the debt that is paid within 30 days after the date on which interest began to accrue. GSA may extend this 30-day period on a case-by-case basis. In addition, GSA may waive interest, penalties, and administrative costs charged under this section, in whole or in part, without regard to the amount of the debt, either under the criteria set forth in these standards for the compromise of debts, or if the Agency determines that collection of these charges resulted from Agency error, is against equity and good conscience, or is not in the best interest of the United States.

(h) Unless a statute or regulation specifically prohibits collection, interest, penalties and administrative costs will continue to accrue for periods during which collection activity has been suspended pending Agency review or waiver consideration.

(i) GSA is authorized to impose interest and related charges on debts not subject to 31 U.S.C. 3717, in accordance with the common law.

§ 105–55.017 Use and disclosure of mailing addresses.

(a) When attempting to locate a debtor in order to collect or compromise a debt under this part or other authority, the General Services Administration (GSA) may send a request to the Secretary (or designee) to obtain a debtor's mailing address from the records of the Internal Revenue Service.

(b) GSA is authorized to use mailing addresses obtained under paragraph (a) of this section to enforce collection of a delinquent debt and may disclose such mailing addresses to other agencies and to collection agencies for collection purposes.

§105–55.018 Exemptions.

(a) The preceding sections of this part, to the extent they reflect remedies or procedures prescribed by the Debt Collection Act of 1982 and the Debt Collection Improvement Act of 1996, such as administrative offset, use of credit bureaus, contracting for collection agencies, and interest and related charges, do not apply to debts arising under, or payments made under, the Internal Revenue Code of 1986, as amended (26 U.S.C. 1 *et seq.*); the Social Security Act (42 U.S.C. 301 *et seq.*), except to the extent provided under 42 U.S.C. 404 and 31 U.S.C. 3716(c); or the tariff laws of the United States. These remedies and procedures, however, may be authorized with respect to debts that are exempt from the Debt Collection Act of 1982 and the Debt Collection Improvement Act of 1996, to the extent they are authorized under some other statute or the common law.

(b) Claims arising from the audit of transportation accounts pursuant to 31 U.S.C. 3726 will be determined, collected, compromised, terminated or settled in accordance with regulation published under the authority of 31 U.S.C. 3726 (see 41 CFR part 101–41, administered by the Director, Office of Transportation Audits) and are otherwise exempted from this part.

§105–55.019 Compromise of claims.

(a) The standards set forth in this section apply to the compromise of debts pursuant to 31 U.S.C. 3711. The General Services Administration (GSA) may exercise such compromise authority for debts arising out of activities of, or referred or transferred for collection services to, the Agency when the amount of the debt then due, exclusive of interest, penalties, and administrative costs, does not exceed $100,000 or any higher amount authorized by the Attorney General. The Administrator may designate other GSA officials to exercise the authorities in this section.

(b) Unless otherwise provided by law, when the principal balance of a debt, exclusive of interest, penalties, and administrative costs, exceeds $100,000 or any higher amount authorized by the Attorney General, the authority to accept the compromise rests with the Department of Justice. GSA will evaluate the compromise offer, using the factors set forth in §105–55.020. If an offer to compromise any debt in excess of $100,000 is acceptable to the Agency, GSA will refer the debt to the Civil Division or other appropriate litigating division in the Department of Justice using a Claims Collection Litigation Report. The referral will include appropriate financial information and a recommendation for the acceptance of the compromise offer. Justice Department approval is not required if GSA rejects a compromise offer.

§105–55.020 Bases for compromise.

(a) The General Services Administration (GSA) may compromise a debt if the full amount cannot be collected because—

(1) The debtor is unable to pay the full amount in a reasonable time, as verified through credit reports or other financial information.

(2) GSA is unable to collect the debt in full within a reasonable time by enforced collection proceedings.

(3) The cost of collecting the debt does not justify the enforced collection of the full amount.

(4) There is significant doubt concerning the Government's ability to prove its case in court.

(b) In determining the debtor's inability to pay, GSA will consider relevant factors such as the following:

(1) Age and health of the debtor.

(2) Present and potential income.

(3) Inheritance prospects.

(4) The possibility that assets have been concealed or improperly transferred by the debtor.

(5) The availability of assets or income that may be realized by enforced collection proceedings.

(c) GSA will verify the debtor's claim of inability to pay by using a credit report and other financial information as provided in paragraph (g) of this section. GSA will consider the applicable exemptions available to the debtor

469

under State and Federal law in determining the Government's ability to enforce collection. GSA also may consider uncertainty as to the price that collateral or other property will bring at a forced sale in determining the Government's ability to enforce collection. A compromise effected under this section will be for an amount that bears a reasonable relation to the amount that can be recovered by enforced collection procedures, with regard to the exemptions available to the debtor and the time that collection will take.

(d) If there is significant doubt concerning the Government's ability to prove its case in court for the full amount claimed, either because of the legal issues involved or because of a bona fide dispute as to the facts, then the amount accepted in compromise of such cases will fairly reflect the probabilities of successful prosecution to judgment, with due regard given to the availability of witnesses and other evidentiary support for the Government's claim. In determining the litigative risks involved, GSA will consider the probable amount of court costs and attorney fees pursuant to the Equal Access to Justice Act, 28 U.S.C. 2412 that may be imposed against the Government if it is unsuccessful in litigation.

(e) GSA may compromise a debt if the cost of collecting the debt does not justify the enforced collection of the full amount. The amount accepted in compromise in such cases may reflect an appropriate discount for the administrative and litigative costs of collection, with consideration given to the time it will take to effect collection. Collection costs may be a substantial factor in the settlement of small debts. In determining whether the cost of collection justifies enforced collection of the full amount, GSA will consider whether continued collection of the debt, regardless of cost, is necessary to further an enforcement principle, such as the Government's willingness to pursue aggressively defaulting and uncooperative debtors.

(f) GSA generally will not accept compromises payable in installments. This is not an advantageous form of compromise in terms of time and administrative expense. If, however, payment of a compromise in installments is necessary, GSA will obtain a legally enforceable written agreement providing that, in the event of default, the full original principal balance of the debt prior to compromise, less sums paid thereon, is reinstated. Whenever possible, GSA will obtain security for repayment in the manner set forth in § 105–55.015.

(g) To assess the merits of a compromise offer based in whole or in part on the debtor's inability to pay the full amount of a debt within a reasonable time, GSA may obtain a current financial statement from the debtor, executed under penalty of perjury, showing the debtor's assets, liabilities, income and expenses. GSA also may obtain credit reports or other financial information to assess compromise offers. GSA may use their own financial information form or may request suitable forms from the Department of Justice or the local United States Attorney's Office.

§ 105–55.021   Enforcement policy.

Pursuant to this section, the General Services Administration may compromise statutory penalties, forfeitures, or claims established as an aid to enforcement and to compel compliance, if the Agency's enforcement policy in terms of deterrence and securing compliance, present and future, will be adequately served by the Agency's acceptance of the sum to be agreed upon.

§ 105–55.022   Joint and several liability.

(a) When two or more debtors are jointly and severally liable, the General Services Administration (GSA) may pursue collection activity against all debtors, as appropriate. GSA will not attempt to allocate the burden of payment between the debtors but will proceed to liquidate the indebtedness as quickly as possible.

(b) GSA will ensure that a compromise agreement with one debtor does not release the Agency's claim against the remaining debtors. The amount of a compromise with one debtor will not be considered a precedent or binding in determining the amount that will be required from other debtors jointly and severally liable on the claim.

§105–55.023 Further review of compromise offers.

If the General Services Administration (GSA) is uncertain whether to accept a firm, written, substantive compromise offer on a debt that is within the Agency's delegated compromise authority, it may refer the offer to the Civil Division or other appropriate litigating division in the Department of Justice (DOJ), using a Claims Collection Litigation Report accompanied by supporting data and particulars concerning the debt. DOJ may act upon such an offer or return it to GSA with instructions or advice.

§105–55.024 Consideration of tax consequences to the Government.

In negotiating a compromise, the General Services Administration (GSA) may consider the tax consequences to the Government. In particular, GSA may consider requiring a waiver of tax-loss-carry-forward and tax-loss-carry-back rights of the debtor. For information on discharge of indebtedness reporting requirements see §105–55.030.

§105–55.025 Mutual releases of the debtor and the Government.

In all appropriate instances, a compromise that is accepted by the General Services Administration may be implemented by means of a mutual release, in which the debtor is released from further non-tax liability on the compromised debt in consideration of payment in full of the compromise amount and the Government and its officials, past and present, are released and discharged from any and all claims and causes of action arising from the same transaction that the debtor may have. In the event a mutual release is not executed when a debt is compromised, unless prohibited by law, the debtor is still deemed to have waived any and all claims and causes of action against the Government and its officials related to the transaction giving rise to the compromised debt.

§105–55.026 Suspending or terminating collection activity.

(a) The standards set forth in §§105–55.027 and 105–55.028 apply to the suspension or termination of collection activity pursuant to 31 U.S.C. 3711 on debts that do not exceed $100,000, or such other amount as the Attorney General may direct, exclusive of interest, penalties, and administrative costs, after deducting the amount of partial payments or collections, if any. Prior to referring a debt to the Department of Justice (DOJ) for litigation, the General Services Administration (GSA) may suspend or terminate collection under this part with respect to debts arising out of activities of, or referred or transferred for collection services to, the Agency.

(b) If, after deducting the amount of any partial payments or collections, the principal amount of a debt exceeds $100,000, or such other amount as the Attorney General may direct, exclusive of interest, penalties, and administrative costs, the authority to suspend or terminate rests solely with DOJ. If GSA believes suspension or termination of any debt in excess of $100,000 may be appropriate, the Agency will refer the debt to the Civil Division or other appropriate litigating division in DOJ, using the Claims Collection Litigation Report. The referral will specify the reasons for the Agency's recommendation. If, prior to referral to DOJ, GSA determines a debt is plainly erroneous or clearly without legal merit, the Agency may terminate collection activity regardless of the amount involved without obtaining DOJ concurrence.

§105–55.027 Suspension of collection activity.

(a) The General Services Administration (GSA) may suspend collection activity on a debt when—

(1) The Agency cannot locate the debtor;

(2) The debtor's financial condition is expected to improve; or

(3) The debtor has requested a waiver or review of the debt.

(b) Based on the current financial condition of the debtor, GSA may suspend collection activity on a debt when the debtor's future prospects justify retention of the debt for periodic review and collection activity and—

(1) The applicable statute of limitations has not expired; or

(2) Future collection can be effected by administrative offset, notwithstanding the expiration of the applicable statute of limitations for litigation of claims, with due regard to the 10-year limitation for administrative offset prescribed by 31 U.S.C. 3716(e)(1); or

(3) The debtor agrees to pay interest on the amount of the debt on which collection will be suspended, and such suspension is likely to enhance the debtor's ability to pay the full amount of the principal of the debt with interest at a later date.

(c)(1) GSA will suspend collection activity during the time required for consideration of the debtor's request for waiver or administrative review of the debt if the statute under which the request is sought prohibits the Agency from collecting the debt during that time.

(2) If the statute under which the request is sought does not prohibit collection activity pending consideration of the request, GSA will use discretion, on a case-by-case basis, to suspend collection. Further, GSA ordinarily will suspend collection action upon a request for waiver or review if the Agency is prohibited by statute or regulation from issuing a refund of amounts collected prior to Agency consideration of the debtor's request. However, GSA will not suspend collection when the Agency determines the request for waiver or review is frivolous or was made primarily to delay collection.

(d) When GSA learns a bankruptcy petition has been filed with respect to a debtor, in most cases the collection activity on a debt will be suspended, pursuant to the provisions of 11 U.S.C. 362, 1201, and 1301, unless the Agency can clearly establish the automatic stay has been lifted or is no longer in effect. GSA will, if legally permitted, take the necessary legal steps to ensure no funds or money are paid by the Agency to the debtor until relief from the automatic stay is obtained.

§ 105–55.028 Termination of collection activity.

(a) The General Services Administration (GSA) may terminate collection activity when—

(1) The Agency is unable to collect any substantial amount through its own efforts or through the efforts of others;

(2) The Agency is unable to locate the debtor;

(3) Costs of collection are anticipated to exceed the amount recoverable;

(4) The debt is legally without merit or enforcement of the debt is barred by any applicable statute of limitations;

(5) The debt cannot be substantiated; or

(6) The debt against the debtor has been discharged in bankruptcy.

(b) Before terminating collection activity, GSA will pursue all appropriate means of collection and determine, based upon the results of the collection activity, that the debt is uncollectible. Termination of collection activity ceases active collection of the debt. The termination of collection activity does not preclude GSA from retaining a record of the account for purposes of—

(1) Selling the debt, if the Secretary determines that such sale is in the best interests of the United States;

(2) Pursuing collection at a subsequent date in the event there is a change in the debtor's status or a new collection tool becomes available;

(3) Offsetting against future income or assets not available at the time of termination of collection activity; or

(4) Screening future applicants of loans and loan guaranties, licenses, permits, or privileges for prior indebtedness.

(c) Generally, GSA will terminate collection activity on a debt that has been discharged in bankruptcy, regardless of the amount. GSA may continue collection activity, however, subject to the provisions of the Bankruptcy Code, for any payments provided under a plan of reorganization. Offset and recoupment rights may survive the discharge of the debtor in bankruptcy and, under some circumstances, claims also may survive the discharge. For example, the claims of GSA that it is a known creditor of a debtor may survive a discharge if the Agency did not receive formal notice of the proceedings.

§ 105–55.029 Exception to termination.

When a significant enforcement policy is involved, or recovery of a judgment is a prerequisite to the imposition of administrative sanctions, the

General Services Administration may refer debts for litigation even though termination of collection activity may otherwise be appropriate.

§ 105–55.030 Discharge of indebtedness; reporting requirements.

(a) Before discharging a delinquent debt (also referred to as a close out of the debt), the General Services Administration (GSA) will take all appropriate steps to collect the debt in accordance with 31 U.S.C. 3711(g), including, as applicable, administrative offset, tax refund offset, Federal salary offset, referral to Treasury, Treasury-designated debt collection centers or private collection contractors, credit bureau reporting, wage garnishment, litigation, and foreclosure. Discharge of indebtedness is distinct from termination or suspension of collection activity and is governed by the Internal Revenue Code. When collection action on a debt is suspended or terminated, the debt remains delinquent and further collection action may be pursued at a later date in accordance with the standards set forth in this part. When GSA discharges a debt in full or in part, further collection action is prohibited. Therefore, GSA will make the determination that collection action is no longer warranted before discharging a debt. Before discharging a debt, GSA will terminate debt collection action.

(b) Section 3711(i), Title 31, United States Code, requires GSA to sell a delinquent non-tax debt upon termination of collection action if the Secretary determines such a sale is in the best interests of the United States. Since the discharge of a debt precludes any further collection action (including the sale of a delinquent debt), GSA may not discharge a debt until the requirements of 31 U.S.C. 3711(i) have been met.

(c) Upon discharge of a debt of more than $600, GSA must report the discharge to the Internal Revenue Service (IRS) in accordance with the requirements of 26 U.S.C. 6050P and 26 CFR 1.6050P–1. GSA may request Treasury or Treasury-designated debt collection centers to file such a discharge report to the IRS on the Agency's behalf.

(d) When discharging a debt, GSA will request the GSA Office of General Counsel to release any liens of record securing the debt.

§ 105–55.031 Prompt referral to the Department of Justice.

(a) The General Services Administration (GSA) will promptly refer to the Department of Justice (DOJ) for litigation debts on which aggressive collection activity has been taken in accordance with § 105–55.009 and that cannot be compromised, or on which collection activity cannot be suspended or terminated, in accordance with §§ 105–55.027 and 105–55.028. GSA may refer those debts arising out of activities of, or referred or transferred for collection services to, the Agency. Debts for which the principal amount is over $1,000,000, or such other amount as the Attorney General may direct, exclusive of interest and penalties, will be referred to the Civil Division or other division responsible for litigating such debts at DOJ, Washington, DC. Debts for which the principal amount is $1,000,000, or less, or such other amount as the Attorney General may direct, exclusive of interest or penalties, will be referred to DOJ's Nationwide Central Intake Facility as required by the Claims Collection Litigation Report instructions. Debts will be referred as early as possible, consistent with aggressive GSA collection activity and the observance of the standards contained in this part, and, in any event, well within the period for initiating timely lawsuits against the debtors. GSA will make every effort to refer delinquent debts to DOJ for litigation within one year of the date such debts last became delinquent. In the case of guaranteed or insured loans, GSA will make every effort to refer these delinquent debts to DOJ for litigation within one year from the date the loan was presented to the Agency for payment or re-insurance.

(b) DOJ has exclusive jurisdiction over the debts referred to it pursuant to this section. GSA, as the referring agency, will immediately terminate the use of any administrative collection activities to collect a debt at the time of the referral of that debt to DOJ. GSA will advise DOJ of the collection activities which have been utilized to date, and their result. GSA will refrain from having any contact with the debtor and will direct all debtor inquiries concerning the debt to DOJ, except as otherwise agreed between GSA and DOJ. GSA will immediately notify DOJ of any payments credited by the Agency to the debtor's account after referral of a debt under this section. DOJ will notify GSA of any payments it receives from the debtor.

§ 105–55.032   Claims Collection Litigation Report.

(a) Unless excepted by the Department of Justice (DOJ), the General Services Administration (GSA) will complete the Claims Collection Litigation Report (CCLR) (see § 105–55.019(b)), accompanied by a signed Certificate of Indebtedness, to refer all administratively uncollectible claims to DOJ for litigation. GSA will complete all sections of the CCLR appropriate to each claim as required by the CCLR instructions and furnish such other information as may be required in specific cases.

(b) GSA will indicate clearly on the CCLR the actions DOJ should take with respect to the referred claim. The CCLR permits the Agency to indicate specifically any of a number of litigative activities which DOJ may pursue, including enforced collection, judgment lien only, renew judgment lien only, renew judgment lien and enforce collection, program enforcement, foreclosure only, and foreclosure and deficiency judgment.

(c) GSA also will use the CCLR to refer claims to DOJ to obtain approval of any proposals to compromise the claims or to suspend or terminate Agency collection activity.

§ 105–55.033   Preservation of evidence.

The General Services Administration (GSA) will take care to preserve all files and records that may be needed by the Department of Justice (DOJ) to prove their claims in court. GSA ordinarily will include certified copies of the documents that form the basis for the claim in the packages referring their claims to DOJ for litigation. GSA will provide originals of such documents immediately upon request by DOJ.

§ 105–55.034   Minimum amount of referrals to the Department of Justice.

(a) The General Services Administration (GSA) will not refer for litigation claims of less than $2,500, exclusive of interest, penalties, and administrative costs, or such other amount as the Attorney General shall from time to time prescribe. The Department of Justice (DOJ) will notify GSA if the Attorney General changes this minimum amount.

(b) GSA will not refer claims of less than the minimum amount unless—

(1) Litigation to collect such smaller claims is important to ensure compliance with the Agency's policies or programs;

(2) The claim is being referred solely for the purpose of securing a judgment against the debtor, which will be filed as a lien against the debtor's property pursuant to 28 U.S.C. 3201 and returned to GSA for enforcement; or

(3) The debtor has the clear ability to pay the claim and the Government effectively can enforce payment, with due regard for the exemptions available to the debtor under State and Federal law and the judicial remedies available to the Government.

(c) GSA will consult with the Financial Litigation Staff of the Executive Office for United States Attorneys in DOJ prior to referring claims valued at less than the minimum amount.

PART 105–56—SALARY OFFSET FOR INDEBTEDNESS OF FEDERAL EMPLOYEES TO THE UNITED STATES

Subpart A—Salary Offset of General Services Administration Employees

Subpart B—Centralized Salary Offset (CSO) Procedures—GSA as Creditor Agency

Subpart C—Centralized Salary Offset (CSO) Procedures—GSA as Paying Agency

AUTHORITY: 5 U.S.C. 5514; 31 U.S.C. 3711; 31 U.S.C. 3716; 5 CFR part 550, subpart K; 31 CFR part 5; 31 CFR 285.7; 31 CFR parts 900–904.

SOURCE: 68 FR 68752, Dec. 10, 2003, unless otherwise noted.

Subpart A—Salary Offset of General Services Administration Employees

§ 105–56.001 Scope.

(a) This subpart covers internal GSA collections under 5 U.S.C. 5514. It applies when certain debts to the United States are recovered by administrative offset from the disposable pay of a GSA employee or a cross-serviced agency employee, except in situations where the employee consents to the recovery.

(b) The collection of any amount under this subpart will be in accordance with the standards promulgated pursuant to the Debt Collection Improvement Act of 1996 (DCIA), 31 U.S.C. 3701 et seq., and the Federal Claims Collection Standards, 31 CFR parts 900 through 904 as amended, or in accordance with any other statutory authority for the collection of claims of the United States or any Federal agency.

§ 105–56.002 Excluded debts or claims.

This subpart does not apply to the following:

(a) Debts or claims arising under the Internal Revenue Code of 1954 as amended (26 U.S.C. 1 et seq.), the Social Security Act (42 U.S.C. 301 et seq.), or the tariff laws of the United States.

(b) Any case where collection of a debt by salary offset is explicitly provided for or prohibited by another statute. Debt collection procedures under other statutory authorities, however, must be consistent with the provisions of the Federal Claims Collection Standards, defined at paragraph (h) of § 105–56.003.

(c) An employee election of coverage or of a change of coverage under a Federal benefits program that requires periodic deductions from pay if the amount to be recovered was accumulated over four pay periods or less. However, if the amount to be recovered was accumulated over more than four pay periods, the procedures under § 105–56.004 of this subpart will apply.

(d) Routine adjustment in pay or allowances that is made to correct an overpayment of pay attributable to clerical or administrative errors or delays in processing pay documents, if the overpayment occurred within the four pay periods preceding the adjustment and, at the time of the adjustment, or as soon after as possible, the employee is provided written notice of the nature and amount of the adjustment.

(e) Any adjustment to collect a debt amounting to $50 or less, if, at the time of the adjustment, or as soon after as possible, the employee is given written notice of the nature and amount of the adjustment and a point of contact for contesting the adjustment.

(f) Debts or claims arising from the accrual of unpaid Health Benefits Insurance (HBI) premiums as the result of an employee's election to continue health insurance coverage during periods of leave without pay (LWOP), or when pay is insufficient to cover premiums. Debt collection procedures for unpaid HBI are covered under 5 CFR part 890, subpart E.

§ 105–56.003   Definitions.

The following definitions apply to this subpart:

(a) *Administrative offset,* as defined in 31 U.S.C. 3701(a)(1), means withholding funds payable by the United States (including funds payable by the United States on behalf of a State government) to, or held by the United States for, a person to satisfy a claim.

(b) *Agency* means a department, agency or sub-agency, court, court administrative office, or instrumentality in the executive, judicial, or legislative branch of the Federal government, including government corporations.

(c) *Business day* means Monday through Friday, excluding Federal legal holidays. For purposes of computation, the last day of the period will be included unless it is a Federal legal holiday.

(d) *Creditor agency* means any agency that is owed a debt, including a debt collection center when acting on behalf of a creditor agency in matters pertaining to the collection of a debt.

(e) *Cross-serviced agency* means an arrangement between GSA and another agency whereby GSA provides financial support services to the other agency on a reimbursable basis. Financial support services can range from simply providing computer and software timesharing services to full-service administrative processing.

(f) *Disposable pay* means the amount that remains from an employee's Federal pay after required deductions for Federal, State and local income taxes; Social Security taxes, including Medicare taxes; Federal retirement programs, including contributions to the Thrift Savings Plan (TSP); premiums for life (excluding amounts deducted for supplemental coverage) and health insurance benefits; Internal Revenue Service (IRS) tax levies; and such other deductions that may be required by law to be withheld.

(g) *Employee* means any individual employed by GSA or a cross-serviced agency of the executive, legislative, or judicial branches of the Federal Government, including Government corporations.

(h) *FCCS* means the Federal Claims Collection Standards jointly published by the Department of Justice and the Department of the Treasury at 31 CFR parts 900 through 904.

(i) *Financial hardship* means an inability to meet basic living expenses for goods and services necessary for the survival of the debtor and his or her spouse and dependents.

(j) For the purposes of the standards in this subpart, unless otherwise stated, the term "Administrator" refers to the Administrator of General Services or the Administrator's delegate.

(k) For the purposes of the standards in this subpart, the terms "claim" and "debt" are synonymous and interchangeable. They refer to an amount of money, funds, or property that has been determined by GSA to be due the United States from an employee of GSA or a cross-serviced agency from sources which include loans insured or guaranteed by the United States and all other amounts due the United States from fees, leases, rents, royalties, services, sales of real or personal property, overpayments, penalties, damages, interest, fines and forfeitures and all other similar sources, including debt administered by a third party as an agent for the Federal Government. For the purposes of administrative offset under 31 U.S.C. 3716, the terms "claim" and "debt" include an amount of money, funds, or property owed by an employee to a State (including past-due support being enforced by a State), the District of Columbia, American Samoa, Guam, the United States Virgin Islands, the Commonwealth of the Northern Mariana Islands, or the Commonwealth of Puerto Rico.

(l) For the purposes of the standards in this subpart, unless otherwise stated, the terms "GSA" and "Agency" are synonymous and interchangeable.

(m) *Hearing official* means a Board Judge of the Civilian Board of Contract Appeals (CBCA).

(n) *Pay* means basic pay, special pay, incentive pay, retired pay, retainer pay, or in the case of an individual not entitled to basic pay, other authorized pay.

(o) *Pre-offset hearing* means a review of the documentary evidence concerning the existence and/or amount of a debt, and/or the terms of a repayment schedule, provided such repayment schedule is established other than by a written agreement entered into pursuant to this subpart. If the hearing official determines that the issues in dispute cannot be resolved solely by review of the written record, such as when the validity of the debt turns on the issue of credibility or veracity, an oral hearing may be provided.

(p) *Program official* means a supervisor or management official of the employee's service, staff office, cross-serviced agency, or other designated Agency officials.

(q) *Reconsideration* means a request by the employee to have a secondary review by GSA of the existence and/or amount of the debt, and/or the proposed offset schedule.

(r) *Salary offset* means an administrative offset to collect a debt under 5 U.S.C. 5514 by deduction(s) at one or more officially established pay intervals from the current pay account of an employee without his or her consent.

(s) *Waiver* means the cancellation, remission, forgiveness, or non-recovery of a debt or debt-related charge as permitted or required by law.

[68 FR 68752, Dec. 10, 2003, as amended at 78 FR 29247, May 20, 2013]

§ 105–56.004 Pre-offset notice.

An employee must be given written notice from the appropriate program official at least 30 days in advance of initiating a deduction from disposable pay informing him or her of—

(a) The nature, origin and amount of the indebtedness determined by GSA or a cross-serviced agency to be due;

(b) The intention of GSA to initiate proceedings to collect the debt through deductions from the employee's current disposable pay and other eligible payments;

(c) The amount (stated as a fixed dollar amount or as a percentage of pay, not to exceed 15 percent of disposable pay), frequency, proposed beginning date, and duration of the intended deductions;

(d) GSA's policy concerning how interest, penalties, and administrative costs are assessed (see 41 CFR part 105–55.017), including a statement that such assessments will be made unless excused under 31 U.S.C. 3717(h) and 31 CFR 901.9(g) and (h);

(e) The employee's right to inspect and copy GSA records relating to the debt, if records of the debt are not attached to the notice, or if the employee or his or her representative cannot personally inspect the records, the right to receive a copy of such records. Any costs associated with copying the records for the debtor will be borne by the debtor. The debtor must give a minimum of three (3) business days notice in advance to GSA of the date on which he or she intends to inspect and copy the records involved;

(f) A demand for repayment providing for an opportunity, under terms agreeable to GSA, for the employee to establish a schedule for the voluntary repayment of the debt by offset or to enter into a written repayment agreement of the debt in lieu of offset;

(g) The employee's right to request a waiver (see § 105–56.005(b) of this subpart);

(h) The employee's right to request reconsideration by the Agency of the existence and/or amount of the debt, and/or the proposed offset schedule;

(i) The employee's right to a pre-offset hearing conducted by a hearing official, arranged by the appropriate program official, if a request is filed as prescribed by § 105–56.006 of this subpart;

(j) The method and time period for requesting a hearing, including a statement that the timely filing of a request for hearing will stay the commencement of collection proceedings;

(k) The issuance of a final decision on the hearing, if requested, at the earliest practicable date, but no later than 60 days after the request for hearing is filed, unless the employee requests and the hearing official grants a delay in the proceedings;

(l) The risk that any knowingly false or frivolous statements, representations, or evidence may subject the employee to—

(1) Disciplinary procedures appropriate under 5 U.S.C. Chapter 75, 5 CFR part 752, or any other applicable statutes or regulations;

(2) Penalties under the False Claims Act, 31 U.S.C. 3729–3731, or any other applicable statutory authority; or

(3) Criminal penalties under 18 U.S.C. 286, 287, 1001, and 1002, or any other applicable statutory authority;

(m) Any other rights and remedies available to the employee under statutes or regulations governing the program for which the collection is being made;

(n) The employee's right to a prompt refund if amounts paid or deducted are later waived or found not owed, unless otherwise provided by law (see § 105–56.012 of this subpart);

(o) The specific address to which all correspondence must be directed regarding the debt.

§ 105–56.005 Employee response.

(a) *Voluntary repayment agreement.* An employee may submit a request to the appropriate program official who signed the pre-offset notice to enter into a written repayment agreement of the debt in lieu of offset. The request must be made within 7 days of receipt of notice under § 105–56.004 of this subpart. The agreement must be in writing, signed by both the employee and the appropriate program official making the notice, and a signed copy must be sent to the appropriate Finance Center serving the program activity. Acceptance of such an agreement is discretionary with the Agency. An employee who enters into such an agreement may, nevertheless, seek a waiver under paragraph (b) of this section.

(b) *Waiver.* An employee may submit a signed waiver request of overpayment of pay or allowances (e.g., 5 U.S.C. 5584, 10 U.S.C. 2774, or 32 U.S.C. 716) to the GSA National Payroll Center (NPC). When an employee requests waiver consideration, further collection on the debt may be suspended until a final administrative decision is made on the waiver request. During the period of any suspension, interest, penalties and administrative charges may be held in abeyance. GSA will not duplicate, for purposes of salary offset, any of the notices/procedures already provided the debtor prior to a request for waiver.

(c) *Reconsideration.* (1) An employee may seek a reconsideration of GSA's determination regarding the existence and/or amount of the debt. The request must be submitted to the appropriate program official indicated in the pre-offset notice, within 7 days of receipt of notice under § 105–56.004 of this subpart. Within 20 days of receipt of this notice, the employee must submit a detailed statement of reasons for reconsideration that must be accompanied by supporting documentation.

(2) An employee may request a reconsideration of the proposed offset schedule. The request must be submitted to the appropriate program official indicated in the pre-offset notice, within 7 days of receipt of notice under § 105–56.004 of this subpart. Within 20 days of receipt of this notice, the employee must submit an alternative repayment schedule accompanied by a detailed statement, supported by documentation, evidencing financial hardship resulting from GSA's proposed schedule. Acceptance of the request is at GSA's discretion. GSA will notify the employee in writing of its decision concerning the request to reduce the rate of an involuntary deduction.

§ 105–56.006 Petition for pre-offset hearing.

(a) The employee may request a pre-offset hearing by filing a written petition with the appropriate program official indicated in the pre-offset notice, within 15 days of receipt of the written notice. The petition must state why the employee believes GSA's determination concerning the existence and/or amount of the debt is in error, set forth any objections to the involuntary repayment schedule, and, if the employee is seeking an oral hearing, set forth reasons for an oral hearing. The timely filing of a petition will suspend the commencement of collection proceedings.

(b) The employee's petition or statement must be signed and dated by the employee.

(c) Petitions for hearing made after the expiration of the 15-day period may be accepted if the employee can show that the delay was because of circumstances beyond his or her control or because of failure to receive notice of the time limit.

(d) If the employee timely requests a pre-offset hearing or the timeliness is waived, the appropriate program official must—

(1) Promptly notify the CBCA and arrange for a hearing official (see § 105–56.003(m) of this subpart). The hearing official will notify the employee whether he or she may have an oral or a "paper hearing," i.e., a review on the written record (see 31 CFR 901.3(e)); and

(2) Provide the hearing official with a copy of all records on which the determination of the debt and any involuntary repayment schedule are based.

(e) If an oral hearing is to be held, the hearing official will notify the appropriate program official and the employee of the date, time, and location of the hearing. The debtor may choose to have the hearing conducted in the hearing official's office located at 1800 M Street NW., 6th Floor, Washington, DC 20036, at another location designated by the hearing official, or by telephone. The debtor and any witnesses are responsible for any personal expenses incurred to arrive at a hearing official's office or other designated location (see § 105–56.007(c)). All telephonic charges incurred during a hearing will be the responsibility of GSA.

(f) If the employee later elects to have the hearing based only on the written submissions, notification must be given to the hearing official and the appropriate program official at least 3 days before the date of the oral hearing. The hearing official may waive the 3-day requirement for good cause.

(g) If either party, without good cause as determined by the hearing official, does not appear at a scheduled oral hearing, the hearing official will make a determination on the claim which takes into account that party's position as presented in writing only.

[68 FR 68752, Dec. 10, 2003, as amended at 78 FR 29247, May 20, 2013]

§ 105–56.007 Pre-offset oral hearing.

(a) The Agency, represented by the appropriate program official or a representative of the Office of General Counsel, and the employee, and/or his or her representative, will explain their case in the form of an oral presentation with reference to the documentation submitted. The employee may testify on his or her own behalf, subject to cross-examination. Other witnesses may be called to testify when the hearing official determines the testimony to be relevant and not redundant. All witnesses will testify under oath, with the oath having been administered by the hearing official. A written transcript of the hearing will be kept and made available to either party in the event of an appeal under the Administrative Procedure Act, 5 U.S.C. 701–706. Arrangements for the taking of the transcript will be made by the hearing official, and all charges associated with the taking of the transcript will be the responsibility of GSA.

(b) The hearing official will—

(1) Conduct a fair and impartial hearing; and

(2) Preside over the course of the hearing, maintain decorum, and avoid delay in the disposition of the hearing.

(c) The employee may represent himself or herself or may be represented by another person of his or her choice at the hearing. GSA will not compensate the employee for representation expenses, including hourly fees for attorneys, travel expenses, and costs for reproducing documents.

(d) Oral hearings are open to the public. However, the hearing official may close all or any portion of the hearing when doing so is in the best interests of the employee or the Agency.

(e) Oral hearings may be conducted by telephone at the request of the employee. All telephonic charges incurred during a hearing will be the responsibility of GSA.

(f) The hearing official may request written submissions and documentation from the employee and the Agency, in addition to considering evidence offered at the hearing.

§ 105–56.008 Pre-offset paper hearing.

If a hearing is to be held only upon written submissions, the hearing official will issue a decision based upon the record and responses submitted by both the Agency and the employee. See § 105–56.006 of this subpart. If either party, without good cause as determined by the hearing official, does not provide written submissions and documentation requested by the hearing official, the hearing official will make a determination on the claim without reference to such submissions and documentation.

§ 105–56.009 Written decision.

(a) Within 60 days of the employee's filing of a petition for a pre-offset hearing, the hearing official will issue a written decision setting forth—

(1) The facts supporting the nature and origin of the debt;

(2) The hearing official's analysis, findings and conclusions as to the employee's or Agency's grounds;

(3) The amount and validity of the debt; and

(4) The repayment schedule, if applicable.

(b) The hearing official's decision will be the final Agency action for the purposes of judicial review under the Administrative Procedure Act (5 U.S.C. 701 *et seq.*).

§ 105–56.010 Deductions.

(a) *When deductions may begin.* Deductions may begin upon the issuance of an Agency decision on a request for reconsideration or waiver (except as provided in § 105–56.005(b) of this subpart) or the issuance of a decision in a pre-offset hearing. In no event will deductions begin sooner than thirty days from the date of the notice letter. If the employee filed a petition for hearing with the appropriate program official before the expiration of the period provided for in § 105–56.006 of this subpart, then deductions will begin after the hearing official has provided the employee with a hearing and the final written decision. The appropriate program official will coordinate with the National Payroll Center to begin offset in accordance with the final written decision.

(b) *Retired or separated employees.* If the employee retires, resigns, or is terminated before collection of the indebtedness is completed, the remaining indebtedness will be offset from any subsequent payments of any nature. If the debt cannot be satisfied from subsequent payments, then the debt will be collected according to the procedures for administrative offset pursuant to § 105–55.011 of this subpart.

(c) *Types of collection.* A debt may be collected in one lump sum or in installments. Collection will be by lump sum unless the employee is able to demonstrate to the program official who signed the notice letter that he or she is financially unable to pay in one lump sum. In these cases, collection will be by installment deductions. Involuntary deductions from pay may not exceed 15 percent of disposable pay.

(d) *Methods of collection.* If the debt cannot be collected in one lump sum, the debt will be collected by deductions at officially established pay intervals from an employee's current pay account, unless the employee and the appropriate program official agree to an alternative repayment schedule. The alternative arrangement must be in writing and signed by both the employee and the appropriate program official.

(1) *Installment deductions.* Installment deductions will be made over the shortest period possible. The size and frequency of installment deductions will bear a reasonable relation to the size of the debt and the employee's ability to pay. However, the amount deducted for any period will not exceed 15 percent of the disposable pay from which the deduction is made, unless the employee has agreed in writing to the deduction of a greater amount. The installment payment normally will be sufficient in size and frequency to liquidate the debt in three (3) years or less, unless circumstances warrant a longer period. Installment payments of less than $100 per pay period will be accepted only in the most unusual circumstances.

(2) *Sources of deductions.* GSA will make salary deductions only from basic pay, special pay, incentive pay, retired pay, retainer pay, or in the case of an employee not entitled to basic pay, other authorized pay.

(e) *Non-Salary payments.* The receipt of collections from salary offsets does not preclude GSA from pursuing other debt collection remedies, including the offset of other Federal payments to satisfy delinquent non-tax debt owed to the United States. GSA will pursue, when appropriate, such debt collection remedies separately or in conjunction with salary offset.

(f) *Interest, penalties and administrative costs.* Interest, penalties and administrative costs on debts under this subpart will be assessed according to the provisions of § 105–55.016 of this subpart.

§ 105–56.011 Non-waiver of rights.

An employee's involuntary payment of all or any portion of a debt being collected under 5 U.S.C. 5514 will not be construed as a waiver of any rights which the employee may have under 5 U.S.C. 5514 or any other provision of contract or law unless there are statutory or contractual provisions to the contrary.

§ 105–56.012 Refunds.

(a) GSA will promptly refund to the employee any amounts offset under these regulations when a debt is waived or otherwise found not owing the United States (unless expressly prohibited by statute or regulation), or GSA is directed by an administrative or judicial order to refund amounts deducted from the employee's current pay or withheld from non-salary payments.

(b) Unless required by Federal law or contract, refunds under this subpart will not bear interest.

§ 105–56.013 Coordinating offset with another Federal agency.

GSA participates in the Centralized Salary Offset (CSO) program (see subparts B and C of this part). In those instances when CSO cannot be utilized (i.e., when another agency does not participate in the program), the following procedures apply:

(a) *When GSA is the creditor agency.* When GSA is owed a debt by an employee of another agency, GSA will provide the paying agency with a written certification that the debtor owes GSA a debt and that GSA has complied with these regulations. This certification will include the amount and basis of the debt, the due date of the payment, or the beginning date of installment payments, if any.

(b) *When another agency is the creditor agency.* (1) GSA may use salary offset against one of its employees or cross-serviced agency employees who is indebted to another agency if requested to do so by that agency. Any such request must be accompanied by a certification from the requesting agency that the person owes the debt, the amount of the debt and that the employee has been given the procedural rights required by 5 U.S.C. 5514 and 5 CFR part 550, subpart K.

(2) The creditor agency must advise GSA of the number of installments to be collected, the amount of each installment, and the beginning date of the first installment if it is not the next established pay period.

(3) If GSA receives an improperly completed request, the creditor agency will be requested to supply the required information before any salary offset begins.

(4) If the claim procedures in paragraph (b)(1) of this section have been properly completed, deductions will begin on the next established pay period unless a different period is requested by the creditor agency.

(5) GSA will not review the merits of the creditor agency's determinations with respect to the amount and/or validity of the debt as stated in the debt claim certification.

(6) If the employee begins separation action before GSA collects the total debt due the creditor agency, the following actions will be taken:

(i) When possible, the balance owed the creditor agency will be liquidated from subsequent payments of any nature due the employee from GSA in accordance with 41 CFR part 105–55.011;

(ii) If the total amount of the debt cannot be recovered, GSA will certify the total amount collected to the creditor agency and the employee;

(iii) If GSA is aware that the employee is entitled to payments from the Civil Service Retirement and Disability Fund, or other similar payments, such information will be provided to the creditor agency so a certified claim can be made against the payments.

(7) If the employee transfers to another Federal agency before GSA collects the total amount due the creditor agency, GSA will certify the total amount collected to the creditor agency and the employee. It is the responsibility of the creditor agency to ensure that collection action is resumed by the new employing agency.

481

Subpart B—Centralized Salary Offset (CSO) Procedures—GSA as Creditor Agency

§ 105–56.014 Purpose and scope.

(a) This subpart establishes procedures for the offset of Federal salary payments, through the Financial Management Service's (FMS) administrative offset program, to collect delinquent debts owed to the Federal Government. This process is known as centralized salary offset. Rules issued by the Office of Personnel Management contain the requirements Federal agencies must follow prior to conducting salary offset and the procedures for requesting offsets directly from a paying agency. See 5 CFR parts 550.1101 through 550.1108.

(b) This subpart implements the requirement under 5 U.S.C. 5514 (a)(1) that all Federal agencies, using a process known as centralized salary offset computer matching, identify Federal employees who owe delinquent non-tax debt to the United States. Centralized salary offset computer matching is the computerized comparison of delinquent debt records with records of Federal employees. The purpose of centralized salary offset computer matching is to identify those debtors whose Federal salaries should be offset to collect delinquent debts owed to the Federal Government.

(c) This subpart specifies the delinquent debt records and Federal employee records that must be included in the salary offset matching process. For purposes of this subpart, delinquent debt records consist of the debt information submitted to FMS for purposes of administrative offset as required under 31 U.S.C. 3716(c)(6). Since GSA submits debts to FMS for purposes of administrative offset, the Agency is not required to submit duplicate information for purposes of centralized salary offset computer matching under 5 U.S.C. 5514(a)(1) and this subpart.

(d) An interagency consortium was established to implement centralized salary offset computer matching on a Governmentwide basis as required under 5 U.S.C. 5514(a)(1). Federal employee records consist of records of Federal salary payments disbursed by members of the consortium.

(e) The receipt of collections from salary offsets does not preclude GSA from pursuing other debt collection remedies, including the offset of other Federal payments to satisfy delinquent non-tax debt owed to the United States. GSA will pursue, when appropriate, such debt collection remedies separately or in conjunction with salary offset.

§ 105–56.015 Definitions.

The following definitions apply to this subpart:

(a) *Administrative offset* means withholding funds payable by the United States to, or held by the United States for, a person to satisfy a debt owed by the payee.

(b) *Agency* means a department, agency or sub-agency, court, court administrative office, or instrumentality in the executive, judicial, or legislative branch of the Federal government, including government corporations.

(c) *Centralized salary offset computer matching* means the computerized comparison of Federal employee records with delinquent debt records to identify Federal employees who owe such debts.

(d) *Consortium* means an interagency group established by the Secretary of the Treasury to implement centralized salary offset computer matching. The group includes all agencies that disburse Federal salary payments.

(e) *Creditor agency* means any agency that is owed a debt, including a debt collection center when acting on behalf of a creditor agency in matters pertaining to the collection of a debt.

(f) *Debt* means any amount of money, funds, or property that has been determined by an appropriate official of the Federal government to be owed to the United States by a person, including debt administered by a third party acting as an agent for the Federal Government. For purposes of this subpart, the term ''debt'' does not include debts arising under the Internal Revenue Code of 1986 (26 U.S.C. 1 *et seq.*).

(g) *Delinquent debt record* means information about a past-due, legally enforceable debt, submitted by GSA to FMS for purposes of administrative offset (including salary offset) in accordance with the provisions of 31 U.S.C.

3716(c)(6) and applicable regulations. Debt information includes the amount and type of debt and the debtor's name, address, and taxpayer identifying number.

(h) *Disbursing official* means an officer or employee designated to disburse Federal salary payments. This includes all disbursing officials of Federal salary payments, including but not limited to, disbursing officials of the Department of the Treasury, the Department of Defense, the United States Postal Service, any government corporation, and any disbursing official of the United States designated by the Secretary.

(i) *Disposable pay* means the amount that remains from an employee's Federal pay after required deductions for Federal, State and local income taxes; Social Security taxes, including Medicare taxes; Federal retirement programs, including contributions to the Thrift Savings Plan (TSP); premiums for life (excluding amounts deducted for supplemental coverage) and health insurance benefits; Internal Revenue Service (IRS) tax levies; and such other deductions that are required by law to be withheld.

(j) *Federal employee* means a current employee of an agency, including a current member of the Armed Forces or a Reserve of the Armed Forces (Reserves), employees of the United States Postal Service, and seasonal and temporary employees.

(k) *Federal employee records* means records of Federal salary payments that a paying agency has certified to a disbursing official for disbursement.

(l) *FMS* means the Financial Management Service, a bureau of the Department of the Treasury.

(m) For the purposes of the standards in this subpart, unless otherwise stated, the term "Administrator" refers to the Administrator of General Services or the Administrator's delegate.

(n) For the purposes of the standards in this subpart, unless otherwise stated, the terms "GSA" and "Agency" are synonymous and interchangeable.

(o) *Pay* means basic pay, special pay, incentive pay, retired pay, retainer pay, or in the case of an individual not entitled to basic pay, other authorized pay.

(p) *Paying agency* means the agency that employs the Federal employee who owes the debt and authorizes the payment of his or her current pay. A paying agency also includes an agency that performs payroll services on behalf of the employing agency.

(q) *Salary offset* means administrative offset to collect a debt owed by a Federal employee from the current pay account of the employee.

(r) *Secretary* means the Secretary of the Treasury or his or her delegate.

(s) *Taxpayer identifying number* means the identifying number described under section 6109 of the Internal Revenue Code of 1986 (26 U.S.C. 6109). For an individual, the taxpayer identifying number is the individual's social security number.

§ 105–56.016   GSA participation.

(a) As required under 5 U.S.C. 5514(a)(1), GSA must participate at least annually in centralized salary offset computer matching. To meet this requirement, GSA will notify FMS of all past-due, legally enforceable debts delinquent for more than 180 days for purposes of administrative offset, as required under 31 U.S.C. 3716(c)(6). Additionally, GSA may notify FMS of past-due, legally enforceable debts delinquent for less than 180 days for purposes of administrative offset.

(b) Prior to submitting a debt to FMS for purposes of collection by administrative offset, including salary offset, GSA will provide written certification to FMS that—

(1) The debt is past-due and legally enforceable in the amount submitted to FMS and that GSA will ensure that collections (other than collections through offset) are properly credited to the debt;

(2) Except in the case of a judgment debt or as otherwise allowed by law, the debt is referred for offset within ten years after GSA's right of action accrues;

(3) GSA has complied with the provisions of 31 U.S.C. 3716 (administrative offset) and related regulations including, but not limited to, the provisions requiring that GSA provide the debtor with applicable notices and opportunities for a review of the debt; and

(4) GSA has complied with the provisions of 5 U.S.C. 5514 (salary offset) and related regulations including, but not limited to, the provisions requiring that GSA provide the debtor with applicable notices and opportunities for a hearing.

(c) FMS may waive the certification requirement set forth in paragraph (b)(4) of this section as a prerequisite to submitting the debt to FMS. If FMS waives the certification requirement, before an offset occurs, GSA will provide the Federal employee with the notices and opportunities for a hearing as required by 5 U.S.C. 5514 and applicable regulations, and will certify to FMS that the requirements of 5 U.S.C. 5514 and applicable regulations have been met.

(d) GSA will notify FMS immediately of any payments credited by GSA to the debtor's account, other than credits for amounts collected by offset, after submission of the debt to FMS. GSA will notify FMS once the debt is paid in its entirety. GSA will also notify FMS immediately of any change in the status of the legal enforceability of the debt, for example, if the Agency receives notice that the debtor has filed for bankruptcy protection.

§ 105–56.017 Centralized salary offset computer match.

(a) Delinquent debt records will be compared with Federal employee records maintained by members of the consortium or paying agencies. The records will be compared to identify Federal employees who owe delinquent debts for purposes of collecting the debt by administrative offset. A match will occur when the taxpayer identifying number and name of a Federal employee are the same as the taxpayer identifying number and name of a debtor.

(b) As authorized by the provisions of 31 U.S.C. 3716(f), FMS, under a delegation of authority from the Secretary, has waived certain requirements of the Computer Matching and Privacy Protection Act of 1988, 5 U.S.C. 552a, as amended, for administrative offset, including salary offset, upon written certification by the Administrator, or the Administrator's delegate, that the requirements of 31 U.S.C. 3716(a) have

been met. Specifically, FMS has waived the requirements for a computer matching agreement contained in 5 U.S.C. 552a(o) and for post-match notice and verification contained in 5 U.S.C. 552a(p). GSA will provide certification in accordance with the provisions of § 105–56.016(b)(3) of this subpart.

§ 105–56.018 Salary offset.

When a match occurs and all other requirements for offset have been met, as required by the provisions of 31 U.S.C. 3716(c), the disbursing official will offset the Federal employee's salary payment to satisfy, in whole or part, the debt owed by the employee. Alternatively, the paying agency, on behalf of the disbursing official, may deduct the amount of the offset from an employee's disposable pay before the employee's salary payment is certified to a disbursing official for disbursement.

§ 105–56.019 Offset amount.

(a) The minimum dollar amount referred for offset under this subpart is $100.

(b) The amount offset from a salary payment under this subpart will be the lesser of—

(1) The amount of the debt, including any interest, penalties and administrative costs; or

(2) Up to 15 percent of the debtor's disposable pay.

(c) Alternatively, the amount offset may be an amount agreed upon, in writing, by the debtor and GSA.

(d) Offsets will continue until the debt, including any interest, penalties, and administrative costs, is paid in full or otherwise resolved to the satisfaction of GSA.

§ 105–56.020 Priorities.

(a) A levy pursuant to the Internal Revenue Code of 1986 (26 U.S.C. 1 et seq.) takes precedence over other deductions under this subpart.

(b) When a salary payment may be reduced to collect more than one debt, amounts offset under this subpart will be applied to a debt only after amounts offset have been applied to satisfy past due child support debts assigned to a State pursuant to the Social Security

Act under 42 U.S.C. 602(a)(26) or 671(a)(17).

§ 105–56.021 Notice.

(a) Before offsetting a salary payment, the disbursing official, or the paying agency on behalf of the disbursing official, will notify the Federal employee in writing of the date deductions from salary will commence and of the amount of such deductions.

(b)(1) When an offset occurs under this subpart, the disbursing official, or the paying agency on behalf of the disbursing official, will notify the Federal employee in writing that an offset has occurred including—

(i) A description of the payment and the amount of offset taken;

(ii) The identity of GSA as the creditor agency requesting the offset; and

(iii) A contact point within GSA that will handle concerns regarding the offset.

(2) The information described in paragraphs (b)(1)(ii) and (b)(1)(iii) of this section does not need to be provided to the Federal employee when the offset occurs if such information was included in a prior notice from the disbursing official or paying agency.

(c) The disbursing official will advise GSA of the names, mailing addresses, and taxpayer identifying numbers of the debtors from whom amounts of past-due, legally enforceable debt were collected and of the amounts collected from each debtor for GSA. The disbursing official will not advise GSA of the source of payment from which the amounts were collected.

§ 105–56.022 Fees.

Agencies that perform centralized salary offset computer matching services may charge a fee sufficient to cover the full cost for such services. In addition, FMS, or a paying agency acting on behalf of FMS, may charge a fee sufficient to cover the full cost of implementing the administrative offset program. FMS may deduct the fees from amounts collected by offset or may bill GSA. Fees charged for offset will be based on actual administrative offsets completed and may be added to the debt as an administrative cost.

§ 105–56.023 Disposition of amounts collected.

(a) The disbursing official conducting the offset will transmit amounts collected for debts, less fees charged under § 105–56.022 of this subpart, to GSA.

(b) If an erroneous offset payment is made to GSA, the disbursing official will notify GSA that an erroneous offset payment has been made.

(1) The disbursing official may deduct the amount of the erroneous offset payment from future amounts payable to GSA; or

(2) Alternatively, upon the disbursing official's request, GSA will promptly return to the disbursing official or the affected payee an amount equal to the amount of the erroneous payment (without regard to whether any other amounts payable to GSA have been paid).

(i) The disbursing official and GSA will adjust the debtor records appropriately.

(ii) Unless required by Federal law or contract, refunds under this subpart will not bear interest.

Subpart C—Centralized Salary Offset (CSO) Procedures— GSA as Paying Agency

§ 105–56.024 Purpose and scope.

(a) This subpart establishes procedures for the offset of Federal salary payments, through the Financial Management Service's (FMS) administrative offset program, to collect delinquent debts owed to the Federal Government. This process is known as salary offset. Rules issued by the Office of Personnel Management contain the requirements Federal agencies must follow prior to conducting salary offset and the procedures for requesting offsets directly from a paying agency. See 5 CFR parts 550.1101 through 550.1108.

(b) This subpart implements the requirement under 5 U.S.C. 5514(a)(1) that all Federal agencies, using a process known as centralized salary computer matching, identify Federal employees who owe delinquent non-tax debt to the United States. Centralized salary offset computer matching is the computerized comparison of delinquent debt records with records of Federal employees. The purpose of centralized salary offset computer matching is to identify those debtors whose Federal salaries should be offset to collect delinquent debts owed to the Federal Government.

(c) This subpart specifies the delinquent debt records and Federal employee records that must be included in the salary offset matching process. For purposes of this subpart, delinquent debt records consist of the debt information submitted to FMS for purposes of administrative offset as required under 31 U.S.C. 3716(c)(6).

(d) An interagency consortium was established to implement centralized salary offset computer matching on a Governmentwide basis as required under 5 U.S.C. 5514(a)(1). Federal employee records consist of records of Federal salary payments disbursed by members of the consortium.

§ 105–56.025 Definitions.

The following definitions apply to this subpart:

(a) *Administrative offset* means withholding funds payable by the United States to, or held by the United States for, a person to satisfy a debt owed by the payee.

(b) *Agency* means a department, agency or sub-agency, court, court administrative office, or instrumentality in the executive, judicial, or legislative branch of the Federal Government, including Government corporations.

(c) *Centralized salary offset computer matching* means the computerized comparison of Federal employee records with delinquent debt records to identify Federal employees who owe such debts.

(d) *Consortium* means an interagency group established by the Secretary of the Treasury to implement centralized salary offset computer matching. The group includes all agencies that disburse Federal salary payments.

(e) *Creditor agency* means any agency that is owed a debt, including a debt collection center when acting on behalf of a creditor agency in matters pertaining to the collection of a debt.

(f) *Cross-serviced agency* means an arrangement between GSA and another agency whereby GSA provides financial support services to the other agency on a reimbursable basis. Financial support services can range from simply providing computer and software timesharing services to full-service administrative processing.

(g) *Debt* means any amount of money, funds, or property that has been determined by an appropriate official of the Federal Government to be owed to the United States by a person, including debt administered by a third party acting as an agent for the Federal Government. For purposes of this subpart, the term "debt" does not include debts arising under the Internal Revenue Code of 1986 (26 U.S.C. 1 *et seq.*).

(h) *Delinquent debt record* means information about a past-due, legally enforceable debt, submitted to GSA by FMS for purposes of administrative offset (including salary offset) in accordance with the provisions of 31 U.S.C. 3716(c)(6) and applicable regulations. Debt information includes the amount and type of debt and the debtor's name, address, and taxpayer identifying number.

(i) *Disbursing official* means an officer or employee designated to disburse Federal salary payments. This includes all disbursing officials of Federal salary payments, including but not limited to, disbursing officials of the Department of the Treasury, the Department of Defense, the United States Postal Service, any government corporation, and any disbursing official of the United States designated by the Secretary.

(j) *Disposable pay* means the amount that remains from an employee's Federal pay after required deductions for Federal, State and local income taxes; Social Security taxes, including Medicare taxes; Federal retirement programs, including contributions to the Thrift Savings Plan (TSP); premiums for life (excluding amounts deducted for supplemental coverage) and health insurance benefits; Internal Revenue Service (IRS) tax levies; and such other deductions that are required by law to be withheld.

(k) *Employee* means any individual employed by GSA or a cross-serviced agency of the executive, legislative, or judicial branches of the Federal Government, including Government corporations.

(1) *Federal employee records* means records of Federal salary payments that a paying agency has certified to a disbursing official for disbursement.

(m) *FMS* means the Financial Management Service, a bureau of the Department of the Treasury.

(n) *Pay* means basic pay, special pay, incentive pay, retired pay, retainer pay, or in the case of an individual not entitled to basic pay, other authorized pay.

(o) *Paying agency* means the agency that employs the Federal employee who owes the debt and authorizes the payment of his or her current pay. A paying agency also includes an agency that performs payroll services on behalf of the employing agency.

(p) *Salary offset* means administrative offset to collect a debt owed by a Federal employee from the current pay account of the employee.

(q) *Secretary* means the Secretary of the Treasury or his or her delegate.

(r) *Taxpayer identifying number* means the identifying number described under section 6109 of the Internal Revenue Code of 1986 (26 U.S.C. 6109). For an individual, the taxpayer identifying number is the individual's social security number.

§ 105–56.026 GSA participation.

(a) As required under 5 U.S.C. 5514(a)(1), creditor agencies must participate at least annually in centralized salary offset computer matching. To meet this requirement, creditor agencies will notify FMS of all past-due, legally enforceable debts delinquent for more than 180 days for purposes of administrative offset, as required under 31 U.S.C. 3716(c)(6). Additionally, creditor agencies may notify FMS of past-due, legally enforceable debts delinquent for less than 180 days for purposes of administrative offset.

(b) Prior to submitting a debt to FMS for purposes of collection by administrative offset, including salary offset, creditor agencies will provide written certification to FMS that—

(1) The debt is past-due and legally enforceable in the amount submitted to FMS and that the creditor agency will ensure that collections (other than collections through offset) are properly credited to the debt;

(2) Except in the case of a judgment debt or as otherwise allowed by law, the debt is referred for offset within ten years after the creditor agency's right of action accrues;

(3) The creditor agency has complied with the provisions of 31 U.S.C. 3716 (administrative offset) and related regulations including, but not limited to, the provisions requiring the creditor agency to provide the debtor with applicable notices and opportunities for a review of the debt; and

(4) The creditor agency has complied with the provisions of 5 U.S.C. 5514 (salary offset) and related regulations including, but not limited to, the provisions requiring the creditor agency to provide the debtor with applicable notices and opportunities for a hearing.

(c) FMS may waive the certification requirement set forth in paragraph (b)(4) of this section as a prerequisite to submitting the debt to FMS. If FMS waives the certification requirement, before an offset occurs, the creditor agency will provide the Federal employee with the notices and opportunities for a hearing as required by 5 U.S.C. 5514 and applicable regulations, and will certify to FMS that the requirements of 5 U.S.C. 5514 and applicable regulations have been met.

(d) The creditor agency will notify FMS immediately of any payments credited by the agency to the debtor's account, other than credits for amounts collected by offset, after submission of the debt to FMS. The creditor agency will notify FMS once the debt is paid in its entirety. The creditor agency will also notify FMS immediately of any change in the status of the legal enforceability of the debt, for example, if the agency receives notice that the debtor has filed for bankruptcy protection.

§ 105–56.027 Centralized salary offset computer match.

(a) Delinquent debt records will be compared with Federal employee records maintained by members of the consortium or paying agencies. The records will be compared to identify Federal employees who owe delinquent debts for purposes of collecting the debt by administrative offset. A match will occur when the taxpayer identifying number and name of a Federal employee are the same as the taxpayer identifying number and name of a debtor.

(b) As authorized by the provisions of 31 U.S.C. 3716(f), FMS, under a delegation of authority from the Secretary, has waived certain requirements of the Computer Matching and Privacy Protection Act of 1988, 5 U.S.C. 552a, as amended, for administrative offset, including salary offset, upon written certification by the creditor agency, that the requirements of 31 U.S.C. 3716(a) have been met. Specifically, FMS has waived the requirements for a computer matching agreement contained in 5 U.S.C. 552a(o) and for post-match notice and verification contained in 5 U.S.C. 552a(p).

§ 105–56.028 Salary offset.

When a match occurs and all other requirements for offset have been met, as required by the provisions of 31 U.S.C. 3716(c), the disbursing official will offset the GSA employee's or cross-serviced agency employee's salary payment to satisfy, in whole or part, the debt owed by the employee. Alternatively, the GSA National Payroll Center, serving as the paying agency, on behalf of the disbursing official, may deduct the amount of the offset from an employee's disposable pay before the employee's salary payment is certified to a disbursing official for disbursement.

§ 105–56.029 Offset amount.

(a) The minimum dollar amount of salary offset under this subpart is $100.

(b) The amount offset from a salary payment under this subpart will be the lesser of—

(1) The amount of the debt, including any interest, penalties and administrative costs; or

(2) Up to 15 percent of the debtor's disposable pay.

(c) Alternatively, the amount offset may be an amount agreed upon, in writing, by the debtor and the creditor agency.

(d) Offsets will continue until the debt, including any interest, penalties, and administrative costs, is paid in full

or otherwise resolved to the satisfaction of the creditor agency.

§ 105–56.030 Priorities.

GSA, acting as the paying agency, on behalf of the disbursing official, will apply the order of precedence when processing debts identified by the centralized salary offset computer match program as follows:

(a) A levy pursuant to the Internal Revenue Code of 1986 (26 U.S.C. 1 *et seq.*) takes precedence over other deductions under this subpart.

(b) When a salary payment may be reduced to collect more than one debt, amounts offset under this subpart will be applied to a debt only after amounts offset have been applied to satisfy past due child support debts assigned to a State pursuant to the Social Security Act under 42 U.S.C. 602(a)(26) or 671(a)(17).

§ 105–56.031 Notice.

(a) The disbursing official will provide GSA an electronic list of the names, mailing addresses, and taxpayer identifying numbers of the debtors from whom amounts of past-due, legally enforceable debt are due other Federal agencies. The disbursing official will identify the creditor agency name and a point of contact that will handle concerns regarding the debt.

(b) Before offsetting a salary payment, the GSA National Payroll Center, acting as the paying agency on behalf of the disbursing official, will notify the debtor in writing of the date deductions from salary will commence and of the amount of such deductions.

(c)(1) When an offset occurs under this subpart, the disbursing official, or the GSA National Payroll Center on behalf of the disbursing official, will notify the debtor in writing that an offset has occurred including—

(i) A description of the payment and the amount of offset taken;

(ii) The identity of the creditor agency identified by the disbursing official requesting the offset; and

(iii) A contact point at the creditor agency identified by the disbursing official that will handle concerns regarding the offset.

(2) The information described in paragraphs (c)(1)(ii) and (c)(1)(iii) of

this section does not need to be provided to the debtor when the offset occurs if such information was included in a prior notice from the disbursing official or the creditor agency.

§ 105–56.032 Fees.

GSA, while performing centralized salary offset computer matching services, may charge a fee sufficient to cover the full cost for such services. In addition, FMS, or GSA acting as the paying agency on behalf of FMS, may charge a fee sufficient to cover the full cost of implementing the administrative offset program. FMS may deduct the fees from amounts collected by offset or may bill the creditor agency. Fees charged for offset will be based on actual administrative offsets completed.

§ 105–56.033 Disposition of amounts collected.

(a) The disbursing official conducting the offset will transmit amounts collected for debts, less fees charged under § 105–56.032 of this subpart, to the creditor agency.

(b) If an erroneous offset payment is made to the creditor agency, the disbursing official will notify the creditor agency that an erroneous offset payment has been made.

(1) The disbursing official may deduct the amount of the erroneous offset payment from future amounts payable to the creditor agency; or

(2) Alternatively, upon the disbursing official's request, the creditor agency will promptly return to the disbursing official or the affected payee an amount equal to the amount of the erroneous payment (without regard to whether any other amounts payable to the creditor agency have been paid). The disbursing official and the creditor agency will adjust the debtor records appropriately.

PART 105–57—ADMINISTRATION WAGE GARNISHMENT

AUTHORITY: 5 U.S.C. 552–553, 31 U.S.C. 3720D, 31 CFR 285.11.

SOURCE: 68 FR 68761, Dec. 10, 2003, unless otherwise noted.

§ 105–57.001 Purpose, authority and scope.

(a) This part provides standards and procedures for GSA to collect money from a debtor's disposable pay by means of administrative wage garnishment to satisfy delinquent non-tax debt owed to the United States.

(b) These standards and procedures are authorized under the wage garnishment provisions of the Debt Collection Improvement Act of 1996, codified at 31 U.S.C. 3720D, and Department of the Treasury Wage Garnishment Regulations at 31 CFR 285.11.

(c) *Scope.* (1) This part applies to any GSA program that gives rise to a delinquent non-tax debt owed to the United States and that pursues recovery of such debt.

(2) This part will apply notwithstanding any provision of State law.

(3) Nothing in this part precludes the compromise of a debt or the suspension or termination of collection action in accordance with applicable law. See, for example, the Federal Claims Collection Standards (FCCS), 31 CFR parts 900 through 904.

(4) The receipt of payments pursuant to this part does not preclude GSA from pursuing other debt collection remedies, including the offset of Federal payments to satisfy delinquent non-tax debt owed to the United States. GSA may pursue such debt collection remedies separately or in conjunction with administrative wage garnishment.

(5) This part does not apply to the collection of delinquent non-tax debt owed to the United States from the wages of Federal employees from their Federal employment. Federal pay is subject to the Federal salary offset procedures set forth in 5 U.S.C. 5514 and

other applicable laws. GSA standards and procedures for offsetting Federal wage payments are stated in 41 CFR part 105–56.

(6) Nothing in this part requires GSA to duplicate notices or administrative proceedings required by contract or other laws or regulations.

§ 105–57.002   Definitions.

(a) *Administrative offset,* as defined in 31 U.S.C. 3701(a)(1), means withholding funds payable by the United States (including funds payable by the United States on behalf of a State government) to, or held by the United States for, a person to satisfy a claim.

(b) *Business day* means Monday through Friday, excluding Federal legal holidays. For purposes of computation, the last day of the period will be included unless it is a Federal legal holiday.

(c) *Day* means calendar day. For purposes of computation, the last day of the period will be included unless it is a Saturday, a Sunday, or a Federal legal holiday.

(d) *Debtor* means an individual who owes a delinquent non-tax debt to the United States.

(e) *"Delinquent" or "past-due" non-tax debt* means any non-tax debt that has not been paid by the date specified in GSA's initial written demand for payment or applicable agreement or instrument (including a post-delinquency payment agreement), unless other satisfactory payment arrangements have been made.

(f) *Disposable pay* means that part of the debtor's compensation (including, but not limited to, salary, bonuses, commissions, and vacation pay) from an employer remaining after the deduction of health insurance premiums and any amounts required by law to be withheld. For purposes of this part, "amounts required by law to be withheld" include amounts for deductions such as social security taxes and withholding taxes, but do not include any amount withheld pursuant to a court order.

(g) *Employer* means a person or entity that employs the services of others and that pays their wages or salaries. The term employer includes, but is not limited to, State and local Governments,

but does not include an agency of the Federal Government as defined by 31 CFR 285.11(c).

(h) *Evidence of service* means information retained by GSA indicating the nature of the document to which it pertains, the date of submission of the document, and to whom the document is being submitted. Evidence of service may be retained electronically or otherwise, so long as the manner of retention is sufficient for evidentiary purposes.

(i) *Financial hardship* means an inability to meet basic living expenses for goods and services necessary for the survival of the debtor and his or her spouse and dependents. See § 105–57.010 of this part.

(j) For the purposes of the standards in this part, unless otherwise stated, the term "Administrator" refers to the Administrator of General Services or the Administrator's delegate.

(k) For the purposes of the standards in this part, the terms "claim" and "debt" are synonymous and interchangeable.

They refer to an amount of money, funds, or property that has been determined by GSA to be due the United States from any person, organization, or entity, except another Federal agency, from sources which include loans insured or guaranteed by the United States and all other amounts due the United States from fees, leases, rents, royalties, services, sales of real or personal property, overpayments, penalties, damages, interest, fines and forfeitures and all other similar sources, including debt administered by a third party as an agent for the Federal Government. For the purposes of administrative offset under 31 U.S.C. 3716, the terms "claim" and "debt" include an amount of money, funds, or property owed by a person to a State (including past-due support being enforced by a State), the District of Columbia, American Samoa, Guam, the United States Virgin Islands, the Commonwealth of the Northern Mariana Islands, or the Commonwealth of Puerto Rico.

(l) For the purposes of the standards in this part, unless otherwise stated, the terms "GSA" and "Agency" are synonymous and interchangeable.

(m) For the purposes of the standards in this part, unless otherwise stated, "Secretary" means the Secretary of the Treasury or the Secretary's delegate.

(n) *Garnishment* means the process of withholding amounts from an employee's disposable pay and the paying of those amounts to GSA in satisfaction of a withholding order.

(o) *Hearing* means a review of the documentary evidence concerning the existence and/or amount of a debt, and/or the terms of a repayment schedule, provided such repayment schedule is established other than by a written agreement entered into pursuant to this part. If the hearing official determines that the issues in dispute cannot be resolved solely by review of the written record, such as when the validity of the debt turns on the issue of credibility or veracity, an oral hearing may be provided.

(p) *Hearing official* means a Board Judge of the Civilian Board of Contract Appeals (CBCA).

(q) *Withholding order* means "Wage Garnishment Order (SF 329B)", issued by GSA. For purposes of this part, the terms "wage garnishment order" and "garnishment order" have the same meaning as "withholding order."

(r) In this part, words in the plural form shall include the singular and vice versa, and words signifying the masculine gender shall include the feminine and vice versa. The terms "includes" and "including" do not exclude matters not listed but do include matters that are in the same general class.

[68 FR 68761, Dec. 10, 2003, as amended at 78 FR 29247, May 20, 2013]

§ 105–57.003 General rule.

Whenever GSA determines a delinquent debt is owed by an individual, the Agency may initiate administrative proceedings to garnish the wages of the delinquent debtor.

§ 105–57.004 Notice requirements.

(a) At least 30 days before the initiation of garnishment proceedings, GSA will send, by first class mail, overnight delivery service, or hand delivery to the debtor's last known address a written notice informing the debtor of—

(1) The nature and amount of the debt;

(2) The intention of GSA to initiate proceedings to collect the debt through deductions from pay until the debt and all accumulated interest, penalties and administrative costs are paid in full; and

(3) The debtor's rights, including those set forth in paragraph (b) of this section, and the time frame within which the debtor may exercise his or her rights.

(b) The debtor will be afforded the opportunity—

(1) To inspect and copy Agency records related to the debt;

(2) To enter into a written repayment agreement with GSA under terms agreeable to the Agency; and

(3) To request a hearing in accordance with § 105-57.005 of this part concerning the existence and/or amount of the debt, and/or the terms of the proposed repayment schedule under the garnishment order. However, the debtor is not entitled to a hearing concerning the terms of the proposed repayment schedule if these terms have been established by written agreement under paragraph (b)(2) of this section.

(c) The notice required by this section may be included with GSA's demand letter required by 41 CFR 105–55.010.

(d) GSA will keep a copy of the evidence of service indicating the date of submission of the notice. The evidence of service may be retained electronically so long as the manner of retention is sufficient for evidentiary purposes.

§ 105–57.005 Hearing.

(a) GSA will provide a hearing, which at the hearing official's option may be oral or written, if within fifteen (15) business days of submission of the notice by GSA, the debtor submits a signed and dated written request for a hearing, to the official named in the notice, concerning the existence and/or amount of the debt, and/or the terms of the repayment schedule (for repayment schedules established other than by written agreement under § 105–57.004(b)(2) of this part). A copy of the request for a hearing must also be sent to the Civilian Board of Contract Appeals (CBCA) at 1800 F Street NW., Washington, DC 20405.

(b) *Types of hearing or review.* (1) For purposes of this section, whenever GSA is required to afford a debtor a hearing, the hearing official will provide the debtor with a reasonable opportunity for an oral hearing when he/she determines that the issues in dispute cannot be resolved by review of the documentary evidence, for example, when the validity of the claim turns on the issue of credibility or veracity.

(2) If the hearing official determines that an oral hearing is appropriate, he/she will establish the time and location of the hearing. An oral hearing may, at the debtor's option, be conducted either in-person or by telephone conference. In-person hearings will be conducted in the hearing official's office located at 1800 M Street NW., 6th Floor, Washington, DC 20036, or at another location designated by the hearing official. All personal and travel expenses incurred by the debtor in connection with an in-person hearing will be borne by the debtor. All telephonic charges incurred during a hearing will be the responsibility of GSA.

(3) The debtor may represent himself or herself or may be represented by another person of his or her choice at the hearing. GSA will not compensate the debtor for representation expenses, including hourly fees for attorneys, travel expenses, or costs for reproducing documents.

(4) In those cases when an oral hearing is not required by this section, the hearing official will nevertheless conduct a "paper hearing", that is, the hearing official will decide the issues in dispute based upon a review of the written record. The hearing official will establish a reasonable deadline for the submission of evidence.

(c) Subject to paragraph (k) of this section, if the debtor's written request is received by GSA on or before the 15th business day after the submission of the notice described in § 105–57.004(a) of this part, the Agency will not issue a withholding order under § 105–57.006 of this part until the debtor has been provided the requested hearing and a decision in accordance with paragraphs (h)

and (i) of this section has been rendered.

(d) If the debtor's written request for a hearing is received by GSA after the 15th business day following the mailing of the notice described in § 105–57.004(a) of this part, GSA may consider the request timely filed and provide a hearing if the debtor can show that the delay was because of circumstances beyond his or her control. However, GSA will not delay issuance of a withholding order unless the Agency determines that the delay in filing the request was caused by factors over which the debtor had no control, or GSA receives information that the Agency believes justifies a delay or cancellation of the withholding order.

(e) After the debtor requests a hearing, the hearing official will notify the debtor of—

(1) The date and time of a telephonic hearing;

(2) The date, time, and location of an in-person oral hearing; or

(3) The deadline for the submission of evidence for a written hearing.

(f) *Burden of proof.* (1) GSA will have the burden of establishing the existence and/or amount of the debt.

(2) Thereafter, if the debtor disputes the existence and/or amount of the debt, the debtor must prove by a preponderance of the evidence that no debt exists or that the amount of the debt is incorrect. In addition, the debtor may present evidence that the terms of the repayment schedule are unlawful, would cause a financial hardship to the debtor, or that collection of the debt may not be pursued due to operation of law.

(g) The hearing official will arrange and maintain a written transcript of any hearing provided under this section. The transcript will be made available to either party in the event of an appeal under the Administrative Procedure Act, 5 U.S.C. 701 through 706. All charges associated with the taking of the transcript will be the responsibility of GSA. A hearing is not required to be a formal evidentiary-type hearing; however, witnesses who testify in oral hearings will do so under oath or affirmation.

(h) The hearing official will issue a written opinion stating his or her decision, as soon as practicable, but not later than sixty (60) days after the date on which the request for such hearing was received by GSA. If the hearing official is unable to provide the debtor with a hearing and render a decision within 60 days after the receipt of the request for such hearing—

(1) GSA will not issue a withholding order until the hearing is held and a decision rendered; or

(2) If GSA had previously issued a withholding order to the debtor's employer, the Agency will suspend the withholding order beginning on the 61st day after the receipt of the hearing request and continuing until a hearing is held and a decision is rendered.

(i) The written decision will include—

(1) A summary of the facts presented;

(2) The hearing official's findings, analysis and conclusions; and

(3) The terms of any repayment schedules, if applicable.

(j) The hearing official's decision will be the final Agency action for the purposes of judicial review under the Administrative Procedure Act (5 U.S.C. 701 *et seq.*).

(k) In the absence of good cause shown, a debtor who fails to appear at a hearing scheduled pursuant to paragraph (e) of this section, or to provide written submissions within the time set by the hearing official, will be deemed to have waived his or her right to appear and present evidence.

[68 FR 68761, Dec. 10, 2003, as amended at 78 FR 29247, May 20, 2013]

§105–57.006 Wage garnishment order.

(a) Unless GSA receives information it believes justifies a delay or cancellation of the withholding order, the Agency will send, by first class mail, overnight delivery service or hand delivery, a SF 329A (Letter to Employer & Important Notice to Employer), a SF 329B (Wage Garnishment Order), a SF 329C (Wage Garnishment Worksheet), and a SF 329D (Employer Certification), to the debtor's employer—

(1) Within 30 days after the debtor fails to make a timely request for a hearing (i.e., within 15 business days

after the mailing of the notice described in §105–57.004(a) of this part); or

(2) If a timely request for a hearing is made by the debtor, within 30 days after a final decision is made by the hearing official to proceed with garnishment.

(b) The withholding order sent to the employer under paragraph (a) of this section will contain the signature of, or the image of the signature of, the Administrator or his or her delegate. The order will contain only the information necessary for the employer to comply with the withholding order. Such information includes the debtor's name, address, and social security number, as well as instructions for withholding and information as to where payments are to be sent.

(c) GSA will retain a copy of the evidence of service indicating the date of submission of the order. The evidence of service may be retained electronically so long as the manner of retention is sufficient for evidentiary purposes.

§105–57.007 Certification by employer.

The employer must complete and return the SF 329D (Employer Certification) to GSA within the time frame prescribed in the instructions to the form. The certification will address matters such as information about the debtor's employment status and disposable pay available for withholding.

§105–57.008 Amounts withheld.

(a) After receipt of the garnishment order issued under this part, the employer shall deduct from all disposable pay paid to the applicable debtor during each pay period the amount of garnishment described in paragraph (b) of this section. The employer may use the SF 329C (Wage Garnishment Worksheet) to calculate the amount to be deducted from the debtor's disposable pay.

(b) Subject to the provisions of paragraphs (c) and (d) of this section, the amount of garnishment will be the lesser of—

(1) The amount indicated on the garnishment order up to 15 percent of the debtor's disposable pay; or

(2) The amount set forth in 15 U.S.C. 1673(a)(2) (Restriction on Garnishment), which is the amount by which a debtor's disposable pay exceeds an amount equivalent to thirty times the minimum wage. See 29 CFR 870.10.

(c) When a debtor's pay is subject to withholding orders with priority, the following will apply:

(1) Unless otherwise provided by Federal law, withholding orders issued under this part will be paid in the amounts set forth under paragraph (b) of this section and will have priority over other withholding orders which are served later in time. Notwithstanding the foregoing, withholding orders for family support will have priority over withholding orders issued under this part.

(2) If amounts are being withheld from a debtor's pay pursuant to a withholding order served on an employer before a withholding order issued pursuant to this part, or if a withholding order for family support is served on an employer at any time, the amounts withheld pursuant to the withholding order issued under this part will be the lesser of—

(i) The amount calculated under paragraph (b) of this section; or

(ii) An amount equal to 25 percent of the debtor's disposable pay less the amount(s) withheld under the withholding order(s) with priority.

(3) If a debtor owes more than one debt to GSA, the Agency may issue multiple withholding orders provided the total amount garnished from the debtor's pay for such orders does not exceed the amount set forth in paragraph (b) of this section.

(d) An amount greater than that set forth in paragraphs (b) and (c) of this section may be withheld upon the written consent of the debtor.

(e) The employer shall promptly pay to GSA all amounts withheld in accordance with the withholding order issued pursuant to this part.

(f) An employer will not be required to vary its normal pay and disbursement cycles in order to comply with the withholding order.

(g) Any assignment or allotment by an employee of his or her earnings will be void to the extent it interferes with or prohibits execution of the withholding order issued under this part, except for any assignment or allotment made pursuant to a family support judgment or order.

(h) The employer will withhold the appropriate amount from the debtor's wages for each pay period until the employer receives notification from GSA to discontinue wage withholding. The garnishment order will indicate a reasonable period of time within which the employer is required to commence wage withholding, usually the first payday after the employer receives the order. However, if the first payday is within ten (10) days after the receipt of the garnishment order, the employer may begin deductions on the second payday.

(i) Payments received through a wage garnishment order will be applied in the following order:

(1) To outstanding penalties.

(2) To administrative costs incurred by GSA to collect the debt.

(3) To interest accrued on the debt at the rate established by the terms of the obligation under which it arose or by applicable law.

(4) To outstanding principal.

§ 105–57.009   Exclusions from garnishment.

GSA will not garnish the wages of a debtor who it knows has been involuntarily separated from employment until the debtor has been reemployed continuously for at least 12 months. The debtor has the burden of informing GSA of the circumstances surrounding an involuntary separation from employment.

§ 105–57.010   Financial hardship.

(a) A debtor whose wages are subject to a wage withholding order under this part, may, at any time, request a review by GSA of the amount garnished, based on materially changed circumstances such as disability, divorce, or catastrophic illness which result in financial hardship.

(b) A debtor requesting a review under paragraph (a) of this section shall submit the basis for claiming the current amount of garnishment results in a financial hardship to the debtor, along with supporting documentation.

(c) If a financial hardship is found, GSA will downwardly adjust, by an amount and for a period of time agreeable to the Agency, the amount garnished to reflect the debtor's financial condition. GSA will notify the employer of any adjustments to the amounts to be withheld.

§ 105–57.011 Ending garnishment.

(a) Once GSA has fully recovered the amounts owed by the debtor, including interest, penalties, and administrative costs consistent with the FCCS, the Agency will send the debtor's employer notification to discontinue wage withholding.

(b) At least annually, GSA will review its debtors' accounts to ensure that garnishment has been terminated for accounts that have been paid in full.

§ 105–57.012 Actions prohibited by the employer.

An employer may not discharge, refuse to employ, or take disciplinary action against the debtor due to the issuance of a withholding order under this part. See 31 U.S.C. 3720D(e).

§ 105–57.013 Refunds.

(a) If a hearing official, at a hearing held pursuant to § 105–57.005 of this part, determines that a debt is not legally due and owing to the United States, GSA will promptly refund any amount collected by means of administrative wage garnishment.

(b) Unless required by Federal law or contract, refunds under this part will not bear interest.

§ 105–57.014 Right of action.

GSA may sue any employer for any amount that the employer fails to withhold from wages owed and payable to an employee in accordance with §§ 105–057.006 and 105–57.008 of this part, plus attorney's fees, costs, and if applicable, punitive damages. However, a suit may not be filed before the termination of the collection action involving a particular debtor, unless earlier filing is necessary to avoid expiration of any applicable statute of limitations period. For purposes of this part, "termination of the collection action" occurs when GSA has terminated collection action in accordance with the FCCS or other applicable standards. In any event, termination of the collection action will have been deemed to occur if GSA has not received any payments to satisfy the debt from the particular debtor whose wages were subject to garnishment, in whole or in part, for a period of one (1) year.

PART 105–60—PUBLIC AVAILABILITY OF AGENCY RECORDS AND INFORMATIONAL MATERIALS

AUTHORITY: 5 U.S.C. 301 and 552; 40 U.S.C. 486(c).

SOURCE: 63 FR 56839, Oct. 23, 1998, unless otherwise noted.

§ 105–60.000 Scope of part.

(a) This part sets forth policies and procedures of the General Services Administration (GSA) regarding public access to records documenting:

(1) Agency organization, functions, decisionmaking channels, and rules and regulations of general applicability;

(2) Agency final opinions and orders, including policy statements and staff manuals;

(3) Operational and other appropriate agency records; and

(4) Agency proceedings.

(b) This part also covers exemptions from disclosure of these records; procedures for the public to inspect or obtain copies of GSA records; and instructions to current and former GSA employees on the response to a subpoena or other legal demand for material or information received or generated in the performance of official duty or because of the person's official status.

(c) Any policies and procedures in any GSA internal or external directive inconsistent with the policies and procedures set forth in this part are superseded to the extent of that inconsistency.

Subpart 105–60.1—General Provisions

§ 105–60.101 Purpose.

This part 105–60 implements the provisions of the Freedom of Information Act (FOIA), as amended, 5 U.S.C. 552. The regulations in this part also implement Executive Order 12600, Predisclosure Notification Procedures for Confidential Commercial Information, of June 23, 1987 (3 CFR, 1987 Comp., p. 235). This part prescribes procedures by which the public may inspect and obtain copies of GSA records under the FOIA, including administrative procedures which must be exhausted before a requester invokes the jurisdiction of an appropriate United States District Court for GSA's failure to respond to a proper request within the statutory time limits, for a denial of agency records or challenge to the adequacy of a search, or for a denial of a fee waiver.

§ 105–60.102 Application.

This part applies to all records and informational materials generated, maintained, and controlled by GSA that come within the scope of 5 U.S.C. 552.

§ 105–60.103 Policy.

§ 105–60.103–1 Availability of records.

The policies of GSA with regard to the availability of records to the public are:

(a) GSA records are available to the greatest extent possible in keeping with the spirit and intent of the FOIA. GSA will disclose information in any existing GSA record, with noted exceptions, regardless of the form or format of the record. GSA will provide the record in the form or format requested if the record is reproducible by the agency in that form or format without significant expenditure of resources. GSA will make reasonable efforts to maintain its records in forms or formats that are reproducible for purposes of this section.

(b) The person making the request does not need to demonstrate an interest in the records or justify the request.

(c) The FOIA does not give the public the right to demand that GSA compile a record that does not already exist. For example, FOIA does not require GSA to collect and compile information from multiple sources to create a new record. GSA may compile records or perform minor reprogramming to extract records from a database or system when doing so will not significantly interfere with the operation of the automated system in question or involve a significant expenditure of resources.

(d) Similarly, FOIA does not require GSA to reconstruct records that have been destroyed in compliance with disposition schedules approved by the Archivist of the United States. However, GSA will not destroy records after a member of the public has requested access to them and will process the request even if destruction would otherwise be authorized.

(e) If the record requested is not complete at the time of the request, GSA may, at its discretion, inform the requester that the complete record will be provided when it is available, with no additional request required, if the record is not exempt from disclosure.

(f) Requests must be addressed to the office identified in § 105–60.402–1.

(g) Fees for locating and duplicating records are listed in § 105–60,305–10.

§ 105–60.103–2 Applying exemptions.

GSA may deny a request for a GSA record if it falls within an exemption under the FOIA outlined in subpart 105–60.5 of this part. Except when a record is classified or when disclosure would violate any Federal statute, the authority to withhold a record from disclosure is permissive rather than mandatory. GSA will not withhold a record unless there is a compelling reason to do so; i.e., disclosure will likely cause harm to a Governmental or private interest. In the absence of a compelling reason, GSA will disclose a record even if it otherwise is subject to exemption. GSA will cite the compelling reason(s) to requesters when any record is denied under FOIA.

§ 105–60.104 Records of other agencies.

If GSA receives a request for access to records that are known to be the primary responsibility of another agency, GSA will refer the request to the agency concerned for appropriate action. For example, GSA will refer requests to the appropriate agency in cases in which GSA does not have sufficient knowledge of the action or matter that is the subject of the requested records to determine whether the records must be released or may be withheld under one of the exemptions listed in Subpart 105–60.5 of this part. If GSA does not have the requested records, the agency will attempt to determine whether the requested records exist at another agency and, if possible, will forward the request to that agency. GSA will inform the requester that GSA has forwarded the request to another agency.

Subpart 105–60.2—Publication of General Agency Information and Rules in the Federal Register

§ 105–60.201 Published information and rules.

In accordance with 5 U.S.C. 552(a)(1), GSA publishes in the FEDERAL REGISTER, for the guidance of the public, the following general information concerning GSA:

(a) Description of the organization of the Central Office and regional offices and the established places at which, the employees from whom, and the methods whereby, the public may obtain information, make submittals or requests, or obtain decisions;

(b) Statements of the general course and method by which its functions are channeled and determined, including the nature and requirements of all formal and informal procedures available;

(c) Rules of procedure, descriptions of forms available or the places where forms may be obtained, and instructions on the scope and contents of all papers, reports, or examinations;

(d) Substantive rules of general applicability adopted as authorized by law, and statements of general policy or interpretations of general applicability formulated and adopted by GSA; and

(e) Each amendment, revision, or repeal of the materials described in this section.

§ 105–60.202 Published materials available for sale to the public.

(a) Substantive rules of general applicability adopted by GSA as authorized by law that this agency publishes in the FEDERAL REGISTER and which are available for sale to the public by the Superintendent of Documents at pre-established prices are: The General Services Administration Acquisition Regulation (48 CFR Ch. 5), the Federal Acquisition Regulation (48 CFR Ch. 1), the Federal Property Management Regulations (41 CFR Ch. 101), and the Federal Travel Regulation (41 CFR Ch. 301–304).

(b) GSA provides technical information, including manuals and handbooks, to other Federal entities, e.g., the National Technical Information Service, with separate statutory authority to make information available to the public at pre-established fees.

(c) Requests for information available through the sources in paragraphs (a) and (b) of this section will be referred to those sources.

Subpart 105–60.3—Availability of Opinions, Orders, Policies, Interpretations, Manuals, and Instructions

§ 105–60.301 General.

GSA makes available to the public the materials described under 5 U.S.C. 552(a)(2), which are listed in § 105–60.302 through an extensive electronic home page, *http://www.gsa.gov/*. A public handbook listing those materials as described in § 105–60.304 is available at GSA's Central Office in Washington, DC, and at the website at *http://www.gsa.gov/staff/c/ca/publ.htm*. Members of the public who do not have the means to access this information electronically, and who are not located in the Washington, DC area, may contact the Freedom of Information Act office in any of the regional offices listed in this regulation. These offices will make arrangements for members of the public to access the information at a computer located at the FOIA office. Reasonable copying services are provided at the fees specified in § 105–60.305.

§ 105–60.302 Available materials.

GSA materials available under this subpart 105–60.3 are as follows:

(a) Final opinions, including concurring and dissenting opinions and orders, made in the adjudication of cases.

(b) Those statements and policy and interpretations that have been adopted by GSA and are not published in the FEDERAL REGISTER.

(c) Administrative staff manuals and instructions to staff affecting a member of the public unless these materials are promptly published and copies offered for sale.

§ 105–60.303 Rules for public inspection and copying.

(a) *Locations.* Selected areas containing the materials available for public inspection and copying, described in this § 105–60.302, are located in the following places:

Central Office (GSA Headquarters),
    General Services Administration, Washington, DC.
    Telephone: 202–501–2262
    FAX: 202–501–2727,
    Email: gsa.foia@gsa.gov
    1800 F Street, NW. (CAI), Washington, DC 20405
Office of the Inspector General
    FOIA Officer, Office of Inspector General (J)
    General Services Administration
    1800 F Street NW., Room 5324
    Washington, DC 20405
New England Region
    General Services Administration (1AB)
    (Comprised of the States of Connecticut, Maine, Massachusetts, New Hampshire, Rhode Island, and Vermont)
    Thomas P. O'Neill, Jr., Federal Building, 10 Causeway Street, Boston, MA 02222
    Telephone: 617–565–8100
    FAX: 617–565–8101
Northeast and Caribbean Region
    (Comprised of the States of New Jersey, New York, the Commonwealth of Puerto Rico, and the Virgin Islands)

General Services Administration (2AR)
26 Federal Plaza, New York, NY 10278
Telephone: 212–264–1234
FAX: 212–264–2760
Mid-Atlantic Region
(Comprised of the States of Delaware, Maryland, Pennsylvania, Virginia, and West Virginia, excluding the Washington, DC metropolitan area)
General Services Administration (3ADS), 100 Penn Square East, Philadelphia, PA 19107
Telephone: 215–656–5530
FAX: 215–656–5590
Southeast Sunbelt Region
(Comprised of the States of Alabama, Florida, Georgia, Kentucky, Mississippi, North Carolina, South Carolina, and Tennessee)
General Services Administration (4E), 401 West Peachtree Street, Atlanta, GA 30365
Telephone: 404–331–5103
FAX: 404–331–1813
Great Lakes Region
(Comprised of the States of Illinois, Indiana, Ohio, Minnesota, Michigan, and Wisconsin)
General Services Administration (5ADB), 230 South Dearborn Street, Chicago, IL 60604
Telephone: 312–353–5383
FAX: 312–353–5385
Heartland Region
(Comprised of the States of Iowa, Kansas, Missouri, and Nebraska)
General Services Administration (6ADB), 1500 East Bannister Road, Kansas City, MO 64131
Telephone: 816–926–7203
FAX: 816–823–1167
Greater Southwest Region
(Comprised of the States of Arkansas, Louisiana, New Mexico, Texas, and Oklahoma)
General Services Administration (7ADQ), 819 Taylor Street, Fort Worth, TX 76102
Telephone: 817–978–3902
FAX: 817–978–4867
Rocky Mountain Region
(Comprised of the States of Colorado, North Dakota, South Dakota, Montana, Utah, and Wyoming)
Business Service Center, General Services Administration (8PB-B), Building 41, Denver Federal Center, Denver, CO 80225
Telephone: 303–236–7408
FAX: 303–236–7403
Pacific Rim Region
(Comprised of the States of Hawaii, California, Nevada, Arizona, Guam, and Trust Territory of the Pacific)
Business Service Center, General Services Administration (9ADB), 525 Market Street, San Francisco, CA 94105
Telephone: 415–522–2715
FAX: 415–522–2705
Northwest/Arctic Region

(Comprised of the States of Alaska, Idaho, Oregon, and Washington)
General Services Administration (10L), GSA Center, 15th and C Streets, SW., Auburn, WA 98002
Telephone: 206–931–7007
FAX: 206–931–7195
National Capital Region
(Comprised of the District of Columbia and the surrounding metropolitan area)
General Services Administration (WPFA-L), 7th and D Streets SW., Washington, DC 20407
Telephone: 202–708–5854
FAX: 202–708–4655.

(b) *Time.* The offices listed above will be open to the public during the business hours of the GSA office where they are located.

(c) *Reproduction services and fees.* The GSA Central Office or the Regional Business Service Centers will furnish reasonable copying and reproduction services for available materials at the fees specified in § 105–60.305.

§ 105–60.304 Public information handbook and index.

GSA publishes a handbook for the public that identifies information regarding any matter described in § 105–60.302. This handbook also lists published information available from GSA and describes the procedures the public may use to obtain information using the Freedom of Information Act (FOIA). This handbook may be obtained without charge from any of the GSA FOIA offices listed in § 105–60.303(a), or at the GSA Internet Homepage (*http://www.gsa.gov/staff/c/ca/cai/links.htm*).

§ 105–60.305 Fees.

§ 105–60.305–1 Definitions.

For the purpose of this part:
(a) A statute specifically providing for setting the level of fees for particular types of records (5 U.S.C. 552(a)(4)(A)(vii)) means any statute that specifically requires a Government agency to set the level of fees for particular types of records, as opposed to a statute that generally discusses such fees. Fees are required by statute to:

(1) Make Government information conveniently available to the public and to private sector organizations;

(2) Ensure that groups and individuals pay the cost of publications and other services which are for their special use so that these costs are not borne by the general taxpaying public;

(3) Operate an information dissemination activity on self-sustaining basis to the maximum extent possible; or

(4) Return revenue to the Treasury for defraying, wholly or in part, appropriated funds used to pay the cost of disseminating Government information.

(b) The term *direct costs* means those expenditures which GSA actually incurs in searching for and duplicating (and in the case of commercial requesters, reviewing and redacting) documents to respond to a FOIA request. Direct costs include, for example, the salary of the employee performing the work (the basic rate of pay for the employee plus 16 percent of that rate to cover benefits), and the cost of operating duplicating machinery. Overhead expenses such as costs of space, and heating or lighting the facility where the records are stored are not included in direct costs.

(c) The term *search* includes all time spent looking for material that is responsive to a request, including line-by-line identification of material within documents. Searches will be performed in the most efficient and least expensive manner so as to minimize costs for both the agency and the requester. Line-by-line searches will not be undertaken when it would be more efficient to duplicate the entire document. *Search* for responsive material is not the same as *review* of a record to determine whether it is exempt from disclosure in whole or in part (see paragraph (e) of this section). Searches may be done manually or by computer using existing programming or new programming when this would not significantly interfere with the operation of the automated system in question.

(d) The term *duplication* means the process of making a copy of a document in response to a FOIA request. Copies can take the form of paper, microform audiovisual materials, or magnetic types or disks. To the extent practicable, GSA will provide a copy of the material in the form specified by the requester.

(e) The term *review* means the process of examining documents located in response to a request to determine if any portion of that document is permitted to be withheld and processing any documents for disclosure. See § 105–60.305–6.

(f) The term *commercial-use request* means a request from or on behalf of one who seeks information for a use or purpose that furthers the commercial, trade, or profit interests of the requester or person on whose behalf the request is made. GSA will determine whether a requester properly belongs in this category by determining how the requester will use the documents.

(g) The term *educational institution* means a preschool, a public or private elementary or secondary school, an institution of graduate higher education, an institution of undergraduate higher education, an institution of professional education, or an institution of vocational education which operates a program or programs of scholarly research.

(h) The term *noncommercial scientific institution* means an institution that is not operated on a "commercial" basis as that term is used in paragraph (f) of this section and which is operated solely for the purpose of conducting scientific research the results of which are not intended to promote any particular product or industry.

(i) The term *representative of the news media* means any person actively gathering news for an entity that is organized and operated to publish or broadcast news to the public. The term *news* means information that is about current events or that would be of current interest to the public. Examples of news media include television or radio stations broadcasting to the public at large, and publishers of periodicals (but only in those instances when they can qualify as disseminators of "news") who make their products available for purchase or subscription by the general public. "Freelance" journalists will be regarded as working for a news organization if they can demonstrate a solid basis for expecting publication through that organization even though they are not actually employed by it.

§ 105–60.305–2 Scope of this subpart.

This subpart sets forth policies and procedures to be followed in the assessment and collection of fees from a requester for the search, review, and reproduction of GSA records.

§ 105–60.305–3 GSA records available without charge.

GSA records available to the public are displayed in the Business Service Center for each GSA region. The address and phone number of the Business Service Centers are listed in § 105–60.303. Certain material related to bids (excluding construction plans and specifications) and any material displayed are available without charge upon request.

§ 105–60.305–4 GSA records available at a fee.

(a) GSA will make a record not subject to exemption available at a time and place mutually agreed upon by GSA and the requester at fees shown in § 105–60.305–10. Waivers of these fees are available under the conditions described in § 105–60.305–13. GSA will agree to:

(1) Show the originals to the requester;

(2) Make one copy available at a fee; or

(3) A combination of these alternatives.

(b) GSA will make copies of voluminous records as quickly as possible. GSA may, in its discretion, make a reasonable number of additional copies for a fee when commercial reproduction services are not available to the requester.

§ 105–60.305–5 Searches.

(a) GSA may charge for the time spent in the following activities in determining "search time" subject to applicable fees as provided in § 105–60.305–10:

(1) Time spent in trying to locate GSA records which come within the scope of the request;

(2) Time spent in either transporting a necessary agency searcher to a place of record storage, or in transporting records to the locations of a necessary agency searcher; and

(3) Direct costs of the use of computer time to locate and extract requested records.

(b) GSA will not charge for the time spent in monitoring a requester's inspection of disclosed agency records.

(c) GSA may assess fees for search time even if the search proves unsuccessful or if the records located are exempt from disclosure.

§ 105–60.305–6 Reviews.

(a) GSA will charge only commercial-use requesters for review time.

(b) GSA will charge for the time spent in the following activities in determining "review time" subject to applicable fees as provided in § 105–60.305–10:

(1) Time spent in examining a requested record to determine whether any or all of the record is exempt from disclosure, including time spent consulting with submitters of requested information; and

(2) Time spent in deleting exempt matter being withheld from records otherwise made available.

(c) GSA will not charge for:

(1) Time spent in resolving issues of law or policy regarding the application of exemptions; or

(2) Review at the administrative appeal level of an exemption already applied. However, records or portions of records withheld in full under an exemption which is subsequently determined not to apply may be reviewed again to determine the applicability of other exemptions not previously considered. GSA will charge for such subsequent review.

§ 105–60.305–7 Assurance of payment.

If fees for search, review, and reproduction will exceed $25 but will be less than $250, the requester must provide written assurance of payment before GSA will process the request. If this assurance is not included in the initial request, GSA will notify the requester that assurance of payment is required before the request is processed. GSA will offer requesters an opportunity to modify the request to reduce the fee.

§ 105–60.305–8 Prepayment of fees.

(a) *Fees over $250.* GSA will require prepayment of fees for search, review, and reproduction which are likely to exceed $250. When the anticipated total fee exceeds $250, the requester will receive notice to prepay and at the same time will be given an opportunity to modify his or her request to reduce the fee. When fees will exceed $250, GSA will notify the requester that it will not start processing a request until payment is received.

(b) *Delinquent payments.* As noted in § 105–6.305–12(d), requesters who are delinquent in paying for previous requests will be required to repay the old debt and to prepay for any subsequent request. GSA will inform the requester that it will process no additional requests until all fees are paid.

§ 105–60.305–9 Form of payment.

Requesters should pay fees by check or money order made out to the General Services Administration and addressed to the official named by GSA in its correspondence. Payment may also be made by means of Mastercard or Visa. For information concerning payment by credit cards, call 816–926–7551.

§ 105–60.305–10 Fee schedule.

(a) When GSA is aware that documents responsive to a request are maintained for distribution by an agency operating a statutory fee based program, GSA will inform the requester of the procedures for obtaining records from those sources.

(b) GSA will consider only the following costs in fees charged to requesters of GSA records:

(1) Review and search fees.

Manual searches by clerical staff: $13 per hour or fraction of an hour.
Manual searches and reviews by professional staff in cases in which clerical staff would be unable to locate the requested records: $29 per hour or fraction of an hour.
Computer searches: Direct cost to GSA.
Transportation or special handling of records: Direct cost to GSA.

(2) Reproduction fees.

Pages no larger than 8½ by 14 inches, when reproduced by routine electrostatic copying: 10¢ per page.
Pages over 8½ by 14 inches: Direct cost of reproduction to GSA.
Pages requiring reduction, enlargement, or other special services: Direct cost of reproduction to GSA.

Reproduction by other than routine electrostatic copying: Direct cost of reproduction to GSA.

(c) Any fees not provided for under paragraph (b) of this section, shall be calculated as direct costs, in accordance with § 105–60.305–1(b).

(d) GSA will assess fees based on the category of the requester as defined in § 105–60.305–1(f)–(1); i.e., commercial-use, educational and noncommercial scientific institutions, news media, and all other. The fees listed in paragraph (b) of this section apply with the following exceptions:

(1) GSA will not charge the requester if the fee is $25 or less as the cost of collection is greater than the fee.

(2) Educational and noncommercial scientific institutions and the news media will be charged for the cost of reproduction alone. These requesters are entitled to the first 100 pages (paper copies) of duplication at no cost. The following are examples of how these fees are calculated:

(i) *A request that results in 150 pages of material.* No fee would be assessed for duplication of 150 pages. The reason is that these requesters are entitled to the first 100 pages at no charge. The charge for the remaining 50 pages would be $5.00. This amount would not be billed under the preceding section.

(ii) *A request that results in 450 pages of material.* The requester in this case would be charged $35.00. The reason is that the requester is entitled to the first 100 pages at no charge. The charge for the remaining 350 pages would be $35.

(3) Noncommercial requesters who are not included under paragraph (d)(2) of this section will be entitled to the first 100 pages (page copies) of duplication at not cost and two hours of search without charge. The term *search time* generally refers to manual search. To apply this term to searches made by computer, GSA will determine the hourly cost of operating the central processing unit and the operator's hourly salary plus 16 percent. When the cost of search (including the operator time and the cost of operating the computer to process a request) reaches the equivalent dollar amount of two hours of the salary of the person performing a manual search, i.e., the operator,

GSA will begin assessing charges for computer search.

(4) GSA will charge commercial-use requesters fees which recover the full direct costs of searching for, reviewing for release, and duplicating the records sought. Commercial-use requesters are not entitled to two hours of free search time.

(e) *Determining category of requester.* GSA may ask any requester to provide additional information at any time to determine what fee category he or she falls under.

§ 105–60.305–11 Fees for authenticated and attested copies.

The fees set forth in § 105–60.305–10 apply to requests for authenticated and attested copies of GSA records.

§ 105–60.305–12 Administrative actions to improve assessment and collection of fees.

(a) *Charging interest.* GSA may charge requesters who fail to pay fees interest on the amount billed starting on the 31st day following the day on which the billing was sent. Interest will be at the rate prescribed in 31 U.S.C. 3717.

(b) *Effect of the Debt Collection Act of 1982.* GSA will take any action authorized by the Debt Collection Act of 1982 (Pub. L. 97–365, 96 Stat. 1749), including disclosure to consumer reporting agencies, use of collection agencies, and assessment of penalties and administrative costs, where appropriate, to encourage payment.

(c) *Aggregating requests.* When GSA reasonably believes that a requester, or group of requesters acting in concert, is attempting to break down a request into a series of requests related to the same subject for the purpose of evading the assessment of fees, GSA will combine any such requests and charge accordingly, including fees for previous requests where charges were not assessed. GSA will presume that multiple requests of this type within a 30-day period are made to avoid fees.

(d) *Advanced payments.* Whenever a requester is delinquent in paying the fee for a previous request (i.e., within 30 days of the date of the billing), GSA will require the requester to pay the full amount owed plus any applicable interest penalties and administrative costs as provided in paragraph (a) of this section or to demonstrate that he or she has, in fact, paid the fee. In such cases, GSA will also require advance payment of the full amount of the estimated fee before the agency begins to process a new request or a pending request from that requester. When advance payment is required under this selection, the administrative time limits in subsection (a)(6) of the FOIA (i.e., 10 working days from receipt of appeals from initial denial plus permissible time extensions) will begin only after GSA has received the fee payments described in § 105–60.305–8.

§ 105–60.305–13 Waiver of fee.

(a) Any request for a waiver or the reduction of a fee should be included in the initial letter requesting access to GSA records under § 105–60.402–1. The waiver request should explain how disclosure of the information would contribute significantly to public's understanding of the operations or activities of the Government and would not be primarily in the commercial interest of the requester. In responding to a requester, GSA will consider the following factors:

(1) Whether the subject of the requested records concerns "the operations or activities of the Government." The subject matter of the requested records must specifically concern identifiable operations or activities of the Federal Government. The connection between the records and the operations or activities must be direct and clear, not remote or attenuated.

(2) Whether the disclosure is "likely to contribute" to an understanding of Government operations or activities. In this connection, GSA will consider whether the requested information is already in the public domain. If it is, then disclosure of the information would not be likely to contribute to an understanding of Government operations or activities, as nothing new would be added to the public record.

(3) Whether disclosure of the requested information will contribute to "public's understanding." The focus here must be on the contribution to public's understanding rather than personal benefit to be derived by the requester. For purposes of this analysis,

the identity and qualifications of the requester should be considered to determine whether the requester is in a position to contribute to public's understanding through the requested disclosure.

(4) Whether the requester has a commercial interest that would be furthered by the requested disclosure; and if so: whether the magnitude of the identified commercial interest of the requester is sufficiently large, in comparison with the public's interest in disclosure, that disclosure is "primarily in the commercial interest of the requester."

(b) GSA will ask the requester to furnish additional information if the initial request is insufficient to evaluate the merits of the request. GSA will not start processing a request until the fee waiver issue has been resolved unless the requester has provided written assurance of payment in full if the fee waiver is denied by the agency.

Subpart 105–60.4—Described Records

§ 105–60.401   General.

(a) Except for records made available in accordance with subparts 105–60.2 and 105–60.3 of this part, GSA will make records available to a requester promptly when the request reasonably describes the records unless GSA invokes an exemption in accordance with subpart 105–60.5 of this part. Although the burden of reasonable description of the records rests with the requester, whenever practical GSA will assist requesters to describe records more specifically.

(b) Whenever a request does not reasonably describe the records requested, GSA may contact the requester to seek a more specific description. The 20-workday time limit set forth in § 105–60.402–2 will not start until the official identified in § 105–60.402–1 or other responding official receives a request reasonably describing the records.

§ 105–60.402   Procedures for making records available.

This subpart sets forth initial procedures for making records available when they are requested, including administrative procedures to be exhausted prior to seeking judicial review by an appropriate United States District Court.

§ 105–60.402–1   Submission of requests.

For records located in the GSA Central Office, the requester must submit a request in writing to the GSA FOIA Officer, General Services Administration (CAI), Washington, DC 20405. Requesters may FAX requests to (202) 501–2727, or submit a request by electronic mail to *gsa.foi@gsa.gov*. For records located in the Office of Inspector General, the requester must submit a request to the FOIA Officer, Office of Inspector General, General Services Administration, 1800 F Street NW., Room 5324, Washington, DC 20405. For records located in the GSA regional offices, the requester must submit a request to the FOIA Officer for the relevant region, at the address listed in § 105–60.303(a). Requests should include the words "Freedom of Information Act Request" prominently marked on both the face of the request letter and the envelope. The 20-workday time limit for agency decisions set forth in § 105–60.402–2 begins with receipt of a request in the office of the official identified in this section, unless the provisions under §§ 105–60.305–8 and 105–60.305–12(d) apply. Failure to include the words "Freedom of Information Act Request" or to submit a request to the official identified in this section will result in processing delays. A requester with questions concerning a FOIA request should contact the GSA FOIA Office, General Services Administration (CAI), 18th and F Streets, NW., Washington, DC 20405, (202) 501–2262.

§ 105–60.402–2   Response to initial requests.

(a) GSA will respond to an initial FOIA request that reasonably describes requested records, including a fee waiver request, within 20 workdays (that is, excluding Saturdays, Sundays, and legal holidays) after receipt of a request by the office of the appropriate official specified in § 105–60.402–1. This letter will provide the agency's decision with respect to disclosure or nondisclosure of the requested records, or, if appropriate, a decision on a request for a fee waiver. If the records to be disclosed are not provided with the initial letter, the records will be sent as soon as possible thereafter.

(b) In unusual circumstances, as described in § 105–60.404, GSA will inform the requester of the agency's need to take an extension of time, not to exceed an additional 10 workdays. This notice will afford requesters an opportunity to limit the scope of the request so that it may be processed within prescribed time limits or an opportunity to arrange an alternative time frame for processing the request or a modified request. Such mutually agreed time frames will supersede the 10 day limit for extensions.

(c) GSA will consider requests for expedited processing from requesters who submit a statement describing a compelling need and certifying that this need is true and correct to the best of such person's knowledge and belief. A *compelling need* means:

(1) Failure to obtain the records on an expedited basis could reasonably be expected to pose an imminent threat to the life or physical safety of an individual; or

(2) The information is urgently needed by an individual primarily engaged in disseminating information in order to inform the public concerning actual or alleged Federal Government activity. An individual primarily engaged in dissmeninating information means a person whose primary activity involves publishing or otherwise disseminating information to the public. "Urgently needed" information has a particular value that will be lost if not disseminated quickly, such as a breaking news story or general public interest. Information of historical interest only, or information sought for litigation or commercial activities would not qualify, nor would a news media publication or broadcast deadline unrelated to the newsbreaking nature of the information.

(d) GSA will decide whether to grant expedited processing within five working days of receipt of the request. If the request is granted, GSA will process the request ahead of non-expedited requests, as soon as practicable. If the request is not granted, GSA will give expeditious consideration to administrative appeals of this denial.

(e) GSA may, at its discretion, establish three processing queues based on whether any requests have been granted expedited status and on the difficulty and complexity of preparing a response. Within each queue, responses will be prepared on a "first in, first out" basis. One queue will be made up of expedited requests; the second, of simple responses that clearly can be prepared without requesting an extension of time; the third, of responses that will require an extension of time.

§ 105–60.403 **Appeal within GSA.**

(a) A requester who receives a denial of a request, in whole or in part, a denial of a request for expedited processing or of a fee waiver request may appeal that decision within GSA. A requester may also appeal the adequacy of the search if GSA determines that it has searched for but has not requested records. The requester must send the appeal to the GSA FOIA Officer, General Services Administration (CAI), Washington, DC 20405, regardless of whether the denial being appealed was made in the Central Office or in a regional office. For denials which originate in the Office of Inspector General, the requester must send the appeal to the Inspector General, General Services Administration, 1800 F Street NW., Washington, DC 20405.

(b) The GSA FOIA Officer must receive an appeal no later than 120 calendar days after receipt by the requester of the initial denial of access or fee waiver.

(c) An appeal must be in writing and include a brief statement of the reasons he or she thinks GSA should release the records or provide expedited processing and enclose copies of the initial request and denial. The appeal letter must include the words "Freedom of Information Act Appeal" on both the face of the appeal letter and on the envelope. Failure to follow these procedures will delay processing of the appeal. GSA has 20 workdays after receipt of a proper appeal of denial of records to issue a determination with respect to the appeal. The 20-workday time limit shall not begin until the GSA FOIA Officer receives the appeal. As noted in § 105–60.404, the GSA FOIA Officer may extend this time limit in unusual circumstances. GSA will process appeals of denials of expedited processing as soon as possible after receiving them.

(d) A requester who receives a denial of an appeal, or who has not received a response to an appeal or initial request within the statutory time frame may seek judicial review in the United States District Court in the district in which the requester resides or has a principal place of business, or where the records are situated, or in the United States District Court for the District of Columbia.

§ 105–60.404 Extension of time limits.

(a) In unusual circumstances, the GSA FOIA Officer or the regional FOIA Officer may extend the time limits prescribed in §§ 105–60.402 and 105–60.403. For purposes of this section, the term *unusual circumstances* means:

(1) The need to search for and collect the requested records from field facilities or other establishments that are separate from the office processing the request;

(2) The need to search for, collect, and appropriately examine a voluminous amount of separate and distinct records which are described in a single request;

(3) The need for consultation, which shall be conducted with all practicable speed, with another agency having a substantial interest in the determination of the request or among two or more components of GSA having substantial subject-matter interest therein; or

(4) The need to consult with the submitter of the requested information.

(b) If necessary, GSA may take more than one extension of time. However, the total extension of time to respond to any single request shall not exceed 10 workdays. The extension may be divided between the initial and appeal stages or within a single stage. GSA will provide written notice to the requester of any extension of time limits.

§ 105–60.405 Processing requests for confidential commercial information.

(a) *General.* The following additional procedures apply when processing requests for confidential commercial information.

(b) *Definitions.* For the purposes of this section, the following definitions apply:

(1) *Confidential commercial information* means records provided to the Government by a submitter that contain material arguably exempt from release under 5 U.S.C. 552(b)(4), because disclosure could reasonably be expected to cause substantial competitive harm.

(2) *Submitter* means a person or entity which provides to the Government information which may constitute confidential commercial information. The term *submitter* includes, but is not limited to, individuals, partnerships, corporations, State governments, and foreign governments.

(c) *Designating confidential commercial information.* Since January 1, 1988, submitters have been required to designate confidential commercial information as such when it is submitted to GSA or at a reasonable time thereafter. For information submitted in connection with negotiated procurements, the requirements of Federal Acquisition Regulation 48 CFR 15.407(c)(8) and 52.215–12 also apply.

(d) *Procedural requirements—consultation with the submitter.* (1) If GSA receives a FOIA request for potentially confidential commercial information, it will notify the submitter immediately by telephone and invite an opinion whether disclosure will or will not cause substantial competitive harm.

(2) GSA will follow up the telephonic notice promptly in writing before releasing any records unless paragraph (f) of this section applies.

(3) If the submitter indicates an objection to disclosure GSA will give the submitter seven workdays from receipt of the letter to provide GSA with a detailed written explanation of how disclosure of any specified portion of the records would be competitively harmful.

(4) If the submitter verbally states that there is no objection to disclosure, GSA will confirm this fact in writing before disclosing any records.

(5) At the same time GSA notifies the submitter, it will also advise the requester that there will be a delay in responding to the request due to the need to consult with the submitter.

(6) GSA will review the reasons for nondisclosure before independently deciding whether the information must be released or should be withheld. If GSA decides to release the requested information, it will provide the submitter with a written statement explaining why his or her objections are not sustained. The letter to the submitter will contain a copy of the material to be disclosed or will offer the submitter an opportunity to review the material in none of GSA's offices. If GSA decides not to release the material, it will notify the submitter orally or in writing.

(7) If GSA determines to disclose information over a submitter's objections, it will inform the submitter the GSA will delay disclosure for 5 workdays from the estimated date the submitter receives GSA's decision before it releases the information. The decision letter to the requester shall state that GSA will delay disclosure of material it has determined to disclose to allow for the notification of the submitter.

(e) *When notice is required.* (1) For confidential commercial information submitted prior to January 1, 1988, GSA will notify a submitter whenever it receives a FOIA request for such information:

(i) If the records are less than 10 years old and the information has been designated by the submitter as confidential commercial information; or

(ii) If GSA has reason to believe that disclosure of the information could reasonably be expected to cause substantial competitive harm.

(2) For confidential commercial information submitted on or after January 1, 1988, GSA will notify a submitter whenever it determines that the agency may be required to disclose records:

(i) That the submitter has previously designated as privileged or confidential; or

(ii) That GSA believes could reasonably be expected to cause substantial competitive harm if disclosed.

(3) GSA will provide notice to a submitter for a period of up to 10 years after the date of submission.

(f) *When notice is not required.* The notice requirements of this section will not apply if:

(1) GSA determines that the information should not be disclosed;

(2) The information has been published or has been officially made available to the public;

(3) Disclosure of the information is required by law other than the FOIA;

(4) Disclosure is required by an agency rule that

(i) Was adopted pursuant to notice and public comment;

(ii) Specifies narrow classes of records submitted to the agency that are to be released under FOIA; and

(iii) Provides in exceptional circumstances for notice when the submitter provides written justification, at the time the information is submitted for a reasonable time thereafter, that disclosure of the information could reasonably be expected to cause substantial competitive harm;

(5) The information is not designated by the submitter as exempt from disclosure under paragraph (c) of this section, unless GSA has substantial reason to believe that disclosure of the information would be competitively harmful; or

(6) The designation made by the submitter in accordance with paragraph (c) of this section appears obviously frivolous; except that, in such cases, the agency must provide the submitter with written notice of any final administrative decision five workdays prior to disclosing the information.

(g) *Lawsuits.* If a FOIA requester sues the agency to compel disclosure of confidential commercial information, GSA will notify the submitter as soon as possible. If the submitter sues GSA to enjoin disclosure of the records, GSA will notify the requester.

Subpart 105–60.5—Exemptions

§ 105–60.501 Categories of records exempt from disclosure under the FOIA.

(a) 5 U.S.C. 552(b) provides that the requirements of the FOIA do not apply to matters that are:

507

(1) Specifically authorized under the criteria established by an executive order to be kept secret in the interest of national defense or foreign policy and are in fact properly classified pursuant to such executive order;

(2) Related solely to the internal personnel rules and practices of an agency;

(3) Specifically exempted from disclosure by statute (other than section 552b of this title), provided that such statute

(i) Requires that the matters be withheld from the public in such a manner as to leave no discretion on the issue; or

(ii) Establishes particular criteria for withholding or refers to particular types of matters to be withheld;

(4) Trade secrets and commercial or financial information obtained from a person and privileged or confidential;

(5) Interagency or intra-agency memorandums or letters which would not be available by law to a party other than an agency in litigation with the agency;

(6) Personnel and medical files and similar files the disclosure of which would constitute a clearly unwarranted invasion of personal privacy;

(7) Records or information compiled for law enforcement purposes, but only to the extent that the production of such law enforcement records or information

(i) Could reasonably be expected to interfere with enforcement proceedings;

(ii) Would deprive a person of a right to a fair trial or an impartial adjudication;

(iii) Could reasonably be expected to constitute an unwarranted invasion of personal privacy;

(iv) Could reasonably be expected to disclose the identity of a confidential source, including a State, local, or foreign agency or authority or any private institution which furnished information on a confidential basis, and, in the case of a record or information compiled by a criminal law enforcement authority in the course of a criminal investigation or by an agency conducting a lawful national security intelligence investigation, information furnished by a confidential source;

(v) Would disclose techniques and procedures for law enforcement investigations or prosecutions, or would disclose guidelines for law enforcement investigations or prosecutions if such disclosure could reasonably be expected to risk circumvention of the law; or

(vi) Could reasonably be expected to endanger the life or physical safety of any individual;

(8) Contained in or related to examination, operating, or condition reports prepared by, on behalf of, or for the use of an agency responsible for the regulation or supervision of financial institutions; or

(9) Geological and geophysical information and data, including maps, concerning wells.

(b) GSA will provide any reasonably segregable portion of a record to a requester after deletion of the portions that are exempt under this section. If GSA must delete information from a record before disclosing it, this information, and the reasons for withholding it, will be clearly described in the cover letter to the requester or in an attachment. Unless indicating the extent of the deletion would harm an interest protected by an exemption, the amount of deleted information shall be indicated on the released portion of paper records by use of brackets or darkened areas indicating removal of information. In the case of electronic deletion, the amount of redacted information shall be indicated at the place in the record where such deletion was made, unless including the indication would harm an interest protected by the exemption under which the exemption was made.

(c) GSA will invoke no exemption under this section to deny access to records that would be available pursuant to a request made under the Privacy Act of 1974 (5 U.S.C. 552a) and implementing regulations, 41 CFR part 105–64, or if disclosure would cause no demonstrable harm to any governmental or private interest.

(d) Pursuant to National Defense Authorization Act of Fiscal Year 1997, Pub. L. No. 104–201, section 821, 110 Stat. 2422, GSA will invoke Exemption 3 to deny access to any proposal submitted by a vendor in response to the requirements of a solicitation for a competitive proposal unless the proposal is set forth or incorporated by reference in a contract entered into between the agency and the contractor that submitted the proposal.

(e) Whenever a request is made which involves access to records described in §105–60.501(a)(7)(i) and the investigation or proceeding involves a possible violation of criminal law, and there is reason to believe that the subject of the investigation or proceeding is not aware of it, and disclosure of the existence of the records could reasonably be expected to interfere with enforcement proceedings, the agency may, during only such time as that circumstance continues, treat the records as not subject to the requirements of this section.

(f) Whenever informant records maintained by a criminal law enforcement agency under an informant's name or personal identifier are requested by a third party according to the informant's name or personal identifier, the agency may treat the records as not subject to the requirements of this section unless the informant's status as an informant has been officially confirmed.

(g) Whenever a request is made that involves access to records maintained by the Federal Bureau of Investigation pertaining to foreign intelligence or counterintelligence, or international terrorism, and the existence of the records is classified information as provided in paragraph (a)(1) of this section, the Bureau may, as long as the existence of the records remains classified information, treat the records are not subject to the requirements of this section.

Subpart 105–60.6—Production or Disclosure by Present or Former General Services Administration Employees in Response to Subpoenas or Similar Demands in Judicial or Administrative Proceedings

§ 105–60.601 Purpose and scope of subpart.

(a) By virtue of the authority vested in the Administrator of General Services by 5 U.S.C. 301 and 40 U.S.C. 486(c) this subpart establishes instructions and procedures to be followed by current and former employees of the General Services Administration in response to subpoenas or similar demands issued in judicial or administrative proceedings for production or disclosure of material or information obtained as part of the performance of a person's official duties or because of the person's official status. Nothing in these instructions applies to responses to subpoenas or demands issued by the Congress or in Federal grand jury proceedings.

(b) This subpart provides instructions regarding the internal operations of GSA and the conduct of its employees, and is not intended and does not, and may not, be relied upon to create any right or benefit, substantive or procedural, enforceable at law by a party against GSA.

§ 105–60.602 Definitions.

For purposes of this subpart, the following definitions apply:

(a) *Material* means any document, record, file or data, regardless of the physical form or the media by or through which it is maintained or recorded, which was generated or acquired by a current or former GSA employee by reason of the performance of that person's official duties or because of the person's official status, or any other tangible item, e.g., personal property possessed or controlled by GSA.

(b) *Information* means any knowledge or facts contained in material, and any knowledge or facts acquired by current or former GSA employee as part of the performance of that person's official duties or because of that person's official status.

(c) *Demand* means any subpoena, order, or similar demand for the production or disclosure of material, information or testimony regarding such material or information, issued by a court or other authority in a judicial or administrative proceeding, excluding congressional subpoenas or demands in Federal grand jury proceedings, and served upon a present or former GSA employee.

(d) *Appropriate authority* means the following officials who are delegated authority to approve or deny responses to demands for material, information or testimony:

(1) The Counsel to the Inspector General for material and information which is the responsibility of the GSA Office of Inspector General or testimony of current or former employees of the Office of the Inspector General;

(2) The Counsel to the Civilian Board of Contract Appeals (CBCA) for material and information which is the responsibility of the CBCA or testimony of current or former CBCA employees;

(3) The GSA General Counsel, Associate General Counsel(s) or Regional Counsel for all material, information, or testimony not covered by paragraphs (d)(1) and (2) of this section.

[63 FR 56839, Oct. 23, 1998, as amended at 78 FR 29247, May 20, 2013]

§ 105–60.603 Acceptance of service of a subpoena duces tecum or other legal demand on behalf of the General Services Administration.

(a) The Administrator of General Services and the following officials are the only GSA personnel authorized to accept service of a subpoena or other legal demand on behalf of GSA: The GSA General Counsel and Associate General Counsel(s) and, with respect to material or information which is the responsibility of a regional office, the Regional Administrator and Regional Counsel. The Inspector General and Counsel to the Inspector General, as well as the Chairman and Vice Chairman of the Civilian Board of Contract Appeals, are authorized to accept service for material or information which are the responsibility of their respective organizations.

(b) A present or former GSA employee not authorized to accept service of a subpoena or other demand for material, information or testimony obtained in an official capacity shall respectfully inform the process server that he or she is not authorized to accept service on behalf of GSA and refer the process server to an appropriate official listed in paragraph (a) of this section.

(c) A Regional Administrator or Regional Counsel shall notify the General Counsel of a demand which may raise policy concerns or affect multiple regions.

[63 FR 56839, Oct. 23, 1998, as amended at 78 FR 29247, May 20, 2013]

§ 105–60.604 Production or disclosure prohibited unless approved by the Appropriate Authority.

No current or former GSA employee shall, in response to a demand, produce any material or disclose, through testimony or other means, any information covered by this subpart, without prior approval of the Appropriate Authority.

§ 105–60.605 Procedure in the event of a demand for production or disclosure.

(a) Whenever service of a demand is attempted in person or via mail upon a current or former GSA employee for the production of material or the disclosure of information covered by this subpart, the employee or former employee shall immediately notify the Appropriate Authority through his or her supervisor or his or her former service, staff office, or regional office. The supervisor shall notify the Appropriate Authority. For current or former employees of the Office of Inspector General located in regional offices, Counsel to the Inspector General shall be notified through the immediate supervisor or former employing field office.

(b) The Appropriate Authority shall require that the party seeking material or testimony provide the Appropriate Authority with an affidavit, declaration, statement, and/or a plan as described in paragraphs (c) (1), (2), and (3) of this section if not included with or described in the demand. The Appropriate Authority may waive this requirement for a demand arising out of proceedings to which GSA or the United States is a party. Any waiver will be coordinated with the United States Department of Justice (DOJ) in proceedings in which GSA, its current or former employees, or the United States are represented by DOJ.

(c)(1) *Oral testimony.* If oral testimony is sought by a demand, the Appropriate Authority shall require the party seeking the testimony or the party's attorney to provide, by affidavit or other statement, a detailed summary of the testimony sought and its relevance to the proceedings. Any authorization for the testimony of a current or former GSA employee shall be limited to the scope of the demand as summarized in such statement or affidavit.

(2) Production of material. When information other than oral testimony is sought by a demand, the Appropriate Authority shall require the party seeking production or the party's attorney to provide a detailed summary, by affidavit or other statement, of the information sought and its relevance to the proceeding.

(3) The Appropriate Authority may require a plan or other information from the party seeking testimony or production of material of all demands reasonably foreseeable, including, but not limited to, names of all current and former GSA employees from whom testimony or production is or will likely be sought, areas of inquiry, for current employees the length of time away from duty anticipated, and identification of documents to be used in each deposition or other testimony, where appropriate.

(d) The Appropriate Authority will notify the current or former employee, the appropriate supervisor, and such other persons as circumstances may warrant, whether disclosure or production is authorized, and of any conditions or limitations to disclosure or production.

(e) Factors to be considered by the Appropriate Authority in responding to demands:

(1) Whether disclosure or production is appropriate under rules of procedure governing the proceeding out of which the demand arose;

(2) The relevance of the testimony or documents to the proceedings;

(3) The impact of the relevant substantive law concerning applicable privileges recognized by statute, common law, judicial interpretation or similar authority;

(4) The information provided by the issuer of the demand in response to requests by the Appropriate Authority pursuant to paragraphs (b) and (c) of this section;

(5) The steps taken by the issuer of the demand to minimize the burden of disclosure or production on GSA, including but not limited to willingness to accept authenticated copies of material in lieu of personal appearance by GSA employees;

(6) The impact on pending or potential litigation involving GSA or the United States as a party;

(7) In consultation with the head of the GSA organizational component affected, the burden on GSA which disclosure or production would entail; and

(8) Any additional factors unique to a particular demand or proceeding.

(f) The Appropriate Authority shall not approve a disclosure or production which would:

(1) Violate a statute or a specific regulation;

(2) Reveal classified information, unless appropriately declassified by the originating agency;

(3) Reveal a confidential source or informant, unless the investigative agency and the source or informant consent;

(4) Reveal records or information compiled for law enforcement purposes which would interfere with enforcement proceedings or disclose investigative techniques and procedures the effectiveness of which would be impaired;

(5) Reveal trade secrets or commercial or financial information which is privileged or confidential without prior consultation with the person from whom it was obtained; or

(6) Be contrary to a recognized privilege.

(g) The Appropriate Authority's determination, including any reasons for denial or limitations on disclosure or production, shall be made as expeditiously as possible and shall be communicated in writing to the issuer of the demand and appropriate current or former GSA employee(s). In proceedings in which GSA, its current or former employees, or the United States are represented by DOJ, the determination shall be coordinated with DOJ which may respond to the issuer of the subpoenas or demand in lieu of the Appropriate Authority.

§ 105–60.606 Procedure where response to demand is required prior to receiving instructions.

(a) If a response to a demand is required before the Appropriate Authority's decision is issued, a GSA attorney designated by the Appropriate Authority for the purpose shall appear with the employee or former employee upon whom the demand has been made, and shall furnish the judicial or other authority with a copy of the instructions contained in this subpart. The attorney shall inform the court or other authority that the demand has been or is being referred for the prompt consideration by the Appropriate Authority. The attorney shall respectfully request the judicial or administrative authority to stay the demand pending receipt of the requested instructions.

(b) The designated GSA attorney shall coordinate GSA's response with DOJ's Civil Division or the relevant Office of the United States Attorney and may request that a DOJ or Assistant United States Attorney appear with the employee in addition to or in lieu of a designated GSA attorney.

(c) If an immediate demand for production or disclosure is made in circumstances which preclude the appearance of a GSA or DOJ attorney on the behalf of the employee or the former employee, the employee or former employee shall respectfully make a request to the demanding authority for sufficient time to obtain advice of counsel.

§ 105–60.607 Procedure in the event of an adverse ruling.

If the court or other authority declines to stay the effect of the demand in response to a request made in accordance with § 105–60.606 pending receipt of instructions, or if the court or other authority rules that the demand must be complied with irrespective of instructions by the Appropriate Authority not to produce the material or disclose the information sought, the employee or former employee upon whom the demand has been made shall respectfully decline to comply, citing these instructions and the decision of the United States Supreme Court in United States ex rel. *Touhy* v. *Ragen*, 340 U.S. 462 (1951).

§ 105–60.608 Fees, expenses, and costs.

(a) In consultation with the Appropriate Authority, a current employee who appears as a witness pursuant to a demand shall ensure that he or she receives all fees and expenses, including travel expenses, to which witnesses are entitled pursuant to rules applicable to the judicial or administrative proceedings out of which the demand arose.

(b) Witness fees and reimbursement for expenses received by a GSA employee shall be disposed of in accordance with rules applicable to Federal employees in effect at the time.

(c) Reimbursement to the GSA for costs associated with producing material pursuant to a demand shall be determined in accordance with rules applicable to the proceedings out of which the demand arose.

PART 105–62—DOCUMENT SECURITY AND DECLASSIFICATION

AUTHORITY: Sec. 205(c), 63 Stat. 390; 40 U.S.C. 486(c); and E.O. 12065 dated June 28, 1978.

SOURCE: 44 FR 64805, Nov. 8, 1979, unless otherwise noted.

§ 105–62.000 Scope of part.

This part prescribes procedures for safeguarding national security information and material within GSA. They explain how to identify, classify, downgrade, declassify, disseminate, and protect such information in the interests of national security. They also supplement and conform with Executive Order 12065 dated June 28, 1978, subject: National Security Information, and the

Implementing Directive dated September 29, 1978, issued through the Information Security Oversight Office.

Subpart 105–62.1—Classified Materials

§ 105–62.101 Security classification categories.

As set forth in Executive Order 12065, official information or material which requires protection against unauthorized disclosure in the interests of the national defense or foreign relations of the United States (hereinafter collectively termed "national security") shall be classified in one of three categories: Namely, Top Secret, Secret, or Confidential, depending on its degree of significance to the national security. No other categories shall be used to identify official information or material as requiring protection in the interests of national security except as otherwise expressly provided by statute. The three classification categories are defined as follows:

(a) *Top Secret.* Top Secret refers to that national security information which requires the highest degree of protection, and shall be applied only to such information as the unauthorized disclosure of which could reasonably be expected to cause exceptionally grave damage to the national security. Examples of exceptionally grave damage include armed hostilities against the United States or its allies, disruption of foreign relations vitally affecting the national security, intelligence sources and methods, and the compromise of vital national defense plans or complex cryptologic and communications systems. This classification shall be used with the utmost restraint.

(b) *Secret.* Secret refers to that national security information or material which requires a substantial degree of protection, and shall be applied only to such information as the unauthorized disclosure of which could reasonably be expected to cause serious damage to the national security. Examples of serious damage include disruption of foreign relations significantly affecting the national security, significant impairment of a program or policy directly related to the national security,

and revelation of significant military plans or intelligence operations. This classification shall be used sparingly.

(c) *Confidential.* Confidential refers to other national security information which requires protection, and shall be applied only to such information as the unauthorized disclosure of which could reasonably be expected to cause identifiable damage to the national security.

§ 105–62.102 Authority to originally classify.

(a) *Top secret, secret, and confidential.* The authority to originally classify information as Top Secret, Secret, or Confidential may be exercised only by the Administrator and is delegable only to the Director, Information Security Oversight Office.

(b) *Limitations on delegation of classification authority.* Delegations of original classification authority are limited to the minimum number absolutely required for efficient administration. Delegated original classification authority may not be redelegated.

[47 FR 5416, Feb. 5, 1982]

§ 105–62.103 Access to GSA-originated materials.

Classified information shall not be disseminated outside the executive branch of the Government without the express permission of the GSA Security Officer except as otherwise provided in this § 105–62.103.

(a) *Access by historical researchers.* Persons outside the executive branch who are engaged in historical research projects, may be authorized access to classified information or material, provided that:

(1) A written determination is made by the Administrator of General Services that such access is clearly consistent with the interests of national security.

(2) Access is limited to that information over which GSA has classification jurisdiction.

(3) The material requested is reasonably accessible and can be located with a reasonable amount of effort.

(4) The person agrees to safeguard the information and to authorize a review of his or her notes and manuscript

for determination that no classified information is contained therein by signing a statement entitled "Conditions Governing Access to Official Records for Historical Research Purposes."

(5) An authorization for access shall be valid for a period of 2 years from the date of issuance and may be renewed under the provisions of this § 105–62.103(a).

(b) *Access by former Presidential appointees.* Persons who previously occupied policymaking positions to which they were appointed by the President may not remove classified information or material upon departure from office as all such material must remain under the security control of the U.S. Government. Such persons may be authorized access to classified information or material which they originated, received, reviewed, signed, or which was addressed to them while in public office, provided that the GSA element having classification jurisdiction for such information or material makes a written determination that access is consistent with the interests of national security, approval is granted by the GSA Security Officer, and the individual seeking access agrees:

(1) To safeguard the information,

(2) To authorize a review of his or her notes for determination that no classified information is contained therein, and

(3) To ensure that no classified information will be further disseminated or published.

(c) *Access during judicial proceedings.* Classified information will not normally be released in the course of any civilian judicial proceeding. In special circumstances however, and upon the receipt of an order or subpoena issued by a Federal court, the Administrator may authorize the limited release of classified information if he or she determines that the interests of justice cannot otherwise be served. Appropriate safeguards will be established to protect such classified material released for use in judicial proceedings.

(d) *Access to material in NARS custody.* The Archivist of the United States prepares procedures governing access to materials transferred to NARS custody. These procedures are issued by the Administrator of General Services in 41 CFR part 105–61.

(e) *Access by the General Accounting Office and congressional committees.* Classified information may be released to the General Accounting Office (GAO) and congressional committees when specifically authorized by the GSA Security Officer except as otherwise provided by law.

Subpart 105–62.2—Declassification and Downgrading

§ 105–62.201 Declassification and downgrading.

(a) *Authority to downgrade and declassify.* The authority to downgrade and declassify national security information or material shall be exercised as follows:

(1) Information or material may be downgraded or declassified by the GSA official authorizing the original classification, by a successor in capacity, by a supervisory official of either, or by the Information Security Oversight Committee on appeal.

(2) Downgrading and declassification authority may also be exercised by an official specifically authorized by the Administrator.

(3) In the case of classified information or material officially transferred to GSA by or under statute or Executive order in conjunction with a transfer of functions and not merely for storage purposes, GSA shall be deemed the originating agency for all purposes under these procedures including downgrading and declassification.

(4) In the case of classified information or material held in GSA not officially transferred under paragraph (a)(3) of this section but originated in an agency which has since ceased to exist, GSA is deemed the originating agency. Such information or material may be downgraded and declassified 30 calendar days after consulting with any other agencies having an interest in the subject matter.

(5) Classified information or material under the final declassification jurisdiction of GSA which has been transferred to NARS for accession into the Archives of the United States may be

downgraded and declassified by the Archivist of the United States in accordance with Executive Order 12065, directives of the Information Security Oversight Office, and the systematic review guidelines issued by the Administrator of General Services.

(6) It is presumed that information which continues to meet classification requirements requires continued protection. In some cases, however, the need to protect such information may be outweighed by the public interest in disclosure of the information, and in these cases the information should be declassified. When such questions arise they shall be referred to the Administrator, the Director of the Information Security Oversight Office, or in accordance with the procedures for mandatory review described in §105–62.202(b).

(b) *Declassification.* Declassification of information shall be given emphasis comparable to that accorded classification. Information classified under Executive Order 12065 and prior orders shall be declassified as early as national security considerations permit. Decisions concerning declassification shall be based on the loss of sensitivity of the information with the passage of time or on the occurrence of an event which permits declassification. When information is reviewed for declassification it shall be declassified unless the declassification authority established in §105–62.202 determines that the information continues to meet the classification requirements prescribed despite the passage of time.

(c) *Downgrading.* Classified information that is marked for automatic downgrading is downgraded accordingly without notification to holders. Classified information that is not marked for automatic downgrading may be assigned a lower classification designation by the originator or by an official authorized to declassify the same information. Notice of downgrading shall be provided to known holders of the information.

§105–62.202 Review of classified materials for declassification purposes.

(a) *Systematic review for declassification.* Except for foreign government information, classified information constituting permanently valuable records

of GSA as defined by 44 U.S.C. 2103, and information in the possession and under control of NARA, under 44 U.S.C. 2107 or 2107 note, shall be reviewed for declassification as it becomes 20 years old. Transition to systematic review at 20 years shall be implemented as rapidly as practicable and shall be completed by December 1, 1988. Foreign government information shall be reviewed for declassification as it becomes 30 years old.

(b) *Mandatory review for declassification.* All classified information upon request by a member of the public or a Government employee or agency to declassify and release such information under the provisions of Executive Order 12065 shall be reviewed by the responsible GSA element for possible declassification in accordance with the procedures set forth in paragraphs (c) through (g) of this section.

(c) *Submission of requests for review.* Requests for mandatory review of classified information shall be submitted in accordance with the following:

(1) Requests originating within GSA shall in all cases be submitted directly to the service or staff office that originated the information.

(2) For expeditious action, requests from other governmental agencies or from members of the public should be submitted directly to the service or staff office that originated the material, or, if the originating element is not known, or no longer exists, the requester shall submit the request to the GSA Security Officer who shall cause such request to be reviewed.

(d) *Requirements for processing.* Requests for declassification review and release of information shall be processed in accordance with the provisions set forth in paragraphs (e) through (h) of this section subject to the following conditions:

(1) The request is in writing and reasonably describes the information sought with sufficient particularity to enable the element to identify it.

(2) The requester shall be asked to correct a request that does not comply with paragraph (d)(1) of this section, to provide additional information.

(3) If within 30 days the requester does not correct the request, describe the information sought with sufficient

particularity or narrow the scope of the request, the element that received the request shall notify the requester and state the reason why no action will be taken on the request.

(e) *Processing of requests.* Requests that meet the foregoing requirements for processing will be acted upon as follows:

(1) GSA action upon the initial request shall be completed within 60 days.

(2) Receipt of the request shall be acknowledged within 7 days.

(3) The designated service or staff office shall determine if the requested information may be declassified and shall make such information available to the requester, unless withholding it is otherwise warranted under applicable law. If the information may not be released in whole or in part, the requester shall be given a brief statement as to the reasons for denial, a notice of the right to appeal the determination to the Deputy Administrator (the notice shall include the Deputy Administrator's name, title, and address), and a notice that such an appeal must be filed with the Deputy Administrator within 60 days in order to be considered.

(f) *Foreign government information.* Except as provided hereinafter, requests for mandatory review for the declassification of classified documents that contain foreign government information shall be processed and acted upon in accordance with the provisions of paragraphs (c) through (e) of this section. If the request involves information that was initially received or classified by GSA, then the corresponding service or staff office shall be designated by the GSA Security Officer to determine whether the foreign government information in the document may be declassified and released in accordance with GSA policy or guidelines, after consulting with other agencies that have subject matter interest as necessary. If GSA is not the agency that received or classified the foreign government information, it shall refer the request to the appropriate agency. In those cases where agency policy or guidelines do not apply, consultation with the foreign originator, through the GSA Security Officer, may be made prior to final action on the request.

(g) *Information classified outside the service or staff office.* When a service or staff office receives a request for declassification of information in a document which is in the custody of the service or staff office but was classified by another service or staff office or by another Government agency, the service or staff office shall refer the request to the classifying service or staff office or Government agency, together with a copy of the document containing the information requested when practicable, and shall notify the requester of the referral, unless the agency that classified the information objects on the grounds that its association with the information requires protection. When a GSA service or staff office receives such a referral, it shall process the request in accordance with the requirements of this paragraph and, if so requested, shall notify the referring service, staff office, or agency of the determination made on the request.

(h) *Action on appeal.* The following procedures shall be followed when denials of requests for declassification are appealed:

(1) The Deputy Administrator shall, within 15 days of the date of the appeal, convene a meeting of the GSA Information Security Oversight Committee (ISOC) that shall include the GSA Security Officer, or his or her representative, and the GSA official who denied the original request (and, at the option of that official, any subordinates or personnel from other agencies that participated in the decision for denial).

(2) The ISOC shall learn from the official the reasons for denying the request, concentrating in particular upon which requirement continued classification is based and the identifiable damage that would result if the information were declassified. The ISOC shall also learn from the official the part or parts of the information that is classified and if by deleting minor segments of the information it might not then be declassified.

(3) The ISOC's decision to uphold or deny the appeal, in whole or in part, shall be based upon the unanimous

opinion of its membership. In the event that unanimity cannot be attained, the matter shall be referred to the Administrator, whose decision shall be final.

(4) Based upon the outcome of the appeal, a reply shall be made to the person making the appeal that either encloses the requested information or part of the information, or explains why the continued classification of the information is required. A copy of the reply shall be sent to the GSA official who originally denied the request for declassification, to the GSA Security Officer, and to any other agency expressing an interest in the decision.

(5) Final action on appeals shall be completed within 30 days of the date of the appeal.

(i) *Prohibition.* No service of staff office in possession of a classified document may refuse to confirm the existence of the document in response to a request for the document under the provisions for mandatory review, unless the fact of its existence would itself be classifiable.

(j) *Presidential papers.* Information less than 10 years old which was originated by the President, by the White House staff, or by committees or commissions appointed by the President, or by others acting on behalf of the President, is exempted from mandatory review for declassification. Such information 10 years old or older is subject to mandatory review for declassification in accordance with procedures developed by the Archivist of the United States which provide for consultation with GSA on matters of primary subject interest to this agency.

PART 105–64—GSA PRIVACY ACT RULES

AUTHORITY: 5 U.S.C. 552a.

SOURCE: 74 FR 66246, Dec. 15, 2009, unless otherwise noted.

§ 105–64.000   What is the purpose of this part?

This part implements the General Services Administration (GSA) rules under the Privacy Act of 1974, 5 U.S.C. 552a, as amended. The rules cover the GSA systems of records from which information is retrieved by an individual's name or personal identifier. These rules set forth GSA's policies and procedures for accessing, reviewing, amending, and disclosing records covered by the Privacy Act. GSA will comply with all existing and future privacy laws.

§ 105–64.001   What terms are defined in this part?

GSA defines the following terms to ensure consistency of use and understanding of their meaning under this part:

Agency means any organization covered by the Privacy Act as defined in 5 U.S.C. 551(1) and 5 U.S.C. 552a (a)(1). GSA is such an agency.

Computer matching program means the computerized comparison of two or more Federal personnel or payroll systems of records, or systems of records used to establish or verify an individual's eligibility for Federal benefits or to recoup delinquent debts.

Disclosure of information means providing a record or the information in a record to someone other than the individual of record.

Exempt records means records exempted from access by an individual under the Privacy Act, subsections (j)(1), Central Intelligence Agency, (j)(2) and (k)(2), law enforcement, (k)(1), Section 552 (b)(1), (k)(3), protective services to the President,(k)(4), statistical records, (k)(5), employee background investigations, (k)(6), federal service disclosure, and (k)(7), promotion in armed services.

Individual means a citizen of the United States or a legal resident alien on whom GSA maintains Privacy Act records. An individual may be addressed as *you* when information is provided for the individual's use.

Personally Identifiable Information (PII) means information about a person that contains some unique identifier, including but not limited to name or Social Security Number, from which the identity of the person can be determined. In OMB Circular M–06–19, the term "Personally Identifiable Information" is defined as any information about an individual maintained by an agency, including, but not limited to, education, financial transactions, medical history, and criminal or employment history and information which can be used to distinguish or trace an individual's identity, such as their name, Social Security Number, date and place of birth, mother's maiden name, biometric records, including any other personal information which can be linked to an individual.

Record means any item, collection, or grouping of information about an individual within a system of records which contains the individual's name or any other personal identifier such as number or symbol, fingerprint, voiceprint, or photograph. The information may relate to education, financial transactions, medical conditions, employment, or criminal history collected in connection with an individual's interaction with GSA.

Request for access means a request by an individual to obtain or review his or her record or information in the record.

Routine use means disclosure of a record outside GSA for the purpose for which it is intended, as specified in the systems of records notices.

Solicitation means a request by an officer or employee of GSA for an individual to provide information about himself or herself for a specified purpose.

System of records means a group of records from which information is retrieved by the name of an individual, or by any number, symbol, or other identifier assigned to that individual.

System manager means the GSA associate responsible for a system of records and the information in it, as noted in the FEDERAL REGISTER systems of records notices.

Subpart 105–64.1—Policies and Responsibilities

§ 105–64.101 Who is responsible for enforcing these rules?

GSA Heads of Services and Staff Offices and Regional Administrators are responsible for ensuring that all systems of records under their jurisdiction meet the provisions of the Privacy Act and these rules. System managers are responsible for the system(s) of records assigned to them. The GSA Privacy Act Officer oversees the GSA Privacy Program and establishes privacy-related policy and procedures for the agency under the direction of the GSA Senior Agency Official for Privacy.

§ 105–64.102 What is GSA's policy on disclosure of information in a system of records?

No information contained in a Privacy Act system of records will be disclosed to third parties without the written consent of you, the individual of record, except under the conditions cited in § 105–64.501.

§ 105–64.103 What is GSA's policy on collecting and using information in a system of records?

System managers must collect information that is used to determine your rights, benefits, or privileges under GSA programs directly from you whenever practical, and use the information only for the intended purpose(s).

§ 105–64.104 What must the system manager tell me when soliciting personal information?

When soliciting information from you or a third party for a system of records, system managers must: Cite the authority for collecting the information; say whether providing the information is mandatory or voluntary; give the purpose for which the information will be used; state the routine uses of the information; and describe the effect on you, if any, of not providing the information. This information is found in the Privacy Act Statement. Any form that asks for personal information will contain this statement.

§ 105–64.105 When may Social Security Numbers (SSNs) be collected?

(a) Statutory or regulatory authority must exist for collecting Social Security Numbers for record systems that use the SSNs as a method of identification. Systems without statutory or regulatory authority implemented after January 1, 1975, will not collect Social Security Numbers.

(b) In compliance with OMB M–07–16 (Safeguarding Against and Responding to the Breach of Personally Identifiable Information) collection and storage of SSN will be limited to systems where no other identifier is currently available. While GSA will strive to reduce the collection and storage of SSN and other PII we recognize that some systems continue to need to collect this information.

§ 105–64.106 What is GSA's policy on information accuracy in a system of records?

System managers will ensure that all Privacy Act records are accurate, relevant, necessary, timely, and complete. All GSA systems are reviewed annually. Those systems that contain Personally Identifiable Information (PII) are reviewed to ensure they are relevant, necessary, accurate, up-to-date, and covered by the appropriate legal or regulatory authority. A listing of GSA Privacy Act Systems can be found at the following link (*http://www.gsa.gov/ Portal/gsa/ep/ contentView.do?contentType= GSA_BASIC&contentId = 21567*).

§ 105–64.107 What standards of conduct apply to employees with privacy-related responsibilities?

(a) Employees who design, develop, operate, or maintain Privacy Act record systems will protect system security, avoid unauthorized disclosure of information, both verbal and written, and ensure that no system of records is maintained without public notice. All such employees will follow the standards of conduct in 5 CFR part 2635, 5 CFR part 6701, 5 CFR part 735, and 5 CFR part 2634 to protect personal information.

(b) Employees who have access to privacy act records will avoid unauthorized disclosure of personal information, both written and verbal, and ensure they have met privacy training requirements. All such employees will follow GSA orders HCO 9297.1 GSA Data Release Policy, HCO 9297.2A GSA Information Breach Notification Policy, HCO 2180.1 GSA Rules of Behavior for Handling Personally Identifiable Information (PII), CIO P 2100.1E CIO P GSA Information Technology (IT) Security Policy, and CIO 2104.1 GSA Information Technology (IT) General Rules of Behavior.

§ 105–64.108 How does GSA safeguard personal information?

(a) System managers will establish administrative, technical, and physical safeguards to ensure the security and confidentiality of records, protect the records against possible threats or hazards, and permit access only to authorized persons. Automated systems will incorporate security controls such as password protection, verification of identity of authorized users, detection of break-in attempts, firewalls, or encryption, as appropriate.

(b) System managers will ensure that employees and contractors who have access to personal information in their system will have the proper background investigation and meet all privacy training requirements.

§ 105–64.109 How does GSA handle other agencies' records?

In cases where GSA has either permanent or temporary custody of other agencies' records, system managers will coordinate with those agencies on any release of information. Office of Personnel Management (OPM) records that are in GSA's custody are subject to OPM's Privacy Act rules.

§ 105–64.110 When may GSA establish computer matching programs?

(a) System managers will establish computer matching programs or agreements for sharing information with other agencies only with the consent and under the direction of the GSA Data Integrity Board that will be established when and if computer matching programs are used at GSA.

(b) GSA will designate which positions comprise the Data Integrity Board and develop a policy that defines the roles and responsibilities of these positions.

§ 105–64.111 What is GSA's policy on directives that may conflict with this part?

These rules take precedence over any GSA directive that may conflict with the requirements stated here. GSA officials will ensure that no such conflict exists in new or existing directives.

Subpart 105–64.2—Access to Records

§ 105–64.201 How do I get access to my records?

You may request access to your record in person or by writing to the system manager or, in the case of geographically dispersed records, to the office maintaining the records (*see* appendix A to this part). Parents or guardians may obtain access to records of minors or when a court has determined that the individual of record is incompetent.

§ 105–64.202 How do I request access in person?

If appearing in person, you must properly identify yourself through photographic identification such as an agency identification badge, passport, or driver's license. Records will be available during normal business hours at the offices where the records are maintained. You may examine the record and be provided a copy on request. If you want someone else to accompany you when reviewing a record, you must first sign a statement authorizing the disclosure of the record; the statement will be maintained with your record.

§ 105–64.203 How do I request access in writing?

If you request access in writing, mark both the envelope and the request letter "Privacy Act Request". Include in the request your full name and address; a description of the records you seek; the title and number of the system of records as published in the FEDERAL REGISTER; a brief description of the nature, time, and place of your association with GSA; and any other information you believe will help in locating the record.

§ 105–64.204 Can parents and guardians obtain access to records?

If you are the parent or guardian of a minor, or of a person judicially determined to be incompetent, you must provide full information about the individual of record. You also must properly identify yourself and provide a copy of the birth certificate of the individual, or a court order establishing guardianship, whichever applies.

§ 105–64.205 Who will provide access to my record?

The system manager will make a record available to you on request, unless special conditions apply, such as for medical, law enforcement, and security records.

§ 105–64.206 How long will it take to get my record?

The system manager will make a record available within 10 workdays after receipt of your request. If a delay of more than 10 workdays is expected, the system manager will notify you in writing of the reason for the delay and when the record will be available. The system manager may ask you for additional information to clarify your request. The system manager will have an additional 10 workdays after receipt of the new information to provide the record to you, or provide another acknowledgment letter if a delay in locating the record is expected.

§ 105–64.207 Are there any fees?

No fees are charged for records when the total fee is less than $25. The system manager may waive the fee above this amount if providing records without charge is customary or in the public interest. When the cost exceeds $25, the fee for a paper copy is 10 cents per page, and the fee for materials other than paper copies is the actual cost of reproduction. For fees above $250, advance payment is required. You should pay by check or money order made payable to the General Services Administration, and provide it to the system manager.

§ 105–64.208 What special conditions apply to release of medical records?

Medical records containing information that may have an adverse effect upon a person will be released only to a physician designated in writing by you, or by your guardian or conservator. Medical records in an Official Personnel Folder (OPF) fall under the jurisdiction of the Office of Personnel Management (OPM) and will be referred to OPM for a response.

§ 105–64.209 What special conditions apply to accessing law enforcement and security records?

Law enforcement and security records are generally exempt from disclosure to individuals except when the system manager, in consultation with legal counsel and the Head of the Service or Staff Office or Regional Administrator or their representatives, determines that information in a record has been used or is being used to deny you any right, privilege, or benefit for which you are eligible or entitled under Federal law. If so, the system manager will notify you of the existence of the record and disclose the information, but only to the extent that the information does not identify a confidential source. If disclosure of information could reasonably be expected to identify a confidential source, the record will not be disclosed to you unless it is possible to delete all such information. A confidential source is a person or persons who furnished information during Federal investigations with the understanding that his or her identity would remain confidential.

Subpart 105–64.3—Denial of Access to Records

§ 105–64.301 Under what conditions will I be denied access to a record?

The system manager will deny access to a record that is being compiled in the reasonable anticipation of a civil action or proceeding or to records that are specifically exempted from disclosure by GSA in its system of records notices, published in the FEDERAL REGISTER. Exempted systems include the Investigation Case Files, Internal Evaluation Case Files, and Security Files. These systems are exempted to maintain the effectiveness and integrity of investigations conducted by the Office of Inspector General, and others, as part of their duties and responsibilities involving Federal employment, contracts, and security.

§ 105–64.302 How will I be denied access?

If you request access to a record in an exempt system of records, the system manager will consult with the Head of Service or Staff Office or Regional Administrator or their representatives, legal counsel, and other officials as appropriate, to determine if all or part of the record may be disclosed. If the decision is to deny access, the system manager will provide a written notice to you giving the reason for the denial and your appeal rights.

§ 105–64.303 How do I appeal a denial to access a record?

If you are denied access to a record in whole or in part, you may file an administrative appeal within 30 days of the denial. The appeal should be in writing and addressed to: GSA Privacy Act Officer (CIB), General Services Administration, 1800 F Street, NW., Washington, DC 20405. Mark both the envelope and the appeal letter "Privacy Act Appeal".

§ 105–64.304 How are administrative appeal decisions made?

The GSA Privacy Act Officer will conduct a review of your appeal by consulting with legal counsel and appropriate officials. The Privacy Act Officer may grant record access if the appeal is granted. If the decision is to reject the appeal, the Privacy Act Officer will provide all pertinent information about the case to the Deputy Administrator and ask for a final administrative decision. The Deputy Administrator may grant access to a record, in which case the Privacy Act Officer will notify you in writing, and the system manager will make the record available to you. If the Deputy Administrator denies the appeal, he or she will notify you in writing of the reason for rejection and of your right to a judicial review. The administrative appeal review will take no longer than 30 workdays after the Privacy Act Officer receives the appeal. The Deputy Administrator may extend the time limit by notifying you in writing of the extension and the reason for it before the 30 days are up.

§ 105–64.305 What is my recourse to an appeal denial?

You may file a civil action to have the GSA administrative decision overturned within two years after the decision is made. You may file in a Federal District Court where you live or have a principal place of business, where the records are maintained, or in the District of Columbia.

Subpart 105–64.4—Amending Records

§ 105–64.401 Can I amend my record?

You may request to amend your record by writing to the system manager with the proposed amendment. Mark both the envelope and the letter "Privacy Act Request to Amend Record".

§ 105–64.402 What records are not subject to amendment?

You may not amend the following records under the law:

(a) Transcripts of testimony given under oath or written statements made under oath.

(b) Transcripts of grand jury proceedings, judicial proceedings, or quasi-judicial proceedings which constitute the official record of the proceedings.

(c) Pre-sentence reports that are maintained within a system of records but are the property of the courts.

(d) Records exempted from amendment by notice published in the FEDERAL REGISTER.

§ 105–64.403 What happens when I submit a request to amend a record?

The system manager will consult with the Head of Service or Staff Office or Regional Administrator or their representatives, and legal counsel. They will determine whether to amend an existing record by comparing its accuracy, relevance, timeliness, and completeness with the amendment you propose. The system manager will notify you within 10 workdays whether your proposed amendment is approved or denied. In case of an expected delay, the system manager will acknowledge receipt of your request in writing and provide an estimate of when you may expect a decision. If your request to amend is approved, the system manager will amend the record and send an amended copy to you and to anyone who had previously received the record. If your request to amend is denied, the system manager will advise you in writing, giving the reason for denial, a proposed alternative amendment if possible, and your appeal rights. The system manager also will notify the GSA Privacy Act Officer of any request for amendment and its disposition. Any amendment to a record may involve a person's Official Personnel Folder (OPF). OPF regulations are governed by OPM regulations, including alternate amendments and appeals of denials, and not GSA regulations.

§ 105–64.404 What must I do if I agree to an alternative amendment?

If you agree to the alternative amendment proposed by the system manager, you must notify the manager in writing of your concurrence. The system manager will amend the record and send an amended copy to you and to anyone else who had previously received the record.

§ 105–64.405 Can I appeal a denial to amend a record?

You may file an appeal within 30 workdays of a denial to amend your record by writing to the: GSA Privacy Act Officer (CIB), General Services Administration, 1800 F Street, NW., Washington, DC 20405. Mark both the envelope and the appeal letter "Privacy Act Amendment Appeal." Appeals to amend records in a GSA employee's official personnel file will be sent to the Office of Personnel Management, Washington, DC 20415.

§ 105–64.406 How will my appeal be handled?

The GSA Privacy Act Officer will consult with legal counsel and appropriate GSA officials concerning your appeal. If they decide to reject your appeal, the Privacy Act Officer will provide the Deputy Administrator with all pertinent information about the case and request a final administrative decision. The Deputy Administrator may approve your amendment, in which case the Privacy Act Officer will notify you in writing, and the system manager will amend the record and send an amended copy to you and anyone who had previously been provided with the record. If the Deputy Administrator denies the appeal, he or she will notify you in writing of the reason for denial, of your right to a judicial review, and of your right to file a Statement of Disagreement. The amendment appeal review will be made within 30 workdays after the Privacy Act Officer receives your appeal. The Deputy Administrator may extend the time limit by notifying you in writing of the reason for the extension before the 30 days are up.

§ 105–64.407 How do I file a Statement of Disagreement?

You may file a Statement of Disagreement with the system manager within 30 days of the denial to amend a record. The statement should explain why you believe the record to be inaccurate, irrelevant, untimely, or incomplete. The system manager will file the statement with your record, provide a copy to anyone who had previously received the record, and include a copy of it in any future disclosure.

§ 105–64.408 What is my recourse to a denial decision?

You may file a civil action to have the GSA decision overturned within two years after denial of an amendment appeal. You may file the civil action in a Federal District Court where you live or have a principal place of business, where the records are maintained, or in the District of Columbia.

Subpart 105–64.5—Disclosure of Records

§ 105–64.501 Under what conditions may a record be disclosed without my consent?

A system manager may disclose your record without your consent under the Privacy Act when the disclosure is: To GSA officials or employees in the performance of their official duties; required by the Freedom of Information Act; for a routine use stated in a FEDERAL REGISTER notice; to the Bureau of the Census for use in fulfilling its duties; for statistical research or reporting, and only when the record is not individually identifiable; to the National Archives and Records Administration (NARA) when the record has been determined to be of historical or other value that warrants permanent retention; to a U.S. law enforcement agency or instrumentality for a civil or criminal law enforcement purpose; under compelling circumstances affecting an individual's health and safety, and upon disclosure a notification will be sent to the individual; to Congress or its committees and subcommittees when the record material falls within their jurisdiction; to the Comptroller General or an authorized representative in the performance of the duties of the Government Accountability Office (GAO); under a court order; or to a consumer reporting agency under the Federal Claims Collection Act of 1966, 31 U.S.C. 3711.

§ 105–64.502 How do I find out if my record has been disclosed?

You may request an accounting of the persons or agencies to whom your record has been disclosed, including the date and purpose of each disclosure, by writing to the system manager. Mark both the envelope and the letter "Privacy Act Accounting Request". The system manager will provide the requested information in the same way as that for granting access to records; see Subpart 105–64.2, providing no restrictions to disclosure or accounting of disclosures applies.

§ 105–64.503 What is an accounting of disclosures?

The system manager maintains an account of each record disclosure for five years or for the life of the record, whichever is longer. The accounting of disclosure information includes the name of the person or agency to whom your record has been provided, the date, the type of information disclosed, and the reason for disclosure. Other pertinent information, such as justifications for disclosure and any written consent that you may have provided, is also included. No accounting needs to be maintained for disclosures to GSA officials or employees in the performance of their duties, or disclosures under the Freedom of Information Act.

§ 105–64.504 Under what conditions will I be denied an accounting of disclosures?

The system manager will deny your request for an accounting of disclosures when the disclosures are to GSA officials or employees in the performance of their duties or disclosures under the Freedom of Information Act, for which no accounting is required; law enforcement agencies for law enforcement activities; and systems of records exempted by notice in the FEDERAL REGISTER. You may appeal a denial using the same procedures as those for denial of access to records, *see* Subpart 105–64.3.

Subpart 105–64.6—Establishing or Revising Systems of Records in GSA

§ 105–64.601 Procedures for establishing system of records.

The following procedures apply to any proposed new or revised system of records:

(a) Before establishing a new or revising an existing system of records, the system manager, with the concurrence of the appropriate Head of Service or Staff Office, will provide to the GSA Privacy Act Officer a proposal describing and justifying the new system or revision.

(b) A Privacy Impact Assessment (PIA) will be filled out to determine if a system notice needs to be completed.

(c) The GSA Privacy Act Officer will work with the program office to create the draft system of notice document.

(d) The GSA Privacy Office will work with various offices to take the draft system notice through the concurrence process.

(e) The GSA Privacy Act Officer will publish in the FEDERAL REGISTER a notice of intent to establish or revise the system of records at least 30 calendar days before the planned system establishment or revision date.

(f) The new or revised system becomes effective 30 days after the notice is published in the FEDERAL REGISTER unless submitted comments result in a revision to the notice, in which case, a new revised notice will be issued.

(g) When publishing a new system notice letters will be sent to the Chairman, Committee on Homeland Security and Governmental Affairs, Chairman, Committee on Oversight and Government Reform, and the Docket Library Office of Information and Regulatory Affairs, Office of Management and Budget.

Subpart 105–64.7—Assistance and Referrals

§ 105–64.701 Submittal of requests for assistance and referrals.

Address requests for assistance involving GSA Privacy Act rules and procedures, or for referrals to system managers or GSA officials responsible for implementing these rules to: GSA Privacy Act Officer (CIB), General Services Administration, 1800 F Street, NW., Washington, DC 20405.

Subpart 105–64.8—Privacy Complaints

§ 105–64.801 How to file a privacy complaint.

E-mail your complaint to *gsa.privacyact@gsa.gov* or send to: GSA Privacy Act Officer (CIB), General Services Administration, 1800 F Street NW., Washington, DC 20405. Please provide as much details about the complaint in the communication. Provide contact information where you prefer all communication to be sent. The Privacy Officer will conduct an investigation and consult with appropriate GSA officials and legal counsel to render a decision within 30 workdays of the complaint being received by the privacy office. The decision will be sent by the method the complaint was received.

§ 105–64.802 Can I appeal a decision to a privacy complaint?

You may file an appeal within 30 workdays of a denial of a privacy complaint by writing to: GSA Privacy Act Officer (CIB), General Services Administration, 1800 F Street NW., Washington, DC 20405. Mark both the envelope and appeal letter "Privacy Act Complaint appeal".

§ 105–64.803 How will my appeal be handled?

The Privacy Act Officer will consult with legal counsel and the appropriate GSA officials concerning your appeal. The decision will be made by the Senior Agency Official for Privacy. The decision will be sent within 30 workdays of the appeal being received by the privacy office. The decision provided in the appeal letter is the final recourse.

Address requests for physically dispersed
records, as noted in the system of records notices, to the Regional Privacy Act Coordinator, General Services Administration, at
the appropriate regional GSA office, as follows:

Great Lakes Region (includes Illinois, Indiana, Michigan, Ohio, Minnesota, and Wisconsin), 230 South Dearborn Street, Chicago,
IL 60604–1696.

Greater Southwest Region (includes Arkansas, Louisiana, Oklahoma, New Mexico, and
Texas), 819 Taylor Street, Fort Worth, TX
76102.

Mid-Atlantic Region (includes Delaware,
Maryland, Pennsylvania, Virginia, and West
Virginia, but excludes the National Capital
Region), The Strawbridge Building, 20 North
8th Street, Philadelphia, PA 19107–3191.

National Capital Region (includes the District of Columbia; the counties of Montgomery and Prince George's in Maryland;
the city of Alexandria, Virginia; and the
counties of Arlington, Fairfax, Loudoun, and
Prince William in Virginia), 7th and D
Streets, SW., Washington, DC 20407.

New England Region (includes Connecticut,
Maine, Massachusetts, New Hampshire,
Rhode Island, and Vermont), 10 Causeway
Street, Boston, MA 02222.

Northeast and Caribbean Region (includes
New Jersey, New York, Puerto Rico, and Virgin Islands), 26 Federal Plaza, New York, NY
10278.

Northwest/Arctic Region (includes Alaska,
Idaho, Oregon, and Washington), 400 15th
Street, SW., Auburn, WA 98001–6599.

Pacific Rim Region (includes Arizona, California, Hawaii, and Nevada), 450 Golden Gate
Avenue, San Francisco, CA 94102–3400.

Rocky Mountain Region (includes Colorado,
Montana, North Dakota, South Dakota,
Utah, and Wyoming), U.S. General Services
Administration, DFC, Bldg. 41, Rm. 210, P.O.
Box 25006, Denver, CO 80225–0006.

Southeast-Sunbelt Region (includes Alabama, Florida, Georgia, Kentucky, Mississippi, North Carolina, South Carolina, and
Tennessee), Office of the Regional Administrator (4A), 77 Forsyth Street, Atlanta, GA
30303.

The Heartland Region (includes Iowa, Kansas, Missouri, and Nebraska), 1500 East Bannister Road, Kansas City, MO 64131–3088.

PART 105–67—SALE OF PERSONAL PROPERTY

Sec.
105–67.100 Scope of subpart.
105–67.101 Debarred, suspended and ineligible contractors.

AUTHORITY: 40 U.S.C. 486(c).

§ 105–67.100 Scope of subpart.

This subpart prescribes policies and
procedures governing the debarment or
suspension of contractors from purchases of Federal personal property
(see FPMR part 101–45).

[51 FR 13500, Apr. 21, 1986]

§ 105–67.101 Debarred, suspended and ineligible contractors.

The policies, procedures and requirements of subpart 509.4 of the General
Services Administration Acquisition
Regulation (GSAR) are incorporated by
reference and made applicable to contracts for, and to contractors who engage in, the purchase of Federal personal property.

[51 FR 13500, Apr. 21, 1986]

PART 105–68—GOVERNMENTWIDE DEBARMENT AND SUSPENSION (NONPROCUREMENT)

Sec.
105–68.25 How is this part organized?
105–68.50 How is this part written?
105–68.75 Do terms in this part have special
meanings?

Subpart A—General

105–68.100 What does this part do?
105–68.105 Does this part apply to me?
105–68.110 What is the purpose of the nonprocurement debarment and suspension
system?
105–68.115 How does an exclusion restrict a
person's involvement in covered transactions?
105–68.120 May we grant an exception to let
an excluded person participate in a covered transaction?
105–68.125 Does an exclusion under the nonprocurement system affect a person's eligibility for Federal procurement contracts?
105–68.130 Does exclusion under the Federal
procurement system affect a person's eligibility to participate in nonprocurement transactions?

105–68.1020 Voluntary exclusion or voluntarily excluded.

Subpart J [Reserved]

APPENDIX TO PART 105–68—COVERED TRANSACTIONS

AUTHORITY: Sec. 2455, Pub. L. 103–355, 108 Stat. 3327; E.O. 12549, 3 CFR, 1986 Comp., p. 189; E.O. 12689, 3 CFR, 1989 Comp., p. 235.

SOURCE: 68 FR 66626, 66627, Nov. 26, 2003, unless otherwise noted.

§ 105–68.25   How is this part organized?

(a) This part is subdivided into ten subparts. Each subpart contains information related to a broad topic or specific audience with special responsibilities, as shown in the following table:

In subpart . . .	You will find provisions related to . . .
A	general information about this rule.
B	the types of GSA transactions that are covered by the Governmentwide nonprocurement suspension and debarment system.
C	the responsibilities of persons who participate in covered transactions.
D	the responsibilities of GSA officials who are authorized to enter into covered transactions.
E	the responsibilities of Federal agencies for the *Excluded Parties List System* (Disseminated by the General Services Administration).
F	the general principles governing suspension, debarment, voluntary exclusion and settlement.
G	suspension actions.
H	debarment actions.
I	definitions of terms used in this part.
J	[Reserved]

(b) The following table shows which subparts may be of special interest to you, depending on who you are:

If you are . . .	See subpart(s) . . .
(1) a participant or principal in a nonprocurement transaction.	A, B, C, and I.
(2) a respondent in a suspension action	A, B, F, G and I.
(3) a respondent in a debarment action	A, B, F, H and I.
(4) a suspending official	A, B, D, E, F, G and I.
(5) a debarring official	A, B, D, E, F, H and I.
(6) a (n) GSA official authorized to enter into a covered transaction.	A, B, D, E and I.
(7) Reserved	J.

§ 105–68.50   How is this part written?

(a) This part uses a "plain language" format to make it easier for the general public and business community to use. The section headings and text,

often in the form of questions and answers, must be read together.

(b) Pronouns used within this part, such as "I" and "you," change from subpart to subpart depending on the audience being addressed. The pronoun "we" always is the General Services Administration.

(c) The "Covered Transactions" diagram in the appendix to this part shows the levels or "tiers" at which the General Services Administration enforces an exclusion under this part.

§ 105–68.75   Do terms in this part have special meanings?

This part uses terms throughout the text that have special meaning. Those terms are defined in Subpart I of this part. For example, three important terms are—

(a) *Exclusion or excluded,* which refers only to discretionary actions taken by a suspending or debarring official under this part or the Federal Acquisition Regulation (48 CFR part 9, subpart 9.4);

(b) *Disqualification or disqualified,* which refers to prohibitions under specific statutes, executive orders (other than Executive Order 12549 and Executive Order 12689), or other authorities. Disqualifications frequently are not subject to the discretion of an agency official, may have a different scope than exclusions, or have special conditions that apply to the disqualification; and

(c) *Ineligibility or ineligible,* which generally refers to a person who is either excluded or disqualified.

Subpart A—General

§ 105–68.100   What does this part do?

This part adopts a governmentwide system of debarment and suspension for GSA nonprocurement activities. It also provides for reciprocal exclusion of persons who have been excluded under the Federal Acquisition Regulation, and provides for the consolidated listing of all persons who are excluded, or disqualified by statute, executive order, or other legal authority. This part satisfies the requirements in section 3 of Executive Order 12549, "Debarment and Suspension" (3 CFR 1986 Comp., p. 189), Executive Order 12689,

"Debarment and Suspension" (3 CFR 1989 Comp., p. 235) and 31 U.S.C. 6101 note (Section 2455, Public Law 103–355, 108 Stat. 3327).

§ 105–68.105 Does this part apply to me?

Portions of this part (see table at § 105–68.25(b)) apply to you if you are a(n)—

(a) Person who has been, is, or may reasonably be expected to be, a participant or principal in a covered transaction;

(b) Respondent (a person against whom the General Services Administration has initiated a debarment or suspension action);

(c) GSA debarring or suspending official; or

(d) GSA official who is authorized to enter into covered transactions with non-Federal parties.

§ 105–68.110 What is the purpose of the nonprocurement debarment and suspension system?

(a) To protect the public interest, the Federal Government ensures the integrity of Federal programs by conducting business only with responsible persons.

(b) A Federal agency uses the nonprocurement debarment and suspension system to exclude from Federal programs persons who are not presently responsible.

(c) An exclusion is a serious action that a Federal agency may take only to protect the public interest. A Federal agency may not exclude a person or commodity for the purposes of punishment.

§ 105–68.115 How does an exclusion restrict a person's involvement in covered transactions?

With the exceptions stated in §§ 105–68.120, 105–68.315, and 105–68.420, a person who is excluded by the General Services Administration or any other Federal agency may not:

(a) Be a participant in a(n) GSA transaction that is a covered transaction under subpart B of this part;

(b) Be a participant in a transaction of any other Federal agency that is a covered transaction under that agency's regulation for debarment and suspension; or

(c) Act as a principal of a person participating in one of those covered transactions.

§ 105–68.120 May we grant an exception to let an excluded person participate in a covered transaction?

(a) The Administrator of General Services may grant an exception permitting an excluded person to participate in a particular covered transaction. If the Administrator of General Services grants an exception, the exception must be in writing and state the reason(s) for deviating from the governmentwide policy in Executive Order 12549.

(b) An exception granted by one agency for an excluded person does not extend to the covered transactions of another agency.

§ 105–68.125 Does an exclusion under the nonprocurement system affect a person's eligibility for Federal procurement contracts?

If any Federal agency excludes a person under its nonprocurement common rule on or after August 25, 1995, the excluded person is also ineligible to participate in Federal procurement transactions under the FAR. Therefore, an exclusion under this part has reciprocal effect in Federal procurement transactions.

§ 105–68.130 Does exclusion under the Federal procurement system affect a person's eligibility to participate in nonprocurement transactions?

If any Federal agency excludes a person under the FAR on or after August 25, 1995, the excluded person is also ineligible to participate in nonprocurement covered transactions under this part. Therefore, an exclusion under the FAR has reciprocal effect in Federal nonprocurement transactions.

§ 105–68.135 May the General Services Administration exclude a person who is not currently participating in a nonprocurement transaction?

Given a cause that justifies an exclusion under this part, we may exclude any person who has been involved, is currently involved, or may reasonably be expected to be involved in a covered transaction.

§ 105–68.140 How do I know if a person is excluded?

Check the *Excluded Parties List System (EPLS)* to determine whether a person is excluded. The General Services Administration (GSA) maintains the *EPLS* and makes it available, as detailed in subpart E of this part. When a Federal agency takes an action to exclude a person under the nonprocurement or procurement debarment and suspension system, the agency enters the information about the excluded person into the *EPLS.*

§ 105–68.145 Does this part address persons who are disqualified, as well as those who are excluded from nonprocurement transactions?

Except if provided for in Subpart J of this part, this part—

(a) Addresses disqualified persons only to—

(1) Provide for their inclusion in the *EPLS;* and

(2) State responsibilities of Federal agencies and participants to check for disqualified persons before entering into covered transactions.

(b) Does not specify the—

(1) GSA transactions for which a disqualified person is ineligible. Those transactions vary on a case-by-case basis, because they depend on the language of the specific statute, Executive order, or regulation that caused the disqualification;

(2) Entities to which the disqualification applies; or

(3) Process that the agency uses to disqualify a person. Unlike exclusion, disqualification is frequently not a discretionary action that a Federal agency takes.

Subpart B—Covered Transactions

§ 105–68.200 What is a covered transaction?

A covered transaction is a nonprocurement or procurement transaction that is subject to the prohibitions of this part. It may be a transaction at—

(a) The primary tier, between a Federal agency and a person (see appendix to this part); or

(b) A lower tier, between a participant in a covered transaction and another person.

§ 105–68.205 Why is it important if a particular transaction is a covered transaction?

The importance of a covered transaction depends upon who you are.

(a) As a participant in the transaction, you have the responsibilities laid out in subpart C of this part. Those include responsibilities to the person or Federal agency at the next higher tier from whom you received the transaction, if any. They also include responsibilities if you subsequently enter into other covered transactions with persons at the next lower tier.

(b) As a Federal official who enters into a primary tier transaction, you have the responsibilities laid out in subpart D of this part.

(c) As an excluded person, you may not be a participant or principal in the transaction unless—

(1) The person who entered into the transaction with you allows you to continue your involvement in a transaction that predates your exclusion, as permitted under § 105–68.310 or § 105–68.415; or

(2) A(n) GSA official obtains an exception from the Administrator of General Services to allow you to be involved in the transaction, as permitted under § 105–68.120.

§ 105–68.210 Which nonprocurement transactions are covered transactions?

All nonprocurement transactions, as defined in § 105–68.970, are covered transactions unless listed in § 105–68.215. (See appendix to this part.)

§ 105–68.215 Which nonprocurement transactions are not covered transactions?

The following types of nonprocurement transactions are not covered transactions:

(a) A direct award to—

(1) A foreign government or foreign governmental entity;

(2) A public international organization;

(3) An entity owned (in whole or in part) or controlled by a foreign government; or

(4) Any other entity consisting wholly or partially of one or more foreign governments or foreign governmental entities.

(b) A benefit to an individual as a personal entitlement without regard to the individual's present responsibility (but benefits received in an individual's business capacity are not excepted). For example, if a person receives social security benefits under the Supplemental Security Income provisions of the Social Security Act, 42 U.S.C. 1301 *et seq.*, those benefits are not covered transactions and, therefore, are not affected if the person is excluded.

(c) Federal employment.

(d) A transaction that the General Services Administration needs to respond to a national or agency-recognized emergency or disaster.

(e) A permit, license, certificate, or similar instrument issued as a means to regulate public health, safety, or the environment, unless the General Services Administration specifically designates it to be a covered transaction.

(f) An incidental benefit that results from ordinary governmental operations.

(g) Any other transaction if the application of an exclusion to the transaction is prohibited by law.

§ 105–68.220 Are any procurement contracts included as covered transactions?

(a) Covered transactions under this part—

(1) Do not include any procurement contracts awarded directly by a Federal agency; but

(2) Do include some procurement contracts awarded by non-Federal participants in nonprocurement covered transactions (see appendix to this part).

(b) Specifically, a contract for goods or services is a covered transaction if any of the following applies:

(1) The contract is awarded by a participant in a nonprocurement transaction that is covered under § 105–68.210, and the amount of the contract is expected to equal or exceed $25,000.

(2) The contract requires the consent of a(n) GSA official. In that case, the contract, regardless of the amount, always is a covered transaction, and it

does not matter who awarded it. For example, it could be a subcontract awarded by a contractor at a tier below a nonprocurement transaction, as shown in the appendix to this part.

(3) The contract is for federally-required audit services.

§ 105–68.225 How do I know if a transaction in which I may participate is a covered transaction?

As a participant in a transaction, you will know that it is a covered transaction because the agency regulations governing the transaction, the appropriate agency official, or participant at the next higher tier who enters into the transaction with you, will tell you that you must comply with applicable portions of this part.

Subpart C—Responsibilities of Participants Regarding Transactions

Doing Business With Other Persons

§ 105–68.300 What must I do before I enter into a covered transaction with another person at the next lower tier?

When you enter into a covered transaction with another person at the next lower tier, you must verify that the person with whom you intend to do business is not excluded or disqualified. You do this by:

(a) Checking the *EPLS;* or

(b) Collecting a certification from that person if allowed by this rule; or

(c) Adding a clause or condition to the covered transaction with that person.

§ 105–68.305 May I enter into a covered transaction with an excluded or disqualified person?

(a) You as a participant may not enter into a covered transaction with an excluded person, unless the General Services Administration grants an exception under § 105–68.120.

(b) You may not enter into any transaction with a person who is disqualified from that transaction, unless you have obtained an exception under the disqualifying statute, Executive order, or regulation.

§ 105–68.310 What must I do if a Federal agency excludes a person with whom I am already doing business in a covered transaction?

(a) You as a participant may continue covered transactions with an excluded person if the transactions were in existence when the agency excluded the person. However, you are not required to continue the transactions, and you may consider termination. You should make a decision about whether to terminate and the type of termination action, if any, only after a thorough review to ensure that the action is proper and appropriate.

(b) You may not renew or extend covered transactions (other than no-cost time extensions) with any excluded person, unless the General Services Administration grants an exception under § 105–68.120.

§ 105–68.315 May I use the services of an excluded person as a principal under a covered transaction?

(a) You as a participant may continue to use the services of an excluded person as a principal under a covered transaction if you were using the services of that person in the transaction before the person was excluded. However, you are not required to continue using that person's services as a principal. You should make a decision about whether to discontinue that person's services only after a thorough review to ensure that the action is proper and appropriate.

(b) You may not begin to use the services of an excluded person as a principal under a covered transaction unless the General Services Administration grants an exception under § 105–68.120.

§ 105–68.320 Must I verify that principals of my covered transactions are eligible to participate?

Yes, you as a participant are responsible for determining whether any of your principals of your covered transactions is excluded or disqualified from participating in the transaction. You may decide the method and frequency by which you do so. You may, but you are not required to, check the *EPLS*.

§ 105–68.325 What happens if I do business with an excluded person in a covered transaction?

If as a participant you knowingly do business with an excluded person, we may disallow costs, annul or terminate the transaction, issue a stop work order, debar or suspend you, or take other remedies as appropriate.

§ 105–68.330 What requirements must I pass down to persons at lower tiers with whom I intend to do business?

Before entering into a covered transaction with a participant at the next lower tier, you must require that participant to—

(a) Comply with this subpart as a condition of participation in the transaction. You may do so using any method(s), unless § 105–68.440 requires you to use specific methods.

(b) Pass the requirement to comply with this subpart to each person with whom the participant enters into a covered transaction at the next lower tier.

DISCLOSING INFORMATION—PRIMARY TIER PARTICIPANTS

§ 105–68.335 What information must I provide before entering into a covered transaction with the General Services Administration?

Before you enter into a covered transaction at the primary tier, you as the participant must notify the GSA office that is entering into the transaction with you, if you know that you or any of the principals for that covered transaction:

(a) Are presently excluded or disqualified;

(b) Have been convicted within the preceding three years of any of the offenses listed in § 105–68.800(a) or had a civil judgment rendered against you for one of those offenses within that time period;

(c) Are presently indicted for or otherwise criminally or civilly charged by a governmental entity (Federal, State or local) with commission of any of the offenses listed in § 105–68.800(a); or

(d) Have had one or more public transactions (Federal, State, or local) terminated within the preceding three years for cause or default.

§ 105–68.340 If I disclose unfavorable information required under § 105–68.335, will I be prevented from participating in the transaction?

As a primary tier participant, your disclosure of unfavorable information about yourself or a principal under § 105–68.335 will not necessarily cause us to deny your participation in the covered transaction. We will consider the information when we determine whether to enter into the covered transaction. We also will consider any additional information or explanation that you elect to submit with the disclosed information.

§ 105–68.345 What happens if I fail to disclose information required under § 105–68.335?

If we later determine that you failed to disclose information under § 105–68.335 that you knew at the time you entered into the covered transaction, we may—

(a) Terminate the transaction for material failure to comply with the terms and conditions of the transaction; or

(b) Pursue any other available remedies, including suspension and debarment.

§ 105–68.350 What must I do if I learn of information required under § 105–68.335 after entering into a covered transaction with the General Services Administration?

At any time after you enter into a covered transaction, you must give immediate written notice to the GSA office with which you entered into the transaction if you learn either that—

(a) You failed to disclose information earlier, as required by § 105–68.335; or

(b) Due to changed circumstances, you or any of the principals for the transaction now meet any of the criteria in § 105–68.335.

DISCLOSING INFORMATION—LOWER TIER
PARTICIPANTS

§ 105–68.355 What information must I provide to a higher tier participant before entering into a covered transaction with that participant?

Before you enter into a covered transaction with a person at the next higher tier, you as a lower tier partici-

pant must notify that person if you know that you or any of the principals are presently excluded or disqualified.

§ 105–68.360 What happens if I fail to disclose the information required under § 105–68.355?

If we later determine that you failed to tell the person at the higher tier that you were excluded or disqualified at the time you entered into the covered transaction with that person, we may pursue any available remedies, including suspension and debarment.

§ 105–68.365 What must I do if I learn of information required under § 105–68.355 after entering into a covered transaction with a higher tier participant?

At any time after you enter into a lower tier covered transaction with a person at a higher tier, you must provide immediate written notice to that person if you learn either that—

(a) You failed to disclose information earlier, as required by § 105–68.355; or

(b) Due to changed circumstances, you or any of the principals for the transaction now meet any of the criteria in § 105–68.355.

Subpart D—Responsibilities of GSA Officials Regarding Transactions

§ 105–68.400 May I enter into a transaction with an excluded or disqualified person?

(a) You as an agency official may not enter into a covered transaction with an excluded person unless you obtain an exception under § 105–68.120.

(b) You may not enter into any transaction with a person who is disqualified from that transaction, unless you obtain a waiver or exception under the statute, Executive order, or regulation that is the basis for the person's disqualification.

§ 105–68.405 May I enter into a covered transaction with a participant if a principal of the transaction is excluded?

As an agency official, you may not enter into a covered transaction with a participant if you know that a principal of the transaction is excluded, unless you obtain an exception under § 105–68.120.

§ 105–68.410 May I approve a participant's use of the services of an excluded person?

After entering into a covered transaction with a participant, you as an agency official may not approve a participant's use of an excluded person as a principal under that transaction, unless you obtain an exception under § 105–68.120.

§ 105–68.415 What must I do if a Federal agency excludes the participant or a principal after I enter into a covered transaction?

(a) You as an agency official may continue covered transactions with an excluded person, or under which an excluded person is a principal, if the transactions were in existence when the person was excluded. You are not required to continue the transactions, however, and you may consider termination. You should make a decision about whether to terminate and the type of termination action, if any, only after a thorough review to ensure that the action is proper.

(b) You may not renew or extend covered transactions (other than no-cost time extensions) with any excluded person, or under which an excluded person is a principal, unless you obtain an exception under § 105–68.120.

§ 105–68.420 May I approve a transaction with an excluded or disqualified person at a lower tier?

If a transaction at a lower tier is subject to your approval, you as an agency official may not approve—

(a) A covered transaction with a person who is currently excluded, unless you obtain an exception under § 105–68.120; or

(b) A transaction with a person who is disqualified from that transaction, unless you obtain a waiver or exception under the statute, Executive order, or regulation that is the basis for the person's disqualification.

§ 105–68.425 When do I check to see if a person is excluded or disqualified?

As an agency official, you must check to see if a person is excluded or disqualified before you—

(a) Enter into a primary tier covered transaction;

(b) Approve a principal in a primary tier covered transaction;

(c) Approve a lower tier participant if agency approval of the lower tier participant is required; or

(d) Approve a principal in connection with a lower tier transaction if agency approval of the principal is required.

§ 105–68.430 How do I check to see if a person is excluded or disqualified?

You check to see if a person is excluded or disqualified in two ways:

(a) You as an agency official must check the *EPLS* when you take any action listed in § 105–68.425.

(b) You must review information that a participant gives you, as required by § 105–68.335, about its status or the status of the principals of a transaction.

§ 105–68.435 What must I require of a primary tier participant?

You as an agency official must require each participant in a primary tier covered transaction to—

(a) Comply with subpart C of this part as a condition of participation in the transaction; and

(b) Communicate the requirement to comply with Subpart C of this part to persons at the next lower tier with whom the primary tier participant enters into covered transactions.

§ 105–68.440 What method do I use to communicate those requirements to participants?

To communicate the requirement, you must include a term or condition in the transaction requiring the participants' compliance with subpart C of this part and requiring them to include a similar term or condition in lower-tier covered transactions.

[68 FR 66627, Nov. 26, 2003]

§ 105–68.445 What action may I take if a primary tier participant knowingly does business with an excluded or disqualified person?

If a participant knowingly does business with an excluded or disqualified person, you as an agency official may refer the matter for suspension and debarment consideration. You may also disallow costs, annul or terminate the transaction, issue a stop work order, or take any other appropriate remedy.

§ 105–68.450 What action may I take if a primary tier participant fails to disclose the information required under § 105–68.335?

If you as an agency official determine that a participant failed to disclose information, as required by § 105–68.335, at the time it entered into a covered transaction with you, you may—

(a) Terminate the transaction for material failure to comply with the terms and conditions of the transaction; or

(b) Pursue any other available remedies, including suspension and debarment.

§ 105–68.455 What may I do if a lower tier participant fails to disclose the information required under § 105–68.355 to the next higher tier?

If you as an agency official determine that a lower tier participant failed to disclose information, as required by § 105–68.355, at the time it entered into a covered transaction with a participant at the next higher tier, you may pursue any remedies available to you, including the initiation of a suspension or debarment action.

Subpart E—Excluded Parties List System

§ 105–68.500 What is the purpose of the Excluded Parties List System (EPLS)?

The *EPLS* is a widely available source of the most current information about persons who are excluded or disqualified from covered transactions.

§ 105–68.505 Who uses the EPLS?

(a) Federal agency officials use the *EPLS* to determine whether to enter into a transaction with a person, as required under § 105–68.430.

(b) Participants also may, but are not required to, use the *EPLS* to determine if—

(1) Principals of their transactions are excluded or disqualified, as required under § 105–68.320; or

(2) Persons with whom they are entering into covered transactions at the

next lower tier are excluded or disqualified.

(c) The *EPLS* is available to the general public.

§ 105–68.510 Who maintains the EPLS?

In accordance with the OMB guidelines, the General Services Administration (GSA) maintains the *EPLS*. When a Federal agency takes an action to exclude a person under the nonprocurement or procurement debarment and suspension system, the agency enters the information about the excluded person into the *EPLS*.

§ 105–68.515 What specific information is in the EPLS?

(a) At a minimum, the *EPLS* indicates—

(1) The full name (where available) and address of each excluded or disqualified person, in alphabetical order, with cross references if more than one name is involved in a single action;

(2) The type of action;

(3) The cause for the action;

(4) The scope of the action;

(5) Any termination date for the action;

(6) The agency and name and telephone number of the agency point of contact for the action; and

(7) The Dun and Bradstreet Number (DUNS), or other similar code approved by the GSA, of the excluded or disqualified person, if available.

(b)(1) The database for the *EPLS* includes a field for the Taxpayer Identification Number (TIN) (the social security number (SSN) for an individual) of an excluded or disqualified person.

(2) Agencies disclose the SSN of an individual to verify the identity of an individual, only if permitted under the Privacy Act of 1974 and, if appropriate, the Computer Matching and Privacy Protection Act of 1988, as codified in 5 U.S.C. 552(a).

§ 105–68.520 Who places the information into the EPLS?

Federal officials who take actions to exclude persons under this part or officials who are responsible for identifying disqualified persons must enter the following information about those persons into the *EPLS*:

(a) Information required by §105–68.515(a);

(b) The Taxpayer Identification Number (TIN) of the excluded or disqualified person, including the social security number (SSN) for an individual, if the number is available and may be disclosed under law;

(c) Information about an excluded or disqualified person, generally within five working days, after—

(1) Taking an exclusion action;

(2) Modifying or rescinding an exclusion action;

(3) Finding that a person is disqualified; or

(4) Finding that there has been a change in the status of a person who is listed as disqualified.

§ 105–68.525 Whom do I ask if I have questions about a person in the EPLS?

If you have questions about a person in the *EPLS*, ask the point of contact for the Federal agency that placed the person's name into the *EPLS*. You may find the agency point of contact from the *EPLS*.

§ 105–68.530 Where can I find the EPLS?

(a) You may access the *EPLS* through the Internet, currently at *http://epls.arnet.gov*.

(b) As of November 26, 2003, you may also subscribe to a printed version. However, we anticipate discontinuing the printed version. Until it is discontinued, you may obtain the printed version by purchasing a yearly subscription from the Superintendent of Documents, U.S. Government Printing Office, Washington, DC 20402, or by calling the Government Printing Office Inquiry and Order Desk at (202) 783–3238.

Subpart F—General Principles Relating to Suspension and Debarment Actions

§ 105–68.600 How do suspension and debarment actions start?

When we receive information from any source concerning a cause for suspension or debarment, we will promptly report and investigate it. We refer the question of whether to suspend or debar you to our suspending or debarring official for consideration, if appropriate.

§ 105–68.605 How does suspension differ from debarment?

Suspension differs from debarment in that—

A suspending official . . .	A debarring official . . .
(a) Imposes suspension as a temporary status of ineligibility for procurement and nonprocurement transactions, pending completion of an investigation or legal proceedings.	Imposes debarment for a specified period as a final determination that a person is not presently responsible.
(b) Must—	Must conclude, based on a *preponderance of the evidence,* that the person has engaged in conduct that warrants debarment.
(1) Have *adequate evidence* that there may be a cause for debarment of a person; and.	
(2) Conclude that *immediate action* is necessary to protect the Federal interest.	
(c) Usually imposes the suspension *first,* and then promptly notifies the suspended person, giving the person an opportunity to contest the suspension and have it lifted.	Imposes debarment *after* giving the respondent notice of the action and an opportunity to contest the proposed debarment.

§ 105–68.610 What procedures does the General Services Administration use in suspension and debarment actions?

In deciding whether to suspend or debar you, we handle the actions as informally as practicable, consistent with principles of fundamental fairness.

(a) For suspension actions, we use the procedures in this subpart and subpart G of this part.

(b) For debarment actions, we use the procedures in this subpart and subpart H of this part.

§ 105–68.615 How does the General Services Administration notify a person of a suspension or debarment action?

(a) The suspending or debarring official sends a written notice to the last known street address, facsimile number, or e-mail address of—

(1) You or your identified counsel; or

(2) Your agent for service of process, or any of your partners, officers, directors, owners, or joint venturers.

(b) The notice is effective if sent to any of these persons.

§ 105–68.620 Do Federal agencies coordinate suspension and debarment actions?

Yes, when more than one Federal agency has an interest in a suspension or debarment, the agencies may consider designating one agency as the lead agency for making the decision. Agencies are encouraged to establish methods and procedures for coordinating their suspension and debarment actions.

§ 105–68.625 What is the scope of a suspension or debarment?

If you are suspended or debarred, the suspension or debarment is effective as follows:

(a) Your suspension or debarment constitutes suspension or debarment of all of your divisions and other organizational elements from all covered transactions, unless the suspension or debarment decision is limited—

(1) By its terms to one or more specifically identified individuals, divisions, or other organizational elements; or

(2) To specific types of transactions.

(b) Any affiliate of a participant may be included in a suspension or debarment action if the suspending or debarring official—

(1) Officially names the affiliate in the notice; and

(2) Gives the affiliate an opportunity to contest the action.

§ 105–68.630 May the General Services Administration impute conduct of one person to another?

For purposes of actions taken under this rule, we may impute conduct as follows:

(a) *Conduct imputed from an individual to an organization.* We may impute the fraudulent, criminal, or other improper conduct of any officer, director, shareholder, partner, employee, or other individual associated with an organization, to that organization when the improper conduct occurred in connection with the individual's performance of duties for or on behalf of that organization, or with the organization's knowledge, approval or acquiescence. The organization's acceptance of the benefits derived from the conduct is evidence of knowledge, approval or acquiescence.

(b) *Conduct imputed from an organization to an individual, or between individuals.* We may impute the fraudulent, criminal, or other improper conduct of any organization to an individual, or from one individual to another individual, if the individual to whom the improper conduct is imputed either participated in, had knowledge of, or reason to know of the improper conduct.

(c) *Conduct imputed from one organization to another organization.* We may impute the fraudulent, criminal, or other improper conduct of one organization to another organization when the improper conduct occurred in connection with a partnership, joint venture, joint application, association or similar arrangement, or when the organization to whom the improper conduct is imputed has the power to direct, manage, control or influence the activities of the organization responsible for the improper conduct. Acceptance of the benefits derived from the conduct is evidence of knowledge, approval or acquiescence.

§ 105–68.635 May the General Services Administration settle a debarment or suspension action?

Yes, we may settle a debarment or suspension action at any time if it is in the best interest of the Federal Government.

§ 105–68.640 May a settlement include a voluntary exclusion?

Yes, if we enter into a settlement with you in which you agree to be excluded, it is called a voluntary exclusion and has governmentwide effect.

§ 105–68.645 Do other Federal agencies know if the General Services Administration agrees to a voluntary exclusion?

(a) Yes, we enter information regarding a voluntary exclusion into the *EPLS*.

(b) Also, any agency or person may contact us to find out the details of a voluntary exclusion.

Subpart G—Suspension

§ 105–68.700 When may the suspending official issue a suspension?

Suspension is a serious action. Using the procedures of this subpart and subpart F of this part, the suspending official may impose suspension only when that official determines that—

(a) There exists an indictment for, or other adequate evidence to suspect, an offense listed under § 105–68.800(a), or

(b) There exists adequate evidence to suspect any other cause for debarment listed under § 105–68.800(b) through (d); and

(c) Immediate action is necessary to protect the public interest.

§ 105–68.705 What does the suspending official consider in issuing a suspension?

(a) In determining the adequacy of the evidence to support the suspension, the suspending official considers how much information is available, how credible it is given the circumstances, whether or not important allegations are corroborated, and what inferences can reasonably be drawn as a result. During this assessment, the suspending official may examine the basic documents, including grants, cooperative agreements, loan authorizations, contracts, and other relevant documents.

(b) An indictment, conviction, civil judgment, or other official findings by Federal, State, or local bodies that determine factual and/or legal matters, constitutes adequate evidence for purposes of suspension actions.

(c) In deciding whether immediate action is needed to protect the public interest, the suspending official has wide discretion. For example, the suspending official may infer the necessity for immediate action to protect the public interest either from the na-ture of the circumstances giving rise to a cause for suspension or from potential business relationships or involvement with a program of the Federal Government.

§ 105–68.710 When does a suspension take effect?

A suspension is effective when the suspending official signs the decision to suspend.

§ 105–68.715 What notice does the suspending official give me if I am suspended?

After deciding to suspend you, the suspending official promptly sends you a Notice of Suspension advising you—

(a) That you have been suspended;

(b) That your suspension is based on—

(1) An indictment;

(2) A conviction;

(3) Other adequate evidence that you have committed irregularities which seriously reflect on the propriety of further Federal Government dealings with you; or

(4) Conduct of another person that has been imputed to you, or your affiliation with a suspended or debarred person;

(c) Of any other irregularities in terms sufficient to put you on notice without disclosing the Federal Government's evidence;

(d) Of the cause(s) upon which we relied under § 105–68.700 for imposing suspension;

(e) That your suspension is for a temporary period pending the completion of an investigation or resulting legal or debarment proceedings;

(f) Of the applicable provisions of this subpart, subpart F of this part, and any other GSA procedures governing suspension decision making; and

(g) Of the governmentwide effect of your suspension from procurement and nonprocurement programs and activities.

§ 105–68.720 How may I contest a suspension?

If you as a respondent wish to contest a suspension, you or your representative must provide the suspending official with information in opposition to the suspension. You may do this orally or in writing, but any information provided orally that you consider important must also be submitted in writing for the official record.

§ 105–68.725 How much time do I have to contest a suspension?

(a) As a respondent you or your representative must either send, or make rrangements to appear and present, the information and argument to the suspending official within 30 days after you receive the Notice of Suspension.

(b) We consider the notice to be received by you—

(1) When delivered, if we mail the notice to the last known street address, or five days after we send it if the letter is undeliverable;

(2) When sent, if we send the notice by facsimile or five days after we send it if the facsimile is undeliverable; or

(3) When delivered, if we send the notice by e-mail or five days after we send it if the e-mail is undeliverable.

§ 105–68.730 What information must I provide to the suspending official if I contest a suspension?

(a) In addition to any information and argument in opposition, as a respondent your submission to the suspending official must identify—

(1) Specific facts that contradict the statements contained in the Notice of Suspension. A general denial is insufficient to raise a genuine dispute over facts material to the suspension;

(2) All existing, proposed, or prior exclusions under regulations implementing E.O. 12549 and all similar actions taken by Federal, state, or local agencies, including administrative agreements that affect only those agencies;

(3) All criminal and civil proceedings not included in the Notice of Suspension that grew out of facts relevant to the cause(s) stated in the notice; and

(4) All of your affiliates.

(b) If you fail to disclose this information, or provide false information, the General Services Administration may seek further criminal, civil or administrative action against you, as appropriate.

§ 105–68.735 Under what conditions do I get an additional opportunity to challenge the facts on which the suspension is based?

(a) You as a respondent will not have an additional opportunity to challenge the facts if the suspending official determines that—

(1) Your suspension is based upon an indictment, conviction, civil judgment, or other finding by a Federal, State, or local body for which an opportunity to contest the facts was provided;

(2) Your presentation in opposition contains only general denials to information contained in the Notice of Suspension;

(3) The issues raised in your presentation in opposition to the suspension are not factual in nature, or are not material to the suspending official's initial decision to suspend, or the official's decision whether to continue the suspension; or

(4) On the basis of advice from the Department of Justice, an office of the United States Attorney, a State attorney general's office, or a State or local prosecutor's office, that substantial interests of the government in pending or contemplated legal proceedings based on the same facts as the suspension would be prejudiced by conducting fact-finding.

(b) You will have an opportunity to challenge the facts if the suspending official determines that—

(1) The conditions in paragraph (a) of this section do not exist; and

(2) Your presentation in opposition raises a genuine dispute over facts material to the suspension.

(c) If you have an opportunity to challenge disputed material facts under this section, the suspending official or designee must conduct additional proceedings to resolve those facts.

§ 105–68.740 Are suspension proceedings formal?

(a) Suspension proceedings are conducted in a fair and informal manner. The suspending official may use flexible procedures to allow you to present matters in opposition. In so doing, the suspending official is not required to follow formal rules of evidence or procedure in creating an official record upon which the official will base a final suspension decision.

(b) You as a respondent or your representative must submit any documentary evidence you want the suspending official to consider.

§ 105–68.745 How is fact-finding conducted?

(a) If fact-finding is conducted—

(1) You may present witnesses and other evidence, and confront any witness presented; and

(2) The fact-finder must prepare written findings of fact for the record.

(b) A transcribed record of fact-finding proceedings must be made, unless you as a respondent and the General Services Administration agree to waive it in advance. If you want a copy of the transcribed record, you may purchase it.

§ 105–68.750 What does the suspending official consider in deciding whether to continue or terminate my suspension?

(a) The suspending official bases the decision on all information contained in the official record. The record includes—

(1) All information in support of the suspending official's initial decision to suspend you;

(2) Any further information and argument presented in support of, or opposition to, the suspension; and

(3) Any transcribed record of fact-finding proceedings.

(b) The suspending official may refer disputed material facts to another official for findings of fact. The suspending official may reject any resulting findings, in whole or in part, only after specifically determining them to be arbitrary, capricious, or clearly erroneous.

§ 105–68.755 When will I know whether the suspension is continued or terminated?

The suspending official must make a written decision whether to continue, modify, or terminate your suspension within 45 days of closing the official record. The official record closes upon the suspending official's receipt of final submissions, information and findings of fact, if any. The suspending official may extend that period for good cause.

§ 105–68.760 How long may my suspension last?

(a) If legal or debarment proceedings are initiated at the time of, or during your suspension, the suspension may continue until the conclusion of those proceedings. However, if proceedings are not initiated, a suspension may not exceed 12 months.

(b) The suspending official may extend the 12 month limit under paragraph (a) of this section for an additional 6 months if an office of a U.S. Assistant Attorney General, U.S. Attorney, or other responsible prosecuting official requests an extension in writing. In no event may a suspension exceed 18 months without initiating proceedings under paragraph (a) of this section.

(c) The suspending official must notify the appropriate officials under paragraph (b) of this section of an impending termination of a suspension at least 30 days before the 12 month period expires to allow the officials an opportunity to request an extension.

Subpart H—Debarment

§ 105–68.800 What are the causes for debarment?

We may debar a person for—

(a) Conviction of or civil judgment for—

(1) Commission of fraud or a criminal offense in connection with obtaining, attempting to obtain, or performing a public or private agreement or transaction;

(2) Violation of Federal or State antitrust statutes, including those proscribing price fixing between competitors, allocation of customers between competitors, and bid rigging;

(3) Commission of embezzlement, theft, forgery, bribery, falsification or destruction of records, making false statements, tax evasion, receiving stolen property, making false claims, or obstruction of justice; or

(4) Commission of any other offense indicating a lack of business integrity or business honesty that seriously and directly affects your present responsibility;

(b) Violation of the terms of a public agreement or transaction so serious as to affect the integrity of an agency program, such as—

(1) A willful failure to perform in accordance with the terms of one or more public agreements or transactions;

(2) A history of failure to perform or of unsatisfactory performance of one or more public agreements or transactions; or

(3) A willful violation of a statutory or regulatory provision or requirement applicable to a public agreement or transaction;

(c) Any of the following causes:

(1) A nonprocurement debarment by any Federal agency taken before October 1, 1988, or a procurement debarment by any Federal agency taken pursuant to 48 CFR part 9, subpart 9.4, before August 25, 1995;

(2) Knowingly doing business with an ineligible person, except as permitted under § 105–68.120;

(3) Failure to pay a single substantial debt, or a number of outstanding debts (including disallowed costs and overpayments, but not including sums owed the Federal Government under the Internal Revenue Code) owed to any Federal agency or instrumentality, provided the debt is uncontested by the debtor or, if contested, provided that the debtor's legal and administrative remedies have been exhausted;

(4) Violation of a material provision of a voluntary exclusion agreement entered into under § 105–68.640 or of any settlement of a debarment or suspension action; or

(5) Violation of the provisions of the Drug-Free Workplace Act of 1988 (41 U.S.C. 701); or

(d) Any other cause of so serious or compelling a nature that it affects your present responsibility.

§ 105–68.805 What notice does the debarring official give me if I am proposed for debarment?

After consideration of the causes in § 105–68.800 of this subpart, if the debarring official proposes to debar you, the official sends you a Notice of Proposed Debarment, pursuant to § 105–68.615, advising you—

(a) That the debarring official is considering debarring you;

(b) Of the reasons for proposing to debar you in terms sufficient to put you on notice of the conduct or transactions upon which the proposed debarment is based;

(c) Of the cause(s) under § 105–68.800 upon which the debarring official relied for proposing your debarment;

(d) Of the applicable provisions of this subpart, subpart F of this part, and any other GSA procedures governing debarment; and

(e) Of the governmentwide effect of a debarment from procurement and nonprocurement programs and activities.

§ 105–68.810 When does a debarment take effect?

A debarment is not effective until the debarring official issues a decision. The debarring official does not issue a decision until the respondent has had an opportunity to contest the proposed debarment.

§ 105–68.815 How may I contest a proposed debarment?

If you as a respondent wish to contest a proposed debarment, you or your representative must provide the debarring official with information in opposition to the proposed debarment. You may do this orally or in writing, but any information provided orally that you consider important must also be submitted in writing for the official record.

§ 105–68.820 How much time do I have to contest a proposed debarment?

(a) As a respondent you or your representative must either send, or make arrangements to appear and present, the information and argument to the debarring official within 30 days after you receive the Notice of Proposed Debarment.

(b) We consider the Notice of Proposed Debarment to be received by you—

(1) When delivered, if we mail the notice to the last known street address, or five days after we send it if the letter is undeliverable;

(2) When sent, if we send the notice by facsimile or five days after we send it if the facsimile is undeliverable; or

(3) When delivered, if we send the notice by e-mail or five days after we send it if the e-mail is undeliverable.

§ 105–68.825 What information must I provide to the debarring official if I contest a proposed debarment?

(a) In addition to any information and argument in opposition, as a respondent your submission to the debarring official must identify—

(1) Specific facts that contradict the statements contained in the Notice of Proposed Debarment. Include any information about any of the factors listed in § 105–68.860. A general denial is insufficient to raise a genuine dispute over facts material to the debarment;

(2) All existing, proposed, or prior exclusions under regulations implementing E.O. 12549 and all similar actions taken by Federal, State, or local agencies, including administrative agreements that affect only those agencies;

(3) All criminal and civil proceedings not included in the Notice of Proposed Debarment that grew out of facts relevant to the cause(s) stated in the notice; and

(4) All of your affiliates.

(b) If you fail to disclose this information, or provide false information, the General Services Administration may seek further criminal, civil or administrative action against you, as appropriate.

§ 105–68.830 Under what conditions do I get an additional opportunity to challenge the facts on which a proposed debarment is based?

(a) You as a respondent will not have an additional opportunity to challenge the facts if the debarring official determines that—

(1) Your debarment is based upon a conviction or civil judgment;

(2) Your presentation in opposition contains only general denials to information contained in the Notice of Proposed Debarment; or

(3) The issues raised in your presentation in opposition to the proposed debarment are not factual in nature, or are not material to the debarring official's decision whether to debar.

(b) You will have an additional opportunity to challenge the facts if the debarring official determines that—

(1) The conditions in paragraph (a) of this section do not exist; and

(2) Your presentation in opposition raises a genuine dispute over facts material to the proposed debarment.

(c) If you have an opportunity to challenge disputed material facts under this section, the debarring official or designee must conduct additional proceedings to resolve those facts.

§ 105–68.835 Are debarment proceedings formal?

(a) Debarment proceedings are conducted in a fair and informal manner. The debarring official may use flexible procedures to allow you as a respondent to present matters in opposition. In so doing, the debarring official is not required to follow formal rules of evidence or procedure in creating an official record upon which the official will base the decision whether to debar.

(b) You or your representative must submit any documentary evidence you want the debarring official to consider.

§ 105–68.840 How is fact-finding conducted?

(a) If fact-finding is conducted—

(1) You may present witnesses and other evidence, and confront any witness presented; and

(2) The fact-finder must prepare written findings of fact for the record.

(b) A transcribed record of fact-finding proceedings must be made, unless you as a respondent and the General Services Administration agree to waive it in advance. If you want a copy of the transcribed record, you may purchase it.

§ 105–68.845 What does the debarring official consider in deciding whether to debar me?

(a) The debarring official may debar you for any of the causes in § 105–68.800. However, the official need not debar you even if a cause for debarment exists. The official may consider the seriousness of your acts or omissions and the mitigating or aggravating factors set forth at § 105–68.860.

(b) The debarring official bases the decision on all information contained in the official record. The record includes—

(1) All information in support of the debarring official's proposed debarment;

(2) Any further information and argument presented in support of, or in opposition to, the proposed debarment; and

(3) Any transcribed record of fact-finding proceedings.

(c) The debarring official may refer disputed material facts to another official for findings of fact. The debarring official may reject any resultant findings, in whole or in part, only after specifically determining them to be arbitrary, capricious, or clearly erroneous.

§ 105–68.850 What is the standard of proof in a debarment action?

(a) In any debarment action, we must establish the cause for debarment by a preponderance of the evidence.

(b) If the proposed debarment is based upon a conviction or civil judgment, the standard of proof is met.

§ 105–68.855 Who has the burden of proof in a debarment action?

(a) We have the burden to prove that a cause for debarment exists.

(b) Once a cause for debarment is established, you as a respondent have the burden of demonstrating to the satisfaction of the debarring official that you are presently responsible and that debarment is not necessary.

§ 105–68.860 What factors may influence the debarring official's decision?

This section lists the mitigating and aggravating factors that the debarring official may consider in determining whether to debar you and the length of your debarment period. The debarring official may consider other factors if appropriate in light of the circumstances of a particular case. The existence or nonexistence of any factor, such as one of those set forth in this section, is not necessarily determinative of your present responsibility. In making a debarment decision, the debarring official may consider the following factors:

(a) The actual or potential harm or impact that results or may result from the wrongdoing.

(b) The frequency of incidents and/or duration of the wrongdoing.

(c) Whether there is a pattern or prior history of wrongdoing. For example, if you have been found by another Federal agency or a State agency to have engaged in wrongdoing similar to that found in the debarment action, the existence of this fact may be used by the debarring official in determining that you have a pattern or prior history of wrongdoing.

(d) Whether you are or have been excluded or disqualified by an agency of the Federal Government or have not been allowed to participate in State or local contracts or assistance agreements on a basis of conduct similar to one or more of the causes for debarment specified in this part.

(e) Whether you have entered into an administrative agreement with a Federal agency or a State or local government that is not governmentwide but is based on conduct similar to one or more of the causes for debarment specified in this part.

(f) Whether and to what extent you planned, initiated, or carried out the wrongdoing.

(g) Whether you have accepted responsibility for the wrongdoing and recognize the seriousness of the misconduct that led to the cause for debarment.

(h) Whether you have paid or agreed to pay all criminal, civil and administrative liabilities for the improper activity, including any investigative or administrative costs incurred by the government, and have made or agreed to make full restitution.

(i) Whether you have cooperated fully with the government agencies during the investigation and any court or administrative action. In determining the extent of cooperation, the debarring official may consider when the cooperation began and whether you disclosed all pertinent information known to you.

(j) Whether the wrongdoing was pervasive within your organization.

(k) The kind of positions held by the individuals involved in the wrongdoing.

(1) Whether your organization took appropriate corrective action or remedial measures, such as establishing ethics training and implementing programs to prevent recurrence.

(m) Whether your principals tolerated the offense.

(n) Whether you brought the activity cited as a basis for the debarment to the attention of the appropriate government agency in a timely manner.

(o) Whether you have fully investigated the circumstances surrounding the cause for debarment and, if so, made the result of the investigation available to the debarring official.

(p) Whether you had effective standards of conduct and internal control systems in place at the time the questioned conduct occurred.

(q) Whether you have taken appropriate disciplinary action against the individuals responsible for the activity which constitutes the cause for debarment.

(r) Whether you have had adequate time to eliminate the circumstances within your organization that led to the cause for the debarment.

(s) Other factors that are appropriate to the circumstances of a particular case.

§ 105–68.865 How long may my debarment last?

(a) If the debarring official decides to debar you, your period of debarment will be based on the seriousness of the cause(s) upon which your debarment is based. Generally, debarment should not exceed three years. However, if circumstances warrant, the debarring official may impose a longer period of debarment.

(b) In determining the period of debarment, the debarring official may consider the factors in § 105–68.860. If a suspension has preceded your debarment, the debarring official must consider the time you were suspended.

(c) If the debarment is for a violation of the provisions of the Drug-Free Workplace Act of 1988, your period of debarment may not exceed five years.

§ 105–68.870 When do I know if the debarring official debars me?

(a) The debarring official must make a written decision whether to debar within 45 days of closing the official record. The official record closes upon the debarring official's receipt of final submissions, information and findings of fact, if any. The debarring official may extend that period for good cause.

(b) The debarring official sends you written notice, pursuant to § 105–68.615 that the official decided, either—

(1) Not to debar you; or

(2) To debar you. In this event, the notice:

(i) Refers to the Notice of Proposed Debarment;

(ii) Specifies the reasons for your debarment;

(iii) States the period of your debarment, including the effective dates; and

(iv) Advises you that your debarment is effective for covered transactions and contracts that are subject to the Federal Acquisition Regulation (48 CFR chapter 1), throughout the executive branch of the Federal Government unless an agency head or an authorized designee grants an exception.

§ 105–68.875 May I ask the debarring official to reconsider a decision to debar me?

Yes, as a debarred person you may ask the debarring official to reconsider the debarment decision or to reduce the time period or scope of the debarment. However, you must put your request in writing and support it with documentation.

§ 105–68.880 What factors may influence the debarring official during reconsideration?

The debarring official may reduce or terminate your debarment based on—

(a) Newly discovered material evidence;

(b) A reversal of the conviction or civil judgment upon which your debarment was based;

(c) A bona fide change in ownership or management;

(d) Elimination of other causes for which the debarment was imposed; or

(e) Other reasons the debarring official finds appropriate.

§ 105–68.885 May the debarring official extend a debarment?

(a) Yes, the debarring official may extend a debarment for an additional period, if that official determines that an extension is necessary to protect the public interest.

(b) However, the debarring official may not extend a debarment solely on the basis of the facts and circumstances upon which the initial debarment action was based.

(c) If the debarring official decides that a debarment for an additional period is necessary, the debarring official must follow the applicable procedures in this subpart, and subpart F of this part, to extend the debarment.

Subpart I—Definitions

§ 105–68.900 Adequate evidence.

Adequate evidence means information sufficient to support the reasonable belief that a particular act or omission has occurred.

§ 105–68.905 Affiliate.

Persons are *affiliates* of each other if, directly or indirectly, either one controls or has the power to control the other or a third person controls or has the power to control both. The ways we use to determine control include, but are not limited to—

(a) Interlocking management or ownership;

(b) Identity of interests among family members;

(c) Shared facilities and equipment;

(d) Common use of employees; or

(e) A business entity which has been organized following the exclusion of a person which has the same or similar management, ownership, or principal employees as the excluded person.

§ 105–68.910 Agency.

Agency means any United States executive department, military department, defense agency, or any other agency of the executive branch. Other agencies of the Federal government are not considered ''agencies'' for the purposes of this part unless they issue regulations adopting the governmentwide Debarment and Suspension system under Executive orders 12549 and 12689.

§ 105–68.915 Agent or representative.

Agent or representative means any person who acts on behalf of, or who is authorized to commit, a participant in a covered transaction.

§ 105–68.920 Civil judgment.

Civil judgment means the disposition of a civil action by any court of competent jurisdiction, whether by verdict, decision, settlement, stipulation, other disposition which creates a civil liability for the complained of wrongful acts, or a final determination of liability under the Program Fraud Civil Remedies Act of 1988 (31 U.S.C. 3801–3812).

§ 105–68.925 Conviction.

Conviction means—

(a) A judgment or any other determination of guilt of a criminal offense by any court of competent jurisdiction, whether entered upon a verdict or plea, including a plea of nolo contendere; or

(b) Any other resolution that is the functional equivalent of a judgment, including probation before judgment and deferred prosecution. A disposition without the participation of the court is the functional equivalent of a judgment only if it includes an admission of guilt.

§ 105–68.930 Debarment.

Debarment means an action taken by a debarring official under subpart H of this part to exclude a person from participating in covered transactions and transactions covered under the Federal Acquisition Regulation (48 CFR chapter 1). A person so excluded is debarred.

§ 105–68.935 Debarring official.

(a) *Debarring official* means an agency official who is authorized to impose debarment. A debarring official is either—

(1) The agency head; or

(2) An official designated by the agency head.

(b) [Reserved]

§ 105–68.940 Disqualified.

Disqualified means that a person is prohibited from participating in specified Federal procurement or nonprocurement transactions as required under a statute, Executive order (other than Executive Orders 12549 and 12689) or other authority. Examples of disqualifications include persons prohibited under—

(a) The Davis-Bacon Act (40 U.S.C. 276(a));

(b) The equal employment opportunity acts and Executive orders; or

(c) The Clean Air Act (42 U.S.C. 7606), Clean Water Act (33 U.S.C. 1368) and Executive Order 11738 (3 CFR, 1973 Comp., p. 799).

§ 105–68.945   Excluded or exclusion.

Excluded or exclusion means—

(a) That a person or commodity is prohibited from being a participant in covered transactions, whether the person has been suspended; debarred; proposed for debarment under 48 CFR part 9, subpart 9.4; voluntarily excluded; or

(b) The act of excluding a person.

§ 105–68.950   Excluded Parties List System

Excluded Parties List System (EPLS) means the list maintained and disseminated by the General Services Administration (GSA) containing the names and other information about persons who are ineligible. The *EPLS* system includes the printed version entitled, "List of Parties Excluded or Disqualified from Federal Procurement and Nonprocurement Programs," so long as published.

§ 105–68.955   Indictment.

Indictment means an indictment for a criminal offense. A presentment, information, or other filing by a competent authority charging a criminal offense shall be given the same effect as an indictment.

§ 105–68.960   Ineligible or ineligibility.

Ineligible or ineligibility means that a person or commodity is prohibited from covered transactions because of an exclusion or disqualification.

§ 105–68.965   Legal proceedings.

Legal proceedings means any criminal proceeding or any civil judicial proceeding, including a proceeding under the Program Fraud Civil Remedies Act (31 U.S.C. 3801–3812), to which the Federal Government or a State or local government or quasi-governmental authority is a party. The term also includes appeals from those proceedings.

§ 105–68.970   Nonprocurement transaction.

(a) *Nonprocurement transaction* means any transaction, regardless of type (except procurement contracts), including, but not limited to the following:

(1) Grants.

(2) Cooperative agreements.

(3) Scholarships.

(4) Fellowships.

(5) Contracts of assistance.

(6) Loans.

(7) Loan guarantees.

(8) Subsidies.

(9) Insurances.

(10) Payments for specified uses.

(11) Donation agreements.

(b) A nonprocurement transaction at any tier does not require the transfer of Federal funds.

§ 105–68.975   Notice.

Notice means a written communication served in person, sent by certified mail or its equivalent, or sent electronically by e-mail or facsimile. (See § 105–68. 615.)

§ 105–68.980   Participant.

Participant means any person who submits a proposal for or who enters into a covered transaction, including an agent or representative of a participant.

§ 105–68.985   Person.

Person means any individual, corporation, partnership, association, unit of government, or legal entity, however organized.

§ 105–68.990   Preponderance of the evidence.

Preponderance of the evidence means proof by information that, compared with information opposing it, leads to the conclusion that the fact at issue is more probably true than not.

§ 105–68.995   Principal.

Principal means—

(a) An officer, director, owner, partner, principal investigator, or other person within a participant with management or supervisory responsibilities related to a covered transaction; or

(b) A consultant or other person, whether or not employed by the participant or paid with Federal funds, who—

(1) Is in a position to handle Federal funds;

(2) Is in a position to influence or control the use of those funds; or,

(3) Occupies a technical or professional position capable of substantially influencing the development or outcome of an activity required to perform the covered transaction.

§ 105–68.1000   Respondent.

Respondent means a person against whom an agency has initiated a debarment or suspension action.

§ 105–68.1005   State.

(a) *State* means—

(1) Any of the states of the United States;

(2) The District of Columbia;

(3) The Commonwealth of Puerto Rico;

(4) Any territory or possession of the United States; or

(5) Any agency or instrumentality of a state.

(b) For purposes of this part, *State* does not include institutions of higher education, hospitals, or units of local government.

§ 105–68.1010   Suspending official.

(a) *Suspending official* means an agency official who is authorized to impose suspension. The suspending official is either:

(1) The agency head; or

(2) An official designated by the agency head.

(b) [Reserved]

§ 105–68.1015   Suspension.

Suspension is an action taken by a suspending official under subpart G of this part that immediately prohibits a person from participating in covered transactions and transactions covered under the Federal Acquisition Regulation (48 CFR chapter 1) for a temporary period, pending completion of an agency investigation and any judicial or administrative proceedings that may ensue. A person so excluded is suspended.

§ 105–68.1020   Voluntary exclusion or voluntarily excluded.

(a) *Voluntary exclusion* means a person's agreement to be excluded under the terms of a settlement between the person and one or more agencies. Voluntary exclusion must have governmentwide effect.

(b) *Voluntarily excluded* means the status of a person who has agreed to a voluntary exclusion.

Subpart J [Reserved]

APPENDIX TO PART 105–68—COVERED TRANSACTIONS

COVERED TRANSACTIONS

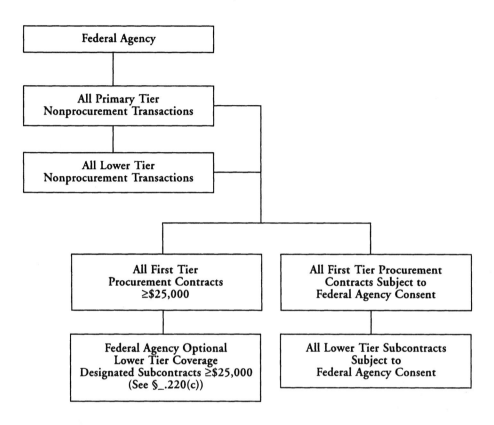

PART 105–69—NEW RESTRICTIONS ON LOBBYING

Subpart A—General

AUTHORITY: Sec. 319, Pub. L. 101–121 (31 U.S.C. 1352); 40 U.S.C. 486(c).

SOURCE: 55 FR 6737, 6753, Feb. 26, 1990, unless otherwise noted.

CROSS REFERENCE: See also Office of Management and Budget notice published at 54 FR 52306, December 20, 1989.

Subpart A—General

§ 105–69.100 Conditions on use of funds.

(a) No appropriated funds may be expended by the recipient of a Federal contract, grant, loan, or cooperative ageement to pay any person for influencing or attempting to influence an officer or employee of any agency, a Member of Congress, an officer or employee of Congress, or an employee of a Member of Congress in connection with any of the following covered Federal actions: the awarding of any Federal contract, the making of any Federal grant, the making of any Federal loan, the entering into of any cooperative agreement, and the extension, continuation, renewal, amendment, or modification of any Federal contract, grant, loan, or cooperative agreement.

(b) Each person who requests or receives from an agency a Federal contract, grant, loan, or cooperative agreement shall file with that agency a certification, set forth in appendix A, that the person has not made, and will not make, any payment prohibited by paragraph (a) of this section.

(c) Each person who requests or receives from an agency a Federal contract, grant, loan, or a cooperative agreement shall file with that agency a disclosure form, set forth in appendix B, if such person has made or has agreed to make any payment using nonappropriated funds (to include profits from any covered Federal action), which would be prohibited under paragraph (a) of this section if paid for with appropriated funds.

(d) Each person who requests or receives from an agency a commitment providing for the United States to insure or guarantee a loan shall file with that agency a statement, set forth in appendix A, whether that person has made or has agreed to make any payment to influence or attempt to influence an officer or employee of any agency, a Member of Congress, an officer or employee of Congress, or an employee of a Member of Congress in connection with that loan insurance or guarantee.

(e) Each person who requests or receives from an agency a commitment providing for the United States to insure or guarantee a loan shall file with that agency a disclosure form, set forth in appendix B, if that person has made or has agreed to make any payment to influence or attempt to influence an officer or employee of any agency, a Member of Congress, an officer or employee of Congress, or an employee of a Member of Congress in connection with that loan insurance or guarantee.

§ 105–69.105 Definitions.

For purposes of this part:

(a) *Agency*, as defined in 5 U.S.C. 552(f), includes Federal executive departments and agencies as well as independent regulatory commissions and Government corporations, as defined in 31 U.S.C. 9101(1).

(b) *Covered Federal action* means any of the following Federal actions:

(1) The awarding of any Federal contract;

(2) The making of any Federal grant;

(3) The making of any Federal loan;

(4) The entering into of any cooperative agreement; and,

(5) The extension, continuation, renewal, amendment, or modification of any Federal contract, grant, loan, or cooperative agreement.

Covered Federal action does not include receiving from an agency a commitment providing for the United States to insure or guarantee a loan. Loan guarantees and loan insurance are addressed independently within this part.

(c) *Federal contract* means an acquisition contract awarded by an agency, including those subject to the Federal Acquisition Regulation (FAR), and any other acquisition contract for real or personal property or services not subject to the FAR.

(d) *Federal cooperative agreement* means a cooperative agreement entered into by an agency.

(e) *Federal grant* means an award of financial assistance in the form of money, or property in lieu of money, by the Federal Government or a direct appropriation made by law to any person. The term does not include technical assistance which provides services instead of money, or other assistance in the form of revenue sharing, loans, loan guarantees, loan insurance, interest subsidies, insurance, or direct United States cash assistance to an individual.

(f) *Federal loan* means a loan made by an agency. The term does not include loan guarantee or loan insurance.

(g) *Indian tribe* and *tribal organization* have the meaning provided in section 4 of the Indian Self-Determination and Education Assistance Act (25 U.S.C. 450B). Alaskan Natives are included under the definitions of Indian tribes in that Act.

(h) *Influencing or attempting to influence* means making, with the intent to influence, any communication to or appearance before an officer or employee or any agency, a Member of Congress, an officer or employee of Congress, or an employee of a Member of Congress in connection with any covered Federal action.

(i) *Loan guarantee* and *loan insurance* means an agency's guarantee or insurance of a loan made by a person.

(j) *Local government* means a unit of government in a State and, if chartered, established, or otherwise recognized by a State for the performance of a governmental duty, including a local public authority, a special district, an intrastate district, a council of governments, a sponsor group representative organization, and any other instrumentality of a local government.

(k) *Officer or employee of an agency* includes the following individuals who are employed by an agency:

(1) An individual who is appointed to a position in the Government under title 5, U.S. Code, including a position under a temporary appointment;

(2) A member of the uniformed services as defined in section 101(3), title 37, U.S. Code;

(3) A special Government employee as defined in section 202, title 18, U.S. Code; and,

(4) An individual who is a member of a Federal advisory committee, as defined by the Federal Advisory Committee Act, title 5, U.S. Code appendix 2.

(1) *Person* means an individual, corporation, company, association, authority, firm, partnership, society, State, and local government, regardless of whether such entity is operated for profit or not for profit. This term excludes an Indian tribe, tribal organization, or any other Indian organization with respect to expenditures specifically permitted by other Federal law.

(m) *Reasonable compensation* means, with respect to a regularly employed officer or employee of any person, compensation that is consistent with the normal compensation for such officer or employee for work that is not furnished to, not funded by, or not furnished in cooperation with the Federal Government.

(n) *Reasonable payment* means, with respect to perfessional and other technical services, a payment in an amount that is consistent with the amount normally paid for such services in the private sector.

(o) *Recipient* includes all contractors, subcontractors at any tier, and subgrantees at any tier of the recipient of funds received in connection with a Federal contract, grant, loan, or cooperative agreement. The term excludes an Indian tribe, tribal organization, or any other Indian organization with respect to expenditures specifically permitted by other Federal law.

(p) *Regularly employed* means, with respect to an officer or employee of a person requesting or receiving a Federal contract, grant, loan, or cooperative agreement or a commitment providing for the United States to insure or guarantee a loan, an officer or employee who is employed by such person for at least 130 working days within one year immediately preceding the date of the submission that initiates agency consideration of such person for receipt of such contract, grant, loan, cooperative agreement, loan insurance commitment, or loan guarantee commitment. An officer or employee who is employed by such person for less than 130 working days within one year immediately preceding the date of the submission that initiates agency consideration of such person shall be considered to be regularly employed as soon as he or she is employed by such person for 130 working days.

(q) *State* means a State of the United States, the District of Columbia, the Commonwealth of Puerto Rico, a territory or possession of the United States, an agency or instrumentality of a State, and a multi-State, regional, or interstate entity having governmental duties and powers.

§ 105–69.110 **Certification and disclosure.**

(a) Each person shall file a certification, and a disclosure form, if required, with each submission that initiates agency consideration of such person for:

(1) Award of a Federal contract, grant, or cooperative agreement exceeding $100,000; or

(2) An award of a Federal loan or a commitment providing for the United States to insure or guarantee a loan exceeding $150,000.

(b) Each person shall file a certification, and a disclosure form, if required, upon receipt by such person of:

(1) A Federal contract, grant, or cooperative agreement exceeding $100,000; or

(2) A Federal loan or a commitment providing for the United States to insure or guarantee a loan exceeding $150,000,

unless such person previously filed a certification, and a disclosure form, if required, under paragraph (a) of this section.

(c) Each person shall file a disclosure form at the end of each calendar quarter in which there occurs any event that requires disclosure or that materially affects the accuracy of the information contained in any disclosure form previously filed by such person under paragraph (a) or (b) of this section. An event that materially affects the accuracy of the information reported includes:

(1) A cumulative increase of $25,000 or more in the amount paid or expected to be paid for influencing or attempting to influence a covered Federal action; or

(2) A change in the person(s) or individual(s) influencing or attempting to influence a covered Federal action; or,

(3) A change in the officer(s), employee(s), or Member(s) contacted to influence or attempt to influence a covered Federal action.

(d) Any person who requests or receives from a person referred to in paragraph (a) or (b) of this section:

(1) A subcontract exceeding $100,000 at any tier under a Federal contract;

(2) A subgrant, contract, or subcontract exceeding $100,000 at any tier under a Federal grant;

(3) A contract or subcontract exceeding $100,000 at any tier under a Federal loan exceeding $150,000; or,

(4) A contract or subcontract exceeding $100,000 at any tier under a Federal cooperative agreement,

shall file a certification, and a disclosure form, if required, to the next tier above.

(e) All disclosure forms, but not certifications, shall be forwarded from tier to tier until received by the person referred to in paragraph (a) or (b) of this section. That person shall forward all disclosure forms to the agency.

(f) Any certification or disclosure form filed under paragraph (e) of this section shall be treated as a material representation of fact upon which all receiving tiers shall rely. All liability arising from an erroneous representation shall be borne solely by the tier filing that representation and shall not be shared by any tier to which the erroneous representation is forwarded. Submitting an erroneous certification or disclosure constitutes a failure to file the required certification or disclosure, respectively. If a person fails to file a required certification or disclosure, the United States may pursue all available remedies, including those authorized by section 1352, title 31, U.S. Code.

(g) For awards and commitments in process prior to December 23, 1989, but not made before that date, certifications shall be required at award or commitment, covering activities occurring between December 23, 1989, and the date of award or commitment. However, for awards and commitments in process prior to the December 23, 1989 effective date of these provisions, but not made before December 23, 1989, disclosure forms shall not be required at time of award or commitment but shall be filed within 30 days.

(h) No reporting is required for an activity paid for with appropriated funds if that activity is allowable under either subpart B or C.

Subpart B—Activities by Own Employees

§ 105–69.200 Agency and legislative liaison.

(a) The prohibition on the use of appropriated funds, in § 105–69.100 (a), does not apply in the case of a payment of reasonable compensation made to an officer or employee of a person requesting or receiving a Federal contract, grant, loan, or cooperative agreement if the payment is for agency and legislative liaison activities not directly related to a covered Federal action.

(b) For purposes of paragraph (a) of this section, providing any information specifically requested by an agency or Congress is allowable at any time.

(c) For purposes of paragraph (a) of this section, the following agency and legislative liaison activities are allowable at any time only where they are not related to a specific solicitation for any covered Federal action:

(1) Discussing with an agency (including individual demonstrations) the qualities and characteristics of the person's products or services, conditions or terms of sale, and service capabilities; and,

(2) Technical discussions and other activities regarding the application or adaptation of the person's products or services for an agency's use.

(d) For purposes of paragraph (a) of this section, the following agencies and legislative liaison activities are allowable only where they are prior to formal solicitation of any covered Federal action:

(1) Providing any information not specifically requested but necessary for an agency to make an informed decision about initiation of a covered Federal action;

(2) Technical discussions regarding the preparation of an unsolicited proposal prior to its official submission; and,

(3) Capability presentations by persons seeking awards from an agency

pursuant to the provisions of the Small Business Act, as amended by Public Law 95–507 and other subsequent amendments.

(e) Only those activities expressly authorized by this section are allowable under this section.

§ 105–69.205 Professional and technical services.

(a) The prohibition on the use of appropriated funds, in § 105–69.100 (a), does not apply in the case of a payment of reasonable compensation made to an officer or employee of a person requesting or receiving a Federal contract, grant, loan, or cooperative agreement or an extension, continuation, renewal, amendment, or modification of a Federal contract, grant, loan, or cooperative agreement if payment is for professional or technical services rendered directly in the preparation, submission, or negotiation of any bid, proposal, or application for that Federal contract, grant, loan, or cooperative agreement or for meeting requirements imposed by or pursuant to law as a condition for receiving that Federal contract, grant, loan, or cooperative agreement.

(b) For purposes of paragraph (a) of this section, "professional and technical services" shall be limited to advice and analysis directly applying any professional or technical discipline. For example, drafting of a legal document accompanying a bid or proposal by a lawyer is allowable. Similarly, technical advice provided by an engineer on the performance or operational capability of a piece of equipment rendered directly in the negotiation of a contract is allowable. However, communications with the intent to influence made by a professional (such as a licensed lawyer) or a technical person (such as a licensed accountant) are not allowable under this section unless they provide advice and analysis directly applying their professional or technical expertise and unless the advice or analysis is rendered directly and solely in the preparation, submission or negotiation of a covered Federal action. Thus, for example, communications with the intent to influence made by a lawyer that do not provide legal advice or analysis directly and

553

solely related to the legal aspects of his or her client's proposal, but generally advocate one proposal over another are not allowable under this section because the lawyer is not providing professional legal services. Similarly, communications with the intent to influence made by an engineer providing an engineering analysis prior to the preparation or submission of a bid or proposal are not allowable under this section since the engineer is providing technical services but not directly in the preparation, submission or negotiation of a covered Federal action.

(c) Requirements imposed by or pursuant to law as a condition for receiving a covered Federal award include those required by law or regulation, or reasonably expected to be required by law or regulation, and any other requirements in the actual award documents.

(d) Only those services expressly authorized by this section are allowable under this section.

§ 105–69.210   Reporting.

No reporting is required with respect to payments of reasonable compensation made to regularly employed officers or employees of a person.

Subpart C—Activities by Other Than Own Employees

§ 105–69.300   Professional and technical services.

(a) The prohibition on the use of appropriated funds, in § 105–69.100 (a), does not apply in the case of any reasonable payment to a person, other than an officer or employee of a person requesting or receiving a covered Federal action, if the payment is for professional or technical services rendered directly in the preparation, submission, or negotiation of any bid, proposal, or application for that Federal contract, grant, loan, or cooperative agreement or for meeting requirements imposed by or pursuant to law as a condition for receiving that Federal contract, grant, loan, or cooperative agreement.

(b) The reporting requirements in § 105–69.110 (a) and (b) regarding filing a disclosure form by each person, if required, shall not apply with respect to professional or technical services rendered directly in the preparation, submission, or negotiation of any commitment providing for the United States to insure or guarantee a loan.

(c) For purposes of paragraph (a) of this section, "professional and technical services" shall be limited to advice and analysis directly applying any professional or technical discipline. For example, drafting or a legal document accompanying a bid or proposal by a lawyer is allowable. Similarly, technical advice provided by an engineer on the performance or operational capability of a piece of equipment rendered directly in the negotiation of a contract is allowable. However, communications with the intent to influence made by a professional (such as a licensed lawyer) or a technical person (such as a licensed accountant) are not allowable under this section unless they provide advice and analysis directly applying their professional or technical expertise and unless the advice or analysis is rendered directly and solely in the preparation, submission or negotiation of a covered Federal action. Thus, for example, communications with the intent to influence made by a lawyer that do not provide legal advice or analysis directly and solely related to the legal aspects of his or her client's proposal, but generally advocate one proposal over another are not allowable under this section because the lawyer is not providing professional legal services. Similarly, communications with the intent to influence made by an engineer providing an engineering analysis prior to the preparation or submission of a bid or proposal are not allowable under this section since the engineer is providing technical services but not directly in the preparation, submission or negotiation of a covered Federal action.

(d) Requirements imposed by or pursuant to law as a condition for receiving a covered Federal award include those required by law or regulation, or reasonably expected to be required by law or regulation, and any other requirements in the actual award documents.

(e) Persons other than officers or employees of a person requesting or receiving a covered Federal action include consultants and trade associations.

(f) Only those services expressly authorized by this section are allowable under this section.

Subpart D—Penalties and Enforcement

§ 105–69.400 Penalties.

(a) Any person who makes an expenditure prohibited herein shall be subject to a civil penalty of not less than $10,000 and not more than $100,000 for each such expenditure.

(b) Any person who fails to file or amend the disclosure form (see appendix B) to be filed or amended if required herein, shall be subject to a civil penalty of not less than $10,000 and not more than $100,000 for each such failure.

(c) A filing or amended filing on or after the date on which an administrative action for the imposition of a civil penalty is commenced does not prevent the imposition of such civil penalty for a failure occurring before that date. An administrative action is commenced with respect to a failure when an investigating official determines in writing to commence an investigation of an allegation of such failure.

(d) In determining whether to impose a civil penalty, and the amount of any such penalty, by reason of a violation by any person, the agency shall consider the nature, circumstances, extent, and gravity of the violation, the effect on the ability of such person to continue in business, any prior violations by such person, the degree of culpability of such person, the ability of the person to pay the penalty, and such other matters as may be appropriate.

(e) First offenders under paragraphs (a) or (b) of this section shall be subject to a civil penalty of $10,000, absent aggravating circumstances. Second and subsequent offenses by persons shall be subject to an appropriate civil penalty between $10,000 and $100,000, as determined by the agency head or his or her designee.

(f) An imposition of a civil penalty under this section does not prevent the United States from seeking any other remedy that may apply to the same conduct that is the basis for the imposition of such civil penalty.

§ 105–69.405 Penalty procedures.

Agencies shall impose and collect civil penalties pursuant to the provisions of the Program Fraud and Civil Remedies Act, 31 U.S.C. sections 3803 (except subsection (c)), 3804, 3805, 3806, 3807, 3808, and 3812, insofar as these provisions are not inconsistent with the requirements herein.

§ 105–69.410 Enforcement.

The head of each agency shall take such actions as are necessary to ensure that the provisions herein are vigorously implemented and enforced in that agency.

Subpart E—Exemptions

§ 105–69.500 Secretary of Defense.

(a) The Secretary of Defense may exempt, on a case-by-case basis, a covered Federal action from the prohibition whenever the Secretary determines, in writing, that such an exemption is in the national interest. The Secretary shall transmit a copy of each such written exemption to Congress immediately after making such a determination.

(b) The Department of Defense may issue supplemental regulations to implement paragraph (a) of this section.

Subpart F—Agency Reports

§ 105–69.600 Semi-annual compilation.

(a) The head of each agency shall collect and compile the disclosure reports (see appendix B) and, on May 31 and November 30 of each year, submit to the Secretary of the Senate and the Clerk of the House of Representatives a report containing a compilation of the information contained in the disclosure reports received during the six-month period ending on March 31 or September 30, respectively, of that year.

(b) The report, including the compilation, shall be available for public inspection 30 days after receipt of the report by the Secretary and the Clerk.

(c) Information that involves intelligence matters shall be reported only to the Select Committee on Intelligence of the Senate, the Permanent Select Committee on Intelligence of the House of Representatives, and the Committees on Appropriations of the Senate and the House of Representatives in accordance with procedures agreed to by such committees. Such information shall not be available for public inspection.

(d) Information that is classified under Executive Order 12356 or any successor order shall be reported only to the Committee on Foreign Relations of the Senate and the Committee on Foreign Affairs of the House of Representatives or the Committees on Armed Services of the Senate and the House of Representatives (whichever such committees have jurisdiction of matters involving such information) and to the Committees on Appropriations of the Senate and the House of Representatives in accordance with procedures agreed to by such committees. Such information shall not be available for public inspection.

(e) The first semi-annual compilation shall be submitted on May 31, 1990, and shall contain a compilation of the disclosure reports received from December 23, 1989 to March 31, 1990.

(f) Major agencies, designated by the Office of Management and Budget (OMB), are required to provide machine-readable compilations to the Secretary of the Senate and the Clerk of the House of Representatives no later than with the compilations due on May 31, 1991. OMB shall provide detailed specifications in a memorandum to these agencies.

(g) Non-major agencies are requested to provide machine-readable compilations to the Secretary of the Senate and the Clerk of the House of Representatives.

(h) Agencies shall keep the originals of all disclosure reports in the official files of the agency.

§ 105–69.605 Inspector General report.

(a) The Inspector General, or other official as specified in paragraph (b) of this section, of each agency shall prepare and submit to Congress each year, commencing with submission of the President's Budget in 1991, an evaluation of the compliance of that agency with, and the effectiveness of, the requirements herein. The evaluation may include any recommended changes that may be necessary to strengthen or improve the requirements.

(b) In the case of an agency that does not have an Inspector General, the agency official comparable to an Inspector General shall prepare and submit the annual report, or, if there is no such comparable official, the head of the agency shall prepare and submit the annual report.

(c) The annual report shall be submitted at the same time the agency submits its annual budget justifications to Congress.

(d) The annual report shall include the following: All alleged violations relating to the agency's covered Federal actions during the year covered by the report, the actions taken by the head of the agency in the year covered by the report with respect to those alleged violations and alleged violations in previous years, and the amounts of civil penalties imposed by the agency in the year covered by the report.

APPENDIX A TO PART 105–69—
CERTIFICATION REGARDING LOBBYING

Certification for Contracts, Grants, Loans, and Cooperative Agreements

The undersigned certifies, to the best of his or her knowledge and belief, that:

(1) No Federal appropriated funds have been paid or will be paid, by or on behalf of the undersigned, to any person for influencing or attempting to influence an officer or employee of an agency, a Member of Congress, an officer or employee of Congress, or an employee of a Member of Congress in connection with the awarding of any Federal contract, the making of any Federal grant, the making of any Federal loan, the entering into of any cooperative agreement, and the extension, continuation, renewal, amendment, or modification of any Federal contract, grant, loan, or cooperative agreement.

(2) If any funds other than Federal appropriated funds have been paid or will be paid to any person for influencing or attempting to influence an officer or employee of any agency, a Member of Congress, an officer or employee of Congress, or an employee of a Member of Congress in connection with this Federal contract, grant, loan, or cooperative agreement, the undersigned shall complete and submit Standard Form-LLL, ''Disclosure

Form to Report Lobbying," in accordance with its instructions.

(3) The undersigned shall require that the language of this certification be included in the award documents for all subawards at all tiers (including subcontracts, subgrants, and contracts under grants, loans, and cooperative agreements) and that all subrecipients shall certify and disclose accordingly.

This certification is a material representation of fact upon which reliance was placed when this transaction was made or entered into. Submission of this certification is a prerequisite for making or entering into this transaction imposed by section 1352, title 31, U.S. Code. Any person who fails to file the required certification shall be subject to a civil penalty of not less than $10,000 and not more than $100,000 for each such failure.

Statement for Loan Guarantees and Loan Insurance

The undersigned states, to the best of his or her knowledge and belief, that:

If any funds have been paid or will be paid to any person for influencing or attempting to influence an officer or employee of any agency, a Member of Congress, an officer or employee of Congress, or an employee of a Member of Congress in connection with this commitment providing for the United States to insure or guarantee a loan, the undersigned shall complete and submit Standard Form-LLL, "Disclosure Form to Report Lobbying," in accordance with its instructions.

Submission of this statement is a prerequisite for making or entering into this transaction imposed by section 1352, title 31, U.S. Code. Any person who fails to file the required statement shall be subject to a civil penalty of not less than $10,000 and not more than $100,000 for each such failure.

APPENDIX B TO PART 105–69—DISCLOSURE FORM TO REPORT LOBBYING

DISCLOSURE OF LOBBYING ACTIVITIES

Approved by OMB
0348-0046

Complete this form to disclose lobbying activities pursuant to 31 U.S.C. 1352
(See reverse for public burden disclosure.)

1. Type of Federal Action:	2. Status of Federal Action:	3. Report Type:
☐ a. contract b. grant c. cooperative agreement d. loan e. loan guarantee f. loan insurance	☐ a. bid/offer/application b. initial award c. post-award	☐ a. initial filing b. material change **For Material Change Only:** year _____ quarter _____ date of last report _____

4. Name and Address of Reporting Entity:	5. If Reporting Entity in No. 4 is Subawardee, Enter Name and Address of Prime:
☐ Prime ☐ Subawardee Tier _____ , if known: **Congressional District,** *if known:*	 **Congressional District,** *if known:*

6. Federal Department/Agency:	7. Federal Program Name/Description: CFDA Number, *if applicable:* _____

8. Federal Action Number, *if known:*	9. Award Amount, *if known:* $

10. a. Name and Address of Lobbying Entity *(if individual, last name, first name, MI):*	b. Individuals Performing Services *(including address if different from No. 10a)* *(last name, first name, MI):*

(attach Continuation Sheet(s) SF-LLL-A, if necessary)

11. Amount of Payment *(check all that apply):* $ _____ ☐ actual ☐ planned	13. Type of Payment *(check all that apply):* ☐ a. retainer ☐ b. one-time fee ☐ c. commission ☐ d. contingent fee ☐ e. deferred ☐ f. other; specify: _____
12. Form of Payment *(check all that apply):* ☐ a. cash ☐ b. in-kind; specify: nature _____ value _____	

14. Brief Description of Services Performed or to be Performed and Date(s) of Service, including officer(s), employee(s), or Member(s) contacted, for Payment Indicated in Item 11:

(attach Continuation Sheet(s) SF-LLL-A, if necessary)

15. Continuation Sheet(s) SF-LLL-A attached: ☐ Yes   ☐ No

16. Information requested through this form is authorized by title 31 U.S.C. section 1352. This disclosure of lobbying activities is a material representation of fact upon which reliance was placed by the tier above when this transaction was made or entered into. This disclosure is required pursuant to 31 U.S.C. 1352. This information will be reported to the Congress semi-annually and will be available for public inspection. Any person who fails to file the required disclosure shall be subject to a civil penalty of not less than $10,000 and not more than $100,000 for each such failure.	Signature: _____ Print Name: _____ Title: _____ Telephone No.: _____ Date: _____

Federal Use Only:	Authorized for Local Reproduction Standard Form - LLL

INSTRUCTIONS FOR COMPLETION OF SF-LLL, DISCLOSURE OF LOBBYING ACTIVITIES

This disclosure form shall be completed by the reporting entity, whether subawardee or prime Federal recipient, at the initiation or receipt of a covered Federal action, or a material change to a previous filing, pursuant to title 31 U.S.C. section 1352. The filing of a form is required for each payment or agreement to make payment to any lobbying entity for influencing or attempting to influence an officer or employee of any agency, a Member of Congress, an officer or employee of Congress, or an employee of a Member of Congress in connection with a covered Federal action. Use the SF-LLL-A Continuation Sheet for additional information if the space on the form is inadequate. Complete all items that apply for both the initial filing and material change report. Refer to the implementing guidance published by the Office of Management and Budget for additional information.

1. Identify the type of covered Federal action for which lobbying activity is and/or has been secured to influence the outcome of a covered Federal action.

2. Identify the status of the covered Federal action.

3. Identify the appropriate classification of this report. If this is a followup report caused by a material change to the information previously reported, enter the year and quarter in which the change occurred. Enter the date of the last previously submitted report by this reporting entity for this covered Federal action.

4. Enter the full name, address, city, state and zip code of the reporting entity. Include Congressional District, if known. Check the appropriate classification of the reporting entity that designates if it is, or expects to be, a prime or subaward recipient. Identify the tier of the subawardee, e.g., the first subawardee of the prime is the 1st tier. Subawards include but are not limited to subcontracts, subgrants and contract awards under grants.

5. If the organization filing the report in item 4 checks "Subawardee", then enter the full name, address, city, state and zip code of the prime Federal recipient. Include Congressional District, if known.

6. Enter the name of the Federal agency making the award or loan commitment. Include at least one organizational level below agency name, if known. For example, Department of Transportation, United States Coast Guard.

7. Enter the Federal program name or description for the covered Federal action (item 1). If known, enter the full Catalog of Federal Domestic Assistance (CFDA) number for grants, cooperative agreements, loans, and loan commitments.

8. Enter the most appropriate Federal identifying number available for the Federal action identified in item 1 (e.g., Request for Proposal (RFP) number; Invitation for Bid (IFB) number; grant announcement number; the contract, grant, or loan award number; the application/proposal control number assigned by the Federal agency). Include prefixes, e.g., "RFP-DE-90-001."

9. For a covered Federal action where there has been an award or loan commitment by the Federal agency, enter the Federal amount of the award/loan commitment for the prime entity identified in item 4 or 5.

10. (a) Enter the full name, address, city, state and zip code of the lobbying entity engaged by the reporting entity identified in item 4 to influence the covered Federal action.

    (b) Enter the full names of the individual(s) performing services, and include full address if different from 10 (a). Enter Last Name, First Name, and Middle Initial (MI).

11. Enter the amount of compensation paid or reasonably expected to be paid by the reporting entity (item 4) to the lobbying entity (item 10). Indicate whether the payment has been made (actual) or will be made (planned). Check all boxes that apply. If this is a material change report, enter the cumulative amount of payment made or planned to be made.

12. Check the appropriate box(es). Check all boxes that apply. If payment is made through an in-kind contribution, specify the nature and value of the in-kind payment.

13. Check the appropriate box(es). Check all boxes that apply. If other, specify nature.

14. Provide a specific and detailed description of the services that the lobbyist has performed, or will be expected to perform, and the date(s) of any services rendered. Include all preparatory and related activity, not just time spent in actual contact with Federal officials. Identify the Federal official(s) or employee(s) contacted or the officer(s), employee(s), or Member(s) of Congress that were contacted.

15. Check whether or not a SF-LLL-A Continuation Sheet(s) is attached.

16. The certifying official shall sign and date the form, print his/her name, title, and telephone number.

Public reporting burden for this collection of information is estimated to average 30 mintues per response, including time for reviewing instructions, searching existing data sources, gathering and maintaining the data needed, and completing and reviewing the collection of information. Send comments regarding the burden estimate or any other aspect of this collection of information, including suggestions for reducing this burden, to the Office of Management and Budget, Paperwork Reduction Project (0348-0046), Washington, D.C. 20503.

DISCLOSURE OF LOBBYING ACTIVITIES
CONTINUATION SHEET

Approved by OMB
0348-0046

Reporting Entity: _____ Page _____ of _____

Authorized for Local Reproduction
Standard Form - LLL-A

PART 105–70—IMPLEMENTATION OF THE PROGRAM FRAUD CIVIL REMEDIES ACT OF 1986

AUTHORITY: 40 U.S.C. 121(c); 31 U.S.C. 3809.

SOURCE: 52 FR 45188, Nov. 25, 1987, unless otherwise noted.

§ 105–70.000 Scope.

This part (a) establishes administrative procedures for imposing civil penalties and assessments against persons who make, submit, or present, or cause to be made, submitted, or presented, false, fictitious, or fraudulent claims or written statements to authorities or to their agents, and (b) specifies the hearing and appeal rights of persons subject to allegations of liability for such penalties and assessments.

§ 105–70.001 Basis.

This part implements the Program Fraud Civil Remedies Act of 1986, Pub. L. No. 99–509, 6101–6104, 100 Stat. 1874 (October 21, 1986), to be codified at 31 U.S.C. 3801–3812. 31 U.S.C. 3809 of the statute requires each authority head to promulgate regulations necessary to implement the provisions of the statute.

§ 105–70.002 Definitions.

The following shall have the meanings ascribed to them below unless the context clearly indicates otherwise:

(a) *ALJ* means an Administrative Law Judge in the Authority appointed pursuant to 5 U.S.C. 3105 or detailed to the Authority pursuant to 5 U.S.C. 3344.

(b) *Authority* means the General Services Administration.

(c) *Authority Head* means the Administrator or Deputy Administrator of General Services.

(d) *Benefit* means, in the context of statements, anything of value, including but not limited to any advantage, preference, privilege, license, permit, favorable decision, ruling, status, or loan guarantee.

(e) *Claim* means any request, demand or submission—

(1) Made to the Authority for property, services, or money (including money representing grants, loans, insurance, or benefits);

(2) Made to a recipient of property, services, or money from the Authority or to a party to a contract with the Authority—

(i) For property or services if the United States—

(A) Provided such property or services;

(B) Provided any portion of the funds for the purchase of such property or services; or

(C) Will reimburse such recipient or party for the purchase of such property or services; or

(ii) For the payment of money (including money representing grants, loans, insurance, or benefits) if the United States—

(A) Provided any portion of the money requested or demanded, or

(B) Will reimburse such recipient or party for any portion of the money paid on such request of demand; or

(3) Made to the Authority which has the effect of decreasing an obligation to pay or account for property, services, or money.

(f) *Complaint* means the administrative complaint served by the reviewing official on the defendant under § 105–70.007.

(g) *Defendant* means any person alleged in a complaint under § 105–70.007 to be liable for a civil penalty or assessment under § 105–70.003.

(h) *Individual* means a natural person.

(i) *Initial Decision* means the written decision of the ALJ required by § 105–70.010 or § 105–70.037, and includes a revised initial decision issued following a remand or a motion for reconsideration.

(j) *Investigating Official* means the Inspector General of the General Services Administration or an officer or employee of the Office of the Inspector General designated by the Inspector General and serving in a position for which the rate of basic pay is not less than the minimum rate of basic pay for grade GS–16 under the General Schedule.

(k) *Knows or has reason to know* means that a person, with respect to a claim or statement—

(1) Has actual knowledge that the claim or statement is false, fictitious, or fraudulent;

(2) Acts in deliberate ignorance of the truth or falsity of the claim or statement; or

(3) Acts in reckless disregard of the truth or falsity of the claim or statement.

(l) *Makes*, wherever it appears, shall include the terms presents, submits, and causes to be made, presented, or submitted. As the context requires, "making" or "made", shall likewise include the corresponding forms of such terms.

(m) *Person* means any individual, partnership, corporation, association, or private organization.

(n) *Representative* means an attorney who is a member in good standing of the bar of any State, Territory, or possession of the United States or of the District of Columbia or the Commonwealth of Puerto Rico. (An individual may appear *pro se;* a corporate officer or an owner may represent a business entity.)

(o) *Reviewing Official* means the General Counsel of the General Services Administration or his designee who is—

(1) Not subject to supervision by, or required to report to, the investigating official; and

(2) Not employed in the organizational unit of the authority in which the investigating official is employed; and

(3) Serving in a position for which the rate of basic pay is not less than the minimum rate of basic pay for grade GS–16 under the General Schedule.

(p) *Statement* means any representation, certification, affirmation, document, record, or accounting or bookkeeping entry made—

(1) With respect to a claim or to obtain the approval or payment of a claim (including relating to eligibility to make a claim); or

(2) With respect to (including relating to eligibility for)—

(i) A contract with, or a bid or proposal for a contract with; or

(ii) A grant, loan, or benefit from, the Authority, or any State, political subdivision of a State, or other party, if the United States Government provides any portion of the money or property under such contract or for such grant, loan, or benefit, or if the Government will reimburse such State, political subdivision, or party for any portion of the money or property under such contract or for such grant, loan, or benefit.

§ 105–70.003 Basis for civil penalties and assessments.

(a) *Claims.* (1) Any person who makes a claim that the person knows or has reason to know—

(i) Is false, fictitious, or fraudulent;

(ii) Includes or is supported by any written statement which asserts a material fact which is false, fictitious, or fraudulent;

(iii) Includes or is supported by any written statement that—

(A) Omits a material fact;

(B) Is false, fictitious, or fraudulent as a result of such omission; and

(C) Is a statement in which the person making such statement has a duty to include such material fact; or

(iv) Is for payment for the provision of property or services which the person has not provided as claimed,

shall be subject, in addition to any other remedy that may be prescribed by law, to a civil penalty of not more than $11,001 for each such claim.

(2) Each voucher, invoice, claim form, or other individual request or demand for property, services, or money constitutes a separate claim.

(3) A claim shall be considered made to the Authority, recipient, or party when such claim is actually made to an agent, fiscal intermediary, or other entity, including any State or political subdivision thereof, acting for or on behalf of the Authority, recipient, or party.

(4) Each claim for property, services, or money is subject to a civil penalty regardless of whether such property, services, or money is actually delivered or paid.

(5) If the Government has made any payment (including transferred property or provided services) on a claim, a person subject to a civil penalty under paragraph (a)(1) of this section shall also be subject to an assessment of not more than twice the amount of such claim or that portion thereof that is determined to be in violation of paragraph (a)(1) of this section. Such assessment shall be in lieu of damages sustained by the Government because of such claim.

(b) *Statements.* (1) Any person who makes a written statement that—

(i) The person knows or has reason to know—

(A) Asserts a material fact which is false, fictitious, or fraudulent; or

(B) Is false, fictitious, or fraudulent because it omits a material fact that the person making the statement has a duty to include in such statement; and

(ii) Contains or is accompanied by an express certification or affirmation of the truthfulness and accuracy of the contents of the statement, shall be subject, in addition to any other remedy that may be prescribed by law, to a civil penalty of not more than $11,001 for each such statement.

(2) Each written representation, certification, or affirmation constitutes a separate statement.

(3) A statement shall be considered made to the Authority when such statement is actually made to an agent, fiscal intermediary, or other entity, including any State or political subdivision thereof, acting for or on behalf of the Authority.

(c) No proof of specific intent to defraud is required to establish liability under this section.

(d) In any case in which it is determined that more than one person is liable for making a claim or statement under this section, each such person may be held liable for a civil penalty under this section.

(e) In any case in which it is determined that more than one person is liable for making a claim under this section on which the Government has made payment (including transferred property or provided services), an assessment may be imposed against any such person or jointly and severally against any combination of such persons.

[52 FR 45188, Nov. 25, 1987, as amended at 61 FR 67235, Dec. 20, 1996; 82 FR 40958, Aug. 29, 2017; 83 FR 1304, Jan. 11, 2018]

§ 105–70.004 Investigation.

(a) If an investigating official concludes that a subpoena pursuant to the authority conferred by 31 U.S.C. 3804(a) is warranted—

(1) The subpoena so issued shall notify the person to whom it is addressed of the authority under which the subpoena is issued and shall identify the records or documents sought;

(2) The investigating official may designate a person to act on his or her

behalf to receive the documents sought; and

(3) The person receiving such subpoena shall be required to tender to the investigating official or the person designated to receive the documents a certification that the documents sought have been produced, or that such documents are not available and the reasons therefor, or that such documents, suitably identified, have been withheld based upon the assertion of an identified privilege, or any combination of the foregoing.

(b) If the investigating official concludes that an action under the Program Fraud Civil Remedies Act may be warranted, the investigating official shall submit a report containing the findings and conclusions of such investigation to the reviewing official.

(c) Nothing in this section shall preclude or limit an investigating official's discretion to refer allegations directly to the Department of Justice for suit under the False Claims Act or other civil relief, or to defer or postpone a report or referral to the reviewing official to avoid interference with a criminal investigation or prosecution.

(d) Nothing in this section modifies any responsibility of an investigating official to report violations of criminal law to the Attorney General.

§ 105–70.005 Review by the reviewing official.

(a) If, based on the report of the investigating official under § 105–70.004(b), the reviewing official determines that there is adequate evidence to believe that a person is liable under § 105–70.003 of this part, the reviewing official shall transmit to the Attorney General a written notice of the reviewing official's intention to issue a complaint under § 105–70.007.

(b) Such notice shall include—

(1) A statement of the reviewing official's reasons for issuing a complaint;

(2) A statement specifying the evidence that supports the allegations of liability;

(3) A description of the claims or statements upon which the allegations of liability are based;

(4) An estimate of the amount of money or the value of property, services, or other benefits requested or demanded in violation of § 105–70.003 of this part;

(5) A statement of any exculpatory or mitigating circumstances that may relate to the claims or statements known by the reviewing official or the investigating official; and

(6) A statement that there is a reasonable prospect of collecting an appropriate amount of penalties and assessments.

§ 105–70.006 Prerequisites for issuing a complaint.

(a) The reviewing official may issue a complaint under § 105–70.007 only if—

(1) The Department of Justice approves the issuance of a complaint in a written statement described in 31 U.S.C. 3803(b)(1), and

(2) In the case of allegations of liability under § 105–70.003(a) with respect to a claim, the reviewing official determines that, with respect to such claim or a group of related claims submitted at the same time such claim is submitted (as defined in paragraph (b) of this section), the amount of money or the value of property or services demanded or requested in violation of § 105–70.003(a) does not exceed $150,000.

(b) For the purposes of this section, a related group of claims submitted at the same time shall include only those claims arising from the same transaction (e.g., grant, loan, application, or contract) that are submitted simultaneously as part of a single request, demand, or submission.

(c) Nothing in this section shall be construed to limit the reviewing official's authority to join in a single complaint against a person claims that are unrelated or were not submitted simultaneously, regardless of the amount of money or the value of property or services demanded or requested.

§ 105–70.007 Complaint.

(a) On or after the date the Department of Justice approves the issuance of a complaint in accordance with 31 U.S.C. 3803(b)(1), the reviewing official may serve a complaint on the defendant, as provided in § 105–70.008.

(b) The complaint shall state—

(1) The allegations of liability against the defendant, including the

statutory basis for liability, an identification of the claims or statements that are the basis for the alleged liability, and the reasons why liability allegedly arises from such claims or statements;

(2) The maximum amount of penalties and assessments for which the defendant may be held liable;

(3) Instructions for filing an answer including a specific statement of the defendant's right to request a hearing by filing an answer and to be represented by a representative; and

(4) That failure to file an answer within 30 days of service of the complaint will result in the imposition of the maximum amount of penalties and assessments without right to appeal, as provided in § 105–70.010.

(c) At the same time the reviewing official serves the complaint, he or she shall serve the defendant with a copy of these regulations.

§ 105–70.008 Service of complaint.

(a) Service of a complaint must be made by certified or registered mail or by delivery in any manner authorized by Rule 4(d) of the Federal Rules of Civil Procedure. Service is complete upon receipt.

(b) Proof of service, stating the name and address of the person on whom the complaint was served, and the manner and date of service, may be made by—

(1) Affidavit of the individual serving the complaint by delivery;

(2) A United States Postal Service return receipt card acknowledging receipt; or

(3) Written acknowledgment of receipt by the defendant or his representative.

§ 105–70.009 Answer.

(a) The defendant may request a hearing by filing an answer with the reviewing official within 30 days of service of the complaint. An answer shall be deemed to be a request for hearing.

(b) In the answer, the defendant—

(1) Shall admit or deny each of the allegations of liability made in the complaint;

(2) Shall state any defense on which the defendant intends to rely;

(3) May state any reasons why the defendant contends that the penalties and assessments should be less than the statutory maximum; and

(4) Shall state the name, address, and telephone number of the person authorized by the defendant to act as defendant's representative, if any.

(c) If the defendant is unable to file an answer meeting the requirements of paragraph (b) of this section within the time provided, the defendant may, before the expiration of 30 days from service of the complaint, file with the reviewing official a general answer denying liability and requesting a hearing, and a request for an extension of time within which to file an answer meeting the requirements of paragraph (b) of this section. The reviewing official shall file promptly with the ALJ the complaint, the general answer denying liability, and the request for an extension of time as provided in § 105–70.011. For good cause shown, the ALJ may grant the defendant up to 30 additional days within which to file an answer meeting the requirements of paragraph (b) of this section.

§ 105–70.010 Default upon failure to file an answer.

(a) If the defendant does not file an answer within the time prescribed in § 105–70.009(a), the reviewing official may refer the complaint to the ALJ.

(b) Upon the referral of the complaint, the ALJ shall promptly serve on the defendant in the manner prescribed in § 105–70.008, a notice that an initial decision will be issued under this section.

(c) The ALJ shall assume the facts alleged in the complaint to be true, and, if such facts establish liability under § 105–70.003, the ALJ shall issue an initial decision imposing the maximum amount of penalties and assessments allowed under the statute.

(d) Except as otherwise provided in this section, by failing to file a timely answer, the defendant waives any right to further review of the penalties and assessments imposed under paragraph (c) of this section, and the initial decision shall become final and binding upon the parties 30 days after it is issued.

(e) If, before such an initial decision becomes final, the defendant files a motion with the ALJ seeking to reopen on the grounds that extraordinary circumstances prevented the defendant from filing an answer, the initial decision shall be stayed pending the ALJ's decision on the motion.

(f) If, on such motion, the defendant can demonstrate extraordinary circumstances excusing the failure to file a timely answer, the ALJ shall withdraw the initial decision in paragraph (c) of this section, if such a decision has been issued, and shall grant the defendant an opportunity to answer the complaint.

(g) A decision of the ALJ denying a defendant's motion under paragraph (e) of this section is not subject to reconsideration under § 105–70.038.

(h) The defendant may appeal to the Authority Head the decision denying a motion to reopen by filing a notice of appeal with the Authority Head within 15 days after the ALJ denies the motion. The timely filing of a notice of appeal shall stay the initial decision until the Authority Head decides the issue.

(i) If the defendant files a timely notice of appeal with the Authority Head, the ALJ shall forward the record of the proceeding to the Authority Head.

(j) The Authority Head shall decide expeditiously whether extraordinary circumstances excuse the defendant's failure to file a timely answer based solely on the record before the ALJ.

(k) If the Authority Head decides that extraordinary circumstances excused the defendant's failure to file a timely answer, the Authority Head shall remand the case to the ALJ with instructions to grant the defendant an opportunity to answer.

(l) If the Authority Head decides that the defendant's failure to file a timely answer is not excused, the Authority Head shall reinstate the initial decision of the ALJ, which shall become final and binding upon the parties 30 days after the Authority Head issues such decision.

§ 105–70.011 Referral of complaint and answer to the ALJ.

Upon receipt of an answer, the reviewing official shall file the complaint and answer with the ALJ.

§ 105–70.012 Notice of hearing.

(a) When the ALJ receives the complaint and answer, the ALJ shall promptly serve a notice of hearing upon the defendant in the manner prescribed by § 105–70.008. At the same time, the ALJ shall send a copy of such notice to the representative for the Government.

(b) Such notice shall include—

(1) The tentative time and place, and the nature of the hearing;

(2) The legal authority and jurisdiction under which the hearing is to be held;

(3) The matters of fact and law to be asserted;

(4) A description of the procedures for the conduct of the hearing;

(5) The name, address, and telephone number of the representative of the Government and of the defendant, if any; and

(6) Such other matters as the ALJ deems appropriate.

§ 105–70.013 Parties to the hearing.

(a) The parties to the hearing shall be the defendant and the Authority.

(b) Pursuant to 31 U.S.C. 3730(c)(5), a private plaintiff under the False Claims Act may participate in these proceedings to the extent authorized by the provisions of that Act.

§ 105–70.014 Separation of functions.

(a) The investigating official, the reviewing official, and any employee or agent of the Authority who takes part in investigating, preparing, or presenting a particular case may not, in such case or a factually related case—

(1) Participate in the hearing as the ALJ;

(2) Participate or advise in the initial decision or the review of the initial decision by the Authority Head, except as a witness or a representative in public proceedings; or

(3) Make the collection of penalties and assessments under 31 U.S.C. 3806.

(b) The ALJ shall not be responsible to, or subject to the supervision or direction of the investigating official or the reviewing official.

(c) Except as provided in paragraph (a) of this section, the representative for the Government may be employed anywhere in the Authority, including in the offices of either the investigating official or the reviewing official.

§ 105–70.015 Ex parte contacts.

No party or person (except employees of the ALJ's office) shall communicate in any way with the ALJ on any matter at issue in a case, unless on notice and opportunity for all parties to participate. This provision does not prohibit a person or party from inquiring about the status of a case or asking routine questions concerning administrative functions or procedures.

§ 105–70.016 Disqualification of reviewing official or ALJ.

(a) A reviewing official or ALJ in a particular case may disqualify himself or herself at any time.

(b) A party may file with the ALJ a motion for disqualification of a reviewing official or an ALJ. Such motion shall be accompanied by an affidavit alleging personal bias or other reason for disqualification.

(c) Such motion and affidavit shall be filed promptly upon the party's discovery of reasons requiring disqualification, or such objections shall be deemed waived.

(d) Such affidavit shall state specific facts that support the party's belief that personal bias or other reason for disqualification exists and the time and circumstances of the party's discovery of such facts. It shall be accompanied by a certificate of the representative of record that it is made in good faith.

(e) Upon the filing of such a motion and affidavit, the ALJ shall proceed not further in the case until he or she resolves the matter of disqualification in accordance with paragraph (f) of this section.

(f)(1) If the ALJ determines that a reviewing official is disqualified, the ALJ shall dismiss the complaint without prejudice.

(2) If the ALJ disqualifies himself or herself, the case shall be reassigned promptly to another ALJ.

(3) If the ALJ denies a motion to disqualify, the authority head may determine the matter only as part of his or her review of the initial decision upon appeal, if any.

§ 105–70.017 Rights of parties.

Except as otherwise limited by this part, all parties may—

(a) Be accompanied, represented, and advised by a representative;

(b) Participate in any conference held by the ALJ;

(c) Conduct discovery;

(d) Agree to stipulations of fact or law, which shall be made part of the record;

(e) Present evidence relevant to the issues at the hearing;

(f) Present and cross-examine witnesses;

(g) Present oral argument at the hearing as permitted by the ALJ; and

(h) Submit written briefs and proposed findings of fact and conclusions of law after the hearing.

§ 105–70.018 Authority of the ALJ.

(a) The ALJ shall conduct a fair and impartial hearing, avoid delay, maintain order, and assure that a record of the proceeding is made.

(b) The ALJ has the authority to—

(1) Set and change the date, time, and place of the hearing upon reasonable notice to the parties;

(2) Continue or recess the hearing in whole or in part for a reasonable period of time;

(3) Hold conferences to identify or simplify the issues, or to consider other matters that may aid in the expeditious disposition of the proceeding;

(4) Administer oaths and affirmations;

(5) Issue subpoenas requiring the attendance of witnesses and the production of documents at depositions or at hearings;

(6) Rule on motions and other procedural matters;

(7) Regulate the scope and timing of discovery;

(8) Regulate the course of the hearing and the conduct of representatives and parties;

(9) Examine witnesses;

(10) Receive, rule on, exclude, or limit evidence;

(11) Upon motion of a party, take official notice of facts;

(12) Upon motion of a party, decide cases, in whole or in part, by summary judgment where there is no disputed issue of material fact;

(13) Conduct any conference, argument, or hearing on motions in person or by telephone; and

(14) Exercise such other authority as is necessary to carry out the responsibility of the ALJ under this part.

(c) The ALJ does not have the authority to find Federal statutes or regulations invalid.

§ 105–70.019 Prehearing conferences.

(a) The ALJ may schedule prehearing conferences as appropriate.

(b) Upon the motion of any party, the ALJ shall schedule at least one prehearing conference at a reasonable time in advance of the hearing.

(c) The ALJ may use prehearing conferences to discuss the following:

(1) Simplification of the issues;

(2) The necessity or desirability of amendments to the pleadings, including the need for a more definite statement;

(3) Stipulations and admissions of fact or as to the contents and authenticity of documents;

(4) Whether the parties can agree to submission of the case on a stipulated record;

(5) Whether a party chooses to waive appearance at an oral hearing and to submit only documentary evidence (subject to the objection of other parties) and written argument;

(6) Limitation of the number of witnesses;

(7) Scheduling dates for the exchange of witness lists and of proposed exhibits;

(8) Discovery;

(9) The time and place for the hearing; and

(10) Such other matters as may tend to expedite the fair and just disposition of the proceedings.

(d) The ALJ may issue an order containing all matters agreed upon by the parties or ordered by the ALJ at a prehearing conference.

§ 105–70.020 Disclosure of documents.

(a) Upon written request to the reviewing official, the defendant may review any relevant and material documents, transcripts, records, and other materials that relate to the allegations set out in the complaint and upon which the findings and conclusions of the investigating official under § 105–70.004(b) are based, unless such documents are subject to a privilege under Federal law. Upon payment of fees for duplication, the defendant may obtain copies of such documents.

(b) Upon written request to the reviewing official, the defendant also may obtain a copy of all exculpatory information in the possession of the reviewing official or investigating official relating to the allegations in the complaint, even if it is contained in a document that would otherwise be privileged. If the document would otherwise be privileged, only that portion containing exculpatory information must be disclosed.

(c) The notice sent to the Attorney General from the reviewing official as described in § 105–70.005 is not discoverable under any circumstances.

(d) The defendant may file a motion to compel disclosure of the documents subject to the provisions of this section. Such a motion may only be filed with the ALJ following the filing of an answer pursuant to § 105–70.009.

§ 105–70.021 Discovery.

(a) The following types of discovery are authorized:

(1) Requests for production of documents for inspection and copying;

(2) Requests for admissions of the authenticity of any relevant document or of the truth of any relevant fact;

(3) Written interrogatories; and

(4) Depositions.

(b) For the purpose of this section and §§ 105–70.022 and 105–70.023, the term "documents" includes information, documents, reports, answers, records, accounts, papers, and other data and documentary evidence. Nothing contained herein shall be interpreted to require the creation of a document.

(c) Unless mutually agreed to by the parties, discovery is available only as ordered by the ALJ. The ALJ shall regulate the timing of discovery.

(d) *Motions for discovery.* (1) A party seeking discovery may file a motion with the ALJ. Such a motion shall be accompanied by a copy of the requested discovery, or in the case of depositions, a summary of the scope of the proposed deposition.

(2) Within ten days of service, a party may file an opposition to the motion and/or a motion for protective order as provided in § 105–70.024.

(3) The ALJ may grant a motion for discovery only if he finds that the discovery sought—

(i) Is necessary for the expeditious, fair, and reasonable consideration of the issues;

(ii) Is not unduly costly or burdensome;

(iii) Will not unduly delay the proceeding; and

(iv) Does not seek privileged information.

(4) The burden of showing that discovery should be allowed is on the party seeking discovery;

(5) The ALJ may grant discovery subject to a protective order under § 105–70.024.

(e) *Depositions.* (1) If a motion for deposition is granted, the ALJ shall issue a subpoena for the deponent, which may require the deponent to produce documents. The subpoena shall specify the time and place at which the deposition will be held.

(2) The party seeking to depose shall serve the subpoena in the manner prescribed in § 105–70.008.

(3) The deponent may file with the ALJ a motion to quash the subpoena or a motion for a protective order within ten days of service.

(4) The party seeking to depose shall provide for the taking of a verbatim transcript of the deposition, which it shall make available to all other parties for inspection and copying.

(f) Each party shall bear its own costs of discovery.

§ 105–70.022 Exchange of witness lists, statements, and exhibits.

(a) At least 15 days before the hearing or at such other time as may be ordered by the ALJ, the parties shall exchange witness lists, copies of prior statements of proposed witnesses, and copies of proposed hearing exhibits, including copies of any written statements that the party intends to offer in lieu of live testimony in accordance with § 105–70.033(b). At the time the above documents are exchanged, any party that intends to rely on the transcript of deposition testimony in lieu of live testimony at the hearing, if permitted by the ALJ, shall provide each party with a copy of the specific pages of the transcript it intends to introduce into evidence.

(b) If a party objects, the ALJ shall not admit into evidence the testimony of any witness whose name does not appear on the witness list or any exhibit not provided to the opposing party as provided above unless the ALJ finds good cause for the failure or that there is no prejudice to the objecting party.

(c) Unless another party objects within the time set by the ALJ, documents exchanged in accordance with paragraph (a) of this section shall be deemed to be authentic for the purpose of admissibility at the hearing.

§ 105–70.023 Subpoena for attendance at hearing.

(a) A party wishing to procure the appearance and testimony of any individual at the hearing may request that the ALJ issue a subpoena.

(b) A subpoena requiring the attendance and testimony of an individual may also require the individual to produce documents at the hearing.

(c) A party seeking a subpoena shall file a written request therefor not less than 15 days before the date fixed for the hearing unless otherwise allowed by the ALJ for good cause shown. Such request shall specify any documents to be produced and shall designate the witnesses and describe the address and location thereof with sufficient particularity to permit such witnesses to be found.

(d) The subpoena shall specify the time and place at which the witness is to appear and any documents the witness is to produce.

(e) The party seeking the subpoena shall serve it in the manner prescribed in § 105–70.008. A subpoena on a party or upon an individual under the control of a party may be served by first class mail.

(f) A party or the individual to whom the subpoena is directed may file with the ALJ a motion to quash the subpoena within ten days after service or on or before the time specified in the subpoena for compliance if it is less than ten days after service.

§ 105–70.024 Protective order.

(a) A party or a prospective witness or deponent may file a motion for a protective order with respect to discovery sought by an opposing party or with respect to the hearing, seeking to limit the availability or disclosure of evidence.

(b) In issuing a protective order, the ALJ may make any order which justice requires to protect a party or person from annoyance, embarrassment, oppression, or undue burden or expense, including one or more of the following:

(1) That the discovery not be had;

(2) That the discovery may be had only on specified terms and conditions, including a designation of the time or place;

(3) That the discovery may be had only through a method of discovery other than that requested;

(4) That certain matters not be inquired into, or that the scope of discovery be limited to certain matters;

(5) That discovery be conducted with no one present except persons designated by the ALJ;

(6) That the contents of discovery or evidence be sealed;

(7) That a deposition after being sealed be opened only by order of the ALJ;

(8) That a trade secret or other confidential research, development, commercial information, or facts pertaining to any criminal investigation, proceeding, or other administrative investigation not be disclosed or be disclosed only in a designated way; or

(9) That the parties simultaneously file specified documents or information enclosed in sealed envelopes to be opened as directed by the ALJ.

§ 105–70.025 Fees.

The party requesting a subpoena shall pay the cost of the fees and mileage of any witness subpoenaed in the amounts that would be payable to a witness in a proceeding in United States District Court. A check for witness fees and mileage shall accompany the subpoena when served, except that when a subpoena is issued on behalf of the Authority, a check for witness fees and mileage need not accompany the subpoena.

§ 105–70.026 Form, filing and service of papers.

(a) *Form.* (1) Documents filed with the ALJ shall include an original and two copies.

(2) Every pleading and paper filed in the proceeding shall contain a caption setting forth the title of the action, the case number assigned by the ALJ, and a designation of the paper (e.g., motion to quash subpoena).

(3) Every pleading and paper shall be signed by, and shall contain the address and telephone number of the party or the person on whose behalf the paper was filed, or his or her representative.

(4) Papers are considered filed when they are mailed. Date of mailing may be established by a certificate from the party or its representative or by proof that the document was sent by certified or registered mail.

(b) *Service.* A party filing a document with the ALJ shall, at the time of filing, serve a copy of such document on every other party. Service upon any party of any document other than those required to be served as prescribed in § 105–70.008 shall be made by delivering a copy or by placing a copy of the document in the United States mail, postage prepaid and addressed to the party's last known address. When a party is represented by a representative, service shall be made upon such representative in lieu of the actual party.

(c) *Proof of service.* A certificate of the individual serving the document by personal delivery or by mail, setting forth the manner of service, shall be proof of service.

§ 105–70.027 Computation of time.

(a) In computing any period of time under this part or in an order issued thereunder, the time begins with the day following the act, event, or default, and includes the last day of the period, unless it is a Saturday, Sunday, or legal holiday observed by the Federal government, in which event it includes the next business day.

(b) When the period of time allowed is less than seven days, intermediate Saturdays, Sundays, and legal holidays observed by the Federal government shall be excluded from the computation.

(c) Where a document has been served or issued by placing it in the mail, an additional five days will be added to the time permitted for any response.

§ 105–70.028 Motions.

(a) Any application to the ALJ for an order or ruling shall be by motion. Motions shall state the relief sought, the authority relied upon, and the facts alleged, and shall be filed with the ALJ and served on all other parties.

(b) Except for motions made during a prehearing conference or at the hearing, all motions shall be in writing. The ALJ may require that oral motions be reduced to writing.

(c) Within 15 days after a written motion is served, or such other time as may be fixed by the ALJ, any party may file a response to such motion.

(d) The ALJ may not grant a written motion before the time for filing responses thereto has expired, except upon consent of the parties or following a hearing on the motion, but may overrule or deny such motion without awaiting a response.

(e) The ALJ shall make a reasonable effort to dispose of all outstanding motions prior to the beginning of the hearing.

§ 105–70.029 Sanctions.

(a) The ALJ may sanction a person, including any party or representative for—

(1) Failing to comply with an order, rule, or procedure governing the proceeding;

(2) Failing to prosecute or defend an action; or

(3) Engaging in other misconduct that interferes with the speedy, orderly, or fair conduct of the hearing.

(b) Any such sanction, including but not limited to those listed in paragraphs (c), (d), and (e) of this section, shall reasonably relate to the severity

and nature of the failure or misconduct.

(c) When a party fails to comply with an order, including an order for taking a deposition, the production of evidence within the party's control, or a request for admission, the ALJ may—

(1) Draw an inference in favor of the requesting party with regard to the information sought;

(2) In the case of requests for admission, deem each matter of which an admission is requested to be admitted;

(3) Prohibit the party failing to comply with such order from introducing evidence concerning, or otherwise relying upon, testimony relating to the information sought; and

(4) Strike any part of the pleadings or other submissions of the party failing to comply with such request.

(d) If a party fails to prosecute or defend an action under this part commenced by service of a notice of hearing, the ALJ may dismiss the action or may issue an initial decision imposing penalties and assessments.

(e) The ALJ may refuse to consider any motion, request, response, brief or other document which is not filed in a timely fashion.

§ 105–70.030 The hearing and burden of proof.

(a) The ALJ shall conduct a hearing on the record in order to determine whether the defendant is liable for a civil penalty or assessment under § 105–70.003 and, if so, the appropriate amount of any such civil penalty or assessment considering any aggravating or mitigating factors.

(b) The authority shall prove defendant's liability and any aggravating factors by a preponderance of the evidence.

(c) The defendant shall prove any affirmative defenses and any mitigating factors by a preponderance of the evidence.

(d) The hearing shall be open to the public unless otherwise ordered by the ALJ for good cause shown.

§ 105–70.031 Determining the amount of penalties and assessments.

In determining an appropriate amount of civil penalties and assessments, the ALJ and the Authority

Head, upon appeal, should evaluate any circumstances presented that mitigate or aggravate the violation and should articulate in their opinions the reasons that support the penalties and assessments they impose.

§ 105-70.032   Location of hearing.

(a) The hearing may be held—

(1) In any judicial district of the United States in which the defendant resides or transacts business;

(2) In any judicial district of the United States in which the claim or statement in issue was made; or

(3) In such other place as may be agreed upon by the defendant and the ALJ.

(b) Each party shall have the opportunity to present arguments with respect to the location of the hearing.

(c) The hearing shall be held at the place and at the time ordered by the ALJ.

§ 105-70.033   Witnesses.

(a) Except as provided in paragraph (b) of this section, testimony at the hearing shall be given orally by witnesses under oath or affirmation.

(b) At the discretion of the ALJ, testimony may be admitted in the form of a written statement or deposition. Any such written statement must be provided to all other parties along with the last known address of such witness, in a manner which allows sufficient time for other parties to subpoena such witness for cross-examination at the hearing. Prior written statements of witnesses proposed to testify at the hearing and deposition transcripts shall be exchanged as provided in § 105-70.022(a).

(c) The ALJ shall exercise reasonable control over the mode and order of interrogating witnesses and presenting evidence so as to—

(1) Make the interrogation and presentation effective for the ascertainment of the truth,

(2) Avoid needless consumption of time, and

(3) Protect witnesses from harassment or undue embarrassment.

(d) The ALJ shall permit the parties to conduct such cross-examination as may be required for a full and true disclosure of the facts.

(e) To the extent permitted by the ALJ, cross-examination on matters outside the scope of direct examination shall be conducted in the manner of direct examination and may proceed by leading questions only if the witness is a hostile witness, an adverse party, or a witness identified with an adverse party.

(f) Upon motion of any party, the ALJ shall order witnesses excluded so that they cannot hear the testimony of other witnesses. This rule does not authorize exclusion of—

(1) A party who is an individual;

(2) In the case of a party that is not an individual, an officer or employee of the party appearing for the entity *pro se* or designated by the party's representative; or

(3) An individual whose presence is shown by a party to be essential to the presentation of its case, including an individual employed by the Government engaged in assisting the representative for the Government.

§ 105-70.034   Evidence.

(a) The ALJ shall determine the admissibility of evidence.

(b) Except as provided in this part, the ALJ shall not be bound by the Federal Rules of Evidence. However, the ALJ may apply the Federal Rules of Evidence where appropriate, e.g., to exclude unreliable evidence.

(c) The ALJ shall exclude irrelevant and immaterial evidence.

(d) Although relevant, evidence may be excluded if its probative value is substantially outweighed by the danger of unfair prejudice, confusion of the issues, or by considerations of undue delay or needless presentation of cumulative evidence.

(e) Although relevant, evidence may be excluded if it is privileged under Federal law.

(f) Evidence concerning offers of compromise or settlement shall be inadmissible to the extent provided in Rule 408 of the Federal Rules of Evidence.

(g) The ALJ shall permit the parties to introduce rebuttal witnesses and evidence.

(h) All documents and other evidence offered or taken for the record shall be open to examination by all parties, unless otherwise ordered by the ALJ pursuant to § 105–70.024.

§ 105–70.035 The record.

(a) The hearing will be recorded and transcribed. Transcripts may be obtained following the hearing from the ALJ at a cost not to exceed the actual cost of duplication.

(b) The transcript of testimony, exhibits and other evidence admitted at the hearing, and all papers and requests filed in the proceeding constitute the record for the decision by the ALJ and the Authority Head.

(c) The record may be inspected and copied (upon payment of a reasonable fee) by anyone, unless otherwise ordered by the ALJ pursuant to § 105–70.024.

§ 105–70.036 Post-hearing briefs.

The ALJ may require the parties to file post-hearing briefs. In any event, any party may file a post-hearing brief. The ALJ shall fix the time for filing such briefs, not to exceed 60 days from the date the parties receive the transcript of the hearing or, if applicable, the stipulated record. Such briefs may be accompanied by proposed findings of fact and conclusions of law. The ALJ may permit the parties to file reply briefs.

§ 105–70.037 Initial decision.

(a) The ALJ shall issue an initial decision based only on the record, which shall contain findings of fact, conclusions of law, and the amount of any penalties and assessments imposed.

(b) The findings of fact shall include a finding on each of the following issues:

(1) Whether the claims or statements identified in the complaint, or any portions thereof, violate § 105–70.003.

(2) If the person is liable for penalties or assessments, the appropriate amount of any such penalties or assessments considering any mitigating or aggravating factors that he or she finds in the case.

(c) The ALJ shall promptly serve the initial decision on all parties within 90 days after the time for submission of post-hearing briefs and reply briefs (if permitted) has expired. The ALJ shall

at the same time serve all parties with a statement describing the right of any defendant determined to be liable for a civil penalty or assessment to file a motion for reconsideration with the ALJ or a notice of appeal with the Authority Head. If the ALJ fails to meet the deadline contained in this paragraph, he or she shall notify the parties of the reason for the delay and shall set a new deadline.

(d) Unless the initial decision of the ALJ is timely appealed to the Authority Head, or a motion for reconsideration of the initial decision is timely filed, the initial decision shall constitute the final decision of the Authority Head and shall be final and binding on the parties 30 days after it is issued by the ALJ.

§ 105–70.038 Reconsideration of initial decision.

(a) Except as provided in paragraph (d) of this section, any party may file a motion for reconsideration of the initial decision within 20 days of receipt of the initial decision. If service was made by mail, receipt will be presumed to be five days from the date of mailing in the absence of contrary proof.

(b) Every such motion must set forth the matters claimed to have been erroneously decided and the nature of the alleged errors. Such motion shall be accompanied by a supporting brief.

(c) Responses to such motions shall be allowed only upon request of the ALJ.

(d) No party may file a motion for reconsideration of an initial decision that has been revised in response to a previous motion for reconsideration.

(e) The ALJ may dispose of a motion for reconsideration by denying it or by issuing a revised initial decision.

(f) If the ALJ denies a motion for reconsideration, the initial decision shall constitute the final decision of the Authority Head and shall be final and binding on the parties 30 days after the ALJ denies the motion, unless the initial decision is timely appealed to the Authority Head in accordance with § 105–70.039.

(g) If the ALJ issues a revised initial decision, that decision shall constitute the final decision of the Authority Head and shall be final and binding on

573

the parties 30 days after it is issued, unless it is timely appealed to the Authority Head in accordance with § 105–70.039.

§ 105–70.039 Appeal to Authority Head.

(a) Any defendant who has filed a timely answer and who is determined in an initial decision to be liable for a civil penalty or assessment may appeal such decision to the Authority Head by filing a notice of appeal with the Authority Head in accordance with this section.

(b)(1) A notice of appeal may be filed at any time within 30 days after the ALJ issues an initial decision. However, if another party files a motion for reconsideration under § 105–70.038, consideration of the appeal shall be stayed automatically pending resolution of the motion for reconsideration.

(2) If a motion for reconsideration is timely filed, a notice of appeal may be filed within 30 days after the ALJ denies the motion or issues a revised initial decision, whichever applies.

(3) The Authority Head may extend the initial 30 day period for an additional 30 days if the defendant files with the Authority Head a request for an extension within the initial 30 day period and shows good cause.

(c) If the defendant files a timely notice of appeal with the Authority Head and the time for filing motions for reconsideration under § 105–70.038 has expired, the ALJ shall forward the record of the proceeding to the Authority Head.

(d) A notice of appeal shall be accompanied by a written brief specifying exceptions to the initial decision and reasons supporting the exceptions.

(e) The representative for the Authority may file a brief in opposition to exceptions within 30 days of receiving the notice of appeal and accompanying brief.

(f) There is no right to appear personally before the Authority Head.

(g) There is no right to appeal any interlocutory ruling by the ALJ.

(h) In reviewing the initial decision, the Authority Head shall not consider any objection that was not raised before the ALJ unless a demonstration is made of extraordinary circumstances causing the failure to raise the objection.

(i) If any party demonstrates to the satisfaction of the Authority Head that additional evidence not presented at such hearing is material and that there were reasonable grounds for the failure to present such evidence at such hearing, the Authority Head shall remand the matter to the ALJ for consideration of such additional evidence.

(j) The Authority Head may affirm, reduce, reverse, compromise, remand, or settle any penalty or assessment, determined by the ALJ in any initial decision.

(k) The Authority Head shall promptly serve each party to the appeal with a copy of the decision of the Authority Head and a statement describing the right of any person determined to be liable for a penalty or assessment to seek judicial review.

(l) Unless a petition for review is filed as provided in 31 U.S.C. 3805 after a defendant has exhausted all administrative remedies under this part and within 60 days after the date on which the Authority Head serves the defendant with a copy of the Authority Head's decision, a determination that a defendant is liable under § 105–70.003 is final and is not subject to judicial review.

§ 105–70.040 Stays ordered by the Department of Justice.

If at any time the Attorney General or an Assistant Attorney General designated by the Attorney General transmits to the Authority Head a written finding that continuation of the administrative process described in this part with respect to a claim or statement may adversely affect any pending or potential criminal or civil action related to such claim or statement, the Authority Head shall stay the process immediately. The Authority Head may order the process resumed only upon receipt of the written authorization of the Attorney General.

§ 105–70.041 Stay pending appeal.

(a) An initial decision is stayed automatically pending disposition of a motion for reconsideration or of an appeal to the Authority Head.

(b) No administrative stay is available following a final decision of the Authority Head.

§ 105–70.042 Judicial review.

Section 3805 of title 31, United States Code, authorizes judicial review by an appropriate United States District Court of a final decision of the Authority Head imposing penalties or assessments under this part and specifies the procedures for such review.

§ 105–70.043 Collection of civil penalties and assessments.

Sections 3806 and 3808(b) of title 31, United States Code, authorize action for collection of civil penalties and assessments imposed under this part and specify the procedures for such actions.

§ 105–70.044 Right to administrative offset.

The amount of any penalty or assessment which has become final, or for which a judgment has been entered under § 105–70.042 or § 105–70.043, or any amount agreed upon in a compromise or settlement under § 105–70.046, may be collected by administrative offset under 30 U.S.C. 3716, except that an administrative offset may not be made under this subsection against a refund of an overpayment of Federal taxes, then or later owing by the United States to the defendant.

§ 105–70.045 Deposit in Treasury of United States.

All amounts collected pursuant to this part shall be deposited as miscellaneous receipts in the Treasury of the United States, except as provided in 31 U.S.C. 3806(g).

§ 105–70.046 Compromise or settlement.

(a) Parties may make offers of compromise or settlement at any time.

(b) The reviewing official has the exclusive authority to compromise or settle a case under this part at any time after the date on which the reviewing official is permitted to issue a complaint and before the date on which the ALJ issues an initial decision.

(c) The Authority Head has exclusive authority to compromise or settle a case under this part at any time after the date on which the ALJ issues an initial decision, except during the pendency of any review under § 105–70.042 or during the pendency of any action to collect penalties and assessments under § 105–70.043.

(d) The Attorney General has exclusive authority to compromise or settle a case under this part during the pendency of any review under § 105–70.042 or of any action to recover penalties and assessments under 31 U.S.C. 3806.

(e) The investigating official may recommend settlement terms to the reviewing official, the Authority Head, or the Attorney General, as appropriate. The reviewing official may recommend settlement terms to the Authority Head, or the Attorney General, as appropriate.

(f) Any compromise or settlement must be in writing.

§ 105–70.047 Limitations.

(a) The Program Fraud Civil Remedies Act of 1986 provides that a hearing shall be commenced within 6 years after the date on which a claim or statement is made. 31 U.S.C. 3808(a). The statute also provides that the hearing is commenced by the mailing or delivery of the presiding officer's (ALJ's) notice. 31 U.S.C. 3803(d)(2)(B). Accordingly, the notice of hearing provided for in § 105–70.012 herein shall be served within 6 years after the date on which a claim or statement is made.

(b) If the defendant fails to file a timely answer, service of a notice under § 105–70.010(b) shall be deemed a notice of hearing for purposes of this section.

PART 105–71—UNIFORM ADMINISTRATIVE REQUIREMENTS FOR GRANTS AND COOPERATIVE AGREEMENTS WITH STATE AND LOCAL GOVERNMENTS

Subpart 105–71.1—General

AUTHORITY: Sec. 205(c), 63 Stat. 390, (40 U.S.C. 486(c)).

SOURCE: 58 FR 43270, Aug. 16, 1993, unless otherwise noted.

Subpart 105–71.1—General

§ 105–71.100 Purpose and scope of this part.

This part establishes uniform administrative rules for Federal grants and cooperative agreements and subawards to State, local and Indian tribal governments.

§ 105–71.101 Scope of §§ 105–71.100 through 105–71.105.

This section contains general rules pertaining to this part and procedures for control of exceptions from this subpart.

§ 105–71.102 Definitions.

As used in this part:

Accrued expenditures mean the charges incurred by the grantee during a given period requiring the provision of funds for: (1) Goods and other tangible property received; (2) services performed by employees, contractors, subgrantees, subcontractors, and other payees; and (3) other amounts becoming owed under programs for which no current services or performance is required, such as annuities, insurance claims, and other benefit payments.

Accrued income means the sum of: (1) Earnings during a given period from services performed by the grantee and goods and other tangible property delivered to purchasers, and (2) amounts becoming owed to the grantee for which no current services or performance is required by the grantee.

Acquisition cost of an item of purchased equipment means the net invoice unit price of the property including the cost of modifications, attachments, accessories, or auxiliary apparatus necessary to make the property usable for the purpose for which it was acquired. Other charges such as the cost of installation, transportation, taxes, duty or protective in-transit insurance, shall be included or excluded from the unit acquisition cost in accordance with the grantee's regular accounting practices.

Administrative requirements mean those matters common to grants in general, such as financial management, kinds and frequency of reports, and retention of records. These are distinguished from *programmatic* requirements, which concern matters that can be treated only on a program-by-program or grant-by-grant basis, such as kinds of activities that can be supported by grants under a particular program.

Awarding agency means (1) with respect to a grant, the Federal agency, and (2) with respect to a subgrant, the party that awarded the subgrant.

Cash contributions means the grantee's cash outlay, including the outlay of money contributed to the grantee or subgrantee by other public agencies and institutions, and private organizations and individuals. When authorized by Federal legislation, Federal funds received from other assistance agreements may be considered as grantee or subgrantee cash constributions.

Contract means (except as used in the definitions for *grant* and *subgrant* in this section and except where qualified by *Federal*) a procurement contract under a grant or subgrant, and means a procurement subcontract under a contract.

Cost sharing or matching means the value of the third party in-kind contributions and the portion of the costs of a federally assisted project or program not borne by the Federal Government.

Cost-type contract means a contract or subcontract under a grant in which the contractor or subcontractor is paid on the basis of the costs it incurs, with or without a fee.

Equipment means tangible, non-expendable, personal property having a useful life of more than one year and an acquisition cost of $5,000 or more per unit. A grantee may use its own definition of equipment provided that such definition would at least include all equipment defined above.

Expenditure report means: (1) For non-construction grants, the SF-269 "Financial Status Report" (or other equivalent report); (2) for construction grants, the SF-271 "Outlay Report and Request for Reimbursement" (or other equivalent report).

Federally recognized Indian tribal government means the governing body or a governmental agency of any Indian tribe, band, nation, or other organized group or community (including any Native village as defined in section 3 of the Alaska Native Claims Settlement Act, 85 Stat. 688) certified by the Secretary of the Interior as eligible for the special programs and services provided by him through the Bureau of Indian Affairs.

Government means a State or local government or a federally recognized Indian tribal government.

Grant means an award of financial assistance, including cooperative agreements, in the form of money, or property in lieu of money, by the Federal Government to an eligible grantee. The term does not include technical assistance which provides services instead of money, or other assistance in the form of revenue sharing, loans, loan guarantees, interest subsidies, insurance, or direct appropriations. Also, the term does not include assistance, such as a fellowship or other lump sum award, which the grantee is not required to account for.

Grantee means the government to which a grant is awarded and which is accountable for the use of the funds provided. The grantee is the entire legal entity even if only a particular component of the entity is designated in the grant award document.

Local government means a county, municipality, city, town, township, local public authority (including any public and Indian housing agency under the United States Housing Act of 1937) school district, special district, intrastate district, council of governments (whether or not incorporated as a nonprofit corporation under State law), any other regional or interstate government entity, or any agency or instrumentality of a local government.

Obligations means the amounts of orders placed, contracts and subgrants awarded, goods and services received, and similar transactions during a given period that will require payment by the grantee during the same or a future period.

OMB means the United States Office of Management and Budget.

Outlays (expenditures) mean charges made to the project or program. They may be reported on a cash or accrual basis. For reports prepared on a cash basis, outlays are the sum of actual cash disbursement for direct charges for goods and services, the amount of indirect expense incurred, the value of in-kind contributions applied, and the amount of cash advances and payments made to contractors and subgrantees. For reports prepared on an accrued expenditure basis, outlays are the sum of actual cash disbursements, the amount of indirect expense incurred, the value of in-kind contributions applied, and the new increase (or decrease) in the amounts owed by the grantee for goods and other property received, for services performed by employees, contractors, subgrantees, subcontractors, and other payees, and other amounts becoming owed under programs for which no current services or performance are required, such as annuities, insurance claims, and other benefit payments.

Percentage of completion method refers to a system under which payments are made for construction work according to the percentage of completion of work, rather than to the grantee's cost incurred.

Prior approval means documentation evidencing consent prior to incurring specific cost.

Real property means land, including land improvements, structures and appurtenances thereto, excluding movable machinery and equipment.

Share, when referring to the awarding agency's portion of real property, equipment or supplies, means the same percentage as the awarding agency's portion of the acquiring party's total costs under the grant to which the acquisition costs under the grant to which the acquisition cost of the property was charged. Only costs are to be counted—not the value of the third-party in-kind contributions.

State means any of the several States of the United States, the District of Columbia, the Commonwealth of Puerto Rico, any territory or possession of the United States, or any agency or instrumentality of a State exclusive of local governments. The term does not include any public and Indian housing under United States Housing Act of 1937.

Subgrant means an award of financial assistance in the form of money, or property in lieu of money, made under a grant by a grantee to an eligible subgrantee. The term includes financial assistance when provided by contractual legal agreement, but does not include procurement purchases, nor does it include any form of assistance which is excluded from the definition of grant in this part.

Subgrantee means the government or other legal entity to which a subgrant is awarded and which is accountable to the grantee for the use of the funds provided.

Supplies means all tangible personal property other than equipment as defined in this part.

Suspension means depending on the context, either (1) temporary withdrawal of the authority to obligate grant funds pending corrective action by the grantee or subgrantee or a decision to terminate the grant, or (2) an action taken by a suspending official in accordance with agency regulations implementing E.O. 12549 to immediately exclude a person from participating in grant transactions for a period, pending completion of an investigation and such legal or debarment proceedings as may ensue.

Termination means permanent withdrawal of the authority to obligate previously-awarded grant funds before that authority would otherwise expire. It also means the voluntary relinquishment of that authority by the grantee or subgrantee.

Termination does not include: (1) Withdrawal of funds awarded on the basis of the grantee's underestimate of the unobligated balance in a prior period; (2) Withdrawal of the unobligated balance as of the expiration of a grant; (3) Refusal to extend a grant or award additional funds, to make a competing or noncompeting continuation, renewal, extension, or supplemental award; or (4) voiding of a grant upon determination that the award was obtained fraudulently, or was otherwise illegal or invalid from inception.

Terms of a grant or subgrant mean all requirements of the grant or subgrant whether in statute, regulations, or the award document.

Third party in-kind contributions mean property or services which benefit a federally assisted project or program and which are contributed by non-Federal third parties without charge to the grantee, or a cost-type contractor under the grant agreement.

Unliquidated obligations for reports prepared on a cash basis mean the amount of obligations incurred by the grantee that has not been paid. For reports prepared on an accrued expenditure basis, they represent the amount of obligations incurred by the grantee for which an outlay has not been recorded.

Unobligated balance means the portion of the funds authorized by the Federal agency that has not been obligated by the grantee and is determined by deducting the cumulative obligations from the cumulative funds authorized.

§ 105-71.103 Applicability.

(a) *General.* Sections 105-71.100 through 105-71.152 of this subpart apply to all grants and subgrants to governments, except where inconsistent with Federal statutes or with regulations authorized in accordance with the exception provision of § 105-71.105 or:

(1) Grants and subgrants to State and local institutions of higher education or State and local hospitals.

(2) The block grants authorized by the Omnibus Budget Reconciliation Act of 1981 (Community Services; Preventive Health and Health Services; Alcohol, Drug Abuse, and Mental Health Services; Maternal and Child Health Services; Social Services; Low-Income Home Energy Assistance; States' Program of Community Development Block Grants for Small Cities; and Elementary and Secondary Education other than programs administered by the Secretary of Education under Title V, subtitle D, chapter 2, section 583—the Secretary's discretionary grant program) and Titles I-III of the Job Training Partnership Act of 1982 and under the Public Health Services Act (section 1921), Alcohol and Drug Abuse Treatment and Rehabilitation Block Grant and part C of Title V. Mental Health Service for the Homeless Block Grant).

(3) Entitlement grants to carry out the following programs of the Social Security Act:

(i) Aid to Needy Families with Dependent Children (Title IV-A of the Act, not including the Work Incentive Program (WIN) authorized by section 402(a)19(G); HHS grants for WIN are subject to this part);

(ii) Child Support Enforcement and Establishment of Paternity (Title IV-D of the Act);

(iii) Foster Care and Adoption Assistance (Title IV-E of the Act);

(iv) Aid to the Aged, Blind, Disabled (Titles I, X, XIV, and XVI-AABD of the Act); and

(v) Medical Assistance (Medicaid) (Title XIX of the Act) not including the State Medical Fraud Control program authorized by section 1903(a)(6)(B).

(4) Entitlement grants under the following programs of The National School Lunch Act:

(i) School Lunch (section 4 of the Act);

(ii) Commodity Assistance (section 6 of the Act);

(iii) Special Meal Assistance (section 11 of the Act);

(iv) Summer Food Service for Children (section 13 of the Act); and

(v) Child Care Food Program (section 17 of the Act).

(5) Entitlement grants under the following programs of The Child Nutrition Act of 1966:

(i) Special Milk (section 3 of the Act), and

(ii) School Breakfast (section 4 of the Act).

(6) Entitlement grants for State Administrative expenses under The Food Stamp Act of 1977 (section 16 of the Act).

(7) A grant for an experimental, pilot, or demonstration project that is also supported by a grant listed in paragraph (a)(3) of this section;

(8) Grant funds awarded under subsection 412(e) of the Immigration and Nationality Act (8 U.S.C. 1522(e)) and subsection 501(a) of the Refugee Education Assistance Act of 1980 (Pub. L. 96-422, 94 Stat. 1809), for cash assistance, medical assistance, and supplemental security income benefits to refugees and entrants and the administrative costs of providing the assistance and benefits;

(9) Grants to local education agencies under 20 U.S.C. 236 through 241-1(a),

and 242 through 244 (portions of the Impact Aid program), except for 20 U.S.C. 238(d)(2)(c) and 240(f) (Entitlement Increase for Handicapped Children); and

(10) Payments under the Veterans Administration's State Home Per Diem Program (38 U.S.C. 641(a)).

(b) *Entitlement programs.* Entitlement programs enumerated above in § 105–71.103(a)(3) through (8) are subject to Subpart—Entitlement.

§ 105–71.104   Effect on other issuances.

All other grants administration provisions of codified program regulations, program manuals, handbooks and other nonregulatory materials which are inconsistent with this part are superseded, except to the extent they are required by statute, or authorized in accordance with the exception provision in § 105–71.105.

§ 105–71.105   Additions and exceptions.

(a) For classes of grants and grantees subject to this part, Federal agencies may not impose additional administrative requirements except in codified regulations published in the FEDERAL REGISTER.

(b) Exceptions for classes of grants or grantees may be authorized only by OMB.

(c) Exceptions on a case-by-case basis and for subgrantees may be authorized by the affected Federal agencies.

Subpart 105–71.11—Pre-Award Requirements

§ 105–71.110   Forms for applying for grants.

(a) *Scope.* (1) This section prescribes forms and instructions to be used by governmental organizations (except hospitals and institutions of higher education operated by a government) in applying for grants. This section is not applicable, however, to formula grant programs which do not require applicants to apply for funds on a project basis.

(2) This section applies only to applications to Federal agencies for grants, and is not required to be applied by grantees in dealing with applicants for subgrants. However, grantees are encouraged to avoid more detailed or burdensome application requirements for subgrants.

(b) *Authorized forms and instructions for governmental organizations.* (1) In applying for grants, applicants shall only use standard application forms or those prescribed by the granting agency with the approval of OMB under the Paperwork Reduction Act of 1980.

(2) Applicants are not required to submit more than the original and two copies of preapplications or applications.

(3) Applicants must follow all applicable instructions that bear OMB clearance numbers. Federal agencies may specify and describe the programs, functions, or activities that will be used to plan, budget, and evaluate the work under a grant. Other supplementary instructions may be issued only with the approval of OMB to the extent required under the Paperwork Reduction Act of 1980. For any standard form, except the SF–424 facesheet, Federal agencies may shade out or instruct the applicant to disregard any line item that is not needed.

(4) When a grantee applies for additional funding (such as a continuation or supplemental award) or amends a previously submitted application, only the affected pages need be submitted. Previously submitted pages with information that is still current need not be resubmitted.

§ 105–71.111   State plans.

(a) *Scope.* The statutes for some programs require States to submit plans before receiving grants. Under regulations implementing Executive Order 12372, "Intergovernmental Review of Federal Programs," States are allowed to simplify, consolidate and substitute plans. This section contains additional provisions for plans that are subject to regulations implementing the Executive order.

(b) *Requirements.* A State need meet only Federal administrative or programmatic requirements for a plan that are in statutes or codified regulations.

(c) *Assurances.* In each plan the State will include an assurance that the State shall comply with all applicable Federal statutes and regulations in effect with respect to the periods for which it receives grant funding. For this assurance and other assurances required in the plan, the State may:

(1) Cite by number the statutory or regulatory provisions requiring the assurances and affirm that it gives the assurances required by those provisions,

(2) Repeat the assurance language in the statutes or regulations, or

(3) Develop its own language to the extent permitted by law.

(d) *Amendments.* A State will amend a plan whenever necessary to reflect:

(1) New or revised Federal statutes or regulations or

(2) A material change in any State law, organization, policy, or State agency operation.

The State will obtain approval for the amendment and its effective date but need submit for approval only the amended portions of the plan.

§ 105–71.112 Special grant or subgrant conditions for "high-risk" grantees.

(a) A grantee or subgrantee may be considered "high risk" if an awarding agency determines that a grantee or subgrantee:

(1) Has a history of unsatisfactory performance, or

(2) Is not financially stable, or

(3) Has a management system which does not meet the management standards set forth in this part, or

(4) Has not conformed to terms and conditions of previous awards, or

(5) Is otherwise not responsible, and if the awarding agency determines that an award will be made, special conditions and/or restrictions shall correspond to the high risk condition and shall be included in the award.

(b) Special conditions or restrictions may include:

(1) Payment on a reimbursement basis;

(2) Withholding authority to proceed to the next phase until receipt of evidence of acceptable performance within a given funding period;

(3) Requiring additional, more detailed financial reports;

(4) Additional project monitoring;

(5) Requiring the grantee or subgrantee to obtain technical or management assistance; or

(6) Establishing additional prior approvals.

(c) If an awarding agency decides to impose such conditions, the awarding official will notify the grantee or subgrantee as early as possible, in writing, of:

(1) The nature of the special conditions/restrictions;

(2) The reason(s) for imposing them;

(3) The corrective actions which must be taken before they will be removed and the time allowed for completing the corrective actions and

(4) The method of requesting reconsideration of the conditions/restrictions imposed.

Subpart 105–71.12—Post-Award Requirements/Financial Administration

§ 105–71.120 Standards for financial management systems.

(a) A State must expand and account for grant funds in accordance with State laws and procedures for expending and accounting for its own funds. Fiscal control and accounting procedures of the State, as well as its subgrantees and cost-type contractors, must be sufficient to—

(1) Permit preparation of reports required by this part and the statutes authorizing the grant, and

(2) Permit the tracing of funds to a level of expenditures adequate to establish that such funds have not been used in violation of the restrictions and prohibitions of applicable statutes.

(b) The financial management systems of other grantees and subgrantees must meet the following standards:

(1) *Financial reporting.* Accurate, current, and complete disclosure of the financial result of financially assisted activities must be made in accordance with the financial reporting requirements of the grant or subgrant.

(2) *Accounting records.* Grantees and subgrantees must maintain records which adequately identify the source and application of funds provided for financially-assisted activities. These records must contain information pertaining to grant or subgrant awards and authorizations, obligations, unobligated balances, assets, liabilities, outlays or expenditures, and income.

581

(3) *Internal control.* Effective control and accountability must be maintained for all grant and subgrant cash, real and personal property, and other assets. Grantees and subgrantees must adequately safeguard all such property and must assure that it is used solely for authorized purposes.

(4) *Budget control.* Actual expenditures or outlays must be compared with budgeted amounts for each grant or subgrant. Financial information must be related to performance or productivity data, including the development of unit cost information whenever appropriate or specifically required in the grant or subgrant agreement. If unit cost data are required, estimates based on available documentation will be accepted whenever possible.

(5) *Allowable cost.* Applicable OMB cost principles, agency program regulations, and the terms of grant and subgrant agreements will be followed in determining the reasonableness, allowability and allocability of costs.

(6) *Source documentation.* Accounting records must be supported by such source documentation as cancelled checks, paid bills, payrolls, time and attendance records, contract and subgrant award documents, etc.

(7) *Cash management.* Procedures for minimizing the time elapsing between the transfer of funds from the U.S. Treasury and disbursement by grantees and subgrantees must be followed whenever advance payment procedures are used. Grantees must establish reasonable procedures to ensure the receipt of reports on subgrantees' cash balances and cash disbursements in sufficient time to enable them to prepare complete and accurate cash transactions reports to the awarding agency. When advances are made by letter-of-credit or electronic transfer of funds methods, the grantee must make drawdowns as close as possible to the time of making disbursements. Grantees must monitor cash drawdowns by their subgrantees to assure that they conform substantially to the same standards of timing and amount as apply to advances to the grantees.

(c) An awarding agency may review the adequacy of the financial management system of any applicant for financial assistance as part of a preaward review or at any time subsequent to award.

§ 105–71.121 **Payment.**

(a) *Scope.* This section prescribes the basic standard and the methods under which a Federal agency will make payments to grantees, and grantees will make payments to subgrantees and contractors.

(b) *Basic standard.* Methods and procedures for payment shall minimize the time elapsing between the transfer of funds and disbursement by the grantee or subgrantee, in accordance with Treasury regulations at 31 CFR part 205.

(c) *Advances.* Grantees and subgrantees shall be paid in advance, provided they maintain or demonstrate the willingness and ability to maintain procedures to minimize the time elapsing between the transfer of the funds and their disbursement by the grantee or subgrantee.

(d) *Reimbursement.* Reimbursement shall be the preferred method when the requirements in paragraph (c) of this section are not met. Grantees and subgrantees may also be paid by reimbursement for any construction grant. Except as otherwise specified in regulation, Federal agencies shall not use the percentage of completion method to pay construction grants. The grantee or subgrantee may use that method to pay its construction contractor, and if it does, awarding agency's payments to the grantee or subgrantee will be based on the grantee's or subgrantee's actual rate of disbursement.

(e) *Working capital advances.* If a grantee cannot meet the criteria for advance payments described in paragraph (c) of this section, and the Federal agency has determined that reimbursement is not feasible because the grantee lacks sufficient working capital the awarding agency may provide cash or a working capital, advance basis. Under this procedure the awarding agency shall advance cash to the grantee to cover its estimated disbursement needs for an initial period generally geared to the grantee's disbursing cycle. Thereafter, the awarding agency shall reimburse the grantee for its actual cash disbursements. The working capital advance method of payment shall not be used by grantees or subgrantees if the reason for using such method is the unwillingness or inability of the grantee to provide timely advances to the subgrantee to meet the subgrantee's actual cash disbursements.

(f) *Effect of program income, refunds and audit recoveries on payment.* (1) Grantees and subgrantees shall disburse repayments to and interest earned on a revolving fund before requesting additional cash payments for the same activity.

(2) Except as provided in paragraph (f)(1) of this section, grantees and subgrantees shall disburse program income, rebates, refunds, contract settlements, audit recoveries and interest earned on such funds before requesting additional cash payments.

(g) *Withholding payments.* (1) Unless otherwise required by Federal statute, awarding agencies shall not withhold payments for proper charges incurred by grantees or subgrantees unless—

(i) The grantee or subgrantee has failed to comply with grant award conditions or

(ii) The grantee or subgrantee is indebted to the United States.

(2) Cash withheld for failure to comply with grant award conditions, but without suspension of the grant, shall be released to the grantee upon subsequent compliance. When a grant is suspended, payment adjustments will be made in accordance with § 105–71.143(c).

(3) A Federal agency shall not make payment to grantees for amounts that are withheld by grantees or subgrantees from payment to contractors to assure satisfactory completion of work. Payments shall be made by the Federal agency when the grantees or subgrantees actually disburse the withheld funds to the contractors or to escrow accounts established to assure satisfactory completion of work.

(h) *Cash depositories.* (1) Consistent with the national goal of expanding the opportunities for minority business enterprises, grantees and subgrantees are encouraged to use minority banks (a bank which is owned at least 50 percent by minority group members). A list of minority owned banks can be obtained from the Minority Business Develop-

ment Agency, Department of Commerce, Washington, DC 20230.

(2) A grantee or subgrantee shall maintain a separate bank account only when required by Federal-State agreement.

(i) *Interest earned on advances.* Except for interest earned on advances of funds exempt under the Intergovernmental Cooperation Act (31 U.S.C. 6501 *et seq.*) and the Indian Self-Determination Act (23 U.S.C. 450), grantees and subgrantees shall promptly, but at least quarterly, remit interest earned on advances to the Federal agency. The grantee or subgrantee may keep interest amounts up to $100 per year for administrative expenses.

§ 105–71.122   Allowable costs.

(a) *Limitation on use of funds.* Grant funds may be used only for:

(1) The allowable costs of the grantees, subgrantees and cost-type contractors, including allowable costs in the form of payments to fixed-price contractors; and

(2) Reasonable fees or profit to cost-type contractors but not any fee or profit (or other increment above allowable costs) to the grantee or subgrantee.

(b) *Applicable cost principles.* For each kind of organization, there is a set of Federal principles for determining allowable costs. Allowable costs will be determined in accordance with the cost principles applicable to the organization incurring the costs. The following chart lists the kinds of organizations and the applicable cost principles:

For the costs of a—	Use the principles in—
State, local or Indian tribal government..	OMB Circular A–87.
Private nonprofit organization other than an (1) institution of higher education, (2) hospital, or (3) organization named in OMB Circular A–122 as not subject to that circular.	OMB Circular A–122.
Educational institutions	OMB Circular A–21
For-profit organization other than a hospital and an organization named in OMB Circular A–122 as not subject to that circular.	48 CFR part 31, Contract Cost Principles and Procedures, or uniform cost accounting standards that comply with cost principles acceptable to the Federal agency.

§ 105–71.123 Period of availability of funds.

(a) *General.* Where a funding period is specified, a grantee may charge to the award only costs resulting from obligations of the funding period unless carryover or unobligated balances are permitted, in which case the carryover balances may be charged for costs resulting from obligations of the subsequent funding period.

(b) *Liquidation of obligations.* A grantee must liquidate all obligations incurred under the award not later than 90 days after the end of the funding period (or as specified in a program regulation) to coincide with the submission of the annual Financial Status Report (SF–269). The Federal agency may extend this deadline at the request of the grantee.

§ 105–71.124 Matching or cost sharing.

(a) *Basic rule: Costs and contributions acceptable.* With the qualifications and exceptions listed in paragraph (b) of this section, a matching or cost sharing requirement may be satisfied by either or both of the following:

(1) Allowable costs incurred by the grantee, subgrantee or cost-type contractor under the assistance agreement. This includes allowable costs borne by non-Federal grants or by other cash donations from non-Federal third parties.

(2) The value of third party in-kind contributions applicable to the period to which the cost sharing or matching requirements apply.

(b) *Qualifications and exceptions*—(1) *Costs borne by other Federal grant agreements.* Except as provided by Federal statute, a cost sharing or matching requirement may not be met by costs borne by another Federal grant. This prohibition does not apply to income earned by a grantee or subgrantee from a contract awarded under another Federal grant.

(2) *General revenue sharing.* For the purpose of this section, general revenue sharing funds distributed under 31 U.S.C. 6702 are not considered Federal grant funds.

(3) *Cost or contributions counted towards other Federal costs-sharing requirements.* Neither costs nor the values of third party in-kind contributions may count towards satisfying a cost sharing or matching requirement of a grant agreement if they have been or will be counted towards satisfying a cost sharing or matching requirement of another Federal grant agreement, a Federal procurement contract or any other award of Federal funds.

(4) *Costs financed by program income.* Costs financed by program income, as defined in § 105–71.125, shall not count towards satisfying a cost sharing or matching requirement unless they are expressly permitted in the terms of the assistance agreement. (This use of general program income is described in § 105–71.125(g).)

(5) *Services or property financed by income earned by contractors.* Contractors under a grant may earn income from the activities carried out under the contract in addition to the amounts earned from the party awarding the contract. No costs of services or property supported by this income may count toward satisfying a cost sharing or matching requirement unless other provisions of the grant agreement expressly permit this kind of income to be used to meet the requirement.

(6) *Records.* Costs and third party in-kind contributions counting towards satisfying a cost sharing or matching requirement must be verifiable from the records of grantees and subgrantee or cost-type contractors. These records must show how the value placed on third party in-kind contributions was derived. To the extent feasible, volunteer services will be supported by the same methods that the organization uses to support the allocability of regular personnel costs.

(7) *Special standards for third party in-kind contributions.* (i) Third party in-kind contributions count towards satisfying a cost sharing or matching requirement only where, if the party receiving the contributions were to pay for them, the payments would be allowable costs.

(ii) Some third party in-kind contributions are goods and services that, if the grantee, subgrantee, or contractor receiving the contribution had to pay for them, the payments would have been an indirect cost. Costs sharing or matching credit for such contributions shall be given only if the grantee, subgrantee, or contractor has established, along with its regular indirect cost rate, a special rate for allocating to individual projects or programs the value of contributions.

(iii) A third party in-kind contribution to a fixed price contract may count towards satisfying a cost sharing or matching requirement only if it results in:

(A) An increase in the services or property provided under the contract (without additional cost to the grantee or subgrantee) or

(B) A cost savings to the grantee or subgrantee.

(iv) The values placed on third party in-kind contributions for cost sharing or matching purposes will conform to the rules in the succeeding sections of this part. If a third party in-kind contribution is a type not treated in those sections, the value placed upon it shall be fair and reasonable.

(c) *Valuation of donated services*—(1) *Volunteer services.* Unpaid services provided to a grantee or subgrantee by individuals will be valued at rates consistent with those ordinarily paid for similar work in the grantee's or subgrantee's organization. If the grantee or subgrantee does not have employees performing similar work, the rates will be consistent with those ordinarily paid by other employers for similar work in the same labor market. In either case, a reasonable amount for fringe benefits may be included in the valuation.

(2) *Employees of other organizations.* When an employer other than a grantee, subgrantee, or cost-type contractor furnishes free of charge the services of an employee in the employee's normal line of work, the services will be valued at the employee's regular rate of pay exclusive of the employee's fringe benefits and overhead costs. If the services are in a different line of work, paragraph (c)(1) of this section applies.

(d) *Valuation of third party donated supplies and loaned equipment or space.* (1) If a third party donates supplies, the contribution will be valued at the market value of the supplies at the time of donation.

(2) If a third party donates the use of equipment or space in a building but retains title, the contribution will be valued at the fair rental rate of the equipment or space.

(e) *Valuation of third party donated equipment, buildings, and land.* If a third party donates equipment, buildings, or land, and the title passes to a grantee or subgrantee, the treatment of the donated property will depend upon the purpose of the grant or subgrant as follows:

(1) *Awards for capital expenditures.* If the purpose of the grant or subgrant is to assist the grantee or subgrantee in the acquisition of property, the market value of that property at the time of donation may be counted as cost sharing or matching.

(2) *Other awards.* If assisting in the acquisition of property is not the purpose of the grant or subgrant, paragraphs (e)(2)(i) and (ii) of this section apply.

(i) If approval is obtained from the awarding agency, the market value at the time of donation of the donated equipment or buildings and the fair rental rate of the donated land may be counted as cost sharing or matching. In the case of a subgrant, the terms of the grant agreement may require that the approval be obtained from the Federal agency as well as the grantee. In all cases, the approval may be given only if a purchase of the equipment or rental of the land would be approved as an allowable direct cost. If any part of the donated property was acquired with Federal funds, only the non-Federal share of the property may be counted as cost sharing or matching.

(ii) If approval is not obtained under paragraph (e)(2)(i) of this section, no amount may be counted for donated land, and only depreciation or use allowances may be counted for donated equipment and buildings. The depreciation or use allowances for this property are not treated as third party in-kind contributions. Instead, they are treated as costs incurred by the grantee or subgrantee. They are computed and allocated (usually as indirect costs) in accordance with the cost principles specified in § 105–71.122, in the same way as depreciation or use allowances for purchased equipment and buildings. The amount of depreciation or use allowances for donated equipment and buildings is based on the property's market value at the time it was donated.

(f) *Valuation of grantee or subgrantee donated real property for construction/acquisition.* If a grantee or subgrantee donates real property for a construction or facilities acquisition project, the current market value of that property may be counted as cost sharing or matching. If any part of the donated property was acquired with Federal funds, only the non-Federal share of the property may be counted as cost sharing or matching.

(g) *Appraisal of real property.* In some cases under paragraphs (d), (e) and (f) of this section, it will be necessary to establish the market value of land or a building or the fair rental rate of land or of space in the building. In these cases, the Federal agency may require the market value or fair rental value be set by an independent appraiser, and that the value or rate be certified by the grantee. This requirement will also be imposed by the grantee on subgrantees.

§ 105–71.125 Program income.

(a) *General.* Grantees are encouraged to earn income to defray program costs. Program income includes income from fees for services performed, from the use or rental of real or personal property acquired with grant funds, from the sale of commodities or items fabricated under a grant agreement, and from payments of principal and interest on loans made with grant funds. Except as otherwise provided in regulations of the Federal agency, program income does not include interest on grant funds, rebates, credits, discounts, refunds, etc. and interest earned on any of them.

(b) *Definition of program income.* Program income means gross income received by the grantee or subgrantee directly generated by a grant supported activity, or earned only as a result of the grant agreement during the grant period. "During the grant period" is the time between the effective date of the award and the ending date of the award reflected in the final financial report.

(c) *Cost of generating program income.* If authorized by Federal regulations or the grant agreement, costs incident to

the generation of program income may be deducted from gross income to determine program income.

(d) *Government revenues.* Taxes, special assessments, levies, fines, and other such revenues raised by a grantee or subgrantee are not program income unless the revenues are specifically identified in the grant agreement or Federal agency regulations as program income.

(e) *Royalties.* Income from royalties and license fees for copyrighted material, patents, and inventions developed by a grantee or subgrantee is program income only if the revenues are specifically identified in the grant agreement or Federal agency regulations as program income. (See § 105–71.134.)

(f) *Property.* Proceeds from the sale of real property or equipment will be handled in accordance with the requirements of §§ 105–71.131 and 105–71.132.

(g) *Use of program income.* Program income shall be deducted from outlays which may be both Federal and non-Federal as described below, unless the Federal agency regulations or the grant agreement specify another alternative (or a combination of the alternatives). In specifying alternatives, the Federal agency may distinguish between income earned by the grantee and income earned by subgrantees and between the sources, kinds, or amounts of income. When Federal agencies authorize the alternatives in paragraphs (g) (2) and (3) of this section, program income in excess of any limits stipulated shall also be deducted from outlays.

(1) *Deduction.* Ordinarily program income shall be deducted from total allowable costs to determine the net allowable costs. Program income shall be used for current costs unless the Federal agency authorizes otherwise. Program income which the grantee did not anticipate at the time of the award shall be used to reduce the Federal agency and grantee contributions rather than to increase the funds committed to the project.

(2) *Addition.* When authorized, program income may be added to the funds committed to the grant agreement by the Federal agency and the grantee. The program income shall be

used for the purposes and under the conditions of the grant agreement.

(3) *Cost sharing or matching.* When authorized, program income may be used to meet the cost sharing or matching requirement of the grant agreement. The amount of the Federal grant award remains the same.

(h) *Income after the award period.* There are no Federal requirements governing the disposition of program income earned after the end of the award period (i.e., until the ending date of the final financial report, see paragraph (a) of this section), unless the terms of the agreement or the Federal agency regulations provide otherwise.

§ 105–71.126 **Non-Federal audit.**

(a) *Basic rule.* Grantees and subgrantees are responsible for obtaining audits in accordance with the Single Audit Act Amendments of 1996 (31 U.S.C. 7501–7507) and revised OMB Circular A–133, "Audits of States, Local Governments, and Non-Profit Organizations." The audits shall be made by an independent auditor in accordance with generally accepted government auditing standards covering financial audits.

(b) *Subgrantees.* State or local governments, as those terms are defined for purposes of the Single Audit Act Amendments of 1996, that provide Federal awards to a subgrantee, which expends $300,000 or more (or other amount as specified by OMB) in Federal awards in a fiscal year, shall:

(1) Determine whether State or local subgrantees have met the audit requirements of the Act and whether subgrantees covered by OMB Circular A–110, "Uniform Administrative Requirements for Grants and Agreements with Institutions of Higher Education, Hospitals, and Other Non-Profit Organizations," have met the audit requirements of the Act. Commercial contractors (private for-profit and private and governmental organizations) providing goods and services to State and local governments are not required to have a single audit performed. State and local governments should use their own procedures to ensure that the contractor has complied with laws and regulations affecting the expenditure of Federal funds;

(2) Determine whether the subgrantee spent Federal assistance funds provided in accordance with applicable laws and regulations. This may be accomplished by reviewing an audit of the subgrantee made in accordance with the Act, Circular A–110, or through other means (e.g., program reviews) if the subgrantee has not had such an audit;

(3) Ensure the appropriate corrective action is taken within six months after receipt of the audit report in instance of noncompliance with Federal laws and regulations;

(4) Consider whether subgrantee audits necessitate adjustment of the grantee's own records; and

(5) Require each subgrantee to permit independent auditors to have access to the records and financial statements.

(c) *Auditor selection.* In arranging for audit services, § 105–71.136 shall be followed.

[58 FR 43270, Aug. 16, 1993, as amended at 62 FR 45939, 45944, Aug. 29, 1997]

Subpart 105–71.13—Post-Award Requirements/Changes, Property, and Subawards

§ 105–71.130 **Changes.**

(a) *General.* Grantees and subgrantees are permitted to rebudget within the approved direct cost budget to meet unanticipated requirements and may make limited program changes to the approved project. However, unless waived by the awarding agency, certain types of post-award changes in budgets and projects shall require the prior written approval of the awarding agency.

(b) *Relation to cost principles.* The applicable cost principles (see § 105–71.122) contain requirements for prior approval of certain types of costs. Except where waived, those requirements apply to all grants and subgrants even if paragraphs (c) through (f) of this section do not.

(c) *Budget changes*—(1) *Non-construction projects.* Except as stated in other regulations or an award document, grantees or subgrantees shall obtain the prior approval of the awarding agency whenever any of the following changes is anticipated under a non-construction award:

(i) Any revision which would result in the need for additional funding.

(ii) Unless waived by the awarding agency, cumulative transfers among direct cost categories, or, if applicable, among separately budgeted programs, projects, functions, or activities which exceed or are expected to exceed ten percent of the current total approved budget, whenever the awarding agency's share exceeds $100,000.

(iii) Transfer of funds allotted for training allowances (i.e., from direct payments to trainees to other expense categories).

(2) *Construction projects.* Grantees and subgrantees shall obtain prior written approval for any budget revision which would result in the need for additional funds.

(3) *Combined construction and non-construction projects.* When a grant or subgrant provides funding for both construction and non-construction activities, the grantee or subgrantee must obtain prior written approval from the awarding agency before making any fund or budget transfer from non-construction to construction or vice versa.

(d) *Programmatic changes.* Grantees or subgrantees must obtain the prior approval of the awarding agency whenever any of the following actions is anticipated:

(1) Any revision of the scope or objectives of the project (regardless of whether there is an associated budget revision requiring prior approval).

(2) Need to extend the period of availability of funds.

(3) Changes in key persons in cases where specified in an application or a grant award. In research projects, a change in the project director or principal investigator shall always require approval unless waived by the awarding agency.

(4) Under non-construction projects, contracting out, subgranting (if authorized by law) or otherwise obtaining the services of a third party to perform activities which are central to the purposes of the award. This approval requirement is in addition to the approval requirements of § 105–71.136 but does not apply to the procurement of equipment, supplies, and general support services.

(e) *Additional prior approval requirements.* The awarding agency may not require prior approval for any budget revision which is not described in paragraph (c) of this section.

(f) *Requesting prior approval.* (1) A request for prior approval of any budget revision will be in the same budget format the grantee used in its application and shall be accomplished by a narrative justification for the proposed revision.

(2) A request for a prior approval under the applicable Federal cost principles (see § 105–71.122) may be made by letter.

(3) A request by a subgrantee for prior approval will be addressed in writing to the grantee. The grantee will promptly review such request and shall approve or disapprove the request in writing. A grantee will not approve any budget or project revision which is inconsistent with the purpose or terms and conditions of the Federal grant to the grantee. If the revision, requested by the subgrantee would result in a change to the grantee's approved project which requires Federal prior approval, the grantee will obtain the Federal agency's approval before approving the subgrantee's request.

§ 105–71.131   **Real property.**

(a) *Title.* Subject to the obligations and conditions set forth in this section, title to real property acquired under a grant or subgrant will vest upon acquisition in the grantee or subgrantee respectively.

(b) *Use.* Except as otherwise provided by Federal statutes, real property will be used for the originally authorized purposes as long as needed for that purpose, and the grantee or subgrantee shall not dispose of or encumber its title or other interests.

(c) *Disposition.* When real property is no longer needed for the originally authorized purpose, the grantee or subgrantee will request disposition instructions from the awarding agency. The instructions will provide for one of the following alternatives.

(1) *Retention of title.* Retain title after compensating the awarding agency.

The amount paid to the awarding agency will be computed by applying the awarding agency's percentage of participation in the cost of the original purchase to the fair market value of the property. However, in those situations where a grantee or subgrantee is disposing of real property acquired with grant funds and acquiring replacement real property under the same program, the net proceeds from the disposition may be used as an offset to the cost of the replacement property.

(2) *Sale of property.* Sell the property and compensate the awarding agency. The amount due to the awarding agency will be calculated by applying the awarding agency's percentage of participation in the cost of the original purchase to the proceeds of the sale after deduction of any actual and reasonable selling and fixing-up expenses. If the grant is still active, the net proceeds from the sale may be offset against the original cost of the property. When a grantee or subgrantee is directed to sell property, sales procedures shall be followed that provide for competition to the extent practicable and result in the highest possible return.

(3) *Transfer of title.* Transfer title to the awarding agency or to a third-party designated/approved by the awarding agency. The grantee or subgrantee shall be paid an amount calculated by applying the grantee or subgrantee's percentage of participation in the purchase of the real property to the current fair market value of the property.

§ 105–71.132   Equipment.

(a) *Title.* Subject to the obligations and conditions set forth in this section, title to equipment acquired under a grant or subgrant will vest upon acquisition in the grantee or subgrantee respectively.

(b) *States.* A State will use, manage, and dispose of equipment acquired under a grant by the State in accordance with State laws and procedures. Other grantees and subgrantees will follow paragraphs (c) through (e) of this section.

(c) *Use.* (1) Equipment shall be used by the grantee or subgrantee in the program or project for which it was ac-

quired as long as needed, whether or not the project or program continues to be supported by Federal funds. When no longer needed for the original program or project, the equipment may be used in other activities currently or previously supported by a Federal agency.

(2) The grantee or subgrantee shall also make equipment available for use on other projects or programs currently or previously supported by the Federal Government, providing such use will not interfere with the work on the projects or program for which it was originally acquired. First preference for other use shall be given to other programs or projects supported by the awarding agency. User fees should be considered if appropriate.

(3) Notwithstanding the encouragement in § 105–71.125(a) to earn program income, the grantee or subgrantee must not use equipment acquired with grant funds to provide services for a fee to compete unfairly with private companies that provide equivalent services, unless specifically permitted or contemplated by Federal statute.

(4) When acquiring replacement equipment, the grantee or subgrantee may use the equipment to be replaced as a trade-in or sell the property and use the proceeds to offset the cost of the replacement property, subject to the approval of the awarding agency.

(d) *Management requirements.* Procedures for managing equipment (including replacement equipment), whether acquired in whole or in part with grant funds, until disposition takes place will, as a minimum, meet the following requirements:

(1) Property records must be maintained that include a description of the property, a serial number or other identification number, the source of property, who holds the title, the acquisition date, and cost of the property, percentage of Federal participation in the cost of the property, the location, use and condition of the property, and any ultimate disposition data including the data of disposal and sale price of the property.

(2) A physical inventory of the property must be taken and the results reconciled with the property records at least once every two years.

(3) A control system must be developed to ensure adequate safeguards to prevent loss, damage or theft of the property. Any loss, damage or theft shall be investigated.

(4) Adequate maintenance procedures must be developed to keep the property in good condition.

(5) If the grantee or subgrantee is authorized or required to sell the property, proper sales procedures must be established to ensure the highest possible return.

(e) *Disposition.* When original or replacement equipment acquired under a grant or subgrant is no longer needed for the original project or program or for other activities currently or previously supported by a Federal agency, disposition of the equipment will be made as follows:

(1) Items of equipment with a current per-unit fair market value of less than $5,000 may be retained, sold or otherwise disposed of with no further obligation to the awarding agency.

(2) Items of equipment with a current per unit fair market value in excess of $5,000 may be retained or sold and the awarding agency shall have a right to an amount calculated by multiplying the current market value or proceeds from sale by the awarding agency's share of the equipment.

(3) In cases where a grantee or subgrantee fails to take appropriate disposition actions, the awarding agency may direct the grantee or subgrantee to take excess and disposition actions.

(f) *Federal equipment.* In the event grantee or subgrantee is provided federally-owned equipment:

(1) Title will remain vested in the Federal Government.

(2) Grantees or subgrantees will manage the equipment in accordance with Federal agency rules and procedures, and submit an annual inventory listing.

(3) When the equipment is no longer needed, the grantee or subgrantee will request disposition instructions from the Federal agency.

(g) *Right to transfer title.* The Federal awarding agency may reserve the right to transfer title to the Federal Government or a third party named by the awarding agency when such a third party is otherwise eligible under existing statutes. Such transfers shall be subject to the following standards:

(1) The property shall be identified in the grant or otherwise made known to the grantee in writing.

(2) The Federal awarding agency shall issue disposition instruction within 120 calendar days after the end of the Federal support of the project for which it was acquired. If the Federal awarding agency fails to issue disposition instructions within the 120 calendar-day period the grantee shall follow § 105–71.132(e).

(3) When title to equipment is transferred, the grantee shall be paid an amount calculated by applying the percentage of participation in the purchase to the current fair market value of the property.

§ 105–71.133 Supplies.

(a) *Title.* Title to supplies acquired under a grant or subgrant will vest, upon acquisition, in the grantee or subgrantee respectively.

(b) *Disposition.* If there is a residual inventory of unused supplies exceeding $5,000 in total aggregate fair market value upon termination or completion of the award, and if the supplies are not needed for any other federally sponsored programs or projects, the grantee or subgrantee shall compensate the awarding agency for its share.

§ 105–71.134 Copyrights.

The Federal awarding agency reserves a royalty-free, nonexclusive, and irrevocable license to reproduce, publish or otherwise use, and to authorize others to use, for Federal Government purposes:

(a) The copyright in any work developed under a grant, subgrant, or contract under a grant or subgrant; and

(b) Any rights of copyright to which a grantee, subgrantee or a contractor purchases ownership with grant support.

§ 105–71.135 Subawards to debarred and suspended parties.

Grantees and subgrantees must not make any award or permit any award (subgrant or contract) at any tier to any party which is debarred or suspended or is otherwise excluded from or ineligible for participation in Federal assistance programs under Executive Order 12549, "Debarment and Suspension".

§ 105–71.136 **Procurement.**

(a) *States.* When procuring property and services under a grant, a State will allow the same policies and procedures it uses for procurements from its non-Federal funds. The State will ensure that every purchase order or other contract includes any clauses required by Federal statutes and executive orders and their implementing regulations. Other grantees and subgrantees will follow paragraphs (b) through (i) in this section.

(b) *Procurement standards.* (1) Grantees and subgrantees will use their own procurement procedures which reflect applicable State and local laws and regulations, provided that the procurements conform to applicable Federal law and the standards identified in this section.

(2) Grantees and subgrantees will maintain a contract administration system which ensures that contractors perform in accordance with the terms, conditions and specifications of their contracts or purchase orders.

(3) Grantees and subgrantees will maintain a written code of standards of conduct governing the performance of their employees engaged in the award and administration of contracts. No employee, officer or agent of the grantee or subgrantee shall participate in selection, or in the award or administration of a contract supported by Federal funds if a conflict of interest, real or apparent, would be involved. Such a conflict would arise when:

(i) The employee, officer or agent,

(ii) Any member of his immediate family,

(iii) His or her partner, or

(iv) An organization which employs, or is about to employ, any of the above, has a financial or other interest in the firm selected for award. The grantee's or subgrantee's officers, employees or agent will neither solicit nor accept gratuities, favors or anything of monetary value from contractors, potential contractors, or parties to subagreements. Grantees and subgrantees may set minimum rules where the fi-

nancial interest is not substantial or the gift is an unsolicited item of nominal intrinsic value. To the extent permitted by State or local law or regulations, such standards of conduct will provide for penalties, sanctions, or other disciplinary actions for violations of such standards by the grantee's officers, employees, or agents, or by contractors or their agents. The awarding agency may in regulation provide additional prohibitions relative to real, apparent, or potential conflicts of interest.

(4) Grantee and subgrantee procedures will provide for a review of proposed procurements to avoid purchase of unnecessary or duplicative items. Consideration should be given to consolidating or breaking out procurements to obtain a more economical purchase. Where appropriate, an analysis will be made of lease versus purchase alternatives, and any other appropriate analysis to determine the most economical approach.

(5) To foster greater economy and efficiency, grantees and subgrantees are encouraged to enter into State and local intergovernmental agreements for procurement or use of common goods and services.

(6) Grantees and subgrantees are encouraged to use Federal excess and surplus property in lieu of purchasing new equipment and property whenever such use is feasible and reduces project costs.

(7) Grantees and subgrantees are encouraged to use value engineering clauses in contracts for construction projects of sufficient size to offer reasonable opportunities for cost reductions. Value engineering is a systematic and creative analysis of each contract item or task to ensure that its essential function is provided at the overall lower cost.

(8) Grantees and subgrantees will make awards only to responsible contractors possessing the ability to perform successfully under the terms and conditions of a proposed procurement. Consideration will be given to such matters as contractor integrity, compliance with public policy, record of past performance, and financial and technical resources.

(9) Grantees and subgrantees will maintain records sufficient to detail the significant history of a procurement. These records will include, but are not necessarily limited to the following: Rationale for the method of procurement, selection of contract type, contractor selection or rejection, and the basis for the contract price.

(10) Grantees and subgrantees will use time and material type contracts only—

(i) After a determination that no other contract is suitable, and

(ii) If the contract includes a ceiling price that the contractor exceeds at its own risk.

(11) Grantees and subgrantees alone will be responsible, in accordance with good administrative practice and sound business judgment, for the settlement of all contractual and administrative issues arising out of procurements. These issues include, but are not limited to source evaluation, protests, disputes and claims. These standards do not relieve the grantee or subgrantee of any contractual responsibilities under its contracts. Federal agencies will not substitute their judgment for that of the grantee or subgrantee unless the matter is primarily a Federal concern. Violations of law will be referred to the local, State or Federal authority having proper jurisdiction.

(12) Grantees and subgrantees will have protest procedures to handle and resolve disputes relating to their procurements and shall in all instances disclose information regarding the protests to the awarding agency. A protestor must exhaust all administrative remedies with the grantee and subgrantee before pursuing a protest with the Federal agency. Reviews of protests by the Federal agency will be limited to:

(i) Violations of Federal law or regulations and the standards of this section (violations of State or local law will be under the jurisdiction of State or local authorities) and

(ii) Violations of grantee's or subgrantee's protest procedures for failure to review a complaint or protest. Protests received by the Federal agency other than those specified above will be referred to the grantee or subgrantee.

(c) *Competition.* (1) All procurement transactions will be conducted in a manner providing full and open competition consistent with the standards of § 105–71.136. Some of the situations considered to be restrictive of competition include but are not limited to:

(i) Placing unreasonable requirements on firms in order for them to qualify to do business,

(ii) Requiring unnecessary experience and excessive bonding,

(iii) Noncompetitive pricing practices between firms or between affiliated companies,

(iv) Noncompetitive awards to consultants that are on retainer contracts,

(v) Organizational conflicts of interest,

(vi) Specifying only a "brand name" product instead of allowing "an equal" product to be offered and describing the performance of other relevant requirements of the procurement, and

(vii) Any arbitrary action in the procurement process.

(2) Grantees and subgrantees will conduct procurements in a manner that prohibits the use of statutorily or administratively imposed in-State or local geographical preferences in the evaluation of bids or proposals, except in those cases where applicable Federal statutes expressly mandate or encourage geographic preference. Nothing in this section preempts State licensing laws. When contracting for architectural and engineering (A/E) services, geographic location may be a selection criteria provided its application leaves an appropriate number of qualified firms, given the nature and size of the project, to compete for the contract.

(3) Grantees will have written selection procedures for procurement transactions. These procedures will ensure that all solicitations:

(i) Incorporate a clear and accurate description of the technical requirements for the material, product, or service to be procured. Such description shall not, in competitive procurements, contain features which unduly restrict competition. The description may include a statement of the qualitative nature of the material, product or service to be procured, and when necessary, shall set forth those minimum essential characteristics and standards to which it must conform if it is to satisfy its intended use. Detailed product specifications should be avoided if at all possible. When it is impractical or uneconomical to make a clear and accurate description of the technical requirements, a "brand name or equal" description may be used as a means to define the performance or other salient requirements of a procurement. The specific features of the named brand which must be met by offerors shall be clearly stated; and

(ii) Identify all requirements which the offerors must fulfill and all other factors to be used in evaluating bids or proposals.

(4) Grantees and subgrantees will ensure that all prequalified lists of persons, firms, or products which are used in acquiring goods and services are current and include enough qualified sources to ensure maximum open and free competition. Also, grantees and subgrantees will not preclude potential bidders from qualifying during the solicitation period.

(d) *Methods of procurement to be followed*—(1) *Procurement by small purchase procedures.* Small purchase procedures are those relatively simple and informal procurement methods for securing services, supplies, or other property that do not cost more than the simplified acquisition threshold fixed at 41 U.S.C. 403(11) (currently set at $100,000). If small purchase procedures are used, price or rate quotations shall be obtained from an adequate number of qualified sources.

(2) Procurement by *sealed bids* (formal advertising). Bids are publicly solicited and a firm-fixed-price contract (lump sum or unit price) is awarded to the responsible bidder whose bid, conforming with all the material terms and conditions of the invitation for bids, is the lowest in price. The sealed bid method is the preferred method for procuring construction, if the conditions in §105–71.136(d)(2)(i) apply.

(i) In order for sealed bidding to be feasible, the following conditions should be present:

(A) A complete, adequate, and realistic specification or purchase description is available;

(B) Two or more responsible bidders are willing and able to compete effectively and for the business; and

(C) The procurement lends itself to a firm fixed price contract and the selection of the successful bidder can be made principally on the basis of price.

(ii) If sealed bids are used, the following requirements apply:

(A) The invitation for bids will be publicly advertised and bids shall be solicited from an adequate number of known suppliers, providing them sufficient time prior to the date set for opening the bids;

(B) The invitation for bids, which will include any specifications and pertinent attachments, shall define the items or services in order for the bidder to properly respond;

(C) All bids will be publicly opened at the time and place prescribed in the invitation for bids;

(D) A firm fixed-price contract award will be made in writing to the lowest responsive and responsible bidder. Where specified in bidding documents, factors such as discounts, transportation cost, and life cycle costs shall be considered in determining which bid is lowest. Payment discounts will only be used to determine the low bid when prior experience indicates that such discounts are usually taken advantage of; and

(E) Any or all bids may be rejected if there is a sound documented reason.

(3) Procurement by *competitive proposals*. The technique of competitive proposals is normally conducted with more than one source submitting an offer, and either a fixed-price or cost-reimbursement type contract is awarded. It is generally used when conditions are not appropriate for the use of sealed bids. If this method is used, the following requirements apply:

(i) Requests for proposals will be publicized and identify all evaluation factors and their relative importance. Any response to publicized requests for proposals shall be honored to the maximum extent practical;

(ii) Proposals will be solicited from an adequate number of qualified sources;

593

(iii) Grantees and subgrantees will have a method for conducting technical evaluations of the proposals received and for selecting awardees;

(iv) Awards will be made to the responsible firm whose proposal is most advantageous to the program, with price and other factors considered; and

(v) Grantees and subgrantees may use competitive proposal procedures for qualifications-based procurement of architectural/engineering (A/E) professional services whereby competitors' qualifications are evaluated and the most qualified competitor is selected, subject to negotiation of fair and reasonable compensation. The method, where price is not used as a selection factor, can only be used in procurement of A/E professional services. It cannot be used to purchase other types of services though A/E firms are a potential source to perform the proposed effort.

(4) Procurement by *noncompetitive proposals* is procurement through solicitation of a proposal from only one source, or after solicitation of a number of sources, competition is determined inadequate.

(i) Procurement by noncompetitive proposals may be used only when the award of a contract is infeasible under small purchase procedures, sealed bids or competitive proposals and one of the following circumstances applies:

(A) The item is available only from a single source;

(B) The public exigency or emergency for the requirement will not permit a delay resulting from competitive solicitation;

(C) The awarding agency authorizes noncompetitive proposals; or

(D) After solicitation of a number of sources, competition is determined inadequate.

(ii) Cost analysis, i.e., verifying the proposed cost data, the projections of the data, and the evaluation of the specific elements of costs and profits, is required.

(iii) Grantees and subgrantees may be required to submit the proposed procurement to the awarding agency for pre-award review in accordance with paragraph (g) of this section.

(e) *Contracting with small and minority firms, women's business enterprise and labor surplus area firms.* (1) The grantee and subgrantee will take all necessary affirmative steps to assure that minority firms, women's business enterprises, and labor surplus area firms are used when possible.

(2) Affirmative steps shall include:

(i) Placing qualified small and minority businesses and women's business enterprises on solicitation lists;

(ii) Assuring that small and minority businesses, and women's business enterprises are solicited whenever they are potential sources;

(iii) Dividing total requirements, when economically feasible, into smaller tasks or quantities to permit maximum participation by small and minority business, and women's business enterprises;

(iv) Establishing delivery schedules, where the requirement permits, which encourage participation by small and minority business, and women's business enterprises;

(v) Using the services and assistance of the Small Business Administration, and the Minority Business Development Agency of the Department of Commerce; and

(vi) Requiring the prime contractor, if subcontracts are to be let, to take the affirmative steps listed in paragraphs (e)(2) (i) through (v) of this section.

(f) *Contract cost and price.* (1) Grantees and subgrantees must perform a cost or price analysis in connection with every procurement action including contract modifications. The method and degree of analysis is dependent on the facts surrounding the particular procurement situation, but as a starting point, grantees must make independent estimates before receiving bids or proposals. A cost analysis must be performed when the offeror is required to submit the elements of his estimated cost, e.g., under professional, consulting, and architectural engineering services contracts. A cost analysis will be necessary when adequate price competition is lacking, and for sole source procurements, including contract modifications or change orders, unless price reasonableness can be established on the basis of a catalog or market price of a commercial product sold in substantial quantities to the general public or based on prices set by law or regulation. A price analysis will be used in all other instances to determine the reasonableness of the proposed contract price.

(2) Grantees and subgrantees will negotiate profit as a separate element of the price for each contract in which there is no price competition and in all cases where cost analysis is performed. To establish a fair and reasonable profit, consideration will be given to the complexity of the work to be performed, the risk borne by the contractor, the contractor's investment, the amount of subcontracting, the quality of its record of past performance, and industry profit rates in the surrounding geographical area for similar work.

(3) Costs or prices based on estimated costs for contracts under grants will be allowable only to the extent that costs incurred or cost estimates included in negotiated prices are consistent with Federal cost principles (see § 105–71.122). Grantees may reference their own cost principles that comply with the applicable Federal cost principles.

(4) The cost plus a percentage of cost and percentage of construction cost methods of contracting shall not be used.

(g) *Awarding agency review.* (1) Grantees and subgrantees must make available, upon request of the awarding agency, technical specifications on proposed procurements where the awarding agency believes such review is needed to ensure that the item and/or service specified is the one being proposed for purchase. This review generally will take place prior to the time the specification is incorporated into a solicitation document. However, if the grantee or subgrantee desires to have the review accomplished after a solicitation has been developed, the awarding agency may still review the specifications, with such review usually limited to the technical aspects of the proposed purchase.

(2) Grantees and subgrantees must on request make available for awarding agency pre-award review procurement documents, such as requests for proposals or invitations for bids, independent cost estimates, etc. when:

(i) A grantee's or subgrantee's procurement procedures or operation fails to comply with the procurement standards in this section; or

(ii) The procurement is expected to exceed the simplified acquisition threshold and is to be awarded without competition or only one bid or offer is received in response to a solicitation; or

(iii) The procurement, which is expected to exceed the simplified acquisition threshold, specifies a "brand name" product; or

(iv) The proposed award is more than the simplified acquisition threshold and is to be awarded to other than the apparent low bidder under a sealed bid procurement; or

(v) A proposed contract modification changes the scope of a contract or increases the contract amount by more than the simplified acquisition threshold.

(3) A grantee or subgrantee will be exempt from the pre-award review in paragraph (g)(2) of this section if the awarding agency determines that its procurement systems comply with the standards of this section.

(i) A grantee or subgrantee may request that its procurement system be reviewed by the awarding agency to determine whether its system meets these standards in order for its system to be certified. Generally, these reviews shall occur where there is a continuous high-dollar funding, and third-party contracts are awarded on a regular basis.

(ii) A grantee or subgrantee may self-certify its procurement system. Such self-certification shall not limit the awarding agency's right to survey the system. Under a self-certification procedure, awarding agencies may wish to rely on written assurances from the grantee or subgrantee that it is complying with these standards. A grantee or subgrantee will cite specific procedures, regulations, standards, etc., as being in compliance with these requirements and have its system available for review.

(h) *Bonding requirements.* For construction or facility improvement contracts or subcontracts exceeding the simplified acquisition threshold, the awarding agency may accept the bonding policy and requirements of the grantee or subgrantee provided the awarding agency has made a determination that the awarding agency's interest is adequately protected. If such a determination has not been made, the minimum requirements shall be as follows:

(1) *A bid guarantee from each bidder equivalent to five percent of the bid price.* The "bid guarantee" shall consist of a firm commitment such as a bid bond, certified check, or other negotiable instrument accompanying a bid as assurance that the bidder will, upon acceptance of his bid, execute such contractual documents as may be required within the time specified.

(2) *A performance bond on the part of the contractor for 100 percent of the contract price.* A "performance bond" is one executed in connection with a contract to secure fulfillment of all the contractor's obligations under such contract.

(3) *A payment bond on the part of the contractor for 100 percent of the contract price.* A "payment bond" is one executed in connection with a contract to assure payment as required by law of all persons supplying labor and material in the execution of the work provided for in the contract.

(i) *Contract provisions.* A grantee's and subgrantee's contracts must contain provisions in paragraph (i) of this section. Federal agencies are permitted to require changes, remedies, changed conditions, access and records retention, suspension of work, and other clauses approved by the Office of Federal Procurement Policy.

(1) Administrative, contractual, or legal remedies in instances where contractors violate or breach contract terms, and provide for such sanctions and penalties as may be appropriate. (Contracts more than the simplified acquisition threshold)

(2) Termination for cause and for convenience by the grantee or subgrantee including the manner by which it will be effected and the basis for settlement. (All contracts in excess of $10,000)

(3) Compliance with Executive Order 11246 of September 24, 1965, entitled "Equal Employment Opportunity," as amended by Executive Order 11375 of October 13, 1967, and as supplemented in Department of Labor regulations (41 CFR chapter 60). (All construction contracts awarded in excess of $10,000 by grantees and their contractors or subgrantees)

(4) Compliance with the Copeland "Anti-Kickback" Act (18 U.S.C. 874) as supplemented in Department of Labor regulations (29 CFR part 3). (All contracts and subgrants for construction or repair)

(5) Compliance with the Davis-Bacon Act (40 U.S.C. 276a to 276a–7) as supplemented by Department of Labor regulations (29 CFR part 5). (Construction contracts in excess of $2000 awarded by grantees and subgrantees when required by Federal grant program legislation)

(6) Compliance with sections 103 and 107 of the Contract Work Hours and Safety Standards Act (40 U.S.C. 327–330) as supplemented by Department of Labor regulations (29 CFR part 5). (Construction contracts awarded by grantees and subgrantees in excess of $2000, and in excess of $2500 for other contracts which involve the employment of mechanics or laborers)

(7) Notice of awarding agency requirements and regulations pertaining to reporting.

(8) Notice of awarding agency requirements and regulations pertaining to patent rights with respect to any discovery or invention which arises or is developed in the course of or under such contract.

(9) Awarding agency requirements and regulations pertaining to copyrights and rights in data.

(10) Access by the grantee, the subgrantee, the Federal grantor agency, the Comptroller General of the United States, or any of their duly authorized representatives to any books, documents, papers, and records of the contractor which are directly pertinent to that specific contract for the purpose of making audit, examination, excerpts, and transcriptions.

(11) Retention of all required records for three years after grantees or subgrantees make final payments and all other pending matters are closed.

(12) Compliance with all applicable standards, orders, or requirements

issued under section 306 of the Clean Air Act (42 U.S.C. 1857(h)), section 508 of the Clean Water Act (33 U.S.C. 1368), Executive Order 11738, and Environmental Protection Agency regulations (40 CFR part 15). (Contracts, subcontracts, and subgrants of amounts in excess of $100,000)

(13) Mandatory standards and policies relating to energy efficiency which are contained in the state energy conservation plan issued in compliance with the Energy Policy and Conservation Act (Pub. L. 94–163, 89 Stat. 871).

[58 FR 43270, Aug. 16, 1993, as amended at 60 FR 19639, 19644, Apr. 19, 1995]

§ 105–71.137 Subgrants.

(a) *States.* States shall follow State law and procedures when awarding and administering subgrants (whether on a cost reimbursement or fixed amount basis) of financial assistance to local and Indian tribal governments. States shall:

(1) Ensure that every subgrant includes any clauses required by Federal statute and executive orders and their implementing regulations;

(2) Ensure that subgrantees are aware of requirements imposed upon them by Federal statute and regulation;

(3) Ensure that a provision for compliance with § 105–71.142 is placed in every cost reimbursement subgrant; and

(4) Conform any advances of grant funds to subgrantees substantially to the same standards of timing and amount that apply to cash advances by Federal agencies.

(b) *All other grantees.* All other grantees shall follow the provisions of this part which are applicable to awarding agencies when awarding and administering subgrants (whether on a cost reimbursement or fixed amount basis) of financial assistance to local and Indian tribal governments. Grantees shall:

(1) Ensure that every subgrant includes a provision for compliance with this part;

(2) Ensure that every subgrant includes any clauses required by Federal statute and executive orders and their implementing regulations; and

(3) Ensure that subgrantees are aware of requirements imposed upon them by Federal statutes and regulations.

(c) *Exceptions.* By their own terms, certain provisions of this part do not apply to the award and administration of subgrants:

(1) Section 105–71.110;

(2) Section 105–71.111;

(3) The letter-of-credit procedures specified in Treasury Regulations at 31 CFR part 205, cited in § 105–71.121; and

(4) Section 105–71.150.

Subpart 105–71.14—Post-Award Requirements/Reports, Records, Retention, and Enforcement

§ 105–71.140 Monitoring and reporting program performance.

(a) *Monitoring by grantees.* Grantees are responsible for managing the day-to-day operations of grant and subgrant supported activities. Grantees must monitor grant and subgrant supported activities to assure compliance with applicable Federal requirements and that performance goals are being achieved. Grantee monitoring must cover each program, function or activity.

(b) *Non-construction performance reports.* The Federal agency may, if it decides that performance information available from subsequent applications contains sufficient information to meet its programmatic needs, require the grantee to submit a performance report only upon expiration or termination of grant support. Unless waived by the Federal agency this report will be due on the same date as the final Financial Status Report.

(1) Grantees shall submit annual performance reports unless the awarding agency requires quarterly or semiannual reports. However, performance reports will not be required more frequently than quarterly. Annual reports shall be due 90 days after the grant year, quarterly or semiannual reports shall be due 30 days after the reporting period. The final performance report will be due 90 days after the expiration or termination of grant support. If a justified request is submitted by a

grantee, the Federal agency may extend the due date for any performance report. Additionally, requirements for unnecessary performance reports may be waived by the Federal agency.

(2) Performance reports will contain, for each grant, brief information on the following:

(i) A comparison of actual accomplishments to the objectives established for the period. Where the output of the project can be quantified, a computation of the cost per unit of output may be required if that information will be useful.

(ii) The reasons for slippage if established objectives were not met.

(iii) Additional pertinent information including, when appropriate, analysis and explanation of cost overruns or high unit costs.

(3) Grantees will not be required to submit more than the original and two copies of performance reports.

(4) Grantees will adhere to the standards in this section in prescribing performance reporting requirements for subgrantees.

(c) *Construction performance reports.* For the most part, on-site technical inspections and certified percentage-of-completion data are relied on heavily by Federal agencies to monitor progress under construction grants and subgrants. The Federal agency will require additional formal performance reports only when considered necessary, and never more frequently than quarterly.

(d) *Significant developments.* Events may occur between the scheduled performance reporting dates which have significant impact upon the grant or subgrant supported activity. In such cases, the grantee must inform the Federal agency as soon as the following types of conditions become known:

(1) Problems, delays, or adverse conditions which will materially impair the ability to meet the objective of the award. This disclosure must include a statement of the action taken, or contemplated, and any assistance needed to resolve the situation.

(2) Favorable developments which enable meeting time schedules and objectives sooner or at less cost than anticipated or producing more beneficial results than originally planned.

(e) Federal agencies may make site visits as warranted by program needs.

(f) *Waivers, extensions.* (1) Federal agencies may waive any performance report required by this part if not needed.

(2) The grantee may waive any performance report from a subgrantee when not needed. The grantee may exend the due date for any performance report from a subgrantee if the grantee will still be able to meet its performance reporting obligations to the Federal agency.

§ 105–71.141 **Financial reporting.**

(a) *General.* (1) Except as provided in paragraphs (a) (2) and (5) of this section, grantees will use only the forms specified in paragraphs (a) through (e) of this section, and such supplementary or other forms as may from time to time be authorized by OMB, for:

(i) Submitting financial reports to Federal agencies, or

(ii) Requesting advances or reimbursements when letters of credit are not used.

(2) Grantees need not apply the forms prescribed in this section in dealing with their subgrantees. However, grantees shall not impose more burdensome requirements on subgrantees.

(3) Grantees shall follow all applicable standard and supplemental Federal agency instructions approved by OMB to the extent required under the Paperwork Reduction Act of 1980 for use in connection with forms specified in paragraphs (b) through (e) of this section. Federal agencies may issue substantive supplementary instructions only with the approval of OMB. Federal agencies may shade out or instruct the grantee to disregard any line item that the Federal agency finds unnecessary for its decision making purposes.

(4) Grantees will not be required to submit more than the original and two copies of forms required under this part.

(5) Federal agencies may provide computer outputs to grantees to expedite or contribute to the accuracy of reporting. Federal agencies may accept the required information from grantees in machine usable format or computer printouts instead of prescribed forms.

(6) Federal agencies may waive any report required by this section if not needed.

(7) Federal agencies may extend the due date on any financial report upon receiving a justified request from a grantee.

(b) *Financial Status Report*—(1) *Form.* Grantees will use Standard Form 269 or 269A, Financial Status Report, to report the status of funds for all non-construction grants and for construction grants when required in accordance with paragraph (e)(2)(iii) of this section.

(2) *Accounting basis.* Each grantee will report program outlays and program income on a cash or accrual basis as prescribed by the awarding agency. If the Federal agency requires accrual information and the grantee's accounting records are not normally kept on the accrual basis, the grantee shall not be required to convert its accounting system but shall develop such accrual information through an analysis of the documentation on hand.

(3) *Frequency.* The Federal agency may prescribe the frequency of the report for each project or program. However, the report will not be required more frequently than quarterly. If the Federal agency does not specify the frequency of the report, it will be submitted annually. A final report will be required upon expiration or termination of grant support.

(4) *Due date.* When reports are required on a quarterly or semiannual basis, they will be due 30 days after the reporting period. When required on an annual basis, they will be due 90 days after the grant year. Final reports will be due 90 days after the expiration or termination of grant support.

(c) *Federal Cash Transactions Report*—(1) *Form.* (i) For grants paid by letter of credit, Treasury check advances or electronic transfer of funds, the grantee will submit the Standard Form 272, Federal Cash Transactions Report, and when necessary, its continuation sheet, Standard Form 272A, unless the terms of the award exempt the grantee from this requirement.

(ii) These reports will be used by the Federal agency to monitor cash advanced to grantees and to obtain disbursement or outlay information for

each grant from grantees. The format of the report may be adapted as appropriated when reporting is to be accomplished with the assistance of automatic data processing equipment provided that the information to be submitted is not changed in substance.

(2) *Forecasts of Federal cash requirements.* Forecasts of Federal cash requirements may be required in the "Remarks" section of the report.

(3) *Cash in hands of subgrantees.* When considered necessary and feasible by the Federal agency, grantees may be required to report the amount of cash advances in excess of three days' needs in the hands of their subgrantees or contractors and to provide short narrative explanations of actions taken by the grantee to reduce the excess balances.

(4) *Frequency and due date.* Grantees must submit the report no later than 15 working days following the end of each quarter. However, where an advance either by letter of credit or electronic transfer of funds is authorized at an annualized rate of one million dollars or more, the Federal agency may require the report to be submitted within 15 working days following the end of each month.

(d) *Request for advance or reimbursement*—(1) *Advance payments.* Requests for Treasury check advance payments will be submitted on Standard Form 270, Request for Advance or Reimbursement. (This form will not be used for drawdowns under a letter of credit, electronic funds transfer or when Treasury check advance payments are made to the grantee automatically on a predetermined basis.)

(2) *Reimbursements.* Requests for reimbursement under non-construction grants will also be submitted on Standard Form 270. (For reimbursement requests under construction grants, see paragraph (e)(1) of this section.)

(3) The frequency for submitting payment requests is treated in §105–71.141(b)(3).

(e) *Outlay report and request for reimbursement for construction programs.* (1) Grants that support construction activities paid by reimbursement method.

(i) Requests for reimbursement under construction grants will be submitted on Standard Form 271, Outlay Report and Request for Reimbursement for Construction Programs. Federal agencies may, however, prescribe the Request for Advance or Reimbursement form, specified in § 105–71.141(d), instead of this form.

(ii) The frequency for submitting reimbursement requests is treated in § 105–71.141(b)(3).

(2) Grants that support construction activities paid by letter of credit, electronic funds transfer or Treasury check advance.

(i) When a construction grant is paid by letter of credit, electronic funds transfer or Treasury check advances, the grantee will report its outlays to the Federal agency using Standard Form 271, Outlay Report and Request for Reimbursement for Construction Programs. The Federal agency will provide any necessary special instruction. However, frequency and due date shall be governed by § 105–71.141(b) (3) and (4).

(ii) When a construction grant is paid by Treasury check advances based on periodic requests from the grantee, the advances will be requested on the form specified in § 105–71.141(d).

(iii) The Federal agency may substitute the Financial Status Report specified in § 105–71.141(b) for the Outlay Report and Request for Reimbursement for Construction Programs.

(3) *Accounting basis.* The accounting basis for the Outlay Report and Request for Reimbursement for Construction Programs shall be governed by § 105–71.141(b)(2).

§ 105–71.142 Retention and access requirements for records.

(a) *Applicability.* (1) This section applies to all financial and programmatic records, supporting documents, statistical records, and other records of grantees of subgrantees or subgrantees which are:

(i) Required to be maintained by the terms of this part, program regulations or the grant agreement, or

(ii) Otherwise reasonably considered as pertinent to program regulations or the grant agreement.

(2) This section does not apply to records maintained by contractors or subcontractors. For a requirement to place a provision concerning records in

certain kinds of contracts, see § 105–71.136(i)(10).

(b) *Length of retention period.* (1) Except as otherwise provided, records must be retained for three years from the starting date specified in paragraph (c) of this section.

(2) If any litigation, claim, negotiation, audit or other action involving the records has been started before the expiration of the 3-year period, the records must be retained until completion of the action and resolution of all issues which arise from it, or until the end of the regular 3-year period, whichever is later.

(3) To avoid duplicate recordkeeping, awarding agencies may make special arrangements with grantees and subgrantees to retain any records which are continuously needed for joint use. The awarding agency will request transfer of records to its custody when it determines that the records possess long-term retention value. When the records are transferred to or maintained by the Federal agency, the 3-year retention requirement is not applicable to the grantee or subgrantee.

(c) *Starting date of retention period*—(1) *General.* When grant support is continued or renewed at annual or other intervals, the retention period for the records of each funding period starts on the day the grantee or subgrantee submits to the awarding agency its single or last expenditure report for that period. However, if grant support is continued or renewed quarterly, the retention period for each year's records starts on the day the grantee submits its expenditure report for the last quarter of the Federal fiscal year. In all other cases, the retention period starts on the day the grantee submits its final expenditure report. If an expenditure report has been waived, the retention period starts on the day the report would have been due.

(2) *Real property and equipment records.* The retention period for real property and equipment records starts from the date of the disposition or replacement or transfer at the direction of the awarding agency.

(3) *Records for income transactions after grant or subgrant support.* In some cases grantees must report income after the period of grant support.

Where there is such a requirement, the retention period for the records pertaining to the earning of the income starts from the end of the grantee's fiscal year in which the income is earned.

(4) *Indirect cost rate proposals, cost allocations plans, etc.* This paragraph applies to the following types of documents, and their supporting records: indirect cost rate computations or proposals, cost allocation plans, and any similar accounting computations of the rates at which a particular group of costs is chargeable (such as computer usage chargeback rates or composite fringe benefit rates).

(i) *If submitted for negotiation.* If the proposal, plan, or other computation is required to be submitted to the Federal Government (or to the grantee) to form the basis for negotiation of the rate, then the 3-year retention period for its supporting records starts from the date of such submission.

(ii) *If not submitted for negotiation.* If the proposal, plan, or other computations are not required to be submitted to the Federal Government (or to the grantee) for negotiation purposes, then the 3-year retention period for the proposal plan, or computation and its supporting records starts from end of the fiscal year (or other accounting period) covered by the proposal, plan, or other computation.

(d) *Substitution of microfilm.* Copies made by microfilming, photocopying, or similar methods may be substituted for the original records.

(e) *Access to records*—(1) *Records of grantees and subgrantees.* The awarding agency and the Comptroller General of the United States, or any of their authorized representatives, shall have the right of access to any pertinent books, documents, papers, or other records of grantees and subgrantees which are pertinent to the grant, in order to make audits, examinations, excerpts, and transcripts.

(2) *Expiration of right of access.* The rights of access in this section must not be limited to the required retention period but shall last as long as the records are retained.

(f) *Restrictions on public access.* The Federal Freedom of Information Act (5 U.S.C. 552) does not apply to records. Unless required by Federal, State, or local law, grantees and subgrantees are not required to permit public access to their records.

§ 105-71.143 **Enforcement.**

(a) *Remedies for noncompliance.* If a grantee or subgrantee materially fails to comply with any term of an award, whether stated in a Federal statute or regulation, an assurance, in a State plan or application, a notice of award, or elsewhere, the awarding agency may take one or more of the following actions, as appropriate in the circumstances:

(1) Temporary withhold cash payments pending correction of the deficiency by the grantee or subgrantee or more severe enforcement action by the awarding agency,

(2) Disallow (that is, deny both use of funds and matching credit for) all or part of the cost of the activity or action not in compliance,

(3) Wholly or partly suspend or terminate the current award for the grantee's or subgrantee's program,

(4) Without further awards for the program, or

(5) Take other remedies that may be legally available,

(b) *Hearings, appeals.* In taking an enforcement action, the awarding agency will provide the grantee or subgrantee an opportunity for such hearing, appeal, or other administrative proceeding to which the grantee or subgrantee is entitled under any statute or regulation applicable to the action involved.

(c) *Effects of suspension and termination.* Costs of grantee or subgrantee resulting from obligations incurred by the grantee or subgrantee during a suspension or after termination of an award are not allowable unless the awarding agency expressly authorizes them in the notice of suspension or termination or subsequently. Other grantee or subgrantee costs during suspension or after termination which are necessary and not reasonably avoidable are allowable if:

(1) The costs result from obligations which were properly incurred by the grantee or subgrantee before the effective date of suspension or termination, are not in anticipation of it, and, in

case of a termination, are noncancellable, and,

(2) The cost would be allowable if the award were not suspended or expired normally at the end of the funding period in which the termination takes effect.

(d) *Relationship to debarment and suspension.* The enforcement remedies identified in this section, including suspension and termination, do not preclude grantee or subgrantee from being subject to "Debarment and Suspension" under E.O. 12549 (see § 105–71.135).

§ 105–71.144 Termination for convenience.

Except as provided in § 105–71.143 awards may be terminated in whole or in part only as follows:

(a) By the awarding agency with the consent of the grantee or subgrantee in which case the two parties shall agree upon the termination conditions, including the effective date and in the case of partial termination, the portion to be terminated, or

(b) By the grantee or subgrantee upon written notification to the awarding agency, setting forth the reasons for such termination, the effective date, and in the case of partial termination, the portion to be terminated. However, if, in the case of a partial termination, the awarding agency determines that the remaining portion of the award will not accomplish the purposes for which the award was made, the awarding agency may terminate the award in its entirety under either § 105–71.143 or paragraph (a) of this section.

Subpart 105–71.15—After-the-Grant Requirements

§ 105–71.150 Closeout.

(a) *General.* The Federal agency will close out the award when it determines that all applicable administrative actions and all required work of the grant has been completed.

(b) *Reports.* Within 90 days after the expiration or termination of the grant, the grantee must submit all financial, performance, and other reports required as a condition of the grant. Upon request by the grantee, Federal

agencies may extend this timeframe. These may include but are not limited to:

(1) Final performance or progress report.

(2) Financial Status Report (SF 269) or Outlay Report and Request for Reimbursement for Construction Programs (SF–271) (as applicable).

(3) Final request for payment (SF–270) (if applicable).

(4) Invention disclosure (if applicable).

(5) Federally-owned property report: In accordance with § 105–71.132(f), a grantee must submit an inventory of all federally owned property (as distinct from property acquired with grant funds) for which it is accountable and request disposition instructions from the Federal agency of property no longer needed.

(c) *Cost adjustment.* The Federal agency will, within 90 days after receipt of reports in paragraph (b) of this section, make upward or downward adjustments to the allowable costs.

(d) *Cash adjustments.* (1) The Federal agency will make prompt payment to the grantee for allowable reimbursable costs.

(2) The grantee must immediately refund to the Federal agency any balance of unobligated (unencumbered) cash advanced that is not authorized to be retained for use on other grants.

§ 105–71.151 Later disallowances and adjustments.

The closeout of a grant does not affect:

(a) The Federal agency's right to disallow costs and recover funds on the basis of a later audit or other review;

(b) The grantee's obligation to return any funds due as a result of later refunds, corrections, or other transactions;

(c) Records retention as required in § 105–71.142;

(d) Property management requirements in §§ 105–71.131 and 105–71.132; and

(e) Audit requirements in § 105–71.126.

§ 105–71.152 Collection of amounts due.

(a) Any funds paid to a grantee in excess of the amount to which the grantee is finally determined to be entitled under the terms of the award constitute a debt to the Federal Government. If not paid within a reasonable period after demand, the Federal agency may reduce the debt by:

(1) Making an administrative offset against other requests for reimbursement,

(2) Withholding advance payments otherwise due to the grantee, or

(3) Other action permitted by law.

(b) Except where otherwise provided by statutes or regulations, the Federal agency will charge interest on an overdue debt in accordance with the Federal Claims Collection Standards (4 CFR Ch. II). The date from which interest is computed is not extended by litigation or the filing of any form of appeal.

Subpart 105-71.16—Entitlements [Reserved]

PART 105-72—UNIFORM ADMINISTRATIVE REQUIREMENTS FOR GRANTS AND AGREEMENTS WITH INSTITUTIONS OF HIGHER EDUCATION, HOSPITALS, AND OTHER NON-PROFIT ORGANIZATIONS

Subpart 105-72.1—General

AUTHORITY: 40 U.S.C. 486(c).

SOURCE: 59 FR 47268, Sept. 15, 1994, unless otherwise noted.

Subpart 105–72.1—General

§ 105–72.100 Purpose.

This part establishes uniform administrative requirements for Federal grants and agreements awarded to institutions of higher education, hospitals, and other non-profit organizations. Federal awarding agencies shall not impose additional or inconsistent requirements, except as provided in §§ 105–72.103, and 105–72.204 or unless specifically required by Federal statute or executive order. Non-profit organizations that implement Federal programs for the States are also subject to State requirements.

§ 105–72.101 Definitions.

(a) *Accrued expenditures* means the charges incurred by the recipient during a given period requiring the provision of funds for:

(1) Goods and other tangible property received;

(2) Services performed by employees, contractors, subrecipients, and other payees; and

(3) Other amounts becoming owed under programs for which no current services or performance is required.

(b) *Accrued income* means the sum of:

(1) Earnings during a given period from

(i) Services performed by the recipient, and

(ii) Goods and other tangible property delivered to purchasers, and

(2) Amounts becoming owed to the recipient for which no current services or performance is required by the recipient.

(c) *Acquisition cost of equipment* means the net invoice price of the equipment, including the cost of modifications, attachments, accessories, or auxiliary apparatus necessary to make the property usable for the purpose for which it was acquired. Other charges, such as the cost of installation, transportation, taxes, duty or protective in-transit insurance, shall be included or excluded from the unit acquisition cost in accordance with the recipient's regular accounting practices.

(d) *Advance* means a payment made by Treasury check or other appropriate payment mechanism to a recipient upon its request either before outlays are made by the recipient or through the use of predetermined payment schedules.

(e) *Award* means financial assistance that provides support or stimulation to accomplish a public purpose. Awards include grants and other agreements in the form of money or property in lieu of money, by the Federal Government to an eligible recipient. The term does not include: technical assistance, which provides services instead of money; other assistance in the form of loans, loan guarantees, interest subsidies, or insurance; direct payments of any kind to individuals; and, contracts which are required to be entered into and administered under procurement laws and regulations.

(f) *Cash contributions* means the recipient's cash outlay, including the outlay of money contributed to the recipient by third parties.

(g) *Closeout* means the process by which a Federal awarding agency determines that all applicable administrative actions and all required work of the award have been completed by the recipient and Federal awarding agency.

(h) *Contract* means a procurement contract under an award or subaward, and a procurement subcontract under a recipient's or subrecipient's contract.

(i) Cost sharing or matching means that portion of project or program costs not borne by the Federal Government.

(j) *Date of completion* means the date on which all work under an award is completed or the date on the award document, or any supplement or amendment thereto, on which Federal sponsorship ends.

(k) *Disallowed* costs means those charges to an award that the Federal awarding agency determines to be unallowable, in accordance with the applicable Federal cost principles or other terms and conditions contained in the award.

(l) *Equipment* means tangible nonexpendable personal property including exempt property charged directly to the award having a useful life of more than one year and an acquisition cost

604

of $5000 or more per unit. However, consistent with recipient policy, lower limits may be established.

(m) *Excess property* means property under the control of any Federal awarding agency that, as determined by the head thereof, is no longer required for its needs or the discharge of its responsibilities.

(n) *Exempt property* means tangible personal property acquired in whole or in part with Federal funds, where the Federal awarding agency has statutory authority to vest title in the recipient without further obligation to the Federal Government. An example of exempt property authority is contained in the Federal Grant and Cooperative Agreement Act (31 U.S.C. 6306), for property acquired under an award to conduct basic or applied research by a non-profit institution of higher education or non-profit organization whose principal purpose is conducting scientific research.

(o) *Federal awarding agency* means the Federal agency that provides an award to the recipient.

(p) *Federal funds* authorized means the total amount of Federal funds obligated by the Federal Government for use by the recipient. This amount may include any authorized carryover of unobligated funds from prior funding periods when permitted by agency regulations or agency implementing instructions.

(q) *Federal share of real property, equipment, or supplies* means that percentage of the property's acquisition costs and any improvement expenditures paid with Federal funds.

(r) *Funding period* means the period of time when Federal funding is available for obligation by the recipient.

(s) *Intangible property and debt instruments* means, but is not limited to, trademarks, copyrights, patents and patent applications and such property as loans, notes and other debt instruments, lease agreements, stock and other instruments of property ownership, whether considered tangible or intangible.

(t) *Obligations* means the amounts of orders placed, contracts and grants awarded, services received and similar transactions during a given period that require payment by the recipient during the same or a future period.

(u) *Outlays or expenditures* means charges made to the project or program. They may be reported on a cash or accrual basis. For reports prepared on a cash basis, outlays are the sum of cash disbursements for direct charges for goods and services, the amount of indirect expense charged, the value of third party in-kind contributions applied and the amount of cash advances and payments made to subrecipients. For reports prepared on an accrual basis, outlays are the sum of cash disbursements for direct charges for goods and services, the amount of indirect expense incurred, the value of in-kind contributions applied, and the net increase (or decrease) in the amounts owed by the recipient for goods and other property received, for services performed by employees, contractors, subrecipients and other payees and other amounts becoming owed under programs for which no current services or performance are required.

(v) *Personal property* means property of any kind except real property. It may be tangible, having physical existence, or intangible, having no physical existence, such as copyrights, patents, or securities.

(w) *Prior approval* means written approval by an authorized official evidencing prior consent.

(x) *Program income* means gross income earned by the recipient that is directly generated by a supported activity or earned as a result of the award (see exclusions in § 105–72.304 (e) and (h)). Program income includes, but is not limited to, income from fees for services performed, the use or rental of real or personal property acquired under federally-funded projects, the sale of commodities or items fabricated under an award, license fees and royalties on patents and copyrights, and interest on loans made with award funds. Interest earned on advances of Federal funds is not program income. Except as otherwise provided in Federal awarding agency regulations or the terms and conditions of the award, program income does not include the receipt of principal on loans, rebates, credits, discounts, etc., or interest earned on any of them.

(y) *Project costs* means all allowable costs, as set forth in the applicable Federal cost principles, incurred by a recipient and the value of the contributions made by third parties in accomplishing the objectives of the award during the project period.

(z) *Project period* means the period established in the award document during which Federal sponsorship begins and ends.

(aa) *Property* means, unless otherwise stated, real property, equipment, intangible property and debt instruments.

(bb) *Real property* means land, including land improvements, structures and appurtenances thereto, but excludes movable machinery and equipment.

(cc) *Recipient* means an organization receiving financial assistance directly from Federal awarding agencies to carry out a project or program. The term includes public and private institutions of higher education, public and private hospitals, and other quasi-public and private non-profit organizations such as, but not limited to, community action agencies, research institutes, educational associations, and health centers. The term may include commercial organizations, foreign or international organizations (such as agencies of the United Nations) which are recipients, subrecipients, or contractors or subcontractors of recipients or subrecipients at the discretion of the Federal awarding agency. The term does not include government-owned contractor-operated facilities or research centers providing continued support for mission-oriented, large-scale programs that are government-owned or controlled, or are designated as federally-funded research and development centers.

(dd) *Research and development* means all research activities, both basic and applied, and all development activities that are supported at universities, colleges, and other non-profit institutions. "Research" is defined as a systematic study directed toward fuller scientific knowledge or understanding of the subject studied. "Development" is the systematic use of knowledge and understanding gained from research directed toward the production of useful materials, devices, systems, or methods, including design and development of prototypes and processes. The term research also includes activities involving the training of individuals in research techniques where such activities utilize the same facilities as other research and development activities and where such activities are not included in the instruction function.

(ee) *Small awards* means a grant or cooperative agreement not exceeding the small purchase threshold fixed at 41 U.S.C. 403(11) (currently $25,000).

(ff) *Subaward* means an award of financial assistance in the form of money, or property in lieu of money, made under an award by a recipient to an eligible subrecipient or by a subrecipient to a lower tier subrecipient. The term includes financial assistance when provided by any legal agreement, even if the agreement is called a contract, but does not include procurement of goods and services nor does it include any form of assistance which is excluded from the definition of "award" in paragraph 105–72.101(e).

(gg) *Subrecipient* means the legal entity to which a subaward is made and which is accountable to the recipient for the use of the funds provided. The term may include foreign or international organizations (such as agencies of the United Nations) at the discretion of the Federal awarding agency.

(hh) *Supplies* means all personal property excluding equipment, intangible property, and debt instruments as defined in this section, and inventions of a contractor conceived or first actually reduced to practice in the performance of work under a funding agreement ("subject inventions"), as defined in 37 CFR part 401, "Rights to Inventions Made by Nonprofit Organizations and Small Business Firms Under Government Grants, Contracts, and Cooperative Agreements."

(ii) *Suspension* means an action by a Federal awarding agency that temporarily withdraws Federal sponsorship under an award, pending corrective action by the recipient or pending a decision to terminate the award by the Federal awarding agency. Suspension of an award is a separate action from suspension under Federal agency regulations implementing E.O.s 12549 and 12689, "Debarment and Suspension."

(jj) *Termination* means the cancellation of Federal sponsorship, in whole or in part, under an agreement at any time prior to the date of completion.

(kk) *Third party in-kind contributions* means the value of noncash contributions provided by non-Federal third parties. Third party in-kind contributions may be in the form of real property, equipment, supplies and other expendable property, and the value of goods and services directly benefiting and specifically identifiable to the project or program.

(ll) *Unliquidated obligations, for financial reports prepared on a cash basis,* means the amount of obligations incurred by the recipient that have not been paid. For reports prepared on an accrued expenditure basis, they represent the amount of obligations incurred by the recipient for which an outlay has not been recorded.

(mm) *Unobligated balance* means the portion of the funds authorized by the Federal awarding agency that has not been obligated by the recipient and is determined by deducting the cumulative obligations from the cumulative funds authorized.

(nn) *Unrecovered indirect cost* means the difference between the amount awarded and the amount which could have been awarded under the recipient's approved negotiated indirect cost rate.

(oo) *Working capital advance* means a procedure where by funds are advanced to the recipient to cover its estimated disbursement needs for a given initial period.

§ 105–72.102   Effect on other issuances.

For awards subject to this regulation, all administrative requirements of codified program regulations, program manuals, handbooks and other nonregulatory materials which are inconsistent with the requirements of this regulation shall be superseded, except to the extent they are required by statute, or authorized in accordance with the deviations provision in § 105–72.103.

§ 105–72.103   Deviations.

The Office of Management and Budget (OMB) may grant exceptions for classes of grants or recipients subject to the requirements of this regulation when exceptions are not prohibited by statute. However, in the interest of maximum uniformity, exceptions from the requirements of this regulation shall be permitted only in unusual circumstances. Federal awarding agencies may apply more restrictive requirements to a class of recipients when approved by OMB. Federal awarding agencies may apply less restrictive requirements when awarding small awards, except for those requirements which are statutory. Exceptions on a case-by-case basis may also be made by Federal awarding agencies.

§ 105–72.104   Subawards.

Unless sections of this regulation specifically exclude subrecipients from coverage, the provisions of this regulation shall be applied to subrecipients performing work under awards if such subrecipients are institutions of higher education, hospitals or other non-profit organizations. State and local government subrecipients are subject to the provisions of regulations implementing the grants management common rule, "Uniform Administrative Requirements for Grants and Cooperative Agreements to State and Local Governments," 41 CFR 105–71.

Subpart 105–72.2—Pre-Award Requirements

§ 105–72.200   Purpose.

Sections 105–72.201 through 105–72.207 prescribes forms and instructions and other pre-award matters to be used in applying for Federal awards.

§ 105–72.201   Pre-award policies.

(a) *Use of grants and cooperative agreements, and contracts.* In each instance, the Federal awarding agency shall decide on the appropriate award instrument (i.e., grant, cooperative agreement, or contract). The Federal Grant and Cooperative Agreement Act (31 U.S.C. 6301–08) governs the use of grants, cooperative agreements and contracts. A grant or cooperative agreement shall be used only when the principal purpose of a transaction is to accomplish a public purpose of support or stimulation authorized by Federal statute. The statutory criterion for choosing between grants and cooperative agreements is that for the latter, "substantial involvement is expected between the executive agency and the State, local government, or other recipient when carrying out the activity contemplated in the agreement." Contracts shall be used when the principal purpose is acquisition of property or services for the direct benefit or use of the Federal Government.

(b) *Public notice and priority setting.* Federal awarding agencies shall notify the public of its intended funding priorities for discretionary grant programs, unless funding priorities are established by Federal statute.

§ 105–72.202 Forms for applying for Federal assistance.

(a) Federal awarding agencies shall comply with the applicable report clearance requirements of 5 CFR part 1320, "Controlling Paperwork Burdens on the Public," with regard to all forms used by the Federal awarding agency in place of or as a supplement to the Standard Form 424 (SF–424) series.

(b) Applicants shall use the SF–424 series or those forms and instructions prescribed by the Federal awarding agency.

(c) For Federal programs covered by E.O. 12372, "Intergovernmental Review of Federal Programs," the applicant shall complete the appropriate sections of the SF–424 (Application for Federal Assistance) indicating whether the application was subject to review by the State Single Point of Contact (SPOC). The name and address of the SPOC for a particular State can be obtained from the Federal awarding agency or the Catalog of Federal Domestic Assistance. The SPOC shall advise the applicant whether the program for which application is made has been selected by that State for review.

(d) Federal awarding agencies that do not use the SF–424 form should indicate whether the application is subject to review by the State under E.O. 12372.

§ 105–72.203 Debarment and suspension.

Federal awarding agencies and recipients shall comply with the nonprocurement debarment and suspension common rule implementing E.O.s 12549 and 12689, "Debarment and Suspension." This common rule restricts subawards and contracts with certain parties that are debarred, suspended or otherwise excluded from or ineligible for participation in Federal assistance programs or activities.

§ 105–72.204 Special award conditions.

If an applicant or recipient:

(a) Has a history of poor performance,

(b) Is not financially stable,

(c) Has a management system that does not meet the standards prescribed in this regulation,

(d) Has not conformed to the terms and conditions of a previous award, or

(e) Is not otherwise responsible;

Federal awarding agencies may impose additional requirements as needed, provided that such applicant or recipient is notified in writing as to: the nature of the additional requirements, the reason why the additional requirements are being imposed, the nature of the corrective action needed, the time allowed for completing the corrective actions, and the method for requesting reconsideration of the additional requirements imposed. Any special conditions shall be promptly removed once the conditions that prompted them have been corrected.

§ 105–72.205 Metric system of measurement.

The Metric Conversion Act, as amended by the Omnibus Trade and Competitiveness Act (15 U.S.C. 205) declares that the metric system is the preferred measurement system for U.S. trade and commerce. The Act requires each Federal agency to establish a date or dates in consultation with the Secretary of Commerce, when the metric system of measurement will be used in the agency's procurements, grants, and other business-related activities. Metric implementation may take longer where the use of the system is initially impractical or likely to cause significant inefficiencies in the accomplishment of federally-funded activities. Federal awarding agencies shall follow the provisions of E.O. 12770, "Metric Usage in Federal Government Programs."

§ 105–72.206 Resource Conservation and Recovery Act.

Under the Resource Conservation and Recovery Act (RCRA) (Pub. L. 94–580 codified at 42 U.S.C. 6962), any State agency or agency of a political subdivision of a State which is using appropriated Federal funds must comply with section 6002. Section 6002 requires that preference be given in procurement programs to the purchase of specific products containing recycled materials identified in guidelines developed by the Environmental Protection Agency (EPA) (40 CFR parts 247 through 254). Accordingly, State and local institutions of higher education, hospitals, and non-profit organizations that receive direct Federal awards or other Federal funds shall give preference in their procurement programs funded with Federal funds to the purchase of recycled products pursuant to the EPA guidelines.

§ 105–72.207 Certifications and representations.

Unless prohibited by statute or codified regulation, each Federal awarding agency is authorized and encouraged to allow recipients to submit certifications and representations required by statute, executive order, or regulation on an annual basis, if the recipients have ongoing and continuing relationships with the agency. Annual certifications and representations shall be signed by responsible officials with the authority to ensure recipients' compliance with the pertinent requirements.

Subpart 105–72.30—Post-Award Requirements/Financial and Program Management

§ 105–72.300 Purpose of financial and program management.

Sections 105–72.301 through 105–72.308 prescribe standards for financial management systems, methods for making payments and rules for: satisfying cost sharing and matching requirements, accounting for program income, budget revision approvals, making audits, determining allowability of cost, and establishing fund availability.

§ 105–72.301 Standards for financial management systems.

(a) Federal awarding agencies shall require recipients to relate financial data to performance data and develop unit cost information whenever practical.

(b) Recipients' financial management systems shall provide for the following.

(1) Accurate, current and complete disclosure of the financial results of each federally-sponsored project or program in accordance with the reporting requirements set forth in § 105–72.602. If a Federal awarding agency requires reporting on an accrual basis from a recipient that maintains its records on other than an accrual basis, the recipient shall not be required to establish an accrual accounting system. These recipients may develop such accrual data for its reports on the basis of an analysis of the documentation on hand.

(2) Records that identify adequately the source and application of funds for federally-sponsored activities. These records shall contain information pertaining to Federal awards, authorizations, obligations, unobligated balances, assets, outlays, income and interest.

(3) Effective control over and accountability for all funds, property and other assets. Recipients shall adequately safeguard all such assets and assure they are used solely for authorized purposes.

(4) Comparison of outlays with budget amounts for each award. Whenever appropriate, financial information should be related to performance and unit cost data.

(5) Written procedures to minimize the time elapsing between the transfer of funds to the recipient from the U.S. Treasury and the issuance or redemption of checks, warrants or payments by other means for program purposes by the recipient. To the extent that the provisions of the Cash Management Improvement Act (CMIA) (Pub. L. 101–453) govern, payment methods of State

agencies, instrumentalities, and fiscal agents shall be consistent with CMIA Treasury-State Agreements or the CMIA default procedures codified at 31 CFR part 205, "Withdrawal of Cash from the Treasury for Advances under Federal Grant and Other Programs."

(6) Written procedures for determining the reasonableness, allocability and allowability of costs in accordance with the provisions of the applicable Federal cost principles and the terms and conditions of the award.

(7) Accounting records including cost accounting records that are supported by source documentation.

(c) Where the Federal Government guarantees or insures the repayment of money borrowed by the recipient, the Federal awarding agency, at its discretion, may require adequate bonding and insurance if the bonding and insurance requirements of the recipient are not deemed adequate to protect the interest of the Federal Government.

(d) The Federal awarding agency may require adequate fidelity bond coverage where the recipient lacks sufficient coverage to protect the Federal Government's interest.

(e) Where bonds are required in the situations described above, the bonds shall be obtained from companies holding certificates of authority as acceptable sureties, as prescribed in 31 CFR part 223, "Surety Companies Doing Business with the United States."

§ 105–72.302 Payment.

(a) Payment methods shall minimize the time elapsing between the transfer of funds from the United States Treasury and the issuance or redemption of checks, warrants, or payment by other means by the recipients. Payment methods of State agencies or instrumentalities shall be consistent with Treasury-State CMIA agreements or default procedures codified at 31 CFR part 205.

(b)(1) Recipients are to be paid in advance, provided they maintain or demonstrate the willingness to maintain:

(i) Written procedures that minimize the time elapsing between the transfer of funds and disbursement by the recipient, and

(ii) Financial management systems that meet the standards for fund con-

trol and accountability as established in § 105–72.301.

(2) Cash advances to a recipient organization shall be limited to the minimum amounts needed and be timed to be in accordance with the actual, immediate cash requirements of the recipient organization in carrying out the purpose of the approved program or project. The timing and amount of cash advances shall be as close as is administratively feasible to the actual disbursements by the recipient organization for direct program or project costs and the proportionate share of any allowable indirect costs.

(c) Whenever possible, advances shall be consolidated to cover anticipated cash needs for all awards made by the Federal awarding agency to the recipient.

(1) Advance payment mechanisms include, but are not limited to, Treasury check and electronic funds transfer.

(2) Advance payment mechanisms are subject to 31 CFR part 205.

(3) Recipients shall be authorized to submit requests for advances and reimbursements at least monthly when electronic fund transfers are not used.

(d) Requests for Treasury check advance payment shall be submitted on SF–270, "Request for Advance or Reimbursement," or other forms as may be authorized by OMB. This form is not to be used when Treasury check advance payments are made to the recipient automatically through the use of a predetermined payment schedule or if precluded by special Federal awarding agency instructions for electronic funds transfer.

(e) Reimbursement is the preferred method when the requirements in paragraph (b) cannot be met. Federal awarding agencies may also use this method on any construction agreement, or if the major portion of the construction project is accomplished through private market financing or Federal loans, and the Federal assistance constitutes a minor portion of the project.

(1) When the reimbursement method is used, the Federal awarding agency shall make payment within 30 days after receipt of the billing, unless the billing is improper.

(2) Recipients shall be authorized to submit request for reimbursement at least monthly when electronic funds transfers are not used.

(f) If a recipient cannot meet the criteria for advance payments and the Federal awarding agency has determined that reimbursement is not feasible because the recipient lacks sufficient working capital, the Federal awarding agency may provide cash on a working capital advance basis. Under this procedure, the Federal awarding agency shall advance cash to the recipient to cover its estimated disbursement needs for an initial period generally geared to the awardee's disbursing cycle. Thereafter, the Federal awarding agency shall reimburse the recipient for its actual cash disbursements. The working capital advance method of payment shall not be used for recipients unwilling or unable to provide timely advances to their subrecipient to meet the subrecipient's actual cash disbursements.

(g) To the extent available, recipients shall disburse funds available from repayments to and interest earned on a revolving fund, program income, rebates, refunds, contract settlements, audit recoveries and interest earned on such funds before requesting additional cash payments.

(h) Unless otherwise required by statute, Federal awarding agencies shall not withhold payments for proper charges made by recipients at any time during the project period unless paragraphs (h)(1) or (2) of this section apply.

(1) A recipient has failed to comply with the project objectives, the terms and conditions of the award, or Federal reporting requirements.

(2) The recipient or subrecipient is delinquent in a debt to the United States as defined in OMB Circular A–129, "Managing Federal Credit Programs." Under such conditions, the Federal awarding agency may, upon reasonable notice, inform the recipient that payments shall not be made for obligations incurred after a specified date until the conditions are corrected or the indebtedness to the Federal Government is liquidated.

(i) Standards governing the use of banks and other institutions as depositories of funds advanced under awards are as follows:

(1) Except for situations described in paragraph (i)(2), Federal awarding agencies shall not require separate depository accounts for funds provided to a recipient or establish any eligibility requirements for depositories for funds provided to a recipient. However, recipients must be able to account for the receipt, obligation and expenditure of funds.

(2) Advances of Federal funds shall be deposited and maintained in insured accounts whenever possible.

(j) Consistent with the national goal of expanding the opportunities for women-owned and minority-owned business enterprises, recipients shall be encouraged to use womenowned and minority-owned banks (a bank which is owned at least 50 percent by women or minority group members).

(k) Recipients shall maintain advances of Federal funds in interest bearing accounts, unless paragraph (k)(1), (2) or (3) of this section apply.

(1) The recipient receives less than $120,000 in Federal awards per year.

(2) The best reasonably available interest bearing account would not be expected to earn interest in excess of $250 per year on Federal cash balances.

(3) The depository would require an average or minimum balance so high that it would not be feasible within the expected Federal and non-Federal cash resources.

(l) For those entities where CMIA and its implementing regulations do not apply, interest earned on Federal advances deposited in interest bearing accounts shall be remitted annually to Department of Health and Human Services, Payment Management System, P.O. Box 6021, Rockville, MD 20852. Interest amounts up to $250 per year may be retained by the recipient for administrative expense. State universities and hospitals shall comply with CMIA, as it pertains to interest. If an entity subject to CMIA uses its own funds to pay pre-award costs for discretionary awards without prior written approval from the Federal awarding agency, it waives its right to recover the interest under CMIA.

(m) Except as noted elsewhere in this regulation, only the following forms shall be authorized for the recipients in requesting advances and reimbursements. Federal agencies shall not require more than an original and two copies of these forms.

(1) *SF–270, Request for Advance or Reimbursement.* Each Federal awarding agency shall adopt the SF–270 as a standard form for all nonconstruction programs when electronic funds transfer or predetermined advance methods are not used. Federal awarding agencies, however, have the option of using this form for construction programs in lieu of the SF–271, "Outlay Report and Request for Reimbursement for Construction Programs."

(2) *SF–271, Outlay Report and Request for Reimbursement for Construction Programs.* Each Federal awarding agency shall adopt the SF–271 as the standard form to be used for requesting reimbursement for construction programs. However, a Federal awarding agency may substitute the SF–270 when the Federal awarding agency determines that it provides adequate information to meet Federal needs.

§ 105–72.303   Cost sharing or matching.

(a) All contributions, including cash and third party in-kind, shall be accepted as part of the recipient's cost sharing or matching when such contributions meet all of the following criteria.

(1) Are verifiable from the recipient's records.

(2) Are not included as contributions for any other federally-assisted project or program.

(3) Are necessary and reasonable for proper and efficient accomplishment of project or program objectives.

(4) Are allowable under the applicable cost principles.

(5) Are not paid by the Federal Government under another award, except where authorized by Federal statute to be used for cost sharing or matching.

(6) Are provided for in the approved budget when required by the Federal awarding agency.

(7) Conform to other provisions of this regulation, as applicable.

(b) Unrecovered indirect costs may be included as part of cost sharing or matching only with the prior approval of the Federal awarding agency.

(c) Values for recipient contributions of services and property shall be established in accordance with the applicable cost principles. If a Federal awarding agency authorizes recipients to donate buildings or land for construction/facilities acquisition projects or long-term use, the value of the donated property for cost sharing or matching shall be the lesser of paragraph (c)(1) or (2) of this section.

(1) The certified value of the remaining life of the property recorded in the recipient's accounting records at the time of donation.

(2) The current fair market value. However, when there is sufficient justification, the Federal awarding agency may approve the use of the current fair market value of the donated property, even if it exceeds the certified value at the time of donation to the project.

(d) Volunteer services furnished by professional and technical personnel, consultants, and other skilled and unskilled labor may be counted as cost sharing or matching if the service is an integral and necessary part of an approved project or program. Rates for volunteer services shall be consistent with those paid for similar work in the recipient's organization. In those instances in which the required skills are not found in the recipient organization, rates shall be consistent with those paid for similar work in the labor market in which the recipient competes for the kind of services involved. In either case, paid fringe benefits that are reasonable, allowable, and allocable may be included in the valuation.

(e) When an employer other than the recipient furnishes the services of an employee, these services shall be valued at the employee's regular rate of pay (plus an amount of fringe benefits that are reasonable, allowable, and allocable, but exclusive of overhead costs), provided these services are in the same skill for which the employee is normally paid.

(f) Donated supplies may include such items as expendable equipment, office supplies, laboratory supplies or workshop and classroom supplies. Value assessed to donated supplies included in the cost sharing or matching share shall be reasonable and shall not exceed the fair market value of the property at the time of the donation.

(g) The method used for determining cost sharing or matching for donated equipment, buildings and land for which title passes to the recipient may differ according to the purpose of the award, if paragraph (g)(1) or (2) of this section apply.

(1) If the purpose of the award is to assist the recipient in the acquisition of equipment, buildings or land, the total value of the donated property may be claimed as cost sharing or matching.

(2) If the purpose of the award is to support activities that require the use of equipment, buildings or land, normally only depreciation or use charges for equipment and buildings may be made. However, the full value of equipment or other capital assets and fair rental charges for land may be allowed, provided that the Federal awarding agency has approved the charges.

(h) The value of donated property shall be determined in accordance with the usual accounting policies of the recipient, with the following qualifications.

(1) The value of donated land and buildings shall not exceed its fair market value at the time of donation to the recipient as established by an independent appraiser (e.g., certified real property appraiser or General Services Administration representative) and certified by a responsible official of the recipient.

(2) The value of donated equipment shall not exceed the fair market value of equipment of the same age and condition at the time of donation.

(3) The value of donated space shall not exceed the fair rental value of comparable space as established by an independent appraisal of comparable space and facilities in a privately-owned building in the same locality.

(4) The value of loaned equipment shall not exceed its fair rental value.

(5) The following requirements pertain to the recipient's supporting records for in-kind contributions from third parties.

(i) Volunteer services shall be documented and, to the extent feasible, supported by the same methods used by the recipient for its own employees.

(ii) The basis for determining the valuation for personal service, material, equipment, buildings and land shall be documented.

§105–72.304   Program income.

(a) Federal awarding agencies shall apply the standards set forth in this section in requiring recipient organizations to account for program income related to projects financed in whole or in part with Federal funds.

(b) Except as provided in paragraph (h) of this section, program income earned during the project period shall be retained by the recipient and, in accordance with Federal awarding agency regulations or the terms and conditions of the award, shall be used in one or more of the ways listed in the following.

(1) Added to funds committed to the project by the Federal awarding agency and recipient and used to further eligible project or program objectives.

(2) Used to finance the non-Federal share of the project or program.

(3) Deducted from the total project or program allowable cost in determining the net allowable costs on which the Federal share of costs is based.

(c) When an agency authorizes the disposition of program income as described in paragraphs (b)(1) or (b)(2), program income in excess of any limits stipulated shall be used in accordance with paragraph (b)(3).

(d) In the event that the Federal awarding agency does not specify in its regulations or the terms and conditions of the award how program income is to be used, paragraph (b)(3) shall apply automatically to all projects or programs except research. For awards that support research, paragraph (b)(1) shall apply automatically unless the awarding agency indicates in the terms and conditions another alternative on the award or the recipient is subject to special award conditions, as indicated in §105–72.204.

(e) Unless Federal awarding agency regulations or the terms and conditions of the award provide otherwise, recipients shall have no obligation to the Federal Government regarding program income earned after the end of the project period.

(f) If authorized by Federal awarding agency regulations or the terms and conditions of the award, costs incident to the generation of program income may be deducted from gross income to determine program income, provided these costs have not been charged to the award.

(g) Proceeds from the sale of property shall be handled in accordance with the requirements of the Property Standards (See §§ 105–72.400 through 105–72.407).

(h) Unless Federal awarding agency regulations or the terms and condition of the award provide otherwise, recipients shall have no obligation to the Federal Government with respect to program income earned from license fees and royalties for copyrighted material, patents, patent applications, trademarks, and inventions produced under an award. However, Patent and Trademark Amendments (35 U.S.C. 18) apply to inventions made under an experimental, developmental, or research award.

§ 105–72.305 Revision of budget and program plans.

(a) The budget plan is the financial expression of the project or program as approved during the award process. It may include either the Federal and non-Federal share, or only the Federal share, depending upon Federal awarding agency requirements. It shall be related to performance for program evaluation purposes whenever appropriate.

(b) Recipients are required to report deviations from budget and program plans, and request prior approvals for budget and program plan revisions, in accordance with this section.

(c) For nonconstruction awards, recipients shall request prior approvals from Federal awarding agencies for one or more of the following program or budget related reasons.

(1) Change in the scope or the objective of the project or program (even if there is no associated budget revision requiring prior written approval).

(2) Change in a key person specified in the application or award document.

(3) The absence for more than three months, or a 25 percent reduction in time devoted to the project, by the approved project director or principal investigator.

(4) The need for additional Federal funding.

(5) The transfer of amounts budgeted for indirect costs to absorb increases in direct costs, or vice versa, if approval is required by the Federal awarding agency.

(6) The inclusion, unless waived by the Federal awarding agency, of costs that require prior approval in accordance with OMB Circular A–21, "Cost Principles for Institutions of Higher Education," OMB Circular A–122, "Cost Principles for Non-Profit Organizations," or 45 CFR part 74 appendix E, "Principles for Determining Costs Applicable to Research and Development under Grants and Contracts with Hospitals," or 48 CFR part 31, "Contract Cost Principles and Procedures," as applicable.

(7) The transfer of funds allotted for training allowances (direct payment to trainees) to other categories of expense.

(8) Unless described in the application and funded in the approved awards, the subaward, transfer or contracting out of any work under an award. This provision does not apply to the purchase of supplies, material, equipment or general support services.

(d) No other prior approval requirements for specific items may be imposed unless a deviation has been approved by OMB.

(e) Except for requirements listed in paragraphs (c)(1) and (c)(4) of this section, Federal awarding agencies are authorized, at their option, to waive cost-related and administrative prior written approvals required by this regulation and OMB Circulars A–21 and A–122. Such waivers may include authorizing recipients to do any one or more of the following.

(1) Incur pre-award costs 90 calendar days prior to award or more than 90 calendar days with the prior approval of the Federal awarding agency. All pre-award costs are incurred at the recipient's risk (i.e., the Federal awarding agency is under no obligation to reimburse such costs if for any reason the recipient does not receive an award or if the award is less than anticipated and inadequate to cover such costs).

(2) Initiate a one-time extension of the expiration date of the award of up to 12 months unless one or more of the following conditions apply. For one-time extensions, the recipient must notify the Federal awarding agency in writing with the supporting reasons and revised expiration date at least 10 days before the expiration date specified in the award. This one-time extension may not be exercised merely for the purpose of using unobligated balances.

(i) The terms and conditions of award prohibit the extension.

(ii) The extension requires additional Federal funds.

(iii) The extension involves any change in the approved objectives or scope of the project.

(3) Carry forward unobligated balances to subsequent funding periods.

(4) For awards that support research, unless the Federal awarding agency provides otherwise in the award or in the agency's regulations, the prior approval requirements described in paragraph (e) are automatically waived (i.e., recipients need not obtain such prior approvals) unless one of the conditions included in paragraph (e)(2) applies.

(f) The Federal awarding agency may, at its option, restrict the transfer of funds among direct cost categories or programs, functions and activities for awards in which the Federal share of the project exceeds $100,000 and the cumulative amount of such transfers exceeds or is expected to exceed 10 percent of the total budget as last approved by the Federal awarding agency. No Federal awarding agency shall permit a transfer that would cause any Federal appropriation or part thereof to be used for purposes other than those consistent with the original intent of the appropriation.

(g) All other changes to nonconstruction budgets, except for the changes described in paragraph (j), do not require prior approval.

(h) For construction awards, recipients shall request prior written approval promptly from Federal awarding agencies for budget revisions whenever paragraphs (h)(1), (2) or (3) of this section apply.

(1) The revision results from changes in the scope or the objective of the project or program.

(2) The need arises for additional Federal funds to complete the project.

(3) A revision is desired which involves specific costs for which prior written approval requirements may be imposed consistent with applicable OMB cost principles listed in § 105-72.307.

(i) No other prior approval requirements for specific items may be imposed unless a deviation has been approved by OMB.

(j) When a Federal awarding agency makes an award that provides support for both construction and nonconstruction work, the Federal awarding agency may require the recipient to request prior approval from the Federal awarding agency before making any fund or budget transfers between the two types of work supported.

(k) For both construction and nonconstruction awards, Federal awarding agencies shall require recipients to notify the Federal awarding agency in writing promptly whenever the amount of Federal authorized funds is expected to exceed the needs of the recipient for the project period by more than $5000 or five percent of the Federal award, whichever is greater. This notification shall not be required if an application for additional funding is submitted for a continuation award.

(l) When requesting approval for budget revisions, recipients shall use the budget forms that were used in the application unless the Federal awarding agency indicates a letter of request suffices.

(m) Within 30 calendar days from the date of receipt of the request for budget revisions, Federal awarding agencies shall review the request and notify the recipient whether the budget revisions have been approved. If the revision is still under consideration at the end of 30 calendar days, the Federal awarding agency shall inform the recipient in writing of the date when the recipient may expect the decision.

§ 105-72.306 Non-Federal audits.

(a) Recipients and subrecipients that are institutions of higher education or other non-profit organizations (including hospitals) shall be subject to the audit requirements contained in the Single Audit Act Amendments of 1996 (31 U.S.C. 7501–7507) and revised OMB Circular A–133, "Audits of States, Local Governments, and Non-Profit Organizations."

(b) State and local governments shall be subject to the audit requirements contained in the Single Audit Act Amendments of 1996 (31 U.S.C. 7501–7507) and revised OMB Circular A–133, "Audits of States, Local Governments, and Non-Profit Organizations."

(c) For-profit hospitals not covered by the audit provisions of revised OMB Circular A–133 shall be subject to the audit requirements of the Federal awarding agencies.

(d) Commercial organizations shall be subject to the audit requirements of the Federal awarding agency or the prime recipient as incorporated into the award document.

[59 FR 47268, Sept. 15, 1994, as amended at 62 FR 45939, 45944, Aug. 29, 1997]

§ 105–72.307 Allowable costs.

For each kind of recipient, there is a set of Federal principles for determining allowable costs. Allowability of costs shall be determined in accordance with the cost principles applicable to the entity incurring the costs. Thus, allowability of costs incurred by State, local or federally-recognized Indian tribal governments is determined in accordance with the provisions of OMB Circular A–87, "Cost Principles for State and Local Governments." The allowability of costs incurred by non-profit organizations is determined in accordance with the provisions of OMB Circular A–122, "Cost Principles for Non-Profit Organizations." The allowability of costs incurred by institutions of higher education is determined in accordance with the provisions of OMB Circular A–21, "Cost Principles for Educational Institutions." The allowability of costs incurred by hospitals is determined in accordance with the provisions of appendix E of 45 CFR part 74, "Principles for Determining Costs Applicable to Research and Development Under Grants and Contracts with Hospitals." The allowability of costs incurred by commercial organizations

and those non-profit organizations listed in Attachment C to Circular A–122 is determined in accordance with the provisions of the Federal Acquisition Regulation (FAR) at 48 CFR part 31.

§ 105–72.308 Period of availability of funds.

Where a funding period is specified, a recipient may charge to the grant only allowable costs resulting from obligations incurred during the funding period and any pre-award costs authorized by the Federal awarding agency.

Subpart 105–72.40—Post-Award Requirements/Property Standards

§ 105–72.400 Purpose of property standards.

Sections 105–72.401 through 105–72.407 set forth uniform standards governing management and disposition of property furnished by the Federal Government whose cost was charged to a project supported by a Federal award. Federal awarding agencies shall require recipients to observe these standards under awards and shall not impose additional requirements, unless specifically required by Federal statute. The recipient may use its own property management standards and procedures provided it observes the provisions of § 105–72.401 through § 105–72.407.

§ 105–72.401 Insurance coverage.

Recipients shall, at a minimum, provide the equivalent insurance coverage for real property and equipment acquired with Federal funds as provided to property owned by the recipient. Federally-owned property need not be insured unless required by the terms and conditions of the award.

§ 105–72.402 Real property.

Each Federal awarding agency shall prescribe requirements for recipients concerning the use and disposition of real property acquired in whole or in part under awards. Unless otherwise provided by statute, such requirements, at a minimum, shall contain the following.

(a) Title to real property shall vest in the recipient subject to the condition that the recipient shall use the real property for the authorized purpose of the project as long as it is needed and shall not encumber the property without approval of the Federal awarding agency.

(b) The recipient shall obtain written approval by the Federal awarding agency for the use of real property in other federally-sponsored projects when the recipient determines that the property is no longer needed for the purpose of the original project. Use in other projects shall be limited to those under federally-sponsored projects (i.e., awards) or programs that have purposes consistent with those authorized for support by the Federal awarding agency.

(c) When the real property is no longer needed as provided in paragraphs (a) and (b), the recipient shall request disposition instructions from the Federal awarding agency or its successor Federal awarding agency. The Federal awarding agency shall observe one or more of the following disposition instructions.

(1) The recipient may be permitted to retain title without further obligation to the Federal Government after it compensates the Federal Government for that percentage of the current fair market value of the property attributable to the Federal participation in the project.

(2) The recipient may be directed to sell the property under guidelines provided by the Federal awarding agency and pay the Federal Government for that percentage of the current fair market value of the property attributable to the Federal participation in the project (after deducting actual and reasonable selling and fix-up expenses, if any, from the sales proceeds). When the recipient is authorized or required to sell the property, proper sales procedures shall be established that provide for competition to the extent practicable and result in the highest possible return.

(3) The recipient may be directed to transfer title to the property to the Federal Government or to an eligible third party provided that, in such cases, the recipient shall be entitled to compensation for its attributable percentage of the current fair market value of the property.

§105–72.403 **Federally-owned and exempt property.**

(a) *Federally-owned property.* (1) Title to federally-owned property remains vested in the Federal Government. Recipients shall submit annually an inventory listing of federally-owned property in their custody to the Federal awarding agency. Upon completion of the award or when the property is no longer needed, the recipient shall report the property to the Federal awarding agency for further Federal agency utilization.

(2) If the Federal awarding agency has no further need for the property, it shall be declared excess and reported to the General Services Administration, unless the Federal awarding agency has statutory authority to dispose of the property by alternative methods (e.g., the authority provided by the Federal Technology Transfer Act (15 U.S.C. 3710 (I)) to donate research equipment to educational and non-profit organizations in accordance with E.O. 12821, "Improving Mathematics and Science Education in Support of the National Education Goals.") Appropriate instructions shall be issued to the recipient by the Federal awarding agency.

(b) *Exempt property.* When statutory authority exists, the Federal awarding agency has the option to vest title to property acquired with Federal funds in the recipient without further obligation to the Federal Government and under conditions the Federal awarding agency considers appropriate. Such property is "exempt property." Should a Federal awarding agency not establish conditions, title to exempt property upon acquisition shall vest in the recipient without further obligation to the Federal Government.

§105–72.404 **Equipment.**

(a) Title to equipment acquired by a recipient with Federal funds shall vest in the recipient, subject to conditions of this section.

(b) The recipient shall not use equipment acquired with Federal funds to provide services to non-Federal outside organizations for a fee that is less than private companies charge for equivalent services, unless specifically authorized by Federal statute, for as long as the Federal Government retains an interest in the equipment.

(c) The recipient shall use the equipment in the project or program for which it was acquired as long as needed, whether or not the project or program continues to be supported by Federal funds and shall not encumber the property without approval of the Federal awarding agency. When no longer needed for the original project or program, the recipient shall use the equipment in connection with its other federally-sponsored activities, in the following order of priority:

(1) Activities sponsored by the Federal awarding agency which funded the original project, then

(2) Activities sponsored by other Federal awarding agencies.

(d) During the time that equipment is used on the project or program for which it was acquired, the recipient shall make it available for use on other projects or programs if such other use will not interfere with the work on the project or program for which the equipment was originally acquired. First preference for such other use shall be given to other projects or programs sponsored by the Federal awarding agency that financed the equipment; second preference shall be given to projects or programs sponsored by other Federal awarding agencies. If the equipment is owned by the Federal Government, use on other activities not sponsored by the Federal Government shall be permissible if authorized by the Federal awarding agency. User charges shall be treated as program income.

(e) When acquiring replacement equipment, the recipient may use the equipment to be replaced as trade-in or sell the equipment and use the proceeds to offset the costs of the replacement equipment subject to the approval of the Federal awarding agency.

(f) The recipient's property management standards for equipment acquired with Federal funds and federally-owned equipment shall include all of the following.

(1) Equipment records shall be maintained accurately and shall include the following information.

(i) A description of the equipment.

(ii) Manufacturer's serial number, model number, Federal stock number, national stock number, or other identification number.

(iii) Source of the equipment, including the award number.

(iv) Whether title vests in the recipient or the Federal Government.

(v) Acquisition date (or date received, if the equipment was furnished by the Federal Government) and cost.

(vi) Information from which one can calculate the percentage of Federal participation in the cost of the equipment (not applicable to equipment furnished by the Federal Government).

(vii) Location and condition of the equipment and the date the information was reported.

(viii) Unit acquisition cost.

(ix) Ultimate disposition data, including date of disposal and sales price or the method used to determine current fair market value where a recipient compensates the Federal awarding agency for its share.

(2) Equipment owned by the Federal Government shall be identified to indicate Federal ownership.

(3) A physical inventory of equipment shall be taken and the results reconciled with the equipment records at least once every two years. Any differences between quantities determined by the physical inspection and those shown in the accounting records shall be investigated to determine the causes of the difference. The recipient shall, in connection with the inventory, verify the existence, current utilization, and continued need for the equipment.

(4) A control system shall be in effect to insure adequate safeguards to prevent loss, damage, or theft of the equipment. Any loss, damage, or theft of equipment shall be investigated and fully documented; if the equipment was owned by the Federal Government, the recipient shall promptly notify the Federal awarding agency.

(5) Adequate maintenance procedures shall be implemented to keep the equipment in good condition.

(6) Where the recipient is authorized or required to sell the equipment, proper sales procedures shall be established which provide for competition to the

extent practicable and result in the highest possible return.

(g) When the recipient no longer needs the equipment, the equipment may be used for other activities in accordance with the following standards. For equipment with a current per unit fair market value of $5000 or more, the recipient may retain the equipment for other uses provided that compensation is made to the original Federal awarding agency or its successor. The amount of compensation shall be computed by applying the percentage of Federal participation in the cost of the original project or program to the current fair market value of the equipment. If the recipient has no need for the equipment, the recipient shall request disposition instructions from the Federal awarding agency. The Federal awarding agency shall determine whether the equipment can be used to meet the agency's requirements. If no requirement exists within that agency, the availability of the equipment shall be reported to the General Services Administration by the Federal awarding agency to determine whether a requirement for the equipment exists in other Federal agencies. The Federal awarding agency shall issue instructions to the recipient no later than 120 calendar days after the recipient's request and the following procedures shall govern.

(1) If so instructed or if disposition instructions are not issued within 120 calendar days after the recipient's request, the recipient shall sell the equipment and reimburse the Federal awarding agency an amount computed by applying to the sales proceeds the percentage of Federal participation in the cost of the original project or program. However, the recipient shall be permitted to deduct and retain from the Federal share $500 or ten percent of the proceeds, whichever is less, for the recipient's selling and handling expenses.

(2) If the recipient is instructed to ship the equipment elsewhere, the recipient shall be reimbursed by the Federal Government by an amount which is computed by applying the percentage of the recipient's participation in the cost of the original project or program to the current fair market value of the equipment, plus any reasonable shipping or interim storage costs incurred.

(3) If the recipient is instructed to otherwise dispose of the equipment, the recipient shall be reimbursed by the Federal awarding agency for such costs incurred in its disposition.

(4) The Federal awarding agency may reserve the right to transfer the title to the Federal Government or to a third party named by the Federal Government when such third party is otherwise eligible under existing statutes. Such transfer shall be subject to the following standards.

(i) The equipment shall be appropriately identified in the award or otherwise made known to the recipient in writing.

(ii) The Federal awarding agency shall issue disposition instructions within 120 calendar days after receipt of a final inventory. The final inventory shall list all equipment acquired with grant funds and federally-owned equipment. If the Federal awarding agency fails to issue disposition instructions within the 120 calendar day period, the recipient shall apply the standards of this section, as appropriate.

(iii) When the Federal awarding agency exercises its right to take title, the equipment shall be subject to the provisions for federally-owned equipment.

§105–72.405 Supplies and other expendable property.

(a) Title to supplies and other expendable property shall vest in the recipient upon acquisition. If there is a residual inventory of unused supplies exceeding $5000 in total aggregate value upon termination or completion of the project or program and the supplies are not needed for any other federally-sponsored project or program, the recipient shall retain the supplies for use on non-Federal sponsored activities or sell them, but shall, in either case, compensate the Federal Government for its share. The amount of compensation shall be computed in the same manner as for equipment.

(b) The recipient shall not use supplies acquired with Federal funds to provide services to non-Federal outside organizations for a fee that is less than private companies charge for equivalent services, unless specifically authorized by Federal statute as long as the Federal Government retains an interest in the supplies.

§ 105–72.406 Intangible property.

(a) The recipient may copyright any work that is subject to copyright and was developed, or for which ownership was purchased, under an award. The Federal awarding agency(ies) reserve a royalty-free, nonexclusive and irrevocable right to reproduce, publish, or otherwise use the work for Federal purposes, and to authorize others to do so.

(b) Recipients are subject to applicable regulations governing patents and inventions, including governmentwide regulations issued by the Department of Commerce at 37 CFR part 401, "Rights to Inventions Made by Nonprofit Organizations and Small Business Firms Under Government Grants, Contracts and Cooperative Agreements."

(c) Unless waived by the Federal awarding agency, the Federal Government has the right to paragraph (c)(1) and (2) of this section.

(1) Obtain, reproduce, publish or otherwise use the data first produced under an award.

(2) Authorize others to receive, reproduce, publish, or otherwise use such data for Federal purposes.

(d) Title to intangible property and debt instruments acquired under an award or subaward vests upon acquisition in the recipient. The recipient shall use that property for the originally-authorized purpose, and the recipient shall not encumber the property without approval of the Federal awarding agency. When no longer needed for the originally authorized purpose, disposition of the intangible property shall occur in accordance with the provisions of § 105–72.404(g).

§ 105–72.407 Property trust relationship.

Real property, equipment, intangible property and debt instruments that are acquired or improved with Federal funds shall be held in trust by the recipient as trustee for the beneficiaries of the project or program under which the property was acquired or improved.

Agencies may require recipients to record liens or other appropriate notices of record to indicate that personal or real property has been acquired or improved with Federal funds and that use and disposition conditions apply to the property.

Subpart 105–72.50—Post-Award Requirements/Procurement Standards

§ 105–72.500 Purpose of procurement standards.

Sections 105–72.501 through 105–72.508 set forth standards for use by recipients in establishing procedures for the procurement of supplies and other expendable property, equipment, real property and other services with Federal funds. These standards are furnished to ensure that such materials and services are obtained in an effective manner and in compliance with the provisions of applicable Federal statutes and executive orders. No additional procurement standards or requirements shall be imposed by the Federal awarding agencies upon recipients, unless specifically required by Federal statute or executive order or approved by OMB.

§ 105–72.501 Recipient responsibilities.

The standards contained in this section do not relieve the recipient of the contractual responsibilities arising under its contract(s). The recipient is the responsible authority, without recourse to the Federal awarding agency, regarding the settlement and satisfaction of all contractual and administrative issues arising out of procurements entered into in support of an award or other agreement. This includes disputes, claims, protests of award, source evaluation or other matters of a contractual nature. Matters concerning violation of statute are to be referred to such Federal, State or local authority as may have proper jurisdiction.

§ 105–72.502 Codes of conduct.

The recipient shall maintain written standards of conduct governing the performance of its employees engaged in the award and administration of contracts. No employee, officer, or agent shall participate in the selection, award, or administration of a contract supported by Federal funds if a real or apparent conflict of interest would be involved. Such a conflict would arise when the employee, officer, or agent, any member of his or her immediate family, his or her partner, or an organization which employs or is about to employ any of the parties indicated herein, has a financial or other interest in the firm selected for an award. The officers, employees, and agents of the recipient shall neither solicit nor accept gratuities, favors, or anything of monetary value from contractors, or parties to subagreements. However, recipients may set standards for situations in which the financial interest is not substantial or the gift is an unsolicited item of nominal value. The standards of conduct shall provide for disciplinary actions to be applied for violations of such standards by officers, employees, or agents of the recipient.

§ 105–72.503 Competition.

All procurement transactions shall be conducted in a manner to provide, to the maximum extent practical, open and free competition. The recipient shall be alert to organizational conflicts of interest as well as noncompetitive practices among contractors that may restrict or eliminate competition or otherwise restrain trade. In order to ensure objective contractor performance and eliminate unfair competitive advantage, contractors that develop or draft specifications, requirements, statements of work, invitations for bids and/or requests for proposals shall be excluded from competing for such procurements. Awards shall be made to the bidder or offeror whose bid or offer is responsive to the solicitation and is most advantageous to the recipient, price, quality and other factors considered. Solicitations shall clearly set forth all requirements that the bidder or offeror shall fulfill in order for the bid or offer to be evaluated by the recipient. Any and all bids or offers may be rejected when it is in the recipient's interest to do so.

§ 105–72.504 Procurement procedures.

(a) All recipients shall establish written procurement procedures. These procedures shall provide for, at a minimum, that paragraphs (a)(1), (2) and (3) of this section apply.

(1) Recipients avoid purchasing unnecessary items.

(2) Where appropriate, an analysis is made of lease and purchase alternatives to determine which would be the most economical and practical procurement for the Federal Government.

(3) Solicitations for goods and services provide for all of the following.

(i) A clear and accurate description of the technical requirements for the material, product or service to be procured. In competitive procurements, such a description shall not contain features which unduly restrict competition.

(ii) Requirements which the bidder/offeror must fulfill and all other factors to be used in evaluating bids or proposals.

(iii) A description, whenever practicable, of technical requirements in terms of functions to be performed or performance required, including the range of acceptable characteristics or minimum acceptable standards.

(iv) The specific features of "brand name or equal" descriptions that bidders are required to meet when such items are included in the solicitation.

(v) The acceptance, to the extent practicable and economically feasible, of products and services dimensioned in the metric system of measurement.

(vi) Preference, to the extent practicable and economically feasible, for products and services that conserve natural resources and protect the environment and are energy efficient.

(b) Positive efforts shall be made by recipients to utilize small businesses, minority-owned firms, and women's business enterprises, whenever possible. Recipients of Federal awards shall take all of the following steps to further this goal.

(1) Ensure that small businesses, minority-owned firms, and women's business enterprises are used to the fullest extent practicable.

(2) Make information on forthcoming opportunities available and arrange timeframes for purchases and contracts to encourage and facilitate participation by small businesses, minority-

621

owned firms, and women's business enterprises.

(3) Consider in the contract process whether firms competing for larger contracts intend to subcontract with small businesses, minority-owned firms, and women's business enterprises.

(4) Encourage contracting with consortiums of small businesses, minority-owned firms and women's business enterprises when a contract is too large for one of these firms to handle individually.

(5) Use the services and assistance, as appropriate, of such organizations as the Small Business Administration and the Department of Commerce's Minority Business Development Agency in the solicitation and utilization of small businesses, minority-owned firms and women's business enterprises.

(c) The type of procuring instruments used (e.g., fixed price contracts, cost reimbursable contracts, purchase orders, and incentive contracts) shall be determined by the recipient but shall be appropriate for the particular procurement and for promoting the best interest of the program or project involved. The "cost-plus-a-percentage-of-cost" or "percentage of construction cost" methods of contracting shall not be used.

(d) Contracts shall be made only with responsible contractors who possess the potential ability to perform successfully under the terms and conditions of the proposed procurement. Consideration shall be given to such matters as contractor integrity, record of past performance, financial and technical resources or accessibility to other necessary resources. In certain circumstances, contracts with certain parties are restricted by agencies' implementation of E.O.s 12549 and 12689, "Debarment and Suspension."

(e) Recipients shall, on request, make available for the Federal awarding agency, pre-award review and procurement documents, such as request for proposals or invitations for bids, independent cost estimates, etc., when any of the following conditions apply.

(1) A recipient's procurement procedures or operation fails to comply with the procurement standards in the Federal awarding agency's implementation of this regulation.

(2) The procurement is expected to exceed the small purchase threshold fixed at 41 U.S.C. 403 (11) (currently $25,000) and is to be awarded without competition or only one bid or offer is received in response to a solicitation.

(3) The procurement, which is expected to exceed the small purchase threshold, specifies a "brand name" product.

(4) The proposed award over the small purchase threshold is to be awarded to other than the apparent low bidder under a sealed bid procurement.

(5) A proposed contract modification changes the scope of a contract or increases the contract amount by more than the amount of the small purchase threshold.

§ 105–72.505   Cost and price analysis.

Some form of cost or price analysis shall be made and documented in the procurement files in connection with every procurement action. Price analysis may be accomplished in various ways, including the comparison of price quotations submitted, market prices and similar indicia, together with discounts. Cost analysis is the review and evaluation of each element of cost to determine reasonableness, allocability and allowability.

§ 105–72.506   Procurement records.

Procurement records and files for purchases in excess of the small purchase threshold shall include the following at a minimum:

(a) Basis for contractor selection,

(b) Justification for lack of competition when competitive bids or offers are not obtained, and

(c) Basis for award cost or price.

§ 105–72.507   Contract administration.

A system for contract administration shall be maintained to ensure contractor conformance with the terms, conditions and specifications of the contract and to ensure adequate and timely follow up of all purchases. Recipients shall evaluate contractor performance and document, as appropriate, whether contractors have met the terms, conditions and specifications of the contract.

§ 105–72.508 Contract provisions.

The recipient shall include, in addition to provisions to define a sound and complete agreement, the following provisions in all contracts. The following provisions shall also be applied to subcontracts.

(a) Contracts in excess of the small purchase threshold shall contain contractual provisions or conditions that allow for administrative, contractual, or legal remedies in instances in which a contractor violates or breaches the contract terms, and provide for such remedial actions as may be appropriate.

(b) All contracts in excess of the small purchase threshold shall contain suitable provisions for termination by the recipient, including the manner by which termination shall be effected and the basis for settlement. In addition, such contracts shall describe conditions under which the contract may be terminated for default as well as conditions where the contract may be terminated because of circumstances beyond the control of the contractor.

(c) Except as otherwise required by statute, an award that requires the contracting (or subcontracting) for construction or facility improvements shall provide for the recipient to follow its own requirements relating to bid guarantees, performance bonds, and payment bonds unless the construction contract or subcontract exceeds $100,000. For those contracts or subcontracts exceeding $100,000, the Federal awarding agency may accept the bonding policy and requirements of the recipient, provided the Federal awarding agency has made a determination that the Federal Government's interest is adequately protected. If such a determination has not been made, the minimum requirements shall be as follows.

(1) A bid guarantee from each bidder equivalent to five percent of the bid price. The "bid guarantee" shall consist of a firm commitment such as a bid bond, certified check, or other negotiable instrument accompanying a bid as assurance that the bidder shall, upon acceptance of his bid, execute such contractual documents as may be required within the time specified.

(2) A performance bond on the part of the contractor for 100 percent of the contract price. A "performance bond" is one executed in connection with a contract to secure fulfillment of all the contractor's obligations under such contract.

(3) A payment bond on the part of the contractor for 100 percent of the contract price. A "payment bond" is one executed in connection with a contract to assure payment as required by statute of all persons supplying labor and material in the execution of the work provided for in the contract.

(4) Where bonds are required in the situations described herein, the bonds shall be obtained from companies holding certificates of authority as acceptable sureties pursuant to 31 CFR part 223, "Surety Companies Doing Business with the United States."

(d) All negotiated contracts (except those for less than the small purchase threshold) awarded by recipients shall include a provision to the effect that the recipient, the Federal awarding agency, the Comptroller General of the United States, or any of their duly authorized representatives, shall have access to any books, documents, papers and records of the contractor which are directly pertinent to a specific program for the purpose of making audits, examinations, excerpts and transcriptions.

(e) All contracts, including small purchases, awarded by recipients and their contractors shall contain the procurement provisions of appendix A to this part, as applicable.

Subpart 105–72.60—Post-Award Requirements/Reports and Records

§ 105–72.600 Purpose of reports and records.

Sections 105–72.601 through 105–72.603 set forth the procedures for monitoring and reporting on the recipient's financial and program performance and the necessary standard reporting forms. They also set forth record retention requirements.

§ 105–72.601 Monitoring and reporting program performance.

(a) Recipients are responsible for managing and monitoring each project, program, subaward, function or activity supported by the award. Recipients shall monitor subawards to ensure subrecipients have met the audit requirements as delineated in § 105–72.306.

(b) The Federal awarding agency shall prescribe the frequency with which the performance reports shall be submitted. Except as provided in paragraph (f) of this section, performance reports shall not be required more frequently than quarterly or, less frequently than annually. Annual reports shall be due 90 calendar days after the grant year; quarterly or semiannual reports shall be due 30 days after the reporting period. The Federal awarding agency may require annual reports before the anniversary dates of multiple year awards in lieu of these requirements. The final performance reports are due 90 calendar days after the expiration or termination of the award.

(c) If inappropriate, a final technical or performance report shall not be required after completion of the project.

(d) When required, performance reports shall generally contain, for each award, brief information on each of the following.

(1) A comparison of actual accomplishments with the goals and objectives established for the period, the findings of the investigator, or both. Whenever appropriate and the output of programs or projects can be readily quantified, such quantitative data should be related to cost data for computation of unit costs.

(2) Reasons why established goals were not met, if appropriate.

(3) Other pertinent information including, when appropriate, analysis and explanation of cost overruns or high unit costs.

(e) Recipients shall not be required to submit more than the original and two copies of performance reports.

(f) Recipients shall immediately notify the Federal awarding agency of developments that have a significant impact on the award-supported activities. Also, notification shall be given in the case of problems, delays, or adverse conditions which materially impair the ability to meet the objectives of the award. This notification shall include a statement of the action taken or contemplated, and any assistance needed to resolve the situation.

(g) Federal awarding agencies may make site visits, as needed.

(h) Federal awarding agencies shall comply with clearance requirements of 5 CFR part 1320 when requesting performance data from recipients.

§ 105–72.602 Financial reporting.

(a) The following forms or such other forms as may be approved by OMB are authorized for obtaining financial information from recipients.

(1) *SF–269 or SF–269A, Financial Status Report.* (i) Each Federal awarding agency shall require recipients to use the SF–269 or SF–269A to report the status of funds for all nonconstruction projects or programs. A Federal awarding agency may, however, have the option of not requiring the SF–269 or SF–269A when the SF–270, Request for Advance or Reimbursement, or SF–272, Report of Federal Cash Transactions, is determined to provide adequate information to meet its needs, except that a final SF–269 or SF–269A shall be required at the completion of the project when the SF–270 is used only for advances.

(ii) The Federal awarding agency shall prescribe whether the report shall be on a cash or accrual basis. If the Federal awarding agency requires accrual information and the recipient's accounting records are not normally kept on the accrual basis, the recipient shall not be required to convert its accounting system, but shall develop such accrual information through best estimates based on an analysis of the documentation on hand.

(iii) The Federal awarding agency shall determine the frequency of the Financial Status Report for each project or program, considering the size and complexity of the particular project or program. However, the report shall not be required more frequently than quarterly or less frequently than annually. A final report shall be required at the completion of the agreement.

(iv) The Federal awarding agency shall require recipients to submit the

SF–269 or SF–269A (an original and no more than two copies) no later than 30 days after the end of each specified reporting period for quarterly and semiannual reports, and 90 calendar days for annual and final reports. Extensions of reporting due dates may be approved by the Federal awarding agency upon request of the recipient.

(2) *SF–272, Report of Federal Cash Transactions.* (i) When funds are advanced to recipients the Federal awarding agency shall require each recipient to submit the SF–272 and, when necessary, its continuation sheet, SF–272a. The Federal awarding agency shall use this report to monitor cash advanced to recipients and to obtain disbursement information for each agreement with the recipients.

(ii) Federal awarding agencies may require forecasts of Federal cash requirements in the "Remarks" section of the report.

(iii) When practical and deemed necessary, Federal awarding agencies may require recipients to report in the "Remarks" section the amount of cash advances received in excess of three days. Recipients shall provide short narrative explanations of actions taken to reduce the excess balances.

(iv) Recipients shall be required to submit not more than the original and two copies of the SF–272, 15 calendar days following the end of each quarter. The Federal awarding agencies may require a monthly report from those recipients receiving advances totaling $1 million or more per year.

(v) Federal awarding agencies may waive the requirement for submission of the SF–272 for any one of the following reasons:

(A) When monthly advances do not exceed $25,000 per recipient, provided that such advances are monitored through other forms contained in this section;

(B) If, in the Federal awarding agency's opinion, the recipient's accounting controls are adequate to minimize excessive Federal advances; or,

(C) When the electronic payment mechanisms provide adequate data.

(b) When the Federal awarding agency needs additional information or more frequent reports, the following shall be observed.

(1) When additional information is needed to comply with legislative requirements, Federal awarding agencies shall issue instructions to require recipients to submit such information under the "Remarks" section of the reports.

(2) When a Federal awarding agency determines that a recipient's accounting system does not meet the standards in § 105–72.301, additional pertinent information to further monitor awards may be obtained upon written notice to the recipient until such time as the system is brought up to standard. The Federal awarding agency, in obtaining this information, shall comply with report clearance requirements of 5 CFR part 1320.

(3) Federal awarding agencies are encouraged to shade out any line item on any report if not necessary.

(4) Federal awarding agencies may accept the identical information from the recipients in machine readable format or computer printouts or electronic outputs in lieu of prescribed formats.

(5) Federal awarding agencies may provide computer or electronic outputs to recipients when such expedites or contributes to the accuracy of reporting.

§ 105–72.603 Retention and access requirements for records.

(a) This section sets forth requirements for record retention and access to records for awards to recipients. Federal awarding agencies shall not impose any other record retention or access requirements upon recipients.

(b) Financial records, supporting documents, statistical records, and all other records pertinent to an award shall be retained for a period of three years from the date of submission of the final expenditure report or, for awards that are renewed quarterly or annually, from the date of the submission of the quarterly or annual financial report, as authorized by the Federal awarding agency. The only exceptions are the following.

(1) If any litigation, claim, or audit is started before the expiration of the 3-year period, the records shall be retained until all litigation, claims or audit findings involving the records

625

have been resolved and final action taken.

(2) Records for real property and equipment acquired with Federal funds shall be retained for 3 years after final disposition.

(3) When records are transferred to or maintained by the Federal awarding agency, the 3-year retention requirement is not applicable to the recipient.

(4) Indirect cost rate proposals, cost allocations plans, etc., as specified in paragraph (g) of this section.

(c) Copies of original records may be substituted for the original records if authorized by the Federal awarding agency.

(d) The Federal awarding agency shall request transfer of certain records to its custody from recipients when it determines that the records possess long term retention value. However, in order to avoid duplicate recordkeeping, a Federal awarding agency may make arrangements for recipients to retain any records that are continuously needed for joint use.

(e) The Federal awarding agency, the Inspector General, Comptroller General of the United States, or any of their duly authorized representatives, have the right of timely and unrestricted access to any books, documents, papers, or other records of recipients that are pertinent to the awards, in order to make audits, examinations, excerpts, transcripts and copies of such documents. This right also includes timely and reasonable access to a recipient's personnel for the purpose of interview and discussion related to such documents. The rights of access in this paragraph are not limited to the required retention period, but shall last as long as records are retained.

(f) Unless required by statute, no Federal awarding agency shall place restrictions on recipients that limit public access to the records of recipients that are pertinent to an award, except when the Federal awarding agency can demonstrate that such records shall be kept confidential and would have been exempted from disclosure pursuant to the Freedom of Information Act (5 U.S.C. 552) if the records had belonged to the Federal awarding agency.

(g) Indirect cost rate proposals, cost allocations plans, etc. Paragraphs (g)(1) and (g)(2) apply to the following types of documents, and their supporting records: indirect cost rate computations or proposals, cost allocation plans, and any similar accounting computations of the rate at which a particular group of costs is chargeable (such as computer usage chargeback rates or composite fringe benefit rates).

(1) If submitted for negotiation. If the recipient submits to the Federal awarding agency or the subrecipient submits to the recipient the proposal, plan, or other computation to form the basis for negotiation of the rate, then the 3-year retention period for its supporting records starts on the date of such submission.

(2) If not submitted for negotiation. If the recipient is not required to submit to the Federal awarding agency or the subrecipient is not required to submit to the recipient the proposal, plan, or other computation for negotiation purposes, then the 3-year retention period for the proposal, plan, or other computation and its supporting records starts at the end of the fiscal year (or other accounting period) covered by the proposal, plan, or other computation.

Subpart 105–72.70—Post-Award Requirements/Termination and Enforcement

§ 105–72.700 Purpose of termination and enforcement.

Section 105–72.701 and § 105–72.702 set forth uniform suspension, termination and enforcement procedures.

§ 105–72.701 Termination.

(a) Awards may be terminated in whole or in part only if paragraph (a)(1), (2) or (3) of this section apply.

(1) By the Federal awarding agency, if a recipient materially fails to comply with the terms and conditions of an award.

(2) By the Federal awarding agency with the consent of the recipient, in which case the two parties shall agree upon the termination conditions, including the effective date and, in the

case of partial termination, the portion to be terminated.

(3) By the recipient upon sending to the Federal awarding agency written notification setting forth the reasons for such termination, the effective date, and, in the case of partial termination, the portion to be terminated. However, if the Federal awarding agency determines in the case of partial termination that the reduced or modified portion of the grant will not accomplish the purposes for which the grant was made, it may terminate the grant in its entirety under either paragraphs (a) (1) or (2).

(b) If costs are allowed under an award, the responsibilities of the recipient referred to in §105–72.801(a), including those for property management as applicable, shall be considered in the termination of the award, and provision shall be made for continuing responsibilities of the recipient after termination, as appropriate.

§105–72.702 Enforcement.

(a) *Remedies for noncompliance.* If a recipient materially fails to comply with the terms and conditions of an award, whether stated in a Federal statute, regulation, assurance, application, or notice of award, the Federal awarding agency may, in addition to imposing any of the special conditions outlined in §105–72.204, take one or more of the following actions, as appropriate in the circumstances.

(1) Temporarily withhold cash payments pending correction of the deficiency by the recipient or more severe enforcement action by the Federal awarding agency.

(2) Disallow (that is, deny both use of funds and any applicable matching credit for) all or part of the cost of the activity or action not in compliance.

(3) Wholly or partly suspend or terminate the current award.

(4) Withhold further awards for the project or program.

(5) Take other remedies that may be legally available.

(b) *Hearings and appeals.* In taking an enforcement action, the awarding agency shall provide the recipient an opportunity for hearing, appeal, or other administrative proceeding to which the recipient is entitled under

any statute or regulation applicable to the action involved.

(c) *Effects of suspension and termination.* Costs of a recipient resulting from obligations incurred by the recipient during a suspension or after termination of an award are not allowable unless the awarding agency expressly authorizes them in the notice of suspension or termination or subsequently. Other recipient costs during suspension or after termination which are necessary and not reasonably avoidable are allowable if paragraph (c) (1) and (2) of this section apply.

(1) The costs result from obligations which were properly incurred by the recipient before the effective date of suspension or termination, are not in anticipation of it, and in the case of a termination, are noncancellable.

(2) The costs would be allowable if the award were not suspended or expired normally at the end of the funding period in which the termination takes effect.

(d) *Relationship to debarment and suspension.* The enforcement remedies identified in this section, including suspension and termination, do not preclude a recipient from being subject to debarment and suspension under E.O.s 12549 and 12689 and the Federal awarding agency implementing regulations (see §105–72.203).

Subpart 105–72.80—After-the-Award Requirements

§105–72.800 Purpose.

Sections 105–72.801 through 105–72.803 contain closeout procedures and other procedures for subsequent disallowances and adjustments.

§105–72.801 Closeout procedures.

(a) Recipients shall submit, within 90 calendar days after the date of completion of the award, all financial, performance, and other reports as required by the terms and conditions of the award. The Federal awarding agency may approve extensions when requested by the recipient.

(b) Unless the Federal awarding agency authorizes an extension, a recipient shall liquidate all obligations incurred under the award not later than 90 calendar days after the funding period or the date of completion as specified in the terms and conditions of the award or in agency implementing instructions.

(c) The Federal awarding agency shall make prompt payments to a recipient for allowable reimbursable costs under the award being closed out.

(d) The recipient shall promptly refund any balances of unobligated cash that the Federal awarding agency has advanced or paid and that is not authorized to be retained by the recipient for use in other projects. OMB Circular A–129 governs unreturned amounts that become delinquent debts.

(e) When authorized by the terms and conditions of the award, the Federal awarding agency shall make a settlement for any upward or downward adjustments to the Federal share of costs after closeout reports are received.

(f) The recipient shall account for any real and personal property acquired with Federal funds or received from the Federal Government in accordance with § 105–72.401 through § 105–72.407.

(g) In the event a final audit has not been performed prior to the closeout of an award, the Federal awarding agency shall retain the right to recover an appropriate amount after fully considering the recommendations on disallowed costs resulting from the final audit.

§ 105–72.802 Subsequent adjustments and continuing responsibilities.

(a) The closeout of an award does not affect any of the following.

(1) The right of the Federal awarding agency to disallow costs and recover funds on the basis of a later audit or other review.

(2) The obligation of the recipient to return any funds due as a result of later refunds, corrections, or other transactions.

(3) Audit requirements in § 105–72.306.

(4) Property management requirements in §§ 105–72.401 through 105–72.407.

(5) Records retention as required in § 105–72.603.

(b) After closeout of an award, a relationship created under an award may be modified or ended in whole or in part with the consent of the Federal awarding agency and the recipient,

provided the responsibilities of the recipient referred to in § 105–72.803(a), including those for property management as applicable, are considered and provisions made for continuing responsibilities of the recipient, as appropriate.

§ 105–72.803 Collection of amounts due.

(a) Any funds paid to a recipient in excess of the amount to which the recipient is finally determined to be entitled under the terms and conditions of the award constitute a debt to the Federal Government. If not paid within a reasonable period after the demand for payment, the Federal awarding agency may reduce the debt by paragraph (a) (1), (2) or (3) of this section.

(1) Making an administrative offset against other requests for reimbursements.

(2) Withholding advance payments otherwise due to the recipient.

(3) Taking other action permitted by statute.

(b) Except as otherwise provided by law, the Federal awarding agency shall charge interest on an overdue debt in accordance with 4 CFR Chapter II, Federal Claims Collection Standards.

APPENDIX A TO PART 105–72—CONTRACT PROVISIONS

All contracts, awarded by a recipient including small purchases, shall contain the following provisions as applicable:

1. *Equal Employment Opportunity*—All contracts shall contain a provision requiring compliance with E.O. 11246, "Equal Employment Opportunity," as amended by E.O. 11375, "Amending Executive Order 11246 Relating to Equal Employment Opportunity," and as supplemented by regulations at 41 CFR part 60, "Office of Federal Contract Compliance Programs, Equal Employment Opportunity, Department of Labor."

2. *Copeland "Anti-Kickback" Act (18 U.S.C. 874 and 40 U.S.C. 276c)*—All contracts and subgrants in excess of $2000 for construction or repair awarded by recipients and subrecipients shall include a provision for compliance with the Copeland "Anti-Kickback" Act (18 U.S.C. 874), as supplemented by Department of Labor regulations (29 CFR part 3, "Contractors and Subcontractors on Public Building or Public Work Financed in Whole or in Part by Loans or Grants from the United States"). The Act provides that each contractor or subrecipient shall be prohibited from inducing, by any means, any person employed in the construction, completion, or

repair of public work, to give up any part of the compensation to which he is otherwise entitled. The recipient shall report all suspected or reported violations to the Federal awarding agency.

3. *Davis-Bacon Act, as amended (40 U.S.C. 276a to a–7)*—When required by Federal program legislation, all construction contracts awarded by the recipients and subrecipients of more than $2000 shall include a provision for compliance with the Davis-Bacon Act (40 U.S.C. 276a to a–7) and as supplemented by Department of Labor regulations (29 CFR part 5, "Labor Standards Provisions Applicable to Contracts Governing Federally Financed and Assisted Construction"). Under this Act, contractors shall be required to pay wages to laborers and mechanics at a rate not less than the minimum wages specified in a wage determination made by the Secretary of Labor. In addition, contractors shall be required to pay wages not less than once a week. The recipient shall place a copy of the current prevailing wage determination issued by the Department of Labor in each solicitation and the award of a contract shall be conditioned upon the acceptance of the wage determination. The recipient shall report all suspected or reported violations to the Federal awarding agency.

4. *Contract Work Hours and Safety Standards Act (40 U.S.C. 327–333)*—Where applicable, all contracts awarded by recipients in excess of $2000 for construction contracts and in excess of $2500 for other contracts that involve the employment of mechanics or laborers shall include a provision for compliance with Sections 102 and 107 of the Contract Work Hours and Safety Standards Act (40 U.S.C. 327–333), as supplemented by Department of Labor regulations (29 CFR part 5). Under Section 102 of the Act, each contractor shall be required to compute the wages of every mechanic and laborer on the basis of a standard work week of 40 hours. Work in excess of the standard work week is permissible provided that the worker is compensated at a rate of not less than 1½ times the basic rate of pay for all hours worked in excess of 40 hours in the work week. Section 107 of the Act is applicable to construction work and provides that no laborer or mechanic shall be required to work in surroundings or under working conditions which are unsanitary, hazardous or dangerous. These requirements do not apply to the purchases of supplies or materials or articles ordinarily available on the open market, or contracts for transportation or transmission of intelligence.

5. *Rights to Inventions Made Under a Contract or Agreement*—Contracts or agreements for the performance of experimental, developmental, or research work shall provide for the rights of the Federal Government and the recipient in any resulting invention in accordance with 37 CFR part 401, "Rights to Inventions Made by Nonprofit Organizations and Small Business Firms Under Government Grants, Contracts and Cooperative Agreements," and any implementing regulations issued by the awarding agency.

6. *Clean Air Act (42 U.S.C. 7401 et seq.) and the Federal Water Pollution Control Act (33 U.S.C. 1251 et seq.), as amended*—Contracts and subgrants of amounts in excess of $100,000 shall contain a provision that requires the recipient to agree to comply with all applicable standards, orders or regulations issued pursuant to the Clean Air Act (42 U.S.C. 7401 *et seq.*) and the Federal Water Pollution Control Act as amended (33 U.S.C. 1251 *et seq.*). Violations shall be reported to the Federal awarding agency and the Regional Office of the Environmental Protection Agency (EPA).

7. *Byrd Anti-Lobbying Amendment (31 U.S.C. 1352)*—Contractors who apply or bid for an award of $100,000 or more shall file the required certification. Each tier certifies to the tier above that it will not and has not used Federal appropriated funds to pay any person or organization for influencing or attempting to influence an officer or employee of any agency, a member of Congress, officer or employee of Congress, or an employee of a member of Congress in connection with obtaining any Federal contract, grant or any other award covered by 31 U.S.C. 1352. Each tier shall also disclose any lobbying with non-Federal funds that takes place in connection with obtaining any Federal award. Such disclosures are forwarded from tier to tier up to the recipient.

8. *Debarment and Suspension (E.O.s 12549 and 12689)*—No contract shall be made to parties listed on the General Services Administration's List of Parties Excluded from Federal Procurement or Nonprocurement Programs in accordance with E.O.s 12549 and 12689, "Debarment and Suspension." This list contains the names of parties debarred, suspended, or otherwise excluded by agencies, and contractors declared ineligible under statutory or regulatory authority other than E.O. 12549. Contractors with awards that exceed the small purchase threshold shall provide the required certification regarding its exclusion status and that of its principal employees.

PART 105–74—GOVERNMENTWIDE REQUIREMENTS FOR DRUG-FREE WORKPLACE (FINANCIAL ASSISTANCE)

Subpart A—Purpose and Coverage

Sec.
105–74.100   What does this part do?
105–74.105   Does this part apply to me?
105–74.110   Are any of my Federal assistance awards exempt from this part?

AUTHORITY: 41 U.S.C. 701 *et seq.*

SOURCE: 68 FR 66627, 66628, Nov. 26, 2003, unless otherwise noted.

Subpart A—Purpose and Coverage

§ 105–74.100 What does this part do?

This part carries out the portion of the Drug-Free Workplace Act of 1988 (41 U.S.C. 701 *et seq.*, as amended) that applies to grants. It also applies the provisions of the Act to cooperative agreements and other financial assistance awards, as a matter of Federal Government policy.

§ 105–74.105 Does this part apply to me?

(a) Portions of this part apply to you if you are either—

(1) A recipient of an assistance award from the General Services Administration; or

(2) A(n) GSA awarding official. (See definitions of award and recipient in §§ 105–74.605 and 105–74.660, respectively.)

(b) The following table shows the subparts that apply to you:

If you are . . .	see subparts . . .
(1) A recipient who is not an individual	A, B and E.
(2) A recipient who is an individual	A, C and E.
(3) A(n) GSA awarding official	A, D and E.

§ 105–74.110 Are any of my Federal assistance awards exempt from this part?

This part does not apply to any award that the Administrator of General Services determines that the application of this part would be inconsistent with the international obligations of the United States or the laws or regulations of a foreign government.

§ 105–74.115 Does this part affect the Federal contracts that I receive?

It will affect future contract awards indirectly if you are debarred or suspended for a violation of the requirements of this part, as described in § 105–74. 510(c). However, this part does not apply directly to procurement contracts. The portion of the Drug-Free Workplace Act of 1988 that applies to Federal procurement contracts is carried out through the Federal Acquisition Regulation in chapter 1 of Title 48 of the Code of Federal Regulations (the drug-free workplace coverage currently is in 48 CFR part 23, subpart 23.5).

Subpart B—Requirements for Recipients Other Than Individuals

§ 105–74.200 What must I do to comply with this part?

There are two general requirements if you are a recipient other than an individual.

(a) First, you must make a good faith effort, on a continuing basis, to maintain a drug-free workplace. You must agree to do so as a condition for receiving any award covered by this part. The specific measures that you must take in this regard are described in more detail in subsequent sections of this subpart. Briefly, those measures are to—

(1) Publish a drug-free workplace statement and establish a drug-free awareness program for your employees (see §§ 105–74.205 through 105–74.220); and

(2) Take actions concerning employees who are convicted of violating drug statutes in the workplace (see § 105–74.225).

(b) Second, you must identify all known workplaces under your Federal awards (see § 105–74.230).

§ 105–74.205 What must I include in my drug-free workplace statement?

You must publish a statement that—

(a) Tells your employees that the unlawful manufacture, distribution, dispensing, possession, or use of a controlled substance is prohibited in your workplace;

(b) Specifies the actions that you will take against employees for violating that prohibition; and

(c) Lets each employee know that, as a condition of employment under any award, he or she:

(1) Will abide by the terms of the statement; and

(2) Must notify you in writing if he or she is convicted for a violation of a criminal drug statute occurring in the workplace and must do so no more than five calendar days after the conviction.

§ 105–74.210 To whom must I distribute my drug-free workplace statement?

You must require that a copy of the statement described in § 105–74.205 be given to each employee who will be engaged in the performance of any Federal award.

§ 105–74.215 What must I include in my drug-free awareness program?

You must establish an ongoing drug-free awareness program to inform employees about—

(a) The dangers of drug abuse in the workplace;

(b) Your policy of maintaining a drug-free workplace;

(c) Any available drug counseling, rehabilitation, and employee assistance programs; and

(d) The penalties that you may impose upon them for drug abuse violations occurring in the workplace.

§ 105–74.220 By when must I publish my drug-free workplace statement and establish my drug-free awareness program?

If you are a new recipient that does not already have a policy statement as described in § 105–74.205 and an ongoing awareness program as described in § 105–74.215, you must publish the statement and establish the program by the time given in the following table:

If . . .	then you . . .
(a) The performance period of the award is less than 30 days	must have the policy statement and program in place as soon as possible, but before the date on which performance is expected to be completed.

If . . .	then you . . .
(b) The performance period of the award is 30 days or more ...	must have the policy statement and program in place within 30 days after award.
(c) You believe there are extraordinary circumstances that will require more than 30 days for you to publish the policy statement and establish the awareness program.	may ask the GSA awarding official to give you more time to do so. The amount of additional time, if any, to be given is at the discretion of the awarding official.

§ 105–74.225 What actions must I take concerning employees who are convicted of drug violations in the workplace?

There are two actions you must take if an employee is convicted of a drug violation in the workplace:

(a) First, you must notify Federal agencies if an employee who is engaged in the performance of an award informs you about a conviction, as required by § 105–74.205(c)(2), or you otherwise learn of the conviction. Your notification to the Federal agencies must—

(1) Be in writing;

(2) Include the employee's position title;

(3) Include the identification number(s) of each affected award;

(4) Be sent within ten calendar days after you learn of the conviction; and

(5) Be sent to every Federal agency on whose award the convicted employee was working. It must be sent to every awarding official or his or her official designee, unless the Federal agency has specified a central point for the receipt of the notices.

(b) Second, within 30 calendar days of learning about an employee's conviction, you must either—

(1) Take appropriate personnel action against the employee, up to and including termination, consistent with the requirements of the Rehabilitation Act of 1973 (29 U.S.C. 794), as amended; or

(2) Require the employee to participate satisfactorily in a drug abuse assistance or rehabilitation program approved for these purposes by a Federal, State or local health, law enforcement, or other appropriate agency.

§ 105–74.230 How and when must I identify workplaces?

(a) You must identify all known workplaces under each GSA award. A failure to do so is a violation of your drug-free workplace requirements. You may identify the workplaces_

(1) To the GSA official that is making the award, either at the time of application or upon award; or

(2) In documents that you keep on file in your offices during the performance of the award, in which case you must make the information available for inspection upon request by GSA officials or their designated representatives.

(b) Your workplace identification for an award must include the actual address of buildings (or parts of buildings) or other sites where work under the award takes place. Categorical descriptions may be used (e.g., all vehicles of a mass transit authority or State highway department while in operation, State employees in each local unemployment office, performers in concert halls or radio studios).

(c) If you identified workplaces to the GSA awarding official at the time of application or award, as described in paragraph (a)(1) of this section, and any workplace that you identified changes during the performance of the award, you must inform the GSA awarding official.

Subpart C—Requirements for Recipients Who Are Individuals

§ 105–74.300 What must I do to comply with this part if I am an individual recipient?

As a condition of receiving a(n) GSA award, if you are an individual recipient, you must agree that—

(a) You will not engage in the unlawful manufacture, distribution, dispensing, possession, or use of a controlled substance in conducting any activity related to the award; and

(b) If you are convicted of a criminal drug offense resulting from a violation occurring during the conduct of any award activity, you will report the conviction:

(1) In writing.

(2) Within 10 calendar days of the conviction.

(3) To the GSA awarding official or other designee for each award that you currently have, unless §105–74.301 or the award document designates a central point for the receipt of the notices. When notice is made to a central point, it must include the identification number(s) of each affected award.

§ 105–74.301 [Reserved]

Subpart D—Responsibilities of GSA Awarding Officials

§ 105–74.400 What are my responsibilities as a(n) GSA awarding official?

As a(n) GSA awarding official, you must obtain each recipient's agreement, as a condition of the award, to comply with the requirements in—

(a) Subpart B of this part, if the recipient is not an individual; or

(b) Subpart C of this part, if the recipient is an individual.

Subpart E—Violations of this Part and Consequences

§ 105–74.500 How are violations of this part determined for recipients other than individuals?

A recipient other than an individual is in violation of the requirements of this part if the Administrator of General Services determines, in writing, that—

(a) The recipient has violated the requirements of subpart B of this part; or

(b) The number of convictions of the recipient's employees for violating criminal drug statutes in the workplace is large enough to indicate that the recipient has failed to make a good faith effort to provide a drug-free workplace.

§ 105–74.505 How are violations of this part determined for recipients who are individuals?

An individual recipient is in violation of the requirements of this part if the Administrator of General Services determines, in writing, that—

(a) The recipient has violated the requirements of subpart C of this part; or

(b) The recipient is convicted of a criminal drug offense resulting from a violation occurring during the conduct of any award activity.

§ 105–74.510 What actions will the Federal Government take against a recipient determined to have violated this part?

If a recipient is determined to have violated this part, as described in §105–74.500 or §105–74.505, the General Services Administration may take one or more of the following actions—

(a) Suspension of payments under the award;

(b) Suspension or termination of the award; and

(c) Suspension or debarment of the recipient under 41 CFR part 105–68, for a period not to exceed five years.

[68 FR 66627, 66628, Nov. 26, 2003]

§ 105–74.515 Are there any exceptions to those actions?

The Administrator of General Services may waive with respect to a particular award, in writing, a suspension of payments under an award, suspension or termination of an award, or suspension or debarment of a recipient if the Administrator of General Services determines that such a waiver would be in the public interest. This exception authority cannot be delegated to any other official.

Subpart F—Definitions

§ 105–74.605 Award.

Award means an award of financial assistance by the General Services Administration or other Federal agency directly to a recipient.

(a) The term award includes:

(1) A Federal grant or cooperative agreement, in the form of money or property in lieu of money.

(2) A block grant or a grant in an entitlement program, whether or not the grant is exempted from coverage under the Governmentwide rule 41 CFR part 105–71 that implements OMB Circular A–102 (for availability, see 5 CFR 1310.3) and specifies uniform administrative requirements.

(b) The term award does not include:

(1) Technical assistance that provides services instead of money.

(2) Loans.

(3) Loan guarantees.

(4) Interest subsidies.

(5) Insurance.

(6) Direct appropriations.

(7) Veterans' benefits to individuals (i.e., any benefit to veterans, their families, or survivors by virtue of the service of a veteran in the Armed Forces of the United States).

[68 FR 66627, 66628, Nov. 26, 2003]

§ 105–74.610   Controlled substance.

Controlled substance means a controlled substance in schedules I through V of the Controlled Substances Act (21 U.S.C. 812), and as further defined by regulation at 21 CFR 1308.11 through 1308.15.

§ 105–74.615   Conviction.

Conviction means a finding of guilt (including a plea of nolo contendere) or imposition of sentence, or both, by any judicial body charged with the responsibility to determine violations of the Federal or State criminal drug statutes.

§ 105–74.620   Cooperative agreement.

Cooperative agreement means an award of financial assistance that, consistent with 31 U.S.C. 6305, is used to enter into the same kind of relationship as a grant (see definition of grant in § 105–74.650), except that substantial involvement is expected between the Federal agency and the recipient when carrying out the activity contemplated by the award. The term does not include cooperative research and development agreements as defined in 15 U.S.C. 3710a.

§ 105–74.625   Criminal drug statute.

Criminal drug statute means a Federal or non-Federal criminal statute involving the manufacture, distribution, dispensing, use, or possession of any controlled substance.

§ 105–74.630   Debarment.

Debarment means an action taken by a Federal agency to prohibit a recipient from participating in Federal Government procurement contracts and covered nonprocurement transactions. A recipient so prohibited is debarred, in accordance with the Federal Acquisition Regulation for procurement contracts (48 CFR part 9, subpart 9.4) and the common rule, Government-wide Debarment and Suspension (Nonprocurement), that implements Executive Order 12549 and Executive Order 12689.

§ 105–74.635   Drug-free workplace.

Drug-free workplace means a site for the performance of work done in connection with a specific award at which employees of the recipient are prohibited from engaging in the unlawful manufacture, distribution, dispensing, possession, or use of a controlled substance.

§ 105–74.640   Employee.

(a) *Employee* means the employee of a recipient directly engaged in the performance of work under the award, including—

(1) All direct charge employees;

(2) All indirect charge employees, unless their impact or involvement in the performance of work under the award is insignificant to the performance of the award; and

(3) Temporary personnel and consultants who are directly engaged in the performance of work under the award and who are on the recipient's payroll.

(b) This definition does not include workers not on the payroll of the recipient (e.g., volunteers, even if used to meet a matching requirement; consultants or independent contractors not on the payroll; or employees of subrecipients or subcontractors in covered workplaces).

§ 105–74.645   Federal agency or agency.

Federal agency or agency means any United States executive department, military department, government corporation, government controlled corporation, any other establishment in the executive branch (including the Executive Office of the President), or any independent regulatory agency.

§ 105–74.650   Grant.

Grant means an award of financial assistance that, consistent with 31 U.S.C. 6304, is used to enter into a relationship—

(a) The principal purpose of which is to transfer a thing of value to the recipient to carry out a public purpose of support or stimulation authorized by a law of the United States, rather than to acquire property or services for the Federal Government's direct benefit or use; and

(b) In which substantial involvement is not expected between the Federal agency and the recipient when carrying out the activity contemplated by the award.

§ 105–74.655 Individual.

Individual means a natural person.

§ 105–74.660 Recipient.

Recipient means any individual, corporation, partnership, association, unit of government (except a Federal agency) or legal entity, however organized, that receives an award directly from a Federal agency.

§ 105–74.665 State.

State means any of the States of the United States, the District of Columbia, the Commonwealth of Puerto Rico, or any territory or possession of the United States.

§ 105–74.670 Suspension.

Suspension means an action taken by a Federal agency that immediately prohibits a recipient from participating in Federal Government procurement contracts and covered nonprocurement transactions for a temporary period, pending completion of an investigation and any judicial or administrative proceedings that may ensue. A recipient so prohibited is suspended, in accordance with the Federal Acquisition Regulation for procurement contracts (48 CFR part 9, subpart 9.4) and the common rule, Government-wide Debarment and Suspension (Nonprocurement), that implements Executive Order 12549 and Executive Order 12689. Suspension of a recipient is a distinct and separate action from suspension of an award or suspension of payments under an award.

CHAPTER 109—DEPARTMENT OF ENERGY PROPERTY MANAGEMENT REGULATIONS

SUBCHAPTER A—GENERAL

PART 109–1—INTRODUCTION

Subpart 109–1.1—Regulation System

Subpart 109–1.50—Personal Property Management Program

Subpart 109–1.51—Personal Property Management Standards and Practices

Subpart 109–1.52—Personal Property Management Program for Designated Contractors

Subpart 109–1.53—Management of High Risk Personal Property

SOURCE: 81 FR 63265, Sept. 14, 2016, unless otherwise noted.

Subpart 109–1.1—Regulation System

§ 109–1.100–50   Scope of subpart.

This subpart sets forth the Department of Energy (DOE) Property Management Regulations (DOE–PMR) which establish uniform DOE property management policies, regulations, and procedures that implement and supplement the Federal Property Management Regulations/Federal Management Regulation. Property management statutory authorities that are unique to the Department (*e.g.*, section 161g of the Atomic Energy Act of 1954 (42 U.S.C. 2201(g)) and section 3155 of the National Defense Authorization Act for Fiscal Year 1994 (42 U.S.C. 72741)) are not addressed in these regulations.

§ 109–1.100–51 Definitions and acronyms.

(a) *Definitions.* As used in this chapter, the terms *personal property* and *property* are synonymous. In addition, the following definitions apply:

Accountable Personal Property includes nonexpendable personal property whose expected useful life is two years or longer and whose acquisition value, as determined by the agency, warrants tracking in the agency's property records, including capitalized and sensitive personal property. 41 CFR 102–35.20.

Administratively controlled items means personal property controlled at the discretion of individual DOE offices, but for which there is no DOE requirement to maintain formal records.

Cannibalization means to remove serviceable parts from one item of equipment in order to install them on another item of equipment (48 CFR Subpart 45.101).

Capitalized Personal Property includes property that is entered on the agency's general ledger records as a major investment or asset. An agency must determine its capitalization thresholds as discussed in Financial Accounting Standard Advisory Board (FASAB) Statement of Federal Financial Accounting Standards No. 6, 41 CFR 102–35.20; DOE Financial Management Handbook.

Controlled Unclassified Information (CUI) means the Unclassified information that is controlled within DOE because its release could cause damage. CUI within DOE encompasses Official Use Only (OUO) and Unclassified Nuclear Information (UCNI). OUO includes information such as Personally Identifiable Information, Export Controlled Information, proprietary information, and other information not covered by other DOE directives. CUI is governed by Executive Order 13556 and is a developing Government-wide policy, Controlled Unclassified Information, which will mandate uniform standards for the control of unclassified information within the Government.

Designated contractors means those on-site DOE contractors to which the DOE–PMR is made applicable when included as a contractual requirement.

The contractors to which these regulations may be made applicable include management and operating (M&O) contractors, environmental management, and other major prime contractors located at DOE sites.

Direct operations means operations conducted by DOE personnel.

Disposal means the process of reutilizing, transferring, donating, selling, abandoning, destroying, or other disposition of Government-owned personal property.

Dual-Use List means nuclear-related material, equipment, and related technology as described in the Nuclear Suppliers Group Dual-Use List as published in International Atomic Energy Agency Information Circular (INFCIRC) 254 Part 2 and as implemented by the Department of Commerce in the U.S. Export Administration Regulations (15 CFR part 774).

Equipment means a tangible asset that is functionally complete for its intended purpose, durable, nonexpendable, and needed for the performance of a contract. Equipment is not intended for sale, and does not ordinarily lose its identity or become a component part of another article when put into use (48 CFR Subpart 45.101).

Especially designed or prepared property means equipment and material designed or prepared especially for use in the nuclear fuel cycle and described in the Nuclear Suppliers Group Trigger List as published in International Atomic Energy Agency INFCIRC 254 Part 1 and as implemented by the Nuclear Regulatory Commission in 10 CFR part 110.

Excess Property means property that is no longer required to carry out the Department of Energy's needs, but for purposes of this regulation, such property has not been reported to the General Services Administration as excess property under 41 CFR 102–36.35.

Export controlled information means unclassified U.S. Government information under DOE cognizance that, if proposed for export by the private sector, would require a U.S. Department of Commerce or U.S. Department of State validated license, or a DOE authorization for export, and which, if given uncontrolled release, could reasonably be expected to adversely affect U.S. national security or nuclear nonproliferation objectives.

Export controlled property means property the export of which is subject to licensing by the U.S. Department of Commerce, the U.S. Department of State, the U.S. Nuclear Regulatory Commission, or authorized by the U.S. Department of Energy.

Hazardous personal property means property that is deemed a hazardous material, chemical substance or mixture, or hazardous waste under the Hazardous Materials Transportation Act (HMTA) (49 U.S.C. 5101), the Resource Conservation and Recovery Act (RCRA) (42 U.S.C. 6901–6981), or the Toxic Substances Control Act (TSCA) (15 U.S.C. 2601–2609). 41 CFR 102–36.40.

High risk personal property means property that, because of its potential impact on public health and safety, the environment, national security interests, or proliferation concerns, must be controlled, and disposed of in other than the routine manner. The categories of high risk property are automatic data processing equipment, especially designed or prepared property, export controlled information, export controlled property, hazardous property, nuclear weapon components or weapon-like components, proliferation sensitive property, radioactive property, special nuclear material, and unclassified controlled nuclear information.

Information Technology. (i) With respect to an executive agency means any equipment or interconnected system or subsystem of equipment, used in the automatic acquisition, storage, analysis, evaluation, manipulation, management, movement, control, display, switching, interchange, transmission, or reception of data or information by the executive agency, if the equipment is used by the executive agency directly or is used by a contractor under a contract with the executive agency that requires the use—

(A) Of that equipment; or

(B) Of that equipment to a significant extent in the performance of a service or the furnishing of a product;

(ii) Includes computers, ancillary equipment (including imaging peripherals, input, output, and storage devices necessary for security and surveillance), peripheral equipment designed to be controlled by the central processing unit of a computer, software, firmware and similar procedures, services (including support services), and related resources; but

(iii) Does not include any equipment acquired by a federal contractor incidental to a federal contract. 40 U.S.C. 11101.

Munitions List Items (MLIs) are commodities (usually defense articles/defense services) listed in the International Traffic in Arms Regulation (22 CFR part 121), published by the U.S. Department of State. 41 CFR 102–36.40.

Nuclear weapon component or weapon-like component means parts of whole war reserve nuclear weapon systems, joint test assemblies, trainers, or test devices, including associated testing, maintenance, and handling equipment; or items that simulate such parts.

Organizational Property Management Officers means establish and administer personal property management programs within their organizations consistent with applicable laws, regulations, practices, and standards.

Personal property means any property, except real property. For purposes of this part, the term excludes records of the Federal Government, and naval vessels of the following categories: Battleships, cruisers, aircraft carriers, destroyers, and submarines. 102–36.40.

Program Secretarial Officer (PSO) Assistant Secretaries/Program Element Heads.

Proliferation-sensitive property means nuclear-related or dual-use equipment, material, or technology as described in the Nuclear Suppliers Group Trigger List and Dual-Use List, or equipment, material or technology used in the research, design, development, testing, or production of nuclear or other weapons.

Property Administrator means an authorized representative of the contracting officer appointed in accordance with agency procedures, responsible for administering the contract requirements and obligations relating to Government property in the possession of a contractor FAR 45–101.

Property management means the system of acquiring, maintaining, using and disposing of the personal property of an organization or entity. 102–35.20.

Radioactive property means any item or material that is contaminated with radioactivity and which emits ionizing radiation in excess of background radiation as measured by appropriate instrumentation.

Sensitive Personal Property includes all items, regardless of value, that require special control and accountability due to unusual rates of loss, theft or misuse, or due to national security or export control considerations. Such property includes weapons, ammunition, explosives, information technology equipment with memory capability, cameras, and communications equipment. These classifications do not preclude agencies from specifying additional personal property classifications to effectively manage their programs. 41 CFR 102–35.20.

Spare equipment/property means items held as replacement spares for equipment in current use in DOE program.

Special nuclear material means plutonium, uranium 233, uranium enriched in the isotope 233 or 235, any other materials which the Nuclear Regulatory Commission pursuant to the Atomic Energy Act of 1954, as amended, determines to be special nuclear material, or any material artificially enriched by any of the foregoing, but does not include source material.

Trigger List means nuclear material, equipment, and related technology as described in International Atomic Energy Agency in INFCIRC 254, Part 1 and as implemented by the Nuclear Regulatory Commission in 10 CFR part 110.

Unclassified controlled nuclear information means U.S. Government information pertaining to atomic energy defense activities as defined in section 148 of the Atomic Energy Act. Such information can relate to aspects of nuclear weapons design, development, testing, physical security, production, or utilization facilities. 10 CFR part 1017.

(b) *Acronyms.* As used in this chapter, the following acronyms apply:

CFR: Code of Federal Regulations
CSC: Customer Supply Center

CUI: Controlled Unclassified Information
DEAR: Department of Energy Acquisition Regulation
DOD: Department of Defense
DOE: Department of Energy
DOE–PMR: Department of Energy Property Management Regulations
DPMO: Departmental Property Management Officer
ECCN: Export Control Classification Number
ECI: Export Controlled Information
EHFFP: Equipment Held For Future Projects
EOQ: Economic Order Quantity
FAR: Federal Acquisition Regulation
FPMR/FMR: Federal Property Management Regulations/Federal Management Regulation
FSC: Federal Supply Classification
FSCG: Federal Supply Classification Group
GAO: General Accounting Office
GSA: General Services Administration
GVWR: Gross Vehicle Weight Rating
INFCIRC: International Atomic Energy Agency Information Circular
IFMS: Interagency Fleet Management System
IT: Information Technology
LEDP: Laboratory Equipment Donation Program
M&O: Management and Operating
MCTL: Military Critical Technologies List
OPMO: Organizational Property Management Officer
OPSEC: Operations Security
PA: Property Administrator
PSO: Program Secretarial Officer (PSO)
SNM: Special Nuclear Material
UCNI: Unclassified Controlled Nuclear Information
U.S.C.: United States Code

§ 109–1.101   Federal Property Management Regulations/Federal Management Regulation System.

§ 109–1.101–50   DOE–PMR System.

The DOE–PMR system described in this subpart is established to provide uniform personal property management policies, standards, and practices within the Department.

§ 109–1.102   Federal Property Management Regulations/Federal Management Regulation.

§ 109–1.102–50   DOE–PMRs.

The DOE–PMRs (41 CFR Ch. 109) implements and supplements the FPMR/FMR (41 CFR Ch. 101) issued by the General Services Administration (GSA), Public Laws, Executive Orders,

Office of Management and Budget directives, and other agency issuances affecting the Department's personal property management program.

§109–1.103 FPMR/FMR temporary regulations.

§109–1.103–50 DOE–PMR temporary policies and bulletins.

(a) Subject to applicable procedural requirements in 41 U.S.C. 1707, 42 U.S.C 7191 and 5 U.S.C 553, Personal Property Letters are authorized for publication of temporary policies that should not be codified in the Code of Federal Regulations (CFR).

(b) DOE–PMR Bulletins are used to disseminate information concerning personal property management matters not affecting policy or to clarify instructions in actions required by the FPMR/FMR or DOE–PMR.

§109–1.104 Publication and distribution of FPMR/FMR.

§109–1.104–50 Publication and distribution of DOE–PMR.

The DOE–PMR will be published in the FEDERAL REGISTER and will appear in the CFR as Chapter 109 of Title 41, Public Contracts and Property Management. Written publications of the DOE–PMR will be distributed to DOE offices.

§109–1.106 Applicability of FPMR/FMR.

§109–1.106–50 Applicability of FPMR/FMR and DOE–PMR.

(a) The FPMR/FMR and DOE–PMR apply to all direct operations.

(b) The DOE–PMR does not apply to facilities and activities conducted under Executive Order 12344 (Naval Nuclear Propulsion Program) and Public Law 98–525.

(c) Unless otherwise provided in the appropriate part or subpart, the FPMR/FMR and DOE–PMR apply to designated contractors.

(d) The Procurement Executive or head of a contracting activity may designate contractors other than designated contractors to which the FPMR/FMR and DOE–PMR apply.

(e) Program Secretarial Officers and other DOE elements are responsible to identify the contracts that involve the life-cycle management of personal property assets. The respective program's Head of Contracting Activity is responsible to issue direction to Contracting Officers to incorporate any and all applicable requirements of the FPMR/FMR and DOE–PMR and any supplemental Program Office guidance into contracts identified with life-cycle management of personal property.

(f) Principal authority and responsibility for the administration of DOE personal property in the custody of its contractors rest with the responsible Contracting Officer.

(g) The FPMR/FMR and DOE–PMR shall be used by contracting officers in the administration of applicable contracts, and in the review, approval, or appraisal of such contractor operations.

(h) Regulations for the management of Government property in the possession of other DOE contractors are contained in the Federal Acquisition Regulation (FAR), 48 CFR part 45, and in the DOE Acquisition Regulation (DEAR), 48 CFR part 945.

(i) Regulations for the management of personal property held by financial assistance recipients are contained in the DOE Financial Assistance Rules (10 CFR part 600) 2 CFR parts 200 and 910 and DOE Order 534.1, Accounting.

§109–1.107–50 Consultation regarding DOE–PMR.

(a) The DOE–PMR shall be fully coordinated with all Departmental elements substantively concerned with the subject matter.

(b) The accountable Under Secretary is responsible for implementation of the DOE PMR through their respective DOE elements.

(c) Program Secretarial Officers and DOE elements with responsibility for personal property, as delegated by their cognizant Under Secretary, may develop program management plans and issue internal program office guidance that is aligned to the requirements in the DOE–PMR and as explicitly authorized by their Under Secretary.

(d) Heads of Contracting Activity designates Organizational Property

Management Officers (OPMO) to establish and administer personal property management programs within their organizations.

(e) Contracting Officers designates Property Administrators (PA) as authorized representatives responsible performing delegated contract administration functions for contract and financial assistance requirements relating to Government personal property.

(f) The Office of Management is responsible for Agency-level management of the contract property program and provides policy and management assistance in support of the policy implementation effort. The Office of Management designates an Agency Property Executive to serve as National Utilization Officer responsible for promoting acquisition and utilization of excess personal property and for establishing policies, standards, and guidance in accordance with applicable laws, regulations and sound personal property management practices and standards.

§ 109–1.108 Agency implementation and supplementation of FPMR/FMR.

(a) The DOE–PMR includes basic and significant Departmental personal property management policies and standards which implement, supplement, or deviate from the FPMR/FMR. In the absence of any DOE–PMR issuance, the basic FPMR/FMR material shall govern.

(b) The DOE–PMR shall be consistent with the FPMR/FMR and shall not duplicate or paraphrase the FPMR/FMR material.

(c) Implementing procedures, instructions, and guides which are necessary to clarify or to implement the DOE–PMR may be issued by Headquarters or field organizations, provided that the implementing procedures, instructions and guides:

(1) Are consistent with the policies and procedures contained in this regulation;

(2) To the extent practicable, follow the format, arrangement, and numbering system of this regulation; and

(3) Contain no material which duplicates, paraphrases, or is inconsistent with the contents of this regulation.

§ 109–1.110–50   Deviation procedures.

(a) Each request for deviation shall contain the following:

(1) A statement of the deviation desired, including identification of the specific paragraph number(s) of the DOE–PMR;

(2) The reason why the deviation is considered necessary or would be in the best interest of the Government;

(3) If applicable, the name of the contractor and identification of the contractor affected;

(4) A statement as to whether the deviation has been requested previously and, if so, circumstances of the previous request;

(5) A description of the intended effect of the deviation;

(6) A statement of the period of time for which the deviation is needed; and

(7) Any pertinent background information which will contribute to a full understanding of the desired deviation.

(b)(1) Requests for deviations from applicable portions of the FPMR/FMR and DOE–PMR (except aviation related portions) shall be forwarded with supporting documentation by the Organizational Property Management Officer (OPMO) to the Office of Management.

(2) Requests for deviations from aviation related portions of the FPMR/FMR and DOE–PMR concerning aviation operations shall be forwarded by the OPMO or on-site DOE Aviation Management Officer with supporting documentation to the DOE Senior Aviation Management Official.

(c) The accountable Under Secretary is authorized to approve documented program-specific or location-specific exemptions, exclusions, and/or deviations from requirements of the DOE PMR based on mission needs, efficiency, and/or efficacy of execution without disregarding federal laws and regulations.

(d) Requests for deviations from the FPMR/FMR will be coordinated with GSA by the Office of Management.

Subpart 109–1.50—Personal Property Management Program

§ 109–1.5000   Scope of subpart.

This subpart supplements the FPMR/FMR, states DOE personal property management policy and program objectives, and prescribes authorities and responsibilities for the conduct of an efficient personal property management program in DOE.

§ 109–1.5001 Policy.

It is DOE policy that a program for the management of personal property shall be established and maintained to meet program needs. Personal property shall be managed efficiently, in accordance with Federal statutes and regulations, and in alignment with mission needs. Personal property must be managed in a safe and secure manor and ensure personal property assets are available to support efficient mission execution. Commercial practices may be used (*i.e.*, industry leading practices, voluntary consensus standards) that are necessary, appropriate, and provide effective and efficient Government property management, except where those practices are inconsistent with law, regulation or otherwise impractical.

§ 109–1.5002 Personal property management program objectives.

The objectives of the DOE personal property management program are to provide:

(a) A system for efficiently managing personal property in the custody or possession of DOE organizations and designated contractors; and

(b) Uniform principles, policies, and standards for efficient management of personal property that are sufficiently broad in scope and flexible in nature to facilitate adaptation to local needs and various kinds of operations.

Subpart 109–1.51—Personal Property Management Standards and Practices

§ 109–1.5100 Scope of subpart.

This subpart provides guidance on DOE standards and practices to be applied in the management of personal property.

§ 109–1.5101 Official use of personal property.

Personal property shall be used only in the performance of official work of the United States Government, except:

(a) In emergencies threatening loss of life or property as authorized by law;

(b) As otherwise authorized by law and approved by the Office of Management; Program Secretarial Officer (PSO) for their respective organizations; or a contracting officer for contractor-held property.

§ 109–1.5102 Maximum use of personal property.

Personal property management practices shall assure the best possible use of personal property. Supplies and equipment shall be generally limited to those items essential for carrying out the programs of DOE efficiently.

§ 109–1.5103 Loan of personal property.

(a) Personal property which is not excess and would otherwise be out of service for temporary periods may be loaned to other DOE offices and contractors, other Federal agencies, and to others for official purposes. The loan request shall be in writing, stating the purpose of the loan and period of time required. The loan shall be executed on DOE Form 4420.2, Personal Property Loan Agreement when approved in writing by the OPMO or on-site DOE property administrator. When approved, a memorandum transmitting the loan agreement shall be prepared identifying the loan period, delivery time, method of payment and transportation, and point of delivery and return, to ensure proper control and protect DOE's interest. The domestic loan period shall not exceed one year, but may be renewed in one year increments. Second renewals of loan agreements shall be reviewed and justified at a level of management at least two levels above that of the individual making the determination to loan the property. Third renewals shall be approved by the head of the field organization or designee.

(b) Requests for loans to foreign Governments and other foreign organizations shall be submitted to the Office of International Affairs for approval, with a copy to the cognizant Headquarters program office.

§ 109–1.5105   Identification marking of personal property.

(a) Personal property shall be marked "U.S. Government property" or "U.S. DOE") subject to the criteria below. The markings shall be securely affixed to the property, legible, and conspicuous. Examples of appropriate marking media are bar code labels, decals, and stamping.

(b) Personal property which by its nature cannot be marked, such as stores items, metal stock, etc., is exempted from this requirement.

(c) To the extent practicable and economical, markings shall be removed prior to disposal outside of DOE. 41 CFR 102–35.30.

§ 109–1.5106   Segregation of personal property.

Generally, contractor-owned personal property shall be segregated from Government personal property. Commingling of Government and contractor-owned personal property may be allowed only when:

(a) The segregation of the property would materially hinder the progress of the work (*i.e.*, segregation is not feasible for reasons such as small quantities, lack of space, or increased costs); and

(b) Control procedures are adequate (*i.e.*, the Government property is specifically marked or otherwise identified as Government property).

§ 109–1.5107   Physical protection of personal property.

Controls such as property pass systems, memorandum records, regular or intermittent gate checks, and/or perimeter fencing shall be established as appropriate to prevent loss, theft, or unauthorized removal of property from the premises on which such personal property is located.

§ 109–1.5108   Personal property records requirements.

The contractor's property control records shall provide the following information for every accountable item of Government personal property in the contractor's possession and any other data elements required by specific contract provisions:

(a) Contract number or equivalent code designation.

(b) Asset type.

(c) Description of item (name, serial number, national stock number (if available)).

(d) Property control number (Government ownership identity).

(e) Unit acquisition cost (including delivery and installation cost, when appropriate, and unit of measure).

(f) Acquisition document reference and date.

(g) Manufacturer's name, model and serial number.

(h) Quantity received, fabricated, issued or on hand.

(i) Location (physical area)

(j) Custodian name and organization code.

(k) Use status (active, storage, excess, etc.)

(l) High risk designation.

(m) Disposition document reference and date.

§ 109–1.5108–1   Equipment.

An individual property record will be developed and maintained for each item of equipment.

§ 109–1.5108–3   Stores inventories.

Perpetual inventory records are to be maintained for stores inventory items.

§ 109–1.5108–4   Precious metals.

Perpetual inventory records are to be maintained for precious metals.

§ 109–1.5108–5   Administratively controlled items.

No formal property management records are required to be maintained for this category of personal property, which includes such items as those controlled for calibration or maintenance purposes, contaminated property, tool crib items, and equipment pool items. Various control records can be employed to help safeguard this property against waste and abuse, including purchase vs. use information, tool crib check-outs, loss and theft reports, calibration records, disposal records, and other similar records. Control techniques would include physical security, custodial responsibility, identification/marking, or other locally established control techniques.

§ 109–1.5110 Physical inventories of personal property.

(a) Physical inventories of those categories of personal property as specified in paragraph (g) of this section shall be conducted at all DOE and designated contractor locations.

(b) Physical inventories shall be performed by the use of personnel other than custodians of the property. Where staffing restraints or other considerations apply, the inventory may be performed by the custodian with verification by a second party.

(c) Detailed procedures for the taking of physical inventories shall be developed for each DOE office and designated contractor. The OPMO/PA shall review and approve the DOE office and contractor procedures.

(d) The conduct of a physical inventory will be observed, or follow-on audits made, by independent representatives, *e.g.*, finance, audit, or property personnel, to the extent deemed necessary to assure that approved procedures are being followed and results are accurate. These observations or audits shall be documented and the documentation retained in the inventory record file.

(e) The DOE capitalization threshold for items acquired prior to October 1, 2011 is $50,000. For items acquired on or after October 1, 2011, the threshold is $500,000.

(f) Procedures that are limited to a check-off of a listing of recorded property without actual verification of the location and existence of such property do not meet the requirements of a physical inventory.

(g) The frequency of physical inventories of personal property shall be as follows:

(1) Equipment—biennial 98%. Inventory accuracy.

(2) Sensitive items—annual 100%. Inventory accuracy.

(3) Stores inventories—annual.

(4) Precious metals—annual 100% Inventory accuracy.

(5) HRPP—annual 100% Inventory accuracy.

(6) All other accountable property every three years 98% Inventory accuracy.

(7) Administratively controlled items—There is no formal Department requirement for the performance of physical inventories of this property. However, OPMOs/PA's determines inventory requirements based on management needs.

(h) Physical inventories shall be performed at intervals more frequently than required when experience at any given location or with any given item or items indicates that this action is necessary for effective property accounting, utilization, or control as directed by OPMO/PA.

(i) Physical inventories of equipment may be conducted by the "inventory by exception" method. The system and procedures for taking physical inventories by this method must be fully documented and approved in writing by the OPMO/PA.

(j) The results of physical inventories shall be reconciled with the property records, and with applicable financial control accounts.

(k) The results of physical inventories shall be reported to the OPMO/PA.

(l) Physical inventories of equipment and stores inventories may be conducted using statistical sampling methods in lieu of the normal wall-to-wall method. The sampling methods employed must be statistically valid and approved in writing by the OPMO. If use of the statistical methods of physical inventory does not produce acceptable results, the wall-to-wall method shall be used to complete the inventories.

§ 109–1.5112 Loss, damage, or destruction of personal property in possession of DOE direct operations.

DOE offices shall establish procedures to provide for the reporting, documentation, and investigation of instances of loss, damage, or destruction of personal property including:

(a) Notification to appropriate DOE organizations and law enforcement offices;

(b) Determination of cause or origin;

(c) Liability and responsibility for repair or replacement; and

(d) Actions taken to prevent further loss, damage, or destruction, and to prevent repetition of similar incidents.

§ 109–1.5113   Loss, damage, or destruction of personal property in possession of designated contractors.

(a) Designated contractors shall report any loss, damage, or destruction of personal property in its possession or control, including property in the possession or control of subcontractors, to the property administrator as soon as it becomes known.

(b) When physical inventories, consumption analyses, or other actions disclose consumption of property considered unreasonable by the property administrator; or loss, damage, or destruction of personal property not previously reported by the contractor, the property administrator shall require the contractor to investigate the incidents and submit written reports.

(c) Reports of physical inventory results and identified discrepancies shall be submitted to the property administrator within 90 days of completion of physical inventories. An acceptable percentage of shrinkage for stores inventories shall be determined by the property administrator on a location-by-location basis, based on type and cost of materials, historical data, and other site-specific factors. This determination shall be in writing and be supported by appropriate documentation.

(d) The contractor's report referenced above shall contain factual data as to the circumstances surrounding the loss, damage, destruction or excessive consumption, including:

(1) The contractor's name and contract number;

(2) A description of the property;

(3) Cost of the property, and cost of repairs in instances of damage (in event actual cost is not known, use reasonable estimate);

(4) The date, time (if pertinent), and cause or origin; and

(5) Actions taken by the contractor to prevent further loss, damage, destruction, or unreasonable consumption, and to prevent repetition of similar incidents.

(e) The property administrator shall ensure that the corrective actions taken by the contractor under paragraph (d)(5) of this section satisfactorily address system weaknesses.

(f) The contracting officer shall make a determination of contractor liability with a copy of the determination furnished to the contractor and the property administrator. Costs may be assessed against a contractor for physical inventory discrepancies or other instances of loss of Government property within the terms of the contract. Credit should only be applied if specific items reported as lost can be uniquely identified. General physical inventory write-ons are not to be used as a credit.

(g) If part of a designated contractor's personal property management system is found to be unsatisfactory, the property administrator shall increase surveillance of that part to prevent, to the extent possible, any loss, damage, destruction or unreasonable consumption of personal property. The property administrator shall give special attention to reasonably ensuring that any loss, damage, destruction or unreasonable consumption occurring during a period when a contractor's personal property management system is not approved is identified before approval or reinstatement of approval.

§ 109–1.5114   Use of non-Government-owned property.

Non-Government-owned personal property shall not be installed in, affixed to, or otherwise made a part of any Government-owned personal property when such action will adversely affect the operation or condition of the Government property.

§ 109–1.5148   Personal property management reports.

Annual personal property reports as required by 41 CFR 102 35.25 and internal DOE personal property reports must be submitted to the Office of Management at a date determined by the Property Executive.

Subpart 109–1.52—Personal Property Management Program for Designated Contractors

§ 109–1.5200   Scope of subpart.

This subpart prescribes policy and responsibilities for the establishment, maintenance, and appraisal of designated contractors' programs for the management of personal property.

§ 109–1.5201 Policy.

(a) Designated contractors shall establish, implement, and maintain a system that provides for an efficient personal property management program. The system shall be consistent with the terms of the contract; prescribed policies, procedures, regulations, statutes, and instructions; and directions from the contracting officer.

(b) Designated contractors' personal property management systems shall not be considered acceptable until reviewed and approved in writing by the cognizant DOE contracting office in accordance with § 109–1.5205 of this subpart.

(c) Designated contractors shall maintain their personal property management systems in writing. Revisions to the systems shall be approved in writing by the cognizant DOE contracting office in accordance with § 109–1.5205 of this subpart.

(d) Designated contractors shall include their personal property management system in their management surveillance or internal review program in order to identify weaknesses and functions requiring corrective action.

(e) Designated contractors are responsible and accountable for all Government personal property in the possession of subcontractors, and shall include appropriate provisions in their subcontracts and property management systems to assure that subcontractors establish and maintain efficient systems for the management of Government personal property in their possession in accordance with § 109–1.5204 of this subpart.

§ 109–1.5202 Establishment of a personal property holdings baseline.

(a) If the contractor is a new designated contractor, the contractor may accept the previous contractor's personal property records as a baseline or may perform a complete physical inventory of all personal property. This physical inventory is to be performed within the time period specified by the contracting officer or the contract, but no later than one year after the execution date of the contract. If the physical inventory is not accomplished within the allotted time frame, the

previous contractor's records will be considered as the baseline.

(b) If any required physical inventories have not been accomplished within the time periods prescribed in § 109–1.5110(f) of this part, the new contractor shall either perform such physical inventories within 120 days of contract renegotiation, or accept the existing property records as the baseline.

§ 109–1.5203 Management of subcontractor-held personal property.

Designated contractors shall require those subcontractors provided Government-owned personal property to establish and maintain a system for the management of such property. As a minimum, a subcontractor's personal property management system shall provide for the following:

(a) Adequate records.

(b) Controls over acquisitions.

(c) Identification as Government-owned personal property.

(d) Physical inventories.

(e) Proper care, maintenance, and protection.

(f) Controls over personal property requiring special handling (*i.e.*, nuclear-related, proliferation-sensitive, hazardous, or contaminated property).

(g) Reporting, redistribution, and disposal of excess and surplus personal property.

(h) Accounting for personal property that is lost, damaged, destroyed, stolen, abandoned, or worn out.

(i) Periodic reports, including physical inventory results and total acquisition cost of Government property.

(j) An internal surveillance program, including periodic reviews, to ensure that personal property is being managed in accordance with established procedures.

§ 109–1.5204 Review and approval of a designated contractor's personal property management system.

(a) An initial review of a designated contractor's personal property management system shall be performed by the property administrator within one year after the execution date of the contract, except for contract extensions or renewals or when an existing contractor has been awarded a follow-on contract. The purpose of the review is

649

to determine whether the contractor's system provides adequate protection, maintenance, utilization, and disposition of personal property, and reasonable assurance that the Department's personal property is safeguarded against waste, loss, unauthorized use, or misappropriation, in accordance with applicable statutes, regulations, contract terms and conditions, programmatic needs, and good business practices. If circumstances preclude completion of the initial review within the "within one year" initial review requirement, the property administrator shall request a deviation from the requirement in accordance with the provisions of § 109–1.110–50 of this part.

(b) If a designated contractor is the successor to a previous designated contractor and the contract award was based in part on the contractor's proposal to overhaul the existing personal property management system(s), the "within one year" initial review requirement may be extended based on:

(1) The scope of the overhaul; and

(2) An analysis of the cost to implement the overhaul within a year versus a proposed extended period.

(c) When an existing contract has been extended or renewed, or the designated contractor has been awarded a follow-on contract, an initial review of the contractor's personal property management system is not required. In such cases, the established appraisal schedule will continue to be followed as prescribed in paragraph (d) of this section.

(d) At a minimum of every three years after the date of approval of a designated contractor's property management system, the OPMO/PA shall make an appraisal of the personal property management operation of the contractor. The purpose of the appraisal is to determine if the contractor is managing personal property in accordance with its previously approved system and procedures, and to establish whether such procedures are efficient. The appraisal may be based on a formal comprehensive appraisal or a series of formal appraisals of the functional segments of the contractor's operation.

(e) A designated contractor's property management system shall be approved, conditionally approved, or dis-

approved in writing by the head of the field organization with advice of the contracting officer, property administrator, OPMO, legal counsel, and appropriate program officials. Approval authority may be redelegated to the contracting officer or OPMO/PA. Conditional approval and disapproval authority cannot be redelegated. When a system is conditionally approved or disapproved, the property administrator or contracting officer shall advise the contractor, in writing, of deficiencies that need to be corrected, and a time schedule established for completion of corrective actions.

(f) Appropriate follow-up will be made by the property administrator to ensure that corrective actions have been initiated and completed.

(g) When a determination has been made by the property administrator that all major system deficiencies identified in the review or appraisal have been corrected, the head of the field organization shall withdraw the conditional approval or disapproval, and approve the system with the concurrence of the OPMO/PA. The approval shall be in writing and addressed to appropriate contractor management.

(h) The property administrator shall maintain a copy of all designated contractor personal property management system appraisals and approvals in such manner as to be readily available to investigative and external review teams.

§ 109–1.5205　Personal property management system changes.

Any proposed significant change to a designated contractor's approved personal property management system shall be reviewed by the property administrator at the earliest possible time. Such changes should then be approved in writing on an interim basis, or disapproved in writing, by the property administrator as appropriate.

Subpart 109–1.53—Management of High Risk Personal Property

§ 109–1.5300　Scope of subpart.

(a) This subpart provides identification, accounting, control, and disposal policy guidance for the following categories of high risk personal property: Especially designed or prepared property, export controlled property, nuclear weapon components or weapon-like components, and proliferation sensitive property. The guidance is intended to ensure that the disposition of these categories of high risk personal property does not adversely affect the national security or nuclear nonproliferation objectives of the United States.

(b) The other categories of high risk personal property are controlled by other life cycle management programs and procedures monitored by other Departmental elements.

§ 109–1.5301 Applicability.

This subpart is applicable to all DOE organizations which purchase, manage or dispose of Government personal property, or contract for the management of Government facilities, programs, or related services, which may directly or indirectly require the purchase, management, or disposal of Government-owned personal property. Using the high-risk personal property control requirements in this subpart as guidance, Program Secretarial Officer (PSO) or OPMOs/PAs shall ensure that designated contractors and financial assistance recipients are responsible for developing a cost effective high-risk property management system, covering all operational responsibilities enumerated in this subpart.

§ 109–1.5302 Policies.

(a) It is the responsibility of DOE organizations and designated contractors to manage and control Government-owned high risk personal property in an efficient manner. High-risk personal property will be managed throughout its life cycle so as to protect public and DOE personnel safety and to advance the national security and the nuclear nonproliferation objectives of the U.S. Government.

(b) The disposition of high risk property is subject to special considerations. Items of high risk property may present significant risks to the national security and nuclear nonproliferation objectives of the Government which must be evaluated. Organizations will identify high risk property and control its disposition to eliminate or mitigate such risks. In no case shall property be transferred or disposed unless it receives a high risk assessment and is handled accordingly.

§ 109–1.5303 Procedures.

(a) *Identification, marking and control.* To ensure the appropriate treatment of property at its disposal and to prevent inadvertent, uncontrolled release of high risk property, property should be assessed and evaluated as high risk property as early in its life cycle as practical.

(1) Newly acquired high risk personal property shall be identified and tracked during the acquisition process and marked upon receipt.

(2) All personal property shall be reviewed for high risk identification, marking, and database entry during regularly scheduled physical inventories, unless access to the property is difficult or impractical because the property is a component of a larger assembly, a complex operating system, or an older facility. The review of this property will be completed, prior to disposition, when replacing components or when operating systems and facilities are decommissioned and dismantling.

(3) High risk personal property which by its nature cannot be marked, such as stores items and metal stock, is exempt from this requirement. However, personal property management programs should contain documentation on the characterization of this property as high risk.

(b) *Disposition of high risk property.* (1) Prior to disposition, all personal property, materials or data will be assessed to determine:

(i) Whether it should be characterized as high risk, and

(ii) What actions are necessary to ensure compliance with applicable national security or nonproliferation controls.

(2) The DOE or designated contractor property management organization may not process high risk personal property into a reutilization/disposal program without performing the reviews prescribed by the local high risk

property management system. The reviews must be properly documented, and all appropriate certifications and clearances received, in accordance with the approved site or facility personal property management program.

(3) The disposition (including demilitarization of items on the Munitions List) and handling of high risk personal property are subject to applicable provisions of subchapter H of the FPMR/FMR, subchapter H of this chapter, and the DOE Guidelines on Export Control and Nonproliferation.

(4) All applicable documentation, including records concerning the property's categorization as high risk, shall be included as part of the property transfer. The documentation shall be included with all transfers within, or external to, DOE.

(5) Unless an alternative disposition option appears to be in the best interest of the Government, surplus Trigger List components, equipment, and materials and nuclear weapon components shall either be sold for scrap after being rendered useless for their originally intended purpose or destroyed, with the destruction verified and documented. Requests for approval of an alternative disposition may be made through the cognizant Assistant Secretary to the Director of the Office of Nonproliferation and National Security.

(6) The following Export Restriction Notice, or approved equivalent notice, shall be included in all transfers, sales, or other offerings:

EXPORT RESTRICTION NOTICE

The use, disposition, export and re-export of this property are subject to all applicable U.S. laws and regulations, including the Atomic Energy Act of 1954, as amended; the Arms Export Control Act (22 U.S.C. 2751 et seq.); the Export Administration Act of 1979 as continued under the International Emergency Economic Powers Act (Title II of Pub. L. 95-223, 91 Stat. 1626, October 28, 1977); Trading with the Enemy Act (50 U.S.C. 4305) as amended by the Foreign Assistance Act of 1961; Assistance to Foreign Atomic Energy Activities (10 CFR part 810); Export and Import of Nuclear Equipment and Material (10 CFR part 110); International Traffic in Arms Regulations (22 CFR parts 120 et seq.); Export Administration Regulations (15 CFR part 730 et seq.);.); and the Espionage Act (37 U.S.C.

791 et seq.) which among other things, prohibit:

a. The making of false statements and concealment of any material information regarding the use or disposition, export or re-export of the property; and

b. Any use or disposition, export or re-export of the property which is not authorized in accordance with the provisions of this agreement.

§ 109-1.5304 Deviations.

(a) Life cycle control determinations. When the PSO approves a contractor program containing controls, other than life cycle control consistent with this subpart, the decision shall be justified in writing and a copy sent to the Office of Management. A PSO's decision not to provide life-cycle control should take into account:

(1) The nature and extent of high risk property typically purchased or otherwise brought to a DOE or designated contractor facility or site;

(2) The projected stability of DOE and designated contractor operations; and

(3) The degree of confidence in the property control measures available at disposition.

(b) Certain transfers, sales, or other offerings of high risk personal property may require special conditions or specific restrictions as determined necessary by the property custodian or cognizant program office.

(c) Requests for deviations from the requirements of this subpart may be made through the cognizant PSO to the Office of Management.

PART 109-6—MISCELLANEOUS REGULATIONS

Subpart 109-6.4—Official Use of Government Passenger Carriers Between Residence and Place of Employment

Sec.
109-6.400 Scope and applicability.
109-6.400-50 Instructions to DOE passenger carrier operators.
109-6.402 Policy.
109-6.450 Statutory provisions.

AUTHORITY: Sec. 205(c), 63 Stat. 390 (40 U.S.C. 121; 31 U.S.C. 1344(e)(1).

SOURCE: 81 FR 63265, Sept. 14, 2016, unless otherwise noted.

Subpart 109–6.4—Official Use of Government Passenger Carriers Between Residence and Place of Employment

§ 109–6.400 Scope and applicability.

(a) With the exception of § 109–6.400–50, the provisions of this subpart and 41 CFR part 102–5 do not apply to designated contractors. Official use provisions applicable to these contractors are contained in § 109–38.3 of this chapter.

(b) When an employee on temporary duty is authorized to travel by Government motor vehicle, and in the interest of the Government, is scheduled to depart before the beginning of regular working hours, or if there will be a significant savings in time, a Government motor vehicle may be issued at the close of the preceding working day. Such authorizations must be submitted to the fleet manager to ensure proper use of motor vehicles during non-duty hours. Similarly, when scheduled to return after the close of working hours, the motor vehicle may be returned the next regular working day. This use of a Government motor vehicle is not regarded as prohibited by 31 U.S.C. 1344 (25 Comp. Gen. 844(1946)).

§ 109–6.400–50 Instructions to DOE passenger carrier operators.

DOE offices shall ensure that DOE employees operating Government motor vehicles are informed concerning:

(a) The statutory requirement that Government motor vehicles shall be used only for official purposes;

(b) Personal responsibility for safe driving and operation of Government motor vehicles, and for compliance with Federal, state, and local laws and regulations, and all accident reporting requirements;

(c) The need to possess a valid state, District of Columbia, or commonwealth operator's license or permit for the type of vehicle to be operated and some form of agency identification. Check for specific details within your state laws regarding vehicle operator's licenses from foreign countries which may be valid in certain States;

(d) The penalties for unauthorized use of Government motor vehicles;

(e) The prohibition against providing transportation to strangers or hitchhikers;

(f) The proper care, control and use of Government credit card and vehicle keys;

(g) Mandatory use of seat belts by each employee operating or riding in a Government motor vehicle;

(h) The prohibition against the use of tobacco products in GSA-Interagency Fleet Management System (IFMS) motor vehicles;

(i) Any other duties and responsibilities assigned to operators with regard to the use, care, operation, and maintenance of Government motor vehicles;

(j) The potential income tax liability when they use a Government motor vehicle for transportation between residence and place of employment; and

(k) Protection for DOE employees under the Federal Tort Claims Act when acting within the scope of their employment.

(l) The prohibition against text messaging while operating a Government vehicle, or any vehicle while on Government business, as set forth under Executive Order 13513; and

(m) See 31 U.S.C. 1344 and 41 CFR 301–10.201 for allowable use of Government vehicles while on temporary duty or official travel orders.

§ 109–6.402 Policy.

(a) It is DOE policy that Government motor vehicles operated by DOE employees are to be used only for official Government purposes or for incidental purposes as prescribed in this section. The Office of Management and Program Secretarial Officer (PSO) for their respective organizations shall establish appropriate controls to ensure that the use of a Government motor vehicle for transportation between an employee's residence and place of employment is in accordance with the provisions of 41 CFR part 102–5 and this subpart.

(b) It is DOE policy that space in a Government motor vehicle used for home-to-work transportation may be shared with a spouse, relative, or friend in accordance with the restrictions contained in 41 CFR 102–5.105.

§ 109–6.450 Statutory provisions.

(a) In accordance with 31 U.S.C. 1349(b), any officer or employee of the Government who willfully uses or authorizes the use of a Government passenger motor vehicle for other than official purposes shall be suspended from duty by the head of the department concerned, without compensation, for not less than one month and shall be suspended for a longer period or summarily removed from office if circumstances warrant.

(b) Under the provisions of 18 U.S.C. 641, any person who knowingly misuses any Government property (including Government motor vehicles) may be subject to criminal prosecution and, upon conviction, to fines or imprisonment.

PART 109–25—GENERAL

Subpart 109–25.1—General Policies

AUTHORITY: Sec. 644, Pub. L. 95–91, 91 Stat. 599 (42 U.S.C. 7254).

SOURCE: 81 FR 63265, Sept. 14, 2016, unless otherwise noted.

Subpart 109–25.1—General Policies

§ 109–25.109–1 Identification of idle equipment.

At a minimum, management walk-throughs shall be conducted to provide for coverage of all operating and storage areas at least once every two years to identify idle and unneeded personal property.

§ 109–25.109–2 Equipment pools.

(a)–(c) [Reserved]

(d) The report on the use and effectiveness of equipment pools shall be submitted to the head of the DOE office at the discretion of that official. However, documentation of evaluations of pools shall be maintained and made available for review by appropriate contractor management, DOE offices, and audit teams.

(e) Program Secretarial Officer (PSO) shall require periodic independent reviews of equipment pool operations.

§ 109–25.302 Office furniture, furnishings, and equipment.

The Director, Office of Management, Program Secretarial Officer (PSO), and designated contractors shall establish criteria for the use of office furniture, furnishings, and equipment.

§ 109–25.350 Furnishing of Government clothing and individual equipment.

(a) Government-owned clothing and individual equipment may be furnished to employees:

(1) For protection from physical injury or occupational disease; or

(2) When employees could not reasonably be required to furnish them as a part of the personal clothing and equipment needed to perform the regular duties of the position to which they are assigned or for which services were engaged.

(b) This section does not apply to uniforms or uniform allowances under the Federal Employees Uniform Allowance Act of 1954, 84 Public Law 37, as amended.

PART 109–26—PROCUREMENT SOURCES AND PROGRAM

Subpart 109–26.2—Federal Requisitioning System

Subpart 109–26.5—GSA Procurement Programs

AUTHORITY: Sec. 644, Pub. L. 95–91, 91 Stat. 599 (42 U.S.C. 7254).

SOURCE: 81 FR 63265, Sept. 14, 2016, unless otherwise noted.

Subpart 109–26.2—Federal Requisitioning System

§ 109–26.203 Activity address codes.

(a) DOE field organizations designated by the Office of Management are responsible for processing routine activity code related transactions for specified groupings of field organizations. Each field organization in a specified grouping will forward their activity address code related transactions to the grouping's lead organization for processing. Each lead organization shall designate a point of contact who will:

(1) Verify the need, purpose, and validity of each transaction; and

(2) Be the specified grouping's authorized point of contact for dealing directly with GSA.

(b) The Office of Management is responsible for:

(1) All policy matters related to the issuance and control of activity address codes within DOE; and

(2) Furnishing the identity of the lead field organization points of contact to GSA.

Subpart 109–26.5—GSA Procurement Programs

§ 109–26.501 Purchase of new motor vehicles.

§ 109–26.501–1 General.

(a) GSA is a mandatory source, under FPMR 101–26.501, for purchase of new non-tactical vehicles.

(b) Under unique circumstances which meet the criteria set forth under FPMR, motor vehicles may be purchased directly rather than through GSA when a waiver has been granted by GSA. The waiver request should be submitted directly to GSA and a copy forwarded to the Office of Management. GSA will grant waivers on a case-by-case basis, in accordance with FPMR 101–26.501(b)(c).

§ 109–26.501–4 Submission of orders.

An original and two copies of requisitions for passenger motor vehicles and law enforcement motor vehicles shall be forwarded with justification for purchase to the Office of Management, for approval and submission to

GSA. Requisitions for all other types of motor vehicles shall be submitted directly to GSA.

§ 109–26.501–50 Authority and allocations for the acquisition of passenger motor vehicles.

(a) Authority for the acquisition of passenger motor vehicles is contained in the Department's annual appropriation act.

(b) DOE offices shall include in their budget submissions the number of passenger motor vehicles to be purchased during the fiscal year. The procurements will be identified as either additions to the motor vehicle fleet or replacement vehicles. A copy of the motor vehicle portion of the submission should be submitted to the Office of Management.

(c) To ensure that DOE does not exceed the number of passenger motor vehicles authorized to be acquired in any fiscal year, the Office of Management or designee shall allocate to and inform the field organizations in writing of the number of passenger motor vehicles which may be acquired under each appropriation. These allocations and the statutory cost limitations imposed on these motor vehicles shall not be exceeded.

(d) The motor vehicle fleet manager shall provide written certification to the OPMO that disposition action has been taken on replaced passenger motor vehicles. Such certification shall be provided no later than 30 days after the disposition of the vehicle. Replaced passenger motor vehicles shall not be retained in service after receipt of the replacement vehicle.

§ 109–26.501–51 Used vehicles.

Normally, DOE does not purchase or authorize contractors to purchase used motor vehicles. However, the Office of Management and Program Secretarial Officer (PSO) may authorize the purchase of used motor vehicles where justified by special circumstances, *e.g.*, when new motor vehicles are in short supply; motor vehicles are to be used for experimental or test purposes; or motor vehicles are acquired from exchange/sale. The statutory passenger motor vehicle allocation requirements shall apply to any purchase of used passenger motor vehicles except in the case of motor vehicles to be used exclusively for experimental or test purposes.

§ 109–26.501–52 Justification for purchase.

(a) Requisitions for additions to the passenger motor vehicle fleet must contain adequate written justification of need. Such justifications shall be prepared by the motor vehicle fleet manager and approved by the OPMO, and should include:

(1) A statement as to why the present fleet size is inadequate to support requirements;

(2) Efforts made to achieve maximum use of on-hand motor vehicles through pool arrangements, shuttle buses, and taxicabs;

(3) The programmatic requirement for the motor vehicles and the impact on the program/project if the requisitions are not filled;

(4) The established DOE or local utilization objectives used to evaluate the utilization of passenger motor vehicles and whether the objectives have been approved by the OPMO; and

(5) The date of the last utilization review and the number of passenger motor vehicles which did not meet the established utilization objectives and the anticipated mileage to be achieved by the new motor vehicles.

(b) Requisitions for replacement passenger motor vehicles should include a statement that utilization, pools, shuttle buses and taxicabs have been considered by the motor vehicle fleet manager and the OPMO. Specific information on the identification, age and mileage of the motor vehicles should be included. When a passenger motor vehicle being replaced does not meet Federal replacement standards, a description of the condition of the vehicle should also be provided.

§ 109–26.501–53 Acquisitions by transfer.

(a) The acquisition of passenger motor vehicles by transfer from another Government agency or DOE organization shall be within the allocations prescribed in § 109–26.501–50 of this subpart.

(b) Passenger motor vehicles may be acquired by transfer provided they are:

(1) Considered as an addition to the motor vehicle fleet of the receiving office;

(2) Acquired for replacement purposes and an equal number of replaced motor vehicles are reported for disposal within 30 days;

(3) For temporary emergency needs exceeding three months and approved in writing by the DPMO; or

(4) For temporary emergency needs of three months or less in lieu of commercial rentals. These transfers will not count toward the allocation.

§ 109–26.501–54 Communications equipment.

Communications equipment considered to be essential for the accomplishment of security and safety responsibilities is exempt from the requirements of 41 CFR 101–26.501. The Fleet Manager shall approve the installation of communications equipment in motor vehicles.

PART 109–27—INVENTORY MANAGEMENT

Subpart 109–27.50—Inventory Management Policies, Procedures, and Guidelines

AUTHORITY: Sec. 644, Pub. L. 95–91, 91 Stat. 599 (42 U.S.C. 7254).

SOURCE: 81 FR 63265, Sept. 14, 2016, unless otherwise noted.

Subpart 109–27.50—Inventory Management Policies, Procedures, and Guidelines

§ 109–27.5008 Control of drug substances.

Effective procedures and practices shall provide for the management and physical security of controlled substances from receipt to the point of use. Such procedures shall, as a minimum, provide for safeguarding, proper use, adequate records, and compliance with applicable laws and regulations.

Subpart 109–27.51—Management of Precious Metals

§ 109–27.5100 Scope of subpart.

This subpart provides policies, principles, and guidelines to be used in the management of purchased and recovered precious metals used to meet research, development, production, and other programmatic needs.

§ 109–27.5101 Definition.

Precious metals means uncommon and highly valuable metals characterized by their superior resistance to corrosion and oxidation. Included are gold, silver, and the platinum group metals—platinum, palladium, rhodium, iridium, ruthenium and osmium.

§ 109–27.5102 Policy.

DOE organizations and contractors shall establish effective procedures and practices for the administrative and physical control of precious metals in accordance with the provisions of this subpart.

§ 109–27.5103 Precious Metals Control Officer.

Each DOE organization and contractor holding precious metals shall designate in writing a Precious Metals Control Officer. This individual shall be the organization's primary point of contact concerning precious metals control and management, and shall be responsible for the following:

(a) Ensuring that the organization's precious metals activities are conducted in accordance with Departmental requirements.

(b) Maintaining an accurate list of the names of precious metals custodians.

(c) Providing instructions and training to precious metals custodians and/or users as necessary to assure compliance with regulatory responsibilities.

(d) Ensuring that physical inventories are performed as required by, and in accordance with, these regulations.

(e) Witnessing physical inventories.

(f) Performing periodic unannounced inspections of a custodian's precious metals inventory and records.

(g) Conducting an annual review of precious metals holdings to determine excess quantities.

(h) Preparing and submitting to the DOE Business Center for Precious Metals Sales and Recovery the annual forecast of anticipated withdrawals from, and returns to, the DOE precious metals pool.

(i) Conducting a program for the recovery of silver from used hypo solution and scrap film in accordance with 41 CFR 101–45.10 and § 109–45.10 of this chapter.

(j) Preparing and submitting of the annual report on recovery of silver from used hypo solution and scrap film as required by § 109–45.1002–2 of this chapter.

(k) Developing and issuing current authorization lists of persons authorized by management to withdraw precious metals from stockrooms.

§ 109–27.5104 Practices and procedures.

§ 109–27.5104–1 Acquisitions.

DOE organizations and contractors shall contact the DOE Business Center for Precious Metals Sales and Recovery to determine the availability of precious metals prior to acquisition on the open market.

§ 109–27.5104–2 Physical protection and storage.

Precious metals shall be afforded exceptional physical protection from time of receipt until disposition. Precious metals not in use shall be stored in a noncombustible combination locked repository with access limited to the designated custodian and an alternate. When there is a change in custodian or alternate having access to the repository, the combination shall be changed immediately.

§ 109–27.5104–3 [Reserved]

§ 109–27.5104–4 Physical inventories.

(a) Physical inventories shall be conducted annually by custodians, and witnessed by the Precious Metals Control Officer or his designee in accordance with 109–1.5110, Physical inventories frequency requirements.

(b) Precious metals not in use shall be inspected and weighed on calibrated scales. The inventoried weight and form shall be recorded on the physical inventory sheets by metal content and percent of metal. Metals in use in an experimental process or contaminated metals, neither of which can be weighed, shall be listed on the physical inventory sheet as observed and/or not observed as applicable.

(c) Any obviously idle or damaged metals should be recorded during the physical inventory. Justification for further retention of idle metals shall be required from the custodian and approved one level above the custodian, or disposed of in accordance with established procedures.

(d) The dollar value of physical inventory results shall be reconciled with the financial records. All adjustments shall be supported by appropriate adjustment reports, and approved by a responsible official.

§ 109–27.5104–5 Control and issue of stock.

Precious metals in stock are metals held in a central location and later issued to individuals when authorized requests are received. The following control procedures shall be followed for such metals:

(a) Stocks shall be held to a minimum consistent with efficient support to programs.

(b) The name and organization number of each individual authorized to withdraw precious metals, and the type and kind of metals, shall be prominently maintained in the stockroom.

This authorization shall be issued by the Precious Metals Control Officer or his designee and updated annually. Issues of metals will be made only to authorized persons.

(c) Accurate records of all receipts, issues, returns, and disposals shall be maintained in the stockroom.

(d) Receipts for metal issues and returns to stock shall be provided to users. Such receipts, signed by the authorized requesting individual and the stockroom clerk, shall list the requesting organization, type and form of metal, quantity, and date of transaction.

§ 109–27.5104–6 Control by using organization.

(a) After receipt, the using organization shall provide necessary controls for precious metals. Materials shall be stored in a non-combustible, combination locked repository at all times except for quantities at the actual point of use.

(b) Each using organization shall maintain a log showing the individual user, type and form of metal, and the time, place, and purpose of each use. The log shall be kept in a locked repository when not in use.

(c) The logs and secured locked storage facilities are subject to review by the Precious Metals Control Officer and other audit or review staffs as required.

(d) Cognizant Departmental managers are responsible for assuring that minimum quantities of precious metals are withdrawn consistent with work requirements and that quantities excess to requirements are promptly returned to the stockroom.

§ 109–27.5105 Management reviews and audits.

(a) Unannounced inspections of custodian's precious metals inventory and records may be conducted between scheduled inventories.

(b) DOE organizations and contractors holding precious metals shall annually review the quantity of precious metals on hand to determine if the quantity is in excess of program requirements. Precious metals which are not needed for current or foreseeable requirements shall be promptly reported to the DOE precious metals pool. The results of this annual review are to be documentèd and entered into the precious metals inventory records.

§ 109–27.5106 Precious metals pool.

§ 109–27.5106–1 Purpose.

The purpose of the precious metals pool is to recycle, at a minimum cost to pool participants, DOE-owned precious metals within the Department and to dispose of DOE-owned precious metals that are excess to DOE needs. However, if the pool is unable to accept any potential precious metal return, the using activity will dispose of the precious metals through the disposal process specified in subchapter H of the FPMR/FMR and this regulation.

§ 109–27.5106–2 Withdrawals.

Pure metals are available through the Business Center for either direct shipment to DOE contractors or facilities to fulfill fabrication requirements. Contact the Business Center for available forms and quantity (*https:// www.y12.doe.gov/missions/pmetal/*).

§ 109–27.5106–3 Returns.

All excess precious metals must be returned to the precious metals pool except as noted in § 109–27.5106–1 of this subpart. The pool is entirely dependent on metal returns; therefore, metal inventories should be maintained on an as-needed basis, and any excess metals must be returned to the pool for recycling. This includes precious metals in any form, including shapes, and scraps. Procedures have been developed by the precious metals pool contractor for metal returns, including storing, packaging, shipping, and security.

§ 109–27.5106–4 Withdrawals/returns forecasts.

The Business Center for Precious Metals Sales and Recovery will request annually from each DOE field organization its long-range forecast of anticipated withdrawals from the pool and returns to the pool.

§ 109–27.5106–5 Assistance.

The Business Center for Precious Metals Sales and Recovery operates the precious metals pool. DOE organizations and contractors may obtain specific information regarding the operation of the precious metals pool (operating contractor's name, address, and telephone number; processing charges; etc.) by contacting the Chief, Property Management Branch.

§ 109–27.5107 Recovery of silver from used hypo solution and scrap film.

The requirements for the recovery of silver from used hypo solution and scrap film are contained in § 109–45.1003 of this chapter.

PART 109–28—STORAGE AND DISTRIBUTION

AUTHORITY: 42 U.S.C. 7254.

SOURCE: 81 FR 63265, Sept. 14, 2016, unless otherwise noted.

§ 109–28.000–50 Policy.

DOE offices and designated contractors shall:

(a) Establish storage space and warehousing services for the receipt, storage, issue, safekeeping and protection of Government property;

(b) Provide storage space and warehousing services in the most efficient manner consistent with program requirements; and

(c) Operate warehouses in accordance with generally accepted industrial management practices and principles.

§ 109–28.000–51 Storage guidelines.

(a) Indoor storage areas should be arranged to obtain proper stock protection and maximum utilization of space within established floor load capacities.

(b) Storage yards for items not requiring covered protection shall be protected by locked fenced enclosures to the extent necessary to protect the Government's interest.

(c) Storage areas shall be prominently posted to clearly indicate that the property stored therein is U.S. Government property, with entrance to such areas restricted to authorized personnel only.

(d) Property in storage must be protected from fire, theft, deterioration, or destruction. In addition certain items require protection from dampness, heat, freezing, or extreme temperature changes. Other items must be stored away from light and odors, protected from vermin infestation, or stored separately because of their hazardous characteristics.

(e) Hazardous or contaminated property, including property having a history of use in an area where exposure to contaminated property may have occurred, shall not be commingled with non-contaminated property, but stored separately in accordance with instructions from the environmental, safety, and health officials.

(f) Unless inappropriate or impractical until declared excess, nuclear-related and proliferation-sensitive property shall be identified as such by use of a certification tag signed by an authorized program official (designated in writing with signature cards on file in the personal property management office). Such personal property shall not be commingled with other personal property, but stored separately in accordance with instructions from the cognizant program office.

Subpart 109–28.3—Customer Supply Centers

§ 109–28.306 Customer supply center (CSC) accounts and related controls.

§ 109–28.306–3 Limitations on use.

DOE offices and designated contractors shall establish internal controls for ensuring that the use of CSC accounts is limited to the purchase of items for official Government use.

§ 109–28.306–5 Safeguards.

DOE offices and designated contractors shall establish internal controls for ensuring that the customer access codes assigned for their accounts are properly protected.

Subpart 109–28.50—Management of Equipment Held for Future Projects

§ 109–28.5000 Scope of subpart.

This subpart provides policies, principles, and guidelines to be used in the management of equipment held for future projects (EHFFP).

§ 109–28.5001 Definition.

Equipment held for future projects means items being retained, based on approved justifications, for a known future use, or for a potential use in planned projects.

§ 109–28.5002 Objective.

The objective of the EHFFP program is to enable DOE offices and contractors to retain equipment not in use in current programs but which has a known or potential use in future DOE programs, while providing visibility on the types and amounts of equipment so retained through review and reporting procedures. It is intended that equipment be retained where economically justifiable for retention, considering cost of maintenance, replacement, obsolescence, storage, deterioration, or future availability; made available for use by others; and promptly excessed when no longer needed.

§ 109–28.5003 Records.

Records of all EHFFP shall be maintained by the holding organization, including a listing of items with original date of classification as EHFFP; initial justifications for retaining EHFFP; rejustifications for retention; and documentation of reviews made by higher levels of management.

§ 109–28.5004 Justification and review procedures.

Procedures shall provide for the following:

(a) The original decision to classify and retain equipment as EHFFP shall be justified in writing, providing sufficient detail to support the need for retention of the equipment. This justification will cite the project for which retained, the potential use to be made of the equipment, or other reasons for retention.

(b) The validity of the initial classification EHFFP shall be reviewed by management at a level above that of the individual making the initial determination.

(c) Retention of equipment as EHFFP must be rejustified annually to ensure that original justifications remain valid. The rejustifications will contain sufficient detail to support retention.

(d) When equipment is retained as EHFFP for longer than one year, the annual rejustification shall be reviewed at a level of management at least two levels above that of the individual making the determination to retain the EHFFP. Equipment retained as EHFFP for longer than three years should be approved by the head of the DOE field organization.

§ 109–28.5005 EHFFP program review.

OPMOs or on-site DOE property administrators shall conduct periodic reviews in accordance 109–1.5110 Physical inventories of personal property frequency requirement to ensure that the EHFFP program is being conducted in accordance with established procedures DOE–FMR. Included in the review will be proper determinations of property as EHFFP, the validity of justifications for retaining EHFFP.

§ 109–28.5006 Utilization.

It is DOE policy that, where practicable and consistent with program needs, EHFFP be considered as a source of supply to avoid or postpone acquisition.

Subpart 109–28.51—Management of Spare Equipment/Property

§ 109–28.5100 Scope of subpart.

This subpart provides policy guidance to be used in the management of spare equipment.

§ 109–28.5101 Definition.

Spare equipment/property means items held as replacement spares for equipment in current use in DOE program.

§ 109–28.5102 Exclusions.

The following categories of equipment will not be considered spare equipment:

(a) Equipment/Property installed for emergency backup, *e.g.*, an emergency power facility, or an electric motor or a pump, any of which is in place and electrically connected.

(b) Equipment items properly classified as stores inventory.

§ 109–28.5103 Management policy.

(a) Procedures shall require the maintenance of records for spare equipment/property, cross-referenced to the location in the facility and the engineering drawing number. The purpose for retention shall be in the records.

(b) Reviews shall be made based on technical evaluations of the continued need for the equipment. The reviews should be held biennially. In addition, individual item levels shall be reviewed when spare equipment/Property is installed for use, the basic equipment is removed from service, or the process supported is changed.

(c) Procedures shall be established to provide for the identification and reporting of unneeded spare equipment/property as excess property.

PART 109–30—FEDERAL CATALOG SYSTEM

AUTHORITY: 42 U.S.C. 7254.

Source: 81 FR 63265, Sept. 14, 2016, unless otherwise noted.

§ 109–30.001–50 Applicability.

The provisions of 41 CFR part 101–30 do not apply to designated contractors.

PART 109–38—MOTOR EQUIPMENT MANAGEMENT

Authority: 42 U.S.C. 7254.

Source: 81 FR 63265, Sept. 14, 2016, unless otherwise noted.

§ 109–38.000 Scope of part.

§ 109–38.000–50 Policy.

Motor vehicles and watercraft shall be acquired, maintained, and utilized in support of DOE programs in the minimum quantity required and in the most efficient manner consistent with program requirements, safety considerations, fuel economy, and applicable laws and regulations.

Subpart 109–38.0—Definition of Terms

§ 109–38.001 Definitions.

Experimental vehicles means vehicles acquired solely for testing and research purposes or otherwise designated for experimental purposes. Such vehicles are to be the object of testing and research as differentiated from those used as vehicular support to testing and research. Experimental vehicles are not to be used for passenger carrying services unless required as part of a testing/evaluation program, and they are not subject to statutory price limitations or authorization limitations.

Motor equipment means any item of equipment which is self-propelled or drawn by mechanical power, including motor vehicles, motorcycles and scooters, construction and maintenance equipment, materials handling equipment, and watercraft.

Motor vehicle means any equipment, self-propelled or drawn by mechanical power, designed to be operated principally on highways in the transportation of property or passengers.

Special purpose vehicles means vehicles which are used or designed for specialized functions. These vehicles include, but are not limited to: Trailers, semi-trailers, other types of trailing equipment; trucks with permanently mounted equipment (such as aerial ladders); construction and other types of equipment set forth in Federal Supply Classification Group (FSCG) 38; material handling equipment set forth in FSCG 39; and firefighting equipment set forth in FSCG 42. For reporting purposes within DOE, motorcycles, motor scooters and all-terrain vehicles will also be reported as special purpose vehicles.

Subpart 109–38.1—Fuel Efficient Motor Vehicles

§ 109–38.104 Fuel efficient passenger automobiles and light trucks.

(a) What size motor vehicles may we obtain? (See 41 CFR 102–34.50).

(b) All requests to obtain passenger automobiles larger than class IA, IB, or II (small, subcompact, or compact) shall be forwarded with justification to the DPMO for approval and certification for compliance with the fuel economy objectives listed in 41 CFR 102–34 subpart B.

(c) Requests to exempt certain light trucks from the fleet average fuel economy calculations shall be forwarded with justification to the Office of Management for approval.

§ 109–38.105 Agency purchase and lease of motor vehicles.

(a) DOE activities shall submit a copy of all motor vehicle leases and purchases not procured through the GSA Automotive Commodity Center to GSA.

(b)–(c) [Reserved]

(d) DOE activities desiring to renew a commercial lease shall submit the requirement in writing to the Office of Management for approval prior to submission by field offices to GSA.

(e) DOE activities shall submit a copy of all lease agreements to GSA.

Subpart 109–38.2—Registration, Identification, and Exemptions

§ 109–38.200 General requirements.

(a)–(e) [Reserved]

(f) Requests made pursuant to 41 CFR 102–34.155 through 102–34.170 for limited exemption from the requirement for displaying U.S. Government tags and other identification on motor vehicles, except for those vehicles exempted in accordance with 41 CFR 102–34.175 and § 109–38.204–1 of this subpart, shall be submitted to the Office of Management for approval. Each approved exemption must be renewed annually, and the Office of Management shall be notified promptly when the need for a previously authorized exemption no longer exists. Copies of certifications and cancellation notices required to be furnished to GSA pursuant to 41 CFR 102–34.160 will be transmitted to GSA.

(g) Requests for temporary removal and substitution of Government markings shall be submitted with justification to the DPMO for review and approval. Copies of the determination and justification required to be furnished to GSA will be transmitted to GSA by the DPMO.

§ 109–38.201 Registration and inspection.

§ 109–38.201–50 Registration in foreign countries.

Motor vehicles used in foreign countries are to be registered and carry license tags in accordance with the existing motor vehicle regulations of the country concerned. The person responsible for a motor vehicle in a foreign country shall make inquiry at the United States Embassy, Legation, or Consulate concerning the regulations that apply to registration, licensing, and operation of motor vehicles and shall be guided accordingly.

§ 109–38.202 Tags.

§ 109–38.202–2 Outside the District of Columbia.

The Office of Management and Program Secretarial Officer (PSO) shall make the determination concerning the use of tags outside the District of Columbia.

§ 109–38.202–3 Records.

(a) The Office of Management assigns "blocks" of U.S. Government license tag numbers to DOE organizations and maintains a current record of such assignments. Additional "blocks" will be assigned upon request.

(b) Each DOE direct operation and designated contractor shall maintain a current record of individual assignments of license tags to the motor vehicles under their jurisdiction.

§ 109–38.202–50 Security.

Unissued license tags shall be stored in a locked drawer, cabinet, or storage area with restricted access to prevent possible fraud or misuse. Tags which are damaged or unusable will be safeguarded until destroyed.

§ 109–38.203 Agency identification.

Standard DOE motor vehicle window decals (DOE Form 1530.1), and door decals to be used only on vehicles without windows (DOE Form 1530.2), are available from the Office of Administrative Services, Logistics Management Division, Headquarters, using DOE Form 4250.2, "Requisition for Supplies, Equipment or Services", or as directed by that office.

§ 109–38.204 Exemptions.

§ 109–38.204–1 Unlimited exemptions.

(a)–(f) [Reserved]

(g) The Office of Management and Program Secretarial Officer (PSO) for their respective organizations may approve exemptions from the requirement for the display of U.S. Government license tags and other official identification for motor vehicles used for security or investigative purposes.

§ 109–38.204–3 Requests for exempted motor vehicles in the District of Columbia.

The Director, Office of Administrative Services is designated to approve requests for regular District of Columbia license tags, and furnishes annually the name and specimen signature of each representative authorized to approve such requests to the District of Columbia Department of Transportation.

§ 109–38.204–4 Report of exempted motor vehicles.

DOE offices shall provide upon request the necessary information to the DPMO to enable that office to submit a report of exempted vehicles.

§ 109–38.204–50 Records of exempted motor vehicles.

The Office of Management and Program Secretarial Officer (PSO) shall maintain records of motor vehicles exempted from displaying U.S. Government license tags and other identification. The records shall contain a listing, by type, of each exempted motor vehicle operated during the previous fiscal year, giving information for each motor vehicle on hand at the beginning of the year and each of those newly authorized during the year, including:

(a) Name and title of authorizing official (including any authorization by Headquarters and GSA);

(b) Date exemption was authorized;

(c) Justification for exemption and limitation on use of the exempted motor vehicle;

(d) Date of discontinuance for any exemption discontinued during the year; and

(e) Probable duration of exemptions for motor vehicles continuing in use.

Subpart 109–38.3—Official Use of Government Motor Vehicles

§109–38.300 Scope.

This subpart prescribes the requirements governing the use of Government motor vehicles for official purposes by designated contractors.

§109–38.301 Authorized use.

The use of Government motor vehicles by officers and employees of the Government is governed by the provisions of 41 CFR 102–34 Subpart D and section 109–6.4 of this chapter.

§109–38.301–1 Contractors' use.

Program Secretarial Officer (PSO) shall ensure that provisions of the FPMR/FMR concerning contractor use of Government motor vehicles are complied with by their designated contractors.

§109–38.301–1.50 Authorization for transportation between residence and place of employment.

(a) Government motor vehicles shall not be used for transportation between residence and place of employment by designated contractor personnel except under extenuating circumstances specifically provided for under the terms of the contract. Examples of circumstances eligible for prior approval of home-to-work motor vehicle use which would be appropriate to include in the terms of the contract include: Use related to safety or security operations, use related to compelling operational considerations, and use determined as cost effective to DOE's interest. Under no circumstances shall the comfort and convenience, or managerial position, of contractor employees be considered justification for authorization of use.

(b) The use of Government motor vehicles for transportation between residence and place of employment (including sporadic use) by designated contractor personnel shall be approved in writing by the Head of the field organization or designee, with delegation no lower than the Director, Office of Management and Program Secretarial Officer (PSO) or the equivalent position at other DOE contracting activities provided that the individual is a warranted contracting officer. The contractor's request for approval shall include the name and title of the employee, the reason for the use, and the expected duration of the use. Each authorization is limited to one year, but can be extended for an unlimited number of additional one-year periods.

§109–38.301–1.51 Emergency use.

(a) Procedures for authorization of designated contractor use of Government motor vehicles in emergencies, including unscheduled overtime situations at remote sites where prior approval is not possible, shall be included in a contractor's approved property management procedures. The procedures shall include examples of emergency situations warranting such use. Records detailing instances of emergency use shall be maintained and review of all such emergency or overtime use must be certified through established audit procedures on at least an annual basis by the OPMO.

(b) In limiting the use of Government motor vehicles to official purposes, it is not intended to preclude their use in emergencies threatening loss of life or property. Such use shall be documented and the documentation retained for three years.

§109–38.301–1.52 Maintenance of records.

Designated contractors shall maintain logs or other records on the use of a Government motor vehicle for transportation between an employee's residence and place of employment. As a minimum, these logs shall indicate the employee's name, date of use, time of departure and arrival, miles driven, and names of other passengers. Cognizant finance offices shall be provided with applicable data on employees who utilize Government motor vehicles for such transportation for purposes of the Deficit Reduction Act of 1984 concerning the taxation of fringe benefits.

§ 109–38.301–1.53 Responsibilities of motor vehicle operators.

Designated contractors shall assure that their employees are aware of their responsibilities, identical to those listed in § 109–6.400–50 of this chapter for DOE employees, concerning the use and operation of Government motor vehicles.

Subpart 109–38.4—Use and Replacement Standards

§ 109–38.401 Use standards.

§ 109–38.401–2 Use of self-service pumps.

It is DOE policy that motor vehicle operators shall use self-service pumps in accordance with the provisions of 41 CFR 101–38.401–2.

§ 109–38.402 Replacement standards.

(a) [Reserved]

(b) Motor vehicles may be replaced without regard to the replacement standards in 41 CFR 102–34 subpart E only after certification by the Office of Management or the Head of the field organization for their respective organizations that a motor vehicle is beyond economical repair due to accident damage or wear caused by abnormal operating conditions.

§ 109–38.402–50 Prompt disposal of replaced motor vehicles.

A replaced motor vehicle shall be removed from service and disposed of prior to or as soon as practicable after delivery of the replacement motor vehicle to avoid concurrent operation of both motor vehicles.

§ 109–38.403 Responsibility for damages.

§ 109–38.403–1 Policy.

The policy for assigning responsibility for vehicle damage is to recover from users the costs for damages which would adversely affect the vehicle's resale.

§ 109–38.403–2 Responsibility.

The designated contractor will charge the using organization all costs resulting from damage, including vandalism, theft and parking lot damage to a DOE vehicle which occurs during the period that the vehicle is assigned to an employee of that organization. The charges recovered by the designated maintenance operation will be used to repair the vehicle. Other examples for which organizations will be charged are as follows:

(a) Damage caused by misuse or abuse inconsistent with normal operation and local conditions; or

(b) Repair costs which are incurred as a result of user's failure to obtain required preventative maintenance; or

(c) Unauthorized purchases or repairs, including credit card misuse, provided there is a clear, flagrant, and documented pattern of such occurrences.

§ 109–38.403–3 Exceptions.

Exceptions to § 109–38.403–2 of this subpart are as follows:

(a) As a result of the negligent or willful act of a party other than the organization or its employee, and the responsible party can be determined; or

(b) As a result of mechanical failure and the employee was not otherwise negligent. Proof of the failure must be provided; or

(c) As a result of normal wear comparable to similar vehicles.

Subpart 109–38.5—Scheduled Maintenance

§ 109–38.502 Guidelines.

§ 109–38.502–50 DOE guidelines.

(a) Whenever practicable and cost effective, commercial service facilities shall be utilized for the maintenance of motor vehicles.

(b) Individual vehicle maintenance records shall be kept to provide records of past repairs, as a control against unnecessary repairs and excessive maintenance, and as an aid in determining the most economical time for replacement.

(c) One-time maintenance and repair limitations shall be established by the motor equipment fleet manager. To exceed repair limitations, approval of the motor equipment fleet manager is required.

(d)(1) Motor vehicles under manufacturer's warranty shall be repaired under the terms of the warranty.

(2) When motor vehicles are maintained in Government repair facilities in isolated locations that are distant from franchised dealer facilities, or when it is not practical to return the vehicles to a dealer, a billback agreement shall be sought from manufacturers to permit warranty work to be performed on a reimbursable basis.

Subpart 109–38.7—Transfer, Storage, and Disposal of Motor Vehicles

§ 109–38.701 Transfer of title for Government-owned motor vehicles.

§ 109–38.701–50 Authority to sign Standard Form 97, The United States Government Certificate to Obtain Title to a Vehicle.

The Standard Form (SF) 97 shall be signed by an appropriate contracting officer. The Director, Office of Management and Program Secretarial Officer (PSO) for their respective organizations may delegate the authority to sign SF 97 to responsible DOE personnel under their jurisdiction.

Subpart 109–38.8—Fleet Credit Card

§ 109–38.800 General.

(a)–(c) [Reserved]

(d) The Office of Management and Program Secretarial Officer (PSO) for their respective organizations shall be responsible for establishing procedures to provide for the administrative control of fleet credit cards. Administrative control shall include, as a minimum:

(1) A reconciliation of on-hand credit cards with the inventory list provided by GSA,

(2) Providing motor vehicle operators with appropriate instructions regarding the use and protection of credit cards against theft and misuse,

(3) The taking of reasonable precautions in the event a fleet credit card is lost or stolen to minimize the opportunity of purchases being made by unauthorized persons, including notification to the paying office of the loss or theft,

(4) Validation of credit card charges to ensure they are for official use only items, and

§ 109–38.801 Obtaining fleet credit card.

A dedicated fleet credit card is issued with each GSA-leased motor vehicle. DOE offices electing to use fleet credit cards for agency-owned vehicles and motor equipment shall request the assignment of new accounts from the Office of Management. Following the assignment, DOE organizations shall submit orders for issuance of fleet credit cards in accordance with the instructions provided by GSA.

Subpart 109–38.9—Federal Motor Vehicle Fleet Report

§ 109–38.902 Records.

The Office of Management and OPMOs for their respective organizations shall establish adequate records for accounting and reporting purposes.

§ 109–38.903 Reporting of data.

§ 109–38.903–50 Reporting DOE motor vehicle data.

See 41 CFR 102–34 subpart J.

Subpart 109–38.51—Utilization of Motor Equipment

§ 109–38.5100 Scope of subpart.

This subpart prescribes policies and procedures concerning the utilization of motor equipment.

§ 109–38.5101 Policy.

It is DOE policy to keep the number of motor vehicles and other motor equipment at the minimum needed to satisfy programmatic requirements. To attain this goal, controls and practices shall be established which will achieve the most practical and economical utilization of motor equipment. These controls and practices apply to all DOE-owned and commercially leased motor equipment and to GSA Interagency Fleet Management System motor vehicles.

§ 109–38.5102 Utilization controls and practices.

Controls and practices to be used by DOE organizations and designated contractors for achieving maximum economical utilization of motor equipment shall include, but not be limited to:

(a) The maximum use of motor equipment pools, taxicabs, shuttle buses, or other common service arrangements;

(b) The minimum, practicable assignment of motor equipment to individuals, groups, or specific organizational components;

(c) The maintenance of individual motor equipment use records, such as trip tickets or vehicle logs, or hours of use, as appropriate, showing sufficiently detailed information to evaluate appropriateness of assignment and adequacy of use being made. If one-time use of a motor vehicle is involved, such as assignments from motor pools, the individual's trip records must, as a minimum, identify the motor vehicle and show the name of the operator, dates, destination, time of departure and return, and mileage;

(d) The rotation of motor vehicles between high and low mileage assignments where practicable to maintain the fleet in the best overall replacement age and mileage balance and operating economy;

(e) The charging, if considered feasible, to the user organization for the cost of operating and maintaining motor vehicles assigned to groups or organizational components. These charge-back costs should include all direct and indirect costs of the motor vehicle fleet operation as determined by the field organization and contractor finance and accounting functions;

(f) The use of dual-purpose motor vehicles capable of hauling both personnel and light cargo whenever appropriate to avoid the need for two motor vehicles when one can serve both purposes. However, truck-type or van vehicles shall not be acquired for passenger use merely to avoid statutory limitations on the number of passenger motor vehicles which may be acquired;

(g) The use of motor scooters and motorcycles in place of higher cost motor vehicles for certain applications within plant areas, such as mail and messenger service and small parts and tool delivery. Their advantage, however, should be weighed carefully from the standpoint of overall economy (comparison with cost for other types of motor vehicles) and increased safety hazards, particularly when mingled with other motor vehicle traffic; and

(h) The use of electric vehicles for certain applications. The use of these vehicles is encouraged wherever it is feasible to use them to further the goal of fuel conservation.

§ 109–38.5103 Motor vehicle utilization standards.

(a) The following average utilization standards are established for DOE as objectives for those motor vehicles operated generally for those purposes for which acquired:

(1) Sedans and station wagons, general purpose use—12,000 miles per year.

(2) Light trucks (4 x 2's) and general purpose vehicles, one ton and under (less than 12,500 GVWR)—10,000 miles per year.

(3) Medium trucks and general purpose vehicles, 1½ ton through 2½ ton (12,500 to 23,999 GVWR)—7,500 miles per year.

(4) Heavy trucks and general purpose vehicles, three ton and over (24,000 GVWR and over)—7,500 miles per year.

(5) Truck tractors—10,000 miles per year.

(6) All-wheel-drive vehicles—7,500 miles per year.

(7) Other motor vehicles—No utilization standards are established for other trucks, ambulances, buses, law enforcement motor vehicles, and special purpose vehicles. The use of these motor vehicles shall be reviewed at least annually by the motor equipment fleet manager and action shall be taken and documented to verify that the motor vehicles are required to meet programmatic, health, safety, or security requirements.

(b) When operating circumstances prevent the above motor vehicle utilization standards from being met, local use objectives must be established and met as prescribed in §109–38.5105 of this subpart.

§109–38.5104 Other motor equipment utilization standards.

No utilization standards are established for motor equipment other than motor vehicles. Each DOE office should establish through an agreement between the fleet manager and the OPMO utilization criteria for other motor equipment including heavy mobile equipment and review, adjust, and approve such criteria annually. Utilization of various classifications of other motor equipment can be measured through various statistics including miles, hours of use, number of trips, and fuel consumption. A utilization review of other motor equipment shall be performed at least annually by the motor equipment fleet manager to justify retainment or disposition of excess equipment not needed to fulfill Departmental, programmatic, health, safety, or security requirements.

§109–38.5105 Motor vehicle local use objectives.

(a) Individual motor vehicle utilization cannot always be measured or evaluated strictly on the basis of miles operated or against any Department-wide mileage standard. For example, light trucks specifically fitted for use by a plumber, welder, etc., in the performance of daily work assignments, would have uniquely tailored use objectives, different from those set forth for a truck used for general purposes. Accordingly, efficient local use objectives, which represent practical units of measurement for motor vehicle utilization and for planning and evaluating future motor vehicle requirements, must be established and documented by the Organizational Motor Equipment Fleet Manager. The objectives should take into consideration past performance, future requirements, geographical disbursement, and special operating requirements.

(b) These objectives shall be reviewed and adjusted as appropriate, but not less often than annually, by the motor equipment fleet manager. The reviews shall be documented. The Organizational Motor Equipment Fleet Manager is responsible for reviewing and approving in writing all proposed local use objectives.

§109–38.5106 Application of motor vehicle use goals.

(a) At least annually, the motor equipment fleet manager will review motor vehicle utilization statistics and all motor vehicles failing to meet the applicable DOE utilization standard or local use objective must be identified.

(b) Prompt action must be initiated to:

(1) Reassign the underutilized motor vehicles;

(2) Dispose of the underutilized motor vehicles; or

(3) Obtain a special justification from users documenting their continued requirement for the motor vehicle and any proposed actions to improve utilization. Any requirement for underutilized motor vehicles which the motor equipment fleet manager proposes to continue in its assignment, must be submitted in writing to the Organizational Motor Equipment Fleet Manager for approval.

(c) Both Department-wide standards and local use objectives should be applied in such a manner that their application does not stimulate motor vehicle use for the purpose of meeting the objective. The ultimate standard against which motor vehicle use must be measured is that the minimum number of motor vehicles will be retained to satisfy program requirements.

Subpart 109–38.52—Watercraft

§109–38.5200 Scope of subpart.

This subpart establishes basic policies and procedures that apply to the management of watercraft operated by DOE organizations and designated contractors. The head of each Departmental organization operating watercraft shall issue such supplemental instructions as may be needed to ensure the efficient use and management of watercraft.

§ 109–38.5201 Definition.

As used in this subpart the following definition applies:

Watercraft means any vessel used to transport persons or material on water.

§ 109–38.5202 Watercraft operations.

(a) No person may operate a watercraft on a waterway until skill of operation and basic watercraft knowledge have been demonstrated.

(b) Operators of watercraft shall check the vessel to ensure that necessary equipment required by laws applicable to the area of operation are present, properly stowed, and in proper working order.

(c) Operators shall comply with all applicable Federal, state, and local laws pertaining to the operation of watercraft.

(d) Operators shall not use watercraft or carry passengers except in the performance of official Departmental assignments.

§ 109–38.5203 Watercraft identification and numbers.

Watercraft in the custody of DOE or designated contractors shall display identifying numbers, whether issued by the U.S. Coast Guard, State, or local field organization, in accordance with applicable requirements.

PART 109–39—INTERAGENCY FLEET MANAGEMENT SYSTEMS

Subpart 109–39.1—Establishment, Modification, and Discontinuance of Interagency Fleet Management Systems

Subpart 109–39.3—Use and Care of GSA Interagency Fleet Management System Vehicles

AUTHORITY: 42 U.S.C. 7254.

SOURCE: 81 FR 63265, Sept. 14, 2016, unless otherwise noted.

Subpart 109–39.1—Establishment, Modification, and Discontinuance of Interagency Fleet Management Systems

§ 109–39.101 Notice of intention to begin a study.

§ 109–39.101–1 Agency cooperation.

The Office of Management and Program Secretarial Officer (PSO) for their respective organizations shall designate representatives to coordinate with GSA concerning the establishment of a GSA fleet management system to serve their organization.

§ 109–39.103 Agency appeals.

The Office of Management and Program Secretarial Officer (PSO) for their respective organizations may appeal, or request exemption from, a determination made by GSA concerning the establishment of a fleet management system. A copy of the appeal or request shall be forwarded to the DPMO.

§ 109–39.105 Discontinuance or curtailment of service.

§ 109–39.105–2 Agency requests to withdraw participation.

Should circumstances arise that would tend to justify discontinuance or curtailment of participation by a DOE organization of a given interagency fleet management system, the participating organization should forward complete details to the DPMO for consideration and possible referral to the Administrator of General Services.

§ 109–39.106 Unlimited exemptions.

The Office of Management and Program Secretarial Officer (PSO) for their respective organizations shall make the determination that an unlimited exemption from inclusion of a motor vehicle in a fleet management system is warranted. A copy of the determination shall be forwarded to GSA and to the Office of Management.

§ 109–39.107 Limited exemptions.

The Office of Management and Program Secretarial Officer (PSO) for their respective organizations shall seek limited exemptions from the fleet management system.

Subpart 109–39.3—Use and Care of GSA Interagency Fleet Management System Vehicles

§ 109–39.300 General.

(a)–(c) [Reserved]

(d) Motor equipment fleet managers shall ensure that operators and passengers in GSA Interagency Fleet Management System (IFMS), agency-owned and agency commercially-leased motor vehicles are aware of the prohibition against the use of tobacco products in these vehicles.

§ 109–39.301 Utilization guidelines.

DOE activities utilizing GSA IFMS motor vehicles will receive and review vehicle utilization statistics in order to determine if miles traveled justify vehicle inventory levels. Activities should retain justification for the retention of vehicles not meeting DOE utilization guidelines or established local use objectives, as appropriate. Those vehicles not justified for retention shall be returned to the issuing GSA interagency fleet management center.

PART 109–40—TRANSPORTATION AND TRAFFIC MANAGEMENT

Subpart 109–40.1—General Provisions

Subpart 109–40.3—Traffic Management

Subpart 109–40.50—Bills of Lading

Subpart 109–40.51—Price-Anderson Coverage Certifications for Nuclear Shipments

AUTHORITY: Sec. 161, as amended, 68 Stat. 948; 42 U.S.C. 2201; sec. 205, as amended, 63 Stat. 390; 40 U.S.C. 121; sec. 644, 91 Stat. 585, 42 U.S.C. 7254.

SOURCE: 81 FR 63265, Sept. 14, 2016, unless otherwise noted.

Subpart 109–40.1—General Provisions

§ 109–40.000 Scope of part.

This part describes DOE regulations governing transportation and traffic management activities. It also covers arrangements for transportation and related services by bill of lading. These regulations are designed to ensure that all transportation and traffic management activities will be carried out in the manner most advantageous to the Government in terms of economy, efficiency, service, environment, safety and security.

§ 109–40.000–50 Applicability to contractors.

DOE–PMR 109–40, Transportation and Traffic Management, should be applied to cost-type contractors' transportation and traffic management activities. Departure by cost-type contractors from the provisions of these regulations may be authorized by the contracting officer provided the practices and procedures followed are consistent with the basic policy objectives in these regulations and DOE Order 460.2, Departmental Materials Transportation and Packaging Management, except to the extent such departure is prohibited by statute or executive order.

§ 109–40.102 Representation before regulatory bodies.

Participation in proceedings related to carrier applications to regulatory bodies for temporary or permanent authority to operate in specified geographical locations shall be confined to statements or testimony in support of a need for service and shall not extend to support of individual carriers or groups of carriers.

§ 109–40.103 Selection of carriers.

§ 109–40.103–1 Domestic transportation.

(a) Preferential treatment, normally, shall not be accorded to any mode of transportation (motor, rail, air, water) or to any particular carrier when arranging for domestic transportation services. However where, for valid reasons, a particular mode of transportation or a particular carrier within that mode must be used to meet specific program requirements and/or limitations, only that mode or carrier shall be considered. Examples of valid reasons for considering only a particular mode or carrier are:

(1) Where only a certain mode of transportation or individual carrier is able to provide the needed service or is able to meet the required delivery date; and

(2) Where the consignee's installation and related facilities preclude or are not conducive to service by all modes of transportation.

(b) The following factors are considered in determining whether a carrier or mode of transportation can meet DOE's transportation service requirements for each individual shipment:

(1) Availability and suitability of carrier equipment;

(2) Carrier terminal facilities at origin and destination;

(3) Pickup and delivery service, if required;

(4) Availability of required or accessorial and special services, if needed;

(5) Estimated time in transit;

(6) Record of past performance of the carrier; and

(7) Availability and suitability of transit privileges.

§ 109–40.103–2 Disqualification and suspension of carriers.

Disqualification and suspension are measures which exclude carriers from participation, for temporary periods of time, in DOE traffic. To ensure that the Government derives the benefits of full and free competition of interested carriers, disqualification and suspension shall not apply for any period of time longer than necessary to protect the interests of the Government.

§ 109–40.103–3 International transportation.

See 49 U.S.C. 41102 for a certificate required in nonuse of U.S. flag vessels or U.S. flag certificated air carriers.

(a) U.S.-flag ocean carriers. Arrangements for international ocean transportation services shall be made in accordance with the provisions of section 901(b) of the Merchant Marine Act of 1936, as amended (46 U.S.C. 1241(b)) concerning the use of privately owned U.S.-flag vessels.

(b) U.S.-flag certificated air carriers. Arrangements for international air transportation services shall be made in accordance with the provisions of section 5(a) of the International Air Transportation Fair Competition Practices Act of 1974 (49 U.S.C. 40118), which requires the use of U.S.-flag certificated air carriers for international travel of persons or property to the extent that services by these carriers is available.

§ 109–40.104 Use of Government-owned transportation equipment.

The preferred method of transporting property for the Government is through use of the facilities and services of commercial carriers. However, Government vehicles may be used when they are available to meet emergencies and accomplish program objectives which cannot be attained through use of commercial carriers.

§ 109–40.109 Utilization of special contracts and agreements.

From time to time special transportation agreements are entered into on a Government-wide or DOE-wide basis and are applicable, generally, to DOE shipments. The HQ DOE Manager, Transportation Operations and Traffic, will distribute information on such agreements to field offices as it becomes available.

§ 109–40.110 Assistance to economically disadvantaged transportation businesses.

§ 109–40.110–1 Small business assistance.

Consistent with the policies of the Government with respect to small businesses, DOE shall place with small business concerns a fair proportion of the total purchases and contracts for transportation and related services such as packing and crating, loading and unloading, and local drayage.

§ 109–40.110–2 Minority business enterprises.

Minority business enterprises shall have the maximum practical opportunity to participate in the performance of Government contracts. DOE shall identify transportation-related minority enterprises and encourage them to provide services that will support DOE's transportation requirements.

§ 109–40.112 Transportation factors in the location of Government facilities.

Transportation rate, charges, and commercial carrier transportation services shall be considered and evaluated prior to the selection of new site locations and during the planning and construction phases in the establishment of leased or relocated Government installations or facilities to ensure that consideration is given to the various transportation factors that may be involved in this relocation or deactivation.

§ 109–40.113 Insurance against transportation hazards.

The policy of the Government with respect to insurance of its property while in the possession of commercial carriers is set forth in 41 CFR 1–19.107.

Subpart 109–40.3—Traffic Management

§ 109–40.301 Traffic management functions administration.

The DOE traffic management functions are accomplished by established field traffic offices under provisions of appropriate Departmental directives and Headquarters' staff traffic management supervision.

§ 109–40.302 Standard routing principle.

(a) Shipments shall be routed using the mode of transportation, or individual carriers within the mode, that can provide the required service at the lowest overall delivered cost to the Government.

(b) When more than one mode of transportation, or more than one carrier within a mode, can provide equally satisfactory service at the same overall cost the traffic shall be distributed as equitably as practicable among the modes and among the carriers within the modes.

§ 109–40.303–3 Most fuel efficient carrier/mode.

When more than one mode, or more than one carrier within a mode, can satisfy the service requirements of a specific shipment at the same lowest aggregate delivered cost, the carrier/mode determined to be the most fuel efficient will be selected. In determining the most fuel efficient carrier/mode, consideration will be given to such factors as use of the carrier's equipment in "turn around" service, proximity of carrier equipment to the shipping activity, and ability of the carrier to provide the most direct service to the destination points.

§ 109–40.304 Rate tenders to the Government.

Under the provisions of the Interstate Commerce Act (49 U.S.C. 10721), common carriers are permitted to submit to the Government tenders which contain rates lower than published tariff rates available to the general public. In addition, rates tenders may be applied to shipments other than those made by the Government provided the total benefits accrue to the Government; that is, provided the Government pays the charges or directly and completely reimburses the party that initially bears the freight charges (323 ICC 347 and 332 ICC 161).

§ 109–40.305–50 [Reserved]

§ 109–40.306–1 Recommended rate tender format.

Only those rate tenders which have been submitted by the carriers in writing shall be considered for use. Carriers should be encouraged to use the format "Uniform Tender of Rates and/or Charges for Transportation Services" when preparing and submitting rate tenders to the Government. Rate tenders that are ambiguous in meaning shall be resolved in favor of the Government.

§ 109–40.306–2 Required shipping documents and annotations.

(a) To qualify for transportation under section 10721 rates, property must be shipped by or for the Government on:

(1) Government bills of lading;

(2) Commercial bills of lading endorsed to show that these bills of lading are to be converted to Government bills of lading after delivery to the consignee;

(3) Commercial bills of lading showing that the Government is either the consignor or the consignee and endorsed with the following statement:

Transportation hereunder is for the U.S. Department of Energy, and the actual total transportation charges paid to the carrier(s) by the consignor or consignee are assignable to, and are to be reimbursed by, the Government.

(b) When a rate tender is used for transportation furnished under a cost-reimbursable contract, the following endorsement shall be used on covering commercial bills of lading:

Transportation hereunder is for the U.S. Department of Energy, and the actual total transportation charges paid to the carrier(s) by the consignor or consignee are to be reimbursed by the Government, pursuant to cost-reimbursable contract number (insert contract number). This may be confirmed by contacting the agency representative at (name and telephone number).

See 332 ICC 161.

(c) To ensure proper application of a Government rate tender on all shipments qualifying for their use, the issuing officer shall show on the bills of lading covering such shipments the applicable rate tender number and carrier identification, such as: "Section 10721 tender, ABC Transportation Company, ICC No. 374." In addition, if commercial bills of lading are used, they shall be endorsed as specified above.

§ 109–40.306–3 Distribution.

Each agency receiving rate tenders shall promptly submit one signed copy to the Transportation and Public Utilities Service (WIT), General Services Administration, Washington, DC 20407. Also, two copies (including at least one signed copy) shall be promptly submitted to the General Services Administration (TA), Chester A. Arthur Building, Washington, DC 20406.

Subpart 109–40.50—Bills of Lading

§ 109–40.5000 Scope of subpart.

This subpart sets forth the requirements under which commercial or Government bills of lading may be used.

§ 109–40.5001 Policy.

Generally DOE cost-type contractors will use commercial bills of lading in making shipments for the account of DOE. Cost-type contractors may be authorized by the contracting officer to use Government bills of lading if such use will be advantageous to the Government. Such authorizations shall be coordinated with the HQ DOE Manager, Transportation Operations and Traffic.

§ 109–40.5002 Applicability.

The policy and procedures set forth in this subpart shall be applied when DOE's cost-type contractors use commercial bills of lading.

§ 109–40.5003 Commercial bills of lading.

(a) DOE's cost-type contractors using commercial bills of lading in making shipments for the account of DOE shall include the following statement on all commercial bills of lading:

This shipment is for the account of the U.S. Government which will assume the freight charges and is subject to the terms and conditions set forth in the standard form of the U.S. Government bills of lading and to any available special rates or charges.

(b) The language in paragraph (a) of this section may be varied without materially changing its substance to satisfy the needs of particular cost-type contractors for the purpose of obtaining the benefit of the lowest available rates for the account of the Government.

(c) Where practicable, commercial bills of lading shall provide for consignment of a shipment to DOE c/o the cost-type contractor or by the contractor "for the DOE."

(d) Commercial bills of lading exceeding $10,000 issued by cost-type contractors shall be annotated with a typewritten, rubber stamp, or similar impression containing the following wording:

Equal Employment Opportunity. All provisions of Executive Order 11246, as amended by Executive Order 11375, and of the rules, regulations, and relevant orders of the Secretary of Labor are incorporated herein.

§ 109–40.5004 Government bills of lading.

In those instances where DOE cost-type contractors are authorized to use Government bills of lading, specific employees of cost-type contractors will be authorized by the contracting officer to issue such Government bills of lading (see Title V, U.S. Government Accounting Office Policy and Procedures Manual for Guidance of Federal Agencies).

§ 109–40.5005 Description of property for shipment.

(a) Each shipment shall be described on the bill of lading or other shipping document as specified by the governing freight classification, carrier's tariff, or rate tender. Shipments shall be described as specifically as possible. Trade names such as "Foamite" or "Formica," or general terms such as "vehicles," "furniture," or "Government supplies," shall not be used as bill of lading descriptions.

(b) A shipment containing hazardous materials, such as explosives, radioactive materials, flammable liquids, flammable solids, oxidizers, or poison A or poison B, shall be prepared for shipment and described on bills of lading or other shipping documents in accordance with the Department of Transportation Hazardous Materials Regulation, 49 CFR, subchapter C.

Subpart 109–40.51—Price-Anderson Coverage Certifications for Nuclear Shipments

§ 109–40.5100 Scope of subpart.

This subpart sets forth the policy for issuance of certifications regarding Price-Anderson coverage of particular shipments of nuclear materials.

§ 109–40.5101 Policy.

Upon request of a carrier, an appropriate certification will be issued by an authorized representative of the DOE to the carrier regarding the applicability of Price-Anderson indemnity to a particular shipment. Copies of such certifications, if performed by a Field Manager or a DOE cost-type contractor, shall be provided to the HQ DOE Manager, Transportation Operations and Traffic.

SUBCHAPTERS B–G [RESERVED]

SUBCHAPTER H—UTILIZATION AND DISPOSAL

PART 109–42—UTILIZATION AND DISPOSAL OF HAZARDOUS MATERIALS AND CERTAIN CATEGORIES OF PROPERTY

Subpart 109–42.11—Special Types of Hazardous Material and Certain Categories of Property

Sec.
109–42.1100.50 Scope of subpart.
109–42.1100.51 Policy.
109–42.1102–8 United States Munitions List items which require demilitarization.
109–42.1102–51 Suspect personal property.
109–42.1102–52 Low level contaminated personal property.

AUTHORITY: 40 U.S.C. 121.

SOURCE: 81 FR 63265, Sept. 14, 2016, unless otherwise noted.

Subpart 109–42.11—Special Types of Hazardous Material and Certain Categories of Property

§ 109–42.1100.50 Scope of subpart.

This subpart sets forth policies and procedures for the utilization and disposal outside of DOE of excess and surplus personal property which has been radioactively or chemically contaminated.

§ 109–42.1100.51 Policy.

When the holding organization determines it is appropriate to dispose of contaminated personal property, it shall be disposed of by DOE in accordance with appropriate Federal regulations governing radiation/chemical exposure and environmental contamination. In special cases where Federal regulations do not exist or apply, appropriate state and local regulations shall be followed.

§ 109–42.1102–8 United States Munitions List items which require demilitarization.

Program Secretarial Officer (PSO) shall determine demilitarization requirements regarding combat material and military personal property using DoD 4160.21–M–1, Defense Demilitarization Manual as a guide.

§ 109–42.1102–51 Suspect personal property.

(a) Excess personal property (including scrap) having a history of use in an area where radioactive or chemical contamination may occur shall be considered suspect and shall be monitored using appropriate instruments and techniques by qualified personnel of the DOE office or contractor generating the excess.

(b) With due consideration to the economic factors involved, every effort shall be made to reduce the level of contamination of excess or surplus personal property to the lowest practicable level. Contaminated personal property that exceeds applicable contamination standards shall not be utilized or disposed outside DOE.

(c) If contamination is suspected and the property is of such size, construction, or location as to make testing for contamination impossible, the property shall not be utilized or disposed outside of DOE.

§ 109–42.1102–52 Low level contaminated personal property.

If monitoring of suspect personal property indicates that contamination does not exceed applicable standards, it may be utilized and disposed of in the same manner as uncontaminated personal property, provided the guidance in § 109–45.5005–1(a) of this chapter has been considered. However, recipients shall be advised where levels of radioactive contamination require specific controls for shipment as provided in Department of Transportation Regulations (49 CFR parts 171–179) for shipment of radioactive personal property. In addition, when any contaminated personal property is screened within DOE, reported to GSA, or otherwise disposed of, the kind and degree of contamination must be plainly indicated on all pertinent documents.

PART 109–43—UTILIZATION OF PERSONAL PROPERTY

AUTHORITY: 40 U.S.C. 121.

SOURCE: 81 FR 63265, Sept. 14, 2016, unless otherwise noted.

§ 109–43.001 Definition.

DOE screening period means the period of time that reportable existing personal property is screened throughout DOE for reutilization purposes and, for selected items, through the Used Laboratory Equipment Donation Program (LEDP).

Subpart 109–43.1—General Provisions

§ 109–43.101 Agency utilization reviews.

DOE offices and designated contractors are responsible for continuously surveying property under their control to assure maximum use, and shall promptly identify property that is excess to their needs and make it available for use elsewhere.

§ 109–43.103 Agency utilization officials.

The Property Executive is designated as the DOE National Utilization Officer.

Subpart 109–43.3—Utilization of Excess

§ 109–43.302 Agency responsibility.

§ 109–43.302–50 Utilization by designated contractors.

Program Secretarial Officer (PSO) may authorize designated contractors to perform the functions pertaining to the utilization of excess personal property normally performed by a Federal agency, provided the designated contractors have written policies and procedures.

§ 109–43.304 Reporting requirements.

§ 109–43.304–1 Reporting.

§ 109–43.304–1.50 DOE reutilization screening.

(a) Personal property must be processed through DOE electronic internal screening prior to reporting excess personal property to GSA.

(b) An additional 30-day screening period shall be allocated for items eligible for screening by educational institutions through LEDP.

(c) Items in FSCG 66 (Instruments and Laboratory Equipment), 70 (General Purpose Information Processing. Equipment (including firmware)), and 99 (Miscellaneous) are reportable.

(d) The Department of Energy National Utilization Officer (NUO) may authorize in exceptional or unusual cases when time is critical, screening of excess property may be accomplished by with due consideration given to the additional costs involved. Examples of situations when this method of screening would be used are when there is a requirement for quick disposal actions due to unplanned contract terminations or facilities closing; to alleviate the paying of storage costs; when storage space is critical; to process exchange/sale transactions; property dangerous to public health and safety; property determined to be classified or otherwise sensitive for reasons of national security (when classified communications facilities are used); or for hazardous materials which may not be disposed of outside of the Department.

(e) Concurrent DOE and Federal agency screening shall not be conducted.

§ 109–43.304–1.51 [Reserved]

§ 109–43.304–2 [Reserved]

§ 109–43.304–4 [Reserved]

§ 109–43.305 [Reserved]

§ 109–43.305–50 Nuclear-related and proliferation-sensitive personal property.

Nuclear-related and proliferation-sensitive property is not reportable and shall not be formally screened within DOE or reported to GSA.

§ 109–43.307 Items requiring special handling.

§ 109–43.307–2 Hazardous materials.

§ 109–43.307–2.50 Monitoring of hazardous personal property.

To provide assurance that hazardous personal property is not being inadvertently released from the site by transfer or sale to the public, all hazardous or suspected hazardous personal property shall be checked for contamination by environmental, safety, and health officials. Contamination-free personal property will be tagged with a certification tag authorizing release for transfer or sale. Contaminated personal property will be referred back to the program office for appropriate action.

§ 109–43.307–2.51 Holding hazardous personal property.

Excess or surplus hazardous personal property shall not be commingled with non-hazardous personal property while waiting disposition action.

§ 109–43.307–50 Export controlled personal property.

(a) When personal property that is subject to export controls is being exported directly by DOE (e.g., a transfer of nuclear equipment or materials as part of a program of cooperation with another country), DOE or the DOE contractor must obtain the necessary export license.

(b) When personal property subject to export controls is transferred under work-for-others agreements, co-operative agreements, or technical programs, the recipients will be informed in writing that:

(1) The property is subject to export controls;

(2) They are responsible for obtaining export licenses or authorizations prior to transferring or moving the property to another country; and

(3) They are required to pass on export control guidance if they transfer the property to another domestic or foreign recipient.

§ 109–43.307–51 Classified personal property.

Classified personal property which is excess to DOE needs shall be stripped of all characteristics which cause it to be classified, or otherwise rendered unclassified, as determined by the cognizant program office, prior to any disposition action. The cognizant program office shall certify that appropriate action has been taken to declassify the personal property as required. Declassification shall be accomplished in a manner which will preserve, so far as practicable, any civilian utility or commercial value of the personal property.

§ 109–43.307–52 Nuclear-related or proliferation-sensitive personal property.

(a) Recognizing that property disposal officials will not have the technical knowledge to identify nuclear-related and proliferation-sensitive personal property, all such personal property shall be physically tagged with a certification signed by an authorized program official at time of determination by the program office of the personal property as excess. Such an authorized official should be designated in writing with signature cards on file in the property office.

(b) Nuclear-related and proliferation-sensitive personal property which is excess to DOE needs shall be stripped of all characteristics which cause it to be nuclear-related or proliferation-sensitive personal property, as determined by the cognizant program office, prior to disposal. The cognizant program office shall certify that appropriate actions have been taken to strip the personal property as required, or shall provide the property disposal office with adequate instructions for stripping the items. Such action shall be accomplished in a manner which will preserve, so far as practicable, any civilian utility or commercial value of the personal property.

§ 109–43.307–53 Information Technology (IT).

All IT shall be sanitized before being transferred into excess to ensure that all data, information, and software has been removed from the equipment. Designated computer support personnel must indicate that the equipment has been sanitized by attaching a certification tag to the item. Sanitized IT will be utilized and disposed in accordance with the provisions of the FPMR/FMR.

§ 109–43.307–54 Unsafe personal property.

Personal property that is considered defective or unsafe must be mutilated prior to shipment for disposal.

§ 109–43.312 Use of excess personal property on cost-reimbursement contracts.

(a) [Reserved]

(b) It is DOE policy for designated contractors to use Government excess personal property to the maximum extent possible to reduce contract costs. However, the determination required in 41 CFR 101–43.312(b) does not apply to such contracts, and a DOE official is not required to execute transfer orders for authorized designated contractors. The procedures prescribed in 41 CFR 101–43.309–5 for execution of transfer orders apply.

§ 109–43.313 Use of excess personal property on cooperative agreements.

(a)–(c) [Reserved]

(d) Program Secretarial Officer (PSO) shall ensure that required records are maintained in a current status.

§ 109–43.314 Use of excess personal property on grants.

(a)–(e) [Reserved]

(f) Program Secretarial Officer (PSO) shall ensure that the records required by 41 CFR 101–43.314(f) are maintained.

Subpart 109–43.5—Utilization of Foreign Excess Personal Property

§ 109–43.502 Holding agency responsibilities.

(a) [Reserved]

(b) Property which remains excess after utilization screening within the general foreign geographical area where the property is located shall be reported to the accountable field office or Headquarters program organization for consideration for return to the United States for further DOE or other Federal utilization. The decision to return property will be based on such factors as acquisition cost, residual value, condition, usefulness, and cost of transportation.

Subpart 109–43.47—Reports

§ 109–43.4701 Performance reports.

(a)–(b) [Reserved]

(c) The annual report of personal property furnished (*e.g.*, transfers, gifts, loans, leases, license agreements, and sales) to non-Federal recipients, including elementary and secondary schools, is furnished to GSA in accordance with 41 CFR 102–38. Internal DOE personal property reports must be submitted to the Office of Management at the date determined by the Property Executive.

Subpart 109–43.50—Utilization of Personal Property Held for Facilities in Standby

§ 109–43.5000 Scope of subpart.

This subpart supplements 41 CFR part 101–43 by providing policies and procedures for the economic and efficient utilization of personal property associated with facilities placed in standby status.

§ 109–43.5001 Definition.

Facility in standby means a complete plant or section of a plant, which is neither in service or declared excess.

§ 109–43.5002 Reviews to determine need for retaining items.

Procedures and practices shall require an initial review at the time the plant is placed in standby to determine which items can be made available for use elsewhere within the established start-up criteria; periodic reviews (no less than biennially) to determine need for continued retention of property; and special reviews when a change in start-up time is made or when circumstances warrant. Such procedures should recognize that:

(a) Equipment, spares, stores items, and materials peculiar to a plant should be retained for possible future operation of the plant;

(b) Where practicable, common-use stores should be removed and used elsewhere; and

(c) Uninstalled equipment and other personal property not required should be utilized elsewhere on-site or be disposed of as excess.

PART 109–44—DONATION OF PERSONAL PROPERTY

Subpart 109–44.7—Donations of Property to Public Bodies

Sec.

AUTHORITY: Sec. 205(c), 63 Stat. 390; 40 U.S.C. 121.

SOURCE: 81 FR 63265, Sept. 14, 2016, unless otherwise noted.

Subpart 109–44.7—Donations of Property to Public Bodies

§ 109–44.701 Findings justifying donation to public bodies.

The Office of Management and Program Secretarial Officer (PSO) shall appoint officials to make required findings and reviews.

§ 109–44.702 Donations to public bodies.

§ 109–44.702–3 Hazardous materials.

The Office of Management and Heads of field organizations) shall be responsible for the safeguards, notifications, and certifications required by 41 CFR part 101–42 and part 109–42 of this chapter, as well as compliance with all other requirements therein.

PART 109–45—SALE, ABANDONMENT, OR DESTRUCTION OF PERSONAL PROPERTY

Subpart 109–45.1—General

Sec.

Subpart 109–45.3—Sale of Personal Property

109–45.309–53 Nuclear-related or proliferation-sensitive property.
109–45.309–54 Information Technology (IT).
109–45.310 Antitrust laws.
109–45.317 Noncollusive bids and proposals.

Subpart 109–45.9—Abandonment or Destruction of Personal Property

109–45.901 Authority to abandon or destroy.
109–45.902 Findings justifying abandonment or destruction.
109–45.902–2 Abandonment or destruction without notice.

Subpart 109–45.10—Recovery of Precious Metals

109–45.1002 Agency responsibilities.
109–45.1002–3 Precious metals recovery program monitor.
109–45.1003 Recovery of silver from precious metals bearing materials.
109–45.1004 Recovery and use of precious metals through the DOD Precious Metals Recovery Program.

Subpart 109–45.47—Reports

109–45.4702 Negotiated sales reports.

Subpart 109–45.50—Excess and Surplus Radioactively and Chemically Contaminated Personal Property

109–45.5005 Disposal.
109–45.5005–1 General.

Subpart 109–45.51—Disposal of Excess and Surplus Personal Property in Foreign Areas

109–45.5100 Scope of subpart.
109–45.5101 Authority.
109–45.5102 General.
109–45.5103 Definitions.
109–45.5104 Disposal.
109–45.5104–1 General.
109–45.5104–2 Methods of disposal.
109–45.5105 Reports.

SOURCE: 81 FR 63265, Sept. 14, 2016, unless otherwise noted.

Subpart 109–45.1—General

§ 109–45.105 Exclusions and exemptions.

§ 109–45.105–3 Exemptions.

GSA, by letter dated May 28, 1965, exempted contractor inventory held by DOE designated contractors from the GSA conducted sales provisions of 41 CFR 101–45.

Subpart 109–45.3—Sale of Personal Property

§ 109–45.300–50 Sales by designated contractors.

Sales of surplus contractor inventory will be conducted by designated contractors when Program Secretarial Officer (PSO) determine that it is in the best interest of the Government. OPMOs and appropriate program officials shall perform sufficient oversight over these sales to ensure that personal property requiring special handling or program office certification is sold in accordance with regulatory requirements.

§ 109–45.301–51 Export/import clause.

The following clause shall be included in all sales invitations for bid:

Personal property purchased from the U.S. Government may or may not be authorized for export/import from/into the country where the personal property is located. If export/import is allowed, the purchaser is solely responsible for obtaining required clearances or approvals. The purchaser also is required to provide to the appropriate party DOE's export control guidance if the property is resold or otherwise disposed.

§ 109–45.302 Sale to Government employees.

§ 109–45.302–50 Sales to DOE employees and designated contractor employees.

(a) DOE employees and employees of designated contractors shall be given the same opportunity to acquire Government personal property as is given to the general public, provided the employees warrant in writing prior to award that they have not either directly or indirectly:
(1) Obtained information not otherwise available to the general public regarding usage, condition, quality, or value of the personal property, or
(2) Participated in:
(i) The determination to dispose of the personal property;
(ii) The preparation of the personal property for sale; and
(iii) Determining the method of sale.
(b) Excess or otherwise unusable special, fitted clothing and other articles of personal property, acquired for the

exclusive use of an individual employee, may be sold to the employee for the best price obtainable when the property is no longer required by the holding organization or the employee is terminated.

§ 109–45.303 Reporting property for sale.

§ 109–45.303–3 Delivery.

(a)–(b) [Reserved]

(c) Guidelines for signature authorization and control of blank copies of Standard Form 97, United States Government Certificate to Obtain Title to a Vehicle are contained in subpart 109–38.7 of this chapter.

§ 109–45.304 Sales methods and procedures.

§ 109–45.304–2 Negotiated sales and negotiated sales at fixed prices.

(a)(1) [Reserved]

(2) The head of each field organization shall designate a responsible person to approve negotiated sales by DOE direct operations.

(3) Requests for prior approval of negotiated sales by DOE direct operations shall be submitted with justification to the OPMO for review and forwarding to GSA for approval.

(b) [Reserved]

§ 109–45.304–2.50 Negotiated sales and negotiated sales at fixed prices by designated contractors.

(a) Negotiated sales by designated contractors of surplus contractor inventory may be made when the DOE contracting officer determines and documents prior to the sale that the use of this method of sale is justified on the basis of the circumstances enumerated below, provided that the Government's interests are adequately protected. These sales shall be at prices which are fair and reasonable and not less than the proceeds which could reasonably be expected to be obtained if the personal property was offered for competitive sale. Specific conditions justifying negotiated sales include:

(1) No acceptable bids have been received as a result of competitive bidding under a suitable advertised sale;

(2) Personal property is of such small value that the proceeds to be derived would not warrant the expense of a formal competitive sale;

(3) The disposal will be to a state, territory, possession, political subdivision thereof, or tax-supported agency therein, and the estimated fair market value of the personal property and other satisfactory terms of disposal are obtained by negotiation;

(4) The specialized nature and limited use potential of the personal property would create negligible bidder interest;

(5) Removal of the personal property would result in a significant reduction in value, or the accrual of disproportionate expense in handling; or

(6) It can be clearly established that such action is in the best interests of the Government.

(b) When determined to be in the best interests of the Government, Program Secretarial Officer (PSO) may authorize fixed-price sales of surplus contractor inventory by designated contractors provided:

(1) The fair market value of the item to be sold does not exceed $15,000;

(2) Adequate procedures for publicizing such sales have been established;

(3) The sales prices are not less than could reasonably be expected if competitive bid sales methods were employed and the prices have been approved by a reviewing authority designated by the head of the field organization; and

(4) The warranty prescribed in § 109–45.302–50(a) of this subpart is obtained when sales are made to employees.

§ 109–45.304–6 Reviewing authority.

The reviewing authority may consist of one or more persons designated by the head of the field organization.

§ 109–45.304–50 Processing bids and awarding of contracts.

The procedures established in 48 CFR 14.4 and 48 CFR 914.4 shall be made applicable to the execution, receipt, safeguarding, opening, abstraction, and evaluation of bids and awarding contracts, except that in evaluating bids and awarding contracts, disposal under conditions most advantageous to the Government based on high bids received shall be the determining factor.

§ 109–45.304–51 Documentation.

Files pertaining to surplus property sales shall contain copies of all documents necessary to provide a complete record of the sales transactions and shall include the following as appropriate:

(a) A copy of the request/invitation for bids if a written request/invitation for bids is employed. A list of items or lots sold, indicating acquisition cost, upset price and sales price indicated.

(b) A copy of the advertising literature distributed to prospective bidders.

(c) A list of prospective bidders solicited.

(d) An abstract of bids received.

(e) Copies of bids received, including Standard Form 119, Contractor's Statement of Contingent or Other Fees, together with other relevant information.

(f) A statement concerning the basis for determination that proceeds constitute a reasonable return for property sold.

(g) When appropriate, full and adequate justification for not advertising the sale when the fair market value of property sold in this manner in any one case exceeds $1,000.

(h) A justification concerning any award made to other than the high bidder.

(i) The approval of the reviewing authority when required.

(j) A copy of the notice of award.

(k) All related correspondence.

(l) In the case of auction or spot bid sales, the following additional information should be included:

(1) A summary listing of the advertising used (*e.g.*, newspapers, radio, television, and public postings).

(2) The names of the prospective bidders who attended the sale.

(3) A copy of any pertinent contract for auctioneering services and related documents.

(4) A reference to files containing record of deposits and payments.

§ 109–45.309 Special classes of property.

§ 109–45.309–2.50 Hazardous property.

Hazardous property shall be made available for sale only after the review

and certification requirements of § 109–43.307–2.50 of this subpart have been met.

§ 109–45.309–51 Export controlled property.

Export controlled property shall be made available for sale only after the export license requirements of § 109–43.307–50 of this subpart have been met.

§ 109–45.309–52 Classified property.

Classified property shall be made available for sale only after the declassification requirements of § 109–43.307–51 of this subpart have been met.

§ 109–45.309–53 Nuclear-related or proliferation-sensitive property.

Nuclear-related or proliferation-sensitive property shall be made available for sale only after the stripping and certification requirements of § 109–43.307–52 of this subpart have been met.

§ 109–45.309–54 Information Technology (IT).

IT shall be made available for sale only after the sanitizing and certification requirements of § 109–43.307–53 of this subpart have been met.

§ 109–45.310 Antitrust laws.

DOE offices shall submit to the Office of Management any request for a proposed sale of a patent, process, technique, or invention, regardless of cost; or of surplus personal property with a fair market value of $3,000,000 or more.

§ 109–45.317 Noncollusive bids and proposals.

(a) [Reserved]

(b) The head of the field organization shall make the determination required in 41 CFR 101–45.317(b). This authority cannot be redelegated.

Subpart 109–45.9—Abandonment or Destruction of Personal Property

§ 109–45.901 Authority to abandon or destroy.

Personal property in the possession of DOE offices or designated contractors may be abandoned or destroyed provided that a written determination has been made by the OPMO/PA that property has no commercial value or the estimated cost of its continued care and handling would exceed the estimated proceeds from its sale.

§ 109–45.902 Findings justifying abandonment or destruction.

§ 109–45.902–2 Abandonment or destruction without notice.

The head of the field organization shall designate an official to make the findings justifying abandonment or destruction without public notice of personal property. The OPMO/PA shall review and coordinate on the findings.

Subpart 109–45.10—Recovery of Precious Metals

§ 109–45.1002 Agency responsibilities.

The Office of Management and Program Secretarial Officer (PSO) are responsible for establishing a program for the recovery of precious metals.

§ 109–45.1002–3 Precious metals recovery program monitor.

The Office of Management shall be the precious metals recovery program monitor.

§ 109–45.1003 Recovery of silver from precious metals bearing materials.

The Office of Management and Program Secretarial Officer (PSO) are responsible for the establishment and maintenance of a program for silver recovery from used hypo solution and scrap film.

§ 109–45.1004 Recovery and use of precious metals through the DOD Precious Metals Recovery Program.

DOE operates its own precious metals pool and therefore does not participate in the DOD Precious Metals Recovery Program. See § 109–27.5106 of this chapter for guidance on operation of the DOE precious metals pool.

Subpart 109–45.47—Reports

§ 109–45.4702 Negotiated sales reports.

The report of negotiated sales shall be submitted by DOE offices to GSA, in accordance with 41 CFR 102–38.

Subpart 109–45.50—Excess and Surplus Radioactively and Chemically Contaminated Personal Property

§ 109–45.5005 Disposal.

§ 109–45.5005–1 General.

(a) Nuclear-related, proliferation-sensitive, low level contaminated property, and classified personal property shall not be transferred, sold, exchanged, leased, donated, abandoned, or destroyed without approval of the cognizant program office. Disposal of this personal property is subject to the restrictions contained in applicable sections of part 109–42 and §§ 109–43.307–50, 109–43.307–51, and 109–43.307–52 of this chapter, and applicable sections of 41 CFR part 101–42.

(b) Personal property that is considered defective or unsafe must be mutilated prior to shipment for disposal.

Subpart 109–45.51—Disposal of Excess and Surplus Personal Property in Foreign Areas

§ 109–45.5100 Scope of subpart.

This subpart sets forth policies and procedures governing the disposal of DOE-owned foreign excess and surplus personal property.

§ 109–45.5101 Authority.

The policies and procedures contained in this subpart are issued pursuant to the provisions of the Federal Property and Administrative Services Act of 1949, former 40 U.S.C. *et seq.*, as amended. Title IV of the Act entitled "Foreign Excess Property" provides that, except where commitments exist under previous agreements, all excess personal property located in foreign areas shall be disposed of by the owning agency, and directs that the head of the agency conform to the foreign policy of the United States in making such disposals in accordance 41 CFR 102–36.

§ 109–45.5102 General.

Disposal of Government-owned personal property in the custody of DOE organizations or its contractors in foreign areas shall be made in an efficient

and economical manner, and in conformance with the foreign policy of the United States.

§ 109–45.5103 Definitions.

As used in this subpart, the following definitions apply:

Foreign means outside the United States, Puerto Rico, American Samoa, Guam, the Trust Territory of the Pacific Islands, and the Virgin Islands.

Foreign service post means the local diplomatic or consular post in the area where the excess personal property is located.

§ 109–45.5104 Disposal.

§ 109–45.5104–1 General.

Foreign excess personal property which is not required for transfer within DOE or to other U.S. Government agencies, except for the personal property identified in § 109–45.5005–1(a) of this part, shall be considered surplus and may be disposed of by transfer, sale, exchange, or lease, for cash, credit, or other property and upon such other terms and conditions as may be deemed proper. Such personal property may also be donated, abandoned, or destroyed under the conditions specified in § 109–45.5105–2 of this subpart. Most foreign governments have indicated to the U.S. State Department that they wish to be consulted before U.S. Government property is disposed of in their countries (except in the case of transfers to other U.S. Government agencies). Matters concerning customs duties and taxes, or similar charges, may require prior agreement with the foreign government involved. The State Department shall be contacted in regard to these issues. Whenever advice or approval of the State Department is required by this subpart, it may be obtained either through the foreign service post in the foreign area involved or from the State Department in Washington, DC. If the issue is to be presented to the State Department in Washington, DC, it shall be referred through appropriate administrative channels to the Office of International Affairs for review, coordination, and handling.

§ 109–45.5104–2 Methods of disposal.

(a) Sales of foreign surplus personal property shall be conducted in accordance with the following guidelines:

(1) Generally, all sales of foreign surplus personal property shall be conducted under the competitive bid process unless it is advantageous and more practicable to the Government not to do so. When competitive bids are not solicited, reasonable inquiry of prospective purchasers shall be made in order that sales may be made on terms most advantageous to the U.S. Government.

(2) In no event shall any personal property be sold in foreign areas without a condition which states that its importation into the United States is forbidden unless the U.S. Secretary of Agriculture (in the case of any agricultural commodity, food, cotton, or woolen goods), or the U.S. Secretary of Commerce (in the case of any other property), has determined that the importation of such property would relieve domestic shortages or otherwise be beneficial to the economy of the United States.

(3) Sales documents shall provide that the purchaser must pay any import duties or taxes levied against personal property sold in the country involved and further provide that the amount of this duty or tax shall not be included as a part of the price paid the U.S. Government for the personal property. In the event the levy is placed upon the seller by law, the buyer will be required to pay all such duties or taxes and furnish the seller copies of his receipts prior to the release of the personal property to him. However, if the foreign government involved will not accept payment from the buyer, the seller will collect the duties or taxes and turn the amounts collected over to the foreign government. Accounting for the amounts collected shall be coordinated with the disbursing officer of the nearest United States foreign service post. The property shall not be released to the purchaser until the disposal officer is satisfied that there is no responsibility for payment by the United States (as contrasted to collection by the United States) of taxes, duties, excises, etc.

(4) Advance approval must be obtained from the State Department for the sale of certain categories of personal property, including small arms and machine guns; artillery and projectiles; ammunition, bombs, torpedoes, rockets and guided missiles; fire control equipment and range finders; tanks and ordnance vehicles; chemical and biological agents, propellants and explosives; vessels of war and special naval equipment; aircraft and all components, parts and accessories for aircraft; military electronic equipment; aerial cameras, military photo-interpretation, stereoscopic plotting and photogrammetry equipment; and all material not enumerated which is included in the United States Munitions List, 22 CFR 121.01, and is subject to disposal restrictions. Therefore, prior to the sale of any of the articles enumerated in the U.S. Munitions List, the foreign service post in the area shall be consulted.

(5) All proposed sales, regardless of the total acquisition cost of personal property involved, which the head of the DOE foreign office believes might have a significant economic or political impact in a particular area, shall be discussed with the foreign service post.

(b) While there is authority for exchange or lease of foreign surplus personal property, such authority shall be exercised only when such action is clearly in the best interests of the U.S. Government. Disposals by exchange are subject to the same requirements as disposals by sale under § 109–45.5105–2 of this subpart.

(c)(1) Foreign excess or surplus personal property (including salvage and scrap) may be donated, abandoned, or destroyed provided:

(i) The property has no commercial value or the estimated cost of its care and handling would exceed the estimated proceeds from its sale; and

(ii) A written finding to that effect is made and approved by the Office of International Affairs.

(2) No personal property shall be abandoned or destroyed if donation is feasible. Donations under these conditions may be made to any agency of the U.S. Government, or to educational, public health, or charitable nonprofit organizations.

(3) Foreign excess personal property may also be abandoned or destroyed when such action is required by military necessity, safety, or considerations of health or security. A written statement explaining the basis for disposal by these means and approval by the Office of International Affairs.

(4) Property shall not be abandoned or destroyed in a manner which is detrimental or dangerous to public health and safety, or which will cause infringement on the rights of other persons.

§ 109–45.5105   Reports.

(a) Proposed sales of foreign surplus personal property shall include all pertinent data, including the following:

(1) The description of personal property to be sold, including:

(i) Identification of personal property (description should be in terms understandable to persons not expert in technical nomenclature). Personal property covered by the U.S. Munitions List and regulations pertaining thereto (as published in 22 CFR 121.1) should be clearly identified;

(ii) Quantity;

(iii) Condition; and

(iv) Acquisition cost.

(2) The proposed method of sale (*e.g.*, sealed bid, negotiated sale, etc.)

(3) Any currency to be received and payment provisions (*i.e.*, U.S. dollars, foreign currency, or credit, including terms of the proposed sale).

(4) Any restrictions on use of personal property to be sold (such as resale of property, disposal as scrap, demilitarization, etc.).

(5) Any special terms or conditions of sale.

(6) The categories of prospective purchasers (*e.g.*, host country, other foreign countries, special qualifications, etc.).

(7) How taxes, excises, duties, etc., will be handled.

(b) [Reserved]

PART 109–46—UTILIZATION AND DISPOSAL OF PERSONAL PROPERTY PURSUANT TO EXCHANGE/SALE AUTHORITY

Sec.
109–46.000 Scope of part.
109–46.000–50 Applicability.

Subpart 109–46.2—Authorization

109–46.202 Restrictions and limitations.
109–46.203 Special authorizations.

AUTHORITY: Sec. 205(c), 63 Stat. 390; 40 U.S.C. 486(c).

SOURCE: 81 FR 63265, Sept. 14, 2016, unless otherwise noted.

§ 109–46.000 Scope of part.

§ 109–46.000–50 Applicability.

(a) Except as set forth in paragraphs (a)(1) through (5) of this section, the requirements of FPMR/FMR part 101–46 and this part are not applicable to designated contractors. Designated contractors shall comply with the following FPMR/FMR requirements:

(1) 101–46.200;

(2) 101–46.201–1;

(3) 101–46.202(b)(2), (3), (4), (5), (6), and (7);

(4) 101–46.202(c)(1), (2), (4), (5), (6), (7), (10), (11), and (12);

(5) 101–46.202(d).

(b) Items in the following Federal Supply Classification Groups (FSCG) are not eligible for processing under the exchange/sale provision. Requests for waivers must be processed through the DPMO to GSA.

DESCRIPTION

FSCG

10 Weapons
11 Nuclear ordnance
12 Fire control equipment
14 Guided missiles
15 Aircraft and airframe structural components (except FSC Class 1560, Airframe structural components)
20 Ship and marine equipment
22 Railway equipment
41 Firefighting, rescue, and safety equipment

Subpart 109–46.2—Authorization

§ 109–46.202 Restrictions and limitations.

(a)–(c)(9) [Reserved]

(10) The Office of Management and Program Secretarial Officer (PSO) for their respective organizations shall designate an official to make the certification that a continuing valid requirement exists for excess personal property acquired and placed in official use for less than one year but no longer required and is to be disposed of under the exchange/sale provisions.

(11) [Reserved]

(12) Program Secretarial Officer (PSO) shall make the determination concerning demilitarization of combat material.

§ 109–46.203 Special authorizations.

(a) [Reserved]

(b) The Office of Management and Program Secretarial Officer (PSO) for their respective organizations shall designate an official to make the certification concerning the exchange of historic items for historical preservation or display..

PART 109–48—UTILIZATION, DONATION, OR DISPOSAL OF ABANDONED AND FORFEITED PERSONAL PROPERTY

Sec.
109–48.000 Scope of part.
109–48.000–50 Applicability.

Subpart 109–48.1—Utilization of Abandoned and Forfeited Personal Property

109–48.101 Forfeited or voluntarily abandoned property.
109–48.101–6 Transfer to other Federal agencies.

AUTHORITY: 40 U.S.C. 121.

SOURCE: 81 FR 63265, Sept. 14, 2016, unless otherwise noted.

§ 109–48.000 Scope of part.

§ 109–48.000–50 Applicability.

This part is applicable to contractor operations where the abandoned or forfeited personal property is found on premises owned or leased by the Government that are managed and operated by designated contractors.

Subpart 109–48.1—Utilization of Abandoned and Forfeited Personal Property

§ 109–48.101 Forfeited or voluntarily abandoned property.

§ 109–48.101–6 Transfer to other Federal agencies.

(a)–(c) [Reserved]

(d) Transfer orders for forfeited or voluntarily abandoned distilled spirits, wine, and malt beverages for medicinal, scientific, or mechanical purposes or any other official purposes for which appropriated funds may be expended by a Government agency shall be forwarded through normal administrative channels for signature by the DPMO and for subsequent forwarding to GSA for release.

(e) [Reserved]

(f) Transfer orders for reportable forfeited drug paraphernalia shall be forwarded through normal administrative channels for signature by the Property Executive and for subsequent forwarding to GSA for approval.

PART 109–50—SPECIAL DOE DISPOSAL AUTHORITIES

AUTHORITY: Sec. 644, Pub. L. 95–91, 91 Stat. 599 (42 U.S.C. 7254); sec. 31, Atomic Energy Act, as amended; Energy Reorganization Act of 1974, secs. 103 and 107; Title III, Department of Energy Organization Act; E.O. 12999; sec. 3710(i), Stevenson-Wydler Technology Innovation Act, as amended (15 U.S.C. 3710(i)); Pub. L. 101–510, Department of Energy Science Education Enhancement Act; Pub. L. 102–245, American Technologies Preeminence Act of 1991 (15 U.S.C. 3701); Office of Science Financial Assistance Program (10 CFR part 605).

SOURCE: 81 FR 63265, Sept. 14, 2016, unless otherwise noted.

§ 109–50.000 Scope of part.

This part provides guidance on the policies, practices, and procedures for the disposal of DOE property under special legislative authorities.

§ 109–50.001 Applicability.

The provisions of this part apply to direct DOE operations and to designated contractors only when specifically provided for in the appropriate subpart.

Subpart 109–50.1—Laboratory Equipment Donation Program Grant Program

§ 109–50.100 Scope of subpart.

This subpart provides guidance on the granting of Laboratory Equipment Donation Program in the LEDP is limited to accredited, post graduate, degree granting institutions including universities, colleges, junior colleges, technical institutes, museums, or hospitals, located in the U.S. and interested in establishing or upgrading energy-oriented educational programs in the life, physical, and environmental sciences and in engineering is eligible to apply. An energy-oriented program is defined as an academic research activity dealing primarily or entirely in energy-related topics.

§ 109–50.101 Applicability.

This subpart is applicable to DOE offices and designated contractors.

§ 109–50.102 General.

DOE, to encourage research and development in the field of energy, awards grants of excess Laboratory Equipment Donation Program to eligible institutions for use in energy-oriented educational programs. Under the Used Laboratory Equipment Donation Program (LEDP) Grant Program, grants of used energy-related equipment excess to the requirements of DOE offices and designated contractors may be made to eligible institutions prior to reporting the equipment to GSA for reutilization screening.

§ 109–50.103 Definitions.

As used in this subpart the following definitions apply: *Book value* means acquisition cost less depreciation. *DOE Financial Assistance Rules* (10 CFR part 600) means the DOE regulation which establishes a uniform administrative system for application, award, and administration of assistance awards, including grants and cooperative agreements.

Eligible institution means any non-profit educational institution of higher learning, such as universities, colleges, junior colleges, hospitals, and technical institutes or museums located in the United States and interested in establishing or upgrading energy-oriented education programs.

Energy-oriented education program means one that deals partially or entirely in energy or energy-related topics.

§ 109–50.104 Equipment which may be granted.

Generally, equipment items classified in FSCG 66, Instruments and Lab-oratory Equipment, are eligible for granting under this program. Other selected items designated by the Office of Workforce Development for Teachers and Scientists (WDTS) and approved by the OPMO, are made available under the program.

§ 109–50.105 Equipment which may not be granted.

Equipment which will not be granted include:

(a) Equipment intended by the DOE institution for use in contractual research projects.

(b) Furniture, such as desks, tables, chairs, typewriters, etc. (exception is such equipment that may be an essential component of and physically attached to an energy-related laboratory equipment system);

(c) General supplies.

§ 109–50.106 Procedure.

(a) After DOE utilization screening through EADS, items eligible for LEDP grants are extracted from the EADS system and Office of Workforce Development for Teachers and Scientists (WDTS).

(b) Office of Workforce Development for Teachers and Scientists (WDTS) to prospective grantees through an automated system.

(c) The following periods have been established during which time equipment will remain available to this program prior to reporting it to GSA for reutilization by other Federal agencies:

(1) Thirty days from the date DOE utilization screening is completed to permit suitable time for eligible institutions to review and earmark the desired equipment.

(2) An additional thirty days after the equipment is earmarked to permit the eligible institutions to prepare and submit an equipment proposal request and to provide time for field organizations to review and evaluate the proposal and take appropriate action.

(d) Upon approval of the proposal, a grant will be issued to the institution upon completion.

(e) A copy of the completed grant, shall be used to transfer title and drop accountability of the granted equipment from the financial records.

(f) The cost of care and handling of personal property incident to the grant shall be charged to the receiving institution. Such costs may consist of packing, crating, shipping and insurance, and are limited to actual costs. In addition, where appropriate, the cost of any repair and/or modification to any equipment shall be borne by the recipient institution.

§ 109–50.107 Reporting.

(a) Gifts made under this program shall be included in the annual report of property transferred to non-Federal recipients, as required by 41 CFR 101–43.4701(c) and 109–43.4701(c).

(b) A copy of each equipment agreement shall be forwarded to the Director, Office of Laboratory Policy and Infrastructure Management.

Subpart 109–50.2—Math and Science Equipment Gift Program

§ 109–50.200 Scope of subpart.

This subpart provides guidance on providing gifts of excess and/or surplus education related and Federal research equipment to elementary and secondary educational institutions or nonprofit organizations for the purpose of improving math and science curricula or conducting of technical and scientific education and research activities.

§ 109–50.201 Applicability.

The provisions of this subpart are applicable to DOE offices and designated contractors.

§ 109–50.202 Definitions.

As used in this subpart the following definitions apply:

DOE Field Organizations means the DOE Federal management activities, including Operations Offices, Field Offices, Area Offices, Site Offices, Energy Technology Centers, and Project Offices staffed by Federal employees.

Education-related and Federal research equipment includes but is not limited to DOE-owned property in FSCG 34, 36, 41, 52, 60, 61, 66, 67, 70, and 74 (See 41 CFR 101–43.4801(d)), and other related equipment, which is deemed appropriate for use in improving math and science curricula or activities for elementary and secondary school education, or for the conduct of technical and scientific education and research activities.

Elementary and secondary schools means individual public or private educational institutions encompassing kindergarten through twelfth grade, as well as public school districts.

Eligible recipient means local elementary and secondary schools and nonprofit organizations.

Facilities under DOE Field Organization cognizance means national laboratories, production plants, and project sites managed and operated by DOE contractors or subcontractors.

§ 109–50.203 Eligible equipment.

(a) Education-related and research equipment will include, but is not limited to the following FSCGs:

FSCG AND DESCRIPTION

34 Metalworking Machinery
36 Special Industry Machinery
41 Refrigeration, Air Conditioning and Air Circulating Equipment
52 Measuring Tools
60 Fiber Optics Materials, Components, Assemblies and Accessories
61 Electric Wire, and Power and Distribution Equipment
66 Instruments and Laboratory Equipment
67 Photographic Equipment
70 General Purpose Automatic Data Processing Equipment (Including Firmware), Software, Supplies and Support Equipment
74 Office Machines, Text Processing Systems and Visible Record Equipment

(b) Other related equipment may be provided if deemed appropriate and approved by the Director, Office of Laboratory Policy and Infrastructure Management.

§ 109–50.204 Limitations.

(a) Excess and/or surplus education-related and Federal research equipment at DOE Field Organizations and cognizant facilities is eligible for transfer as a gift under this program. However, safety, environmental, and health matters must be considered.

(b) Title to the equipment will transfer upon the recipient's written acknowledgement of receipt.

(c) The Office of Workforce Development for Teachers and Scientists

(WDTS) may authorize gifts of excess and/or surplus education-related and Federal research equipment by signature on the appropriate gift instrument where the book value of an item of equipment exceeds $25,000 or the cumulative book value of the gifts under this program to any one institution exceeds $25,000. HCA or designee may authorize gifts of excess and/or surplus education-related and Federal research equipment of lesser individual and cumulative book value by signature on the appropriate gift instrument. Delegations by the HCA to authorize gifts of excess and/or surplus education-related and Federal research equipment shall be in writing to a specific individual, for a specified period of time, and for a specified (or unlimited) level of authority.

(d) Gifts shall be serviceable and in working order. Disposal Condition Codes 1 and 4, as defined in 41 CFR 101–43.4801(e), meet this criteria. Serviceability of equipment should be verified before the gift is made to the eligible recipient.

§ 109–50.205 **Procedure.**

(a) The DOE facility will set aside an appropriate amount of excess and/or surplus education-related and Federal research equipment for transfer under this program.

(b) A list of available education-related and Federal research equipment will be prepared and distributed to eligible recipients and the chief State School Board Officer.

(c) Precollege institutions with partnership arrangements with the DOE or its facilities (*e.g.*, an adopted school) may receive gifts of equipment in support of the partnership.

(d) Precollege institutions not in a partnership with DOE may receive equipment at the recommendation of the chief State School Board Officer. The Chief State School Board Officer will determine which schools within the state will receive which equipment. Consideration for placement of the equipment should be based on:

(1) The elementary or secondary schools determined to have the greatest need; or

(2) Recipients of federally funded math and science projects where the

equipment would further enhance the progress of the project.

(e) Eligible·recipients will have 30 days to select and freeze, on a first come, first serve basis, the items desired and submit a request for selected items stating:

(1) Why the gift is needed; and

(2) How the gift will be used to improve math and science curricula or in the conduct of technical and scientific education and research activities.

(f) The cost of shipping should be minimal and not more than the actual equipment value.

(g) An Equipment Gift Agreement will be prepared and used to provide the gift to eligible recipients. The gift agreement will be in the format provided in section 109–50.4801 of this subchapter. The agreement shall be numbered for control purposes, and signed by the Office of Science's Office of Workforce Development for Teachers and Scientists (WDTS) or the HCA or designee, as appropriate, and an appropriate official representing the eligible recipient.

§ 109–50.206 **Reporting.**

(a) Gifts made under this program shall be included in the annual report of property transferred to non-Federal recipients, as required by 41 CFR 101–43.4701(c) and § 109–43.4701(c) of this chapter.

(b) A copy of each equipment agreement shall be forwarded to the Office of Workforce Development for Teachers and Scientists (WDTS).

Subpart 109–50.3 [Reserved]

Subpart 109–50.4—Programmatic Disposal to Contractors of DOE Property in a Mixed Facility

§ 109–50.400 **Scope of subpart.**

This subpart contains policy to be followed when it is proposed to sell or otherwise transfer DOE personal property located in a mixed facility to the contractor who is the operator of that facility.

§ 109–50.401 Definitions.

As used in this subpart, the following definitions apply;

Contractor means the operator of the mixed facility.

DOE property means DOE-owned personal property located in a mixed facility.

Mixed facility means a partly DOE-owned and partly contractor-owned facility. For purposes of this subpart, however, this definition does not apply to such a facility operated by an educational or other nonprofit institution under a basic research contract with DOE.

§ 109–50.402 Submission of proposals.

Proposals involving programmatic disposals of DOE personal property located in mixed facilities to contractors operating that facility shall be forwarded through the appropriate program organization to the Property Executive, for review and processing for approval. Each such request shall include all information necessary for a proper evaluation of the proposal. The proposal shall include, as a minimum:

(a) The purpose of the mixed facility;

(b) The description, condition, acquisition cost, and present use of the DOE personal property involved.

(c) The programmatic benefits which could accrue to DOE from the disposal to the contractor (including the considerations which become important if the disposal is not made);

(d) The appraised value of the DOE personal property (preferably by independent appraisers); and

(e) The proposed terms and conditions of disposal including:

(1) Price;

(2) Priority to be given work for DOE requiring the use of the transferred property, and including the basis for any proposed charge to DOE for amortizing the cost of plant and equipment items;

(3) Recapture of the property if DOE foresees a possible future urgent need; and

(4) Delivery of the property, whether "as is-where is," etc.

§ 109–50.403 Need to establish DOE program benefit.

When approval for a proposed programmatic disposal of DOE personal property in a mixed facility is being sought, it must be established that the disposal will benefit a DOE program. For example, approval might be contingent on showing that:

(a) The entry of the contractor as a private concern into the energy program is important and significant from a programmatic standpoint; and

(b) The sale of property to the contractor will remove obstacles which otherwise discourage entry into the field.

Subpart 109–50.48—Exhibits

§ 109–50.4800 Scope of subpart.

This subpart exhibits information referenced in the text of part 109–50 of this chapter that is not suitable for inclusion elsewhere in that part.

§ 109–50.4801 Equipment Gift Agreement.

(a) The following Equipment Gift Agreement format will be used to provide gifts of excess and/or surplus equipment to eligible recipients under the Math and Science Equipment Gift Program (see subpart 109–50.2 of this chapter).

EQUIPMENT GIFT AGREEMENT

(Reference Number)

BETWEEN THE U.S. DEPARTMENT OF ENERGY
AND

(Name of Eligible Recipient)

I. PURPOSE

The Department of Energy shall provide as a gift, excess and/or surplus education-related and Federal research equipment to (Name of Eligible Recipient), hereafter referred to as the Recipient, for the purpose of improving the Recipient's math and science education curricula or for the Recipient's conduct of technical and scientific education and research activities.

II. AUTHORITY

Federal agencies have been directed, to the maximum extent permitted by law, to give highest preference to elementary and secondary schools in the transfer or donation of education-related Federal equipment, at the lowest cost permitted by law. Furthermore, subsection 11(i) of the Stevenson Wydler Technology Innovation Act of 1980, as amended (15 U.S.C. 3710 (i)), authorizes the Director of a laboratory, or the head of any Federal agency or department to give excess research equipment to an educational institution or nonprofit organization for the conduct of technical and scientific education and research activities.

III. AGREEMENT

A. The Department of Energy agrees to provide the equipment identified in the attached equipment gift list, as a gift for the purpose of improving the Recipient's math and science curricula or for the Recipient's conduct of technical and scientific education and research activities.

B. Title to the education-related and Federal research equipment, provided as a gift under this agreement, shall vest with the Recipient upon the Recipient's written acknowledgement of receipt of the equipment. The acknowledgement shall be provided to (Name of the DOE signatory) at (address).

C. The Recipient will be responsible for any repair and modification costs to any equipment received under this gift.

D. The Recipient hereby releases and agrees to hold the Government, the Department of Energy, or any person acting on behalf of the Department of Energy harmless, to the extent allowable by State law, for any and all liability of every kind and nature whatsoever resulting from the receipt, shipping, installation, operation, handling, use, and maintenance of the education-related and Federal Research equipment provided as a gift under this agreement.

E. The Recipient agrees to use the gift provided herein for the primary purpose of improving the math and science curricula or for the conduct of technical and scientific education and research activities.

F. The Recipient agrees to provide for the return of the equipment if such equipment, while still usable, has not been placed in use for its intended purpose within one year after receipt from the Department of Energy.

(U.S. Department of Energy Office)

(Name and Address of Recipient)

(Signature of HCA or Designee)

(Signature of Official)

(Typed Name)

(Typed Name)

(Typed Title)

(Typed Title)

(Date)

(Date)

(b) The list of gifts that accompanies the Equipment Gift Agreement shall contain the Gift Agreement reference number, name of the eligible recipient, and the name of the DOE office. In addition, the following information shall be provided for each line item provided as a gift: DOE ID number, description (name, manufacturer, model number, serial number, etc.), FSC code, quantity, location, acquisition date, and acquisition cost.

CHAPTER 114—DEPARTMENT OF THE INTERIOR

PART 114–51—GOVERNMENT FURNISHED QUARTERS

AUTHORITY: 5 U.S.C. 301.

Subpart 114–51.1—General

§ 114–51.100 Departmental Quarters Handbook.

The Office of Acquisition and Property Management (PAM) has prepared the Departmental Quarters Handbook (DQH), 400 DM, which provides detailed guidelines governing administration, management and rental rate establishment activities relating to Government furnished quarters (GFQ). Officials responsible for administration and management of quarters shall implement and comply with the provisions of the DQH, and shall ensure its availability for examination by all employees.

[60 FR 3555, Jan. 18, 1995]

CHAPTER 115—ENVIRONMENTAL PROTECTION AGENCY

PART 115-1—INTRODUCTION

Subpart 115-1.1—Regulation System

AUTHORITY: Sec. 205(c), 63 Stat. 377, as amended; 40 U.S.C. 486(c).

SOURCE: 36 FR 8568, May 8, 1971, unless otherwise noted.

Subpart 115-1.1—Regulation System

§ 115-1.100 Scope of subpart.

This subpart establishes the Environmental Protection Agency Property Management Regulations (EPPMR), chapter 115 of the Federal Property Management Regulations System (FPMR) (41 CFR chapter 101); states its relationship to the FPMR, and provides instructions governing the property management policies and procedures of the Environmental Protection Agency (EPA).

§ 115-1.103 Temporary-type FPMR.

§ 115-1.103-50 Temporary-type changes to EPPMR.

Where required, temporary changes will be published as EPPMR-Temporary Regulations. Temporary Regulations will be cross-referenced to related EPPMR subparts and will indicate dates for compliance with, and cancellation of each issuance.

§ 115-1.104 Publication of FPMR.

§ 115-1.104-50 Publication of EPPMR.

(a) Material published in the EPPMR will generally not be of interest to nor directly affect the public. Therefore, most EPPMR material will not be published in the FEDERAL REGISTER.

(b) Arrows printed in the margin of a page indicate material changed, deleted, or added by the EPPMR Trans-mittal Notice cited at the bottom of that page. (See GSA, FPMR Amendment Transmittal pages for illustrations.)

§ 115-1.106 Applicability of FPMR.

The FPMR apply to all EPA activities unless otherwise specified, or unless a deviation is approved.

§ 115-1.108 Agency implementation and supplementation of FPMR.

(a) EPPMR implements and supplements the FPMR and follows the FPMR in style, arrangement and numbering sequence. Except to assure continuity and understanding FPMR material will not be repeated or paraphrased in the EPPMR.

(b) Implementing material expands upon related material in the FPMR. Supplementing material deals with subject material not covered in the FPMR.

§ 115-1.109 Numbering in FPMR system.

(a) The numbering system used in EPPMR conforms to that of the FPMR except for the chapter number. The first three digits represent the Chapter number assigned to this Agency in title 41, Code of Federal Regulations (CFR). In FPMR the chapter number is 101 and in EPPMR the Chapter number is 115.

(b) Where EPA Chapter 115 implements Chapter 101 the material will be numbered and captioned to correspond to the FPMR part, subpart, section or subsection, e.g., 115-1.106 "Applicability of FPMR" implements 101-1.106 of FPMR.

(c) Where Chapter 115 supplements the FPMR and deals with subject matter not contained in the FPMR, the EPPMR material is numbered to follow that which is most closely related to similar material in the FPMR, Supplementing material is numbered "50" or higher.

§ 115-1.110 Deviations.

Where deemed necessary that regulations set forth in the FPMR or EPPMR be changed in the interest of program effectiveness, a proposed revision will be submitted in accordance with FPR § 1-1.009, to the Division of Data and

Support Systems (DSSD) for review
and consideration.

CHAPTER 128—DEPARTMENT OF JUSTICE

PART 128-1—INTRODUCTION

Subpart 128-1.1—Regulation System

AUTHORITY: 5 U.S.C. 301, 40 U.S.C. 121(c), 41 CFR 101–1.108, and 28 CFR 0.75(j), unless otherwise noted.

SOURCE: 41 FR 45987, Oct. 19, 1976, unless otherwise noted.

Subpart 128-1.1—Regulation System

§ 128-1.100 Scope of subpart.

This subpart introduces the Department of Justice Property Management Regulations (JPMR) as part of the Federal Property Management Regulations System (FPMR) (41 CFR part 101); states its relationship to the FPMR; and provides instructions for the issuance and use of these property management policies and procedures of the Department of Justice.

§ 128-1.101 Justice Property Management Regulations.

The JPMR, established in this subpart, implement and supplement, as necessary, the FPMR provisions governing the acquisition, utilization, management, and disposal of real and personal property. The JPMR are issued to establish uniform property management policies, regulations, and, as necessary, procedures in the Department of Justice.

§ 128-1.105 Authority for JPMR.

The Department of Justice Property Management Regulations are prescribed by the Assistant Attorney General for Administration under authority of 5 U.S.C. 301, 40 U.S.C. 486(c), 41 CFR 101–1.108, and 28 CFR 0.75(j).

§ 128-1.152 Citation.

The JPMR will be cited in accordance with the FEDERAL REGISTER standards applicable to the FPMR. Accordingly, when this section is referred to formally in official documents, it should be cited as "41 CFR 128-1.152." When a section of the JPMR is referred to informally, however, it may be identified simply by "JPMR" followed by the complete paragraph reference number, e.g., "JPMR 128-1.152."

Subpart 128-1.50—Authorities and Responsibilities for Personal Property Management

§ 128-1.5001 Scope of subpart.

This subpart sets forth general definitions of terms used throughout the JPMR and states responsibilities and authorities within the Department of

Justice as they pertain to personal property management functions.

§ 128–1.5002   Definitions.

§ 128–1.5002–1   Acquire.

To procure, purchase, or obtain in any manner, except by lease, including transfer, donation or forfeiture, manufacture, or production at Government-owned plants or facilities.

§ 128–1.5002–2   Department.

The Department of Justice, including all its Bureaus and their respective field operations in all locations.

§ 128–1.5002–3   Head of the Agency/Department.

The Attorney General of the United States.

§ 128–1.5002–4   Bureau.

The Federal Bureau of Investigation; the Law Enforcement Assistance Administration; the Immigration and Naturalization Service; the Drug Enforcement Administration; the Bureau of Prisons; the Federal Prison Industries, Incorporated; and the Operations Support Staff (OSS) of the Office of Management and Finance. The OSS has authority and is responsible for all personal property management functions for the Offices, Boards, and Divisions of the Department, the United States Marshals Service, and the United States Parole Commission.

§ 128–1.5002–5   Personal property.

Property of any kind or interest therein, except real and related property (as defined in FPMR 41 CFR 101–43.104–15), records of the Federal Government, and naval vessels, cruisers, aircraft-carriers, destroyers, and submarines (FPMR 41 CFR 101–43.104–13). For management and accounting control, personal property is categorized as follows:

(a) "Expendable personal property" is that which, by its nature or function, is consumed in use; is used as repair parts or components of an end product considered nonexpendable; or has an expected service life of less than one year.

(b) "Non-expendable personal property" is that which is complete within itself, does not lose its identity or become a component part of another article when put into use, and is of a durable nature with an expected service life one or more years.

(c) "Controlled personal property" is that personal property for which good management practice dictates that it would be in the interest of the Government to assign and record accountability to assure the proper use, maintenance, protection and disposal of property for which the Government is responsible. Includes, but is not restricted to property which:

(1) Is leased by, in the custody of, or is loaned to or from the Department.

(2) Due to inherent attractiveness and/or portability is subject to a high probability of theft or misuse.

(3) Is warranted, requires knowledge of age and/or previous repair data when determining whether repair or replacement is appropriate.

§ 128–1.5002–6   Personal property management.

A system for controlling the acquisition, receipt, storage issue, utilization, maintenance, protection, accountability, and disposal of personal property to best satisfy the program needs of the Department.

§ 128–1.5002–7   Property management officer (PMO).

An individual responsible for the overall administration, coordination, and control of the personal property management program of a bureau. The designation as PMO may or may not correspond to the individual's official job title.

§ 128–1.5002–8   Property custodian (PC).

An individual responsible for the immediate physical custody of all personal property under his control and for providing documentation as required on all actions affecting the personal property within his jurisdiction. The designation as PC may or may not correspond to the individual's official job title.

§ 128–1.5002–9 Supply support system.

The sum of all actions taken in providing buildings, equipment, supplies, and services to support program areas.

§ 128–1.5003 Primary authority and responsibility.

(a) The Attorney General of the United States has the primary authority and responsibility for providing direction, leadership, and general supervision in the development and administration of an effective and efficient supply support system for the Department, to include:

(1) The establishment of Department-wide policies, directions, regulations, and procedures satisfying the requirements of law, regulations, and sound management practice; and

(2) The review, evaluation, and improvement of personal property management programs, functions, operations, and procedures throughout the Department.

(b) Pursuant to 28 CFR 0.75 and subject to the general supervision of the Attorney General and the direction of the Deputy Attorney General, the functions described above are assigned to the Assistant Attorney General for Administration as delegations of authority.

§ 128–1.5004 Basis for delegations of authority and assignment of responsibilities.

Certain personal property management functions can be performed by an individual only under a specific grant of authority to that individual. Other functions may be performed simply on the basis of general instructions or directions or by virtue of an individual occupying the position to which the responsibility for the function is assigned. In either situation, to eliminate excessive delay and to reduce unnecessary involvement of multiple management levels, it is considered generally desirable to place authority and responsibility for and to exercise property management actions at the lowest organizational unit practical. Accordingly, specific redelegations of the authority vested in the Assistant Attorney General for Administration are made to the heads of bureaus for the personal property management functions listed in § 128–1.5005 below. The authority to prescribe and issue Department-wide policies, regulations, and procedures for personal property management is not redelegated and remains solely within the jurisdiction of the Assistant Attorney General for Administration.

§ 128–1.5005 Delegations of authority.

§ 128–1.5005–1 Primary delegations.

The following authorities are redelegated to the heads of bureaus for use within their respective jurisdictions and shall be exercised in accordance with the policies and procedures established by the Assistant Attorney General for Administration.

(a) Designating the PMO, for the bureau, within the following limitations:

(1) Only one PMO is to be designated for the bureau, at the bureau level. Neither the title designation nor the responsibilities of the PMO are to be delegated below that level.

(2) One or more PC's also may be designated for the bureau, depending upon the size and complexity of the organizational structure. Each PC is responsible solely for that property within his respective jurisdiction. The number and distribution of PC's designated is entirely at the option of the head of the bureau.

(3) There is no restriction on designating a single individual as PMO and PC providing that the functions and responsibilities are compatible and are within the capabilities of a single person.

(b) Authorizing exceptions to the FPMR use and replacement standards for office machines, furniture, furnishings and typewriters specified in §§ 101–25.3 and 101–25.4.

(c) Authorizing exceptions to FPMR replacement standards for materials handling equipment specified in § 101–25.304.

(d) Authorizing the procurement of passenger motor vehicles with additional systems or equipment or the procurement of additional systems or equipment for passenger motor vehicles already owned or operated by the Government, in conformance with Federal Standards No. 122 and § 101–25.304.

(e) Authorizing the retention for official use by the bureau of abandoned or other unclaimed personal property and of personal property which is voluntarily abandoned or forfeited other than by court decree.

(f) Determining when personal property becomes excess and reporting the excess property to the General Services Administration (GSA).

(g) Assigning or transferring excess personal property within the bureau to other bureaus of the Department, other Federal agencies, the Legislative Branch to the Judicial Branch, to wholly-owned or mixed-ownership Government corporations, to cost-reimbursable type contractors, or to authorized grantees.

(h) Transferring property forfeited to the Government to other authorized recipients or requesting judicial transfer of such property from others to the bureau.

(i) Determining fair market value of abandoned and other unclaimed property retained for official use by the bureau, for deposit to a special fund for reimbursement of owners.

(j) Approving claims and reimbursing, less direct costs, former owners of abandoned or other unclaimed personal property which has been sold or retained for official use.

(k) Recommending non-Federal grantee excess property screeners to GSA as required in FPMR 101–43.320(h).

(l) When authorized by statutory authority, vesting title to Government-furnished personal property in contractors or grantees.

(m) Acquiring excess personal property from other bureaus and from other Federal agencies.

§ 128–1.5005–2 Redelegations of authority.

(a) The authorities delegated by the Assistant Attorney General for Administration to heads of bureaus may, in turn, be redelegated as necessary to enable personal property management functions to be performed at the organizational level best equipped to handle such functions, unless otherwise prohibited by this regulation.

(b) Such redelegations can be made without the specific approval of the Assistant Attorney General for Administration to deputies, principal administrative officers, heads of field offices and installations and their respective deputies. Such redelegations shall not conflict with the duties or responsibilities assigned to the PMO, or PC under the JPMR.

(c) Existing delegations of authority by the Assistant Attorney General for Administration in matters of personal property management which are not covered in this section shall continue in effect until modified or revoked.

(d) Redelegations of authorities made in accordance with this section shall be in writing and shall be made available for audits, surveys, or as otherwise appropriate.

§ 128–1.5006 General responsibilities.

§ 128–1.5006–1 Head of bureau.

The head of a bureau is responsible for establishing and administering a property management program within his respective operation which will provide for:

(a) The planning and scheduling of property requirements to assure that supplies, equipment, and space are readily available to satisfy program needs while minimizing operating costs and inventory levels.

(b) The creation and maintenance of complete, accurate inventory control and accountability record systems.

(c) The maximum utilization of available property for official purposes.

(d) The proper care and securing of property, to include storage, handling, preservation, and preventative maintenance.

(e) The identification of property excess to the needs of the bureau which must be made available to other Departmental activities and reported to GSA for transfer, donation, or disposal, as appropriate, under the provisions of the FPMR and JPMR.

(f) The submission of required property management reports.

(g) The conducting of periodic management reviews within the activity to assure compliance with prescribed policies, regulations, and procedures and to determine additional guidance or training needs.

(h) Advising all bureau employees of their responsibilities for Government property.

(i) Supporting general ledger control accounts for personal property by establishing subsidiary accounts and records as prescribed by the bureau in accordance with the provisions of DOJ Order 2110.1, Paragraph 4(b)(c).

§ 128–1.5006–2 Property management officer (PMO).

The property management officer of a bureau is responsible for coordinating and conducting the activities of the personal property management program and for performing the following functions:

(a) Providing the required leadership, guidance, and operating procedures for personal property management functions.

(b) Ensuring general ledger control accounts for personal property are supported by property records in accordance with DOJ Order 2110.1, Paragraph 6.103b(4).

(c) Ensuring bureau compliance with the personal property management requirements of the FPMR and JPMR.

(d) Designating items of controlled personal property within the bureau.

(e) Ensuring records of controlled personal property are created and maintained by personnel other than property custodians.

§ 128–1.5006–3 Department employees.

Each employee of the Department who has use of, supervises the use of, or has control over Government property is responsible for that property. This responsibility may take either or both of the following forms:

(a) Supervisory responsibility, in which an officer-in-charge, and administrative officer, or a supervisor is obligated to establish and enforce necessary administrative and security measures to ensure proper preservation and use of all Government property under his jurisdiction.

(b) Personal responsibility, in which each employee of the Department is obligated to properly care for, handle, use, and protect Government property issued to or assigned for the employee's use at or away from the office or station.

§ 128–1.5007 Reproduction of departmental and bureau seals.

(a) Requests for permission to reproduce the Departmental seal for commercial, educational, ornamental or other purposes by other government agencies or private entities shall be referred to the Assistant Attorney General for Administration for decision.

(b) Requests for permission to reproduce the seals of the Federal Bureau of Investigation, the Bureau of Prisons, the Federal Prison Industries, the Immigration and Naturalization Service, the Board of Parole, the Drug Enforcement Administration, and the United States Marshals Service for such purposes by other government agencies or private entities shall be referred to the head of the respective Departmental organization for decision.

(c) The decision whether to grant such a request shall be made on a case-by-case basis, with consideration of any relevant factors, which may include the benefit or cost to the government of granting the request; the unintended appearance of endorsement or authentication by the Department; the potential for misuse; the effect upon Departmental security; the reputability of the use; the extent of control by the Department over the ultimate use; and the extent of control by the Department over distribution of any products or publications bearing a Departmental seal.

[45 FR 55727, Aug. 21, 1980]

§ 128–1.5009 Authorization for use of the Federal Bureau of Investigation anti-piracy warning seal.

(a) *Purpose.* The Federal Bureau of Investigation (FBI) Anti-Piracy Warning Seal ("APW Seal") is an official insignia of the FBI and the United States Department of Justice. The purpose of the APW Seal is to help detect and deter criminal violations of United States intellectual property laws by educating the public about the existence of these laws and the authority of the FBI to enforce them.

(b) The APW Seal is a modified image of the Official FBI Seal with the words "FBI ANTI-PIRACY WARNING" displayed horizontally across its center in an enclosed border, whether rendered in color, black and white, outline, or otherwise.

(c) The APW Seal has been approved by the Attorney General as an official insignia of the FBI within the meaning of Title 18, United States Code, Section 701, which provides criminal sanctions for unauthorized uses of such insignia.

(d)(1) The regulations in this section authorize use of the APW Seal by copyright holders on copyrighted works including, but not limited to films, audio recordings, electronic media, software, books, photographs, etc., subject to the terms and conditions set forth in this section.

(2) Use of the APW Seal or of the authorized warning language in a manner not authorized under this section may be punishable under Title 18, United States Code, Sections 701, 709, or other applicable law.

(e) *Conditions regarding use of the APW Seal.* (1) The APW Seal shall only be used on copyrighted works subject to protection under United States Criminal Code provisions such as those in Title 18, United States Code, Sections 2319, 2319A, and 2319B.

(2) The APW Seal shall only be used immediately adjacent to the authorized warning language. "Authorized warning language" refers to the language set forth in paragraph (e)(2)(i) of this section, or alternative language specifically authorized in writing for this purpose by the Director of the FBI or his or her designee and posted on the FBI's official public Internet Web site (*http://www.fbi.gov*). Except as authorized pursuant to paragraph (f)(1), the APW Seal and authorized warning language shall be enclosed by a plain box border at all times that other text or images appear on the same screen or page.

(i) "The unauthorized reproduction or distribution of a copyrighted work is illegal. Criminal copyright infringement, including infringement without monetary gain, is investigated by the FBI and is punishable by fines and federal imprisonment."

(ii) [Reserved]

(3) The APW Seal image must be obtained from the FBI's official public Internet Web site (*http://www.fbi.gov*). The APW Seal image shall not be animated or altered except that it may be rendered in outline, black and white, or grayscale.

(4) In programming or reproducing the APW Seal in or on a work, users are encouraged to employ industry-recognized copyright anti-circumvention or copy protection techniques to discourage copying of the FBI APW Seal, except that such techniques need not be used if no other content or advertising programmed into the same work on the same media utilizes such copyright anti-circumvention or copy protection techniques.

(f) *Prohibitions regarding use of the APW Seal.* (1) The APW Seal shall not be used in a manner indicating FBI approval, authorization, or endorsement of any communication other than the authorized warning language. No other text or image that appears on the same screen, page, package, etc., as the APW Seal or authorized warning language shall reference, contradict, or be displayed in a manner that appears to be associated with, the APW Seal or authorized warning language, except as authorized in writing by the Director of the FBI or his or her designee and posted on the FBI's official public Internet Web site (*http://www.fbi.gov*).

(2) The APW Seal shall not be used on any work whose production, sale, public presentation, or distribution by mail or in or affecting interstate commerce would violate the laws of the United States including, but not limited to, those protecting intellectual property and those prohibiting child pornography and obscenity.

(3) The APW Seal shall not be forwarded or copied except as necessary to display it on an eligible work.

(4) The APW Seal shall not be used in any manner:

(i) Indicating that the FBI has approved, authorized, or endorsed any work, product, production, or private entity, including the work on which it appears;

(ii) Indicating that the FBI has determined that a particular work or portion thereof is entitled to protection of the law; or,

(iii) Indicating that any item or communication, except as provided herein, originated from, on behalf of, or in coordination with the FBI, whether for enforcement purposes, education, or otherwise.

[77 FR 41320, July 13, 2012]

Subpart 128–1.80—Seismic Safety Program

AUTHORITY: 42 U.S.C. 7701 et seq., E.O. 12699 (3 CFR, 1990 Comp., p. 269).

SOURCE: 58 FR 42876, Aug. 12, 1993; 59 FR 33439, June 29, 1994, unless otherwise noted.

§ 128–1.8000 Scope.

This subpart establishes a Seismic Safety Program for the Department of Justice and sets forth the policies and procedures for obtaining compliance with Executive Order 12699 (Executive Order), "Seismic Safety of Federal and Federally Assisted or Regulated New Building Construction."

§ 128–1.8001 Background.

The Earthquake Hazards Reduction Act of 1977 (Act), 42 U.S.C. 7701, et seq., as amended, directs the Federal government to establish and maintain an effective earthquake hazards reduction program to reduce the risks to life and property from future earthquakes. Executive Order 12699 implements certain provisions of the Act by requiring Federal agencies responsible for the design and construction of new buildings to develop and implement a seismic safety program. The regulations in this subpart implement the Executive Order, and apply to buildings designed and constructed under the responsibility of the Department of Justice. These regulations do not apply to buildings used by the Department and obtained, through purchase or lease, by the General Services Administration or other Federal agencies.

§ 128–1.8002 Definitions of terms.

(a) *Construction documents*—Detailed plans and specifications for the construction of a building.

(b) *Building*—Any structure, fully or partially enclosed, used or intended for sheltering persons or property.

(c) *New building*—A building, or an addition to an existing building, for which development of construction documents was initiated after January 5, 1990.

(d) *Leased building*—A new building constructed expressly for lease by the Department of Justice, and for which the Department contracted with the lessor or owner to develop construction documents to meet the specifications of the Department.

(e) *Purchased building*—A new building constructed expressly for purchase by the Department, and for which the Department contracted with the owner/developer to develop construction documents meeting the specifications of the Department.

(f) *Assisted or regulated building*—A new building designed and constructed with funding assistance from the Department through Federal grants or loans, or guarantees of financing, through loan or mortgage insurance programs.

(g) *Covered building*—a new building owned, leased, purchased, or assisted or regulated by the Department of Justice.

§ 128–1.8003 Objective.

The Department shall comply with Executive Order 12699 for the purpose of reducing the risks to lives of occupants of new buildings owned by the Department, leased for Department uses, or purchased and constructed with assistance from the Department, and to other persons who would be affected by the failure of such buildings in earthquakes; improving the capability of essential new Department buildings to function during or after an earthquake; and protecting public investments in all covered buildings; all in a cost-effective manner.

§ 128–1.8004 Seismic Safety Coordinators.

(a) The Justice Management Division shall designate an individual with technical training, engineering experience and a seismic background as the Department of Justice Seismic Safety Coordinator who shall provide overall guidance for the implementation of the Seismic Safety Program for the Department. The Department Seismic Safety Coordinator shall, at a minimum:

(1) Monitor the execution and results of the efforts of the Department to upgrade the seismic safety of the Department's new construction activities;

(2) Implement seismic safety program changes, as required;

(3) Act as a point-of-contact for the Department in maintaining necessary records, and consolidate data pertaining to the seismic safety activities in the Department;

(4) Monitor and record the cost, construction and other consequences attributable to compliance with the Executive Order;

(5) Notify each Component Seismic Coordinator about what information he must maintain under the Seismic Safety Program and what reports he must prepare;

(6) Prepare and forward for submission all reports, as required by law and regulation;

(7) Manage the Seismic Safety Program for all components of the Department, with the exception of the components listed in paragraph (b) of this section.

(b) The Component Head for the Bureau of Prisons, the Drug Enforcement Administration, the Federal Bureau of Investigation, the Immigration and Naturalization Service, and the United States Marshals Service, shall designate a Component Seismic Safety Coordinator for his/her respective component. Each of these Component Seismic Safety Coordinators shall manage and implement the seismic safety policies and activities within the component. The Component Seismic Safety Coordinators shall, at a minimum:

(1) Provide guidance to component employees who undertake building activity;

(2) Maintain and provide data about the Seismic Safety Program, as requested by the Department Seismic Safety Coordinator;

(3) Monitor and record the cost, construction and other consequences attributable to compliance with the Executive Order; and

(4) Submit an annual Seismic Safety Program status report as directed by the Department Seismic Safety Coordinator.

§ 128–1.8005 Seismic safety standards.

(a) To meet the building and construction requirements of this subpart, the Department, except as noted, adopts as its seismic safety standards the seismic safety levels set forth in the model building codes that the Interagency Committee on Seismic Safety in Construction (ICSSC) recognizes and recommends as appropriate for implementing the Executive Order. The ICSSC, as of the date of this rule, recognizes and recommends:

(1) The 1991 International Conference of Building Officials (ICBO) Uniform Building Code (UBC);

(2) The 1992 Supplement to the Building Officials and Code Administrators International (BOCA) National Building Code (NBC); and

(3) The 1992 Amendments to the Southern Building Code Congress (SBCC) Standard Building Code (SBC).

(b) The seismic design and construction of a covered building shall conform to the model code applicable in the locality where the building is constructed, unless:

(1) The building code for the locality provides a higher level of seismic safety than provided by the appropriate model code, in which case the local code shall be utilized as the standard; or

(2) The locality does not have seismic safety building requirements, in which case the ICSSC model building code appropriate for that geographic area shall be utilized as the standard.

§ 128–1.8006 Seismic Safety Program requirements.

The Department Seismic Safety Coordinator and each Component Seismic Safety Coordinator shall ensure that an individual familiar with seismic design provisions of the Seismic Safety Standards (appropriate standards), or a professional, licensed engineer shall conduct the reviews required under this section, as appropriate.

(a) *New building projects.* Construction documents initiated after August 12, 1993, and which apply to new construction projects, shall comply with the appropriate standards and shall be reviewed for compliance. Once the reviewer determines that the documents comply, the reviewer shall affix his/her signature and seal (if a licensed engineer) to the approved documents and provide a statement certifying compliance with the appropriate standards.

(b) *Existing building projects.* For new buildings with construction documents that were initiated prior to August 12, 1993, the documents shall be reviewed to determine whether they comply with the appropriate standards. If the reviewer determines that the documents comply with the standard, the reviewer shall affix his/her signature and seal (if a licensed engineer) to the approved documents and provide a statement certifying compliance with the appropriate standards. If the reviewer determines that seismic deficiencies exist, the appropriate Component Head shall ensure completion of one of the following:

(1) For a new building project for which a contract for construction has not been awarded, the construction documents shall be revised to incorporate the appropriate standards. The revised construction documents shall then be reviewed for compliance. Once the reviewer determines that the documents comply with the standard, the reviewer shall affix his/her signature and seal (if a licensed engineer) to the approved documents and provide a statement certifying compliance with the Department standards.

(2) For a new building under construction, or for which construction has been completed, a corrective action plan shall be devised to bring the building into compliance with the appropriate standards. The plan shall then be reviewed for compliance. Once the reviewer determines that the plan complies with the standard, the reviewer shall affix his/her signature and seal (if a licensed engineer) to the approved documents and provide a statement certifying compliance with the Department standards. The Component Head shall ensure implementation of the approved plan.

(3) For an addition to an existing building, the review shall account for, in addition to the requirements provided in paragraphs (b) (1) or (2) of this section, as appropriate, any effect the addition will have on the seismic resistance of the existing portion of the structure. If the reviewer determines

that the addition will decrease the level of seismic resistance of the existing building, the appropriate Component Head shall develop a plan of corrective action to restore the seismic integrity of the existing structure. Once the plan of corrective action has been accomplished, the reviewer shall verify that the current level of seismic resistance of the existing building at least equals the seismic resistance level of the building before the addition.

(c) The Department Seismic Safety Coordinator and each Component Seismic Safety Coordinator shall ensure that statements verifying compliance made under this subpart have been completed and retained by the appropriate contracting officer when the Department contracted for design or design review services, or by an individual designated by the Component Head where the Department has not contracted for either design or design review.

§ 128–1.8007 **Reporting.**

The Department shall file reports on the execution of the Executive Order as required under the Order, and as required by the Federal Emergency Management Agency.

§ 128–1.8008 **Exemptions.**

The Executive Order exempts from the regulations in this subpart only those categories of buildings exempted by the "National Earthquake Hazards Reduction Program Recommended Provisions for the Development of Seismic Regulations for New Buildings." The Department Seismic Safety Coordinator shall maintain the latest version of this document.

§ 128–1.8009 **Review of Seismic Safety Program.**

The Department shall review and, as necessary, revise the Seismic Safety Program once every three years from August 12, 1993.

§ 128–1.8010 **Judicial review.**

Nothing in this subpart is intended to create any right or benefit, substantive or procedural, enforceable at law by a party against the Department of Justice, its Seismic Safety Coordinators, its officers, or any employee of the Department.

PART 128–18—ACQUISITION OF REAL PROPERTY

Subpart 128–18.50—Uniform Relocation Assistance and Real Property Acquisition for Federal and Federally Assisted Programs

AUTHORITY: Sec. 213, Uniform Relocation Assistance and Real Property Acquisition Policies Act of 1970, Pub. L. 91–646, 84 Stat. 1894 (42 U.S.C. 4601) as amended by the Surface Transportation and Uniform Relocation Assistance Act of 1987, Title IV of Pub. L. 100–17, 101 Stat. 246–256 (42 U.S.C. 4601 note).

§ 128–18.5001–1　Uniform relocation assistance and real property acquisition.

Regulations and procedures for complying with the Uniform Relocation Assistance and Real Property Acquisition Policies Act of 1970 (Pub. L. 91–646, 84 Stat. 1894, 42 U.S.C. 4601), as amended by the Surface Transportation and Uniform Relocation Assistance Act of 1987 (Title IV of Pub. L. 100–17, 101 Stat. 246–255, 42 U.S.C. 4601 note) are set forth in 49 CFR part 25.

[52 FR 48025, Dec. 17, 1987]

PART 128–48—UTILIZATION, DONATION, OR DISPOSAL OF ABANDONED AND FORFEITED PERSONAL PROPERTY

Sec.
128–48.001　Definitions.
128–48.001–5　Forfeited property.
128–48.001–50　Administrative or summary process.

Subpart 128–48.1—Utilization of Abandoned and Forfeited Personal Property

128–48.102–1　Vesting of title in the United States.
128–48.102–4　Proceeds.
128–48.150　Determination of type of property.

Subpart 128–48.3—Disposal of Abandoned and Forfeited Personal Property

128–48.305–1　Abandoned or other unclaimed property.

Subpart 128–48.50—Proper Claims for Abandoned or Other Unclaimed Personal Property

128–48.500　Scope of subpart.
128–48.501　Definitions.
128–48.501–1　Determining official.
128–48.501–2　Claimant.
128–48.501–3　Owner.
128–48.501–4　Person.
128–48.502　Procedures relating to claims.
128–48.503　General procedures.

AUTHORITY: 41 CFR 128–1.105.

SOURCE: 43 FR 3279, Jan. 24, 1978, unless otherwise noted.

§ 128–48.001　Definitions.

§ 128–48.001–5　Forfeited property.

Personal property acquired by a bureau, either by administrative process or by order of a court of competent jurisdiction pursuant to any law of the United States.

§ 128–48.001–50　Administrative or summary process.

Forfeiture is achieved by direction of the seizing bureau in lieu of the courts. The phrase shall be interpreted to mean by administrative process.

Subpart 128–48.1—Utilization of Abandoned and Forfeited Personal Property

§ 128–48.102–1　Vesting of title in the United States.

(a) Abandoned or other unclaimed property, subject to the provisions of section 203(m) of the Federal Property and Administrative Services Act of 1949, as amended (40 U.S.C. 484(m)), shall remain in the custody of and be the responsibility of the bureau finding such property.

(b) If the owner of such property is known, the owner shall be notified within 20 days of finding such property by certified mail at the owner's address of record that the property may be claimed by the owner or his designee and that if the property is not claimed within 30 days from the date the letter of notification is postmarked, the title of the property will vest in the United States.

(c) If the owner of such property is not known and the estimated value of the property exceeds $100, the bureau shall post notice within 20 days of finding such property, which contains the following information:

(1) A description of the property including model or serial numbers, if known.

(2) A statement of the location where the property was found and the office that has custody of it.

(3) A statement that any person desiring to claim the property must file with the bureau within 30 days from the date of first publication a claim for said property.

(4) A complete mailing address is to be provided as a point of contact within the bureau for any person to obtain additional information concerning the property or the procedures involved in filing a claim.

Notice must be published once a week for at least three successive weeks. Sound judgment and discretion must be used in selecting the publication medium. Advertisements should be placed in a publication of general circulation within the judicial district where the property was found.

(d) Property, as described in paragraphs (b) and (c) of this section, shall be held for a period of 30 days from the date of the first publication of notice. Upon the expiration of this 30-day period, title to such property vests in the United States, except that title reverts to the owner where a proper claim is filed within three years from the date of vesting of title in the United States, but if the property has been in official use, transferred for official use, or sold at the time the proper claim is approved, title shall not revert back to the former owner. The former owner shall instead obtain reimbursement in accordance with 41 CFR 101–48.102–4 or 101–48.305–1.

(e) If the owner of such property is unknown and the estimated value of the property is $100 or less, no notice is required, and the property shall be held for a period of 30 days from the date of finding the property. Upon expiration

of this 30-day period, title to such property vests in the United States.

§ 128–48.102–4   Proceeds.

(a) Records of abandoned or other unclaimed property will be maintained in such a manner as to permit identification of the property with the original owner, if known, when such property is put into official use or transferred for official use by the finding bureau. Records will be maintained until the three-year period for filing claims has elapsed to enable the bureau to determine the amount of reimbursement due to a former owner who has filed a proper claim for abandoned or other unclaimed property.

(b) Reimbursement for official use by the finding bureau or transfer for official use of abandoned or other unclaimed property that has been placed in a special fund by the bureau for more than three years shall be deposited in the Treasury of the United States as miscellaneous receipts, or in such other bureau accounts as provided by law.

§ 128–48.150   Determination of type of property.

If a bureau is unable to determine whether the personal property in its custody is abandoned or voluntarily abandoned, the bureau shall contact the regional office of the General Services Administration for the region in which the property is located for such a determination.

Subpart 128–48.3—Disposal of Abandoned and Forfeited Personal Property

§ 128–48.305–1   Abandoned or other unclaimed property.

Proceeds from the sale of abandoned or other unclaimed property that have been placed in a special fund by a bureau for more than three years shall be deposited in the Treasury of the United States as miscellaneous receipts, or in such other bureau accounts as provided by law.

Subpart 128–48.50—Proper Claims for Abandoned or Other Unclaimed Personal Property

§ 128–48.500 Scope of subpart.

This subpart sets forth the policies in regard to proper claims for abandoned or other unclaimed property.

§ 128–48.501 Definitions.

§ 128–48.501–1 Determining official.

The official who has the authority to grant or deny the claim for the abandoned or other unclaimed property.

§ 128–48.501–2 Claimant.

The person who submitted the claim for the abandoned or other unclaimed property.

§ 128–48.501–3 Owner.

The person who has primary and direct title to property (see 28 CFR 9.2(e)).

§ 128–48.501–4 Person.

An individual, partnership, corporation, joint venture, or other entity capable of owning property (see 28 CFR 9.2(f)).

§ 128–48.502 Procedures relating to claims.

(a) Upon receipt of a claim, an investigation shall be conducted to determine the merits of the claim, and the investigation's report shall be submitted to the determining official.

(b) The determining official shall be designated by the head of a bureau.

(c) Upon receipt of a claim and the report thereon by the determining official, he shall make a ruling based upon the claim and the investigation's report.

(d) Notice of the granting or denial of a claim for abandoned or other unclaimed property shall be mailed to the claimant or his attorney. If the claim is granted, the conditions of relief and the procedures to be followed to obtain the relief shall be set forth. If the claim is denied, the claimant shall be advised of the reason for such denial.

(e) A request for reconsideration of the claim may be submitted within 10 days from the date of the letter denying the claim. Such request shall be addressed to the head of the bureau and shall be based on evidence recently developed or not previously considered.

§ 128–48.503 General procedures.

(a) Claims shall be sworn and shall include the following information in clear and concise terms:

(1) A complete description of the property including serial numbers, if any.

(2) The interest of the claimant in the property, as owner, mortgagee, or otherwise, to be supported by bills of sale, contracts, mortgages, or other satisfactory documentary evidence.

(3) The facts and circumstances, to be established by satisfactory proof, relied upon by the claimant to justify the granting of the claim.

(b) If the claim is filed before title has vested in the United States, the determining official shall not grant the claim for the abandoned or other unclaimed property unless the claimant establishes a valid, good faith interest in the property.

(c) If the claim is filed after title has vested in the United States, the determining official shall not grant the claim for abandoned or other unclaimed property unless the claimant:

(1) Establishes that he would have a valid, good faith interest in the property had not title vested in the United States; and

(2) Establishes that he had no actual or constructive notice, prior to the vesting of title in the United States, that the property was in the custody of a bureau and that title, after the appropriate time period, would vest in the United States. A claimant shall be presumed to have constructive notice upon publication in a suitable medium concerning the property unless he was in such circumstances as to prevent him from knowing of the status of the property or having the opportunity to see the notice.

PART 128–50—SEIZED PERSONAL PROPERTY

Sec.
128–50.000 Scope of part.
128–50.001 Definitions.
128–50.001–1 Seized personal property.

Subpart 128–50.1—Storage and Care of Seized Personal Property

128–50.100 Storage and care.
128–50.101 Inventory records.
128–50.102 Periodic reviews.
128–50.103 Investigation of any discrepancy.

AUTHORITY: 41 CFR 128–1.105.

SOURCE: 43 FR 3279, Jan. 24, 1978, unless otherwise noted.

§ 128–50.000 Scope of part.

This part prescribes the policies for the storage and care of seized personal property; the preparation and maintenance of inventory records of its seized personal property; the conducting of periodic internal reviews; and the investigation of any discrepancy between the inventory records and the actual amount of its seized personal property.

§ 128–50.001 Definitions.

§ 128–50.001–1 Seized personal property.

Personal property for which the Government does not have title but which the Government has obtained custody or control of in accordance with 15 U.S.C. 1177; 18 U.S.C. 924(d), 1955(d), 2513, 3611, 3612, 3615; 19 U.S.C. 1595a; 21 U.S.C. 881; 22 U.S.C. 401; Fed. R. Crim. P. 41(b); 28 CFR 0.86, 0.89, 0.111(j), 3.5, 3.6, 8.1, 8.2, 9a.1, 9a.2; or other statutory authority.

Subpart 128–50.1—Storage and Care of Seized Personal Property

§ 128–50.100 Storage and care.

(a) Each bureau shall be responsible for providing that its seized personal property storage facilities meet the safeguarding standards applicable to the type of property being stored.

(b) Each bureau shall be responsible for performing care on its seized personal property to prevent the unnecessary deterioration of such property. In particular, a bureau preparing a seized vehicle for storage should be at a minimum;

(1) Protect the cooling system from freezing;

(2) Protect the battery by assuring it is properly watered;

(3) Protect the tires by inflating to correct pressure;

(4) Remove all articles found in the vehicle's interior (for example, easily removable radios, tape players, and speakers) and all exterior accessories (for example, wheel covers) that are subject to pilferage and properly store them; and

(5) Shut all windows and lock all doors and compartments that have locks.

§ 128–50.101 Inventory records.

Each bureau shall be responsible for establishing and maintaining inventory records of its seized personal property to ensure that:

(a) The date the property was seized is recorded;

(b) All of the property associated with a case is recorded together under the case name and number;

(c) The location of storage of the property is recorded;

(d) A well documented chain of custody is kept; and

(e) All information in the inventory records is accurate and current.

§ 128–50.102 Periodic reviews.

Each bureau shall be responsible for performing an independent accountability review at least once a year to ensure compliance with this subpart and with the bureau's procedures for the handling, storage, and disposal of its seized personal property. In particular, a bureau conducting a review shall verify that the inventory records are accurate, current, and are being kept in accordance with established inventory procedures.

§ 128–50.103 Investigation of any discrepancy.

(a) Upon discovery of any discrepancy between the inventory records and the bureau's actual amount of seized personal property, a board of survey shall conduct an investigation in accordance with 41 CFR 128–51.1.

(b) If the discrepancy cannot be eliminated and involves a shortage, the bureau shall notify the U.S. attorney in charge of the litigation involving the missing property of the shortage as soon as possible.

(c) If the discrepancy cannot be eliminated and involves an overage, the bureau shall determine if the property has any evidentiary value. If the property does have evidentiary value, the property shall be properly stored and inventoried. If the property does not have any evidentiary value, the bureau shall determine whether the property is forfeitable to the United States, voluntarily abandoned, or abandoned. Proper proceedings shall be commenced as soon as possible to vest title of the forfeitable property in the United States. The voluntarily abandoned and abandoned property shall be kept in custody in accordance with 41 CFR 101–48 and any applicable Justice property management regulations.

CHAPTERS 129–200 [RESERVED]

Subtitle D—Other Provisions Relating to Property Management [Reserved]

FINDING AIDS

A list of CFR titles, subtitles, chapters, subchapters and parts and an alphabetical list of agencies publishing in the CFR are included in the CFR Index and Finding Aids volume to the Code of Federal Regulations which is published separately and revised annually.

Table of CFR Titles and Chapters
Alphabetical List of Agencies Appearing in the CFR
List of CFR Sections Affected

Table of CFR Titles and Chapters

(Revised as of July 1, 2019)

Title 1—General Provisions

Title 2—Grants and Agreements

Title 2—Grants and Agreements—Continued

Title 3—The President

Title 4—Accounts

Title 5—Administrative Personnel

Title 8—Aliens and Nationality

Title 9—Animals and Animal Products

Title 10—Energy

Title 11—Federal Elections

Title 12—Banks and Banking

Title 15—Commerce and Foreign Trade—Continued

Title 16—Commercial Practices

Title 17—Commodity and Securities Exchanges

Title 18—Conservation of Power and Water Resources

Title 19—Customs Duties

Title 20—Employees' Benefits

Title 23—Highways—Continued

Title 24—Housing and Urban Development

Title 25—Indians

Title 26—Internal Revenue

Title 27—Alcohol, Tobacco Products and Firearms

Title 28—Judicial Administration

Title 29—Labor

733

Title 29—Labor—Continued

Title 30—Mineral Resources

Title 31—Money and Finance: Treasury

Title 34—Education—Continued

Title 35 [Reserved]

Title 36—Parks, Forests, and Public Property

Title 37—Patents, Trademarks, and Copyrights

Title 38—Pensions, Bonuses, and Veterans' Relief

Title 39—Postal Service

Title 40—Protection of Environment

Title 41—Public Contracts and Property Management

737

Title 41—Public Contracts and Property Management—Continued

Title 42—Public Health

Title 43—Public Lands: Interior

Title 44—Emergency Management and Assistance

Title 45—Public Welfare

Title 45—Public Welfare—Continued

Title 46—Shipping

Title 47—Telecommunication

Title 48—Federal Acquisition Regulations System

Title 49—Transportation

Title 50—Wildlife and Fisheries

Alphabetical List of Agencies Appearing in the CFR
(Revised as of July 1, 2019)

Agency	CFR Title, Subtitle or Chapter
Administrative Conference of the United States	1, III
Advisory Council on Historic Preservation	36, VIII
Advocacy and Outreach, Office of	7, XXV
Afghanistan Reconstruction, Special Inspector General for	5, LXXXIII
African Development Foundation	22, XV
Federal Acquisition Regulation	48, 57
Agency for International Development	2, VII; 22, II
Federal Acquisition Regulation	48, 7
Agricultural Marketing Service	7, I, IX, X, XI
Agricultural Research Service	7, V
Agriculture, Department of	2, IV; 5, LXXIII
Advocacy and Outreach, Office of	7, XXV
Agricultural Marketing Service	7, I, IX, X, XI
Agricultural Research Service	7, V
Animal and Plant Health Inspection Service	7, III; 9, I
Chief Financial Officer, Office of	7, XXX
Commodity Credit Corporation	7, XIV
Economic Research Service	7, XXXVII
Energy Policy and New Uses, Office of	2, IX; 7, XXIX
Environmental Quality, Office of	7, XXXI
Farm Service Agency	7, VII, XVIII
Federal Acquisition Regulation	48, 4
Federal Crop Insurance Corporation	7, IV
Food and Nutrition Service	7, II
Food Safety and Inspection Service	9, III
Foreign Agricultural Service	7, XV
Forest Service	36, II
Grain Inspection, Packers and Stockyards Administration	7, VIII; 9, II
Information Resources Management, Office of	7, XXVII
Inspector General, Office of	7, XXVI
National Agricultural Library	7, XLI
National Agricultural Statistics Service	7, XXXVI
National Institute of Food and Agriculture	7, XXXIV
Natural Resources Conservation Service	7, VI
Operations, Office of	7, XXVIII
Procurement and Property Management, Office of	7, XXXII
Rural Business-Cooperative Service	7, XVIII, XLII
Rural Development Administration	7, XLII
Rural Housing Service	7, XVIII, XXXV
Rural Telephone Bank	7, XVI
Rural Utilities Service	7, XVII, XVIII, XLII
Secretary of Agriculture, Office of	7, Subtitle A
Transportation, Office of	7, XXXIII
World Agricultural Outlook Board	7, XXXVIII
Air Force, Department of	32, VII
Federal Acquisition Regulation Supplement	48, 53
Air Transportation Stabilization Board	14, VI
Alcohol and Tobacco Tax and Trade Bureau	27, I
Alcohol, Tobacco, Firearms, and Explosives, Bureau of	27, II
AMTRAK	49, VII
American Battle Monuments Commission	36, IV
American Indians, Office of the Special Trustee	25, VII
Animal and Plant Health Inspection Service	7, III; 9, I

745

Agency	CFR Title, Subtitle or Chapter
Indian Arts and Crafts Board	25, II
Indian Health Service	25, V
Industry and Security, Bureau of	15, VII
Information Resources Management, Office of	7, XXVII
Information Security Oversight Office, National Archives and Records Administration	32, XX
Inspector General	
Agriculture Department	7, XXVI
Health and Human Services Department	42, V
Housing and Urban Development Department	24, XII, XV
Institute of Peace, United States	22, XVII
Inter-American Foundation	5, LXIII; 22, X
Interior, Department of	2, XIV
American Indians, Office of the Special Trustee	25, VII
Endangered Species Committee	50, IV
Federal Acquisition Regulation	48, 14
Federal Property Management Regulations System	41, 114
Fish and Wildlife Service, United States	50, I, IV
Geological Survey	30, IV
Indian Affairs, Bureau of	25, I, V
Indian Affairs, Office of the Assistant Secretary	25, VI
Indian Arts and Crafts Board	25, II
Land Management, Bureau of	43, II
National Indian Gaming Commission	25, III
National Park Service	36, I
Natural Resource Revenue, Office of	30, XII
Ocean Energy Management, Bureau of	30, V
Reclamation, Bureau of	43, I
Safety and Enforcement Bureau, Bureau of	30, II
Secretary of the Interior, Office of	2, XIV; 43, Subtitle A
Surface Mining Reclamation and Enforcement, Office of	30, VII
Internal Revenue Service	26, I
International Boundary and Water Commission, United States and Mexico, United States Section	22, XI
International Development, United States Agency for	22, II
Federal Acquisition Regulation	48, 7
International Development Cooperation Agency, United States	22, XII
International Joint Commission, United States and Canada	22, IV
International Organizations Employees Loyalty Board	5, V
International Trade Administration	15, III; 19, III
International Trade Commission, United States	19, II
Interstate Commerce Commission	5, XL
Investment Security, Office of	31, VIII
James Madison Memorial Fellowship Foundation	45, XXIV
Japan–United States Friendship Commission	22, XVI
Joint Board for the Enrollment of Actuaries	20, VIII
Justice, Department of	2, XXVIII; 5, XXVIII; 28, I, XI; 40, IV
Alcohol, Tobacco, Firearms, and Explosives, Bureau of	27, II
Drug Enforcement Administration	21, II
Federal Acquisition Regulation	48, 28
Federal Claims Collection Standards	31, IX
Federal Prison Industries, Inc.	28, III
Foreign Claims Settlement Commission of the United States	45, V
Immigration Review, Executive Office for	8, V
Independent Counsel, Offices of	28, VI
Prisons, Bureau of	28, V
Property Management Regulations	41, 128
Labor, Department of	2, XXIX; 5, XLII
Employee Benefits Security Administration	29, XXV
Employees' Compensation Appeals Board	20, IV
Employment and Training Administration	20, V
Employment Standards Administration	20, VI
Federal Acquisition Regulation	48, 29
Federal Contract Compliance Programs, Office of	41, 60

Agency	CFR Title, Subtitle or Chapter
Federal Procurement Regulations System	41, 50
Labor-Management Standards, Office of	29, II, IV
Mine Safety and Health Administration	30, I
Occupational Safety and Health Administration	29, XVII
Public Contracts	41, 50
Secretary of Labor, Office of	29, Subtitle A
Veterans' Employment and Training Service, Office of the Assistant Secretary for	41, 61; 20, IX
Wage and Hour Division	29, V
Workers' Compensation Programs, Office of	20, I, VII
Labor-Management Standards, Office of	29, II, IV
Land Management, Bureau of	43, II
Legal Services Corporation	45, XVI
Libraries and Information Science, National Commission on	45, XVII
Library of Congress	36, VII
Copyright Royalty Board	37, III
U.S. Copyright Office	37, II
Local Television Loan Guarantee Board	7, XX
Management and Budget, Office of	5, III, LXXVII; 14, VI; 48, 99
Marine Mammal Commission	50, V
Maritime Administration	46, II
Merit Systems Protection Board	5, II, LXIV
Micronesian Status Negotiations, Office for	32, XXVII
Military Compensation and Retirement Modernization Commission	5, XCIX
Millennium Challenge Corporation	22, XIII
Mine Safety and Health Administration	30, I
Minority Business Development Agency	15, XIV
Miscellaneous Agencies	1, IV
Monetary Offices	31, I
Morris K. Udall Scholarship and Excellence in National Environmental Policy Foundation	36, XVI
Museum and Library Services, Institute of	2, XXXI
National Aeronautics and Space Administration	2, XVIII; 5, LIX; 14, V
Federal Acquisition Regulation	48, 18
National Agricultural Library	7, XLI
National Agricultural Statistics Service	7, XXXVI
National and Community Service, Corporation for	2, XXII; 45, XII, XXV
National Archives and Records Administration	2, XXVI; 5, LXVI; 36, XII
Information Security Oversight Office	32, XX
National Capital Planning Commission	1, IV, VI
National Counterintelligence Center	32, XVIII
National Credit Union Administration	5, LXXXVI; 12, VII
National Crime Prevention and Privacy Compact Council	28, IX
National Drug Control Policy, Office of	2, XXXVI; 21, III
National Endowment for the Arts	2, XXXII
National Endowment for the Humanities	2, XXXIII
National Foundation on the Arts and the Humanities	45, XI
National Geospatial-Intelligence Agency	32, I
National Highway Traffic Safety Administration	23, II, III; 47, VI; 49, V
National Imagery and Mapping Agency	32, I
National Indian Gaming Commission	25, III
National Institute of Food and Agriculture	7, XXXIV
National Institute of Standards and Technology	15, II; 37, IV
National Intelligence, Office of Director of	5, IV; 32, XVII
National Labor Relations Board	5, LXI; 29, I
National Marine Fisheries Service	50, II, IV
National Mediation Board	5, CI; 29, X
National Oceanic and Atmospheric Administration	15, IX; 50, II, III, IV, VI
National Park Service	36, I
National Railroad Adjustment Board	29, III
National Railroad Passenger Corporation (AMTRAK)	49, VII
National Science Foundation	2, XXV; 5, XLIII; 45, VI
Federal Acquisition Regulation	48, 25
National Security Council	32, XXI

749

Agency	CFR Title, Subtitle or Chapter
National Security Council and Office of Science and Technology Policy	47, II
National Technical Information Service	15, XI
National Telecommunications and Information Administration	15, XXIII; 47, III, IV, V
National Transportation Safety Board	49, VIII
Natural Resources Conservation Service	7, VI
Natural Resource Revenue, Office of	30, XII
Navajo and Hopi Indian Relocation, Office of	25, IV
Navy, Department of	32, VI
Federal Acquisition Regulation	48, 52
Neighborhood Reinvestment Corporation	24, XXV
Northeast Interstate Low-Level Radioactive Waste Commission	10, XVIII
Nuclear Regulatory Commission	2, XX; 5, XLVIII; 10, I
Federal Acquisition Regulation	48, 20
Occupational Safety and Health Administration	29, XVII
Occupational Safety and Health Review Commission	29, XX
Ocean Energy Management, Bureau of	30, V
Oklahoma City National Memorial Trust	36, XV
Operations Office	7, XXVIII
Overseas Private Investment Corporation	5, XXXIII; 22, VII
Patent and Trademark Office, United States	37, I
Payment From a Non-Federal Source for Travel Expenses	41, 304
Payment of Expenses Connected With the Death of Certain Employees	41, 303
Peace Corps	2, XXXVII; 22, III
Pennsylvania Avenue Development Corporation	36, IX
Pension Benefit Guaranty Corporation	29, XL
Personnel Management, Office of	5, I, XXXV; 5, IV; 45, VIII
Human Resources Management and Labor Relations Systems, Department of Homeland Security	5, XCVII
Federal Acquisition Regulation	48, 17
Federal Employees Group Life Insurance Federal Acquisition Regulation	48, 21
Federal Employees Health Benefits Acquisition Regulation	48, 16
Pipeline and Hazardous Materials Safety Administration	49, I
Postal Regulatory Commission	5, XLVI; 39, III
Postal Service, United States	5, LX; 39, I
Postsecondary Education, Office of	34, VI
President's Commission on White House Fellowships	1, IV
Presidential Documents	3
Presidio Trust	36, X
Prisons, Bureau of	28, V
Privacy and Civil Liberties Oversight Board	6, X
Procurement and Property Management, Office of	7, XXXII
Public Contracts, Department of Labor	41, 50
Public and Indian Housing, Office of Assistant Secretary for	24, IX
Public Health Service	42, I
Railroad Retirement Board	20, II
Reclamation, Bureau of	43, I
Refugee Resettlement, Office of	45, IV
Relocation Allowances	41, 302
Research and Innovative Technology Administration	49, XI
Rural Business-Cooperative Service	7, XVIII, XLII
Rural Development Administration	7, XLII
Rural Housing Service	7, XVIII, XXXV
Rural Telephone Bank	7, XVI
Rural Utilities Service	7, XVII, XVIII, XLII
Safety and Environmental Enforcement, Bureau of	30, II
Saint Lawrence Seaway Development Corporation	33, IV
Science and Technology Policy, Office of	32, XXIV
Science and Technology Policy, Office of, and National Security Council	47, II
Secret Service	31, IV
Securities and Exchange Commission	5, XXXIV; 17, II

List of CFR Sections Affected

All changes in this volume of the Code of Federal Regulations (CFR) that were made by documents published in the FEDERAL REGISTER since January 1, 2014 are enumerated in the following list. Entries indicate the nature of the changes effected. Page numbers refer to FEDERAL REGISTER pages. The user should consult the entries for chapters, parts and subparts as well as sections for revisions.

For changes to this volume of the CFR prior to this listing, consult the annual edition of the monthly List of CFR Sections Affected (LSA). The LSA is available at *www.govinfo.gov*. For changes to this volume of the CFR prior to 2001, see the "List of CFR Sections Affected, 1949–1963, 1964–1972, 1973–1985, and 1986–2000" published in 11 separate volumes. The "List of CFR Sections Affected 1986–2000" is available at *www.govinfo.gov*.